Arizona & New Mexico

W9-CJF-485

Published by AAA Publishing
1000 AAA Drive, Heathrow, FL 32746-5063
Copyright AAA 2015, All rights reserved

Advertising Rate and Circulation Information: (407) 444-8280

Printed in the USA by Quad/Graphics

This book is printed on paper certified by third-party standards for sustainably managed forestry and production.

Printed on recyclable paper.
Please recycle whenever possible.

Stock #4602

CONTENTS

Attractions, hotels, restaurants and other travel experience information are all grouped under the alphabetical listing of the city in which those experiences are physically located—or the nearest recognized city.

Arizona

■ Phoenix 125-191

■ Tucson 255-296

New Mexico

Featured Information

Going the Extra Mile

Every year AAA experts travel North America to check out places for members to see, stay, dine and play.

Professional Inspectors - conduct in-person hotel and restaurant evaluations, providing ratings, notes and tips to guide your decisions.

Seasoned Travel Writers - gather destination insight, providing itineraries and top picks including AAA GEM attractions.

A to Z City Listings

Cities and places are listed alphabetically within each state or province. Attractions, hotels and restaurants are listed once — under the city in which they are physically located.

Cities that are considered part of a larger destination city or area have an expanded city header. The header identifies the larger region and cross-references pages that contain shared trip planning resources:

- Destination map – outline map of the cities that comprise a destination city or area
- Attraction spotting map – regional street map marked with attraction locations
- Hotel/restaurant spotting map and index – regional street map numbered with hotel and restaurant locations identified in an accompanying index

Cities that are not considered part of a larger destination city or area but have a significant number of listings may have these resources within the individual city section:

- Attraction spotting map
- Hotel/restaurant spotting map and index

Location Abbreviations

Directions are from the center of town unless otherwise specified, using these highway abbreviations:

Bus. Rte.=business route
CR=county road
FM=farm to market
FR=forest road
Hwy.=Canadian highway
I=interstate highway
LR=legislative route
R.R.=rural route
SR/PR=state or provincial route
US=federal highway

Maps

Use the navigable road maps and accompanying legend in the Atlas Section for route planning. Check the destination maps for general location reference. In select cities only, refer to the mass transit overview maps to cross-reference station names and numbers. For attraction and hotel/restaurant spotting maps, see the legend below to identify symbols and color coding.

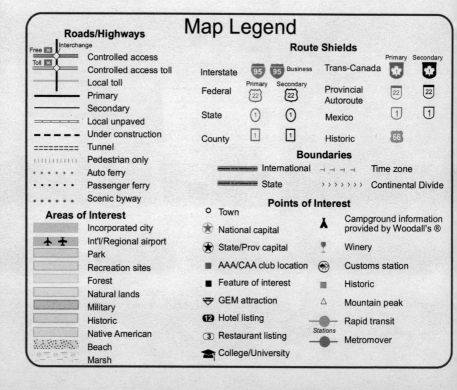

Map Legend

Roads/Highways

Free / Interchange	
Toll	
	Controlled access
	Controlled access toll
	Local toll
	Primary
	Secondary
	Local unpaved
	Under construction
	Tunnel
	Pedestrian only
	Auto ferry
	Passenger ferry
	Scenic byway

Areas of Interest

	Incorporated city
✈ ✈	Int'l/Regional airport
	Park
	Recreation sites
	Forest
	Natural lands
	Military
	Historic
	Native American
	Beach
	Marsh

Route Shields

	Primary	Secondary
Interstate	95	95 Business
Federal	22	22
State	1	1
County	1	1

	Primary	Secondary
Trans-Canada		
Provincial Autoroute	22	22
Mexico	1	1
Historic	66	

Boundaries

International	Time zone	
State	Continental Divide	

Points of Interest

○ Town	⚲ Campground information provided by Woodall's ®
⊛ National capital	⚑ Winery
⊛ State/Prov capital	⊛ Customs station
■ AAA/CAA club location	Historic
■ Feature of interest	△ Mountain peak
⬇ GEM attraction	Rapid transit
12 Hotel listing	Stations
3 Restaurant listing	Metromover
College/University	

About Listed Establishments

AAA/CAA Approved hotels and restaurants are listed on the basis of merit alone after careful evaluation and approval by full-time, professionally trained AAA/CAA inspectors. An establishment's decision to advertise in the TourBook guide has no bearing on its evaluation or rating; nor does inclusion of advertising imply AAA endorsement of products and services.

Information in this guide was believed accurate at the time of publication. However, since changes inevitably occur between annual editions, please contact your AAA travel professional, visit AAA.com or download the AAA mobile app to confirm prices and schedules.

Attraction Listings

ATTRACTION NAME, 3 mi. n. off SR 20A (Main Ave.), consists of 250 acres with Olmsted-designed gardens, a 205-foot marble and coquina bell tower and a Mediterranean-style mansion. One of the state's oldest attractions, the tower and gardens were dedicated to the American people in 1929 by President Calvin Coolidge on behalf of their founder, a Dutch immigrant.

Hours: Gardens daily 8-6. Last admission 1 hour before closing. Visitor center daily 9-5. Estate tours are given at noon and 2. Carillon concerts are given at 1 and 3. Phone ahead to confirm schedule. **Cost:** $10; $3 (ages 5-12). Gardens and estate $16; $8 (ages 5-12). **Phone:** (555) 555-5555.
🔌 GT 🍴 🎪 🚇 Dupont Circle,13

AAA/CAA travel experts may designate an attraction of exceptional interest and quality as a AAA GEM — a *Great Experience for Members®*. See GEM Attraction Index (listed on CONTENTS page) for a complete list of locations.

Consult the online travel guides at AAA.com or visit AAA Mobile for additional things to do if you have time.

Cost

Prices are quoted without sales tax in the local currency (U.S. or Canadian dollars). Children under the lowest age specified are admitted free when accompanied by an adult. Most establishments accept credit cards, but a small number require cash, so please call ahead to verify.

Adventure Travel

Activities such as air tours, hiking, skiing and white-water rafting are listed to provide member information and do not imply AAA/CAA endorsement. For your safety, be aware of inherent risks and adhere to all safety instructions.

Icons

SAVE AAA Discounts & Rewards® member discount

🔌 Electric vehicle charging station on premises. Domestic station information provided by the U.S. Department of Energy. Canadian station information provided by Plug'n Drive Ontario.

GT Guided Tours available

🅐 Camping facilities

🍴 Food on premises

🎾 Recreational activities

🐾 Pets on leash allowed

🎪 Picnicking allowed

In select cities only:

🚇 Mass transit station within 1 mile. Icon is followed by station name and AAA/CAA designated station number within listing.

Information-Only Attraction Listings

Bulleted listings, which include the following categories, are listed for informational purposes as a service to members:

- **Gambling establishments** (even if located in a AAA/CAA Approved hotel)
- **Participatory recreational activities** (those requiring physical exertion or special skills)
- **Wineries that offer tours and tastings**

Mobile Tags

 Scan QR codes throughout the TourBook guide to see online offers, menus, videos and more on your smartphone or tablet. If you need a QR scanner app, download one for free from your app store.

If you see a non-QR code in an ad, check the nearby text for details on which app you'll need to scan it.

Hotel and Restaurant Listings

1 Diamond Rating – AAA/CAA Approved hotels and restaurants are assigned a rating of one to five Diamonds. Red Diamonds distinguish establishments that participate in the AAA/CAA logo licensing program. For details, see p. 11 or AAA.com/Diamonds.

fyi indicates hotels and restaurants that are not AAA/CAA Approved and/or Diamond Rated but are listed to provide additional choices for members:

- **Hotels** may be unrated if they are too new to rate, under construction, under major renovation or have not yet been evaluated; or if they do not meet all AAA requirements. Hotels that do not meet all AAA requirements may be included if they offer member value or are the only option; details are noted in the listing.
- **Restaurants** may be unrated if they have not yet been evaluated by AAA.

2 Classification or Cuisine Type – Noted after the Diamond Rating.

- **Hotel Classifications** indicate the style of operation, overall concept and service level. Subclassifications may also be added. (See p. 12.)
- **Restaurant Cuisine Types** identify the food concept from more than 100 categories. If applicable, a classification may also be added. (See p. 13.)

3 Dollar Amounts – Quoted without sales tax in the local currency (U.S. or Canadian dollars), rounded up to the nearest dollar. Most establishments accept credit cards, but a small number require cash, so please call ahead to verify.

- **Hotel Rates** indicate the publicly available two-person rate or rate range for a standard room, applicable all year.
- **Restaurant Prices** represent the minimum and maximum entrée cost per person. Exceptions may include one-of-a-kind or special market priced items.

4 Spotting Symbol – Ovals containing numbers correspond with numbered location markings on hotel and restaurant spotting maps.

5 Parking – Unless otherwise noted, parking is free, on-site self parking.

6 Hotel Value Nationwide – Blue boxes highlight member benefits available at AAA/CAA Approved locations across a hotel chain. (See Just For Members section for details.)

7 Hotel Unit Limited Availability – Unit types, amenities and room features preceded by "some" are available on a limited basis, potentially as few as one.

8 Hotel Terms – Cancellation and minimum stay policies are listed. Unless otherwise noted, most properties offer a full deposit refund with cancellations received at least 48 hours before standard check-in. Properties that require advance payment may not refund the difference for early departures. "Resort fee" indicates a charge may apply above and beyond the quoted room rate.

9 Hotel Check-in/Check-out – Unless otherwise noted, check-in is after 3 p.m. and check-out is before 10 a.m.

10 Restaurant Dress Code – Unless otherwise noted, dress is casual or dressy casual.

11 Restaurant Menu – Where indicated, menus may be viewed in a secure online environment at AAA.com or, if a mobile tag is provided, via the restaurant's website.

12 Hotel Icons – May be preceded by CALL and/or SOME UNITS.

Member Information:

SAVE Member rates: discounted standard room rate or lowest public rate available at time of booking for dates of stay.

ECO Eco-certified by government or private organization.

⊑ Electric vehicle charging station on premises. Domestic station information provided by the U.S. Department of Energy. Canadian station information provided by Plug'n Drive Ontario.

☒ Smoke-free premises

In select cities only:

🚇 Mass transit station within 1 mile. Icon is followed by station name and AAA/CAA designated station number within listing.

Services:

✈ Airport transportation

🐾 Pets allowed (Call property for restrictions.)

S🐾 Pets allowed (Call property for restrictions and fees.)

🍴 Restaurant on premises

🍴⁺ Restaurant off premises

🍽 Room service for 2 or more meals

🍸 Full bar

HOTEL LISTING

HOTEL NAME   (555)555-5555 **50**

◆◆◆ Hotel
$109-$199

LOGO **AAA Benefit:** Members save a minimum 5% off the best available rate.

Address: 300 Main St 55555 **Location:** I-275 exit 31 southbound; exit 30 northbound, 1.6 mi w on SR 688 (Oak Rd). Dupont Circle, 13. **Facility:** 149 units, some efficiencies. 3 stories, interior corridors. **Parking:** on-site (fee). **Terms:** check-in 4 pm, cancellation fee imposed, resort fee. **Amenities:** video games. **Pool(s):** heated outdoor. **Activities:** hot tub, exercise room. **Guest Services:** valet and coin laundry. **Featured Amenity:** continental breakfast.

RESTAURANT LISTING

RESTAURANT NAME   555/555-5555

◆◆◆ Continental Fine Dining
$15-$35

AAA Inspector Notes: *Historic.* A romantic aura punctuates the modern and casual dining room, which is accented with floral arrangements and dramatic, freshly cut branches. The menu features seasonal ingredients. The pastry chef's decadent creations are popular. Semiformal attire. **Features:** full bar, patio dining, happy hour. **Address:** 26 N Main St 55555 **Location:** SR A1A southbound, 2.7 mi s of jct SR 520. Dupont Circle, 13.
Menu on AAA.com

Child care

BIZ Business area

Accessible features (Call property for available services and amenities.)

Activities:
Full-service casino
Pool
Health club on premises

In-Room Amenities:
HS High-speed Internet service
SHS High-speed Internet service (Call property for fees.)
Wireless Internet service
Wireless Internet service (Call property for fees.)
No wireless Internet service
Pay movies
Refrigerator
Microwave
Coffee maker
No air conditioning
No TV
No telephones

13 Restaurant Icons
SAVE AAA Discounts & Rewards® member discount
ECO Eco-certified by government or private organization.
Electric vehicle charging station on premises. Domestic station information provided by the U.S. Department of Energy. Canadian station information provided by Plug'n Drive Ontario.
No air conditioning
Accessible features (Call property for available services and amenities.)
Designated smoking section
B Breakfast
L Lunch
D Dinner
24 Open 24 hours
LATE Open after 11 p.m.
Pet-friendly (Call property for restrictions.)

In select cities only:
Mass transit station within 1 mile. Icon is followed by station name and AAA/CAA designated station number within listing.

Just For Members

Understanding the Diamond Ratings

Hotel and restaurant evaluations are unscheduled to ensure our professionally trained inspectors encounter the same experience members do.

- When an establishment is Diamond Rated, it means members can expect a good fit with their needs. The inspector assigns a rating that indicates the type of experience to expect.
- While establishments at high levels must offer increasingly complex personalized services, establishments at every level are subject to the same basic requirements for cleanliness, comfort and hospitality. Learn more at AAA.com/Diamonds.

Hotels

Budget-oriented, offering basic comfort and hospitality.

Affordable, with modestly enhanced facilities, décor and amenities.

Distinguished, multifaceted with enhanced physical attributes, amenities and guest comforts.

Refined, stylish with upscale physical attributes, extensive amenities and high degree of hospitality, service and attention to detail.

Ultimate luxury, sophistication and comfort with extraordinary physical attributes, meticulous personalized service, extensive amenities and impeccable standards of excellence.

Restaurants

Simple, economical food, often self-service, in a functional environment.

Familiar food, often cooked to order, served in relaxed surroundings.

Popular cuisine, skillfully prepared and served, with expanded beverage options, in enhanced setting.

Imaginative, market-fresh food creatively prepared and skillfully served, often with wine steward, amid upscale ambience.

Cutting-edge cuisine of the finest ingredients, uniquely prepared by an acclaimed chef, served by expert service staff led by maître d' in extraordinary surroundings.

What's the difference?

Red Diamonds mark establishments that participate in the AAA/CAA logo licensing program for increased visibility to members.

Black Diamonds identify all other AAA/CAA Approved and Diamond Rated establishments.

Hotel Classifications

Quality and comfort are usually consistent across each Diamond Rating level, but décor, facilities and service levels vary by classification.

Berry Manor Inn, Rockland, ME

Bed & Breakfast — Typically owner-operated with a high degree of personal touches. Guests are encouraged to interact during evening and breakfast hours. A continental or full, hot breakfast is included in the room rate.

Killarney Lodge, Algonquin Provincial Park, ON

Cabin — Often located in wooded, rural or waterfront locations. Freestanding units are typically rustic and of basic design. As a rule, essential cleaning supplies, kitchen utensils and complete bed and bath linens are supplied.

Hyatt Regency Clearwater Beach Resort & Spa, Clearwater Beach, FL

Condominium — Apartment-style accommodations of varying design or décor, units often contain one or more bedrooms, a living room, full kitchen and an eating area. As a rule, essential cleaning supplies, kitchen utensils and complete bed and bath linens are supplied.

Montpelier Plantation and Beach, St. Kitts and Nevis

Cottage — Often located in wooded, rural, or waterfront locations. Freestanding units are typically home-style in design and décor. As a rule, essential cleaning supplies, kitchen utensils and complete bed and bath linens are supplied.

Nottoway Plantation & Resort, White Castle, LA

Country Inn — Although similar in definition to a bed and breakfast, country inns are usually larger in scale with spacious public areas and offer a dining facility that serves breakfast and dinner.

The Shores Resort & Spa, Daytona Beach Shores, FL

Hotel — Typically a multistory property with interior room entrances and a variety of guest unit styles. The magnitude of the public areas is determined by the overall theme, location and service level, but may include a variety of facilities such as a restaurant, shops, a fitness center, a spa, a business center and meeting rooms.

All Star Vacation Homes, Kissimmee, FL

House — Freestanding units of varying home-style design. Typically larger scale, often containing two or more bedrooms, a living room, a full kitchen, a dining room and multiple bathrooms. As a rule, essential cleaning supplies, kitchen utensils and complete bed and bath linens are supplied.

Bryce View Lodge, Bryce Canyon City, UT

Motel — A one- or two-story roadside property with exterior room entrances and drive up parking. Public areas and facilities are often limited in size and/or availability.

Vista Verde Guest Ranch, Clark, CO

Ranch — Typically a working ranch featuring an obvious rustic, Western theme, equestrian-related activities and a variety of guest unit styles.

Hotel Subclassifications

These additional descriptives may be added to the classification for more information:

- **Boutique** — Often thematic, typically informal yet highly personalized; may have a luxurious or quirky style that is fashionable or unique.
- **Casino** — Extensive gambling facilities are available, such as blackjack, craps, keno and slot machines.
- **Classic** — Renowned and landmark properties, older than 50 years, well known for their unique style and ambience.
- **Contemporary** — Overall theme reflects characteristics of present mainstream trends.
- **Extended Stay** — Offers a predominance of long-term accommodations with a designated full-service kitchen area within each unit.
- **Historic** — More than 75 years old with one of the following documented historical features: Maintains the integrity of the historical nature, listed on the National Register of Historic Places, designated a National Historic Landmark or located in a National Register Historic District.
- **Resort** — Extensive recreational facilities and programs may include golf, tennis, skiing, fishing, water sports, spa

treatments or professionally guided activities.
- **Retro** — Overall theme reflects a contemporary design that reinterprets styles from a past era.
- **Vacation Rental** — Typically houses, condos, cottages or cabins; these properties are "home away from home" self-catering accommodations.
- **Vintage** — Overall theme reflects upon and maintains the authentic traits and experience of a past era.

Restaurant Classifications

If applicable, in addition to the cuisine type noted under the Diamond Rating, restaurant listings may also include one or both classifications:

- **Classic** — Renowned and landmark operation in business for 25 plus years; unique style and ambience.
- **Historic** — Meets one of the following: Listed on National Register of Historic Places, designated a National Historic Landmark or located in a National Register Historic District.

Service Animals

Under the Americans with Disabilities Act (ADA), U.S. businesses that serve the public must allow people with disabilities to bring their service animals into all areas of the facility where customers are normally allowed to go.

Businesses may ask if an animal is a service animal and what tasks the animal has been trained to perform. Businesses may not ask about the person's disability, require special identification for the animal or request removal of the animal from the premises except in limited cases that require alternate assistance. Businesses may not charge extra fees for service animals, including standard pet fees, but may charge for damage caused by service animals if guests are normally charged for damage they cause.

Call the U.S. Department of Justice ADA Information Line: (800) 514-0301 or TTY (800) 514-0383, or visit ada.gov. Regulations may differ in Canada.

AAA/CAA Approved Hotels

For members, AAA/CAA Approved means quality assured.

- Only properties that meet basic requirements for cleanliness, comfort and hospitality pass inspection.
- Approved hotels receive a Diamond Rating that tells members the type of experience to expect.

Guest Safety

Inspectors view a sampling of rooms during evaluations and, therefore, AAA/CAA cannot guarantee the presence of working locks and operational fire safety equipment in every guest unit.

Member Rates

AAA/CAA members can generally expect to pay no more than the maximum TourBook listed rate for a standard room. Member discounts apply to rates quoted within the rate range and are applicable at the time of booking. Listed rates are usually based on last standard room availability. Rates may fluctuate within the range and vary by season and room type. Obtain current AAA/CAA member rates and make reservations at AAA.com.

Exceptions

- Rates for properties operating as concessionaires for the U.S. National Park Service are not guaranteed due to governing regulations.
- Special advertised rates and short-term promotional rates below the rate range are not subject to additional member discounts.
- During special events, hotels may temporarily increase room rates, not recognize discounts or modify pricing policies. Special events may include Mardi Gras, the Kentucky Derby (including pre-Derby events), college football games, holidays, holiday periods and state fairs. Although some special events are listed in the TourBook guides and on AAA.com, it's always wise to check in advance with AAA travel professionals for specific dates.

If you are charged more than the maximum TourBook listed rate, question the additional charge. If an exception is not in effect and management refuses to adhere to the published rate, pay for the room and contact AAA/CAA. The amount paid above the stated maximum will be refunded if our investigation indicates an unjustified charge.

Reservations and Cancellations

When making your reservation, identify yourself as a AAA/CAA member and request written confirmation of your room type, rate, dates of stay, and cancellation and refund policies. At registration, show your membership card.

To cancel, contact the hotel, your AAA/CAA club office or AAA.com, depending on how you booked your reservation. Request a cancellation number or proof of cancellation.

If your room is not as specified and you have written confirmation of your reservation for a specific room type, you should be given the option of choosing a different room or receiving a refund. If management refuses to issue a refund, contact AAA/CAA.

Contacting AAA/CAA About Approved Properties

If your visit to a AAA/CAA Approved attraction, hotel or restaurant doesn't meet your expectations, please tell us about it — **during your visit or within 30 days.** Be sure to save your receipts and other documentation for reference.

Use the easy online form at AAA.com/TourBookComments to send us the details.

Alternatively, you can email your comments to: memberrelations@national.aaa.com or submit them via postal mail to: AAA Member Comments, 1000 AAA Dr., Box 61, Heathrow, FL 32746.

AAA/CAA Preferred Hotels

All AAA/CAA Approved hotels are committed to providing quality, value and member service. In addition, those designated as AAA/CAA Preferred Hotels also offer these extra values at Approved locations nationwide. Valid AAA/CAA membership required.

- **Best AAA/CAA member rates for your dates of stay**.
- **Seasonal promotions and special member offers.** Visit AAA.com to view current offers.
- **Member benefit.** See the blue boxes in hotel listings for the chains shown in the right-hand column below to find values offered at AAA/CAA Approved locations nationwide, subject to availability. Details valid at the time of publication and may change without notice.

- **Total satisfaction guarantee.** If you book your stay with AAA/CAA Travel and your stay fails to meet your expectations, you can apply for a full refund. Bring the complaint to the hotel's attention during the stay and request resolution; if the complaint is not resolved by the hotel, ask your AAA/CAA travel agent to request resolution through the AAA/CAA Assured Stay program.

DISCOUNTS »REWARDS

PREFERRED HOTELS

Rewards

PREFERRED HOTELS

ASSURED STAY
Total Satisfaction Guarantee

BEST WESTERN®, BEST WESTERN PLUS®, EXECUTIVE RESIDENCY, Vib, BEST WESTERN PREMIER® and BW Premier Collection℠

Hilton Hotels & Resorts, Waldorf Astoria™ Hotels & Resorts, Conrad® Hotels & Resorts, Canopy by Hilton, Curio - A Collection by Hilton™, DoubleTree by Hilton™, Embassy Suites Hotels™, Hilton Garden Inn™, Hampton Inn™, Homewood Suites by Hilton™, Home2 Suites by Hilton™ and Hilton Grand Vacations™

Park Hyatt®, Andaz®, Grand Hyatt®, Hyatt Centric®, Hyatt®, Hyatt Regency®, Hyatt Place®, HYATT house®, Hyatt Zilara® and Hyatt Ziva®

JW Marriott®, Autograph Collection® Hotels, Renaissance® Hotels, Marriott Hotels®, Delta Hotels and Resorts®, Gaylord Hotels®, AC Hotels by Marriott®, Courtyard®, Residence Inn®, SpringHill Suites®, Fairfield Inn & Suites® and TownePlace Suites®

MGM RESORTS INTERNATIONAL

Bellagio®, ARIA®, Vdara®, MGM Grand®, The Signature at MGM Grand®, Mandalay Bay®, Delano™ Las Vegas, The Mirage®, Monte Carlo™, New York-New York®, Luxor®, Excalibur® and Circus Circus® Las Vegas

starwood Hotels and Resorts

St. Regis®, The Luxury Collection®, W®, Westin®, Le Méridien®, Sheraton®, Four Points® by Sheraton, Aloft®, element® and Tribute Portfolio™

Member Discounts

Visit AAA.com/searchfordiscounts to find locations and available member discounts. Your AAA/CAA club may offer even greater discounts on theme park tickets. Amtrak and theme park discounts may be used for up to six tickets; restaurant savings may be used for up to six patrons. Other restrictions may apply. All offers subject to change. For complete restrictions, visit your AAA office or AAA.com/restrictions.

ATTRACTIONS

Six Flags

- Save on admission at the gate, participating AAA/CAA offices or AAA.com/SixFlags.

- Save 10% on merchandise of $15 or more at in-park stores.

Universal Orlando Resort and Universal Studios Hollywood

- Save on tickets at select AAA/CAA offices or AAA.com/Universal. In-park savings available in FL.

- Save 10% on Blue Man Group tickets and at select food and merchandise venues at Universal CityWalk®.

DINING

Hard Rock Cafe

- Save 10% on food, nonalcoholic beverages and merchandise at all locations in the U.S. and Canada, plus select international locations. Visit AAA.com/HardRock for full listing.

Landry's Seafood House, The Crab House, Chart House, Oceanaire, Saltgrass Steak House, Muer Seafood Restaurants and Aquarium Restaurants

- Save 10% on food and nonalcoholic beverages at all of the above restaurants.

- Save 10% on merchandise at Aquarium, Downtown Aquarium and Rainforest Cafe restaurants.

SHOPPING

adidas Outlet

- Save 20% on the entire purchase. Visit AAA.com/adidasoutlet for list of locations.

Reebok & Rockport Outlet

- Save 20% on the entire purchase. Visit AAA.com/Reebok for list of locations.

Tanger Outlet Centers

- Receive a free coupon book with discounts up to 50% at select merchants.

TRANSPORTATION

Amtrak

- Save 10% on rail fare booked at least three days in advance of travel date at AAA.com/Amtrak.

El Monte RV

- Save up to 10% on nightly rates booked at least 24 hours in advance of pickup at AAA.com/ElMonteRV or (800) 337-2156.

Hertz

- Save on daily, weekend, weekly and monthly rentals at AAA.com/Hertz or (800) 654-3080.

RACK UP THE REWARDS

Make membership an even more rewarding experience.

The AAA Member Rewards Visa® credit card lets you earn reward points on all of your purchases. Apply for an account today and let the rewards start rolling in!

 Earn 1 point for every $1 in purchases with your AAA Member Rewards Visa® card!*

 Earn 2X points for gas, grocery and drug store purchases!

 Earn 3X points on qualifying AAA and travel purchases!

 Redeem for cash or get a AAA Voucher that gives you up to 40% more value!**

 Exclusive rewards to make you smile!

VISIT AAA.com/creditcard   **STOP BY** any AAA branch

Grand Canyon National Park

Arizona

Close your eyes and think about Arizona. Chances are the images that first come to mind are those of the Old West—cowboys, Native Americans, deserts, cacti—stuff straight out of TV Westerns.

Cowboys still do exist here, but they're more likely to be found assisting city slickers at modern guest ranches than lassoing cattle on a trail drive.

Native Americans, the first Arizonans, though a small percentage of today's population, are a major influence in everyday life. Reminders of their heritage are evident in national monuments, tribal parks and historic sites that preserve their ancient dwellings, customs and crafts.

As for the deserts, well, the sand and the intricate rock formations are still there, but their expanse is now broken by major metropolitan areas like Phoenix and Tucson and golf courses that seem strangely out of place. And rare species of cactus, such as

Taliesin West, Scottsdale

the organ pipe and saguaro, are protected in their own preserves.

The Grand Canyon State

"Did the government build it?"

More than one flabbergasted visitor has asked this upon first seeing Arizona's Grand Canyon. Though it may sound preposterous, it's a question you'll find less naive after gazing at these myriad erosion-carved columns, arches and windows—a virtual cityscape of landforms that would make a Manhattanite feel at home.

No doubt Uncle Sam would love to claim responsibility for the Grand Canyon, but only Father Time can take credit for this natural wonder. Over millions of years geologic upheaval forced a former sea bottom into the sky, allowing wind and water to work their rock-sculpting magic. The result: a spectacle so awesome that some 5 million people from all over the world visit each year.

The South Rim area boasts many of the best vantage points from which to gape at the canyon in all its multihued glory. What's more, the tall pine trees here hide the great chasm from view until you are almost at its edge. Confronting this breathtaking scene as you emerge from the forest is an unforgettable experience.

In the early morning and late afternoon, colors dance along canyon walls in the rapidly changing sunlight. If a storm comes your way, don't despair: Shadows of rain clouds can create striking patterns of darkness as they drift across the canyon's depths.

But even after visiting the Grand Canyon, don't think you've seen it all. An equally spectacular play of color and light awaits you at Monument Valley Navajo Tribal Park. Here you just might feel like you're walking through a Hollywood set, and with good reason: The valley, with its rose-tinted buttes and mesas, has served as backdrop for countless Westerns and car commercials.

Grand Canyon visitors frequently overlook another Arizona jewel—Sedona's Red Rock territory. Oak Creek Canyon has its own collection of buttes, spires and sheer rock walls that shimmer with shades of beige, ocher, salmon and scarlet. Beat the heat and go with Oak Creek's flow at Slide Rock State Park, where a waterslide—natural, not man-made—splashes from pool to pool.

"Married to the Ground"

Ancient cliff dwellings at Montezuma Castle, Canyon de Chelly and Navajo national monuments blend with their environs so well, they seem to have sprouted from the precipices they're perched upon.

Centuries after these towns in the sky were abandoned, architect Frank Lloyd Wright designed buildings—notably Taliesin West, his former home and studio in Scottsdale—according to his belief that they should harmoniously coexist with their surroundings.

Wright once encapsulated his design philosophy by saying his buildings were "married to the ground." It's easy to see why he chose Arizona as his studio's setting. Here the terrain seems a willing companion to man's handiwork: mesas rise from the desert like skyscrapers and pinnacles soar like church spires.

Recreation

Canyons. Mountains. Forests. Lakes. The extensive Colorado River. Arizona, derived from the Native American word meaning "little spring," is a veritable fountain of fun for outdoor types.

Hopefully you packed your putter. With more than 350 golf courses to choose from, people drive from all over the country to chip and putt. But watch out for hazards—Mesa, Phoenix, northern Scottsdale and Tucson are chock-full of challenging fairways.

Then there's *the* Canyon, the grandest of them all. For a bird's-eye view, try a helicopter or airplane tour; or capture that Old West spirit of adventure on a train ride from Williams. Peer off the edge while hiking along the South Rim Trail—the panorama will

knock your socks off.

If you're more adventurous, follow Bright Angel Trail into the depths of the gorge. The South Kaibab and North Kaibab trails also are good treks on foot or on hoof: Mule rides are available for 2-day jaunts (advance reservations are required). Since it takes a full day to reach the canyon floor, camping is a popular option; contact Trip Planner, (928) 638-7888, for a backcountry permit.

Despite Arizona's arid landscape, there are plenty of places to find refreshment. Dip your toes, skis, jet ski, sailboard or speedboat into Glen Canyon National Recreation Area's Lake Powell or Lake Mead National Recreation Area's lakes Mead and Mojave. Why not explore the Colorado River on a peaceful float trip or an adrenaline-pumping ride through white-water rapids?

If fishing is your sport, head for the waters of the White Mountains, where you can hook all sorts of trout and bass. For information about hunting trophy elk or other game, contact the Arizona Game and Fish Department.

When it gets chilly, skiing at the Arizona Snowbowl, north of Flagstaff in the Coconino National Forest, is the cool thing to do. Other places to catch a chairlift are Sunrise Park, in Greer; Mount Lemmon, north of Tucson; and Elk Ridge Ski and Outdoor Recreation Area, in Williams.

Glen Canyon National Recreation Area's Lake Powell

Historic Timeline

1539	Franciscan friar Marcos de Niza searches unsuccessfully for the fabled Seven Cities of Cíbola throughout the Southwest.
1853	The Gadsden Purchase brings a portion of present-day southern Arizona and southern New Mexico under U.S. control.
1889	Phoenix is chosen as the territorial capital.
1911	The completion of the Roosevelt Dam on the Salt River delivers much-needed water to the area.
1912	Arizona enters the Union as the 48th state.
1919	Grand Canyon is designated a national park.
1966	The Miranda vs. Arizona ruling stipulates that arrested persons must be informed of their rights before any questioning occurs.
1973	Construction begins on the Central Arizona Project to bring Colorado River water to dry parts of the state.
1981	Arizonan Sandra Day O'Connor is appointed as the first woman member of the U.S. Supreme Court.
1991	Eight scientists researching ecosystem sustainability begin living in the glass-enclosed biomes of Biosphere 2 in Oracle.
2001	In just their fourth season, the Arizona Diamondbacks defeat the New York Yankees in the World Series.

What To Pack

Temperature Averages Maximum/Minimum	JANUARY	FEBRUARY	MARCH	APRIL	MAY	JUNE	JULY	AUGUST	SEPTEMBER	OCTOBER	NOVEMBER	DECEMBER
Flagstaff	41/14	44/17	48/20	57/27	67/33	76/40	81/50	78/49	74/41	63/31	51/22	43/16
Grand Canyon NP	41/17	45/20	51/24	59/30	69/37	81/45	83/52	80/51	75/45	64/34	53/26	44/17
Kingman	57/31	61/34	66/37	75/42	82/49	94/57	97/67	96/65	90/57	79/47	67/38	56/31
Phoenix	65/38	69/41	74/45	84/52	93/60	101/68	105/77	102/76	98/70	88/57	75/45	66/38
Tucson	63/38	67/40	71/44	81/50	90/57	98/66	98/74	95/72	93/67	84/56	72/49	65/39
Yuma	68/43	73/46	78/50	86/57	93/64	101/71	106/81	104/81	100/74	90/62	76/50	68/44

From the records of The Weather Channel Interactive, Inc.

Good Facts To Know

ABOUT THE STATE

POPULATION: 6,392,017.

AREA: 113,990 square miles; ranks 6th.

CAPITAL: Phoenix.

HIGHEST POINT: 12,643 ft., Humphreys Peak.

LOWEST POINT: 70 ft., Colorado River.

TIME ZONE(S): Mountain. DST on Navajo Reservation only.

GAMBLING

MINIMUM AGE FOR GAMBLING: 21.

REGULATIONS

TEEN DRIVING LAWS: No more than one unrelated passenger under age 18 is permitted for the first six months unless accompanied by a parent or legal guardian. Driving is not permitted midnight-5 a.m. The minimum age for an unrestricted driver's license is 16 years, 6 months. Phone (800) 251-5866.

SEAT BELT/CHILD RESTRAINT LAWS: Seat belts are required for driver and front-seat passengers ages 16 and over. Children ages 8-16 are required to be properly restrained by a booster seat or seat belt. Children ages 5-8 and 57 inches or less in height must use a booster seat. Child restraints are required for children under age 5. AAA recommends seat belts/child restraints for driver and all passengers.

CELLPHONE RESTRICTIONS: Cellphone regulations vary by county and/or city. Phoenix and Tucson ban texting while driving.

HELMETS FOR MOTORCYCLISTS: Required for riders under age 18.

RADAR DETECTORS: Permitted.

MOVE OVER LAW: Driver is required to slow down and vacate the lane nearest stopped police, fire and rescue vehicles using audible or flashing signals. The law also applies to recovery vehicles, such as tow trucks.

FIREARMS LAWS: Varies. Contact the Law Library of Arizona, 1700 W. Washington St., 3rd Floor, Phoenix, AZ 85007; phone (602) 926-3948.

HOLIDAYS

HOLIDAYS: Jan. 1 ■ Martin Luther King Jr. Day, Jan. (3rd Mon.) ■ Presidents Day, Feb. (3rd Mon.) ■ Memorial Day, May (last Mon.) ■ July 4 ■ Labor Day, Sept. (1st Mon.) ■ Columbus Day, Oct. (2nd Mon.) ■ Veterans Day, Nov. 11 ■ Thanksgiving, Nov. (4th Thurs.) ■ Christmas, Dec. 25.

MONEY

TAXES: Arizona's statewide sales tax is 5.6 percent, along with local taxes on goods and services, including lodgings.

VISITOR INFORMATION

INFORMATION CENTERS: Lupton off I-40 westbound exit 359 is a state welcome center that provides details about attractions, accommodations, parks and events.

DAYLIGHT-SAVING TIME:
The Navajo Reservation is the only area in the state to observe daylight-saving time.

NATIVE AMERICAN RESERVATIONS:
Reservations are regarded as sovereign nations, making and enforcing laws pertaining to their land. The following rules are the most relevant to visitors: Alcoholic beverages (including transportation and use) are prohibited; leaving established roadways and hiking cross-country is prohibited unless permission is obtained from the local tribal office; seat belts must be worn by motorists; and helmets must be worn by motorcyclists.

FURTHER INFORMATION FOR VISITORS:
Arizona Office of Tourism
1110 W. Washington St., Suite 155
Phoenix, AZ 85007
(602) 364-3700
(866) 275-5816
Phoenix Visitor Center
125 N. 2 St., Suite 120
Phoenix, AZ 85004
(602) 254-6500

NATIONAL FOREST INFORMATION:
Southwestern Region
Public Affairs Office
333 Broadway Blvd. S.E.
Albuquerque, NM 87102
(505) 842-3292
(877) 444-6777 (reservations)

FISHING AND HUNTING REGULATIONS:
Arizona Game and Fish Department
5000 W. Carefree Hwy.
Phoenix, AZ 85086-5000
(602) 942-3000

RECREATION INFORMATION:
Arizona State Parks Board
1300 W. Washington St.
Phoenix, AZ 85007
(602) 542-4174 *(See ad p. 85.)*
Arizona BLM Information Center
1 N. Central Ave., Suite 800
Phoenix, AZ 85004
(602) 417-9300

Arizona Annual Events
Please call ahead to confirm event details.

JANUARY

- Brian Lebel's High Noon Show and Auction / Mesa
480-779-9378
- Arizona National Horse Show / Scottsdale
602-258-8568
- Native American Art Festival Litchfield Park
623-935-9040

FEBRUARY

- Gold Rush Days Wickenburg
928-684-5479
- Cochise Cowboy Poetry and Music Gathering Sierra Vista
520-549-3868
- Arizona Matsuri / Phoenix
602-262-5029

MARCH

- Arizona State Open Chili Championship Casa Grande
520-560-2256
- Heard Museum Guild Indian Fair and Market Phoenix
602-252-8840
- Midnight at the Oasis Festival / Yuma
928-343-1715

APRIL

- Maricopa County Fair Phoenix
602-252-0717
- Scottsdale Culinary Festival Scottsdale
480-945-7193
- Rose Tree Festival Tombstone
520-457-3326

MAY

- Cinco de Mayo Celebration and Chihuahua Races Chandler
480-782-2665
- Peach Festival Queen Creek
480-987-3100, ext. 1006
- Wyatt Earp Days Tombstone
520-457-3451

JUNE

- Made in the Shade Beer Tasting Festival / Flagstaff
928-779-1775
- Fiber and Wool Festival at Flagstaff / Flagstaff
928-774-6272
- Strawberry Festival / Pine
928-476-3655

JULY

- Fabulous Phoenix Fourth Phoenix
602-261-8645
- Hopi Festival of Arts and Culture / Flagstaff
928-774-5213
- July 4th Tempe Town Lake Festival / Tempe
480-350-5189

AUGUST

- World's Oldest Continuous Rodeo / Payson
928-474-4515
- Eagar Daze / Eagar
928-333-4128, ext. 251
- Summer Series Race Phoenix
602-684-1496

SEPTEMBER

- Navajo Nation Fair Rodeo Window Rock
928-871-6478
- Bisbee Blues Festival Bisbee
520-227-6547
- Oktoberfest / Sierra Vista
520-417-6980

OCTOBER

- Wild Western Festival Glendale
623-521-3856
- Arizona Exposition & State Fair / Phoenix
602-252-6771
- Helldorado Days Tombstone
520-378-5117

NOVEMBER

- Quicken Loans Race For Heroes 500 / Avondale
623-463-5400
- Colorado River Crossing Balloon Festival / Yuma
928-343-1715
- Tucson Celtic Festival and Scottish Highland Games Tucson
520-349-4345

DECEMBER

- Boat Parade of Lights Lake Havasu City
928-680-4652
- Tempe Fall Festival of the Arts / Tempe
602-997-2601
- Pueblo Grande Museum Indian Market / Phoenix
602-495-0901

Tumacácori National Historical
Park

Downtown Phoenix

Cactus in the Sonoran
Desert

Petrified Forest National Park

Grand Canyon Railway, Williams

Index: Great Experience for Members

AAA editor's picks of exceptional note

Arizona Capitol Museum

Heard Museum

Musical Instrument Museum

Phoenix Art Museum

See Orientation map on p. 34 for corresponding grid coordinates, if applicable.

Tuzigoot National Monument (C-3)
Tuzigoot National Monument *(See p. 297.)*

Walnut Canyon National Monument (C-4)
Walnut Canyon National Monument *(See p. 297.)*

Williams (C-3)
Grand Canyon Railway *(See p. 301.)*

Winslow (C-5)
Meteor Crater *(See p. 305.)*

Wupatki National Monument (B-4)
Wupatki National Monument *(See p. 306.)*

Arizona Atlas Section

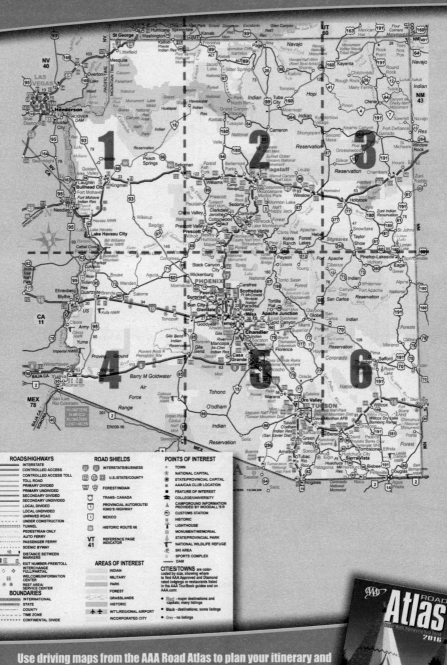

ROADS/HIGHWAYS
- INTERSTATE
- CONTROLLED ACCESS
- CONTROLLED ACCESS TOLL
- TOLL ROAD
- PRIMARY DIVIDED
- PRIMARY UNDIVIDED
- SECONDARY DIVIDED
- SECONDARY UNDIVIDED
- LOCAL DIVIDED
- LOCAL UNDIVIDED
- UNPAVED ROAD
- UNDER CONSTRUCTION
- TUNNEL
- PEDESTRIAN ONLY
- AUTO FERRY
- PASSENGER FERRY
- SCENIC BYWAY
- DISTANCE BETWEEN MARKERS
- EXIT NUMBER-FREE/TOLL
- INTERCHANGE FULL/PARTIAL
- WELCOME/INFORMATION CENTER
- REST AREA/ SERVICE CENTER

BOUNDARIES
- INTERNATIONAL
- STATE
- COUNTY
- TIME ZONE
- CONTINENTAL DIVIDE

ROAD SHIELDS
- INTERSTATE/BUSINESS
- U.S./STATE/COUNTY
- FOREST/INDIAN
- TRANS-CANADA
- PROVINCIAL AUTOROUTE/ KING'S HIGHWAY
- MEXICO
- HISTORIC ROUTE 66
- VT 41 REFERENCE PAGE INDICATOR

AREAS OF INTEREST
- INDIAN
- MILITARY
- PARK
- FOREST
- GRASSLANDS
- HISTORIC
- INT'L/REGIONAL AIRPORT
- INCORPORATED CITY

POINTS OF INTEREST
- TOWN
- NATIONAL CAPITAL
- STATE/PROVINCIAL CAPITAL
- AAA/CAA CLUB LOCATION
- FEATURE OF INTEREST
- COLLEGE/UNIVERSITY
- CAMPGROUND INFORMATION PROVIDED BY WOODALL'S®
- CUSTOMS STATION
- HISTORIC
- LIGHTHOUSE
- MONUMENT/MEMORIAL
- STATE/PROVINCIAL PARK
- NATIONAL WILDLIFE REFUGE
- SKI AREA
- SPORTS COMPLEX
- DAM

CITIES/TOWNS
are color-coded by size, showing where to find AAA Approved and Diamond rated lodgings or restaurants listed in the AAA TourBook guides and on AAA.com:
- Red - major destinations and capitals; many listings
- Black - destinations; some listings
- Grey - no listings

Atlas ROAD 2016

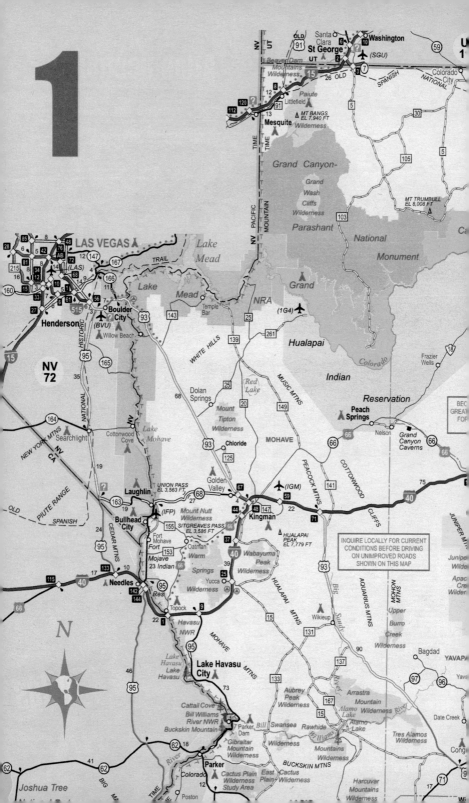

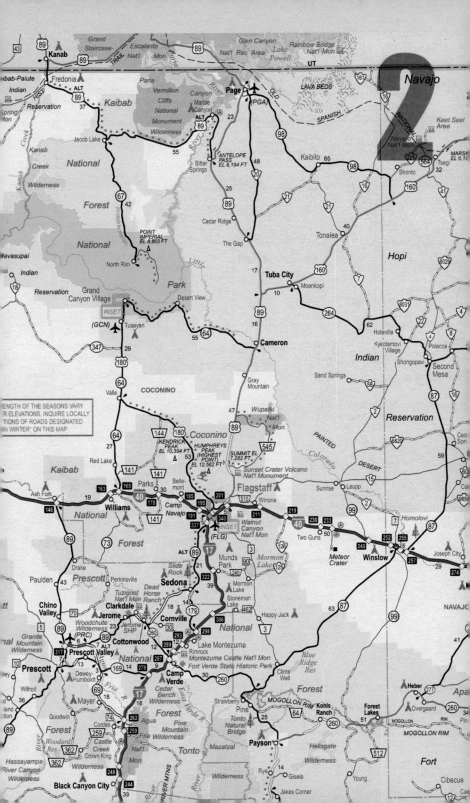

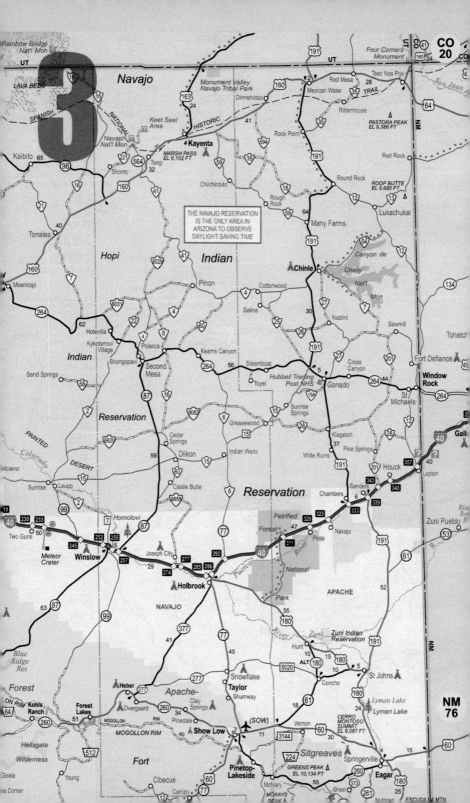

3

Rainbow Bridge Nat'l Mon

UT

LAVA BEDS

SPANISH

Navajo

Kaibito 65

98

21

40

Tonalea

160

7

Moenkopi

264

62

Hotevilla

Kykotsmovi Village

Shongopavi

Polacca

Second Mesa

Sand Springs

58

Reservation

PAINTED

Colorado

DESERT

Sunrise

Leupp

99

19

40 230 233

Two Guns 50

245 252

Meteor Crater

Winslow

257

63 87

99

Blue Ridge Res

Forest

ON RIM Kohls Ranch

64 260

51

Hellsgate Wilderness

Gisela

Young

Navajo Nat'l Mon

Shonto

221 564

Tsegi 32

Keet Seel Area

HISTORIC

Monument Valley Navajo Tribal Park

163

24

MARSH PASS EL 6,102 FT

Kayenta

18

41

Chilchinbito

Dinnehotso

160

Rock Point

Rough Rock

59

64

Many Farms

191

THE NAVAJO RESERVATION IS THE ONLY AREA IN ARIZONA TO OBSERVE DAYLIGHT SAVING TIME

Pinon

6029

Hopi

Indian

8031

22

4

8

60

Keams Canyon

264

56

Toyei

Steamboat

Hubbell Trading Post NHS

9062

6

Greasewood

15

Cedar Springs

6820

59

Dilkon

15

Indian Wells

15

Sunrise Springs

28

60

Castle Butte

9859

6

Reservation

Hornolovi

7

87

Joseph City

29

277

274

292

285 286

Holbrook

NAVAJO

41

377

77

45

Snowflake

Taylor

Shumway

5020

ALT 180

Forest Lakes

Overgaard

277

260

MOGOLLON

34

Pinedale

RIM

RD

Clay Springs

Apache-

512

Cibecue

Fort

60

Carrizo

77

Pinetop-Lakeside

McNary

MCKAYS PEAK

GREENS PEAK EL 10,134 FT

Show Low

3

(SOW)

11

Vernon

3144

61

Concho

St Johns

180

Lyman Lake

Lyman Lake

24

CERRO MONTOSO SUMMIT EL 8,087 FT

60

30

Sitgreaves

224

Springerville

Greer

261

Eagar

260

373

Nutrioso

180

60

15

4

ESCUDILLA MTN

UT

160

24

Four Corners Monument

Red Mesa

28

Teec Nos Pos

TRAIL

35

Mexican Water

Rittenhouse

PASTORA PEAK EL 9,386 FT

Round Rock

ROOF BUTTE EL 9,685 FT

12

Lukachukai

Canyon de Chelly Nat'l Mon

Chinle

Cottonwood

Salina

30

Nazlini

Sawmill

27

Tohatchi

134

191

Cross Canyon

5

Ganado

264

44

St Michaels

Window Rock

264

12

Klagetoh

37

Pine Springs

Wide Ruins

191

201

Houck

343

Sanders

6

357

40

Lupton

348

339

333

Chambers

52

APACHE

180

35

Zuni

River

Hunt

10

15

180

10

5

Zuni Indian Reservation

191

53

Zuni Pueblo

61

Gall

40

2

NM

San Juan R

64

Red Rock

594

18

Rock Point

635

64

Petrified

Forest

47

320 325

311

Pinta

Navajo

National

Park

Puerco

River

Blue Ro

R

Kaibito 65

Tsegi

24

Kayenta

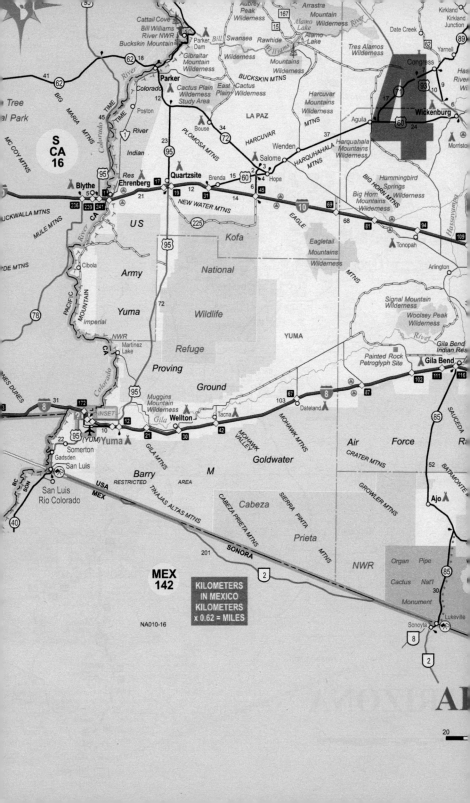

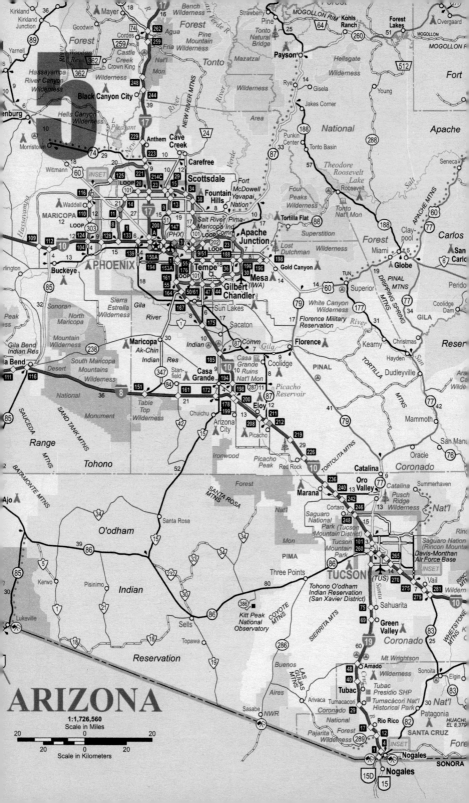

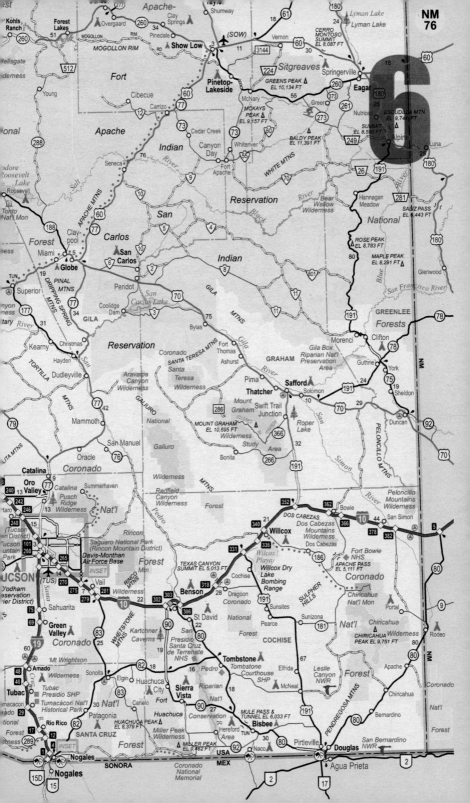

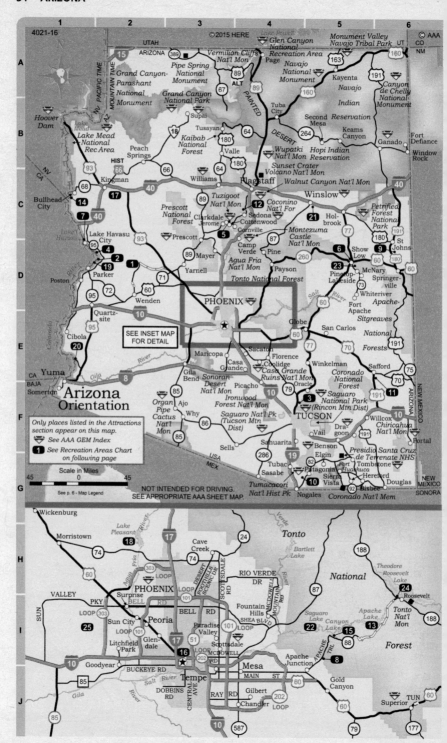

Recreation Areas Chart

The map location numerals in column 2 show an area's location on the preceding map.

	MAP LOCATION	CAMPING	PICNICKING	HIKING TRAILS	BOATING	BOAT RAMP	BOAT RENTAL	FISHING	SWIMMING	PETS ON LEASH	BICYCLE TRAILS	WINTER SPORTS	VISITOR CENTER	LODGE/CABINS	FOOD SERVICE
NATIONAL PARKS *(See place listings.)*															
Grand Canyon (A-3) 1,218,376 acres.		•	•	•				•		•		•	•	•	•
Saguaro (F-5) 91,000 acres.		•	•	•						•	•	•	•		
NATIONAL FORESTS *(See place listings.)*															
Apache-Sitgreaves (D-6) 2.1 million acres. East-central Arizona.		•	•	•	•	•		•	•	•	•	•			•
Coconino (C-4) 1,821,495 acres. Northern Arizona.		•	•	•	•	•	•	•	•	•	•	•		•	•
Coronado (E-5) 1,780,196 acres. Southeastern Arizona.		•	•	•	•	•	•	•	•	•	•	•	•		
Kaibab (B-3) 1.6 million acres. Northern Arizona.		•	•	•	•	•		•		•	•	•		•	•
Prescott (C-3) 1,238,154 acres. Central Arizona. Electric boat motors only. Horse rental.		•	•	•	•	•	•	•	•	•	•	•			
Tonto (H-4) 2,900,000 acres. Central Arizona.		•	•	•	•	•	•	•	•	•					•
NATIONAL RECREATION AREAS *(See place listings.)*															
Glen Canyon (A-4) 1,250,000 acres.		•	•	•	•	•	•	•	•	•				•	•
Lake Mead (B-1) 1,500,000 acres. Southeastern Nevada. Scuba diving.		•	•	•	•	•	•	•	•	•	•			•	•
STATE															
Alamo Lake (D-2) 2,858 acres 38 mi. n. of US 60 via a paved road. *(See Wenden p. 298.)*	**1**	•	•	•	•	•		•		•	•		•		•
Buckskin Mountain (D-2) 1,677 acres 11 mi. n. off SR 95. *(See Parker p. 119.)*	**2**	•	•	•	•	•	•	•	•	•	•		•		•
Catalina (F-5) 5,500 acres 9 mi. n. off SR 77. *(See Tucson p. 266.)*	**3**	•	•	•					•	•	•		•		
Cattail Cove (D-2) 2,375 acres off SR 95. *(See Lake Havasu City p. 101.)*	**4**	•	•	•	•	•		•	•	•					•
Dead Horse Ranch (C-3) 423 acres off 10th St. Bird-watching; horse trails. *(See Cottonwood p. 55.)*	**5**	•	•	•	•	•		•	•	•	•		•		
Fool Hollow Lake (D-5) 686 acres 2 mi. n. of US 60 off SR 260, then e. on Old Linden Rd. to 32nd Ave. *(See Show Low p. 238.)*	**6**	•	•	•	•	•	•	•	•	•					
Lake Havasu (C-1) 928 acres n. of London Bridge off London Bridge Rd. *(See Lake Havasu City p. 101.)*	**7**	•	•	•	•	•	•	•	•	•					
Lost Dutchman (I-5) 320 acres 5 mi. n.e. off SR 88. *(See Apache Junction p. 39.)*	**8**	•	•	•						•	•	•			
Lyman Lake (D-6) 1,200 acres 14 mi. n. off US 60 onto US 180/191, then just off SR 81. *(See St. Johns p. 200.)*	**9**	•	•	•	•	•	•	•	•	•	•				•
Patagonia Lake (G-5) 2,659 acres 7 mi. s.w. on SR 82, then 5 mi. w. following signs. *(See Patagonia p. 120.)*	**10**	•	•	•	•	•	•	•	•	•					•
Roper Lake (F-6) 339 acres .5 mi. s. off US 191. *(See Safford p. 198.)*	**11**	•	•	•	•	•		•	•	•	•			•	•
Slide Rock (C-4) 55 acres 7 mi. n. off SR 89A within Oak Creek Canyon. *(See Sedona p. 222.)*	**12**		•	•				•	•	•	•				
OTHER															
Apache Lake (I-5) 2,656 acres 30 mi. n.e. on SR 88. *(See Apache Junction p. 38.)*	**13**	•	•	•	•	•	•	•	•	•				•	•
Bullhead (C-1) 20 acres .25 mi. s. of Bullhead City. No tent camping.	**14**		•		•	•		•	•	•					
Canyon Lake (I-5) 950 acres 16 mi. n.e. on SR 88. *(See Apache Junction p. 38.)*	**15**	•	•	•	•	•	•	•	•	•					•
Encanto (I-3) 66 acres at 2605 N. 15th Ave. Golf (nine and 18 holes). *(See Phoenix p. 135.)*	**16**		•	•					•	•					
Hualapai Mountain (C-2) 2,200 acres 12 mi. s.e. of Kingman. *(See Kingman p. 97.)*	**17**	•	•	•					•	•				•	•
Lake Pleasant (H-2) 24,500 acres 29 mi. e. on SR 74, then 2 mi. n. off Castle Hot Springs Rd. *(See Morristown p. 112.)*	**18**	•	•	•	•	•	•	•	•	•			•		•
La Paz County (D-2) 165 acres 8 mi. n. of Parker via SR 95.	**19**	•	•		•	•		•	•	•					
Martinez Lake (E-1) 600 acres 25 mi. n. of Yuma. Water skiing.	**20**	•	•		•	•		•	•	•				•	•

Recreation Areas Chart

The map location numerals in column 2 show an area's location on the preceding map.

	MAP LOCATION	CAMPING	PICNICKING	HIKING TRAILS	BOATING	BOAT RAMP	BOAT RENTAL	FISHING	SWIMMING	PETS ON LEASH	BICYCLE TRAILS	WINTER SPORTS	VISITOR CENTER	LODGE/CABINS	FOOD SERVICE
McHood (C-5) 160 acres 5 mi. s.e. of Winslow off SR 99.	21	•	•	•	•	•		•	•	•					
Saguaro Lake (I-5) 1,280 acres 25 mi. n.e. of Mesa via US 60 and Bush Hwy. *(See Mesa p. 107.)*	22		•		•	•	•	•	•					•	•
Show Low Lake (D-5) 100 acres 5.5 mi. s.e. of Show Low via SR 260.	23	•	•	•	•	•	•	•							•
Theodore Roosevelt Lake (H-6) 17,315 acres 29 mi. n.w. of Globe via SR 88. *(See Roosevelt p. 198.)*	24	•	•	•	•	•	•	•	•	•			•	•	•
White Tank Mountain (I-1) 26,337 acres 8 mi. s. of Surprise via SR 303, then 4 mi. w. on Olive Ave. Horse trails. *(See Surprise p. 242.)*	25	•	•	•					•	•	•		•		•

Dream.
Plan.
Go.

Picture yourself on the ideal road trip. Make it real with **TripTik® Travel Planner**.

Online: AAA.com/ttp | On the go: AAA or CAA Mobile app

AGUA FRIA NATIONAL MONUMENT (D-4)

North of Phoenix off I-17 exit 259 to Bloody Basin Road or off exit 256 to Badger Springs, Agua Fria National Monument embraces 71,000 acres including the Agua Fria River canyon between Black Canyon City and Cordes Lakes.

The river canyon, at an elevation of 2,150 feet above sea level, and Perry and Black mesas are the primary formations; elevations in the northern hills reach 4,500 feet. The monument preserves thousands of prehistoric sites with more than 450 surveyed and recorded. Petroglyphs, terraced landscapes and pueblo ruins suggest the area was heavily populated A.D. 1250-1450 by an agrarian society skilled at growing food and sustaining life in the desert.

Semidesert grasslands and a riparian forest support abundant wildlife, including pronghorn, mountain lions, javelinas and white-tailed deer.

Camping, hiking and picnicking are permitted. Because the terrain is rugged and rocky, a high-clearance, four-wheel-drive vehicle is recommended in most locations. For further information contact the Monument Manager, Phoenix District, Bureau of Land Management, 21605 N. 7th Ave., Phoenix, AZ 85027; phone (623) 580-5500.

AJO (F-3) pop. 3,304, elev. 1,747'

The name Ajo comes either from the Tohono O'odham word for "paint" or the Spanish name for "garlic." Home to the first copper mine in the state, Ajo did not boom until ore-refining methods made the mining of low-grade ore profitable in the early 1900s.

In 1906 Col. John Greenway formed the New Cornelia Copper Co., which was eventually purchased by one of the nation's largest copper companies, Dodge Corp., in 1921. Visitors to the town can view the New Cornelia Open Pit Mine on Indian Village Road. The mine, which was shut down in 1984, is nearly 2 miles in diameter and 1,000 feet deep. Open October through May, its visitor center features a video and display of the mining operations as well as an observation area; phone (520) 387-7742.

Organ Pipe Cactus National Monument (see place listing p. 115), 32 miles south of Ajo, preserves a portion of the Sonoran Desert; its inhabitants include the statuesque organ pipe cactus as well as such desert foliage as saguaro, paloverde and ocotillo.

As in much of the southwest, the Spanish and Native American influences can be seen in Ajo's Spanish Colonial Revival town square surrounded by a park, mission churches and Southwestern-style buildings. The Ajo Historical Museum, 160 W. Mission St., is housed in a mission church built in the 1930s; phone (520) 387-7105. Other historic buildings include the 1919 Curley School, 201 W. Esperanza Ave., and the historic 1916 Ajo Train Depot,

formerly used by the Tucson, Cornelia and Gila Bend Railroad and now housing the chamber of commerce visitor center, 1 W. Plaza St.

Ajo Chamber of Commerce: 1 W. Plaza St., Ajo, AZ 85321. Phone: (520) 387-7742.

CABEZA PRIETA NATIONAL WILDLIFE REFUGE is at 1611 N. Second Ave.; an entry permit must be obtained at the visitor center. Created in 1939 for the conservation and development of natural wildlife resources and to protect Sonoran Desert wildlife, the 860,000-acre refuge protects desert bighorn sheep and such endangered species as the Sonoran pronghorn, ferruginous pygmy-owl and lesser long-nosed bat. During spring and fall migration periods, visitors may see warblers, swallows, hawks, towhees and falcons.

Note: A four-wheel-drive vehicle is required on most of the refuge. Firearms are legal but shooting is not permitted. Campfires are allowed at three designated campsites: Papago Well, Tule Well and Christmas Pass Camp. At all other campsites, campers (except backpackers) must use charcoal with a ground pan or a propane cookstove. Hours: Mon.-Fri. 8-4. Cost: Free. Phone: (520) 387-6483.

GUEST HOUSE INN   520/387-6133
▼▼▼▼ Historic Bed & Breakfast $89-$99 Address: 700 W Guest House Rd 85321 Location: SR 85, 0.5 mi sw; from town plaza, take La Mina Ave and Hospital Dr. Located in a residential area. Facility: Built in 1925 as a home for visiting mine directors, this inn offers expansive rooms and two enclosed porches. 4 units. 1 story, interior corridors. Terms: 3 day cancellation notice.

LA SIESTA MOTEL & RV RESORT   520/387-6569
▼ Motel $63-$68 Address: 2561 N Ajo-Gila Bend Hwy 85321 Location: On SR 85, 1.8 mi n of town plaza. Facility: 31 units. 1 story, exterior corridors. Terms: cancellation fee imposed. Pool(s): heated outdoor. Activities: hot tub, tennis, picnic facilities. Guest Services: coin laundry.

WHERE TO EAT

100 ESTRELLA RESTAURANT & LOUNGE   520/387-3110
▼▼ American. Casual Dining. $6-$14 AAA Inspector Notes: Situated alongside the historic town square in sleepy Ajo is this family friendly spot known for its gourmet burgers, panini, pizza and an impressive beer selection on tap. Features: beer & wine. Address: 100 W Estrella St 85321 Location: Center. [L] [D]

AMADO pop. 295
• Restaurants p. 38

AMADO TERRITORY B & B   520/398-8684
▼▼▼ Bed & Breakfast. Rates not provided. Address: 3001 E Frontage Rd 85645 Location: I-19 exit 48, just e, then just s. Located on the grounds of Territory Ranch. Facility: A two-story stone fireplace and a sunny breakfast room looking across a dry wash create a charming environment. 10 units, some houses. 2 stories (no elevator), interior corridors. Activities: picnic facilities.

WHERE TO EAT

COW PALACE RESTAURANT & BAR   520/398-8000

WW Steak. Casual Dining. $8-$22 **AAA Inspector Notes:** Besides the grilled steaks, diners can order Mexican dishes, Italian specialties, fresh salads, baby back ribs and grilled or fried fish at this restaurant. Established more than 50 years ago, this has been a frequent stop for travelers heading south from Tucson. **Features:** full bar, happy hour. **Address:** 28802 S Nogales Hwy 85645 **Location:** I-19 exit 48, just w, then just n. [B] [L] [D]

ANTHEM pop. 21,700

HAMPTON INN AT ANTHEM   (623)465-7979

WWW Hotel $89-$249 **Address:** 42415 N 41st Dr 85086 **Location:** I-17 exit 229 (Anthem Way), just w. **Facility:** 76 units. 3 stories, interior corridors. **Terms:** 1-7 night minimum stay, cancellation fee imposed. **Pool(s):** heated outdoor. **Activities:** hot tub, picnic facilities, exercise room. **Guest Services:** coin laundry.

AAA Benefit: Members save up to 10%!

WHERE TO EAT

SHANGHAI CLUB   623/465-3225

WWW Chinese. Casual Dining. $7-$18 **AAA Inspector Notes:** Diners will find traditional Chinese favorites like mu shu pork, sesame chicken, and walnut shrimp, all served in a friendly, casual atmosphere. Service is noticeably speedy. **Features:** full bar. **Address:** 3434 W Anthem Way 85086 **Location:** I-17 exit 229 (Anthem Way), 0.7 mi e. [L] [D]

APACHE JUNCTION (J-5) pop. 35,840, elev. 1,715'
• Part of Phoenix area — see map p. 126

As its name implies, Apache Junction—the western terminus of the Apache Trail—is at the junction of US 60 and SR 88. The surrounding desert, lakes and mountains make Apache Junction a natural recreation site. Hiking, horseback riding, picnicking, rockhounding and water sports facilities are available.

At the junction of Old West Highway and SR 88 stands a monument to the memory of Jacob Waltz, purported discoverer of the Lost Dutchman Gold Mine, which is said to be in the nearby Superstition Mountains.

For eight consecutive weekends from the first Saturday in February through the last Sunday in March, the Arizona Renaissance Festival and Artisan Marketplace is held 7 miles east on US 60. Jousting tournaments, wandering musicians, theatrical productions and demonstrations of period crafts are all part of this event re-creating a 16th-century European village at play.

Apache Junction Chamber of Commerce: 567 W. Apache Tr., P.O. Box 1747, Apache Junction, AZ 85217. **Phone:** (480) 982-3141 or (800) 252-3141.

APACHE LAKE, 30 mi. n.e. on SR 88, is part of the Salt River chain of lakes. A popular recreation area, it is surrounded by the Tonto National Forest (see

place listing p. 251). To the south lies the Superstition Wilderness. See Recreation Areas Chart. **Phone:** (928) 467-3200.

APACHE TRAIL (SR 88) starts at Apache Junction and proceeds for 39 mi., climbing past the famed Superstition Mountains, passing through Fish Creek Canyon and skirting the southern edges of Apache, Saguaro, Canyon and Roosevelt lakes, ending at Globe. The trail was created in 1905 to transport supplies from Phoenix and Globe to the construction site of Roosevelt Dam. The road parallels the ancient route of the Apaches through the canyons of the Salt River.

Note: The 25-mile portion of Apache Trail between Tortilla Flat and Roosevelt is a narrow, winding gravel road. It is not recommended during rainy weather, for inexperienced drivers or for vehicles more than 35 feet. West-to-east travel from Apache Junction to Globe will put you on the inside lane and grant all passengers the security of rock walls rather than the steep cliffs on the other side. **Phone:** (480) 610-3300 or (928) 467-3200.

Fish Creek Canyon is approximately 25 mi. n.e. of Apache Junction on the Apache Trail. The canyon is noted for massive, vividly colored walls rising as much as 2,000 feet above the highway. Formed by Fish Creek, which runs from the center of the Superstition Mountains northwest towards the Salt River, the canyon floor is lush with saguaro cacti, trees, bushes, reeds and waterfalls. **Phone:** (480) 610-3300.

CANYON LAKE, 16 mi. n.e. on SR 88, is one of a series of lakes on the Salt River. Impounded by the Mormon Flat Dam, Canyon Lake twists for 10 miles through a magnificent gorge to Horse Mesa Dam. See Recreation Areas Chart. **Phone:** (480) 610-3300.

GOLDFIELD GHOST TOWN & MINE TOURS, 5 mi. n.e. on SR 88, passing Milepost 200 to 4650 E. Mammoth Mine Rd., offers mine tours, gold panning and specialty shops within view of the spectacular Superstition Mountains. Gunfights are performed November through April. A museum features a large exhibit of antique mining equipment. In the Mystery Shack, guests can walk at a 45-degree angle and iron balls roll uphill. A scenic narrow-gauge railroad also encompasses the town.

Hours: Daily 10-5. Gunfights Sat.-Sun. noon-4, Nov.-Apr. Closed Thanksgiving and Christmas. **Cost:** Town free. Mine tour $8; $7 (ages 60+). Train ride $8; $7 (ages 60+); $5 (ages 5-12). Museum $1. Mystery Shack $5; $4 (ages 60+); $3 (ages 6-12). **Phone:** (480) 983-0333.

Apache Trail Tours depart from Goldfield Ghost Town. Participants partake in 1- to 8-hour guided jeep tours of the Apache Trail, the Superstition Mountains and the Four Peaks Wilderness. Climate-controlled SUVs are available. Two-hour gold-panning experiences also are offered.

Hours: Tours daily by reservation. Closed Thanksgiving and Christmas. **Cost:** Two-hour tour $75; $65 (ages 3-15). Four-hour tour $100. Phone for other tour rates. Two-hour tour requires a minimum of two people; 4-hour tour requires a minimum of four people. Reservations are required. **Phone:** (480) 982-7661.

LOST DUTCHMAN STATE PARK, 5 mi. n.e. off SR 88 to 6109 N. Apache Tr., offers 320 acres of hiking trails, camping and picnicking areas. Special moonlight hikes are offered monthly and guided hikes and campfire programs are offered weekly November through March. *See Recreation Areas Chart.* **Hours:** Daily dawn-10 p.m. Office daily 7-4; hours vary in summer. **Cost:** $7 (per private vehicle, up to four passengers); $3 (per additional adult passenger in vehicle or individual arriving on foot or bicycle). Electric campsites Jan.-Mar. $30 (per private vehicle); rest of year $25. Nonelectric camping Jan.-Mar. $17 (per private vehicle); rest of year $15. **Phone:** (480) 982-4485, or (520) 586-2283 for camping reservations.

SUPERSTITION MOUNTAIN MUSEUM, 4087 N. Apache Tr., contains exhibits and artifacts depicting local history and folklore. You'll find maps of the mythical Lost Dutchman Gold Mine; exhibits about Native Americans, geology and natural history; the Elvis Memorial Chapel and Apacheland Barn, featured in Western movies filmed at the Apacheland Movie Ranch; a military exhibit about the Buffalo Soldiers; and reproductions of 19th-century buildings. The Superstition Mountain Railroad display, housed in its own building, is a G-scale model train set-up that depicts life in late 1800s-early 1900s Arizona, complete with towns, mines and mining camps, brothels, ranches and a working stamp mill. Nature trails traverse the 12-acre grounds.

 Time: Allow 1 hour minimum. **Hours:** Daily 9-4. Closed Jan. 1, Thanksgiving and Christmas. **Cost:** $5; $4 (ages 55+); $2 (students ages 17+ with ID); free (ages 0-16 with paying adult). **Phone:** (480) 983-4888.

SUPERSTITION MOUNTAINS, e. of town off Apache Trail (SR 88), were named for the many legends surrounding them. The fabled Lost Dutchman Gold Mine lies somewhere in these mountains. Whether the mine really exists is uncertain, but at least eight men were killed because of it and many others died searching for it. Monuments at Roosevelt Dam and Apache Junction commemorate Jacob Waltz, who allegedly discovered the mine.

APACHE JUNCTION MOTEL   480/982-7702

Motel
$49-$89

Address: 1680 W Apache Tr 85120 **Location:** US 60 exit 195, 2 mi n, then just w. **Facility:** 15 units. 1 story, exterior corridors. *Bath:* shower only. **Terms:** 3 day cancellation notice-fee imposed.

/ SOME UNITS

BEST WESTERN APACHE JUNCTION INN

(480)982-9200

Hotel
$90-$180

AAA Benefit: Save 10% or more every day and earn 10% bonus points!

Address: 1101 W Apache Tr 85220 **Location:** US 60 exit 195, 2 mi n to W Apache Tr, then 0.4 mi e. **Facility:** 40 units. 2 stories (no elevator), interior/exterior corridors. **Terms:** 2 night minimum stay - seasonal and/or weekends. **Pool(s):** heated outdoor. **Activities:** hot tub. **Guest Services:** coin laundry. **Featured Amenity: full hot breakfast.**

WHERE TO EAT

DIRTWATER SPRINGS   480/983-3478

Steak. Casual Dining. $8-$27 **AAA Inspector Notes:** Steaks and ribs are favorites, but diners should not miss the classic Mexican-style dishes at this restaurant, owned and operated by friendly folks since 1987. Casual decor incorporates Western and hunting elements, including a few mounted animal heads. **Features:** full bar, patio dining, happy hour. **Address:** 586 W Apache Tr 85220 **Location:** Center.

HISTORIC MINING CAMP RESTAURANT & DUTCHMAN'S HIDE-OUT   480/982-3181

American. Family Dining. $15-$28 **AAA Inspector Notes:** Established in 1961, this restaurant sits at the base of the Superstition Mountains. At lunch, diners can choose from the a la carte menu featuring USDA Choice cuts of meat. All-you-can-eat dinners include roast chicken, baked ham and barbecue ribs served in the style of an early mining camp cook shanty. **Features:** beer & wine, senior menu. **Address:** 6100 E Mining Camp St 85219 **Location:** US 60 exit 196 (Idaho Rd/SR 88 E), 2.2 mi n to Apache Tr, 2.9 mi n, then 1 mi e and n, via Nodak Rd and Mining Camp St, follow signs.

APACHE-SITGREAVES NATIONAL FORESTS (D-6)

Elevations in the forests range from 3,500 ft. in the Upper Sonoran Desert to 11,500 ft. at Mount Baldy. Refer to AAA maps for additional elevation information.

Along the south rim of the Colorado Plateau in east-central Arizona, the Apache-Sitgreaves national forests comprise nearly 2.1 million acres. They are named, respectively, for the Apaches and for Lt. Lorenzo Sitgreaves, who in 1851 led the first military topographical mapping expeditions across Arizona. The forests include the Mount Baldy, Bear Wallow and Escudilla wilderness areas and the Blue Range Primitive Area.

Hunting is permitted in season. Numerous lakes and streams offer trout fishing. Boats with motors larger than 8 horsepower are prohibited; on some lakes only electric motors are permitted. Trails are available for varying interests, including horseback riding, mountain biking, and hiking as well as for off-roading vehicles. Picnic facilities are available in summer. Winter activities include cross-country skiing, snowmobiling, snowshoeing and ice fishing.

Visitor centers are at Big Lake and on the Mogollon Rim near Heber. Visitor information also is available in summer from attendants at developed campgrounds in the forests and district ranger offices.

The Coronado Trail Scenic Byway (US 191), 127 miles long and ranging from 3,500 to 9,000 feet high, connects the cities of Clifton/Morenci to Springerville/Eagar. The present Coronado Trail (US 191) commemorates portions of the historic route followed by Francisco Vázquez de Coronado when he sought the fabled Seven Cities of Cíbola in 1540. The road traverses areas that remain much as they were more than 450 years ago.

From Clifton the road climbs a corkscrew grade up Rose Peak to an elevation of 8,550 feet. Near this point a Forest Service lookout tower affords a magnificent panorama. Continuing northward, the trail rises to an elevation of 9,200 feet at Blue Vista. The steep, narrow road is not recommended for vehicles pulling trailers more than 20 feet long.

From the rim northward the road is noted for its spectacular autumn coloring. The named portion of the trail ends at Springerville, where US 191 joins US 60.

The White Mountains Scenic Byway is a series of connecting roads that forms a loop through the White Mountains of the Apache-Sitgreaves national forests. The 123-mile loop includes parts of SRs 73, 260, 273 and 373.

For more information contact the Forest Supervisor's Office, Apache-Sitgreaves National Forests, 30 S. Chiricahua Dr., P.O. Box 640, Springerville, AZ 85938; phone (928) 333-4301 or (877) 444-6777 for reservations. *See Recreation Areas Chart.*

AVONDALE pop. 76,238
- **Hotels & Restaurants map & index p. 154**
- **Part of Phoenix area — see map p. 126**

HILTON GARDEN INN PHOENIX/AVONDALE
623/882-3351 **35**

▼▼▼ **Hotel.** Rates not provided. **Address:** 11460 W Hilton Way 85323 **Location:** I-10 exit 131 (Avondale Blvd), just s. **Facility:** 123 units. 4 stories, interior corridors. **Terms:** check-in 4 pm. **Pool(s):** heated outdoor. **Activities:** hot tub, exercise room. **Guest Services:** valet and coin laundry, area transportation.

AAA Benefit:
Members save up to 10%!

HOMEWOOD SUITES BY HILTON PHOENIX/AVONDALE
623/882-3315 **36**

▼▼▼ **Extended Stay Hotel.** Rates not provided. **Address:** 11450 W Hilton Way 85323 **Location:** I-10 exit 131 (Avondale Blvd), just s. **Facility:** 123 efficiencies, some two bedrooms. 4 stories, interior corridors. **Terms:** check-in 4 pm. **Pool(s):** heated outdoor. **Activities:** hot tub, picnic facilities, exercise room. **Guest Services:** valet and coin laundry, area transportation.

AAA Benefit:
Members save up to 10%!

AAA Vacations® packages ...
exciting itineraries and exclusive values

BELLEMONT

DAYS INN BELLEMONT
928/556-9599

▼ **Hotel.** Rates not provided. **Address:** 12380 I-40 86015 **Location:** I-40 exit 185, just n. **Facility:** 60 units. 2 stories (no elevator), interior corridors. **Guest Services:** coin laundry.

BENSON (F-5) pop. 5,105, elev. 3,581'

On the Southern Pacific Railroad route, Benson grew as a distribution center for copper and silver mined in the San Pedro Valley. When railroad transportation began to decline in the 1920s, the town welcomed a new breed of traveler, fledgling motorists out to discover the Southwest. Benson's mining, ranching and railroad history is recalled at the Benson Area Museum; phone (520) 586-3134.

For a breed of a different kind, visit The Oasis Sanctuary at 5411 N. Teran Rd. Open by appointment only, the facility is an exotic bird sanctuary that permanently houses rescued psittacines (parrot-type) birds; phone (520) 212-4737.

Benson/San Pedro Valley Chamber of Commerce/Visitor Center: 168 E. 4th St., Benson, AZ 85602. **Phone:** (520) 265-8031.

KARTCHNER CAVERNS STATE PARK, 9 mi. s. of I-10 exit 302 off SR 90, contains one of the world's few living wet caves open for viewing. The guided 1.5-hour Rotunda/Throne Room Tour takes visitors through rooms that contain more than 30 types of colorful formations growing for more than 200,000 years out of the limestone beneath the Whetstone Mountains. The guided 1.75-hour Big Room Tour features striking calcite formations and giant boulders. Formations include stalactites, stalagmites, canopies, bacon-colored draperies, helictites and rimstone dams. Turnip shield and birdsnest quartz needle formations also may be found. The guided 1.25-hour Headlight and Helmet Tour allows guests to experience the cave as discoverers did in 1974 using only the light provided by their helmet's headlamp.

Discovered in 1974, the 7-acre cave system holds the world's second-longest soda straw formation and "Kubla Khan," a 58-foot-high column. The skeleton of a Shasta ground sloth from the Pleistocene period is among the fossil finds. Within the 550-acre park are a discovery center with exhibits and interactive displays, an interpretive nature path and 5 miles of hiking trails.

Note: Cameras are not permitted in the cave. **Time:** Allow 2 hours, 30 minutes minimum. **Hours:** Park open daily 7 a.m.-10 p.m. Visitor Center daily 8-6, Oct.-May; 9-5, rest of year. Rotunda/Throne Room tours are offered all year and Big Room tours are offered Oct. 15-Apr. 15. Headlight and Helmet Tour on Sat. Times vary, phone ahead. Closed Christmas.

Cost: $6 (per private vehicle, up to four passengers); $3 (per additional adult passenger in vehicle or individual arriving on foot or bicycle); free (with our reservation). Rotunda/Throne Room tour $23; $13 (ages 7-13). Big Room tour $22.95; $12.95 ages 7-13). Ages 0-6 are not permitted on Big Room tour. Headlight and Helmet Tour $30. Ages 0-9 are not permitted on Headlight and Helmet tour. Rates may vary; phone ahead. Reservations are recommended. **Phone:** (520) 586-4100 for information, or (520) 586-2283 for tour and camping reservations.

BEST WESTERN QUAIL HOLLOW INN   (520)586-3646

Hotel
$65-$105

 AAA Benefit: Save 10% or more every day and earn 10% bonus points!

Address: 699 N Ocotillo Rd 85602 **Location:** I-10 exit 304 (Ocotillo Rd), just s. **Facility:** 82 units. 1-2 stories (no elevator), exterior corridors. **Pool(s):** heated outdoor. **Activities:** hot tub, picnic facilities, exercise room. **Guest Services:** coin laundry.

WHERE TO EAT

G & F PIZZA PALACE   520/586-9449

Italian. Family Dining. $4-$22 **AAA Inspector Notes:** This family-friendly pizza joint serves up delicious pizza, wings, sandwiches and Italian favorites in a fun and casual setting. Kids can enjoy the arcade games. **Features:** beer & wine. **Address:** 114 E 5th St 85602 **Location:** Southeast corner of Patagonia and 5th sts; downtown. L D

MAGALY'S MEXICAN RESTAURANT   520/720-6530

Mexican. Casual Dining. $7-$13 **AAA Inspector Notes:** Friendly staff members serve economical and hearty Sonoran dishes prepared by the chef-owner. The neat and tidy dining room is decorated with Mexican handicrafts, which may be purchased. **Features:** beer & wine. **Address:** 675 W 4th St 85602 **Location:** I-10 exit 304 (Ocotillo Rd), 0.5 mi s, then just w. L D

PALATIANO'S FAMILY RESTAURANT   520/586-3523

American. Family Dining. $7-$18 **AAA Inspector Notes:** This popular local eatery serves a blend of classic Italian and American dishes including great burgers, seafood diavolo and a roast beef dinner. The special dessert is "my mother's bread pudding," served warm. **Features:** wine only. **Address:** 601 W 4th St 85602 **Location:** I-10 exit 304 (Ocotillo Rd), 0.6 mi s; center. B L D

BISBEE (G-5) pop. 5,575, elev. 5,300'
• Restaurants p. 42

Bisbee became internationally renowned during the 1880s mining rush, with the discovery of the Copper Queen Lode. Bisbee mines, nestled in the foothills of the Mule Mountains in southeast Arizona, have produced more than $2 billion in copper, gold, lead, silver and zinc. By 1900 Bisbee was the largest cosmopolitan center between St. Louis and San Francisco. Besides operating several stock exchanges, the town was a major venue for rodeos, circus, vaudeville, theater and lectures.

By the early 1970s most of the mines had closed, and artists' studios replaced the miners' shacks. Bisbee is now home to numerous art galleries and studios and serves as an enclave for more than 100 resident artists and artisans as well as actors, dancers, writers, musicians and photographers. Events and cultural activities are held throughout the year; contact the visitor center for further information.

Artifacts and period furnishings of early Bisbee are displayed at the Muheim Heritage House Museum at 207 Youngblood Hill; phone (520) 432-7698. The house was completed in 1915 by a prominent local businessman. Another museum that preserves Bisbee's past through artifacts, clothing and memorabilia is the Bisbee Restoration Museum at 37 Main St. Historic Warren Ballpark, on Old Bisbee Road, is one of the oldest ballparks in the country; phone (520) 432-3554.

Bisbee Visitor Center: 478 N. Dart Rd., Bisbee, P.O. Box 1642, AZ 85603. **Phone:** (520) 432-3554 or (866) 224-7233.

Shopping: The downtown section known as Old Bisbee has several specialty shops that sell antiques, assorted crafts, gifts, jewelry, turquoise and Western items.

BISBEE MINING AND HISTORICAL MUSEUM, 5 Copper Queen Plaza, jct. Main St. and Brewery Gulch, is in the building that served as the headquarters of the Copper Queen Consolidated Mining Co. An affiliate of the Smithsonian Institution, the museum examines local history and culture beginning in 1877. The exhibit Digging In tells the story of copper. The archival library contains photographs, manuscripts, documents and research books about state history and the copper mining era.

Hours: Daily 10-4. Closed Thanksgiving and Christmas. **Cost:** $7.50; $6.50 (ages 60+); $3 (ages 3-16). **Phone:** (520) 432-7071.

QUEEN MINE, on SR 80 near The Lavender Pit mine, offers 1.25-hour tours by mine car into an underground copper mine. The tours are conducted by former miners. **Note:** Sweaters or jackets are recommended. **Hours:** Tours depart daily at 9, 10:30, noon, 2 and 3:30. Closed Thanksgiving and Christmas. **Cost:** $13; $5.50 (ages 4-12). Reservations are recommended. **Phone:** (520) 432-2071 or (866) 432-2071.

AMERICAS BEST VALUE INN & SUITES   520/432-2293

Motel
Rates not provided

Address: 1372 Hwy 92 85603 **Location:** 0.8 mi w of jct Naco Hwy; southwest of downtown. **Facility:** 35 units, some two bedrooms, efficiencies and kitchens. 1-2 stories (no elevator), exterior corridors. **Activities:** picnic facilities. **Guest Services:** coin laundry.

AUDREY'S INN   (520)227-6120

♦♦♦ **Condominium** $105-$145 **Address:** 20 Brewery Ave 85603 **Location:** Just ne of Main St; in historic district. **Facility:** Originally a gentleman's club in the early 1900s, this historic building now houses modern guest suites and two-level units, each with a full kitchen. 6 condominiums. 3 stories (no elevator), interior corridors. **Parking:** on-site and street. **Terms:** 2 night minimum stay - weekends, cancellation fee imposed. **Guest Services:** coin laundry.

⊞ 🛜 ✖ 🗄 🖥 🖥 / SOME UNITS 🔇

CANYON ROSE SUITES   (520)432-5098

♦♦♦ **Historic Condominium** $109-$195 **Address:** 27 Subway St 85603 **Location:** Corner of Shearer Ave; in historic district. **Facility:** This historic building, located just off Main Street, features spacious condo-style rooms with modern conveniences. 7 condominiums. 2 stories (no elevator), interior corridors. **Parking:** street only. **Terms:** cancellation fee imposed. **Guest Services:** coin laundry. ⊞ 🛜 ✖ 🔇 🗄 🖥 🖥

THE JONQUIL MOTEL   520/432-7371

♦ **Motel.** Rates not provided. **Address:** 317 Tombstone Canyon Rd 85603 **Location:** SR 80 exit towards Old Bisbee, left on Main St, 0.6 mi nw. **Facility:** 7 units, some two bedrooms. 1 story, exterior corridors. *Bath:* shower only.

⊞ 🛜 ✖ 🔇 / SOME UNITS 🗄 🖥 🖥

LETSON LOFT HOTEL   520/432-3210

♦♦♦ **Historic Bed & Breakfast.** Rates not provided. **Address:** 26 Main St 85603 **Location:** Center. **Facility:** Located in the historic downtown area, this converted hotel offers charming, individually decorated guest rooms as well as a communal lounge. Check-in is between 3-6 pm, or by appointment. 8 units. 3 stories (no elevator), interior corridors. **Parking:** street only. **Terms:** age restrictions may apply.

⊞ BIZ 🛜 ✖ 🔇 / SOME UNITS 🗄 🖥 🖥

SAN JOSE LODGE   (520)432-5761

♦♦♦
Motel
$55-$180

Address: 2102 Naco Hwy 85603 **Location:** SR 92 W, 1.5 mi s. **Facility:** 43 units, some kitchens. 1 story, exterior corridors. **Terms:** 3 day cancellation notice-fee imposed. **Pool(s):** outdoor.

Activities: picnic facilities. **Guest Services:** coin laundry.

SAVE ⊞ 🍸 🏊 🛜 🗄 🖥 🖥 / SOME UNITS 🐾

COPPER QUEEN HOTEL   520/432-2216

fyi Not evaluated. **Address:** 11 Howell Ave 85603 **Location:** Corner of Brewery Ave; in historic district. Facilities, services, and décor characterize a mid-scale property. This charming hotel dates from the early 1900s and features attractively furnished rooms and modern baths.

WHERE TO EAT

BISBEE BREAKFAST CLUB   520/432-5885

♦♦ American. Family Dining. $5-$9 **AAA Inspector Notes:** One of the more popular spots in town for both locals and tourists, guests might have a bit of a wait for a table but the tasty food and friendly servers more than make up for it. Be sure to try one of the delicious pies for dessert. **Address:** 75 Erie St 85603 **Location:** Jct SR 80, 1.5 mi se from center. **Parking:** street only. B L

BISBEE'S TABLE   520/432-6788

♦♦♦
American
Casual Dining
$11-$24

AAA Inspector Notes: Located in the center of the historic mining town, this grill is a popular casual lunch and dinner spot for both visitors and locals. Choose from grilled steaks, burgers, seafood and pasta dishes. **Features:** full bar. **Reservations:** suggested. **Address:** 2 Copper Queen Plaza 85603 **Location:** Center; in Copper Queen Plaza. **Parking:** street only. L D

CAFE CORNUCOPIA   520/432-482

♦ Deli. Casual Dining. $6-$9 **AAA Inspector Notes:** *Historic* The small space of this sidewalk delicatessen does not limit the bi taste from homemade soups, sandwiches, quiche and fresh-bake desserts. **Address:** 14 Main St 85603 **Location:** In historic district **Parking:** street only. L

CAFE ROKA   520/432-515

♦♦♦
New
American
Casual Dining
$14-$28

AAA Inspector Notes: This popular up scale eatery is located in a restore 1907 building with multiple levels and a lively central bar. The chef/owner serves up expertly prepared New American cui sine using fresh, seasonal ingredients. Live jazz is offered every Friday. **Fea tures:** full bar. **Reservations:** sug gested. **Address:** 35 Main St 85603 **Location:** SR 80, just n; i historic district. **Parking:** street only. D

HIGH DESERT MARKET & CAFE   520/432-6775

♦♦ American. Quick Serve. $5-$10 **AAA Inspector Notes:** Tucked away on the high end of Main Street is this casual market and eatery featuring sidewalk dining where guests can watch those passing by while enjoying freshly-made soups, organic salads and gourmet sandwiches. Evening dinners are available for take-out. Also available is a coffee and smoothie bar. **Features:** patio dining. **Address:** 203 Tombstone Canyon 85603 **Location:** 0.5 mi ne of jct SR 80 W and 80 E via Main St; across from courthouse. B L D

SCREAMING BANSHEE PIZZA   520/432-1300

♦♦ Pizza. Casual Dining. $9-$17 **AAA Inspector Notes:** Come join the fun at this eclectic and artsy bistro. Savory specialty pizza is fired up in a pecan wood-burning oven. Locally grown, organic ingredients are used whenever possible. Wash it all down with a homemade sangria or margarita. **Features:** full bar, patio dining, Sunday brunch. **Address:** 200 Tombstone Canyon 85603 **Location:** 0.5 mi ne of jct SR 80 W and 80 E via Main St; next to courthouse. **Parking:** on-site and street. L D

BLACK CANYON CITY   pop. 2,837

CHILLEEN'S ON 17   623/374-5552

♦♦ Steak. Casual Dining. $8-$18 **AAA Inspector Notes:** The country barbecue, grilled steaks, roasted chicken and desserts served here are large enough to share. Live entertainment is featured on the weekends. Featured on Spike TVs "Bar Rescue." **Features:** full bar. **Address:** 33150 Coldwater Rd 85324 **Location:** I-17 exit 244, just e. L D

ROCK SPRINGS CAFE   623/374-5794

♦♦ American. Family Dining. $8-$20 **AAA Inspector Notes:** Famous for its pies, this country store, saloon and café has been a popular rest stop for weary travelers along the busy I-17 corridor for decades. Enjoy a hearty breakfast of chicken-fried steak, or just stop in to grab a delicious fruit pie or an Old West souvenir. **Features:** full bar. **Address:** 35769 Old Black Canyon Hwy 85324 **Location:** I-17 exit 242, just w. B L D

BUCKEYE   pop. 50,876
• Part of Phoenix area — see map p. 126

DAYS INN-BUCKEYE   (623)386-5400

♦♦♦
Hotel
$110-$270

Address: 25205 W Yuma Rd 85326 **Location:** I-10 exit 114 (Miller Rd), just sw. **Facility:** 60 units. 2 stories (no elevator), exterior corridors. **Terms:** cancellation fee imposed. **Pool(s):** outdoor. **Activities:** hot tub. **Guest Services:** coin laundry. **Featured Amenity:** continental breakfast.

SAVE ⊞ 🏊 BIZ HS 🛜 🗄 🖥 🖥 / SOME UNITS 🐾

BULLHEAD CITY (C-1) pop. 39,540, elev. 540'

Established originally as a supply and support base for builders of the Davis Dam, which impounds Lake Mojave in the Lake Mead National Recreation Area *(see place listing p. 104)*, Bullhead City has evolved into a vacation community. The city's accommodations industry thrives on the thousands of visitors drawn to the mild winter weather and the casinos across the river in Laughlin, Nev. Two bridges connect the towns, and a free river ferry is available.

Bullhead Area Chamber of Commerce: 1251 SR 95, Bullhead City, AZ 86429. **Phone:** (928) 754-4121 or (800) 987-7457.

COLORADO RIVER MUSEUM is at 2201 SR 68. Exhibits feature Mojave Indian artifacts, a Native American village display, the first telephone switchboard used in Bullhead City, a replica of 1885 Fort Mojave, a gold mine replica, minerals and gemstones and steamboat models. Special activities also are offered; phone for details. **Time:** Allow 30 minutes minimum. **Hours:** Tues.-Sat. 10-4, Sept.-June. Closed Jan. 1, Easter, Thanksgiving and Christmas. **Cost:** $2; free (ages 0-12). **Phone:** (928) 754-3399.

BEST WESTERN BULLHEAD CITY INN   (928)754-3000

Hotel
$70

AAA Benefit: Save 10% or more every day and earn 10% bonus points!

Address: 1126 Hwy 95 86429 **Location:** 1.8 mi s of Laughlin Bridge. **Facility:** 88 units. 2 stories, exterior corridors. **Terms:** check-in 4 pm. **Amenities:** safes. **Pool(s):** outdoor. **Activities:** hot tub. **Guest Services:** coin laundry. **Featured Amenity: continental breakfast.**

LAKE MOHAVE RESORT MOTEL   (928)754-3245

 Motel $95-$170 **Address:** 2690 E Katherine Spur Rd 86429 **Location:** Jct SR 95, 1.5 mi e on SR 68, 1 mi n, then 5.4 mi e; at Katherine Landing; in Lake Mead National Recreation Area. **Facility:** 49 units, some efficiencies. 2 stories (no elevator), exterior corridors. **Terms:** 3 day cancellation notice-fee imposed, resort fee. **Activities:** marina, fishing, trails.

BLACK BEAR DINER   928/763-2477
Comfort Food. Family Dining. $8-$19 **AAA Inspector Notes:** A homey atmosphere characterizes this family-oriented restaurant. Familiar comfort foods, such as meatloaf with mashed potatoes, are at the heart of the menu and are served in generous portions. **Features:** beer & wine. **Address:** 1751 W Hwy 95, Suite 25 86442 **Location:** 3.6 mi s of Laughlin Bridge.
B   L   D

COLIANNO'S ITALIAN RESTAURANT   928/758-7104
Italian. Casual Dining. $9-$30 **AAA Inspector Notes:** The feeling here is decidedly Old World, complete with cozy checkered tablecloths. The menu lists steak, seafood and pasta dishes as well as specialty pizza. Carry-out service is available from the on-premises delicatessen. **Features:** beer & wine. **Address:** 1884 Hwy 95 86442 **Location:** 4.1 mi s of Laughlin Bridge.   L   D

EL PALACIO   928/763-2494
Mexican. Casual Dining. $6-$31 **AAA Inspector Notes:** In addition to assorted Mexican dishes and seafood dishes, the menu lists more familiar burritos, enchiladas and tamales. The atmosphere is festive, with bright and colorful appointments. **Features:** full bar, happy hour. **Address:** 1885 Hwy 95 86442 **Location:** 4.1 mi s of Laughlin Bridge.   L   D

CAMERON pop. 885
• Part of Grand Canyon National Park area — see map p. 82

CAMERON TRADING POST MOTEL, RESTAURANT & GIFT SHOP   928/679-2231

Motel
$79-$119

Address: 466 N Hwy 89 86020 **Location:** 1 mi from east gate turn off. **Facility:** 66 units. 2-3 stories (no elevator), exterior corridors. **Terms:** check-in 4 pm. **Dining:** Cameron Trading Post Restaurant, see separate listing. *(See ad on inside front cover, p. 89, p. 302.)*

CAMERON TRADING POST RESTAURANT
928/679-2231

Southwestern Casual Dining
$6-$19

AAA Inspector Notes: Located at a busy intersection outside the Grand Canyon entrance, this restaurant is attached to a trading post and a motel, making it very convenient for travelers. Casual, friendly, helpful staff members deliver steaks, chicken and Mexican cuisine amid Native American decor. **Address:** 466 N Hwy 89 86020 **Location:** 1 mi from east gate turn off; in Cameron Trading Post Motel, Restaurant & Gift Shop.   B   L   D

CAMP VERDE (C-4) pop. 10,873, elev. 3,160'
• Hotels p. 44

Camp Verde was founded as Camp Lincoln in 1866 by Arizona Volunteers to defend pioneers from Apache raids. The fort was renamed Fort Verde a few years later by the U.S. Army. As the area became more peaceful, residents turned their energies toward cattle raising and farming, the two major industries in the broad Verde Valley. Native American ruins and cliff dwellings may be seen at nearby Montezuma Castle National Monument *(see place listing p. 111)* and Montezuma Well.

The Fort Verde Days event in October celebrates the town's cowboy and pioneer history with reenactments, parade and live entertainment around Fort Verde State Historic Park.

FORT VERDE STATE HISTORIC PARK is 3 mi. e. of I-17. In one of the four restored structures of the old fort are Native American, pioneer and military artifacts. Officers' quarters, bachelor's housing and the doctor's quarters are furnished in period. Historic reenactments take place in February, April and October. **Time:** Allow 1 hour minimum. **Hours:** Thurs.-Mon. 9-5. Closed Christmas. **Cost:** $5; $2 (ages 7-13). Hours and rates may vary; phone ahead. **Phone:** (928) 567-3275.

[SAVE] **OUT OF AFRICA WILDLIFE PARK** is, from I-17 exit 287, 3 mi. w. on SR 260, following signs to park entrance. The Wildlife Preserve features several photography platforms to allow for unobstructed pictures of lions, tigers and wolves. Visitors may interact with giraffes and camels during the narrated African Bush Safari tour, attend a Predator Feed show, and watch caretakers activate the instinct of play at a Tiger Splash show. Special tour options include a 1-hour Unimog Adventure and a 3-hour Behind the Scenes VIP tour.

Time: Allow 1 hour minimum. **Hours:** Park open daily 9:30-5. Predator Feed Sun., Wed. and Fri. at 3. Tiger Splash daily at 1:15. Unimog Adventure departs daily at 11 and 2. Behind the Scenes VIP tour departs daily at 10. Last admission 1 hour before closing. Closed Thanksgiving and Christmas. **Cost:** $29.95; $27.95 (ages 65+); $14.95 (ages 3-12). Unimog Adventure $20 (park admission not included for ages 5+). Behind the Scenes VIP tour $149; $125 (ages 3-12). Rates may vary; phone ahead. Behind the Scenes VIP tour and Unimog Adventure reservations must be made 24 hours in advance. Reservations are required. **Phone:** (928) 567-2840. [¶]

GAMBLING ESTABLISHMENTS

- **Cliff Castle Casino** is off I-17 exit 289 at 555 Middle Verde Rd. **Hours:** Daily 24 hours. **Phone:** (928) 567-7900 or (800) 381-7568.

RECREATIONAL ACTIVITIES
White-water Rafting

- **AAM's Mild to Wild Rafting & Jeep Tours Inc.** departs from Super 8 Motel at 1550 W. SR 260. Other activities are offered. **Hours:** Tours depart daily 8-6 at various times. **Phone:** (970) 247-4789 or (800) 567-6745.

CLIFF CASTLE CASINO HOTEL   928/567-6611

Hotel
Rates not provided

Address: 333 Middle Verde Rd 86322 **Location:** I-17 exit 289, 0.4 mi se. **Facility:** Two miles south of Montezuma Castle National Monument, the hotel offers spacious, but basic rooms. The well-appointed, hilltop casino is the main draw for this hotel. 80 units. 2 stories (no elevator), exterior corridors. **Terms:** check-in 4 pm. **Pool(s):** heated outdoor. **Activities:** hot tub. **Guest Services:** area transportation. **Featured Amenity:** continental breakfast.

[SAVE] [icons] [BIZ] [HS] [icons] [X] / SOME UNITS [icons]

SUPER 8-CAMP VERDE   (928)567-2622

Hotel $60-$80 **Address:** 1550 W Hwy 260 86322 **Location:** I-17 exit 287, just e. **Facility:** 44 units. 2 stories (no elevator), interior corridors. **Terms:** cancellation fee imposed. **Pool(s):** heated indoor. **Activities:** hot tub.

[icons] / SOME UNITS [icons]

[GEM] CANYON DE CHELLY NATIONAL MONUMENT (B-6)

In the Navajo Reservation 3 miles east of Chinle, Canyon de Chelly (d'-SHAY) National Monument is reached from Gallup or Shiprock, N.M., and Chambers, Holbrook, Winslow or Tuba City, Ariz. Five periods of Native American culture (Archaic, Basket Makers, early Pueblo, Hopi and Navajo), dating from 2500 B.C. to present, are represented within the 83,849-acre monument.

Archaic, Basket Makers and early Pueblo groups successively occupied the canyons until a reduction in population in A.D. 1275. During the 14th and 15th centuries the Hopis utilized the canyons. The Navajo arrived sometime in the 17th century and continue to live in the canyons, growing corn and herding livestock.

The 26-mile-long Canyon de Chelly is joined by the 25-mile-long Canyon del Muerto; red sandstone walls rise from 30 to 1,000 feet in a sheer, remarkably smooth ascent. Pictographs painted on the walls date from the earliest occupation to the Navajo era.

The principal area ruins are White House, Antelope House and Mummy Cave. White House was first explored in 1848, and its architecture may indicate connections with Chaco Canyon. Antelope House is named for the large pictograph of running antelopes that appears there. Mummy Cave, in which some well-preserved human remains were discovered, has a three-story tower. The architecture of these ancient villages suggests connections with Chaco Canyon and Mesa Verde.

Independent companies registered with the Navajo Parks and Recreation Department offer vehicle, horseback and hiking canyon tours led by an authorized guide. Arrangements for tours are made directly with the companies. For individuals with their own four-wheel-drive vehicles, authorized guides are available at the visitor center. Other regulations apply; *see Good Facts To Know.*

Cottonwood Campground is managed by the Navajo Nation and offers primitive campsites for tent and group camping. Restroom facilities are on-site; no showers or hookups are available. Limited services are offered in winter. A nightly fee is required. Phone (928) 674-2106.

Except for a self-guiding trail from White House Overlook to the White House Ruin, all visitors within the canyons *must* be accompanied by a park ranger or an authorized guide. Fees and permits are required; phone (928) 674-2106.

Two scenic drives traverse both sides of the canyon, affording views of most major ruins from overlooks. Allow 2 hours for each drive if stopping at all of the 10 overlooks. There is one restroom along the rim on South Rim Dr. at White House Overlook. Food and gas are available in Chinle. Pets must be on a leash at all times and are permitted in the parking lots and campground. Pets are not allowed in the canyon or on tours.

The visitor center is open daily 8-5; closed Jan. 1, Thanksgiving and Christmas. The Navajo Reservation observes daylight-saving time, unlike the rest of the state; times listed reflect this when applicable. Monument admission free. For further information contact Canyon de Chelly National Monument, P.O. Box 588, Chinle, AZ 86503; phone (928) 674-5500.

CAREFREE pop. 3,363
• Part of Phoenix area — see map p. 126

BOULDERS RESORT & SPA, A CURIO COLLECTION BY HILTON   480/488-9009

WWW WWW **Resort Hotel.** Rates not provided. **Address:** 34631 N Tom Darlington Dr 85377 **Location:** Jct Scottsdale and Bell rds, 11 mi n. **Facility:** Nestled in the Sonora Desert, this distinctive resort with its oversized casita rooms uses the natural topography of dramatic boulders in its design. 220 units, some houses. 1-2 stories (no elevator), exterior corridors. **Parking:** on-site and valet. **Amenities:** safes. **Dining:** 6 restaurants. **Pool(s):** heated outdoor. **Activities:** sauna, hot tub, steamroom, regulation golf, tennis, recreation programs, bicycles, trails, spa. **Guest Services:** valet laundry, area transportation.

AAA Benefit: Members save 5% or more!

CAREFREE RESORT & CONFERENCE CENTER
(480)488-5300

WWWW
Resort Hotel
$69-$870

Address: 37220 Mule Train Rd 85377 **Location:** SR 101 exit 36 (Pima Rd), 12.2 mi n to Cave Creek Rd, 1 mi w, then 0.4 mi n. **Facility:** Spacious rooms in the main building and expansive, well-appointed condominium units all overlook the lovely landscaped pool area or the pristine Sonoran desert. 220 units, some kitchens and condominiums. 1-3 stories (no elevator), interior/exterior corridors. **Parking:** on-site and valet. **Terms:** check-in 4 pm, 3 day cancellation notice-fee imposed, resort fee. **Pool(s):** heated outdoor. **Activities:** hot tub, tennis, recreation programs, bicycles, exercise room, spa. **Guest Services:** valet laundry, area transportation.

CAFE BINK   480/488-9796

WWW American. Casual Dining. $10-$32 **AAA Inspector Notes:** The little sister to Binkley's just up the street, this intimate bistro serves delicious comfort fare including buttermilk fried chicken, pork osso buco and salmon and succotash using only the freshest ingredients. The outdoor patio is a fine place to enjoy a leisurely meal overlooking the surrounding mountains. **Features:** full bar, patio dining, Sunday brunch, happy hour. **Reservations:** suggested. **Address:** 36899 N Tom Darlington Dr 85377 **Location:** Jct Cave Creek Rd, 0.4 mi s. L D

ENGLISH ROSE TEA ROOM   480/488-4812

WWW Specialty. Casual Dining. $7-$25 **AAA Inspector Notes:** The setting is tiny in space, but the charming decor is classic tea room. The friendly staff even offer a selection of hats guests may wear to make their luncheon or high tea a special experience. **Reservations:** required. **Address:** 201 Easy St, Unit 103 85377 **Location:** From Tom Darlington Dr, just e on Wampum Way, just n; center. **Parking:** street only. L

CASA GRANDE (E-4) pop. 48,571, elev. 1,387'
• Restaurants p. 46

Casa Grande, founded in 1879, was named for the Ancestral Desert People Indian ruins *(see Casa Grande Ruins National Monument p. 46)* 20 miles northeast of town.

Greater Casa Grande Chamber of Commerce: 575 N. Marshall St., Casa Grande, AZ 85122. **Phone:** (520) 836-2125 or (800) 916-1515.

THE MUSEUM OF CASA GRANDE, 110 W. Florence Blvd., has exhibits relating to regional and state history. Highlights include period rooms; Native American artifacts; European settlement, mining and agricultural exhibits; antique fire engines; and railroad displays. Historic properties include an early 20th century church, a 1930s era African-American school house and a historic cemetery. Educational programs, entertainment and special events are offered throughout the year.

Hours: Thurs.-Sun. noon-4, Sept. 15-May 15. Closed major holidays. **Cost:** $5; $4 (ages 60+); free (ages 0-16). **Phone:** (520) 836-2223.

BEST WESTERN PLUS CASA GRANDE   (520)836-1600

WWW
Hotel
$50-$150

Best Western PLUS

AAA Benefit: Save 10% or more every day and earn 10% bonus points!

Address: 665 N Via del Cielo Rd 85222 **Location:** I-10 exit 194 (SR 287), 1 mi w. Across from regional medical center. **Facility:** 80 units. 2 stories (no elevator), exterior corridors. **Terms:** cancellation fee imposed. **Pool(s):** heated outdoor. **Activities:** hot tub, picnic facilities, exercise room. **Guest Services:** valet and coin laundry, area transportation. **Featured Amenity:** full hot breakfast.

COMFORT INN CASA GRANDE
(520)421-9878

Hotel
$59-$119

Address: 2145 E Florence Blvd 85222 **Location:** I-10 exit 194 (SR 287), 0.5 mi w. **Facility:** 65 units. 2 stories (no elevator), interior corridors. **Amenities:** safes. **Pool(s):** heated outdoor. **Activities:** hot tub, picnic facilities, exercise room. **Guest Services:** valet and coin laundry. **Featured Amenity:** breakfast buffet.

FRANCISCO GRANDE HOTEL & GOLF RESORT
520/836-6444

Hotel. Rates not provided. **Address:** 12684 W Gila Bend Hwy 85193 **Location:** I-8 exit 172 (Thornton Rd), 3.5 mi n, then 4.2 mi w. **Facility:** 64 units, some kitchens. 2-9 stories, exterior corridors. **Dining:** Legend's Restaurant, see separate listing. **Pool(s):** heated outdoor. **Activities:** hot tub, regulation golf, exercise room, massage. **Guest Services:** valet and coin laundry.

HOLIDAY INN EXPRESS & SUITES CASA GRANDE
(520)509-6333

Hotel
$99-$149

Address: 805 N Cacheriss Ct 85122 **Location:** I-10 exit 194 (SR 287), 0.6 mi w. **Facility:** 77 units. 3 stories, interior corridors. **Pool(s):** heated outdoor. **Activities:** hot tub, exercise room. **Guest Services:** valet and coin laundry. **Featured Amenity:** breakfast buffet.

HOLIDAY INN HOTEL CASA GRANDE
(520)426-3500

Hotel
$79-$159

Address: 777 N Pinal Ave 85122 **Location:** I-10 exit 194 (SR 287), 3.9 mi w. **Facility:** 176 units. 4 stories, interior corridors. **Pool(s):** heated outdoor. **Activities:** hot tub, exercise room. **Guest Services:** valet and coin laundry, area transportation. **Featured Amenity:** breakfast buffet.

MAINSTAY SUITES CASA GRANDE
(520)426-1177

Extended Stay Hotel $50-$100 **Address:** 851 N Henness Rd 85222 **Location:** I-10 exit 194 (SR 287), 1 mi w, then just n. **Facility:** 70 efficiencies. 2 stories (no elevator), interior corridors. **Activities:** exercise room. **Guest Services:** coin laundry.

SUPER 8
(520)836-8800

Hotel
$59-$79

Address: 2066 E Florence Blvd 85222 **Location:** I-10 exit 194 (SR 287), 0.6 mi w. **Facility:** 41 units. 2 stories (no elevator), interior corridors. **Pool(s):** outdoor. **Guest Services:** coin laundry. **Featured Amenity:** continental breakfast.

WHERE TO EAT

BEDILLON'S CACTUS GARDEN RESTAURANT
520/836-2045
Southwestern. Casual Dining. $9-$40 AAA Inspector **Notes:** This 80-year-old restored home enables visitors to visit a Western museum, walk through a cactus garden and devour a luscious meal. Creative sides such as jicama salad and fruit salsa enhance any sandwich, seafood or meat dish. **Features:** full bar, happy hour. **Reservations:** suggested. **Address:** 800 N Park Ave 85222 **Location:** I-10 exit 194 (SR 287), 3.8 mi n, then just n.

CAFÉ DE MANUEL
520/421-3199
Mexican. Family Dining. $7-$14 AAA Inspector **Notes:** This friendly, casual eatery serves fresh, traditional fare. Such made-to-order dishes as enchilada salad, creamed chimichangas and carne asada are worth the wait. Breakfast includes rellenos and eggs with machaca. **Features:** full bar. **Address:** 1300 N Pinal Ave 85222 **Location:** Jct SR 84 and 287, 0.4 mi n on SR 387 (Pinal Ave).

LEGEND'S RESTAURANT
520/836-6444
Western American. Casual Dining. $10-$25 AAA Inspector **Notes:** This Southwest-style dining room and bar area serve up casual American favorites including seared Alaskan salmon, St. Louis barbecue ribs, lamb sirloin and crispy fish and chips. On nice days, diners can sit outside overlooking the expansive valley and distant mountains. **Features:** full bar, patio dining. **Address:** 12684 W Gila Bend Hwy 85293 **Location:** I-8 exit 172 (Thornton Rd), 3.5 mi n, then 4.2 mi w; in Francisco Grande Hotel & Golf Resort.

SEÑOR SUSHI
520/836-5529
Japanese Fusion. Casual Dining. $8-$14 AAA Inspector **Notes:** This high-energy spot features a fun and eclectic menu that combines Asian and Latin flavors. Try the Latino roll which is filled with bacon, avocado, chihuahua cheese and spicy peppers. A traditional sushi menu also is available. Live music is offered on the weekends. **Features:** full bar, patio dining, happy hour. **Address:** 1601 E Florence Blvd 85122 **Location:** I-10 exit 194 (Florence Blvd), 1.8 mi w.

◆ CASA GRANDE RUINS NATIONAL MONUMENT (E-4)

Off SR 87/287, Casa Grande Ruins National Monument lies within the city limits of Coolidge (see place listing p. 54). The Casa Grande (Big House) was built prior to 1350 A.D. by Ancestral Desert People, the prehistoric peoples formerly known as Hohokam. The four-story structure was constructed of layers of caliche mud and represent the height of the period's architectural advancement. Around the main building are the remains of a walled village. A viewing platform overlooking a prehistoric ball court is behind the picnic area.

The Ancestral Desert People lived in the area for many centuries prior to the construction of the Casa Grande. Sometime around 1450 Casa Grande was abandoned for unknown reasons after the Ancestral Desert People had used it for only a century. The ruins were seen and named in 1694 by Father Eusebio Francisco Kino, a missionary who was led to the site by local Akimel O'odham Indians.

The visitor center features a museum and theater with a 22-minute film. Self-guiding tours and picnic facilities are available year-round. Guided tours are available November through March. Allow 1 hour minimum. Monument open daily 9-5; closed Thanksgiving and Christmas. Admission $5; free (ages

0-15). For further information contact the Superintendent, Casa Grande Ruins National Monument, 1100 W. Ruins Dr., Coolidge, AZ 85128; phone (520) 723-3172.

CATALINA pop. 7,569
• Part of Tucson area — see map p. 256

CATALINA INN   520/818-9500
🚩🚩 **Hotel.** Rates not provided. **Address:** 15691 N Oracle Rd 85739 **Location:** 4.6 mi n of Tangerine Rd. **Facility:** 48 units. 2 stories (no elevator), interior/exterior corridors. **Pool(s):** outdoor. **Guest Services:** coin laundry.

MIRAVAL ARIZONA RESORT & SPA   520/825-4000
[fyi] Not evaluated. **Address:** 5000 E Via Estancia Miraval 85739. Facilities, services, and décor characterize an upscale property.

WHERE TO EAT

MI TIERRA RESTAURANTE   520/825-3040
🚩🚩 Mexican. Casual Dining. $11-$24 **AAA Inspector Notes:** The friendly staff, bright Mexican decor and traditional Sonoran dishes warm diners' hearts and satisfy their craving for a comfort meal. **Features:** full bar. **Address:** 16238 N Oracle Rd 85739 **Location:** 5.3 mi n of Tangerine Rd. [L] [D]

CAVE CREEK (H-3) pop. 5,015, elev. 2,129'
• Part of Phoenix area — see map p. 126

Cave Creek was originally home to the Ancestral Desert People, who irrigated their fields with water from Cave Creek. In 1870 a road was built to link the newly formed town of Cave Creek to Fort McDowell on the Verde River. The late 1800s saw the establishment of numerous mining camps in the surrounding mountains, and permanent settlers who followed took to ranching and farming.

Recreational activities abound in Cave Creek with the Tonto National Forest (see place listing p. 251) as its neighbor. Six lakes in the forest offer numerous opportunities for swimming, fishing and boating.

Carefree-Cave Creek Chamber of Commerce: 748 Easy St., Suite 2 and 4, P.O. Box 734, Carefree, AZ 85377. **Phone:** (480) 488-3381.

CAVE CREEK MUSEUM is at 6140 E. Skyline Dr. Exhibits depict archeological sites as well as what life was like for area pioneers, miners and ranchers. The museum features artifacts attributed to Ancestral Puebloan, Hohokam and Mogollon Indian cultures. A cabin from a tuberculosis sanitarium operating nearby in the 1920s is on the grounds as well as the first church in Cave Creek and the operational Golden Reef Stamp Mill. **Time:** Allow 30 minutes minimum. **Hours:** Wed.-Thurs. and Sat.-Sun. 1-4:30, Fri. 10-4:30, Oct.-May. **Cost:** $5; $3 (ages 55+ and students with ID); $2 (ages 0-12). **Phone:** (480) 488-2764.

RECREATIONAL ACTIVITIES
Horseback Riding
• **Cave Creek Trail Rides** departs from 37109 N. 32nd St. in Cave Creek Recreation Area. Other activities are offered. **Hours:** Rides depart daily at 9, 11, 1 and 3, Oct.-May. Sunset rides offered daily. **Phone:** (623) 742-6700.

BINKLEY'S RESTAURANT   480/437-1072
🚩🚩🚩 🚩🚩🚩 New American. Fine Dining. $40-$95 **AAA Inspector Notes:** Innovative, ambitious and exceptional cuisine is created by chef Kevin Binkley and his team at this posh Cave Creek hideaway. It is worth the drive to sample the chef's tasting menu, which changes daily and features exotic flavors such as crispy seared foie gras, potato-crusted black cod or Guinea hen with parsnip puree and black truffles. **Features:** full bar, patio dining. **Reservations:** suggested. **Address:** 6920 E Cave Creek Rd 85331 **Location:** Jct Scottsdale Rd, 0.5 mi e. [D]

EL ENCANTO MEXICAN RESTAURANT   480/488-1752
🚩🚩 Mexican. Casual Dining. $7-$19 **AAA Inspector Notes:** An outdoor dining area features a mission-style garden with a pond and lots of shade trees. Southwestern, Mexican and Sonoran Mexican cuisine is featured in this relaxing oasis set in a scenic Western town. **Features:** full bar, patio dining, Sunday brunch. **Address:** 6248 E Cave Creek Rd 85331 **Location:** Center. [L] [D]

THE HORNY TOAD RESTAURANT   480/488-9542
🚩🚩 American. Casual Dining. $9-$24 **AAA Inspector Notes:** Built like a Western-style barn, this restaurant has fun decor befitting its casual, friendly service. Guests can savor freshly prepared, mesquite-grilled meats and ample-size desserts. A patio is open when the weather cooperates. **Features:** full bar, patio dining. **Address:** 6738 E Cave Creek Rd 85331 **Location:** Jct Scottsdale Rd and Tom Darlington Dr, 0.8 mi w. [L] [D]

TONTO BAR & GRILL   480/488-0698
🚩🚩🚩 American. Casual Dining. $13-$40 **AAA Inspector Notes:** The casual setting, in an old dude ranch, and views of a golf course do not detract from the upscale, eclectic cuisine that award-winning chef Flatt prepares. The seasonally changing menu takes advantage of the freshest regional foods available. **Features:** full bar, patio dining, happy hour. **Reservations:** suggested. **Address:** 5736 E Rancho Mañana Blvd 85331 **Location:** Jct Carefree Hwy, 2.4 mi n on Cave Creek Rd, just w; at Rancho Mañana Golf Resort. [L] [D]

CHANDLER (J-4) pop. 236,123
• Hotels p. 48 • Restaurants p. 51
• Hotels & Restaurants map & index p. 164
• Part of Phoenix area — see map p. 126

Chandler was founded by Dr. Alexander J. Chandler, a veterinary surgeon who bought 80 acres of land in the Salt River Valley in 1891 and created a series of canals. By 1900 his ranch covered 18,000 acres; in 1912, Chandler sold $50,000 worth of land to 300 speculators and the city was born. In the beginning, Chandler's chief industry was agriculture; alfalfa, cotton and grain were common crops. Today agriculture, while still in the picture, takes a back seat to manufacturing and electronics.

With their restored facades and colonnades, buildings in historic downtown Chandler add to the area's original character, giving it a distinct early-1900s ambience. A host of shopping and dining establishments as well as event opportunities are available to visitors year-round.

Shopping: Downtown Chandler, south of Chandler Boulevard on Arizona Avenue, offers an eclectic mix of stores ranging from trendy clothing boutiques to the home and gift items at Sibley's West—The Chandler Arizona Gift Shop, specializing in made-in-Arizona items. Just 3 miles west of downtown,

(See map & index p. 164.)

Chandler Fashion Center features such name-brand stores as Eddie Bauer, Nordstrom and Victoria's Secret.

Chandler Pavilions/Casa Paloma, an upscale shopping center east of US 10 on Ray Road, features a combination of national stores and distinctive shops including Francesca's Collection, Katy Bug Faye Boutique and Sur La Table.

HUHUGAM HERITAGE CENTER is at 4759 N. Maricopa Rd. Exhibits including art and archeological collections share the history and culture of the Gila River Indian Community. Educational classes and programs also are offered. **Time:** Allow 1 hour minimum. **Hours:** Wed.-Fri. 10-4. Closed major and tribal holidays. **Cost:** $6; $4 (ages 65+ and students with ID); $2 (ages 6-12); free (Native Americans). **Phone:** (520) 796-3500.

SAVE **RAWHIDE WESTERN TOWN & STEAK-HOUSE AT WILD HORSE PASS,** 5700 W. North Loop Rd., is a replica of an 1880s frontier town. Craftsmen sell their wares in antique buildings and shops. The family-style entertainment includes stunt and comedy shows, sundown cookouts, burro rides, gold panning, and stagecoach and train rides.

Hours: Wed.-Fri. 5-10 p.m., Sat. noon-10, Sun. noon-8. Closed Christmas. Phone ahead to confirm schedule. **Cost:** Western town free. Single-attraction tickets $5. One-day Town Pass unlimited use ticket $15. Prices may vary; phone ahead to confirm. **Parking:** $5. **Phone:** (480) 502-5600. [T]

BEST WESTERN INN OF CHANDLER

(480)814-8600 **76**

Motel
$80-$130

AAA Benefit: Save 10% or more every day and earn 10% bonus points!

Address: 950 N Arizona Ave 85225 **Location:** Just s of Ray Rd. **Facility:** 47 units. 2 stories (no elevator), exterior corridors. **Pool(s):** outdoor. **Activities:** hot tub. **Guest Services:** valet laundry. **Featured Amenity:** full hot breakfast.

COMFORT INN CHANDLER-PHOENIX SOUTH

(480)857-4969 **74**

Hotel
$59-$199

Address: 7400 W Boston St 85226 **Location:** I-10 exit 160 (Chandler Blvd), just s on Southgate Dr. **Facility:** 129 units. 4 stories, interior corridors. **Terms:** resort fee. **Amenities:** safes. **Pool(s):** heated outdoor. **Activities:** exercise room. **Guest Services:** valet laundry. **Featured Amenity:** full hot breakfast.

COURTYARD BY MARRIOTT PHOENIX CHANDLER

(480)763-9500 **68**

Hotel
$71-$258

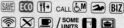
COURTYARD *Marriott* **AAA Benefit:** Members save 5% or more!

Address: 920 N 54th St 85226 **Location:** I-10 exit 159, just e on Ray Rd, then just s. **Facility:** 156 units. 3 stories, interior corridors. **Pool(s):** heated outdoor. **Activities:** hot tub, exercise room. **Guest Services:** valet and coin laundry, boarding pass kiosk.

COURTYARD BY MARRIOTT PHOENIX CHANDLER/FASHION CENTER

(480)855-8600 **84**

Hotel $82-$233 **Address:** 1100 S Price Rd 85286 **Location:** SR 202 exit 50B (Price Rd), just s. **Facility:** 150 units. 6 stories, interior corridors. **Pool(s):** heated outdoor. **Activities:** hot tub, exercise room. **Guest Services:** valet and coin laundry, boarding pass kiosk, area transportation.

AAA Benefit: Members save 5% or more!

CROWNE PLAZA SAN MARCOS GOLF RESORT

(480)812-0900 **81**

Historic Resort Hotel $99-$309 **Address:** 1 N San Marcos Pl 85225 **Location:** Jct Chandler Blvd, just s on Arizona Ave, then just w on Buffalo St; in historic downtown. **Facility:** The resort, dating from 1912, sits on 123 acres with extensively landscaped grounds, including wisteria-covered arbors. All of the newly renovated rooms have balconies or patios. 248 units. 4 stories, exterior corridors. **Terms:** cancellation fee imposed, resort fee. **Amenities:** video games. **Pool(s):** heated outdoor. **Activities:** hot tub, regulation golf, tennis, exercise room. **Guest Services:** valet laundry, rental car service, area transportation.

FAIRFIELD INN & SUITES BY MARRIOTT PHOENIX CHANDLER

(480)940-0099 **72**

Hotel
$64-$180

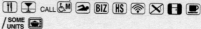
FAIRFIELD INN & SUITES *Marriott* **AAA Benefit:** Members save 5% or more!

Address: 7425 W Chandler Blvd 85226 **Location:** I-10 exit 160 (Chandler Blvd), just e, then just s on Southgate Dr. **Facility:** 64 units. 3 stories, interior corridors. **Pool(s):** heated outdoor. **Activities:** hot tub, exercise room. **Guest Services:** valet and coin laundry, boarding pass kiosk. **Featured Amenity:** breakfast buffet.

FAIRFIELD INN & SUITES BY MARRIOTT PHOENIX CHANDLER/FASHION CENTER

(480)963-5300 **83**

Hotel $71-$213 **Address:** 1100 S Price Rd 85286 **Location:** SR 202 exit 50B (Price Rd), just s. **Facility:** 110 units. 6 stories, interior corridors. **Pool(s):** heated outdoor. **Activities:** hot tub, exercise room. **Guest Services:** valet and coin laundry, area transportation.

AAA Benefit: Members save 5% or more!

(See map & index p. 164.)

HAMPTON INN & SUITES PHOENIX/CHANDLER FASHION CENTER
(480)917-9500 **86**

▼▼▼ **Hotel** $79-$179 **Address:** 1231 S Spectrum Blvd 85286 **Location:** SR 202 exit 50B (Price Rd), just s. **Facility:** 153 units. 4 stories, interior corridors. **Terms:** 1-7 night minimum stay, cancellation fee imposed. **Pool(s):** heated outdoor. **Activities:** hot tub, exercise room. **Guest Services:** valet and coin laundry, area transportation.

AAA Benefit: Members save up to 10%!

[icons]

HAMPTON INN PHOENIX-CHANDLER
(480)753-5200 **70**

▼▼▼ **Hotel** $89-$189 **Address:** 7333 W Detroit St 85226 **Location:** I-10 exit 160 (Chandler Blvd), just e, just n on 54th St, then just w. **Facility:** 101 units. 6 stories, interior corridors. **Terms:** 1-7 night minimum stay, cancellation fee imposed. **Pool(s):** heated outdoor. **Activities:** hot tub, exercise room. **Guest Services:** valet laundry.

AAA Benefit: Members save up to 10%!

[icons]

HAWTHORN SUITES BY WYNDHAM-CHANDLER
(480)705-8881 **75**

▼▼ ▼ **Extended Stay Hotel** $79-$219 **Address:** 5858 W Chandler Blvd 85226 **Location:** I-10 exit 160 (Chandler Blvd), 1.5 mi e. **Facility:** 100 efficiencies, some two bedrooms. 2 stories (no elevator), interior corridors. **Pool(s):** heated outdoor. **Activities:** hot tub, picnic facilities, exercise room. **Guest Services:** valet and coin laundry.

[icons]

HILTON PHOENIX CHANDLER
(480)899-7400 **80**

▼▼▼ **Hotel** $99-$279 **Address:** 2929 W Frye Rd 85224 **Location:** SR 202 exit 50B (Price Rd), 0.4 mi n, then just e. **Facility:** 197 units. 6 stories, interior corridors. **Terms:** 1-7 night minimum stay, cancellation fee imposed. **Amenities:** safes. **Pool(s):** heated outdoor. **Activities:** hot tub, exercise room. **Guest Services:** valet laundry, area transportation.

AAA Benefit: Members save 5% or more!

[icons]

HOLIDAY INN AT OCOTILLO
480/203-2121 **88**

▼▼▼ **Hotel** **Rates not provided**

Address: 1200 W Ocotillo Rd 85248 **Location:** I-10 exit 164 (Queen Creek Rd), 5.5 mi e, 1.1 mi s on Alma School Rd, then just w. **Facility:** 106 units. 4 stories, interior corridors. **Pool(s):** heated outdoor. **Activities:** hot tub, bicycles, exercise room. **Guest Services:** valet and coin laundry, area transportation. **Featured Amenity:** full hot breakfast.

[icons]

HOMEWOOD SUITES BY HILTON PHOENIX-CHANDLER
(480)753-6200 **69**

▼▼▼ **Extended Stay Hotel** $104-$189 **Address:** 7373 W Detroit St 85226 **Location:** I-10 exit 160 (Chandler Blvd), 0.4 mi e, n on 54th St, then just w. **Facility:** 83 efficiencies, some two bedrooms. 3 stories, interior corridors. **Terms:** 1-7 night minimum stay, cancellation fee imposed. **Pool(s):** heated outdoor. **Activities:** hot tub, picnic facilities, exercise room. **Guest Services:** valet and coin laundry.

AAA Benefit: Members save up to 10%!

[icons]

HOMEWOOD SUITES BY HILTON-PHOENIX/CHANDLER FASHION CENTER
(480)963-5700 **85**

▼▼▼ **Extended Stay Hotel** $99-$209 **Address:** 1221 S Spectrum Blvd 85286 **Location:** SR 202 exit 50B (Price Rd), just s. **Facility:** 133 efficiencies, some two bedrooms. 4 stories, interior corridors. **Terms:** 1-7 night minimum stay, cancellation fee imposed. **Pool(s):** heated outdoor. **Activities:** hot tub, picnic facilities, exercise room. **Guest Services:** valet and coin laundry, area transportation.

AAA Benefit: Members save up to 10%!

[icons]

HYATT PLACE PHOENIX CHANDLER FASHION CENTER
(480)812-9600 **79**

▼▼▼ **Hotel** $89-$299

HYATT PLACE
AAA Benefit: Members save 10%!

Address: 3535 W Chandler Blvd 85226 **Location:** I-10 exit 160 (Chandler Blvd), 4 mi e. Located at Chandler Fashion Center Mall. **Facility:** 129 units. 3 stories, interior corridors. **Terms:** cancellation fee imposed. **Pool(s):** heated outdoor. **Activities:** hot tub, exercise room. **Guest Services:** valet and coin laundry, area transportation. **Featured Amenity:** breakfast buffet.

[icons]

QUALITY INN
(480)705-0922 **73**

▼▼▼ **Hotel** $59-$249

Address: 255 N Kyrene Rd 85226 **Location:** I-10 exit 160 (Chandler Blvd), 1.5 mi e, then just n. **Facility:** 70 units. 3 stories, interior corridors. **Pool(s):** outdoor. **Guest Services:** valet and coin laundry. **Featured Amenity:** breakfast buffet.

[icons]

RADISSON PHOENIX-CHANDLER
(480)961-4444 **71**

▼▼▼ **Hotel** $65-$229

Address: 7475 W Chandler Blvd 85226 **Location:** I-10 exit 160 (Chandler Blvd), just e, then just s on Southgate Dr. Located in a commercial area. **Facility:** 159 units. 4 stories, interior corridors. **Terms:** 3 day cancellation notice-fee imposed. **Amenities:** Some: safes. **Pool(s):** heated outdoor. **Activities:** hot tub, exercise room. **Guest Services:** valet and coin laundry, area transportation.

[icons]

RESIDENCE INN BY MARRIOTT-CHANDLER FASHION CENTER
(480)782-1551 **78**

▼▼▼ **Extended Stay Hotel** $100-$270 **Address:** 200 N Federal St 85226 **Location:** I-10 exit 160 (Chandler Blvd), 4.2 mi e, just n on N Metro Blvd, then just e. Across from Chandler Fashion Center Mall. **Facility:** 102 units, some two bedrooms, efficiencies and kitchens. 3 stories, interior corridors. **Pool(s):** heated outdoor. **Activities:** hot tub, picnic facilities, exercise room. **Guest Services:** valet and coin laundry.

AAA Benefit: Members save 5% or more!

[icons]

(See map & index p. 164.)

SHERATON WILD HORSE PASS RESORT & SPA
(602)225-0100

Resort Hotel
$99-$369

AAA Benefit: Members save up to 15%, plus Starwood Preferred Guest® benefits!

Address: 5594 W Wild Horse Pass Blvd 85226 **Location:** I-10 exit 162, 2.4 mi w. **Facility:** Wild horses roam the desert areas nearby, while the property's extensive grounds offer views of the golf course and mountains. 500 units. 4 stories, interior corridors. **Parking:** on-site and valet. **Terms:** check-in 4 pm, resort fee. **Amenities:** safes. **Dining:** 4 restaurants, also, Kai, see separate listing. **Pool(s):** heated outdoor. **Activities:** sauna, hot tub, steamroom, regulation golf, tennis, recreation programs, kids club, trails, spa. **Guest Services:** valet laundry, area transportation. *(See ad this page.)*

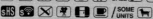

Enjoy great member rates

and benefits at AAA/CAA

Preferred Hotels

SPRINGHILL SUITES BY MARRIOTT-CHANDLER FASHION CENTER
(480)726-7666 **77**

Hotel $83-$240 **Address:** 225 N Metro Blvd 85226 **Location:** I-10 exit 160 (Chandler Blvd), 4.2 mi e, then just n. Across from Chandler Fashion Center Mall. **Facility:** 101 units. 3 stories, interior corridors. **Pool(s):** heated outdoor. **Activities:** hot tub, exercise room. **Guest Services:** valet and coin laundry.

AAA Benefit: Members save 5% or more!

WILD HORSE PASS HOTEL & CASINO
(520)796-7777 **82**

Contemporary Hotel
$59-$229

Address: 5040 W Wild Horse Pass Blvd 85226 **Location:** I-10 exit 162, 2.4 mi w. **Facility:** Located within the Gila River Indian Community, this large luxury resort boasts many entertainment options, including a nightclub, theater, upscale dining and 36 holes of golf. 242 units. 10 stories, interior corridors. **Parking:** on-site and valet. **Terms:** check-in 4 pm, cancellation fee imposed. **Amenities:** safes. **Dining:** 5 restaurants, also, Ling & Louie's Asian Bar & Grill, Shula's America's Steak House, see separate listings, nightclub, entertainment. **Pool(s):** heated outdoor. **Activities:** hot tub, regulation golf, exercise room. **Guest Services:** valet laundry, area transportation. *(See ad p. 182.)*

▼ See AAA listing this page ▼

(See map & index p. 164.)

WHERE TO EAT

BRUNCHIE'S 480/899-5036 **55**
▼▼ American. Family Dining. $6-$17 AAA Inspector Notes: A casual and homey spot in downtown Chandler's historic district, this eatery serves breakfast and lunch classics as well as Mexican specialties. Enjoy the weather and view from the sidewalk seating area. Features: beer & wine. Address: 17 E Boston St 85225 Location: Southeast corner of Arizona Ave and Boston St. [B] [L]

C-FU GOURMET 480/899-3888 **46**
▼▼ Chinese. Casual Dining. $5-$19 AAA Inspector Notes: Among favorite choices are moo goo gai pan and chicken lo mein, as well as the reasonably priced dim sum. Diners can choose live seafood from tanks and have it prepared in the style of their choice. Features: full bar. Address: 2051 W Warner Rd 85224 Location: Southwest corner of Warner and Dobson rds. [L] [D]

CHOU'S KITCHEN 480/821-2888 **50**
▼▼ Northern Chinese. Casual Dining. $5-$13 AAA Inspector Notes: Authentic northern Chinese cuisine is served by a friendly staff at this no-frills storefront establishment. Sample the clay pots, lamb skewers, stir-fry noodles, beef pies, homemade dumplings and noodle dishes for a unique culinary experience. Address: 910 N Alma School Rd 85224 Location: SR 101 exit 59 (Ray Rd), 2.1 mi e; southwest corner of Ray and Alma School rds; in Alma School Village Shopping Center. [L] [D]

CYCLO VIETNAMESE CUISINE 480/963-4490 **52**
▼▼ Vietnamese. Casual Dining. $6-$13 AAA Inspector Notes: In a small shopping plaza, this cozy, modern eatery has food bursting with flavor and freshness. Such dishes as chicken pineapple curry and jasmine tea-scented crème brûlée made without eggs are favorites. Local chefs often visit to relax and enjoy the savory foods. Address: 1919 W Chandler Blvd, Suite 2 85224 Location: Just e of Dobson Rd. [L] [D]

DC STEAKHOUSE 480/899-4400 **54**
▼▼▼ Steak. Casual Dining. $12-$41 AAA Inspector Notes: This lively spot serves fresh steaks, chops, ribs and seafood in an up-scale casual environment. The friendly staff makes diners feel at home. Features: full bar, patio dining, happy hour. Address: 98 S San Marcos Pl 85225 Location: Loop 202 exit 47 (Arizona Ave), 1 mi n, just w on Boston St, then just n. Parking: street only. [D]

FLEMING'S PRIME STEAKHOUSE & WINE BAR
480/940-1900 **55**
▼▼▼▼ Steak. Fine Dining. $19-$57 AAA Inspector Notes: The warm, clubby atmosphere is the ideal setting for perfectly grilled steaks and seafood. Side dishes come in hearty portions, and salads are fresh and crisp. More than 100 wine selections are available. Features: full bar, happy hour. Reservations: suggested. Address: 905 N 54th St 85226 Location: I-10 exit 159 (Ray Rd), just e, then just s. [D]

KAI 602/385-5726 **59**
▼▼▼▼▼
Southwestern
Fine Dining
$35-$175

AAA Inspector Notes: Using Native American indigenous foods, this eatery's renowned chefs have created a seasonally-changing tasting menu. Meats, game and seafood are enhanced by vegetable and herb sauces developed from native seeds. Sunset views against the mountain backdrop and wild horses roaming the area create a breathtaking scene. Features: full bar, patio dining. Reservations: suggested. Semiformal attire. Address: 5594 W Wild Horse Pass Blvd 85226 Location: I-10 exit 162, 2.4 mi w; in Sheraton Wild Horse Pass Resort & Spa. Parking: on-site and valet.

(See ad p. 50.) [D]

KEEGAN'S GRILL 480/814-0003
▼▼▼ American. Casual Dining. $7-$22 AAA Inspector Notes: A decor featuring witty quotes painted on the walls and huge wooden columns welcomes diners to this bistro. Friendly staff members serve dishes ranging from such comfort foods as meatloaf and barbecue ribs to more eclectic creations, including prosciutto-wrapped shrimp and Pacific Rim grilled chicken salad. Features: full bar. Address: 1095 W Queen Creek Rd 85248 Location: I-10 exit 164 (Queen Creek Rd), 5.2 mi e. [L] [D]

LA STALLA 480/855-9990 **53**
▼▼▼ Italian. Casual Dining. $8-$26 AAA Inspector Notes: This cozy, rustic kitchen offers a taste of Old World Italy in downtown Chandler. Pasta dishes, specialty pizzas and chicken, veal and seafood entrées line the menu. Sidewalk seating is an option in pleasant weather. Features: full bar, patio dining, happy hour. Address: 68 W Buffalo St 85225 Location: Jct Chandler Blvd, just s on Arizona Ave, just w. [L] [D] [🐾]

LING & LOUIE'S ASIAN BAR & GRILL 520/796-7281 **57**
▼▼ Asian. Casual Dining. $11-$17 AAA Inspector Notes: Located just off the casino floor, this high-energy spot offers a modern twist on Asian favorites. Try the sizzling blackened chicken and pork platter or fresh seafood in a hot pot simmering in green coconut curry sauce. Features: full bar, patio dining, happy hour. Address: 5040 Wild Horse Pass Blvd 85226 Location: I-10 exit 162, 2.4 mi w; in Wild Horse Pass Hotel & Casino. Parking: on-site and valet. [L] [D]

P.F. CHANG'S CHINA BISTRO 480/899-0472 **51**
▼▼▼ Chinese. Fine Dining. $9-$25 AAA Inspector Notes: Trendy, upscale decor provides a pleasant backdrop for New Age Chinese dining. Appetizers, soups and salads are a meal by themselves. Vegetarian plates and sides, noodles, chow meins, chicken and meat dishes are created from exotic, fresh ingredients. Features: full bar, happy hour. Reservations: suggested. Address: 3255 W Chandler Blvd 85226 Location: SR 101 exit 60 (Chandler Blvd), just e; across from Chandler Fashion Center Mall. [L] [D] CALL [✆M]

PITA JUNGLE 480/855-3232 **49**
▼▼ Mediterranean. Casual Dining. $7-$16 AAA Inspector Notes: The atmosphere is casual in the dining area and on the lakeside patio of this eatery. The menu lists hot and cold pita wraps, pizza, falafel, spanakopita, salads and burgers, as well as healthful, natural vegetarian offerings. Features: full bar, patio dining, happy hour. Address: 1949 W Ray Rd 85224 Location: Jct Dobson Rd; southeast corner. [L] [D]

RAWHIDE STEAKHOUSE 480/502-5600 **58**
▼▼ Steak. Casual Dining. $14-$65 AAA Inspector Notes: Part of a Western town venue, this eatery offers hearty meals of mesquite-grilled steaks, ribs and chicken. Rich fruit or pecan pie desserts finish off your meal, and there is live entertainment nightly. Features: full bar, patio dining. Address: 5700 W North Loop Rd 85226 Location: I-10 exit 162, 0.8 mi w to 48th St, just s, then w. [D]

RUBIO'S FRESH MEXICAN GRILL
▼ Mexican. Quick Serve. $4-$10 AAA Inspector Notes: Freshly prepared and healthful foods, bright decor and friendly staff are found in this upscale fast-food spot. A special treat, the salsa bar lines up four styles and flavors. Bar: beer only. [L] [D]

For additional information, visit AAA.com

LOCATIONS:
Address: 5055 W Ray Rd 85226 Location: Jct Rural Rd; southwest corner. Phone: 480/753-0633
Address: 3111 W Chandler Blvd 85226 Location: SR 101 exit 60 (Chandler Blvd), just w; in Chandler Fashion Center Mall. Phone: 480/812-9460

SAIGON PHO & SEAFOOD 480/786-8828 **48**
▼▼ Vietnamese. Casual Dining. $6-$13 AAA Inspector Notes: Dishes are prepared with fresh vegetables, herbs, beef, seafood, chicken and pork. From hot pot soups to fresh fish pulled from an on-site tank, this casual storefront eatery's offerings are infused with Eastern flavors. Address: 1381 N Alma School Rd 85224 Location: Jct Warner Rd, 0.5 mi s. [L] [D]

(See map & index p. 164.)

SERRANO'S MEXICAN RESTAURANT   480/899-3318

♦♦ Mexican. Casual Dining. $7-$17 **AAA Inspector Notes:** A pleasant stop for lunch or dinner, the local chain is known for consistently good food and attractive, upscale Mexican-style décor. The warm bean dip starter stirs the appetite for traditional dishes such as chiles rellenos or seafood enchiladas prepared with fresh ingredients. Service is friendly. **Features:** full bar. **Address:** 141 S Arizona Ave 85225 **Location:** 3 mi e on Chandler Blvd from jct SR 101, 0.3 mi s. [L] [D]

SHULA'S AMERICA'S STEAK HOUSE   520/796-1972 [56]

♦♦♦♦ Steak. Fine Dining. $25-$68 **AAA Inspector Notes:** Comfortable and club-like, the dining room is decorated with Dolphins football memorabilia. Finish off the 48-ounce porterhouse steak and be recognized on a plaque. The lamb chops and seafood are good, too, as is the to-die-for seven-layer chocolate cake. **Features:** full bar. **Reservations:** suggested. **Address:** 5040 Wild Horse Pass Blvd 85226 **Location:** I-10 exit 162, 2.4 mi w; in Wild Horse Pass Hotel & Casino. **Parking:** on-site and valet. [D]

Z'TEJAS SOUTHWESTERN GRILL   480/893-7550 [47]

♦♦♦ Southwestern. Casual Dining. $7-$25 **AAA Inspector Notes:** The young, friendly staff at this grill welcomes diners with smiles. Attractively presented entrées are prepared in a Southwestern style with influences from Texas, Louisiana and Arizona. Banana cream pie is among the show-stopping desserts. **Features:** full bar, patio dining, Sunday brunch, happy hour. **Address:** 7221 W Ray Rd 85226 **Location:** I-10 exit 158, just e. [L] [D]

CHINLE pop. 4,518

BEST WESTERN CANYON DE CHELLY INN
(928)674-5874

♦♦
Motel
$110-$120

AAA Benefit:
Save 10% or more every day and earn 10% bonus points!

Address: 100 Main St, Indian Rt 7 86503 **Location:** US 191, just e. **Facility:** 104 units. 2 stories (no elevator), exterior corridors. **Dining:** Junction Restaurant, see separate listing. **Pool(s):** heated indoor. **Activities:** sauna, exercise room.

[SAVE] [♦] [≈] [BIZ] [♦] [✕] [♦]
[♦] / SOME UNITS [♦]

HOLIDAY INN CANYON DE CHELLY   928/674-5000
♦♦
Hotel
Rates not provided

Address: Indian Rt 7 86503 **Location:** US 191, 2.5 mi e; at entrance to Canyon de Chelly National Monument. **Facility:** 108 units. 2 stories (no elevator), interior corridors. **Dining:** Garcia's Restaurant, see separate listing. **Pool(s):** heated outdoor. **Activities:** exercise room. **Guest Services:** coin laundry.

[SAVE] [♦] [♦] [≈] [BIZ] [♦] [✕]
[♦] [♦]

SACRED CANYON LODGE   928/674-5841
♦♦ Motel. Rates not provided. **Address:** Indian Rt 7 86503 **Location:** US 191, 3.5 mi e; just e of visitor center. Located in Canyon de Chelly National Monument. **Facility:** 67 units. 1 story, exterior corridors. **Dining:** Thunder Bird Cafeteria, see separate listing.
[♦] [♦] [✕]

WHERE TO EAT

GARCIA'S RESTAURANT   928/674-2511

♦♦ American. Family Dining. $5-$22 **AAA Inspector Notes:** Located right off the lobby, this casual restaurant offers basic service, a salad bar and American cuisine along with a few Navajo specialties. **Address:** Indian Rt 7 86503 **Location:** US 191, 2.5 mi e; at entrance to Canyon de Chelly National Monument; in Holiday Inn Canyon de Chelly. [B] [L] [D]

JUNCTION RESTAURANT   928/674-8443

♦♦ American. Family Dining. $5-$18 **AAA Inspector Notes:** This family restaurant lines up a good selection of beef, chicken, pork, sandwiches and such Navajo favorites as mutton stew and fry bread. Local Native American arts and crafts are displayed. The dining patio opens seasonally. **Features:** patio dining. **Address:** 100 Main St, Rt 7 86503 **Location:** US 191, just e; in BEST WESTERN Canyon de Chelly Inn. [B] [L] [D]

THUNDER BIRD CAFETERIA   928/674-5841

♦ American. Cafeteria. $6-$15 **AAA Inspector Notes:** Among this cafeteria's comfort foods are some Mexican entrées and Navajo fry bread. Some steak and other dishes are prepared to order and delivered to the table. **Address:** Indian Rt 7 86503 **Location:** US 191, 3.5 mi e; just e of visitor center; in Sacred Canyon Lodge.
[B] [L] [D]

CHINO VALLEY pop. 10,817

DAYS INN CHINO VALLEY   (928)636-0311

♦♦ Hotel $76-$113 **Address:** 688 Fletcher Ct 86323 **Location:** Center. **Facility:** 55 units. 2 stories (no elevator), interior corridors. **Pool(s):** heated indoor. **Activities:** hot tub. **Guest Services:** valet laundry.

[♦] CALL [♦M] [≈] [BIZ] [HS] [♦] [✕] [♦] [♦] [♦]
/ SOME UNITS [♦]

◈ CHIRICAHUA NATIONAL MONUMENT (F-6)
GEM

Approximately 70 miles northeast of Douglas via US 191 and SR 181 or 36 miles southeast of Willcox via SR 186 and SR 181, Chiricahua (cheer-ee-KAH-wah) National Monument, also called the "Wonderland of Rocks," is in the Chiricahua Mountains at an elevation ranging from 5,180 to 7,310 feet. Nine miles of the 21-mile county road that runs south from Bowie across Apache Pass to SR 186 are unpaved and rough in places. Unseasoned mountain drivers and cars pulling trailers should avoid the narrow, winding route from Portal; it is closed in winter.

The 11,985-acre area encompasses lands once controlled by the Chiricahua Apaches under Cochise, who led the Native Americans' resistance to the white man during the 1860s.

The Chiricahua Mountains rise above the surrounding grasslands, providing shady forests and glens that harbor Mexican chickadees, raccoon-like coatimundis, javelinas and a number of other wildlife species. Among the monument's outstanding features are gigantic, erosion-sculptured monoliths of volcanic ash.

Current research indicates that about 27 million years ago violent eruptions from the nearby Turkey Creek caldera took place, covering the area with white-hot ash. After the ash fused and cooled into an almost 2,000-foot layer of rock, the forces of erosion sculpted it into the odd array of shapes that can be seen.

Formations include the Totem Pole, 137 feet high and only a yard thick at its narrowest point; the Mushroom; and Big Balanced Rock, weighing 1,000 tons and resting on a base about 4 feet thick. In some places canyon walls rise as much as 1,000 feet. Many areas can be reached only on foot.

Among the first pioneers to settle in the area were Ja Hu Stafford and Neil and Emma Erickson. By the 1920s one of the Erickson daughters, Lillian, and her husband, Ed Riggs, had turned the homestead into a guest ranch, built trails into the rocks and were the driving force in the creation of Chiricahua National Monument. Today Faraway Ranch is preserved as a historic site with tours offered *(see attraction listing this page)*.

Picnicking, camping and parking areas are available near the visitor center in Bonita Canyon. Reached from the visitor center by 6 miles of paved mountain road, 6,780-foot Massai Point offers an overlook and an exhibit building. More than 17 miles of trails lead to all parts of the monument. Campground programs are conducted in spring and fall. Contact the visitor center, (520) 824-3560, for an updated schedule.

Vehicles longer than 29 feet are not permitted beyond the visitor center. A hiker's shuttle departs to the high country daily; phone for schedule. Visitor center daily 8:30-4:30; closed Christmas. Park entrance and shuttle free. Campers must register at the campground. Camping fee per night $12; $6 (ages 62+). Fees may vary; phone ahead. Campgrounds will not accommodate travel trailers or motor homes more than 29 feet long.

For further information contact the Superintendent, Chiricahua National Monument, 12856 E. Rhyolite Creek Rd., Willcox, AZ 85643; phone (520) 824-3560, ext. 302.

FARAWAY RANCH, 1.5 mi. w. of the monument visitor center, is the homestead of pioneers Neil and Emma Erickson. The home was built in 1888 and additions were made through 1915. By the 1920s the Ericksons' daughter Lillian and her husband had turned the homestead into a working cattle and guest ranch.

Time: Allow 1 hour minimum. **Hours:** Homestead site accessible daily dawn-dusk. Guided tours of the home are given depending on staff availability.

Phone ahead to confirm schedule. **Cost:** Free. **Phone:** (520) 824-3560, ext. 302. GT

CHLORIDE pop. 271
• Part of Grand Canyon National Park area — see map p. 82

DIGGER DAVES   928/565-3283
◈ Burgers Sandwiches. Casual Dining. $7-$10 **AAA Inspector Notes:** This small 1920s building is run by a fun and friendly couple. The menu is limited to basic burgers, sandwiches and corn dogs. Root beer floats are the specialty dessert and the pulled-pork sandwich is hearty. **Features:** full bar. **Address:** 4962 Tennessee Ave W 86431 **Location:** Center. **Parking:** street only. [B] [L]

CIBOLA (E-1) pop. 250, elev. 240'

CIBOLA NATIONAL WILDLIFE REFUGE is 17 mi. s. on Neighbors Blvd., across the Cibola Bridge, then 3.5 mi. s. to 66600 Cibola Lake Rd. Home to many wildlife species including more than 288 species of birds as well as desert tortoises, mule deer and bobcats, the refuge has a visitor center with interpretive displays. A 1-mile nature trail winds through three native habitats: cottonwood, mesquite and willow.

From an elevated observation deck, winter visitors can view flocks of geese, ducks and sandhill cranes on a 20-acre pond. **Time:** Allow 30 minutes minimum. **Hours:** Refuge daily 8-4:30. Visitors center Mon.-Fri. 8-4:30, Sept.-Apr. Wildlife is best viewed Nov.-Feb. Closed major holidays. **Cost:** Free. **Phone:** (928) 857-3253. 🏕

CLARKDALE (C-3) pop. 4,097, elev. 3,545'
• Restaurants p. 54

Clarkdale was named after its founder, William Andrews Clark, who purchased the United Verde Copper Co. in Jerome in 1888. In 1911, the mine's smelter was relocated and Clarkdale was created to house the company's 7,000 employees. Clark controlled every detail of the town's construction and incorporated modern details including a sewer system and hardwood flooring in every home.

The town's proximity to Tuzigoot National Monument *(see place listing p. 297)*, Prescott National Forest *(see place listing p. 196)* and Coconino National Forest allows for such outdoor activities as hiking and bird-watching.

VERDE CANYON RAILROAD, 300 N. Broadway, offers a 4-hour scenic ride through the Verde Canyon, adjacent to the Sycamore Wilderness Area near Sedona. Visitors can see Sinagua Indian ruins and such desert fauna as American bald eagles, great blue herons, red-tailed hawks, javelinas and deer. The open-air viewing cars are available to all.

Hours: Trains depart daily at 1. Special event and holiday rides are offered throughout the year; phone for details. Phone ahead to confirm schedule. **Cost:** First-class fare $89.95 (all ages). Coach fare $64.95; $59.95 (ages 65+); $44.95 (ages 2-12). Reservations are required. **Phone:** (928) 639-0010 or (877) 800-7326.

SU CASA OF CLARKDALE   928/634-2771
▼▼ ▼▼ Mexican. Family Dining. $7-$14 **AAA Inspector Notes:** Friendly service complements well-prepared dishes made to order from the freshest ingredients. The comfortable eatery is welcoming to families. **Features:** full bar, patio dining. **Address:** 1000 S Main St 86324 **Location:** Center. [L] [D]

COCONINO NATIONAL FOREST (C-4)

Elevations in the forest range from 2,600 ft. at Fossil Creek in the Verde Valley to 12,643 ft. at the San Francisco Peaks. Refer to AAA maps for additional elevation information.

Surrounding Flagstaff and Sedona, Coconino National Forest covers 1,821,495 acres. In the south the forest is cut by deep canyons; in the north the San Francisco Peaks attain the highest elevation in Arizona. These peaks, including Mount Humphreys, the state's highest point, and Mount Agassiz, are some of the places in Arizona where alpine conditions exist. Many roads provide scenic drives.

Outstanding features include the Mogollon Rim, at an altitude of 7,600 feet, and Oak Creek Canyon *(see Sedona p. 221).* Among the recreational facilities within the forest is the Arizona Snowbowl winter sports area *(see Flagstaff p. 60).* Lake Mary offers good fishing, boating and waterfowl hunting. Camping facilities are available in the area Memorial Day-Labor Day, with some facilities open throughout the year; an $8-$20 per night fee is charged. Campfire restrictions may be in effect.

For additional information contact the Forest Service, 1824 S. Thompson St., Flagstaff, AZ 86001, phone (928) 527-3600; or the Flagstaff Ranger District Office, 5075 N. SR 89, Flagstaff, AZ 86004, phone (928) 526-0866. *See Recreation Areas Chart.*

COOLIDGE (E-4) pop. 11,825, elev. 1,430'

Coolidge is east of the entrance to Casa Grande Ruins National Monument *(see place listing p. 46)* and just west of Pinal Pioneer Parkway (SR 79), a scenic route south to Tucson.

GOLDEN ERA TOY AND AUTO MUSEUM, off SR 87 at 297 W. Central Ave., features a collection of antique toys, dolls and model trains as well as restored automobiles. **Hours:** Sat.-Sun. 11-5, Jan.-May. **Cost:** $6; $2 (ages 3-12). **Phone:** (480) 948-9570 or (520) 723-5044.

CORNVILLE (C-4) pop. 3,280, elev. 3,304'

PAGE SPRINGS FISH HATCHERY is 5 mi. n. on Page Springs Rd. Rainbow trout are raised here for release into the Verde River and Oak Creek as well as other lakes and rivers statewide. Visitors can take a walking tour of the facility, stroll along a nature trail and view exhibits at a visitors center. **Hours:** Daily 7-3:30. Closed Thanksgiving and Christmas. **Cost:** Free. **Phone:** (928) 634-4805.

THE MANZANITA RESTAURANT   928/634-885¹
▼▼ ▼▼ Continental. Fine Dining. $15-$32 **AAA Inspector Notes** Chef Albert Kramer III prides himself on old-fashioned healthy cooking. Fresh local produce is used when available to accompany fresh meats, seafood, and wild game. The dining room has an old world ambiance. Set in Verde Valley wine country, this restaurant provides for a relaxing and enjoyable overall experience. **Features:** full bar. **Reservations:** suggested. **Address:** 11425 E Cornville Rd 86325 **Location:** 4.5 mi e of jct SR 89A. [L] [D]

CORONADO NATIONAL FOREST (E-5)
• Attractions map p. 265

Elevations in the forest range from 3,000 ft. in the Santa Catalina Mountains to 10,720 ft. in the Pinaleno Mountains. Refer to AAA maps for additional elevation information.

In southeastern Arizona and southwestern New Mexico, Coronado National Forest's 12 widely scattered sections cover 1,780,000 acres. Named for Spanish explorer Francisco Vázquez de Coronado, who journeyed through southern Arizona in 1540, the forest's varied plant and animal life reflects the area's extremes of elevation: Flat deserts of cacti and paloverde give way to rugged, heavily forested mountains known as the Madrean Sky Islands that are covered with oak, juniper, pine, fir and spruce, depending on the elevation.

Within the forest's boundaries are five fishing lakes. Mount Lemmon, northeast of Tucson, is one of the southernmost ski areas in the continental United States. More than 1,100 miles of trails offer hiking opportunities.

Madera Canyon, nestled in the Santa Rita Mountains, is a popular bird-watching spot with more than 200 species, including hummingbirds, woodpeckers and swallows. Hiking trails, a nature trail, picnic areas and campgrounds complete the area.

Scenic drives include Swift Trail in the Pinaleno Mountains (Mount Graham), Ruby Road in the Tumacácori Mountains, Onion Saddle Road and Rucker Canyon Road in the Chiricahua Mountains and SRs 82 and 83. The winding 28-mile Sky Island Scenic Byway begins at Tanque Verde Road in the desert just outside the Tucson city limits and extends to the top of Mount Lemmon in the Santa Catalina Mountains. Pullouts provide opportunities to observe the contrasts of the lower and upper regions.

Legend has it that Cochise's grave is somewhere within the Cochise Stronghold Recreation Area in the Dragoon Mountains. A natural rock fortress, the stronghold is where the Chiricahua Apache leader hid from his enemies. Camping and picnicking are permitted, and interpretive trails are available.

Picnicking and camping fees range from $10-$20. Day pass $5. Further information can be obtained at district offices in Douglas, (520) 364-3468; Nogales, (520) 281-2296; Safford, (928) 428-4150; Sierra Vista, (520) 378-0311; and Tucson, (520) 749-8700; or contact the Supervisor, Coronado National Forest, Federal Building, 300 W. Congress St., Tucson, AZ 85701; phone (520) 388-8300. *See Recreation Areas Chart.*

WHIPPLE OBSERVATORY is atop Mount Hopkins in the Santa Rita Mountains. The visitor center is accessible from I-19 exit 56 (Canoa Rd.); from Canoa Rd. turn e. to Frontage Rd., 3 mi. s. to Elephant Head Rd., 1 mi. e. to Mount Hopkins Rd., then 7 mi. s.e. The observatory houses one of the world's largest mirrored telescopes for conducting interstellar investigations. A visitor center has exhibits about astronomy, astrophysics and natural science as well as scenic views. A 6-hour guided tour of the observatory is available by appointment; phone for more information.

Hours: Visitor center open Mon.-Fri. 8:30-4:30. Tours depart Mon., Wed. and Fri. at 9, Mar.-Nov. Closed major holidays. **Cost:** Visitor center free. Observatory tour $10; $5 (ages 6-12). Ages 0-7 are not recommended. Reservations are required. **Phone:** (520) 879-4407.

CORONADO NATIONAL MEMORIAL (G-5)

Lying 22 miles south of Sierra Vista and 5 miles off SR 92, Coronado National Memorial was established to commemorate Francisco Vázquez de Coronado's exploration of the Southwest. The expedition, the first European venture across what is now the U.S.-Mexican border, began in February 1540 when the viceroy of Mexico sent young Coronado northward in search of gold from the fabled Seven Cities of Cibola.

Coronado led an expedition of more than 1,400 soldiers and natives as well as 1,500 animals. Five months of hard travel brought the party not to the gold of the fabled cities but to the rock and adobe pueblos of the Zuni Indians near Zuni, N.M. After traveling as far east as central Kansas, the expedition gave up its search and retraced the route to Mexico in 1542.

Although they never found the city of gold, Coronado and his men found the Grand Canyon as well as many Hopi, Zuni and other villages. Besides paying tribute to Coronado's journey, the memorial's 4,750 acres provide a natural habitat for a variety of plants and animals.

The park, at the southern end of the Huachuca Mountains, is mostly oak woodland sprinkled with yucca, cholla and bear grass, which bloom from April to August. The mountains and canyons harbor wildlife ranging from bobcats to golden eagles. Three miles west of the visitor center, an overlook provides a sweeping view of the San Rafael Valley, the San Pedro Valley and the San Jose Peak in Mexico.

An alternative to driving to the pass is the 3-mile-long Joe's Canyon Trail, which begins near the visitor center. A half-mile hiking trail, with benches for resting and exhibits explaining the significance of Coronado's expedition extends from the pass to Coronado Peak. The visitor center has a 14-foot-long window wall for viewing birds and wildlife. Picnic facilities are available dawn-dusk.

The visitor center is open daily 8-4; closed Christmas. Free. For further information contact the Visitor Center, Coronado National Memorial, 4101 E. Montezuma Canyon Rd., Hereford, AZ 85615; phone (520) 366-5515.

CORONADO CAVE is accessible via a steep half-mile trail w. of the visitor center. The cave, which remains in its natural state with no lighting or guardrails, features two chambers connected by a narrow passageway. Several short tunnels branch from the main cavern and require some crawling. **Note:** Visitors must be equipped with one flashlight per person. Comfortable walking shoes and water also are recommended. **Hours:** Daily dawn-dusk. **Cost:** Free. **Phone:** (520) 366-5515.

COTTONWOOD (C-3) pop. 11,265, elev. 3,314'
• Hotels p. 56 • Restaurants p. 56

One of two Arizona towns called Cottonwood, this Cottonwood is in the center of the 1,500-square-mile Verde Valley, which contributed to its development as a commerce center for the area. In 1874 soldiers from nearby Camp Verde were quartered in town. Settlers eventually arrived and named the community for a nearby stand of 16 large cottonwood trees. Cottonwood is about 2 miles southeast of Tuzigoot National Monument (see place listing p. 297).

Cottonwood Chamber of Commerce: 1010 S. Main St., Cottonwood, AZ 86326. **Phone:** (928) 634-7593.

BLAZIN' M RANCH is 1 mi. n. on 10th St. to 1875 Mabery Ranch Rd., following signs from Main St. Cowboy-style entertainment and a chuck wagon supper are offered in a re-created Western town with boutiques, a museum and farm animals. There also is a tractor pull, roping lessons, a shooting gallery and a saloon.

Time: Allow 2 hours minimum. **Hours:** Performances are given Wed.-Sat. at 7:30 p.m. Gates open at 5, and the dinner bell rings at 6:30. **Cost:** $35.95; $32.95 (ages 65+); $19.95 (ages 3-12). Reservations are recommended. **Phone:** (928) 634-0334 or (800) 937-8643.

CLEMENCEAU HERITAGE MUSEUM is at jct. Willard St. and Mingus Ave. at 1 N. Willard St. The museum is housed in a former schoolhouse built 1923-24. Seven railroads that operated in the Verde Valley 1895-1953 are depicted in a working railroad diorama. The diorama also depicts farming and ranching. Exhibits on permanent display include a typical 1920s bedroom, kitchen and dining room as well as a schoolroom. **Time:** Allow 30 minutes minimum. **Hours:** Fri.-Sun. 11-3, Wed. 9-noon. **Cost:** Donations. **Phone:** (928) 634-2868.

DEAD HORSE RANCH STATE PARK is at 675 Dead Horse Ranch Rd. The Ireys family, who bought the ranch in the late 1940s, chose the name after finding a horse skeleton on the property. Once the stomping grounds of Native Americans and

Spanish conquistadors, the park now features Quetta Seed Pine Orchard; three stocked fishing ponds; trails for hiking, biking and horseback riding; and picnic areas overlooking the Verde River. *See Recreation Areas Chart.*

Cabins, camping and trail rides are available. Boating is permitted; as the park does not provide boats, visitors may bring nonmotorized personal watercraft. **Hours:** Park open daily dawn-dusk. Ranger station 8-4:30; closed Christmas. **Cost:** $7 (per private vehicle, up to four passengers); $3 (per additional adult passenger in vehicle or individual arriving on foot or bicycle). Camping $15-$30 (per private vehicle). Cabins $55. Trail rides $65-$205 (per person). Reservations are required for cabins and group sites. **Phone:** (928) 634-5283, or (520) 586-2283 for camping reservations.

WINERIES

• **Alcantara Vineyards** is at 3445 S. Grapevine Way. **Hours:** Tours Fri.-Sat. at 11:30 and by appointment. Tastings daily 11-5. **Phone:** (928) 649-8463. GT

AZ PINES MOTEL   (928)634-9975

Motel $75-$159 **Address:** 920 S Camino Real 86326 **Location:** Jct SR 260, just nw on SR 89A, then just s. **Facility:** 25 units, some efficiencies. 2 stories (no elevator), exterior corridors. **Pool(s):** heated outdoor. **Guest Services:** coin laundry.

BEST WESTERN COTTONWOOD INN   (928)634-5575

Hotel
$105-$180

AAA Benefit: Save 10% or more every day and earn 10% bonus points!

Address: 993 S Main St 86326 **Location:** On SR 89A, at SR 260. Across from a shopping center. **Facility:** 77 units. 1-2 stories (no elevator), exterior corridors. **Pool(s):** heated outdoor. **Activities:** hot tub. **Guest Services:** coin laundry. **Featured Amenity:** breakfast buffet.

QUALITY INN   (928)634-4207

Hotel
$80-$95

Address: 301 W SR 89A 86326 **Location:** 2.8 mi sw of jct SR 260. Across from Verde Valley Medical Center. **Facility:** 51 units. 2 stories (no elevator), exterior corridors. **Amenities:** safes. **Pool(s):** outdoor. **Activities:** hot tub. **Featured Amenity:** continental breakfast.

SUPER 8 COTTONWOOD   (928)639-1888

Hotel $62-$80 **Address:** 800 S Main St 86326 **Location:** On SR 89A, 0.4 mi nw of jct SR 260. **Facility:** 52 units. 2 stories (no elevator), exterior corridors. **Terms:** cancellation fee imposed. **Pool(s):** outdoor. **Activities:** hot tub.

THE VIEW MOTEL   928/634-7581

Motel
$59-$150

Address: 818 S Main St 86326 **Location:** On SR 89A, 0.4 mi nw of jct SR 260. **Facility:** 35 units, some three bedrooms and kitchens. 1 story, exterior corridors. **Pool(s):** heated outdoor. **Activities:** hot tub.

WHERE TO EAT

MAI THAI ON MAIN   928/649-2999

Thai. Casual Dining. $10-$15 **AAA Inspector Notes:** Dishes ranging from classic pad thai to choices of curry, including panang, red, mussamon and green, are served by friendly and helpful staff members who guide guests through the heat levels. Many vegetarian dishes are on the menu. **Features:** full bar. **Address:** 157 S Main St 86326 **Location:** 1.1 mi nw of jct SR 260.
L D

NIC'S ITALIAN STEAK & CRAB HOUSE   928/634-9626

Steak Seafood. Casual Dining. $11-$36 **AAA Inspector Notes:** This local favorite seems to be packed every night for the fresh and reasonably priced seafood and steaks. The service is very casual and other tasty pasta and chicken dishes are offered. There are great deals at the bar on wine and set menu items. **Features:** full bar. **Address:** 925 N Main St 86326 **Location:** Center. D

THE TAVERN GRILLE   928/634-6669

American. Gastropub. $9-$25 **AAA Inspector Notes:** This small restaurant is very popular and gets packed daily for the happy hour specials. The red brick walls are covered with flat-screen TVs making it a great place to enjoy the game. The menu serves upscale bar favorites such as ahi tuna sashimi, burgers, sandwiches, New York steak and pasta dishes. **Features:** full bar, patio dining, happy hour. **Address:** 914 N Main St 86326 **Location:** Center. **Parking:** street only. L D

DOUGLAS (G-6) pop. 17,378, elev. 3,955'

Douglas, on the Mexican border, began as the site of annual roundups for surrounding ranches. The town was founded in 1901 by a copper-smelting company and is now a center for commerce, manufacturing, agriculture and tourism.

The Gadsden Hotel, 1046 G Ave., was built in 1906 and has a high-ceilinged lobby with a mural of Tiffany stained glass and a curving staircase. Of interest in the vicinity are many ghost towns and mining camps as well as shopping and sightseeing opportunities in nearby Agua Prieta, Mexico.

Douglas Visitors Center: 345 16th St., Douglas, AZ 85607. **Phone:** (520) 417-7344.

Self-guiding tours: Maps detailing self-guiding historical tours of Douglas are available at the visitor center.

SLAUGHTER RANCH MUSEUM (SAN BERNARDINO RANCH NATIONAL HISTORIC LANDMARK), 16 mi. e. on 15th St. (which turns into Geronimo Tr.), was the home of John Slaughter. The former Texas Ranger and sheriff of Cochise County developed the property he purchased in 1884 into a vast cattle ranch. Now restored, the opulent main house contains many original family photographs and furnishings. Also on the ranch are a car shed, granary, barn, icehouse and washhouse. Near the ranch is a military outpost originally established by Spaniards and later used by the U.S. Army in the early 1900s.

Time: Allow 2 hours minimum. **Hours:** Wed.-Sun. 9:30-3:30. Closed Jan. 1 and Christmas. **Cost:** $5; free (ages 0-17). **Phone:** (520) 678-7935 or (520) 678-7596.

BEST WESTERN DOUGLAS INN & SUITES

(520)364-5000

Hotel
$99-$139

AAA Benefit: Save 10% or more every day and earn 10% bonus points!

Address: 199 E 7th St 85607 **Location:** Jct SR 80, 0.6 mi s on Pan American Ave. **Facility:** 69 units. 3 stories, interior corridors. **Pool(s):** heated outdoor. **Activities:** hot tub, exercise room. **Guest Services:** coin laundry.

THE GADSDEN HOTEL   520/364-4481

[fyi] Hotel Did not meet all AAA rating requirements for locking devices in some guest rooms at time of last evaluation on 12/11/2013. **Address:** 1046 G Ave 85607 **Location:** Center. Facilities, services, and décor characterize an economy property. This charming historic hotel has a lobby with 40 feet of Tiffany stained glass, a wide central staircase and huge marble columns.

DRAGOON (F-5) pop. 209, elev. 4,615'

AMERIND MUSEUM AND RESEARCH CENTER, I-10, exit 318, 1 mi. s. on Dragoon Rd. to 2100 N. Amerind Rd., is an extension of the Amerind (an amalgamated name formed from the words American and Indian) Foundation's archeological research facility. Featured are artifacts, crafts, art and photographs documenting Native American peoples from Alaska to South America.

An art gallery contains works with Western themes by such well-known artists as Carl Oscar Borg, William Leigh and Frederic Remington as well as a variety of contemporary paintings and furnishings dating from the 17th century. **Time:** Allow 1 hour, 30 minutes minimum. **Hours:** Tues.-Sun. 10-4. Closed major holidays. **Cost:** $10; $9 (ages 60+); $8 (ages 12-18 and students with ID). **Phone:** (520) 586-3666.

EAGAR pop. 4,885

BEST WESTERN SUNRISE INN   (928)333-2540

Motel
$96-$115

AAA Benefit: Save 10% or more every day and earn 10% bonus points!

Address: 128 N Main St 85925 **Location:** Jct SR 260, just n; jct US 60, 1.5 mi s. **Facility:** 41 units. 2 stories (no elevator), exterior corridors. **Activities:** sauna, exercise room. **Guest Services:** coin laundry. **Featured Amenity:** continental breakfast.

Best Western

Gateway to the White Mountains! Located next to Bashas' Grocery and Trail Riders Restaurant.

EHRENBERG pop. 1,470

BEST WESTERN DESERT OASIS   (928)923-9711

Hotel
$100-$189

AAA Benefit: Save 10% or more every day and earn 10% bonus points!

Address: S Frontage Rd 85334 **Location:** I-10 exit 1, just s; 0.5 mi e of Colorado River. Located at Flying J Travel Plaza. **Facility:** 83 units. 2 stories (no elevator), interior corridors. **Pool(s):** outdoor. **Activities:** hot tub, picnic facilities, exercise room. **Guest Services:** coin laundry. **Featured Amenity:** full hot breakfast.

ELGIN (G-5) pop. 161, elev. 4,700'

WINERIES

• **Sonoita Vineyards,** 3 mi. s. on Elgin/Canelo Rd. **Hours:** Daily 10-4. Closed major holidays. **Phone:** (520) 455-5893. GT

ELOY pop. 16,631

MOTEL 6 #1263   (520)836-3323

Motel $45-$61 **Address:** 4965 S Sunland Gin Rd 85231 **Location:** I-10 exit 200, just w. **Facility:** 97 units. 2 stories (no elevator), exterior corridors. **Pool(s):** outdoor. **Guest Services:** coin laundry.

FLAGSTAFF (C-4) pop. 65,870, elev. 6,905'
• Hotels p. 63 • Restaurants p. 68
• Hotels & Restaurants map & index p. 61
• Part of Grand Canyon National Park area — see map p. 82

Flagstaff rests on the Colorado Plateau under the gaze of the San Francisco Peaks amid ponderosa pine forests, high deserts and lakes. Dusted with snow in winter and wildflowers in summer, the mountains provide a scenic backdrop for what was once a mere rest stop.

The town was established in 1881. The name Flagstaff is believed to refer to a ponderosa pine tree that was stripped of its branches and used as a flagstaff by members of an exploration party during Fourth of July celebrations in 1876. The flagstaff, visible from afar, remained in place to serve as a landmark for wagon trains bound for California; transients knew that they would find a good place to camp when they spotted it.

Shepherd Thomas F. McMillan, said to be the town's first permanent resident, deemed the land perfect for raising sheep when he arrived in 1876. Early industry revolved around timber, sheep and cattle, but when the Atlantic and Pacific Railway Co. (now the Santa Fe) decided to merge with the Southern Pacific line, settlers again put out their welcome mats, providing water and supplies to the railroad crews. The railroad reached Flagstaff in 1882. The Flagstaff Railroad Depot, on SR 66 between S. San Francisco and S. Beaver streets, opened in 1926. Impressive with its Revival Tudor style, it now houses the Flagstaff Visitor Center and an Amtrak station.

Downtown Flagstaff, which grew up around the railroad depot, contains many historic buildings dating from the late 1800s to early 1900s. Plaques and seasonal tours give insight to buildings' former functions.

The Northern Arizona Normal School, established in 1899, was renamed Northern Arizona University in 1966. The university contributes to Flagstaff's college town feel. NAU's north campus, which encompasses 140 acres, boasts numerous restored buildings constructed 1894-1935 of local sandstone. This area reputedly contains the largest number of restored sandstone buildings in the Southwest.

In the 1920s, Route 66 brought travelers through town; they stayed briefly yet contributed to the economy. Money from tourism helped Flagstaff become an incorporated city in 1928, and the route continues to attract visitors.

Another popular drive is the 54-mile scenic stretch of SR 89A that begins in Flagstaff, winds its way south through Oak Creek Canyon and ends in Jerome. (The steep, narrow road is not recommended for vehicles pulling trailers more than 40 feet long.)

The city remains a good home base for many day trips. Within the boundaries of Coconino County, the second largest in the country, visitors will find Grand Canyon National Park *(see place listing p. 82)*, Meteor Crater *(see attraction listing p. 305)*, Oak Creek Canyon *(see Sedona p. 221)*, Sunset Crater Volcano National Monument *(see place listing p. 242)*, Walnut Canyon National Monument *(see place listing p. 297)* and Wupatki National Monument *(see place listing p. 306)*. The landscape varies from deep green woodlands to rugged, rocky escarpments and provides for nearly every recreational pursuit, from skiing and hiking to camping, hunting and fishing.

Flagstaff Convention & Visitors Bureau: 211 W. Aspen Ave., Flagstaff, AZ 86001. **Phone:** (928) 213-2901 or (800) 217-2367. *(See ad p. 59.)*

Flagstaff Visitor Center: 1 E. Rte. 66, Historic Train Station, Flagstaff, AZ 86001. **Phone:** (928) 213-2951 or (800) 842-7293.

Self-guiding tours: Maps outlining walking tours of Flagstaff's historic downtown area, Route 66 and supposedly haunted locations are available at the Flagstaff Visitor Center in the historic train station on Route 66. The center also sells Grand Canyon Park entry passes.

Shopping: Flagstaff Mall and The Marketplace, 6 miles east at 4650 SR 89N, has more than 70 stores, including Dillard's, JCPenney and Sears. Flagstaff's downtown historic district also offers shopping opportunities.

THE ARBORETUM AT FLAGSTAFF, off SR 66 to Woody Mountain Rd., then 4 mi. s., highlights more than 750 species of native plants in natural settings. One of the country's largest collections of mountain wildflowers may be seen; peak wildflower season is July through August. A nature trail traverses meadows and a ponderosa pine forest. A guided garden tour is offered, and a presentation features falcons, hawks and owls native to the Southwest.

Time: Allow 2 hours minimum. **Hours:** Wed.-Mon. 9-4, May-Oct. Garden tour daily at 11 and 1. Raptor program Wed.-Thurs. and Sat.-Mon. at noon and 2, May-Sept. **Cost:** $8.50; $6 (senior citizens); $3 (ages 6-17). **Phone:** (928) 774-1442.

ARIZONA HISTORICAL SOCIETY PIONEER MUSEUM is 2 mi. n.w. at 2340 N. Fort Valley Rd. (US 180). The museum is in a former hospital for the indigent built in 1908 and contains interpretive historical exhibits about livestock, medicine, domestic life and the lumbering industry in northern Arizona. A 1908 homesteader's cabin, a 1929 Baldwin articulated locomotive and a 1940s Santa Fe caboose are on the premises. Festivals and programs take place throughout the year.

Time: Allow 1 hour minimum. **Hours:** Mon.-Sat. 9-5; closed Jan. 1, Martin Luther King Jr. Day, Presidents Day, Columbus Day, Veterans Day, Thanksgiving and Christmas. **Cost:** $6; $5 (ages 65+ and students with ID); $3 (ages 7-17). Prices may vary; phone ahead. **Phone:** (928) 774-6272. 🕎

(See map & index p. 61.)

LOWELL OBSERVATORY is 1 mi. w. of downtown via Santa Fe Ave. to 1400 W. Mars Hill Rd., following signs. The observatory was founded in 1894 by Percival Lowell. Discoveries made here include Lowell's observations about the planet Mars, the basis for the theory of the expanding universe and the discovery of Pluto in 1930. The Putnam Collection Center houses equipment and archives. Traveling exhibits change every few months.

Daytime tours explore the Rotunda Museum and the Pluto Discovery Telescope, the instrument used when Pluto was first identified here in 1930. At night, you can use the observatory's telescopes to catch a glimpse of planets, the moon and other celestial wonders. Research continues at the observatory with the operation of seven modern telescopes, including the Discovery Channel Telescope.

Hours: Mon.-Sat. 10-10, Sun. 10-5 (also Sun. before Mon. holidays 5-10). Closed major holidays. **Cost:** $12; $11 (ages 65+ and college students with ID); $6 (ages 5-17). **Phone:** (928) 774-3358.

MUSEUM OF NORTHERN ARIZONA is 3 mi. n. to 3101 N. Fort Valley Rd. (US 180). The museum contains displays about artistic traditions, native cultures and natural science, including exhibits about anthropology, biology and geology. A reproduction of

▼ See AAA listing p. 58 ▼

(See map & index p. 61.)

a kiva—a meeting place and ceremonial room—also is featured. Recreation programs and festivals are offered in summer.

Hours: Mon.-Sat. 10-5, Sun. noon-5. Closed Jan. 1, Thanksgiving and Christmas. **Cost:** $10; $9 (ages 65+); $7 (students with ID); $6 (Native Americans and ages 10-17). **Phone:** (928) 774-5213.

NORTHERN ARIZONA UNIVERSITY ART MUSEUM is at 321 Mc Mullen Cir., jct. Tormey St. and Knoles Dr., building #10 on campus. Five galleries, two with permanent collections and three with changing exhibits, feature oil paintings on canvas, sculptures, contemporary art and American antiques. **Time:** Allow 30 minutes minimum. **Hours:** Tues.-Sat. noon-5. **Cost:** Donations. **Phone:** (928) 523-3471.

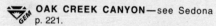 **OAK CREEK CANYON**—see Sedona p. 221.

RIORDAN MANSION STATE HISTORIC PARK is .5 mi. n. of jct. I-17 and I-40 (off Milton Rd.) at 409 W. Riordan Rd. Built in 1904, the 40-room mansion was home to prominent lumbermen Timothy and Michael Riordan and their families. The rustic exterior incorporates log-slab siding, volcanic stone arches and hand-split wood shingles. The lavish Arts and Crafts-style interior contains handcrafted and Stickley furniture, a Steinway piano, stained-glass windows and personal family items, which can be seen via a guided tour. The park's visitor center has exhibits and a children's "touch table."

Time: Allow 1 hour minimum. **Hours:** Grounds daily 9:30-5, May-Oct.; Thurs.-Mon. 10:30-5, rest of year. Guided tours of the mansion are given on the hour daily 10-4, May-Oct.; 11-4, rest of year. Closed

Thanksgiving and Christmas. Phone ahead to confirm schedule. **Cost:** $10; $5 (ages 7-13). Reservations are recommended for guided tours. **Phone:** (928) 779-4395. GT

SCHULTZ PASS ROAD (FR 420) leads n. off US 180 and offers a scenic drive through Schultz Pass between the San Francisco Peaks and Elden Mountain. Travelers may also access the road via bicycle and horseback, often catching a glimpse of such resident animals as mule deer and elk.

Note: Portions of the road may be closed due to fire activity or inclement weather; snow closes the road during winter months. Passenger vehicles are not permitted during these conditions. **Phone:** (928) 526-0866 for current road condition updates from the Peaks Ranger Station or (928) 527-3600.

RECREATIONAL ACTIVITIES
Skiing

- **Arizona Snowbowl**, in the San Francisco Peaks, is 7 mi. n. on Fort Valley Rd. (US 180), then 7 mi. n. on Snowbowl Rd. Other activities are offered. **Hours:** Skiing is available daily 9-4, late Nov.-early Apr. Scenic SkyRide Fri.-Sun. and holidays 10-4, Memorial Day to mid-Oct. **Phone:** (928) 779-1951.
- **Flagstaff Nordic Center**, in the San Francisco Peaks, is on US 180 at mile marker 232. Other activities are offered. **Hours:** Daily 9-4 (weather permitting). Phone ahead to confirm schedule. **Phone:** (928) 220-0550.
- **Wing Mountain Snow Play Area**, in the San Francisco Peaks, is on US 180 n. to mile marker 226, then left on FR 222B. Other activities are offered. **Hours:** Daily 9-4, Dec.-Mar. (weather permitting). Phone ahead to confirm schedule. **Phone:** (602) 923-3555.

▼ See AAA listing p. 305 ▼

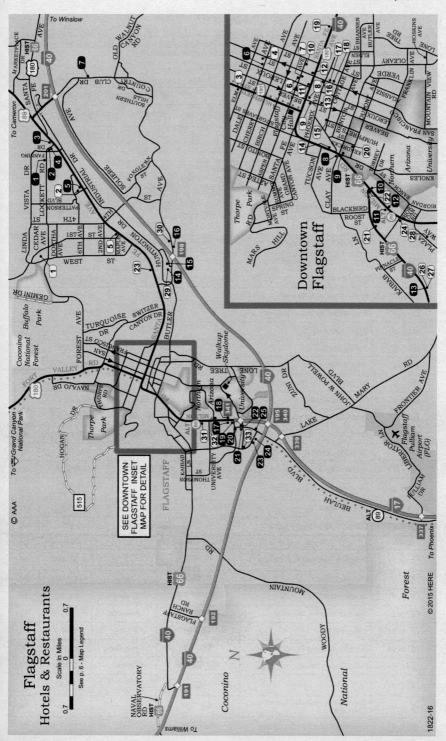

Flagstaff
Hotels & Restaurants

Scale in Miles

See p. 6 - Map Legend

Downtown Flagstaff

© AAA

©2015 HERE

1822-16

Flagstaff

This index helps you "spot" where approved hotels and restaurants are located on the corresponding detailed maps. Hotel daily rate range is for comparison only. Restaurant price range is a combination of lunch and/or dinner. Turn to the listing page for more detailed rate and price information and consult display ads for special promotions.

FLAGSTAFF

Map Page	Hotels	Diamond Rated	Rate Range	Page
1 p. 61	Starlight Pines, A Bed & Breakfast	◆◆◆	$159-$179	68
2 p. 61	Country Inn & Suites By Carlson, Flagstaff	◆◆	Rates not provided	63
3 p. 61	**Super 8-Flagstaff Mall**	◆◆	$50-$102 SAVE	68
4 p. 61	**Days Inn & Suites** *(See ad p. 64.)*	◆◆	$63-$150 SAVE	64
5 p. 61	**BEST WESTERN Pony Soldier Inn & Suites**	◆◆	$79-$199 SAVE	63
6 p. 61	The Inn at 410 Bed & Breakfast	◆◆◆	$180-$260	66
7 p. 61	**Sonesta ES Suites Flagstaff**	◆◆◆	Rates not provided SAVE	68
8 p. 61	**Highland Country Inn**	◆◆	$49-$159 SAVE	65
9 p. 61	Drury Inn & Suites-Flagstaff	◆◆◆	$100-$240	65
10 p. 61	Embassy Suites by Hilton Flagstaff	◆◆◆	$129-$329	65
11 p. 61	**Budget Inn**	◆◆	$49-$149 SAVE	63
12 p. 61	**Econo Lodge-University**	◆◆	$50-$185 SAVE	65
13 p. 61	**DoubleTree by Hilton Flagstaff** *(See ad p. 65.)*	◆◆◆	$119-$249 SAVE	64
14 p. 61	**Days Hotel Flagstaff**	◆◆	$56-$87 SAVE	64
15 p. 61	Holiday Inn Express	◆◆◆	$99-$229	66
16 p. 61	**Little America Hotel** *(See ad p. 67.)*	◆◆◆	$99-$269 SAVE	68
17 p. 61	Baymont Inn & Suites Flagstaff	◆◆	$99-$209	63
18 p. 61	Quality Inn University	◆◆	$60-$150	68
19 p. 61	**Hilton Garden Inn** *(See ad p. 66.)*	◆◆◆	$99-$309 SAVE	65
20 p. 61	Comfort Inn I-17/I-40	◆◆◆	$90-$190	63
21 p. 61	SpringHill Suites by Marriott	◆◆◆	$98-$244	68
22 p. 61	Hampton Inn & Suites	◆◆◆	$139-$289	65
23 p. 61	Motel 6-Flagstaff West #1000	◆	Rates not provided	68
24 p. 61	**Ramada West**	◆◆	$54-$97 SAVE	68
25 p. 61	Courtyard by Marriott-Flagstaff	◆◆◆	$96-$251	64

Map Page	Restaurants	Diamond Rated	Cuisine	Price Range	Page
1 p. 61	**Brandy's Restaurant & Bakery**	◆◆	Breakfast Sandwiches	$5-$10	69
2 p. 61	Mamma Luisa	◆◆	Italian	$12-$21	70
3 p. 61	**Josephine's**	◆◆◆	American	$10-$27	69
4 p. 61	Brix Restaurant & Wine Bar	◆◆◆	American	$15-$36	69
5 p. 61	Salsa Brava	◆◆	Mexican	$7-$17	70
6 p. 61	Monsoon Chinese Bistro & Sushi	◆◆	Asian Sushi	$10-$28	70
7 p. 61	Pasto Cucina Italiana	◆◆◆	Italian	$9-$26	70
8 p. 61	La Bellavia	◆	Breakfast Sandwiches	$5-$9	70
9 p. 61	Beaver Street Brewery & Whistle Stop Cafe	◆◆	American	$9-$13	68
10 p. 61	Swaddee Authentic Thai Cuisine	◆◆	Thai	$11-$16	70

Map Page	Restaurants (cont'd)	Diamond Rated	Cuisine	Price Range	Page
⑪ p. 61	**Karma Sushi Bar Grill**	◆◆	Japanese Sushi	$9-$26	69
⑫ p. 61	Majerle's Sports Grill	◆◆	American	$8-$14	70
⑬ p. 61	Macy's European Coffee House & Bakery	◆	Breads/Pastries Coffee/Tea	$7-$8	70
⑮ p. 61	**Cottage Place Restaurant**	◆◆◆	Continental	$21-$37	69
⑯ p. 61	Lumberyard Brewing Company	◆◆	American	$8-$16	70
⑰ p. 61	Dara Thai Restaurant	◆◆	Thai	$7-$14	69
⑱ p. 61	Tinderbox Kitchen	◆◆◆	Northern American	$20-$35	70
⑲ p. 61	Kachina Restaurant	◆	Mexican	$7-$26	69
⑳ p. 61	**1899 Bar & Grill**	◆◆◆	American	$8-$33	68
㉑ p. 61	Galaxy Diner	◆◆	Comfort Food	$5-$12	69
㉒ p. 61	Bun Huggers	◆	American	$5-$8	69
㉓ p. 61	China Star	◆	Chinese	$7-$9	69
㉔ p. 61	Little Thai Kitchen	◆	Thai	$6-$14	70
㉖ p. 61	**Sakura Restaurant** *(See ad p. 65.)*	◆◆	Japanese	$10-$29	70
㉗ p. 61	**Woodlands Restaurant** *(See ad p. 65.)*	◆◆	American	$7-$24	70
㉘ p. 61	Hiro's Sushi Bar & Japanese Restaurant	◆◆	Japanese	$10-$21	69
㉙ p. 61	**The Northern Pines Restaurant**	◆◆	American	$8-$27	70
㉚ p. 61	**Black Bart's Steak House & Musical Revue**	◆◆	Steak	$12-$42	69
㉛ p. 61	Hickory's Smokehouse BBQ	◆	Barbecue	$9-$20	69
㉜ p. 61	Buster's	◆◆	American	$9-$26	69
㉝ p. 61	Delhi Palace	◆◆	Indian	$9-$20	69

BAYMONT INN & SUITES FLAGSTAFF (928)773-1300
◆◆ Hotel $99-$209 **Address:** 2005 S Milton Rd 86001 **Location:** I-40 exit 195, 0.5 mi n. **Facility:** 130 units. 3 stories, interior/exterior corridors. **Pool(s):** heated outdoor. **Activities:** hot tub, exercise room. **Guest Services:** valet laundry.

BEST WESTERN PONY SOLDIER INN & SUITES
(928)526-2388

Hotel
$79-$199

AAA Benefit: Save 10% or more every day and earn 10% bonus points!

Address: 3030 E Route 66 86004 **Location:** I-40 exit 201, just n, then 1 mi w. Next to railroad tracks. **Facility:** 75 units, some two bedrooms. 2 stories (no elevator), interior corridors. **Pool(s):** heated indoor. **Activities:** hot tub. **Featured Amenity:** breakfast buffet.

BUDGET INN (928)774-5038
◆◆
Motel
$49-$149

Address: 913 S Milton Rd 86001 **Location:** I-40 exit 195, 1.2 mi n. **Facility:** 38 units. 2 stories (no elevator), exterior corridors. **Terms:** 3 day cancellation notice-fee imposed.

COMFORT INN I-17/I-40 (928)774-2225 ⑳
◆◆ Hotel $90-$190 **Address:** 2355 S Beulah Blvd 86001 **Location:** I-40 exit 195, just n to Forest Meadows St, then 1 blk w. **Facility:** 85 units. 2 stories, interior corridors. **Pool(s):** heated outdoor. **Activities:** hot tub, exercise room. **Guest Services:** valet and coin laundry.

COUNTRY INN & SUITES BY CARLSON, FLAGSTAFF
928)526-1885
◆◆ Hotel. Rates not provided. **Address:** 3501 E Lockett Rd 86004 **Location:** I-40 exit 201, 0.5 mi w on I-40 business loop, then just n on Fanning Dr. **Facility:** 50 units. 2 stories, interior corridors. **Pool(s):** heated indoor. **Activities:** hot tub, exercise room. **Guest Services:** valet laundry.

(See map & index p. 61.)

COURTYARD BY MARRIOTT-FLAGSTAFF
(928)774-5800 **25**

▼▼▼ Hotel $96-$251 **Address:** 2650 S Beulah Blvd 86001 **Location:** I-40 exit 195, just n to Forest Meadows St, just w to Beulah Blvd, then just s. **Facility:** 164 units. 4 stories, interior corridors. **Pool(s):** heated indoor. **Activities:** hot tub, exercise room. **Guest Services:** valet and coin laundry.

AAA Benefit: Members save 5% or more!

DAYS HOTEL FLAGSTAFF
(928)779-6944 **14**

▼▼▼ Hotel $56-$87

Address: 2200 E Butler Ave 86004 **Location:** I-40 exit 198 (Butler Ave), just n. **Facility:** 100 units. 3 stories, interior corridors. **Amenities:** safes. **Dining:** The Northern Pines Restaurant, see separate listing. **Pool(s):** heated indoor. **Activities:** sauna, hot tub, exercise room. **Guest Services:** coin laundry.

Visit AAA.com/searchfordiscounts to save on travel, shopping, dining and attractions

DAYS INN & SUITES
(928)527-1477 **4**

▼▼▼ Hotel $63-$150

Address: 3601 E Lockett Rd 86004 **Location:** I-40 business loop, then just n on Fanning Dr. **Facility:** 54 units. 3 stories, interior corridors. **Amenities:** safes. **Pool(s):** heated indoor. **Activities:** hot tub, exercise room. **Guest Services:** valet and coin laundry. **Featured Amenity:** full hot breakfast. *(See ad this page.)*

DOUBLETREE BY HILTON FLAGSTAFF
(928)773-8888 **13**

▼▼▼ Hotel $119-$249

AAA Benefit: Members save 5% or more!

Address: 1175 W Route 66 86001 **Location:** I-40 exit 195, 1.5 mi n on SR 89A (Milton Rd), then 0.5 mi w. **Facility:** 183 units. 3-4 stories, interior corridors. **Terms:** check-in 4 pm, 1-7 night minimum stay, cancellation fee imposed. **Amenities:** safes. **Dining:** Sakura Restaurant, Woodlands Restaurant, see separate listings. **Pool(s):** heated outdoor. **Activities:** sauna, hot tub, exercise room. **Guest Services:** valet and coin laundry, area transportation. *(See ad p. 65.)*

▼ See AAA listing this page ▼

(See map & index p. 61.)

DRURY INN & SUITES-FLAGSTAFF (928)773-4900 **9**

 Hotel $100-$240 **Address:** 300 S Milton Rd 86001 **Location:** I-40 exit 195, 1.8 mi n on SR 89A (Milton Rd). **Facility:** 160 units, some two bedrooms. 6 stories, interior corridors. **Terms:** cancellation fee imposed. **Pool(s):** heated indoor. **Activities:** hot tub, exercise room. **Guest Services:** valet and coin laundry.

[ECO] [†↑] CALL [&M] [≈] [BIZ] [≈] [✕] [☐] [☐] [▭] / SOME UNITS [☐]

ECONO LODGE-UNIVERSITY (928)774-7326 **12**

Motel
$50-$185

Address: 914 S Milton Rd 86001 **Location:** I-40 exit 195, 1.2 mi n on SR 89A (Milton Rd). **Facility:** 66 units. 2 stories (no elevator), exterior corridors. **Pool(s):** heated outdoor. **Guest Services:** coin laundry. **Featured Amenity:** continental breakfast.

[SAVE] [†↑] [≈] [≈] [✕] [☐] [☐] [▭] / SOME UNITS [☐]

EMBASSY SUITES BY HILTON FLAGSTAFF (928)774-4333 **10**

Hotel $129-$329 **Address:** 706 S Milton Rd 86001 **Location:** I-40 exit 195, 1.5 mi n on SR 89A (Milton Rd). Adjacent to Northern Arizona University. **Facility:** 119 units, some two bedrooms. 3 stories, interior corridors. **Terms:** check-in 4 pm, 1-7 night minimum stay, cancellation fee imposed. **Pool(s):** heated indoor. **Activities:** hot tub, exercise room. **Guest Services:** valet and coin laundry.

AAA Benefit: Members save 5% or more!

[ECO] [†↑] [♿] [Y] [≈] [BIZ] [≈] [☐] [☐] [▭]

HAMPTON INN & SUITES (928)913-0900 **22**

 Hotel $139-$289 **Address:** 2400 S Beulah Blvd 86001 **Location:** I-40 exit 195, just n to Forest Meadows St, just w, then just s. **Facility:** 126 units, some efficiencies. 5 stories, interior corridors. **Terms:** 1-7 night minimum stay, cancellation fee imposed. **Pool(s):** heated indoor. **Activities:** hot tub, exercise room. **Guest Services:** valet and coin laundry.

AAA Benefit: Members save up to 10%!

[†↑] CALL [&M] [≈] [BIZ] [HS] [≈] [✕] [▭] / SOME UNITS [☐] [☐]

HIGHLAND COUNTRY INN (928)774-5041 **8**

Motel
$49-$159

Address: 223 S Beulah Blvd 86001 **Location:** I-40 exit 195, 1.8 mi n on SR 89A (Milton Rd). **Facility:** 42 units. 2 stories (no elevator), exterior corridors. **Terms:** 3 day cancellation notice-fee imposed. **Guest Services:** coin laundry.

[SAVE] [†↑] [≈] [☐] [☐]

HILTON GARDEN INN (928)226-8888 **19**

Hotel
$99-$309

 Hilton Garden Inn

AAA Benefit: Members save up to 10%!

Address: 350 W Forest Meadows St 86001 **Location:** I-40 exit 195, 0.5 mi n on SR 89A (Milton Rd), then just w. **Facility:** 89 units. 3 stories, interior corridors. **Terms:** 1-7 night minimum stay, cancellation fee imposed. **Pool(s):** heated indoor. **Activities:** sauna, hot tub, exercise room. **Guest Services:** valet and coin laundry. (See ad p. 66.)

[SAVE] [†↑] CALL [&M] [≈] [BIZ] [HS] [≈] [☐] [☐] [▭]

▼ See AAA listing p. 64 ▼

(See map & index p. 61.)

HOLIDAY INN EXPRESS   (928)714-1000 **15**
▼▼▼▼ **Hotel** $99-$229 **Address:** 2320 E Lucky Ln 86004 **Location:** I-40 exit 198 (Butler Ave), just n, then just e. **Facility:** 155 units. 5 stories, interior corridors. **Pool(s):** heated outdoor, heated indoor. **Activities:** hot tub, exercise room. **Guest Services:** valet and coin laundry.

THE INN AT 410 BED & BREAKFAST   (928)774-0088 **6**
▼▼▼▼ **Historic Bed & Breakfast** $180-$260 **Address:** 410 N Leroux St 86001 **Location:** Just n of Cherry Ave. **Facility:** A garden gazebo accents the grounds of this charming 1907 Craftsman home, which is comfortably furnished with antiques and Southwestern touches. 10 units. 2 stories (no elevator), interior/exterior corridors. **Terms:** 2 night minimum stay - seasonal and/or weekends, age restrictions may apply, 14 day cancellation notice-fee imposed. **Guest Services:** complimentary laundry.

▼ *See AAA listing p. 65* ▼

- Free Wi-Fi • Free Parking
- Indoor Pool and Spa
- Breakfast Buffet • Beer & Wine Bar
- 24/7 Pavilion Pantry Snack Shop
- Fitness Center
- Guest Laundry

Hilton **Garden Inn**®
Flagstaff

350 W Forest Meadows Street
Flagstaff, AZ 86001
928-226-8888
Reservations: 1-800-333-0785
FLAGSTAFF.HGI.COM

Approved
▼▼▼

Take your imagination to new destinations
with the online AAA/CAA Travel Guides

(See map & index p. 61.)

Stay connected with #AAA and #CAA

on your favorite social media sites

(See map & index p. 61.)

LITTLE AMERICA HOTEL (928)779-7900 16

Hotel
$99-S269

Address: 2515 E Butler Ave 86004 **Location:** I-40 exit 198 (Butler Ave), just s. **Facility:** 247 units, some two bedrooms and kitchens. 2 stories (no elevator), interior corridors. **Terms:** check-in 4 pm, cancellation fee imposed. **Amenities:** safes. **Pool(s):** heated outdoor. **Activities:** hot tub, playground, trails, exercise room. **Guest Services:** valet and coin laundry, area transportation. *(See ad p. 67.)*

MOTEL 6-FLAGSTAFF WEST #1000 928/779-3757 23

Motel. Rates not provided. **Address:** 2745 S Woodlands Village Blvd 86001 **Location:** I-40 exit 195, just n to Forest Meadows St, w to Beulah Blvd, just s, then just w. **Facility:** 150 units. 3 stories, exterior corridors. **Pool(s):** heated outdoor. **Guest Services:** coin laundry.

QUALITY INN UNIVERSITY (928)774-8771 18

Hotel $60-$150 **Address:** 2000 S Milton Rd 86001 **Location:** I-40 exit 195, just n to Forest Meadows St, then right. **Facility:** 96 units. 2 stories (no elevator), interior corridors. **Pool(s):** heated outdoor.

RAMADA WEST (928)773-1111 24

Hotel
$54-$97

Address: 2755 S Woodlands Village Blvd 86001 **Location:** I-40 exit 195, just n to Forest Meadows St, w to Beulah Blvd, just s, then w. **Facility:** 90 units. 2 stories (no elevator), exterior corridors. **Pool(s):** heated outdoor. **Activities:** hot tub, exercise room. **Guest Services:** valet and coin laundry. **Featured Amenity:** breakfast buffet.

SONESTA ES SUITES FLAGSTAFF 928/526-5555 7

Extended Stay
Hotel
Rates not provided

Address: 1400 N Country Club Dr 86004 **Location:** I-40 exit 201, 0.5 mi s. **Facility:** 102 kitchen units, some two bedrooms. 2 stories (no elevator), interior/exterior corridors. **Terms:** check-in 4 pm. **Amenities:** safes. **Pool(s):** heated outdoor. **Activities:** hot tub, picnic facilities, exercise room. **Guest Services:** valet and coin laundry.

SPRINGHILL SUITES BY MARRIOTT (928)774-8042 21

Contemporary Hotel $98-$244 **Address:** 2455 S Beulah Blvd 86001 **Location:** I-40 exit 195, just n to Forest Meadows St, then 1 blk w. **Facility:** 112 units. 5 stories, interior corridors. **Pool(s):** heated indoor. **Activities:** exercise room. **Guest Services:** valet and coin laundry.

AAA Benefit: Members save 5% or more!

STARLIGHT PINES, A BED & BREAKFAST (928)527-1912 1

Bed & Breakfast $159-$179 **Address:** 3380 E Lockett Rd 86004 **Location:** I-40 exit 201, 0.5 mi w on I-40 business loop, then just n. **Facility:** Bathrooms in this stately Victorian-style home feature vintage claw-foot tubs as well as showers with handmade soap. Rooms have a wood-burning fireplace or a porch. 4 units. 2 stories (no elevator), interior corridors. **Terms:** check-in 4 pm, 14 day cancellation notice-fee imposed.

SUPER 8-FLAGSTAFF MALL (928)526-0818 3

Hotel
$50-$102

Address: 3725 N Kasper Ave 86004 **Location:** I-40 exit 201, just n, 0.5 mi w on I-40 business loop, then just n. Located on a busy commercial street. **Facility:** 89 units. 2 stories (no elevator), interior corridors. **Terms:** cancellation fee imposed. **Guest Services:** coin laundry. **Featured Amenity:** continental breakfast.

TWIN ARROWS NAVAJO CASINO RESORT (928)856-7200

Contemporary
Resort Hotel
$89-$219

Address: 22181 Resort Blvd 86004 **Location:** I-40 exit 219, 0.5 mi ne. **Facility:** Influenced by Navajo culture, this desert hotel is bright and vibrant. Large rooms offer elegant amenities, including social media access through the televisions. 200 units. 5 stories, interior corridors. **Parking:** on-site and valet. **Terms:** check-in 4 pm, cancellation fee imposed. **Amenities:** video games, safes. **Dining:** 5 restaurants, entertainment. **Pool(s):** heated indoor. **Activities:** hot tub, game room, exercise room.

WHERE TO EAT

1899 BAR & GRILL 928/523-1899 20

American
Fine Dining
$8-$33

AAA Inspector Notes: Named after the opening year of the Arizona College, this large and impressive dining room gives a visual surprise as each guest enters. The food goes right along with the contemporary decor by offering such vibrant items as summer salads, filet mignon, red trout and shrimp scampi. Check the schedule for entertainment some evenings. **Features:** full bar, patio dining. **Address:** 307 W Dupont Ave 86001 **Location:** I-40 exit 195, 1.8 mi n on SR 89A (Milton Rd), then just e. L D CALL

BEAVER STREET BREWERY & WHISTLE STOP CAFE 928/779-0079 9

American. Gastropub. $9-$13 **AAA Inspector Notes:** Among offerings at the casual restaurant are soups, fondues, salads, sandwiches and wood-fired pizza, as well as a selection of entrées at dinner. Several ales and beers are brewed on the premises. Patio dining is a nice option in pleasant weather. **Features:** full bar, patio dining. **Address:** 11 S Beaver St, Suite 1 86001 **Location:** I-40 exit 195, 2 mi n to Santa Fe Ave, just e, then just s. L D

Recommend places

you'd like us to inspect at

AAA.com/TourBookComments

(See map & index p. 61.)

BLACK BART'S STEAK HOUSE & MUSICAL REVUE
928/779-3142 **30**

Steak
Casual Dining
$12-$42

AAA Inspector Notes: Located adjacent to an RV park, the freeway and lodging, this spot is convenient for those looking for a meal. A musical revue provides nightly entertainment at this rustic, casual restaurant. Oak-broiled steak, seafood, chicken and prime rib delight the palate. Full service is provided by an attentive staff casually attired fitting the theme of the restaurant. The staff doubles as entertainers providing the nightly musical revue. **Features:** full bar. **Reservations:** suggested, weekends. **Address:** 2760 E Butler Ave 86004 **Location:** I-40 exit 198 (Butler Ave), just se.

D ⚞

BRANDY'S RESTAURANT & BAKERY
928/779-2187 **1**

Breakfast
Sandwiches
Casual Dining
$5-$10

AAA Inspector Notes: Operating since 1993, this popular establishment serves breakfast dishes including 10 variations of eggs Benedict, 3-egg omelets and made-from-scratch pancakes. Lunch stand-outs are albacore tuna melts, reubens, burgers, grilled salmon and grilled Portobello sandwiches. **Features:** beer & wine. **Address:** 1500 E Cedar Ave, Suite 40 86004 **Location:** Route 66, 0.8 mi n on 4th St, then just w; in strip mall.

Menu on AAA.com B L

BRIX RESTAURANT & WINE BAR
928/213-1021 **4**

American. Fine Dining. $15-$36 **AAA Inspector Notes:** Contemporary American cuisine is served in this historic 1900s carriage house with a charming décor. The menu is created around fresh local farmed and organic items such as artisan cheese, Manila clams, steak frites and seasonal fish. Guests also like to sit at the bar and enjoy the large wine selection. **Features:** full bar. **Reservations:** suggested. **Address:** 413 N San Francisco St 86001 **Location:** 2 blks n of downtown. D

BUN HUGGERS
928/779-3743 **22**

American. Quick Serve. $5-$8 **AAA Inspector Notes:** This casual burger joint serves hearty burgers, chicken sandwiches and chili fries. After ordering be prepared for a wait before your name is called. **Features:** beer only. **Address:** 901 S Milton Rd 86001 **Location:** I-40 exit 195, 1.5 mi n. L D

BUSTER'S
928/774-5155 **32**

American. Casual Dining. $9-$26 **AAA Inspector Notes:** For casual dining in a lively atmosphere, this restaurant is a favorite with students of nearby Northern Arizona University. Contemporary furnishings provide a selection of tables and booths with a view from large windows, perfect to enjoy the sunset. Salads and sandwiches are popular lunch offerings, while dinners typically revolve around steaks, chicken and a daily selection of fresh seafood. Portions are large, cooked to order and colorfully garnished. The staff is professional and cordial. **Features:** full bar, happy hour. **Address:** 1800 S Milton Rd 86001 **Location:** I-40 exit 195, 0.5 mi n; in Green Tree Village. L D

CHINA STAR
928/774-8880 **23**

Chinese. Quick Serve. $7-$9 **AAA Inspector Notes:** Two large self-service buffet lines display soups, salads, fruits and desserts. You'll also find a variety of chicken, beef and rice entrées, including moo goo gai pan. Parking is plentiful around the restaurant, which stands alone in front of a small shopping center. **Address:** 1802 E Route 66 86004 **Location:** I-40 exit 198 (Butler Ave), just w, just n on Enterprise Rd, then just e. L D

COTTAGE PLACE RESTAURANT
928/774-8431 **15**

Continental
Fine Dining
$21-$37

AAA Inspector Notes: Classical background music and contemporary decor highlight works by local artists in the cozy, restored 1909 bungalow set in an old downtown neighborhood. A cordial, formally attired staff presents a nice selection of international entrées as well as a prix fixe dinner with wine parings. **Features:** beer & wine, patio dining. **Reservations:** suggested. **Address:** 126 W Cottage Ave 86001 **Location:** Just s of downtown; just w of Beaver St. **Parking:** on-site and street. D

DARA THAI RESTAURANT
928/774-8390 **17**

Thai. Casual Dining. $7-$14 **AAA Inspector Notes:** Enjoy fresh, popular Thai dishes in a relaxed and unpretentious Thai-themed dining room. The basil garlic chicken is refreshing and I loved the Thai tea with vodka. Spice levels are adjusted to suit each diner's taste. **Features:** full bar. **Address:** 14 S San Francisco St 86001 **Location:** Corner of W Phoenix Ave and S San Francisco St; downtown. **Parking:** street only. L D

DELHI PALACE
928/556-0019 **33**

Indian. Casual Dining. $9-$20 **AAA Inspector Notes:** Located in a strip mall, this eatery serves fresh traditional Indian cuisine such as tandoori chicken, shish kebabs and a large assortment of breads (naan). The service is casual and friendly, and the staff is eager to help guests understand Indian cuisine. Wash it all down with Indian tea or a mango milkshake. **Features:** beer & wine. **Address:** 2700 S Woodlands Village Blvd 86001 **Location:** I-40 exit 195, just n to Forest Meadows St, w to Beulah Blvd, just s, then just w. L D

GALAXY DINER
928/774-2466 **21**

Comfort Food. Casual Dining. $5-$12 **AAA Inspector Notes:** On the west side of town on Historic Route 66, this diner welcomes patrons with 1950s-era music and photographs of movie stars decorating the walls. On the menu are burgers, chicken-fried steak and roast beef. Shakes, malts and ice cream in a variety of flavors are among sweet choices. **Features:** beer & wine. **Address:** 931 W Route 66 86001 **Location:** I-40 exit 195, 1.5 mi n on SR 89A (Milton Rd), then just w. B L D

HICKORY'S SMOKEHOUSE BBQ
928/774-2278 **31**

Barbecue. Quick Serve. $9-$20 **AAA Inspector Notes:** This spot serves up classic barbecue in a sleek, contemporary dining room. The baby back ribs and beef brisket are the top sellers, but do not forget about the homemade macaroni and cheese and funnel cakes. **Features:** beer only, happy hour. **Address:** 1435 S Milton Rd 86001 **Location:** I-40 exit 195, 1 mi n. L D CALL 🖰Ⓜ

HIRO'S SUSHI BAR & JAPANESE RESTAURANT
928/226-8030 **28**

Japanese. Casual Dining. $10-$21 **AAA Inspector Notes:** Fresh sushi, tempura and other traditional dishes are served in a laid-back atmosphere. On the way out, be sure to peruse the small Japanese shop for distinctive gifts. **Features:** beer & wine. **Address:** 1312 S Plaza Way 86001 **Location:** I-40 exit 195, 1 mi n on SR 89A (Milton Rd), then just sw. L D

JOSEPHINE'S
928/779-3400 **3**

American
Fine Dining
$10-$27

AAA Inspector Notes: This renovated historic home provides a casually comfortable setting. The eclectic menu is a showcase for steak, seafood, chicken, lamb and pork dishes prepared with European, Asian, Pan American and Southwestern influences. **Features:** full bar, patio dining, Sunday brunch. **Reservations:** suggested. **Address:** 503 N Humphrey's St 86001 **Location:** Just n of jct Old Route 66. *Menu on AAA.com* L D

KACHINA RESTAURANT
928/779-1944 **19**

Mexican. Casual Dining. $7-$26 **AAA Inspector Notes:** Sporting vintage decor, this popular restaurant prepares varied enchiladas, burritos, tamales and other traditional Mexican dishes, as well as tempting daily specials. Friendly servers are very attentive. **Features:** full bar. **Address:** 522 E Route 66 86001 **Location:** Just e; downtown. L D

KARMA SUSHI BAR GRILL
928/774-6100 **11**

Japanese
Sushi
Casual Dining
$9-$26

AAA Inspector Notes: This small eatery puts a contemporary American twist on fresh Japanese ingredients. It seems to always be packed, yet the laid-back service can be slow at times. **Features:** full bar, happy hour. **Address:** 6 E Route 66 86001 **Location:** Downtown. **Parking:** street only.

L D

(See map & index p. 61.)

LA BELLAVIA 928/774-8301 8

🍷 Breakfast Sandwiches. Casual Dining. $5-$9 **AAA Inspector Notes:** Cozy, comfortable and daily specials are featured at this spot near the old downtown area of Flagstaff and convenient to shopping and other eateries. Providing breakfast as the foot traffic goes by, stop here for the house specialty—Swedish oat pancakes. Full service is provided by a casually attired, attentive staff. **Address:** 18 S Beaver St 86001 **Location:** Just s of Old Route 66; downtown. **Parking:** street only. B L

LITTLE THAI KITCHEN 928/226-9422 24

🍷 Thai. Casual Dining. $6-$14 **AAA Inspector Notes:** The fresh cuisine packs a big punch in this little dining room with minimal decorations. All sauces and desserts are made in house. I loved the ginger chicken, pad thai and fried bananas with homemade coconut ice cream. **Address:** 1051 S Milton Rd 86001 **Location:** I-40 exit 195, 1.1 mi n. L D

LUMBERYARD BREWING COMPANY 928/779-2739 16

🍷🍷 American. Gastropub. $8-$16 **AAA Inspector Notes:** Seasonal brewed beers and casual pub fare are featured at this fun brewpub. Guests flock into the lounge for football games, while others head into the dining room for the great burgers and tri-tip. The servers are casual, but friendly. **Features:** full bar, patio dining, happy hour. **Address:** 5 S Francisco St 86001 **Location:** Downtown. L D CALL 🚗M

MACY'S EUROPEAN COFFEE HOUSE & BAKERY 928/774-2243 13

🍷 Breads/Pastries Coffee/Tea. Quick Serve. $7-$8 **AAA Inspector Notes:** While the perfect place to stop in for a specialty coffee, they also offer fresh vegetarian cuisine including sandwiches, soups and baked goods. **Address:** 14 S Beaver St 86001 **Location:** Just s of Old Route 66; in historic town center. **Parking:** street only. B L D

MAJERLE'S SPORTS GRILL 928/774-6463 12

🍷🍷 American. Casual Dining. $8-$14 **AAA Inspector Notes:** The legendary Phoenix Suns basketball player Dan Majerle has opened a fun, sports-oriented restaurant. Guests can enjoy the games on many TVs while munching on casual pub grub. Signature items include the "slam dunk shrimp," Asian chicken salad and "9's teriyaki chicken and rice." **Features:** full bar, happy hour. **Address:** 102 E Route 66 86001 **Location:** Jct N San Francisco St; downtown. **Parking:** street only. L D LATE

MAMMA LUISA 928/526-6809 2

🍷🍷 Italian. Casual Dining. $12-$21 **AAA Inspector Notes:** This small, cozy eatery appeals to those seeking a good Italian meal in a casual Old World atmosphere. The family restaurant prides itself on fresh Italian recipes and friendly service. **Reservations:** suggested. **Address:** 2710 N Steves Blvd 86004 **Location:** On US 180 and 89, just n of E Route 66; in Kachina Square Shopping Center. D

MONSOON CHINESE BISTRO & SUSHI 928/226-8844 6

🍷🍷 Asian Sushi. Casual Dining. $10-$28 **AAA Inspector Notes:** Located in the heart of downtown, this eatery offers a sushi bar and an open dining room with a flat-screen TV. The menu includes a variety of such Asian items as ahi tuna, pad thai noodles, kung pao chicken and honey lemon shrimp. The bar is popular and the service is casual and friendly. **Features:** full bar. **Address:** 6 E Aspen Ave 86001 **Location:** Corner of Aspen Ave and Leroux St; downtown. **Parking:** street only. L D

THE NORTHERN PINES RESTAURANT
928/266-1929 29

American
Casual Dining
$8-$27

AAA Inspector Notes: This inviting diner boasts several stack stone walls and tasty, traditional food. The casual and friendly staff members joke with the locals as they serve hearty items such as french toast, chicken-fried steak and even filet mignon. **Features:** full bar, happy hour. **Address:** 2200 E Butler Ave 86004 **Location:** I-40 exit 198 (Butler Ave), just n; in Days Hotel Flagstaff. B L D CALL 🚗M

PASTO CUCINA ITALIANA 928/779-1937 7

🍷🍷🍷 Italian. Fine Dining. $9-$26 **AAA Inspector Notes:** In historic downtown, this casual, yet elegant, bistro features contemporary Italian cuisine that has won much local praise. The menu lists beef, seafood, chicken and pasta choices, all prepared with ingredients sourced from local farms. **Features:** beer & wine. **Reservations:** suggested. **Address:** 19 E Aspen Ave 86001 **Location:** Route 66, just n on Leroux St, then just e; downtown. **Parking:** street only. L D

PICAZZO'S ORGANIC ITALIAN KITCHEN 928/226-1000

🍷🍷 Italian. Casual Dining. $10-$27 **AAA Inspector Notes:** This upscale pizzeria, close to NAU, offers fresh pizza with homemade dough along with other casual Italian dishes. **Features:** full bar. **Address:** 1300 S Milton Rd, Suite 101 86001 **Location:** I-40 exit 195, 0.8 mi n on SR 89A (Milton Rd). L D

SAKURA RESTAURANT 928/773-9118 26

🍷🍷 🔷🔷

Japanese
Casual Dining
$10-$29

AAA Inspector Notes: Teppanyaki-style cooking is prepared in a traditional Japanese steakhouse atmosphere. A sushi bar also is offered. **Features:** full bar. **Address:** 1175 W Route 66 86001 **Location:** I-40 exit 195, 1.5 mi n on SR 89A (Milton Rd), then 0.5 mi w; in DoubleTree by Hilton Flagstaff. (See ad p. 65.) L D

SALSA BRAVA 928/779-5293 5

🍷🍷 Mexican. Casual Dining. $7-$17 **AAA Inspector Notes:** On Historic Route 66, this restaurant serves a variety of Mexican dishes. Most folks order the Baja fish wraps, for which this place is known. **Features:** full bar, patio dining. **Address:** 2220 E Route 66 86001 **Location:** I-40 exit 201, 0.5 mi n, then 2.7 mi w. L D CALL 🚗M

SWADDEE AUTHENTIC THAI CUISINE 928/773-1122 10

🍷🍷 Thai. Casual Dining. $11-$16 **AAA Inspector Notes:** This small ding room is accented with dark wood and upscale Thai artwork. A variety of fresh Thai items are served such as pad thai, red curry, chicken satay and coconut sherbet. The coconut princess bursts with flavors and you can never go wrong with a Thai tea. **Features:** beer & wine. **Address:** 115 E Aspen Ave 86001 **Location:** Jct N San Francisco St, just e; downtown. **Parking:** street only. L D

TINDERBOX KITCHEN 928/226-8400 18

🍷🍷 Northern American. Fine Dining. $20-$35 **AAA Inspector Notes:** This fun and contemporary restaurant specializes in fresh and seasonal cuisine, such as venison over sweet potato risotto, Colorado lamb, and amazing house-made chocolate cake. There is an upscale separate bar area that is a little more casual and serves a smaller menu and a huge selection of specialty beers and cocktails. **Features:** full bar. **Address:** 34 S San Francisco St 86001 **Location:** Between Phoenix and Cottage aves; downtown. **Parking:** street only. D

WOODLANDS RESTAURANT 928/773-9118 27

🍷🍷 🍷🍷

American
Casual Dining
$7-$24

AAA Inspector Notes: This casual restaurant shares a kitchen with a Japanese restaurant. Although there are several Asian influences, the menu consists of mainly American cuisine such as basic steak cuts, salmon and halibut cakes. Great for a casual and relaxing meal. **Features:** full bar, Sunday brunch. **Address:** 1175 W Route 66 86001 **Location:** I-40 exit 195, 1.5 mi n on SR 89A (Milton Rd), then 0.5 mi w; in DoubleTree by Hilton Flagstaff. (See ad p. 65.) B L D CALL 🚗M

FLORENCE (E-4) pop. 25,536, elev. 1,493'

One of Arizona's oldest towns and the seat of Pinal County, Florence was founded by Levi Ruggles in 1866. Many historic homes and buildings perpetuate its frontier atmosphere.

Scenic desert highways from Florence include Kelvin Highway, a county road running east to Kelvin, and the Pinal Pioneer Parkway, a part of SR 79 leading southeast to Oracle Junction. Markers along the parkway identify desert wildlife.

Florence Visitor Center: 24 W. Ruggles St., P.O. Box 109, Florence, AZ 85132. **Phone:** (520) 868-4496.

PINAL COUNTY HISTORICAL MUSEUM, 715 S. Main St., displays Native American artifacts from the Southwest, blacksmith equipment, antique woodworking tools, cactus furniture and documents relating to the county's history. Farm machinery, an 1884 square piano, a collection of Tom Mix memorabilia and an Arizona state prison exhibit featuring hanging nooses also are offered.

Time: Allow 1 hour minimum. **Hours:** Tues.-Sat. 11-4, Sun. noon-4, Sept. 1-July 14. Closed major holidays. **Cost:** Donations. **Phone:** (520) 868-4382.

BLUE MIST MOTEL · (520)868-5875

Motel
$55-$75

Address: 40 S Pinal Pkwy 85132 **Location:** On SR 79, at SR 287. **Facility:** 22 units, some efficiencies. 1 story, exterior corridors. **Terms:** 3 day cancellation notice-fee imposed. **Pool(s):** outdoor.

RANCHO SONORA INN · (520)868-8000

Country Inn $89-$225 **Address:** 9198 N Hwy 79 85232 **Location:** 5 mi s of SR 287. **Facility:** In a quiet desert location, the inn's adobe-style buildings and casitas face a charming shaded patio with fountains and mature plantings. 8 units, some two bedrooms, kitchens and cottages. 1 story, exterior corridors. **Terms:** 3 day cancellation notice-fee imposed. **Pool(s):** outdoor. **Activities:** hot tub, lawn sports, picnic facilities. **Guest Services:** coin laundry.

WHERE TO EAT

L & B INN · 520/868-9981

Mexican. Casual Dining. $8-$16 **AAA Inspector Notes:** Family owned for more than 30 years, this friendly establishment features authentic, Sonoran-style food along with great margaritas. **Features:** full bar, happy hour. **Address:** 695 S Main St 85132 **Location:** Center. **Parking:** on-site and street. B L D

MOUNT ATHOS RESTAURANT & CAFE · 520/868-0735

Greek. Casual Dining. $10-$18 **AAA Inspector Notes:** From breakfast to dinner, the busy restaurant's friendly staff pleases patrons with hearty portions of delicious Greek and Italian dishes. Gyros made with skewered beef and lamb are popular. A wide selection of crispy salads, sandwiches and pasta dishes means everyone will be satisfied. **Features:** full bar, patio dining, happy hour. **Address:** 444 N Pinal Pkwy (SR 79) 85232 **Location:** Just s of jct SR 287 and 79. B L D

FOREST LAKES

FOREST LAKES LODGE · (928)535-4727

Motel
$67-$89

Address: 2823 SR 260 85931 **Location:** Between MM 288 and 289. Located in a quiet area. **Facility:** 20 units. 2 stories (no elevator), exterior corridors. **Activities:** picnic facilities. **Featured Amenity: continental breakfast.**

FORT APACHE (D-5) pop. 143

FORT APACHE AND THEODORE ROOSEVELT SCHOOL NATIONAL HISTORIC LANDMARK, s. off SR 73, is a 288-acre site featuring 27 buildings dated 1870-1930, including officers' quarters; a guardhouse; stables; dormitories; the White Mountain Apache Cultural Center and Museum; a military cemetery; ancient petroglyphs; and Kinishba Ruins, a partially restored Pueblo village.

Hours: Park open daily 7 a.m.-dusk. Guided tours are available by reservation. **Cost:** (Includes White Mountain Apache Cultural Center and Museum and Kinishba Ruins) $5; $3 (ages 64+ and students with ID); free (ages 0-6). **Phone:** (928) 338-4625. GT

White Mountain Apache Cultural Center and Museum, s. off SR 73 to Indian Rte. 46, following signs, provides visitor orientation for Fort Apache and Theodore Roosevelt School National Historic Landmark. The museum features two permanent exhibits: The Fort Apache Legacy and Footprints of the Apache, as well as changing exhibits. Video presentations about the Apache creation story and cultural topics are available. Cultural and historical relics such as clothing, weapons and dolls are on display, as are works by local artists.

Time: Allow 1 hour minimum. **Hours:** Mon.-Sat. 8-5, Sun. 11-3, May-Sept.; Mon.-Fri. 8-5, rest of year. Closed major holidays. **Cost:** Included in Fort Apache and Theodore Roosevelt School National Historic Landmark admission of $5; $3 (ages 64+ and students with ID); free (ages 0-6). **Phone:** (928) 338-4625.

FORT DEFIANCE (B-6) pop. 3,624, elev. 6,862'

Fort Defiance lies at the mouth of Canyon Bonito, or Blue Canyon, in the Navajo Reservation. In some places sheer walls overhang the canyon floor. Established in 1851, Fort Defiance saw action in the Navajo wars that occurred during the 1860s. For many years it has been the headquarters of the Bureau of Indian Affairs, Fort Defiance Agency.

Navajos on the reservation maintain much of their traditional way of life. They engage in agriculture, stock raising, employment on the reservation and seasonal off-reservation work. Many still dwell in hogans, circular log and earth huts. Distinctive Navajo blankets, rugs and silver and turquoise jewelry are crafted.

FORT HUACHUCA (G-5)

In southeastern Arizona, Fort Huachuca (wa-CHOO-ka) was founded in 1877 to combat raids by Native Americans and outlaws. In 1954 the fort became the site of the Army Electronic Proving Ground. The 73,272-acre fort is headquarters of the U.S. Army Information Systems Command, the U.S. Army Intelligence Center and various other military organizations. The Old Post retains many of the original buildings constructed in the late 19th century.

Note: Each visitor must be a U.S. citizen and present photo identification to gain admittance to the fort. Foreign nationals must be escorted by public affairs personnel. Proof of vehicle registration and insurance must be provided for each vehicle entering the premises.

FORT HUACHUCA MUSEUM is 3.6 mi. n.w. of Fort Huachuca's main gate in the Old Post area at Boyd and Grierson aves. Southwest history and the U.S. Army's activities in the area are depicted through exhibits in three buildings. **Hours:** Tues.-Sat. 9-4; closed Federal holidays. **Cost:** Donations. **Phone:** (520) 533-4946.

FOUNTAIN HILLS (I-4) pop. 22,489, elev. 1,600'
• Part of Phoenix area — see map p. 126

Fountain Hills is named for its rolling terrain and celebrated fountain. The community provides a number of recreation and vacation opportunities.

Fountain Hills Chamber of Commerce: 16837 E. Palisades Blvd., Fountain Hills, AZ 85268. **Phone:** (480) 837-1654.

THE FOUNTAIN is off Saguaro Blvd. in 64-acre Fountain Park. Within a 29-acre lake, the fountain shoots a jet of water 330 feet into the air for 15 minutes at a time. On special occasions, the town turns on all three pumps for a spectacular plume that reaches 560 feet high. Sustained winds of more than 10 mph may prevent operation. **Hours:** Park open daily 6 a.m.-11 p.m. Fountain show daily on the hour 9-9. **Cost:** Free. **Phone:** (480) 816-5100.

RIVER OF TIME MUSEUM, adjacent to the library at 12901 N. La Montana Blvd., includes multimedia displays, historical and cultural programs, and activities educating visitors about the vital role of water in the Lower Verde River Valley. Conditions in this part of the High Sonoran Desert forced such inhabitants as Native American tribes and early ranchers to invent ways to control water. Visitors learn about ancient canals and more recent dam projects as well as the area's developments in housing. The museum also houses a scale model of Fort McDowell.

Time: Allow 30 minutes minimum. **Hours:** Tues.-Fri. 1-4, Sat. 10-4, Sept.-May; Fri. 1-4, Sat. 10-4, rest of year. Closed major holidays. Phone ahead to confirm schedule. **Cost:** $5; $4 (ages 60+); $3 (ages 5-18); $12 (family). **Phone:** (480) 837-2612. [GT]

INN AT EAGLE MOUNTAIN   480/816-3000
▼▼▼▼ **Hotel.** Rates not provided. **Address:** 9800 N Summer Hill Blvd 85268 **Location:** Loop 101 exit 41, 7.3 mi e on Shea Blvd, 0.3 mi e on Eagle Mountain Pkwy, then just w. **Facility:** 42 units. 2 stories (no elevator), exterior corridors. **Pool(s):** heated outdoor. **Activities:** hot tub, regulation golf, spa. **Guest Services:** coin laundry.

GANADO (B-6) pop. 1,210, elev. 6,386'

Ganado is one of the traditional meeting and trading centers of the Pueblo Colorado Valley. For centuries the valley has been a favored Native American gathering place, first for the Ancestral Puebloans and now for the Navajo. When John Hubbell bought the original trading post, he christened it Ganado to honor his Navajo friend Ganado Mucho and to distinguish the community from Pueblo, Colo.

Visitors to the reservation should be aware of certain travel restrictions; see Good Facts To Know.

HUBBELL TRADING POST NATIONAL HISTORIC SITE, .5 mi. w. via SR 264, is the oldest continuously operated trading post in the Navajo Nation. In 1878 John L. Hubbell bought the

trading post and established himself as a leading trader. Hubbell's collection of Western art and Native American crafts is displayed in his furnished house on the site.

The trading post and the Hubbell home depict the role of trading in the history of the Southwest and the life of a trader's family. The trading post conducts business much as it did when the Hubbell family ran it. Members of the Navajo, Hopi, Zuni and other tribes sell and trade such crafts as hand-woven rugs, jewelry, baskets and pottery. Ranger-led programs, guided house tours and weaving demonstrations are offered.

Time: Allow 1 hour minimum. **Hours:** Daily 8-6, May-Sept.; 8-5, rest of year. **Note:** In summer the reservation observes daylight-saving time, which is an hour later than outside the reservation. Closed Jan. 1, Thanksgiving and Christmas. **Cost:** Donations. Hubbell home tour $2. Prices may vary; phone ahead. **Phone:** (928) 755-3475.

GILA BEND (E-3) pop. 1,922, elev. 735'

Gila Bend is the center for a prosperous stock-raising and farming region in the Gila River Valley. The first farms were established in 1699 by Jesuit missionary Father Eusebio Francisco Kino. Just west of town is the site of the infamous 1851 Oatman Massacre, where all but three children of a westward-bound family were killed by Apaches. Exhibits about area history are displayed in a museum at the information center.

Gila Bend Tourist Information Center and Chamber of Commerce: 644 W. Pima, P.O. Box CC, Gila Bend, AZ 85337. **Phone:** (928) 420-1964.

BEST WESTERN SPACE AGE LODGE   (928)683-2273

Motel
$109-$169

AAA Benefit: Save 10% or more every day and earn 10% bonus points!

Address: 401 E Pima St 85337 **Location:** Business Loop I-8; center. **Facility:** 41 units. 1 story, exterior corridors. **Terms:** 3 day cancellation notice. **Dining:** Space Age Restaurant, see separate listing. **Pool(s):** outdoor. **Activities:** hot tub.

Request roadside assistance

in a click — online or using

the AAA or CAA apps

SPACE AGE RESTAURANT   928/683-2761

American Family Dining
$5-$15

AAA Inspector Notes: Friendly servers dish up good food at this kitschy diner with a hard-to-miss spaceship design outside and a unique atmosphere inside. **Address:** 401 E Pima St 85337 **Location:** Business Loop I-8; center; in BEST WESTERN Space Age Lodge.

B L D

American/Mexican Dining-Original Space Murals-Gift Shop

GILBERT (J-4) pop. 208,453

- Hotels & Restaurants map & index p. 164
- Part of Phoenix area — see map p. 126

GILBERT HISTORICAL MUSEUM, 10 S. Gilbert Rd., relates the history of the town. Housed in a 1913 school building, the museum has nine themed galleries. Highlights include a model train exhibit, a collection of military uniforms and a courtyard with antique farm and firefighting equipment. The museum also hosts quilting bees and an annual quilting show March through May.

Time: Allow 1 hour minimum. **Hours:** Tues.-Sat. 9-4. Closed major holidays. **Cost:** $5; $4 (ages 60+); $3 (ages 5-12). **Phone:** (480) 926-1577. GT

THE RIPARIAN PRESERVE AT WATER RANCH is at 2757 E. Guadalupe Rd. The 110-acre preserve features interpretive exhibits, an observatory, a floating boardwalk, trails and children's play areas. A great spot for bird-watching, the area is home to more than 200 species. Visitors can also fish (with a license) and camp on the grounds.

Ramadas can be rented by the hour. **Time:** Allow 1 hour minimum. **Hours:** Preserve daily dawn-dusk. Fishing lake daily dawn-10 p.m. Phone for observatory hours. **Cost:** Free. Camping $30-$40. Phone for other activity fees. Campsites must be reserved. **Phone:** (480) 797-2019, or (480) 503-6200 for camping reservations.

HAMPTON INN & SUITES PHOENIX/GILBERT
          (480)543-1500 **65**

Hotel $75-$225 **Address:** 3265 S Market St 85297 **Location:** Loop 202 exit 42 (Val Vista Dr), just n, then just e. **Facility:** 96 units. 4 stories, interior corridors. **Terms:** 1-7 night minimum stay, cancellation fee imposed. **Pool(s):** heated outdoor. **Activities:** hot tub, exercise room. **Guest Services:** valet and coin laundry, area transportation.

AAA Benefit: Members save up to 10%!

(See map & index p. 164.)

HYATT PLACE PHOENIX/GILBERT   (480)899-5900 64

Hotel
$69-$229

H HYATT PLACE

AAA Benefit: Members save 10%!

Address: 3275 S Market St 85297 **Location:** Loop 202 exit 42 (Val Vista Dr), just n, then just e. **Facility:** 127 units. 6 stories, interior corridors. **Terms:** cancellation fee imposed. **Pool(s):** heated outdoor. **Activities:** exercise room. **Guest Services:** valet laundry, area transportation. **Featured Amenity:** breakfast buffet.

SAVE 🔚 🍴 CALL ⬅M 🛁 BIZ

HS 📶 ✕ 🐾 🔌 💻 /SOME UNITS 🔊

RESIDENCE INN BY MARRIOTT PHOENIX GILBERT   (480)699-4450 63

Extended Stay Hotel
$118-$338 **Address:** 3021 E Banner Gateway Dr 85234 **Location:** US 60 exit 186 (Higley Rd), just s, then just w. **Facility:** 100 units, some two bedrooms, efficiencies and kitchens. 4 stories, interior corridors. **Pool(s):** heated outdoor. **Activities:** hot tub, picnic facilities, exercise room. **Guest Services:** valet and coin laundry, area transportation.

AAA Benefit: Members save 5% or more!

🔚 🍴 CALL ⬅M 🛁 BIZ HS 📶 ✕ 🔌 💻 💻 /SOME UNITS 🔊

WHERE TO EAT

CANTINA LAREDO   480/782-6777 43

Mexican
Casual Dining
$10-$25

AAA Inspector Notes: Sophisticated yet relaxed, this eatery features authentic Mexican fare with a creative twist. A great starter is the top-shelf guacamole, which is prepared tableside and primes the palate for the entree. The menu features traditional favorites such as tacos, enchiladas, fajitas, carnitas and chiles rellenos. Also featured are vegetarian and gluten-free dishes. **Features:** full bar, patio dining, Sunday brunch, happy hour. **Address:** 2150 E Williams Field Rd 85295 **Location:** Loop 202 exit 40, 0.5 mi w. L D

Gourmet Mexican food, fresh-squeezed lime margaritas

THE FARMHOUSE RESTAURANT   480/926-0676 42

Breakfast Sandwiches. Casual Dining. $4-$9 **AAA Inspector Notes:** This small, casual breakfast and lunch spot is always bustling no matter what time of day. In a simple stroke of genius, and because of a little lovely Arizona weather, patrons are never distracted by the crowd gathering just outside the door. Cinnamon rolls with cream cheese frosting are an absolute must here, and they do sell out quickly, so it's not uncommon to see people ordering these as soon as they get inside. Breakfast is served hot and fresh. Lunch is quick and tasty. **Features:** Sunday brunch. **Address:** 228 N Gilbert Rd 85234 **Location:** Jct W Page Ave and Gilbert Rd; downtown. **Parking:** street only. B L

FLANCER'S CAFE   480/926-9077 39

American. Family Dining. $7-$20 **AAA Inspector Notes:** This café's sandwiches are not made, they are created—and incredible sandwiches they are. Try the award-winning green chile turkey prepared with avocado slices, sizzling bacon and zippy green chile mayonnaise or the perfect prickly pear with a chicken breast baked in prickly pear glaze. A good variety of burgers highlight the menu. Everything from the breads to the desserts is homemade and delicious. Pizza, pasta and salads also figure on the menu. **Features:** beer & wine, happy hour. **Address:** 610 N Gilbert Rd, Suite 300 85234 **Location:** US 60 (Superstition Frwy) exit 182 (Gilbert Rd), 1.6 mi s. L D

JOE'S REAL BBQ   480/503-3805 41

Barbecue
Quick Serve
$8-$19

AAA Inspector Notes: Pecan-grilled meats, barbecue beans, root beer made on site and fresh desserts are favorites at this family joint. The serve-yourself setting and optional patio seating lend to a fun atmosphere. **Features:** patio dining. **Address:** 301 N Gilbert Rd 85234 **Location:** US 60 (Superstition Frwy) exit 182 (Gilbert Rd), 2.1 mi s. **Parking:** street only. *Menu on AAA.com*

L D

PATSY GRIMALDI'S COAL BRICK-OVEN PIZZERIA   480/814-7722

Pizza. Casual Dining. $9-$18 **AAA Inspector Notes:** Fresh ingredients and a coal-fired brick oven are the features at this New York style pizzeria. **Features:** beer & wine. **Address:** 2168 E Williams Field Rd, Suite 502 85295 **Location:** Loop 202 exit 40, 0.7 mi w; in San Tan Village. L D

POSTINO GILBERT WINECAFE   480/632-6363 40

Small Plates Sandwiches. Casual Dining. $9-$14 **AAA Inspector Notes:** This upscale, casual wine bar is great for small groups getting together for drinks and having some delicious small bites at the same time. Guests can pick from four different crostinis they want to sample, all are distinctive and delicious. The paninis offer a bit of a heartier dining option, while the prosciutto with Brie and fig is highly recommended. Bellini's, wines and craft beers are a must. **Features:** beer & wine, patio dining, Sunday brunch, happy hour. **Address:** 302 N Gilbert Rd 85234 **Location:** Jct W Page Ave and Gilbert Rd; downtown. **Parking:** street only. L D

SERRANO'S MEXICAN RESTAURANT   480/507-5027

Mexican. Casual Dining. $7-$17 **AAA Inspector Notes:** A pleasant stop for lunch or dinner, the local chain is known for consistently good food and attractive, upscale Mexican-style décor. The warm bean dip starter stirs the appetite for traditional dishes such as chiles rellenos or seafood enchiladas prepared with fresh ingredients. Service is friendly. **Features:** full bar, happy hour. **Address:** 959 N Val Vista Dr 85234 **Location:** US 60 (Superstition Hwy) exit 184 (Val Vista Dr), 1.4 mi s. L D

💎 GLEN CANYON NATIONAL RECREATION AREA (A-4)

Along the Colorado River from Grand Canyon National Park in far north-central Arizona to Canyonlands National Park in southeastern Utah, Glen Canyon National Recreation Area is home to one of the highest dams in the United States. Part of the Colorado River storage project, the Glen Canyon Dam generates hydroelectric power that is distributed to cities and industries throughout the West; the dam's main purpose is water storage.

Reaching out to hidden canyons, sandy coves and inlets, and winding through towering red cliffs, 186-mile-long Lake Powell presents an ever-changing array of scenery and such recreational opportunities as water skiing, boating and fishing. Amenities include campsites, marinas, and boat rentals and tours. A copy of fishing regulations can be obtained at the Carl Hayden Visitor Center, the Navajo Bridge Interpretive Center, the Bullfrog Visitor Center or at the administration offices in Page, Ariz.; phone (928) 608-6200.

The Bullfrog Visitor Center, at the Bullfrog Marina in Utah, exhibits the natural and cultural history of Glen Canyon and includes a life-size slot canyon model. The visitor center is open seasonally as staffing allows; phone (435) 684-7423. The Navajo Bridge Interpretive Center, on US 89A near Lees Ferry, Ariz., features a historic pedestrian bridge over the Colorado River at Marble Canyon and outdoor exhibits highlighting the early river crossings. The interpretive center is open daily 9-5, Apr.-Oct., as staffing allows; phone (928) 355-2319.

Exhibits in the Carl Hayden Visitor Center, next to US 89, Glen Canyon Dam and Glen Canyon Bridge in Page illustrate the construction of the dam and bridge and include a relief model of the canyon country. Guided tours of the dam are available throughout the year. The center is open daily 8-6, Memorial Day-Labor Day; 8-5, Mar. 1-day before Memorial Day; 8:30-4:30, rest of year. Closed Jan. 1, Thanksgiving and Christmas. Phone (928) 608-6404.

Ranger-led interpretive programs are offered Memorial Day through Labor Day; phone ahead or stop by the Carl Hayden Visitor Center for program times and locations.

Arrangements for boat tours on Lake Powell can be made at Wahweap Lodge and Marina; facilities, including public launching ramps, boat rentals, camping and boat and automobile fuel, are provided at Wahweap and at four other marinas on the lake. All facilities may not be available year-round. A boat ramp providing access to 15 miles of the Colorado River below Glen Canyon Dam is available at Lees Ferry, 5 miles north of Marble Canyon.

Boat excursions, which last from 4 to 6.5 hours, are available through Colorado River Discovery; phone (928) 645-9175 or (888) 522-6644. The tours begin near the Glen Canyon Dam and conclude at Lees Ferry. One-day raft trips on the Colorado River below the dam can be arranged in Page. Half-day and full-day trips are available to Rainbow Bridge National Monument, Utah, which is about 50 miles from Wahweap. Trips on the San Juan River leave from Mexican Hat and Bluff, Utah.

Admission, valid for up to 7 days, is $20 (per private vehicle); $10 (per person arriving by foot or bicycle). An annual pass is $40. An additional use fee of $20 is charged for one motorized water vessel and is valid for up to 7 days.

Admission prices are scheduled to increase January 1, 2016, after which admission, valid for up to 7 days, will be $25 (per private vehicle); $12 (per person arriving by foot or bicycle). An annual pass will be $50. An additional use fee of $25 is charged for one motorized water vessel and is valid for up to 7 days.

For further information contact the Superintendent, Glen Canyon National Recreation Area; phone (928) 608-6200. *See Recreation Areas Chart.*

GLENDALE (I-2) pop. 226,721, elev. 1,154'
- **Restaurants p. 78**
- **Attractions map p. 138**
- **Hotels & Restaurants map & index p. 154**
- **Part of Phoenix area — see map p. 126**

Established in 1892, Glendale retains much of its turn-of-the-20th-century charm. A tree-lined town square, red brick sidewalks and gaslights form an appropriate setting for the abundance of boutique and antique shops around shady Murphy Park in the city's historic downtown. Cerreta Candy Company, about half a mile east of Murphy Park at 5345 W. Glendale Ave., provides behind-the-scenes guided tours of its candy- and chocolate-making operations; phone (623) 930-9000.

In a more modern vein, Glendale also is home to Thunderbird, The American Graduate School of International Management and the jet fighter wing at Luke Air Force Base, purportedly the world's largest F-16 training base. Major League Baseball's Los Angeles Dodgers and Chicago White Sox play their

▼ See AAA listing p. 117 ▼

(See map & index p. 154.)

spring training games at Camelback Ranch-Glendale, while the Arizona Cardinals football and Arizona Coyotes hockey teams call the city home.

In late December, the 🏈 Fiesta Bowl, one of the nation's largest college bowl games, is played at The University of Phoenix Stadium, which also is the home stadium for the National Football League's Arizona Cardinals. In early February, chocoholics flock to Murphy Park for the 🏈 Glendale Chocolate Affaire, which features chocolate purveyors from across the country.

During the holiday season, 🏈 Glendale Glitters jazzes up downtown in festive multicolored lights.

Glendale Visitor Center: 5800 W. Glenn Dr., Suite 140, Glendale, AZ 85301. **Phone:** (623) 930-4500 or (877) 800-2601.

Shopping: Known as the Antique Capital of Arizona, more than 90 antique stores, specialty shops and restaurants are concentrated around Glendale's town square, Murphy Park, at the intersection of Glendale and 58th avenues. Old Towne Glendale and the Historic Catlin Court Shops District specialize in arts, crafts, furniture, dolls, jewelry, period clothing and Western memorabilia. Arrowhead Towne Center contains 170 stores, including Dillard's and JCPenney. More than 90 stores draw deal-seekers to [SAVE] Tanger Outlets Westgate, off Loop 101 at Glendale Avenue exit.

ARIZONA DOLL AND TOY MUSEUM, 5847 W. Myrtle Ave., exhibits antique dolls and toys from around the world. One exhibit is devoted to a late 19th-century schoolroom, featuring the dolls as students. **Time:** Allow 30 minutes minimum. **Hours:** Tues.-Sat. 10-4. Closed major holidays. **Cost:** $5; $1 (children). **Phone:** (623) 939-6186.

SAHUARO RANCH PARK HISTORIC AREA is 2.5 mi. n. of Glendale Ave. to 9802 N. 59th Ave.; or take I-10 exit 138, then go n. 7.6 mi. on N. 59th Ave. Seventeen acres of a model fruit and animal farm developed by William Henry Bartlett in 1885 feature 13 historic structures, including an adobe house, a foreman's house, a barnyard, the main house and a fruit packing shed. A lavish rose garden planted in 1890, several citrus groves and free-roaming peacocks enhance the fenced grounds.

Time: Allow 1 hour minimum. **Hours:** Grounds daily 6 a.m.-dusk. Phone for guided tour schedule. Closed major holidays. Phone ahead to confirm schedule. **Cost:** Grounds free. Tours by donation. Admission is charged for some special events. **Phone:** (623) 930-4200. [GT]

[SAVE] **WET 'N' WILD PHOENIX,** 4243 W. Pinnacle Peak Rd., is a 30-plus-acre water park featuring more than 30 attractions. Slides include the Maximum Velocity and the high-speed Constrictor raft ride as well as the Tornado, which catapults guests through a swirling 45-foot tunnel. Monsoon Bay is a 700,000-gallon wave pool. Wet 'n' Wild Jr., a children's water park, features miniature versions of the park's most popular attractions for youngsters.

Changing rooms and showers are on the premises; lockers, cabanas and tubes can be rented. **Hours:** Open at 10, mid-May through Sept. 30; at 11, Mar. 1 to mid-May. Closing times vary. Phone ahead to confirm schedule. **Cost:** $39.99; $29.99 (ages 65+ and under 42 inches tall); free (ages 0-2). **Parking:** $8. **Phone:** (623) 201-2000. [T]

COMFORT SUITES GLENDALE UNIVERSITY OF PHOENIX
STADIUM AREA   (623)271-9005 [32]
▼▼▼ Hotel $99-$499 **Address:** 9824 W Camelback Rd 85305 **Location:** SR 101 exit 5 (Camelback Rd), just w to 99th St, then just n. **Facility:** 100 units. 4 stories, interior corridors. **Pool(s):** heated outdoor. **Activities:** hot tub, exercise room. **Guest Services:** valet and coin laundry, area transportation.
[🛏+] CALL [ℓM] [🔁] [BIZ] [HS] [📶] [✕] [🍴] [📷] [💻]
/ SOME UNITS [🛏]

HAMPTON INN & SUITES GLENDALE/WESTGATE
                                      (623)271-7771 [31]
▼▼▼ Hotel $129-$299 **Address:**   **AAA Benefit:**
6630 N 95th Ave 85305 **Location:** SR   Members save up to
101 exit 7 (Glendale Ave), just e, then 0.4   10%!
mi s. **Facility:** 149 units. 4 stories, interior corridors. **Terms:** 1-7 night minimum stay, cancellation fee imposed. **Pool(s):** heated outdoor. **Activities:** hot tub, exercise room. **Guest Services:** complimentary and valet laundry, area transportation.
[🛏+] CALL [ℓM] [🔁] [BIZ] [HS] [📶] [✕] [🍴] [💻]
/ SOME UNITS [📷]

HOLIDAY INN EXPRESS & SUITES PHOENIX/GLENDALE
                                      623/939-8888 [29]
▼▼▼ Hotel. Rates not provided. **Address:** 9310 W Cabela Dr 85305 **Location:** SR 101 exit 7 (Glendale Ave), 0.6 mi e to N Zanjero Blvd, then just n. **Facility:** 96 units. 3 stories, interior corridors. **Pool(s):** heated outdoor. **Activities:** hot tub, picnic facilities, exercise room. **Guest Services:** valet laundry.
[🛏+] [🔁] [BIZ] [HS] [📶] [✕] [📷] [💻]
/ SOME UNITS [🍴] [📷]

RENAISSANCE GLENDALE HOTEL & SPA
                                      (623)937-3700 [30]

▼▼▼ ▼▼ ◆   R   **AAA Benefit:**
Hotel   Members save 5%
$118-$293   RENAISSANCE° or more!
            HOTELS

Address: 9495 W Coyotes Blvd 85305 **Location:** SR 101 exit 7 (Glendale Ave), just e to N 95th Ave, just n, then just e. **Facility:** A few steps from Glendale Stadium, this hotel offers well-decorated rooms and public areas with bright, desert colors and upscale amenities. 320 units. 11 stories, interior corridors. **Parking:** on-site and valet. **Terms:** check-in 4 pm. **Amenities:** safes. **Dining:** 2 restaurants, also, Soleil, see separate listing. **Pool(s):** heated outdoor, heated indoor. **Activities:** hot tub, steamroom, exercise room, spa. **Guest Services:** valet and coin laundry.
[SAVE] [✈+] [🍴] [🧖] [🍸] CALL [ℓM] [🔁] [BIZ] [sHS] [s📶]
[✕] [🐾] [🍴] [💻] / SOME UNITS [🛏] [📷]

(See map & index p. 154.)

RESIDENCE INN BY MARRIOTT PHOENIX GLENDALE SPORTS & ENTERTAINMENT DISTRICT (623)772-8900 **26**

▼▼▼▼ Extended Stay Hotel $114-$263 **Address:** 7350 W Zanjero Blvd 85305 **Location:** SR 101 exit 7 (Glendale Ave), then e. **Facility:** 126 units, some two bedrooms, efficiencies and kitchens. 4 stories, interior corridors. **Pool(s):** heated outdoor. **Activities:** hot tub, picnic facilities, exercise room. **Guest Services:** valet and coin laundry.

AAA Benefit: Members save 5% or more!

[icons] CALL M ≈ BIZ HS 🛜 ✕ 🎥 🖥 📺 / SOME UNITS 🐾

▼ See AAA listing p. 106 ▼

SPRINGHILL SUITES BY MARRIOTT GLENDALE/ PEORIA (623)878-6666 **25**

▼▼▼ Hotel $77-$198

SPRINGHILL SUITES Marriott

AAA Benefit: Members save 5% or more!

Address: 7810 W Bell Rd 85308 **Location:** SR 101 exit 14 (Bell Rd), 0.3 mi e. Adjacent to Arrowhead Towne Center. **Facility:** 88 units. 4 stories, interior corridors. **Pool(s):** heated outdoor. **Activities:** hot tub, exercise room. **Guest Services:** valet and coin laundry. **Featured Amenity:** breakfast buffet.

[icons] SAVE 🍴 ≈ BIZ 🛜 ✕ 🖥 📺 🖥

SPRINGHILL SUITES BY MARRIOTT PHOENIX GLENDALE SPORTS & ENTERTAINMENT DISTRICT (623)772-9200 **27**

▼▼▼ Hotel $98-$244 **Address:** 7370 N Zanjero Blvd 85305 **Location:** SR 101 exit 7 (Glendale Ave), 0.6 mi e, then just n. **Facility:** 120 units. 4 stories, interior corridors. **Pool(s):** heated outdoor. **Activities:** hot tub, picnic facilities, exercise room. **Guest Services:** valet and coin laundry.

AAA Benefit: Members save 5% or more!

[icons] CALL M ≈ BIZ 🛜 ✕ 🎥 🖥 📺 🖥

STAYBRIDGE SUITES PHOENIX/GLENDALE 623/842-0000 **28**

▼▼▼ Extended Stay Hotel. Rates not provided. **Address:** 9340 W Cabela Dr 85305 **Location:** SR 101 exit 7 (Glendale Ave), 0.6 mi e to N Zanjero Blvd, then just n. **Facility:** 116 efficiencies, some two bedrooms. 4 stories, interior corridors. **Pool(s):** heated outdoor. **Activities:** hot tub, picnic facilities, exercise room. **Guest Services:** complimentary and valet laundry.

[icons] CALL M ≈ BIZ HS 🛜 ✕ 🎥 🖥 📺 🖥 / SOME UNITS 🐾

WHERE TO EAT

BETTY'S NOSH 623/561-6674 **16**

▼▼ American. Casual Dining. $8-$23 **AAA Inspector Notes:** There is much to choose from at this eclectic eatery, including a mushroom bar with gourmet fillings, small plates, pasta and such entrées as grilled salmon and top sirloin. There even is a pastry and coffee bar for breakfast. **Features:** full bar, happy hour. **Address:** 6685 W Beardsley Rd 85308 **Location:** SR 101 exit 18 (67th Ave), just e along frontage road. [L] [D]

HAUS MURPHY'S 623/939-2480 **23**

▼▼ German. Casual Dining. $8-$20 **AAA Inspector Notes:** As is the case in many favorite neighborhood pubs, the walls of this eatery are covered in photographs and memorabilia. The hearty food is freshly prepared and a selection of German beers is available to wash down the crispy schnitzels and plump sausages. **Features:** full bar, patio dining. **Reservations:** suggested. **Address:** 5739 W Glendale Ave 85301 **Location:** Just e of Grand Ave (US 60); center. **Parking:** street only. [D]

MACAYO MEXICAN KITCHEN 602/298-8080

▼▼ Mexican. Casual Dining. $7-$19 **AAA Inspector Notes:** The colorfully furnished Mexican-style eatery prepares Sonoran Mexican dishes. Friendly and efficient staffers serve traditional and lighter dishes flavored with this place's own chili peppers, which are grown near Tucson. **Features:** full bar, patio dining, happy hour. **Address:** 6012 W Bell Rd 85308 **Location:** Just e of 59th Ave. [L] [D]

Visit the AAA/CAA senior driver sites for resources to help you drive safely longer

(See map & index p. 154.)

MAMA GINA'S PIZZERIA   623/872-0300 ⓴

▼▼ Italian. Casual Dining. $8-$21 **AAA Inspector Notes:** Come before or after a game at the nearby sports stadiums to taste New York style pizza, stromboli and calzones. The relaxed atmosphere here also features several flat-screen TVs and a large covered patio great for people watching. The tiramisu and cannolis are delicious. **Features:** full bar, patio dining. **Address:** 9380 W Westgate Blvd, Suite D101 85305 **Location:** SR 101 exit 7 (Glendale Ave), just e; in Westgate City Center. Ⓛ Ⓓ

PITA JUNGLE   623/486-2615 ⓲

▼▼ Mediterranean. Casual Dining. $7-$16 **AAA Inspector Notes:** The atmosphere is hip and super-casual in the dining area and on the patio. The menu offers a wide variety of hot and cold pita wraps, pizza, falafel, spanakopita, salads and burgers, as well as natural, healthful vegetarian offerings. **Features:** full bar, patio dining, happy hour. **Address:** 7530 W Bell Rd, Suite 106 85308 **Location:** SR 101 exit 14 (Bell Rd), 1 mi e. Ⓛ Ⓓ

RUBIO'S FRESH MEXICAN GRILL   623/376-9868

▼ Mexican. Quick Serve. $4-$10 **AAA Inspector Notes:** Freshly prepared and healthful foods, bright decor and friendly staff are found in this upscale fast-food spot. A special treat, the salsa bar lines up four styles and flavors. **Features:** beer only. **Address:** 20210 N 59th Ave 85308 **Location:** SR 101 exit 19 (59th Ave), just n. Ⓛ Ⓓ

SAKANA SUSHI & GRILL   623/566-3595 ⓯

▼▼ Japanese. Casual Dining. $8-$17 **AAA Inspector Notes:** This grill serves up some of the freshest sushi around. The menu includes classic sushi and sashimi choices as well as Japanese favorites and full teppanyaki dinners. **Features:** beer & wine. **Address:** 20250 N 59th Ave 85308 **Location:** SR 101 exit 19 (59th Ave), just n. Ⓛ Ⓓ

SOLEIL   623/937-3700 ⓴①

▼▼ Regional American. Casual Dining. $12-$35 **AAA Inspector Notes:** A tempting range of mouthwatering selections are offered at this upscale eatery. Beef, pork, chicken, fish and even antelope are prepared with a Southwestern flair. The menu is sure to please every palate. **Features:** full bar, patio dining, happy hour. **Address:** 9495 W Coyotes Blvd 85305 **Location:** SR 101 exit 7 (Glendale Ave), just e to N 95th Ave, just n, then just e; in Renaissance Glendale Hotel & Spa. **Parking:** on-site and valet.

Ⓑ Ⓛ Ⓓ CALL Ⓜ

THEE PITT'S "AGAIN"   602/996-7488 ⓳

▼▼ Barbecue. Casual Dining. $9-$20 **AAA Inspector Notes:** Diners can sample award-winning barbecue that has a distinct flavor. In addition to the standard Memphis-style pork, chicken, brisket and sausage pit-cooked over mesquite, the menu lists burgers, salads and sides, including coleslaw, potato salad, beans and corn on the cob. The diner displays colorful pig artwork. **Features:** beer & wine. **Address:** 5558 W Bell Rd 85308 **Location:** N on 55th Ave, then w; opposite Honeywell. Ⓛ Ⓓ CALL Ⓜ

ZANG ASIAN BISTRO   623/847-8892 ⓴②

▼▼ Asian Fusion. Casual Dining. $9-$15 **AAA Inspector Notes:** A gem in downtown Glendale, this friendly spot serves delicious regional Asian specialties like Singapore rice noodles, Hong Kong sweet and sour pork, and Thai seafood curry. **Features:** full bar. **Address:** 6835 N 58th Dr 85301 **Location:** Just e of Grand Ave (US 60); center. **Parking:** street only. Ⓛ Ⓓ

GLOBE (E-5) pop. 7,532, elev. 3,517'
• Hotels p. 80 • Restaurants p. 80

Named for a globe-shaped piece of almost pure silver reputedly found nearby, Globe has a colorful history punctuated by mining discoveries. It began as a mining community in 1876. The town's first boom was silver; the second was copper, which is still mined in large quantities. Globe also serves as a trading center for the San Carlos Apache Reservation (see San Carlos p. 200) 4 miles east.

Salt River Canyon, traversed by US 60 about 45 miles northeast, is 1,500 to 2,000 feet deep. About 5 miles wide at the top, the vertical-walled canyon winds for many miles with sedimentary rock layers visible from the road. At the foot of the canyon is a state roadside park. Running westward from Globe, scenic US 60 traverses Devil's Canyon before reaching Superior (see place listing p. 242).

Globe is the eastern terminus of yet another scenic highway, the Apache Trail (SR 188). The road runs northwest to Roosevelt and Theodore Roosevelt Lake Recreation Area (see Recreation Areas Chart) before turning southwest (SR 88) toward Apache Junction (see attraction listing p. 38 for an advisory about driving this route).

Globe-Miami Regional Chamber of Commerce: 1360 N. Broad St., Globe, AZ 85501. **Phone:** (928) 425-4495 or (800) 804-5623.

BESH-BA-GOWAH ARCHAEOLOGICAL PARK, 1324 Jesse Hayes Rd., is a 300-room pueblo inhabited 1225-1400 by Salado Indians. Several rooms are restored and furnished in period. Artifacts from the ruins are displayed in the museum, and an ethnobotanical garden illustrating how native plants were used by the Salado is featured. A video presentation also is available. **Hours:** Daily 9-4:30, Oct.-June; Wed.-Sun. 9-4:30, rest of year. Closed Jan. 1, Thanksgiving and Christmas. **Cost:** $5; $4 (ages 65+); free (ages 0-11 with adult). **Phone:** (928) 425-0320.

COBRE VALLEY CENTER FOR THE ARTS, 101 N. Broad St., is housed in the 1906 Old Gila County Courthouse. The center presents sculptures, photography, paintings, ceramics, jewelry, quilts and other art forms created by local and other artists. The Rose Mofford room exhibits memorabilia donated to the museum by the state's first female governor, who was originally from Globe.

A working stained-glass studio may be seen. The Copper City Community Players present live performance pieces in the center's theater; phone for schedule and admission information.

Time: Allow 30 minutes minimum. **Hours:** Mon.-Sat. 10-5, Sun. noon-4, Memorial Day-Labor Day; Mon.-Sat. 10-4, Sun. noon-4, rest of year. Closed major holidays. **Cost:** Donations. **Phone:** (928) 425-0884.

DEVIL'S CANYON, w. on US 60, is noted for its sharp ridges, rock strata and cathedral-like tower formations that illustrate the enormous geological pressures exerted on the region. The mineral wealth of the area is credited mainly to these forces. The Queen Creek Gorge, Bridge and Tunnel are on the drive through the canyon. **Phone:** (602) 225-5200 or (928) 402-6200.

THEODORE ROOSEVELT DAM AND LAKE—see Roosevelt p. 198.

RECREATIONAL ACTIVITIES
White-water Rafting

- **AAM's Mild to Wild Rafting & Jeep Tours Inc.** is 40 mi. n. off US 60/SR 77, following signs. **Hours:** Daily late Feb.-late May (weather permitting). **Phone:** (970) 247-4789 or (800) 567-6745.
- **Arizona Rafting** is 45 mi. e. off US 60 at the bridge over the Salt River. **Hours:** Daily, Mar. 1-early May. **Phone:** (719) 395-2112 or (800) 231-7238.

BEST WESTERN COPPER HILLS INN   (928)425-7575

Hotel
$110-$129

AAA Benefit: Save 10% or more every day and earn 10% bonus points!

Address: 1565 E South St 85501 **Location:** On US 60, 1 mi e of town. Adjacent to Round Mountain Park. **Facility:** 51 units. 2 stories, exterior corridors. **Amenities:** *Some:* safes. **Pool(s):** outdoor. **Activities:** hot tub, exercise room. **Featured Amenity:** full hot breakfast.

WHERE TO EAT

GUAYO'S ON THE TRAIL   928/425-9969

▼▼ Mexican. Casual Dining. $6-$14 **AAA Inspector Notes:** For an array of traditional favorites-including menudo, crunchy salads and burritos-try this eatery with a friendly atmosphere. It's been serving locals for the past 40 years. **Features:** full bar, senior menu. **Address:** 14239 S Hwy 188 85501 **Location:** Jct US 60, 1.3 mi n.

GOLD CANYON (J-5) elev. 1,839'

RECREATIONAL ACTIVITIES
Horseback Riding

- **Donnelly's D-Spur Riding Stables** is e. on US 60 to Peralta Rd. (between Mileposts 204 and 205), 1 mi. n.e. to a gravel road, then 1 mi. e. to 15371 E. Ojo Rd. **Hours:** Mon.-Sat. year-round. Closed major holidays. **Phone:** (602) 810-7029.

BEST WESTERN GOLD CANYON INN & SUITES
          (480)671-6000

Hotel
$85-$169

AAA Benefit: Save 10% or more every day and earn 10% bonus points!

Address: 8333 E Sunrise Sky Dr 85118 **Location:** US 60 exit Kings Ranch Rd, just n, then just e; 7 mi e of Apache Junction. **Facility:** 68 units. 2 stories, interior corridors. **Pool(s):** heated outdoor. **Activities:** hot tub, game room, exercise room. **Guest Services:** coin laundry. **Featured Amenity:** full hot breakfast.

WHERE TO EAT

KOKOPELLI'S   480/671-5517

▼▼▼ American. Fine Dining. $8-$33 **AAA Inspector Notes:** Views of the Superstition Mountains and over the adjacent golf course enhance the dining experience at this restaurant. The well-trained staff assists with choices of specialty steaks or preparations of seafood, chicken and veal. Gold Canyon mousse is a must for dessert. **Features:** full bar, patio dining, Sunday brunch, happy hour. **Address:** 6100 S Kings Ranch Rd 85219 **Location:** US 60 exit Kings Ranch Rd, 1 mi n; in Gold Canyon Golf Resort. **Parking:** on-site and valet. B L D 🛒

GOODYEAR (I-2) pop. 65,275, elev. 1,000'
- **Hotels & Restaurants map & index p. 154**
- **Part of Phoenix area — see map p. 126**

In the early 1900s Goodyear Tire & Rubber Company obtained tracts of land in the Salt River Valley, with the intent of growing Egyptian cotton, a component in tire cords. The small farms established on this land evolved into company towns, including one named for its originator. Just 14 miles west of Phoenix, the town is now a suburban residential community. Goodyear Ballpark, 1933 S. Ballpark Way, is the spring training center for Major League Baseball's Cleveland Indians and Cincinnati Reds.

Southwest Valley Chamber of Commerce: 289 N. Litchfield Rd., Goodyear, AZ 85338. **Phone:** (623) 932-2260.

ESTRELLA MOUNTAIN REGIONAL PARK, off I-10 Estrella Pkwy. S. exit, contains 19,840 acres of rugged desert terrain; more than 40 miles of trails for hiking, horseback riding and mountain biking; and an 18-hole golf course. Educational programs are offered; equestrian events are held throughout the year. **Hours:** Park Mon.-Fri. 8-8, Sat.-Sun. 8 a.m.-10 p.m. Nature Center daily 8-4. **Cost:** $6 (per private vehicle); $2 (per person arriving on foot, horseback or bicycle). Camping $12-$40. **Phone:** (623) 932-3811.

RECREATIONAL ACTIVITIES
Horseback Riding

- **Corral West Horse Adventures** departs from 14401 W. Arena Dr. in Estrella Regional Park. Other activities are offered. **Hours:** Daily Oct.-Apr. **Phone:** (623) 882-3808.

BEST WESTERN PHOENIX GOODYEAR INN
          (623)932-3210 53

Hotel
$80-$210

AAA Benefit: Save 10% or more every day and earn 10% bonus points!

Address: 55 N Litchfield Rd 85338 **Location:** I-10 exit 128, 0.8 mi s. **Facility:** 85 units. 1-2 stories (no elevator), interior/exterior corridors. **Terms:** check-in 4 pm. **Pool(s):** heated outdoor. **Activities:** exercise room. **Guest Services:** valet and coin laundry.

(See map & index p. 154.)

COMFORT SUITES GOODYEAR (623)266-2884 **48**

Hotel $79-$169 **Address:** 15575 W Roosevelt St 85338 **Location:** I-10 exit 126, just s on Estrella Pkwy, then just w. **Facility:** 84 units. 3 stories, interior corridors. **Pool(s):** heated outdoor. **Activities:** hot tub, exercise room. **Guest Services:** valet and coin laundry.

HAMPTON INN & SUITES GOODYEAR (623)536-1313 **47**

Hotel $109-$209 **Address:** 2000 N Litchfield Rd 85395 **Location:** I-10 exit 128, 0.5 mi n. **Facility:** 110 units, some efficiencies. 3 stories, interior corridors. **Terms:** check-in 4 pm, 1-7 night minimum stay, cancellation fee imposed. **Pool(s):** heated outdoor. **Activities:** hot tub, picnic facilities, exercise room. **Guest Services:** valet and coin laundry, rental car service.

> **AAA Benefit:** Members save up to 10%!

HOLIDAY INN & SUITES GOODYEAR (623)547-1313 **50**

Hotel $139-$229 **Address:** 1188 N Dysart Rd 85395 **Location:** I-10 exit 129 (Dysart Rd), just n. **Facility:** 100 units. 4 stories, interior corridors. **Amenities:** video games, safes. **Pool(s):** heated outdoor. **Activities:** hot tub, exercise room. **Guest Services:** valet and coin laundry.

HOLIDAY INN EXPRESS WEST PHOENIX/GOODYEAR (623)535-1313 **49**

Hotel $109-$259 **Address:** 1313 N Litchfield Rd 85395 **Location:** I-10 exit 128, just n. **Facility:** 90 units. 3 stories, interior corridors. **Terms:** check-in 4 pm, 7 day cancellation notice-fee imposed. **Pool(s):** heated outdoor. **Activities:** hot tub, exercise room. **Guest Services:** valet and coin laundry.

QUALITY INN & SUITES GOODYEAR (623)932-9191 **51**

Hotel $65-$180 **Address:** 950 N Dysart Rd 85338 **Location:** I-10 exit 129 (Dysart Rd), just s. **Facility:** 158 units. 2 stories (no elevator), exterior corridors. **Amenities:** safes. **Pool(s):** heated outdoor. **Activities:** hot tub, picnic facilities, exercise room. **Guest Services:** valet and coin laundry.

RESIDENCE INN BY MARRIOTT (623)866-1313 **46**

Extended Stay Hotel $99-$244 **Address:** 2020 N Litchfield Rd 85395 **Location:** I-10 exit 128, 0.6 mi n. **Facility:** 78 units, some two bedrooms, efficiencies and kitchens. 3 stories, interior corridors. **Pool(s):** heated outdoor. **Activities:** hot tub, picnic facilities, exercise room. **Guest Services:** valet and coin laundry.

> **AAA Benefit:** Members save 5% or more!

TOWNEPLACE SUITES BY MARRIOTT PHOENIX/ GOODYEAR (623)535-5009 **52**

Extended Stay Hotel $84-$238

TownePlace SUITES Marriott

> **AAA Benefit:** Members save 5% or more!

Address: 13971 W Celebrate Life Way 85338 **Location:** I-10 exit 128, just s, then just w. **Facility:** 118 efficiencies, some two bedrooms. 4 stories, interior corridors. **Terms:** check-in 4 pm. **Pool(s):** heated outdoor. **Activities:** hot tub, picnic facilities, exercise room. **Guest Services:** valet and coin laundry. **Featured Amenity:** continental breakfast.

WHERE TO EAT

BELLA LUNA RISTORANTE 623/535-4642 **31**

Italian. Casual Dining. $10-$26 **AAA Inspector Notes:** Italian dishes freshly made to entice guests include shrimp and crab in a fra diavolo sauce over linguine and veal cutlet in a special white wine sauce with onions and peas. The light and delicate preparations are served by friendly staff in a modern setting. **Features:** full bar, patio dining, happy hour. **Address:** 14175 W Indian School Rd 85338 **Location:** I-10 exit 128 (Litchfield Rd), 1.9 mi n. L D

MACAYO MEXICAN KITCHEN 623/209-7000

Mexican. Casual Dining. $7-$19 **AAA Inspector Notes:** The colorfully furnished Mexican-style eatery prepares Sonoran Mexican dishes. Friendly and efficient staffers serve traditional and lighter dishes flavored with this place's own chili peppers, which are grown near Tucson. **Features:** full bar, happy hour. **Address:** 1474 N Litchfield Rd 85338 **Location:** I-10 exit 128, just n. L D

P.F. CHANG'S CHINA BISTRO 623/536-3222 **32**

Chinese. Fine Dining. $8-$25 **AAA Inspector Notes:** Trendy, upscale decor provides a pleasant backdrop for New Age Chinese dining. Appetizers, soups and salads are a meal by themselves. Vegetarian plates and sides, noodles, chow meins, chicken and meat dishes are created from exotic, fresh ingredients. **Features:** full bar, patio dining, happy hour. **Address:** 14681 W McDowell Rd 85395 **Location:** I-10 exit 127 (Bullard Ave), just n, then just w. L D

ROYAL JASMINE THAI 623/236-3362 **30**

Thai. Casual Dining. $8-$15 **AAA Inspector Notes:** This West Valley gem is tucked away in an unassuming strip mall, but the food is filled with flavor and the service is helpful and helpful. The different curries are delicious, as is the tom yum soup. **Features:** beer & wine, happy hour. **Address:** 14970 W Indian School Rd 85395 **Location:** I-10 exit 127 (Bullard Ave), 1.7 mi n, then 0.6 mi w. L D

TOMO JAPANESE CUISINE 623/935-2031 **34**

Japanese. Casual Dining. $8-$27 **AAA Inspector Notes:** This small and intimate shopping plaza sushi spot serves fresh fish and authentic Japanese favorites. **Features:** full bar, happy hour. **Address:** 1550 N Dysart Rd, Suite A7 85338 **Location:** I-10 exit 129 (Dysart Rd), 0.3 mi n; southwest corner of McDowell and Dysart rds. L D

GRAND CANYON NATIONAL PARK (A-3)

• Hotels p. 90 • Restaurants p. 92
• Attractions map p. 84

Elevations in the park range from 1,100 ft. in the lower part of the canyon to about 9,000 ft. at the North Rim. Refer to AAA maps for additional elevation information.

The Grand Canyon of the Colorado River is so magnificent, so humbling, you'll never forget the sensation you feel at first sight. And yes, if you visit in summer, the South Rim is so crowded you'll be griping about the crush of tourists for years to come. But this 277-mile-long canyon, sculpted by the mighty Colorado, is without question America's number one natural wonder.

Viewing aerial IMAX footage simply can't compare to finding a solitary spot somewhere, anywhere, in this mile-deep gorge, and silently watching a raven glide on the breeze above a vast panorama of pyramidal buttes, lonely mesas, rust-colored cliffs and shadowy side canyons.

Of course, not everyone who visits the canyon is compelled to wax poetic like a talking head in a Ken Burns documentary. In the early 19th century, James Ohio Pattie, the first American to lay eyes on the immense chasm, called it "horrid." Following an 1857 Army expedition, Lt. Joseph Ives deemed it a "profitless locality." If he could only witness the 5 million visitors a year who fill the hotels, ride the mules to Phantom Ranch, light up the gift shop cash registers and buzz over the canyon on helicopter tours.

As the hawk flies, it's 10 miles from the South Rim Village to the North Rim lodge. To grasp the canyon's geologic scope, a bit of textbook-speak is necessary. Eons of time are on display in the layer-cake-like strata of the canyon walls. Though scientists estimate the canyon is relatively young (6 million years old), the rock layers at the bottom, near the Colorado River, date back some 2 billion years.

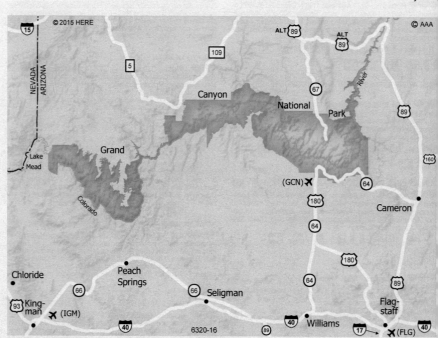

This map shows cities in Grand Canyon National Park where you will find attractions, hotels and restaurants. Cities are listed alphabetically in this book on the following pages.

Put in perspective, the 270-million-year-old Permian Period layer (formed just prior to the age of the dinosaurs) is what you're standing on at the rim. No wonder they call the canyon "grand."

General Information and Activities

North Rim visitor services and facilities are open mid-May to late October; heavy snow closes the road to the North Rim during the winter (November 1 to mid-May). For road conditions and weather information phone (928) 638-7888.

South Rim visitor services and facilities are open all year. During the winter South Rim trails into the canyon are open; however, they can be dangerously icy from November through April. Trail conditions should be verified at the Backcountry Information Center or at Grand Canyon Visitor Center. Hikers are advised not to hike from the rim to the river and back in one day. If you attempt to do so, you may find yourself stranded overnight, or at the very least, exhausted. Since nights are cool even in summer, pack warm clothing. However, be prepared for high daytime summer temperatures within the canyon. The area also is subject to monsoon weather with dangerous lightning in July and August.

Maps, trail descriptions, lists of ranger-led activities, seasonal information and shuttle schedules are available at all entrance stations as well as at visitor centers and local hotels.

Backpacking anywhere in the park or camping below the canyon rim requires a permit from the Backcountry Information Center, Permits Office, 1824 S. Thompson St., Suite 201, Flagstaff, AZ 86001. Permit requests and backcountry camping reservations are accepted by mail, fax or in person up to 4 months in advance. A limited number of last minute walk-up permits are available at the South Rim and/or North Rim Backcountry Information Center for Corridor Campgrounds (Indian Garden, Bright Angel and Cottonwood campgrounds). These permits are issued in person only, are for one or two consecutive nights and cannot be purchased more than one day prior to the start of a hike. For more information phone (928) 638-7875, Mon.-Fri. 1-5 or fax (928) 638-2125.

Four campgrounds are inside the park, and there are several located outside the park and in the adjacent national forests. There is only one RV campground within the park with full hook-ups, which is in Grand Canyon Village on the South Rim. Desert View Campground, on the South Rim of the park and 25 miles to the east of Grand Canyon Village, is first-come, first-served only. No reservations are accepted. The campground is open seasonally, May through mid-October. Reservations for National Park Service-operated campgrounds on the North and South rims can be made up to 6 months in advance by phoning (877) 444-6777 or TTY (877) 833-6777. *See Recreation Areas Chart.*

Trans-Canyon Shuttle provides one-way and round-trip van transportation once daily to each of the canyon's rims from mid-May to mid-October. The 4.5-hour shuttle ride departs for the South Rim

at 7 a.m. and begins its return to the North Rim at 1:30 p.m. The fare is $85 for a one-way ride; $160 for a round-trip ride. Reservations are required; phone (928) 638-2820 for information and reservations.

Flagstaff Shuttle, Charter and Tours offers transportation to and from the park and its environs in Sedona, Flagstaff and Phoenix. From Flagstaff to the South Rim, the fare is $150 for up to three people; $595 from Phoenix to the South Rim for up to three; and $450 for up to three to the North Rim from Flagstaff or the South Rim. An additional fare of $45 is assessed for each passenger above three. Children ages 0-16 ride free with a paying adult. Admission to the park is $8 each. Prices may vary; phone (888) 215-3105 for information and reservations.

Buses departing from Yavapai Lodge, Maswik Lodge and Bright Angel Lodge & Cabins take visitors on a variety of sightseeing tours. The 2-hour Hermits Rest Tour is $25; free (ages 0-16 with paying adult). The 3.75-hour Desert View Tour is $42; free (ages 0-16 with paying adult). The 90-minute Sunrise and Sunset tours each are $20; free (ages 0-16 with paying adult). A Combination Tour ($57) and a Railway Express Tour ($65) also are available.

For bus tour information and advance reservations, contact Xanterra Parks & Resorts at (888) 297-2757. For same-day reservations, phone (928) 638-2631.

Flightseeing tours are offered from the South Rim and from several nearby cities, including Page, Phoenix, Sedona, Williams and Las Vegas, Nev.

Another way to glimpse the Grand Canyon from overlooks is on a four-wheel-drive tour. These backroad sightseeing trips through the Kaibab National Forest are led by guides well-versed in the ecology of the canyon, its history, wildlife and legends. Contact Grand Canyon Jeep Tours & Safaris at (928) 638-5337 or (800) 320-5337.

ADMISSION to the park, valid for both rims for up to 7 days, is $30 (per private vehicle); $25 (per person arriving by motorcycle); $15 (per person arriving by other means); free (military with ID).

PETS are permitted in the park only if they are leashed, crated or otherwise physically restrained at all times. Pets are excluded entirely from backcountry areas, are not allowed below the rim and are not permitted on shuttle buses. Kennels are available; reservations are recommended. Restrictions do not apply to service animals. Phone (928) 638-0534.

ADDRESS inquiries to the Superintendent, Grand Canyon National Park, P.O. Box 129, Grand Canyon, AZ 86023; phone (928) 638-7888. Information also is available from the Grand Canyon Chamber of Commerce, P.O. Box 3007, Grand Canyon, AZ 86023; phone (888) 472-2696 or (928) 638-2901.

Grand Canyon National Park Attractions

GRAND CANYON NATIONAL PARK - SOUTH RIM (A-3)

Hotels p. 90 • Restaurants p. 92
Attractions map p. 84

One superb canyon vista after another is what you'll see along the South Rim's paved roads. The 25-mile Desert View Drive (open year-round to private vehicles) connects the East Entrance Station with Grand Canyon Village, winding through a ponderosa pine forest and passing a half-dozen viewpoints (Grandview is a standout) along the way.

West of the village, Hermit Road leads to more overlooks (including the phenomenal Hopi Point) on its way to Hermit's Rest, where you'll find restrooms, a snack bar and a gift shop. The road is closed to private vehicles March through November but can be accessed by the park's free shuttle bus during these months.

In peak summer travel season, brace yourself for crowds. In most areas of Grand Canyon Village, parking is scarce. Free shuttles run year round at the village, and it's often wise to park at the visitor center and use the shuttle to get around. To avoid parking headaches all together, consider riding the free shuttle from Tusayan (the park's gateway town); service is available June through September.

If you're driving into the park through the South Entrance Station (near Tusayan), take note: There are five entry gates with one gate dedicated to prepaid passes. This is a very popular point of entry and crowds can be large, so paying admission outside the park at the National Geographic Visitor Center Grand Canyon (see attraction listing p. 86) is a smart move when traffic is heavy. Passes also can be purchased at most Tusayan hotels and at visitor centers in Williams and Flagstaff. Of course, the most obvious way to avoid possible delays is to get an early start.

Both helicopter and airplane tours of the canyon are available from the Grand Canyon National Park Airport in Tusayan, 5 miles south of the park headquarters. For information and reservations contact Grand Canyon Airlines, (888) 235-9422; Grand Canyon Helicopters, (928) 638-2764; Maverick Helicopters, (928) 638-2622 or (800) 962-3869; or

Papillon Grand Canyon Helicopters, (928) 638-2419 or (800) 528-2418.

BRIGHT ANGEL TRAIL starts just w. of Bright Angel Lodge & Cabins. Descending 4,460 feet to the Colorado River, the trail leads 9 miles to the river and Phantom Ranch. From Indian Garden, 4.4 miles below the trailhead, a branch trail leads 1.5 miles across the Tonto Platform to Plateau Point, offering a grand view of the Colorado River. To view the depths from the rim, telescopes are available near Bright Angel Lodge & Cabins and at Desert View Watchtower.

Note: Hikers should check park publications for the latest information about the trail. Overnight hikers must obtain a camping permit. Water and other hiking necessities must be carried on all canyon trails.

DESERT VIEW WATCHTOWER is 25 mi. e. of Grand Canyon Village at Desert View. Built in 1932, the 70-ft. tower built of stone and mortar was inspired by prehistoric towers found in the Four Corners region. From the brink of the canyon wall, the tower commands views of the river, the canyon, the Painted Desert and Kaibab National Forest (see place listing p. 96); telescopes extend the view far into the Navajo Reservation and to the Colorado River.

Also at Desert View are food concessions, an information desk, a seasonal campground and a gas station. **Hours:** Daily 8-dusk, day before Memorial Day-Labor Day; 9-6, day after Labor Day-Nov. 30; 9-5, Dec.-Feb.; 8-6, rest of year. **Cost:** Free. 🍽

GRAND CANYON CAVERNS—see Peach Springs p. 122.

GRAND CANYON RAILWAY—see Williams p. 301.

GRAND CANYON SKYWALK—see Kingman p. 98.

GRAND CANYON VISITOR CENTER is 5 mi. n. of the South Entrance Station near Mather Point. The center can be reached via a free shuttle bus from various locations in Grand Canyon Village. The visitor center is at an altitude of 6,950 feet and features indoor displays, a theater with a film, outdoor

▼ See AAA listing p. 21 ▼

exhibits, an information center and views of the canyon from nearby observation points.

Note: Inquire at the center about local road conditions. **Hours:** Daily 8-6, Memorial Day-Labor Day; 8-5, rest of year. Ranger programs are presented. Hours may vary; consult park publications for details. **Cost:** Free. **Phone:** (928) 638-7888.

 HAVASU CANYON—see Supai p. 242.

KOLB STUDIO, just w. of Bright Angel Lodge & Cabins, was built as a photography studio in 1904 for brothers Ellsworth and Emery Kolb, who took photos of tourists descending Bright Angel Trail *(see attraction listing)* on mules. The building now serves as both a bookstore and a gallery with changing Grand Canyon-related exhibits. Antique photographic equipment used by the Kolb brothers is on display, and you can snap your own photos from a small outdoor viewing area. **Time:** Allow 30 minutes minimum. **Hours:** Daily 8-8, Memorial Day-Labor Day; 8-6, day after Labor Day-Oct. 31 and Feb. 1-day before Memorial Day; 8-5, rest of year. Hours may vary; consult *The Guide* newspaper for details. **Cost:** Free. **Phone:** (928) 638-2481.

LIPAN POINT, along Desert View Dr., has an elevation of 7,360 feet and offers a fine view of the river, the Unkar Delta and the San Francisco Peaks.

NATIONAL GEOGRAPHIC VISITOR CENTER

GRAND CANYON, 9 mi. s. of Grand Canyon Village at 450 SR 64 in Tusayan, features exhibits about Grand Canyon history, explorers, geology and wildlife. Visitors wishing to visit Grand Canyon National Park can obtain trip-planning information, purchase park passes and book tours. **Hours:** Daily 8 a.m.-10 p.m., Mar.-Oct.; 9-8, rest of year. **Cost:** Free. **Phone:** (928) 638-2468. *(See ad p. 87.)*

 IMAX Theater is within the National Geographic Visitor Center Grand Canyon, 9 mi. s. of Grand Canyon Village at 450 SR 64 in Tusayan. Equipped with a seven-story screen and surround system, the theater presents "Grand Canyon: The Hidden Secrets," a 34-minute IMAX film that depicts the beauty of this geologic formation and 4,000 years of its history. The film also shows parts of the canyon that can't be seen on tours.

Time: Allow 45 minutes minimum. **Hours:** The film is shown daily every hour on the half-hour 8:30-8:30, Mar.-Oct.; 9-6:30, rest of year. **Cost:** Film $12.50; $11.50 (senior citizens and military with ID); $9.50 (ages 6-10). **Phone:** (928) 638-2468. *(See ad p. 87.)*

▼ *See AAA listing p. 300* ▼

PINK JEEP TOURS GRAND CANYON depart from the IMAX Theater, 9 mi. s. of Grand Canyon Village at 450 SR 64 in Tusayan. Board a distinctively colored jeep for a professionally guided ride along the South Rim with several stops during the tour to take photos of the Grand Canyon's incredible vistas. **Time:** Allow 2 hours minimum. **Hours:** Tours depart daily every hour on the quarter hour 7:15-dusk, Mar.-Nov.; 8:15-dusk, rest of year. Closed Christmas. **Cost:** Grand Entrance Tour $74; $55 (ages 18 months-15 years). Other tours are available. All tours include admission to IMAX Theater for the "Grand Canyon: The Hidden Secrets" IMAX film. Reservations are recommended. **Phone:** (800) 873-3662. GT

PHANTOM RANCH, at the bottom of the Grand Canyon, is reached by hiking *(see Bright Angel Trail)* or mule ride *(see South Rim Mule Trips).* The only lodging available below the rim, it provides dormitory accommodations, cabins and a dining room. Dormitories and cabins are available to hikers; cabin lodging is included with overnight mule trips. **Cost:** Dorm space $46.33 per person. Cabins $148.66 (for four people). Reservations are required for lodging and meals and must be made well in advance, especially during summer and holidays. **Phone:** (303) 297-2757 or (888) 297-2757.

RIM TRAIL extends 13 mi. along the rim of the canyon from Hermits Rest to South Kaibab Trailhead (near Yaki Point). A paved section starting at Pima Point and extending east for about 1.7 miles accommodates wheelchairs and is suitable for walking and biking. The trail is steeply downhill from Maricopa Point to Grand Canyon Village, then relatively flat. The paved 5.4-mile section from Maricopa Point to Pipe Creek Vista is better for children and casual hikers than the park's other more strenuous canyon trails. Pamphlets about the biology and geology of the canyon can be obtained from boxes along the trail.

SOUTH KAIBAB TRAIL begins near Yaki Point, 3.5 mi. e. of Grand Canyon Village. This is a steep, 7-mile trail to a Colorado River suspension bridge. A good 3-mile round-trip day hike leads from the head of South Kaibab Trail to Cedar Ridge, where beautiful views of the canyon may be seen.

Note: Visitors should not attempt to hike from the South Rim to the river and back in 1 day. The Kaibab Trail is strenuous and not recommended for hiking out of the canyon. The trip is recommended only for hardy individuals. Hikers should carry water (1 gallon per person per day), since none is available along the trail. The road to the trailhead is closed to private vehicles and may be reached by shuttle bus. **Hours:** Conducted hikes to Cedar Ridge are scheduled early on summer mornings.

SOUTH RIM MULE TRIPS depart from a point near the trailhead of the Bright Angel Trail. Offered through Grand Canyon National Parks Lodges,

guided overnight mule trips take visitors along the Bright Angel Trail to Phantom Ranch in the bottom of the canyon. There also is the 3-hour Canyon Vistas mule ride through Kaibab Forest along the canyon rim.

Note: For safety purposes, riders must be fluent in English, be taller than 4 feet 7 inches, and weigh less than 200 pounds when fully dressed (including equipment) for the Phantom Ranch ride or 225 pounds for the Canyon Vistas ride. The trips are strenuous and should be undertaken only by those in good physical condition; pregnant women are not permitted on the trips.

Hours: Trips depart daily year-round. **Cost:** Rates vary; phone ahead. Reservations are required and must be made well in advance, particularly during summer and holidays. **Phone:** (888) 297-2757.

TUSAYAN MUSEUM AND RUIN is 22 mi. e. of Grand Canyon Village on a short spur leading off Desert View Dr. The museum traces the development of the Native American culture at the canyon. Exhibits include a painting of the ruin, displays about modern tribes and such Ancestral Puebloan artifacts as pottery, twig figurines and rock drawings.

Tusayan Ruin is a U-shaped, prehistoric pueblo inhabited 1185-1225 by two generations of Ancestral Puebloans; it contains about 15 rooms and about 30 people lived there. The Ancestral Puebloans are believed to be the ancestors of the Hopi as well as other Pueblo tribes.

An adjacent .1-mile paved trail runs around the pueblo. A self-guiding brochure is available at the trailhead. **Note:** Inclement weather may result in winter closures; phone ahead. **Hours:** Daily 9-5. **Cost:** Free. **Phone:** (928) 638-7888. (GT)

YAVAPAI GEOLOGY MUSEUM, 1.5 mi. e. of Grand Canyon Village, offers exhibits and programs that explain the geologic history of the region. A panoramic view of the canyon is visible through the building's windows. **Hours:** Daily 8-8, Memorial Day-Labor Day; 8-7, Mar. 1-Wed. before Memorial Day and day after Labor Day-Nov. 30; 8-6, rest of year. **Cost:** Free.

RECREATIONAL ACTIVITIES
Bicycling
- **Bright Angel Bicycle Rentals** departs from the Grand Canyon Visitor Center. Tours and rentals are offered. **Hours:** Daily 8-6, May 1-Sept. 15. **Phone:** (928) 638-3055. (¶)

Horseback Riding
- **Apache Stables** is 1 mi. n. of Tusayan off SR 64, then .25 mi. w. on FR 328/Moqui Dr. **Hours:** Daily, Mar.-Nov. (weather permitting). Phone for schedule details. **Phone:** (928) 638-2891.

White-water Rafting
- **Raft Trips** is on the Colorado River. **Hours:** Trips operate Mar.-Oct. **Phone:** (928) 526-4575 or (800) 473-4576.

▼ See AAA listing p. 43 ▼

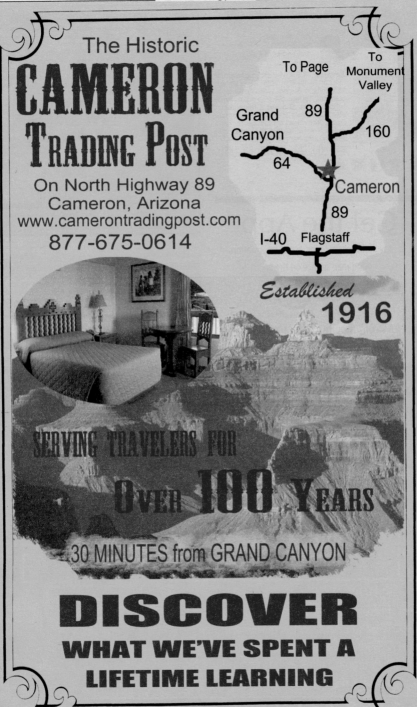

BEST WESTERN PREMIER GRAND CANYON SQUIRE INN   (928)638-2681

Hotel
$99-$399

Best Western PREMIER

AAA Benefit: Save 10% or more every day and earn 10% bonus points!

Address: 74 SR 64 86023 **Location:** 2 mi s of South Rim entrance. **Facility:** 250 units. 1-3 stories, interior/exterior corridors. **Terms:** check-in 4 pm. **Amenities:** safes. **Dining:** 2 restaurants, also, Coronado Room, see separate listing. **Activities:** hot tub, game room, exercise room. **Guest Services:** coin laundry, area transportation.

Get the App

Stay mobile with maps, travel information and road service on the go.

AAA.com/mobile · CAA.ca/mobile

CANYON PLAZA GRAND CANYON   (928)638-2673

Hotel
$109-$309

Address: 406 Canyon Plaza Ln 86023 **Location:** On SR 64; 2 mi s of South Rim entrance. Located behind Imax Theater. **Facility:** 232 units. 3 stories, interior/exterior corridors. **Terms:** cancellation fee imposed. **Pool(s):** heated outdoor. **Activities:** hot tub, exercise room. **Guest Services:** coin laundry.

Canyon Plaza
RESORT
GRAND CANYON

7 minutes from Grand Canyon National Park South Rim. Lush Indoor Garden Atrium, Buffet or Menu Dining.

EL TOVAR HOTEL   303/297-2757

Classic Historic Resort Hotel. Rates not provided. **Address:** South Rim 86023 **Location:** At Grand Canyon Village South Rim. **Facility:** Built in 1905, this hotel along the canyon rim features a lodge-style lobby and varying room sizes. A second-story seating area provides many electrical outlets and complimentary board games. 127 units. 2-4 stories (no elevator), interior corridors. **Terms:** check-in 4 pm. **Amenities:** safes. **Dining:** El Tovar Hotel Dining Room, see separate listing.

▼ See AAA listing p. 91 ▼

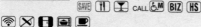

GRAND CANYON

Holiday Inn Express & Suites
GRAND CANYON

164 GUEST ROOMS
—
35 SUITES

□ Indoor Pool & Spa
□ FREE **Express Start**® Breakfast
□ Walk to **IMAX**® & Local Restaurants
□ 2 Bedroom **Kid's Suites** with Video Games
□ 1 Bedroom Suites with Refrigerator, Coffeemaker, Microwave & Cable TV
□ **Totally new look!**

1-888-473-2269 ▪ **www.gcanyon.com**

THE GRAND HOTEL AT THE GRAND CANYON
(928)638-3333

Hotel
$99-$410

Address: 149 State Hwy 64 86023 **Location:** 2 mi s of South Rim entrance. **Facility:** 121 units. 3 stories, interior corridors. **Terms:** check-in 4 pm, cancellation fee imposed. **Amenities:** safes. **Dining:** Canyon Star, see separate listing, entertainment. **Pool(s):** heated indoor. **Activities:** hot tub, exercise room. **Guest Services:** coin laundry, area transportation.

HOLIDAY INN EXPRESS HOTEL & SUITES-GRAND CANYON
928/638-3000

Hotel. Rates not provided. **Address:** 226 SR 64 86023 **Location:** 2 mi s of South Rim entrance. **Facility:** 196 units. 3 stories, interior corridors. **Terms:** check-in 4 pm. **Pool(s):** heated indoor. **Activities:** hot tub, exercise room. *(See ad p. 90.)*

MASWIK LODGE
303/297-2757

Motel. Rates not provided. **Address:** South Rim 86023 **Location:** At Grand Canyon Village South Rim. **Facility:** 250 units. 2 stories (no elevator), exterior corridors. **Terms:** check-in 4 pm. **Amenities:** *Some:* safes.

▼ See AAA listing p. 92 ▼

RED FEATHER LODGE   (928)638-2414

Hotel
$75-$350

Address: 300 SR 64 86023 **Location:** 2 mi s of South Rim entrance. **Facility:** 227 units, some kitchens. 2-3 stories, interior/exterior corridors. **Terms:** check-in 4 pm, cancellation fee imposed. **Amenities:** video games. **Pool(s):** heated outdoor. **Activities:** hot tub. **Guest Services:** coin laundry. *(See ad p. 91.)*

[SAVE] [❚❙] CALL [&M] [⟱] [BIZ]
[📶] [⊗] [🏋]
/SOME UNITS [S⟋] [🔒] [▤]

THUNDERBIRD LODGE   303/297-2757
Hotel. Rates not provided. **Address:** South Rim 86023 **Location:** At Grand Canyon Village South Rim. **Facility:** 55 units. 2 stories (no elevator), interior/exterior corridors. **Terms:** check-in 4 pm. **Amenities:** safes. [❚❙+] CALL [&M] [📶] [✕] [🔒] [▤]

YAVAPAI LODGE   928/638-4001
Motel $141-$175 **Address:** South Rim 86023 **Location:** 1 mi e of Grand Canyon Village South Rim. Located in a quiet area. **Facility:** 358 units. 1-2 stories (no elevator), interior/exterior corridors. **Terms:** cancellation fee imposed. **Amenities:** *Some:* safes.

[❚❙] CALL [&M] [BIZ] [📶] [✕] [🔒] [▤] /SOME UNITS [S⟋] [Ж]

BRIGHT ANGEL LODGE & CABINS   303/297-2757
[fyi] Not evaluated. **Address:** Hwy 64, South Rim 86023 **Location:** At Grand Canyon Village South Rim. Facilities, services, and décor characterize an economy property.

WHERE TO EAT

THE ARIZONA ROOM AT BRIGHT ANGEL LODGE
928/638-2631
American. Casual Dining. $8-$29 **AAA Inspector Notes:** Everyone can enjoy a panoramic view of the Grand Canyon, while feasting on such American fare as organic chicken breast, salmon, buffalo burgers and even prime rib. Try a local brewed beer for lunch or dinner. **Features:** full bar. **Address:** 10 South Rim Ave 86023 **Location:** At Grand Canyon Village South Rim; between Bright Angel Lodge & Cabins and Thunderbird Lodge. [L] [D]

BIG E STEAKHOUSE & SALOON   928/638-0333

American
Casual Dining
$12-$39

AAA Inspector Notes: Enjoy a great selection of savory steaks plus seafood, poultry, pastas, vegetarian and gluten-free entrées. Live entertainment is offered nightly on a stage that features a dazzling 200 square foot video wall. **Features:** full bar, patio dining, happy hour. **Address:** 395 SR 64 86023 **Location:** 1 mi s of South Rim entrance. [L] [D]

BRIGHT ANGEL RESTAURANT   928/638-2631
American. Casual Dining. $9-$26 **AAA Inspector Notes:** This restaurant presents an eclectic menu with many healthy and sustainable items such as natural Angus beef burgers, pork loin and salmon filets. **Features:** full bar. **Address:** South Rim 86023 **Location:** At Grand Canyon Village South Rim; in Bright Angel Lodge & Cabins. [B] [L] [D] CALL [&M]

CANYON STAR   928/638-3333

American
Casual Dining
$8-$45

AAA Inspector Notes: Featuring a Southwestern menu with steaks and a seasonal buffet, the restaurant also entertains guests with Native American dancers and singing cowboys. **Features:** full bar, happy hour. **Address:** Hwy 64 86023 **Location:** 2 mi s of South Rim entrance; in The Grand Hotel at the Grand Canyon. [B] [L] [D]

CORONADO ROOM   928/638-2681
Steak Seafood. Casual Dining. $15-$30 **AAA Inspector Notes:** The menu features a nice selection of steaks, seafood, pastas and Mexican dishes. **Features:** full bar, early bird specials, happy hour. **Address:** 74 SR 64 86023 **Location:** 2 mi s of South Rim entrance; in BEST WESTERN PREMIER Grand Canyon Squire Inn. [D]

EL TOVAR HOTEL DINING ROOM   928/638-2631
Continental. Fine Dining. $11-$35 **AAA Inspector Notes:** The very attractive dining room is the setting for a nice selection of veal, beef, seafood, chicken and vegetarian entrées. **Features:** full bar. **Reservations:** suggested, for dinner. **Address:** South Rim 86023 **Location:** At Grand Canyon Village South Rim; in El Tovar Hotel. [B] [L] [D]

WE COOK PIZZA & PASTA   928/638-2278

Italian
Pizza
Quick Serve
$10-$29

AAA Inspector Notes: After a long day exploring the canyon, locals and visitors congregate here for beer and pizza. Although specialty pizzas are the most popular choices, the menu also lists sandwiches, simple pasta dishes, calzones and a salad bar. **Features:** beer & wine, patio dining. **Address:** 605 N Hwy 64 86023 **Location:** 2 mi s of South Rim entrance. [L] [D]

◤GEM◢ GRAND CANYON NATIONAL PARK - NORTH RIM (A-3)
• Attractions map p. 84

Less visited than the South Rim, the North Rim is not as extensively developed. The views from the North and South rims differ considerably. Observers at Bright Angel Point on the North Rim can see the San Francisco Peaks, which are 80 miles south of the South Rim.

From Grand Canyon Village on the South Rim, it is 215 miles to Grand Canyon North Rim Lodge via SR 64 to Cameron, US 89 to its junction with US 89A at Bitter Springs, US 89A to Jacob Lake and scenic SR 67 to the North Rim Entrance Station. The 5-hour drive passes through the Navajo reservation, the Painted Desert and Kaibab National Forest.

A road runs 22 miles southeast from the Grand Canyon North Rim Lodge road to Point Imperial, Vista Encantada and Cape Royal. Point Imperial, at 8,803 feet, is the highest point on the canyon rim. These points all afford splendid views. Reservations for the North Rim Campground can be made up to 6 months in advance by phoning Reserve America at (877) 444-6777. *See Recreation Areas Chart.*

GRAND CANYON CAVERNS—see Peach Springs p. 122.

◤GEM◢ **GRAND CANYON RAILWAY**—see Williams p. 301.

GRAND CANYON SKYWALK—see Kingman p. 98.

MARBLE CANYON, at the n.e. end of the park, is traversed by US 89A via the Navajo Bridge, which is 616 feet long and 467 feet high. The Colorado River lies in a 500-foot-deep gorge that cuts across the level plain on which the highway sits.

NORTH KAIBAB TRAIL starts at the head of Roaring Springs Canyon. This 14.2-mile trail descends 5,850 feet to the river and Phantom Ranch, following Bright Angel Creek. **Note:** Only experienced hikers in good physical condition should use the trail. Check park publications, for the latest information about the trail. Overnight hikers must obtain a camping permit and make camping reservations.

NORTH RIM MULE RIDES depart from a point near the trailhead of the North Kaibab Trail. Offered through Grand Canyon Trail Rides, half-day muleback trips take visitors through the canyon to the Supai Tunnel. A 1-hour trip along the North Rim and a half-day trip to Uncle Jim's Point are available. Trips do not go to the Colorado River.

Note: For safety purposes, riders must be fluent in English; they also must weigh less than 200 pounds when fully dressed (including equipment) for the half-day trip to the Supai Tunnel and less than 220 pounds when fully dressed for the 1-hour rim trip and the half-day trip to Uncle Jim's Point. All riding levels can participate.

Hours: Half-day trips depart daily at 7:30 and 12:30, mid-May to mid-Oct. One-hour trips depart daily 8:30-1:30, mid-May to mid-Oct. **Cost:** Half-day trips $80. One-hour trip $40. Ages 0-9 are not permitted on half-day trips; ages 0-6 are not permitted on 1-hour trip. **Phone:** (435) 679-8665.

TUWEEP AREA is in the n.w. corner, via SR 389 and a 60-mile dirt road west of Fredonia. Also known as Toroweap, the remote area embraces 40 miles of the Grand Canyon between Kanab Creek and the Uinkaret Mountains. Toroweap Overlook offers exceptional views of the Grand Canyon's inner gorge and of Lava Falls rapids. Vulcans Throne, a cinder cone, is on the Esplanade just west of Toroweap Overlook.

Note: Due to a lack of accommodations, the trip should not be attempted without adequate preparation and equipment. Water, gasoline and camping supplies are not available. Limited camping is offered south of the Tuweep Ranger Station; electricity and water are not available. The 60-mile dirt road is impassable when wet. A high-clearance, four-wheel-drive vehicle is required.

GRAND CANYON NORTH RIM LODGE   928/638-2611

fyi Not evaluated. **Address:** North Rim 86052 **Location:** At Bright Angel Point. Facilities, services, and décor characterize a mid-scale property.

KAIBAB LODGE   928/638-2389

fyi Not evaluated. **Address:** SR 67 86003 **Location:** 26 mi s of jct SR 67 and Alternate Rt US 89. Facilities, services, and décor characterize a mid-scale property.

GRAND CANYON-PARASHANT NATIONAL MONUMENT (A-2)

In the northwestern corner of the state, Grand Canyon-Parashant National Monument comprises more than 1 million undeveloped acres bordered on the west by Nevada and on the south by Grand Canyon National Park *(see place listing p. 82)*.

Exposed in the remote, unspoiled canyons and mesas are layers representing nearly 1.7 billion years of the earth's formation. Human occupation can be traced through such archeological finds as petroglyphs, pit houses and villages, with evidence pointing to habitation by hunter-gatherers as early as the Paleo-Indian and Archaic periods, and later by Puebloan and Southern Paiute cultures. Abandoned homesteads, ranches and mining camps are among the 19th- and 20th-century ruins preserved.

Wildlife is as diverse as the scenery. Two extreme ecological regions, the Mojave Desert and the Colorado Plateau, intersect within the boundaries of the monument, which is inhabited by bighorn sheep, coyotes, mule deer, turkeys and Kaibab squirrels as well as the endangered California condor.

Hiking, picnicking and primitive camping are permitted. There are no paved roads, services or developed recreation sites. Graded dirt roads are passable by two-wheel drive vehicles when dry but become impassable when wet. Use four-wheel drive vehicles with full-sized spare tires to travel alternative routes. Be prepared for adverse and isolated conditions; most of the monument has no cellphone coverage. For maps and further information contact the Arizona Strip District Field Office, Bureau of Land Management, 345 E. Riverside Dr., St. George, UT 84790; phone (435) 688-3200.

GREEN VALLEY pop. 21,391

- Restaurants p. 94
- Hotels & Restaurants map & index p. 282
- Part of Tucson area — see map p. 256

BEST WESTERN GREEN VALLEY INN   (520)625-2250

Hotel
$89-$129

AAA Benefit: Save 10% or more every day and earn 10% bonus points!

Address: 111 S La Canada Dr 85614 **Location:** I-19 exit 65, just w, then just s. **Facility:** 105 units. 2 stories, interior corridors. **Pool(s):** heated outdoor. **Activities:** hot tub, exercise room. **Guest Services:** coin laundry. **Featured Amenity:** full hot breakfast.

COMFORT INN   (520)399-3736

Hotel
$90-$175

Address: 90 W Esperanza Blvd 85614 **Location:** I-19 exit 65, just w. **Facility:** 55 units. 2 stories, interior corridors. **Pool(s):** outdoor. **Activities:** hot tub, exercise room. **Guest Services:** coin laundry. **Featured Amenity:** full hot breakfast.

HOLIDAY INN EXPRESS   520/625-0900

 Hotel. Rates not provided. **Address:** 19200 S I-19 Frontage Rd 85614 **Location:** I-19 exit 69 (Duval Mine Rd), west side of interstate, then just s. **Facility:** 60 units. 3 stories, interior corridors. **Pool(s):** heated indoor. **Activities:** hot tub. **Guest Services:** coin laundry.

(See map & index p. 282.)

INN AT SAN IGNACIO CONDO HOTEL 520/393-5700  **4**
**Condominium.** Rates not provided. **Address:** 1861 W Demetrie Loop 85622 **Location:** I-19 exit 56 (Canoa Rd), 0.5 mi n on Frontage Rd, 0.3 mi w on Calle Tres, then just n on Camino Del Sol, follow signs. **Facility:** 84 condominiums. 1 story, exterior corridors. **Pool(s):** heated outdoor. **Activities:** hot tub, regulation golf, picnic facilities. **Guest Services:** complimentary and valet laundry.

WYNDHAM CANOA RANCH RESORT
(520)382-0450 **5**

Resort
Condominium
$92-$207

Address: 5775 S Camino Del Sol 85622 **Location:** I-19 exit 56 (Canoa Rd), just w, 0.5 mi n on Frontage Rd to Calle Tres, just w, then 1 mi s. **Facility:** Located across from the golf club and restaurant, the property's well-appointed rooms offer views of the mountains and valleys. 96 condominiums. 3 stories, interior corridors. **Terms:** 3 day cancellation notice-fee imposed. **Pool(s):** heated outdoor. **Activities:** hot tub, regulation golf, exercise room. **Guest Services:** complimentary laundry. **Featured Amenity: full hot breakfast.**

AGAVE AT DESERT DIAMOND CASINO 520/342-2328 **1**
Regional American. Casual Dining. $10-$28 **AAA Inspector Notes:** After a show or an evening in the casino, patrons can relax and enjoy friendly service and such dishes as Sea of Cortez cabrilla with cremini and green chiles. Char-grilled steaks are a specialty. **Features:** full bar, patio dining. **Reservations:** suggested. **Address:** 1100 W Pima Mine Rd 85629 **Location:** I-19 exit 80, just e; in Desert Diamond Casino. **Parking:** on-site and valet.
L D

GRILL AT QUAIL CREEK 520/393-5806 **2**
American. Casual Dining. $8-$29 **AAA Inspector Notes:** Attractive contemporary decor surrounds this dining room, where guests eat overlooking the golf course. Friendly servers bring out freshly made and attractively presented beef, pork and seafood dishes. **Features:** full bar, patio dining, Sunday brunch, happy hour. **Address:** 1490 N Quail Range Loop, Bldg 3 85614 **Location:** I-19 exit 63, 3.9 mi e, n on Continental Rd/Old Nogales Hwy, then 1.5 mi s. L D

GRILL ON THE GREEN AT CANOA RANCH GOLF CLUB
520/393-1933 **4**
American. Casual Dining. $9-$30 **AAA Inspector Notes:** Located in the Canoa Ranch Clubhouse, this casual spot offers great views across the putting green and valley to the Santa Rita Mountains. Feast on Australian grilled lamb with winter berry sauce or pistachio-crusted salmon. **Features:** full bar, patio dining, happy hour. **Address:** 5800 S Camino Del Sol 85614 **Location:** I-19 exit 56 (Canoa Rd), just w, 0.5 mi n on Frontage Rd, 0.3 mi w on Calle Tres, then 1 mi s. B L D

LAVENDER 520/648-0205 **3**
French. Casual Dining. $10-$29 **AAA Inspector Notes:** A surprise is in store at this attractive bistro overlooking the golf course. The classically trained chef has adapted recipes using regional ingredients to create dishes that blend flavors and textures. Enjoyable dishes include rack of lamb with herbes de Provence crust or east coast-style crab cakes. **Features:** full bar, Sunday brunch. **Reservations:** suggested. **Address:** 77 E Paseo de Golf 85614 **Location:** I-19 exit 69, just e to Abrego Dr, then 2 mi s; in Country Club of Green Valley. L D

HEBER

BEST WESTERN SAWMILL INN (928)535-505?

Hotel
$70-$120

AAA Benefit:
Save 10% or more every day and earn 10% bonus points!

Address: 1877 Hwy 260 85928 **Location:** 0.5 mi e of center. **Facility:** 42 units. 2 stories (no elevator), exterior corridors. **Terms:** cancellation fee imposed. **Activities:** exercise room. **Guest Services:** coin laundry.

WHERE TO EAT

RED ONION LOUNGE 928/535-4433
American. Casual Dining. $5-$23 **AAA Inspector Notes:** The popular burgers served here are made from fresh Choice USDA ground chuck and cooked over an open flame. Great finger food appetizers, homemade soups, prime rib, baked ham steak, mesquite grilled chicken and hand-cut french fried potatoes are among choices at this lively, yet laid-back, sports bar. **Features:** full bar. **Address:** 1931 Hwy 260 85933 **Location:** SR 260, east of town.
L D

HEREFORD (G-5) elev. 7,587'

THE NATURE CONSERVANCY'S RAMSEY CANYON PRESERVE is 5.9 mi. s. on SR 92 from jct. SR 90, then 3.5 mi. w. to 27 E. Ramsey Canyon Rd. The 380-acre preserve serves as a sanctuary for more than 400 species of plants; 170 species of birds, including hummingbirds and painted redstarts; various species of butterflies; and other wildlife, including black bears and Yarrow's spiny lizards. A natural history interpretive center is available.

Note: Parking is limited. Picnicking is permitted only at the headquarters. Pets are not permitted. **Hours:** Thurs.-Mon. 8-5, Mar.-Oct.; 9-4, rest of year. Closed Jan. 1, Thanksgiving and Christmas. **Cost:** (Valid for 1 week) $6; free (ages 0-5 and first Sat. of the month). **Phone:** (520) 378-2785.

HOLBROOK (C-5) pop. 5,053, elev. 5,080'

Holbrook was founded in 1881 when the Atlantic and Pacific Railroad reached this point. Once called the "town too tough for women and churches," the community was named for Henry R. Holbrook, chief engineer of the railroad project. The seat of Navajo County, Holbrook is close to Petrified Forest National Park *(see place listing p. 123)* and several reservations.

The Little Colorado River's sweeping turns traverse westward through town, and the terrain consists of flat plains, rugged hills and small buttes. Official U.S. mail is delivered to Scottsdale in early February when the Pony Express rides from Holbrook.

The Navajo County Historic Courthouse, 100 E. Arizona St., is the center of Wild West Days the second weekend in July. Native American and Mexican folkloric dances are held Mon.-Sat. evenings in June and July at Gillespie Park, at the junction of Navajo and Hopi blvds. Phone the chamber of commerce to confirm schedule. A parade of lights is held the second weekend in December.

Holbrook Chamber of Commerce: 100 E. Arizona St., Holbrook, AZ 86025. **Phone:** (928) 524-6558.

Self-guiding tours: A self-guiding tour including the Navajo County Courthouse/Museum is available. Brochures can be obtained at the chamber of commerce.

BEST WESTERN ARIZONIAN INN   (928)524-2611

Hotel
$70-$140

AAA Benefit: Save 10% or more every day and earn 10% bonus points!

Address: 2508 Navajo Blvd 86025 **Location:** I-40 exit 289, 0.5 mi w. **Facility:** 72 units. 2 stories (no elevator), exterior corridors. **Pool(s):** heated outdoor.

 / SOME UNITS

DAYS INN   (928)524-6949

Motel
$60-$85

Address: 2601 Navajo Blvd 86025 **Location:** I-40 exit 289, 0.3 mi w. **Facility:** 55 units. 2 stories (no elevator), exterior corridors. **Pool(s):** heated indoor. **Activities:** hot tub. **Guest Services:** coin laundry. **Featured Amenity:** continental breakfast.

HOWARD JOHNSON   (928)524-2566

Hotel
$59-$89

Address: 2608 E Navajo Blvd 86025 **Location:** I-40 exit 289, just w. **Facility:** 40 units. 2 stories (no elevator), exterior corridors. **Pool(s):** heated indoor. **Activities:** hot tub, exercise room. **Guest Services:** coin laundry. **Featured Amenity:** breakfast buffet.

/ SOME UNITS

LEXINGTON INN HOLBROOK   (928)524-1466

Hotel
$99-$149

Address: 1308 E Navajo Blvd 86025 **Location:** I-40 exit 286, just e. **Facility:** 59 units. 2 stories (no elevator), interior corridors. **Pool(s):** heated indoor. **Activities:** hot tub. **Guest Services:** coin laundry. **Featured Amenity:** full hot breakfast.

/ SOME UNITS

QUALITY INN   928/524-6131

Hotel
$75-$92

Address: 2602 Navajo Blvd 86025 **Location:** I-40 exit 289, just w. **Facility:** 60 units. 2 stories (no elevator), exterior corridors. **Pool(s):** outdoor. **Featured Amenity:** full hot breakfast.

/ SOME UNITS

TRAVELODGE   (928)524-6815

Hotel $55-$90 **Address:** 2418 E Navajo Blvd 86025 **Location:** I-40 exit 289, 0.8 mi s. **Facility:** 33 units. 2 stories (no elevator), exterior corridors. **Amenities:** safes. **Pool(s):** heated indoor. **Activities:** hot tub. **Guest Services:** coin laundry.

WIGWAM MOTEL   928/524-3048

fyi Not evaluated. **Address:** 811 W Hopi Dr 86025. Facilities, services, and décor characterize an economy property. Owned and operated by the same family since its opening in 1950, these concrete and steel teepee units feature many of the original furnishings.

WHERE TO EAT

BUTTERFIELD STAGE CO. STEAK HOUSE   928/524-3447

Steak. Casual Dining. $9-$30 **AAA Inspector Notes:** Western decor and a nice selection of steaks are offered here. A soup and salad bar also are available. **Features:** full bar. **Address:** 609 W Hopi Dr 86025 **Location:** I-40 exit 285, 1 mi e on US 180 (Hopi Dr).

MANDARIN BEAUTY RESTAURANT   928/524-3663

Chinese. Casual Dining. $6-$13 **AAA Inspector Notes:** This no-frills restaurant serves traditional Chinese dishes in a casual atmosphere. A lunch buffet is offered, along with a limited choice of American favorites. **Features:** beer & wine. **Address:** 2218 E Navajo Blvd 86025 **Location:** I-40 exit 286, 1 mi e.

MESA ITALIANA RESTAURANT   928/524-6696

Italian. Casual Dining. $9-$17 **AAA Inspector Notes:** Featuring a nice selection of traditional Italian dishes, this restaurant appeals to those looking for something different in a small Western town. An attached casual bar with a smaller menu is a great place to have a drink before or after dinner. **Features:** full bar. **Address:** 2318 E Navajo Blvd 86025 **Location:** I-40 exit 286, 1.3 mi e.

IRONWOOD FOREST NATIONAL MONUMENT (F-3)

Northwest of Tucson 25 miles via I-10 to Avra Valley Road, Ironwood Forest National Monument contains the highest density of ironwood trees in the Sonoran Desert. The diverse ironwood provides food and shelter for a variety of wildlife, including desert bighorn sheep, tortoises and hawks.

For further information contact the Tucson Field Office, Bureau of Land Management, 3201 E. Universal Way, Tucson, AZ 85756; phone (520) 258-7200.

JACOB LAKE

JACOB LAKE INN   928/643-7232
fyi Not evaluated. **Address:** Jct SR 89A & 67 86002. Facilities, services, and décor characterize an economy property.

JEROME (C-3) pop. 444, elev. 5,435'

In 1582 Spanish missionaries exploring the Verde Valley recorded that natives were using the copper mines near what is now Jerome. The missionaries' description of the mines was identical to the workings found in 1883 by the United Verde Co. Eugene Jerome of New York agreed to finance the mining project on condition the camp be named for him. In 1886 a smelter arrived by rail from Ash Fork and operations began in earnest.

Once a city with a population of 15,000, Jerome became a virtual ghost town when the United Verde Branch copper mines of the Phelps Dodge Corp. closed in 1953. Since then, shops, galleries, studios and museums, some housed in former brothels and saloons, have been established in the restored town which clings to Cleopatra Hill on the side of Mingus Mountain. Some of the restored homes are open during the Home Tour in May.

A 54-mile scenic stretch of SR 89A begins in Flagstaff and winds its way south through Oak Creek Canyon (see Sedona p. 221) and ends in Jerome. The steep, narrow road is not recommended for vehicles pulling trailers more than 40 feet long. The nearby mountains are ideal for camping, fishing and hunting.

Jerome Chamber of Commerce: 310 Hull Ave., Box K, Jerome, AZ 86331. **Phone:** (928) 634-2900.

JEROME STATE HISTORIC PARK is off SR 89A. The park museum in the 1916 adobe brick Douglas Mansion traces the history of local mining and the family of James S. Douglas, developer of the rich United Verde Extension Mine in the early 1900s. A movie highlighting the history of Jerome is shown continuously. **Time:** Allow 1 hour minimum. **Hours:** Park daily 8:30-5. Museum daily 8:30-4:45. Closed Christmas. **Cost:** (Includes museum) $5; $2 (ages 7-13). **Phone:** (928) 634-5381. 🎫

MINE MUSEUM, 200 Main St., depicts Jerome's history through mine artifacts and equipment. **Hours:** Daily 9-4:30. Closed Jan. 1, Thanksgiving and Christmas. **Cost:** $2; $1 (ages 60+); free (ages 0-12). **Phone:** (928) 634-5477.

CONNOR HOTEL OF JEROME   928/634-5006
🏩🏩 **Historic Hotel** $105-$165 **Address:** 160 S Main St 86331 **Location:** Center. **Facility:** This historic 1898 hotel offers charming rooms filled with period pieces and modern tiled baths. Some rooms are small, but have amazing views. 12 units. 2 stories (no elevator), interior corridors. **Parking:** street only. **Terms:** 3 day cancellation notice-fee imposed.

THE ASYLUM RESTAURANT   928/639-3197
🏩🏩💎💎
American
Casual Dining
$10-$32

AAA Inspector Notes: Billed as fun, fine dining, the experience at this cozy restaurant includes relaxed service and spectacular views. The wide selection of wines, interesting sauces and creative combinations, such as roast maple leaf duck breast on green chili brown rice with plum serrano salsa, add up to fine dining. **Features:** full bar, patio dining. **Reservations:** suggested. **Address:** 200 Hill St 86331 **Location:** 0.3 mi s on SR 89A, just s on Cobblestone Rd; center; in Jerome Grand Hotel. L D

GRAPES   928/639-8477
🏩🏩 Pizza. Casual Dining. $10-$19 **AAA Inspector Notes:** The menu here offers a range of such items as pizza, sandwiches, entrée salads and full dinners. The wine theme is carried through with different wines used in preparing the food and a selection of wine flights available for tasting. A nice outdoor dining patio makes a good rest stop. **Features:** full bar, patio dining. **Address:** 111 Main St 86331 **Location:** Center. **Parking:** street only. L D

JEROME PALACE/HAUNTED HAMBURGER   928/634-0554
🏩🏩 American. Casual Dining. $7-$19 **AAA Inspector Notes:** Guests should arrive here before they are hungry, as there always is a line waiting to wolf down the great burgers and comfort food. In a historic house overlooking the valley, this restaurant is a good spot to rest and recuperate after the steep street walking tour. **Features:** full bar, patio dining. **Address:** 410 Clark St 86331 **Location:** Center. **Parking:** street only. L D

KAIBAB NATIONAL FOREST (B-3)
• Attractions map p. 84

Elevations in the forest range from 3,000 ft. to 10,418 ft. at Kendrick Peak. Refer to AAA maps for additional elevation information.

Comprised of three districts north and south of Grand Canyon National Park (see place listing p. 82), Kaibab National Forest covers 1.6 million acres. The portion north of the canyon includes Grand Canyon National Game Preserve, a thickly forested, domed limestone plateau. The Kaibab Plateau is the only known home of the Kaibab squirrel, a dark gray squirrel with a white tail and tufted ears. The southernmost of the three districts contains volcanic cones and scattered forested peaks.

Big game animals can be seen in roadside meadows and throughout the forest. Fishing can be enjoyed at several lakes. Recreational opportunities within the national forest include camping, hiking, mountain biking, horseback riding and cross-country skiing.

The Kaibab Plateau-North Rim Scenic Byway has been described as the most beautiful 42 miles in the United States. The scenic parkway begins at Jacob Lake and winds through dense forests and alpine meadows to culminate at the North Rim of the Grand Canyon; the road is closed mid-October through May.

For further information contact the Kaibab Plateau Visitor Center (mid-May through Sept. 30), US 89A and SR 67, Jacob Lake, AZ 86022, phone (928) 643-7298; or the Williams and Forest Service Visitor

KAYENTA (A-5) pop. 5,189, elev. 5,641'

Kayenta grew from a trading post that John Wetherill established in 1910. He first called it Oljeto, but eventually changed the name to Kayenta after a deep spring nearby. The area's uranium and coal deposits are important in the town's economy. Scenic US 163, beginning at US 160, passes through Kayenta before running 22 miles north to the Utah border and the entrance to Monument Valley Navajo Tribal Park *(see place listing p. 112)*.

Crawley's Monument Valley Tours offers back-country trips into areas of the park. For further information about the tours and the area contact Crawley's Monument Valley Tours, P.O. Box 187, Kayenta, AZ 86033; phone (928) 278-8533.

HAMPTON INN OF KAYENTA   (928)697-3170

▼▼▼ Hotel $89-$129 **Address:** Hwy 160 86033 **Location:** Just w of US 163. **Facility:** 73 units. 3 stories, interior corridors. **Terms:** check-in 4 pm, 1-7 night minimum stay, cancellation fee imposed. **Dining:** Reuben Heflin Restaurant, see separate listing. **Pool(s):** heated outdoor. **Activities:** limited exercise equipment. **Guest Services:** coin laundry.

AAA Benefit: Members save up to 10%!

🍽️ 👤 CALL 🅛Ⓜ ⊠ BIZ 🛜 ✕ 🖵 / SOME UNITS 🐾

WETHERILL INN   (928)697-3231

▼▼▼

Hotel

$97-$165

Address: US Hwy 163 86033 **Location:** 1 mi n of jct US 160. **Facility:** 54 units. 2 stories (no elevator), exterior corridors. **Terms:** cancellation fee imposed. **Pool(s):** heated indoor. **Guest Services:** coin laundry. **Featured Amenity: continental breakfast.**

SAVE 🍽️ ⊠ BIZ 🛜 ✕ 🗎
🖵

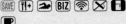

WHERE TO EAT

REUBEN HEFLIN RESTAURANT   928/697-3170

▼▼ Regional American. Family Dining. $9-$24 **AAA Inspector Notes:** The décor is decidedly Southwestern in this eatery with an exposed beam ceiling and a warm fireplace, all opening up to the hotel lobby. The menu centers on steak, seafood and Southwestern dishes. **Features:** patio dining. **Address:** Hwy 160 86033 **Location:** Just w of US 163; in Hampton Inn of Kayenta.

Ⓑ Ⓓ CALL 🅛Ⓜ

KEAMS CANYON (B-5) pop. 304, elev. 6,184'

Keams Canyon is within the Hopi Reservation that occupies a large tract in the center of the vast Navajo Reservation of northeastern Arizona. The reservation is crossed by SR 264, which runs between US 491, 8 miles north of Gallup, N.M., and US 160 at Tuba City. Noted for weaving, pottery and jewelry, the Hopi also farm and raise livestock. Information about Hopi ceremonies can be obtained from the Hopi Indian Agency in Keams Canyon, (928) 738-2228, or from the Hopi tribal headquarters in Kykotsmovi, (928) 734-3100.

Of particular interest are the villages of Old Oraibi and Walpi on First Mesa. High on a narrow, rocky mesa, Old Oraibi is possibly the oldest of the present Hopi villages; it is thought to be one of the oldest continuously inhabited cities in the country. A trading post and schools are in each village, and the main tribal headquarters is at nearby Kykotsmovi. Walpi occupies the end of a high mesa, where ancestors of the present inhabitants began building about 1680. You can learn about Hopi history and culture on a guided 1-hour walking tour of the First Mesa villages; for information phone First Mesa Tour, (928) 737-2670.

No photography, painting, recording or sketching are permitted while on the Hopi Reservation. Primitive campgrounds are at Second Mesa, next to the Hopi Cultural Center; phone (928) 734-2401.

KINGMAN (C-2) pop. 28,068, elev. 3,334'
• Hotels p. 98 • Restaurants p. 100
• Part of Grand Canyon National Park area — see map p. 82

Kingman, the county seat of Mohave County, is located between Las Vegas and the Grand Canyon and was established in the early 1880s with the arrival of the railroad. It also serves as a transportation corridor to Grand Canyon National Park South Rim *(see place listing p. 85)* as well as the Grand Canyon Skywalk *(see attraction listing)* in the western area.

Kingman's popularity is maintained as the main stop on the longest existing stretch of Historic Route 66—the first completely paved national highway in the country. Linking hundreds of towns and cities between Chicago and Los Angeles, Route 66 formed the main street of towns along its route, thus its nickname "Main Street of America." Today travelers can traverse some 158 miles of historic roadway beginning west of Ashfork, continuing through Seligman, Peach Springs, Valentine, Truxton, Hackberry and on to Kingman and through Oatman to Topock. For a self-guiding driving tour brochure contact the Historic Route 66 Association of Arizona, 120 W. Andy Devine Ave., Kingman, AZ 86401; phone (928) 753-5001.

Some 800 classic cars start their engines in Seligman and head 140 miles to Topock/Golden Shores during the 🚩 Historic Route 66 Fun Run, held the first weekend in May. Communities along the route celebrate with food and entertainment.

At the junction of I-40 and US 93, Kingman is an access point to lakes Mead, Mohave and Havasu. Ghost towns surround this former gold-mining community. Towns such as Oatman and Chloride were business and social centers for surrounding mining camps during the early 20th century. With many of their original buildings still standing, Oatman and Chloride draw both filmmakers and tourists. In Oatman, visitors may even hand-feed the burros—descendants of those left behind by early-day miners—that roam the town's streets. From Kingman, Oatman is reached by SR 66 (Old Route 66). Chloride is north of Kingman on SR 93 at mile marker 53, 4 miles off the highway on CR 125.

Hualapai Mountain Park (pronounced Wal-lah-pie) is 12 miles southeast. It is named for the Native Americans who inhabited the mountains until the 1870s. Mountain elevations range from 5,000 to 8,500 feet, and a variety of native wildlife lives here, including deer, eagles, elk, foxes, hawks, rabbits and squirrels. *See Recreation Areas Chart.*

Kingman Visitor Center: 120 W. Andy Devine Ave., Kingman, AZ 86401. **Phone:** (928) 753-6106 or (866) 427-7866.

BONELLI HOUSE is e. off I-40 exit 48, then .2 mi. n. to 430 E. Spring St. Built in 1915, Bonelli House depicts the lifestyle of a prominent Arizona family in the early 20th century. It is outfitted with original furnishings and other period pieces similar to those used by the Bonelli family.

Features include a Victorian-style cupola where the children acted as sentries for their father's arrival from work, and a large wall clock that was once the only clock in town. **Time:** Allow 1 hour minimum. **Hours:** Mon.-Fri. 11-3. Closed major holidays. **Cost:** (includes pass to Historic Route 66 Museum and Mohave Museum of History and Arts)$4; $3 (ages 60+); free (ages 0-11 with adult). House only by donation. **Phone:** (928) 753-3195.

GRAND CANYON SKYWALK is at the far western end of the Grand Canyon; from Kingman, go north on CR 20 (Stockton Hill Rd.) about 42 mi. to CR 25 (Pierce Ferry Rd.), CR 25 n. about 7 mi. to CR 261 (Diamond Bar Rd.) and Diamond Bar Rd. 21 mi. to Grand Canyon West (the Hualapai Indian tribe's recreation area), an approximate 100-minute drive. Drivers should follow the road to the parking lot by Grand Canyon West Airport.

Staunch environmentalists protested when the Hualapai tribe built this horseshoe-shaped, glass-floored "sky bridge" on their reservation land in 2007. Extending 70 feet out from the canyon rim, the skywalk is suspended 4,000 feet above the canyon bottom and the Colorado River far, far below. Weighing 1.2 million pounds, it's unquestionably an architectural wonder and a unique engineering feat, and the views—as long as you don't suffer from acrophobia—are jaw-dropping. Grand Canyon National Park visitors should keep in mind that the location is remote, easily a 4.5-hour drive from the park's South Rim.

Note: To stroll on the skywalk you must first purchase a Grand Canyon West tour package; the fee includes hop-on, hop-off bus transportation to the skywalk, a faux Native American village, a mock cowboy town and the Guano Point overlook. Personal items are not permitted on the skywalk (free lockers are available for storage). Cameras are strictly prohibited; you will be searched. Allow 2-4 hours minimum to view the skywalk and take the Grand Canyon West tour.

Hours: Daily 7-7, Apr.-Sept.; 8-5, rest of year (weather permitting). Last admission 2 hours before closing. **Cost:** Grand Canyon West Legacy Gold Package (includes skywalk admission, permitting fee and hop-on, hop-off shuttle transportation to the Native American village, Hualapai Ranch and the Guano Point overlook) $75.54. **Phone:** (928) 769-2636 or (888) 868-9378.

HISTORIC ROUTE 66 MUSEUM is at 120 W. Andy Devine Ave. Dioramas, murals and photos depict the history of historic Route 66 from its early use by Native Americans and pioneers to the travelers of the 1950s. The Route 66 EV (electric vehicle) Museum is on the first floor. A reading room and archive are available. **Time:** Allow 30 minutes minimum. **Hours:** Daily 9-5. Closed Jan. 1, Easter, Thanksgiving and Christmas. **Cost:** (includes pass to Bonelli House and Mohave Museum of History and Arts)$4; $3 (ages 60+); free (ages 0-11 with adult). **Phone:** (928) 753-3195.

MOHAVE MUSEUM OF HISTORY AND ARTS is off I-40 exit 48 .25 mi. s.e. to 400 W. Beale St. (US 93). Collections of turquoise, re-created Mohave and Hualapai dwellings and local artifacts and artwork depict the history of northwest Arizona. Other exhibits feature Andy Devine memorabilia, Lawrence Williams' portraits of presidents and first ladies and Mohave County ranching history. A re-created copper mine outfitted with original mining equipment depicts miners at work. A 1923 all-wood caboose also is on display.

Hours: Mon.-Fri. 9-5, Sat. 1-5. Closed major holidays. **Cost:** (includes pass to Historic Route 66 Museum and Bonelli House) $4; $3 (ages 60+); free (ages 0-11 with adult). **Phone:** (928) 753-3195.

GET REAL

REAL INSPECTORS, REAL RATINGS

AAA's in-person inspections ensure the places you select provide what you expect.

AAA.com/Diamonds

BEST WESTERN PLUS KING'S INN & SUITES
(928)753-6101

Hotel
$105-$120

AAA Benefit:
Save 10% or more every day and earn 10% bonus points!

Address: 2930 E Andy Devine Ave 86401 **Location:** I-40 exit 53, just w on Route 66. **Facility:** 100 units, some two bedrooms and efficiencies. 2 stories, exterior corridors. **Pool(s):** heated outdoor. **Activities:** hot tub, exercise room. **Guest Services:** valet and coin laundry. **Featured Amenity:** breakfast buffet.

The hospitality of "the mother road," with all the modern features, and a Free Hot Breakfast Buffet!

COMFORT INN   (928)718-1717

Hotel $75-$129 **Address:** 3129 E Andy Devine Ave 86401 **Location:** I-40 exit 53, just w on Route 66. **Facility:** 60 units. 3 stories, interior corridors. **Pool(s):** heated indoor. **Activities:** hot tub, exercise room. **Guest Services:** coin laundry.

HOLIDAY INN EXPRESS HOTEL & SUITES
(928)718-4343

Hotel
$109-$129

Address: 3031 E Andy Devine Ave 86401 **Location:** I-40 exit 53, just w on Route 66. **Facility:** 75 units, some two bedrooms. 3 stories, interior corridors. **Pool(s):** heated indoor. **Activities:** hot tub, exercise room. **Guest Services:** valet and coin laundry. **Featured Amenity:** breakfast buffet.

SPRINGHILL SUITES BY MARRIOTT
(928)753-8766

Hotel
$117-$190

AAA Benefit:
Members save 5% or more!

Address: 3101 E Andy Devine Ave 86401 **Location:** I-40 exit 53, just w on Route 66. **Facility:** 73 units. 4 stories, interior corridors. **Pool(s):** heated indoor. **Activities:** exercise room. **Guest Services:** valet and coin laundry.

▼ See AAA listing p. 98 ▼

Let Your Voice Be Heard
If your visit to a TourBook-listed property doesn't meet your expectations, tell us about it.
AAA.com/TourBookComments

WHERE TO EAT

ABC RESTAURANT   928/753-6363

Chinese. Casual Dining. $7-$15 **AAA Inspector Notes:** American and Chinese dishes can be ordered from the menu, while a buffet is available for both lunch and dinner. **Features:** full bar. **Address:** 2890 E Andy Devine Ave 86401 **Location:** I-40 exit 53, just sw. L D

DAMBAR & STEAKHOUSE   928/753-3523

Steak
Casual Dining
$9-$28
L D

AAA Inspector Notes: The menu here incorporates a good selection of steak, ribs, sandwiches and salads. The atmosphere is casually rustic. **Features:** full bar. **Address:** 1960 E Andy Devine Ave 86401 **Location:** I-40 exit 53, 1.2 mi sw.

EL PALACIO   928/718-0018

Mexican. Family Dining. $9-$15 **AAA Inspector Notes:** Located in a more than 100-year-old building on Route 66 in downtown Kingman, this family spot serves traditional fresh Mexican items highlighting chimichangas, burritos and marimba served in a fun and colorful dining room. **Features:** full bar, happy hour. **Address:** 401 E Andy Devine Ave 86401 **Location:** Jct 4th St. **Parking:** on-site and street. L D

KINGMAN CO. STEAKHOUSE   928/718-2292

Steak. Casual Dining. $12-$26 **AAA Inspector Notes:** Just off the interstate, this steakhouse is convenient for travelers. Casual, rustic decor incorporates antiques and stories of old settlers along the walls. The menu focuses on large cowboy-style steaks. **Features:** full bar. **Address:** 3157 Stockton Hill Rd 86401 **Location:** I-40 exit 51, just s. L D

MATTINA'S RISTORANTE & STEAKHOUSE   928/753-7504

Italian. Casual Dining. $13-$25 **AAA Inspector Notes:** Located in an intimate, yet casual, cottage in historic downtown, this family-owned and -operated bistro features aged Premium steaks cut when ordered, as well as fresh seafood and Italian pasta dishes. The homemade tiramisu is a personal favorite. They close early on slower evenings. **Features:** full bar, patio dining. **Address:** 318 E Oak St 86401 **Location:** Between 3rd and 4th sts; downtown. **Parking:** street only. D

MR. D'Z ROUTE 66 DINER   928/718-0066

American. Casual Dining. $5-$16 **AAA Inspector Notes:** Nestled along Historic Route 66, patrons at this traditional 1950s-style diner can select seating at the counter or in pink and turquoise vinyl booths. Traditional diner fare is served such as burgers, chicken sandwich, chicken fried steak, all-day breakfast items and, of course, homemade desserts. **Address:** 105 E Andy Devine Ave 86401 **Location:** Jct Old Route 66 and 1st St; downtown. B L D

REDNECK'S SOUTHERN PIT BBQ   928/757-8227

Southern Barbecue. Quick Serve. $5-$22 **AAA Inspector Notes:** Located in the heart of Kingman, this spot offers Memphis-style barbecue in a fun cafeteria style dining room. Large picnic tables allow for community dining and many local brewed beers are featured. **Features:** beer only. **Address:** 420 E Beale St 86401 **Location:** Between 3rd and 4th sts; downtown. L D

KOHLS RANCH pop. 46

KOHL'S RANCH LODGE   (928)478-4211

Resort Condominium $89-$149 **Address:** 202 S Kohl's Ranch Lodge Rd 85541 **Location:** SR 87, 16.6 mi e on US 260, between MM 238-239. **Facility:** Charming, attractively appointed lodge rooms and creekside cabins, ranging from cozy to spacious, await guests at this high mountain resort. 66 units, some condominiums. 1 story, interior/exterior corridors. **Terms:** check-in 4 pm, cancellation fee imposed, resort fee. **Amenities:** safes. **Pool(s):** heated outdoor. **Activities:** hot tub, fishing, tennis, recreation programs, playground, game room, lawn sports, picnic facilities, trails, exercise room. **Guest Services:** complimentary laundry.

LAKE HAVASU CITY (D-1) pop. 52,527, elev. 482'
• Restaurants p. 102

Lake Havasu City takes its name from the lake by which it lies. (Havasu is a Mohave Indian word meaning "blue-green water.") Formed by the impoundment of Parker Dam in 1938, Lake Havasu is fed by the Colorado River. The 45-mile-long lake has a maximum width of 3 miles and supplies water to Arizona, Los Angeles and intermediate cities.

In 1963 industrialist Robert P. McCulloch Sr. purchased a 3,500-acre former Army Air Corps landing strip and rest camp on Pittsburg Point, a peninsula jutting into the Colorado River. After expanding the area by another 13,000 acres, McCulloch teamed up with Disneyland developer C.V. Wood to create a planned community and tourist destination.

The new town captured the world's attention in 1968 when McCulloch bought the London Bridge *(see attraction listing)*. Originally built in 1831 by architect John Rennie, the multi-arch bridge resided over the Thames River until 1968, when it began to sink into the river. Dismantled stone by stone, the bridge was brought over from London and reconstructed on Pittsburg Point. A man-made canal (known today as Bridgewater Channel) was dug underneath, separating Pittsburg Point from the land and forming an island.

Just over the bridge and along the island side of Bridgewater Channel, London Bridge Beach (1340 McCulloch Blvd.) has basketball and sand volleyball courts, playgrounds, picnicking facilities and a dog park. On the opposite side of the channel, Rotary Community Park (1400 S. Smoketree Ave.) features volleyball and bocce courts, a skate park, playgrounds, picnicking facilities, a buoyed swimming area and a shaded walkway.

Lake Havasu provides a setting for all types of water-related activities. Fishing is excellent, especially for striped and large-mouth bass, catfish and panfish; several public fishing docks and piers are available. Numerous public companies rent canoes, kayaks, houseboats, pontoon boats, sailboats and other watercraft for use on the lake; contact the convention and visitors bureau for more information.

Believe it or not, lighthouses exist in landlocked Arizona. Twenty-four functioning one-third-scale replicas of famous U.S. lighthouses stand along the shoreline of Lake Havasu, providing navigational aid *and* a conversation piece.

In December a fleet of illuminated boats on the lake makes the Boat Parade of Lights a dazzling sight spectators won't soon forget.

Lake Havasu City Convention and Visitors Bureau: 422 English Village, Lake Havasu City, AZ 86403. **Phone:** (928) 453-3444 or (800) 242-8278.

Shopping: The English Village, Island Fashion Mall, Havasu Downtown District and Shops at Lake Havasu all provide shopping opportunities in the London Bridge area.

CATTAIL COVE STATE PARK, 15 mi. s. off SR 95, is named after the numerous cattails in the park's cove. Water activities abound in the park. *See Recreation Areas Chart.* Hiking and camping also are available. **Hours:** Daily 8-4:30. **Cost:** Mon.-Thurs. $10 (per private vehicle, up to four passengers); $3 (per additional adult passenger in vehicle or individual arriving on foot or bicycle). Fri.-Sun. $15 (per private vehicle). Camping $26 (per private vehicle). Boat-in campsites $20. Overnight trailer parking $15-$20. **Phone:** (928) 855-1223, or (520) 586-2283 for camping reservations.

HAVASU NATIONAL WILDLIFE REFUGE is off I-40 exit 1, following signs. The refuge consists of two areas: Topock Gorge, south of junction I-40 and the Colorado River, and Topock Marsh, north of I-40 on the Arizona side of the river. Topock Gorge includes the 18,000-acre Havasu Wilderness Area. The 37,515-acre refuge is home to the southwestern willow flycatcher, the Yuma clapper rail, migratory birds, beavers and bighorn sheep. The refuge headquarters is in Needles, Calif.

Note: The gorge is accessible only by boat. Hunting and fishing (in season) are permitted, as is boating in designated areas. **Hours:** Refuge open daily 24 hours. Office open Mon.-Fri. 7:30-3:30. Closed major holidays. **Cost:** Free. **Phone:** (760) 326-3853.

LAKE HAVASU STATE PARK, n. of London Bridge off SR 95 and London Bridge Rd., stretches along the river. *See Recreation Areas Chart.* Camping and hiking are available. **Hours:** Daily dawn-10 p.m. Campsites daily Oct.-Apr. **Cost:** Day use fee Mon.-Thurs. $10 (per private vehicle, up to four passengers); $3 (per additional adult passenger in vehicle or individual arriving on foot or bicycle). Day use fee

Fri.-Sun. $15 (per private vehicle). Camping (per private vehicle) beachfront sites, $35; overflow lot, $20. **Phone:** (928) 855-2784, or (520) 586-2283 for camping reservations.

LONDON BRIDGE, off US 95 along the Colorado River, was the famed span on the Thames River in London from 1831 to 1968, and now crosses the man-made Bridgewater Channel of the Colorado River in the Arizona desert. The channel created an island from Pittsburgh Point, a former peninsula, that now contains recreational facilities, including a golf course, marina, walking/bicycling trails and a campground. Transported stone by stone from England and reassembled at this location in its original form, the bridge is a striking landmark in this community. **Cost:** Tours $10 (over age 12). **Phone:** (928) 855-5655 for tour reservations, (928) 453-3444, or (800) 242-8278 for the Lake Havasu Convention and Visitors Bureau. GT

DAYS INN LAKE HAVASU (928)855-7841

Motel
$65-$129

Address: 1700 McCulloch Blvd N 86403 **Location:** Just ne of Lake Havasu Ave; center. **Facility:** 89 units. 2 stories (no elevator), exterior corridors. **Pool(s):** heated outdoor. **Activities:** hot tub, picnic facilities. **Guest Services:** coin laundry. **Featured Amenity:** continental breakfast.

▼ See AAA listing p. 102 ▼

HAMPTON INN LAKE HAVASU   (928)855-4071

WWW Hotel $107-$215 Address: 245 London Bridge Rd 86403 Location: 0.5 mi n of London Bridge. Facility: 162 units. 4 stories, interior/exterior corridors. Terms: 1-7 night minimum stay, cancellation fee imposed. Pool(s): heated outdoor. Activities: hot tub, bicycles, picnic facilities, exercise room. Guest Services: valet and coin laundry, area transportation.

AAA Benefit: Members save up to 10%!

HAVASU TRAVELODGE   (928)680-9202

WWW
Motel
$60-$270

Address: 480 London Bridge Rd 86403 Location: 1 mi n of London Bridge. Facility: 41 units, some efficiencies. 2 stories (no elevator), interior corridors. Terms: 3 day cancellation notice. Amenities: safes. Activities: hot tub. Featured Amenity: continental breakfast.

ISLAND SUITES   (928)855-7333

WW Extended Stay Hotel $60-$150 Address: 236 S Lake Havasu Ave 86403 Location: Just s of jct McCulloch Blvd. Facility: 45 efficiencies. 2 stories (no elevator), interior corridors. Terms: 3 day cancellation notice-fee imposed. Pool(s): heated outdoor. Activities: hot tub, boat dock.

LONDON BRIDGE RESORT   (928)855-0888

WWWW
Resort Hotel
$99-$629

Address: 1477 Queens Bay 86403 Location: Waterfront. SR 95, just sw on Swanson Ave. Facility: Located adjacent to London Bridge, this waterfront hotel offers many recreational facilities and large, comfortable suites. 122 efficiencies, some two bedrooms. 3 stories, interior corridors. Terms: check-in 4 pm, cancellation fee imposed, resort fee. Amenities: video games. Dining: 2 restaurants, also, Martini Bay, see separate listing, nightclub. Pool(s): heated outdoor. Activities: hot tub, boat dock, fishing, scuba diving, snorkeling, regulation golf, tennis, picnic facilities, exercise room, massage. Guest Services: valet and coin laundry. Featured Amenity: continental breakfast. (See ad p. 101.)

THE NAUTICAL BEACHFRONT RESORT   928/855-2141

WW Resort Hotel. Rates not provided. Address: 1000 McCulloch Blvd N 86403 Location: Waterfront. 1.4 mi w of London Bridge, follow signs. Facility: The rooms vary at this spread-out resort, but they all have amazing views of Lake Havasu. Along with the lake, the large pool and beach areas are a huge draw. 139 units, some two bedrooms and efficiencies. 3 stories (no elevator), exterior corridors. Terms: check-in 4 pm. Dining: The Turtle Grill, see separate listing. Pool(s): heated outdoor. Activities: boat dock, fishing, regulation golf. Guest Services: coin laundry.

QUALITY INN & SUITES   (928)855-1111

WWW Hotel $70-$160 Address: 271 S Lake Havasu Ave 86403 Location: SR 95, just e on Swanson Ave, just s. Facility: 177 units. 3 stories (no elevator), exterior corridors. Pool(s): heated outdoor. Guest Services: valet and coin laundry.

RODEWAY INN & SUITES   (928)453-4656

WWW Hotel $60-$212 Address: 335 London Bridge Rd 86403 Location: 0.8 mi n of London Bridge. Facility: 43 units, some efficiencies. 2 stories (no elevator), interior corridors. Parking: winter plug-ins. Amenities: safes. Pool(s): heated indoor. Activities: hot tub. Guest Services: coin laundry.

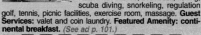

WHERE TO EAT

ANGELINA'S ITALIAN CUISINE   928/680-3868

WWW Italian. Family Dining. $11-$25 AAA Inspector Notes: This small family-run restaurant is busy and they do their best to make everyone feel comfortable. The menu consists of traditional fresh Italian items such as spaghetti, chicken parmigiana, fried calamari and gourmet pizza. Take out also is popular. Features: beer & wine, patio dining. Address: 1530 El Camino Dr 86403 Location: Just w of SR 95; 1.2 mi n of London Bridge. [D]

BARLEY BROS. RESTAURANT & BREWERY   928/505-7837

WW American. Casual Dining. $9-$24 AAA Inspector Notes: Guests can enjoy a mixture of fun pub grub and gourmet cuisine at this brewery. This is a perfect spot to enjoy grand views of the London Bridge or watch a game on the many TVs. Features: full bar, happy hour. Address: 1425 McCulloch Blvd N 86403 Location: West side of London Bridge. [L] [D]

BBQ BILL'S BIG EASY BISTRO AND GATOR LOUNGE   928/680-1100

WW American. Casual Dining. $8-$18 AAA Inspector Notes: This casual bistro serves up slow-cooked barbecue items along with burgers, catfish and peach cobbler. The bar decor is fun as is the friendly staff. Features: full bar. Address: 3557 Maricopa Ave 86406 Location: Jct McCulloch Blvd, just nw. [B] [L] [D]

CASA SERRANO   928/854-5500

WW Mexican. Casual Dining. $8-$16 AAA Inspector Notes: Friendly staffers welcome diners into a brightly colored dining room. Fresh ingredients in the wide variety of dishes will satisfy the most discriminating diner. Features: full bar. Address: 150 Swanson Ave 86403 Location: Jct SR 95, just sw. [L] [D]

CHA' BONES   928/854-5554

WWW Steak. Casual Dining. $8-$39 AAA Inspector Notes: Just north of London Bridge, this upscale eatery serves cooked-to-perfection steak and a wide range of tapas dishes for lighter meals. Tall fountains at the entry give an atmosphere of freshness to the attractive room. Features: full bar, happy hour. Address: 112 London Bridge Rd 86403 Location: Jct SR 95, 0.3 mi nw. [L] [D]

FARRELL'S GOLDEN HORSESHOE STEAKHOUSE   928/764-3800

WW Steak. Casual Dining. $7-$40 AAA Inspector Notes: The Western theme is carried out in everything from buckets of peanuts on the table to such steak names as cowboy cut or cattle baron. Patrons can enjoy live entertainment while feasting on a choice of beef, seafood or pasta. Save room for the six-layer carrot cake. Features: full bar, happy hour. Address: 4501 N London Bridge Rd 86404 Location: SR 95, 6.1 mi n. [L] [D]

JAVELINA CANTINA   928/855-8226

♦♦ Mexican. Casual Dining. $5-$18 **AAA Inspector Notes:** Adding to this cantina's trendy decor are curved metal dividers, brightly colored tile walls and mounted plasma televisions so diners can watch sports while they eat. On a riverside patio, a misting system cools the summer heat while patrons enjoy classic, freshly prepared south-of-the-border cuisine. Wednesday nights feature $1 taco specials, and the place tends to get mobbed. **Features:** full bar, patio dining. **Address:** 1420 McCulloch Blvd N 86403 **Location:** West side of London Bridge. [L] [D]

JUICY'S RIVER CAFE   928/855-8429

American
Casual Dining
$7-$19

AAA Inspector Notes: Serving hearty, homemade food for more than two decades, owner Mike Bradley even stops by guests' tables to be sure they are satisfied. Breakfast dishes are popular with locals, and the award-winning café also offers a wide selection of sandwiches, salads and specials such as Pop's favorite meatloaf. **Features:** beer & wine, patio dining. **Address:** 42 Smoketree Ave S 86403 **Location:** Jct Smoketree Ave, just e; uptown.

[B] [L] [D]

KRYSTAL'S STEAK HOUSE AND SEAFOOD   928/453-2999

♦♦ Steak. Casual Dining. $13-$32 **AAA Inspector Notes:** Familiar selections of chicken, seafood and beef, including rib-eye, filet mignon and prime rib cuts are prepared in a simple, yet tasty, fashion. Chicken comes barbecued or broiled, while dominant seafood choices range from shrimp scampi to mahi mahi to the fisherman's platter-a must for those with hearty appetites. There are hints of formalized service. **Features:** full bar, early bird specials. **Reservations:** suggested. **Address:** 460 El Camino Way 86403 **Location:** Just w of SR 95; 1.2 mi n of London Bridge. [D]

MARIO'S ITALIAN RESTAURANT & LOUNGE   928/854-3223

♦♦ Italian. Casual Dining. $10-$20 **AAA Inspector Notes:** This is a fun, retro-style dining spot with all the traditional Italian dishes alongside well-prepared steaks. The chicken parmigiana and the linguini with clam sauce are local favorites. **Features:** full bar. **Address:** 350 London Bridge Rd 86403 **Location:** 1 mi n of London Bridge. [D]

MARTINI BAY   928/855-0888

International
Casual Dining
$10-$32

AAA Inspector Notes: High-gloss decor and fun music make this a happening place. Thankfully, the food is just as enjoyable as the surroundings. Mediterranean-inspired dishes include plates of freshly grilled steaks and seafood as well as cold, crisp salads. Plenty of hearty appetizers await, including marinated beef filet skewers to lighter options like smoked chicken quesadillas. **Features:** full bar, patio dining, happy hour. **Address:** 1477 Queens Bay 86403 **Location:** SR 95, just sw on Swanson Ave; in London Bridge Resort. [D]

MONTANA STEAK HOUSE   928/855-3736

♦♦ Steak. Casual Dining. $13-$27 **AAA Inspector Notes:** Western décor sets the stage at this casual family restaurant. Steaks, including filet mignon, New York strip and rib-eye, are the house specialty. Meals come with the usual accompaniments of soup or salad and a starch. **Features:** full bar, happy hour. **Reservations:** suggested. **Address:** 3301 Maricopa Ave 86406 **Location:** 4.7 mi s of London Bridge; just off SR 95 on east side. [D]

MUDSHARK BREWING CO   928/453-2981

♦♦ American. Casual Dining. $9-$23 **AAA Inspector Notes:** This casual eatery offers tasty pub fare with a number of sandwiches, burgers, pizzas and pasta dishes. Don't forget to enjoy one of the brewmaster's handcrafted ales and lager, such as the dry heat hefeweizen or skyline stout. If guests would like to escape the ever-present sunshine, take a break in the outdoor shaded bier garden, which features cooling mists and sounds of a relaxing waterfall. **Features:** full bar, patio dining, happy hour. **Address:** 210 Swanson Ave 86403 **Location:** Jct SR 95, just sw. [L] [D]

THE RED ONION   928/505-0302

♦♦ American. Casual Dining. $7-$11 **AAA Inspector Notes:** This casual spot offers an open-air dining room. Serving up breakfast and lunch with such items as burgers and sandwiches, diners will find the service friendly and helpful. **Features:** full bar, patio dining. **Address:** 2013 McCulloch Blvd N 86403 **Location:** Jct Smoketree Ave, just e; uptown. **Parking:** on-site and street. [B] [L]

SCOTTY'S BROASTED CHICKEN & RIBS   928/680-4441

♦ Chicken. Casual Dining. $6-$24 **AAA Inspector Notes:** This small restaurant specializes in broasted chicken and ribs. The service is very friendly and there is indoor and outdoor seating. **Address:** 410 El Camino Way 86403 **Location:** Just w of SR 95, 1.2 mi n of London Bridge. [L] [D]

SHO-GUN JAPANESE CUISINE   928/680-6668

♦♦ Japanese. Casual Dining. $9-$46 **AAA Inspector Notes:** There is something for everyone at this fun and popular spot. Diners can enjoy the teppanyaki menu while watching the chefs perform, or dine in the main dining room and enjoy fresh nigiri, sashimi, specialty rolls or flavorful Asian fusion selections. **Features:** full bar, happy hour. **Address:** 90 Swanson Ave 86403 **Location:** SR 95, just se on Swanson Ave. [L] [D]

SHUGRUE'S   928/453-1400

♦♦ Steak. Casual Dining. $13-$32 **AAA Inspector Notes:** Overlooking the channel to Lake Havasu and London Bridge, this restaurant bakes pastries and bread on the premises. Fresh seafood is offered daily, and Pacific Rim dishes are available Thursday evenings. **Features:** full bar, early bird specials, Sunday brunch, happy hour. **Reservations:** suggested. **Address:** 1425 McCulloch Blvd N 86403 **Location:** West side of London Bridge. [L] [D]

TACO HACIENDA   928/855-8932

♦♦ Mexican. Casual Dining. $7-$15 **AAA Inspector Notes:** High above the lake, this small eatery offers views from its outdoor patio and some indoor tables. Friendly owners set a pleasant tone for the staff, who serve classics along the lines of enchiladas with green chiles, seafood burritos and MJ's chicken and rice. **Features:** full bar, patio dining. **Address:** 2200 Mesquite Ave 86403 **Location:** Jct SR 95, 1.5 mi e. [L] [D]

THE TURTLE GRILL   928/855-1897

♦♦ American. Casual Dining. $9-$38 **AAA Inspector Notes:** Diners may choose between watching one of the 14 large TV screens, or gazing at the beautiful lake and mountain views from this waterfront eatery. Island chicken penne, Caribbean Caesar and barbecue ribs are among choices that will make your mouth water. Create-your-own pizza gives guests a chance to unleash their creativity. **Features:** full bar, patio dining, Sunday brunch, happy hour. **Address:** 1000 McCulloch Blvd N 86403 **Location:** 1.4 mi w of London Bridge, follow signs; in The Nautical Beachfront Resort.

[B] [L] [D] [🛏]

LAKE MEAD NATIONAL RECREATION AREA (B-1)

This 1.5 million-acre recreation area, established in 1964, was created around Lake Mead, the massive Colorado River reservoir resulting from the construction of Hoover Dam. Exit wild river rapids. Enter motorboating, water skiing and fishing on a placid lake. Further downstream, the completion of Davis Dam in 1951 impounded Lake Mohave, another popular spot with the boat and Jet Ski set. In all, the recreation area extends about 140 miles along the Colorado River from the west end of Grand Canyon National Park, Ariz., down to Bullhead City, Ariz., and its neighbor across the river, Laughlin, Nev.

Though man remodeled nature to suit his thirst for water and hydroelectric power, that doesn't mean the native desert bighorn sheep, mountain lions, mule deer, coyotes, foxes, bobcats, lizards, snakes and tortoises were going to take a hike. Not by a long shot. They're all still here, where three of America's four desert ecosystems—the Mojave, the Great Basin and the Sonoran deserts—meet against a starkly beautiful backdrop of desert mountains, cliffs, canyons and plateaus.

If you're here on a day trip from Vegas and water sports aren't in the cards, point your ride down scenic Lakeshore Road (SR 166). A good starting point is at the junction of Lakeshore and US 93, next to the Alan Bible Visitor Center. Skirting the shores of Lake Mead, the road winds through desert terrain, passing beaches, boat marinas and several nice viewpoints, some with sheltered picnic tables. From the suggested starting point to the Lake Mead Parkway entrance station, with a few short stops, budget about 30 to 40 minutes.

From fall through spring (soaring summer temps can spell heat stroke), go for a hike. One of the area's best hiking paths is the Redstone Dune Trail, off the Northshore Road at Mile Marker 27. From the Lake Mead Parkway entrance station, it's a good half-hour drive, but well worth it. Sandy walking trails snake past huge, jumbled red rock formations similar to what you'll see at nearby Valley of Fire State Park. The difference is this hidden gem usually lacks the crowds you'll find up the road. Rock scrambling and photography opportunities are outstanding. Pack plenty of water, and perhaps, a lunch; there's a picnic area with shaded tables.

Back at the lakes, whip out your rod and reel. Striped and largemouth bass are the chief catches in Lake Mead; crappie and catfish are common in the waters of Callville Bay. Wherever you cast off, remember that either a Nevada or an Arizona fishing license is required.

If boats, kayaks and personal watercraft are too much fuss, go for a swim. There's a long, kid-friendly strand at Lake Mead's Boulder Beach. The lake bottom here is a bit rocky; those with sensitive tootsies should wear water shoes or sport sandals. **Note:** No lifeguards are on duty at Boulder Beach or anywhere else in the recreation area. Life jackets are recommended.

Most areas are open daily 24 hours; signs are posted for areas that close earlier. Headquarters visitor center open daily 8-4:30. Alan Bible Visitor Center daily 9-4:30. Closed Jan. 1, Thanksgiving and Christmas. Food is available. Admission $10 (per private vehicle or motorcycle); $5 (per person arriving by other means). Lake-use fee $16 (per boat). Passes are valid for up to 7 days. For further information contact Lake Mead National Recreation Area, 601 Nevada Way, Boulder City, NV 89005. Phone (702) 293-8990 for the Alan Bible Visitor Center. *See Recreation Areas Chart.*

HOOVER DAM is along SR 172 (Hoover Dam Access Rd.), about 8 mi. n.e. of Boulder City. Soaring 726 feet high (about 60 stories), this curved wall of concrete is one of the highest dams ever constructed. It's also a hugely popular day trip from Vegas, and with good reason. The Depression-era engineering marvel (built 1931-35) sits in Black Canyon, a ruggedly dramatic Colorado River chasm that's home to the dam, its mega-wattage hydroelectric power plant and a visitor center/tourist complex with all the bells and whistles.

Hoover Dam was lucky enough to be born in the 1930s, the peak of the Art Deco craze. Witness the dam's main plaza, a Deco-style beauty graced with terrazzo floor-embedded celestial diagrams and the twin, 30-foot-high bronze sculptures, the Winged Figures of the Republic (casino gamblers take note: rubbing the statues' toes will reputedly bring you good luck). Walking across the top of the dam, take time to admire the beautiful bas-relief panels adorning the elevator towers.

The Hoover Dam Visitor Center is a glass-and-steel building perched on the upper cliffs of Black Canyon; feel free to wander the excellent, upper level exhibits, many of them high-tech, interactive affairs. Once you tire of learning about turbines, transformers and penstocks, step out on the top level's outdoor observation platform for dizzying photo-ops, both of the dam and the downstream Mike O'Callaghan-Pat Tillman Memorial Bridge *(see attraction listing p. 105).* The Old Exhibit Building, built in the 1940s and located across the dam roadway, displays a vintage, raised-relief topographical map of the entire desert Southwest, a must-see for cartography geeks.

For the full, in-depth experience, the guided 30-minute Powerplant Tour begins 530 feet underground and visits eight of the plant's 17 generators. The Dam Tour is a 1-hour guided visit to the generators, tunnels and inspection points.

Note: Before reaching the dam you'll pass through a vehicle inspection station. Upon entering the visitor center, expect an airport-style security search. Food, weapons, knives and oversize backpacks and purses are prohibited; however, bottled water is permitted.

Hours: Visitor center daily 9-5. Last admission 45 minutes before closing. Parking structure daily 8-6. Closed Thanksgiving and Christmas. **Cost:** Dam Tour $30. Powerplant Tour $15; $12 (ages 4-16, ages 62+ and military with ID); free (ages 0-3 and active military in uniform). Visitor center $10; free (ages 0-3). The availability of either guided tour is subject to elevator malfunctions and power plant maintenance; phone ahead for updates. The Dam Tour is conducted on a first-come, first-served basis; a maximum of 20 people are allowed on each tour. Under 8 and the physically impaired are not permitted on the Dam Tour. **Parking:** $10. **Phone:** (702) 494-2517 or (866) 730-9097. GT ⑪

LAKE MEAD, extending behind Hoover Dam, is 110 miles long, averages 200 feet deep at normal capacity and has a 550-mile shoreline. Due to recent drought conditions, the lake's surface elevation is 1,081 feet (1,229 feet is considered a full pool).

Nevada recreational centers with marinas and launch facilities include Hemenway Harbor, 4 miles northeast of Boulder City; and Callville Bay, 22 miles east of North Las Vegas. An additional Arizona center is about 80 miles north of Kingman at Temple Bar. The lake also offers numerous primitive launch ramps without services.

Exhibits and a film about natural and cultural history are offered at the Alan Bible Visitor Center, 4 miles east of Boulder City at US 93 and Lakeshore Road (SR 166), overlooking Lake Mead. A botanical and cactus garden surrounds the visitor center. *See Recreation Areas Chart.*

Hours: Alan Bible Visitor Center daily 9-4:30. Closed Jan. 1, Thanksgiving and Christmas. **Cost:** $10 (per private vehicle or motorcycle); $5 (per person arriving by other means). Passes are valid for up to 7 days. Motorized boat $16. **Phone:** (702) 293-8990 for the Alan Bible Visitor Center.

Lake Mead Cruises depart from the Lake Mead Cruises Landing at Hemenway Harbor at 490 Horsepower Rd., just off Lakeshore Rd. (SR 166). Excursion cruises on a Mississippi-style paddlewheeler include a narration about area history and the construction of Hoover Dam. Brunch and dinner cruises also are available April through October. **Note:** Visitors traveling to Hemenway Harbor must pay the Lake Mead National Recreation Area access fee of $10 per private vehicle or motorcycle or $5 per person arriving by other means. **Hours:** Ninety-minute round-trip excursion cruises depart daily at noon and 2. **Cost:** $26; $13 (ages 2-11). Reservations are recommended. **Phone:** (702) 293-6180 or (866) 292-9191. ⑪

LAKE MOHAVE extends 67 mi. s. from Hoover Dam to Davis Dam. Launching ramps, trailer sites, refreshment concessions, boat rentals and overnight accommodations are available at Katherine Landing, about 35 miles west of Kingman, Ariz., and at Cottonwood Cove, 14 miles east of Searchlight. Accommodations also are available a short distance away in Needles, Calif., and Bullhead City, Ariz. Willow Beach, 28 miles east of Boulder City on US 93, offers a launch ramp and concession facilities. Information about recreational facilities is available at all three sites.

MIKE O'CALLAGHAN-PAT TILLMAN MEMORIAL BRIDGE is along US 93, about 5.5 mi. n.e. of Boulder City. Linking Nevada and Arizona, this arched, 1,900-foot-long concrete-and-steel span is some 1,500 feet downstream from Hoover Dam. Opened in 2010, the bridge was built to replace a longstanding traffic bottleneck: the two-lane section of US 93 that crossed the Colorado River atop Hoover Dam (now SR 172).

Thanks to a 6-foot-wide pedestrian sidewalk running its length, the bridge—which honors former Nevada Governor Mike O'Callaghan and Afghanistan war hero Pat Tillman—has become a major attraction. Lined with etched information panels, the sidewalk is accessible only from the Nevada side (it dead-ends at the Arizona side); follow signs to the Hoover Dam Access Road (SR 172) exit. The parking lot for visitors is about 2 miles down the road; if the bridge lot is full, an overflow lot is a couple hundred yards further down.

From this lofty perch you'll have a grand view of the Hoover Dam, not to mention a jaw-dropping (and stomach-churning, for those afraid of heights) perspective of the turquoise Colorado River 900 feet below, wedged between the rock cliffs that form Black Canyon. Prime time for photography is mid- to late-afternoon.

Note: Before reaching the bridge and Hoover Dam area you'll pass through a vehicle inspection security station. A switchback trail with 70 steps (and paved, wheelchair-accessible ramps) provides access to the pedestrian sidewalk. **Time:** Allow 45 minutes minimum. **Hours:** Daily dawn-dusk. **Cost:** Free.

FOX SMOKEHOUSE BBQ   702/489-2211

🔻 Barbecue. Quick Serve. $9-$26 **AAA Inspector Notes:** The Fox family is doing barbecue right with Certified Angus beef brisket and tri-tip. Do not forget about the ribs, creamy macaroni and cheese, sweet cornbread and homemade desserts. Competition trophies are displayed throughout the small dining room showing that this barbecue has proved itself time and time again. **Features:** beer only. **Address:** 1007 Elm St 89005 **Location:** Just w; center.
Ⓛ Ⓓ

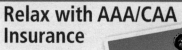

LAVEEN

VEE QUIVA HOTEL & CASINO   (520)946-4452

Hotel
$59-$259

Address: 15091 S Komatke Ln 85339 **Location:** I-10 exit 139 (51st Ave), 10 mi s. **Facility:** Located in the foothills just south of the city, this boutique-style property offers upscale state-of-the-art guest rooms along with multiple dining and entertainment options. 90 units. 3 stories, interior corridors. *Bath:* shower only. **Parking:** on-site and valet. **Terms:** check-in 4 pm, 3 day cancellation notice-fee imposed. **Dining:** 7 restaurants, nightclub. **Pool(s):** heated outdoor. **Activities:** hot tub, exercise room. **Guest Services:** valet laundry.

(See ad p. 78.)

LITCHFIELD PARK (I-2) pop. 5,476
• Hotels & Restaurants map & index p. 154
• Part of Phoenix area — see map p. 126

WILDLIFE WORLD ZOO, AQUARIUM & SAFARI PARK, s.e. corner of SR 303 at 16501 W. Northern Ave., presents more than 500 rare and exotic species of animals including giraffes, lions, rhinoceroses, tigers, crocodiles, sharks, penguins, fish and tropical birds along with 85 aquarium exhibits. A tram takes visitors through the 15-acre safari park, home to wildebeests, kudu antelopes, baboons, a white lion, gazelles and watusi cattle. The attraction features lory parrot feedings, stingray feedings, giraffe feedings, a safari train ride, a boat ride, a sky ride, a log-flume ride, a sea lion show and other wildlife encounter shows.

Hours: Zoo daily 9-6. Aquarium daily 9-9. **Cost:** Zoo, safari park and aquarium $32.50; $30 (ages 60+ on Tues.); $15 (ages 3-12). Aquarium after 5 p.m. $16.99; $14.99 (ages 60+ on Tues.); $8.99 (ages 3-12). Prices may vary; phone ahead. **Phone:** (623) 935-9453.

THE WIGWAM   623/935-3811 39

Historic
Retro Hotel
Rates not provided

Address: 300 Wigwam Blvd 85340 **Location:** I-10 exit 128 (Litchfield Rd), 2.4 mi n, then 0.4 mi e. **Facility:** This gracious resort, which opened in 1929, offers beautifully renovated public areas, a golf course by Robert Trent Jones Sr., lushly landscaped grounds and oversize rooms. 331 units, some two bedrooms. 1-2 stories (no elevator), exterior corridors. **Parking:** on-site and valet. **Terms:** check-in 4 pm. **Amenities:** safes. **Dining:** 2 restaurants, also, Litchfield's, see separate listing. **Pool(s):** heated outdoor. **Activities:** sauna, hot tub, steamroom, regulation golf, tennis, recreation programs, bicycles, game room, lawn sports, exercise room, spa. **Guest Services:** valet laundry, boarding pass kiosk, area transportation.

BLU SUSHI LOUNGE & GRILL   623/935-9730 27

Sushi. Casual Dining. $10-$27 **AAA Inspector Notes:** Fresh, classic sushi choices along with distinctive rolls, noodles, tempura and teriyaki are served in this sleek, trendy atmosphere. **Features:** full bar, patio dining, happy hour. **Address:** 118 N Old Litchfield Rd 85340 **Location:** I-10 exit 128 (Litchfield Rd), 2.5 mi n, 0.3 mi e on Wigwam Blvd, then just n. **Parking:** on-site and street.

LITCHFIELD'S   623/935-3811 26

New American. Casual Dining. $16-$29 **AAA Inspector Notes:** The menu at this upscale, casual dining room features many local, farm-to-table ingredients including Arizona trout with pecan sage butter, Double Check Ranch grass-fed tenderloin and Santa Fe lamb stew. If weather permits, enjoy a table outside overlooking the manicured grounds. **Features:** full bar, patio dining, happy hour. **Reservations:** suggested. **Address:** 300 Wigwam Blvd 85340 **Location:** I-10 exit 128 (Litchfield Rd), 2.4 mi n, then 0.4 mi e; in The Wigwam. **Parking:** on-site and valet.

MARANA pop. 34,961
• Hotels & Restaurants map & index p. 274
• Part of Tucson area — see map p. 256

BEST WESTERN PLUS GOLD POPPY INN
(520)579-7202 53

Hotel
$70-$170

AAA Benefit: Save 10% or more every day and earn 10% bonus points!

Address: 4930 W Ina Rd 85743 **Location:** I-10 exit 248 (Ina Rd), just w. **Facility:** 60 units. 3 stories, interior corridors. **Pool(s):** outdoor. **Activities:** hot tub, exercise room.

COMFORT INN & SUITES   (520)579-1099 50

Hotel $125-$146 **Address:** 8425 N Cracker Barrel Rd 85743 **Location:** I-10 exit 246 (Cortaro Rd), just w. **Facility:** 65 units. 3 stories, interior corridors. **Pool(s):** outdoor. **Activities:** hot tub, exercise room. **Guest Services:** valet and coin laundry.

HOLIDAY INN EXPRESS & SUITES   520/572-4777 52

Hotel. Rates not provided. **Address:** 8373 N Cracker Barrel Rd 85743 **Location:** I-10 exit 246 (Cortaro Rd), just w, then just n. **Facility:** 83 units. 3 stories, interior corridors. **Pool(s):** heated outdoor. **Activities:** hot tub, exercise room. **Guest Services:** valet and coin laundry.

LA QUINTA INN & SUITES NW TUCSON MARANA
(520)572-4235 51

Hotel $64-$258 **Address:** 6020 W Hospitality Rd 85743 **Location:** I-10 exit 246 (Cortaro Rd), just w, then just n. **Facility:** 65 units, some kitchens. 3 stories, interior corridors. **Pool(s):** outdoor. **Activities:** hot tub, picnic facilities, exercise room. **Guest Services:** coin laundry.

(See map & index p. 274.)

THE RITZ-CARLTON, DOVE MOUNTAIN   520/572-3000

Resort Hotel
Rates not provided

AAA Benefit:
Unequaled service at special member savings!

Address: 15000 N Secret Springs Dr 85658 **Location:** I-10 exit 240 (Tangerine Rd), 5 mi e to Dove Mountain Dr, then 4.5 mi n, follow signs. **Facility:** Nestled into the Tortolita Mountains, this elegant resort features rooms with expansive views and luxurious baths as well as world-class golf facilities. 253 units. 1-5 stories, interior corridors. **Parking:** valet only. **Terms:** check-in 4 pm. **Amenities:** video games, safes. **Dining:** 4 restaurants, also, Core Kitchen & Wine Bar, see separate listing. **Pool(s):** heated outdoor. **Activities:** sauna, hot tub, steamroom, regulation golf, tennis, recreation programs, kids club, bicycles, lawn sports, trails, spa. **Guest Services:** valet laundry, area transportation.

WHERE TO EAT

CORE KITCHEN & WINE BAR   520/572-3000

Regional American. Fine Dining. $24-$36 **AAA Inspector Notes:** The talented chefs creates unique, creative and memorable regional dishes at this elegant, yet casual spot. Diners can sample such dishes as chili-lacquered New York strip with nopales relish, prickly pear barbecue quail and buffalo tenderloin with three chili aioli. **Features:** full bar, patio dining. **Reservations:** suggested. **Address:** 15000 N Secret Springs Dr 85658 **Location:** I-10 exit 240 (Tangerine Rd), 5 mi e to Dove Mountain Dr, then 4.5 mi n, follow signs; in The Ritz-Carlton, Dove Mountain. **Parking:** on-site and valet. B D

LA OLLA MEXICAN CAFE   520/579-0950   73

Mexican. Casual Dining. $9-$16 **AAA Inspector Notes:** Fresh salsa and homemade guacamole will help start the meal while rich sauces and baked calabacitas, squash cooked with corn and tomatoes, enhance most entrées. Everything, from the chipotle shrimp and pork to the carne con chili rojo, is freshly made. Friendly staff will make this a comfortable dining experience. **Features:** full bar, happy hour. **Address:** 8553 N Silverbell Rd 85743 **Location:** I-10 exit 246 (Cortaro Rd), 0.9 mi w, then 1.4 mi n. L D

LI'L ABNER'S STEAKHOUSE   520/744-2800   74

Steak. Casual Dining. $16-$39 **AAA Inspector Notes:** An area institution, this restaurant grills steaks, ribs and chicken on an outdoor pit. Young servers are energetic. The funky, Western-style building sports years of guest graffiti on the walls. **Features:** full bar. **Reservations:** suggested. **Address:** 8501 N Silverbell Rd 85743 **Location:** I-10 exit 246 (Cortaro Rd), 0.9 mi w, then 1.3 mi n. D

MARICOPA (E-3) pop. 43,482, elev. 1,177'

Prevalent clear blue skies beckon fans of soaring to Maricopa. This area at the foot of the Sierra Estrella Mountains is noted for its thermal conditions. Arizona Soaring, (520) 568-2318, is at 22548 N. Sailport Way.

GAMBLING ESTABLISHMENTS

• **Harrah's Phoenix Ak-Chin Casino,** 1 mi. s. on SR 347 to 15406 Maricopa Rd. **Hours:** Daily 24 hours. **Phone:** (480) 802-5000 or (800) 427-7247.

HARRAH'S AK-CHIN CASINO RESORT   480/802-5000

 Hotel. Rates not provided. **Address:** 15406 Maricopa Rd 85239 **Location:** Jct SR 238, 4.5 mi s on SR 347. **Facility:** Guests can lounge under palm trees in the courtyard or cool off in the pool, which features a swim-up cocktail bar. 300 units. 2-5 stories, interior/exterior corridors. **Terms:** check-in 4 pm. **Amenities:** safes. **Dining:** 5 restaurants. **Pool(s):** heated outdoor. **Activities:** hot tub.

MAYER (D-3) pop. 1,497, elev. 4,402'

ARCOSANTI is off I-17 exit 263, then 2.5 mi. n.e. on a dirt road, following signs. The prototype city is the urban design vision of the late architect Paolo Soleri based on his philosophy of arcology (architecture plus ecology). The town, which still is under construction, will be a pedestrian-oriented city with a goal of reducing urban sprawl and its impact on the environment. A display of Soleri's bells is featured along with tours of the construction site. Educational workshops are held throughout the year. Monthly concerts take place in the Colly Soleri Music Center, except in winter; phone for schedule.

Note: Tours include some stairs. **Hours:** Visitor center daily 9-5. One-hour tours are conducted daily on the hour 10-11 and 1-4. Closed Jan. 1, Thanksgiving and Christmas. **Cost:** Donations. Visitor center free. **Phone:** (928) 632-7135.

MCNARY (D-5) pop. 528, elev. 7,309'

RECREATIONAL ACTIVITIES
Skiing

• **Sunrise Ski Area** is 15 mi. e. on SR 260, then 7 mi. s. on SR 273. Other activities are offered. **Hours:** Daily 9-4, Dec.-Apr. and Memorial Day-Labor Day (weather permitting). **Phone:** (928) 735-7669 or (855) 735-7669.

MESA (J-4) pop. 439,041, elev. 1,234'

• Hotels p. 109 • Restaurants p. 111
• Attractions map p. 138
• Hotels & Restaurants map & index p. 164
• Part of Phoenix area — see map p. 126

Mesa (Spanish for "tabletop") is in the center of the Salt River Valley on a plateau. The area has long been inhabited by Native Americans, including the Ancestral Desert People, or "the Departed Ones." The resourceful tribe realized the need for water for irrigation and dug some 125 miles of canals around 700 B.C. Some of these irrigation ditches are still in use and can be seen at the Park of the Canals and Mesa Grande Ruins.

In 1883 the founding Mormon community discovered the ancient canal system and used it to irrigate the thousands of acres of fertile farmland above the Salt River. Alfalfa, cotton, wheat and grapes were the major crops; citrus was introduced in 1897. Agriculture carried the town into the 20th century; today, the aviation, education and health care industries play a big role in Mesa's economy.

Recreation areas, mostly east and north of the city, are easily accessible from bike-friendly Mesa.

(See map & index p. 164.)

Rafting and other water sports on the Salt River are popular, as are varied activities available within the Apache Lake and Canyon Lake recreation areas *(see attraction listings p. 38)* and on Theodore Roosevelt Lake *(see attraction listing p. 198)* and Saguaro Lake. *See Recreation Areas Chart.*

Mesa also hosts major league baseball at two stadiums: Sloan Park, the spring training home of the Chicago Cubs, and Hohokam Stadium, home of the Oakland A's, which reopened in 2015 after a major renovation.

Visit Mesa: 120 N. Center St., Mesa, AZ 85201. **Phone:** (480) 827-4700 or (800) 283-6372.

Shopping: The largest indoor shopping centers in the city are Fiesta Mall, US 60 and Alma School Road, which offers Dillard's Clearance Center and Sears; and Superstition Springs Center, at US 60 and Superstition Springs Boulevard, which offers Dillard's, JCPenney, Macy's and Sears. When it comes to open-air destination shopping, Dana Park Village Square, at Val Vista Drive and Baseline Road, offers such stores as Ann Taylor Loft, Anthropologie, Chico's and Talbot's. Mesa Riverview, at Dobson Road and Loop 202 Freeway, includes Bass Pro Shops Outdoor World, Rue 21 and Shepler's Western Wear.

Bargain hunters can find discounted name-brand merchandise at Power Square Mall, a half-mile south of US 60 at Power and Baseline roads. The Mesa Market Place and Swap Meet boasts more than 1,500 vendors offering new and used merchandise at its shaded facility at 10550 E. Baseline Rd.

ARIZONA MUSEUM OF NATURAL HISTORY, 53 N. Macdonald St., covers the history of Arizona from the days of the dinosaurs to the 21st century. Permanent and temporary exhibits focus on Arizona's prehistoric life, featuring animated dinosaurs, dinosaur skeletons and other fossil specimens. Archeology displays highlight the life of Arizona's ancient Ancestral Desert People, while reminders of old Mesa's past include territorial jail cells and the Lost Dutchman's Gold Mine.

Time: Allow 1 hour minimum. **Hours:** Tues.-Fri. 10-5, Sat. 11-5, Sun. 1-5; closed state and major holidays. **Cost:** $12; $10 (ages 65+); $9 (students with ID); $7 (ages 3-12). **Phone:** (480) 644-2230.

ARIZONA TEMPLE VISITORS' CENTER is at 525 E. Main St. The center presents dioramas and audiovisual programs that explain the purpose of the temple and the history of the Church of Jesus Christ of Latter-Day Saints; paintings and statues are featured. Free guided and self-guiding tours of the visitors' center are available. A pageant is presented during the 2 weeks before Easter, and a holiday lights display is featured the day after Thanksgiving through New Year's Eve. **Time:** Allow 1 hour minimum. **Hours:** Daily 9-9. Guided tours are given daily. **Cost:** Free. **Phone:** (480) 964-7164. GT

COMMEMORATIVE AIR FORCE-AIRBASE ARIZONA, e. on SR 202 to 2017 N. Greenfield Rd. at jct. McKellips Rd. (adjoining Falcon Field), is dedicated to celebrating our heritage of freedom through education, flight, exhibits and memorabilia. The 30,000-square-foot hangar features exhibits and aircraft dedicated to the history of flight and is home to the World War II B-17 Flying Fortress *Sentimental Journey.*

Time: Allow 1 hour minimum. **Hours:** Daily 10-4, Oct.-May; Wed.-Sun. 9-3, rest of year. *Sentimental Journey* is on display late fall-early summer. Closed Jan. 1, Thanksgiving and Christmas. **Cost:** Oct.-May $15; $12 (ages 62+); $3 (ages 5-12). Rest of year $12; $10 (ages 62+); $3 (ages 5-12). **Phone:** (480) 924-1940.

GOLFLAND/SUNSPLASH, 155 W. Hampton Ave., is a 15-acre miniature golf and water park complex that offers more than 30 attractions, including the Master Blaster, the four-person Stormrider, a wave pool and a lazy river. Year-round attractions include three miniature golf courses, bumper boats, go-carts, a video arcade and laser tag. Changing rooms and lockers are available.

Hours: Sunsplash Sun.-Thurs. 11-7, Fri.-Sat. 11-11, Memorial Day-Labor Day. Golfland Mon.-Thurs. 11-10, Fri. 11 a.m.-midnight, Sat. 10 a.m.-midnight, Sun. 11-9. Phone ahead to confirm schedule. **Cost:** Sunsplash $29.99; $19.99 (ages 55+, under 48 inches tall, active military and after 4 p.m.); $3 (ages 0-2). Golfland free. Fees apply for golf, go-carts, bumper boats and other activities. Prices may vary; phone ahead. **Phone:** (480) 834-8319. [T]

I.D.E.A. MUSEUM, 150 W. Pepper Pl., offers children the opportunity to view, create and explore various forms of art. Six new exhibitions are introduced each year, and workshops teach a variety of skills from cartooning to printmaking. ArtVille, a permanent gallery, highlights art activities for children ages 0-4. **Time:** Allow 1 hour minimum. **Hours:** Tues.-Sat. 9-4, Sun. noon-4. The main gallery is closed periodically for exhibit installation. Closed major holidays. Phone ahead to confirm schedule. **Cost:** $8; free (ages 0-1). **Phone:** (480) 644-2467.

MESA HISTORICAL MUSEUM is at 51 E. Main St. The museum features changing exhibits and programs about Mesa history and the history of baseball spring training in the city. **Time:** Allow 30 minutes minimum. **Hours:** Wed.-Sat. 10-4. Closed major holidays. **Cost:** $5; $4 (ages 65+); $3 (ages 3-12). **Phone:** (480) 835-2286. [□] [↟]

ROCKIN' R RANCH, 6136 E. Baseline Rd., is a re-creation of a Western town where you can pan for gold. All-you-can-eat chuck wagon suppers are served cowboy style. A stage show has songs and humor of the Old West; a gunfight is staged after the show.

Hours: Doors open at 5:30. Meal precedes stage show and gunfight. Times vary; phone ahead. **Cost:**

(See map & index p. 164.)

$32; $22 (ages 3-12). Reservations are required. **Phone:** (480) 832-1539.

RECREATIONAL ACTIVITIES
Tubing

- **Salt River Tubing and Recreation** is 15 mi. n. of US 60 on Power Rd. **Hours:** Daily 9-6:30, late Apr.-Sept. 30 (weather and water level permitting). **Phone:** (480) 984-3305.

BAYMONT INN & SUITES MESA   (480)621-6375 **45**
▼▼▼ Hotel $70-$190 **Address:** 651 E Main St 85203 **Location:** US 60 (Superstition Frwy) exit 180 (Mesa Dr), 2 mi e, then 0.4 mi e. **Facility:** 48 units. 2 stories, interior corridors. **Amenities:** safes. **Pool(s):** heated outdoor. **Activities:** hot tub.

BEST WESTERN LEGACY INN & SUITES
                                   (480)457-8181 **60**

Hotel
$75-$179

AAA Benefit:
Save 10% or more every day and earn 10% bonus points!

Address: 4470 S Power Rd 85212 **Location:** Santan Frwy (Loop 202) exit Power Rd, just n. **Facility:** 110 units. 3 stories, interior corridors. **Pool(s):** heated outdoor. **Activities:** hot tub, exercise room. **Guest Services:** valet and coin laundry, area transportation.

BEST WESTERN PLUS MESA   (480)926-3600 **55**

Hotel
$69-$199

AAA Benefit:
Save 10% or more every day and earn 10% bonus points!

Address: 1563 S Gilbert Rd 85204 **Location:** US 60 (Superstition Frwy) exit 182 (Gilbert Rd), just n. **Facility:** 115 units. 4 stories, interior corridors. **Amenities:** video games. **Pool(s):** heated outdoor. **Activities:** hot tub, exercise room. **Guest Services:** valet and coin laundry.

BEST WESTERN SUPERSTITION SPRINGS INN
                                   (480)641-1164 **57**

Hotel
$69-$149

AAA Benefit:
Save 10% or more every day and earn 10% bonus points!

Address: 1342 S Power Rd 85206 **Location:** Just n of US 60 (Superstition Frwy) exit 188 (Power Rd); northwest corner of Power Rd and Hampton Ave. Next to Superstition Springs Mall and Leisure World. **Facility:** 59 units, some kitchens. 2 stories (no elevator), exterior corridors. **Pool(s):** heated outdoor. **Activities:** hot tub, limited exercise equipment. **Guest Services:** coin laundry. **Featured Amenity:** full hot breakfast.

COUNTRY INN & SUITES BY CARLSON   (480)641-8000 **59**
▼▼▼▼ Hotel $75-$199 **Address:** 6650 E Superstition Springs Blvd 85206 **Location:** Just s of US 60 (Superstition Frwy) exit 188 (Power Rd), just sw. **Facility:** 126 units. 4 stories, interior corridors. **Terms:** check-in 4 pm, cancellation fee imposed. **Pool(s):** heated outdoor. **Activities:** hot tub, picnic facilities, exercise room. **Guest Services:** valet and coin laundry, area transportation.

COURTYARD BY MARRIOTT-MESA   (480)461-3000 **47**

Hotel
$60-$220

COURTYARD
Marriott

AAA Benefit: Members save 5% or more!

Address: 1221 S Westwood 85210 **Location:** US 60 (Superstition Frwy) exit 178 (Alma School Rd), 0.4 mi n, just e on Southern Ave, then just s. **Facility:** 149 units. 3 stories, interior corridors. **Pool(s):** heated outdoor. **Activities:** hot tub, exercise room. **Guest Services:** valet and coin laundry, boarding pass kiosk, area transportation.

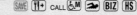

DAYS HOTEL MESA COUNTRY CLUB   (480)844-8900 **54**
▼▼ Hotel $66-$160 **Address:** 333 W Juanita Ave 85210 **Location:** US 60 (Superstition Frwy) exit 179 (Country Club Dr), just s, then just e. **Facility:** 120 units. 3 stories, interior corridors. **Amenities:** safes. **Pool(s):** heated outdoor. **Activities:** hot tub, exercise room. **Guest Services:** valet and coin laundry.

DAYS INN-EAST MESA   (480)981-8111 **46**
▼▼ Hotel $55-$120 **Address:** 5531 E Main St 85205 **Location:** 0.4 mi e of Higley Rd. **Facility:** 61 units. 2 stories (no elevator), exterior corridors. **Pool(s):** heated outdoor.

ECONO LODGE INN & SUITES MESA   480/833-1231 **43**
▼▼ Hotel. Rates not provided. **Address:** 951 W Main St 85201 **Location:** US 60 (Superstition Frwy) exit 178 (Alma School Rd), 2 mi n to Main St, then just e. **Facility:** 90 units. 2 stories (no elevator), interior corridors. **Pool(s):** outdoor. **Activities:** hot tub, exercise room. **Guest Services:** valet and coin laundry.

FAIRFIELD INN & SUITES BY MARRIOTT PHOENIX MESA
                                  (480)668-8000 **50**

Hotel
$58-$163

FAIRFIELD
INN & SUITES
Marriott

AAA Benefit: Members save 5% or more!

Address: 1405 S Westwood 85210 **Location:** Just n of US 60 (Superstition Frwy) exit 178 (Alma School Rd), just e on Grove St, then just s. **Facility:** 64 units. 3 stories, interior corridors. **Pool(s):** heated outdoor. **Activities:** hot tub, exercise room. **Guest Services:** valet laundry. **Featured Amenity:** breakfast buffet.

(See map & index p. 164.)

HILTON PHOENIX/MESA　　(480)833-5555　**51**

Hotel
$79-$269

AAA Benefit: Members save 5% or more!

Address: 1011 W Holmes Ave 85210 **Location:** US 60 (Superstition Frwy) exit 178 (Alma School Rd), just n, then just e. Across from Fiesta Mall. **Facility:** 260 units. 8 stories, interior corridors. **Terms:** 1-7 night minimum stay, cancellation fee imposed. **Amenities:** safes. **Pool(s):** heated outdoor. **Activities:** hot tub, exercise room. **Guest Services:** valet laundry, area transportation.

HOLIDAY INN & SUITES PHOENIX-MESA/CHANDLER
480/964-7000　**53**

 Hotel. Rates not provided. **Address:** 1600 S Country Club Dr 85210 **Location:** US 60 (Superstition Frwy) exit 179 (Country Club Dr), just s. **Facility:** 246 units. 6 stories, interior/exterior corridors. **Pool(s):** heated outdoor. **Activities:** hot tub, exercise room. **Guest Services:** valet and coin laundry.

HYATT PLACE PHOENIX/MESA　　(480)969-8200　**41**

Hotel
$69-$229

HYATT PLACE
AAA Benefit: Members save 10%!

Address: 1422 W Bass Pro Dr 85201 **Location:** Loop 202 exit 10 (Dobson Rd), just s, then just e. **Facility:** 152 units. 4 stories, interior corridors. **Terms:** cancellation fee imposed. **Pool(s):** heated outdoor. **Activities:** hot tub, exercise room. **Guest Services:** valet and coin laundry, area transportation. **Featured Amenity:** breakfast buffet.

LA QUINTA INN & SUITES MESA SUPERSTITION SPRINGS
(480)654-1970　**58**

 **Hotel** $75-$273 **Address:** 6530 E Superstition Springs Blvd 85206 **Location:** US 60 (Superstition Frwy) exit 187 (Superstition Springs Blvd) eastbound, just se; exit 188 (Power Rd) westbound, just sw. **Facility:** 107 units. 4 stories, interior corridors. **Pool(s):** heated outdoor. **Activities:** hot tub, exercise room. **Guest Services:** valet and coin laundry, area transportation.

LA QUINTA INN & SUITES PHOENIX MESA WEST
(480)844-8747　**48**

 **Hotel** $64-$246 **Address:** 902 W Grove Ave 85210 **Location:** US 60 (Superstition Frwy) exit 178 (Alma School Rd), just n, then just e. **Facility:** 125 units. 7 stories, interior corridors. **Pool(s):** heated outdoor. **Activities:** hot tub, exercise room. **Guest Services:** valet and coin laundry.

Visit AAA.com/searchfordiscounts to save
on travel, shopping, dining and attractions

MEZONA INN　　(480)834-9233　**44**

Hotel
$59-$170

Address: 250 W Main St 85201 **Location:** Just e of Country Club Dr; downtown. **Facility:** 128 units. 2 stories (no elevator), exterior corridors. **Terms:** cancellation fee imposed. **Pool(s):** heated outdoor. **Activities:** hot tub, picnic facilities. **Guest Services:** coin laundry. **Featured Amenity:** full hot breakfast.

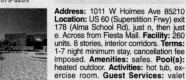
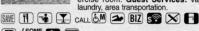

PHOENIX MARRIOTT MESA　　(480)898-8300　**42**

Hotel
$73-$220

AAA Benefit: Members save 5% or more!

Address: 200 N Centennial Way 85201 **Location:** US 60 (Superstition Frwy) exit 180 (Mesa Dr), 2 mi n, just w on Main St, then just n. **Facility:** 274 units. 12 stories, interior corridors. **Terms:** check-in 4 pm. **Pool(s):** heated outdoor. **Activities:** hot tub, picnic facilities, exercise room. **Guest Services:** valet and coin laundry, boarding pass kiosk, area transportation.

QUALITY INN MESA - SUPERSTITION SPRINGS
(480)807-7760　**56**

 Hotel $90-$130 **Address:** 6347 E Southern Ave 85206 **Location:** US 60 (Superstition Frwy) exit 188 (Power Rd), 0.8 mi n, then 0.4 mi w to mall entrance. Located at west end of Superstition Springs Mall. **Facility:** 84 units. 3 stories, interior corridors. **Pool(s):** heated outdoor. **Activities:** hot tub. **Guest Services:** coin laundry.

RAMADA MESA PHOENIX EAST AREA　　(480)831-7000　**52**

Hotel $40-$94 **Address:** 1666 S Dobson Rd 85202 **Location:** Just s of US 60 (Superstition Frwy) exit 177 (Dobson Rd). **Facility:** 213 units. 2 stories, interior/exterior corridors. **Terms:** check-in 4 pm. **Pool(s):** heated outdoor. **Activities:** hot tub, limited exercise equipment. **Guest Services:** coin laundry.

RESIDENCE INN BY MARRIOTT PHOENIX MESA
(480)610-0100　**49**

Extended Stay Hotel
$85-$273

Residence Inn **Marriott**
AAA Benefit: Members save 5% or more!

Address: 941 W Grove Ave 85210 **Location:** US 60 (Superstition Frwy) exit 178 (Alma School Rd), just n, then just e. **Facility:** 117 units, some two bedrooms, efficiencies and kitchens. 3 stories, interior corridors. **Pool(s):** heated outdoor. **Activities:** hot tub, picnic facilities, exercise room. **Guest Services:** valet and coin laundry. **Featured Amenity:** full hot breakfast.

WESTGATE PAINTED MOUNTAIN GOLF RESORT
480/654-3611

fyi Not evaluated. **Address:** 6302 E McKellips Rd 85215 **Location:** Loop 202 E exit 12 (McKellips Rd), 9.1 mi e; adjacent to golf course. Facilities, services, and décor characterize a mid-scale property.

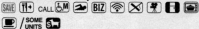

(See map & index p. 164.)

WHERE TO EAT

BLUE ADOBE GRILLE   480/962-1000   **28**

♦♦ Mexican. Casual Dining. $9-$20 **AAA Inspector Notes:** Becoming a local favorite in the Southwestern dining scene, this restaurant prepares regional cuisine using red and green chiles from New Mexico. Bold flavors infuse the interesting and diverse dishes, including the honey pork tamale, pecan-roasted chicken quesadilla and tenderloin chiles rellenos. **Features:** full bar. **Reservations:** suggested. **Address:** 144 N Country Club Dr 85201 **Location:** US 60 (Superstition Frwy) exit 179 (Country Club Dr), 2.1 mi n.

L   D

FLANCER'S   480/396-0077   **27**

♦ Pizza. Casual Dining. $7-$13 **AAA Inspector Notes:** Fun, friendly and casual best describe this East Valley pizza joint. Fresh, handmade New York-style pizza, calzones and pasta choices are some of the tasty items available. Framed concert posters of old rock bands line the walls and help create a "hip" environment. **Features:** beer & wine, happy hour. **Address:** 1902 N Higley Rd 85205 **Location:** SR 202 exit 21 (Higley Rd), 2.1 mi s.   L   D

THE LANDMARK RESTAURANT   480/962-4652   **29**

♦♦ American. Casual Dining. $8-$27 **AAA Inspector Notes:** Dine in a restored church building amid Victorian décor. A varied menu and a soup and salad 'room' are featured as well as an extensive display of Mesa historical photographs. **Features:** full bar. **Address:** 809 W Main St 85201 **Location:** US 60 (Superstition Frwy) exit 179 (Country Club Dr), 2 mi n, then 0.5 mi w.   L   D

LITTLE MESA CAFE   480/830-6201   **31**

♦ American. Family Dining. $7-$17 **AAA Inspector Notes:** Some patrons might just start with the home-baked pies, which are as good as Grandma's, before digging into a fresh salad and such dishes as chicken-fried steak and center-cut pork chops. The casual decor and smiling servers put guests at ease. **Address:** 3929 E Main St 85205 **Location:** US 60 (Superstition Frwy) exit 184 (Val Vista Rd), 2 mi n, then just e.   B   L   D

LOS DOS MOLINOS   480/969-7475   **30**

♦♦ Mexican. Casual Dining. $4-$14 **AAA Inspector Notes:** This popular valley eatery has been serving up delicious New Mexico-style Mexican food for more than two decades. Specializing in spicy chili dishes like shrimp Veracruz and carne adovada, there is a good reason why their motto is "some like it hot." **Features:** full bar, patio dining, Sunday brunch. **Address:** 260 S Alma School Rd, Suite 137 85210 **Location:** US 60 (Superstition Frwy) exit 178 (Alma School Rd), 1.7 mi n. 🚇 Sycamore/Main, 32.

L   D   🚇

MACAYO MEXICAN KITCHEN   480/820-0237

♦♦ Mexican. Casual Dining. $9-$19 **AAA Inspector Notes:** The colorfully furnished Mexican-style eatery prepares Sonoran Mexican dishes. Friendly and efficient staffers serve traditional and lighter dishes flavored with this place's own chili peppers, which are grown near Tucson. **Features:** full bar, happy hour. **Address:** 1920 S Dobson Rd 85202 **Location:** Baseline and Dobson rds; northwest corner.   L   D

MI AMIGOS MEXICAN GRILL   480/892-6822   **32**

♦♦ Mexican. Casual Dining. $7-$19 **AAA Inspector Notes:** Bright and cheerful decor is welcoming at this casual grill, where the food is freshly prepared. Patrons savor the flavors in all the dishes, from tortilla soup to sizzling fajitas. **Features:** full bar, patio dining, happy hour. **Address:** 1264 S Gilbert Rd 85204 **Location:** US 60 (Superstition Frwy) exit 182 (Gilbert Rd), 0.4 mi n.   L   D

MY BIG FAT GREEK RESTAURANT   480/981-0010   **33**

♦♦ Greek. Casual Dining. $7-$20 **AAA Inspector Notes:** Employing friendly staff members, this eatery dishes up all the favorite Greek classics, like lamb souvlaki and moussaka, in large portions. An expanded menu pleases a wide range of patrons with such items as rib-eye, calzones and pizza. Baklava cheesecake and rich chocolate cake are tempting meal-enders. **Features:** full bar, patio dining. **Address:** 6447 E Southern Ave 85206 **Location:** 0.4 mi w of Power Rd.   L   D

P.F. CHANG'S CHINA BISTRO   480/218-4900   **35**

♦♦♦ Chinese. Fine Dining. $8-$25 **AAA Inspector Notes:** Trendy, upscale decor provides a pleasant backdrop for New Age Chinese dining. Appetizers, soups and salads are a meal by themselves. Vegetarian plates and sides, noodles, chow meins, chicken and meat dishes are created from exotic, fresh ingredients. **Features:** full bar, happy hour. **Address:** 6610 E Superstition Springs Blvd 85206 **Location:** US 60 (Superstition Frwy) exit 188 (Power Rd), just s, then just w.   L   D

PINK PEPPER THAI CUISINE   480/839-9009   **34**

♦♦ Thai. Casual Dining. $8-$14 **AAA Inspector Notes:** A wide selection of dishes, including nicely spiced jumping shrimp with vegetables, demonstrates the chef's expertise. Soft décor colors are a pleasant backdrop for the vivid flavors of the food. To cool the palate, savor homemade tropic-flavored ice cream or sticky rice with mango. **Features:** full bar. **Address:** 1941 W Guadalupe Rd, #105 85202 **Location:** US 60 (Superstition Frwy) exit 177 (Dobson Rd), 1.6 mi s.   L   D

RUBIO'S FRESH MEXICAN GRILL

♦ Mexican. Quick Serve. $4-$10 **AAA Inspector Notes:** Freshly prepared and healthful foods, bright decor and friendly staff are found in this upscale fast-food spot. A special treat, the salsa bar lines up four styles and flavors. **Bar:** beer only.   L   D

For additional information, visit AAA.com

LOCATIONS:

Address: 6736 E Baseline Rd 85206 **Location:** US 60 (Superstition Frwy) exit 188 (Power Rd), just s. **Phone:** 480/830-2247

Address: 1649 S Stapley Rd 85204 **Location:** US 60 (Superstition Frwy) exit 181 (Stapley Rd), just s. **Phone:** 480/633-3119

Address: 884 W Warner Rd 85234 **Location:** Jct Cooper Rd; northwest corner. **Phone:** 480/539-8919

SAKANA SUSHI & GRILL   480/218-1023   **36**

♦♦ Sushi. Casual Dining. $8-$34 **AAA Inspector Notes:** With four locations throughout the Valley, this grill serves up some of the freshest sushi around. The menu includes classic sushi and sashimi choices as well as Japanese favorites and full teppanyaki dinners. **Features:** beer & wine, patio dining. **Address:** 1853 S Power Rd 85206 **Location:** US 60 (Superstition Frwy) exit 188 (Power Rd), just s.   L   D

SERRANO'S MEXICAN RESTAURANT

♦♦ Mexican. Casual Dining. $9-$18 **AAA Inspector Notes:** A pleasant stop for lunch or dinner, the local chain is known for consistently good food and attractive, upscale Mexican-style décor. The warm bean dip starter stirs the appetite for traditional dishes such as chiles rellenos or seafood enchiladas prepared with fresh ingredients. Service is friendly. **Bar:** full bar.   L   D

For additional information, visit AAA.com

LOCATIONS:

Address: 1021 S Power Rd 85205 **Location:** Just n of Southern Blvd. **Phone:** 480/854-7455

Address: 1964 E McKellips Rd 85203 **Location:** Northeast corner of Gilbert and McKellips rds. **Phone:** 480/649-3503

⬥GEM MONTEZUMA CASTLE NATIONAL MONUMENT (C-4)

Off I-17 exit 289 on Montezuma Castle Hwy., Montezuma Castle National Monument contains remains of an early cliff dwelling. Built in the 12th and 13th centuries, it is among the best preserved dwellings of its type. The foundation is in a vertical cliff 46 feet above the talus slope. The five-story castle, believed to be inhabited by the Ancestral Puebloan people referred to as the Sinagua, contains 20 rooms and was once accessible only by ladders. Other pueblos dot the cliffs and hilltops around Beaver Creek.

As a preservative measure, tours into Montezuma Castle are not allowed, but a self-guiding trail offers good views of the castle and displays a scale model of its interior. The .34-mile trail is handicap accessible. The visitor center contains artifacts found in the area. Picnicking is permitted in designated areas. Allow 1 hour minimum. Visitor center and monument open daily 8-5. Closed Christmas. Admission $5; free (ages 0-15). Prices may vary; phone ahead. Phone (928) 567-3322, ext. 221.

MONTEZUMA WELL, about 11 mi. n.e., is a detached portion of the monument. The limestone sinkhole, 470 feet wide and more than 55 feet deep, is rimmed by pueblos and cliff dwellings. A source of water to the fields of ancient peoples, some of the ditches dug A.D. 1200-1300 are still visible. A self-guiding trail is available (not recommended for wheelchairs). **Time:** Allow 1 hour minimum. **Hours:** Daily 8-5. **Cost:** Free. **Phone:** (928) 567-4521. ⛩

⬖ MONUMENT VALLEY NAVAJO TRIBAL PARK (A-5)

Reached via scenic US 163, Monument Valley Navajo Tribal Park is a colorful region covering several thousand square miles within the Navajo Indian Reservation. The park contains Mystery Valley, where isolated monoliths of red sandstone tower as much as 1,000 feet above the valley floor.

The visitor center, 4 miles southeast of US 163, provides information about self-guiding tours. Guided tours from the center are offered daily; picnicking is permitted.

Horseback and four-wheel-drive trips through the vicinity can be arranged through agencies in Arizona at Kayenta and in Utah at Bluff, Mexican Hat and Monument Valley. Overnight accommodations also are available in Kayenta, Mexican Hat and Monument Valley; reservations are recommended.

Visitors should not photograph the Navajo people, their homes or their possessions without asking permission; a gratuity is usually requested. Other restrictions apply. For more information contact Monument Valley Navajo Tribal Park, P.O. Box 360289, Monument Valley, UT 84536.

The park is open daily 6 a.m.-8 p.m., May-Sept.; 8-4:30, rest of year (weather permitting). Closed Jan. 1, Thanksgiving and Christmas. Last admission 30 minutes before closing. Recreational vehicles more than 25 feet long and motorcycles are not permitted on the self-guiding tour. A 4-day pass is $20 (per vehicle with 1-4 people; $6 each additional person). Phone (435) 727-5870.

VISITOR CENTER, 4 mi. s.e. of US 163 near the Arizona/Utah border, offers an impressive panorama of the Mitten and Merrick buttes; exhibits about Native Americans; an auditorium; an outdoor amphitheater; a patio; a library; and a Navajo hogan, the traditional housing structure of the Navajo people.

Departing from the center are various guided tours led by Navajo tour operators, who take visitors down into the valley and backcountry. **Time:** Allow 2 hours, 30 minutes minimum. **Hours:** Daily 8-5.

Hours may be extended in summer; phone to confirm schedule. Closed Jan. 1, Thanksgiving and Christmas. **Cost:** Free. **Phone:** (435) 727-5870. ⛩ ⛩

MORMON LAKE

MORMON LAKE LODGE   928/354-2227

fyi Not evaluated. **Address:** 1 Main St 86038 **Location:** I-17 exit 339, 30 mi s of Flagstaff via Lake Mary and Mormon Lake rds; follow brown signs. Facilities, services, and décor characterize an economy property.

MORRISTOWN (H-1) elev. 1,971'

LAKE PLEASANT REGIONAL PARK, 12 mi. e. on SR 74, then 2 mi. n. off Castle Hot Springs Rd., encompasses more than 24,500 acres. A 10-lane boat ramp and a visitor center are available at the main entrance, and a four-lane ramp is at the north entrance. Books, brochures and exhibits about the Central Arizona Project, Waddell Dam and the lake are offered at the visitor center. *See Recreation Areas Chart.*

Hours: Daily 24 hours. **Cost:** $6 (per private vehicle). Watercraft $2-$4 each. Camping $10-$35 (per private vehicle). **Phone:** (928) 501-1710. ⛩ ⛩ ⛩ ⛩ ⛩

Waddell Dam, at the southern end of Lake Pleasant, impounds Lake Pleasant. On the Agua Fria River, the earthen dam completed in 1992 is 4,700 feet long and 300 feet high.

NAVAJOLAND

Encompassing some 27,000 square miles, Navajoland includes parts of Arizona, Utah and New Mexico. Larger than the state of West Virginia, the sovereign nation is the largest Native American nation in the country.

From the stark monoliths of Monument Valley Navajo Tribal Park *(see place listing this page)* and the sheer walls of Canyon de Chelly National Monument *(see place listing p. 44)* to the ancient ruins of Navajo National Monument *(see place listing p. 113)*, Navajoland is home to more than a dozen national monuments. The area also contains the Petrified Forest National Park *(see place listing p. 123)*, 186-mile-long Lake Powell and various tribal parks and historic sites.

Heritage is important to the Navajo, and singing and dancing give the Navajo a chance to wear their traditional attire. Tribal dress includes knee-high moccasins, velvet vests, concho belts and silver and turquoise jewelry for both men and women. Pow-wows often are performed throughout the Navajo nation and visitors are invited to observe.

The Navajo, or Dineh, consider themselves an extension of Mother Earth and therefore treat nature with great respect. Not only rich in culture, the Navajo live in an area rich in minerals; oil, gas, coal and uranium lie beneath the arid desert. The discovery of oil in the 1920s prompted the Navajo to form their own tribal government to help handle the encroachment of mining companies.

Reorganized in 1991, the Navajo government consists of an elected president, vice president and 88 council delegates representing 110 local units of government. Council meetings take place four times a year in Window Rock (see place listing p. 304); visitors are welcome.

Tradition also can be seen in the Navajo's arts and crafts, particularly the distinctive style of their vibrantly-colored rugs and blankets as well silver pieces, basketry and sand paintings. Visitors to the area can purchase Navajo wares at various shops throughout the area.

The following places in Navajoland are listed separately under their individual names: Fort Defiance, Ganado, Kayenta, Keams Canyon, Page, Second Mesa, Tuba City and Window Rock. Visitors should be aware of certain restrictions while in Navajoland; see Good Facts To Know.

Navajo Tourism Department-Navajoland: P.O. Box 663, Window Rock, AZ 86515. **Phone:** (928) 810-8501.

◆ NAVAJO NATIONAL MONUMENT (A-4)

Reached via US 160 and a 9-mile paved road (SR 564), Navajo National Monument preserves some of the largest and most intact of Arizona's known cliff dwellings in perhaps the most awe-inspiring area in the Southwest. There are two areas that can be visited by ranger-guided tours, each of which contains a remarkable 13th-century Pueblo ruin.

The monument lies within the Navajo Indian Reservation. Traveling off paved roads is not permitted. Most of the unmarked dirt-surfaced roads on the reservation are private driveways; private Navajo property is not open to visitors. Visitors should be aware of certain restrictions; see Good Facts To Know.

Free year-round camping and picnicking are permitted near the monument headquarters. The 41 campsites are available on a first-come first-served basis and are usually filled by dusk during the summer; vehicles must be no longer than 30 feet in length. Accommodations are available at Kayenta; reservations are recommended. Gas and grocery services are not available in the park; the nearest services are 9 miles south at the junction of SR 564 and US 160.

Note: In summer the Navajo Reservation observes daylight-saving time, which is an hour later than outside the reservation.

At an elevation of approximately 7,300 feet, the visitor center at the monument headquarters offers exhibits of ancestral Native American artifacts, a 20-minute video tour of the Betatakin ruins, and a 25-minute video about the prehistoric culture. Check for fire restrictions at the campgrounds. Visitor center open daily 8-5, Memorial Day-Labor Day; 9-5, rest of year. Closed Jan. 1, Thanksgiving and Christmas. Free. Phone (928) 672-2700.

BETATAKIN AREA is 2.5 mi. from monument headquarters by way of a strenuous 5-mi. round-trip trail. This is the monument's most accessible area. Ranger-guided tours depart daily at 8:15 a.m. and 10 a.m. from Memorial Day through Labor Day (weather permitting). Hikers should arrive early to ensure a spot on these popular tours. The early tour is limited to 25 people per day on a first-come, first-served basis. The second tour at 10 a.m., which takes a different trail, is limited to 15 people. The cliff dwelling also can be viewed across the canyon from the end of the Sandal Trail year-round via a 1-mile round-trip self-guiding walk.

Note: Sturdy shoes and 2 quarts of water are recommended; the high altitude, heat and steep grade of the trail make good physical condition a requirement. Allow 3-5 hours for tour. **Hours:** Daily 8-5, Memorial Day-Labor Day; 9-5, rest of year. **Cost:** Tour free. **Phone:** (928) 672-2700 for information and schedule updates. GT

KEET SEEL AREA is accessible by hiking a difficult 17-mi. round-trip trail. The area contains the largest and best-preserved cliff dwellings in the vicinity, which date 1250-1300. To protect these fragile ruins there is a daily limit of 20 people.

Note: This trip is not recommended for inexperienced hikers. Hikers are required to attend a trail briefing to receive a permit and are advised to bring sufficient bottled water. Primitive campgrounds are available for hikers. **Hours:** Trail open Memorial Day-Labor Day. Schedules for tours of the ruins vary. **Cost:** Free. Check with rangers at the visitor center for reservations, which can be confirmed 1 week prior. Reservations are required and can be made beginning in January for the year. **Phone:** (928) 672-2700 for reservations, information and schedule updates.

NOGALES (G-4) pop. 20,837, elev. 3,865'
• Hotels p. 114 • Restaurants p. 114

Nogales (noh-GAH-lehs) is rich in history; Franciscan missionary Fray Marcos de Niza entered Santa Cruz County as early as 1539. Hollywood actors made cowboy films in the area during the 1940s.

Mexico's Pacific Highway, a four-lane divided highway, starts in Nogales and continues through Guadalajara, Mexico, with connecting roads to Mexico City. Nogales is a popular port of entry for U.S. travelers as well as for more than 75 percent of winter fruits and vegetables shipped throughout the United States and Canada. Retail and wholesale trade with northern Mexico also is an important industry in the town. Passports are required for visitors planning to cross into Mexico.

Nogales-Santa Cruz County Chamber of Commerce and Visitor Center: 123 W. Kino Park Way, Nogales, AZ 85621. **Phone:** (520) 287-3685.

BEST WESTERN SONORA INN & SUITES

(520)375-6500

Hotel
$121-$201

AAA Benefit: Save 10% or more every day and earn 10% bonus points!

Address: 750 W Shell Rd 85621 **Location:** I-19 exit 4, just w to Frank Reed Rd, then just nw. **Facility:** 65 units. 3 stories, interior corridors. **Terms:** 2 night minimum stay - seasonal and/or weekends, cancellation fee imposed. **Pool(s):** heated outdoor. **Activities:** hot tub, picnic facilities, exercise room. **Guest Services:** valet and coin laundry. **Featured Amenity:** full hot breakfast.

 CALL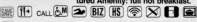

CANDLEWOOD SUITES   (520)281-1111

Extended Stay Hotel $99-$159 **Address:** 875 N Frank Reed Rd 85621 **Location:** I-19 exit 4, just w to Frank Reed Rd, then just nw. **Facility:** 83 efficiencies. 3 stories, interior corridors. **Terms:** cancellation fee imposed. **Activities:** picnic facilities, exercise room. **Guest Services:** valet and coin laundry.

HOLIDAY INN EXPRESS HOTEL NOGALES   (520)281-0123

Hotel $99-$249 **Address:** 850 W Shell Rd 85621 **Location:** I-19 exit 4, just w to Frank Reed Rd, then just nw. **Facility:** 99 units. 3 stories, interior corridors. **Terms:** cancellation fee imposed. **Pool(s):** outdoor. **Activities:** hot tub, bicycles, exercise room. **Guest Services:** valet and coin laundry.

WHERE TO EAT

LAS VIGAS STEAK RANCH   520/287-6641

Mexican Steak. Casual Dining. $8-$22 **AAA Inspector Notes:** A taste of the Old West greets diners in this long-standing Mexican-style steak house just a few blocks from the border. For starters, the queso fundido cannot be beat, and the juicy steaks are grilled to perfection. **Features:** full bar, Sunday brunch. **Address:** 180 W Loma St 85621 **Location:** Downtown. **Parking:** on-site and street. L D

MR. C'S RESTAURANT & SUPPER CLUB   520/281-9000

Steak. Casual Dining. $8-$46 **AAA Inspector Notes:** Classic. Views through tall windows in this hilltop eatery enhance meals that incorporate wonderfully tasty steaks, seafood and pasta, along with a salad bar filled with crispy ingredients. Mexican favorites also are available. **Features:** full bar. **Address:** 282 W View Point Dr 85621 **Location:** I-19 exit 4, 0.7 mi e to W Mastick Way, just s, then just w to top of hill. L D

Visiting Mexico
Personal Safety

Thousands of Americans routinely cross the border into Mexico on a daily basis for business and personal reasons without incident, and crimes directed at tourists are unlikely. The possibility does exist, however, particularly in cities that are centers

of activity for Mexican drug cartels. This violence grabs news headlines and adversely affects the daily lives of many Mexicans.

But for the casual visitor, safety almost always boils down to good old common sense. Stash traveler's checks and cash in different places; for example, in money belts and extra pockets sewn inside clothing. Keep photocopies of passports, credit cards and other documents in a separate place from the originals. Use parking lots or garages whenever possible. Legal parking is designated by a sign showing a red circle with a capital "E" inside; no-parking zones have signs with a diagonal red line through the "E."

Nearby Mexico

NOGALES, SONORA pop. 220,292, elev. 3,674'

Note: For current information about safety/security issues in Nogales, refer to the U.S. State Department website (travel.state.gov).

The border city of Nogales (noh-GAH-lehs) is sometimes referred to as Ambos Nogales ("both Nogales") in recognition of the sister city of Nogales, Ariz. on the other side of the international boundary fence. Established in 1882, the city is not only significantly larger than its U.S. counterpart but also retains a strong sense of Mexican identity.

The gateway into northwestern mainland Mexico and points south is primarily a day visit for tourists. A tourist permit is not needed for in-town stays of less than 72 hours, but proof of citizenship is required.

Mexican and U.S. Customs and Border Protection offices are open 24 hours daily. For southbound motorists, the official immigration checkpoint is 21 kilometers (13 miles) south of Nogales on Mex. 15. You can obtain a tourist permit here if you don't already have one, and must present a federal temporary vehicle importation permit or an "Only Sonora" temporary vehicle importation permit (if you intend to stay within the state of Sonora) and accompanying windshield sticker.

A vehicle permit is not required for travel to the following destinations in the state of Sonora: Rocky Point (Puerto Peñasco), Guaymas, San Carlos, Bahía Kino and other locations west of Mex. 15, as well as cities along Mex. 15 (Magdalena, Santa Ana, Hermosillo). An "Only Sonora" permit is required if driving within Sonora east of Mex. 15 as well as south of Empalme (about 350 miles south of the U.S. border). The permit can be obtained at Banjercito offices in Agua Prieta (opposite Douglas, Ariz.), Cananea (southwest of Agua Prieta on Mex. 2) and Empalme (on Mex. 15 at Km marker 98, just south of the Guaymas bypass).

From Tucson, I-19 south ends at Nogales, Ariz.; signs point the way to the border crossing. Mex. 15 begins at the border, but the downtown Nogales crossing passes through the most congested part of the city. Motorists intending to bypass Nogales for points south can save time by using the international truck crossing, known as the Mariposa crossing; take exit 4 off I-19, then proceed west on SR 189 (Mariposa Road), following signs that say "Border Truck Route" and "International Border." This route reconnects with Mex. 15 south of Nogales at the 21-kilometer (13-mile) immigration checkpoint. The charge at the toll booth approximately 6 miles south of the border is about $2 (U.S.).

If you're driving through downtown Nogales back to the United States, watch for the sign that says "Linea International"; follow the directions for the road that leads to the border crossing.

Since almost all of the tourist-oriented shopping is within easy walking distance of the border, it is recommended that day visitors park on the Arizona side and head into Mexico on foot. From the Nogales-Santa Cruz County Chamber of Commerce and Visitor Center, 123 W. Kino Park Way (just off the intersection of Grand Avenue and US 82) in Nogales, Ariz., it's about a 1.5-mile drive south to a series of guarded lots; all-day parking fees average about $8, and cash is expected. The turnstiles to Mexico are at the foot of the Port of Entry.

Shops and vendor stalls catering to tourists are concentrated along north-south Avenida Obregón. They sell pottery, baskets, fabrics, ceramics, leather goods, glassware, carved pine furniture, rugs, jewelry and more. Most business is conducted in English, bargaining is acceptable and even expected, and American currency is preferred. More exclusive establishments have fixed prices and carry crafts and gift items from all over Mexico. When buying at stalls or from street vendors, always check for quality.

Along with shopping, Nogales offers such standard tourist experiences as having your picture taken astride a donkey and listening to mariachi bands. And like other Mexican border cities, it's a place to get prescriptions filled at a cost that is often far less than stateside.

La Roca Restaurant is just across the border on a side street off Avenida Ruiz Cortines (look for the large magnolia trees in front of the restaurant). Built into the base of a cliff, it has an elegant atmosphere, expert service by white-jacketed waiters and a menu emphasizing Sonoran specialties.

This ends the Nogales section and resumes the alphabetical city listings for Arizona.

ORACLE (F-5) pop. 3,686, elev. 4,513'
• Part of Tucson area — see map p. 256

Oracle is named for the ship which carried the town's founder, Albert Weldon, to the United States in the late 1800s. A local miner, Weldon built a brush camp where the town now stands. Originally a copper mining town, Oracle's present-day economy is based on tourism, electronics and arts and crafts. In the foothills of the Santa Catalina Mountains, 35 miles northeast of Tucson, Oracle's high altitude

provides visitors a respite from the heat of the desert.

UNIVERSITY OF ARIZONA-BIOSPHERE 2, 5 mi. n.e. of jct. SRs 79 and 77 to 32540 S. Biosphere Rd., is a glass and steel structure that encompasses some 3 acres and five biomes: rain forest, ocean, savanna, desert and marsh. The biosphere is a learning, teaching and research center for determining an ecosystem's ability to recycle air, water and nutrients in order to sustain human, plant and animal life.

The guided Under the Glass tour provides visitors a closer look at the interior of the facility, including its rainforest, savanna, ocean, lung and technological systems. The tour begins with a film presentation and includes a walking tour inside the Biosphere 2.

Note: The interior portion of the tour involves ascending and descending 150 steps and is not accessible by wheelchair or baby stroller. Comfortable walking shoes are recommended. **Time:** Allow 2 hours minimum. **Hours:** Daily 9-4. Tours are given daily. Closed Thanksgiving and Christmas. Phone ahead to confirm schedule. **Cost:** $20; $18 (ages 62+ and military with ID); $13 (ages 6-12). **Phone:** (520) 838-6200.

ORGAN PIPE CACTUS NATIONAL MONUMENT (F-2)

In southwestern Arizona, Organ Pipe Cactus National Monument preserves a diverse and relatively undisturbed sample of the Sonoran Desert of particular interest to desert aficionados. The organ pipe cactus thrives within the United States primarily in this 516-square-mile preserve. The spectacular saguaro cacti, along with the paloverde, ironwood and ocotillo, also contribute to the desert landscape.

The monument contains two scenic drives. The 21-mile Ajo Mountain Drive begins near the visitor center, and conditions are generally good for car travel. The drive is closed occasionally because of adverse weather conditions or construction; phone ahead. No trailers or recreational vehicles more than 25 feet are permitted on this park road. A high-clearance vehicle is recommended for the 41-mile Puerto Blanco Loop. Check conditions at the visitor center.

The Kris Eggle Visitor Center, at Milepost 75 on scenic SR 85 (34 miles south of Ajo), is open daily 8:30-4:30; closed Thanksgiving and Christmas. Exhibits interpret the monument's flora, fauna and cultural history. A 15-minute introductory slide program is shown upon request. Ranger-led interpretive programs are offered January through March. Self-guiding interpretive trails are near the visitor center and the campground area ($12 per night).

Admission is by 7-day permit. The cost is $8 per private vehicle. Fees may vary; phone ahead. For further information contact the Superintendent, Organ Pipe Cactus National Monument, 10 Organ Pipe Dr., Ajo, AZ 85321; phone (520) 387-6849.

ORO VALLEY pop. 41,011

- Hotels & Restaurants map & index p. 274
- Part of Tucson area — see map p. 256

FAIRFIELD INN & SUITES BY MARRIOTT TUCSON NORTH/ ORO VALLEY (520)202-4000

 Hotel $96-$197 **Address:** 10150 N Oracle Rd 85737 **Location:** 3.9 mi n of jct Ina Rd. **Facility:** 89 units. 2 stories, interior corridors. **Pool(s):** heated outdoor. **Activities:** hot tub, picnic facilities, exercise room. **Guest Services:** valet and coin laundry.

AAA Benefit:
Members save 5% or more!

HILTON TUCSON EL CONQUISTADOR GOLF & TENNIS RESORT (520)544-5000

Resort Hotel
$89-$299

AAA Benefit:
Members save 5% or more!

Address: 10000 N Oracle Rd 85704 **Location:** I-10 exit 248 (Ina Rd); jct Ina Rd, 4.4 mi n. Located in a quiet area. **Facility:** The large resort, located at the base of Catalina Mountains, has spacious rooms around a landscaped pool area. 428 units, some two bedrooms. 1-3 stories, interior/exterior corridors. **Parking:** on-site and valet. **Terms:** check-in 4 pm, 1-7 night minimum stay, cancellation fee imposed. **Amenities:** safes. **Dining:** 4 restaurants. **Pool(s):** heated outdoor. **Activities:** sauna, hot tub, regulation golf, tennis, bicycles, lawn sports, trails, massage. **Guest Services:** valet and coin laundry, area transportation.

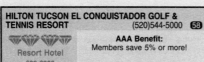

Hilton
HOTELS & RESORTS

Hilton Tucson El Conquistador Resort offers unparalleled service amongst breathtaking mountain views.

HOLIDAY INN EXPRESS HOTEL & SUITES ORO VALLEY-TUCSON NORTH 520/544-2100

 Hotel. Rates not provided. **Address:** 11075 N Oracle Rd 85737 **Location:** 1.8 mi s of Tangerine Rd. **Facility:** 105 units. 3 stories, interior corridors. **Amenities:** safes. **Pool(s):** heated outdoor. **Activities:** hot tub, exercise room. **Guest Services:** valet and coin laundry.

THE CONDOS AT VISTOSO 520/877-7924

(fyi) Not evaluated. **Address:** 655 W Vistoso Highlands Dr 85755 **Location:** Jct Tangerine Rd, 2.2 mi n on Rancho Vistoso Blvd, then just w. Facilities, services, and décor characterize a mid-scale property.

WHERE TO EAT

CAFFE TORINO RISTORANTE ITALIANO 520/219-2994 (79)

Italian. Casual Dining. $9-$24 **AAA Inspector Notes:** This popular spot allows guests to savor an omelet and coffee while enjoying mountain views from the front patio. Lunchtime choices include freshly made salads and hearty panini sandwiches that melt in the mouth. The dinner menu features Italian classics featuring such ingredients as veal, ravioli and gnocchi. **Features:** full bar, patio dining. **Address:** 10325 N La Canada Dr, Suite 151 85739 **Location:** Jct Lambert Ln.

DRAGON VILLAGE RESTAURANT 520/229-0388 (77)

Chinese. Casual Dining. $6-$13 **AAA Inspector Notes:** This casual eatery serves freshly prepared classic meals and healthy foods. The sesame chicken is a local favorite, and soups are hearty and warm. Expect friendly service and large portions at this spot. **Features:** full bar. **Address:** 12152 N Rancho Vistoso Blvd, Suite 180 85737 **Location:** Jct Tangerine Rd; northwest corner.

HARVEST 520/731-1100 (78)

Regional American. Casual Dining. $9-$21 **AAA Inspector Notes:** Sustainable, locally grown and seasonal are some of the words to describe the contemporary American fare at this upscale, modern yet comfortable dining spot. With a menu that changes seasonally, diners can expect fresh, organic offerings like the farmer's market medley of vegetables, empanadas made with local organic beef and tempting homemade desserts such as the chocolate truffle beignets. **Features:** full bar, Sunday brunch. **Reservations:** suggested. **Address:** 10355 N La Canada Dr 85737 **Location:** Southwest corner of La Canada and Rancho Sonora drs.

RUBIO'S FRESH MEXICAN GRILL 520/297-9551

Mexican. Quick Serve. $4-$10 **AAA Inspector Notes:** Freshly prepared and healthful foods, bright decor and friendly staff are found in this upscale fast-food spot. A special treat, the salsa bar lines up four styles and flavors. **Features:** beer only. **Address:** 10509 N Oracle Rd 85739 **Location:** Jct N 1st Ave, just s.

PAGE (A-4) pop. 7,247, elev. 4,281'

Established to provide housing and facilities for workers on the Glen Canyon Dam project, Page was named for John Chatfield Page, the commissioner of reclamation who devoted many years to the development of the upper Colorado River. The town is a center for outfitters who provide trips into Antelope Canyon and the Glen Canyon National Recreation Area *(see place listing p. 75)*.

Scenic flights over Lake Powell and the surrounding Navajo country as well as to the Grand Canyon depart from the Page airport.

Page-Lake Powell Chamber of Commerce: 5 Lake Powell Blvd., Unit #3, P.O. Box 727, Page, AZ 86040. **Phone:** (928) 645-2741.

ANTELOPE CANYON NAVAJO TRIBAL PARK, 1 mi. e. on SR 98, comprises two slot canyons with graceful, swirling red sandstone walls carved by wind and rain over thousands of years. Visitors are driven 3.5 miles to the canyons and must tour the canyons with a licensed guide. Access to Lower Antelope Canyon requires a climb down ladders bolted to the canyon walls. On the Upper Antelope Canyon tour visitors walk right into the canyon.

Time: Allow 1 hour minimum. **Hours:** Entrance fee station daily 8-5, late Mar.-Nov. 30; 9-3, rest of year. Phone ahead to confirm schedule. **Cost:** $8; free (ages 0-7). Guided tour fees vary; phone ahead. **Phone:** (928) 698-2808.

GLEN CANYON NATIONAL RECREATION AREA—see place listing p. 75.

JOHN WESLEY POWELL MEMORIAL MUSEUM AND VISITOR INFORMATION CENTER, Lake Powell Blvd. and N. Navajo Dr., contains exhibits relating to area development, Native American culture, geology, paleontology, the Colorado River and John Wesley Powell, the river's first modern scientist-explorer. The museum staff can book Lake Powell, Colorado River and scenic air tours.

Nearby slot canyons may be viewed by guided tours only; tickets are available at the museum. **Hours:** Mon.-Fri. 9-5, mid-Feb. to mid-Dec. (alsoSat. 9-5, mid-May to mid-Sept.). Closed major holidays. Phone ahead to confirm schedule. **Cost:** $3; $2 (ages 62+); $1 (ages 5-15). **Phone:** (928) 645-9496. GT

AMERICAS BEST VALUE INN   928/645-2858

Motel
Rates not provided

Address: 75 S 7th Ave 86040 **Location:** 1 mi e of US 89 via Loop 89; just n of Lake Powell Blvd. **Facility:** 38 units. 2 stories (no elevator), exterior corridors.

BEST WESTERN PLUS AT LAKE POWELL
(928)645-5988

Hotel
$89-$299

AAA Benefit: Save 10% or more every day and earn 10% bonus points!

Address: 208 N Lake Powell Blvd 86040 **Location:** 0.8 mi e of US 89 via Loop 89. **Facility:** 130 units. 4 stories, interior corridors. **Terms:** check-in 3:30 pm, cancellation fee imposed. **Pool(s):** heated outdoor. **Activities:** hot tub, exercise room. **Guest Services:** coin laundry. **Featured Amenity:** full hot breakfast.

BEST WESTERN VIEW OF LAKE POWELL HOTEL
(928)645-8868

Hotel
$79-$309

AAA Benefit: Save 10% or more every day and earn 10% bonus points!

Address: 716 Rimview Dr 86040 **Location:** 0.7 mi e of US 89 via Loop 89. **Facility:** 102 units. 3 stories, interior corridors. **Bath:** shower only. **Terms:** cancellation fee imposed. **Pool(s):** heated outdoor. **Activities:** hot tub, exercise room. **Featured Amenity:** full hot breakfast.

COMFORT INN & SUITES PAGE LAKE POWELL
(928)645-6931

 Hotel $90-$350 **Address:** 890 Haul Rd 86040 **Location:** Jct US 89, just e. **Facility:** 68 units, some two bedrooms. 3 stories, interior corridors. **Pool(s):** heated indoor. **Activities:** hot tub, exercise room. **Guest Services:** coin laundry.

COURTYARD BY MARRIOTT   (928)645-5000

Hotel
$84-$320

COURTYARD Marriott **AAA Benefit:** Members save 5% or more!

Address: 600 Clubhouse Dr 86040 **Location:** On Loop 89, jct US 89. **Facility:** 153 units. 2-4 stories, interior corridors. **Amenities:** safes. **Dining:** Pepper's, see separate listing. **Pool(s):** heated outdoor. **Activities:** hot tub, exercise room. **Guest Services:** valet and coin laundry.

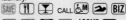

HOLIDAY INN EXPRESS & SUITES PAGE-LAKE POWELL AREA
(928)645-9900

 Hotel $59-$599 **Address:** 643 S Lake Powell Blvd 86040 **Location:** On Loop 89, just e of US 89. **Facility:** 103 units, some two bedrooms. 3 stories, interior corridors. **Terms:** cancellation fee imposed. **Pool(s):** heated outdoor. **Activities:** hot tub, exercise room. **Guest Services:** valet and coin laundry.

LAKE POWELL DAYS INN & SUITES   (928)645-2800

Hotel
$70-$330

Address: 961 N Hwy 89 86040 **Location:** On US 89, just s. **Facility:** 81 units. 3 stories, interior corridors. **Amenities:** safes. **Pool(s):** heated outdoor. **Activities:** hot tub. **Guest Services:** coin laundry. **Featured Amenity:** full hot breakfast.

LAKE POWELL RESORT AND MARINA   928/645-2433

 Resort Hotel. Rates not provided. **Address:** 100 Lakeshore Dr 86040 **Location:** Waterfront. 4 mi n of Glen Canyon Dam via US 89. **Facility:** Located in the Glen Canyon National Recreation Area, this hotel provides direct access to all sorts of water sports on Lake Powell. The rooms are modest with some modern amenities. 348 units. 2 stories (no elevator), interior corridors. **Terms:** check-in 4 pm. **Dining:** 3 restaurants, also, Rainbow Room, see separate listing. **Pool(s):** heated outdoor. **Activities:** sauna, hot tub, marina, exercise room. **Guest Services:** valet laundry, area transportation. *(See ad p. 76.)*

(See ad p. 76.)

 WHERE TO EAT

BLUE BUDDHA SUSHI & TEPPANYAKI   928/645-0007

Japanese
Casual Dining
$8-$38

AAA Inspector Notes: Walking up to the restaurant's hidden entrance, guests would not guess the interior would be so modern and trendy. Once inside diners find a trendy ultra lounge décor and fun Japanese favorites. Some menu items include shrimp tempura, chicken teriyaki, pork dumplings, and, of course, fresh sushi. Specialty sake drinks are a big hit. **Features:** full bar, happy hour. **Address:** 644 N Navajo Dr, Suite G 86040 **Location:** 0.6 mi n of US 89 via Loop 89; in shopping center. D

BONKERS RESTAURANT　　　928/645-2706

American. Casual Dining. $9-$22 **AAA Inspector Notes:** Near downtown, this family-oriented restaurant prepares a variety of American favorites including burgers, Angus beef steaks and Idaho trout. Also offered are some Italian options. Several large murals depicting the area adorn the walls. **Features:** beer & wine, early bird specials, happy hour. **Address:** 810 N Navajo Dr 86040 **Location:** 1 mi s of US 89 via Loop 89, just ne of Lake Powell Blvd. D

THE DAM BAR & GRILLE　　　928/645-2161

American
Casual Dining
$9-$27

AAA Inspector Notes: Located in a small shopping center, this casual, sports-bar restaurant is convenient to other eateries and lodgings. The dining room is separated from the sports bar by a half-wall and hallway. On the menu is a nice selection of steak, chicken, seafood and pasta dishes, as well as an assortment of sandwiches. The staff provides full service in a cordial and attentive fashion. **Features:** full bar, patio dining, happy hour. **Address:** 644 N Navajo Dr, Suite C 86040 **Location:** 0.6 mi n of US 89 via Loop 89. L D

KEN'S OLD WEST RESTAURANT & LOUNGE　928/645-5160

Steak. Casual Dining. $10-$26 **AAA Inspector Notes:** This restaurant features a selection of cooked-to-order steak, seafood and prime rib entrées. Daily, live country and Western music lends an upbeat atmosphere to this rustic, downtown spot near Lake Powell and Glen Canyon National Park. A small salad bar welcomes self-service, and a cordial staff provides assistance. **Features:** full bar. **Address:** 718 Vista Ave 86040 **Location:** 0.8 mi e of US 89 via Loop 89, just n. D

MANDARIN GOURMET CHINESE CUISINE　928/645-5516

Chinese. Casual Dining. $6-$20 **AAA Inspector Notes:** The restaurant offers a variety of traditional Chinese dishes in a casual atmosphere. An extensive buffet is a good lunchtime option. **Address:** 683 S Lake Powell Blvd 86040 **Location:** Jct US 89. L D

PEPPER'S　　　928/645-5000

Southwestern. Casual Dining. $14-$32 **AAA Inspector Notes:** Near Lake Powell, this upscale and comfortable restaurant is enlivened by Southwestern décor and prepares a nice variety of Southwestern and American entrées. Seasonal patio dining is available. Limited self service is complemented by a cordial and attentive staff. **Features:** full bar, patio dining. **Address:** 600 Clubhouse Dr 86040 **Location:** On Loop 89, jct US 89; in Courtyard by Marriott. B D

RAINBOW ROOM　　　928/645-1162

American. Casual Dining. $7-$29 **AAA Inspector Notes:** This dining room affords beautiful views of Lake Powell from every table. The lunch menu offers a selection of sandwiches, salads and entrées with a Southwestern flair. The dinner menu centers on fresh fish and flame-broiled steaks. **Features:** full bar, patio dining. **Address:** 100 Lakeshore Dr 86040 **Location:** 4 mi n of Glen Canyon Dam via US 89; in Lake Powell Resort and Marina. B L D

RANCH HOUSE GRILLE　　　928/645-1420

Breakfast Sandwiches. Casual Dining. $6-$16 **AAA Inspector Notes:** Locals frequent this casual restaurant to satisfy cravings for hearty portions of comfort food. **Address:** 819 N Navajo Dr 86040 **Location:** Jct Loop 89, just n. B L

STROMBOLLI'S ITALIAN RESTAURANT & PIZZERIA
928/645-2605

Italian. Casual Dining. $9-$16 **AAA Inspector Notes:** When in need of a break from the outdoors, stop here for homemade pizza and pasta. The fresh tasting pizza and calzones make up for the casual, no-frills atmosphere. **Features:** beer & wine, patio dining. **Address:** 711 N Navajo Dr 86040 **Location:** 1 mi s of US 89 via Loop 89; just ne of Lake Powell Blvd. L D

PARADISE VALLEY (I-3) pop. 12,820,
elev. 1,340'
• Attractions map p. 138
• Hotels & Restaurants map & index p. 158
• Part of Phoenix area — see map p. 126

COSANTI, 6433 E. Doubletree Ranch Rd., is the studio and workshop of architect-craftsman Paolo Soleri, who came to the area to study with Frank Lloyd Wright. Designated as an Arizona Historic Site, this landmark features experimental earth-formed concrete structures that incorporate terraced landscapes constructed 1956 to 1970. Soleri's prototype urban design, Arcosanti *(see Mayer p. 107)*, is based on his philosophy of arcology (architecture plus ecology). Most weekday mornings, visitors can watch bronze pours. Soleri's sculptures and wind bells can be viewed throughout the property. **Time:** Allow 1 hour minimum. **Hours:** Mon.-Sat. 9-5, Sun. 11-5. Closed major holidays. **Cost:** Free. **Phone:** (480) 948-6145 or (800) 752-3187.

HERMOSA INN　　　602/955-8614　61

Boutique Hotel. Rates not provided. **Address:** 5532 N Palo Cristi Rd 85253 **Location:** 1 mi s of Lincoln Dr; corner of Stanford Dr. Located in a quiet residential area. **Facility:** This historic home of cowboy artist Lon Megargee offers a variety of intimate guest rooms housed in different buildings scattered throughout the beautifully landscaped grounds. 34 units. 1 story, exterior corridors. **Amenities:** safes. **Dining:** Lon's at the Hermosa, see separate listing. **Pool(s):** heated outdoor. **Activities:** hot tub, bicycles, massage. **Guest Services:** valet laundry.

OMNI SCOTTSDALE RESORT & SPA AT MONTELUCIA
480/627-3200　60

Resort Hotel
Rates not provided

Address: 4949 E Lincoln Dr 85253 **Location:** Southeast corner of Lincoln Dr and Tatum Blvd, enter from Lincoln Dr. **Facility:** The resort features large, luxurious guest rooms and baths along with attractive, spacious grounds located at the foot of Camelback Mountain. A man-made cave and waterfall enhance the main pool. 293 units, some two bedrooms. 1-3 stories, interior/exterior corridors. **Parking:** on-site and valet. **Terms:** check-in 4 pm. **Amenities:** safes. **Dining:** 3 restaurants, also, Prado, see separate listing. **Pool(s):** heated outdoor. **Activities:** sauna, hot tub, steamroom, recreation programs, bicycles, lawn sports, spa. **Guest Services:** valet laundry.

(See map & index p. 158.)

SANCTUARY CAMELBACK MOUNTAIN

(480)948-2100 **62**

▼▼▼▼ ▼▼▼▼
Resort Hotel
$339-$829

Address: 5700 E McDonald Dr 85253 **Location:** SR 101 exit McDonald Dr, 3.9 mi w; 1.8 mi w of jct Scottsdale Rd. **Facility:** This quiet retreat offers luxurious rooms and amenities, some with fireplaces and panoramic views. 112 units, some efficiencies, kitchens and houses. 1 story, exterior corridors. **Parking:** on-site and valet. **Terms:** check-in 4 pm, 7 day cancellation notice-fee imposed, resort fee. **Amenities:** safes. **Dining:** Elements, see separate listing. **Pool(s):** heated outdoor. **Activities:** hot tub, steamroom, tennis, recreation programs, bicycles, spa. **Guest Services:** valet laundry.

WHERE TO EAT

EL CHORRO

480/948-5170 **81**

▼▼▼▼ Continental. Fine Dining. $19-$49 **AAA Inspector Notes:** *Classic.* Serving the local area since 1937, this charming restaurant has a nice selection of steaks, lamb and fresh seafood preparations. Complimentary sticky buns are a specialty. Outdoor seating is a pleasant option with mountain views and a warming fireplace for chilly nights. **Features:** full bar, patio dining, Sunday brunch, happy hour. **Reservations:** suggested. **Address:** 5550 E Lincoln Dr 85253 **Location:** 2 mi w of Scottsdale Rd; north side of Lincoln Dr. **Parking:** on-site and valet.

ELEMENTS

480/607-2300 **83**

▼▼▼▼
Fusion
Fine Dining
$16-$45

AAA Inspector Notes: Using local farm-fresh organic vegetables and a wide selection of meat and seafood, chef Beau MacMillan creates Asian-inspired seasonal menus that satisfy the most discerning gourmet. Stunning views of the valley and sunsets enhance the experience. A private chef's tasting room is available. **Features:** full bar, patio dining, Sunday brunch. **Reservations:** suggested. **Address:** 5700 E McDonald Dr 85253 **Location:** SR 101 exit McDonald Dr, 3.9 mi w; 1.8 mi w of jct Scottsdale Rd; in Sanctuary Camelback Mountain. **Parking:** valet only.

LON'S AT THE HERMOSA

602/955-7878 **82**

▼▼▼▼ ▼▼▼▼
American
Fine Dining
$27-$70

AAA Inspector Notes: Coming here for dinner is like returning to the "home ranch" in Arizona territorial days. The excellent menu selection centers on natural and organic foods, some grown on the premises. Choices include seafood, steak and fowl preparations, delivered with casual yet attentive service. **Features:** full bar, patio dining, Sunday brunch, happy hour. **Reservations:** suggested. **Address:** 5532 N Palo Cristi Rd 85253 **Location:** 1 mi s of Lincoln Dr; corner of Stanford Dr; in Hermosa Inn. **Parking:** on-site and valet.

PRADO

480/627-3004 **80**

▼▼▼▼ ▼▼▼▼
Italian
Fine Dining
$13-$30

AAA Inspector Notes: The menu is inspired by old world Europe. Savory, fresh, local ingredients are used with a Mediterranean influence. If weather permits, dine al fresco with a stunning view of Camelback Mountain. **Features:** full bar, patio dining, happy hour. **Reservations:** suggested. **Address:** 4949 E Lincoln Dr 85253 **Location:** Southeast corner of Lincoln Dr and Tatum Blvd, enter from Lincoln Dr; in Omni Scottsdale Resort & Spa at Montelucia. **Parking:** on-site and valet.

PARKER (D-1) pop. 3,083, elev. 1,642'

• Hotels p. 120 • Restaurants p. 120

Parker, founded in 1908, was named for Ely Parker, the first Native American commissioner for the U.S. government. The city originally was south of its current location but was moved to accommodate the Santa Fe Railroad. Parker is a trade center for the surrounding Native American communities and a water recreation destination attracting nearly 1 million visitors each year.

The Parker Dam and Power Plant, 17 miles north on SR 95, is considered the world's deepest because 65 percent of its structural height is below the riverbed. Overlooks on top of the dam provide views of Lake Havasu and the Colorado River. Just north of town on SR 95 is La Paz County Park *(see Recreation Areas Chart).*

Parker Area Chamber of Commerce: 1217 California Ave., Parker, AZ 85344. **Phone:** (928) 669-2174.

BILL WILLIAMS RIVER NATIONAL WILDLIFE REFUGE is off SR 95 (between Mileposts 160 and 161) at the delta of the Bill Williams River at its confluence with Lake Havasu (the Colorado River). A 9-mile corridor along the river encompasses desert riparian and upland habitat. Named after a trapper who explored the area in the 1800s, the 6,000-acre refuge preserves the last remaining flood-regenerated riparian habitat in the Lower Colorado River Valley.

The refuge is home to beavers, bobcats, foxes, mule deer, bighorn sheep, raccoons and 360 species of birds. Fishing and limited hunting are permitted (in season). Camping is prohibited. A high-clearance, four-wheel-drive vehicle is recommended. **Hours:** Office open Mon.-Fri. 8-4. Visitor center Mon.-Fri. 8-4, Sat.-Sun. 9-2. **Cost:** Free. **Phone:** (928) 667-4144.

BUCKSKIN MOUNTAIN STATE PARK, 11 mi. n. off SR 95, is the state's "water playground" on the Colorado River. Activities include hiking, swimming, boating and fishing. River Island State Park offers campsites, a boat ramp and a sandy beach. It is 1 mile north of Buckskin Mountain State Park. *See Recreation Areas Chart.* **Hours:** Daily 9-4:30. **Cost:** $10 (per private vehicle, up to four passengers); $3 (per additional adult passenger in vehicle or individual arriving on foot or bicycle). Camping $30 (per private vehicle). **Phone:** (928) 667-3231, or (520) 586-2283 for camping reservations.

COLORADO RIVER INDIAN TRIBES MUSEUM is at 1007 Arizona Ave. The museum houses the Beebe Brown Basket Collection and historical and modern material about local tribes. **Time:** Allow 1 hour minimum. **Hours:** Mon.-Fri. 8-5, Sat. 10-2, Oct.-Apr. Closed major holidays. **Cost:** Free. **Phone:** (928) 669-8970.

GAMBLING ESTABLISHMENTS

- **Blue Water Resort & Casino,** 1 mi. n.e. on SR 95 to 11300 Resort Dr. **Hours:** Daily 24 hours. **Phone:** (928) 669-7000 or (888) 243-3360.

BEST WESTERN PARKER INN   (928)669-6060

Hotel
$110-$160

AAA Benefit: Save 10% or more every day and earn 10% bonus points!

Address: 1012 Geronimo Ave 85344 **Location:** Jct SR 95, just e. **Facility:** 44 units. 2 stories (no elevator), interior corridors. **Pool(s):** outdoor. **Activities:** picnic facilities, exercise room. **Guest Services:** coin laundry.

BLUE WATER RESORT & CASINO   928/669-7000

Resort Hotel
$60-$260

Address: 11300 Resort Dr 85344 **Location:** Waterfront. Jct SR 62, 1.3 mi nw on SR 95. **Facility:** Attractive rooms with balconies overlooking the marina and Colorado River make for a pleasant vacation or weekend getaway. There are also a movie theater, indoor water slide and video game arcade on site. 200 units. 5 stories, exterior corridors. **Parking:** on-site and valet. **Terms:** 3 day cancellation notice-fee imposed, resort fee. **Dining:** 3 restaurants, also, River Willow Fine Dining, see separate listing. **Pool(s):** heated indoor. **Activities:** hot tub, limited beach access, cabanas, marina, fishing, miniature golf, playground, game room, picnic facilities, exercise room.

WHERE TO EAT

RIVER WILLOW FINE DINING   928/669-7000

Continental
Casual Dining
$18-$36

AAA Inspector Notes: Diners can enjoy a Prime steak, veal topped with crab meat and scallops with pasta all served in a casual yet upscale setting. **Features:** full bar. **Reservations:** suggested. **Address:** 11300 Resort Dr 85344 **Location:** Jct SR 62, 1.3 mi nw on SR 95; in Blue Water Resort & Casino. **Parking:** on-site and valet.

STROKES STEAK HOUSE   928/667-2366

 American. Casual Dining. $10-$45 **AAA Inspector Notes:** A great place to unwind after a day on the river, this family-run establishment offers delicious steaks, seafood and lighter fare served by a friendly staff. Nightly specials include prime rib, corned beef and chicken pot pie. **Features:** full bar, patio dining, happy hour. **Reservations:** suggested. **Address:** 8010 Riverside Dr 85344 **Location:** Jct SR 95, 3 mi ne.

PATAGONIA (G-5) pop. 913, elev. 4,057'

PATAGONIA LAKE STATE PARK, 7 mi. s.w. on SR 82, then 4 mi. w. following signs, is home to southeastern Arizona's largest lake. Bird-watching is a popular activity. Pontoon boat tours are available early October through April. Adjacent to the park is Sonoita Creek State Natural Area, which offers nature hikes and educational programs. *See Recreation Areas Chart.*

Gas, boating, fishing and swimming are available. Jet boats and jet skis are prohibited. **Hours:** Daily 4 a.m.-10 p.m. Phone ahead to confirm schedule. **Cost:** $10-$15 (per private vehicle, up to four passengers); $3 (per additional adult passenger in vehicle or individual arriving on foot or bicycle). Camping $17-$28 (per private vehicle). **Phone:** (520) 287-6965, (520) 287-2791 for pontoon tour information, or (520) 586-2283 for camping reservations.

PATAGONIA-SONOITA CREEK PRESERVE, w. off SR 82 onto 4th St., then 1.7 mi. s. on Pennsylvania Ave., is home to more than 300 species of birds as well as mountain lions, bobcats, deer, javelinas, coyotes and turtles. The preserve also protects the cottonwood-willow riparian forest containing some of the largest and oldest Fremont cottonwood trees in the world. A self-guiding nature trail and a visitor center are available.

Hours: Wed.-Sun. 6:30-4, Apr.-Sept.; 7:30-4, rest of year. Closed Jan. 1, Thanksgiving, day after Thanksgiving and Christmas. **Cost:** $6; free (ages 0-15). **Phone:** (520) 394-2400.

PAYSON (D-4) pop. 15,301, elev. 4,887'

Known by such names as Green Valley, Long Valley, Big Valley and Union City, Payson was first settled by prospectors who came to the area seeking wealth. Payson's mines produced little, and cattle and lumber soon became the community's livelihood. With the help of Senator Payson of Chicago, the early residents helped establish a post office and named it and the town in his honor.

Surrounded by the lakes and dense woodlands of Tonto National Forest *(see place listing p. 251)* and the nearby Mogollon Rim, Payson has become a convenient getaway for visitors, with Phoenix only 90 minutes away.

Rim Country Regional Chamber of Commerce: 100 W. Main St., P.O. Box 1380, Payson, AZ 85547. **Phone:** (928) 474-4515 or (800) 672-9766.

RIM COUNTRY MUSEUM, 1 mi. w. on Main St. from jct. SR 87, then just n. to 700 S. Green Valley Pkwy., is comprised of several historic structures. A replica of the turn-of-the-20th-century Herron Hotel contains exhibits about the ancient cultures that developed around the Mogollon Rim as well as a 1908 kitchen, blacksmith shop and gold mine. Payson's original forest ranger's station and residence, built in 1907, depict the life of the forest ranger. Firefighting equipment also is featured. The 40-acre Green Valley Park neighbors the museum.

Time: Allow 30 minutes minimum. **Hours:** Mon. and Wed.-Sat. 10-4, Sun. 1-4. Closed Jan. 1, hanksgiving and Christmas. **Cost:** (includes admit-ance to the Zane Grey Cabin) $5; $4 (ages 55+); $3 (ges 12-18). **Phone:** (928) 474-3483. 🏛

ane Grey Cabin is at 700 S. Green Valley Pkwy. he replica cabin and the adjoining Rim Country useum house the personal belongings and memo-ibilia of adventurer and "Riders of the Purple age" author Zane Grey. The original cabin was de-royed in the 1990 Dude Fire; exhibits in the mu-eum focus on Grey's literary contributions and areer achievements. Displays also document the story of the Payson community, which Grey fre-uented from 1918-29.

Hours: Mon. and Wed.-Sat. 10-4, Sun. 1-4. losed Jan. 1, Thanksgiving and Christmas. **Cost:** ncludes admittance to the Rim Country Museum) 5; $4 (ages 55+); $3 (ages 12-18). **Phone:** (928) 74-3483. 🏛

ONTO NATURAL BRIDGE STATE PARK, 10 mi. .w. off SR 87, is bordered by Tonto National Forest. he bridge, among the world's largest natural trav-rtine structures, reaches a height of 183 feet; the pening beneath is 150 feet wide and 400 feet long. historic lodge (available for overnight stays) is fur-ished with antiques that were lowered into the anyon using ropes and mules. There are four easily ccessible viewpoints from which to see the bridge; he walk to each is less than a half-mile.

Note: Four trails lead into the canyon; all are steep and difficult for many persons to negotiate. ets are not permitted on canyon trails but are per-itted at viewpoints. **Hours:** Daily 9-5. Last admis-ion 1 hour before closing. Closed Christmas. **Cost:** 5; $2 (ages 7-13). **Phone:** (928) 476-4202. 🗙 🐾 🏛

GAMBLING ESTABLISHMENTS

- **Mazatzal Casino,** .5 mi. s. on SR 87 (Beeline Hwy.) at Milepost 251. **Hours:** Daily 24 hours. **Phone:** (928) 474-6044 or (800) 777-7529.

AMERICAS BEST VALUE INN   (928)474-2283
  🏆 **Motel** $60-$125 **Address:** 811 S Beeline Hwy 85541 **Loc**ation: SR 87, 0.7 mi s of SR 260. **Facility:** 20 units. 1-2 stories (no el-evator), interior/exterior corridors. **Terms:** cancellation fee imposed.

COMFORT INN   (928)472-7484

Hotel
$90-$130

Address: 206 S Beeline Hwy 85541 **Lo**cation: SR 87, just s of SR 260. **Fa**cility: 44 units. 3 stories, interior corridors. **Pool(s):** heated indoor. **Activities:** hot tub. **Guest Services:** coin laundry. **Featured Amenity:** breakfast buffet.

SAVE 🍽 🏊 BIZ 🛜 🗙 🗄

DAYS INN & SUITES   (928)474-9800
🏆🏆🏆
Hotel
$41-$99

Address: 301 S Beeline Hwy Ste A 85541 **Location:** SR 87, just s of SR 260. **Facility:** 48 units. 2 stories (no ele-vator), interior corridors. **Pool(s):** heated indoor. **Activities:** hot tub. **Guest Ser**vices: coin laundry. **Featured Amenity:** continental breakfast.

SAVE 🍽 🏊 BIZ 🛜 🗙 🗄 📠 💻

MAZATZAL HOTEL & CASINO   928/474-6044
🏆🏆🏆 **Hotel** $160 **Address:** Hwy 87, MM 251 85547 **Location:** 1.5 mi s of SR 260. **Facility:** The hotel offers well-appointed rooms with comfortable furnishings and spacious bathrooms with marble and granite accents. 40 units, some two bedrooms. 3 stories, interior corridors. **Terms:** resort fee. **Pool(s):** heated indoor. **Activities:** hot tub, game room, exercise room.
🎰 🍽 🕴 🍸 🏊 BIZ 🛜 🗙 🎥 🗄 💻

QUALITY INN PAYSON   (928)474-3241
🏆🏆 **Hotel** $80-$210 **Address:** 801 N Beeline Hwy 85541 **Lo**cation: SR 87, 0.6 mi n of SR 260. **Facility:** 98 units, some two bed-rooms. 2 stories (no elevator), exterior corridors. **Terms:** check-in 4 pm. **Pool(s):** outdoor. **Activities:** hot tub, exercise room. **Guest Ser**vices: coin laundry.
🍽 🏊 BIZ 🛜 🗙 💻
/ SOME UNITS 🛎 HS 🗄 📠

SUPER 8 INN & SUITES OF PAYSON   (928)474-5241
🏆🏆 **Motel** $70-$150 **Address:** 809 E Hwy 260 85541 **Locatio**n: 0.7 mi e of SR 87. **Facility:** 39 units. 2 stories (no elevator), ex-terior corridors. **Pool(s):** outdoor. **Activities:** hot tub.
🍽 🏊 BIZ 🛜 🗙 🗄 📠 💻

WOODEN NICKEL CABINS   928/478-4519
🏆🏆 **Cabin.** Rates not provided. **Address:** 165 S Hunter Creek Dr 85541 **Location:** SR 87, 22 mi e on SR 260, 0.7 mi n; just w of MM 275, follow signs. **Facility:** 6 units, some efficiencies, kitchens, houses and cabins. 1-2 stories (no elevator), exterior corridors. **Ac**tivities: playground, picnic facilities, trails.
🛜 🗙 🕿 🗄 📠 💻 / SOME UNITS 🛎

WHERE TO EAT

CROSSWINDS RESTAURANT   928/474-1613
🏆🏆 American. Family Dining. $7-$16 **AAA Inspector Notes:** Reservations are suggested for the popular breakfasts, but heartier burgers and fried chicken for lunch also satisfy. Patrons enjoy great views of small planes taking off and landing on the adjacent airstrip. **Features:** Sunday brunch. **Address:** 800 W Airport Rd 85541 **Loca**tion: Jct SR 260, 1.1 mi n on SR 87, then 0.9 mi w.
B L D

FARGO'S STEAKHOUSE   928/474-7455
🏆🏆 Steak. Casual Dining. $14-$31 **AAA Inspector Notes:** The setting here is much like a comfortable lakefront lodge, and the warm welcome from staff starts off a pleasant dining experience. Steaks and seafood may be combined for a hearty meal. **Features:** full bar, patio dining, happy hour. **Address:** 620 E Hwy 260 85541 **Location:** 0.5 mi e of SR 87. L D

GERARDO'S FIREWOOD CAFE   928/468-6500
🏆🏆 Italian. Casual Dining. $11-$24 **AAA Inspector Notes:** The pleasant trattoria-style restaurant serves rustic homemade Italian food. Included on the menu are hand-tossed pizza cooked in wood-burning ovens, panini and traditional pasta preparations. Fish dishes are a favorite of the locals. A salad buffet is offered at lunch. **Fea**tures: full bar, patio dining. **Address:** 512 N Beeline Hwy 85541 **Lo**cation: SR 87, 0.5 mi n of SR 260. L D

MACKY'S GRILL 928/474-7411

 American. Casual Dining. $6-$18 **AAA Inspector Notes:** Diners will feel right at home in this friendly and casual eatery. Grab one of the specialty hamburgers such as the spicy fireside or savory guacamole burger. Relax afterwards and enjoy a slice of homemade pie or cheesecake while chatting with the locals. **Features:** beer & wine, patio dining. **Address:** 201 W Main St 85541 **Location:** Jct SR 87 and 260, 0.7 mi s, just w. L D

PEACH SPRINGS (B-2) pop. 1,090, elev. 4,788'

• Part of Grand Canyon National Park area — see map p. 82

Peach Springs is the trading center and headquarters for the Hualapai Indian Reservation, which covers nearly a million acres between the town and the Colorado River. The town serves as one of the transportation corridors to the western parts of Grand Canyon National Park (see place listing p. 82). Fishing is allowed on the river and at small ponds on the reservation. Primitive camping also is available.

GRAND CANYON CAVERNS, 12 mi. e. of Peach Springs at SR 66 Milepost 115, is reached by a 21-story elevator descent during the 45-minute standard tour or the 3-hour Explorers tour. The temperature is 56 degrees Fahrenheit throughout the year. Nearly a mile of lighted trails highlights colorful mineral formations. An abbreviated tour is available for the physically impaired. A Ghost Walk is held daily after dark; payment must be made before 4 p.m.

Note: Children under 13 are not permitted on the Ghost Walk. **Hours:** Daily 9-5, Mar.-Oct.; 10-4, rest of year. Closed Christmas. **Cost:** Explorers tour $54.95. Standard tour $19.95; $12.95 (ages 5-17). Ghost walk $21.95; $15.95 (ages 13-17). Reservations for Explorers tour are required 72 hours in advance. **Phone:** (928) 422-4565.

GRAND CANYON SKYWALK—see Kingman p. 98.

HUALAPAI LODGE 928/769-2230

Hotel
Rates not provided

Address: 900 Route 66 86434 **Location:** Center. Located near train tracks. **Facility:** 54 units. 2 stories, interior corridors. **Dining:** Diamond Creek Restaurant, see separate listing. **Pool(s):** heated outdoor. **Activities:** hot tub, exercise room. **Guest Services:** coin laundry. **Featured Amenity:** continental breakfast.

SAVE CALL M BIZ

WHERE TO EAT

DIAMOND CREEK RESTAURANT 928/769-2800

Regional American Casual Dining $6-$19

AAA Inspector Notes: Although this restaurant serves traditional American offerings, there are Native American-influenced options as well. Items include a Hualapai taco (a traditional taco served on fry bread), Hualapai stew and an Indian fry bread dessert. Equally loved are the half-pound charbroiled hamburgers, sandwiches, and pizza. The homemade desserts are a huge hit. **Address:** 900 Route 66 86434 **Location:** Center; in Hualapai Lodge. B L D

PEORIA (I-2) pop. 154,065, elev. 1,138'

• Hotels & Restaurants map & index p. 154
• Part of Phoenix area — see map p. 126

SAVE **CHALLENGER SPACE CENTER** is 3.2 mi. on 91st Ave., 1 mi. e. on Lake Pleasant Blvd, then .3 mi. n. to 21170 N. 83rd Ave. An affiliate of the Smithsonian Institution, the center features permanent and temporary space exhibits as well as star gazing events, Lego building workshops, rocket launching events and classes and camps. A highlight is the 2-hour simulated space mission, including launching and docking. The mission control room is based on the design of the Johnson Space Center; the spacecraft simulates a room on the International Space Station.

Time: Allow 1 hour minimum. **Hours:** Mon.-Sat. 10-4. Space missions are held monthly; phone for schedule. Closed Jan. 1, Thanksgiving, Christmas Eve, Christmas and Dec. 31. Other holiday hours vary; phone ahead. **Cost:** $8; $7 (ages 55+ and military with ID); $6 (ages 3-12). Space mission $22.50; $19.50 (ages 10-17 and 55+). Students below sixth grade must be with a ticketed adult on space mission. The space mission Rendezvous with a Comet is not recommended for students below fourth grade. The space mission Voyage to Mars is not recommended for students below sixth grade. Reservations are required for space mission. **Phone** (623) 322-2001.

BLUEGREEN VACATION CIBOLA VISTA RESORT AND SPA, AN ASCEND RESORT COLLECTION MEMBER
623/889-6700

Condominium
Rates not provided

Address: 27501 N Lake Pleasant Pkwy 85383 **Location:** SR 101 exit 16 (Beardsley Rd), 0.5 mi w, then 6.6 mi nw. **Facility:** Tucked into the outer desert foothills of the northwest section of the Valley, this family-oriented resort features large pool areas, an activities center and horseback riding. 248 condominiums. 1-4 stories, interior/exterior corridors. **Terms:** check-in 4 pm. **Amenities:** safes. **Pool(s):** heated outdoor. **Activities:** hot tub, cabanas, tennis, recreation programs, picnic facilities, exercise room, spa. **Guest Services:** complimentary laundry.

SAVE CALL M BIZ

COMFORT SUITES BY CHOICE HOTELS/PEORIA SPORTS COMPLEX (623)334-3993 **13**

 Hotel $79-$209 **Address:** 8473 W Paradise Ln 85382 **Location:** SR 101 exit 14 (Bell Rd), just e to 83rd Ave, just s, then just w. **Facility:** 79 units. 3 stories, interior corridors. **Amenities:** safes. **Pool(s):** heated outdoor. **Activities:** hot tub, picnic facilities, exercise room. **Guest Services:** valet and coin laundry.

BIZ /SOME UNITS

DAYS HOTEL PEORIA GLENDALE AREA (623)979-7200 **19**

 Hotel $53-$113 **Address:** 8955 W Grand Ave 85345 **Location:** SR 101 exit 11 (Grand Ave), 0.5 mi n. **Facility:** 100 units, some efficiencies. 1-2 stories (no elevator), interior corridors. **Pool(s):** heated outdoor. **Activities:** exercise room. **Guest Services:** coin laundry.

BIZ

/SOME UNITS

(See map & index p. 154.)

EXTENDED STAY AMERICA PEORIA   623/487-0020   [18]

▼▼ **Extended Stay Hotel.** Rates not provided. **Address:** 8345 W Bell Rd 85382 **Location:** SR 101 exit 14 (Bell Rd), 1.2 mi e. **Facility:** 101 efficiencies. 3 stories, interior corridors. **Guest Services:** coin laundry.

[icons] /SOME UNITS

HAMPTON INN   (623)486-9918   [17]

▼▼▼ **Hotel** $89-$369 **Address:** 8408 W Paradise Ln 85382 **Location:** SR 101 exit 14 (Bell Rd), just e to 83rd Ave, just s, then just w. Across from Peoria Sports Complex. **Facility:** 112 units. 5 stories, interior corridors. **Terms:** 1-7 night minimum stay, cancellation fee imposed. **Pool(s):** heated outdoor. **Activities:** hot tub, exercise room. **Guest Services:** valet and coin laundry.

| AAA Benefit: |
| Members save up to 10%! |

[icons]

HOLIDAY INN EXPRESS HOTEL & SUITES PEORIA NORTH-GLENDALE   623/853-1313   [14]

▼▼▼ **Hotel.** Rates not provided. **Address:** 16771 N 84th Ave 85382 **Location:** SR 101 exit 14 (Bell Rd), just w, then just s. Located in a busy commercial area. **Facility:** 98 units. 4 stories, interior corridors. **Pool(s):** heated outdoor. **Activities:** exercise room. **Guest Services:** valet and coin laundry.

[icons] /SOME UNITS

LA QUINTA INN & SUITES PHOENIX WEST/PEORIA   (623)487-1900   [15]

▼▼▼ **Hotel** $68-$631 **Address:** 16321 N 83rd Ave 85382 **Location:** SR 101 exit 14 (Bell Rd), just e, then just s. Adjacent to Peoria Sports Complex. **Facility:** 108 units. 5 stories, interior corridors. **Pool(s):** heated outdoor. **Activities:** hot tub, exercise room. **Guest Services:** coin laundry.

[icons] /SOME UNITS

RESIDENCE INN BY MARRIOTT GLENDALE/PEORIA   (623)979-2074   [16]

▼▼▼ **Extended Stay Hotel** $104-$278 **Address:** 8435 W Paradise Ln 85382 **Location:** SR 101 exit 14 (Bell Rd), just e to 83rd Ave, just s, then just w. Across from Peoria Sports Complex. **Facility:** 90 units, some two bedrooms, efficiencies and kitchens. 3 stories, interior corridors. **Pool(s):** heated outdoor. **Activities:** hot tub, picnic facilities, exercise room. **Guest Services:** valet and coin laundry.

| AAA Benefit: |
| Members save 5% or more! |

[icons] /SOME UNITS

WHERE TO EAT

AH-SO STEAK & SUSHI   623/487-8862   [11]

▼▼ **Japanese. Casual Dining.** $7-$38 **AAA Inspector Notes:** Guests can find it all here, from a fresh sushi bar to dining tables to teppan grill tables with chefs ready to put on a show. The menu lists the standard combinations of chicken, steak and seafood along with a large selection of rolls, sushi and sashimi. **Features:** full bar, happy hour. **Address:** 16610 N 75th Ave, Suite 104 85381 **Location:** Just s of Bell Rd. [L] [D]

DILLON'S RESTAURANT   623/979-5353   [12]

▼▼ **American. Casual Dining.** $10-$25 **AAA Inspector Notes:** The barbecue on this restaurant's menu is popular with local folks. Friendly, young servers bring out a selection of grilled meat, poultry and fish dishes along with homemade desserts large enough to share. The attractive decor has a country cottage feel. **Features:** full bar. **Address:** 8706 W Thunderbird Rd 85381 **Location:** SR 101 exit 12, just w. [L] [D]

GOOD CHINA   623/572-8838   [9]

▼▼ ▼▼ **Chinese. Casual Dining.** $8-$17 **AAA Inspector Notes:** Great classics like kung pao chicken and moo goo gai pan are served in this modern setting by friendly servers. Trendy Asian-influenced décor adds to the dining experience. **Features:** full bar. **Address:** 9180 W Union Hills Dr 85382 **Location:** SR 101 exit 15 (Union Hills Dr), 1.4 mi w. [L] [D]

PATSY GRIMALDI'S COAL BRICK-OVEN PIZZERIA   623/486-4455

▼▼ **Pizza. Casual Dining.** $9-$18 **AAA Inspector Notes:** Fresh ingredients and a coal-fired brick oven are the features at this New York style pizzeria. **Features:** beer & wine, patio dining. **Address:** 9788 W Northern Ave, Suite 1440 85345 **Location:** SR 101 N exit 8 (Northern Ave), 0.3 mi w; in Park West Center. [L] [D]

P.F. CHANG'S CHINA BISTRO   623/412-3335   [10]

▼▼▼ **Chinese. Fine Dining.** $8-$25 **AAA Inspector Notes:** Trendy, upscale decor provides a pleasant backdrop for New Age Chinese dining. Appetizers, soups and salads are a meal by themselves. Vegetarian plates and sides, noodles, chow meins, chicken and meat dishes are created from exotic, fresh ingredients. **Features:** full bar, happy hour. **Address:** 16170 N 83rd Ave 85382 **Location:** Just s of Bell Rd. [L] [D]

RUBIO'S FRESH MEXICAN GRILL   623/773-0998

▼ **Mexican. Quick Serve.** $4-$10 **AAA Inspector Notes:** Freshly prepared and healthful foods, bright decor and friendly staff are found in this upscale fast-food spot. A special treat, the salsa bar lines up four styles and flavors. **Features:** beer only. **Address:** 7407 W Bell Rd 85345 **Location:** Jct 75th Ave; southeast corner. [L] [D]

◈GEM PETRIFIED FOREST NATIONAL PARK (C-6)

> Elevations in the park range from 5,300 ft. at the Puerco River to 6,235 ft. at Pilot Rock. Refer to AAA maps for additional elevation information.

East of Holbrook, Petrified Forest National Park contains an abundance of petrified logs. Most of the brilliantly colored trees in the 140,000-acre park are prone, and many are in fragments. Early dinosaurs and other reptiles once roamed the area, and numerous fossil bones and fossil plants have been discovered in the park.

More than 200 million years ago trees clinging to eroding riverbanks fell into streams and were buried in the floodplains. The trees were buried under river sediments in ground water that included volcanic ash rich in silica; a replacement process began to take place. Silica replaced the wood until the logs were virtually turned to stone. Iron oxide and other minerals stained the silica to produce rainbow colors.

In more recent times, the area was uplifted as part of the Colorado Plateau, and erosion exposed some logs; many more probably remain buried to a depth of 300 feet. There are five areas with heavy concentrations of petrified wood in the park: Blue Mesa, Jasper Forest, Crystal Forest, Rainbow Forest (comprising Long Logs and Giant Logs near US 180) and Black Forest. The first four are accessible by the park road. Black Forest, in a designated wilderness area, can be reached from the parking lot at Kachina Point, down a switchback unimproved trail to the desert floor. The Rainbow Forest area contains the most colorful concentration of petrified wood.

General Information and Activities

The park is open daily 8-5; closed Christmas. Hours may vary; phone to confirm schedule.

The 28-mile drive through the park offers breathtaking views of the Painted Desert from Pintado Point and Kachina Point. Other scenic overlooks include Chinde, Nizhoni, Tawa, Tiponi and Whipple points. Petrified logs are common in the southern part of the park.

Westbound motorists on I-40 should use the northern entrance to avoid backtracking. Visitors can view the Painted Desert *(see attraction listing this page)*, ancient pueblos and petroglyphs, petrified log deposits and the Rainbow Forest Museum *(see attraction listing this page)*. Motorists should exit on US 180 and continue west to Holbrook. Eastbound motorists can use the southern (Rainbow Forest) entrance off US 180, 19 miles from Holbrook, to see the same attractions in reverse order, then exit onto I-40 east. Allow 3 hours minimum.

Within the park it is unlawful to gather plants, sand, rocks or specimens of petrified wood of any size whatsoever; archeological and other paleontological material is likewise protected. Violations are punishable by heavy fines and imprisonment. Curio stores sell a variety of polished specimens collected from privately owned land outside the park.

There are no overnight accommodations in the park; backpack camping is allowed by free permit only for hikers staying overnight in one of the park's two designated wilderness areas. Picnic sites are near the Rainbow Forest Museum and on the Painted Desert rim at Chinde Point. Gas, oil and food services are available next to the Painted Desert Visitor Center.

ADMISSION to the park is $20 per private vehicle, $10 per person arriving by other means.

PETS are permitted in the park only if they are leashed, crated or otherwise physically restricted at all times. With the exception of service animals, pets are not permitted in park buildings.

ADDRESS inquiries to the Superintendent, Petrified Forest National Park, P.O. Box 2217, Petrified Forest National Park, AZ 86028; phone (928) 524-6228.

AGATE BRIDGE, at a stopping point on the park road in Petrified Forest National Park, is a nearly 140-foot-long petrified log that spans a 40-foot-wide ravine. **Hours:** Park open daily 8-5. Closed Christmas. Phone ahead to confirm schedule. **Cost:** Included in Petrified Forest National Park admission of $20 per private vehicle; $10 per person arriving by other means. **Phone:** (928) 524-6228.

NEWSPAPER ROCK, via a short side road 1 mi. s. of Puerco Pueblo in Petrified Forest National Park, bears prehistoric petroglyphs that can be viewed through spotting scopes from an overlook. **Hours:** Park open daily 8-5. Hours may be extended Mar.-Sept. Closed Christmas. Phone ahead to confirm schedule. **Cost:** Included in park admission of $1 per private vehicle; $5 per person arriving by other means. **Phone:** (928) 524-6228.

PAINTED DESERT, partially contained i the northern part of Petrified Forest National Park, is an area of colorful badlands that displays variety of hues. Representing more than 200-million-year-old-soil layers and river channels turned re from oxidation of iron minerals and then to stone the desert's colorful erosion effects were create over the millennia by sculpturing from wind an water. Overlooks with an especially scenic view in clude Chinde Point, Kachina Point, Pintado Point Tawa Point and Tiponi Point.

The Painted Desert Visitor Center offers a 20 minute film that explains park resources, including how wood is petrified. **Hours:** Visitor center open daily 8-5. Closed Christmas. Phone ahead to confirm schedule. **Cost:** Free. **Phone:** (928) 524-6228.

PUERCO PUEBLO, s. of the Puerco River in Petrified Forest National Park, is the visible remains of a Native American village that was utilized more than 6 centuries ago. Petroglyphs can be seen along a short (.3-mile), paved loop trail.

RAINBOW FOREST MUSEUM, near the s. entrance of Petrified Forest National Park, contains fossils and exhibits telling the story of the early dinosaurs, giant reptiles and the Triassic forest ecosystem. A 20-minute film explains park resources, including how wood is petrified. **Time:** Allow 30 minutes minimum. **Hours:** Daily 8-5. Phone ahead to confirm schedule. **Cost:** Free. **Phone:** (928) 524-6822.

Phoenix

Then & Now

In Phoenix, if you don't drink plenty of water, a golf stroke is promptly followed by heat stroke. Precious H20. Piped in from the Colorado, Salt and Verde rivers, it's what makes this ultrahot metropolis possible. Lush resorts, posh spas, superb museums and excellent restaurants surrounded by a starkly beautiful landscape, Phoenix is Arizona's big city-vacation oasis.

If your mental picture of Arizona is one of a Marlboro man riding merrily across the saguaro cactus-studded desert, that's here, too. Rising behind the downtown skyscrapers is Camelback Mountain, the go-to spot for desert-style hiking. East of the city, beyond the spill of cookie-cutter suburbs, are the rugged Superstition Mountains.

Of course, from late spring to late summer when daytime temps spike past the century mark for weeks on end, the only hiking you'll be doing is from Nordstrom to Neiman Marcus at the Scottsdale Fashion Square mall. Located about 10 miles northeast of downtown, Scottsdale—with its golf resorts, upscale eateries, hip nightlife and art galleries galore—is the state capital's tourist hot spot.

Downtown Phoenix, which has been spruced up over the past few decades, is where you can see the Arizona Diamondbacks turn double plays in their retractable-roofed stadium, listen to a Brahms concerto at Symphony Hall or watch a Phoenix Suns point guard hit an outside jump shot at Talking Stick Resort Arena (formerly US Airways Center).

The downtown core is loaded with restaurants and lively bars, especially in the streets surrounding the sports venues. But unless you get a charge out of staring up at modern glass-and-steel towers inhabited by the likes of Chase and U.S. Bank, this isn't exactly the stuff of walking tour brochures. A few exceptions include the 1929 Art Deco-style Luhrs Tower (at the corner of First Avenue and Jefferson Street) and Heritage Square, where the city's original Victorian brick buildings house small museums and a pair of popular restaurants.

Greater Phoenix, often maligned for its housing tracts full of stucco schlock, boasts many architectural jewels. Frank Lloyd Wright chose Scottsdale for the site of his gorgeous Taliesin West retreat. Wright also influenced the Mayan textile block design of the Arizona Biltmore Resort & Spa, A Waldorf Astoria Hotel.

In the older neighborhoods surrounding the downtown core you'll drive down broad, sunbaked boulevards lined with ranch-style homes and aging strip

The Phoenix skyline

(Continued on p. 127.)

Destination Phoenix

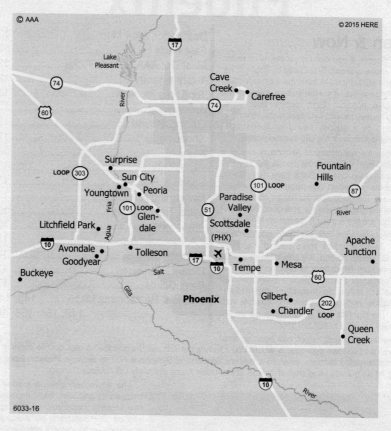

This map shows cities in the Phoenix vicinity where you will find attractions, hotels and restaurants. Cities are listed alphabetically in this book on the following pages.

Fast Facts

ABOUT THE CITY

POP: 1,445,632 ■ **ELEV:** 1,117 ft.

MONEY

SALES TAX: Arizona's statewide sales tax is 5.6 percent; an additional 2 percent is added in Phoenix and an additional 0.7 percent is added in Maricopa County. There is a hotel/motel tax of 12.27 percent. Rental cars incur a 10.3 percent tax, plus an 11.11 percent concession fee. There is a stadium tax of 3.25 percent. Parking at the airport includes a daily surcharge of 4.5 percent.

WHOM TO CALL

EMERGENCY: 911

POLICE (non-emergency): (602) 262-6151

HOSPITALS: Banner Good Samaritan Medical Center, (602) 839-2000 ■ Maryvale Hospital, (623) 848-5000 ■ St. Joseph's Hospital and Medical Center, (602) 406-3000.

WHERE TO LOOK AND LISTEN

NEWSPAPERS: The city's daily newspaper is *The Arizona Republic,* published in the morning.

RADIO: Phoenix radio station KTAR (92.3 FM) is a news/talk/traffic station ■ KJZZ (91.5 FM) is a member of National Public Radio.

VISITOR INFORMATION

Visit Phoenix: 125 N. 2nd St., Suite 120, Phoenix, AZ 85004. **Phone:** (602) 254-6500 or (877) 225-5749. Visit Phoenix distributes the helpful *Official Travel Guide to Greater Phoenix* and *Downtown Phoenix Dining Guide.*

TRANSPORTATION

AIR TRAVEL: Phoenix Sky Harbor International Airport (PHX), 4 miles southeast of downtown, is served by 17 major airlines. SuperShuttle is a 24-hour shared-ride service; phone (602) 244-9000 in metro Phoenix, or (800) 258-3826 outside Arizona. ExecuCar also is available from SuperShuttle; phone (602) 232-4600 or (800) 410-4444.

Airport limousine service, independent of the hotels, costs $40-$90. Some companies that serve the airport and certain downtown hotels are Arizona Limousines, (602) 267-7097 or (800) 678-0033; Carey Limousine, (602) 996-1955 or (800) 336-4646; and Desert Rose Limousine Service, (623) 780-0159 or (800) 716-8660. Cab service to downtown averages 20 minutes and costs an average of $20; traffic delays will increase the drive time and fare.

RENTAL CARS: Several rental car companies serve the Phoenix metropolitan area. At the airport, Hertz, (602) 267-8822 or (800) 654-3080, offers discounts to AAA members.

BUSES: Greyhound Lines Inc. has terminals at 2115 E. Buckeye Rd., (602) 389-4200, and 2647 W. Glendale Ave., (602) 246-0907, (800) 231-2222, or (800) 531-5332 (Spanish).

TAXIS: Taxi companies serving the greater Phoenix area include AAA Yellow Cab, (602) 252-5252 ■ Discount Cab, (602) 200-2000 ■ and VIP Taxi, (602) 300-3000.

PUBLIC TRANSPORTATION: METRO Light Rail connects downtown Phoenix to the neighboring communities of Tempe and Mesa. To reach Sky Harbor International Airport, get off at the station at 44th and Washington streets. From there, the free PHX Sky Train connects to the East Economy parking area and Terminals 3 and 4. At Terminal 4, shuttle buses provide transportation to Terminals 2 and 3.

METRO Light Rail fares are $2 per ride or $4 for an all-day pass; self-serve ticket machines located at all stations accept cash and credit cards. The light rail operates 4:40 a.m.-midnight, with extended hours on Friday and Saturday. More information and printed route maps are available at downtown's Central Station (on Van Buren St. between Central and 1st avenues), or by phoning (602) 253-5000.

(Continued from p. 125.)

malls. In these areas you'll find several outstanding Mexican eateries and a handful of small joints dishing up cheap and tasty Native American food.

The Ancestral Desert People were the first to settle in the Valley of the Sun (as the Phoenix area is known). They built a network of irrigation canals, farmed the beautiful wasteland and created a great city. But around the mid-1400s, they mysteriously vanished. The 1860s saw a new frontier town begin to take shape atop the old site. This rebirth, like the mythical Phoenix rising from the ashes, is what gives the city its name.

Now crisscrossed by a network of wide L.A.-style freeways, the greater metro area is home to some 4.3 million residents, making it the largest city in the desert Southwest.

One reason behind the explosive growth of the past 20 years is that the weather isn't always comparable to an oven set on broil. In the often warm, mild months of late fall, winter and early spring, when D.C. and NYC are bracing for the next "Snowmageddon," Phoenix residents are wearing shorts and reserving tee times.

Must Do: AAA Editor's Picks

- Touch scarlet cactus fruit, marvel at the iridescent wings of hummingbirds and watch butterflies touch down on wildflowers and giant saguaro cacti at the ⇳ **Desert Botanical Garden** (1201 N. Galvin Pkwy.), where you'll find plenty of Sonoran Desert wonders to admire.

- Hike to the summit of Camelback Mountain, the double-humped peak that soars above Paradise Valley and Arcadia. A strenuous trail beginning in **Echo Canyon Recreation Area** (4925 E. McDonald Dr.) is called—for good reason—the "Scenic Stairmaster." This is no casual amble. At the top, scan the spectacular panorama of metropolitan Phoenix and the Sonoran Desert beyond.

- Pamper yourself in one of the spa capitals of the world. Walking through the tranquil lobby of the **Arizona Biltmore, A Waldorf Astoria Resort** (2400 E. Missouri Ave.)—with its architecture inspired by Frank Lloyd Wright—is a great way to begin your luxurious experience. At the spa, tie on a thick robe and delight in a rose quartz facial or a Sonoran stone massage.

- Go power shopping in Scottsdale. In the **Scottsdale Arts District** (7056 E. Main St.) you can browse art galleries galore. Nearby in **Old Town Scottsdale** (3900 N. Scottsdale Rd.)—with its Wild West-themed wooden storefronts—you'll find touristy trinket emporiums and dealers of authentic Native American crafts. Funky clothing boutiques and one-of-a-kind shops line 5th Avenue. And for those addicted to brand-name designer threads, there's the behemoth,

three-story **Scottsdale Fashion Square** mall (7014 E. Camelback Rd.).

- Be a cowpoke for a day and ride a horse throug Sonoran Desert country. In the foothills of **Soutl Mountain Park** (1346 E. South Mountain Ave.) you can trot and canter along more than 40 mile of trails. Hire horses and guides through Ponderosa Stables (10215 S. Central Ave.), or contact the Greater Phoenix Convention and Visitors Bureau.

- Take an art walk on **Roosevelt Row** (1200 E. Roosevelt St.) on the first Friday of every month Galleries and art studios stay open late, and the sidewalks are crowded with families, bohemian hipsters and street performers. This culture clash is a Phoenix rarity.

- "Batter up!" If it's late February or March, catch **spring training** with Major League Baseball's Cactus League. In the autumn, check out the Arizona Fall League, a proving ground for Major League farm teams. Phoenix is a hot place for sports—this is the hometown of the **NBA Suns, NHL Coyotes, NFL Cardinals** and **MLB Diamondbacks.**

- Hear bells at **Cosanti** (6433 E. Doubletree Ranch Rd.) in Paradise Valley. Paolo Soleri, an architect, sculptor and protégé of Frank Lloyd Wright, founded this site to further his organically inspired architecture. An hour north of Phoenix is Soleri's experimental community, **Arcosanti** (13555 S. Cross L Rd.), where you can observe his distinctive spiraling, swooping edifices—there aren't any box-shaped buildings here. Sales from the foundation's renowned wind-bells support the community's structural innovations, and most weekday mornings you can watch foundry workers pour the bronze bells.

Desert Botanical Garden

- Search for the fabled Lost Dutchman Gold Mine in the rugged **Superstition Mountains** east of the city. Even if you don't find the mine (no one has in more than 110 years), the scenery alone is a rich payoff. Stop at **Goldfield Ghost Town & Mine Tours** (4650 N. Mammoth Mine Rd.) for some cheesy Wild West fun. Go hiking in nearby **Lost Dutchman State Park** (6109 N. Apache Tr.). And then drive the windy but incredibly scenic **Apache Trail** road (SR 88) to **Canyon Lake** and beyond (the road is unpaved but suitable for cars).

- Up, up and away—in a **hot air balloon.** From high in the clouds, marvel at the immensity of metro Phoenix and the stark beauty of its desert surroundings. The convention and visitors bureau can provide a list of ballooning companies.

Phoenix 1-day Itinerary

AAA editors suggest these activities for a great short vacation experience. Those staying in the area for a longer visit can access a 3-day itinerary at AAA.com/TravelGuide.

Morning

- Start your trip by communing with nature at the ⚜ **Desert Botanical Garden** (1201 N. Galvin Pkwy.) in 1,200-acre **Papago Park** on the east side of town. This is where visitors really come to understand the majesty of the Sonoran Desert and Phoenix's arid climate. You'll see native and exotic cacti, aloes and other plant species that thrive in desertlike conditions. Take the loop trail leading to the wildflower exhibits. This area is lovely no matter what time of year you visit, but it's bursting with color in March and April.

- Next, drive south in Papago Park and enjoy the scenery—sandstone buttes dramatically jut skyward. Stop at the **Phoenix Zoo** (455 N. Galvin Pkwy.) and meet a Galapagos tortoise, a reticulated giraffe, a Grevy's zebra, a ring-tailed lemur and other heat-loving animals that live in replicas of their own natural habitats. Visitors craving up-close animal encounters can touch stingrays, feed a giraffe or ride a camel.

Arizona Capitol Museum

Afternoon

- For lunch, head west toward downtown, where you'll spend the rest of the day. North of town, inhale a barbecue sandwich or a slab of ribs slathered in a special, spicy tomato-based sauce at **Honey Bear's BBQ** (2824 N. Central Ave.). The tasty side dishes complete the Honey Bear's experience, so try the mac & cheese or the chunky potato salad, and if you love sweet potato fries, this is the place!

- Now duck indoors away from the desert heat at the ⚜ **Heard Museum** (2301 N. Central Ave.) and immerse yourself in Native American culture and arts. Stroll through the museum's 10 exhibit galleries and view baskets, drawings, paintings, photographs, pottery, jewelry, Kachina dolls, sculpture and textiles of the past and present. You can try your hand at bead looming, watch audiovisual presentations and unwind in the serene courtyards. Hit up the Heard Museum Shop on your way out if you're in the market for authentic Native American arts and crafts.

- You can peruse the masters: Boucher, Rodin and Monet. Stop at the ⚜ **Phoenix Art Museum** (1625 N. Central Ave.) for some high art. You'll find more than 17,000 works from many art periods, ancient to contemporary. If you have a passion for high fashion, the Fashion Design collection is a must-see; if architecture and interior design interest you, don't miss the Thorne Miniature Rooms exhibit. Even the kids will enjoy this place—there's a family-friendly, hands-on gallery, and elementary schoolers are given packs stuffed with puzzles and other activities that correspond with art displays.

- A visit to the ⚜ **Arizona Capitol Museum** (1700 W. Washington St.), about 3 miles southwest of the N. Central Avenue museums, will definitely satisfy history buffs who want to learn more about the state's fascinating beginnings. The museum is housed in the old state capitol building, built of tuff stone and granite and capped with a copper dome. Inside you'll explore former government officials' offices and the House and Senate chambers and view all sorts of historical and political memorabilia.

Evening

- For dinner in the area, check out **Pizzeria Bianco** (623 E. Adams St.). It may take awhile to be seated, but the wood-fired oven pizza is worth the wait. When it comes time to order your pie, opt for the Rosa, topped with Parmigiano-Reggiano cheese, red onion, rosemary and Arizona pistachios; or the Wiseguy, which has a tasty combination of fennel sausage, smoked mozzarella and roasted onion on top.

- If you have a hankering for "modern Mexican," head to **Barrio Café** (2814 N. 16th St.). This offbeat joint's chef-owner puts an innovative spin on traditional Mexican dishes like *cochinita pibil* (slow-roasted pork), chicken in mole sauce, tacos and enchiladas. The guacamole, whipped up tableside with fresh avocados, spices and pomegranate seeds, is to die for. Wash it all down with a tequila-infused specialty drink—or, if you dare, *just* tequila. For dessert try the dangerously delectable *churros* (sugar-coated, tube-shaped fritters filled with *cajeta*, a sweet caramel flavoring made from goat's milk).

Top Picks for Kids

Under 13

- Start the day with an fun-filled visit to the **Arizona Science Center** (600 E. Washington St.). Five themed galleries feature more than 300 hands-on exhibits, including a rock-climbing wall and the Evans Family SkyCycle, which allows riders to pedal along a 90-foot cable suspended in midair. There's also an IMAX and a planetarium, giving you enough choices to fill an entire afternoon with educational activities!

- Fans of G.I. Joe and antique dolls alike should head to the **Arizona Doll and Toy Museum** (5847 W. Myrtle Ave.). There are figurines and even a classroom filled with porcelain students. Meanwhile, parents should get a kick out of seeing toys they recognize, such as a rare Vinyl Cape Jawa from "Star Wars."

- At the ▽▽ **Phoenix Art Museum** (1625 N. Central Ave.), kids can frame their art experiences easily; just ask for a children's pack, which includes activities and puzzles sure to capture the imagination and explain a thing or two about art.

- The **Hard Rock Cafe** (3 S. 2nd St.) proves perfect for eating and sightseeing. Order the usual kid-friendly staples and look around. You'll see Justin Timberlake's stage costume from his 'N Sync days, a purple Prince costume and Stevie Nicks' black cloak with silver stitches. Then, after eating, you can always buy a guitar-emblazoned T-shirt or mug.

Teens

- Walk down **Roosevelt Row** (1200 E. Roosevelt St.), the hip heart of the Downtown Arts District. Showcasing galleries, boutiques, restaurants and live music, it's a walkable, artsy epicenter for gathering those hard-to-find objects you never knew you needed. If vintage is your thing, scratch some vinyl at **Revolver Records** (918 N. 2nd St.) or shop at **Annie Boomer Vintage** (908 N. 6th St.), which offers fashion from the 1920s to the 1980s.

- The renowned ▽▽ **Heard Museum** (2301 N. Central Ave.) highlights Native American culture and art. With audiovisual guides and interactive exhibits, you can develop a greater appreciation for the region's culture. You can even step inside a traditional Navajo hogan and think about how different it is from your own home.

- Continue your time-traveling at the **Center for Archaeology & Society: Deer Valley Petroglyph Preserve** (3711 W. Deer Valley Rd.), a 30-minute drive to the Hedgpeth Hills, to see firsthand examples of Native American heritage. More than 1,500 petroglyphs, or carved symbols, cover the black basalt boulders. Walk the quarter-mile Petroglyph Trail, visit the museum to learn about the people and culture behind the petroglyphs or just enjoy the scenery. You may even see roadrunners and coyotes (not necessarily giving chase).

- The nearby **Pioneer Arizona Living History Museum** (3901 W. Pioneer Rd.) adds to the state's story with a pioneer village from the late 19th century. Costumed interpreters fill the old buildings—complete with an opera house, blacksmith shop and jail—with new life by reenacting historical events.

All Ages

- Closer to the airport, there's **Pueblo Grande Museum** (4619 E. Washington St.) with its ruins of a 1,500-year-old Hohokam village. Along with an ancient ball court and platform mound, you'll find an updated theater and galleries, including a hands-on children's section.

- The **Phoenix Zoo** (455 N. Galvin Pkwy.) shows off more than 1,300 animals across 125 acres in the area known as Papago Park. With five trails—or themed areas—explaining the different zoo environments, it offers exhibits for both adults and children. The Children's Trail, for example, displays kid-friendly farming methods and a petting zoo.

- The ▽▽ **Desert Botanical Garden** (1201 N. Galvin Pkwy.) features collections of the growing sort, including Australian, Baja California and South American areas—all artistically arranged. Kids will enjoy following the main trail's discovery stations, while parents will enjoy the photo opportunities along the way.

Visit the Phoenix Zoo

Arriving

By Car

Major highways make Phoenix readily accessible from all directions. The main route from Flagstaff and other points north is I-17, while the main route from the south and southeast is I-10. US 60, coming from the east, joins I-10 just north of Baseline Road.

In Phoenix I-10 intersects I-17 at 20th Street and leads west to Los Angeles. West of Phoenix, SR 85 intersects with I-10 and continues south to Gila Bend; I-8 can then be followed to Yuma and San Diego.

Getting Around

Street System

The streets in Phoenix form an orderly grid. Numbered streets run north and south, intersected by named streets going east and west. The axis is formed by Washington Street, which divides the city north and south, and Central Avenue, which determines the east and west sections. All avenues run west of Central; all streets, east.

Unless otherwise posted the speed limit on most streets is 25 mph. A right turn on red after a complete stop is legal unless otherwise posted. During rush hours the center turn lanes of 7th Avenue and 7th Street are reverse traffic flow lanes: morning rush hour one way into the city and evening rush hour one way out of the city. Try to avoid rush hours, 7-9 a.m. and 4-6 p.m.

Parking

Parking is regulated by meters, which are enforced Mon.-Fri. 8-5, Sat.-Sun. 8 a.m.-10 p.m. (including holidays) with an hourly rate of $1 to $1.50. During business hours and in the downtown area certain one-way streets have restricted parking hours. Rates at public lots start at $1.50 per hour.

Shopping

If your monthly credit card statements read like shopping mall directories, this is your kinda town. The metro Phoenix phone book lists some two dozen major shopping malls.

At the high end is **Biltmore Fashion Park,** 2502 E. Camelback Rd., an open-air affair loaded with budget-busting names like Saks and Ralph Lauren; however, its expansion called **Union** possesses a dozen boutique-style shops such as **Lilly and Framed Ewe** and **Paris Envy** as part of a plan to pair chains and locally owned businesses. **Desert Sky Mall,** west of downtown at 7611 W. Thomas Rd., is more akin to the all-purpose suburban center you'll find back home (think Hot Topic, Sunglass Hut and Orange Julius). Try **Desert Ridge Marketplace,** 21001 N. Tatum Blvd., for an open-air shopping center.

The **Outlets at Anthem,** SR 17 and Anthem Way, are a good 30 minutes north of the city center, but if you're crazy for Ann Taylor and Calvin Klein at cut-rate prices, it's worth the drive.

CityScape Phoenix

In the shadow of office buildings, downtown's open-air **Arizona Center,** at 400 E. Van Buren between 3rd and 5th streets, offers apparel and a handful of tourist souvenir stores. Even if you keep the Visa card holstered, it's worth wandering around the nicely landscaped courtyards and fountains.

CityScape Phoenix, bounded by Washington and Jefferson streets and First Avenue, features an entertainment complex filled with hip dining and shopping options. Plus, after you exercise your buying power, you can get a workout in the on-site gym.

For authentic Native American arts and crafts, there's no topping the **Heard Museum Shop,** 2301 N. Central Ave. From high-quality jewelry and weavings to pottery and Kachina dolls, everything is purchased directly from Native American artists. The shop also stocks an extensive selection of books on the Southwest.

Vintage vinyl LPs are protected from the wax-melting Phoenix heat in the air-conditioned cocoon of **Revolver Records,** 918 N. 2nd St., at the corner of 2nd and Roosevelt streets. In addition to collectible punk, metal, jazz, blues and classic rock platters, you'll also find a wide selection of new and used CDs and DVDs.

The pedestrian-friendly **Roosevelt Row,** Roosevelt Street between 7th Street and Grand Avenue, is the heart of the **Downtown Arts District.** Once a run-down part of town, it's now home to several indie art galleries. If cutting-edge art is your thing, it's a must. If not, stick to Scottsdale *(see p. 200),* where you'll find galleries of all kinds, as well as the valley's best shopping in general.

Nightlife

You'll find most of the valley's nocturnal action in Scottsdale *(see p. 200)* and Tempe *(see p. 243)*, but Phoenix proper is no slouch when it comes to live music, cocktail lounges and casual bars. Pick up the free weekly *Phoenix New Times* for a comprehensive roundup of club and concert listings.

The downtown streets are brimming with sports bars that get wild on big game nights. Located behind **Talking Stick Resort Arena,** and only a few blocks from **Chase Field, Alice Cooper'stown** (owned by the heavy metal shockmeister), 101 E. Jackson St., is loaded with flat-screen TVs, Cooper memorabilia and die-hard D-backs fans. Drinks are cheap and the pub grub menu features the 22-inch "Big Unit" hot dog. Welcome to your nightmare.

Stand Up Live at **CityScape Phoenix** is the latest place to catch top comedy acts in the CityScapes complex. Nearby **Lucky Strike** combines state-of-the-art bowling with an upscale menu and full-service bar-definitely not your daddy's bowling alley.

Everyone knows what to expect from [SAVE] **Hard Rock Cafe,** 3 S. 2nd St., and the Phoenix branch near **Talking Stick Resort Arena** holds no surprises. But it's still a fun spot to grab a pre- or post-game brew. **Majerle's Sports Grill,** 24 N. 2nd St., is owned by ex-Suns great Dan Majerle and draws big crowds during the NBA season.

If suds and ESPN SportsCenter aren't your scene, the city has several classy cocktail bars where you can sip a $12 appletini and chill in style. SoHo meets the Southwest at **MercBar,** 2525 E. Camelback Rd., a dark, sexy lounge across the street from Biltmore Fashion Park. A few minutes northwest of downtown is **SideBar,** 1514 N. 7th Ave., a snug watering hole with swank décor and bartenders who know their business.

Chivas Regal on the rocks is best enjoyed while gazing out at twinkling city lights. The upscale **Jade Bar,** 5700 E. McDonald Dr., obliges with outstanding nighttime views from its lofty locale at the Sanctuary on Camelback Mountain resort.

The Rhythm Room, 1019 E. Indian School Rd., is the place to catch live blues, roots rock and R&B. In the Downtown Arts District, the **Crescent Ballroom,** 308 N. 2nd Ave., hosts live jazz several nights a week. For country music and line dancing, you'll need to saddle up for Scottsdale *(see p. 200).*

Big Events

What are New Year's festivities without college football? Starting in mid-November enjoy a hole-in-one golf tournament and a block party that leads up to the 🏈 **Fiesta Bowl,** held at The University of Phoenix Stadium in **Glendale,** on New Year's Day. The excitement continues the following day with **Phoenix's** annual 🏈 **National Bank of Arizona Fiesta Bowl Parade,** one of the country's largest. It proceeds down Central Avenue and includes marching bands from around the country, gussied-up horses, lavish floats and colorful balloons.

The college football fervor continues just a few days later with the 🏈 **Cactus Bowl** in early January, hosted at Chase Field. The pregame fun includes a party near the stadium with marching bands, pep rallies and live music.

In March, the **Heard Museum Guild Indian Fair and Market** brings together the finest Native American artists in the Southwest. You'll see pottery, carved Kachina dolls, baskets, jewelry, photography and paintings—along with talented musicians, drummers and feather-costumed dancers. Be sure to try the fry bread and posole stew.

The Valley of the Sun knows how to put on a party for Independence Day, and the **Fabulous Phoenix Fourth** lives up to its name. Enjoy live entertainment by local acts, amusement rides, a classic car exhibit and lots of food. The party wraps up with a spectacular fireworks display at Steele Indian School Park.

After a long, sizzling summer the heat finally breaks in October, just in time for the **Arizona Exposition & State Fair.** If you're into livestock shows, carnival games, live tunes, handmade quilts or homemade jellies, you'll love this kind of old-fashioned fun. The grandstand is home to rodeos, a stunt show and a demolition derby. Ride the Ferris wheel, test your aim at the shooting gallery or visit the Home Arts Building to see if you agree with the judges' blue ribbon choices.

The bratwurst's steaming, the accordion's jamming and the tap's open at Tempe's annual **Oktoberfest at Tempe Town Lake.** Knockwurst and

Shop for baskets and pottery at the Indian Fair and Market in March

otato latkes are on the menu, and so is your favorite brew. Sitting is verboten, so boogie to an R&B band, feel irie with a reggae outfit or oompah into the night with polka players.

In December, more than 3.5 million lights transform the **Phoenix Zoo** into a twinkling holiday wonderland. **ZooLights** features fantastic creatures and light sculptures, including an 18-foot-long rattlesnake and a life-size talking giraffe. For holiday shopping, don't miss the **Pueblo Grande Museum Indian Market,** held on the museum grounds. One-of-a-kind crafts by more than 100 top artisans make perfect gifts for friends and family.

From late November to late December you can experience Christmas lights the old-fashioned way at the Desert Botanical Garden's **Las Noches de las Luminarias.** A Southwestern Christmas tradition, luminarias are sand-weighted paper bags holding a candle, and they're typically spaced along walkways and rooflines. In the botanical garden, thousands of luminarias light the paths and cast a radiant glow on beautiful desert flora. Stroll the garden and enjoy musical entertainment, and sip on a glass of wine or warm cider to keep the December chill at bay.

Sports & Rec

Phoenix's mild winters make it an all-year sports paradise. For spectators the winter months mean **horse racing** at Turf Paradise from October through early May; phone (602) 942-1101.

Note: Policies vary concerning admittance of children to pari-mutuel betting facilities. Phone for information.

During **baseball** season the Arizona Diamondbacks, 2001 World Series champs, play at the retractable-roofed Chase Field, 401 E. Jefferson St. in downtown Phoenix; phone (602) 462-6500. Both the Diamondbacks and the Colorado Rockies conduct spring training at Salt River Fields at Talking Stick in Scottsdale; phone (480) 270-5000.

Other teams with spring training sites in the Phoenix area include the Milwaukee Brewers at Maryvale Baseball Park in Phoenix, (800) 933-7890; Oakland Athletics at Hohokam Stadium in Mesa, (480) 644-1466; the Los Angeles Angels of Anaheim at Tempe Diablo Stadium in Tempe, (480) 350-5205; the Kansas City Royals and the Texas Rangers at Surprise Stadium in Surprise, (623) 222-2222; the San Diego Padres and the Seattle Mariners at Peoria Sports Complex in Peoria, (623) 773-8700 or (623) 773-8720; the Los Angeles Dodgers and the Chicago White Sox at Camelback Ranch in Glendale, (623) 302-5000; the Cleveland Indians and the Cincinnati Reds at the Goodyear Ballpark in Goodyear, (623) 882-3120; and the San Francisco Giants at Scottsdale Stadium in Scottsdale, (480) 312-2580; and the Chicago Cubs at Sloan Park (formerly the Cubs Stadium) in Mesa, (480) 668-0500.

Talking Stick Resort Arena (formerly the US Airways Center), 201 E. Jefferson St., is the site of many of Phoenix's sporting events. It is the home

Play golf all year in Arizona

court of the NBA Phoenix Suns **basketball** team November through April; phone (602) 379-7867. The WNBA's Phoenix Mercury take over the arena's court May through August; phone (602) 252-9622. April through August the arena also houses the Arizona Rattlers, Phoenix's professional **arena football** team; phone (480) 985-3292. September through April the Gila River Arena, 9400 W. Maryland Ave., is the home of the Phoenix Coyotes, the city's National **Hockey** League team; phone (480) 563-7825.

Professional **football** is played in Glendale, where the NFL Arizona Cardinals take the field at The University of Phoenix Stadium, 1 Cardinals Dr.; phone (602) 379-0102. The ᗐ Fiesta Bowl football classic at the stadium is a late December highlight.

National Hot Rod Association **drag racing** as well as **dragboat racing** are at Firebird Raceway, about 8 miles south of Phoenix at Maricopa Road and I-10; phone (602) 268-0200. Indy cars, NASCAR **stock cars and trucks,** and Grand Am sports cars race at Phoenix International Raceway; phone (623) 463-5400 *(see attraction listing p. 141).*

Licensed drivers can experience race car driving at Bob Bondurant School of High Performance Driving, I-10 and Maricopa Road; phone (480) 403-7600 or (800) 842-7223.

Play **golf** all year in Arizona. There are more than 300 golf courses in the state, both public and private, appealing to all levels of proficiency. Phone (602) 237-9601 to reserve a tee time at one of six city courses.

Public and private courses include Club West, (480) 460-4400, at 16400 S. 14th Ave.; Encanto,

(602) 253-3963, at 2745 N. 15th Ave.; The Foothills, (480) 460-4653, at 2201 E. Clubhouse Dr.; Maryvale, (623) 846-4022, at 5902 W. Indian School Rd.; Papago, (602) 275-8428, in Papago Park at 5595 E. Moreland St.; The Arizona Grand Golf Resort, (602) 431-6480, at 8000 S. Arizona Grand Pkwy.; Lookout Mountain Golf Club, (602) 866-6356, at 11111 N. 7th St.; and Stonecreek, (602) 953-9110, at 4435 E. Paradise Village Pkwy. S.

Golf courses in nearby Mesa include: Dobson Ranch, (480) 644-2291, at 2155 S. Dobson Rd.; Red Mountain Ranch, (480) 981-6501, at 6425 E. Teton Cir.; and Superstition Springs, (480) 985-5622, at 6542 E. Baseline Rd.

Courses in Scottsdale include: Marriott's Camelback, (480) 596-7050, at 7847 N. Mockingbird Ln.; McCormick Ranch, (480) 948-0260, at 7505 E. McCormick Pkwy.; Starfire at Scottsdale Country Club, (480) 948-6000, at 11500 N. Hayden Rd.; TPC Scottsdale, (480) 585-4334, at 17020 N. Hayden Rd.; and Troon North, (480) 585-5300, at 10320 E. Dynamite Blvd.

Other area courses include: Gold Canyon, (480) 982-9090, at 6100 S. Kings Ranch Rd. in Apache Junction; Hillcrest, (623) 584-1500, at 20002 N. Star Ridge Dr. in Sun City West; The Legend at Arrowhead, (623) 561-1902, at 21027 N. 67th Ave. in Glendale; Ocotillo, (480) 917-6660, at 3751 S. Clubhouse Dr. in Chandler; We-Ko-Pa, (480) 836-9000, at 18200 East Toh Vee Cir. in Fort McDowell; and The Wigwam Resort, (623) 935-3811, at 300 E. Wigwam Blvd. in Litchfield Park. In Tempe are ASU-Karsten, (480) 921-8070, at 1125 E. Rio Salado

Hot air balloon rides

Pkwy.; and Ken McDonald, (480) 350-5250, at 800 E. Divot Dr.

Tennis courts open to the public are plentiful at several high schools and park areas, including Encanto Park, 15th Avenue and Encanto Drive, and Granada Park, 6505 N. 20th St. The Phoenix Tennis Center, (602) 249-3712, at 6330 N. 21st Ave., has 25 lighted courts and reasonable rates; reservations are accepted.

The valley's beautiful desert country lends itself to **horseback riding.** Ponderosa Stables, (602) 268-1261, at 10215 S. Central Ave., offers trail rides.

Trails for **hiking** and **biking** are plentiful. A favorite hike is the 1-mile scenic trek to the summit of Piestewa Peak. Formerly known as Squaw Peak, the peak was renamed in honor of Lori Piestewa, an American servicewoman and Hopi who was killed in combat during Operation Iraqi Freedom in 2003. Hike In Phoenix, LLC *(see Scottsdale p. 202)* offers guided hiking trips along several mountain trails in Phoenix and Scottsdale; phone (877) 445-3749.

The Phoenix Parks and Recreation Department, (602) 534-6587, operates a number of parks; some have municipal **swimming** pools. Saguaro Lake and Canyon Lake *(see Recreation Areas Chart)* offer **water skiing, boating** and **fishing.** The Salt River is popular with **tubing** enthusiasts. Salt River Tubing and Recreation *(see Mesa p. 109)*, (480) 984-3305, rents tubes and also provides shuttle-bus service along the Salt River.

For the **shooting** enthusiast, the Ben Avery Shooting Range, (623) 582-8313, 25 miles north of Phoenix off I-17 exit 223, offers pistol, rifle and archery ranges and trap and skeet fields.

The suburb of Tempe boasts inland **surfing** at Big Surf *(see Tempe p. 245)*, (480) 994-2297; and **ice skating** at the Oceanside Ice Arena, (480) 941-0944, at 1520 N. McClintock Dr.

Hot air balloon rides over the metropolitan area and the Sonora Desert are available through several companies. Balloon rides average 1 hour and are usually followed by a champagne brunch. Many companies operate October through May, but some offer flights year-round. Prices range from $145 to $225 per person. Companies include: Aerogelic Ballooning, (480) 247-7813 or (866) 359-8329; Hot Air Expeditions, (480) 502-6999 or (800) 831-7610; and Unicorn Balloon Co., (480) 991-3666 or (800) 755-0935. **Soaring** is available at Turf Soaring School, (602) 439-3621, at 8700 W. Carefree Hwy. in Peoria.

Performing Arts

Phoenix's rapid growth has been cultural as well as industrial. The following theaters present a mix of classic and contemporary drama: **Herberger Theater Center,** (602) 254-7399, 222 E. Monroe; **Phoenix Theatre,** (602) 254-2151, 100 E. McDowell Rd.; **Greasepaint Youtheatre,** (480) 949-7529, 7020 E. 2nd St. in Scottsdale; and **TheaterWorks,** (623) 815-7930, at 8355 W. Peoria Ave. in Peoria.

Arizona's professional state theater group, the **Arizona Theater Co.**, (602) 256-6995, performs at the **Herberger Theater Center** during its October to June season.

The historic **Orpheum Theatre**, (602) 262-6225, at 203 W. Adams St., was originally built for vaudeville acts and movies in 1929. Scheduled to be condemned, the city bought the theater and in 1997 reopened it as a 1,400-seat performing arts center. Free guided tours of the Spanish Baroque Revival building are available; phone (602) 534-5600.

For music and dance lovers, the **Arizona Opera, Ballet Arizona** and **Phoenix Symphony** offer performances throughout the year. The symphony performs in the striking **Symphony Hall**, Phoenix Civic Plaza, 75 N. Second St.; phone (602) 262-7272.

Cabarets, special concerts, big-name entertainment, shows and lectures are presented at the Herberger Theater Center, (602) 254-7399, 222 E. Monroe; and the **ASU Gammage**, (480) 965-3434, on the campus of Arizona State University at Mill Avenue and Apache Boulevard in Tempe.

Other special performance areas include **Talking Stick Resort Arena**, (602) 379-7800, 201 E. Jefferson St.; **Arizona Veterans Memorial Coliseum**, (602) 252-6771, 1826 W. McDowell Rd.; **Celebrity Theatre**, (602) 267-1600, 440 N. 32nd St.; **Ak-Chin Pavilion**, (602) 254-7200, 2121 N. 83rd Ave.; and the **Comerica Theatre**, (602) 379-2800, 400 W. Washington St. In Mesa are the **Mesa Arts Center**, (480) 644-6500, 1 E. Main St.; and the **Mesa Amphitheater**, (480) 644-2560, 263 N. Center St.

⚑ ATTRACTIONS

ARIZONA CAPITOL MUSEUM is in the Arizona Capitol building at 1700 W. Washington St. The Capitol is built of tuff stone from Kirkland Junction and granite from the Salt River Mountains. Opened in 1901, the four-story building served as the territorial capitol until statehood came in 1912; it then became the state capitol.

The museum, located in the center of the Capitol Complex, is designed to connect Arizonans to their state government and reveals how Arizona was established as a territory, how it transitioned to a state and how the people continue to shape their government after more than 100 years of statehood.

Hours: Mon.-Fri. 9-4 (also Sat. 10-2, Sept.-May). Closed state holidays. Guided tours are available by reservation. **Cost:** Free admission to museum and free parking at Wesley Bolin Park. **Phone:** (602) 926-3620. GT

CENTER FOR ARCHAEOLOGY & SOCIETY: DEER VALLEY PETROGLYPH PRESERVE is off I-17 exit Deer Valley Road W., then 2 mi. w. to 3711 W. Deer Valley Rd. The center consists of a museum, archeological site and 47-acre Sonoran Desert preserve. It has the largest concentration of

Native American petroglyphs in the Phoenix area. A .25-mile trail provides a view of 1,500 hillside petroglyphs made between 500 and 7,000 years ago.

The museum emphasizes preservation, connection and respect for cultural heritage sites and desert environments and is managed by one of the top archeology programs in the country, the School of Human Evolution and Social Change in the College of Liberal Arts and Sciences at Arizona State University.

Time: Allow 1 hour, 30 minutes minimum. **Hours:** Tues.-Sat. 9-5, Oct.-Apr.; Tues.-Sat. 8-2, rest of year. Last admission 30 minutes before closing. Closed Jan. 1, July 4, Thanksgiving and Christmas. Phone ahead to confirm schedule. **Cost:** $7; $4 (ages 62+, military with ID and students with ID); $3 (ages 6-12); free (ages 0-5). **Phone:** (623) 582-8007.

CHASE FIELD is at 401 E. Jefferson St. Opened in 1998, this multipurpose ballpark is home to the Arizona Diamondbacks, the state's first Major League Baseball team. The facility also serves as a venue for other sporting events as well as concerts, temporary exhibitions and trade shows.

A 75-minute guided tour of the Diamondbacks' stadium encompasses the rotunda, a luxury suite, the dugout, and the visiting team's clubhouse or press box. **Hours:** Mon.-Sat. at 9:30, 11 and 12:30. **Cost:** $7; $5 (ages 60+); $3 (ages 4-6). **Phone:** (602) 514-8400. 🚇 3rd St/Jefferson, 16

ECHO CANYON RECREATION AREA, 4925 E. McDonald Dr., is where you will find the trailhead for the 1.3-mile Echo Canyon Trail to the top of 2,704-foot Camelback Mountain, a challenging hike that gains nearly 1,200 feet in elevation. Hikers who reach the summit are treated to excellent views of Phoenix and the surrounding Sonoran Desert.

Note: This extremely popular trail lures large crowds, especially in winter and spring and during weekends. When the parking lot is full, rangers close the entry gate, and cars are not permitted to idle at the gate while waiting for it to be reopened. Dogs are not allowed in the Echo Canyon area. **Hours:** Daily 5:30 a.m.-10. **Cost:** Free. **Phone:** (602) 261-8318, or (602) 534-5867 for Camelback Mountain gatehouse.

ENCANTO PARK, 2605 N. 15th Ave., has a lagoon and islands that serve as a waterfowl refuge; unusual trees and shrubs also can be seen. A children's amusement park with a carousel, train rides and bumper boats is on one of the islands. Tennis, basketball, racquetball and volleyball courts, boat rentals, a swimming pool and nature trails are available. *See Recreation Areas Chart.*

Hours: Daily 5:30 a.m.-11 p.m. **Cost:** Park free. Amusement park ride prices vary; phone ahead. **Phone:** (602) 261-8991, or (602) 261-8443 for sports complex and reservations. 🍴 🎿 🎯 🎪

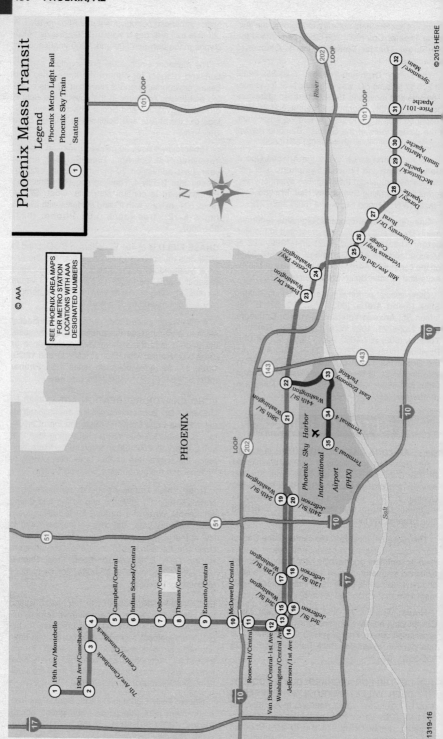

Phoenix Mass Transit

Legend

Phoenix Metro Light Rail

Phoenix Sky Train

① Station

SEE PHOENIX AREA MAPS FOR METRO STATION LOCATIONS WITH AAA DESIGNATED NUMBERS

© AAA

PHOENIX

① 19th Ave/Montebello
② 19th Ave/Camelback
③ 7th Ave/Camelback
④ Central/Camelback
⑤ Campbell/Central
⑥ Indian School/Central
⑦ Osborn/Central
⑧ Thomas/Central
⑨ Encanto/Central
⑩ McDowell/Central
⑪ Roosevelt/Central
⑫ Van Buren/Central-1st Ave
⑬ Washington/Central Ave
⑭ Jefferson/1st Ave
⑮ 3rd St/Washington
⑯ 3rd St/Jefferson
⑰ 12th St/Washington
⑱ 12th St/Jefferson
⑲ 24th St/Washington
⑳ 24th St/Jefferson
㉑ 38th St/Washington
㉒ 44th St/Washington
㉓ Priest Dr/Washington
㉔ Center Pkwy/Washington
㉕ Mill Ave/3rd St
㉖ Veterans Way/College
㉗ University Dr/Rural
㉘ Dorsey/Apache
㉙ McClintock/Apache
㉚ Smith-Martin/Apache
㉛ Price-101/Apache
㉜ Sycamore/Main
㉝ East Economy Parking
㉞ Terminal 4
㉟ Terminal 3

Phoenix Sky Harbor International Airport (PHX)

© 2015 HERE

1319-16

HALL OF FLAME FIRE MUSEUM, 6101 E. Van Buren St., houses one of the largest collections of firefighting equipment dating from 1725. A 10-minute video presentation introduces visitors to the museum's exhibits, which include hand- and horse-drawn pumpers, hook-and-ladder wagons and vehicles dating 1800-1969.

A wildland firefighting gallery explains the history and techniques of fighting wildfires. Other displays include fire marks, helmets, badges, patches, an interactive fire safety exhibit and play area for children, and artwork depicting major events in the history of fire service.

The National Firefighting Hall of Heroes recognizes firefighters who died in the line of duty and were decorated for bravery. **Time:** Allow 2 hours, 30 minutes minimum. **Hours:** Mon.-Sat. 9-5, Sun. noon-4. Closed Jan. 1, Thanksgiving and Christmas. **Cost:** $7; $6 (ages 62+); $5 (ages 6-17); $2 (ages 3-5). **Phone:** (602) 275-3473.

Priest Dr/Washington, 23

HEARD MUSEUM, 2301 N. Central Ave., is a museum of native cultures and art. Among the exhibits in its 12 galleries are contemporary, ethnological and historical materials of Southwestern Native Americans; Native American basketry, jewelry and pottery; and Kachina dolls.

Visitors are greeted with colorful images as they enter the exhibit area. The architecture, foods, culture and spirituality of more than 20 tribes from desert, uplands and the Colorado Plateau regions are examined. Interactive exhibits allow visitors to work on a bead loom and experience re-created geographic settings of Native Americans. Changing exhibits and audiovisual presentations also are featured.

Time: Allow 1 hour minimum. **Hours:** Mon.-Sat. 9:30-5, Sun. 11-5. Guided tours are given daily at noon, 1, 2 and 3. Closed Easter, July 4, Thanksgiving and Christmas. **Cost:** $18; $13.50 (ages 65+); $7.50 (ages 6-12); free (Native Americans). **Phone:** (602) 252-8848 or (602) 252-8840.

GT Encanto/Central, 9

HERITAGE AND SCIENCE PARK is on Monroe St. between 5th and 7th sts. The park includes Heritage Square, comprised of 10 late 19th-century structures that were part of the original site of Phoenix; they contain exhibits, museums and restaurants. The modern Lath House Pavilion serves as a community meeting area, botanical garden and festival site.

Validated parking is available in the garage at Fifth and Monroe sts. **Hours:** Buildings open Wed.-Sat. 10-4, Sun. noon-4, day after Labor Day through mid-Aug. Phone ahead to confirm schedule. **Cost:** Grounds free. Admission fees are charged at some museums and historical buildings. **Parking:** $1-$12. **Phone:** (602) 262-5029.

3rd St/Washington, 15

Arizona Science Center, in Heritage and Science Park at 600 E. Washington St., offers more than 300 hands-on displays that allow visitors to explore such topics as biology, physics, psychology and digital communications in a fun and educational environment. Demonstrations, a rock-climbing wall, a Sky-Cycle ride, an IMAX theater and a planetarium also are featured. **Hours:** Daily 10-5. Closed Thanksgiving and Christmas. **Cost:** $16.95; $14.95 (ages 62+); $11.95 (ages 3-17). Planetarium shows $8; $7 (ages 3-12). IMAX show $9; $8 (ages 3-17). Sky-Cycle ride $5. **Phone:** (602) 716-2000.

3rd St/Jefferson, 16

Rosson House Museum, 113 N. 6th St. in Heritage and Science Park, was built in 1895 for Dr. Roland Lee Rosson, mayor of Phoenix 1895-96. The restored Victorian mansion, constructed in 6 months at a cost of $7,525, features lathe-worked posts on the veranda, pressed-tin ceilings, parquet floors, an elaborately carved staircase and period furnishings. Various events are presented throughout the year.

Hours: Guided tours are given Wed.-Sat. 10-4, Sun. noon-4. Last tour begins 1 hour before closing. Closed major holidays. **Cost:** $7.50; $6.50 (ages 62+, students and military with ID); $4 (ages 6-12). **Phone:** (602) 262-5070.

GT 3rd St/Washington, 15

JAPANESE FRIENDSHIP GARDEN OF PHOENIX is at 1125 N. 3rd Ave. Japanese landscape architects made some 60 visits from Himeji, Japan, Phoenix's sister city, to build an authentic Japanese garden and teahouse. The 3.5 acres of the gardens—known as Ro Ho En—contain 50 desert-tolerant plants, a gazebo, koi pond, pavilion, decorative bridges and a 12-foot waterfall. The name, Ro Ho En, combines the Japanese words for Heron (*Ro*), Himeji's symbol; with *Ho*, for the mythical Phoenix bird; and *En* for garden.

Note: Reservations are required for tea ceremonies. **Hours:** Tues.-Sun. 10-5, Oct.-May. Phone ahead to confirm schedule. **Cost:** $5; $4 (ages 6-17, ages 62+ and military with ID). Public tea ceremony and garden $22; $18 (ages 62+). Guided tour $7. **Phone:** (602) 256-3204, (602) 274-8700 or TTY (602) 262-6713. GT Roosevelt/Central, 11

MUSICAL INSTRUMENT MUSEUM is at 4725 E. Mayo Blvd. The museum boasts an extensive collection of more than 15,000 musical instruments and associated objects, at least 6,000 of which are on display at any given time. Upon arrival you'll don a wireless headset that picks up signals transmitted from each exhibit; as you walk toward an exhibit you'll hear the sounds of the instruments displayed.

In the Orientation Gallery on the ground floor, the exhibit "Guitars. Many Forms, Many Countries" features 22 wall-mounted guitars and 8 displayed on stands, including an 1800 English lute guitar. Just beyond the guitars you'll see a 12-foot tall octobass, a sūrbahār, an alphorn, a saxello, an accordion and

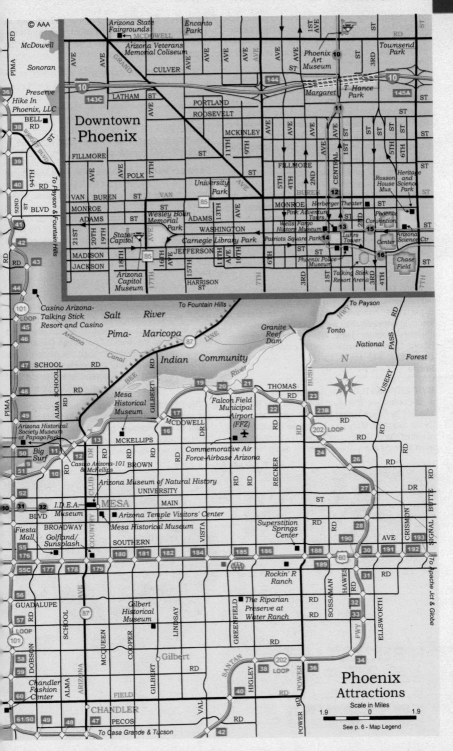

© AAA

McDowell
Sonoran

Preserve
Hike In
Phoenix, LLC

Arizona State Fairgrounds
Arizona Veterans Memorial Coliseum

Encanto Park

Phoenix Art Museum **10**

Townsend Park

CULVER

Downtown Phoenix

LATHAM ST

PORTLAND
ROOSEVELT
MCKINLEY

FILLMORE

POLK

University Park

VAN BUREN ST

MONROE
ADAMS

State Capitol

MADISON
JACKSON

Arizona Capitol Museum

Wesley Bolin Memorial Park

Carnegie Library Park

ADAMS
WASHINGTON
JEFFERSON

HARRISON

Margaret T. Hance Park

11

FILLMORE

MONROE
Pink Adventure Tours **12**
Herberger Theater
Wells Fargo History Museum
Patriots Square Park **14**
Phoenix Police Museum

13 **15**

Luhrs Tower **16**

Rosson House and Science Mus
Heritage and Science Park

Phoenix Convention Center

Arizona Science Ctr

Chase Field

Talking Stick Resort Arena

Casino Arizona-Talking Stick Resort and Casino

Salt   River

Pima-   Maricopa

Indian   Community

Arizona Canal

BEE LINE

Granite Reef Dam

Tonto

National

Forest

N

USERY PASS

Mesa Historical Museum

Arizona Historical Society Museum at Papago Park

Big Surf

Casino Arizona-101 & McKellips

Arizona Museum of Natural History

MESA

I.D.E.A. Museum

Fiesta Mall

Golfland/ Sunsplash

GUADALUPE

Gilbert Historical Museum

Falcon Field Municipal Airport (FFZ)

THOMAS RD

Commemorative Air Force-Airbase Arizona

UNIVERSITY
MAIN

Arizona Temple Visitors' Center
Mesa Historical Museum

BROADWAY
SOUTHERN

Rockin' R Ranch

Superstition Springs Center

The Riparian Preserve at Water Ranch

CHANDLER
PECOS

Chandler Fashion Center

Gilbert

**Phoenix
Attractions**

Scale in Miles
1.9   0   1.9

See p. 6 - Map Legend

To Fountain Hills
To Payson
To Payson & Fountain Hills
To Casa Grande & Tucson
To Apache Jct & Globe

other instruments accompanied by identification plaques that explain each instrument's construction. Upstairs in the Rock and Roll exhibit are a 12-string Rickenbacker 360 (think The Beatles) and a 1978 Ibanez Iceman (think KISS).

You can test your music-making skills in the Experience Gallery, admire instruments donated by or on loan from renowned musicians in the Artist Gallery and view temporary exhibits in the Target Gallery. The Elvis exhibit in the Artist Gallery, done in conjunction with Elvis Presley Enterprises, features a changing array of instruments and artifacts centering on The King.

Upstairs, five galleries are divided almost continentally: Africa and the Middle East, Asia and Oceania, Latin America (including Mexico and the Caribbean), North America (U.S. and Canada) and Europe. Each gallery has displays devoted to the music of individual countries. Asian *dombras* and *dutars* (long-necked lutes), Guatemalan *marimbas*, Tibetan *dungchen* (giant copper trumpets), and an enormous exhibit of Fender guitars are among the many instruments on display.

A 300-seat theater brings live performances and workshops to kids and adults. For a more intimate experience, however, find a musician giving a teaching demonstration as part of the Museum Encounters program. **Time:** Allow 2 hours minimum. **Hours:** Daily 9-5. Phone ahead to confirm schedule. **Cost:** $20; $15 (ages 13-19); $10 (ages 4-12). **Phone:** (480) 478-6000. ⊓

MYSTERY CASTLE, near South Mountain Park, is s. on Central Ave. then e. to 800 E. Mineral Rd. Built 1930-45 by Boyce Luther Gulley as his dream castle for his daughter, Mary Lou, the house is constructed of native stone. Gulley abandoned his family in 1930 upon learning of his illness; after his death his family discovered the castle and Mary Lou moved in. **Time:** Allow 30 minutes minimum. **Hours:** Thurs.-Sun. 11-4, Oct.-May. **Cost:** $10; $5 (ages 5-12). **Phone:** (602) 268-1581.

NORTH MOUNTAIN PARK, 9 mi. n. at 10600 N. 7th St., accesses more than 7,000 acres of the Phoenix Mountains Preserve. The park has various hiking trails, including the Penny Howe Barrier-Free Nature Trail, as well as picnic areas and a playground. **Hours:** Parking lot daily 5 a.m.-7 p.m. Trail 5 a.m.-11 p.m. **Cost:** Free. **Phone:** (602) 495-5458, or (602) 262-7901 (ranger office).

PAPAGO PARK, jct. Galvin Pkwy. and Van Buren St., covers 1,200 acres and features fishing lagoons, bicycle paths, nature trails and picnic areas. There also is a golf course on the park grounds. A popular attraction is Hole-in-the-Rock, a sandstone formation offering good views of the city to the west. Hunt's Tomb, a white pyramid, is the burial place of Governor George Wiley Paul Hunt, Arizona's first governor. **Hours:** Daily 6 a.m.-7 p.m. **Cost:** Free. **Phone:** (602) 495-5458.

Ⓟ Priest Dr/Washington, 23

◥GEM◣ **Desert Botanical Garden,** 1201 N. Galvin Pkwy., covers more than 145 acres in Papago Park. The garden is devoted exclusively to arid land plants of the world. The paved Desert Discovery Trail leads visitors through the garden; other walkways include the Plants and People of the Sonoran Desert Trail, the Sonoran Desert Nature Trail and the Harriet K. Maxwell Desert Wildflower Trail.

The majority of the garden's plants are succulents and include cacti, aloes and century plants. The height of the wildflower blooming season is March through May. Special programs, including bird walks, flashlight tours and children's ecology camps,

▼ See AAA listing p. 202 ▼

are offered. **Time:** Allow 2 hours minimum. **Hours:** Daily 7 a.m.-8 p.m., May-Sept.; 8-8, rest of year. **Cost:** $22; $20 (ages 60+); $12 (ages 13-18 and students with ID); $10 (ages 3-12). Phone ahead to confirm rates. **Phone:** (480) 941-1225.

[SAVE] **Phoenix Zoo,** off N. Galvin Pkwy. in Papago Park, exhibits more than 1,400 mammals, birds and reptiles. The 125-acre zoo features four trails and is home to Southwestern animals, African lions, Sumatran tigers, Bornean orangutans, Asian elephants, Masai giraffes, Komodo dragons and Andean bears. Encounters, tours and experiences include Monkey Village, Stingray Bay, Giraffe Encounter, 4-D Theater, Discovery Farm and the Safari Train. Feel the Difference, an exhibit for the visually impaired, includes life-size sculptures of such animals as elephants, fish and insects. The displays are labeled in Braille.

Time: Allow 2 hours minimum. **Hours:** Daily 7-2, June-Aug.; 9-4 during Zoolights Nov. 4-Jan. 10; 9-5, rest of year. Closed Christmas. Phone ahead to confirm schedule. **Cost:** $20; $14 (ages 3-13). **Phone:** (602) 273-1341.

Priest Dr/Washington, 23

GEM [SAVE] **PHOENIX ART MUSEUM,** 1625 N. Central Ave., features more than 18,000 works of American, European, Asian, Latin American, Western American and contemporary art as well as photography and fashion design. Changing exhibits may include works by such renowned artists as Pablo Picasso, Frida Kahlo, Claude Monet, Kehinde Wiley, Yayoi Kusama and Louisa McElwain. Among the highlights are photography exhibitions from the Center for Creative Photography at the University of Arizona as well as traveling national and international exhibits and the Dorrance Sculpture Garden. Families can enjoy PhxArtKids, an interactive gallery filled with hands-on exhibits. Also featured are the Thorne Miniature Rooms of historic interiors and a collection of works by Arizona artist Philip C. Curtis.

Time: Allow 1 hour minimum. **Hours:** Wed.-Sat. 10-5 (also Wed. 5-9), Sun. noon-5. Closed major holidays. **Cost:** $15; $12 (ages 65+); $10 (full-time college students with ID); $6 (ages 6-17). **Phone:** (602) 257-1880. GT McDowell/Central, 10

PHOENIX INTERNATIONAL RACEWAY is w. off I-10 to exit 131 (Avondale Blvd.), then 5.6 mi. s. to 7602 S. Avondale Blvd. Opened in 1964 at the foot of the Estrella Mountains, the raceway took off in 1988 with the arrival of the NASCAR Sprint Cup Series (formerly NASCAR Winston Cup Series).

Two annual NASCAR Sprint Cup Series weekends are the raceway's main draws. The facility has reserved seats for 76,000. With hillside and infield seating surrounding the 1-mile oval paved racetrack, the raceway can accommodate more than 100,000 fans. **Hours:** Two major race weekends take place

Phoenix International Raceway

in Mar. and Nov. **Phone:** (623) 463-5400 for track information, (866) 408-7223, or TTY (866) 472-8725 for tickets.

PHOENIX POLICE MUSEUM is at 17 S. 2nd Ave. Exhibits include antique police cars, motorcycles, uniforms, guns and badges. The Miranda Rights features photos, a signed confession and other items relating to the case that changed the relationship between law enforcement and suspects in the United States and many places around the world. Other highlights include 1880s and 1930s jail cells, the city's first police helicopter bought in 1973 and a 1919 Ford Model T police car. A memorial room pays tribute to police officers killed in the line of duty. **Time:** Allow 30 minutes minimum. **Hours:** Mon.-Sat. 9-3; closed city holidays. **Cost:** Free. **Phone:** (602) 534-7278. Jefferson/1st Ave, 14

PIONEER ARIZONA LIVING HISTORY MUSEUM is off I-17 exit 225 to 3901 W. Pioneer Rd. More than 26 original and reconstructed buildings, spread over 92 acres, replicate the territorial days of the Southwest 1863-1912. Costumed interpreters re-enact life in territorial Arizona during themed special events held monthly. **Hours:** Wed-Sun 9-4. **Cost:** $9; $8 (ages 55+ and military with ID); $7 (ages 6-18). **Phone:** (623) 465-1052.

PUEBLO GRANDE MUSEUM, 4619 E. Washington St., contains a prehistoric Hohokam village ruin that includes a platform mound, ball court and irrigation canals. Outdoor exhibits include full-size replicas of Hohokam pit houses and adobe compound houses. Interactive museum exhibits center on archeology and the life of the Hohokam. Changing exhibits and tours also are available. Ancient Tech Day is held the second Saturday in March and a Native American market is offered in December.

Time: Allow 1 hour minimum. **Hours:** Mon.-Sat. 9-4:45, Sun. 1-4:45, Oct.-Apr.; Tues.-Sat. 9-4:45, rest of year. Closed Martin Luther King Jr. Day, Memorial Day, July 4, Labor Day, Thanksgiving and Christmas. **Cost:** $6; $5 (ages 55+); $3 (ages 6-17). **Phone:** (602) 495-0901 or (877) 706-4408. 🚇 44th St/Washington, 22

SHEMER ART CENTER AND MUSEUM, 5005 E. Camelback Rd., is in the first house built in the Arcadia section of Phoenix; the house was completed in early 1919. The restored Santa Fe Mission-style building with adobe walls contains changing exhibits of fine art; seasonal classes also are available. A highlight is a walk-through sculpture garden. The landscaped grounds feature creative orchards. **Hours:** Tues.-Sat. 10-3 (also Thurs. 6:30-8:30 p.m.). Closed city and major holidays. Schedule varies seasonally; phone ahead. **Cost:** Donations. A fee is charged for special shows. **Phone:** (602) 262-4727.

SOUTH MOUNTAIN PARK, 8 mi. s. at 10919 S. Central Ave., contains more than 16,000 acres of peaks, canyons and strange rock formations as well as native Arizona flora. The park also features Native American petroglyphs. There are some 50 miles of trails for hiking, horseback riding and mountain biking. Dobbins Lookout, accessible by road and trail, affords an excellent view. The Pima Canyon park entrance (9904 S. 4th St.) offers convenient access to many of the hiking trails. **Hours:** Parking lot open daily 5 a.m.-7 p.m. Trails close at 11 p.m. **Cost:** Free. **Phone:** (602) 495-5458. 🐾 🏕

WELLS FARGO HISTORY MUSEUM is at 145 W. Adams St. Exhibits portray Arizona stagecoach history beginning in the mid-1850s. An 1860 stagecoach and Western art by such artists as Frederic Remington and N.C. Wyeth are on display. **Time:** Allow 1 hour

minimum. **Hours:** Mon.-Fri. 9-5. **Cost:** Free. **Phone:** (602) 378-1852. 🚇 Jefferson/1st Ave, 14

THE WRIGLEY MANSION is at 2501 E. Telawa Tr. Completed in 1932, the Mediterranean-style mansion was built by chewing-gum magnate William Wrigley Jr. as a 50th wedding anniversary gift for his wife, Ada. Guided tours of the house provide a glimpse into the family's history. **Time:** Allow 1 hour minimum. **Hours:** Guided tours are given Tues.-Sat. at 10, noon, 1 and 3, Sun. at 2:15, mid-Sept. to mid-June. Closed Jan. 1 and Christmas. **Cost:** $15 (plus $5 private club membership). Reservations are required. **Phone:** (602) 955-4079. 🄶🅃

Sightseeing
Bus, Four-wheel-drive and Van Tours

A tour is the best way to get an overall view of the city. Several companies offer four-wheel-drive or van tours of the desert: Open Road Tours, (602) 997-6474 or (800) 766-7117; Vaughan's Southwest Custom Tours, (602) 971-1381 or (800) 513-1381; and Wayward Wind Tours Inc., (602) 867-7825 or (800) 804-0480.

PINK ADVENTURE TOURS picks up passengers at most metro Phoenix area hotels. The tour provider offers a variety of off-road excursions through the Sonoran Desert characterized by beautiful mountain scenery, rocky creek beds and diverse plant life, including saguaro and cholla cactuses and ocotillo. Professional tour guides narrate the drive, describing local history as well as the area's plant and animal life. Day trips to the Grand Canyon and Sedona also are offered. **Time:** Allow 2 hours minimum. **Hours:** Tours depart daily 7 a.m.-dusk. Closed Christmas. **Cost:** $84; $63 (ages 3-12). Children under 3 are not permitted. Reservations are required. **Phone:** (855) 298-3070. 🄶🅃 🚇 Washington/Central Ave, 13

Plane Tours

Westwind Air Service provides scenic tours of the Grand Canyon. For flight arrangements phone (480) 991-5557 or (888) 869-0866.

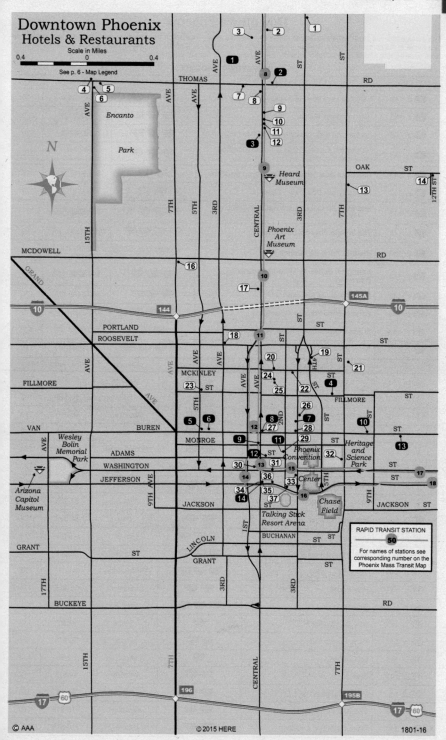

Downtown Phoenix

This index helps you "spot" where approved hotels and restaurants are located on the corresponding detailed maps. Hotel daily rate range is for comparison only. Restaurant price range is a combination of lunch and/or dinner. Turn to the listing page for more detailed rate and price information and consult display ads for special promotions.

DOWNTOWN PHOENIX

Map Page	Hotels	Diamond Rated	Rate Range	Page
1 p. 143	Hampton Inn-Phoenix/Midtown (Downtown Area)	◆◆◆	$99-$259	170
2 p. 143	Hilton Phoenix Suites	◆◆◆	$89-$289	170
3 p. 143	Fairfield Inn & Suites by Marriott Phoenix Midtown	◆◆◆	$92-$263	170
4 p. 143	Holiday Inn Express Hotel & Suites- Downtown Ball Park	◆◆◆	Rates not provided	170
5 p. 143	**Americas Best Value Inn-Downtown Phoenix**	◆◆	$59-$169 SAVE	170
6 p. 143	**Rodeway Inn Downtown Phoenix**	◆◆	$55-$110 SAVE	170
7 p. 143	**Sheraton Phoenix Downtown Hotel** *(See ad p. 171.)*	◆◆◆	$99-$500 SAVE	171
8 p. 143	**The Westin Phoenix Downtown**	◆◆◆	$109-$399 SAVE	172
9 p. 143	**Historic Hotel San Carlos**	◆◆	Rates not provided SAVE	170
10 p. 143	**SpringHill Suites by Marriott Phoenix Downtown**	◆◆◆	$94-$280 SAVE	171
11 p. 143	**Hyatt Regency Phoenix**	◆◆◆	$99-$499 SAVE	170
12 p. 143	**Renaissance Phoenix Downtown**	◆◆◆	$124-$364 SAVE	170
13 p. 143	**Super 8-Downtown Phoenix/Convention Center**	◆◆	$70-$150 SAVE	172
14 p. 143	Hotel Palomar Phoenix-CityScape	◆◆◆◆	$119-$439	170

Map Page	Restaurants	Diamond Rated	Cuisine	Price Range	Page
① p. 143	China Chili	◆◆	Chinese	$7-$26	172
② p. 143	Duck and Decanter	◆	Deli	$6-$10	173
③ p. 143	The Good Egg	◆◆	American	$6-$10	173
④ p. 143	Mu Shu Asian Grill	◆◆	Asian	$9-$17	173
⑤ p. 143	Persian Garden Café	◆◆	Middle Eastern	$10-$35	173
⑥ p. 143	The Original Hamburger Works	◆	American	$4-$7	173
⑦ p. 143	Pino's Pizza Al Centro	◆◆	Italian	$6-$17	174
⑧ p. 143	Honey Bear's BBQ	◆	Barbecue	$7-$25	173
⑨ p. 143	**The Wild Thaiger**	◆◆	Thai	$8-$22	174
⑩ p. 143	**Durant's**	◆◆◆	Steak	$14-$64	173
⑪ p. 143	Switch Restaurant & Wine Bar	◆◆◆	Comfort Food	$9-$25	174
⑫ p. 143	Corduroy	◆◆◆	Small Plates	$11-$17	172
⑬ p. 143	Rice Paper	◆◆	Vietnamese	$8-$16	174
⑭ p. 143	Tuck Shop	◆◆	Comfort Food	$10-$35	174
⑯ p. 143	How Do You Roll?	◆	Sushi	$4-$7	173
⑰ p. 143	Pizza People Pub	◆◆	Pizza	$8-$15	174
⑱ p. 143	Lola Coffee	◆	Coffee/Tea	$2-$6	173
⑲ p. 143	Bliss	◆◆	American	$9-$17	172
⑳ p. 143	Matt's Big Breakfast	◆◆	American	$5-$9	173
㉑ p. 143	Mother Bunch Brewing	◆◆	American	$10-$15	173
㉒ p. 143	Moira Sushi Bar & Kitchen	◆◆	Japanese	$10-$15	173

Map Page	Restaurants (cont'd)	Diamond Rated	Cuisine	Price Range	Page
㉓ p. 143	Cibo Urban Pizzeria Cafe	▼▼	Italian	$9-$17	172
㉔ p. 143	Pomo Pizzeria Napoletana	▼▼	Italian	$10-$17	174
㉕ p. 143	The Breadfruit Authentic Jamaican Grill	▼▼	Jamaican	$9-$28	172
㉖ p. 143	Sam's Cafe at the Arizona Center	▼▼	Southwestern	$9-$21	174
㉗ p. 143	Province Urban Kitchen & Bar	▼▼▼	American	$18-$35	174
㉘ p. 143	District American Kitchen & Wine Bar *(See ad p. 171.)*	▼▼▼	American	$9-$24	173
㉙ p. 143	Compass Arizona Grill	▼▼▼	American	$27-$40	172
㉚ p. 143	Tom's Tavern & 1929 Grill	▼▼	American	$11-$23	174
㉛ p. 143	Duck and Decanter	▼	Deli	$6-$10	173
㉜ p. 143	Pizzeria Bianco	▼▼	Pizza	$13-$18	174
㉝ p. 143	Kincaid's Fish, Chop & Steak House	▼▼▼	Steak Seafood	$17-$49	173
㉞ p. 143	Blue Hound Kitchen & Cocktails	▼▼▼	American	$10-$36	172
㉟ p. 143	The Breakfast Club	▼▼	American	$6-$14	172
㊱ p. 143	The Arrogant Butcher	▼▼▼	American	$12-$34	172
㊲ p. 143	Hard Rock Cafe	▼▼	American	$9-$21 [SAVE]	173

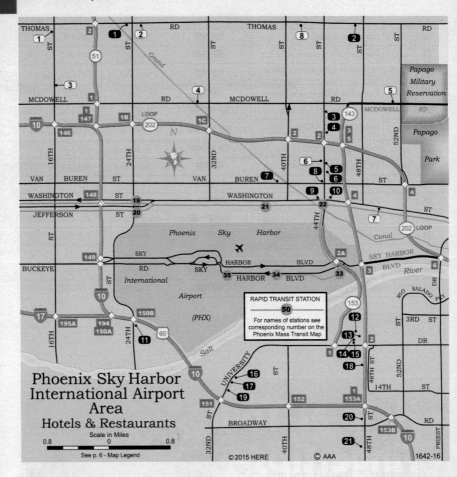

Phoenix Sky Harbor
International Airport
Area
Hotels & Restaurants

Scale in Miles
0.8   0   0.8

See p. 6 - Map Legend

RAPID TRANSIT STATION
50
For names of stations see
corresponding number on the
Phoenix Mass Transit Map

© 2015 HERE   © AAA   1642-16

✈ Airport Hotels

Map Page	PHOENIX SKY HARBOR INTERNATIONAL (Maximum driving distance from airport: 4.6 mi)	Diamond Rated	Rate Range	Page
10 p. 146	Aloft Phoenix Airport Hotel, 2.6 mi	◈◈◈	Rates not provided [SAVE]	175
11 p. 146	BEST WESTERN Airport Inn, 2.9 mi	◈◈	$70-$180 [SAVE]	175
14 p. 146	Courtyard by Marriott Phoenix Airport, 3.0 mi	◈◈◈	$80-$301 [SAVE]	176
9 p. 146	Crowne Plaza Phoenix Airport, 2.4 mi	◈◈◈	$79-$249 [SAVE]	176
8 p. 146	DoubleTree Suites by Hilton Phoenix, 2.6 mi	◈◈◈	$169-$399 [SAVE]	177
19 p. 146	Drury Inn & Suites Phoenix Airport, 4.6 mi	◈◈◈	$80-$210	177
15 p. 146	Fairfield Inn & Suites by Marriott Phoenix Airport, 3.0 mi	◈◈◈	$69-$238 [SAVE]	178
5 p. 146	Hampton Inn Phoenix Airport North, 2.9 mi	◈◈◈	$99-$179	179
17 p. 146	Hilton Garden Inn Phoenix Airport, 4.4 mi	◈◈◈	$89-$269	179
7 p. 146	Hilton Garden Inn Phoenix Airport North, 3.2 mi	◈◈◈	$89-$289	179
12 p. 146	Hilton Phoenix Airport, 3.2 mi	◈◈◈	$139-$229	180
18 p. 146	Holiday Inn & Suites Phoenix Airport, 3.4 mi	◈◈◈	$79-$289	180
3 p. 146	Holiday Inn & Suites Phoenix Airport North, 3.5 mi	◈◈◈	$119-$309 [SAVE]	180
16 p. 146	Holiday Inn Express & Suites Phoenix Airport, 4.3 mi	◈◈◈	$79-$249	180
4 p. 146	Phoenix Airport Marriott, 3.3 mi	◈◈◈	$111-$346	181
6 p. 146	Radisson Hotel Phoenix Airport, 2.7 mi	◈◈◈	$85-$299 [SAVE]	182
13 p. 146	Sleep Inn Airport, 3.1 mi	◈◈	$70-$200	183
2 p. 164	Hyatt Place Tempe/Phoenix Airport, 3.9 mi	◈◈◈	$69-$259 [SAVE]	247
8 p. 164	La Quinta Inn Phoenix Sky Harbor Airport South, 3.1 mi	◈◈	$64-$251	247
5 p. 164	SpringHill Suites by Marriott Phoenix Tempe Airport, 3.6 mi	◈◈◈	$71-$248 [SAVE]	248

Phoenix Sky Harbor International Airport

This index helps you "spot" where approved hotels and restaurants are located on the corresponding detailed maps. Hotel daily rate range is for comparison only. Restaurant price range is a combination of lunch and/or dinner. Turn to the listing page for more detailed rate and price information and consult display ads for special promotions.

PHOENIX

Map Page	Hotels	Diamond Rated	Rate Range	Page
1 p. 146	Embassy Suites by Hilton Phoenix Airport at 24th St	◈◈◈	$99-$269 [SAVE]	177
2 p. 146	La Quinta Inn Phoenix-Arcadia	◈◈	$64-$207	181
3 p. 146	Holiday Inn & Suites Phoenix Airport North	◈◈◈	$119-$309 [SAVE]	180
4 p. 146	Phoenix Airport Marriott	◈◈◈	$111-$346	181
5 p. 146	Hampton Inn Phoenix Airport North	◈◈◈	$99-$179	179
6 p. 146	Radisson Hotel Phoenix Airport	◈◈◈	$85-$299 [SAVE]	182
7 p. 146	Hilton Garden Inn Phoenix Airport North	◈◈◈	$89-$289	179
8 p. 146	DoubleTree Suites by Hilton Phoenix	◈◈◈	$169-$399 [SAVE]	177
9 p. 146	Crowne Plaza Phoenix Airport	◈◈◈	$79-$249 [SAVE]	176
10 p. 146	Aloft Phoenix Airport Hotel	◈◈◈	Rates not provided [SAVE]	175
11 p. 146	BEST WESTERN Airport Inn	◈◈	$70-$180 [SAVE]	175

PHOENIX (cont'd)

Map Page	Hotels (cont'd)	Diamond Rated	Rate Range	Page
12 p. 146	Hilton Phoenix Airport	◆◆◆	$139-$229	180
13 p. 146	Sleep Inn Airport	◆◆	$70-$200	183
14 p. 146	**Courtyard by Marriott Phoenix Airport**	◆◆◆	$80-$301 (SAVE)	176
15 p. 146	**Fairfield Inn & Suites by Marriott Phoenix Airport**	◆◆◆	$69-$238 (SAVE)	178
16 p. 146	Holiday Inn Express & Suites Phoenix Airport	◆◆◆	$79-$249	180
17 p. 146	Hilton Garden Inn Phoenix Airport	◆◆◆	$89-$269	179
18 p. 146	Holiday Inn & Suites Phoenix Airport	◆◆◆	$79-$289	180
19 p. 146	Drury Inn & Suites Phoenix Airport	◆◆◆	$80-$210	177
20 p. 146	Country Inn & Suites By Carlson, Phoenix Airport South	◆◆◆	Rates not provided	176
21 p. 146	Homewood Suites by Hilton Phoenix Airport South	◆◆◆	$159-$299	180

Map Page	Restaurants	Diamond Rated	Cuisine	Price Range	Page
1 p. 146	**Barrio Cafe**	◆◆	New Mexican	$10-$26	184
2 p. 146	Wild Game Grill	◆◆	American	$9-$24	190
3 p. 146	La Condesa Gourmet Taco Shop	◆	Mexican	$4-$9	186
4 p. 146	Red Devil Restaurant & Pizzeria	◆◆	Italian	$8-$26	188
5 p. 146	Indian Delhi Palace	◆◆	Indian	$8-$21	186
6 p. 146	Szechwan Palace	◆◆	Chinese	$7-$20	190
7 p. 146	Stockyards Restaurant & 1889 Saloon	◆◆◆	Steak	$8-$75	190
8 p. 146	SaBai Modern Thai	◆◆	Thai	$10-$18	189

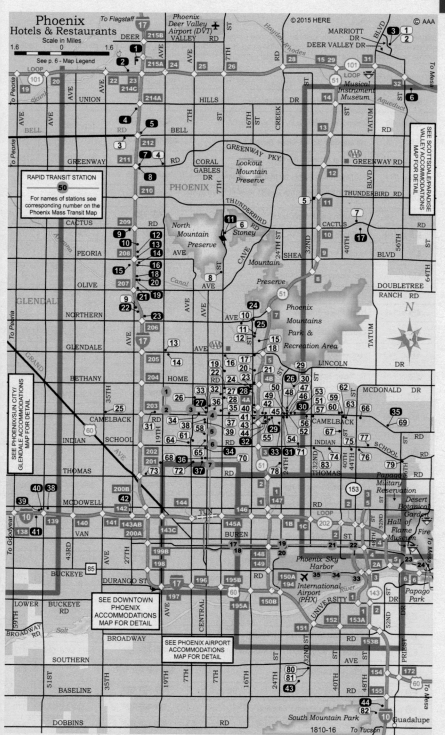

Phoenix
Hotels & Restaurants

Scale in Miles

1.6   0   1.6

See p. 6 - Map Legend

© 2015 HERE   © AAA

RAPID TRANSIT STATION

50

For names of stations see
corresponding number on the
Phoenix Mass Transit Map

SEE SCOTTSDALE/PARADISE
VALLEY ACCOMMODATIONS
MAP FOR DETAIL

SEE PHOENIX/SUN CITY/
GLENDALE ACCOMMODATIONS
MAP FOR DETAIL

SEE DOWNTOWN
PHOENIX
ACCOMMODATIONS
MAP FOR DETAIL

SEE PHOENIX AIRPORT
ACCOMMODATIONS
MAP FOR DETAIL

1810-16

Phoenix

This index helps you "spot" where approved hotels and restaurants are located on the corresponding detailed maps. Hotel daily rate range is for comparison only. Restaurant price range is a combination of lunch and/or dinner. Turn to the listing page for more detailed rate and price information and consult display ads for special promotions.

PHOENIX

Map Page	Hotels	Diamond Rated	Rate Range	Page
1 p. 149	Extended Stay America Phoenix-Deer Valley	♦♦	Rates not provided	178
2 p. 149	Country Inn & Suites By Carlson, Deer Valley	♦♦♦	Rates not provided	176
3 p. 149	**JW Marriott Desert Ridge Resort & Spa**	♦♦♦♦	$160-$538 SAVE	181
4 p. 149	**Sleep Inn Phoenix North**	♦♦	$59-$179 SAVE	183
5 p. 149	**Fairfield Inn & Suites by Marriott Phoenix North**	♦♦♦	$58-$163 SAVE	178
6 p. 149	**Phoenix Residence Inn Desert View at Mayo Clinic by Marriott**	♦♦♦	$98-$361 SAVE	181
7 p. 149	La Quinta Inn Phoenix North	♦♦	$64-$251	181
8 p. 149	Embassy Suites by Hilton Phoenix North	♦♦♦	$99-$229	177
9 p. 149	Holiday Inn North Phoenix	♦♦♦	Rates not provided	180
10 p. 149	Candlewood Suites Phoenix	♦♦	Rates not provided	175
11 p. 149	**Pointe Hilton Tapatio Cliffs Resort**	♦♦♦	$89-$329 SAVE	182
12 p. 149	**Hyatt Place Phoenix-North**	♦♦♦	$64-$229 SAVE	181
13 p. 149	**Crowne Plaza Phoenix North**	♦♦♦	Rates not provided SAVE	177
14 p. 149	Homewood Suites by Hilton Phoenix Metrocenter	♦♦♦	Rates not provided	180
15 p. 149	Radisson Hotel Phoenix North	♦♦♦	Rates not provided	182
16 p. 149	Comfort Suites Phoenix North	♦♦	$84-$139	176
17 p. 149	**Embassy Suites by Hilton Phoenix-Scottsdale at Stonecreek Golf Club** (See ad p. 178.)	♦♦♦	$109-$229 SAVE	177
18 p. 149	**Courtyard by Marriott Phoenix North**	♦♦♦	$71-$200 SAVE	176
19 p. 149	SpringHill Suites by Marriott Phoenix North	♦♦♦	$66-$182	183
20 p. 149	TownePlace Suites by Marriott Phoenix North	♦♦♦	$61-$183	184
21 p. 149	**Sheraton Crescent Hotel**	♦♦♦	$89-$349 SAVE	183
22 p. 149	Residence Inn by Marriott Phoenix	♦♦♦	$89-$248	183
23 p. 149	**BEST WESTERN Phoenix I-17 MetroCenter Inn**	♦♦	$59-$189 SAVE	175
24 p. 149	**BEST WESTERN InnSuites Phoenix Hotel & Suites**	♦♦♦	$79-$159 SAVE	175
25 p. 149	**Pointe Hilton Squaw Peak Resort**	♦♦♦	$109-$359 SAVE	182
26 p. 149	**Arizona Biltmore, A Waldorf Astoria Resort**	♦♦♦♦	$119-$429 SAVE	175
27 p. 149	Maricopa Manor Bed & Breakfast Inn	♦♦♦	$119-$239	181
28 p. 149	Extended Stay America Phoenix-Biltmore	♦♦	Rates not provided	177
29 p. 149	**Courtyard by Marriott-Camelback**	♦♦♦	$89-$335 SAVE	176
30 p. 149	**Embassy Suites by Hilton Phoenix Biltmore**	♦♦♦	$109-$409 SAVE	177
31 p. 149	The Ritz-Carlton, Phoenix	♦♦♦♦	Rates not provided	183
32 p. 149	Homewood Suites by Hilton Phoenix-Biltmore	♦♦♦	$94-$239	180
33 p. 149	Hampton Inn Phoenix Biltmore	♦♦♦	$89-$279	179
34 p. 149	Hilton Garden Inn Phoenix Midtown	♦♦♦	$79-$399	179

PHOENIX (cont'd)

Map Page	Hotels (cont'd)	Diamond Rated	Rate Range	Page
35 p. 149	**Royal Palms Resort and Spa**	◆◆◆◆	$149-$799 SAVE	183
36 p. 149	Wyndham Garden Phoenix Midtown	◆◆◆	$67-$147	184
37 p. 149	Extended Stay America Phoenix/Midtown	◆◆	Rates not provided	178
38 p. 149	La Quinta Inn & Suites Phoenix I-10 West	◆◆◆	$69-$977	181
39 p. 149	**Red Roof Inn Phoenix West**	◆◆	$50-$126 SAVE	183
40 p. 149	Holiday Inn Phoenix West	◆◆◆	$89-$149	180
41 p. 149	Super 8-Phoenix West	◆◆	$55-$80	184
42 p. 149	Comfort Inn I-10 West/Central	◆◆	$120-$190	176
43 p. 149	**The Legacy Golf Resort**	◆◆◆	$99-$499 SAVE	181
44 p. 149	**Arizona Grand Resort & Spa**	◆◆◆◆	Rates not provided SAVE	175

Map Page	Restaurants	Diamond Rated	Cuisine	Price Range	Page
1 p. 149	Meritage Steakhouse	◆◆◆	American	$24-$55	187
2 p. 149	Roy's Desert Ridge	◆◆◆	Hawaiian	$20-$30	189
3 p. 149	India Palace	◆◆	Indian	$11-$16	186
4 p. 149	Chino Bandido	◆	Fusion	$7-$10	185
5 p. 149	**Original Breakfast House**	◆◆	American	$6-$13	187
6 p. 149	**Different Pointe of View**	◆◆◆◆	New American	$29-$42	185
7 p. 149	Yasu Sushi Bistro	◆◆◆	Japanese	$9-$26	191
8 p. 149	Scramble	◆◆	American	$6-$10	189
9 p. 149	Bobby Q	◆◆	Barbecue	$9-$36	184
10 p. 149	THIRTEENORTH grille	◆◆	American	$9-$23	190
11 p. 149	Rico's American Grill	◆◆◆	American	$12-$32	189
12 p. 149	Tutti Santi Ristorante	◆◆◆	Italian	$14-$27	190
13 p. 149	Restaurant Atoyac Estilo Oaxaca	◆	Mexican	$4-$9	188
14 p. 149	Silver Dragon Chinese Restaurant	◆◆	Chinese	$8-$12	189
15 p. 149	Aunt Chilada's Hideaway	◆◆	Mexican	$6-$18	184
16 p. 149	Sierra Bonita Grill	◆◆◆	Southwestern	$12-$28	189
17 p. 149	Babbo Italian Eatery	◆◆	Italian	$9-$15	184
18 p. 149	Moto	◆◆	Asian Fusion	$7-$19	187
19 p. 149	Christo's	◆◆	Italian	$8-$30	185
20 p. 149	Richardson's of New Mexico	◆◆	Southwestern	$13-$35	189
21 p. 149	The Vig Uptown	◆◆	American	$11-$17	190
22 p. 149	Fuego Bistro	◆◆	Latin American	$10-$30	186
23 p. 149	Zipps Sports Grill	◆◆	American	$6-$15	191
24 p. 149	Phoenix City Grille	◆◆◆	American	$12-$32	188
25 p. 149	Great Wall Hong Kong Cuisine	◆◆	Chinese	$8-$25	186
26 p. 149	Hana Japanese Eatery	◆◆	Japanese	$9-$36	186
27 p. 149	Little Cleo's Seafood Legend	◆◆◆	Seafood	$14-$38	187
28 p. 149	Scott's Generations Deli	◆◆	Deli	$5-$18	189

Map Page	Restaurants (cont'd)	Diamond Rated	Cuisine	Price Range	Page
㉙ p. 149	Frank & Albert's	♦♦♦	American	$16-$42	185
㉚ p. 149	Wright's at the Biltmore	♦♦♦♦	American	$29-$46	190
㉛ p. 149	Pepe's Taco Villa	♦♦	Mexican	$7-$16	188
㉜ p. 149	Windsor	♦♦	American	$12-$20	190
㉝ p. 149	Postino Central WineCafe	♦♦	American Small Plates Sandwiches	$10-$14	188
㉞ p. 149	Southern Rail	♦♦♦	Southern American	$7-$27	189
㉟ p. 149	Ticoz Resto-Bar	♦♦♦	Southwestern	$10-$20	190
㊱ p. 149	St. Francis	♦♦♦	New American	$12-$28	189
㊲ p. 149	Cherryblossom Noodle Cafe	♦♦	Noodles	$7-$15	185
㊳ p. 149	Maizie's Cafe & Bistro	♦♦	American	$10-$18	187
㊴ p. 149	Hula's Modern Tiki	♦♦	Polynesian	$10-$26	186
㊵ p. 149	Blue Water Grill	♦♦♦	Seafood	$15-$49	184
㊶ p. 149	Duck and Decanter	♦	Deli	$6-$10	185
㊷ p. 149	The Parlor Pizzeria	♦♦	Pizza	$10-$31	188
㊸ p. 149	Greekfest	♦♦♦	Greek	$7-$28	186
㊹ p. 149	Miracle Mile Delicatessen	♦	Deli	$9-$14	187
㊺ p. 149	True Food Kitchen	♦♦♦	American	$10-$26	190
㊻ p. 149	Forge Handcrafted Pizza	♦♦	Pizza	$12-$17	185
㊼ p. 149	Blanco Tacos & Tequila	♦♦	Mexican	$8-$20	184
㊽ p. 149	Zinburger	♦♦	Burgers	$10-$16	191
㊾ p. 149	Christopher's Restaurant & Crush Lounge	♦♦♦	French	$12-$68	185
㊿ p. 149	The Capital Grille	♦♦♦	Steak	$11-$49	184
51 p. 149	Hillstone Restaurant	♦♦♦	American	$16-$45	186
52 p. 149	Stingray Sushi	♦♦♦	Sushi	$9-$30	190
53 p. 149	Omaha Steakhouse	♦♦	American	$9-$38	187
54 p. 149	Bistro 24	♦♦♦	Continental	$16-$36	184
55 p. 149	Pizzeria Bianco	♦♦♦	Italian Pizza	$13-$23	188
56 p. 149	Donovan's Steak & Chop House	♦♦♦	Steak	$28-$55	185
57 p. 149	Tarbell's	♦♦♦	American	$11-$35	190
58 p. 149	Pane Bianco	♦	Specialty	$9-$16	188
59 p. 149	Chelsea's Kitchen	♦♦♦	American	$10-$27	185
60 p. 149	Vincent on Camelback	♦♦♦	French	$26-$38	190
61 p. 149	Harley's Italian Bistro	♦♦	Italian	$9-$22	186
62 p. 149	The Grind	♦♦	American	$8-$28	186
63 p. 149	North Italian Farmhouse	♦♦♦	Italian	$10-$33	187
64 p. 149	The Fry Bread House	♦	Regional Specialty	$3-$8	185
65 p. 149	The Clever Koi	♦♦	Asian	$10-$15	185
66 p. 149	The Henry	♦♦♦	New American	$10-$28	186
67 p. 149	Postino WineCafe	♦♦	American	$10-$14	188

Map Page	Restaurants (cont'd)	Diamond Rated	Cuisine	Price Range	Page
68 p. 149	La Pinata	◈◈	Mexican	$8-$18	186
69 p. 149	**T. Cook's**	◈◈◈◈	Mediterranean	$16-$44	190
70 p. 149	Alexi's Grill	◈◈◈	Northern Italian	$7-$29	184
71 p. 149	Giuseppe's on 28th	◈◈	Italian	$9-$27	186
72 p. 149	Mi Patio Mexican Food	◈◈	Mexican	$5-$14	187
73 p. 149	Pizza a Metro	◈◈	Italian	$10-$15	188
74 p. 149	Nook Kitchen	◈◈	American	$11-$28	187
75 p. 149	The Yacht Club	◈◈◈	American	$12-$31	191
76 p. 149	Sushi Brokers	◈◈	Japanese	$11-$16	190
77 p. 149	Over Easy Cafe	◈◈	American	$5-$12	187
78 p. 149	Mejico	◈◈	Regional Mexican	$15-$23	187
79 p. 149	Kitchen 56	◈◈◈	American	$10-$26	186
80 p. 149	Quiessence	◈◈◈◈	New American	$20-$40	188
81 p. 149	**Farm Kitchen at The Farm at South Mountain**	◈	American	$10-$12	185
82 p. 149	**Rustler's Rooste**	◈◈	Steak	$15-$31	189
83 p. 149	Desert Jade	◈◈	Chinese	$11-$26	185

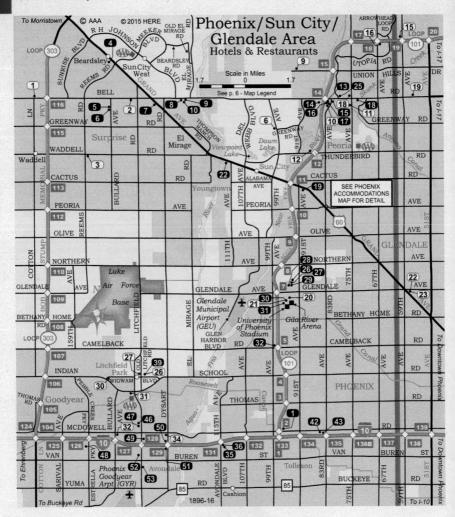

Phoenix/Sun City/Glendale Area

This index helps you "spot" where approved hotels and restaurants are located on the corresponding detailed maps. Hotel daily rate range is for comparison only. Restaurant price range is a combination of lunch and/or dinner. Turn to the listing page for more detailed rate and price information and consult display ads for special promotions.

PHOENIX

Map Page	Hotel	Diamond Rated	Rate Range	Page
1 this page	Courtyard by Marriott Phoenix West-Avondale	▽▽▽	$93-$221	176

SURPRISE

Map Page	Hotels	Diamond Rated	Rate Range	Page
4 this page	**Hampton Inn & Suites Surprise**	▽▽▽	$79-$159 SAVE	243
5 this page	Holiday Inn Express & Suites	▽▽▽	Rates not provided	243
6 this page	Residence Inn by Marriott Phoenix NW Surprise	▽▽▽	$113-$280	243
7 this page	Comfort Inn & Suites of Surprise	▽▽▽	$70-$210	243
8 this page	**Windmill Suites in Surprise**	▽▽	Rates not provided SAVE	243

SURPRISE (cont'd)

Map Page	Hotels (cont'd)	Diamond Rated	Rate Range	Page
9 p. 154	Days Inn & Suites Surprise	♦♦	$44-$134	243
10 p. 154	Quality Inn & Suites of Sun Cities	♦♦	$59-$209	243

Map Page	Restaurants	Diamond Rated	Cuisine	Price Range	Page
1 p. 154	Amuse Bouche	♦♦	American	$10-$26	243
2 p. 154	Saigon Kitchen	♦♦	Vietnamese	$6-$15	243
3 p. 154	Vogue Bistro	♦♦♦	New American	$10-$26	243

PEORIA

Map Page	Hotels	Diamond Rated	Rate Range	Page
13 p. 154	Comfort Suites by Choice Hotels/Peoria Sports Complex	♦♦	$79-$209	122
14 p. 154	Holiday Inn Express Hotel & Suites Peoria North-Glendale	♦♦	Rates not provided	123
15 p. 154	La Quinta Inn & Suites Phoenix West/Peoria	♦♦♦	$68-$631	123
16 p. 154	Residence Inn by Marriott Glendale/Peoria	♦♦♦	$104-$278	123
17 p. 154	Hampton Inn	♦♦♦	$89-$369	123
18 p. 154	Extended Stay America Peoria	♦♦	Rates not provided	123
19 p. 154	Days Hotel Peoria Glendale Area	♦♦	$53-$113	122

Map Page	Restaurants	Diamond Rated	Cuisine	Price Range	Page
9 p. 154	Good China	♦♦	Chinese	$8-$17	123
10 p. 154	P.F. Chang's China Bistro	♦♦♦	Chinese	$8-$25	123
11 p. 154	Ah-So Steak & Sushi	♦♦	Japanese	$7-$38	123
12 p. 154	Dillon's Restaurant	♦♦	American	$10-$25	123

YOUNGTOWN

Map Page	Hotel	Diamond Rated	Rate Range	Page
22 p. 154	**BEST WESTERN Inn & Suites of Sun City**	♦♦	$69-$159 [SAVE]	306

GLENDALE

Map Page	Hotels	Diamond Rated	Rate Range	Page
25 p. 154	**SpringHill Suites by Marriott Glendale/Peoria**	♦♦♦	$77-$198 [SAVE]	78
26 p. 154	Residence Inn by Marriott Phoenix Glendale Sports & Entertainment District	♦♦♦	$114-$263	78
27 p. 154	SpringHill Suites by Marriott Phoenix Glendale Sports & Entertainment District	♦♦♦	$98-$244	78
28 p. 154	Staybridge Suites Phoenix/Glendale	♦♦♦	Rates not provided	78
29 p. 154	Holiday Inn Express & Suites Phoenix/Glendale	♦♦♦	Rates not provided	77
30 p. 154	**Renaissance Glendale Hotel & Spa**	♦♦♦♦	$118-$293 [SAVE]	77
31 p. 154	Hampton Inn & Suites Glendale/Westgate	♦♦♦	$129-$299	77
32 p. 154	Comfort Suites Glendale University of Phoenix Stadium Area	♦♦♦	$99-$499	77

Map Page	Restaurants	Diamond Rated	Cuisine	Price Range	Page
15 p. 154	Sakana Sushi & Grill	♦♦	Japanese	$8-$17	79
16 p. 154	Betty's Nosh	♦♦	American	$8-$23	78
18 p. 154	Pita Jungle	♦♦	Mediterranean	$7-$16	79
19 p. 154	Thee Pitt's "Again"	♦♦	Barbecue	$9-$20	79
20 p. 154	Mama Gina's Pizzeria	♦♦	Italian	$8-$21	79

Map Page	Restaurants (cont'd)	Diamond Rated	Cuisine	Price Range	Page
21 p. 154	Soleil	◆◆◆	Regional American	$12-$35	79
22 p. 154	Zang Asian Bistro	◆◆	Asian Fusion	$9-$15	79
23 p. 154	Haus Murphy's	◆◆	German	$8-$20	78

AVONDALE

Map Page	Hotels	Diamond Rated	Rate Range	Page
35 p. 154	Hilton Garden Inn Phoenix/Avondale	◆◆◆	Rates not provided	40
36 p. 154	Homewood Suites by Hilton Phoenix/Avondale	◆◆◆	Rates not provided	40

LITCHFIELD PARK

Map Page	Hotel	Diamond Rated	Rate Range	Page
39 p. 154	**The Wigwam**	◆◆◆◆	Rates not provided SAVE	106

Map Page	Restaurants	Diamond Rated	Cuisine	Price Range	Page
26 p. 154	Litchfield's	◆◆◆	New American	$16-$29	106
27 p. 154	Blu Sushi Lounge & Grill	◆◆	Sushi	$10-$27	106

TOLLESON

Map Page	Hotels	Diamond Rated	Rate Range	Page
42 p. 154	**BEST WESTERN Tolleson-Phoenix Hotel**	◆◆	$100 SAVE	250
43 p. 154	Premier Inns	◆◆	Rates not provided	250

GOODYEAR

Map Page	Hotels	Diamond Rated	Rate Range	Page
46 p. 154	Residence Inn by Marriott	◆◆◆	$99-$244	81
47 p. 154	Hampton Inn & Suites Goodyear	◆◆◆	$109-$209	81
48 p. 154	Comfort Suites Goodyear	◆◆◆	$79-$169	81
49 p. 154	Holiday Inn Express West Phoenix/Goodyear	◆◆	$109-$259	81
50 p. 154	Holiday Inn & Suites Goodyear	◆◆◆	$139-$229	81
51 p. 154	Quality Inn & Suites Goodyear	◆◆	$65-$180	81
52 p. 154	**TownePlace Suites by Marriott Phoenix/Goodyear**	◆◆◆	$84-$238 SAVE	81
53 p. 154	**BEST WESTERN Phoenix Goodyear Inn**	◆◆	$80-$210 SAVE	80

Map Page	Restaurants	Diamond Rated	Cuisine	Price Range	Page
30 p. 154	Royal Jasmine Thai	◆◆	Thai	$8-$15	81
31 p. 154	Bella Luna Ristorante	◆◆◆	Italian	$10-$26	81
32 p. 154	P.F. Chang's China Bistro	◆◆◆	Chinese	$8-$25	81
34 p. 154	Tomo Japanese Cuisine	◆◆	Japanese	$8-$27	81

SUN CITY

Map Page	Restaurant	Diamond Rated	Cuisine	Price Range	Page
6 p. 154	Little Bite of Italy	◆◆	Italian	$8-$16	242

Ask your AAA/CAA club about travel money
and other financial services for travelers

EXCITING ITINERARIES | ENGAGING EXPERIENCES | EXCLUSIVE VALUES

A world of choices!

AAA Vacations® offers members unsurpassed amenities, 24/7 Member Care and a Best Price Guarantee.*

Call your AAA/CAA Travel Agent or visit

AAA.com/AAAVacations
CAA.ca/AAAVacations

* If you book a qualifying *AAA Vacations*® cruise or tour package and you find a valid better rate for the exact itinerary within 24 hours of your booking, *AAA Vacations*® will match the lower rate and send you a $50 future travel credit certificate. Certain restrictions apply. Visit AAA.com/AAAVacations for full details.

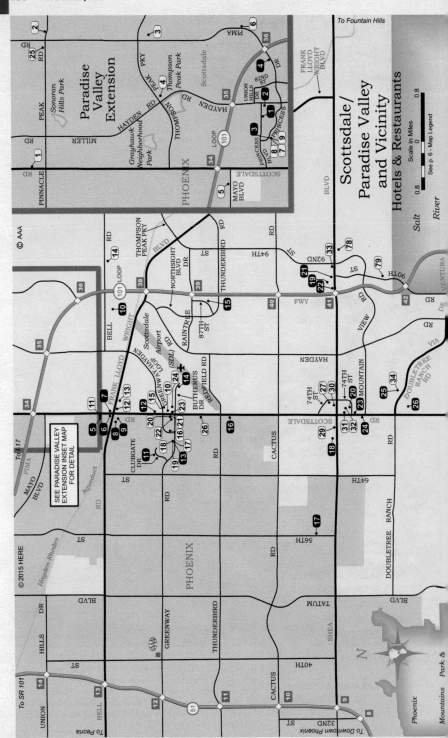

Scottsdale/
Paradise Valley
and Vicinity
Hotels & Restaurants

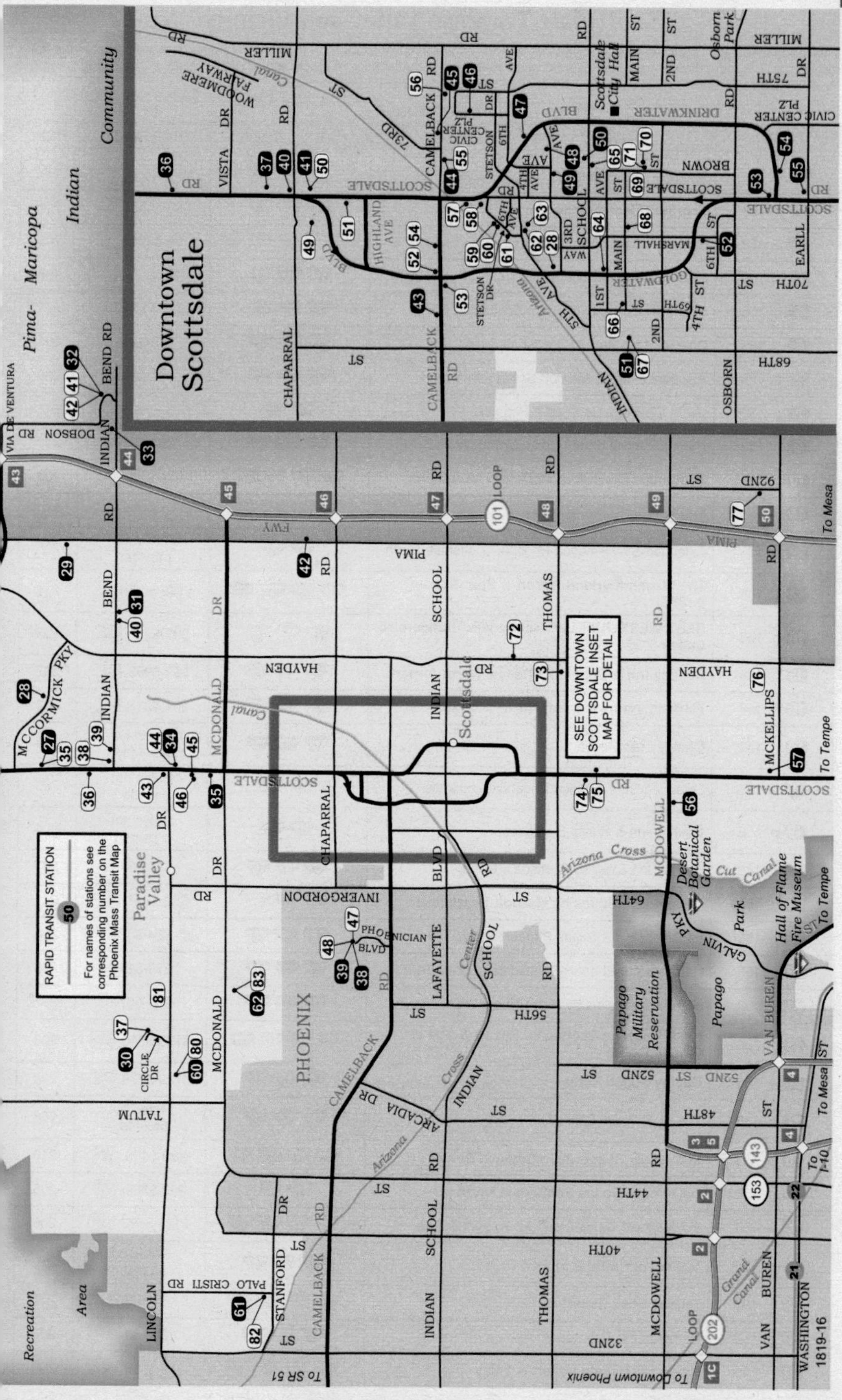

Pima- Maricopa Indian Community

Downtown Scottsdale

Recreation Area

RAPID TRANSIT STATION
50
For names of stations see corresponding number on the Phoenix Mass Transit Map

SEE DOWNTOWN SCOTTSDALE INSET MAP FOR DETAIL

Paradise Valley

PHOENIX

Desert Botanical Garden

Papago Park

Papago Military Reservation

Hall of Flame Fire Museum

Scottsdale City Hall

To Mesa

To Tempe

To Downtown Phoenix

To SR 51

Scottsdale/Paradise Valley and Vicinity

This index helps you "spot" where approved hotels and restaurants are located on the corresponding detailed maps. Hotel daily rate range is for comparison only. Restaurant price range is a combination of lunch and/or dinner. Turn to the listing page for more detailed rate and price information and consult display ads for special promotions.

SCOTTSDALE

Map Page	Hotels	Diamond Rated	Rate Range	Page
1 p. 158	Scottsdale Villa Mirage	◆◆◆	Rates not provided	210
2 p. 158	**Sheraton Desert Oasis**	◆◆◆	$99-$449 [SAVE]	211
3 p. 158	**Fairmont Scottsdale Princess**	◆◆◆◆	$169-$3099 [SAVE]	205
4 p. 158	Hilton Garden Inn Scottsdale North	◆◆◆	$109-$399	206
5 p. 158	SpringHill Suites by Marriott-Scottsdale North	◆◆◆	$74-$313	211
6 p. 158	Courtyard by Marriott/Scottsdale North	◆◆◆	$79-$342	204
7 p. 158	Residence Inn by Marriott Scottsdale North	◆◆◆	$98-$297	208
8 p. 158	Sleep Inn North Scottsdale/Phoenix	◆◆	$69-$259	211
9 p. 158	Hampton Inn & Suites Phoenix/Scottsdale	◆◆◆	$84-$399	206
10 p. 158	**Scottsdale Marriott at McDowell Mountains**	◆◆◆	$132-$392 [SAVE]	209
11 p. 158	**The Westin Kierland Villas**	◆◆◆◆	$159-$659 [SAVE]	212
12 p. 158	Extended Stay America-Phoenix-Scottsdale-North	◆◆	Rates not provided	205
13 p. 158	**The Westin Kierland Resort & Spa** *(See ad p. 210.)*	◆◆◆◆	$149-$709 [SAVE]	211
14 p. 158	**BEST WESTERN PLUS Scottsdale Thunderbird Suites**	◆◆◆	$99-$219 [SAVE]	203
15 p. 158	**Holiday Inn & Suites Scottsdale North-Airpark**	◆◆◆	$99-$999 [SAVE]	207
16 p. 158	**Fairfield Inn by Marriott North Scottsdale**	◆◆◆	$65-$233 [SAVE]	205
17 p. 158	Orange Tree Resort	◆◆◆	Rates not provided	208
18 p. 158	Extended Stay America Phoenix-Scottsdale	◆◆	Rates not provided	205
19 p. 158	Country Inn & Suites By Carlson	◆◆	Rates not provided	204
20 p. 158	Holiday Inn Express Scottsdale North	◆◆◆	$79-$349	207
21 p. 158	**TownePlace Suites by Marriott Scottsdale**	◆◆◆	$82-$341 [SAVE]	211
22 p. 158	La Quinta Inn & Suites Phoenix Scottsdale	◆◆◆	$64-$339	208
23 p. 158	Hampton Inn Phoenix-Scottsdale at Shea Blvd	◆◆◆	$89-$299	206
24 p. 158	Homewood Suites by Hilton Phoenix/Scottsdale	◆◆◆	$89-$379	207
25 p. 158	**Hyatt Regency Scottsdale Resort & Spa at Gainey Ranch**	◆◆◆◆	$139-$850 [SAVE]	208
26 p. 158	**Gainey Suites Hotel**	◆◆◆	$129-$279 [SAVE]	206
27 p. 158	The McCormick Scottsdale	◆◆◆	Rates not provided	208
28 p. 158	**Scottsdale Resort & Conference Center**	◆◆◆◆	$89-$449 [SAVE]	210
29 p. 158	**Days Inn & Suites Scottsdale North**	◆◆	$89-$389 [SAVE]	205
30 p. 158	**JW Marriott Camelback Inn Resort & Spa**	◆◆◆◆	$135-$577 [SAVE]	208
31 p. 158	Scottsdale Resort & Athletic Club	◆◆◆	Rates not provided	210
32 p. 158	**Talking Stick Resort**	◆◆◆	$119-$459 [SAVE]	211
33 p. 158	Hampton Inn & Suites Scottsdale Riverwalk	◆◆◆	$99-$349	206
34 p. 158	**Hilton Scottsdale Resort & Villas**	◆◆◆◆	$89-$499 [SAVE]	206

SCOTTSDALE (cont'd)

Map Page	Hotels (cont'd)	Diamond Rated	Rate Range	Page
35 p. 158	Residence Inn by Marriott, Scottsdale/Paradise Valley	◆◆◆	$101-$337 SAVE	209
36 p. 158	DoubleTree Resort by Hilton Paradise Valley-Scottsdale	◆◆◆◆	$79-$479 SAVE	205
37 p. 158	Days Hotel Scottsdale	◆◆	$59-$260 SAVE	204
38 p. 158	The Phoenician, A Luxury Collection Resort, Scottsdale (See ad p. 209.)	◆◆◆◆◆	$199-$599 SAVE	208
39 p. 158	The Canyon Suites at The Phoenician, A Luxury Collection Resort, Scottsdale (See ad p. 203.)	◆◆◆◆	Rates not provided SAVE	204
40 p. 158	Chaparral Suites Scottsdale	◆◆◆	Rates not provided SAVE	204
41 p. 158	FireSky Resort & Spa, A Kimpton Hotel	◆◆◆◆	$109-$419 SAVE	205
42 p. 158	Courtyard by Marriott Scottsdale Salt River	◆◆◆	$80-$281 SAVE	204
43 p. 158	Motel 6 Scottsdale #29	◆	Rates not provided	208
44 p. 158	W Scottsdale	◆◆◆◆	$149-$909 SAVE	212
45 p. 158	BEST WESTERN PLUS Sundial	◆◆◆	$99-$299 SAVE	203
46 p. 158	Hotel Indigo Scottsdale	◆◆◆	Rates not provided SAVE	207
47 p. 158	HYATT house Scottsdale/Old Town	◆◆◆	$79-$359 SAVE	207
48 p. 158	Hyatt Place Scottsdale/Old Town	◆◆◆	$79-$399 SAVE	207
49 p. 158	Scottsdale Marriott Suites Old Town	◆◆◆	$120-$404 SAVE	210
50 p. 158	Hilton Garden Inn Scottsdale Old Town	◆◆◆	$75-$399	206
51 p. 158	Hotel Valley Ho	◆◆◆◆	$119-$499 SAVE	207
52 p. 158	Extended Stay America-Phoenix-Scottsdale-Old Town	◆◆	Rates not provided	205
53 p. 158	Courtyard by Marriott Scottsdale Old Town	◆◆◆	$85-$358 SAVE	204
54 p. 158	Comfort Suites by Choice Hotels-Old Town	◆◆	$99-$219	204
55 p. 158	Holiday Inn Express Hotel & Suites-Scottsdale Old Town	◆◆◆	Rates not provided	207
56 p. 158	Magnuson Hotel Papago Inn	◆◆◆	$70-$300	208
57 p. 158	Hospitality Suite Resort	◆◆	$59-$299	207

Map Page	Restaurants	Diamond Rated	Cuisine	Price Range	Page
1 p. 158	Jade Palace	◆◆	Chinese	$15-$39	214
2 p. 158	Mastro's Steakhouse	◆◆◆	Steak	$27-$90	215
3 p. 158	Fleming's Prime Steakhouse & Wine Bar	◆◆◆	Steak	$30-$60	214
4 p. 158	Pure Sushi Bar & Dining	◆◆◆	Japanese Sushi	$12-$26	216
5 p. 158	The White Chocolate Grill	◆◆◆	American	$11-$28	218
6 p. 158	Lush Burger	◆◆	American	$8-$12	214
7 p. 158	Bourbon Steak	◆◆◆◆	Steak	$22-$175	212
8 p. 158	Toro	◆◆◆	Latin American Small Plates Fusion	$22-$39	218
9 p. 158	La Hacienda	◆◆◆	Mexican	$12-$31	214
10 p. 158	True Food Kitchen	◆◆	American	$10-$20	218
11 p. 158	Persian Room	◆◆◆	Middle Eastern	$9-$35	216
12 p. 158	The Capital Grille	◆◆◆	Steak	$11-$49	213

Map Page	Restaurants (cont'd)	Diamond Rated	Cuisine	Price Range	Page
⑬ p. 158	**Cantina Laredo**	▽▽	Mexican	$10-$25	213
⑭ p. 158	Over Easy Cafe	▽▽	American	$6-$16	215
⑮ p. 158	Eddie V's Prime Seafood	▽▽▽	Seafood	$19-$49	213
⑯ p. 158	Mastro's Ocean Club	▽▽▽	Seafood	$27-$78	215
⑰ p. 158	Brittlebush Bar & Grill	▽▽▽	American	$12-$16	212
⑱ p. 158	Nellie Cashman's Monday Club Cafe	▽▽▽	New American	$9-$28	215
⑲ p. 158	**Deseo**	▽▽▽▽	New Latin American	$27-$38	213
⑳ p. 158	Zinc Bistro	▽▽▽	French	$10-$36	218
㉑ p. 158	NoRTH	▽▽▽	New Italian	$8-$28	215
㉒ p. 158	P.F. Chang's China Bistro	▽▽▽	Chinese	$8-$25	216
㉓ p. 158	Dominick's Steakhouse	▽▽▽	Steak	$28-$58	213
㉔ p. 158	Stingray Sushi	▽▽▽	Sushi	$13-$30	217
㉕ p. 158	Preston's Steakhouse	▽▽▽	Steak	$28-$79	216
㉖ p. 158	Sapporo	▽▽▽	Japanese	$11-$45	217
㉗ p. 158	Pita Jungle	▽▽	Mediterranean	$7-$16	216
㉘ p. 158	EVO	▽▽▽	Italian	$11-$30	213
㉙ p. 158	Sushi On Shea	▽▽	Japanese	$8-$35	217
㉚ p. 158	Squid Ink Sushi	▽▽	Sushi	$11-$25	217
㉛ p. 158	Razz's Restaurant	▽▽▽	New American	$24-$38	216
㉜ p. 158	Takeda Thai	▽▽	Thai	$14-$43	217
㉝ p. 158	Jade Palace	▽▽	Chinese	$10-$23	214
㉞ p. 158	Alto Ristorante & Bar	▽▽▽	Italian	$20-$32	212
㉟ p. 158	Piñon Grill	▽▽▽	Southwestern	$15-$40	216
㊱ p. 158	Remington's	▽▽▽	American	$13-$30	216
㊲ p. 158	**BLT Steak**	▽▽▽▽	Steak	$26-$92	212
㊳ p. 158	ShinBay	▽▽▽	Japanese	$16-$30	217
㊴ p. 158	Ruth's Chris Steak House	▽▽▽	Steak	$31-$40	217
㊵ p. 158	OC Seven Restaurant & Bar	▽▽	American	$8-$26	215
㊶ p. 158	Orange Sky	▽▽▽	Seafood Steak	$24-$56	215
㊷ p. 158	Ocean Trail	▽▽	Creole	$17-$20	215
㊸ p. 158	Sumo Maya Mexican Asian Kitchen	▽▽▽	Fusion	$10-$32	217
㊹ p. 158	Fleming's Prime Steakhouse & Wine Bar	▽▽▽	Steak	$18-$57	214
㊺ p. 158	Rancho Pinot	▽▽▽	American	$22-$31	216
㊻ p. 158	Blanco Tacos + Tequila	▽▽	Mexican	$11-$20	212
㊼ p. 158	**Il Terrazzo**	▽▽▽	Italian	$14-$34	214
㊽ p. 158	**J&G Steakhouse**	▽▽▽▽	Steak	$17-$66	214
㊾ p. 158	Roaring Fork	▽▽▽	Western American	$13-$34	216
㊿ p. 158	Taggia	▽▽▽	Italian	$15-$32	217
51 p. 158	Posh Improvisational Cuisine	▽▽▽▽	International	$50-$140	216

Map Page	Restaurants (cont'd)	Diamond Rated	Cuisine	Price Range	Page
52 p. 158	P.F. Chang's China Bistro	◈◈◈	Chinese	$8-$25	216
53 p. 158	Mastro's City Hall Steakhouse	◈◈◈	Steak	$27-$78	215
54 p. 158	Kona Grill	◈◈◈	Pacific Rim Fusion	$10-$30	214
55 p. 158	Sushi Roku	◈◈◈	Japanese	$10-$35	217
56 p. 158	Don and Charlie's	◈◈	American	$12-$43	213
57 p. 158	Stax Burger Bistro	◈◈	American	$4-$7	217
58 p. 158	The Breakfast Club	◈◈	Breakfast	$6-$16	212
59 p. 158	Cowboy Ciao	◈◈◈	American	$13-$35	213
60 p. 158	The Herb Box	◈◈	American	$15-$32	214
61 p. 158	Marcellino Ristorante	◈◈◈	Italian	$21-$40	215
62 p. 158	Citizen Public House	◈◈◈	American	$12-$38	213
63 p. 158	F n B Restaurant	◈◈◈	New American	$22-$35	214
64 p. 158	Arcadia Farms	◈◈	American	$11-$17	212
65 p. 158	Tommy V's Urban Kitchen and Bar	◈◈◈	Italian	$15-$26	218
66 p. 158	Old Town Tortilla Factory	◈◈	Mexican	$15-$33	215
67 p. 158	Cafe Zu Zu	◈◈◈	American	$10-$30	213
68 p. 158	Malee's Thai On Main	◈◈	Regional Thai	$10-$21	215
69 p. 158	Bandera	◈◈◈	American	$14-$41	212
70 p. 158	Jewel of the Crown	◈◈	Indian	$12-$18	214
71 p. 158	The Mission	◈◈◈	Latin American	$23-$32	215
72 p. 158	Carlsbad Tavern	◈◈	Southwestern	$11-$22	213
73 p. 158	Tottie's Asian Fusion	◈◈	Asian	$8-$14	218
74 p. 158	Los Sombreros	◈◈	Mexican	$10-$37	214
75 p. 158	Atlas Bistro	◈◈◈	International	$25-$35	212
76 p. 158	The Salt Cellar Restaurant	◈◈◈	Seafood	$30-$75	217
77 p. 158	Cholla Prime Steakhouse	◈◈◈	Regional Steak	$10-$29	213
78 p. 158	Ling & Louie's Asian Bar & Grill	◈◈	Asian	$9-$18	214
79 p. 158	Hiro Sushi	◈◈	Sushi	$10-$21	214

PARADISE VALLEY

Map Page	Hotels	Diamond Rated	Rate Range	Page
60 p. 158	**Omni Scottsdale Resort & Spa at Montelucia**	◈◈◈◈	Rates not provided SAVE	118
61 p. 158	Hermosa Inn	◈◈◈	Rates not provided	118
62 p. 158	**Sanctuary Camelback Mountain**	◈◈◈◈	$339-$829 SAVE	119

Map Page	Restaurants	Diamond Rated	Cuisine	Price Range	Page
80 p. 158	**Prado**	◈◈◈◈	Italian	$13-$30	119
81 p. 158	El Chorro	◈◈◈	Continental	$19-$49	119
82 p. 158	**Lon's at the Hermosa**	◈◈◈◈	American	$27-$70	119
83 p. 158	**Elements**	◈◈◈◈	Fusion	$16-$45	119

Get maps, travel information and road service with the AAA and CAA Mobile apps

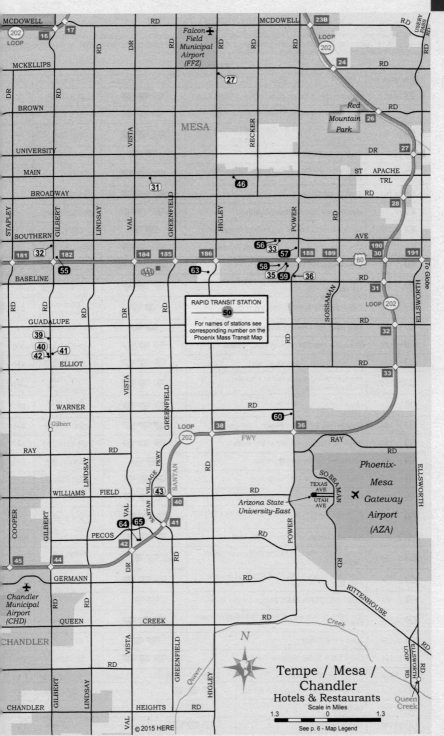

RAPID TRANSIT STATION

50

For names of stations see
corresponding number on the
Phoenix Mass Transit Map

Falcon Field Municipal Airport (FFZ)

MESA

Red Mountain Park

Phoenix-Mesa Gateway Airport (AZA)

Arizona State University-East

Chandler Municipal Airport (CHD)

Tempe / Mesa / Chandler
Hotels & Restaurants
Scale in Miles

See p. 6 - Map Legend

© 2015 HERE

Tempe/Mesa/Chandler

This index helps you "spot" where approved hotels and restaurants are located on the corresponding detailed maps. Hotel daily rate range is for comparison only. Restaurant price range is a combination of lunch and/or dinner. Turn to the listing page for more detailed rate and price information and consult display ads for special promotions.

TEMPE

Map Page	Hotels	Diamond Rated	Rate Range	Page
❶ p. 164	Hampton Inn & Suites Phoenix/Tempe-ASU Area	◆◆◆	$179-$259	246
❷ p. 164	Red Lion Inn & Suites Phoenix/Tempe - ASU	◆◆◆	$79-$159	247
❸ p. 164	Country Inn & Suites By Carlson, Phoenix Airport at Tempe	◆◆◆	$69-$229	246
❹ p. 164	**BEST WESTERN Inn of Tempe**	◆◆	$69-$149 [SAVE]	245
❺ p. 164	**SpringHill Suites by Marriott Phoenix Tempe Airport**	◆◆◆	$71-$248 [SAVE]	248
❻ p. 164	**Aloft Hotel Tempe**	◆◆◆	$99-$209 [SAVE]	245
❼ p. 164	**Hyatt Place Tempe/Phoenix Airport**	◆◆◆	$69-$259 [SAVE]	247
❽ p. 164	La Quinta Inn Phoenix Sky Harbor Airport South	◆◆	$64-$251	247
❾ p. 164	**Courtyard by Marriott-Downtown Tempe**	◆◆◆	$86-$314 [SAVE]	246
❿ p. 164	**Tempe Mission Palms Hotel**	◆◆◆◆	$119-$359 [SAVE]	248
⓫ p. 164	**Residence Inn by Marriott Tempe Downtown/University**	◆◆◆	$115-$376 [SAVE]	247
⓬ p. 164	Extended Stay America-Phoenix/Airport/Tempe	◆◆	Rates not provided	246
⓭ p. 164	**Red Roof Inn Phoenix Airport**	◆◆	$49-$118 [SAVE]	247
⓮ p. 164	**Sheraton Phoenix Airport Hotel Tempe**	◆◆◆	$69-$299 [SAVE]	248
⓯ p. 164	**Comfort Suites Phoenix Airport**	◆◆◆	$74-$189 [SAVE]	245
⓰ p. 164	Holiday Inn Express & Suites Phoenix Tempe-University	◆◆◆	Rates not provided	246
⓱ p. 164	Hotel 1333	◆◆◆	Rates not provided	247
⓲ p. 164	**DoubleTree by Hilton Phoenix-Tempe**	◆◆◆	$79-$249 [SAVE]	246
⓳ p. 164	**Phoenix Marriott Tempe at the Buttes**	◆◆◆	$121-$311 [SAVE]	247
⓴ p. 164	**Hawthorn Suites by Wyndham**	◆◆	$70-$135 [SAVE]	246
㉑ p. 164	Residence Inn by Marriott Tempe	◆◆◆	$90-$324	247
㉒ p. 164	Embassy Suites by Hilton Phoenix-Tempe	◆◆◆	$129-$149	246
㉓ p. 164	Holiday Inn Express Hotel & Suites Tempe Arizona Mills	◆◆◆	$99-$169	246
㉔ p. 164	**Ramada Tempe at Arizona Mills Mall**	◆◆◆	$50-$100 [SAVE]	247
㉕ p. 164	Hotel Tempe Phoenix Airport InnSuites Hotel & Suites	◆◆	Rates not provided	247
㉖ p. 164	SpringHill Suites by Marriott Tempe at Arizona Mills Mall	◆◆◆	$74-$214	248
㉗ p. 164	**BEST WESTERN PLUS Tempe by the Mall**	◆◆	$70-$140 [SAVE]	245
㉘ p. 164	TownePlace Suites by Marriott Tempe at Arizona Mills Mall	◆◆◆	$79-$229	248
㉙ p. 164	Days Inn & Suites	◆◆	$69-$99	246
㉚ p. 164	Drury Inn & Suites Phoenix Tempe	◆◆◆	$80-$210	246

Map Page	Restaurants	Diamond Rated	Cuisine	Price Range	Page
① p. 164	Gordon Biersch Brewery Restaurant	◆◆◆	American	$10-$28	249
② p. 164	La Bocca	◆◆	Pizza	$8-$16	249
③ p. 164	House of Tricks	◆◆◆	American	$23-$49	249

Map Page	Restaurants (cont'd)	Diamond Rated	Cuisine	Price Range	Page
④ p. 164	P.F. Chang's China Bistro	◈◈◈	Chinese	$8-$25	249
⑤ p. 164	Cafe Lalibela	◈◈	Ethiopian	$6-$15	248
⑥ p. 164	Casey Moore's Oyster House	◈◈	American	$6-$28	248
⑦ p. 164	Sushi 101	◈◈	Sushi	$5-$25	249
⑧ p. 164	Republic Ramen	◈◈	Asian Noodles	$6-$8	249
⑨ p. 164	Tasty Kabob	◈◈	Middle Eastern	$7-$31	249
⑩ p. 164	Pita Jungle	◈◈	Mediterranean	$6-$15	249
⑪ p. 164	Cafe Istanbul & Market	◈◈	Middle Eastern	$6-$14	248
⑫ p. 164	Haji Baba Middle Eastern Food	◈◈	Middle Eastern	$7-$14	249
⑬ p. 164	**The Dhaba**	◈◈	Indian	$10-$21	248
⑭ p. 164	Top of the Rock Restaurant	◈◈◈	American	$14-$35	249
⑮ p. 164	Lemon Grass Thai Cuisine	◈◈	Thai	$6-$16	249
⑯ p. 164	Royal Taj	◈◈	Indian	$9-$17	249
⑰ p. 164	Byblos Restaurant	◈◈	Greek	$8-$19	248
⑱ p. 164	Tom's BBQ Chicago Style	◈	Barbecue	$8-$25	249

PHOENIX

Map Page	Hotels	Diamond Rated	Rate Range	Page
33 p. 164	**Clarion Hotel Phoenix-Chandler**	◈◈	$49-$199 [SAVE]	176
34 p. 164	**Four Points by Sheraton Phoenix South**	◈◈◈	Rates not provided [SAVE]	179
35 p. 164	Extended Stay America-Phoenix-Chandler	◈◈	Rates not provided	178
36 p. 164	**Holiday Inn Express & Suites Phoenix-Chandler**	◈◈◈	Rates not provided [SAVE]	180
37 p. 164	La Quinta Inn & Suites Phoenix Chandler	◈◈◈	$64-$251	181
38 p. 164	Extended Stay America Phoenix-Chandler-E Chandler Blvd	◈◈	Rates not provided	178

Map Page	Restaurants	Diamond Rated	Cuisine	Price Range	Page
㉑ p. 164	Caffe Boa	◈◈◈	Italian	$11-$27	184
㉒ p. 164	Sakana Sushi and Grill	◈◈	Sushi	$8-$17	189
㉓ p. 164	Pacific Gardens Asian Bistro	◈◈	Asian Fusion	$8-$17	187
㉔ p. 164	Ruffino Italian Cuisine	◈◈◈	Italian	$13-$35	189

MESA

Map Page	Hotels	Diamond Rated	Rate Range	Page
41 p. 164	**Hyatt Place Phoenix/Mesa**	◈◈◈	$69-$229 [SAVE]	110
42 p. 164	**Phoenix Marriott Mesa**	◈◈◈	$73-$220 [SAVE]	110
43 p. 164	Econo Lodge Inn & Suites Mesa	◈◈	Rates not provided	109
44 p. 164	**Mezona Inn**	◈◈	$59-$170	110
45 p. 164	Baymont Inn & Suites Mesa	◈◈◈	$70-$190	109
46 p. 164	Days Inn-East Mesa	◈◈	$55-$120	109
47 p. 164	**Courtyard by Marriott-Mesa**	◈◈◈	$60-$220 [SAVE]	109
48 p. 164	La Quinta Inn & Suites Phoenix Mesa West	◈◈	$64-$246	110
49 p. 164	**Residence Inn by Marriott Phoenix Mesa**	◈◈◈	$85-$273 [SAVE]	110
50 p. 164	**Fairfield Inn & Suites by Marriott Phoenix Mesa**	◈◈◈	$58-$163 [SAVE]	109

MESA (cont'd)

Map Page	Hotels (cont'd)	Diamond Rated	Rate Range	Page
51 p. 164	**Hilton Phoenix/Mesa**	◆◆◆	$79-$269 SAVE	110
52 p. 164	Ramada Mesa Phoenix East Area	◆◆	$40-$94	110
53 p. 164	Holiday Inn & Suites Phoenix-Mesa/Chandler	◆◆◆	Rates not provided	110
54 p. 164	Days Hotel Mesa Country Club	◆◆	$66-$160	109
55 p. 164	**BEST WESTERN PLUS Mesa**	◆◆◆	$69-$199 SAVE	109
56 p. 164	Quality Inn Mesa - Superstition Springs	◆◆	$90-$130	110
57 p. 164	**BEST WESTERN Superstition Springs Inn**	◆◆	$69-$149 SAVE	109
58 p. 164	La Quinta Inn & Suites Mesa Superstition Springs	◆◆◆	$75-$273	110
59 p. 164	Country Inn & Suites By Carlson	◆◆◆	$75-$199	109
60 p. 164	**BEST WESTERN Legacy Inn & Suites**	◆◆◆	$75-$179 SAVE	109

Map Page	Restaurants	Diamond Rated	Cuisine	Price Range	Page
27 p. 164	Flancer's	◆◆	Pizza	$7-$13	111
28 p. 164	Blue Adobe Grille	◆◆	Mexican	$9-$20	111
29 p. 164	The Landmark Restaurant	◆◆	American	$8-$27	111
30 p. 164	Los Dos Molinos	◆◆	Mexican	$4-$14	111
31 p. 164	Little Mesa Cafe	◆	American	$7-$17	111
32 p. 164	Mi Amigos Mexican Grill	◆◆	Mexican	$7-$19	111
33 p. 164	My Big Fat Greek Restaurant	◆◆	Greek	$7-$20	111
34 p. 164	Pink Pepper Thai Cuisine	◆◆	Thai	$8-$14	111
35 p. 164	P.F. Chang's China Bistro	◆◆◆	Chinese	$8-$25	111
36 p. 164	Sakana Sushi & Grill	◆◆	Sushi	$8-$34	111

GILBERT

Map Page	Hotels	Diamond Rated	Rate Range	Page
63 p. 164	Residence Inn by Marriott Phoenix Gilbert	◆◆◆	$118-$338	75
64 p. 164	**Hyatt Place Phoenix/Gilbert**	◆◆◆	$69-$229 SAVE	75
65 p. 164	Hampton Inn & Suites Phoenix/Gilbert	◆◆	$75-$225	74

Map Page	Restaurants	Diamond Rated	Cuisine	Price Range	Page
39 p. 164	Flancer's Cafe	◆◆	American	$7-$20	75
40 p. 164	Postino Gilbert WineCafe	◆◆	Small Plates Sandwiches	$9-$14	75
41 p. 164	**Joe's Real BBQ**	◆	Barbecue	$8-$19	75
42 p. 164	The Farmhouse Restaurant	◆◆	Breakfast Sandwiches	$4-$9	75
43 p. 164	**Cantina Laredo**	◆◆	Mexican	$10-$25	75

CHANDLER

Map Page	Hotels	Diamond Rated	Rate Range	Page
68 p. 164	**Courtyard by Marriott Phoenix Chandler**	◆◆◆	$71-$258 SAVE	48
69 p. 164	Homewood Suites by Hilton Phoenix-Chandler	◆◆◆	$104-$189	49
70 p. 164	Hampton Inn Phoenix-Chandler	◆◆◆	$89-$189	49
71 p. 164	**Radisson Phoenix-Chandler**	◆◆◆	$65-$229 SAVE	49
72 p. 164	**Fairfield Inn & Suites by Marriott Phoenix Chandler**	◆◆◆	$64-$180 SAVE	48
73 p. 164	**Quality Inn**	◆◆	$59-$249 SAVE	49

CHANDLER (cont'd)

Map Page	Hotels (cont'd)	Diamond Rated	Rate Range	Page
74 p. 164	**Comfort Inn Chandler-Phoenix South**	◆◆◆	$59-$199 [SAVE]	48
75 p. 164	Hawthorn Suites by Wyndham-Chandler	◆◆	$79-$219	49
76 p. 164	**BEST WESTERN Inn of Chandler**	◆◆	$80-$130 [SAVE]	48
77 p. 164	SpringHill Suites by Marriott-Chandler Fashion Center	◆◆◆	$83-$240	50
78 p. 164	Residence Inn by Marriott-Chandler Fashion Center	◆◆◆	$100-$270	49
79 p. 164	**Hyatt Place Phoenix Chandler Fashion Center**	◆◆◆	$89-$299 [SAVE]	49
80 p. 164	Hilton Phoenix Chandler	◆◆◆	$99-$279	49
81 p. 164	Crowne Plaza San Marcos Golf Resort	◆◆◆	$99-$309	48
82 p. 164	**Wild Horse Pass Hotel & Casino** (See ad p. 182.)	◆◆◆◆	$59-$229 [SAVE]	50
83 p. 164	Fairfield Inn & Suites by Marriott Phoenix Chandler/Fashion Center	◆◆◆	$71-$213	48
84 p. 164	Courtyard by Marriott Phoenix Chandler/Fashion Center	◆◆◆	$82-$233	48
85 p. 164	Homewood Suites by Hilton-Phoenix/Chandler Fashion Center	◆◆◆	$99-$209	49
86 p. 164	Hampton Inn & Suites Phoenix/Chandler Fashion Center	◆◆◆	$79-$179	49
87 p. 164	**Sheraton Wild Horse Pass Resort & Spa** (See ad p. 50.)	◆◆◆◆	$99-$369 [SAVE]	50
88 p. 164	**Holiday Inn at Ocotillo**	◆◆◆	Rates not provided [SAVE]	49

Map Page	Restaurants	Diamond Rated	Cuisine	Price Range	Page
46 p. 164	C-Fu Gourmet	◆◆	Chinese	$5-$19	51
47 p. 164	Z'Tejas Southwestern Grill	◆◆◆	Southwestern	$7-$25	52
48 p. 164	Saigon Pho & Seafood	◆◆	Vietnamese	$6-$13	51
49 p. 164	Pita Jungle	◆◆	Mediterranean	$7-$16	51
50 p. 164	Chou's Kitchen	◆◆	Northern Chinese	$5-$13	51
51 p. 164	P.F. Chang's China Bistro	◆◆◆	Chinese	$9-$25	51
52 p. 164	Cyclo Vietnamese Cuisine	◆◆	Vietnamese	$6-$13	51
53 p. 164	La Stalla	◆◆◆	Italian	$8-$26	51
54 p. 164	DC Steakhouse	◆◆◆	Steak	$12-$41	51
55 p. 164	Brunchie's	◆◆	American	$6-$17	51
55 p. 164	Fleming's Prime Steakhouse & Wine Bar	◆◆◆	Steak	$19-$57	51
56 p. 164	Shula's America's Steak House	◆◆◆	Steak	$25-$68	52
57 p. 164	Ling & Louie's Asian Bar & Grill	◆◆	Asian	$11-$17	51
58 p. 164	Rawhide Steakhouse	◆◆	Steak	$14-$65	51
59 p. 164	Kai (See ad p. 50.)	◆◆◆◆◆	Southwestern	$35-$175	51

Use travel time to share driving tips

and rules of the road with your teens

DOWNTOWN PHOENIX

- Restaurants p. 172
- Hotels & Restaurants map & index p. 143

AMERICAS BEST VALUE INN-DOWNTOWN PHOENIX
(602)257-8331 **5**

Motel
$59-$169

Address: 424 W Van Buren St 85003 **Location:** Corner of 5th Ave; center. Van Buren/Central-1st Ave, 12. **Facility:** 37 units. 2 stories (no elevator), exterior corridors. **Terms:** cancellation fee imposed. **Guest Services:** coin laundry. **Featured Amenity: continental breakfast.**

FAIRFIELD INN & SUITES BY MARRIOTT PHOENIX MIDTOWN
(602)716-9900 **3**

Hotel $92-$263 **Address:** 2520 N Central Ave 85004 **Location:** I-10 exit 145 (7th St), 0.8 mi n to Virginia Ave, 0.4 mi w, then 0.7 mi n. Located in a commercial area. Encanto/Central, 9. **Facility:** 107 units. 4 stories, interior corridors. **Amenities:** safes. **Pool(s):** heated outdoor. **Activities:** hot tub, exercise room. **Guest Services:** valet and coin laundry, area transportation.

AAA Benefit: Members save 5% or more!

HAMPTON INN-PHOENIX/MIDTOWN (DOWNTOWN AREA)
(602)200-0990 **1**

Hotel $99-$259 **Address:** 160 W Catalina Dr 85013 **Location:** Jct Thomas Rd, just n on Central Ave, then 0.3 mi w. Opposite St. Joseph's Hospital/Barrow Institute. Thomas/Central, 8. **Facility:** 99 units. 4 stories, interior corridors. **Terms:** 1-7 night minimum stay, cancellation fee imposed. **Pool(s):** heated outdoor. **Activities:** hot tub, exercise room. **Guest Services:** valet and coin laundry.

AAA Benefit: Members save up to 10%!

HILTON PHOENIX SUITES
(602)222-1111 **2**

Hotel $89-$289 **Address:** 10 E Thomas Rd 85012 **Location:** Just e of Central Ave; in Phoenix Plaza. Thomas/Central, 8. **Facility:** 226 units. 11 stories, interior corridors. **Parking:** on-site (fee) and valet. **Terms:** 1-7 night minimum stay, cancellation fee imposed. **Amenities:** video games, safes. **Pool(s):** heated indoor. **Activities:** hot tub, exercise room. **Guest Services:** valet and coin laundry, area transportation.

AAA Benefit: Members save 5% or more!

HISTORIC HOTEL SAN CARLOS
602/253-4121 **9**

Historic Hotel
Rates not provided

Address: 202 N Central Ave 85004 **Location:** Just n of Washington St; center. Van Buren/Central-1st Ave, 12. **Facility:** Located along the light rail line, this charming historic hotel offers themed suites and attractive guest rooms. 128 units. 7 stories, interior corridors. **Parking:** valet only. **Pool(s):** heated outdoor. **Activities:** exercise room. **Guest Services:** boarding pass kiosk.

HOLIDAY INN EXPRESS HOTEL & SUITES- DOWNTOWN BALL PARK
602/452-2020 **4**

Hotel. Rates not provided. **Address:** 620 N 6th St 85004 **Location:** I-10 exit 145 (7th St), 0.5 mi s, then 1 blk w on Fillmore St. 3rd St/Washington, 15. **Facility:** 90 units. 3 stories, interior corridors. **Pool(s):** heated outdoor. **Activities:** hot tub, exercise room. **Guest Services:** valet and coin laundry.

HOTEL PALOMAR PHOENIX-CITYSCAPE
(602)253-6633 **14**

Contemporary Hotel $119-$439 **Address:** 2 E Jefferson St 85004 **Location:** Northeast corner of Central Ave and Jefferson St. Jefferson/1st Ave, 14. **Facility:** Located within the CityScape complex, this beautifully designed property is a short stroll to upscale shops, restaurants, sports and cultural facilities. The rooftop pool and bar command sweeping skyline views. 242 units. 10 stories, interior corridors. **Parking:** on-site (fee) and valet. **Terms:** cancellation fee imposed. **Amenities:** safes. **Dining:** Blue Hound Kitchen & Cocktails, see separate listing. **Pool(s):** heated outdoor. **Activities:** bicycles. **Guest Services:** valet laundry, boarding pass kiosk.

HYATT REGENCY PHOENIX
(602)252-1234 **11**

Hotel
$99-$499

HYATT REGENCY

AAA Benefit: Members save 10%!

Address: 122 N 2nd St 85004 **Location:** Just n of Washington St; at Civic Plaza. 3rd St/Washington, 15. **Facility:** 693 units, some two bedrooms. 24 stories, interior corridors. **Parking:** on-site and valet. **Terms:** cancellation fee imposed. **Amenities:** safes. **Dining:** 3 restaurants, also, Compass Arizona Grill, see separate listing. **Pool(s):** heated outdoor. **Activities:** hot tub, exercise room. **Guest Services:** valet laundry, boarding pass kiosk.

RENAISSANCE PHOENIX DOWNTOWN
(602)333-0000 **12**

Hotel
$124-$364

R
RENAISSANCE HOTELS

AAA Benefit: Members save 5% or more!

Address: 50 E Adams St 85004 **Location:** Just w of 1st St; between 1st St and Central Ave. Washington/Central Ave, 13. **Facility:** 527 units. 18 stories, interior corridors. **Parking:** valet only. **Terms:** check-in 4 pm. **Amenities:** safes. **Dining:** 2 restaurants. **Pool(s):** heated outdoor. **Activities:** exercise room. **Guest Services:** valet laundry, boarding pass kiosk.

RODEWAY INN DOWNTOWN PHOENIX
(602)254-7247 **6**

Motel
$55-$110

Address: 402 W Van Buren St 85003 **Location:** Just w of Central Ave; center. Van Buren/Central-1st Ave, 12. **Facility:** 38 units. 2 stories (no elevator), interior/exterior corridors. **Terms:** cancellation fee imposed, resort fee.

(See map & index p. 143.)

SHERATON PHOENIX DOWNTOWN HOTEL
(602)262-2500 **7**

Hotel
$99-$500

S Sheraton HOTELS & RESORTS

AAA Benefit: Members save up to 15%, plus Starwood Preferred Guest® benefits!

Address: 340 N 3rd St 85004 **Location:** I-10 exit 145A (7th St), 0.5 mi s to Fillmore St, just w, then just s. 🅿 Van Buren/Central-1st Ave, 12. **Facility:** Upscale and spacious public areas, refined service and well-appointed guest rooms make this downtown property a good choice for either business or leisure travel. 1000 units. 31 stories, interior corridors. **Parking:** on-site (fee) and valet. **Terms:** cancellation fee imposed. **Amenities:** safes. **Dining:** 2 restaurants, also, District American Kitchen & Wine Bar, see separate listing. **Pool(s):** heated outdoor. **Activities:** hot tub, exercise room. **Guest Services:** valet laundry. *(See ad this page.)*

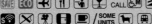

SPRINGHILL SUITES BY MARRIOTT PHOENIX DOWNTOWN
(602)307-9929 **10**

Hotel
$94-$280

SPRINGHILL SUITES Marriott

AAA Benefit: Members save 5% or more!

Address: 802 E Van Buren St 85006 **Location:** I-10 exit 145 (7th St), just s, then just e. 🅿 12th St/Washington, 17. **Facility:** 121 units. 6 stories, interior corridors. **Pool(s):** heated outdoor. **Activities:** hot tub, exercise room. **Guest Services:** valet and coin laundry, area transportation. **Featured Amenity:** breakfast buffet.

 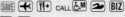

▼ See AAA listing this page ▼

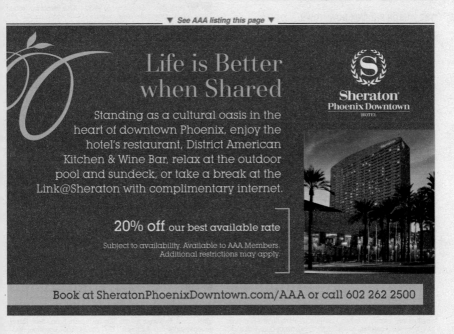

Life is Better when Shared

Standing as a cultural oasis in the heart of downtown Phoenix, enjoy the hotel's restaurant, District American Kitchen & Wine Bar, relax at the outdoor pool and sundeck, or take a break at the Link@Sheraton with complimentary internet.

Sheraton Phoenix Downtown HOTEL

20% off our best available rate

Subject to availability. Available to AAA Members. Additional restrictions may apply.

Book at SheratonPhoenixDowntown.com/AAA or call 602 262 2500

Remember, car seats, booster seats
and seat belts save lives

(See map & index p. 143.)

SUPER 8-DOWNTOWN PHOENIX/CONVENTION CENTER
(602)252-6823 **13**

Motel
$70-$150

Address: 965 E Van Buren St 85006 **Location:** I-10 exit 145 (7th St), just s, then just e. Located in a light-commercial area. 12th St/Washington, 17. **Facility:** 59 units. 2 stories (no elevator), exterior corridors. **Pool(s):** outdoor. **Guest Services:** coin laundry.

Walking distance to Convention Center, Chase Field and Talking Stick Resort Arena.

THE WESTIN PHOENIX DOWNTOWN
(602)429-3500 **8**

Hotel
$109-$399

WESTIN HOTELS & RESORTS **AAA Benefit:** Members save up to 15%, plus Starwood Preferred Guest® benefits!

Address: 333 N Central Ave 85004 **Location:** Northeast corner of Central Ave and Van Buren St. Van Buren/Central-1st Ave, 12. **Facility:** Spacious, modern and elegant guest rooms with sweeping views are the showcase of this downtown property. 242 units. 26 stories, interior corridors. **Parking:** valet and street only. **Amenities:** safes. **Dining:** Province Urban Kitchen & Bar, see separate listing. **Pool(s):** heated outdoor. **Activities:** exercise room, massage. **Guest Services:** valet laundry.

WHERE TO EAT

THE ARROGANT BUTCHER
602/324-8502 **36**

American. Gastropub. $12-$34 **AAA Inspector Notes:** Upscale comfort food meets hand-crafted specialty cocktails at this trendy downtown hot spot. Try the charcuterie for a mix of smoked meats and gourmet cheeses, or one of the daily specials including meatloaf and mashed potatoes, slow-roasted prime rib and Kurobuta baby back ribs. **Features:** full bar, patio dining, happy hour. **Reservations:** suggested. **Address:** 2 E Jefferson St, #150 85004 **Location:** Northwest corner of Jefferson and 1st sts; in CityScape. Washington/Central Ave, 13. **Parking:** on-site (fee) and street.

BLISS
602/795-1792 **19**

American. Casual Dining. $9-$17 **AAA Inspector Notes:** Hip and casual, this hot spot boasts a large outdoor bar and dining terrace overlooking downtown. Comfort food is served late, with such favorites as mama's pot roast, loaded macaroni and cheese and double-cut pork chops. **Features:** full bar, patio dining, Sunday brunch, happy hour. **Address:** 901 N 4th St 85004 **Location:** Just s of Roosevelt St. Roosevelt/Central, 11. **Parking:** street only.

BLUE HOUND KITCHEN & COCKTAILS
602/258-0231 **34**

American. Casual Dining. $10-$36 **AAA Inspector Notes:** The focus is on fresh, sustainable and organic at this stylish pub-style spot. Menu items include charred pork belly sliders, jerk cured Scottish salmon and goat cheese stuffed squash blossoms. Ask the server to suggest craft cocktails to match the dishes. **Features:** full bar, patio dining, Sunday brunch, happy hour. **Address:** 2 E Jefferson St 85004 **Location:** Northeast corner of Central Ave and Jefferson St; in Hotel Palomar Phoenix-CityScape. Jefferson/1st Ave, 14. **Parking:** on-site (fee) and valet.

THE BREADFRUIT AUTHENTIC JAMAICAN GRILL
602/267-1266 **25**

Jamaican. Casual Dining. $9-$28 **AAA Inspector Notes:** This intimate modern storefront serves authentic Jamaican cuisine using fresh, organic ingredients. The jerk-rubbed chicken and escovitch tilapia are favorites. **Features:** patio dining, happy hour. **Reservations:** suggested. **Address:** 108 E Pierce St 85004 **Location:** Jct Central Ave, just e. Roosevelt/Central, 11. **Parking:** street only.

THE BREAKFAST CLUB
602/354-7284 **35**

American. Casual Dining. $6-$14 **AAA Inspector Notes:** This modern, comfortable diner located in CityScape is popular with visitors and downtown workers for its fresh food and fast, friendly service. **Address:** 2 E Jefferson St, Suite 213 85004 **Location:** In CityScape. Jefferson/1st Ave, 14. **Parking:** on-site (fee) and street.

CHINA CHILI
602/266-4463 **1**

Chinese. Casual Dining. $7-$26 **AAA Inspector Notes:** This popular lunch spot features classic Chinese favorites served in a comfortable family-friendly setting. **Features:** beer & wine. **Address:** 302 E Flower St 85012 **Location:** At 3rd St. Osborn/Central, 7.

CIBO URBAN PIZZERIA CAFE
602/441-2697 **23**

Italian. Casual Dining. $9-$17 **AAA Inspector Notes:** Located downtown in a historic house, this intimate Italian cafe serves fresh made pizza, calzones, gourmet salads, and delicious nutella crepes for dessert. The patio is a great space when the weather is nice. **Features:** beer & wine, patio dining, Sunday brunch, happy hour. **Address:** 603 N 5th Ave 85003 **Location:** Corner of Fillmore St; downtown. Van Buren/Central-1st Ave, 12. **Parking:** valet and street only.

COMPASS ARIZONA GRILL
602/440-3166 **29**

American. Fine Dining. $27-$40 **AAA Inspector Notes:** This revolving restaurant on the 24th floor offers panoramic views of the city. Innovative presentations of seafood, beef, lamb and chicken combine artistic color with tempting accompaniments to make a delightful meal. **Features:** full bar, Sunday brunch, happy hour. **Reservations:** suggested. **Address:** 122 N 2nd St 85004 **Location:** Just n of Washington St; at Civic Plaza; in Hyatt Regency Phoenix. 3rd St/Washington, 15. **Parking:** valet and street only.

CORDUROY
602/374-7585 **12**

Small Plates. Casual Dining. $11-$17 **AAA Inspector Notes:** With a sophisticated, yet comfortable setting, this midtown hot spot features creative shareable plates like the chicken piri piri with a spicy glaze, or roasted mussels with bacon, tomato and garlic in a white wine broth, as well as salads and sandwiches. The young, energetic staff is more than happy to assist with the extensive cocktail and wine selections. **Features:** full bar, patio dining, Sunday brunch, happy hour. **Reservations:** suggested. **Address:** 2601 N Central Ave 85004 **Location:** SE corner of N Central and E Virginia aves. Encanto/Central, 9.

(See map & index p. 143.)

DISTRICT AMERICAN KITCHEN & WINE BAR
602/817-5400 (28)

▼▼▼ American. Casual Dining. $9-$24 **AAA Inspector Notes:** Creative twists on American cuisine are attractively presented, and guests are even treated to cotton candy at the end of the meal. The spacious dining area has large windows overlooking the busy downtown street. There also is an energetic bar and lounge area with live entertainment on the weekends. **Features:** full bar, patio dining, happy hour. **Reservations:** suggested. **Address:** 320 N 3rd St 85004 **Location:** I-10 exit 145A (7th St), 0.5 mi s to Fillmore St, just w, then just s; in Sheraton Phoenix Downtown Hotel. Ⓟ 3rd St/Washington, 15. **Parking:** on-site (fee) and valet. *(See ad p. 171.)* Ⓑ Ⓛ Ⓓ ⓁⒶⓉⒺ CALL ⓒ̲ⓜ̲ 🚇

DUCK AND DECANTER
602/234-3656 (2)

▼ Deli. Quick Serve. $6-$10 **AAA Inspector Notes:** This eatery cannot be beat for a quick, delicious lunch consisting of sandwiches and soups. Dinners may include wine, and can be selected from an excellent list. The baked goodies are excellent for dessert or to take home for an after-meal snack. **Features:** wine only. **Address:** 3111 N Central Ave 85008 **Location:** Just n of Earll Dr. Ⓟ Osborn/Central, 7. Ⓑ Ⓛ 🚇

DUCK AND DECANTER
602/266-6637 (31)

▼ Deli. Quick Serve. $6-$10 **AAA Inspector Notes:** Located close to downtown attractions, this popular lunch spot is good for gourmet deli sandwiches and a nice selection of wines. **Features:** beer & wine, patio dining. **Address:** 1 N Central Ave 85004 **Location:** Corner of N 1st and E Washington sts. Ⓟ Washington/Central Ave, 13. **Parking:** street only. Ⓑ Ⓛ Ⓓ CALL ⓒ̲ⓜ̲ 🚇

DURANT'S
602/264-5967 (10)

▼▼▼
Steak
Casual Dining
$14-$64

AAA Inspector Notes: *Classic.* For great steaks, a classic club atmosphere and accomplished service, this restaurant fits the bill. The well-trained staff strives to provide guests a special dining experience. When entering from the parking area, diners may meet the grill chef as they walk through the kitchen. **Features:** full bar. **Reservations:** suggested. **Address:** 2611 N Central Ave 85004 **Location:** 0.8 mi n of McDowell Rd. Ⓟ Thomas/Central, 8. **Parking:** on-site and valet. *Menu on AAA.com* Ⓛ Ⓓ 🚇

THE GOOD EGG
602/248-3897 (3)

▼▼ American. Casual Dining. $6-$10 **AAA Inspector Notes:** This popular, Midtown breakfast spot is as well known for its delicious food as it is for great people-watching out on the patio. **Address:** 3110 N Central Ave 85012 **Location:** In Park Central Shopping Center. Ⓟ Osborn/Central, 7. Ⓑ Ⓛ 🚇

HARD ROCK CAFE
602/261-7625 (37)

▼▼ American. Casual Dining. $9-$21 **AAA Inspector Notes:** Rock 'n' roll memorabilia decorates the walls of the popular theme restaurant. Live music on the weekends contributes to the bustling atmosphere. On the menu is a wide variety of American cuisine—from burgers and sandwiches to seafood, steaks and pasta. **Features:** full bar. **Address:** 3 S 2nd St, Suite 117 85004 **Location:** At Jackson St; in Collier Center. Ⓟ 3rd St/Washington, 15. **Parking:** street only. Ⓢ̲Ⓐ̲Ⓥ̲Ⓔ̲ Ⓛ Ⓓ 🚇

HONEY BEAR'S BBQ
602/279-7911 (8)

▼ Barbecue. Quick Serve. $7-$25 **AAA Inspector Notes:** Barbecue sandwiches and ribs are slathered in a special, spicy tomato-based sauce at this popular eatery. **Features:** beer & wine, patio dining. **Address:** 2824 N Central Ave 85004 **Location:** Jct Central Ave and Thomas Rd, just s. Ⓟ Thomas/Central, 8. Ⓛ Ⓓ 🚇

HOW DO YOU ROLL?
602/254-1442 (16)

▼ Sushi. Quick Serve. $4-$7 **AAA Inspector Notes:** Diners can choose from a variety of fresh fillings and sauces to create personalized sushi rolls, assembly-line style. Also available are miso soup, calamari salad, edamame and mochi ice cream. **Features:** beer & wine. **Address:** 1515 N 7th Ave, Suite 100 85007 **Location:** I-10 exit 144 (7th Ave), just n. Ⓟ McDowell/Central, 10. Ⓛ Ⓓ 🚇

KINCAID'S FISH, CHOP & STEAK HOUSE
602/340-0000 (33)

▼▼▼ Steak Seafood. Fine Dining. $17-$49 **AAA Inspector Notes:** This popular restaurant has a bustling, warm ambience. The varied menu includes seafood, steak and excellent prime rib. Ample wine and dessert choices round out the meal. **Features:** full bar, patio dining, happy hour. **Address:** 2 S 3rd St 85004 **Location:** Southwest corner of 3rd and Washington sts; in Collier Center. Ⓟ 3rd St/Washington, 15. **Parking:** on-site and street. Ⓛ Ⓓ 🚇

LOLA COFFEE
602/252-2265 (18)

▼ Coffee/Tea. Quick Serve. $2-$6 **AAA Inspector Notes:** Delectable homemade pastries and savory quiche are the backdrops at this uptown chic coffee house. The real star is the fresh roasted coffee, where every espresso shot is hand-crafted from vintage machines. **Features:** patio dining. **Address:** 1001 N 3rd Ave 85003 **Location:** Corner of Roosevelt St. Ⓟ Roosevelt/Central, 11. **Parking:** on-site and street. Ⓑ Ⓛ Ⓓ 🚇

MATT'S BIG BREAKFAST
602/254-1074 (20)

▼▼ American. Casual Dining. $5-$9 **AAA Inspector Notes:** A popular spot for breakfast, this diner features fresh, local ingredients and hearty favorites like salami scramble or Belgian-style waffles with thick-cut bacon. Be prepared for a wait if you show up late on weekend mornings. **Address:** 825 N 1st St 85004 **Location:** Northeast corner of McKinley and 1st sts. Ⓟ Roosevelt/Central, 11. **Parking:** on-site and street. Ⓑ Ⓛ 🚇

MOIRA SUSHI BAR & KITCHEN
602/254-5085 (22)

▼▼ Japanese. Casual Dining. $10-$15 **AAA Inspector Notes:** An intimate, modern space welcomes diners who may choose from a blend of the traditional sushi and sashimi choices to more eclectic dishes such as intense red curry with kaffir lime leaves and pineapple. **Features:** full bar, happy hour. **Address:** 215 E McKinley St 85004 **Location:** Jct 3rd St, just w. Ⓟ Roosevelt/Central, 11. **Parking:** street only. Ⓛ Ⓓ 🚇

MOTHER BUNCH BREWING
602/368-3580 (21)

▼▼ American. Casual Dining. $10-$15 **AAA Inspector Notes:** This trendy brewpub sports an open, industrial interior and a young, fun waitstaff. Several signature beers are on tap, as well as others from around the state. Try the green chile burger if you like it spicy. **Features:** full bar, Sunday brunch, happy hour. **Address:** 825 N 7th St 85006 **Location:** I-10 exit 7th St, just s. Ⓟ Roosevelt/Central, 11. Ⓛ Ⓓ 🚇

MU SHU ASIAN GRILL
602/277-9867 (4)

▼▼ Asian. Casual Dining. $9-$17 **AAA Inspector Notes:** At this eatery, diners can choose from classic Szechuan-style dishes, a popular lunch buffet, or create-your-own stir-fry all served in a friendly and comfortable setting. **Features:** beer & wine. **Address:** 1502 W Thomas Rd 85015 **Location:** Corner of 15th Ave and Thomas Rd. Ⓛ Ⓓ

THE ORIGINAL HAMBURGER WORKS
602/263-8693 (6)

▼ American. Casual Dining. $4-$7 **AAA Inspector Notes:** This spot truly has been a Phoenix original for more than 25 years. Burgers are grilled while diners watch and a salad cart is filled with fresh ingredients to accompany each sandwich. Other choices include crispy Arizona fries, zucchini or onion rings and honey hot barbecue wings. **Features:** full bar, patio dining, happy hour. **Address:** 2801 N 15th Ave 85013 **Location:** Just s of Thomas Rd. Ⓛ Ⓓ

PERSIAN GARDEN CAFÉ
602/263-1915 (5)

▼ Middle Eastern. Casual Dining. $10-$35 **AAA Inspector Notes:** From the hummus, baba ghanoush and falafel to gyros and lamb or chicken kebabs, diners can be completely satisfied with the flavors and portions served here. There are many vegetarian choices as well. Consider Persian ice cream as a decadent finish. **Address:** 1335 W Thomas Rd 85013 **Location:** Just e of 15th Ave. Ⓟ Thomas/Central, 8. Ⓛ Ⓓ 🚇

(See map & index p. 143.)

PINO'S PIZZA AL CENTRO   602/279-3237   (7)

♦♦♦ Italian. Casual Dining. $6-$17 **AAA Inspector Notes:** It is all about the food at this casual, no-frills Italian bistro in Midtown. The owner, Pino, always is in house and creates some of the tastiest Italian classics west of the Mississippi. The meatballs, handmade pasta and calzones are outstanding, as is the tiramisu. At lunch, line up for delicious pizza by the slice. **Features:** beer & wine. **Address:** 139 W Thomas Rd 85013 **Location:** Just w of Central Ave. ⓐ Thomas/Central, 8. [L] [D] [🚐]

PIZZA PEOPLE PUB   602/795-7954   (17)

♦♦♦ Pizza. Casual Dining. $8-$15 **AAA Inspector Notes:** An abundance of comfort foods like various styles of macaroni and cheese, along with piggies in blankets complement the delicious artisanal pizza and salads. Beer lovers can enjoy the abundant tap selection. **Features:** full bar, patio dining, happy hour. **Address:** 1326 N Central Ave 85004 **Location:** Jct Central Ave and McDowell Rd, just s. ⓐ McDowell/Central, 10. [L] [D] [🚐]

PIZZERIA BIANCO   602/258-8300   (32)

♦♦ Pizza. Casual Dining. $13-$18 **AAA Inspector Notes:** Be prepared to wait for a table in order to sample what some critics have judged as the best pizza in the country. The freshly made, wood-fired pies come with a selection of fresh toppings. The dining room exudes casual energy, and the adjacent building provides a spot to wait and enjoy special wine and beer selections. **Features:** beer & wine. **Address:** 623 E Adams St 85004 **Location:** I-10 exit 145 (7th St), 0.5 mi s, then just w. ⓐ 3rd St/Jefferson, 16. [L] [D] [🚐]

POMO PIZZERIA NAPOLETANA   602/795-2555   (24)

♦♦ Italian. Casual Dining. $10-$17 **AAA Inspector Notes:** Diners feel like they are transported to Italy when entering this stylish pizzeria which offers certified authentic Neapolitan pizza. There are more than 15 different pies to choose from, along with antipasti, insalate, savory homemade desserts and cappuccino. **Features:** full bar, patio dining. **Reservations:** suggested. **Address:** 705 N 1st St 85004 **Location:** Jct Roosevelt St; just s. ⓐ Roosevelt/Central, 11. **Parking:** on-site (fee) and street. [L] [D] CALL[♿M] [🚐]

PROVINCE URBAN KITCHEN & BAR   602/429-3600   (27)

♦♦♦ American. Fine Dining. $18-$35 **AAA Inspector Notes:** The cuisine at this modern, upscale dining spot is American with global influences. The menu changes seasonally and features farm-to-table, local ingredients. Try the homemade pasta, fresh seafood selections or the petite filet. **Features:** full bar, patio dining, Sunday brunch, happy hour. **Reservations:** suggested. **Address:** 333 N Central Ave 85004 **Location:** Northeast corner of Central Ave and Van Buren St; in The Westin Phoenix Downtown. ⓐ Van Buren/Central-1st Ave, 12. **Parking:** valet and street only. [B] [L] [D] CALL[♿M] [🚐]

RICE PAPER   602/252-3326   (13)

♦♦ Vietnamese. Casual Dining. $8-$16 **AAA Inspector Notes:** This chic eatery along the up and coming 7th Street corridor specializes in Vietnamese rice paper rolls, stuffed with such items as tempura crab, mango, avocado, pork and shrimp. Spicy hot pots also are popular, along with traditional banh mi sandwiches and pho. An extensive, hand-crafted cocktail menu is worth perusing. **Features:** full bar, happy hour. **Address:** 2221 N 7th St 85006 **Location:** I-10 exit 145 (7th St), 0.7 mi n. ⓐ Encanto/Central, 9. [L] [D] [🚐]

SAM'S CAFE AT THE ARIZONA CENTER   602/252-3545   (26)

♦♦ Southwestern. Casual Dining. $9-$21 **AAA Inspector Notes:** Those who are hungry after shopping, sports events or the theater will appreciate this restaurant's Southwestern fare. Applewood-smoked pecan salmon, adobo chicken pasta and steaming fajitas are sure to satisfy the hungriest patrons. **Features:** full bar. **Reservations:** suggested. **Address:** 455 N 3rd St, Suite 114 85004 **Location:** Northwest corner of Van Buren and 3rd sts. ⓐ Van Buren/Central-1st Ave, 12. **Parking:** street only. [L] [D] [🚐]

SWITCH RESTAURANT & WINE BAR   602/264-2295   (11)

♦♦♦ Comfort Food. Casual Dining. $9-$25 **AAA Inspector Notes:** Popular with the eclectic crowd for its specialty cocktails and late night dining, this urban hot spot feels like an intimate lounge. The menu ranges from galettes and crepes to such sophisticated entrées as blueberry duck breast and Provence chicken with risotto. **Features:** full bar, patio dining, Sunday brunch, happy hour. **Address:** 2603 N Central Ave 85004 **Location:** Northeast corner of Central and Virginia aves. ⓐ Encanto/Central, 9. [L] [D] [LATE] [🚐]

TOM'S TAVERN & 1929 GRILL   602/257-1688   (30)

♦♦ American. Casual Dining. $11-$23 **AAA Inspector Notes:** A Phoenix institution since 1929, this historic downtown spot serves traditional pub fare including burgers, salads, soups, fish and chips, and meatloaf. Come in during the busy lunch hour and mingle with the influential crowd as the state capitol is a short distance away. **Features:** full bar, happy hour. **Address:** 2 N Central Ave, Suite 102 85004 **Location:** Northeast corner of Washington St and 1st Ave; in One Renaissance Square. ⓐ Washington/Central Ave, 13. **Parking:** street only. [L] [D] [🚐]

TUCK SHOP   602/354-2980   (14)

♦♦♦ Comfort Food. Casual Dining. $10-$35 **AAA Inspector Notes:** Tucked away in a historic neighborhood, this stylish bistro serves American classic comfort food with a fresh new twist. The menu items include citrus-brined fried chicken with white cheddar waffles, Medjool dates stuffed with chorizo and bananas Foster for dessert. **Features:** full bar. **Address:** 2245 N 12th St 85006 **Location:** At Oak St. [D] CALL[♿M]

THE WILD THAIGER   602/241-8995   (9)

♦♦♦
Thai
Casual Dining
$8-$22

AAA Inspector Notes: The friendly staff at this eatery presents classic, made-to-order dishes that are marked by attractive presentations. Popular choices include hot pots that serve two, a variety of curries and many vegetarian options. The intimate, casual setting is located along the Central Corridor and offers streetside dining. **Features:** full bar, patio dining, happy hour. **Address:** 2631 N Central Ave 85004 **Location:** Just s of Thomas Rd. ⓐ Thomas/Central, 8. *Menu on AAA.com* [L] [D] [🚐]

PHOENIX (D-3)

- Restaurants p. 184
- Hotels & Restaurants map & index p. 146, 149, 154, 158, 164

ALOFT PHOENIX AIRPORT HOTEL 602/275-6300

Hotel
Rates not provided

AAA Benefit: Members save up to 15%, plus Starwood Preferred Guest® benefits!

Address: 4450 E Washington St 85034 **Location:** SR 143 exit Washington St, just w. 44th St/Washington, 22. **Facility:** 143 units. 6 stories, interior corridors. *Bath:* shower only. **Amenities:** safes. **Pool(s):** heated outdoor. **Activities:** exercise room. **Guest Services:** valet and coin laundry, area transportation.

ARIZONA BILTMORE, A WALDORF ASTORIA RESORT
(602)955-6600

Historic Retro Resort Hotel
$119-$429

AAA Benefit: Members save 5% or more!

Address: 2400 E Missouri Ave 85016 **Location:** Jct Camelback Rd, 0.5 mi n on 24th St, then 0.4 mi e. Located in a residential area. **Facility:** This venerable valley resort is noted for its attentive staff, Frank Lloyd Wright-inspired design, elegant guest rooms and expansive grounds with lush landscaping. 738 units, some kitchens and condominiums. 2-4 stories, interior/exterior corridors. **Parking:** on-site and valet. **Terms:** check-in 4 pm, 1-7 night minimum stay, cancellation fee imposed. **Amenities:** safes. **Dining:** 3 restaurants, also, Frank & Albert's, Wright's at the Biltmore, see separate listings. **Pool(s):** heated outdoor. **Activities:** sauna, hot tub, steamroom, regulation golf, tennis, recreation programs, kids club, bicycles, playground, lawn sports, spa. **Guest Services:** valet laundry, boarding pass kiosk, area transportation.

ARIZONA GRAND RESORT & SPA 602/438-9000

Resort Hotel
Rates not provided

Address: 8000 S Arizona Grand Pkwy 85044 **Location:** I-10 exit 155 (Baseline Rd), just w, then just s. **Facility:** Water plays a key role at this six-acre property, which features fountains, adult and children's pools, a waterslide and a simulated lazy river. 744 units, some kitchens. 2-5 stories, exterior corridors. **Parking:** on-site and valet. **Terms:** check-in 4 pm. **Amenities:** video games, safes. **Dining:** 3 restaurants, also, Rustler's Rooste, see separate listing, entertainment. **Pool(s):** heated outdoor. **Activities:** hot tub, steamroom, regulation golf, recreation programs, trails, spa. **Guest Services:** valet and coin laundry, boarding pass kiosk, area transportation.

BEST WESTERN AIRPORT INN (602)273-7251

Hotel
$70-$180

AAA Benefit: Save 10% or more every day and earn 10% bonus points!

Address: 2425 S 24th St 85034 **Location:** I-10 exit 150B (24th St) westbound, just s; exit 151 (University Dr) eastbound, just n to I-10 westbound, 1 mi w to exit 150B (24th St), then just s. **Facility:** 117 units. 2 stories (no elevator), interior/exterior corridors. **Terms:** check-in 4 pm. **Amenities:** *Some:* safes. **Pool(s):** heated outdoor. **Activities:** sauna, hot tub, exercise room. **Guest Services:** coin laundry, area transportation.

BEST WESTERN INNSUITES PHOENIX HOTEL & SUITES (602)997-6285

Hotel
$79-$159

AAA Benefit: Save 10% or more every day and earn 10% bonus points!

Address: 1615 E Northern Ave 85020 **Location:** SR 51 exit 7, 0.6 mi w. **Facility:** 111 units, some efficiencies. 3 stories (no elevator), exterior corridors. **Terms:** check-in 4 pm. **Pool(s):** heated outdoor. **Activities:** hot tub, picnic facilities, exercise room. **Guest Services:** valet and coin laundry.

BEST WESTERN PHOENIX I-17 METROCENTER INN (602)864-6233

Hotel
$59-$189

AAA Benefit: Save 10% or more every day and earn 10% bonus points!

Address: 8101 N Black Canyon Hwy 85021 **Location:** I-17 exit 206 (Northern Ave), just e, then just n; on east side of freeway. **Facility:** 147 units. 3 stories, exterior corridors. **Terms:** cancellation fee imposed. **Amenities:** safes. **Pool(s):** heated outdoor. **Activities:** hot tub. **Guest Services:** valet and coin laundry.

CANDLEWOOD SUITES PHOENIX 602/861-4900

 Extended Stay Hotel. Rates not provided. **Address:** 11411 N Black Canyon Hwy 85029 **Location:** I-17 exit 208 (Peoria Ave), just e, then 0.4 mi n. Adjacent to Saguaro Sports Park. **Facility:** 98 efficiencies. 3 stories, interior corridors. **Pool(s):** heated outdoor. **Activities:** hot tub, picnic facilities, exercise room. **Guest Services:** valet and coin laundry.

(See maps & indexes p. 146, 149, 154, 158, 164.)

CLARION HOTEL PHOENIX-CHANDLER

(480)893-3900 **33**

Hotel
$49-$199

Address: 5121 E La Puenta Ave 85044 **Location:** I-10 exit 157 (Elliot Rd), just w, just n on 51st St, then just e. **Facility:** 188 units. 4 stories, exterior corridors. **Pool(s):** heated outdoor. **Activities:** hot tub, picnic facilities, exercise room. **Guest Services:** valet and coin laundry, area transportation. **Featured Amenity: full hot breakfast.**

COMFORT INN I-10 WEST/CENTRAL

(602)415-1623 **42**

Hotel $120-$190 **Location:** I-10 exit 27th Ave eastbound, just n; exit 141 (35th Ave) westbound, just n, 1 mi e on McDowell Rd, then s. Located in a busy commercial area. **Facility:** 65 units. 3 stories, interior corridors. **Pool(s):** heated outdoor. **Activities:** hot tub, exercise room. **Guest Services:** coin laundry.

COMFORT SUITES PHOENIX NORTH

(602)861-3900 **16**

Hotel $84-$139 **Address:** 10210 N 26th Dr 85021 **Location:** I-17 exit 208 (Peoria Ave), just e, just s on 25th Ave, then 0.3 mi w on W Beryl Ave. **Facility:** 60 units. 3 stories, interior corridors. **Amenities:** safes. **Pool(s):** heated indoor. **Activities:** limited exercise equipment. **Guest Services:** valet and coin laundry.

COUNTRY INN & SUITES BY CARLSON, DEER VALLEY

623/879-9000 **2**

Hotel. Rates not provided. **Address:** 20221 N 29th Ave 85027 **Location:** I-17 exit 215A (Rose Garden Ln), just w to 27th Ave, 0.4 mi s, then just w on Frontage Rd. **Facility:** 126 units. 4 stories, interior corridors. **Terms:** check-in 4 pm. **Pool(s):** heated outdoor. **Activities:** hot tub, picnic facilities, exercise room. **Guest Services:** valet and coin laundry, area transportation.

COUNTRY INN & SUITES BY CARLSON, PHOENIX AIRPORT SOUTH

602/438-8688 **20**

Hotel. Rates not provided. **Address:** 4234 S 48th St 85040 **Location:** I-10 exit 153 (48th St/Broadway Rd), just s; exit 153B (52nd St/Broadway Rd) westbound, 0.4 mi w. **Facility:** 106 units. 4 stories, interior corridors. **Pool(s):** heated outdoor. **Activities:** hot tub, exercise room. **Guest Services:** valet and coin laundry, area transportation.

COURTYARD BY MARRIOTT-CAMELBACK

(602)955-5200 **29**

Hotel
$89-$335

COURTYARD Marriott **AAA Benefit:** Members save 5% or more!

Address: 2101 E Camelback Rd 85016 **Location:** Jct 20th St and Camelback Rd. Located in Town and Country Shopping Center. **Facility:** 155 units. 4 stories, interior corridors. **Pool(s):** heated outdoor. **Activities:** hot tub, exercise room. **Guest Services:** valet and coin laundry, boarding pass kiosk.

/ SOME UNITS

COURTYARD BY MARRIOTT PHOENIX AIRPORT

(480)966-4300 **14**

Hotel
$80-$301

COURTYARD Marriott **AAA Benefit:** Members save 5% or more!

Address: 2621 S 47th St 85034 **Location:** I-10 exit 151 (University Dr), 2 mi n, then just w. East Economy Parking, 33. **Facility:** 145 units. 4 stories, interior corridors. **Pool(s):** heated outdoor. **Activities:** hot tub, exercise room. **Guest Services:** valet and coin laundry, boarding pass kiosk, area transportation.

COURTYARD BY MARRIOTT PHOENIX NORTH

(602)944-7373 **18**

Hotel
$71-$200

COURTYARD Marriott **AAA Benefit:** Members save 5% or more!

Address: 9631 N Black Canyon Hwy 85021 **Location:** I-17 exit 207 (Dunlap Ave), just e, then 0.4 mi n. **Facility:** 146 units. 3 stories, interior corridors. **Pool(s):** heated outdoor. **Activities:** exercise room. **Guest Services:** valet and coin laundry, boarding pass kiosk.

COURTYARD BY MARRIOTT PHOENIX NORTH/HAPPY VALLEY

(623)580-8844

Hotel $75-$228 **Address:** 2029 W Whispering Wind Dr 85085 **Location:** I-17 exit 218 (Happy Valley Rd), 0.4 mi e to 23rd Ave, just s, then just e. **Facility:** 164 units. 5 stories, interior corridors. **Pool(s):** heated outdoor. **Activities:** hot tub, exercise room. **Guest Services:** valet and coin laundry, area transportation.

AAA Benefit: Members save 5% or more!

COURTYARD BY MARRIOTT PHOENIX WEST-AVONDALE

(623)271-7660 **1**

Hotel $93-$221 **Address:** 1650 N 95th Ln 85037 **Location:** I-10 exit 133 (99th Ave) eastbound, just n to McDowell Rd, 0.5 mi e, then just n; exit 134 (91st Ave) westbound, just n to McDowell Rd, just w, then just n. **Facility:** 127 units. 4 stories, interior corridors. **Pool(s):** heated outdoor. **Activities:** hot tub, exercise room. **Guest Services:** valet and coin laundry, boarding pass kiosk, area transportation.

AAA Benefit: Members save 5% or more!

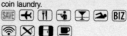

CROWNE PLAZA PHOENIX AIRPORT

(602)273-7778 **9**

Hotel
$79-$249

Address: 4300 E Washington St 85034 **Location:** SR 202 exit 2 (44th St), 0.7 mi s. 44th St/Washington, 22. **Facility:** 290 units. 10 stories, interior corridors. **Parking:** on-site and valet. **Amenities:** Some: safes. **Pool(s):** heated outdoor. **Activities:** hot tub, exercise room. **Guest Services:** valet and coin laundry.

(See maps & indexes p. 146, 149, 154, 158, 164.)

CROWNE PLAZA PHOENIX NORTH   602/943-2341

Hotel
Rates not provided

Address: 2532 W Peoria Ave 85029 **Location:** I-17 exit 208 (Peoria Ave), just e, then just n on 25th Ave. **Facility:** 248 units. 4 stories, interior corridors. **Pool(s):** heated outdoor, heated indoor. **Activities:** hot tub, exercise room. **Guest Services:** complimentary and valet laundry. **Featured Amenity:** full hot breakfast.

DOUBLETREE SUITES BY HILTON PHOENIX
(602)225-0500

Hotel
$169-$399

DOUBLETREE
BY HILTON

AAA Benefit: Members save 5% or more!

Address: 320 N 44th St 85008 **Location:** SR 202 exit 2 (44th St), 0.5 mi s. 44th St/Washington, 22. **Facility:** 242 units. 6 stories, exterior corridors. **Terms:** 1-7 night minimum stay, cancellation fee imposed. **Amenities:** safes. **Pool(s):** heated outdoor. **Activities:** hot tub, exercise room. **Guest Services:** valet and coin laundry, boarding pass kiosk, area transportation.

DRURY INN & SUITES PHOENIX AIRPORT
(602)437-8400

Hotel $80-$210 **Address:** 3333 E University Dr 85034 **Location:** I-10 exit 151 (University Dr), just e, then just s on Elwood St. **Facility:** 162 units. 6 stories, interior corridors. **Terms:** cancellation fee imposed. **Pool(s):** heated outdoor. **Activities:** hot tub, exercise room. **Guest Services:** valet and coin laundry, area transportation.

DRURY INN & SUITES PHOENIX HAPPY VALLEY
(623)879-8800

Hotel $70-$200 **Address:** 2335 W Pinnacle Peak Rd 85027 **Location:** I-17 exit 217 (Pinnacle Peak Rd), just e. **Facility:** 178 units. 7 stories, interior corridors. **Terms:** cancellation fee imposed. **Pool(s):** heated outdoor, heated indoor. **Activities:** hot tub, exercise room. **Guest Services:** valet and coin laundry.

EMBASSY SUITES BY HILTON PHOENIX AIRPORT AT 24TH ST
(602)957-1910

Hotel
$99-$269

EMBASSY SUITES
by HILTON

AAA Benefit: Members save 5% or more!

Address: 2333 E Thomas Rd 85016 **Location:** SR 51 exit 2 (44th St), just e. **Facility:** 182 units. 4 stories, exterior corridors. **Parking:** on-site (fee). **Terms:** 1-7 night minimum stay, cancellation fee imposed. **Pool(s):** heated outdoor. **Activities:** hot tub, picnic facilities, exercise room. **Guest Services:** valet and coin laundry, area transportation. **Featured Amenity:** full hot breakfast.

EMBASSY SUITES BY HILTON PHOENIX BILTMORE
(602)955-3992

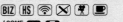
Hotel
$109-$409

E
EMBASSY SUITES

AAA Benefit: Members save 5% or more!

Address: 2630 E Camelback Rd 85016 **Location:** Just n of Camelback Rd, on 26th St. Adjacent to Biltmore Fashion Park. **Facility:** 232 units. 5 stories, interior corridors. **Parking:** on-site (fee). **Terms:** 1-7 night minimum stay, cancellation fee imposed. **Dining:** Omaha Steakhouse, see separate listing. **Pool(s):** heated outdoor. **Activities:** hot tub, exercise room. **Guest Services:** valet and coin laundry, area transportation. **Featured Amenity:** full hot breakfast.

EMBASSY SUITES BY HILTON PHOENIX NORTH
(602)375-1777

Hotel $99-$229 **Address:** 2577 W Greenway Rd 85023 **Location:** I-17 exit 211, just e. **Facility:** 314 units, some two bedrooms. 3 stories, exterior corridors. **Terms:** 1-7 night minimum stay, cancellation fee imposed. **Pool(s):** heated outdoor. **Activities:** hot tub, tennis, exercise room. **Guest Services:** valet and coin laundry, area transportation.

AAA Benefit: Members save 5% or more!

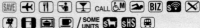

EMBASSY SUITES BY HILTON PHOENIX-SCOTTSDALE AT STONECREEK GOLF CLUB
(602)765-5800

Hotel
$109-$229

E
EMBASSY SUITES

AAA Benefit: Members save 5% or more!

Address: 4415 E Paradise Village Pkwy S 85032 **Location:** Just s of Cactus Rd; just w of Tatum Blvd. **Facility:** 270 units. 6 stories, interior corridors. **Terms:** 1-7 night minimum stay, cancellation fee imposed. **Amenities:** safes. **Pool(s):** heated outdoor. **Activities:** hot tub, regulation golf, exercise room. **Guest Services:** valet and coin laundry, area transportation. *(See ad p. 178.)*

EXTENDED STAY AMERICA PHOENIX-BILTMORE
602/265-6800

Extended Stay Hotel. Rates not provided. **Address:** 5235 N 16th St 85016 **Location:** Jct SR 51, just w on Camelback Rd, then just n. **Facility:** 112 efficiencies. 3 stories, interior corridors. **Pool(s):** heated outdoor. **Activities:** hot tub, picnic facilities, limited exercise equipment. **Guest Services:** coin laundry.

(See maps & indexes p. 146, 149, 154, 158, 164.)

EXTENDED STAY AMERICA-PHOENIX-CHANDLER
480/785-0464 **35**

Extended Stay Hotel. Rates not provided. **Address:** 14245 S 50th St 85044 **Location:** I-10 exit 159, just w on Ray Rd, just s, then just e. **Facility:** 101 efficiencies. 3 stories, interior corridors. **Guest Services:** coin laundry.

EXTENDED STAY AMERICA PHOENIX-CHANDLER-E CHANDLER BLVD 480/753-6700 **38**

Extended Stay Hotel. Rates not provided. **Address:** 5035 E Chandler Blvd 85048 **Location:** I-10 exit 160 (Chandler Blvd), just w. **Facility:** 129 efficiencies. 2 stories (no elevator), exterior corridors. **Pool(s):** heated outdoor. **Activities:** picnic facilities, limited exercise equipment. **Guest Services:** coin laundry.

EXTENDED STAY AMERICA PHOENIX-DEER VALLEY
623/879-6609 **1**

Extended Stay Hotel. Rates not provided. **Address:** 20827 N 27th Ave 85027 **Location:** I-17 exit 215A, just w. **Facility:** 104 efficiencies. 3 stories, interior corridors. **Guest Services:** coin laundry.

EXTENDED STAY AMERICA PHOENIX/MIDTOWN
602/279-9000 **37**

Extended Stay Hotel. Rates not provided. **Address:** 217 W Osborn Rd 85013 **Location:** Just w of Central Ave; between Indian School and Thomas rds. **Facility:** 129 efficiencies. 3 stories, interior corridors. **Pool(s):** heated outdoor. **Activities:** picnic facilities, exercise room. **Guest Services:** coin laundry.

FAIRFIELD INN & SUITES BY MARRIOTT PHOENIX AIRPORT (480)829-0700 **15**

Hotel
$69-$238

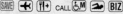

AAA Benefit: Members save 5% or more!

Address: 4702 E University Dr 85034 **Location:** I-10 exit 151 (University Dr), 2 mi n, then e. East Economy Parking, 33. **Facility:** 88 units. 3 stories, interior corridors. **Pool(s):** heated outdoor. **Activities:** hot tub, exercise room. **Guest Services:** valet and coin laundry. **Featured Amenity:** breakfast buffet.

FAIRFIELD INN & SUITES BY MARRIOTT PHOENIX NORTH (602)548-8888 **5**

Hotel
$58-$163

AAA Benefit: Members save 5% or more!

Address: 17017 N Black Canyon Hwy 85023 **Location:** I-17 exit 212, just e, then just n; on east side of freeway. **Facility:** 64 units. 3 stories, interior corridors. **Pool(s):** heated outdoor. **Activities:** hot tub, exercise room. **Guest Services:** valet and coin laundry. **Featured Amenity:** breakfast buffet.

▼ See AAA listing p. 177 ▼

Choose real ratings you can trust
from professional inspectors who've been there

(See maps & indexes p. 146, 149, 154, 158, 164.)

FOUR POINTS BY SHERATON PHOENIX SOUTH
480/893-3000 **34**

Hotel
Rates not provided

AAA Benefit: Members save up to 15%, plus Starwood Preferred Guest® benefits!

Address: 10831 S 51st St 85044 **Location:** I-10 exit 157 (Elliott Rd), just w, then just s. **Facility:** 160 units. 6 stories, interior corridors. **Amenities:** safes. **Pool(s):** heated outdoor. **Activities:** hot tub, tennis, picnic facilities, exercise room, spa. **Guest Services:** valet laundry, area transportation.

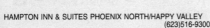

 / SOME UNITS

HAMPTON INN & SUITES PHOENIX NORTH/HAPPY VALLEY
(623)516-9300

Hotel $109-$239 **Address:** 2550 W Charlotte Dr 85085 **Location:** I-17 exit 217 (Pinnacle Peak Rd), 0.6 mi n on Frontage Rd. **Facility:** 125 units. 4 stories, interior corridors. **Terms:** 1-7 night minimum stay, cancellation fee imposed. **Pool(s):** heated outdoor. **Activities:** hot tub, exercise room. **Guest Services:** valet and coin laundry, area transportation.

AAA Benefit: Members save up to 10%!

/ SOME UNITS

HAMPTON INN PHOENIX AIRPORT NORTH
(602)267-0606 **5**

Hotel $99-$179 **Address:** 601 N 44th St 85008 **Location:** SR 202 exit 2 (44th St), 0.3 mi s. Across from Chinese Cultural Center. 44th St/Washington, 22. **Facility:** 106 units. 4 stories, interior corridors. **Terms:** 1-7 night minimum stay, cancellation fee imposed. **Pool(s):** heated outdoor. **Activities:** picnic facilities, exercise room. **Guest Services:** valet and coin laundry, area transportation.

AAA Benefit: Members save up to 10%!

HAMPTON INN PHOENIX BILTMORE
(602)956-5221 **33**

Hotel $89-$279 **Address:** 2310 E Highland Ave 85016 **Location:** Just sw of Camelback Rd and 24th St. **Facility:** 120 units. 4 stories, interior corridors. **Terms:** 1-7 night minimum stay, cancellation fee imposed. **Pool(s):** heated outdoor. **Activities:** hot tub, exercise room. **Guest Services:** valet laundry, area transportation.

AAA Benefit: Members save up to 10%!

HILTON GARDEN INN PHOENIX AIRPORT
(602)470-0500 **17**

Hotel $89-$269 **Address:** 3422 E Elwood St 85040 **Location:** I-10 exit 151 (University Dr), just n. **Facility:** 93 units, some efficiencies. 3 stories, interior corridors. **Terms:** 1-7 night minimum stay, cancellation fee imposed. **Pool(s):** heated outdoor. **Activities:** hot tub, exercise room. **Guest Services:** valet and coin laundry, area transportation.

AAA Benefit: Members save up to 10%!

HILTON GARDEN INN PHOENIX AIRPORT NORTH
(602)306-2323 **7**

Hotel $89-$289 **Address:** 3838 E Van Buren St 85008 **Location:** SR 202 exit 2 (40th St), 0.5 mi s, then just w. 38th St/Washington, 21. **Facility:** 192 units. 10 stories, interior corridors. **Terms:** 1-7 night minimum stay, cancellation fee imposed. **Amenities:** safes. **Pool(s):** heated outdoor. **Activities:** hot tub, exercise room. **Guest Services:** valet and coin laundry, area transportation.

AAA Benefit: Members save up to 10%!

HILTON GARDEN INN PHOENIX MIDTOWN
(602)279-9811 **34**

Hotel $79-$399 **Address:** 4000 N Central Ave 85012 **Location:** 0.3 mi s of Indian School Rd, just w on Clarendon Ave. Located in a commercial area. Indian School/Central, 6. **Facility:** 156 units. 3-7 stories, interior corridors. **Terms:** 1-7 night minimum stay, cancellation fee imposed. **Pool(s):** heated outdoor. **Activities:** hot tub, exercise room. **Guest Services:** valet and coin laundry, area transportation.

AAA Benefit: Members save up to 10%!

HILTON GARDEN INN PHOENIX NORTH /HAPPY VALLEY
(623)434-5556

Hotel $80-$249 **Address:** 1940 W Pinnacle Peak Rd 85027 **Location:** I-17 exit 217 (Pinnacle Peak Rd), 0.8 mi e. **Facility:** 126 units. 4 stories, interior corridors. **Terms:** 1-7 night minimum stay, cancellation fee imposed. **Pool(s):** heated outdoor. **Activities:** hot tub, exercise room. **Guest Services:** valet and coin laundry, area transportation.

AAA Benefit: Members save up to 10%!

(See maps & indexes p. 146, 149, 154, 158, 164.)

HILTON PHOENIX AIRPORT   (480)894-1600   **12**

▼▼▼▼ **Hotel** $139-$229 **Address:** 2435 S 47th St 85034 **Location:** I-10 exit 151 (University Dr), 2 mi n, then just w. ⬛ East Economy Parking, 33. **Facility:** 259 units. 4 stories, interior corridors. **Terms:** 1-7 night minimum stay, cancellation fee imposed. **Amenities:** safes. **Pool(s):** heated outdoor. **Activities:** hot tub, exercise room. **Guest Services:** valet laundry, area transportation.

AAA Benefit: Members save 5% or more!

HOLIDAY INN & SUITES PHOENIX AIRPORT   (480)543-1700   **18**

▼▼▼▼ **Hotel** $79-$289 **Address:** 3220 S 48th St 85040 **Location:** SR 143 exit 2 (University Dr), just w, then just s. **Facility:** 114 units. 5 stories, interior corridors. **Terms:** cancellation fee imposed. **Pool(s):** heated outdoor. **Activities:** hot tub, exercise room. **Guest Services:** valet and coin laundry, area transportation.

HOLIDAY INN & SUITES PHOENIX AIRPORT NORTH
(602)244-8800   **3**

▼▼▼
Hotel
$119-$309

Address: 1515 N 44th St 85008 **Location:** SR 202 exit 2 (44th St), 0.3 mi n. **Facility:** 228 units, some efficiencies. 4 stories, exterior corridors. **Terms:** cancellation fee imposed. **Pool(s):** heated outdoor. **Activities:** hot tub, exercise room. **Guest Services:** valet and coin laundry, area transportation.

HOLIDAY INN EXPRESS & SUITES PHOENIX AIRPORT   (602)453-9900   **16**

▼▼▼▼ **Hotel** $79-$249 **Address:** 3401 E University Dr 85034 **Location:** I-10 exit 151 (University Dr), just n. **Facility:** 114 units. 4 stories, interior corridors. **Terms:** cancellation fee imposed. **Pool(s):** heated outdoor. **Activities:** hot tub, exercise room. **Guest Services:** valet and coin laundry, area transportation.

HOLIDAY INN EXPRESS & SUITES PHOENIX-CHANDLER
480/785-8500   **36**

▼▼▼
Hotel
Rates not provided

Address: 15221 S 50th St 85044 **Location:** I-10 exit 160 (Chandler Blvd), just w, then just n. **Facility:** 125 units. 4 stories, interior corridors. **Pool(s):** heated outdoor. **Activities:** hot tub, exercise room. **Guest Services:** valet and coin laundry. **Featured Amenity:** breakfast buffet.

HOLIDAY INN NORTH PHOENIX   602/548-6000   **9**

▼▼▼ **Hotel.** Rates not provided. **Address:** 12027 N 28th Dr 85029 **Location:** I-17 exit 209 (Cactus Rd), just w, then just s. **Facility:** 174 units. 4 stories, interior corridors. **Amenities:** safes. **Pool(s):** heated outdoor. **Activities:** hot tub, exercise room. **Guest Services:** valet and coin laundry.

HOLIDAY INN PHOENIX WEST   (602)484-9009   **40**

▼▼▼▼ **Hotel** $89-$149 **Address:** 1500 N 51st Ave 85043 **Location:** I-10 exit 139 (51st Ave), just n. **Facility:** 144 units. 4 stories, interior corridors. **Terms:** 3 day cancellation notice. **Pool(s):** heated outdoor. **Activities:** hot tub, exercise room. **Guest Services:** valet and coin laundry.

HOMEWOOD SUITES BY HILTON PHOENIX AIRPORT SOUTH
(602)470-2100   **21**

▼▼▼ **Extended Stay Hotel** $159-$299 **Address:** 4750 E Cotton Center Blvd 85040 **Location:** I-10 exit 153 (48th St/Broadway Rd E), 0.4 mi s, then just w. **Facility:** 125 efficiencies, some two bedrooms. 4 stories, interior corridors. **Terms:** 1-7 night minimum stay, cancellation fee imposed. **Pool(s):** heated outdoor. **Activities:** hot tub, picnic facilities, exercise room. **Guest Services:** valet and coin laundry, area transportation.

AAA Benefit: Members save up to 10%!

HOMEWOOD SUITES BY HILTON PHOENIX-BILTMORE
(602)508-0937   **32**

▼▼▼ **Extended Stay Hotel** $94-$239 **Address:** 2001 E Highland Ave 85016 **Location:** Just e of 20th St. **Facility:** 124 efficiencies, some two bedrooms. 4 stories, interior corridors. **Terms:** 1-7 night minimum stay, cancellation fee imposed. **Pool(s):** heated outdoor. **Activities:** picnic facilities, limited exercise equipment. **Guest Services:** valet and coin laundry, area transportation.

AAA Benefit: Members save up to 10%!

HOMEWOOD SUITES BY HILTON PHOENIX METROCENTER
602/674-8900   **14**

▼▼▼ **Extended Stay Hotel.** Rates not provided. **Address:** 2536 W Beryl Ave 85021 **Location:** I-17 exit 208 (Peoria Ave), just e, just s on 25th Ave, then just w. **Facility:** 126 efficiencies, some two bedrooms. 5 stories, interior corridors. **Pool(s):** heated outdoor. **Activities:** picnic facilities, exercise room. **Guest Services:** valet and coin laundry.

AAA Benefit: Members save up to 10%!

HOMEWOOD SUITES PHOENIX NORTH/HAPPY VALLEY
(623)580-1800

▼▼▼ **Extended Stay Hotel** $109-$239 **Address:** 2470 W Charlotte Dr 85085 **Location:** I-17 exit 217 (Pinnacle Peak Rd), 0.6 mi n on Frontage Rd. **Facility:** 135 efficiencies, some two bedrooms. 4 stories, interior corridors. **Terms:** 1-7 night minimum stay, cancellation fee imposed. **Pool(s):** heated outdoor. **Activities:** hot tub, picnic facilities, exercise room. **Guest Services:** valet and coin laundry, area transportation.

AAA Benefit: Members save up to 10%!

(See maps & indexes p. 146, 149, 154, 158, 164.)

HYATT PLACE PHOENIX-NORTH   (602)997-8800 [12]

Hotel
$64-$229

HYATT PLACE
AAA Benefit: Members save 10%!

Address: 10838 N 25th Ave 85029 Location: I-17 exit 208 (Peoria Ave), just e, then 0.3 mi n. Facility: 127 units. 4 stories, interior corridors. Terms: cancellation fee imposed. Pool(s): heated outdoor. Activities: exercise room. Guest Services: valet laundry, area transportation. Featured Amenity: breakfast buffet.

JW MARRIOTT DESERT RIDGE RESORT & SPA   (480)293-5000 [3]

Resort Hotel
$160-$538

JW MARRIOTT.
AAA Benefit: Members save 5% or more!

Address: 5350 E Marriott Dr 85054 Location: SR 101 exit 31 (Tatum Blvd), 0.4 mi n to Deer Valley Dr, then 0.5 mi e. Facility: This expansive destination resort has activities for families or groups. A tri-level lobby opens to a courtyard with pools, water play areas and a flowing lazy river. 950 units. 6 stories, interior corridors. Parking: on-site (fee) and valet. Terms: check-in 4 pm, 3 day cancellation notice, resort fee. Amenities: video games, safes. Dining: 4 restaurants, also, Meritage Steakhouse, Roy's Desert Ridge, see separate listings. Pool(s): heated outdoor. Activities: sauna, hot tub, steamhouse, regulation golf, tennis, recreation programs, kids club, bicycles, lawn sports, spa. Guest Services: complimentary and valet laundry, boarding pass kiosk, area transportation.

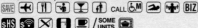

LA QUINTA INN & SUITES PHOENIX CHANDLER   (480)961-7700 [37]

Hotel $64-$251 Address: 15241 S 50th St 85044 Location: I-10 exit 160 (Chandler Blvd), just w, then just n. Located in a light-commercial area. Facility: 117 units. 4 stories, interior corridors. Pool(s): heated outdoor. Activities: hot tub, exercise room. Guest Services: valet and coin laundry.

LA QUINTA INN & SUITES PHOENIX I-10 WEST   (602)595-7601 [38]

Hotel $69-$977 Address: 4929 W McDowell Rd 85035 Location: I-10 exit 139 (51st Ave), just n, then just e. Facility: 66 units, some two bedrooms and kitchens. 3 stories, interior corridors. Pool(s): heated outdoor. Activities: hot tub, exercise room. Guest Services: coin laundry.

LA QUINTA INN PHOENIX-ARCADIA   (602)956-6500 [2]

Hotel $64-$207 Address: 4727 E Thomas Rd 85018 Location: Just w of 48th St. Facility: 160 units. 2 stories, interior/exterior corridors. Amenities: safes. Pool(s): heated outdoor. Activities: hot tub, picnic facilities, exercise room. Guest Services: coin laundry.

LA QUINTA INN PHOENIX NORTH   (602)993-0800 [7]

Hotel $64-$251 Address: 2510 W Greenway Rd 85023 Location: I-17 exit 211, just e. Facility: 146 units. 2 stories (no elevator), exterior corridors. Pool(s): heated outdoor. Activities: hot tub, exercise room. Guest Services: coin laundry.

THE LEGACY GOLF RESORT   (602)305-5500 [43]

Resort Condominium
$99-$499

Address: 6808 S 32nd St 85042 Location: I-10 exit 155 (Baseline Rd), 2.4 mi w, then 0.4 mi n. Facility: Spacious rooms and baths, along with a golf course designed by Gary Panks, await you in this contemporary desert setting. 328 condominiums. 2 stories (no elevator), exterior corridors. Terms: check-in 4 pm, 2 night minimum stay, cancellation fee imposed. Amenities: safes. Pool(s): heated outdoor. Activities: hot tub, regulation golf, tennis, recreation programs, playground, picnic facilities, exercise room, massage. Guest Services: complimentary laundry.

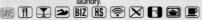

MARICOPA MANOR BED & BREAKFAST INN   (602)264-9200 [27]

Classic Bed & Breakfast $119-$239 Address: 15 W Pasadena Ave 85013 Location: Just n of Camelback Rd; w of Central Ave. Located in a residential area. Central/Camelback, 4. Facility: This 1928 Spanish mission home has elegantly decorated suites with patios, and some with a gas or wood-burning fireplace. The walled-in courtyard boasts extensive mature landscaping. 6 units. 1 story, interior/exterior corridors. Pool(s): outdoor. Activities: hot tub, picnic facilities.

PHOENIX AIRPORT MARRIOTT   (602)273-7373 [4]

Hotel $111-$346 Address: 1101 N 44th St 85008 Location: SR 202 exit 2 (44th St), just n. 44th St/Washington, 22. Facility: 345 units. 12 stories, interior corridors. Amenities: video games. Pool(s): heated outdoor. Activities: exercise room. Guest Services: valet and coin laundry, boarding pass kiosk.

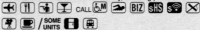

PHOENIX RESIDENCE INN DESERT VIEW AT MAYO CLINIC BY MARRIOTT   (480)563-1500 [6]

Extended Stay Hotel
$98-$361

Residence Inn Marriott
AAA Benefit: Members save 5% or more!

Address: 5665 E Mayo Blvd 85054 Location: SR 101 exit 32 (56th St), just s, then just e. Facility: 208 units, some two bedrooms, efficiencies and kitchens. 6 stories, interior corridors. Terms: 3 day cancellation notice. Pool(s): heated outdoor. Activities: picnic facilities, exercise room. Guest Services: valet and coin laundry, boarding pass kiosk, area transportation.

▼ See AAA listing p. 50 ▼

POINTE HILTON SQUAW PEAK RESORT
(602)997-2626 **25**

Resort Hotel
$109-$359

AAA Benefit: Members save 5% or more!

Address: 7677 N 16th St 85020 **Location:** SR 51 exit Glendale Ave, 0.4 mi w, then 0.6 mi n. **Facility:** The resort's suites and large casitas are scattered throughout extensive grounds featuring shaded pool areas and courtyards with tiered fountains. 563 units, some houses. 3-4 stories, exterior corridors. **Terms:** check-in 4 pm, 1-7 night minimum stay, cancellation fee imposed. **Amenities:** safes. **Dining:** 2 restaurants, also, Rico's American Grill, see separate listing. **Pool(s):** heated outdoor. **Activities:** sauna, hot tub, steamroom, miniature golf, tennis, recreation programs, kids club, playground, spa. **Guest Services:** valet and coin laundry, area transportation.

POINTE HILTON TAPATIO CLIFFS RESORT
(602)866-7500 **11**

Resort Hotel
$89-$329

AAA Benefit: Members save 5% or more!

Address: 11111 N 7th St 85020 **Location:** I-17 exit 207 (Dunlap Ave), 3 mi e, then 2 mi n. **Facility:** On extensive, nicely landscaped hillside grounds with sweeping views across the valley, this property offers spacious one-bedroom suites housed in several buildings. 584 units. 2-5 stories, exterior corridors. **Parking:** on-site and valet. **Terms:** check-in 4 pm, 1-7 night minimum stay, cancellation fee imposed. **Amenities:** safes. **Dining:** 3 restaurants, also, Different Pointe of View, see separate listing. **Pool(s):** heated outdoor. **Activities:** sauna, hot tub, regulation golf, tennis, recreation programs, trails, exercise room, spa. **Guest Services:** complimentary and valet laundry, area transportation.

RADISSON HOTEL PHOENIX AIRPORT
(602)220-4400 **6**

Hotel
$85-$299

Address: 427 N 44th St 85008 **Location:** SR 202 exit 2 (44th St), 0.5 mi s. 44th St/Washington, 22. **Facility:** 204 units. 7 stories, interior corridors. **Terms:** 3 day cancellation notice-fee imposed. **Amenities:** Some: safes. **Pool(s):** heated outdoor. **Activities:** hot tub, exercise room. **Guest Services:** valet laundry, area transportation.

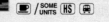

RADISSON HOTEL PHOENIX NORTH
602/997-5900 **15**

Hotel. Rates not provided. **Address:** 10220 N Metro Pkwy E 85051 **Location:** I-17 exit 208 (Peoria Ave), 0.3 mi w to 28th Dr, just s, then just e. **Facility:** 284 units. 5 stories, interior corridors. **Bath:** shower only. **Amenities:** Some: safes. **Pool(s):** heated outdoor. **Activities:** hot tub, exercise room. **Guest Services:** valet and coin laundry, area transportation.

(See maps & indexes p. 146, 149, 154, 158, 164.)

RED ROOF INN PHOENIX WEST (602)233-8004

Hotel
$50-$126

Address: 5215 W Willetta St 85043 **Location:** I-10 exit 139 (51st Ave), just n, just e on McDowell Rd, then just s. **Facility:** 133 units. 4 stories, interior corridors. **Amenities:** safes. **Pool(s):** heated outdoor.

RESIDENCE INN BY MARRIOTT PHOENIX
(602)864-1900

Extended Stay Hotel $89-$248 **Address:** 8242 N Black Canyon Hwy 85051 **Location:** I-17 exit 207 (Dunlap Ave), just n, 0.8 mi s; on frontage road. **Facility:** 168 efficiencies, some two bedrooms. 2 stories (no elevator), interior/exterior corridors. **Pool(s):** heated outdoor. **Activities:** playground, picnic facilities, exercise room. **Guest Services:** valet and coin laundry.

AAA Benefit: Members save 5% or more!

RESIDENCE INN BY MARRIOTT PHOENIX NORTH/HAPPY VALLEY (623)580-8833

Extended Stay Hotel $87-$254 **Address:** 2035 W Whispering Wind Dr 85085 **Location:** I-17 exit 128 (Happy Valley Rd), 0.4 mi e to 23rd Ave, just s, then just e. **Facility:** 129 units, some two bedrooms, efficiencies and kitchens. 5 stories, interior corridors. **Pool(s):** heated outdoor. **Activities:** hot tub, picnic facilities, exercise room. **Guest Services:** valet and coin laundry, area transportation.

AAA Benefit: Members save 5% or more!

THE RITZ-CARLTON, PHOENIX
602/468-0700

Hotel. Rates not provided. **Address:** 2401 E Camelback Rd 85016 **Location:** Southeast corner of Camelback Rd and 24th St. Across from Biltmore Fashion Park. **Facility:** Catering to both business and leisure travelers, this elegant, service-oriented hotel has well-appointed guest rooms and large meeting spaces. 281 units. 11 stories, interior corridors. **Parking:** valet only. **Amenities:** safes. **Dining:** Bistro 24, see separate listing, entertainment. **Pool(s):** heated outdoor. **Activities:** sauna, exercise room, massage. **Guest Services:** valet laundry, area transportation.

AAA Benefit: Unequaled service at special member savings!

Get maps, travel information

and road service with the

AAA and CAA Mobile apps

ROYAL PALMS RESORT AND SPA (602)840-3610

Boutique Hotel
$149-$799

Address: 5200 E Camelback Rd 85018 **Location:** Just e of 52nd St. Located in a quiet residential area. **Facility:** Originally built as a private residence in the 1920s, this nine-acre hideaway nestled into the base of Camelback Mountain has extensive grounds dotted with fountains and outdoor fireplaces. 119 units. 1-2 stories, interior/exterior corridors. **Parking:** on-site and valet. **Terms:** check-in 4 pm, 7 day cancellation notice-fee imposed, resort fee. **Amenities:** safes. **Dining:** T. Cook's, see separate listing. **Pool(s):** heated outdoor. **Activities:** hot tub, steamroom, recreation programs, lawn sports, exercise room, spa. **Guest Services:** valet laundry, boarding pass kiosk.

SHERATON CRESCENT HOTEL (602)943-8200

Hotel
$89-$349

Sheraton

AAA Benefit: Members save up to 15%, plus Starwood Preferred Guest® benefits!

Address: 2620 W Dunlap Ave 85021 **Location:** I-17 exit 207 (Dunlap Ave), just e. **Facility:** 342 units. 8 stories, interior corridors. **Terms:** cancellation fee imposed. **Amenities:** safes. **Dining:** 2 restaurants. **Pool(s):** heated outdoor. **Activities:** sauna, hot tub, tennis, playground. **Guest Services:** valet laundry, area transportation.

SLEEP INN AIRPORT (480)967-7100

Hotel $70-$200 **Address:** 2621 S 47th Pl 85034 **Location:** I-10 exit 151 (University Dr), 2 mi n, then just w. East Economy Parking, 33. **Facility:** 104 units. 3 stories, interior corridors. *Bath:* shower only. **Pool(s):** heated outdoor. **Activities:** hot tub, picnic facilities, exercise room. **Guest Services:** valet and coin laundry, area transportation.

SLEEP INN PHOENIX NORTH (602)504-1200

Hotel
$59-$179

Address: 18235 N 27th Ave 85053 **Location:** I-17 exit 214A (Union Hills Dr), just w, then just s. **Facility:** 61 units. 2 stories, interior corridors. *Bath:* shower only. **Amenities:** safes. **Pool(s):** heated outdoor. **Activities:** hot tub, limited exercise equipment. **Guest Services:** valet and coin laundry. **Featured Amenity:** full hot breakfast.

SPRINGHILL SUITES BY MARRIOTT PHOENIX NORTH (602)943-0010

Hotel $66-$182 **Address:** 9425 N Black Canyon Frwy 85021 **Location:** I-17 exit 207 (Dunlap Ave), just e, then 0.3 mi n. **Facility:** 81 units. 3 stories, interior corridors. **Pool(s):** heated outdoor. **Activities:** hot tub, exercise room. **Guest Services:** valet laundry.

AAA Benefit: Members save 5% or more!

(See maps & indexes p. 146, 149, 154, 158, 164.)

SUPER 8-PHOENIX WEST   (602)415-0888   41

WW WW Hotel $55-$80 Address: 1242 N 53rd Ave 85043 Location: I-10 exit 139 (51st Ave), just s to Latham Rd, then just w. Facility: 67 units. 2 stories (no elevator), interior corridors. Pool(s): outdoor. Guest Services: coin laundry.

[icons]

TOWNEPLACE SUITES BY MARRIOTT PHOENIX NORTH
(602)943-9510   20

WWWW **Extended Stay Hotel** $61-$183 Address: 9425 N Black Canyon Frwy 85021 Location: I-17 exit 207 (Dunlap Ave), just e, then 0.3 mi n. Facility: 93 efficiencies, some two bedrooms. 3 stories, interior corridors. Pool(s): heated outdoor. Activities: exercise room. Guest Services: valet and coin laundry.

AAA Benefit: Members save 5% or more!

[icons]

WYNDHAM GARDEN PHOENIX MIDTOWN
(602)604-4900   36

WWW Hotel $67-$147 Address: 3600 N 2nd Ave 85013 Location: Just n of Osborn Rd, 0.5 mi s of Indian School Rd. Osborn/Central, 7. Facility: 160 units. 6 stories, interior/exterior corridors. Pool(s): heated outdoor. Activities: tennis, playground, exercise room. Guest Services: valet and coin laundry, area transportation.

[icons]

WHERE TO EAT

AH-SO SUSHI & STEAK   623/869-7700

WW Japanese. Casual Dining. $10-$40 AAA Inspector Notes: You can find it all here: a fresh sushi bar, dining tables and teppan grills with chefs ready to put on a show. The standard combinations of chicken, steak and seafood are available, along with a large selection of sushi, rolls and sashimi. Features: full bar, patio dining, happy hour. Address: 2450 W Happy Valley Rd 85085 Location: I-17 exit 218 (Happy Valley Rd), just e. L D

ALEXI'S GRILL   602/279-0982   70

WW Northern Italian. Casual Dining. $7-$29 AAA Inspector Notes: Whether for a business lunch, a celebration or an intimate dinner, the friendly staff and eclectic foods prepared with a Mediterranean flair are sure to delight. The signature rack of lamb is highly recommended. Features: full bar, patio dining, happy hour. Reservations: suggested. Address: 3550 N Central Ave 85012 Location: Just n of Osborn Rd. Osborn/Central, 7.

L D

AUNT CHILADA'S HIDEAWAY   602/944-1286   15

WW Mexican. Casual Dining. $6-$18 AAA Inspector Notes: Colorful decor, Mexican memorabilia and several patios, including one that is dog-friendly, enhance the rooms of this historic, hacienda-style building. Guests can select from traditional favorites such as chimichangas, enchiladas and fajitas (the house specialty). Live entertainment is on hand some evenings. Features: full bar, patio dining, Sunday brunch, happy hour. Address: 7330 N Dreamy Draw Dr 85020 Location: SR 51 exit 5 (Glendale Ave), 0.4 mi w to 16th St, 0.6 mi to Morten Ave, then just e. Parking: on-site and street.

L D

BABBO ITALIAN EATERY   602/279-1500   17

WW Italian. Casual Dining. $9-$15 AAA Inspector Notes: Classic Italian favorites are served up in a casual, modern setting. Try the spicy shrimp fra diavolo or the manicotti with a choice of sauce. Monday and Tuesday feature a spaghetti and meatball special. Features: full bar, patio dining. Address: 6855 N 16th St 85016 Location: SR 51 exit 5 (Glendale Ave), just w, then just s.

L D

BARRIO CAFE   602/636-0240   1

New Mexican Casual Dining $10-$26

AAA Inspector Notes: This hot spot in the heart of town serves what the award-winning chef calls modern Mexican cuisine. Using creative blends of traditional sauces, she enhances such dishes as enchiladas with chicken and fish grilled in a banana leaf. Many vegetarian dishes are also offered. Features: full bar, Sunday brunch, happy hour. Address: 2814 N 16th St 85006 Location: Just s of Thomas Rd. L D

BISTRO 24   602/952-2424   54

WWW Continental. Fine Dining. $16-$36 AAA Inspector Notes: A seasonally changing menu at this upscale bistro features the freshest of ingredients with choices like crispy risotto croquettes or truffle pappardelle pasta. A friendly, attentive waitstaff oversees the elegant, yet casual dining room. Features: full bar, patio dining, happy hour. Reservations: suggested. Address: 2401 E Camelback Rd 85016 Location: Southeast corner of Camelback Rd and 24th St; in The Ritz-Carlton, Phoenix. Parking: valet only.

B L D

BLANCO TACOS & TEQUILA   602/429-8000   47

WW Mexican. Casual Dining. $8-$20 AAA Inspector Notes: This popular spot serves modern Mexican cuisine in a festive setting. Familiar items like tacos, cheese crisps and burritos are dressed up with fresh, distinctive ingredients. The energetic staff recommends tequilas from their selection of more than 30 premium choices. Features: full bar, patio dining, happy hour. Address: 2502 E Camelback Rd 85016 Location: Corner of 24th St and Camelback Rd; in Biltmore Fashion Park. Parking: on-site and valet. L D

BLUE WATER GRILL   602/277-3474   40

WWW Seafood. Casual Dining. $15-$49 AAA Inspector Notes: Fresh seafood and friendly service are the main attractions at this comfortable dining spot. The seafood cioppino is hearty and delicious. Features: full bar, patio dining, happy hour. Address: 1720 E Camelback Rd 85016 Location: Jct 16th St and Camelback Rd, just e. L D

BOBBY Q   602/995-5982   9

WW Barbecue. Casual Dining. $9-$36 AAA Inspector Notes: Located in a popular shopping area, this lively barbecue spot serves up the classics with a choice of mild or spicy sauce. Try the famous Q rolls to start, followed by the tender brisket and finish with homemade peach cobbler. Stick around for late night revelry in the adjacent club. Features: full bar, patio dining, happy hour. Address: 8501 N 27th Ave 85051 Location: I-17 exit 206 (Northern Ave), just w, then just n; on west side of freeway. L D

CAFFE BOA   480/893-3331   21

WW Italian. Casual Dining. $11-$27 AAA Inspector Notes: The highlight here is the upscale presentations that include rich, thick soups such as shrimp bisque and grilled salmon with basmati rice. The menu includes pasta dishes like rigatoni puttanesca, as well as preparations of beef, chicken and seafood. Indoor and outdoor seating is offered. Features: full bar, patio dining, happy hour. Address: 5063 E Elliot Rd 85044 Location: I-10 exit 157 (Elliot Rd), 1 blk w; in Ahwatukee Plaza. L D

THE CAPITAL GRILLE   602/952-8900   50

WWW Steak. Fine Dining. $11-$49 AAA Inspector Notes: Cherry wood and red leather assist in making this clubby dining room a beautiful spot to dine on excellent cuts of dry-aged beef. The staff is highly attentive and knowledgeable. Features: full bar. Address: 2502 E Camelback Rd, Suite 199 85016 Location: Jct Camelback Rd and 26th St, just e; in Biltmore Fashion Park; on south side. L D

CARLOS O'BRIENS MEXICAN RESTAURANT   602/274-5881

WW Mexican. Casual Dining. $9-$16 AAA Inspector Notes: This attractively decorated restaurant serves traditional northern Mexican fare in hearty portions. Both the food and the margaritas make this spot popular with the locals. Features: full bar, happy hour. Address: 1133 E Northern Ave 85020 Location: SR 51 exit Northern Ave, 1.4 mi w; sw of 12th St. L D LATE

(See maps & indexes p. 146, 149, 154, 158, 164.)

CHELSEA'S KITCHEN   602/957-2555 59

WWWW American. Casual Dining. $10-$27 **AAA Inspector Notes:** A high-energy atmosphere, helpful and knowledgeable waitstaff and cooked-to-order foods distinguish this upscale eatery in east Phoenix. Custom burgers, ahi tuna and veggie options are featured as well as freshly-made desserts. A nice selection of wines by the glass are offered. **Features:** full bar, patio dining, Sunday brunch, happy hour. **Address:** 5040 N 40th St 85018 **Location:** Just n of Camelback Rd. **Parking:** on-site and valet. [L] [D]

CHERRYBLOSSOM NOODLE CAFE   602/248-9090 37

WW Noodles. Casual Dining. $7-$15 **AAA Inspector Notes:** It is difficult to decide between the different styles of noodles at this distinctive fusion concept café. Try a steaming bowl of spicy pork ramen, hot or cold Japanese noodle dishes or such Italian favorites as shrimp cappelini and eggplant primavera. Interesting saki cocktails are offered. **Features:** beer & wine, happy hour. **Address:** 914 E Camelback Rd 85014 **Location:** Northwest corner of 10th St and Camelback Rd. [railcar] Central/Camelback, 4. [L] [D] [railcar]

CHINO BANDIDO   602/375-3639 4

W Fusion. Quick Serve. $7-$10 **AAA Inspector Notes:** Diners can choose from a list of Chinese and Mexican favorites, so there are more than 42 combination possibilities, including egg foo yong burritos, emerald chicken with black beans and spicy jerk chicken with fried rice. The atmosphere is basic, so takeout is a great option. **Address:** 15414 N 19th Ave 85023 **Location:** I-17 exit 211 (Greenway Rd), 1 mi e to 19th Ave, then just n. [L] [D]

CHRISTOPHER'S RESTAURANT & CRUSH LOUNGE
602/522-2344 49

WWWW French. Fine Dining. $12-$68 **AAA Inspector Notes:** This restaurant is located in an upscale modern space in the Biltmore Fashion Park. Diners will be delighted by regional American cuisine with classic French preparations. **Features:** full bar, patio dining, happy hour. **Reservations:** suggested. **Address:** 2502 E Camelback Rd 85016 **Location:** Just e of 24th St; in Biltmore Fashion Park. **Parking:** on-site and valet. [L] [D]

CHRISTO'S   602/264-1784 19

WW Italian. Fine Dining. $8-$30 **AAA Inspector Notes:** This popular restaurant serves an excellent variety of traditional Italian dishes, including fettuccine Monte casino, chicken Florentine and shrimp diavolo. The waitstaff, all dressed in tuxedo shirts, serves the meal with casual and friendly commentary. **Features:** full bar. **Address:** 6327 N 7th St 85014 **Location:** Just s of Maryland Ave. [L] [D]

CLAIM JUMPER   623/581-8595

WW American. Casual Dining. $8-$37 **AAA Inspector Notes:** Great menu variety makes this place a good stop for parties with diverse tastes. Choices include specialty appetizers, salads, rotisserie chicken and barbecue items, not to mention good comfort foods, such as traditional pot pie. Hearty portions satisfy big appetites. The atmosphere is fun and lively. **Features:** full bar, happy hour. **Address:** 3063 W Agua Fria Frwy 85027 **Location:** I-17 exit 214A (Yorkshire Dr), 0.4 mi w; in Deer Valley Plaza. [L] [D]

THE CLEVER KOI   602/222-3474 65

WW Asian. Casual Dining. $10-$15 **AAA Inspector Notes:** An eclectic Neo-Asian menu features such items as pig face dumplings, kimchi fried rice and Peking duck buns. Equally interesting are the craft cocktails served in the modern, trendy décor. **Features:** full bar, patio dining. **Address:** 4236 N Central Ave 85012 **Location:** Jct Indian School Rd, just n. [railcar] Indian School/Central, 6. [L] [D] [railcar]

DESERT JADE   602/954-0048 83

WW Chinese. Casual Dining. $11-$26 **AAA Inspector Notes:** This cozy neighborhood spot has a lodge-like feel and serves all the favorites such as kung pao chicken, Mongolian beef and chow mein. The service is friendly and attentive. **Features:** full bar. **Address:** 3215 E Indian School Rd 85018 **Location:** Jct 32nd St; just e. [L] [D]

DIFFERENT POINTE OF VIEW   602/866-6350 6

WWWW
New American Fine Dining
$29-$42

AAA Inspector Notes: The panoramic views of the valley are truly spectacular at this mountain-top restaurant, which offers indoor and outdoor dining areas. The menu, created by chef Anthony DeMuro reflects New American cuisine, incorporating natural and organic ingredients. The restaurant boasts an award-winning, international wine list. **Features:** full bar, patio dining. **Reservations:** suggested. **Address:** 11111 N 7th St 85020 **Location:** I-17 exit 207 (Dunlap Ave), 3 mi e, then 2 mi n; in Pointe Hilton Tapatio Cliffs Resort. **Parking:** on-site and valet. [D]

DONOVAN'S STEAK & CHOP HOUSE   602/955-3666 56

WWW Steak. Fine Dining. $28-$55 **AAA Inspector Notes:** A dark, clubby atmosphere sets the tone for top-notch USDA Prime steaks, chops and fresh seafood. The polished staff can guide guests through the extensive wine list. **Features:** full bar, happy hour. **Reservations:** suggested. **Address:** 3101 E Camelback Rd 85016 **Location:** Jct 32nd St, just w. **Parking:** valet only. [D]

DUCK AND DECANTER   602/274-5429 41

W Deli. Quick Serve. $6-$10 **AAA Inspector Notes:** This eatery cannot be beat for a quick, delicious lunch consisting of sandwiches, salads and soups. Dinners may include wine, which can be selected from an excellent list. Giftware featuring their duck logo as well as coffee beans are available for purchase. **Features:** beer & wine. **Address:** 1651 E Camelback Rd 85016 **Location:** Just e of 16th St. [B] [L] [D]

FARM KITCHEN AT THE FARM AT SOUTH MOUNTAIN
602/276-6545 81

WWW
American Quick Serve
$10-$12

AAA Inspector Notes: Dining outdoors is a picnic, with meals in a basket given to patrons who can seek refuge under canvas awnings or shady trees. Take a seat at one of the checkered-cloth covered picnic tables scattered among the brick-covered patio and enjoy cool salads and warming soups along with homemade pies, cookies and cakes. **Features:** patio dining. **Address:** 6106 S 32nd St 85042 **Location:** I-10 exit 151 (University Dr/32nd St), 1.4 mi s, then just s of Southern Ave. *Menu on AAA.com*
[L] [X]

FORGE HANDCRAFTED PIZZA   602/955-0334 46

WW Pizza. Casual Dining. $12-$17 **AAA Inspector Notes:** This is a delicious pit stop during a day of shopping. Brick-oven pizza, along with tasty salads and sandwiches and tempting starters like crispy Brussels sprouts or cheese curds line the menu. There is also an ample selection of wines by the glass and tap beers available. **Features:** full bar, patio dining, happy hour. **Address:** 2502 E Camelback Rd 85016 **Location:** Just e of 24th St; in Biltmore Fashion Park. **Parking:** on-site and valet. [L] [D]

FRANK & ALBERT'S   602/381-7632 29

WWWW American. Casual Dining. $16-$42 **AAA Inspector Notes:** This is the perfect spot to have a well-prepared comfort meal in a beautiful setting with an attentive staff. The extensive breakfast buffet is popular, as are the special holiday meals served throughout the year. The daily happy hour features discounts on specialty drinks and small plates. **Features:** full bar, patio dining, happy hour. **Reservations:** suggested. **Address:** 2400 E Missouri Ave 85016 **Location:** Jct Camelback Rd, 0.5 mi n on 24th St, then 0.4 mi e; in Arizona Biltmore Resort & Spa, A Waldorf Astoria Hotel. **Parking:** on-site and valet. [B] [L] [D]

THE FRY BREAD HOUSE   602/351-2345 64

W Regional Specialty. Quick Serve. $3-$8 **AAA Inspector Notes:** For something unusual and a true Native American food, try the tasty fry-bread tacos with any of varied fillings. The honey-covered dessert fry bread is decadent. **Address:** 4140 N 7th Ave 85013 **Location:** Just n of Indian School Rd. [railcar] Indian School/Central, 6. [L] [D] [railcar]

(See maps & indexes p. 146, 149, 154, 158, 164.)

FUEGO BISTRO 602/277-1151 (22)

♦♦♦♦ Latin American. Casual Dining. $10-$30 **AAA Inspector Notes:** Patrons can feast upon authentic Cuban, Puerto Rican and Latin American favorites at this bistro including pernil asado, ropa vieja and arroz con gandules. The intimate dining room is complemented by a large outdoor patio featuring live entertainment on the weekends. **Features:** full bar, patio dining, happy hour. **Reservations:** suggested. **Address:** 713 E Palo Verde Dr 85014 **Location:** Jct 7th St and Bethany Home Rd, just s, just e. **Parking:** on-site and street. [L] [D]

GIUSEPPE'S ON 28TH 602/381-1237 (71)

♦♦♦♦ Italian. Casual Dining. $9-$27 **AAA Inspector Notes:** Similar to a neighborhood café one would find in Europe, this tiny family-owned eatery features an impressive selection of wines to accompany the ever-changing menu of fresh made pastas, sauces and desserts. The squid ink pasta with clams and veal osso buco are standouts. **Features:** beer & wine, patio dining. **Address:** 2824 E Indian School Rd 85016 **Location:** SR 51 exit 3 (Indian School Rd), 1.5 mi e. [L] [D]

GREAT WALL HONG KONG CUISINE 602/973-1112 (25)

♦♦ Chinese. Casual Dining. $8-$25 **AAA Inspector Notes:** Authentic dim sum is served daily during lunch hours in this large, unassuming dining room. Choose from a wide variety of small plates including delicious pork buns, siu mai and shrimp dumplings. An extensive a la carte menu also is available. **Features:** full bar. **Address:** 3446 W Camelback Rd 85017 **Location:** Jct 35th Ave. [L] [D]

GREEKFEST 602/265-2990 (43)

♦♦♦ Greek. Casual Dining. $7-$28 **AAA Inspector Notes:** Traditional Greek favorites are served in a taverna setting complete with whitewashed walls, arched windows and Greek music. The cheerful spot employs a polished staff. Choose from classic salads, souvlaki and moussaka, and follow your choice with baklava and strong Greek coffee. **Features:** full bar. **Reservations:** suggested. **Address:** 1940 E Camelback Rd 85016 **Location:** Jct Camelback Rd and 20th St; northwest corner. [L] [D]

THE GRIND 602/954-7463 (62)

♦♦ American. Casual Dining. $8-$28 **AAA Inspector Notes:** Modern and intimate, this gourmet burger joint is the latest addition to trendy eats in the neighborhood. The menu features fresh ingredients, all coal-fired in custom-made ovens. Try the sweet and spicy burger with candied jalapenos, followed by doughnuts with salted butterscotch. **Features:** full bar, happy hour. **Address:** 3961 E Camelback Rd 85018 **Location:** Southwest corner of 40th St and Camelback Rd. [L] [D]

HANA JAPANESE EATERY 602/973-1238 (26)

♦♦ Japanese. Casual Dining. $9-$36 **AAA Inspector Notes:** This cozy spot serves traditional Japanese eats including bento and hibachi as well as fresh sushi. Save room for such desserts as mochi or tempura ice cream. **Address:** 5524 N 7th Ave 85013 **Location:** Jct 7th Ave and Camelback Rd, 0.6 mi n. 🚇 7th Ave/Camelback, 3. **Parking:** on-site and street. [L] [D] 🚇

HARLEY'S ITALIAN BISTRO 602/234-0333 (61)

♦♦ Italian. Casual Dining. $9-$22 **AAA Inspector Notes:** A Phoenix staple for more than 60 years, this casual dining room is cozy and inviting. Menu favorites include ravioli, gnocchi and sautéed salmon over penne in a light tomato sauce. **Features:** full bar, patio dining, Sunday brunch, happy hour. **Address:** 4221 N 7th Ave 85013 **Location:** I-10 exit 144, 2.2 mi n. 🚇 Indian School/Central, 6. [L] [D] 🚇

THE HENRY 602/429-8020 (66)

♦♦♦ New American. Casual Dining. $10-$28 **AAA Inspector Notes:** Perfectly prepared meals with an emphasis on garden fresh ingredients make the menu here much more interesting than their simple neighborhood restaurant slogan suggests. Urbanites love the retro chic atmosphere with curios to bewilder in every nook. Hunter green velvet upholstered booths, butcher block tables and a view into the pristine kitchen complete the inspiring, yet comfy, feel. **Features:** full bar, patio dining, Sunday brunch, happy hour. **Reservations:** suggested, weekends. **Address:** 4455 E Camelback Rd 85018 **Location:** Just e of 44th St. [L] [D] CALL[♿M]

HILLSTONE RESTAURANT 602/957-9700 (51)

♦♦♦ American. Casual Dining. $16-$45 **AAA Inspector Notes:** Modern and trendy, the setting here is perfect for a date night or corporate meeting. The servers are attentive and will suggest the fresh, seasonal options on the menu, which includes sushi selections, thick steaks and the famous grilled artichoke. **Features:** full bar, patio dining, happy hour. **Reservations:** suggested. **Address:** 2650 E Camelback Rd 85016 **Location:** Jct 24th St and Camelback Rd; just e. [L] [D]

HULA'S MODERN TIKI 602/265-8454 (39)

♦♦ Polynesian. Casual Dining. $10-$26 **AAA Inspector Notes:** Diners at this hip and fun Polynesian-style joint may start with the poke or the coconut shrimp rolls, then choose from the blackened ahi burger or Hawaiian jerk chicken or pork, and wash it all down with such signature cocktails as a mai tai or zombie. **Features:** full bar, patio dining, Sunday brunch, happy hour. **Address:** 4700 N Central Ave 85012 **Location:** Jct Camelback Rd, just s. 🚇 Central/Camelback, 4. [L] [D] [LATE] 🚇

INDIAN DELHI PALACE 602/244-8181 (5)

♦♦ Indian. Casual Dining. $8-$21 **AAA Inspector Notes:** Classic Indian cuisine includes freshly made sauces, hot breads and spicy flavors. Local businesspeople favor the luncheon buffet. **Features:** full bar. **Address:** 5104 E McDowell Rd 85008 **Location:** 0.5 mi e of SR 143. [L] [D]

INDIA PALACE 602/942-4224 (3)

♦♦ Indian. Casual Dining. $11-$16 **AAA Inspector Notes:** Using fresh ingredients and spices, the eatery features such southern Indian foods as karahi chicken, beef or lamb rubbed with special spices and stir-fried with onion and bell pepper. A large selection of vegetarian dishes and tandoori breads are available. **Features:** full bar, Sunday brunch. **Address:** 2941 W Bell Rd 85032 **Location:** I-17 exit 212, just w to Holmes Rd; southwest corner. [L] [D]

KEEGAN'S GRILL

♦♦ American. Casual Dining. $7-$22 **AAA Inspector Notes:** Patrons are treated like family in this neighborhood pub, which serves great sandwiches, freshly made soups and the house specialty: tender baby back ribs. **Bar:** full bar. [L] [D]

For additional information, visit AAA.com

LOCATIONS:

Address: 3114 E Camelback Rd 85016 **Location:** Just w of 32nd St. **Phone:** 602/955-6616

Address: 4723 E Ray Rd 85044 **Location:** I-10 exit 159 (Ray Rd), 0.5 mi w. **Phone:** 480/705-0505

KITCHEN 56 480/994-5656 (79)

♦♦♦ American. Casual Dining. $10-$26 **AAA Inspector Notes:** Casual American comfort food is on the menu at this gathering spot. Enjoy a wide variety of choices including charcuterie boards, pizza, pasta and such entrées as Cabernet-braised short ribs or ahi tuna with eggplant caponata—all while sipping hand-crafted cocktails and conversing with the locals. **Features:** full bar, patio dining, happy hour. **Reservations:** suggested. **Address:** 3433 N 56th St 85018 **Location:** Southeast corner of 56th St and Indian School Rd. [L] [D]

LA CONDESA GOURMET TACO SHOP 602/254-6330 (3)

♦ Mexican. Quick Serve. $4-$9 **AAA Inspector Notes:** Inspired by the cuisine of their native country, the owners of this gourmet taqueria have blended regional Mexican fare with their own family recipes to create delicious, fresh tacos, quesas, burros and house-favorite cochinita pibil. The salsa bar features more than a dozen homemade choices. **Features:** full bar. **Address:** 1919 N 16th St 85006 **Location:** I-10 exit 1, jct McDowell Rd, just n. [L] [D]

LA PINATA 602/279-1763 (68)

♦♦ Mexican. Casual Dining. $8-$18 **AAA Inspector Notes:** Known as the home of the chimichanga, this festive spot has been a valley favorite for more than 40 years. Classic, Sonoran-style comfort food is served in large portions. Favorites are the queso fundido, seafood enchiladas and, of course, the chimichangas. **Features:** full bar. **Address:** 3330 N 19th Ave 85015 **Location:** I-17 exit 201 (Thomas Rd), 0.7 mi e, then 0.4 mi n. [L] [D]

(See maps & indexes p. 146, 149, 154, 158, 164.)

LITTLE CLEO'S SEAFOOD LEGEND   602/680-4044   27

▼▼▼▼ Seafood. Casual Dining. $14-$38 **AAA Inspector Notes:** This trendy spot features the freshest seafood with a New Orleans influence. Friendly servers help with wine selections while blues plays in the background. **Features:** full bar. **Reservations:** suggested. **Address:** 5632 N 7th St 85014 **Location:** Jct Bethany Home Rd; just s. Central/Camelback, 4. **Parking:** valet and street only.

D   ⊞

MACAYO MEXICAN KITCHEN

▼▼ Mexican. Casual Dining. $10-$19 **AAA Inspector Notes:** The colorfully furnished Mexican-style eatery prepares Sonoran Mexican dishes. Friendly and efficient staffers serve traditional and lighter dishes flavored with this place's own chili peppers, which are grown near Tucson. **Bar:** full bar.

For additional information, visit AAA.com

LOCATIONS:

Address: 7829 W Thomas Rd 85033 **Location:** 0.5 mi w of 75th Ave; adjacent to Desert Sky Mall. **Phone:** 623/873-0313

Address: 4001 N Central Ave 85012 **Location:** Just n of Indian School Rd. Indian School/Central, 6. **Phone:** 602/264-6141

Address: 12637 S 48th St 85044 **Location:** Just s of Warner Rd. **Phone:** 480/598-5101

MAIZIE'S CAFE & BISTRO   602/274-2828   38

▼▼ American. Casual Dining. $10-$18 **AAA Inspector Notes:** This urban eatery is located in the uptown district steps from the light rail. The impressive wine list and unique signature cocktails complement eclectic salads, panini, gourmet pizzas and homemade desserts. The weekend brunch is very popular. **Features:** full bar, patio dining, Sunday brunch, happy hour. **Address:** 4750 N Central Ave 85012 **Location:** Just s of Camelback Rd. Central/Camelback, 4. L   D   ⊞

MEJICO   602/956-4420   78

▼▼ Regional Mexican. Casual Dining. $15-$23 **AAA Inspector Notes:** This fun, cozy neighborhood café features expertly prepared regional cuisine like shrimp relleno with jalapeño cream sauce, mole de pollo and slow-simmered pork chile verde. The extensive wine list includes selections from Mexico. **Features:** full bar, patio dining. **Address:** 2333 E Osborn Rd 85016 **Location:** Corner of 24th St and Osborn Rd. L   D

MERITAGE STEAKHOUSE   480/293-5000   1

▼▼▼▼ American. Fine Dining. $24-$55 **AAA Inspector Notes:** With classic style, the steaks and chops are grilled to perfection and the seafood is delicately sauced. Crisp salads and sides, such as sautéed asparagus and mushrooms, round out a meal served by attentive and courteous staff. **Features:** full bar, patio dining, happy hour. **Reservations:** suggested. **Address:** 5350 E Marriott St 85054 **Location:** SR 101 exit 31 (Tatum Blvd), 0.4 mi n to Deer Valley Dr, then 0.5 mi e; in JW Marriott Desert Ridge Resort & Spa. **Parking:** on-site and valet. L   D

MI PATIO MEXICAN FOOD   602/277-4831   72

▼▼ Mexican. Casual Dining. $5-$14 **AAA Inspector Notes:** The atmosphere here is fun and energetic, while fresh and tasty describe the food. Try some interesting dishes like green corn tamales or carne asada picado burrito with marinated fresh vegetables. **Features:** full bar, happy hour. **Address:** 3347 N 7th Ave 85013 **Location:** Southeast corner of Osborn Rd and 7th Ave. Osborn/Central, 7. L   D   ⊞

MIRACLE MILE DELICATESSEN   602/776-0992   44

▼ Deli. Quick Serve. $9-$14 **AAA Inspector Notes:** Since 1949, this New York-style deli has served delicious hot pastrami and corned beef sandwiches, along with other delicatessen favorites and daily entrée specials, including stuffed cabbage, homemade meatloaf and chicken noodle casserole. **Features:** beer & wine. **Address:** 1949 E Camelback Rd 85016 **Location:** SR 51 exit 3 (Indian School Rd); just w to 16th st, then 0.5 mi n. L   D

MOTO   602/263-5444   18

▼▼ Asian Fusion. Casual Dining. $7-$19 **AAA Inspector Notes:** Asian-fusion cuisine reigns supreme at this lively neighborhood spot. Try the Vietnamese pork tacos or wonton nachos. The owner's signature dessert has become a local legend. A full sushi menu also is available. **Features:** full bar, patio dining, happy hour. **Address:** 6845 N 16th St 85016 **Location:** SR 51 exit 5 (Glendale Ave), 0.5 mi w. L   D

NOOK KITCHEN   602/651-1390   74

▼▼ American. Casual Dining. $11-$28 **AAA Inspector Notes:** Tucked into a small shopping center, this stylish and friendly spot focuses on fresh, house-made ingredients. Along with the delicious wood-fired pizzas, the chicken Marsala and the halibut tacos are excellent choices. **Features:** full bar, happy hour. **Address:** 3623 E Indian School Rd 85018 **Location:** SR 51 exit 3 (Indian School Rd), 2.4 mi e; in Gaslight Square Shopping Center. D

NORTH ITALIAN FARMHOUSE   602/324-5600   63

▼▼▼ Italian. Casual Dining. $10-$33 **AAA Inspector Notes:** A newer addition to the hip Arcadia neighborhood, this trendy, lively bistro focuses on Italian country cuisine. There is a salumi and cheese selection, enticing antipasti, wood-fired pizza and such entrées as gnocchi and braised short rib in horseradish cream. **Features:** full bar, patio dining, Sunday brunch, happy hour. **Reservations:** suggested. **Address:** 4925 N 40th St 85018 **Location:** Jct Camelback Rd, just s. **Parking:** on-site and valet. L   D   🐾

OMAHA STEAKHOUSE   602/553-8970   53

▼▼▼ American. Casual Dining. $9-$38 **AAA Inspector Notes:** This traditional steakhouse, with an upscale yet casual atmosphere, features certified Midwestern corn-fed beef. Also on the varied menu are pasta, seafood, lamb and pork dishes. After 10 meals, diners have their name engraved on a steak knife that sits in a display case to await their next meal. **Features:** full bar, happy hour. **Reservations:** suggested. **Address:** 2630 E Camelback Rd 85020 **Location:** Just n of Camelback Rd, on 26th St; in Embassy Suites by Hilton Phoenix-Biltmore. L   D

OREGANO'S PIZZA BISTRO   602/241-0707

▼▼ Italian Pizza. Casual Dining. $7-$15 **AAA Inspector Notes:** The high-energy eatery, with its young and attentive waitstaff, serves hearty, oversized portions of delicious pizza, salads, pasta and baked sandwiches. When the weather permits, the patio is a happening spot. **Features:** full bar, patio dining. **Address:** 1008 E Camelback Rd 85014 **Location:** Just e of 7th St. Central/Camelback, 4. L   D   ⊞

ORIGINAL BREAKFAST HOUSE   602/482-2328   5

◆◆◆
American
Casual Dining
$6-$13

AAA Inspector Notes: Featuring locally sourced items and organic choices, this cozy neighborhood spot boasts friendly servers and home-style cooking. Try the S.O.S—it's the house favorite. **Address:** 13623 N 32nd St 85032 **Location:** SR 51 exit 11 (Thunderbird Rd), just w, then just s. B   L

OVER EASY CAFE   602/468-3447   77

▼▼ American. Casual Dining. $5-$12 **AAA Inspector Notes:** On weekends, prepare to wait for a table at this very popular breakfast and lunch spot featuring such comfort foods as chicken fried steak, jalapeño cheddar biscuits with sausage gravy and homemade corned beef hash—all served up in a friendly, retro-style setting. **Features:** full bar. **Address:** 4730 E Indian School Rd 85018 **Location:** Northwest corner of 48th St and Indian School Rd. B   L

PACIFIC GARDENS ASIAN BISTRO   602/795-3333   23

▼▼ Asian Fusion. Casual Dining. $8-$17 **AAA Inspector Notes:** For those who have a hard time deciding what to order, there are plenty of choices from the nice selection of Thai, Chinese and Japanese items available here. A sushi bar also is offered. **Features:** full bar, happy hour. **Address:** 4747 E Elliott Rd 85044 **Location:** I-10 exit 157 (Elliott Rd), 0.6 mi w; in Ahwatukee Mercado shopping center. L   D

(See maps & indexes p. 146, 149, 154, 158, 164.)

PANE BIANCO   602/234-2100   [58]
Specialty. Casual Dining. $9-$16 **AAA Inspector Notes:** Pizza, pasta and seasonally changing entrées are available at this eatery. All ingredients are of the highest quality. A complimentary mini-dessert is a homemade caramel. Imported bottled beverages and specialty food items like gourmet olive oils and pasta also are available. **Features:** patio dining. **Address:** 4404 N Central Ave 85012 **Location:** 0.4 mi n of Indian School Rd. Campbell/Central, 5.
L D CALL

PAPPADEAUX SEAFOOD KITCHEN   602/331-3434
Cajun Seafood. Casual Dining. $12-$50 **AAA Inspector Notes:** A seafood lover's delight, the restaurant taps into a little bit of New Orleans with its Cajun dishes and elaborate menu selections. Patrons might start off with a creative choice of blackened oyster and shrimp fondeaux with crayfish and let the feast begin. While music plays in the background, patrons can dig into dirty rice or spicy gumbo loaded with seafood. Well-seasoned shrimp and fish are prepared in varied ways. **Features:** full bar, happy hour. **Address:** 11051 N Black Canyon Hwy 85029 **Location:** I-17 exit 208 (Peoria Ave), 0.6 mi n on Frontage Rd. L D

THE PARLOR PIZZERIA   602/248-2480   [42]
Pizza. Casual Dining. $10-$31 **AAA Inspector Notes:** Housed in a former beauty parlor, this chic spot serves up delicious wood-fired pizza, gourmet salads and sandwiches. **Features:** full bar, patio dining, happy hour. **Address:** 1916 E Camelback Rd 85016 **Location:** Just w of 20th St. L D

PEPE'S TACO VILLA   602/2420379   [31]
Mexican. Casual Dining. $7-$16 **AAA Inspector Notes:** A down home atmosphere, with friendly servers and deliciously simple authentic food are the staples at this long-standing west side eatery. Specialties include mole poblano, tacos Monterrey and delectable flan for dessert. **Features:** full bar. **Address:** 2108 W Camelback Rd 85015 **Location:** I-17 exit 203 (Camelback Rd), 0.5 mi w. 19 Ave/Camelback, 2. B L D

P.F. CHANG'S CHINA BISTRO   623/707-4495
Chinese. Fine Dining. $8-$25 **AAA Inspector Notes:** Trendy, upscale decor provides a pleasant backdrop for New Age Chinese dining. Appetizers, soups and salads are a meal by themselves. Vegetarian plates and sides, noodles, chow meins, chicken and meat dishes are created from exotic, fresh ingredients. **Features:** full bar, patio dining, happy hour. **Address:** 2420 W Happy Valley Rd 85085 **Location:** I-17 exit 218 (Happy Valley Rd), just e.
L D

PHOENIX CITY GRILLE   602/266-3001   [24]
American. Casual Dining. $12-$32 **AAA Inspector Notes:** This friendly, comfortable neighborhood place employs capable servers who bring out traditional salads, sandwiches, pasta and chicken. Cedar-plank salmon is a favorite, and mesquite-smoked barbecue pork ribs are lean and tasty. **Features:** full bar, patio dining, Sunday brunch, happy hour. **Address:** 5816 N 16th St 85016 **Location:** 0.8 mi n of Camelback Rd. L D

PITA JUNGLE   623/587-5572
Mediterranean. Casual Dining. $7-$16 **AAA Inspector Notes:** The atmosphere here is super-casual and fun in the dining area and on the patio. On the menu is a wide variety of hot and cold pita wraps, pizza, falafel, spanakopita, salads and burgers, as well as natural, healthful vegetarian offerings. **Features:** full bar, happy hour. **Address:** 2530 W Happy Valley Rd 85085 **Location:** I-17 exit 218 (Happy Valley Rd), just e; in The Shops at Norterra.
L D

PIZZA A METRO   602/262-9999   [73]
Italian. Casual Dining. $10-$15 **AAA Inspector Notes:** This unassuming storefront in a strip mall belies the authentic culinary delights inside. The wood-fired pizza is available by the meter, as the name implies, and other Italian specialties including homemade gnocchi, stuffed ravioli and creamy tiramisu are equally as delicious. **Features:** beer & wine. **Address:** 2336 W Thomas Rd 85015 **Location:** I-17 exit 201 (Thomas Rd), just e. L D

PIZZERIA BIANCO   602/368-3273   [55]
Italian Pizza. Casual Dining. $13-$23 **AAA Inspector Notes:** This is chef Chris Bianco's second Phoenix location, and diners have even more options at this tucked-away location. The menu features handmade pasta and mozzarella cheese, creative desserts, and of course, the signature mouth-watering artisanal pizza this place has become famous for. **Features:** beer & wine, patio dining. **Reservations:** suggested. **Address:** 4743 N 20th St 85016 **Location:** Corner of 20th St and Camelback Rd; in Town & Country Shopping Center. L D

POSTINO CENTRAL WINECAFE   602/274-5144   [33]
American Small Plates Sandwiches. Casual Dining. $10-$14 **AAA Inspector Notes:** The light fare served in this mid-century modern building incorporates Mediterranean blends and flavors, such as bruschetta toppings of roasted artichoke or ricotta with pistachios. The varied sandwich and salad menu continues through the evening. Several beers are available on tap. **Features:** beer & wine, patio dining, Sunday brunch, happy hour. **Address:** 5144 N Central Ave 85012 **Location:** Jct Camelback Rd, just n. Central/Camelback, 4. **Parking:** on-site and valet.
L D

POSTINO WINECAFE   602/852-3939   [67]
American. Casual Dining. $10-$14 **AAA Inspector Notes:** The light fare served in the recycled post office building incorporates Mediterranean blends and flavors, including bruschetta toppings of roasted artichoke or ricotta with pistachios. The varied sandwich and salad menu continues through the evening. **Features:** beer & wine, patio dining, happy hour. **Address:** 3939 E Campbell Ave 85018 **Location:** 0.5 mi n of Indian School Rd on 40th St, just w. **Parking:** on-site and valet. L D

QUIESSENCE   602/276-0601   [80]
New American. Fine Dining. $20-$40 **AAA Inspector Notes:** Nestled into the backdrop of the Farm at South Mountain, the hand-crafted New American cuisine is the real star here. With a focus on local, market fresh ingredients, the menu never fails to impress. The seasonal chef's tasting menu is an excellent way to sample the wide array of choices like handmade pappardelle duck confit pasta and Alaskan halibut with carrot couscous. Finish with a chocolate hazelnut pie. **Features:** full bar, patio dining. **Reservations:** suggested. **Address:** 6106 S 32nd St 85042 **Location:** I-10 exit 151 (University Dr/32nd St), 1.4 mi s; at Farm at South Mountain. D

RA SUSHI BAR RESTAURANT   480/940-1111
Japanese Sushi. Casual Dining. $8-$20 **AAA Inspector Notes:** Innovatively-designed seafood dishes are served by a casual, efficient staff at this upscale sushi bar located in a busy shopping plaza. Try the spinach gyoza followed by the signature tempura cinnamon ice cream (serves three or four folks). **Features:** full bar, happy hour. **Address:** 4921 E Ray Rd, Suite B1 85044 **Location:** I-10 exit 159 (Ray Rd), just w. L D LATE

RED DEVIL RESTAURANT & PIZZERIA   602/267-1036   [4]
Italian. Casual Dining. $8-$26 **AAA Inspector Notes:** A family-owned valley tradition since 1960, diners still flock to this old-school, traditional pizza joint. The outdoor take-out window is very popular and can have a line of patrons waiting for delicious thin-crust pies, spicy wings or the house specialty, red devil trio—fettuccine Alfredo, stuffed rigatoni and chicken parmigiana. **Features:** full bar. **Address:** 3102 E McDowell Rd 85008 **Location:** Loop 202 exit 1C (32nd St), just n, then just w. L D

RESTAURANT ATOYAC ESTILO OAXACA   602/864-2746   [13]
Mexican. Quick Serve. $4-$9 **AAA Inspector Notes:** The location may be hard to find, but big flavors in the food are not. Authentic Oaxacan-style street fare is the specialty at this tiny taqueria. Sample the carne asada, pastor and chorizo tacos, shrimp burrito or crispy quesadillas. Wash it all down with a fresh horchata and finish with warm churros. **Features:** patio dining. **Address:** 1830 W Glendale Ave 85021 **Location:** I-17 exit 205 (Glendale Ave), 0.8 mi e. L D

(See maps & indexes p. 146, 149, 154, 158, 164.)

RICHARDSON'S OF NEW MEXICO   602/287-8900   20
WW Southwestern. Casual Dining. $13-$35 AAA Inspector Notes: This Phoenix institution has been brought back to life after a fire destroyed the original building in 2009. The beloved New Mexico-style menu is the same, as is the dining room, which is an exact replica of the original. Favorite menu items are the carne adobado, red chile pork tamales and the relleno platter. Features: full bar, patio dining, Sunday brunch, happy hour. Address: 6335 N 16th St 85016 Location: SR 5 exit 4B, just w on E Bethany Home Rd, then 0.5 mi n. Parking: on-site and valet. [L] [D] [LATE]

RICO'S AMERICAN GRILL   602/997-5850   11
WWWW American. Casual Dining. $12-$32 AAA Inspector Notes: This popular and attractive restaurant offers seasonal patio dining, friendly staff and comfort foods prepared with Southwestern influences. Sharing space on the menu are a variety of fresh salads, seasonal soups, gourmet sandwiches and a nice selection of dinner entrées. Features: full bar, patio dining, happy hour. Address: 7677 N 16th St 85020 Location: SR 51 exit Glendale Ave, 0.4 mi w, then 0.6 mi n; in Pointe Hilton Squaw Peak Resort. Parking: on-site and valet. [B] [L] [D]

ROY'S DESERT RIDGE   480/419-7697   2
WWW Hawaiian. Casual Dining. $20-$30 AAA Inspector Notes: An attractive setting and tropical motif blend well with friendly and attentive service. Widely varied seafood dishes, which change based on availability, are expertly prepared. Examples might include basil-seared ono, herb-crusted yellowtail and butterfish. Chocolate souffle is a house specialty. Features: full bar, patio dining, happy hour. Reservations: suggested. Address: 5350 E Marriott Dr 85054 Location: SR 101 exit 31 (Tatum Blvd), 0.4 mi n to Deer Valley Dr, then 0.5 mi e; in JW Marriott Desert Ridge Resort & Spa. Parking: on-site and valet. [D]

RUBIO'S FRESH MEXICAN GRILL
W Mexican. Quick Serve. $4-$10 AAA Inspector Notes: Freshly prepared and healthful foods, bright decor and friendly staff are found in this upscale fast-food spot. A special treat, the salsa bar lines up four styles and flavors. Bar: beer only. [L] [D]

For additional information, visit AAA.com
LOCATIONS:
Address: 4340 E Indian School Rd, Suite 1 85018 Location: Just w of 44th St. Phone: 602/508-1732
Address: 21001 N Tatum Blvd, Suite 34-1130 85050 Location: Just n of SR 101; in Desert Ridge Marketplace. Phone: 480/473-9225
Address: 4747 E Bell Rd 85032 Location: Jct Tatum Blvd; northeast corner. Phone: 602/867-1454
Address: 4905 E Ray Rd 85044 Location: I-10 exit 159 (Ray Rd), 0.4 mi w to 48th St, then just s; southeast corner.
Phone: 480/961-0621

RUFFINO ITALIAN CUISINE   480/893-8544   24
WWW Italian. Fine Dining. $13-$35 AAA Inspector Notes: A quiet and relaxing space in the busy city awaits you at this Italian eatery. Known for seafood specialties, more traditional dishes such as rigatoni bolognese and veal saltimbocca are offered. The attentive waitstaff welcome diners and guide them through a pleasant and satisfying dining experience. Features: full bar, happy hour. Reservations: suggested. Address: 4902 E Warner Rd 85044 Location: I-10 exit 158, 0.5 mi w. [D]

RUSTLER'S ROOSTE   602/431-6474   82

Steak
Casual Dining
$15-$31
AAA Inspector Notes: Overlooking the city, this popular Western-style restaurant prepares a nice selection of steak, seafood and barbecue specialties. A band performs nightly. Features: full bar, patio dining, happy hour. Reservations: suggested. Address: 8383 S 48th St 85044 Location: I-10 exit 155 (Baseline Rd), just w, then just s; in Arizona Grand Resort & Spa. [D]

SABAI MODERN THAI   602/954-8774   8
WW Thai. Casual Dining. $10-$18 AAA Inspector Notes: Small and modern with a friendly vibe, this neighborhood secret has some of the best Thai food around. The jalapeño curry packs a flavor punch, and the chicken lettuce wraps with peanut sauce are worth the trip. Features: full bar, happy hour. Address: 4121 E Thomas Rd 85018 Location: Jct 40th St; just e. [L] [D]

ST. FRANCIS   602/200-8111   36
WWWW New American. Casual Dining. $12-$28 AAA Inspector Notes: Seasonal American fare is served up in a modern chic setting. Patrons can choose from such wood-fired specialties as green chile pork stew and pork chop with fresh corn polenta, sweet peppers and whole grain mustard sauce. Homemade desserts include toffee pudding with sweet cream gelato. Features: full bar, patio dining, Sunday brunch, happy hour. Address: 111 E Camelback Rd 85012 Location: Jct Central Ave, just e. [M] Central/Camelback, 4. Parking: on-site and valet. [L] [D] [M]

SAKANA SUSHI AND GRILL   480/598-0506   22
WWW Sushi. Casual Dining. $8-$17 AAA Inspector Notes: One of four locations in the Valley, this restaurant is known for serving the freshest sushi in the area. The menu includes classic sushi and sashimi choices as well as Japanese favorites and full teppanyaki dinners. Features: beer & wine, happy hour. Address: 5061 E Elliot Rd 85044 Location: I-10 exit 157 (Elliot Rd), 0.3 mi w; in Ahwatukee Plaza. [L] [D]

SAUCE   602/216-2400
WW Italian. Casual Dining. $6-$11 AAA Inspector Notes: This restaurant's selections could be characterized as gourmet fast food. Among choices are sausage and caramelized onion or chicken and broccoli rabe pizza. Lasagna and fresh salads also are on the menu. The clean modern décor lends to a fun experience. Features: beer & wine. Address: 742 E Glendale Ave 85020 Location: Jct 7th St; northeast corner. [L] [D]

SCOTT'S GENERATIONS DELI   602/277-5662   28
WW Deli. Family Dining. $5-$18 AAA Inspector Notes: The Snyder family has been serving authentic New York-style deli favorites to Valley regulars since 1988. The bagels are fresh, and homemade potato latkes are the real deal. For lunch the corned beef and pastrami are piled high on delicious rye bread, complemented with beet borscht or matzo ball soup. Features: patio dining. Address: 5555 N 7th St, Suite 108 85014 Location: Jct 7th St and Missouri Ave; northeast corner; in Cinema Park Shopping Center. [M] Central/Camelback, 4. [B] [L] [M]

SCRAMBLE   602/374-2294   8
WW American. Quick Serve. $6-$10 AAA Inspector Notes: This very popular breakfast and lunch café specializes in fresh, local ingredients. The brizza, or breakfast pizza, is a crowd favorite, as are the Santa Fe eggs Benedict served on jalapeño corn bread with a chipotle hollandaise. Features: patio dining. Address: 9832 N 7th St 85020 Location: I-17 exit 207 (Dunlap Ave), 3 mi e to 7th St, then 0.6 mi n. [B] [L]

SIERRA BONITA GRILL   602/264-0700   16
WWWW Southwestern. Casual Dining. $12-$28 AAA Inspector Notes: Southwest flavors are highlighted at this comfortable and sophisticated neighborhood spot. Menu choices range from wood-grilled burgers and marinated carne asada tacos to buttermilk chicken with Oaxacan chile mashed potatoes and New Mexican-style stacked enchiladas. An extensive wine list is available. Features: full bar, patio dining, Sunday brunch, happy hour. Reservations: suggested. Address: 6933 N 7th St 85014 Location: I-17 exit 295 (Glendale Ave), 2.7 mi e, then just s. [L] [D]

SILVER DRAGON CHINESE RESTAURANT   623/841-1346   14
WWW Chinese. Casual Dining. $8-$12 AAA Inspector Notes: This unassuming spot features such popular Americanized dishes as kung pao chicken and Mongolian beef, but for something more exotic, ask for the Hong Kong menu. This place gets busy at lunch. Address: 1739 W Glendale Ave 85021 Location: I-17 exit 205 (Glendale Ave), 1 mi e. [L] [D]

SOUTHERN RAIL   602/200-0085   34
WWWW Southern American. Casual Dining. $7-$27 AAA Inspector Notes: Inspired by regional Southern-style cooking, local chef Justin Beckett has created a warm, inviting and lively atmosphere complementing such comfort food choices as smoked chicken and andouille gumbo, cornbread salad with grilled cauliflower and smoked trout with sweet pea cakes. Try the red velvet cake or beignets to finish. Features: full bar, patio dining, Sunday brunch, happy hour. Address: 300 W Camelback Rd 85013 Location: Jct Central Ave and Camelback Rd, 0.3 mi w. [M] Central/Camelback, 4.
[L] [D] [M]

(See maps & indexes p. 146, 149, 154, 158, 164.)

STINGRAY SUSHI 602/955-2008 ⑤②

▼▼▼ Sushi. Casual Dining. $9-$30 **AAA Inspector Notes:** Bright colors and lively music set the stage at this sushi spot attracting a younger, trendy crowd enjoying a large selection of sushi, salads, bento and tasty main courses. Creative rolls, such as the Godzilla and lollipop are packed with fresh ingredients and topped with creative glazes like sweet eels or unagi (freshwater eels). **Features:** full bar, patio dining, happy hour. **Address:** 2502 E Camelback Rd 85018 **Location:** Just e of 24th St; in Biltmore Fashion Park. **Parking:** on-site and valet. [L] [D] [LATE]

STOCKYARDS RESTAURANT & 1889 SALOON
602/273-7378 ⑦

▼▼▼ Steak. Casual Dining. $8-$75 **AAA Inspector Notes:** *Classic.* Since 1947, this restaurant has been serving a nice selection of steak, prime rib and other entrées. The warm and inviting décor features an attractive stone dual-sided fireplace. **Features:** full bar, happy hour. **Reservations:** suggested. **Address:** 5009 E Washington St, Suite 115 85034 **Location:** 0.5 mi e of 48th St. 44th St/Washington, 22. [L] [D] [▥]

SUSHI BROKERS 480/515-5000 ⑦⑥

▼▼ Japanese. Casual Dining. $11-$16 **AAA Inspector Notes:** A great choice in the neighborhood for sushi rolls, sashimi, tempura and other favorites, along with fun music and friendly service. **Features:** full bar, happy hour. **Address:** 4419 E Indian School Rd 85018 **Location:** Jct 44th St, just e. [L] [D]

SZECHWAN PALACE 602/685-0888 ⑥

▼▼ Chinese. Casual Dining. $7-$20 **AAA Inspector Notes:** Located within the Chinese Cultural Center, this traditional establishment serves such favorites as kung pao chicken, Mongolian beef and shrimp in lobster sauce. **Features:** full bar. **Address:** 668 N 44th St, Suite 108 85008 **Location:** SR 202 exit 2 (44th St), just s; in Chinese Cultural Center. 44th St/Washington, 22. [L] [D] [▥]

TARBELL'S 602/955-8100 ⑤⑦

▼▼▼ American. Casual Dining. $11-$35 **AAA Inspector Notes:** This lively restaurant's monthly changing selection of creative dishes are complemented with organic local produce and a variety of poultry, fish and beef. An open kitchen allows glimpses of the preparation process. The over-sized desserts are fit to share with bread pudding with Kentucky bourbon sauce being a sure winner. **Features:** full bar. **Reservations:** suggested. **Address:** 3213 E Camelback Rd 85018 **Location:** Just e of 32nd Ave. **Parking:** on-site and valet. [D]

T-BONE STEAKHOUSE 602/276-0945

▼▼ Steak. Casual Dining. $11-$45 **AAA Inspector Notes:** Friendly staff serves mesquite-broiled steaks and chicken. The dining room and outdoor patio afford panoramic views of the city skyline and Camelback Mountain. **Features:** full bar, patio dining. **Address:** 10037 S 19th Ave 85041 **Location:** 1.5 mi s of Baseline Rd. [D]

T. COOK'S 602/808-0766 ⑥⑨

▼▼▼ ▼▼◆
Mediterranean
Fine Dining
$16-$44

AAA Inspector Notes: *Classic.* Accomplished staffers serve a nice selection of Mediterranean-inspired entrées in elegant surroundings. Grab a specialty cocktail and enjoy the piano music in the adjacent lounge after dinner. Patio seating is an option, weather permitting. **Features:** full bar, patio dining, Sunday brunch, happy hour. **Reservations:** suggested. **Address:** 5200 E Camelback Rd 85018 **Location:** Just e of 52nd St; in Royal Palms Resort and Spa. **Parking:** on-site and valet. [B] [L] [D]

THIRTEENORTH GRILLE 602/795-1397 ⑩

▼▼ American. Casual Dining. $9-$23 **AAA Inspector Notes:** This is a great neighborhood place with great daily specials and a friendly staff. Try the rib-eye, or the mussels and shrimp with linguine. **Features:** full bar, patio dining, Sunday brunch, happy hour. **Address:** 1301 E Northern Ave 85020 **Location:** SR 51 exit 7 (Northern Ave), 1.1 mi w. [L] [D]

TICOZ RESTO-BAR 602/200-0160 ③⑤

▼▼▼ Southwestern. Casual Dining. $10-$20 **AAA Inspector Notes:** Modern and lively, this uptown bistro serves a variety of comfort foods with a focus on Southwest flavors and festive cocktails in a casual contemporary setting. **Features:** full bar, patio dining, Sunday brunch, happy hour. **Address:** 5114 N 7th St 85014 **Location:** Just n of Camelback Rd. Central/Camelback, 4. **Parking:** on-site and valet. [L] [D] [LATE] [▥]

TRUE FOOD KITCHEN 602/774-3488 ④⑤

▼▼▼ American. Casual Dining. $10-$26 **AAA Inspector Notes:** With many vegetarian, vegan and gluten-free options, this stylish eatery emphasizes healthy eating without sacrificing taste. Try the Tuscan kale salad with steelhead salmon, or miso-glazed black cod with bok choy and Asian mushrooms. Fresh, hand-made sodas loaded with antioxidants are distinctive and tasty. **Features:** full bar, patio dining, Sunday brunch. **Address:** 2502 E Camelback Rd 85016 **Location:** Jct Camelback Rd and 24th St; in Biltmore Fashion Park. **Parking:** on-site and valet. [L] [D]

TUTTI SANTI RISTORANTE 602/216-0336 ⑫

▼▼▼ Italian. Casual Dining. $14-$27 **AAA Inspector Notes:** Vaulted ceilings, large framed artwork, fresh pasta and an outdoor terrace distinguish this family-operated local favorite. **Features:** full bar. **Address:** 7575 N 16th St, Suite 5 85254 **Location:** SR 51 exit 5 (Glendale Ave), just w, then 0.5 mi n; in Centre Pointe Shoppes. [D]

THE VIG UPTOWN 602/633-1187 ②①

▼▼ American. Casual Dining. $11-$17 **AAA Inspector Notes:** This local hangout serves up simple and delicious comfort food, while patrons play bocce ball out on the patio, listening to their favorite live music. **Features:** full bar, patio dining, Sunday brunch, happy hour. **Address:** 6015 N 16th St 85014 **Location:** Jct Bethany Home Rd, just n. **Parking:** on-site and valet. [L] [D] [LATE]

VINCENT ON CAMELBACK 602/224-0225 ⑥⓪

▼▼▼ French. Fine Dining. $26-$38 **AAA Inspector Notes:** Prepared with a French flair, the fresh seafood, lobster, duck confit, veal, rack of lamb, beef and Cornish hen all are attractively presented at this restaurant. Attentive, accomplished service is achieved in each of several intimate dining rooms, which are surrounded by fresh orchids. **Features:** full bar, patio dining, happy hour. **Reservations:** suggested. **Address:** 3930 E Camelback Rd 85018 **Location:** Just w of 40th St, on north side of Camelback Rd. **Parking:** valet only. [D]

WILD GAME GRILL 602/955-1142 ②

▼▼ American. Casual Dining. $9-$24 **AAA Inspector Notes:** There are plenty of TVs to watch your favorite sporting event at this grill, but the real star is the eclectic menu filled with exotic items like rabbit sloppy joes, jackalope meatloaf and the ever-popular Rocky Mountain oysters. **Features:** full bar, patio dining, happy hour. **Address:** 2445 E Thomas Rd 85016 **Location:** SR 51 exit 2 (Thomas Rd), 0.3 mi e. [L] [D]

WINDSOR 602/279-1111 ③②

▼▼ American. Casual Dining. $12-$20 **AAA Inspector Notes:** Upscale bar food and specialty cocktails delight the eclectic, lively crowd at this trendy North Central hot spot. Check out the fondue with pulled pork and sausage, the crab cake BLT and the Chicago-style tender belly hot dog. **Features:** full bar, patio dining, Sunday brunch. **Address:** 5223 N Central Ave 85012 **Location:** Jct Camelback Rd and Central Ave, 0.3 mi n. Central/Camelback, 4. **Parking:** on-site and valet. [L] [D] CALL [⌖M] [▥]

WRIGHT'S AT THE BILTMORE 602/381-7668 ③⓪

▼▼▼ American. Fine Dining. $29-$46 **AAA Inspector Notes:** *Historic.* Elegant, attentive servers bring eye-pleasing and palate-satisfying dishes that take advantage of seasonally fresh ingredients. Menu selections range from the freshest seafood to aged steaks. The signature chocolate soufflé is well worth the wait. **Features:** full bar, patio dining, Sunday brunch. **Reservations:** suggested. **Address:** 2400 E Missouri Ave 85016 **Location:** Jct Camelback Rd, 0.5 mi n on 24th St, 0.4 mi e; in Arizona Biltmore, A Waldorf Astoria Resort. **Parking:** on-site and valet. [D]

(See maps & indexes p. 146, 149, 154, 158, 164.)

THE YACHT CLUB   602/368-2088 (75)
▼▼▼ American. Casual Dining. $12-$31 **AAA Inspector Notes:** Located in the Arcadia neighborhood, this preppy, nautical-themed bistro features New England-style fare with a Southwest flair. Try the lobster roll two ways, Baja fish tacos or the seared duck breast with vanilla-citrus confit. **Features:** full bar, happy hour. **Reservations:** suggested. **Address:** 4231 E Indian School Rd 85018 **Location:** Jct 44th St and Indian School Rd; just w. **Parking:** valet only. [D]

YASU SUSHI BISTRO   602/787-9181 (7)
▼▼▼ Japanese. Casual Dining. $9-$26 **AAA Inspector Notes:** Classic Japanese preparations at this bistro include abundant sushi selections, tempura and sumibiyaki for delicious grilled meats and seafood. Also, Chef Yasu creates such delectable small plates and entrees as creamy bacon wrapped scallops and homemade grilled chicken meatballs. **Features:** full bar, patio dining, happy hour. **Reservations:** suggested. **Address:** SR 51 exit 10 (Cactus Rd), 1.2 mi e. [L] [D]

ZINBURGER   602/424-9500 (48)
▼▼ Burgers. Casual Dining. $10-$16 **AAA Inspector Notes:** The high energy of this popular bistro is apparent from the moment guests enter. Serving a selection of gourmet burgers including Kobe beef and Clint's almost famous veggie option, they also offer salads and fun floats and shakes for dessert. **Features:** full bar, patio dining, happy hour. **Address:** 2502 E Camelback Rd 85016 **Location:** Jct Camelback Rd and 24th St; in Biltmore Fashion Park. **Parking:** on-site (fee) and valet. [L] [D]

ZIPPS SPORTS GRILL   602/266-1600 (23)
▼▼ American. Casual Dining. $6-$15 **AAA Inspector Notes:** The perfect place to watch a favorite sports team on one of the more than 30 plasma screens. A casual bar menu consisting of crispy buffalo wings, nachos, chicken fingers, pizza, burgers and chili is available late. Several premium beers are offered on tap. **Features:** full bar, patio dining, happy hour. **Address:** 1515 E Bethany Home Rd 85014 **Location:** Jct 16th St; southwest corner.
[L] [D] [LATE]

PICACHO (E-4) pop. 471, elev. 1,607'

PICACHO PEAK STATE PARK, .5 mi. s. off I-10 exit 219, is the site of Arizona's westernmost Civil War battle. In 1862 a dozen Union soldiers defeated 10 Confederate cavalrymen. The park is home to the 1,500-foot peak that was used as a landmark for settlers traveling between New Mexico and California. The Mormon Battalion constructed the road used by the forty-niners and the Butterfield Overland Stage.

Today trails meander throughout the park and to the top of the peak. A Civil War reenactment is held each spring. **Hours:** Daily dawn-dusk; **Cost:** $7 (per private vehicle, up to four passengers); $3 (per individual arriving on foot or bicycle). Camping $15-$25. **Phone:** (520) 466-3183, or (520) 586-2283 for camping reservations. [A] [🏕] [⛺]

PINE (D-4) pop. 1,963

PINE-STRAWBERRY MUSEUM is on SR 87 between Hardscrabble Rd. and Randall Dr. The museum houses artifacts from prehistoric Native American cultures and the Spanish, Anglo and Mormon pioneers who first settled the area. Exhibits include World War II memorabilia, farming implements, furnishings and clothing from the late 1800s. **Time:** Allow 1 hour minimum. **Hours:** Wed.-Sat. 10-2, mid-May to mid-Oct; Thurs.-Sat. 10-2, rest of

year. Closed Jan. 1, Easter, Thanksgiving and Christmas. Phone ahead to confirm schedule. **Cost:** $1. **Phone:** (928) 476-3547.

PINETOP-LAKESIDE (D-5) pop. 4,282, elev. 6,960'
• Restaurants p. 192

Lakeside originally was named Fairview in 1880 by Mormon pioneers. Pinetop, also founded by Mormons, began in 1878 with a sawmill and ranching on the open range of the White Mountains. Before tourism, logging and ranching were the mainstays of the area. The twin towns were incorporated in 1984 as a resort area.

Pinetop-Lakeside, on the edge of the White Mountain Apache Reservation, is 10 miles southeast of Show Low on SR 260 on the edge of Mogollon Rim. The elevation makes the area cool in summer for trout fishing, camping and other activities. Winter sports such as snowmobiling, skiing and ice fishing are popular in the Apache-Sitgreaves National Forests *(see place listing p. 39)* and on the reservation. Fishing also is permitted by fee on the reservation.

Pinetop-Lakeside Chamber of Commerce: 518 W. White Mountain Blvd. in Lakeside, P.O. Box 4220, Pinetop, AZ 85935. **Phone:** (928) 367-4290 or (800) 573-4031.

GAMBLING ESTABLISHMENTS
• **Hon-Dah Resort Casino and Conference Center,** 3 mi. e. at jct. SRs 260 and 73. **Hours:** Daily 24 hours. **Phone:** (928) 369-0299 or (800) 929-8744.

BEST WESTERN INN OF PINETOP   (928)367-6667

Motel
$75-$149

AAA Benefit:
Save 10% or more every day and earn 10% bonus points!

Address: 404 E White Mountain Blvd 85935 **Location:** On SR 260, east end of town. Located in Pinetop. **Facility:** 41 units. 2 stories (no elevator), exterior corridors. **Activities:** hot tub. **Guest Services:** coin laundry. **Featured Amenity: full hot breakfast.**
[SAVE] [📶] [🐾] [BIZ] [🛜] [📱] [🍽]
[💻] / SOME UNITS [🐕] [HS]

EXECUTIVE INN & SUITES   (928)367-4146
▼▼ Motel $56-$135 **Address:** 1023 E White Mountain Blvd 85935 **Location:** On SR 260; east end of town. Located in Pinetop. **Facility:** 24 units. 2 stories (no elevator), exterior corridors. **Terms:** cancellation fee imposed. **Activities:** miniature golf.
[📶] [🛜] [✖] [📱] [🍽] [💻] / SOME UNITS [🐕]

HOLIDAY INN EXPRESS   928/367-6077
▼▼▼ Hotel. Rates not provided. **Address:** 431 E White Mountain Blvd 85935 **Location:** On SR 260, east end of town. Located in Pinetop. **Facility:** 73 units. 2 stories, interior corridors. **Pool(s):** heated indoor. **Activities:** sauna, hot tub. **Guest Services:** coin laundry.
[📶] CALL [🄼] [🚗] [🐾] [BIZ] [🛜] [✖] [📱] [🍽] [💻]
/ SOME UNITS [HS]

HON-DAH RESORT CASINO AND CONFERENCE CENTER
928/369-0299

Hotel
$129-$199

Address: 777 Hwy 260 85935 **Location:** Jct SR 260 and 73; east end of town. Located in White Mountain Apache Reservation of Pinetop. **Facility:** The surrounding acres of the wooded reservation, cool weather and outdoor sports are as enticing here as the casino. A beautiful covered outdoor pool and unique rock grand staircase are showcased. 128 units. 2 stories, interior corridors. **Terms:** check-in 4 pm. **Dining:** nightclub, entertainment. **Pool(s):** heated outdoor. **Activities:** sauna, hot tub, game room. **Guest Services:** coin laundry.

NORTHWOODS RESORT
928/367-2966

Cabin. Rates not provided. **Address:** 165 E White Mountain Blvd 85935 **Location:** On SR 260, MM 352. Located in Lakeside. **Facility:** 14 units, some houses and cabins. 1-2 stories (no elevator), exterior corridors. **Activities:** hot tub, playground. **Guest Services:** coin laundry.

QUALITY INN PINETOP
(928)367-3636

Motel $80-$130 **Address:** 458 E White Mountain Blvd 85935 **Location:** On SR 260; east end of town. Located in Pinetop. **Facility:** 42 units. 2 stories (no elevator), exterior corridors.

TIMBERLODGE INN
(928)367-4463

Motel $49-$99 **Address:** 1078 E White Mountain Blvd 85935 **Location:** On SR 260; east end of town. Located in Pinetop. **Facility:** 29 units. 1-2 stories (no elevator), exterior corridors. **Terms:** 2-3 night minimum stay - seasonal and/or weekends, 72 day cancellation notice-fee imposed.

WHERE TO EAT

THE CHALET RESTAURANT & SHARKY'S SUSHI BAR
928/367-1514

American. Casual Dining. $8-$26 **AAA Inspector Notes:** An attractive country decor welcomes guests at this casual restaurant, which appeals to both locals and travelers. The menu has a variety of steak, seafood and chicken selections, and a sushi bar, the only one in the county, is a big hit. A kind, efficient staff dons semiformal, black-and-white uniforms. **Features:** full bar, early bird specials. **Address:** 348 W White Mountain Blvd 85929 **Location:** On SR 260; in Lakeside.

CHARLIE CLARK'S STEAK HOUSE
928/367-4900

Steak. Casual Dining. $14-$35 **AAA Inspector Notes:** An informal, Western atmosphere characterizes the popular, long-established restaurant on the city's main thoroughfare. Saddles and chuckwagon-style utensils adorn the dining room, where patrons nosh on prime rib, seafood and mesquite-broiled steak. Lunch is served in the bar and on the patio by friendly staffers. **Features:** full bar, patio dining, early bird specials, happy hour. **Address:** 1701 E White Mountain Blvd **Location:** On SR 260; east end of town; in Pinetop.

DARBI'S CAFE
928/367-6556

American. Casual Dining. $6-$17 **AAA Inspector Notes:** This roadside eatery serves specialty hot and cold sandwiches, salads, wraps, pasta plates, burgers, fish and chips, homemade chili con carne, homemade meatloaf and luscious desserts. The friendly staff is a plus. **Features:** beer & wine, patio dining. **Address:** 235 E White Mountain Blvd 85935 **Location:** On SR 260; east end of town; in Pinetop.

EL RANCHO RESTAURANT
928/367-4557

Mexican. Casual Dining. $7-$20 **AAA Inspector Notes:** The Chavez family recipes go back 60 years, but the friendly staff and owners of today contribute to a pleasant family dining experience. After noshing on traditional dishes, guests can savor flan or churros for dessert. **Features:** full bar. **Address:** 1523 E White Mountain Blvd 85935 **Location:** On SR 260; in Pinetop.

LOS CORRALES
928/367-5585

Mexican. Casual Dining. $7-$17 **AAA Inspector Notes:** This bright and lively family eatery is colorfully decorated in oranges, reds and yellows. The three-dimensional tabletops are sunny and fun. Otherwise ordinary Mexican dishes alive with freshness and flavor are presented by a well-groomed waitstaff. The margaritas are not to be missed! **Features:** full bar. **Address:** 845 E White Mountain Blvd 85935 **Location:** On SR 260, east end of town; in Pinetop.

MOUNTAIN THAI RESTAURANT
928/368-4166

Thai. Casual Dining. $8-$15 **AAA Inspector Notes:** In a ramshackle little building, not without its charm, this spot is known for true authentic recipes from Thailand, including delicious yam wun sen (a spicy dish of clear bean thread noodles with cucumbers and cabbage). Delicious soups are made with lemon grass and coconut milk. Everything is homemade, right down to the coconut ice cream. **Features:** full bar. **Address:** 2741 Hwy 260 85929 **Location:** West on SR 260; in Lakeside.

THE PASTA HOUSE
928/367-2782

Italian. Casual Dining. $14-$24 **AAA Inspector Notes:** Diners will feel as if they are in Old Italy at this intimate, cozy eatery featuring American Italian specialties such as chicken Jerusalem, sorrentino and piccata, scaloppine of veal and jumbo shrimp, linguine with clams in white or red sauce and shrimp McAngelo with roasted pimentos, shallots and mushrooms. There always is a daily chef's special. Homemade desserts feature a variety of attractively presented cheesecakes, bananas Foster and crème brûlée. **Features:** full bar, patio dining. **Address:** 2188 E White Mountain Blvd 85935 **Location:** On SR 260; east end of town; in Pinetop.

VILLAGE GRILL
928/368-2424

Burgers. Quick Serve. $4-$12 **AAA Inspector Notes:** This simple restaurant serves fresh, made-to-order all-beef burgers, hot dogs and chicken. It is mostly self service, but the food tastes great and is offered at an affordable price. **Features:** patio dining. **Address:** 1477 W White Mountain Blvd, Suite 4 85929 **Location:** Jct Woodland Rd; in Lakeside.

PIPE SPRING NATIONAL MONUMENT (A-3)

Off SR 389 15 miles west of Fredonia, Pipe Spring National Monument preserves a life-sustaining water source that Paiute Indians called Mu-tum-wa-va, or Dripping Rock. In the early 1870s, Mormon pioneers built a compound over the springs consisting of a sandstone fort and ranch house. Tours of the fort, named Winsor Castle, are offered. Pipe Spring has long served as a way station for weary travelers. The visitor center offers exhibits and a movie about Kaibab and pioneer culture and history.

Allow 1 hour minimum. Daily 8-5. Closed Jan. 1, Thanksgiving and Christmas. Tours of Winsor Castle are given daily generally on the half-hour. Admission $7; free (ages 0-15). Phone (928) 643-7105.

PORTAL (F-6) elev. 4,773'

Portal received its name because it is at the entrance to Cave Creek Canyon. The town became a popular summer vacation spot for those seeking cool, high altitudes and such recreational pastimes as camping, fishing, hiking and hunting.

CAVE CREEK CANYON, s.w. via a paved road, displays brilliant colors and rugged towering cliffs of red rhyolite rising from the canyon floor. The Southwestern Research Station of the American Museum of Natural History in New York City is at the upper end of the canyon; its laboratories are closed to the public. Bird-watching and hiking opportunities are available. **Hours:** Visitor center open Fri.-Sun. 8:30-4, Memorial Day-Labor Day. Phone ahead to confirm schedule. **Phone:** (520) 558-2221 or (520) 364-6800. 🅰

POSTON (D-1) pop. 285, elev. 335'

The remains of a Japanese-American internment camp as well as a memorial may be found in Poston on Mohave Road. From May 1942 to November 1945, the 17,000-acre camp housed more than 17,000 Japanese-Americans, removed by executive order from California and southern Arizona during World War II.

The Poston Memorial Monument is a 30-foot concrete pillar representing unity of spirit; its hexagonal base represents a Japanese lantern. Twelve small pillars stand in a circle around the monument forming a working sundial. A kiosk, also in the shape of a lantern, holds plaques that relate the story of the camp.

PRESCOTT (C-3) pop. 39,843, elev. 5,346'
• Hotels p. 194 • Restaurants p. 195

The area around Prescott was first settled in 1864 by miners prospecting for gold. It was the presence of gold that prompted the cash-poor Union to designate Arizona as a territory in 1863. In 1867 the capitol was moved south to Tucson. However, Prescott briefly became capital again in 1877, a title it lost to Phoenix in 1889.

Named to honor historian William Hickling Prescott, the town was incorporated in 1883. Because of the surrounding pine forests, wooden structures rather than the typical adobe buildings were built. Fire devastated Prescott in 1900, but determined townsfolk rebuilt and developed a water system utilizing Del Rio Springs.

Surrounded by mountain ranges and nearly encircled by the 1.2-million-acre Prescott National Forest, the mile-high town is now a resort community. Outdoor enthusiasts can indulge in more than 450 miles of multiuse groomed trails, four lakes and five golf courses. Camping, horseback riding, hiking, fishing, rockhounding and picnicking are popular activities. A robust arts community helps facilitate year-round activities, events and festivals, many of which are held on Prescott's charming, tree-lined Courthouse Plaza.

Prescott Chamber of Commerce and Visitor Information Center: 117 W. Goodwin St., Prescott, AZ 86303. **Phone:** (928) 445-2000 or (800) 266-7534.

Self-guiding tours: Maps of mountain biking areas along with a leaflet outlining a self-guiding walking tour of Prescott's Victorian-era neighborhoods can be obtained at the chamber of commerce and visitor information center.

Shopping: Dillard's, JCPenney and Sears anchor the Prescott Gateway Mall, 3250 Gateway Blvd. near SR 69 and Lee Boulevard. Whiskey Row/Courthouse Square, downtown off SR 89 and Cortez Street, offers antique, souvenir and clothes shopping opportunities as well as several eateries.

BUCKY O'NEILL MONUMENT, on Courthouse Plaza, was created by Solon H. Borglum. It pays tribute to the First U.S. Volunteer Cavalry (Roosevelt's Rough Riders) and Capt. William O'Neill, the first volunteer in the Spanish-American War and organizer of the Rough Riders.

GRANITE BASIN, just inside Prescott National Forest about 12 mi. n.w., is a 7-acre lake lying at the foot of Granite Mountain. A recreation area offers hiking, horse trails and facilities, camping and fishing. **Cost:** Camping $18. **Parking:** Day use $5. **Phone:** (928) 443-8000.

GRANITE DELLS (Point of Rocks RV Campground), 4 mi. n. on SR 89, is a summer playground on Watson Lake. Picnicking, rock climbing and fishing are popular activities. Granite formations line the highway for 2 miles. Recreational vehicle camping only (no tent camping). **Cost:** Camping fee $33.50 (1-2 visitors); $3 per each additional visitor. **Phone:** (928) 445-9018.

HERITAGE PARK ZOOLOGICAL SANCTUARY, 6 mi. n. via SR 89, off Willow Creek Rd. in Heritage Park, presents exotic and native wild animals in their natural settings. **Hours:** Daily 9-5 (also Sat. 5-8, June-Aug.), May-Oct.; 10-4, rest of year. **Cost:** $8; $7 (ages 65+); $5 (ages 3-12). **Phone:** (928) 778-4242.

PHIPPEN MUSEUM—ART AND HERITAGE OF THE AMERICAN WEST, 6 mi. n.e. at 4701 SR 89 N., displays permanent and changing exhibitions by prominent Western artists. The 16,900-square-foot facility also displays contemporary artwork depicting the American West. **Time:** Allow 30 minutes minimum. **Hours:** Tues.-Sat. 10-4, Sun. 1-4. **Cost:** $7; $5 (students with ID); free (ages 0-11). **Phone:** (928) 778-1385.

SHARLOT HALL MUSEUM, downtown at 415 W. Gurley St., contains 4 acres of exhibits, historic buildings and gardens. The highlight is the Territorial Governor's Mansion, which was the home and center of government for Arizona's first territorial officials. It was later restored by poet and historian Sharlot M. Hall. Hall filled the mansion with Native American and pioneer artifacts and opened it as a museum in 1928.

Additional historic buildings and several exhibits trace the area's heritage including Fort Misery, the oldest surviving log cabin in Arizona (1864), which was used as a store, boarding house and residence; a replica of the first school house in Prescott which began operation in 1867; the John C. Frémont and the William Bashford houses both classic Victorian-style homes built in the 1870s; the Lawler Exhibit Center featuring exhibits tracing Arizona history from prehistoric beasts to the Clovis native people through territorial days to U.S. statehood; the Sharlot Hall Building, built in 1936 as a CWA project, and housing many of the museum's historical exhibits and dioramas; and the library and archives for historical and academic research.

Time: Allow 1 hour minimum. **Hours:** Mon.-Sat. 10-5, Sun. noon-4, May-Sept.; Mon.-Sat. 10-4, Sun. noon-4, rest of year. Weekend events are held May-Oct.; phone ahead for information. Closed Jan. 1, Thanksgiving and Christmas. **Cost:** $7; free (ages 0-17). **Phone:** (928) 445-3122.

Governor's Mansion, part of the Sharlot Hall Museum complex, was completed in 1864 for John N. Goodwin, Arizona's first territorial governor. The mansion's furnishings and artifacts depict the period 1864-67. The exhibit Behind Whiskey Row tells the story of Prescott's second-class citizens, including its Chinese workers, during the late 1800s. **Hours:** Mon.-Sat. 10-5, Sun. noon-4, May-Sept.; Mon.-Sat. 10-4, Sun. noon-4, rest of year. Weekend events are held May-Oct.; phone ahead for information. Closed Jan. 1, Thanksgiving and Christmas. **Cost:** $7; free (ages 0-17). **Phone:** (928) 445-3122.

John C. Frémont House, part of the Sharlot Hall Museum complex at 415 W. Gurley St., was built in 1875 from locally milled lumber. It served as the home of the celebrated "Pathfinder" during his term as fifth territorial governor of Arizona. The furnishings and artifacts depict the period 1875-81. **Hours:** Mon.-Sat. 10-5, Sun. noon-4, May-Sept.; Mon.-Sat. 10-4, Sun. noon-4, rest of year. Weekend events are held May-Oct.; phone ahead for information. Closed Jan. 1, Thanksgiving and Christmas. **Cost:** $7; free (ages 0-17).

William C. Bashford House, part of the Sharlot Hall Museum complex at 415 W. Gurley St., was built in 1877 and represents the late Victorian style. The home is furnished in period. **Hours:** Mon.-Sat. 10-5, Sun. noon-4, May-Sept.; Mon.-Sat. 10-4, Sun. noon-4, rest of year. Weekend events are held May-Oct.; phone ahead for information. Closed Jan. 1, Thanksgiving and Christmas. **Cost:** $7; free (ages 0-17).

SMOKI MUSEUM, n. of Gurley St. at 147 N. Arizona Ave., is patterned after early Pueblo structures both in architecture and interior design. The museum contains art and artifacts pertaining to Native American pre-history, history and modern culture. Ceramics, baskets, beaded ornaments, clothing, jewelry and paintings are among the items displayed. **Hours:** Mon.-Sat. 10-4, Sun. 1-4 (also 10-1 Christmas Eve and Christmas). Closed Easter and

Thanksgiving. **Cost:** $7; $6 (ages 56+); $5 (students with ID); free (ages 0-12 and Native Americans). **Phone:** (928) 445-1230.

THUMB BUTTE, 4 mi. w., is a rugged outcropping of granite. Extensive views are offered from the summit, which can be reached on foot. **Cost:** $5. **Phone:** (928) 443-8000.

GAMBLING ESTABLISHMENTS
- **Bucky's Casino,** in the Prescott Resort at 1500 E. SR 69, just e. of jct. SR 89. **Hours:** Daily 24 hours. **Phone:** (928) 776-5695 or (800) 756-8744.

BEST WESTERN PRESCOTTONIAN (928)445-3096

 Motel $90-$149

 AAA Benefit: Save 10% or more every day and earn 10% bonus points!

Address: 1317 E Gurley St 86301 **Location:** On SR 89, just s of jct SR 69. **Facility:** 121 units, some two bedrooms. 2-3 stories (no elevator), exterior corridors. **Pool(s):** heated outdoor. **Guest Services:** valet and coin laundry. **Featured Amenity:** breakfast buffet.

HAMPTON INN PRESCOTT (928)443-5500

 Hotel $89-$239

 AAA Benefit: Members save up to 10%!

Address: 3453 Ranch Dr 86303 **Location:** Jct SR 69 and Lee Blvd, just s. **Facility:** 76 units, 3 stories, interior corridors. **Terms:** 1-7 night minimum stay, cancellation fee imposed. **Pool(s):** heated indoor. **Activities:** hot tub, exercise room. **Guest Services:** valet and coin laundry. **Featured Amenity:** full hot breakfast.

HASSAYAMPA INN 928/778-9434

 Historic Hotel. Rates not provided. **Address:** 122 E Gurley St 86301 **Location:** Jct Marina St; downtown. **Facility:** Dating from 1927, the historic inn delivers the charm of yesteryear with a stenciled beamed lobby ceiling and original manual elevator. The rooms are cozy, comfortable, and each has a small bathroom. 67 units. 3 stories, interior corridors. **Terms:** check-in 4 pm. **Dining:** Peacock Dining Room, see separate listing. **Activities:** exercise room. **Guest Services:** valet laundry.

HOLIDAY INN EXPRESS PRESCOTT 928/445-8900

Hotel. Rates not provided. **Address:** 3454 Ranch Dr 86303 **Location:** Jct SR 69 and Lee Blvd, just s. **Facility:** 76 units. 3 stories, interior corridors. **Pool(s):** heated indoor. **Activities:** sauna, hot tub, exercise room. **Guest Services:** valet and coin laundry.

HOTEL ST. MICHAEL   (928)776-1999

WWW **Historic Hotel** $89-$169 **Address:** 205 W Gurley St 86301 **Location:** Center. **Facility:** Across from the courthouse square, this historic building is filled with charm and offers pleasant guest rooms and small baths. 70 units. 2 stories, interior corridors. **Terms:** 2 night minimum stay - seasonal and/or weekends, cancellation fee imposed. **Dining:** Bistro St. Michael, see separate listing.

[icons]

HOTEL VENDOME   (928)776-0900

WWW **Historic Hotel.** Rates not provided. **Address:** 230 S Cortez St 86303 **Location:** South of Gurley St; downtown. **Facility:** This small 1880s historic hotel is a short distance from old Courthouse Square and has two porches where you can rock in a chair as you watch passersby. 20 units. 2 stories (no elevator), interior corridors. [icons]

LA QUINTA INN & SUITES   (928)777-0770

WWW **Hotel** $79-$323 **Address:** 4499 E SR 69 86301 **Location:** 3.6 mi e of jct SR 89. **Facility:** 82 units. 2 stories, interior corridors. **Dining:** Black Canyon Grille, see separate listing. **Pool(s):** heated indoor. **Activities:** hot tub, exercise room. **Guest Services:** coin laundry.

[icons]

PLEASANT STREET INN BED & BREAKFAST   928/445-4774

WWW **Bed & Breakfast** $135-$199 **Address:** 142 S Pleasant St 86303 **Location:** Just s of Gurley St; downtown. **Facility:** This Victorian house, built in 1906 and renovated in recent decades is just three blocks from Courthouse Plaza in the historic district. The two-story home sits on a corner lot in a residential area. 4 units. 2 stories (no elevator), interior corridors. **Parking:** street only. **Terms:** 10 day cancellation notice-fee imposed. [icons]

PRESCOTT CABIN RENTALS-LYNX CREEK FARM

928/778-9573

WWW **Cabin** $87-$309 **Address:** 5555 Onyx Dr 86303 **Location:** Jct SR 89, 5 mi e on SR 69, 0.4 mi s on dirt/gravel road. Located in a quiet rural area. **Facility:** 8 cabins. 1 story, exterior corridors. **Terms:** check-in 4 pm, 2 night minimum stay - weekends, 31 day cancellation notice-fee imposed. **Activities:** playground, trails.

[icons]

QUALITY INN   (928)776-1282

WW **Motel** $79-$169 **Address:** 1105 E Sheldon St 86301 **Location:** 0.4 mi e of jct SR 89. **Facility:** 66 units. 2 stories, interior corridors. **Pool(s):** heated outdoor. **Guest Services:** valet and coin laundry.

[icons]

RESIDENCE INN BY MARRIOTT   (928)775-2232

WWW **Extended Stay Hotel** $123-$236 **Address:** 3599 Lee Cir 86301 **Location:** Jct SR 69, just n on Lee Blvd, then just e. **Facility:** 92 kitchen units, some two bedrooms. 3 stories, interior corridors. **Pool(s):** heated outdoor. **Activities:** hot tub, exercise room. **Guest Services:** valet and coin laundry.

AAA Benefit: Members save 5% or more!

[icons]

SPRINGHILL SUITES BY MARRIOTT   (928)776-0998

WWW **Hotel** $103-$221 **Address:** 200 E Sheldon St 86301 **Location:** On SR 89; at Marina St. **Facility:** 105 units. 3 stories, interior corridors. **Pool(s):** heated indoor. **Activities:** hot tub, exercise room. **Guest Services:** valet and coin laundry.

AAA Benefit: Members save 5% or more!

[icons]

WHERE TO EAT

BARBUDO'S BURRITO COMPANY   928/443-0102

W Mexican. Quick Serve. $3-$9 **AAA Inspector Notes:** This small taco shop is great for a quick lunch. The bright and inviting surfer décor gives a feeling like the beach is right outside. **Features:** beer & wine, patio dining. **Address:** 1042 Willow Creek Rd 86301 **Location:** Jct Whipple St, just n; in Willow Creek Shopping Center. [B] [L]

THE BARLEY HOUND   928/237-4506

WWWW American. Gastropub. $10-$25 **AAA Inspector Notes:** People pack into the small dining room and huge patio for the fun, distinctive menu and drink items. The hand-ground burgers are popular along with duck-fat fries, shishito peppers and beet confit. **Features:** patio dining, Sunday brunch. **Address:** 234 S Cortez St 86303 **Location:** Just s of Gurley St; downtown. **Parking:** street only. [D]

BISTRO ST. MICHAEL   928/778-2500

WWW American. Casual Dining. $6-$18 **AAA Inspector Notes:** Historic. The service is friendly in this restored 1901 bistro featuring with a casual setting. **Features:** full bar. **Address:** 100 S Montezuma St 86301 **Location:** Center; in Hotel St. Michael. **Parking:** on-site and street. [B] [L]

BLACK CANYON GRILLE   928/777-0770

WWW American. Casual Dining. $6-$18 **AAA Inspector Notes:** The lounge area here has been turned into the main dining room, where patrons can partake of small pub-like, menu items. The manager is very hands-on, serving and checking on tables. It is a nice set-up for a casual, quick meal or to watch a game. **Features:** full bar, patio dining, happy hour. **Address:** 4499 E SR 69 86301 **Location:** 3.6 mi e of jct SR 89; in La Quinta Inn & Suites. [L] [D] CALL[icons]

EL GATO AZUL   928/445-1070

WWW Mediterranean Small Plates. Casual Dining. $9-$20 **AAA Inspector Notes:** Enjoy leisurely lunches by the creek or cozy patio or terrace dining at this unique, darkly decorated restaurant. Try the rotating tapas and wine selections along with nightly features. **Features:** full bar, patio dining, happy hour. **Address:** 316 W Goodwin St 86303 **Location:** Just e of Granite St. **Parking:** street only. [L] [D]

GENOVESE'S   928/541-9089

WWW Italian. Casual Dining. $8-$25 **AAA Inspector Notes:** Just around the corner from the park is a charmingly decorated Italian bistro where attentive staff members assist you through a meal that might include eggplant Milanese or chicken parmigiana. Hand-rolled pizza, calzones and panini attract those with a lighter appetite. **Features:** beer & wine. **Address:** 217 W Gurley St 86301 **Location:** Just w of SR 89; center. **Parking:** street only. [L] [D]

GURLEY STREET GRILL   928/445-3388

WW American. Casual Dining. $8-$20 **AAA Inspector Notes:** Inside this resorted 1901 red brick building you can dine in a lively atmosphere on pizza, burgers, steak, pasta, seafood and spit-roasted chicken. **Features:** full bar. **Address:** 230 W Gurley St 86301 **Location:** Just w of SR 89. **Parking:** street only. [L] [D]

MACAYO MEXICAN KITCHEN   928/776-7711

WW Mexican. Casual Dining. $10-$19 **AAA Inspector Notes:** The colorfully furnished Mexican-style eatery prepares Sonoran Mexican dishes. Friendly and efficient staffers serve traditional and lighter dishes flavored with this place's own chili peppers, which are grown near Tucson. **Features:** full bar, happy hour. **Address:** 3250 Gateway Blvd, Suite 516 86303 **Location:** In Prescott Gateway Mall. [L] [D]

MURPHY'S RESTAURANT   928/445-4044

WW American. Casual Dining. $16-$36 **AAA Inspector Notes:** Historic. Restored to depict the era in which it was built, the historic 1890 mercantile now accommodates this restaurant, which serves mesquite-broiled seafood, steak and prime rib. Breads are baked daily on the premises. The pleasant waitstaff guides patrons through their casual dining experience. **Features:** full bar. **Reservations:** suggested. **Address:** 201 N Cortez St 86301 **Location:** Downtown. **Parking:** street only. [L] [D]

THE OFFICE RESTAURANT & BAR 928/445-1211

▼▼ Southwestern. Casual Dining. $7-$16 **AAA Inspector Notes:** Patrons will not fool anyone by saying, "I'm going to the office," but they will find a nice selection of Southwestern dishes, including tortilla soup thick with chicken, and burgers with toppings from caramelized onions to green chiles. The warm cookie dessert is too tempting to share. **Features:** full bar. **Address:** 128 N Cortez St 86301 **Location:** Just n of Gurley St; center. **Parking:** street only.

[L] [D]

THE PALACE RESTAURANT AND SALOON 928/541-1996

▼▼ American. Casual Dining. $9-$33 **AAA Inspector Notes:** Historic. Guests can enjoy casual, relaxed dining in Arizona's oldest bar and amid a restored 1880s decor. **Features:** full bar. **Address:** 120 S Montezuma St 86301 **Location:** Just s of Gurley St; downtown. **Parking:** street only. [L] [D]

PAPA'S ITALIAN RESTAURANT 928/776-4880

▼ Italian. Casual Dining. $10-$17 **AAA Inspector Notes:** This family-run restaurant serves classic Italian favorites, many made from great family recipes. The dining room, featuring red brick walls and tapestries, can get a little crowded. **Features:** beer & wine. **Reservations:** suggested. **Address:** 129-1/2 N Cortez St 86303 **Location:** Just n of Gurley St; center. [D]

PEACOCK DINING ROOM 928/778-9434

▼▼▼ American. Fine Dining. $8-$37 **AAA Inspector Notes:** Historic. In a historic 1927 hotel, this elegant dining room is named for what was once a brightly colored tile wall entry called Peacock Alley. The sophisticated menu lists pasta, steak, seafood and veal dishes, in addition to other specialties. **Features:** full bar, patio dining, happy hour. **Address:** 122 E Gurley St 86301 **Location:** Jct Marina St; downtown; in Hassayampa Inn. [B] [L] [D]

PRESCOTT BREWING COMPANY 928/771-2795

▼▼
American
Gastropub
$7-$25

AAA Inspector Notes: Enjoy the on-site brewery and in-house bakery at this casual restaurant. **Features:** full bar, happy hour. **Address:** 130 W Gurley St, Suite A 86301 **Location:** Between Cortez and Montezuma sts; downtown. **Parking:** street only.

[L] [D]

RAVEN CAFE 928/717-0009

▼▼ Natural/Organic. Quick Serve. $8-$18 **AAA Inspector Notes:** This local hot spot prides itself on serving fresh organic, vegetarian and vegan items. The open-wood café decor is fun with distinctive local art along the walls. There are some self service aspects but the servers are very friendly and eager to please in this bustling atmosphere. **Features:** beer & wine, patio dining, Sunday brunch, happy hour. **Address:** 142 N Cortez St 86301 **Location:** Jct Willis St; downtown. **Parking:** street only. [B] [L] [D]

SHANNON'S GOURMET CHEESECAKES 928/776-0133

▼ American. Casual Dining. $5-$8 **AAA Inspector Notes:** An amazingly fresh assortment of cheesecakes and wraps is offered at this fun, family-run restaurant. Many wraps are named after a family member or employee. I love the caramel pumpkin cheesecake and club wrap. **Address:** 208 W Gurley St 86301 **Location:** Center. **Parking:** street only. [L] [D]

TAJ MAHAL 928/445-5752

▼▼ Northern Indian. Casual Dining. $10-$19 **AAA Inspector Notes:** North Indian dishes, such as chicken tikka and lamb madras are on the menu, as well as tandoori, curry and other traditional selections. A vegan buffet is available on Wednesday evening. Entertainment of live ethnic music and belly dancing often is scheduled. **Features:** full bar, Sunday brunch. **Address:** 124 N Montezuma St 86301 **Location:** Jct Gurley St, just n; center. [L] [D]

THE WAFFLE IRON 928/445-9944

▼ Breakfast Sandwiches. Casual Dining. $6-$10 **AAA Inspector Notes:** Come enjoy great simple breakfast items and sandwiches in one of Prescott's oldest buildings. The fruit covered buckwheat waffles are the signature dish, but guests cannot go wrong with any of the fresh items. **Features:** Sunday brunch. **Address:** 420 E Sheldon St 86301 **Location:** On SR 89; at N Mt Vernon Ave. [B] [L]

ZEKE'S EATIN' PLACE 928/776-4602

▼▼ American. Casual Dining. $7-$12 **AAA Inspector Notes:** A popular stop with locals for a hearty breakfast or lunch, this casual spot is known for its ample portions. The omelets and breakfast burritos will carry you through a long morning of work or touring. Its many movie posters feature famous Western actors. **Address:** 1781 E Hwy 69, Suite 35 86301 **Location:** 1.2 mi e; in Frontier Village Center.

[B] [L]

PRESCOTT NATIONAL FOREST (C-3)

Elevations in the forest range from 3,071 ft. in the Verde Valley to 7,971 ft. at Mount Union. Refer to AAA maps for additional elevation information.

Accessed via SR 89, SR 89A and SR 69 off I-17 in central Arizona, Prescott National Forest encompasses two long mountain ranges with varying elevations. In addition to its major access routes, other scenic but primitive roads not recommended for low-clearance vehicles penetrate the 1,238,154-acre forest. Phone ahead for current road condition updates.

Developed recreation areas are at Mingus Mountain and in Prescott Basin. The forest also contains Granite Mountain Trail (a National Recreation Trail), and Lynx Lake where boating and fishing take place all year. Camping, picnicking, hiking, backpacking, mountain biking and horseback riding are popular recreational pursuits in the forest; many trails can be enjoyed year-round. Groom Creek is an equestrian-only campground. Most campgrounds are first-come, first-served; Lynx Campground and Groom Creek accept reservations. Some popular day-use areas in Prescott have a $5 parking fee. Hunting is permitted in season with the appropriate state game license obtained from the Game and Fish Department (Kingman office); phone (928) 692-7700.

For further information contact Prescott National Forest, 344 S. Cortez St., Prescott, AZ 86303; phone (928) 443-8000 Mon.-Fri. 8-4:30. *See Recreation Areas Chart.*

PRESCOTT VALLEY pop. 38,822

AMERICAS BEST VALUE INN (928)772-2200

▼▼
Hotel
$59-$155

Address: 8383 E SR 69 86314 **Location:** Just w of N Navajo Dr. **Facility:** 50 units. 2 stories (no elevator), interior corridors. **Pool(s):** heated indoor. **Activities:** hot tub. **Guest Services:** coin laundry. **Featured Amenity:** continental breakfast.

ARIZONA INN OF PRESCOTT VALLEY (928)772-8600

▼▼ Hotel $69-$125 **Address:** 7875 E Hwy 69 86314 **Location:** Corner of Windsong Rd. **Facility:** 78 units. 2 stories (no elevator), exterior corridors. **Pool(s):** heated outdoor. **Guest Services:** coin laundry.

COMFORT SUITES PRESCOTT VALLEY   (928)771-2100

Hotel
$119-$199

Address: 2601 N Crownpointe Dr 86314 **Location:** Just w on SR 69, just n on Market St. **Facility:** 100 units. 4 stories, interior corridors. **Pool(s):** heated outdoor. **Activities:** hot tub, exercise room. **Guest Services:** valet and coin laundry. **Featured Amenity: continental breakfast.**

HAMPTON INN & SUITES BY HILTON PRESCOTT VALLEY
(928)772-1800

Hotel $89-$249 **Address:** 2901 N Glassford Rd 86314 **Location:** Jct SR 69, just n. **Facility:** 118 units. 4 stories, interior corridors. **Terms:** check-in 4 pm, 1-7 night minimum stay, cancellation fee imposed. **Pool(s):** heated outdoor. **Activities:** hot tub, exercise room. **Guest Services:** valet and coin laundry.

AAA Benefit: Members save up to 10%!

SUPER 8   (928)775-5888

Hotel
$90-$110

Address: 7801 E SR 69 86314 **Location:** 0.4 mi w of Robert Rd. **Facility:** 54 units. 2 stories (no elevator), interior corridors. **Terms:** cancellation fee imposed. **Pool(s):** heated outdoor. **Guest Services:** coin laundry. **Featured Amenity: continental breakfast.**

Enjoy the beauty and culture of the Old West with easy access to the Grand Canyon National Park.

WHERE TO EAT

GARCIA'S MEXICAN RESTAURANT   928/759-9499

Mexican. Casual Dining. $9-$19 **AAA Inspector Notes:** The eatery serves classic preparations of all the favorites, including fajitas, burritos and tacos. The chicken enchilada with sour cream is excellent. Also on the menu are some lighter options. **Features:** full bar. **Address:** 2992 Park Ave, Suite B 86314 **Location:** Jct SR 69, just n on Centre Ct, then just e; behind theater. [L] [D]

TARA THAI 2 CUISINE   928/772-3249

Thai. Casual Dining. $9-$17 **AAA Inspector Notes:** Fresh, cooked-to-order food makes up the menu at this modest eatery. Widely varied curries and specialties come with fragrantly scented rice and crispy vegetables. Homemade ice cream is a perfect end to the meal. **Features:** beer & wine. **Address:** 6170 E SR 69, Suite 100 86314 **Location:** Just w of Prescott Hwy; west side of town. [L] [D]

PRESIDIO SANTA CRUZ DE TERRENATE NATIONAL HISTORIC SITE (F-5)

Presidio Santa Cruz de Terrenate National Historic Site is 4 miles north of Tombstone on SR 80, 6 miles west on SR 82 to Fairbank, .75 miles west to In Balance Ranch Road, then 2 miles north in the San Pedro Riparian National Conservation Area. Established by the Spanish in 1776 on the banks of the San Pedro River, the presidio was built to protect the overland route east of Tucson. Because of the frequent Apache raids as well as the lack of proper supplies, Terrenate was abandoned less than 5 years after its establishment.

The site, once consisting of seven structures built around a central courtyard, contains signs showing what each of the structures originally looked like. Many of the adobe walls that surrounded the presidio are eroded and only a few remain. They were planned to be 15 feet tall, but were built to only 12 feet due to lack of funds. In addition, the bastion/gunpowder storehouse was never completed, and less than one-fourth of the planned barracks were never constructed because of insufficient funding.

The historic site is fragile, and visitors are instructed by signs to stay on the trails and not to touch the remaining structures. A 1.2-mile dirt trail leads from the parking lot to the presidio. Camping is permitted. Visitors should bring their own food and water as no facilities are available. Site admission free. Camping $2 per person per night. Phone (520) 439-6400.

QUARTZSITE (D-1) pop. 3,677, elev. 876'

A settler named Charles Tyson built a fort on this site in 1856 for protection against Native Americans. Because of a good water supply it soon became a stagecoach stop on the Ehrenburg-to-Prescott route. As the stage lines vanished, Fort Tyson, or Tyson's Wells (as it became known), was abandoned. A small mining boom in 1897 revitalized the area, and the settlement revived as Quartzsite.

The winter population of this desert town swells to 1 million during January and February because of the gem and mineral shows in the area. The Pow Wow Rock and Mineral Show began the rockhound winter migration to town in 1965; now 10 major shows entice gem enthusiasts, collectors and jewelers to Quartzsite to buy and sell. In an event that has attained international scope, thousands of dealers offer raw and handcrafted merchandise throughout January and February.

Quartzsite Tourism Bureau: P.O. Box 619, Quartzsite, AZ 85346. **Phone:** (928) 916-1090 or (888) 878-2202.

HI JOLLY MEMORIAL, e. on I-10 in the old cemetery, honors Hadji Ali. Nicknamed Hi Jolly by soldiers and pioneers, the Arab came to Arizona in 1856 with an Army consignment of camels. The camels adapted well to their new environment but were never used successfully, partly because the sight of them caused horses, mules and cattle to stampede. **Hours:** Daily 24 hours. **Cost:** Free. **Phone:** (928) 916-1090.

SUPER 8-QUARTZSITE   (928)927-8080
▼▼ **Motel** $70-$140 **Address:** 2050 Dome Rock Rd 85359 **Location:** I-10 exit 17, just s to Frontage Rd, then 0.6 mi w. **Facility:** 51 units. 2 stories (no elevator), interior corridors. **Terms:** 3 day cancellation notice-fee imposed. **Guest Services:** coin laundry.

QUEEN CREEK pop. 26,361
• **Part of Phoenix area — see map p. 126**

SERRANO'S MEXICAN RESTAURANT   480/987-0192
▼▼ Mexican. Casual Dining. $7-$17 **AAA Inspector Notes:** A pleasant stop for lunch or dinner, the local chain is known for consistently good food and attractive, upscale Mexican-style décor. The warm bean dip starter stirs the appetite for traditional dishes such as chiles rellenos or seafood enchiladas prepared with fresh ingredients. Service is friendly. **Address:** 22701 S Ellsworth Rd 85242 **Location:** SR 202 exit 36, s to E Ocotillo Rd, then just s. L D

RIO RICO pop. 18,962

NONNA VIVI PIZZERIA   520/761-2825
▼▼ Pizza. Casual Dining. $10-$14 **AAA Inspector Notes:** Tucked inside a shopping center, this family-owned bistro offers delicious wood-fired gourmet pizzas, fresh salads, panini and a nice selection of wines by the glass. If weather permits, grab a table on the large patio. **Features:** beer & wine, patio dining. **Address:** 1060 Yavapai Dr 85648 **Location:** I-19 exit 17 (Yavapai Dr), 0.3 mi w. L D

SAN CAYETANO   520/281-1901
▼▼▼ Regional American. Casual Dining. $9-$25 **AAA Inspector Notes:** Diners at this eatery enjoy the casual atmosphere and stunning views across the valley to the mountains beyond. Specialties include steaks, seafood, sandwiches and soups. **Features:** full bar, patio dining, early bird specials, happy hour. **Reservations:** suggested. **Address:** 1069 Camino Caralampi 85648 **Location:** I-19 exit 17 (Rio Rico Dr), just w to Camino Caralampi, then just s; in Esplendor Resort at Rio Rico. B L D

ROOSEVELT (I-6) pop. 28, elev. 2,215'

THEODORE ROOSEVELT DAM AND LAKE is reached via SR 188 or SR 88 (the Apache Trail), a dirt road. Natives A.D. 1000 built 150 miles of stone-lined canals to irrigate their fields. Modern Arizona's reclamation of the Salt River Valley began with the completion of the Roosevelt Dam in 1911. Unlike other dams, the Roosevelt was made with thousands of hand-hewn stones.

As the first major federal reclamation project, the dam provides water to one of the state's richest agricultural regions. Many recreational opportunities are available on the lake. *See Recreation Areas Chart.* **Cost:** $6 per motorized vehicle; $4 per boat. Prices may vary; phone ahead. **Phone:** (928) 467-3200.

SACATON (E-4) pop. 2,672, elev. 1,127'

Sacaton, first visited by Spanish missionaries in 1696, was even then an ancient Pima Indian settlement; currently the town is the headquarters for the Pima Reservation. American pioneers noted the abundance of very tall grass, from which the town derived the town name.

Japanese-American internment camp memorials and their sites may be found 9 miles west of Sacaton on Gila River Indian Tribal land. From July 1942 to November 1945, the 17,000-acre Gila River Relocation Center housed more than 13,000 Japanese-Americans, removed by executive order from California during World War II. The center consisted of two camps named Butte and Canal. Today, memorial markers and concrete slab foundations are basically all that remain of the camps.

The Butte Camp markers are near a monument that lists the Japanese-American soldiers killed in World War II. The Canal Camp marker includes a map, photograph and descriptive information. Visitors must obtain a permit from the Gila River Indian Tribe to visit the sites.

SAFFORD (E-6) pop. 9,566, elev. 2,920'

The first American colony in the Gila Valley, Safford was founded in 1874 by farmers whose previous holdings had been washed away by the Gila River. From Safford the Swift Trail winds 36 miles to the top of 10,720-foot Mount Graham. En route the trail traverses five of the seven ecological zones in Western North America. Camping, hiking and picnicking are permitted. Gila Box Riparian National Conservation Area, 15 miles northeast, offers seasonal river floating opportunities.

The region south of Safford is known for its hot mineral water baths. Information about area spas is available from the chamber of commerce. One popular spot is Hot Well Dunes, which has two artesian mineral wells now turned into hot tubs. The area also is popular with off-road enthusiasts.

For seekers of fire agates and other semiprecious stones, there are two rockhound areas administered and maintained by the U.S. Bureau of Land Management. Black Hills Back Country Byway is a 21-mile scenic drive through the Black Hills. The drive is a graded dirt road with sharp turns and steep drops.

Round Mountain Rockhound Area, featuring chalcedony roses and fire agates, is 12 miles south of Duncan on US 70, west at Milepost 5.6, 7.1 miles to the BLM sign, then 2.5 miles south to the first collection area. A second collection area is 4.5 miles south using the left fork in the road. **Note:** The road is not maintained and is very rough. Because of the area's remote location, visitors should bring along plenty of water and gasoline. Phone ahead for road conditions. Information about these areas can be obtained by contacting the Bureau of Land Management, 711 14th Ave., Safford, AZ 85546; phone (928) 348-4400.

Graham County Chamber of Commerce: 1111 Thatcher Blvd., Safford, AZ 85546. **Phone:** (928) 428-2511 or (888) 837-1841.

EASTERN ARIZONA COLLEGE DISCOVERY PARK CAMPUS is at 1651 W. Discovery Park Blvd. Located at the base of Mount Graham, this site offers both nature and science enthusiasts an interactive experience. Trail paths with viewing areas feature diverse wildlife and ponds while the Gov Aker Observatory contains exhibits relating to time and space. **Note:** Rattlesnakes and Gila monsters roam the trails; use caution when walking. **Time:** Allow 30 minutes minimum. **Hours:** Campus open Mon.-Fri. 8-5, Sat. 4-9:30. Last shuttle Mon.-Thurs. at 4. Closed major holidays. **Cost:** Free. **Phone:** (928) 428-6260. 🅰

ROPER LAKE STATE PARK, 1 mi. s. off US 191, is at the base of Mount Graham. A great place to hike, camp, swim and picnic, this park features a rock-lined pool filled with water from the natural mineral hot springs. *See Recreation Areas Chart.* **Hours:** Daily 6 a.m.-10 p.m. Phone ahead to confirm schedule. **Cost:** $7 (per private vehicle, up to four adult passengers); $3 (per additional adult passenger in vehicle or individual arriving on foot or bicycle). Camping $15-$25 (per private vehicle). Cabins $55-$65. **Phone:** (928) 428-6760, or (520) 586-2283 for camping reservations.

BEST WESTERN DESERT INN   (928)428-0521

Motel
$85

AAA Benefit: Save 10% or more every day and earn 10% bonus points!

Address: 1391 W Thatcher Blvd 85546 **Location:** US 191, 1 mi w on US 70. **Facility:** 66 units. 2 stories (no elevator), exterior corridors. **Pool(s):** outdoor. **Guest Services:** coin laundry.

COMFORT INN & SUITES SAFFORD   928/348-9400

[fyi] Not evaluated. **Address:** 415 Entertainment Ave 85541 **Location:** US 191, 0.5 mi e. Facilities, services, and décor characterize a mid-scale property.

WHERE TO EAT

CASA MAÑANA   928/428-3170

♦♦ Mexican. Casual Dining. $7-$16 **AAA Inspector Notes:** Guests sit down amid simple, yet bright and cheerful décor while friendly staff members bring out a selection of salsas. Diners can peruse the menu for such classic dishes as homemade pork tamales, grilled chicken or beef fajitas. **Features:** beer & wine. **Address:** 502 S 1st Ave 85546 **Location:** Jct US 70 and 191; center.

L | D

MANOR HOUSE   928/428-7148

♦♦ American. Casual Dining. $9-$25 **AAA Inspector Notes:** The family-style warmth offered by the staff reflects the owner's friendly manner. In addition to sandwiches, hearty dinners include Mexican, pasta, steaks and seafood dishes. A large gift shop is on the premises. **Features:** full bar, patio dining, senior menu. **Address:** 415 E Hwy 70 85546 **Location:** US 191, 0.5 mi e.

B | L | D

SAGUARO NATIONAL PARK (F-5)
- Attractions map p. 265
- Part of Tucson area — see map p. 256

> Elevations in the park range from 2,500ft. on the desert floor along the loop roads to 8,666 ft. at Mica Mountain. Refer to AAA maps for additional elevation information.

Separated by the city of Tucson *(see place listing p. 255)*, Saguaro National Park is divided into two districts: Rincon Mountain (Saguaro East) is about 15 miles east of Tucson via Old Spanish Trail, and Tucson Mountain (Saguaro West) is 15 miles west via Speedway Boulevard. Both districts typify the Sonoran arboreal desert and contain stands of saguaro cacti, known for their sometimes humanlike shapes.

The saguaro grows only in southern Arizona, in California along the Colorado River and in the northern Mexican state of Sonora. It can live more than 200 years, attaining heights of 30 to 40 feet; a few exceptional ones exceed 50 feet. Its blossom, the state flower, appears in May and June. Native Americans use its fruit for food and as a beverage base.

In addition to protecting the saguaro and other desert vegetation of the Sonoran Desert, the park's Saguaro West district has rock formations decorated with Native American petroglyphs and designs.

At the park headquarters in Saguaro East a visitor center contains plant and animal exhibits and offers nature programs; phone (520) 733-5153. The 8-mile Cactus Forest Drive begins at the visitor center parking lot. Picnic facilities are available. Saguaro West's unpaved 5-mile Bajada Loop Drive winds through dense stands of saguaro cacti. A visitor center has exhibits, a slide show and interpretive programs; phone (520) 733-5158.

Saguaro East and Saguaro West are open daily 7 a.m.-dusk. Visitor centers open daily 9-5; closed Christmas. Admission to Saguaro East or Saguaro West is by 7-day or annual permit; 7-day permits cost $10 per private vehicle or $5 for persons arriving by other means. Backcountry backpacking is by permit only in Saguaro East; no drive-in camping permitted. For additional information contact the Superintendent, Saguaro National Park, 3693 S. Old Spanish Tr., Tucson, AZ 85730-5601; phone (520) 733-5153. *See Recreation Areas Chart.*

SAHUARITA (F-4) pop. 25,259, elev. 2,702'
- Part of Tucson area — see map p. 256

ASARCO MINERAL DISCOVERY CENTER, off I-19 exit 80 to 1421 W. Pima Mine Rd., features hands-on exhibits about mining and minerals. A theater offers presentations about mining, mineral resources and reclamation. A 1-hour tour provides a look inside an operating open-pit copper mine.

Time: Allow 1 hour, 30 minutes minimum. **Hours:** Mon.-Sat. 9-5, in Feb.; Tues.-Sat. 9-5, Mar.-Apr. and Sept.-Jan.; Tues.-Fri. 9-3, Sat. 9-5, rest of year. Mine tours daily Oct.-May. Closed major holidays. **Cost:** Center free. Mine tour $9; $7 (ages 62+ and active military with ID); $6 (ages 5-12). Reservations are recommended. **Phone:** (520) 625-8233 for tour reservations.

TITAN MISSILE MUSEUM, .75 mi. w. of I-19 exit 69 at 1580 Duval Mine Rd., is a formerly active Intercontinental Ballistic Missile (ICBM) complex preserved as a museum. Of the 54 Titan II ICBM sites in the U.S. weapon system, all except the missile museum have been destroyed. Special tours are offered, including Beyond the Blast Doors, Titan Top to Bottom, Moonlight MADness (a summer Saturday evening celebration), Crew Tour, Director's Tour and Titan Overnight Experience.

Note: The basic tour includes descending/ascending 55 steps and may be cumbersome for the physically challenged or those with a heart condition. Arrangements may be made for the use of an elevator for the physically challenged. **Time:** Allow 1 hour minimum. **Hours:** Daily 8:45-5. Tours are given on the hour. Last admission 1 hour before closing. Closed Thanksgiving and Christmas. **Cost:** $9.50; $8.50 (ages 62+ and active military with ID); $6 (ages 7-12). **Phone:** (520) 625-7736. ▣ GT

GAMBLING ESTABLISHMENTS

• **Desert Diamond Casino,** 1100 W. Pima Mine Rd. **Hours:** Daily 24 hours. **Phone:** (520) 294-7777 or (866) 332-9467.

ST. JOHNS (C-6) pop. 3,480, elev. 5,650'

APACHE COUNTY HISTORICAL SOCIETY MUSEUM, .25 mi. w. of jct. US 191 and SR 61 at 180 W. Cleveland St., displays pioneer artifacts, mammoth bones, Native American artifacts, miniature replicas of early St. Johns homes, and antique guns and slot machines. **Time:** Allow 30 minutes minimum. **Hours:** Tues., Thurs. and Sat. 10-2, Mar.-Oct. Closed major holidays. **Cost:** Donations. **Phone:** (928) 337-4737. GT

LYMAN LAKE STATE PARK is 14 mi. n. off US 60 onto US180/191, then just off SR 81, following signs. This 1,200-acre park is a great place for camping, hiking, swimming, fishing, water skiing and wildlife viewing. A marked trail leads to the ruins of Rattlesnake Point Pueblo, a village constructed and occupied by ancestors of the Hopi tribe during the 1300s. *See Recreation Areas Chart.*

Cabins and group campsites are available by reservation. **Hours:** Daily 8-5, mid-May to mid-Sept. **Cost:** $7 (per private vehicle, up to four adult passengers); $3 (per additional adult passenger in vehicle or individual arriving on foot or bicycle). Cabins $55. Camping $20-$30 (per private vehicle). **Phone:** (928) 337-4441, or (928) 586-2283 for camping reservations. ▣ ▣ ▣ ▣

SAN CARLOS (E-5) pop. 4,038, elev. 2,432'

San Carlos, north of Coolidge Dam, is a trading center and headquarters for the San Carlos Indian

Agency. The Apaches operate one of the largest cattle ranches in this area. The San Carlos Apache Reservation offers some of the best trophy-hunting and fishing in the state; permits are required. For permit information contact the San Carlos Recreation and Wildlife Department, P.O. Box 97, San Carlos, AZ 85550; phone (928) 475-2343.

Coolidge Dam, about 9 miles southeast on the Gila River, impounds the waters that irrigate the Casa Grande Valley. Construction of the dam was delayed until a solution satisfactory to the Apache Indians was found concerning the disturbance of tribal burial grounds. Once it was agreed that a concrete slab would cover the cemetery, construction resumed.

APACHE GOLD HOTEL   (928)475-7600
▼▼▼ **Hotel** $99-$169 **Address:** San Carlos Ave 85550 **Location:** Jct SR 77 S, 4.2 mi e. **Facility:** 146 units, some two bedrooms. 2 stories, interior corridors. **Terms:** 3 day cancellation notice-fee imposed. **Dining:** 3 restaurants. **Pool(s):** heated outdoor. **Activities:** hot tub, regulation golf, trails, exercise room.
▣ ▣ CALL ▣ ▣ BIZ HS ▣ ▣ ▣
/ SOME UNITS ▣ ▣

SASABE (G-4) elev. 3,560'

BUENOS AIRES NATIONAL WILDLIFE REFUGE, 7 mi. n. on SR 286 at Milepost 8/37257 S. Sasabe Hwy., is a 118,000-acre refuge established to preserve the endangered masked bobwhite quail and other grassland wildlife. The refuge contains extensive grasslands, seasonal streams and ponds. It is home to nearly 340 species of birds, including gray hawks, vermilion flycatchers and golden eagles. Other wildlife include coyotes, deer, foxes, javelinas, pronghorn antelope and bobcats. Trails are on the eastern side near the town of Arivaca. Guided hikes are offered.

Time: Allow 4 hours minimum. **Hours:** Refuge open daily 24 hours. Visitor center daily 7:30-4, Aug. 15-May 31; Mon.-Fri. 7:30-4, rest of year. Guided bird walks on the Arivaca Cienega Trail are offered Sat. at 8 a.m., Nov.-Apr. Guided hikes in Brown Canyon are offered the second and fourth Sat. of the month, Nov.-Apr. Closed Jan. 1, Thanksgiving and Christmas. **Cost:** Refuge free. Guided bird walks free. Brown Canyon guided hikes $5. Reservations are required for Brown Canyon guided hikes. **Phone:** (520) 823-4251.

SCOTTSDALE (I-3) pop. 217,385, elev. 1,259'

• Hotels p. 203 • Restaurants p. 212
• Hotels & Restaurants map & index p. 158
• Part of Phoenix area — see map p. 126

Scottsdale was named for Chaplain Winfield Scott, Civil War veteran and retired military man who in 1888 purchased some farmland near the center of present-day Scottsdale. The city's slogan, "The West's Most Western Town," certainly applies to the wooden storefronts and hitching posts of Old Town Scottsdale. But the rest of the city is better described as "South Beach meets the Sonoran Desert."

Chic and sophisticated, Scottsdale is home to more than 100 art galleries, an array of specialty stores, fine dining, hip nightlife, plush resorts and

See map & index p. 158.)

olf courses galore. In short, this is the Valley of the Sun's tourist hot spot.

Indian Bend Wash Greenbelt along Hayden Road offers 7 miles of trails for bicyclists and runners. McCormick-Stillman Railroad Park, 7301 E. Indian Bend Rd., (480) 312-2312, offers 1-mile rides on a scale train. Several full-size railroad cars, a 1907 locomotive, playgrounds and an operating 1950s carousel are in the park. Picnic facilities are available.

The free Scottsdale trolley is a handy way to get around the downtown area. Following a route that includes stops at Old Town, the Arts District and Scottsdale Fashion Square, the trolley operates daily (except January 1, Memorial Day, July 4, Labor Day, Thanksgiving and Christmas) 11-6 (also Thurs. 6-9 p.m.) and runs every 15 minutes. For route maps and more information check hotel brochure racks, or phone (800) 782-1117.

Scottsdale Convention & Visitors Bureau: 4343 N. Scottsdale Rd., Suite 170, Scottsdale, AZ 85251. Phone: (480) 421-1004 or (800) 782-1117.

Self-guiding tours: Maps detailing self-guiding walking tours of Scottsdale's Old Town are available from the convention and visitors bureau. There's also a self-serve information kiosk loaded with maps and brochures at the corner of Main Street and Brown Avenue.

Shopping: Arizona's answer to Santa Fe, New Mexico, downtown Scottsdale is one of the biggest art gallery centers in the Southwest. Fine art collectors armed with high-limit plastic will want to head for the Arts District, along palm-lined Main Street (just w. of Scottsdale Rd.) and Marshall Way (between Main St. and 5th Ave.)

The Biltmore Galleries of Scottsdale (7113 E. Main St.) specializes in works by big-name American West painters (think Charles Russell and Olaf Wieghorst). Obviously, this is museum-quality art that'll put a serious dent in your bank account. The Knox Artifacts Gallery (7056 E. Main St.) is a must for collectors of Pre-Columbian and Native American art.

If your taste leans more toward abstract squiggles on a huge white canvas, the Gebert Contemporary Art Gallery (7160 E. Main St.) deals in cutting-edge paintings and sculptures by established international artists. For modern art that's a bit more accessible to the masses, Xanadu Gallery (7039 E. Main St., #101) sells beautiful glass art, jewelry, paintings, photography and intriguing contemporary sculptures; some of it is surprisingly affordable.

The weekly Scottsdale ArtWalk (held Thursdays 7 p.m.-9 p.m.) is a fun way to get acquainted with the area. Many of the galleries stay open late for this "open house" event, which occasionally features live music and artist demonstrations.

If souvenirs are more your speed, Old Town Scottsdale (a four-block area bounded by Scottsdale Road, Indian School Road, Brown Avenue and 2nd Street) is loaded with trinket shops selling everything from fridge magnets to toy tomahawks. For authentic Native American crafts, try Bischoff's Shades of West (7247 E. Main St.) or Gilbert Ortega Galleries (3925 N. Scottsdale Rd.).

Old Town's wooden storefronts may very well put you in the mood to don Western duds. Saba's Famous Texas Boots (7254 Main St.) stocks brand names like Tony Lama and Nocona. Az-Tex Hats & Gifts (3903 N. Scottsdale Rd.) has a nice selection of quality cowboy hats and straw sun hats but, beware, prices are steep.

For clothes you might actually wear back home, head for the funky boutiques and shops lining 5th Avenue (between Scottsdale Rd. and Marshall Way). A relaxed shady lane, the 5th Avenue shopping district also has jewelry stores, art galleries and a sprinkling of casual sidewalk cafes.

Just north of 5th Avenue is the Scottsdale Waterfront, a five-acre mixed-use development spread along the banks of the Arizona Canal. The complex features a handful of mall stores (High Point, Urban Outfitters), restaurants and the Ellie & Michael Ziegler Fiesta Bowl Museum (7135 E. Camelback Rd., #190), a must-visit for college football fans; phone (480) 350-0900.

A massive three-story mall, Scottsdale Fashion Square (at the corner of Camelback and Scottsdale roads) has more than 250 stores, including upscale anchors like Barneys New York and Prada. Scottsdale Quarter (15279 N. Scottsdale Rd.) is a 28-acre shopping district featuring retail, restaurant and entertainment options as well as office space. Retailers include Apple Store, H & M, Lululemon, Nike, Pottery Barn and Sephora.

Shopping Tours: Spree! The Art of Shopping is an upscale shopping service and experience for those who want to channel their inner Carrie Bradshaw. Several round-trip tour packages are available and power shoppers have the choice of being picked up in either a limousine or luxury sedan. Tours run approximately 3 hours and advance reservations of at least 24 hours are required; phone (480) 661-1080 for more information or to make reservations.

Nightlife: Scottsdale lays claim to the valley's hottest dance club scene. You'll find the trendiest spots in the dozen-or-so city blocks southeast of the intersection of Scottsdale and Camelback roads.

For those with country in their hearts and a love of live music, there's the Rusty Spur Saloon (7245 E. Main St.). Scottsdale's last real cowboy saloon is housed in the former Farmers Bank of Scottsdale. Celebrities including Clint Eastwood, John Wayne, Vince Vaughn and Jennifer Anniston have walked through its swinging doors.

For a good old Budweiser-fueled, boot-scootin' night on the town, head for Handlebar J (7116 E. Becker Ln.). A Scottsdale landmark since 1966, the club has live country music nightly, plus free country

(See map & index p. 158.)

dance lessons every Wednesday, Thursday and Sunday night at 7; phone (480) 948-0110.

SCOTTSDALE CIVIC CENTER AND MALL, at Drinkwater Blvd. and 2nd St., includes a library, municipal buildings, a park, fountains, sculptures, a pond and landscaped lawns. Also on the mall is the Scottsdale Center for the Performing Arts, a forum for the visual and performing arts. **Cost:** Free. **Phone:** (480) 499-8587.

Scottsdale Historical Museum, 7333 E. Civic Center Mall, is housed in a 1909 red brick grammar school furnished in period. A replica of a barbershop, complete with a barber chair and tools, and an old-fashioned kitchen are featured. Other exhibits include a display of town memorabilia and a replica of a 1900 schoolroom. Rotating exhibits change every 2 to 3 months. **Time:** Allow 30 minutes minimum. **Hours:** Wed.-Sat. 10-5, Sun. noon-4, Oct.-May; Wed.-Sun. 10-2 in June and Sept. **Cost:** Donations. **Phone:** (480) 945-4499.

Scottsdale Museum of Contemporary Art, 7374 E. 2nd St. in the Scottsdale Civic Center and Mall, features works by contemporary artists from Arizona and around the world. Displays focusing on modern architecture and design also are offered. **Hours:** Tues.-Sun. noon-5 (also Thurs.-Sat. 5-9). Closed major holidays. **Cost:** $7; $5 (students with ID); free (ages 0-15 and for all Thurs. and Fri.-Sat. 5-9). **Phone:** (480) 874-4666.

TALIESIN WEST, 12345 N. Taliesin Dr., was the winter home and studio of architect Frank Lloyd Wright. On nearly 600 acres of Sonoran Desert at the foothills of the McDowell Mountains, the complex of buildings is connected by gardens, terraces and walkways. Taliesin West is the international headquarters for the Frank Lloyd Wright Foundation.

Tours include a 1-hour Panorama Tour, a 90-minute Insights Tour, a 3-hour Extended Insights Tour and a 2-hour Night Lights Tour. The Panorama Tour provides a basic introduction to the complex and Wright's theories of architecture. The Insights Tour encompasses the famed Living Room and Wright's private living quarters. The Extended Insights Tour includes tea in the colorful dining room. The Night Lights Tour shows visitors the home at night. Other tours are available.

Note: Tours may be canceled due to inclement weather; phone ahead to confirm. Walking shoes and sun protection are recommended. **Time:** Allow 1 hour minimum. **Hours:** Panorama Tour departs daily at 10:15 and 2:15, Sept.-May; Thurs.-Mon. at 10:15, rest of year. Insights Tour departs every 30 minutes daily 9-4, Nov.-Apr.; every hour daily 9-4 in May and Sept.-Oct.; every hour Thurs.-Mon. 9-2, rest of year. Extended Insights Tour departs Mon., Thurs. and Sat. at 9:15. Night Lights Tour departs Fri. at 6:30, 7 and 7:15 p.m., May-Oct.; Fri. at 6,

6:30 and 7 p.m., Feb.-Apr. Closed Easter, Thanksgiving and Christmas. Phone ahead to confirm schedule.

Cost: Panorama Tour $28; $24 (ages 60+, active military with ID and students with ID); $10 (ages 4-12). Insights Tour $36; $32 (ages 60+, active military with ID and students with ID); $17 (ages 4-12) Extended Insights Tour $70; reservations are required. Night Lights Tour $35; $30 (ages 60+, active military with ID and students with ID); reservations are required. Rates may vary and combination rates may be available; phone ahead. Tours not recommended for children ages 0-5, unless in strollers or parents' arms. Reservations are recommended **Phone:** (480) 860-2700, ext. 5462 for recorded tour information, or (888) 516-0811.

WESTERN SPIRIT: SCOTTSDALE'S MUSEUM OF THE WEST, 3830 N. Marshall Way, tells the story of the West through the works of artists in various media and interactive programs. Exhibitions of paintings, historical photos and artifacts focus on regional history, and visitors can enjoy interactive experiences such as Story Circle or relax amid desert plantings while viewing exhibits in the Sculpture Courtyard. **Hours:** Tues.-Sat. 9:30-5, Sun. 11-5. Scottsdale Artwalk Thurs. 9:30-9. **Cost:** $13; $11 (senior citizens and active military with ID); $8 (students with ID); free (ages 0-5). **Phone:** (480) 686-9539.

GAMBLING ESTABLISHMENTS
- **Casino Arizona—101 & McKellips** is at Loop 101 and McKellips Rd. **Hours:** Daily 24 hours. **Phone:** (480) 850-7777 or (877) 724-4687.
- **Casino Arizona—Talking Stick Resort and Casino** is at Loop 101 and Indian Bend Rd. **Hours:** Daily 24 hours. **Phone:** (480) 850-7777 or (877) 724-4687.

RECREATIONAL ACTIVITIES
Hiking
- **Hike In Phoenix, LLC** departs from various locations in Phoenix, Scottsdale and other Phoenix metro locations; transportation to and from most local hotels can be arranged. **Hours:** Phone reservations taken daily 6 a.m.-10 p.m., mid-Mar. to early Nov.; 5 a.m.-9 p.m., rest of year. **Phone:** (602) 492-6867 or (877) 445-3749.

Hot Air Ballooning
- **Rainbow Ryders, Inc. Hot Air Balloon Co.** departs from various locations for flights over the Sonoran Desert. **Hours:** Daily at dawn and dusk (weather permitting), Nov.-Mar.; daily at dawn, rest of year. **Phone:** (877) 771-0776. *(See ad p. 140.)*

(See map & index p. 158.)

BEST WESTERN PLUS SCOTTSDALE THUNDERBIRD SUITES
(480)951-4000

Hotel
$99-$219

AAA Benefit:
Save 10% or more every day and earn 10% bonus points!

Address: 7515 E Butherus Dr 85260 **Location:** 0.5 mi e of jct Scottsdale Rd. Located at Scottsdale Municipal Airport. **Facility:** 120 units. 4 stories, interior/exterior corridors. **Terms:** cancellation fee imposed. **Pool(s):** heated outdoor. **Activities:** hot tub, exercise room. **Guest Services:** valet and coin laundry, area transportation.

BEST WESTERN PLUS SUNDIAL
(480)994-4170

Hotel
$99-$299

AAA Benefit:
Save 10% or more every day and earn 10% bonus points!

Address: 7320 E Camelback Rd 85251 **Location:** Just e of Scottsdale Rd. **Facility:** 54 units. 3 stories, exterior corridors. **Bath:** shower only. **Pool(s):** heated outdoor. **Activities:** hot tub, exercise room. **Guest Services:** valet and coin laundry. **Featured Amenity:** continental breakfast.

        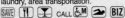

▼ See AAA listing p. 204 ▼

(See map & index p. 158.)

THE CANYON SUITES AT THE PHOENICIAN, A LUXURY COLLECTION RESORT, SCOTTSDALE
480/423-2880 **39**

Resort Hotel
Rates not provided

THE LUXURY COLLECTION
Hotels & Resorts

AAA Benefit: Members save up to 15%, plus Starwood Preferred Guest® benefits!

Address: 6000 E Camelback Rd 85251 **Location:** 0.5 mi w of 64th St; in The Phoenician, A Luxury Collection Resort, Scottsdale. **Facility:** This elegant resort is nestled at the base of Camelback Mountain. Ambassadors tend to every guest's needs with such comforts as nightly wine tastings and a "tub turn down" with scented bath water. 60 units, some kitchens. 2 stories, interior corridors. **Terms:** check-in 4 pm. **Amenities:** safes. **Pool(s):** heated outdoor. **Activities:** hot tub, kids club, bicycles, lawn sports, trails, spa. **Guest Services:** valet laundry, rental car service, luggage security pick-up, area transportation. Affiliated with The Luxury Collection. *(See ad p. 203.)*

CHAPARRAL SUITES SCOTTSDALE 480/949-1414 **40**

Hotel
Rates not provided

Address: 5001 N Scottsdale Rd 85250 **Location:** At Chaparral Rd. **Facility:** 312 units, some two bedrooms. 4 stories, exterior corridors. **Amenities:** safes. **Pool(s):** heated outdoor. **Activities:** hot tub, tennis, exercise room. **Guest Services:** valet and coin laundry.

COMFORT SUITES BY CHOICE HOTELS-OLD TOWN
(480)946-1111 **54**

Hotel $99-$219 **Address:** 3275 N Drinkwater Blvd 85251 **Location:** N of Thomas Rd; just e of Scottsdale Rd. **Facility:** 60 units. 3 stories, interior corridors. **Amenities:** safes. **Pool(s):** heated indoor. **Activities:** hot tub, limited exercise equipment. **Guest Services:** valet and coin laundry.

COUNTRY INN & SUITES BY CARLSON 480/314-1200 **19**

Hotel. Rates not provided. **Address:** 10801 N 89th Pl 85260 **Location:** SR 101 exit 41 (Shea Blvd), just e, then just n. **Facility:** 162 units. 3 stories, interior corridors. **Pool(s):** heated outdoor. **Activities:** hot tub, picnic facilities, exercise room. **Guest Services:** valet and coin laundry, area transportation.

COURTYARD BY MARRIOTT SCOTTSDALE AT MAYO CLINIC
(480)860-4000

Hotel
$101-$345

COURTYARD
Marriott

AAA Benefit: Members save 5% or more!

Address: 13444 E Shea Blvd 85259 **Location:** SR 101 exit 41 (Shea Blvd), 5.8 mi e. Located at entrance to Mayo Clinic. **Facility:** 124 units. 2 stories, interior corridors. **Pool(s):** heated outdoor. **Activities:** hot tub, exercise room. **Guest Services:** valet and coin laundry, area transportation.

COURTYARD BY MARRIOTT/SCOTTSDALE NORTH
(480)922-8400 **6**

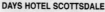
Hotel $79-$342 **Address:** 17010 N Scottsdale Rd 85255 **Location:** Just n of Frank Lloyd Wright Blvd. **Facility:** 153 units. 3 stories, interior corridors. **Amenities:** safes. **Pool(s):** heated

AAA Benefit: Members save 5% or more!

outdoor. **Activities:** hot tub, exercise room. **Guest Services:** valet and coin laundry, boarding pass kiosk, area transportation.

COURTYARD BY MARRIOTT SCOTTSDALE OLD TOWN
(480)429-7785 **5**

Hotel
$85-$358

COURTYARD
Marriott

AAA Benefit: Members save 5% or more!

Address: 3311 N Scottsdale Rd 85251 **Location:** Jct Drinkwater Blvd. **Facility:** 180 units. 5 stories, interior corridors. **Pool(s):** heated outdoor. **Activities:** hot tub, exercise room. **Guest Services:** valet and coin laundry, boarding pass kiosk.

COURTYARD BY MARRIOTT SCOTTSDALE SALT RIVER
(480)745-8200 **42**

Hotel
$80-$281

COURTYARD
Marriott

AAA Benefit: Members save 5% or more!

Address: 5201 N Pima Rd 85250 **Location:** SR 101 exit 46 (Chaparral Rd), just w, then just n. **Facility:** 158 units. 4 stories, interior corridors. **Pool(s):** heated outdoor. **Activities:** hot tub, exercise room. **Guest Services:** valet and coin laundry, boarding pass kiosk, area transportation.

DAYS HOTEL SCOTTSDALE
(480)945-4392 **37**

Hotel
$59-$260

Address: 5101 N Scottsdale Rd 85250 **Location:** Just n of Chaparral Rd. **Facility:** 211 units. 2 stories (no elevator), exterior corridors. **Terms:** cancellation fee imposed. **Dining:** nightclub. **Pool(s):** heated outdoor. **Activities:** hot tub, bicycles, picnic facilities, exercise room. **Guest Services:** coin laundry, area transportation.

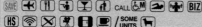

Visit AAA.com/searchfordiscounts

to save on travel, shopping,

dining and attractions

(See map & index p. 158.)

DAYS INN & SUITES SCOTTSDALE NORTH
(480)948-3800 **29**

Hotel
$89-$389

Address: 7330 N Pima Rd 85258 **Location:** 0.4 mi n of Indian Bend Rd; on west side of Pima Rd. **Facility:** 104 units. 2 stories, interior/exterior corridors. **Terms:** cancellation fee imposed. **Pool(s):** heated outdoor. **Activities:** hot tub, bicycles, picnic facilities, exercise room. **Guest Services:** valet and coin laundry, area transportation.

[icons]

DOUBLETREE RESORT BY HILTON PARADISE VALLEY-SCOTTSDALE
(480)947-5400 **36**

Resort Hotel
$79-$479

AAA Benefit: Members save 5% or more!

Address: 5401 N Scottsdale Rd 85250 **Location:** Just n of Chaparral Rd; on east side of Scottsdale Rd. **Facility:** Guests will enjoy beautiful manicured grounds, luxurious pool areas, a basketball court and spacious guest rooms. All rooms have great views from a balcony or patio. 378 units. 2 stories, exterior corridors. **Parking:** on-site and valet. **Terms:** check-in 4 pm, 1-7 night minimum stay, cancellation fee imposed. **Amenities:** safes. **Dining:** 2 restaurants. **Pool(s):** heated outdoor. **Activities:** sauna, hot tub, steamroom, tennis, playground, massage. **Guest Services:** valet laundry, rental car service, area transportation.

[icons]

EXTENDED STAY AMERICA PHOENIX-SCOTTSDALE
(480)483-1333 **18**

Extended Stay Hotel. Rates not provided. **Address:** 10660 N 69th St 85254 **Location:** Jct Scottsdale Rd, just w on Shea Blvd, then just n. Located in Agua Caliente Center. **Facility:** 106 efficiencies. 3 stories, interior corridors. **Pool(s):** heated outdoor. **Activities:** hot tub, picnic facilities, exercise room. **Guest Services:** coin laundry.

[icons]

EXTENDED STAY AMERICA-PHOENIX-SCOTTSDALE-NORTH
480/607-3767 **12**

Extended Stay Hotel. Rates not provided. **Address:** 15501 N Scottsdale Rd 85254 **Location:** SR 101 exit 38 (Frank Lloyd Wright Blvd), 2 mi w, 0.5 mi s on Scottsdale Rd, then just e on Tierra Buena Ln. **Facility:** 120 efficiencies. 3 stories, exterior corridors. **Guest Services:** coin laundry.

[icons]

EXTENDED STAY AMERICA-PHOENIX-SCOTTSDALE-OLD TOWN
480/994-0297 **52**

Extended Stay Motel. Rates not provided. **Address:** 3560 N Marshall Way 85251 **Location:** Just w of Scottsdale Rd on Goldwater Blvd, just s. **Facility:** 121 efficiencies. 2 stories (no elevator), exterior corridors. **Pool(s):** heated outdoor. **Activities:** picnic facilities. **Guest Services:** coin laundry.

[icons]

FAIRFIELD INN BY MARRIOTT NORTH SCOTTSDALE
(480)483-0042 **16**

Hotel
$65-$233

AAA Benefit: Members save 5% or more!

Address: 13440 N Scottsdale Rd 85254 **Location:** Just s of Thunderbird Rd; on west side of Scottsdale Rd. **Facility:** 131 units. 3 stories, interior/exterior corridors. **Pool(s):** heated outdoor. **Activities:** hot tub, picnic facilities, exercise room. **Guest Services:** valet and coin laundry. **Featured Amenity:** full hot breakfast.

[icons]

FAIRMONT SCOTTSDALE PRINCESS
(480)585-4848 **3**

Resort Hotel
$169-$3099

Address: 7575 E Princess Dr 85255 **Location:** SR 101 exit 34 (Scottsdale Rd), 0.8 mi s, then just e; 0.6 mi n of Bell Rd. **Facility:** Each spacious unit at this expansive 450-acre luxury resort features a balcony or terrace. A world-class spa and elaborate pool areas add to the abundance of recreational and leisure activities. 649 units. 1-4 stories, interior/exterior corridors. **Parking:** on-site and valet. **Terms:** check-in 4 pm, 7 day cancellation notice-fee imposed, resort fee. **Amenities:** safes. **Dining:** 3 restaurants, also, Bourbon Steak, La Hacienda, Toro, see separate listings. **Pool(s):** heated outdoor. **Activities:** sauna, hot tub, steamroom, fishing, regulation golf, recreation programs, kids club, bicycles, playground, game room, lawn sports, trails, spa. **Guest Services:** valet laundry, area transportation.

[icons]

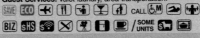

Fairmont
SCOTTSDALE PRINCESS
Located in North Scottsdale overlooking the TPC Stadium, Golf Course and majestic McDowell Mountains

FIRESKY RESORT & SPA, A KIMPTON HOTEL
(480)945-7666 **41**

Hotel
$109-$419

Address: 4925 N Scottsdale Rd 85251 **Location:** Southeast corner of Scottsdale and Chaparral rds. **Facility:** Guest rooms have modern, elegant furnishings and bedding. Fountains in the gardens, a pool with a sand bottom and small foot bridge all set the scene for a sense of escape. 204 units. 2 stories (no elevator), interior corridors. **Parking:** on-site and valet. **Terms:** check-in 4 pm, 3 day cancellation notice-fee imposed, resort fee. **Amenities:** safes. **Dining:** Taggia, see separate listing. **Pool(s):** heated outdoor. **Activities:** hot tub, bicycles, exercise room, spa. **Guest Services:** valet laundry, area transportation.

[icons]

(See map & index p. 158.)

FOUR SEASONS RESORT SCOTTSDALE AT TROON NORTH
480/515-5700

Resort Hotel
Rates not provided

Address: 10600 E Crescent Moon Dr 85262 **Location:** SR 101 exit 36 (Pima Rd), 4.7 mi n, 2 mi e on Happy Valley Rd, then 1.5 mi n on Alma School Rd. **Facility:** Well-designed landscaping seamlessly blends with the desert surroundings, allowing for striking views from the territorial-style casitas. 210 units, some two bedrooms. 1-3 stories, exterior corridors. **Parking:** on-site and valet. **Terms:** check-in 4 pm. **Amenities:** video games, safes. **Dining:** 2 restaurants, also, Talavera, see separate listing. **Pool(s):** heated outdoor. **Activities:** sauna, hot tub, steamroom, regulation golf, tennis, recreation programs, kids club, trails, spa. **Guest Services:** valet laundry, boarding pass kiosk, area transportation.

SAVE ⊞ ⊞ ⊞ ⊞ ⊞ CALL ⊞M ⊞ ⊞ BIZ
$HS ⊞ ⊞ ⊞ ⊞ ⊞ / SOME UNITS ⊞ ⊞

GAINEY SUITES HOTEL
(480)922-6969 **26**

Hotel
$129-$279

Address: 7300 E Gainey Suites Dr 85258 **Location:** Just e of Scottsdale Rd. **Facility:** 162 efficiencies, some two bedrooms. 2-3 stories, interior corridors. **Terms:** cancellation fee imposed. **Amenities:** safes. **Pool(s):** heated outdoor. **Activities:** hot tub, exercise room. **Guest Services:** valet and coin laundry, area transportation. **Featured Amenity: breakfast buffet.**

SAVE ⊞ ⊞ BIZ ⊞ ⊞
⊞ ⊞ ⊞ ⊞ / SOME UNITS ⊞

GAINEY SUITES HOTEL

**Style & Value in best part of Scottsdale
• Includes full hot breakfast + evening
social. 10% AAA Disc**

HAMPTON INN & SUITES PHOENIX/SCOTTSDALE
(480)348-9280 **9**

⊞⊞⊞ Hotel $84-$399 **Address:** 16620 N Scottsdale Rd 85254 **Location:** Just s of Bell Rd, just w. **Facility:** 123 units, some efficiencies. 3 stories, interior corridors. **Terms:** 1-7 night minimum stay, cancellation fee imposed. **Pool(s):** heated outdoor. **Activities:** hot tub, picnic facilities, exercise room. **Guest Services:** valet and coin laundry, area transportation.

AAA Benefit: Members save up to 10%!

⊞ CALL ⊞M ⊞ BIZ ⊞ ⊞ ⊞ ⊞ ⊞ ⊞

HAMPTON INN & SUITES SCOTTSDALE RIVERWALK
(480)270-5393 **33**

⊞⊞⊞ Hotel $99-$349 **Address:** 9550 E Indian Bend Rd 85256 **Location:** SR 101 exit 44 (Indian Bend Rd), just e. **Facility:** 101 units. 4 stories, interior corridors. **Terms:** 1-7 night minimum stay, cancellation fee imposed. **Activities:** exercise room. **Guest Services:** valet and coin laundry, area transportation.

AAA Benefit: Members save up to 10%!

⊞ CALL ⊞M ⊞ BIZ ⊞ ⊞ ⊞ ⊞
/ SOME UNITS ⊞ ⊞ ⊞

HAMPTON INN PHOENIX-SCOTTSDALE AT SHEA BLVD
(480)443-3233 **23**

⊞⊞⊞ Hotel $89-$299 **Address:** 10101 N Scottsdale Rd 85253 **Location:** Just s of Shea Blvd. **Facility:** 130 units. 2 stories, interior corridors. **Terms:** 1-7 night minimum stay, cancellation fee imposed. **Pool(s):** heated outdoor. **Activities:** hot tub, exercise room. **Guest Services:** valet and coin laundry, boarding pass kiosk, area transportation.

AAA Benefit: Members save up to 10%!

⊞ CALL ⊞M ⊞ BIZ ⊞ ⊞ ⊞ ⊞ ⊞ ⊞
/ SOME UNITS ⊞

HILTON GARDEN INN SCOTTSDALE NORTH
(480)515-4944 **4**

⊞⊞⊞ Hotel $109-$399 **Address:** 8550 E Princess Dr 85255 **Location:** SR 101 exit 36 (Princess Dr/Pima Rd), just w. **Facility:** 122 units. 3 stories, interior corridors. **Terms:** check-in 4 pm, 1-7 night minimum stay, cancellation fee imposed. **Pool(s):** heated outdoor. **Activities:** hot tub, exercise room. **Guest Services:** valet and coin laundry.

AAA Benefit: Members save up to 10%!

⊞ ⊞ CALL ⊞M ⊞ BIZ ⊞ ⊞ ⊞ ⊞ ⊞
⊞ ⊞

HILTON GARDEN INN SCOTTSDALE OLD TOWN
(480)481-0400 **50**

⊞⊞⊞ Hotel $75-$399 **Address:** 7324 E Indian School Rd 85251 **Location:** Just e of Scottsdale Rd. **Facility:** 199 units. 7 stories, interior corridors. **Terms:** 1-7 night minimum stay, cancellation fee imposed. **Pool(s):** heated outdoor. **Activities:** bicycles, exercise room. **Guest Services:** valet and coin laundry.

AAA Benefit: Members save up to 10%!

⊞ ⊞ CALL ⊞M ⊞ BIZ ⊞ ⊞ ⊞ ⊞ ⊞
⊞

HILTON SCOTTSDALE RESORT & VILLAS
(480)948-7750 **34**

Hotel
$89-$499

Hilton HOTELS & RESORTS

AAA Benefit: Members save 5% or more!

Address: 6333 N Scottsdale Rd 85250 **Location:** SR 101 exit 45, 2.1 mi w on McDonald Dr, then 0.3 mi n. **Facility:** Chic, modern décor is highlighted in the lobby and framed by high ceilings and large windows. Relax and enjoy the tropical pool area, complete with a lounge and poolside food and beverage service. 235 units, some two bedrooms and kitchens. 2-3 stories, interior corridors. **Parking:** on-site and valet. **Terms:** check-in 4 pm, 1-7 night minimum stay, cancellation fee imposed. **Amenities:** safes. **Dining:** 3 restaurants. **Pool(s):** heated outdoor. **Activities:** sauna, hot tub, steamroom, bicycles, massage. **Guest Services:** valet laundry, area transportation.

SAVE ⊞ ⊞ ⊞ CALL ⊞M ⊞ ⊞ BIZ ⊞ ⊞
⊞ ⊞ / SOME UNITS ⊞ ⊞ ⊞

Keep your focus safely

on the road when driving

(See map & index p. 158.)

HOLIDAY INN & SUITES SCOTTSDALE NORTH-AIRPARK
(480)922-6500 **15**

Hotel
$99-$999

Address: 14255 N 87th St 85260 **Location:** SR 101 exit 39 (Raintree Dr), just w, then 0.3 mi s. **Facility:** 117 units, some two bedrooms and efficiencies. 4 stories, interior corridors. **Terms:** cancellation fee imposed. **Amenities:** safes. **Pool(s):** heated outdoor. **Activities:** hot tub, exercise room. **Guest Services:** valet and coin laundry, area transportation.

SAVE 🍴 🖥 🍸 🏊 BIZ HS
📶 ✕ 🧺 🛗 🖨

HOLIDAY INN EXPRESS HOTEL & SUITES-SCOTTSDALE OLD TOWN
480/675-7665 **55**

Hotel. Rates not provided. **Address:** 3131 N Scottsdale Rd 85251 **Location:** Northeast corner of Scottsdale Rd and Earll Dr. **Facility:** 169 units. 3 stories, interior corridors. **Pool(s):** heated outdoor. **Activities:** hot tub, exercise room. **Guest Services:** valet and coin laundry, area transportation.

🖐 🍴 CALL ᴹ 🏊 BIZ 📶 ✕ 🛗 🖨 🖥
/SOME UNITS 🛏 HS

HOLIDAY INN EXPRESS SCOTTSDALE NORTH
(480)596-6559 **20**

Hotel $79-$349 **Address:** 7350 E Gold Dust Ave 85258 **Location:** Just e of Scottsdale Rd; just s of Shea Blvd; on north side of Gold Dust Ave. Located in a light-commercial area. **Facility:** 122 units. 3 stories, interior corridors. **Terms:** cancellation fee imposed. **Pool(s):** heated outdoor. **Activities:** hot tub, picnic facilities, exercise room. **Guest Services:** valet and coin laundry, area transportation.

🍴 CALL ᴹ 🏊 BIZ 📶 ✕ 🛗 🖨 /SOME UNITS 🛏

HOMEWOOD SUITES BY HILTON PHOENIX/SCOTTSDALE
(480)368-8705 **24**

Extended Stay Hotel $89-$379 **Address:** 9880 N Scottsdale Rd 85253 **Location:** 0.5 mi s of Shea Blvd. **Facility:** 114 efficiencies, some two bedrooms. 3 stories, interior corridors. **Terms:** 1-7 night minimum stay, cancellation fee imposed. **Pool(s):** heated outdoor. **Activities:** picnic facilities, exercise room. **Guest Services:** valet and coin laundry, area transportation.

AAA Benefit: Members save up to 10%!

🖐 🏊 BIZ 📶 🏀 🛗 🖨 🖥 /SOME UNITS 🛏

HOSPITALITY SUITE RESORT
(480)949-5115 **57**

Hotel $59-$299 **Address:** 409 N Scottsdale Rd 85257 **Location:** Just n of McKellips Rd; on east side of Scottsdale Rd. Located in a light-commercial and residential area. **Facility:** 210 units, some two bedrooms, efficiencies and kitchens. 2-3 stories (no elevator), exterior corridors. **Terms:** cancellation fee imposed. **Amenities:** video games. **Pool(s):** heated outdoor. **Activities:** hot tub, tennis, picnic facilities. **Guest Services:** valet and coin laundry, area transportation.

🖐 🍴 🍸 🏊 BIZ 📶 ✕ 🛗 🖨 🖥 /SOME UNITS 🛏

HOTEL INDIGO SCOTTSDALE
480/941-9400 **46**

Hotel
Rates not provided

Address: 4415 N Civic Center Plaza 85251 **Location:** Scottsdale Rd, just e on Camelback Rd, just s on 75th St. **Facility:** 126 units. 5 stories, interior/exterior corridors. **Parking:** valet only. **Pool(s):** heated outdoor. **Activities:** exercise room. **Guest Services:** valet laundry, area transportation.

SAVE 🍴 🖥 🍸 CALL ᴹ 🏊
BIZ 📶 ✕ 🏀 🖥
/SOME UNITS 🛏 🛗 🖨

HOTEL VALLEY HO
(480)248-2000 **51**

Boutique Contemporary Retro Hotel
$119-$499

Address: 6850 E Main St 85251 **Location:** 0.4 mi w of Scottsdale Rd, just s of Indian School Rd; on north side of Main St. **Facility:** Maintaining the flavor of its 1950s origins, this classic gem offers fully retro-fitted trendy rooms with oversize posh baths. The tower suites offer full kitchens and oversize balconies with sweeping views. 238 units, some kitchens and condominiums. 2-6 stories, interior/exterior corridors. **Parking:** on-site and valet. **Terms:** check-in 4 pm, cancellation fee imposed. **Amenities:** safes. **Dining:** Cafe Zu Zu, see separate listing. **Pool(s):** heated outdoor. **Activities:** sauna, hot tub, bicycles, spa. **Guest Services:** valet laundry. Affiliated with Preferred Hotels & Resorts.

SAVE ECO 🍴 🖥 🏀 🏊 🖐 BIZ HS 📶 ✕
🎦 🛗 🖨 🖥 /SOME UNITS 🛏 🖨

HYATT HOUSE SCOTTSDALE/OLD TOWN
(480)946-7700 **47**

Extended Stay Hotel
$79-$359

H HYATT house™

AAA Benefit: Members save 10%!

Address: 4245 N Drinkwater Blvd 85251 **Location:** 0.3 mi e of Scottsdale Rd. **Facility:** 164 units, some two bedrooms, efficiencies and kitchens. 3 stories (no elevator), exterior corridors. **Terms:** check-in 4 pm, cancellation fee imposed. **Pool(s):** heated outdoor. **Activities:** hot tub, picnic facilities, exercise room. **Guest Services:** valet and coin laundry, area transportation. **Featured Amenity:** breakfast buffet.

SAVE 🖐 CALL ᴹ 🏊 BIZ HS 📶 ✕ 🛗 🖨
🖥 /SOME UNITS 🛏

HYATT PLACE SCOTTSDALE/OLD TOWN
(480)423-9944 **48**

Hotel
$79-$399

📶 HYATT PLACE®

AAA Benefit: Members save 10%!

Address: 7300 E 3rd Ave 85251 **Location:** Just e of Scottsdale Rd. **Facility:** 126 units. 6 stories, interior corridors. **Terms:** cancellation fee imposed. **Amenities:** safes. **Pool(s):** heated outdoor. **Activities:** exercise room. **Guest Services:** valet laundry. **Featured Amenity:** breakfast buffet.

SAVE 🍴 🖥 CALL ᴹ 🏊 BIZ
📶 ✕ 🏀 🛗 🖥
/SOME UNITS 🛏 HS

(See map & index p. 158.)

HYATT REGENCY SCOTTSDALE RESORT & SPA AT GAINEY RANCH
(480)444-1234 **25**

Resort Hotel
$139-$850

HYATT REGENCY

AAA Benefit: Members save 10%!

Address: 7500 E Doubletree Ranch Rd 85258 **Location:** SR 101 exit 43, 2.6 mi w on Via de Ventura. **Facility:** The resort has a man-made beach, waterslide, spa and many family-friendly recreational activities along with upscale, spacious rooms. A learning center offers cultural programs. 493 units, some two bedrooms. 4 stories, interior/exterior corridors. **Parking:** on-site and valet. **Terms:** check-in 4 pm, 3 day cancellation notice-fee imposed, resort fee. **Amenities:** safes. **Dining:** 5 restaurants, also, Alto Ristorante & Bar, see separate listing, entertainment. **Pool(s):** heated outdoor. **Activities:** sauna, hot tub, steamroom, regulation golf, tennis, recreation programs, kids club, bicycles, playground, game room, exercise room, spa. **Guest Services:** valet laundry, boarding pass kiosk, area transportation.

JW MARRIOTT CAMELBACK INN RESORT & SPA
(480)948-1700 **30**

Resort Hotel
$135-$577

JW MARRIOTT

AAA Benefit: Members save 5% or more!

Address: 5402 E Lincoln Dr 85253 **Location:** 0.5 mi e of Tatum Blvd; on north side of Lincoln Dr. **Facility:** This lovely resort, dating back to 1936, occupies 125 scenic acres and boasts elegant Southwestern décor with mountain views. Some of the Pueblo-style casitas have a private pool. 453 units, some efficiencies. 1-2 stories, exterior corridors. **Parking:** on-site and valet. **Terms:** check-in 4 pm, 3 day cancellation notice, resort fee. **Amenities:** video games, safes. **Dining:** 6 restaurants, also, BLT Steak, see separate listing, entertainment. **Pool(s):** heated outdoor. **Activities:** sauna, hot tub, steamroom, regulation golf, tennis, recreation programs, bicycles, playground, lawn sports, spa. **Guest Services:** complimentary and valet laundry, boarding pass kiosk, area transportation.

LA QUINTA INN & SUITES PHOENIX SCOTTSDALE
(480)614-5300 **22**

Hotel $64-$339 **Address:** 8888 E Shea Blvd 85260 **Location:** SR 101 exit 41 (Shea Blvd); northeast corner. **Facility:** 140 units. 3 stories, interior corridors. **Pool(s):** heated outdoor. **Activities:** hot tub, exercise room. **Guest Services:** valet and coin laundry, area transportation.

MAGNUSON HOTEL PAPAGO INN
(480)947-7335 **56**

Hotel $70-$300 **Address:** 7017 E McDowell Rd 85257 **Location:** From Scottsdale Rd, just w. Located in a busy commercial area. **Facility:** 58 units. 2 stories (no elevator), interior/exterior corridors. **Terms:** cancellation fee imposed. **Pool(s):** heated outdoor. **Activities:** exercise room. **Guest Services:** valet and coin laundry.

Discover a wealth of savings and offers on the AAA/CAA travel websites

THE MCCORMICK SCOTTSDALE
480/948-5050 **27**

Hotel. Rates not provided. Address: 7401 N Scottsdale Rd 85253 **Location:** 0.8 mi n of Indian Bend Rd. **Facility:** 136 units some two bedrooms, three bedrooms and kitchens. 3 stories, interior/exterior corridors. **Terms:** check-in 4 pm. **Dining:** Piñon Grill, see separate listing. **Pool(s):** heated outdoor. **Activities:** boat dock, fishing, regulation golf, tennis, bicycles, exercise room. **Guest Services:** valet laundry, area transportation.

MOTEL 6 SCOTTSDALE #29
480/946-2280 **43**

Motel. Rates not provided. Address: 6848 E Camelback Rd 85251 **Location:** Just w of Scottsdale Rd. **Facility:** 122 units. 2 stories (no elevator), exterior corridors. **Pool(s):** heated outdoor. **Activities:** hot tub. **Guest Services:** coin laundry.

ORANGE TREE RESORT
480/948-6100 **17**

Resort Hotel. Rates not provided. Address: 10601 N 56th St 85254 **Location:** SR 101 exit 41 (Shea Blvd), 4.1 mi w, then just n. **Facility:** Clustered buildings form lovely courtyards with citrus trees and shaded barbecue areas. Rooms, some overlooking the golf course, are spacious and feature a large bath. 162 units. 2 stories (no elevator), exterior corridors. **Terms:** check-in 4 pm. **Amenities:** safes. **Pool(s):** heated outdoor. **Activities:** hot tub, regulation golf, recreation programs, lawn sports, picnic facilities, exercise room. **Guest Services:** complimentary and valet laundry.

THE PHOENICIAN, A LUXURY COLLECTION RESORT, SCOTTSDALE
(480)941-8200 **38**

Resort Hotel
$199-$599

THE LUXURY COLLECTION
Hotels & Resorts

AAA Benefit: Members save up to 15%, plus Starwood Preferred Guest® benefits!

Address: 6000 E Camelback Rd 85251 **Location:** 0.5 mi w of 64th St. **Facility:** Tucked at the base of Camelback Mountain, this venerable resort features extensive landscaping, sweeping valley views, world-class dining and golf, a tropical lagoon and elegant rooms. 583 units, some two bedrooms and kitchens. 3-4 stories, interior/exterior corridors. **Parking:** on-site and valet. **Terms:** check-in 4 pm, 7 day cancellation notice-fee imposed, resort fee. **Amenities:** safes. **Dining:** 4 restaurants, also, Il Terrazzo, J&G Steakhouse, see separate listings, entertainment. **Pool(s):** heated outdoor. **Activities:** sauna, hot tub, steamroom, regulation golf, tennis, recreation programs, kids club, bicycles, playground, lawn sports, spa. **Guest Services:** valet laundry, rental car service, luggage security pick-up, area transportation. Affiliated with The Luxury Collection. *(See ad p. 209.)*

RESIDENCE INN BY MARRIOTT SCOTTSDALE NORTH
(480)563-4120 **7**

Extended Stay Hotel $98-$297 **Address:** 17011 N Scottsdale Rd 85255 **Location:** SR 101 exit 34 (Scottsdale Rd), 1.1 mi s; northeast corner of Frank Lloyd Wright Blvd and Scottsdale Rd.

AAA Benefit: Members save 5% or more!

Facility: 120 units, some two bedrooms, efficiencies and kitchens. 3 stories, interior corridors. **Pool(s):** heated outdoor. **Activities:** hot tub, picnic facilities, exercise room. **Guest Services:** valet and coin laundry, area transportation.

(See map & index p. 158.)

RESIDENCE INN BY MARRIOTT, SCOTTSDALE/PARADISE VALLEY   (480)948-8666

Extended Stay Hotel
$101-S337

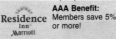 Residence Inn Marriott

AAA Benefit: Members save 5% or more!

Address: 6040 N Scottsdale Rd 85253 **Location:** Just n of McDonald Dr. **Facility:** 122 efficiencies, some two bedrooms. 2 stories (no elevator), interior/exterior corridors. **Pool(s):** heated outdoor. **Activities:** hot tub, exercise room. **Guest Services:** valet and coin laundry. **Featured Amenity:** breakfast buffet.

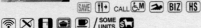
SAVE [†↓] CALL &M ➳ BIZ HS

 ✕ 📱 📷 📺 / SOME UNITS 🐾

SCOTTSDALE MARRIOTT AT MCDOWELL MOUNTAINS
(480)502-3836

Hotel
$132-S392

 MARRIOTT

AAA Benefit: Members save 5% or more!

Address: 16770 N Perimeter Dr 85260 **Location:** SR 101 exit 36 (Princess Dr/Pima Rd), just w to N Perimeter Dr, then 0.6 mi s. **Facility:** Adjacent to the TPC Scottsdale golf course, golfers and business travelers alike will appreciate the ideal location. The upscale resort features expansive public areas and all-suite guest rooms. 266 units. 4 stories, interior corridors. **Parking:** on-site and valet. **Terms:** check-in 4 pm. **Pool(s):** heated outdoor. **Activities:** hot tub, exercise room. **Guest Services:** valet and coin laundry, boarding pass kiosk, area transportation.

SAVE [†↓] [†↓] ¥ CALL &M ➳ BIZ sHS 🔁 ✕
🎥 📱 📺 / SOME UNITS 🐾

▼ See AAA listing p. 208 ▼

(See map & index p. 158.)

SCOTTSDALE MARRIOTT SUITES OLD TOWN
(480)945-1550 **49**

Hotel
$120-$404

MARRIOTT

AAA Benefit: Members save 5% or more!

Address: 7325 E 3rd Ave 85251 **Location:** Just e of Scottsdale Rd. **Facility:** 243 units. 8 stories, interior corridors. **Parking:** on-site (fee) and valet. **Amenities:** video games. **Pool(s):** heated outdoor. **Activities:** hot tub, exercise room. **Guest Services:** valet and coin laundry, boarding pass kiosk.

SCOTTSDALE RESORT & ATHLETIC CLUB
480/344-0600 **31**

▼▼▼ **Hotel.** Rates not provided. **Address:** 8235 E Indian Bend Rd 85250 **Location:** 1.5 mi e of Scottsdale Rd. **Facility:** 85 units, some kitchens. 2 stories (no elevator), exterior corridors. **Dining:** OC Seven Restaurant & Bar, see separate listing. **Pool(s):** heated outdoor. **Activities:** sauna, hot tub, tennis, picnic facilities, spa. **Guest Services:** coin laundry.

SCOTTSDALE RESORT & CONFERENCE CENTER
(480)991-9000 **28**

Resort Hotel
$89-$449

Address: 7700 E McCormick Pkwy 85258 **Location:** Just w of Hayden Rd; 0.7 mi e of Scottsdale Rd. **Facility:** Hacienda-style rooms, shaded courtyards and spacious public areas are all graciously appointed. 326 units. 2-3 stories, interior/exterior corridors. **Parking:** on-site and valet. **Terms:** 3 day cancellation notice, resort fee. **Amenities:** safes. **Dining:** 3 restaurants. **Pool(s):** heated outdoor. **Activities:** sauna, hot tub, tennis, bicycles, spa. **Guest Services:** valet laundry, area transportation.

SCOTTSDALE VILLA MIRAGE
480/473-4000 **1**

▼▼▼ **Condominium.** Rates not provided. **Address:** 7887 E Princess Blvd 85255 **Location:** SR 101 exit 34, 0.7 mi s on Scottsdale Rd, then 0.7 mi e. **Facility:** These garden-style condominiums are pleasantly appointed and convenient to shops, attractions and sports centers. Some guest rooms have fireplaces that add to their overall appeal. 224 condominiums. 3 stories (no elevator), exterior corridors. **Terms:** check-in 4 pm. **Amenities:** *Some:* safes. **Pool(s):** heated outdoor. **Activities:** sauna, hot tub, steamroom, tennis, recreation programs, playground, game room, lawn sports, picnic facilities, exercise room, massage. **Guest Services:** complimentary and valet laundry.

▼ See AAA listing p. 211 ▼

(See map & index p. 158.)

SHERATON DESERT OASIS   (480)515-5888   2

Condominium
$99-$449

Sheraton
HOTELS & RESORTS

AAA Benefit: Members save up to 15%, plus Starwood Preferred Guest® benefits!

Address: 17700 N Hayden Rd 85255 **Location:** SR 101 exit 35 (Hayden Rd), 0.5 mi s. **Facility:** Waterfalls spilling over boulders into pools, charming garden areas with tall palm trees and attractive, well-appointed rooms combine to create an oasis. 300 condominiums. 2-3 stories (no elevator), exterior corridors. **Terms:** check-in 4 pm, 3 day cancellation notice-fee imposed. **Amenities:** safes.

Pool(s): heated outdoor. **Activities:** hot tub, recreation programs, playground, picnic facilities, exercise room. **Guest Services:** complimentary laundry.

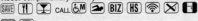

SLEEP INN NORTH SCOTTSDALE/PHOENIX
(480)998-9211   8

Hotel $69-$259 **Address:** 16630 N Scottsdale Rd 85254 **Location:** Just s of Bell Rd. **Facility:** 107 units. 3 stories, interior corridors. *Bath:* shower only. **Pool(s):** heated outdoor. **Activities:** hot tub, picnic facilities, exercise room. **Guest Services:** valet and coin laundry, area transportation.

SPRINGHILL SUITES BY MARRIOTT-SCOTTSDALE NORTH
(480)922-8700   5

Hotel $74-$313 **Address:** 17020 N Scottsdale Rd 85255 **Location:** Just n of Frank Lloyd Wright Blvd. Located in a commercial area. **Facility:** 121 units. 4 stories, interior corridors.

AAA Benefit: Members save 5% or more!

Amenities: safes. **Pool(s):** heated outdoor. **Activities:** hot tub, exercise room. **Guest Services:** valet and coin laundry, area transportation.

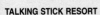

TALKING STICK RESORT   (480)850-7777   32

Resort Hotel
$119-$459

Address: 9800 E Indian Bend Rd 85256 **Location:** SR 101 exit 44 (E Indian Bend Rd), just e. **Facility:** This expansive, upscale resort and casino combines outstanding entertainment, fine dining and luxurious guest rooms to bring a taste of Vegas to the Valley of the Sun. 496 units. 15 stories, interior corridors. **Parking:** on-site and valet. **Terms:** check-in 4 pm, 3 day cancellation notice-fee imposed. **Amenities:** safes. **Dining:** 4 restaurants, also, Ocean Trail, Orange Sky, see separate listings, nightclub, entertainment. **Pool(s):** heated outdoor. **Activities:** hot tub, steamroom, regulation golf, game room, exercise room, spa. **Guest Services:** valet laundry, boarding pass kiosk.

TOWNEPLACE SUITES BY MARRIOTT SCOTTSDALE
(480)551-1100   21

Extended Stay Hotel
$82-$341

TownePlace
SUITES
Marriott

AAA Benefit: Members save 5% or more!

Address: 10740 N 90th St 85260 **Location:** SR 101 exit 41 (Shea Blvd), just e to 90th St, then just n. **Facility:** 130 efficiencies, some two bedrooms. 3 stories, interior corridors. **Pool(s):** heated outdoor. **Activities:** picnic facilities, limited exercise equipment. **Guest Services:** valet and coin laundry, area transportation. **Featured Amenity: continental breakfast.**

WE-KO-PA RESORT AND CONFERENCE CENTER
(480)789-5300

Resort Hotel
$79-$269

Address: 10438 N Ft. McDowell Rd 85264 **Location:** Jct Shea Blvd, 1.6 mi ne on SR 87. Located in a rural area with mountain views. **Facility:** Situated on the lands of Fort McDowell Yavapai Nation, this property boasts elegant guest rooms and baths reflecting Native American design. 246 units. 5 stories, interior corridors. **Parking:** on-site and valet. **Terms:** check-in 4 pm, cancellation fee imposed, resort fee. **Amenities:** safes. **Dining:** 7 restaurants, also, Ah-nala, see separate listing. **Pool(s):** heated outdoor. **Activities:** hot tub, regulation golf, lawn sports, trails, exercise room, spa. **Guest Services:** valet laundry, area transportation.

THE WESTIN KIERLAND RESORT & SPA
(480)624-1000   13

Resort Hotel
$149-$709

WESTIN
HOTELS & RESORTS

AAA Benefit: Members save up to 15%, plus Starwood Preferred Guest® benefits!

Address: 6902 E Greenway Pkwy 85254 **Location:** 0.5 mi w of Scottsdale Rd. **Facility:** Located adjacent to two high-end shopping areas in North Scottsdale, this upscale resort offers spectacular golf course and mountain views. 732 units. 11 stories, interior corridors. **Parking:** on-site and valet. **Terms:** check-in 4 pm, 7 day cancellation notice-fee imposed, resort fee.

Amenities: safes. **Dining:** 4 restaurants, also, Brittlebush Bar & Grill, Deseo, Nellie Cashman's Monday Club Cafe, see separate listings. **Pool(s):** heated outdoor. **Activities:** sauna, hot tub, steamroom, regulation golf, tennis, recreation programs, kids club, bicycles, playground, lawn sports, trails, exercise room, spa. **Guest Services:** valet laundry, area transportation. *(See ad p. 210.)*

Stay connected with #AAA and #CAA

on your favorite social media sites

(See map & index p. 158.)

THE WESTIN KIERLAND VILLAS   (480)624-1700 🔟

Vacation Rental
Condominium
$159-$659

WESTIN HOTELS & RESORTS **AAA Benefit:** Members save up to 15%, plus Starwood Preferred Guest® benefits!

Address: 15620 N Clubgate Dr 85254 **Location:** Jct Scottsdale Rd, 0.6 mi w on Greenway Pkwy, then just n. **Facility:** Elegant, attractively furnished rooms feature kitchens and balconies or patios, some overlooking the golf course. 298 condominiums. 3-4 stories, exterior corridors. **Terms:** check-in 4 pm, 3 day cancellation notice-fee imposed. **Amenities:** safes. **Pool(s):** heated outdoor. **Activities:** sauna, hot tub, steamroom, regulation golf, tennis, recreation programs, kids club, bicycles, playground, lawn sports, picnic facilities, trails, exercise room, spa. **Guest Services:** valet and coin laundry, area transportation.

SAVE 🍴 🛎 🍸 🧺 🏋 CALL 🕭M 🌊 BIZ HS 📶 ✕ 🛏 📷

W SCOTTSDALE   (480)970-2100 44

Hotel
$149-$909

W HOTELS **AAA Benefit:** Members save up to 15%, plus Starwood Preferred Guest® benefits!

Address: 7277 E Camelback Rd 85251 **Location:** Just e of Scottsdale Rd. **Facility:** This trendy hotel offers a zen garden as well as "whatever-whenever" service levels. Upscale rooms feature attractive bedding and spacious work areas. 230 units. 7 stories, interior corridors. **Parking:** on-site (fee) and valet. **Terms:** cancellation fee imposed. **Amenities:** safes. **Dining:** Sushi Roku, see separate listing. **Pool(s):** heated outdoor. **Activities:** exercise room, spa. **Guest Services:** valet laundry, area transportation.

SAVE 🍴 🛎 🍸 🧺 CALL 🕭M BIZ SHS 📷 ✕ 📽 🛏 /SOME UNITS 🔧

THE SCOTTSDALE PLAZA RESORT   480/948-5000

[fyi] Not evaluated. **Address:** 7200 N Scottsdale Rd 85253 **Location:** Just n of Indian Bend Rd. Facilities, services, and décor characterize an upscale property.

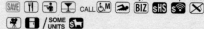

WHERE TO EAT

AHNALA   480/836-5305

▼▼▼▼ Regional Southwestern. Fine Dining. $22-$38 **AAA Inspector Notes:** Attention here is paid to presenting innovative dishes that showcase local ingredients, such as Idaho trout crusted with Fort McDowell pecans. The chef enjoys chatting with diners as well as creating such savory dishes as main lobster empanadas. Ahnala (mesquite grilled) items feature wood obtained from the local Yavapai tribe. **Features:** full bar, patio dining, happy hour. **Reservations:** suggested. **Address:** 10438 N Ft. McDowell Rd 85264 **Location:** Jct Shea Blvd, 1.6 mi ne on SR 87; in We-Ko-Pa Resort & Conference Center. **Parking:** on-site and valet. B L D

ALTO RISTORANTE & BAR   480/444-1234 34

▼▼▼▼ Italian. Casual Dining. $20-$32 **AAA Inspector Notes:** A modern, elegant space, friendly staff and excellent food attract patrons to this dining spot. Enjoy trying the delicate homemade pasta, including ravioli de mozzarella. Desserts range from flavorful sorbets to hearty chocolate hazelnut mousse cake. **Features:** full bar, patio dining. **Address:** 7500 E Doubletree Ranch Rd 85258 **Location:** SR 101 exit 43, 2.6 mi w on Via de Ventura; in Hyatt Regency Scottsdale Resort & Spa at Gainey Ranch. **Parking:** on-site and valet. D

ARCADIA FARMS   480/941-5665 64

▼▼▼ American. Casual Dining. $11-$17 **AAA Inspector Notes:** The cheery garden décor delights guests' eyes in this popular eatery in Old Town Scottsdale. Lush salads, thick sandwiches and desserts tempt any appetite. Patio seating is an option. **Features:** beer & wine. **Reservations:** suggested. **Address:** 7014 E 1st Ave 85251 **Location:** Just w of Scottsdale Rd. **Parking:** valet and street only. B L

ATLAS BISTRO   480/990-2433 75

▼▼▼ International. Fine Dining. $25-$35 **AAA Inspector Notes:** The setting can be described as simple, yet intimate. With an ever-changing menu, diners may see such exotic choices as crispy veal sweetbreads, California squab or Cape Cod skate. The cozy spot is BYOB (Bring Your Own Bottle), but is conveniently attached to a wine shop. **Reservations:** suggested. **Address:** 2515 N Scottsdale Rd 85257 **Location:** Jct Thomas Rd, 0.4 mi s. D

BANDERA   480/994-3524 69

▼▼▼ American. Casual Dining. $14-$41 **AAA Inspector Notes:** Rotisserie chicken and comfort foods are the highlights of this upscale, yet casual spot in the heart of Old Town. Friendly servers make guests feel right at home. **Features:** full bar. **Reservations:** suggested. **Address:** 3821 N Scottsdale Rd 85251 **Location:** Jct 1st St and Scottsdale Rd; in Old Town. **Parking:** street only. D

BLANCO TACOS + TEQUILA   480/305-6692 46

▼▼ Mexican. Casual Dining. $11-$20 **AAA Inspector Notes:** This popular spot serves modern Mexican cuisine in a festive setting. Familiar items like tacos, cheese crisps and burritos are dressed up with fresh, distinctive ingredients. The energetic staff recommends tequilas from the selection of more than 30 premium choices. **Features:** full bar, patio dining, happy hour. **Address:** 6166 N Scottsdale Rd 85253 **Location:** Jct Lincoln Rd, 0.3 mi s. L D

BLT STEAK   480/905-7979 37

▼▼▼ Steak Fine Dining $26-$92

AAA Inspector Notes: Created by chef Laurent Tourondel, this sophisticated steakhouse combines Southwest flavors, outstanding cuts of beef including Kobe strip and Wagyu rib-eye, seafood selections, and seasonings from the restaurant's own organic herb garden. The atmosphere is casual yet elegant, with sweeping views of the mountains. **Features:** full bar, patio dining, happy hour. **Reservations:** suggested. **Address:** 5402 E Lincoln Dr 85253 **Location:** 0.5 mi e of Tatum Blvd; on north side of Lincoln Dr; in JW Marriott Camelback Inn Resort & Spa. **Parking:** on-site and valet. D

BOURBON STEAK   480/513-6002 7

▼▼▼▼ Steak Fine Dining $22-$175

AAA Inspector Notes: Acclaimed chef Michael Mina's Bourbon Steak offers a diverse range of delectable menu selections. Along with the tender Kobe and all-natural USDA Prime beef, diners will find Colorado lamb, Kurobuta pork, Maine lobster, ahi tuna and Scottish salmon, to name a few. An incredible dining experience awaits. **Features:** full bar, patio dining, happy hour. **Reservations:** suggested. **Address:** 7575 E Princess Dr 85255 **Location:** SR 101 exit 34 (Scottsdale Rd), 0.8 mi s, then just e; 0.6 mi n of Bell Rd; in Fairmont Scottsdale Princess. **Parking:** on-site and valet. D CALL 🕭M

THE BREAKFAST CLUB   480/222-2582 58

▼▼ Breakfast. Casual Dining. $6-$16 **AAA Inspector Notes:** Breakfast choices will satisfy any sleepy patron wanting to jump-start the day. Wide-awake staffers quickly serve fresh coffee, eggs of any style, juices and homemade baked goods. Lunch salads and sandwiches are hearty. **Address:** 4400 N Scottsdale Rd 85251 **Location:** Northwest corner of Stetson Dr and Scottsdale Rd. B L

BRITTLEBUSH BAR & GRILL   480/624-1000 17

▼▼ American. Casual Dining. $12-$16 **AAA Inspector Notes:** Dine while overlooking the golf greens at this relaxed eatery located at the golf shop. Friendly service, hearty salads and sandwiches with soups will please everyone. **Features:** full bar, patio dining. **Reservations:** suggested. **Address:** 6902 E Greenway Pkwy 85254 **Location:** 0.5 mi w of Scottsdale Rd; in The Westin Kierland Resort & Spa. **Parking:** on-site and valet. 💳 B L

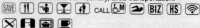

(See map & index p. 158.)

CAFE ZU ZU 480/421-7997 67
▼▼▼ American. Casual Dining. $10-$30 **AAA Inspector Notes:** Chef Wiley delights the palate with such delectable dishes as orange-basted breast of duck or chicken piccata with lemon caper butter. Also on the menu are such comfort foods as meatloaf and macaroni and cheese. The décor is reminiscent of a trendy, upscale version of a 1960s diner. **Features:** full bar, patio dining, Sunday brunch, happy hour. **Address:** 6850 E Main St 85251 **Location:** 0.4 mi w of Scottsdale Rd, just s of Indian School Rd; on north side of Main St; in Hotel Valley Ho. **Parking:** on-site and valet.
B L D CALL M

CANTINA LAREDO 480/951-3807 13
◇◇◇
Mexican
Casual Dining
$10-$25
AAA Inspector Notes: Sophisticated yet relaxed, this eatery features authentic Mexican fare with a creative twist. A great starter is the top-shelf guacamole, which is prepared tableside and primes the palate for the entree. The menu features traditional favorites such as tacos, enchiladas, fajitas, carnitas and chiles rellenos. Also featured are vegetarian and gluten-free dishes. **Features:** full bar, patio dining, Sunday brunch, happy hour. **Address:** 7361 E Frank Lloyd Wright Blvd 85260 **Location:** Just e of Scottsdale Rd. L D

Gourmet Mexican food, fresh-squeezed lime margaritas

THE CAPITAL GRILLE 480/348-1700 12
▼▼▼ Steak. Fine Dining. $11-$49 **AAA Inspector Notes:** Cherry wood and red leather assist in making this clubby dining room a beautiful spot to dine on excellent cuts of dry-aged beef. The staff is highly attentive and knowledgeable. **Features:** full bar, patio dining. **Reservations:** suggested. **Address:** 16489 N Scottsdale Rd 85254 **Location:** SR 101 exit 34 (Scottsdale Rd), 1.5 mi s; in Scottsdale Promenade Shopping Center. **Parking:** on-site and valet.
L D

CARLOS O'BRIENS MEXICAN RESTAURANT 480/367-0469
▼▼ Mexican. Casual Dining. $9-$16 **AAA Inspector Notes:** This family restaurant serves all the classic Mexican favorites: fajitas, enchiladas and Spanish chicken. Attentive servers take guests through the meal, from chips and salsa to the sweet desserts, which are served in ample portions. **Features:** full bar, happy hour. **Address:** 7111 E Bell Rd 85254 **Location:** Just w of Scottsdale Rd.
L D

CARLSBAD TAVERN 480/970-8164 72
▼▼ Southwestern. Casual Dining. $11-$22 **AAA Inspector Notes:** There are no bats here. Instead, guests find great regional dishes served by a helpful staff. A newspaper menu offers horoscopes and fun reading, along with such choices as tequila shrimp and flan with prickly pear sauce. A pond and bridge highlight the outdoor patio area. **Features:** full bar, Sunday brunch, happy hour. **Address:** 3313 N Hayden Rd 85251 **Location:** Just s of Osborn Rd.
L D LATE

CHOLLA PRIME STEAKHOUSE 480/850-7736 77
▼▼▼ Regional Steak. Fine Dining. $10-$29 **AAA Inspector Notes:** This fine-dining establishment has an elegant decor with Native American art adding sparks of color to the soft grays of the quiet room. Specialty items such as barbecue-spiced buffalo tenderloin join beef steaks, seafood and lamb on the menu. Fresh salads and tasty desserts complement any selection. **Features:** full bar. **Reservations:** suggested. **Address:** 524 N 92nd St 85256 **Location:** SR 101 exit 50 (McKellips Rd), just ne; in Casino Arizona. **Parking:** on-site and valet. D CALL M

CITIZEN PUBLIC HOUSE 480/398-4208 62
▼▼▼ American. Gastropub. $12-$38 **AAA Inspector Notes:** Enjoy the upscale and lively atmosphere of this gastro pub featuring an innovative menu with choices including fair trade coffee-charred short ribs and kilt-lifter fondue with hunter's sausage. Wash it all down with a hand-crafted classic cocktail. **Features:** full bar, patio dining, happy hour. **Reservations:** suggested. **Address:** 7111 E 5th Ave 85251 **Location:** Jct Scottsdale Rd, just w. **Parking:** street only.
D

COWBOY CIAO 480/946-3111 59
▼▼▼ American. Casual Dining. $13-$35 **AAA Inspector Notes:** Eclectic, artsy décor sets the stage for fun dining. Among wine-friendly dishes are peppercorn-seared sea bass with pan-fried penne and pig and pudding, a preparation of pulled pork in chipotle and balsamic barbecue sauce over chili grits. Try warm bread pudding or Mexican chocolate pot de crème for a satisfying meal-ender. **Features:** full bar, Sunday brunch. **Reservations:** suggested. **Address:** 7133 E Stetson Dr 85251 **Location:** Just w of Scottsdale Rd; downtown. **Parking:** valet and street only. L D

DESEO 480/624-1202 19
◇◇◇ ◇◇◇
New
Latin American
Fine Dining
$27-$38
AAA Inspector Notes: With influences spanning the Caribbean and South America, expert chefs prepare a savory selection of ceviche, creative seafood entrées and marinated meats. The open kitchen allows for interaction among diners and chefs. Resident Cuban artist Nelson Miranda-Garcia demonstrates his talents five days a week in the dining room, and his work is available for purchase. **Features:** full bar, patio dining, happy hour. **Reservations:** suggested. **Address:** 6902 E Greenway Pkwy 85254 **Location:** 0.5 mi w of Scottsdale Rd; in The Westin Kierland Resort & Spa. **Parking:** on-site and valet.
D

DOMINICK'S STEAKHOUSE 480/272-7271 23
▼▼▼ Steak. Fine Dining. $28-$58 **AAA Inspector Notes:** Elegant surroundings, live music and top-notch steaks set the stage at this North Scottsdale hotspot. Polished servers attend to every need. The rooftop poolside dining area is a distinctive setting for a special occasion. **Features:** full bar, happy hour. **Reservations:** suggested. **Address:** 15169 N Scottsdale Rd 85254 **Location:** Jct Greenway Pkwy, just s; in Scottsdale Quarter. **Parking:** on-site and valet.
D

DON AND CHARLIE'S 480/990-0900 56
▼▼ American. Casual Dining. $12-$43 **AAA Inspector Notes:** This restaurant appeals to the comfort zone with a casual atmosphere, relaxed staff and a varied menu. Sports fans will enjoy the photographs of ball players, signed baseball bats and framed jerseys. Their specialty is barbecue ribs featuring a rich, delicious sauce. Other menu items include broasted chicken and Momo's spaghetti marinara as well as an extensive steak list. Chocolate lovers will delight in the triple-layer cake, served with a gravy boat of chocolate sauce. **Features:** full bar. **Reservations:** suggested. **Address:** 7501 E Camelback Rd 85251 **Location:** Jct Scottsdale Rd, 0.3 mi e. **Parking:** on-site and valet. D

EDDIE V'S PRIME SEAFOOD 480/730-4800 15
▼▼▼ Seafood. Fine Dining. $19-$49 **AAA Inspector Notes:** Fresh seafood, steaks and tempting desserts will please any palate at this upscale dining spot. Seasonal fresh seafood selections might include Gulf snapper, swordfish, Jonah crab and West Australian lobster tails. A flaming butter cake topped with bananas Foster is a festive way to finish. **Features:** full bar, happy hour. **Reservations:** suggested. **Address:** 15323 N Scottsdale Rd 85254 **Location:** Jct Greenway Haven Loop; in Scottsdale Quarter. **Parking:** on-site and valet. D

EVO 480/265-9814 28
▼▼▼ Italian. Casual Dining. $11-$30 **AAA Inspector Notes:** Dark and modern, this cozy spot in Old Town serves eclectic Italian-inspired dishes made with the freshest ingredients. The warm EVO salad is a standout, as are the homemade pastas. **Features:** full bar, happy hour. **Reservations:** suggested. **Address:** 4175 N Goldwater Blvd 85251 **Location:** Jct Indian School Rd, just n; in Old Town. **Parking:** on-site and street. D LATE

Let Your Voice Be Heard

(See map & index p. 158.)

FLEMING'S PRIME STEAKHOUSE & WINE BAR

▼▼▼▼ Steak. Fine Dining. $30-$60 **AAA Inspector Notes:** The warm, clubby atmosphere is the ideal setting for perfectly grilled steaks and seafood. Side dishes come in hearty portions, and salads are fresh and crisp. More than 100 wine selections are available. **Bar:** full bar. D

For additional information, visit AAA.com
LOCATIONS:
Address: 6333 N Scottsdale Rd 85250 **Location:** SR 101 exit 45, 2.1 mi w on McDonald Dr, then 0.3 mi n; adjacent to Hilton Scottsdale Resort & Villas. **Phone:** 480/596-8265 44

Address: 20753 N Pima Rd 85255 **Location:** SR 101 exit 36 (Pima Rd), 2.1 mi n. **Phone:** 480/538-8000 3

F N B RESTAURANT   480/284-4777 63

▼▼▼▼ New American. Casual Dining. $22-$35 **AAA Inspector Notes:** The focus is on fresh, local, quality ingredients. Diners can watch the chef whip up delicious and eclectic comfort food from an ever-changing menu. Try the roasted Jidori chicken with spaetzle and blue lake green beans, or the grilled lamb tenderloin with eggplant, carrots and mint. The wine list features outstanding selections from local wineries. **Features:** full bar, patio dining. **Reservations:** suggested. **Address:** 7125 E 5th Ave 85251 **Location:** Just w of Scottsdale Rd; downtown. **Parking:** valet and street only. L D

THE HERB BOX   480/289-6160 60

▼▼▼▼ American. Casual Dining. $15-$32 **AAA Inspector Notes:** A perfect spot for an upscale lunch date, this country chic spot features garden-fresh salads, homemade soups, and a variety of entrées with a Southwestern flair. **Features:** full bar, patio dining, Sunday brunch, happy hour. **Address:** 7134 E Stetson Dr 85251 **Location:** Jct Scottsdale Rd, just w; in Southbridge District.

L D 🐾

HIRO SUSHI   480/314-4215 79

▼▼ Sushi. Casual Dining. $10-$21 **AAA Inspector Notes:** Tucked away in an unassuming shopping center, this cozy neighborhood sushi spot serves some of the freshest fish around. Fresh crispy tempura, specialty rolls, and nigiri are all expertly made by a father and son team. **Features:** beer & wine. **Address:** 9393 N 90th St 85258 **Location:** SR 101 exit 42, just e. L D

IL TERRAZZO   480/423-2530 47

**Italian
Casual Dining
$14-$34**

AAA Inspector Notes: Upscale Italian dishes boast artisan cheese, handcrafted pasta, the freshest organic vegetables and specially aged olive oil. Guests may dine indoors with a garden view or on the covered terrace. The accomplished staff is friendly and knowledgeable. **Features:** full bar, patio dining, happy hour. **Reservations:** suggested. **Address:** 6000 E Camelback Rd 85251 **Location:** 0.5 mi w of 64th St; in The Phoenician, A Luxury Collection Resort, Scottsdale. **Parking:** on-site and valet.

B L D CALL 🅖M

JADE PALACE   480/391-0607 33

▼▼ Chinese. Casual Dining. $10-$23 **AAA Inspector Notes:** In a strip mall across from the hospital, this restaurant is a friendly place to dine. On the menu are traditional favorites, as well as specialty dinners and healthy choices. Reasonably priced lunches include soup, crab puff, spring roll and fried rice. **Features:** full bar. **Address:** 9160 E Shea Blvd 85260 **Location:** SR 101 exit 41 (Shea Blvd), 0.4 mi e. L D

JADE PALACE   480/585-6630 1

▼▼ Chinese. Casual Dining. $15-$39 **AAA Inspector Notes:** Classic Szechuan and Cantonese dishes are served in this modern, comfortable setting with friendly service. The shrimp with lobster sauce, lemon chicken and spare ribs are crowd favorites. **Features:** full bar, patio dining. **Address:** 23623 N Scottsdale Rd 85255 **Location:** SR 101 exit 34 (Scottsdale Rd), 2.9 mi n. L D

JEWEL OF THE CROWN   480/949-8000 70

▼▼ Indian. Casual Dining. $12-$18 **AAA Inspector Notes:** In a garden setting, this colorfully decorated eatery offers specialties from Goa, India, including fiery vindaloo and a creamy spinach with yogurt sauce to drizzle over chicken or lamb. **Features:** full bar, patio dining. **Reservations:** suggested. **Address:** 7373 E Scottsdale Mall, Suite 1 85251 **Location:** Jct Scottsdale Rd, just e on 2nd St to Wells Fargo Ave, then just n to parking garage; in Scottsdale Civic Center Mall. **Parking:** street only. L D

J&G STEAKHOUSE   480/214-8000 48

**Steak
Fine Dining
$17-$66**

AAA Inspector Notes: The first of many upscale steakhouses from chef Jean-Georges Vongerichten, this restaurant has commanding views of the valley. Fresh, local ingredients combine with premium cuts of meat and global seafood selections to create a memorable experience. **Features:** full bar, patio dining, happy hour. **Reservations:** suggested. **Address:** 6000 E Camelback Rd 85251 **Location:** 0.5 mi w of 64th St; in The Phoenician, A Luxury Collection Resort, Scottsdale. **Parking:** on-site and valet.

D CALL 🅖M

KONA GRILL   480/429-1100 54

▼▼▼▼ Pacific Rim Fusion. Casual Dining. $10-$30 **AAA Inspector Notes:** The eclectic menu reflects Pacific influences. In addition to noodle dishes and sushi, it lists specialties of macadamia nut chicken and lemon grass-encrusted swordfish. The dining room has a large aquarium, a private area and a sushi bar. The patio opens during warm weather. **Features:** full bar, patio dining, happy hour. **Address:** 7014 E Camelback Rd 85251 **Location:** Just w of Scottsdale Rd; in Scottsdale Fashion Square Mall, ground level. L D CALL 🅖M

LA HACIENDA   480/585-4848 9

▼▼▼▼ Mexican. Fine Dining. $12-$31 **AAA Inspector Notes:** Modern Mexican cuisine is served in an upscale, elegant setting. Led by executive chef Richard Sandoval, the culinary team expertly blends creative, bold flavors of the Southwest with traditional European cooking techniques. A certified Tequila specialist is on staff to offer knowledge and suggestions on the close to 200 varieties of in-house tequila. **Features:** full bar, patio dining, happy hour. **Reservations:** suggested. **Address:** 7575 E Princess Dr 85255 **Location:** SR 101 exit 34 (Scottsdale Rd), 0.8 mi s, then just e; 0.6 mi n of Bell Rd; in Fairmont Scottsdale Princess. **Parking:** on-site and valet. D

LING & LOUIE'S ASIAN BAR & GRILL   480/767-5464 78

◆◆ Asian. Casual Dining. $9-$18 **AAA Inspector Notes:** This fun and lively spot offers a modern twist on Asian favorites. Try the sizzling blackened chicken and pork platter or fresh seafood in a hot pot simmering in green coconut curry sauce. **Features:** full bar, patio dining, happy hour. **Address:** 9397 E Shea Blvd 85260 **Location:** Loop 101 exit 41 (Shea Blvd), 0.7 mi e. L D

LOS SOMBREROS   480/994-1799 74

▼▼ Mexican. Casual Dining. $10-$37 **AAA Inspector Notes:** Located in a historic home, this small, colorful Mexican restaurant specializes in authentic Oaxacan cuisine with a French influence. **Features:** full bar, patio dining, happy hour. **Address:** 2534 N Scottsdale Rd 85257 **Location:** Just s of Thomas St. D

LUSH BURGER   480/686-8908 6

▼▼ American. Casual Dining. $8-$12 **AAA Inspector Notes:** Gourmet burgers, shakes and fresh salads are served in a hip, upscale diner setting. The large, shaded patio is perfect for warm weather. **Features:** beer & wine, patio dining. **Address:** 18251 N Pima Rd 85255 **Location:** SR 101 exit 36 (Princess Dr/Pima Rd), 0.5 mi e; in DC Ranch Crossing. L D

MACAYO MEXICAN KITCHEN   480/596-1181

▼▼ Mexican. Casual Dining. $10-$19 **AAA Inspector Notes:** The colorfully furnished Mexican-style eatery prepares Sonoran Mexican dishes. Friendly and efficient staffers serve traditional and lighter dishes flavored with this place's own chili peppers, which are grown near Tucson. **Features:** full bar, happy hour. **Address:** 11107 N Scottsdale Rd 85254 **Location:** Just n of Shea Blvd. L D

(See map & index p. 158.)

MALEE'S THAI ON MAIN   480/947-6042   68

▼▼▼ Regional Thai. Casual Dining. $10-$21 **AAA Inspector Notes:** The food at this casual, popular restaurant is a showcase for interesting combinations of flavors and sauces. Yum woon sen blends chicken, shrimp, cilantro and lime. In the heart of the Old Scottsdale art district, this place also offers patio seating, weather permitting. Staff will happily make suggestions concerning good combinations and flavorful accents. **Features:** full bar, patio dining. **Reservations:** suggested. **Address:** 7131 E Main St 85251 **Location:** Just s of Indian School Rd; just w of Scottsdale Rd; on south side of Main St. **Parking:** street only. L D

MARCELLINO RISTORANTE   480/990-9500   61

▼▼▼ Italian. Fine Dining. $21-$40 **AAA Inspector Notes:** A sophisticated, warm ambience and a helpful, polished staff create a welcoming atmosphere in which to enjoy wonderful homemade pasta dishes, including several with mussels, clams, shrimp or scallops. Veal, chicken, pork and beef round out classic selections that feature special taste twists. For example, the sauteed veal slices are drizzled with a tangy Gorgonzola sauce. **Features:** full bar. **Reservations:** suggested. **Address:** 7114 E Stetson Dr 85251 **Location:** Just w of Scottsdale Rd; downtown. L D

MASTRO'S CITY HALL STEAKHOUSE   480/941-4700   53

▼▼▼ Steak. Fine Dining. $27-$78 **AAA Inspector Notes:** For a purely sophisticated dining experience, it does not get much better than this special occasion steakhouse. Hand-cut USDA Prime steaks are served by an attentive staff that anticipates every need. Live entertainment and dancing create a festive scene in the lounge. **Features:** full bar. **Reservations:** suggested. **Address:** 6991 E Camelback Rd 85251 **Location:** Corner of Goldwater Blvd. **Parking:** on-site and valet. D

MASTRO'S OCEAN CLUB   480/443-8555   16

▼▼▼ Seafood. Fine Dining. $27-$78 **AAA Inspector Notes:** For a purely sophisticated dining experience, it does not get much better than this spot. Perfect for special occasions, this is where the well-heeled go to see and be seen. The freshest seafood selections are served by an attentive and accomplished staff. People watching always is fun in the lounge featuring live entertainment. **Features:** full bar, patio dining. **Reservations:** suggested. **Address:** 15045 N Kierland Blvd 85254 **Location:** Northwest corner of Scottsdale Rd and Greenway Pkwy; in Kierland Commons Shopping Center. **Parking:** on-site and valet. D

MASTRO'S STEAKHOUSE   480/585-9500   2

▼▼▼ Steak. Fine Dining. $27-$90 **AAA Inspector Notes:** For a purely sophisticated dining experience, it does not get much better than this steakhouse. Perfect for special occasions, this is where the well-heeled go to see and be seen. Hand-cut USDA Prime steaks are served by attentive staff that anticipates every need. Live entertainment provides the willing an opportunity to dance. **Features:** full bar, Sunday brunch. **Reservations:** suggested. **Address:** 8852 E Pinnacle Peak Rd 85260 **Location:** SR 101 exit 36 (Pima Rd), 3.7 mi n; in La Mirada Shopping Center. **Parking:** on-site and valet. D

THE MISSION   480/636-5005   71

▼▼▼ Latin American. Casual Dining. $23-$32 **AAA Inspector Notes:** Right in the heart of Old Town, this trendy, casual, and sophisticated hot spot serves modern Latin cuisine featuring such items as crispy cola pork and green chile duck confit. **Features:** full bar, patio dining, Sunday brunch. **Address:** 3815 N Brown Ave 85251 **Location:** In Old Town Scottsdale. L D

NELLIE CASHMAN'S MONDAY CLUB CAFE   480/624-1000   18

▼▼▼▼ New American. Casual Dining. $9-$28 **AAA Inspector Notes:** The namesake's history is worth reading at the comfortable cafe. Casually modern surroundings afford views to the courtyard, and artful dish presentations contribute to an enjoyable dining experience. **Features:** full bar, patio dining, Sunday brunch. **Address:** 6902 E Greenway Pkwy 85254 **Location:** 0.5 mi w of Scottsdale Rd; in The Westin Kierland Resort & Spa. **Parking:** on-site and valet. B L D

NORTH   480/948-2055   21

▼▼▼ New Italian. Casual Dining. $8-$28 **AAA Inspector Notes:** In the trendy Kierland shopping district, this upscale, modern eatery delights palates with fresh, innovative, Italian-based creations. Wood-fired pizza is a nice beginning. **Features:** full bar, patio dining, happy hour. **Address:** 15024 N Scottsdale Rd, #160 85254 **Location:** Just w on Greenway Pkwy; in Kierland Commons. **Parking:** street only. L D 🐾

OCEAN TRAIL   480/850-7777   42

▼▼ Creole. Casual Dining. $17-$20 **AAA Inspector Notes:** Traditional Creole-inspired dishes are made to order in the open air kitchen of this eatery. Diners can watch as chefs prepare spicy gumbo, hand-shucked oysters and other seafood specialties. Open to the casino floor, the atmosphere is loud and lively. **Features:** full bar, senior menu, happy hour. **Address:** 9800 E Indian Bend Rd 85256 **Location:** SR 101 exit 44 (E Indian Bend Rd), just e; in Talking Stick Resort. **Parking:** on-site and valet. L D

OC SEVEN RESTAURANT & BAR   480/991-1571   40

▼▼ American. Casual Dining. $8-$26 **AAA Inspector Notes:** For a casual meal between tennis matches or for an intimate dinner, this bistro offers upscale dishes with regional and Pacific Rim touches. Hearty soups, wrap sandwiches and grilled steaks are among the choices. **Features:** full bar, patio dining, happy hour. **Address:** 8225 E Indian Bend Rd 85250 **Location:** 1.5 mi e of Scottsdale Rd; in Scottsdale Resort & Athletic Club. L D

OLD TOWN TORTILLA FACTORY   480/945-4567   66

▼▼ Mexican. Casual Dining. $15-$33 **AAA Inspector Notes:** Diners can enjoy the expansive outdoor dining patio with fountains and mature plantings at this eatery. Menu items range from traditional enchiladas and tamales to more refined steak and seafood dishes. This place prides itself on its varied margaritas and homemade tortillas. **Features:** full bar, patio dining. **Address:** 6910 E Main St 85251 **Location:** Just w of Goldwater Blvd. D

ORANGE SKY   480/850-7777   41

▼▼▼ Seafood Steak. Fine Dining. $24-$56 **AAA Inspector Notes:** Located on the 15th floor with panoramic views of the valley, this spacious restaurant boasts a modern, yet elegant, interior. Attentive service and a classic menu featuring steaks and seafood is offered. **Features:** full bar, patio dining. **Reservations:** suggested. **Address:** 9800 E Indian Bend Rd 85256 **Location:** SR 101 exit 44 (E Indian Bend Rd), just e; in Talking Stick Resort. **Parking:** on-site and valet. D

OREGANO'S PIZZA BISTRO   480/348-0500

▼▼ Italian Pizza. Casual Dining. $7-$15 **AAA Inspector Notes:** This high-energy eatery, with its young and attentive waitstaff, serves hearty, over-sized portions of delicious pizza, salads, pasta and baked sandwiches. The patio is the happening spot. **Features:** wine only, patio dining. **Address:** 7215 E Shea Blvd 85260 **Location:** Just e of Scottsdale Rd. L D

OVER EASY CAFE   480/270-3447   14

▼▼ American. Casual Dining. $6-$16 **AAA Inspector Notes:** On weekends, prepare to wait for a table at this very popular breakfast and lunch spot featuring comfort foods including chicken fried steak, jalapeño cheddar biscuits with sausage gravy and home-made corned beef hash. **Address:** 9375 E Bell Rd 85260 **Location:** Loop 101 northbound exit 38, 1.2 mi n on Pima Rd, then 0.5 mi e; Loop 101 southbound exit 36, 0.4 mi s on Pima Rd, then 0.5 mi e. B L

PATSY GRIMALDI'S COAL BRICK-OVEN PIZZERIA

▼▼ Pizza. Casual Dining. $9-$18 **AAA Inspector Notes:** Fresh ingredients and a coal-fired brick oven are the features at this New York-style pizzeria. Diners can enjoy pizza, salads and calzones all served in a lively atmosphere. **Bar:** beer & wine.

L D

For additional information, visit AAA.com

LOCATIONS:

Address: 4000 N Scottsdale Rd 85251 **Location:** Jct Indian School Rd, just s. **Phone:** 480/994-1100

Address: 20715 N Pima Rd, Suite F115 85255 **Location:** SR 101 exit 36 (Pima Rd), 2 mi n; in Village at Market Street. **Phone:** 480/515-5588

(See map & index p. 158.)

PERSIAN ROOM
480/614-1414 [11]

WWWW Middle Eastern. Fine Dining. $9-$35 AAA Inspector Notes: The owner's classic, traditionally prepared Persian dishes include marinated chicken shish kebab, koobideh kebab (ground beef) and dolma (stuffed grape leaves). Fragrant jasmine rice and crisp salads with the house yogurt dressing complete meals, which the owner puts together in classic presentations with large sprigs of fresh basil and mint along with slices of mild onion to cleanse the palate. Gilt-accented columns enhance the elegant dining room. **Features:** full bar, patio dining, happy hour. **Address:** 17040 N Scottsdale Rd 85255 **Location:** Jct Bell Rd, just n. [L] [D] [🏠]

P.F. CHANG'S CHINA BISTRO

WWW Chinese. Fine Dining. $8-$25 AAA Inspector Notes: Trendy, upscale decor provides a pleasant backdrop for New Age Chinese dining. Appetizers, soups and salads are a meal by themselves. Vegetarian plates and sides, noodles, chow meins, chicken and meat dishes are created from exotic, fresh ingredients. **Bar:** full bar. [L] [D]

For additional information, visit AAA.com

LOCATIONS:
Address: 7135 E Camelback Rd, Suite 101 85251
Location: Southwest corner of Scottsdale Rd.
Phone: 480/949-2610 [52]
Address: 7132 E Greenway Pkwy 85254 **Location:** 1 mi s of Bell Rd at Scottsdale Rd; in Kierland Commons.
Phone: 480/367-2999 [22]

PIÑON GRILL
480/948-5050 [35]

WWW Southwestern. Casual Dining. $15-$40 AAA Inspector Notes: Two seating options are offered at this grill—the intimate dining room or the patio which affords a view over the lake to the golf course. Distinctive Southwestern Rim preparations of chicken, seafood, veal, steak and wild game are accompanied by succulent vegetables and sauces. **Features:** full bar, patio dining, happy hour. **Reservations:** suggested. **Address:** 7401 N Scottsdale Rd 85253 **Location:** 0.8 mi n of Indian Bend Rd; in The McCormick Scottsdale. **Parking:** on-site and valet. [B] [L] [D]

PITA JUNGLE
480/922-7482 [27]

WW Mediterranean. Casual Dining. $7-$16 AAA Inspector Notes: A casual atmosphere envelops the dining area and large patio. The menu offers a wide variety of hot and cold pita wraps, pizza, falafel, spanakopita, salads and burgers, as well as natural, healthful vegetarian offerings. The red pepper hummus is a great starter, with a light delicate flavor. **Features:** full bar, patio dining, happy hour. **Address:** 7366 E Shea Blvd 85260 **Location:** Just e of jct Scottsdale Rd; in Shea Scottsdale East Plaza. [L] [D]

POSH IMPROVISATIONAL CUISINE
480/663-7674 [51]

WWW WWW International. Fine Dining. $50-$140 AAA Inspector Notes: Diners will not see a menu at this chic dining spot, but what they will see is amazingly creative dishes, presented beautifully, in a modern and elegant setting. Chef Joshua Hebert creates improvisational tasting menus based on exotic, market-fresh ingredients tailored to the preferences of each patron. A sampling of dishes may include Kobe beef with pickled ramps, halibut cheeks with lemon aioli or mushroom braised veal. Desserts are equally impressive. **Features:** full bar. **Reservations:** suggested. **Address:** 7167 E Rancho Vista Dr, Suite 111 85251 **Location:** Jct Scottsdale Rd, just w. **Parking:** on-site and valet. [D]

PRESTON'S STEAKHOUSE
480/629-5087 [25]

WWW Steak. Fine Dining. $28-$79 AAA Inspector Notes: The upscale steakhouse features premium cuts of meat, fresh seafood and locally sourced ingredients. The atmosphere is comfortable and classy, with a fireplace inside and excellent sunset views outside. Service is professional and personalized. **Features:** full bar. **Reservations:** suggested. **Address:** 8700 E Pinnacle Peak Rd 85255 **Location:** Loop 101 exit 36 (Pima Rd), 3.7 mi n to Pinnacle Peak Rd; northwest corner. [D]

PURE SUSHI BAR & DINING
480/355-0999 [4]

WWW WW Japanese Sushi. Casual Dining. $12-$26 AAA Inspector Notes: Chic and modern, this neighborhood spot is known for fresh sushi selections, along with specialty rolls, soups and noodle dishes. Try the creamy baked lobster roll; it will not disappoint. **Features:** full bar, patio dining, happy hour. **Reservations:** suggested. **Address:** 20567 N Hayden Rd 85255 **Location:** Loop 101 exit 35 (Hayden Rd), just n. [L] [D]

RANCHO PINOT
480/367-8030 [45]

WWWW American. Fine Dining. $22-$31 AAA Inspector Notes: Taking advantage of seasonally fresh items here as the menu changes frequently to bring diners an excellent variety of fresh meat, poultry and seafood. The high-energy dining room looks into the open kitchen, where chefs use a mesquite grill for many of the dishes. **Features:** full bar. **Reservations:** suggested. **Address:** 6208 N Scottsdale Rd 85253 **Location:** Just s of Lincoln Dr; in Lincoln Plaza Shopping Center. [D]

RA SUSHI BAR RESTAURANT
480/990-9256

WWW Japanese Sushi. Casual Dining. $6-$20 AAA Inspector Notes: Fresh sushi creations are the specialty at this busy, bistro-style restaurant. Crunchy tempura is available for the less daring. Artful, tasty creations can be accented with seaweed, squid salad or rice. **Features:** full bar, patio dining, happy hour. **Address:** 3815 N Scottsdale Rd 85251 **Location:** Corner of 1st St; in historic downtown. **Parking:** on-site and valet. [L] [D]

RA SUSHI BAR RESTAURANT
480/951-5888

WWW Japanese Sushi. Casual Dining. $6-$20 AAA Inspector Notes: Fresh sushi creations are the specialty at this busy, bistro-style restaurant. Crunchy tempura is available for the less daring. Artful, tasty creations can be accented with seaweed, squid salad or rice. **Features:** full bar, patio dining, happy hour. **Address:** 7012 E Greenway Pkwy, Suite 100 85254 **Location:** SR 101 exit 34 (Scottsdale Rd), 2.5 mi s, then just w; in Kierland Commons. **Parking:** on-site and street. [L] [D]

RAZZ'S RESTAURANT
480/905-1308 [31]

WWW WW New American. Casual Dining. $24-$38 AAA Inspector Notes: An eclectic menu with French, Asian and many other influences makes for a unique dining experience. The menu features items like pork tenderloin schnitzel, spicy bouillabaisse, and a tracoe-roasted duck breast with lingonberry sauce. The attentive staff is very helpful with selections. **Features:** full bar. **Reservations:** suggested. **Address:** 10315 N Scottsdale Rd 85254 **Location:** Southeast corner of Shea Blvd and Scottsdale Rd. [D]

REMINGTON'S
480/951-5101 [36]

WWW American. Casual Dining. $13-$30 AAA Inspector Notes: Favorites on this restaurant's menu include USDA Prime cuts of beef, mesquite-grilled chicken and braised veal osso buco. The well-trained staff assists with any celebration or casual dinner. Patio dining is available weather permitting. **Features:** full bar, patio dining, happy hour. **Address:** 7200 N Scottsdale Rd 85253 **Location:** Just n of Indian Bend Rd; in The Scottsdale Plaza Resort. [L] [D]

ROARING FORK
480/947-0795 [49]

WWWW Western American. Casual Dining. $13-$34 AAA Inspector Notes: Known for its excellent, award-winning food by chef McGrath, this restaurant is a repeated recipient of the notable James Beard award. Its spacious, upscale dining room is ideal for any special occasion. Service is consistently friendly and accomplished, and the salmon cooked campfire-style is among the signature dishes. **Features:** full bar, patio dining, happy hour. **Reservations:** suggested. **Address:** 4800 N Scottsdale Rd, Suite 1700 85251 **Location:** Southwest corner of Chaparral and Scottsdale rds. [D]

RUBIO'S FRESH MEXICAN GRILL

WWW Mexican. Quick Serve. $4-$10 AAA Inspector Notes: Freshly prepared and healthful foods, bright decor and friendly staff are found in this upscale fast-food spot. A special treat, the salsa bar lines up four styles and flavors. **Bar:** beer only. [L] [D]

For additional information, visit AAA.com

LOCATIONS:
Address: 32415 N Scottsdale Rd 85262 **Location:** Just n of Asher Hills Rd; in Target Plaza. **Phone:** 480/575-7280
Address: 15705 N Pima Rd 85260 **Location:** SR 101 exit 38 (Frank Lloyd Wright Blvd), just w, then just s. **Phone:** 480/348-0195

(See map & index p. 158.)

RUTH'S CHRIS STEAK HOUSE   480/991-5988   **39**

🔻🔻🔻 Steak. Fine Dining. $31-$40 **AAA Inspector Notes:** The main fare is steak, which is prepared from several cuts of Prime beef and cooked to perfection, but the menu also lists lamb, chicken and seafood dishes. Guests should come hungry because the side dishes, which are among the a la carte offerings, could make a meal in themselves. **Features:** full bar, happy hour. **Reservations:** suggested. **Address:** 7001 N Scottsdale Rd 85253 **Location:** Northeast corner of Scottsdale and Indian Bend rds; in Seville Shopping Center. **D**

THE SALT CELLAR RESTAURANT   480/947-1963   **76**

🔻🔻🔻 Seafood. Casual Dining. $30-$75 **AAA Inspector Notes:** This popular, underground cellar displays marine motif prints and carries a large selection of seafood which is flown in daily, as well as the turf to accompany it. The energetic waitstaff is knowledgeable and will offer to crack crabs table-side. The restaurant has been in this location for more than three decades. **Features:** full bar, happy hour. **Reservations:** suggested. **Address:** 550 N Hayden Rd 85257 **Location:** Jct McDowell Rd, just s. **D**

SAPPORO   480/607-1114   **26**

🔻🔻🔻🔻 Japanese. Casual Dining. $11-$45 **AAA Inspector Notes:** Seated amid a trendy decor with waterfalls and jellyfish tanks, diners can indulge their whims for sushi and Pacific Rim foods. The knowledgeable waitstaff provides guidance through a large selection of fish and Kobe beef. **Features:** full bar, patio dining, happy hour. **Reservations:** suggested. **Address:** 14344 N Scottsdale Rd 85254 **Location:** Just n of Thunderbird Rd. **L D**

SASSI RISTORANTE   480/502-9095

💎💎💎💎

Southern
Italian
Fine Dining
$28-$38

AAA Inspector Notes: Set high in the desert foothills, this Tuscan-style villa is the perfect setting for any special occasion or romantic dinner. Take in the magnificent views while enjoying fresh and creative menu options inspired by Southern Italian cooking such as handmade ricotta gnocchi with wild mushroom ragu and vanilla bean panna cotta with cherry reduction. **Features:** full bar, patio dining, happy hour. **Reservations:** suggested. **Address:** 10455 E Pinnacle Peak Pkwy 85255 **Location:** SR 101 exit 36 (Pima Rd), 4.7 mi n, 2 mi e on Happy Valley Rd, 1 mi n on Alma School Rd, then just e. **Parking:** on-site and valet. **D**

SAUCE   480/321-8800

🔻🔻 Italian. Quick Serve. $6-$11 **AAA Inspector Notes:** This restaurant's selections could be characterized as gourmet fast food. Among choices are sausage and caramelized onion or chicken and broccoli rabe pizza, as well as fresh salads and lasagna. Clean, modern decor makes for a fun dining experience. Diners can sit indoors or on a patio. **Features:** beer & wine, patio dining. **Address:** 14418 N Scottsdale Rd 85254 **Location:** Just n of Thunderbird Rd; in Thunderbird Square. **L D**

SHINBAY   480/664-0180   **38**

🔻🔻🔻 Japanese. Casual Dining. $16-$30 **AAA Inspector Notes:** Discreetly tucked away in the back of a shopping center, this intimate spot specializes in omakase, or chef's choice tasting menus. Very fresh, exotic ingredients like grouper carpaccio, kusshi oysters, Madagascar prawns and sea urchin are highlighted with delicate sauces and artful presentations. **Features:** beer & wine. **Address:** 7001 N Scottsdale Rd 85253 **Location:** Northeast corner of Scottsdale and Indian Bend rds; in Scottsdale Seville Shopping Center. **D CALL 🅼**

SQUID INK SUSHI   480/922-5566   **30**

🔻🔻 Sushi. Casual Dining. $11-$25 **AAA Inspector Notes:** The sleek modern interior of this restaurant opens to an expansive patio area—the perfect place to enjoy the music and energetic atmosphere. Fresh sushi, sashimi, rolls and yakitori selections are enhanced by a creative cocktail list. **Features:** full bar, patio dining, happy hour. **Reservations:** suggested. **Address:** 7318 E Shea Blvd 85260 **Location:** Jct Scottsdale Rd and Shea Blvd. **L D**

STAX BURGER BISTRO   480/946-4222   **57**

🔻🔻 🔻🔻 American. Casual Dining. $4-$7 **AAA Inspector Notes:** This tiny modern hot spot features sliders with such exotic meats as kangaroo, antelope and wild boar. Mix and match the sliders, then add a loaded macaroni and cheese for a tasty side. **Features:** full bar, happy hour. **Address:** 4400 N Scottsdale Rd, Suite 12 85251 **Location:** Just s of Camelback Rd; in Old Town. **L D**

STINGRAY SUSHI   480/427-2011   **24**

🔻🔻🔻 Sushi. Casual Dining. $13-$30 **AAA Inspector Notes:** Bright colors and lively music set the stage at this sushi spot attracting a younger, trendy crowd enjoying a large selection of sushi, salads, bento and tasty main courses. Creative rolls, like the Godzilla and the lollipop are packed with fresh ingredients and topped with creative glazes such as sweet eel or unagi (freshwater eel). **Features:** full bar, patio dining, happy hour. **Address:** 15027 N Scottsdale Rd 85260 **Location:** SR 101 exit 34 (Scottsdale Rd), 2.2 mi s; in Scottsdale Quarter. **Parking:** on-site and valet. **L D LATE 🐕**

SUMO MAYA MEXICAN ASIAN KITCHEN   480/397-9520   **43**

🔻🔻🔻 Fusion. Casual Dining. $10-$30 **AAA Inspector Notes:** The distinctive blending of Mexican and Asian influences creates an exciting culinary experience at this high-energy hot spot. The distinctive fusion menu incorporates sushi, street-style tacos and noodle and rice dishes, along with salsa, guacamole and ceviche—a little something for everyone. **Features:** full bar, patio dining, happy hour. **Address:** 6560 N Scottsdale Rd 85253 **Location:** Northwest corner of Scottsdale and Lincoln rds. **Parking:** on-site and valet. **L D**

SUSHI ON SHEA   480/483-7799   **29**

🔻🔻 Japanese. Casual Dining. $8-$35 **AAA Inspector Notes:** This fun, casually elegant restaurant includes two saltwater aquariums and an expansive sushi bar. Patrons can enjoy fresh sushi, tempura, noodles and specialty dishes, such as sesame-crusted salmon or chicken katsu. **Features:** full bar. **Address:** 7000 E Shea Blvd, #1510 85254 **Location:** Just w of Scottsdale Rd. **L D**

SUSHI ROKU   480/970-2121   **55**

🔻🔻🔻 Japanese. Casual Dining. $10-$35 **AAA Inspector Notes:** Seating at this spot is available in the chic, contemporary dining room or on the casual, second-floor poolside lounge area. The menu features a wide mix of skillfully prepared sushi as well as tempura, teriyaki and grilled meat selections. **Features:** full bar, patio dining, happy hour. **Reservations:** suggested. **Address:** 7277 E Camelback Rd 85251 **Location:** Just e of Scottsdale Rd; in W Scottsdale. **Parking:** on-site (fee) and valet. **B L D**

TAGGIA   480/945-7666   **50**

🔻🔻🔻 Italian. Casual Dining. $15-$32 **AAA Inspector Notes:** This bistro prepares coastal Italian food using the freshest seafood, local and organic vegetables and homemade pasta. The chef may circulate through the dining room, checking on tables. Innovative desserts include the trio of brûlée with vanilla, chocolate and orange. **Features:** full bar, patio dining, happy hour. **Reservations:** suggested. **Address:** 4925 N Scottsdale Rd 85251 **Location:** Southeast corner of Scottsdale and Chaparral rds; in FireSky Resort & Spa, A Kimpton Hotel. **Parking:** on-site and valet. **B L D**

TAKEDA THAI   480/483-5006   **32**

🔻🔻 Thai. Casual Dining. $14-$43 **AAA Inspector Notes:** Delicious curry and noodle dishes, along with many Thai specialties, are served in this intimate, sophisticated spot tucked away in an unassuming shopping center. **Features:** full bar, patio dining. **Address:** 10271 N Scottsdale Rd 85253 **Location:** Southeast corner of Scottsdale Rd and Shea Blvd. **L D**

(See map & index p. 158.)

TALAVERA   480/513-5086

▼▼▼▼ ▼▼▼▼
American
Fine Dining
S28-S72

AAA Inspector Notes: Chefs Mecinas and Goldstein have created a forum for dining that is exceptional. Using the freshest ingredients and specialty items, they offer Arizona grass-fed and Australian Wagyu beef prepared with regional flavors such as chorizo bread pudding and chipotle honeycomb polenta. Tasting menus change weekly. **Features:** full bar, patio dining. **Reservations:** suggested. **Address:** 10600 E Crescent Moon Dr 85262 **Location:** SR 101 exit 36 (Pima Rd), 4.7 mi n, 2 mi e on Happy Valley Rd, then 1.5 mi n on Alma School Rd; in Four Seasons Resort Scottsdale at Troon North. **Parking:** valet only. [D] CALL [&M]

TOMMY V'S URBAN KITCHEN AND BAR   480/427-2264 (65)

▼▼▼▼ Italian. Casual Dining. $15-$26 **AAA Inspector Notes:** Sleek and sophisticated, this Old Town eatery makes a splash with such dishes as the popular pasta trio plate, and the mushroom risotto with roasted shallots, truffle and toasted hazelnuts. The attentive staff is helpful with selections and wine pairings. **Address:** 7303 E Indian School Rd 85251 **Location:** Jct Scottsdale Rd, just e. [L] [D] [🐾]

TORO   480/585-4848 (8)

▼▼▼▼ Latin American Small Plates Fusion. Gastropub. $22-$39 **AAA Inspector Notes:** Overlooking the 18th green at TPC golf course, this restaurant offers beautiful views. Wonderful flavor profiles combine varying textures and tastes. The lamb antichucho skewers are an excellent example with a crunchy cucumber/onion relish and yogurt dipping sauce. **Features:** full bar, patio dining, happy hour. **Reservations:** suggested. **Address:** 7575 E Princess Dr 85253 **Location:** SR 101 exit 34 (Scottsdale Rd), 0.8 mi s, then just e; 0.6 mi n of Bell Rd; in Fairmont Scottsdale Princess. [B] [L] [D] [🐾]

TOTTIE'S ASIAN FUSION   480/970-0633 (73)

▼▼ ▼▼ Asian. Casual Dining. $8-$14 **AAA Inspector Notes:** Authentic Thai, Vietnamese, Laotian and Chinese styles of cooking can all be found at this casual and friendly eatery. In the evenings, the sushi bar adds another dimension to the already vast array of menu options. **Features:** full bar. **Address:** 7901 E Thomas Rd 85251 **Location:** Southwest corner of Hayden and Thomas rds. [L] [D]

TRUE FOOD KITCHEN   480/265-4500 (10)

▼▼ ▼▼ American. Casual Dining. $10-$20 **AAA Inspector Notes:** The focus here is on healthy, well-balanced food with many vegetarian and gluten-free options. The trendy, colorful setting is perfect for a leisurely lunch while out shopping. Try one of the fresh-pressed fruit and vegetable elixirs—they are delicious. **Features:** full bar. **Address:** 15191 N Scottsdale Rd 85254 **Location:** SR 101 exit 34 (Scottsdale Rd), 2.5 mi s; in Scottsdale Quarter. **Parking:** on-site and valet. [L] [D]

THE WHITE CHOCOLATE GRILL   480/563-3377 (5)

▼▼▼▼ American. Casual Dining. $11-$28 **AAA Inspector Notes:** This popular contemporary American dining spot features a diverse menu with fresh chopped salads, gourmet sandwiches and burgers, fresh seafood and wood-grilled steaks. Do not miss the famous desserts, most of which feature white chocolate. **Features:** full bar, patio dining, happy hour. **Reservations:** suggested. **Address:** 7000 E Mayo Blvd 85251 **Location:** SR 101 exit 34 (Scottsdale Rd), just s, then just w; in Scottsdale 101 Shopping Center. [L] [D]

ZINC BISTRO   480/603-0922 (20)

▼▼▼▼ French. Casual Dining. $10-$36 **AAA Inspector Notes:** This French bistro prepares steak, roasted pork, lamb, chicken, seafood and some pasta dishes. A nice selection of salads and sandwiches appeals to those who want a lighter meal. **Features:** full bar, patio dining, Sunday brunch. **Address:** 15034 N Scottsdale Rd, Suite 140 85254 **Location:** Just w of jct N Scottsdale Rd and Greenway-Hayden Loop; in Kierland Commons. **Parking:** street only. [L] [D] [🐾]

DU JOUR RESTAURANT   480/603-1066

[fyi] Not evaluated. This is the on-campus training facility for students of the Arizona Culinary Institute. The dining room overlooks the bakery kitchen where mouthwatering goodies are prepared. **Address:** 10585 N 114th St 85251 **Location:** Jct Shea Blvd, just s on 116th St.

SECOND MESA (B-5) pop. 962, elev. 5,680'

Second Mesa, near the junction of SRs 264 and 87, is within a Hopi Reservation that occupies a large tract in the center of the vast Navajo Reservation of northeastern Arizona. The mesa is home to three Hopi villages: Shungopavi, where most of the tribe's religious and ceremonial activities originated; Sipaulovi, the last village founded after the Pueblo Revolt of 1680; and Mishongnovi. Resident basketmakers specialize in coiled basketry, which involves wrapping, weaving and stitching colorful grasses and yucca together.

HOPI CULTURAL CENTER MUSEUM, 5 mi. w. of SR 87 on SR 264, displays basketry, weaving, jewelry and other artifacts depicting the history of the Hopi. Kachina dolls, representations of divine ancestral spirits, also are featured. **Time:** Allow 1 hour minimum. **Hours:** Mon.-Fri. 8-5, Sat.-Sun. 9-3. **Cost:** $3; $1 (ages 0-13). **Phone:** (928) 734-6650.

SEDONA (C-4) pop. 10,031, elev. 4,400'
• Hotels p. 228 • Restaurants p. 235
• Hotels & Restaurants map & index p. 225

Sedona is nestled between the massive, fire-hued rocks of Red Rock State Park and the lush gorges of Oak Creek Canyon *(see attraction listing p. 221)*. The dusty, semi-arid topography is the base for giant, striped monoliths that take on shades from bright red to pale sand and seem to change color with each passing cloud or ray of sunshine. Since most of the rock is sedimentary, the portrait is constantly eroding and changing shape. Verdant Oak Creek Canyon, with juniper and cypress trees lining a clear stream, provides a sharp contrast.

So prominent are the buttes and pinnacles that locals have named them. Some of the more popular rock stars are Bell Rock, Cathedral Rock, Chimney Rock, Coffeepot Rock, Courthouse Butte and Snoopy Rock. Formations in the shape of a castle or merry-go-round also can be spotted. Conveniently, two nuns overlook a chapel. And close by, a submarine surfaces near a mushroom cap.

Sedona's rugged red rocks and canyons have even shared the screen with Hollywood movie stars. The area has served as a backdrop for dozens of Western movies. Some popular titles filmed here include "Angel and the Badman," "Broken Arrow," "Firecreek," "Midnight Run" and "The Quick and the Dead."

Mother Nature was kind to Sedona, blessing her with sharp light, bright blue skies, colorful terrain, picturesque sunsets and animated clouds. Inspired painters, sculptors and other creative souls flocked to Sedona and now call the area home. In 1965 the Cowboy Artists of America, a successful art organization, was founded in what is now Uptown; its goals remain to ensure accurate portrayal of Western scenes in art. An established art colony, Sedona boasts ubiquitous galleries and studios that display residents' artistic endeavors: Pottery, sculpture, paintings and jewelry embody a variety of styles, from Western and Southwestern to modern.

Tlaquepaque Arts and Crafts Village, on SR 179 just south of SR 89A, is a shopping village modeled after a small Mexican village. Notable for its architectural features alone, it houses a theater, a collection of galleries and restaurants as well as a chapel; musicians often perform in the courtyards.

Alongside artists live spiritualists, who embrace the energy set forth by such natural splendor. Sedona is purportedly home to several vortices, specific fields that emit energy upward or inward from or to the earth. First channeled and defined by Page Bryant in 1980, a vortex is said to emanate three types of energy: electrical (masculine), magnetic (feminine) or electromagnetic (neutral). Found at various locations, these natural power fields are thought to energize and inspire.

Sedona is said to contain a curiously high number of vortexes and is one of the few places in the world that possesses all three types of energy. Countless businesses in Sedona specialize in alternative medicine, and many offer vortex or spiritual tours. Visitors may find vortexes at Bell Rock, Cathedral Rock and Boynton Canyon. At Airport Mesa, the attraction is twofold: Guests may locate an electric force as well as a great spot from which to view a spectacular sunset.

The town received its name in 1902 from T. Carl Schnebly, one of the first settlers in the area. Schnebly wanted to establish a post office, yet both names he submitted to the postmaster general—Schnebly Station and Oak Creek Crossing—were deemed too long for a cancellation stamp. At the suggestion of his brother, he suggested his wife's name, and it stuck.

The Schneblys weren't the first ones to reside in Sedona. Ancient cliff dwellings found in the area were constructed by the Southern Sinagua people (Spanish for "without water") around A.D. 1130-1300. Two of the largest cliff dwellings, Honanki and Palatki *(see attraction listings)*, still retain a number of pictographs in the shapes of animals, people and various designs.

Sedona is the starting point for hikes and scenic drives through the Red Rock Country. From the vista point on the Mogollon Rim to Sedona, Oak Creek Canyon Drive (SR 89A) winds through the canyon, offering a continuous display of natural beauty, including the area's signature colored rock formations as well as sudden changes in vegetation. Oak Creek flows between 1,200-foot-tall canyon walls toward the red rocks of Sedona.

A Red Rock Pass is required for parking when visiting or hiking the many scenic areas in Sedona. Passes may be purchased at the Sedona Chamber of Commerce. A daily pass is $5; a weekly pass is $15. Federal Inter-agency passes are available at self-serve machines at various trailheads, at the Sedona Chamber of Commerce Visitor Center, the Red Rock Ranger Station Visitor Center and Oak Creek Overlook. Some restrictions may apply.

Red Rock Country is just the spot for an exhilarating, hang-on-tight jeep adventure. Guided tours of the backcountry are offered by Red Rock Western Jeep Tours; phone (928) 282-6826 or (800) 848-7728.

Great West Adventure Co. provides transportation and tours to the Grand Canyon and the Hopi Reservation as well as scenic tours of Sedona via 14-passenger buses; Colorado River rafting trips also are available. Phone (928) 204-5506 or (877) 367-2383.

Sedona Chamber of Commerce and Tourism Bureau: 331 Forest Rd., Sedona, AZ 86336. **Phone:** (928) 282-7722 or (800) 288-7336.

Shopping: Art galleries and restaurants intermingle with specialty shops at Tlaquepaque Arts and Crafts Village, just south of Uptown on SR 179. Oakcreek Factory Outlets, 7 miles south on SR 179, offers 16 outlet stores. Other areas featuring galleries and shops are Hillside Sedona, Hozho Center and along SR 89A near the Village of Oak Creek.

ARIZONA HELICOPTER ADVENTURES, departing from the Sedona Airport, offers a variety of in-flight, narrated sightseeing tours of Sedona and environs,

(See map & index p. 225.)

including the Native American ruins of Boynton Canyon and the area's scenic red rock formations. **Hours:** Daily 9-5. Length of tours varies. Closed Christmas. **Cost:** $115-$265; $95-$245 (ages 2-11). Reservations are recommended. **Phone:** (928) 282-0904 or (800) 282-5141.

ARIZONA SAFARI JEEP TOURS, .3 mi. n. of jct. SRs 179 and 89A to 335 Jordan Rd., offers a variety of tours of Sedona, the Colorado Plateau and the Sonoran Desert. All tours include narration by educated guides with backgrounds in biology, geology and game and range management; hands-on animal demonstrations are featured. **Time:** Allow 2 hours minimum. **Hours:** Daily dawn-dusk. **Cost:** $39-$199; $35.75-$145 (ages 0-12). **Phone:** (928) 282-3012.

CHAPEL OF THE HOLY CROSS, .8 mi. s. off SR 179 on Chapel Rd., stands on a small mountain that provides scenic views. The contemporary Catholic shrine is constructed on the area's noted red rock. Built in 1956, the chapel is between two large red sandstone peaks with a ramp leading to the entrance. A 90-foot cross dominates the structure. **Time:** Allow 30 minutes minimum. **Hours:** Daily 9-6, Apr.-Oct.; 9-5, rest of year. **Cost:** Free. **Phone:** (928) 282-4069.

A DAY IN THE WEST JEEP TOURS is at 252 N. SR 89A, .3 mi. n.e. from jct. SR 179. Comprehensive

▼ See AAA listing p. 223 ▼

(See map & index p. 225.)
jeep tours of Sedona's red rock canyons, rock formations and trails are offered. Guides in old-fashioned cowboy garb dispense photography tips and provide information about local animals, geology, history and vegetation. Winery tours and horseback rides also are offered.

Note: Comfortable walking shoes are recommended. Inquire about weather policies. **Time:** Allow 1 hour minimum. **Hours:** Tours daily 8-dusk. **Cost:** $55-$85; $43-$65 (ages 18 months-12 years). Ages 0-18 months and pregnant women are not permitted. Reservations are recommended. **Phone:** (928) 282-4320 or (800) 973-3662. 🍴

GREAT VENTURE TOURS, with pickup from hotels in Phoenix, Sedona and Flagstaff, offers narrated coach tours into the south rim of the Grand Canyon. Highlights include the Painted Desert and the Navajo Indian Reservation. Colorado River float trips and white-water adventures also are offered; phone for information. **Hours:** Daily 7-7. Phone ahead to confirm schedule. **Cost:** $44-$599; $37-$599 (ages 3-15). Fares may vary; phone ahead to confirm. Reservations are required. **Phone:** (928) 282-4451 or (800) 578-2643.

HONANKI SOUTHERN SINAGUA CLIFF DWELLINGS, 9 mi. s.w. on SR 89A to Milepost 365, .5 mi. s. to FR 525, then 10.2 mi. n. via FR 525 (a dirt road), is one of the largest ruins of Southern Sinagua cliff dwellings in the Red Rock area; occupation is estimated A.D. 1100-1300. The earliest pictographs on the rock walls predate Sinagua habitation.

Note: Phone the Red Rock Ranger District, (928) 203-7500, for information about road conditions prior to visiting the site. **Hours:** Daily 9:30-5:30. Closed Jan. 1, Thanksgiving and Christmas. **Cost:** A Red Rock Pass (Day Pass $5, Weekly Pass $15 or Annual Pass $20) is required for admission. National Federal Pass also accepted. **Phone:** (928) 282-4119.

OAK CREEK CANYON, n. on SR 89A, is traversed by a scenic stretch of that road. About 16 miles long and rarely more than 1 mile wide, the canyon is known for its spectacularly colored white, yellow and red cliffs dotted with pine, cypress and juniper. Rocky gorges, unusual rock formations and buttes add interest to the drive.

Oak Creek is noted for trout fishing; throughout the canyon are Forest Service camping and picnicking grounds. Area maps are available from the chambers of commerce in Flagstaff and Sedona.

PALATKI RUINS AND RED CLIFFS ROCK ART SITE is 9 mi. s. on SR 89A, then 8 mi. n. via FRs 525 and 795 (dirt roads), following signs. Pictographs dating from the Archaic period of Native American culture are preserved in rock alcoves. It is believed that nearby cliff dwellings were occupied A.D. 1100-1300 by the Southern Sinagua people. Docents are available on site.

Note: Sites are reached via walking trails; comfortable shoes are recommended. Parking is limited. **Time:** Allow 1 hour, 30 minutes minimum. **Hours:** Daily 9:30-3. Closed Jan. 1, Thanksgiving and Christmas. **Cost:** A Red Rock Pass (Day Pass $5, Weekly Pass $15 or Annual Pass $20) is required for admission. National Federal Pass also accepted. Reservations are recommended. **Phone:** (928) 282-3854.

PINK JEEP TOURS is at 204 N. SR 89A, .4 mi. n.e. from jct. SR 179. Passengers experience a true four-wheel-drive adventure on and over Sedona red rocks. Well-trained guides share lore about local flora, fauna, geology and Native American history and legends. Other tours are available.

Time: Allow 1 hour, 30 minutes minimum. **Hours:** Departures require a minimum of 2 people. Tours daily 7-dusk, Mar.-Sept.; 8-dusk, rest of year. Closed Christmas. **Cost:** Fare $52-$185; $39-$165 (ages 18 months-12 years). Children ages 0-17 months are not permitted. Rates may vary; phone ahead. **Phone:** (928) 282-5000 or (800) 873-3662. *(See ad p. 87.)* GT

RED ROCK STATE PARK, 3 mi. s. off SR 89A on Lower Red Rock Loop Rd., features 286 acres of a riparian ecosystem. Oak Creek runs through the park creating a diverse riparian habitat that abounds with plants and wildlife. Displays in the visitor center highlight the ecology and conservation of Oak Creek. Nature hikes, bird walks, theater presentations and other planned activities are offered; phone for schedule.

Hours: Park open daily 8-5. Visitor center open daily 9-5. **Cost:** $5 (per private vehicle, up to four adult passengers); $3 (per additional adult passenger in vehicle or individual arriving on foot or bicycle); free (ages 0-13). **Phone:** (928) 282-6907.

REDSTONE TOURS, with pickup from Sedona and Flagstaff hotels, provides van tours led by naturalist guides. The 2.5-hour Sedona tour takes guests to such sites as the Airport overlook, Bell Rock, Tlaquepaque and the Sedona Heritage Museum. The full-day Grand Canyon tour includes the South and East Rims; views of the Painted Desert; Ancestral Puebloan ruins and a Navajo Indian reservation; lunch is provided. A Colorado River float trip, a Grand Canyon tour with ruins and volcanoes, a Grand Canyon day hike, a Monument Valley tour and a trip to the Hopi reservation also are available.

Hours: Daily 8-6. **Cost:** Fare $38-$219; $32-$199 (ages 3-12). Reservations are required. **Phone:** (928) 203-0396 or (866) 473-3786.

SEDONA AIR TOURS, 1 mi. w. of SR 179 on SR 89A, then s. to 1225 Airport Rd., offers various aerial tours over Sedona and the Grand Canyon as well as destination tours. Passengers can view from the air

(See map & index p. 225.)

ancient Native American dwellings not accessible by foot or vehicle. **Hours:** Bi-plane, helicopter and sky safari tours daily 8-6. **Cost:** Fare $99-$800. **Phone:** (928) 204-5939 or (888) 866-7433.

SEDONA HERITAGE MUSEUM is .1 mi. n. of jct. SR 179 and SR 89A, then .6 mi. n. to 735 N. Jordan Rd. in Jordan Park. The museum features a restored one-room cabin built in 1931; additional rooms were added 1937-47. One exhibit is dedicated to more than 80 movies made in Sedona (mainly Westerns) and another depicts the lifestyle of the cowboy. A restored telegraph office used in the John Wayne movie "Angel and the Bad Man" is outside the museum in Jordan Park. A 1940 apple grading machine and a 1942 fire truck are on display. **Time:** Allow 1 hour minimum. **Hours:** Daily 11-3. Closed Jan. 1, Easter, July 4, Thanksgiving and Christmas. **Cost:** $5; free (ages 0-12). Audio tour $2. **Phone:** (928) 282-7038. 🏕

SEDONA OFFROAD ADVENTURES is at 336 SR 179, Suite F-103. Experienced guides take passengers on jeep excursions to Bear Wallow Canyon, the Red Rock Outback or Sedona vortexes. Hummer tours go to the Colorado Plateau and the Western and Cliffhanger trails. **Time:** Allow 1 hour minimum. **Hours:** Daily 8-8, May 1-Labor Day; 8-6, rest of year. **Cost:** $35-$97; $30-$77 (ages 1-12). **Phone:** (928) 282-6656.

SEDONA TROLLEY is at 276 N. SR 89A in uptown Sedona. Drivers provide sightseeing narration of the Sedona area. Two 55-minute tours are available. Tour A covers the south side of Sedona, including a stop at the Chapel of the Holy Cross. Tour B covers the west side of town into the Seven Canyons area and includes two stops for picture taking.

Time: Allow 1 hour minimum. **Hours:** Tour A departs daily at 10, noon, 2 and 4. Tour B departs daily at 9, 11, 1, 3 and 5 (also at 6, Memorial Day-Labor Day). Closed Thanksgiving and Christmas. Phone ahead to confirm schedule. **Cost:** One tour $15; $10 (ages 0-12). Two tours $25; $20 (ages 0-12). **Phone:** (928) 282-4211.

SLIDE ROCK STATE PARK is 7 mi. n. on SR 89A to 6871 N. SR 89A, within Oak Creek Canyon. Developed around a natural 70-foot waterslide, the park is the site of the historic Pendley homestead and an apple orchard. Activities include swimming and picnicking. *See Recreation Areas Chart.*

Note: Pets, glass containers and fires are not permitted. **Hours:** Daily 8-7, Memorial Day-Labor Day; 8-6, May 1-day before Memorial Day and day after Labor Day-Sept. 30; 8-5, rest of year. Closed Christmas. Phone ahead to confirm schedule. **Cost:** Memorial Day-Labor Day $20 (per private vehicle, up to four passengers); $3 (each additional passenger ages 13+ and each individual arriving on foot or bicycle). Rest of year $10 (per private vehicle, up to four passengers). Fees may vary; phone ahead. **Phone:** (928) 282-3034. 🅰 🍴 🚫 🏕

V-BAR-V RANCH PETROGLYPH SITE, 3 mi. e. off I-17 exit 298, following signs, contains 13 panels with more than 1,000 petroglyphs representing the Beaver Creek style of rock art. It is believed that the images of snakes, turtles, coyotes, stick-figured humans and palmlike trees were chiseled into the rock walls by members of the Ancestral Puebloan people referred to as the Sinagua. A docent is on the

(See map & index p. 225.)

grounds. **Time:** Allow 1 hour minimum. **Hours:** Fri.-Mon. 9:30-3. Closed Jan. 1, Thanksgiving and Christmas. **Cost:** Red Rock day pass $5 per vehicle; $15 (week pass); free (national park pass holders). **Phone:** (928) 282-4119. 🏕

RECREATIONAL ACTIVITIES
Hot Air Ballooning
- **Northern Light Balloon Expeditions** provides transportation to the departure point. **Hours:**

Tours depart daily at dawn (weather permitting). **Phone:** (928) 282-2274 or (800) 230-6222. **(See ad p. 220.)**
- **Red Rock Balloon Adventures** picks up from local hotels. **Hours:** Tours depart daily at dawn (weather permitting). **Phone:** (928) 284-0040 or (800) 258-3754. **(See ad this page.)**

Jeep Tours (Self-driving)
- **Barlow Jeep Rentals** is at 3009 W. SR 89A. **Hours:** Daily 8-6. Closed Christmas. **Phone:** (928) 282-8700 or (888) 928-5337.

▼ See AAA listing this page ▼

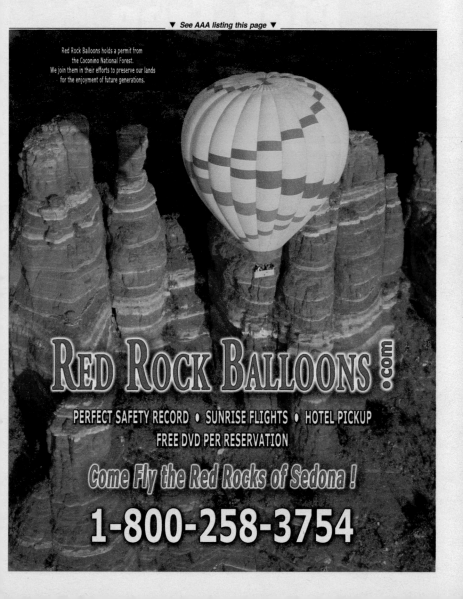

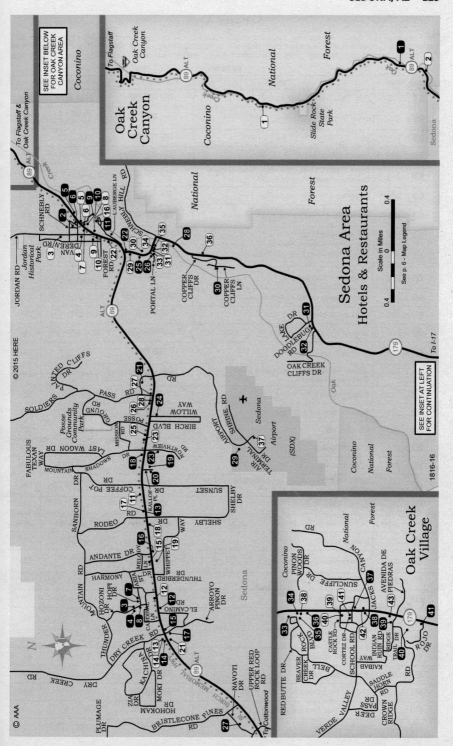

Sedona Area
Hotels & Restaurants

Sedona Area

This index helps you "spot" where approved hotels and restaurants are located on the corresponding detailed maps. Hotel daily rate range is for comparison only. Restaurant price range is a combination of lunch and/or dinner. Turn to the listing page for more detailed rate and price information and consult display ads for special promotions.

SEDONA

Map Page	Hotels	Diamond Rated	Rate Range	Page
① p. 225	Briar Patch Inn Bed & Breakfast	▼▼▼	$239-$425	230
② p. 225	Rose Tree Inn	▼	Rates not provided	233
③ p. 225	Alma de Sedona Inn B&B	▼▼▼	$159-$309	228
④ p. 225	Casa Sedona Inn	▼▼▼	$199-$349 SAVE	231
⑤ p. 225	BEST WESTERN PLUS Arroyo Roble Hotel & Creekside Villas (See ad p. 229.)	▼▼▼	$189-$500 SAVE	228
⑥ p. 225	Matterhorn Inn (See ad p. 233.)	▼▼▼	$109-$199 SAVE	232
⑦ p. 225	Boots & Saddles Romantic Bed & Breakfast	▼▼▼	Rates not provided	230
⑧ p. 225	Adobe Grand Villas	▼▼▼▼	$429-$875 SAVE	228
⑨ p. 225	Amara Resort and Spa, a Kimpton Hotel	▼▼▼▼	Rates not provided	228
⑩ p. 225	Orchards Inn of Sedona	▼▼▼	Rates not provided SAVE	232
⑪ p. 225	L'Auberge de Sedona Inn and Spa	▼▼▼▼	$225-$1150 SAVE	232
⑫ p. 225	Days Inn Sedona	▼▼	$80-$110 SAVE	231
⑬ p. 225	Sedona Rouge Hotel & Spa	▼▼▼	$209-$279 SAVE	234
⑭ p. 225	Southwest Inn at Sedona	▼▼	Rates not provided	234
⑮ p. 225	Arroyo Pinion Hotel, an Ascend Hotel Collection Member	▼▼▼	$99-$219 SAVE	228
⑯ p. 225	Sedona Super 8	▼▼	$80-$200	234
⑰ p. 225	Sedona Real Inn & Suites	▼▼▼	$99-$240 SAVE	234
⑱ p. 225	Hampton Inn	▼▼	$189-$239	231
⑲ p. 225	Villas of Sedona	▼▼▼	$175-$250	234
⑳ p. 225	The Lodge at Sedona	▼▼▼	$189-$349	232
㉑ p. 225	BEST WESTERN PLUS Inn of Sedona (See ad p. 230.)	▼▼▼	$129-$299 SAVE	230
㉒ p. 225	Cedars Resort	▼▼	$99-$159	231
㉓ p. 225	Sedona Springs Resort	▼▼▼	$125-$300	234
㉔ p. 225	Baby Quail Inn	▼▼	$95-$125	228
㉕ p. 225	Sedona Motel	▼▼	Rates not provided SAVE	233
㉖ p. 225	El Portal Sedona Hotel	▼▼▼▼	$229-$399 SAVE	231
㉗ p. 225	Sedona Summit Resort	▼▼▼	$159-$489	234
㉘ p. 225	The Inn Above Oak Creek	▼▼▼	Rates not provided	232
㉙ p. 225	Sky Ranch Lodge	▼▼	$120-$299	234
㉚ p. 225	Creekside Inn at Sedona	▼▼▼	$199-$329	231
㉛ p. 225	Poco Diablo Resort	▼▼▼	$149-$299 SAVE	232
㉜ p. 225	Villas at Poco Diablo	▼▼▼	$155-$195	234
㉝ p. 225	Canyon Villa Bed & Breakfast Inn of Sedona	▼▼▼	$199-$359 SAVE	230
㉞ p. 225	Wildflower Inn	▼▼	$79-$279 SAVE	234

SEDONA (cont'd)

Map Page	Hotels (cont'd)	Diamond Rated	Rate Range	Page
35 p. 225	Village Lodge	◆	$59-$99	234
36 p. 225	Holiday Inn Express-Sedona	◆◆	$69-$192	232
37 p. 225	The Views Inn Sedona	◆◆	Rates not provided	234
38 p. 225	Desert Quail Inn	◆◆	Rates not provided	231
39 p. 225	**Hilton Sedona Resort at Bell Rock**	◆◆◆	$179-$329 SAVE	232
40 p. 225	Diamond Resorts International-The Ridge on Sedona Golf Resort	◆◆◆	Rates not provided	231
41 p. 225	Adobe Hacienda Bed & Breakfast	◆◆◆	Rates not provided	228

Map Page	Restaurants	Diamond Rated	Cuisine	Price Range	Page
1 p. 225	The Table at Junipine	◆◆	American	$8-$29	237
2 p. 225	India Palace Cuisine	◆◆	Indian	$9-$16	235
3 p. 225	Takashi Japanese Restaurant	◆◆	Japanese	$9-$25	237
4 p. 225	Sedona Memories Bakery & Cafe	◆	Breads/Pastries Sandwiches	$7-$10	237
5 p. 225	Open Range Grill & Tavern	◆◆	American	$14-$30	236
6 p. 225	Canyon Breeze	◆	Deli	$8-$17	235
7 p. 225	Oaxaca Restaurant	◆◆	Mexican	$10-$20	236
8 p. 225	TAOS Cantina	◆◆	Mexican	$9-$22	237
9 p. 225	Thai Palace Uptown	◆◆	Thai	$11-$21	237
10 p. 225	Cowboy Club	◆◆	American	$9-$37	235
11 p. 225	Coffee Pot Restaurant	◆◆	Breakfast Comfort Food	$6-$10	235
12 p. 225	Nick's on the West Side	◆◆	American	$8-$20	236
13 p. 225	Euro Deli	◆	Deli	$9-$10	235
14 p. 225	Famous Pizza	◆	Pizza	$8-$22	235
15 p. 225	Barking Frog Grille	◆◆◆	American	$13-$30	235
16 p. 225	**L'Auberge Restaurant on Oak Creek**	◆◆◆◆	American	$18-$95	236
17 p. 225	**Red's**	◆◆◆	American	$8-$34	236
18 p. 225	Dahl & DiLuca Ristorante Italiano	◆◆◆	Italian	$13-$32	235
19 p. 225	Thai Spices Natural Restaurant	◆◆	Thai	$11-$15	237
21 p. 225	Relics Restaurant at Rainbow's End	◆◆	Steak	$20-$32	236
22 p. 225	Wildflower Bread Company	◆	Breads/Pastries Sandwiches	$7-$9	237
23 p. 225	Shallot's Cafe	◆◆	American	$15-$29	237
25 p. 225	The Heartline Cafe	◆◆◆	American	$8-$30	235
26 p. 225	Szechuan Chinese Restaurant & Sushi Bar	◆◆	Asian	$10-$20	237
27 p. 225	Judi's Restaurant	◆◆	American	$11-$31	235
28 p. 225	New York Bagels and Deli	◆	Deli Pizza	$3-$8	236
29 p. 225	**Red Rock BBQ**	◆◆	Barbecue	$7-$23	236
30 p. 225	Creekside Restaurant	◆◆◆	American	$12-$37	235
31 p. 225	El Rincon Restaurante Mexicano	◆◆	Mexican	$7-$18	235
32 p. 225	Oak Creek Brewery & Grill	◆◆	American	$11-$28	236

Map Page	Restaurants (cont'd)	Diamond Rated	Cuisine	Price Range	Page
㉝ p. 225	Spoke & Wheel Tavern and Eatery	◆◆	American	$12-$26	237
㉞ p. 225	**Rene At Tlaquepaque**	◆◆◆	Continental	$9-$42	236
㉟ p. 225	The Secret Garden Cafe	◆◆	American	$7-$13	237
㊱ p. 225	Elote Cafe	◆◆◆	Mexican	$19-$26	235
㊲ p. 225	Mesa Grill	◆◆	Italian	$10-$29	236
㊳ p. 225	Tara Thai	◆◆	Thai	$8-$18	237
㊴ p. 225	Pago's Pizzeria & Italian Cuisine	◆◆	Italian	$5-$20	236
㊵ p. 225	Maria's Restaurant & Cantina	◆◆	Mexican	$8-$19	236
㊶ p. 225	PJ's Village Pub	◆◆	American	$8-$15	236
㊷ p. 225	Marketplace Cafe	◆◆	American	$9-$28	236
㊸ p. 225	**Cucina Rustica**	◆◆◆	Mediterranean	$20-$34	235

ADOBE GRAND VILLAS (928)203-7616 **8**

◆◆◆◆ Boutique Bed & Breakfast $429-$875

Address: 35 Hozoni Dr 86336 **Location:** Jct SR 179, 2 mi w on SR 89A, just nw on Tortilla and Southwest drs, then just nw. Located in West Sedona residential area. **Facility:** This boutique-style B&B has spacious villas offering luxurious appointments; rooms have custom-designed furnishings and a private balcony or patio. 16 units, some two bedrooms and kitchens. 2 stories (no elevator), exterior corridors. **Terms:** 2 night minimum stay - seasonal and/or weekends, 15 day cancellation notice-fee imposed. **Amenities:** safes. **Pool(s):** outdoor. **Activities:** hot tub, spa. **Guest Services:** valet laundry. **Featured Amenity: full hot breakfast.**

SAVE BIZ HS

ADOBE HACIENDA BED & BREAKFAST 928/284-2020 **41**

◆◆◆ **Bed & Breakfast.** Rates not provided. **Address:** 10 Rojo Dr 86351 **Location:** Jct SR 89A, 7.5 mi s on SR 179. Located in Village of Oak Creek. **Facility:** This adobe-style building is set in a quiet neighborhood. Guest rooms reflect varied Southwest themes, and some have golf course views. 6 units. 1 story, exterior corridors. **Activities:** regulation golf. **Guest Services:** complimentary laundry.

ALMA DE SEDONA INN B&B (928)282-2737 **3**

◆◆◆ **Bed & Breakfast** $159-$309 **Address:** 50 Hozoni Dr 86336 **Location:** Jct SR 179, 3 mi w on SR 89A, then 3 blks nw via Tortilla and Southwest drs. Located in a quiet residential area. **Facility:** Guest rooms at this traditional Southwestern pueblo-style inn are elegantly appointed with couches and flat panel TV's. Some units have a balcony or patio with views of the area's scenic red rocks. 12 units. 2 stories (no elevator), exterior corridors. **Terms:** 2 night minimum stay - seasonal and/or weekends, 15 day cancellation notice-fee imposed. **Pool(s):** heated outdoor.

CALL BIZ

AMARA RESORT AND SPA, A KIMPTON HOTEL 928/282-4828 **9**

◆◆◆◆ **Hotel.** Rates not provided. **Address:** 100 Amara Ln 86336 **Location:** Jct SR 179, 0.4 mi ne; center. **Facility:** This property's upscale, modern rooms boast elegant appointments and amazing views. The central garden courtyard, with sculptures, ample seating, fire pits and an infinity pool, sits along Oak Creek. 100 units. 2 stories, interior corridors. **Parking:** on-site and valet. **Terms:** check-in 4 pm. **Amenities:** safes. **Dining:** entertainment. **Pool(s):** heated outdoor. **Activities:** hot tub, fishing, bicycles, exercise room, spa. **Guest Services:** valet laundry, area transportation.

CALL BIZ / SOME UNITS

ARROYO PINION HOTEL, AN ASCEND HOTEL COLLECTION MEMBER (928)204-1146 **15**

◆◆◆ Hotel $99-$219

Address: 3119 W Hwy 89A 86336 **Location:** Jct SR 179, 3 mi w. Located in business section of West Sedona. **Facility:** 45 units, some kitchens. 2 stories (no elevator), exterior corridors. **Amenities:** safes. **Pool(s):** heated outdoor. **Activities:** hot tub, limited exercise equipment. **Guest Services:** coin laundry. **Featured Amenity: breakfast buffet.**

SAVE CALL / SOME UNITS

BABY QUAIL INN (928)282-2835 **24**

◆◆ **Motel** $95-$125 **Address:** 50 Willow Way 86336 **Location:** Jct SR 179, 1.4 mi w on SR 89A, just s. Located in a residential area. **Facility:** 12 units. 2 stories (no elevator), exterior corridors. **Terms:** cancellation fee imposed. **Activities:** hot tub.

CALL

BEST WESTERN PLUS ARROYO ROBLE HOTEL & CREEKSIDE VILLAS (928)282-4001 **5**

◆◆◆ Hotel $189-$500

Best Western PLUS

AAA Benefit: Save 10% or more every day and earn 10% bonus points!

Address: 400 N SR 89A 86336 **Location:** Jct SR 179, 0.5 mi ne. **Facility:** 65 units, some two bedrooms, kitchens and cottages. 5 stories, exterior corridors. **Amenities:** safes. **Pool(s):** heated outdoor, heated indoor. **Activities:** sauna, hot tub, steamroom, tennis, playground, game room, exercise room. **Guest Services:** coin laundry. **Featured Amenity: breakfast buffet.** (See ad p. 229.)

SAVE BIZ HS / SOME UNITS

Best Western PLUS
Arroyo Roble Hotel & Creekside Villas

On Oak Creek . . . In the Heart of Uptown Sedona!
Walk to Shops, Galleries, & Restaurants

THE VIEWS
Standard hotel rooms offer fabulous red rock views. Town view rooms also available.

A PEACEFUL RETREAT
Creekside Villas, located on the banks of sparkling Oak Creek, offer 2 bedrooms, 2 1/2 baths, full kitchen, 2 fireplaces, private balconies & patios.

COMFORTABLE UPGRADES
North Signature Rooms feature a fireplace and magnificent red rock views.

As our guest, you'll enjoy...

- Spectacular red rock views
- Free full hot breakfast buffet
- Private balconies and/or patios
- Over 600 feet of private frontage on Oak Creek
- Free Wi-Fi
- Free clubhouse access with in and outdoor pools, whirlpools, steam room, sauna, game room, and more!

> BOOK YOUR RESERVATION. CALL TO RECEIVE SPECIAL PRICING FOR AAA MEMBERS*

bestwesternsedona.com ◆ For reservations 800-773-3662

400 N. STATE ROUTE 89A ◆ SEDONA, AZ 86336

(See map & index p. 225.)

BEST WESTERN PLUS INN OF SEDONA
(928)282-3072

 Hotel
$129-$299

 AAA Benefit:
Save 10% or more every day and earn 10% bonus points!

Address: 1200 W SR 89A 86336 **Location:** Jct SR 179, 1.2 mi w. **Facility:** 110 units. 1-3 stories (no elevator), exterior corridors. **Terms:** cancellation fee imposed. **Pool(s):** heated outdoor. **Activities:** hot tub, exercise room. **Guest Services:** coin laundry, area transportation. **Featured Amenity: full hot breakfast.** *(See ad this page.)*

BOOTS & SADDLES ROMANTIC BED & BREAKFAST
928/282-1944

 **Bed & Breakfast.** Rates not provided. **Address:** 2900 Hopi Dr 86336 **Location:** Jct SR 179 W, 2.7 mi w on SR 89A, n on Tortilla Dr, 1 blk w on Southwest Dr, 1 blk n on Hozoni Dr, then just e. **Facility:** The casual Western décor of this property lends a fun ambiance to its guest rooms, all of which have a gas fireplace and a patio or balcony. 6 units. 2 stories (no elevator), interior/exterior corridors.

BRIAR PATCH INN BED & BREAKFAST
928/282-2342

Cottage $239-$425 **Address:** 3190 N SR 89A 86336 **Location:** Jct SR 179, 3.4 mi ne. Located in Oak Creek Canyon. **Facility:** Many of the comfortable, rustic cottages have a fireplace at this property situated on nine tree-shaded acres bordering Oak Creek. A massage gazebo is on the grounds. 19 units, some houses and cottages. 1 story, exterior corridors. **Terms:** 2 night minimum stay - weekends, 14 day cancellation notice-fee imposed. **Activities:** fishing, massage.

CANYON VILLA BED & BREAKFAST INN OF SEDONA
(928)284-1226

 Bed & Breakfast
$199-$359

Address: 40 Canyon Circle Dr 86351 **Location:** Jct SR 179, just w on Bell Rock Blvd, then just n. Located in Village of Oak Creek. **Facility:** A nearby desert provides outdoor interest at this upscale Spanish-Mission compound overlooking the red rocks. The modern, Southwestern-style building houses spacious guest rooms and common areas. 11 units. 2 stories (no elevator), interior/exterior corridors. **Terms:** 14 day cancellation notice-fee imposed. **Pool(s):** outdoor. **Featured Amenity: full hot breakfast.**

▼ See AAA listing this page ▼

Visit the AAA/CAA senior driver sites
for resources to help you drive safely longer

(See map & index p. 225.)

CASA SEDONA INN
(928)282-2938 **4**

Boutique Hotel
$199-$349

Address: 55 Hozoni Dr 86336 **Location:** Jct SR 179, 3 mi w on SR 89A, then 3 blks nw via Tortilla, Southwest and Hozoni drs. Located in a quiet residential area. **Facility:** Décor at this Southwest-style inn includes custom beds and all rooms feature a balcony, patio or terrace. 15 units. 2 stories (no elevator), interior/exterior corridors. **Terms:** 3 day cancellation notice. **Amenities:** safes. **Activities:** hot tub, massage. **Featured Amenity:** full hot breakfast.

CEDARS RESORT
(928)282-7010 **22**

Hotel $99-$159 **Address:** 20 W SR 89A 86339 **Location:** Jct SR 179, southeast corner. **Facility:** 38 units. 1-2 stories (no elevator), exterior corridors. **Terms:** check-in 4 pm, cancellation fee imposed. **Pool(s):** outdoor. **Activities:** hot tub, exercise room.

CREEKSIDE INN AT SEDONA
(928)282-4992 **30**

Bed & Breakfast $199-$329 **Address:** 99 Copper Cliffs Dr 86336 **Location:** Jct SR 89A, 0.7 mi s on SR 179, then just w. **Facility:** The sights and sounds behind this elegant B&B of Oak Creek create a soothing ambiance. The back patio is a perfect setting for breakfast. Many of the guest rooms are quite spacious. 7 units. 1 story, interior/exterior corridors. **Terms:** 2 night minimum stay - weekends, 14 day cancellation notice-fee imposed. **Activities:** fishing, massage.

DAYS INN SEDONA
(928)282-9166 **12**

Motel
$80-$110

Address: 2991 W Hwy 89A 86336 **Location:** Jct SR 179, 3 mi w. **Facility:** 66 units, some two bedrooms. 2 stories (no elevator), exterior corridors. **Pool(s):** heated outdoor. **Activities:** hot tub. **Featured Amenity:** continental breakfast.

DESERT QUAIL INN
928/284-1433 **38**

Hotel. Rates not provided. **Address:** 6626 SR 179 86351 **Location:** Jct Bell Rock Blvd, 0.9 mi s. Across from factory outlet center. **Facility:** 40 units. 2 stories (no elevator), exterior corridors. **Pool(s):** heated outdoor. **Guest Services:** coin laundry.

DIAMOND RESORTS INTERNATIONAL-THE RIDGE ON SEDONA GOLF RESORT
928/284-1200 **40**

Condominium. Rates not provided. **Address:** 55 Sunridge Cir 86351 **Location:** Jct SR 89A, 7.4 mi s on SR 179, just w on Ridge Trail Dr, then just s. **Facility:** The resort's pueblo-style buildings house attractively furnished suites and standard rooms. Some units overlook the golf course and others have red rock views. 236 condominiums. 2 stories (no elevator), exterior corridors. **Terms:** check-in 4 pm. **Amenities:** safes. **Pool(s):** outdoor. **Activities:** hot tub, recreation programs, exercise room. **Guest Services:** complimentary laundry.

EL PORTAL SEDONA HOTEL
(928)203-9405 **26**

Hotel
$229-$399

Address: 95 Portal Ln 86336 **Location:** Jct SR 89A, just s on SR 179, just w. Adjacent to Tlaquepaque Plaza. **Facility:** Built to replicate early 1900s Southwestern buildings, the hotel features elegantly appointed guest rooms that graciously surround a courtyard. 12 units. 2 stories (no elevator), interior/exterior corridors. **Terms:** 2 night minimum stay - weekends, 15 day cancellation notice-fee imposed, resort fee. **Activities:** massage. **Guest Services:** valet laundry, area transportation.

ENCHANTMENT RESORT AND MII AMO SPA
928/282-2900

Resort Hotel
Rates not provided

Address: 525 Boynton Canyon Rd 86336 **Location:** Jct SR 89A, 5 mi n on Dry Creek Rd and FR 152C. Located in a quiet rural area. **Facility:** Tucked into spectacular Boynton Canyon with overhanging red rock cliffs, the property offers one- to two-bedroom suites in adobe-style casitas. The facilities are spread out over several acres. 234 units, some two bedrooms, efficiencies and kitchens. 1 story, exterior corridors. **Terms:** check-in 4 pm. **Amenities:** safes. **Dining:** 4 restaurants, also, Che-Ah-Chi, see separate listing, entertainment. **Pool(s):** heated outdoor, heated indoor. **Activities:** sauna, hot tub, tennis, recreation programs, kids club, bicycles, trails, spa. **Guest Services:** complimentary and valet laundry, area transportation.

HAMPTON INN
(928)282-4700 **18**

Hotel $189-$239 **Address:** 1800 W Hwy 89A 86336 **Location:** Jct SR 179, 2 mi w. **Facility:** 55 units. 2 stories, interior corridors. **Terms:** 1-7 night minimum stay, cancellation fee imposed.

AAA Benefit: Members save up to 10%!

Pool(s): heated outdoor. **Activities:** hot tub, exercise room. **Guest Services:** valet laundry.

(See map & index p. 225.)

HILTON SEDONA RESORT AT BELL ROCK
(928)284-4040   **39**

Resort Hotel
$179-$329

AAA Benefit:
Members save 5% or more!

Address: 90 Ridge Trail Dr 86351 **Location:** Jct SR 89A, 7.3 mi s on SR 179. Located in Village of Oak Creek. **Facility:** Beautiful red rock views can be enjoyed from some of these well-appointed guest rooms with a patio and fireplace. 219 units. 3 stories, interior corridors. **Terms:** check-in 4 pm, 1-7 night minimum stay, cancellation fee imposed. **Amenities:** safes. **Dining:** 2 restaurants. **Pool(s):** heated outdoor. **Activities:** hot tub, regulation golf, tennis, spa. **Guest Services:** complimentary and valet laundry.

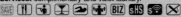
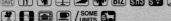

Hilton
SEDONA RESORT AT BELL ROCK

Newly renovated resort offering on-site golf and spa in the heart of Sedona's Red Rock Country.

HOLIDAY INN EXPRESS-SEDONA
(928)284-0711   **36**

Hotel $69-$192 **Address:** 6176 SR 179 86351 **Location:** Jct Bell Rock Blvd, just s. Located in Village of Oak Creek. **Facility:** 100 units. 2 stories, interior corridors. **Pool(s):** heated outdoor. **Activities:** hot tub, exercise room. **Guest Services:** coin laundry.

THE INN ABOVE OAK CREEK
928/282-7896   **28**

Boutique Hotel. Rates not provided. **Address:** 556 SR 179 86336 **Location:** Jct SR 89A, 0.5 mi s. **Facility:** The inn is walking distance to Tlaquepaque shopping area. The guest can enjoy an open living area and deck overlooking Oak Creek as they enter. All rooms offer fireplaces. 13 units. 2 stories (no elevator), interior corridors.

L'AUBERGE DE SEDONA INN AND SPA
(928)282-1661   **11**

Hotel
$225-$1150

Address: 301 L'Auberge Ln 86336 **Location:** Jct SR 179, just n on SR 89A, then ne; down the hill. Located in a secluded area. **Facility:** A lodge and individual cottages are nestled on several acres of landscaped and tree-shaded grounds along Oak Creek. A country French décor, king canopy beds and fireplaces are offered in the cottages. 88 units, some two bedrooms and cottages. 1-2 stories (no elevator), interior/exterior corridors. **Parking:** valet only. **Terms:** 2-3 night minimum stay - seasonal and/or weekends, 7 day cancellation notice-fee imposed, resort fee. **Amenities:** safes. **Dining:** L'Auberge Restaurant on Oak Creek, see separate listing. **Pool(s):** heated outdoor. **Activities:** hot tub, fishing, recreation programs, exercise room, spa. **Guest Services:** valet laundry, boarding pass kiosk, area transportation.

THE LODGE AT SEDONA
(928)204-1942   **20**

Bed & Breakfast $189-$349 **Address:** 125 Kallof Pl 86336 **Location:** Jct SR 179, 1.8 mi w on SR 89A, then just s. Located in a secluded area. **Facility:** This elegant Mission-style inn sits on three acres and offers warmly decorated public areas. Many units feature a gas fireplace, and most include a private deck; one unit has an outdoor shower. 14 units. 1-2 stories (no elevator), interior/exterior corridors. **Terms:** age restrictions may apply, 30 day cancellation notice-fee imposed.

MATTERHORN INN
928/282-7176   **6**

Motel
$109-$199

Address: 230 Apple Ave 86336 **Location:** Jct SR 179, just ne on SR 89A; uptown. Located in a central shopping district. **Facility:** 23 units. 2 stories (no elevator), exterior corridors. **Pool(s):** heated outdoor. **Activities:** hot tub. *(See ad p. 233.)*

ORCHARDS INN OF SEDONA
928/282-2405   **10**

Hotel
Rates not provided

Address: 254 N SR 89A 86336 **Location:** Jct SR 179, just ne. Located in Uptown Sedona shopping area. **Facility:** 70 units. 2-3 stories (no elevator), exterior corridors. **Dining:** TAOS Cantina, see separate listing. **Pool(s):** heated outdoor. **Activities:** hot tub. **Guest Services:** coin laundry. **Featured Amenity:** breakfast buffet.

POCO DIABLO RESORT
(928)282-7333   **31**

Resort Hotel
$149-$299

Address: 1752 State Route 179 86336 **Location:** Jct SR 179, 2 mi s of SR 89A. **Facility:** The resort's multiple buildings are spread across several acres featuring ponds, cool streams, lush landscape and an outdoor fireplace. Some of the spacious rooms have either a patio or balcony and some also feature a fireplace. 137 units. 2 stories (no elevator), exterior corridors. **Terms:** check-in 4 pm, cancellation fee imposed, resort fee. **Pool(s):** heated outdoor. **Activities:** hot tub, regulation golf, tennis, bicycles, exercise room, massage. **Guest Services:** valet and coin laundry.

POCO DIABLO RESORT

Spacious Rooms, Dog Friendly, Restaurant, Tennis, 9 Hole Exec Golf, Wi-Fi, Fitness Center & Spa.

(See map & index p. 225.)

ROSE TREE INN 928/282-2065 **2**

Motel. Rates not provided. **Address:** 376 Cedar St 86336 **Location:** Jct SR 179, 0.4 mi ne on SR 89A, just nw on Apple Ave, then just ne. Located in a quiet area. **Facility:** 5 units, some kitchens. 1 story, exterior corridors. **Guest Services:** complimentary laundry.

SEDONA MOTEL 928/282-7187 **25**

Motel

Rates not provided

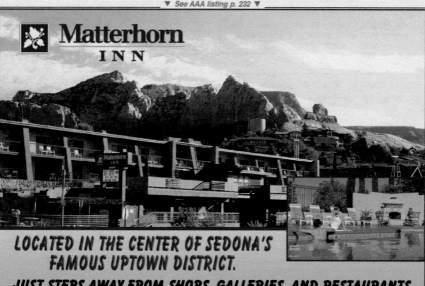

Address: 218 SR 179 86336 **Location:** Jct SR 89A, just s. Located in a busy area. **Facility:** 16 units. 1 story, exterior corridors. **Amenities:** safes.

▼ See AAA listing p. 232 ▼

(See map & index p. 225.)

SEDONA REAL INN & SUITES (928)282-1414 **17**

Hotel
$99-$240

Address: 95 Arroyo Pinon Dr 86336 **Location:** Jct SR 179, 3.4 mi w on SR 89A, just sw. Located in West Sedona. **Facility:** 89 units. 2 stories (no elevator), exterior corridors. **Pool(s):** heated outdoor. **Activities:** hot tub, exercise room. **Guest Services:** valet and coin laundry. **Featured Amenity:** full hot breakfast.

Sedona Real
INN & SUITES

Great Sedona location! Stay with us and enjoy free wi-fi, a hot breakfast and warm friendly service!

SEDONA ROUGE HOTEL & SPA (928)203-4111 **13**

Hotel
$209-$279

Address: 2250 W Hwy 89A 86336 **Location:** Jct SR 179, 2 mi w. **Facility:** 72 units. 2-3 stories, interior/exterior corridors. **Terms:** 2 night minimum stay - seasonal and/or weekends, 3 day cancellation notice-fee imposed, resort fee. **Dining:** Red's, see separate listing. **Pool(s):** heated outdoor. **Activities:** hot tub, steamroom, exercise room, spa. **Guest Services:** valet laundry.

Sedona
Rouge
HOTEL & SPA

Hotel & Spa located in West Sedona. Conveniently located near all local attractions.

SEDONA SPRINGS RESORT (928)204-3400 **23**

Condominium $125-$300 **Address:** 55 Northview Rd 86336 **Location:** Jct SR 179, 1.6 mi w on SR 89A, then just e. Located in West Sedona. **Facility:** Many of the spacious units at this apartment-style complex surrounding a central courtyard with pools feature garden-style hot tubs and showers. 40 condominiums. 2 stories (no elevator), exterior corridors. **Terms:** check-in 4 pm, 14 day cancellation notice-fee imposed. **Amenities:** safes. **Pool(s):** outdoor, heated indoor. **Activities:** hot tub, playground, game room, exercise room. **Guest Services:** coin laundry.

SEDONA SUMMIT RESORT (928)204-3100 **27**

Condominium $159-$489 **Address:** 4055 Navoti Dr 86336 **Location:** Jct SR 179, 3.8 mi w on SR 89A, then on Bristlecone Pine Dr. **Facility:** The Santa Fe-style buildings offer some red rock views. Choose from spacious suites or standard rooms in a garden setting with a lush courtyard. 417 condominiums. 1-2 stories (no elevator), exterior corridors. **Terms:** check-in 4 pm, cancellation fee imposed, resort fee. **Amenities:** safes. **Pool(s):** heated outdoor. **Activities:** hot tub, recreation programs, exercise room. **Guest Services:** complimentary and valet laundry.

SEDONA SUPER 8 (928)282-1533 **16**

Hotel $80-$200 **Address:** 2545 W Hwy 89A 86336 **Location:** Jct SR 179, 2.4 mi w. **Facility:** 66 units. 3 stories, interior corridors. **Terms:** cancellation fee imposed. **Pool(s):** heated outdoor. **Guest Services:** coin laundry.

SKY RANCH LODGE (928)282-6400 **29**

Motel $120-$299 **Address:** 1105 Airport Rd 86336 **Location:** Jct SR 179, 1 mi w on SR 89A, then 1 mi s. **Facility:** 94 units, some cottages. 1-2 stories (no elevator), exterior corridors. **Terms:** check-in 4 pm, 2 night minimum stay - weekends, cancellation fee imposed. **Pool(s):** heated outdoor. **Activities:** hot tub. **Guest Services:** coin laundry.

SOUTHWEST INN AT SEDONA 928/282-3344 **14**

Hotel. Rates not provided. **Address:** 3250 W Hwy 89A 86336 **Location:** Jct SR 179, 3.5 mi w. Located in West Sedona. **Facility:** 28 units. 2 stories (no elevator), exterior corridors. **Pool(s):** heated outdoor. **Activities:** hot tub, exercise room.

THE VIEWS INN SEDONA 928/284-2487 **37**

Hotel. Rates not provided. **Address:** 65 E Cortez Dr 86351 **Location:** Jct Bell Rock Blvd, 0.9 mi s on SR 179, just e. Located in Village of Oak Creek. **Facility:** 39 units. 2 stories (no elevator), exterior corridors. **Pool(s):** heated outdoor. **Activities:** hot tub. **Guest Services:** coin laundry.

VILLAGE LODGE 928/284-3626 **35**

Motel $59-$99 **Address:** 105 Bell Rock Plaza 86351 **Location:** Jct SR 179, just w. Located in Village of Oak Creek. **Facility:** 17 units. 2 stories (no elevator), interior/exterior corridors. **Terms:** 2 night minimum stay - weekends, 3 day cancellation notice-fee imposed.

VILLAS AT POCO DIABLO (928)204-3300 **32**

Condominium $155-$195 **Address:** 1752 SR 179 86336 **Location:** Jct SR 89A, 2 mi s. Located in a quiet area. **Facility:** Nestled between a rocky creek and a resort golf course, these spacious villas offer welcoming views and a shady retreat from the desert heat. This intimate complex has a central pool. 33 condominiums. 1 story, exterior corridors. **Terms:** check-in 4 pm, 14 day cancellation notice-fee imposed. **Amenities:** safes. **Pool(s):** heated outdoor. **Activities:** hot tub. **Guest Services:** coin laundry.

VILLAS OF SEDONA (928)204-3400 **19**

Condominium $175-$250 **Address:** 120 Kallof Pl 86336 **Location:** Jct SR 179, 1.6 mi w on SR 89A, then just s. Located in West Sedona. **Facility:** This apartment-style complex with spacious townhouse units surrounds a central courtyard and pool. Most units have a private outdoor hot tub. 40 condominiums. 2 stories (no elevator), exterior corridors. **Terms:** check-in 4 pm, 14 day cancellation notice-fee imposed. **Amenities:** safes. **Pool(s):** outdoor, heated indoor. **Activities:** sauna, hot tub, playground, game room, exercise room. **Guest Services:** coin laundry.

WILDFLOWER INN (928)284-3937 **34**

Hotel
$79-$279

Address: 6086 SR 179 86351 **Location:** Jct SR 179 and Bell Rock Blvd. Located in Village of Oak Creek. **Facility:** 29 units. 2 stories (no elevator), exterior corridors. **Terms:** cancellation fee imposed. **Guest Services:** coin laundry. **Featured Amenity:** continental breakfast.

JUNIPINE RESORT 928/282-3375

[fyi] Not evaluated; management refused inspection. **Address:** 8351 N SR 89A 86336 **Location:** Jct SR 179, 9 mi ne. Facilities, services, and décor characterize a mid-scale property.

(See map & index p. 225.)

WHERE TO EAT

BARKING FROG GRILLE
928/204-2000 (15)

WWW American. Casual Dining. $13-$30 AAA Inspector Notes: Enjoy an upbeat atmosphere at this lovely Southwestern-style restaurant with its brick and stucco walls adorned with colorful rugs, pottery and pictures. Several dining sections including attractive patios, some enhanced with a fireplace. The menu is extensive with items ranging from ribs, steaks, rotisserie chicken and pork, to blackened halibut tacos, plantain-encrusted swordfish and caramelized scallops. A lighter menu with sandwiches, burgers and French dip also is available. Features: full bar, patio dining, happy hour. Address: 2620 W Hwy 89A 86336 Location: Jct SR 179, 2.4 mi w.
L D

CANYON BREEZE
928/282-2112 (6)

W Deli. Quick Serve. $8-$17 AAA Inspector Notes: Catering to foot traffic, this large cafeteria-style deli serves quick bites such as pizza, panini, coffee and ice cream. There is a full bar that overlooks the beautiful red rocks. Features: full bar, patio dining. Address: 300 N Hwy 89A 86336 Location: Jct SR 179, just ne; uptown. Parking: street only. B L D

CHE-AH-CHI
928/204-6000

WWWW
American
Fine Dining
$15-$58

AAA Inspector Notes: While taking in stunning views of Boynton Canyon, patrons can savor contemporary local game and organic dishes at this spot. The elegant service and décor complete a truly distinguished dining experience. The Sunday champagne brunch is exceptional with a variety of traditional and Southwestern dishes. Features: full bar, patio dining, Sunday brunch. Reservations: suggested. Address: 525 Boynton Canyon Rd 86336 Location: Jct SR 179, 3.5 mi w on SR 89A, 5 mi n on Dry Creek Rd and FR 152C; in Enchantment Resort and Mii amo Spa.
B D

COFFEE POT RESTAURANT
928/282-6626 (11)

WW Breakfast Comfort Food. Casual Dining. $6-$10 AAA Inspector Notes: If you love omelets, there are 101 varieties at this neighborhood favorite. The large dining room has a comfortable, casual feel with gigantic Southwest murals and servers know many guests by name. The distinctive clay coffee mugs make drinking coffee a fun experience. Address: 2050 W Hwy 89A 86336 Location: Jct SR 179, 1.9 mi w. B L

COWBOY CLUB
928/282-4200 (10)

WW American. Casual Dining. $9-$37 AAA Inspector Notes: One of the more popular restaurants in Sedona, the menu is this eatery revolves around buffalo meat. There are buffalo burgers, flank steak, tenderloin and soup. Try the buffalo flank steak, a super tender meat served in an amazing sweet-brown sauce. There also are more traditional items such as burgers, cedar plank salmon and beef steaks for the non-adventurous. The casual country decor is fun with lively servers. A long wooden bar is fully stocked and serves locally-brewed beer. Features: full bar, patio dining. Address: 241 N Hwy 89A 86336 Location: SR 179, 0.5 mi n. L D

CREEKSIDE RESTAURANT
928/282-1705 (30)

WWW American. Casual Dining. $12-$37 AAA Inspector Notes: Mouth-watering cuisine and eye-popping views are the focus at this casual restaurant. The pork belly appetizer's barbecue flavor is fantastic and the spicy prawns have the perfect amount of kick. Features: full bar, patio dining, Sunday brunch. Address: 251 Highway 179 86336 Location: Jct SR 89A, just s.
B L D

CUCINA RUSTICA
928/284-3010 (43)

WWW
Mediterranean
Fine Dining
$20-$34

AAA Inspector Notes: Boasting a decor akin to that of an elegant seaside villa, this eatery prepares such hearty dishes as marinated and grilled pork loin and roast chicken in lemon-garlic sauce. Features: full bar, patio dining, happy hour. Reservations: suggested. Address: 7000 Hwy 179, Suite 126A 86351 Location: Just s of Bell Rock Blvd. Menu on AAA.com D

DAHL & DILUCA RISTORANTE ITALIANO
928/282-5219 (18)

WWW Italian. Fine Dining. $13-$32 AAA Inspector Notes: In West Sedona, this spot features Italian-style food with Tuscan influences, including delicious seafood, steak, veal and chicken dishes with creative touches using creamy and wine sauces dashed with various herbs. Examples of the refined, traditional entrées include piatto Milanese and linguine carbonara. Quiet tones present a feeling of an outdoor garden. Professional, yet casual, service is offered from a staff in black and white formal attire. Features: full bar. Reservations: suggested. Address: 2321 W Hwy 89A 86336 Location: Jct SR 179, 3 mi w; in West Sedona. D

ELOTE CAFE
928/203-0105 (36)

WWW Mexican. Casual Dining. $19-$26 AAA Inspector Notes: Many homemade Mexican items are served in this small, casual café. The popular restaurant does not take reservations for parties less than five, so be prepared to wait. Features: full bar. Address: 771 SR 179 86336 Location: 0.7 mi s of jct SR 89A; in Arabella Hotel Sedona. D

EL RINCON RESTAURANTE MEXICANO
928/282-4648 (31)

WW Mexican. Casual Dining. $7-$18 AAA Inspector Notes: The casual eatery serves freshly prepared classics and specialty chimichangas that are robust meals for hungry art shoppers. Patio dining also is available. Features: full bar, patio dining. Reservations: suggested. Address: 336 S Hwy 179 86336 Location: Just s of jct SR 179 and 89A; in Tlaquepaque Plaza. L D

EURO DELI
928/282-4798 (13)

W Deli. Quick Serve. $9-$10 AAA Inspector Notes: This eatery is a casual deli that serves European style sandwiches for breakfast and lunch. While guests wait they can shop for European style foods. Features: patio dining. Address: 3190 W Hwy 89A 86336 Location: Jct SR 179, 3 mi w. B L

FAMOUS PIZZA
928/282-5464 (14)

W Pizza. Quick Serve. $8-$22 AAA Inspector Notes: This small, New York-style pizzeria offers a large counter and a few small tables. A perfect place for a quick bite or to relax and enjoy a beer. Features: beer only. Address: 3190 W Hwy 89A, Suite 300 86336 Location: Jct SR 179, 3.4 mi w. L D

THE HEARTLINE CAFE
928/282-0785 (25)

WWW American. Fine Dining. $8-$30 AAA Inspector Notes: The warm, intimate interior and pleasant waitstaff complement the imaginative selection of very fresh cuisine. There are many vegetarian and vegan options available. Features: full bar, patio dining. Reservations: suggested. Address: 1600 W Hwy 89A 86336 Location: On SR 89A, 1.5 mi s of jct SR 179.
B L D 🍴

INDIA PALACE CUISINE
928/204-2300 (2)

WW Indian. Casual Dining. $9-$16 AAA Inspector Notes: Competent and friendly waitstaff serve an extensive offering ranging from various tandoori entrées to seafood, chicken, lamb and vegetable dishes. The daily lunch buffet is filling. Features: full bar. Address: 1910 W SR 89A, Suite 102 86336 Location: Jct SR 179, 1.8 mi w. L D

JAVELINA CANTINA
928/282-1313

WW Mexican. Casual Dining. $5-$16 AAA Inspector Notes: In a popular and upscale shopping area with art galleries and shops nearby, the relaxed eatery affords spectacular views of the red rock from inside or on the covered patio. Large portions of fresh food are served in a festive setting punctuated by bright glass lamps, punched-tin sconces and tall windows. The energetic staff is quick to meet service needs. Features: full bar, patio dining, happy hour. Address: 671 Hwy 179 86336 Location: SR 89A, 0.8 mi s; in Hillside Courtyard and Marketplace, Bldg F, ground level. L D

JUDI'S RESTAURANT
928/282-4449 (27)

WW American. Casual Dining. $11-$31 AAA Inspector Notes: Antiques and beamed ceilings contribute to the comfortable, cozy atmosphere. The menu centers on chicken, pasta, seafood and steak dishes. A favorite choice is barbecue baby back ribs. A shady courtyard offers additional seating. Features: full bar, patio dining, early bird specials. Reservations: suggested. Address: 40 Soldier's Pass Rd 86336 Location: Jct SR 179, 1 mi w on SR 89A; northeast corner. L D 🍴

(See map & index p. 225.)

L'AUBERGE RESTAURANT ON OAK CREEK
928/282-1661 16

American
Fine Dining
$18-$95

AAA Inspector Notes: This restaurant offers elegant surroundings and formal service. The talented chef offers a tasting menu for dinner with modern international elements. The terrace allows for seasonal creekside dining. **Features:** full bar, patio dining, Sunday brunch. **Reservations:** suggested. **Address:** 301 L'Auberge Ln 86336 **Location:** Jct SR 179, just n on SR 89A, then ne; down the hill; in L'Auberge de Sedona Inn and Spa. **Parking:** valet only.

B L D

MARIA'S RESTAURANT & CANTINA 928/284-3739 40

Mexican. Casual Dining. $8-$19 **AAA Inspector Notes:** This eatery offers classic Mexican dishes along with specialty appetizers such as rattlesnake eggs, which are cheese-stuffed jalapeños that test your tongue for pepper-hot heat. **Features:** full bar, happy hour. **Address:** 6446 Hwy 179, #212 86351 **Location:** 0.5 mi s of Bell Rock Blvd. B L D

MARKETPLACE CAFE 928/284-5478 42

American. Casual Dining. $9-$28 **AAA Inspector Notes:** This spacious restaurant is decorated in local artwork offering booth and table seating, and a vast array of menu options. Food is very well prepared and portions are ample. Their intriguing cocktail list is a crowd pleaser. **Features:** full bar, patio dining, happy hour. **Address:** 6645 SR 179 86351 **Location:** Jct Jacks Canyon Rd; in Village of Oak Creek Outlet Mall Shopping Complex. L D

MESA GRILL 928/282-2400 37

Italian. Casual Dining. $10-$29 **AAA Inspector Notes:** This is an amazing place to grab a flavorful Italian dish while enjoying the planes on the runway. The dining room is bright and contemporary while the service is very casual. The lunch sandwiches feature a distinctive twist on traditional favorites utilizing great flavors. **Features:** full bar, patio dining, happy hour. **Address:** 1185 Airport Rd 86336 **Location:** Jct SR 179, 1 mi w on SR 89A, 1 mi s.

B L D CALL &M

NEW YORK BAGELS AND DELI 928/204-1242 28

Deli Pizza. Quick Serve. $3-$8 **AAA Inspector Notes:** This small deli is family run by native New Yorkers. Bagels are the specialty, but it's a full deli and pizza is served for lunch and dinner. **Features:** patio dining. **Address:** 1650 W SR 89A 86336 **Location:** Jct SR 179, 1.3 mi w. B L D

NICK'S ON THE WEST SIDE 928/204-2088 12

American. Casual Dining. $8-$20 **AAA Inspector Notes:** Locally popular for breakfast, this restaurant draws in folks for its eggs Judi dish, which outsells its French toast. For lunch or dinner, barbecue and Mexican dishes are hearty options. **Features:** full bar. **Address:** 2920 W Hwy 89A 86336 **Location:** 2.7 mi w of jct SR 179. B L D

OAK CREEK BREWERY & GRILL 928/282-3300 32

American. Gastropub. $11-$28 **AAA Inspector Notes:** The microbrewery's owner, who trained in Germany, designs the prize-winning, freshly brewed beers. Accompaniments include crisp salads, hearty sandwiches, pizza, steaks and ribs. **Features:** full bar, happy hour. **Address:** 336 Hwy 179, Suite D201 86336 **Location:** Jct SR 89A, 0.3 mi s; in Tlaquepaque Arts & Crafts Village. L D

OAXACA RESTAURANT 928/282-4179 7

Mexican. Family Dining. $10-$20 **AAA Inspector Notes:** This family-friendly place serves dishes from the Mexican region of the same name. For more than 20 years, the family has prepared foods, being conscious of dietary concerns, using vegetable oils and no additives. **Features:** full bar, early bird specials, Sunday brunch. **Address:** 321 N SR 89A 86336 **Location:** Jct Apple Rd and SR 89A. L D

OPEN RANGE GRILL & TAVERN 928/282-0002 5

American. Casual Dining. $14-$30 **AAA Inspector Notes:** The large two-story windows display panoramic views of the red rocks for which Sedona is known. The casual dining room offers an open kitchen and minimal decorations. The menu offers fresh Southwestern American cuisine-the blackened salmon is great. The service is friendly. **Features:** full bar. **Address:** 320 N SR 89A 86336 **Location:** Jct SR 179, just ne. **Parking:** street only. L D

PAGO'S PIZZERIA & ITALIAN CUISINE 928/284-1939 39

Italian. Casual Dining. $5-$20 **AAA Inspector Notes:** This small family-owned-and-operated restaurant features traditional fresh Italian cuisine including pizza, chicken parmigiana, veal Marsala, spaghetti and other favorites. **Address:** 6446 SR 179 86351 **Location:** Jct Bell Rock Blvd, just s; in Village of Oak Creek. L D

PICAZZO'S ORGANIC ITALIAN KITCHEN 928/282-4140

Italian. Casual Dining. $10-$27 **AAA Inspector Notes:** This upscale pizzeria offers fresh gourmet pizza with homemade dough. Many gluten-free, vegetarian and vegan dishes are served along with large salads and succulent desserts. The skillet brownie is super rich and impressive. **Features:** full bar. **Address:** 1855 W Hwy 89A 86336 **Location:** Jct SR 179, 2 mi w. L D

PJ'S VILLAGE PUB 928/284-2250 41

American. Casual Dining. $8-$15 **AAA Inspector Notes:** For those looking for great tasting pub grub in a fun casual atmosphere, this is the place. Many large TVs show all of the games. Menu items are fresh and flavorful—be sure to try the fried zucchini and the steak salad. **Features:** full bar, patio dining, happy hour. **Address:** 40 W Cortez Dr 86351 **Location:** Jct SR 179; just w. L D

RED ROCK BBQ 928/204-5975 29

Barbecue
Casual Dining
$7-$23

AAA Inspector Notes: Guests can taste the love that goes into the fresh meat and homemade sauce at this vibrant Southwestern dining room. The pulled pork melted in my mouth while I enjoyed the jaw dropping panoramic mountain view. **Features:** beer & wine, patio dining. **Address:** 150 Hwy 179, Suite 1 86336 **Location:** Jct SR 89A, just s. L D

RED'S 928/340-5321 17

American
Casual Dining
$8-$34

AAA Inspector Notes: The trendy California décor of this eatery fits well in this red rock town and attentive staff watch over the tables. Chef Ron Moler creates his own delectable version of meatloaf, grilled seafood and salads such as honey-spiced pecans that will simply delight. **Features:** full bar, patio dining, happy hour. **Reservations:** suggested. **Address:** 2250 W Hwy 89A 86336 **Location:** Jct SR 179, 2 mi w; in Sedona Rouge Hotel & Spa. B L D

RELICS RESTAURANT AT RAINBOW'S END 928/282-1593 21

Steak. Casual Dining. $20-$32 **AAA Inspector Notes:** A former homestead from the early 1900s and the oldest restaurant in Sedona, the spot is filled with antiques and memorabilia. The eatery is known for prime steaks, barbecue and seafood as well as its pleasant staff. **Features:** full bar, patio dining, happy hour. **Address:** 3235 W SR 89A 86336 **Location:** Jct SR 179, 3.1 mi w. D

RENE AT TLAQUEPAQUE 928/282-9225 34

Continental
Fine Dining
$9-$42

AAA Inspector Notes: Tucked into an upscale, art-filled shopping plaza, this quietly elegant dining room is where diners are treated to attentive service and Continental and American favorites. Entertainers perform on weekends and the efficient staff works as a team to quietly meet all dining needs. The antelope tenderloin and the tableside flambé is amazing. **Features:** full bar, patio dining, happy hour. **Reservations:** suggested. **Address:** 336 Hwy 179, B-118 86336 **Location:** SR 89A, 0.3 mi s; in Tlaquepaque Arts & Crafts Village. L D

(See map & index p. 225.)

THE SECRET GARDEN CAFE   928/203-9564 35
WWW American. Casual Dining. $7-$13 AAA Inspector Notes:
Just off the Tlaquepaque courtyard, this casual eatery serves fresh
salads, homemade soups and such innovative sandwiches as the
turkey salad croissant. The dessert showcase holds mile-high carrot
or chocolate cake, pies and other delicacies that will tempt even a
staunch dieter. Features: full bar, patio dining. Address: 336 Hwy
179, Suite F101 86336 Location: Jct SR 89A, 0.3 mi s; at north end
of Tlaquepaque Arts & Crafts Village. B L

SEDONA MEMORIES BAKERY & CAFE   928/282-0032 4
W Breads/Pastries Sandwiches. Quick Serve. $7-$10 AAA Inspector Notes: The huge, fresh and amazing sandwiches draw
guests daily to this super small bakery. The seating and indoor free
floor space is limited but there is ample outdoor seating. Features:
patio dining. Address: 321 Jordan Rd 86336 Location: Jct SR 179,
0.4 mi ne on SR 89A, then just n. L

SHALLOT'S CAFE   928/554-4805 23
WW American. Casual Dining. $15-$29 AAA Inspector Notes:
Fun and distinctive spins are put on traditional favorites at this intimate dining room filled with local artwork. Check out the chicken-fried
prime rib, steak Diane rib-eye and signature roasted shallots covered
with mozzarella and balsamic vinegar. Bringing your own alcohol is
encouraged, but there is a corkage fee. Address: 1650 SR 89A
86336 Location: 1.5 mi s of jct SR 179. L D

SPOKE & WHEEL TAVERN AND EATERY   928/203-5334 33
WWW American. Casual Dining. $12-$26 AAA Inspector Notes:
Upscale decor characterizes the warm interior of this popular sports
bar. The menu varies from simple pub grub to salmon filets, offering
something for everyone. The attentive staff serves guests with smiles
and ease while the many TVs broadcast sporting events. Features:
full bar, patio dining, happy hour. Address: 160 Portal Ln 86336 Location: Jct SR 89A, just s on SR 179, then just w; in Los Abrigados
Resort & Spa. B L D 🐾

SZECHUAN CHINESE RESTAURANT & SUSHI BAR
                                                    928/282-9288 26
WW Asian. Casual Dining. $10-$20 AAA Inspector Notes:
This casual restaurant specializes in such traditional Chinese dishes
as orange chicken, Mongolian beef and cashew shrimp. A full fresh
sushi bar also is available. The attached martini lounge is a popular
place for a pre- or post-dinner drink. Features: full bar, patio dining,
happy hour. Address: 1350 W Hwy 89A, Suite 21 86336 Location:
Jct SR 179, 1.3 mi w. L D 🐾

THE TABLE AT JUNIPINE   928/282-7406 1
WW American. Casual Dining. $8-$29 AAA Inspector Notes:
Located north of town along Oak Creek Canyon, this cozy and very
casual eatery with simple rustic decor serves a nice variety of beef,
chicken, seafood and pasta. Outdoor dining is available, weather permitting. Photographs and paintings by local artists displayed on the
walls is available for purchase. Features: full bar, patio dining. Address: 8351 N SR 89A 86336 Location: Jct SR 179, 9 mi ne; in Junipine Resort. B L D

TAKASHI JAPANESE RESTAURANT   928/282-2334 3
WW Japanese. Casual Dining. $9-$25 AAA Inspector Notes:
This restaurant offers an excellent selection of Japanese appetizers,
entrées and sushi in a dining room with attractive decor. Sake and
Japanese beer are available. Outdoor dining is offered, weather per-
mitting. Features: full bar, patio dining. Reservations: suggested.
Address: 465 Jordan Rd 86336 Location: SR 89A, 0.4 mi n; in north
Uptown Sedona area. D

TAOS CANTINA   928/282-7200 8
WW Mexican. Casual Dining. $9-$22 AAA Inspector Notes:
From the day's start to the finish, this popular eatery provides such
well-cooked dishes as eggs Benedict, hearty burgers and sand-
wiches as well as Mexican regional dishes. The staff is friendly. Fea-
tures: full bar, patio dining. Address: 254 N SR 89A 86336
Location: Jct SR 179, just ne; in Orchards Inn of Sedona.
L D

TARA THAI   928/284-9167 38
WW WW Thai. Casual Dining. $8-$18 AAA Inspector Notes: This
local favorite serves authentic, made-to-order Thai dishes spiced to
diners' preference. The small restaurant has a very casual atmosphere and friendly service. Features: beer & wine. Address: 34 Bell
Rock Plaza 86351 Location: Jct Bell Rock Blvd, just s; in Bell Rock
Plaza Village. L D

THAI PALACE UPTOWN   928/282-8424 9
WW WW Thai. Casual Dining. $11-$21 AAA Inspector Notes: This
contemporary restaurant serves such fresh Thai favorites as pad thai,
fried rice and coconut soup. The servers exude a proud demeanor
and promote the fresh ingredients. On comfortable days and nights,
the outdoor patio featuring a large fountain is a popular spot. Features: full bar. Address: 260 Van Deren Rd 86336 Location: Jct SR
89A, just nw on Jordan Rd, then just e. Parking: on-site and street.
L D

THAI SPICES NATURAL RESTAURANT   928/282-0599 19
WW WW Thai. Casual Dining. $11-$15 AAA Inspector Notes: This
small eatery serves fresh Thai favorites and prides itself on serving
organic vegetables. The atmosphere is very casual and a perfect
place for a care-free lunch or dinner. Address: 2611 W SR 89A
86336 Location: Jct SR 179, 2.5 mi w. L D

WILDFLOWER BREAD COMPANY   928/204-2223 22
W Breads/Pastries Sandwiches. Quick Serve. $7-$9 AAA Inspector Notes: This bright and vibrant dining room with a huge
pastry showcase and glass flower statue lures guests right in. All
items are fresh including amazing turkey sandwiches and distinctive
cakes. All is self service, and a great place to get a tasty, quick meal.
Address: 101 N Hwy 89A 86336 Location: Jct SR 179.
B L D

SELIGMAN pop. 445
• Restaurants p. 238
• Part of Grand Canyon National Park area — see
map p. 82

CANYON LODGE   928/422-3255
W Motel. Rates not provided. Address: 22340 Old Hwy 66
86337 Location: I-40 exit 121, 1 mi n, then 0.7 mi e. Facility: 16
units, some kitchens. 2 stories (no elevator), exterior corridors. Bath:
shower only.
📶 🛜 ✕ 🔲 🖼 🖵 / SOME UNITS 🕭

DELUXE INN MOTEL   (928)422-3244

▼▼▼
Vintage Motel
$62-$72

Address: 22295 Old Hwy 66 86337 Location: I-40 exit 121, 1 mi n,
then 0.7 mi e; exit 123 westbound, just
ne on I-40 business loop, then 2.4 mi w.
Facility: The small motel has old historic
Route 66 charm with a large mural on
the outside wall, neon sign and gravel
parking lot. This basic lodging is very
well cared for by its owner/operator. 15
units. 1 story, exterior corridors. Terms:
cancellation fee imposed.
SAVE 📶 🛜 ✕ 🔲 🖼
/ SOME UNITS 🕭

HISTORIC ROUTE 66 MOTEL   928/422-3204

▼▼▼
Vintage Motel
$62-$82

Address: 22750 W Old Hwy 66 86337
Location: I-40 exit 121, 1 mi n, then just
e. Facility: A throwback to lodging from
a bygone era, the property offers varied-
size guest units with many homey nice-
ties. All have a Route 66 décor, including
bedspreads with prints of the motel. 16
units. 1 story, exterior corridors. Bath:
shower only. Terms: cancellation fee
imposed.
SAVE 📶 🛜 ✕ 🔲 🖵

SUPAI MOTEL
(928)422-4153

Motel
$62-$74

Address: 22450 Old Hwy 66 86337 **Location:** I-40 exit 121, 1 mi n, then 0.7 mi e. **Facility:** 15 units. 1 story, exterior corridors. **Terms:** cancellation fee imposed.

WHERE TO EAT

DELGADILLOS SNOW CAP DRIVE-IN   928/422-3291

Burgers Desserts. Quick Serve. $2-$8 **AAA Inspector Notes:** Known to be a highlight on Route 66, guests can enjoy old cars, trucks and an antique setting throughout a courtyard at this spot. The cheeseburger with cheese, "girl" cheese and root beer floats are some favorites. Be alert for the staffs' pranks and humor. Kids and adults are sure to enjoy their visit. **Features:** beer only, patio dining. **Address:** 301 W Chino Ave 86337 **Location:** I-40 exit 121, 1 mi n, then 0.7 mi e. Ⓛ Ⓚ 🐄 🛏

ROADKILL 66 CAFE AND OK SALOON   928/422-3554

American Casual Dining $5-$16

AAA Inspector Notes: Enjoy this distinctive eatery with stuffed animal trophies and Route 66 charm. Casual American items, served with fun, local attitudes, include sandwiches, burgers and basic cuts of steak. **Features:** full bar. **Address:** 22830 W Hwy 66 86337 **Location:** I-40 exit 121, 1 mi n, then just e. Ⓑ Ⓛ Ⓓ

SELLS (F-4) pop. 2,495, elev. 2,379'

Originally known as Indian Oasis, Sells was renamed in 1918 in honor of Indian commissioner Cato Sells. The dependable water supply made the area a popular stop for travelers, even in prehistoric times.

Sells is the headquarters of the Tohono O'odham Indian Reservation. In addition to this vast reservation west of Tucson, a smaller tract is south of Tucson at the site of Mission San Xavier del Bac (see Tucson p. 267). Mainly farmers and ranchers, the Tohono O'odham are known for their handcrafted baskets and pottery.

KITT PEAK NATIONAL OBSERVATORY IS 20 mi. e. on SR 86, then 12 mi. s. on SR 386, within the Tohono O'odham reservation in the Quinlan Mountains. The facility conducts astronomical research and contains 27 telescopes, including the world's largest solar telescope and the Mayall 4-meter telescope. Exhibits, special programs and a nightly stargazing program are featured.

Travelers are advised to check on weather and road conditions. **Hours:** Visitor center daily 9-4. Guided tours of the facility are offered at 10, 11:30 and 1:30. Nightly stargazing program begins at dusk, Sept. to mid-July. Closed Jan. 1, Thanksgiving and Christmas.

Cost: Visitor center free. Guided tours $7.75; $3 (ages 7-12). All-day pass $9.75; $3.25 (ages 7-12). Night observation program $49; $45 (ages 62+, students with ID and military with ID). Reservations are

required for night observation program and should be made 1 month in advance. **Phone:** (520) 318-8726. GT 🎏

SHOW LOW (D-5) pop. 10,660, elev. 6,347'

Show Low took its name from the winning hand in a poker game between Native American scout Col. Croyden E. Cooley and his friend Marion Clark. The town's main street, Deuce of Clubs, was named after the winning card.

On the edge of the Mogollon Rim, the town offers numerous recreational pursuits, including fishing, camping, hiking and horseback riding.

Show Low Chamber of Commerce: 81 E. Deuce of Clubs, Show Low, AZ 85901. **Phone:** (928) 537-2326 or (888) 746-9569.

FOOL HOLLOW LAKE RECREATION AREA, 2 mi. n. of US 60 off SR 260, then e. on Old Linden Rd. to park entrance, offers fishing and boating in a lake covering the old town site of Adair. Camping among the 100-foot-tall pine trees also is available. See Recreation Areas Chart. **Hours:** Park daily 5 a.m.-10 p.m. Office daily 8-4:30. **Cost:** Mar. 15-Oct. 15 $7 (per private vehicle, up to four passengers); $3 (per additional adult passenger in vehicle or individual arriving on foot or bicycle). Rest of year $3 (per private vehicle). Camping Mar. 15-Oct. 15 $17-$30 (per private vehicle). Camping rest of year $15-$25 (per private vehicle). **Phone:** (928) 537-3680, or (520) 586-2283 for camping reservations. 🏕 ⊠ 🎣 🎏

SHOW LOW HISTORICAL SOCIETY MUSEUM is at 561 E. Deuce of Clubs. The 17-room museum is housed in Show Low's former city hall, police department and jail building. You'll see an original jail cell, a railroad display, a quilt room, a kitchen filled with items from the 1800s and early 1900s, and photos of the town and its well-known residents and visitors. **Time:** Allow 30 minutes minimum. **Hours:** Wed.-Sat. 10-3 (weather permitting), Mar.-Dec. **Cost:** Donations. **Phone:** (928) 532-7115.

BEST WESTERN PAINT PONY LODGE   (928)537-5773

Motel $89-$199

AAA Benefit: Save 10% or more every day and earn 10% bonus points!

Address: 581 W Deuce of Clubs Ave 85901 **Location:** On US 60 and SR 260. **Facility:** 50 units. 2 stories (no elevator), exterior corridors. **Guest Services:** coin laundry. **Featured Amenity: full hot breakfast.**

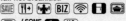

DAYS INN   (928)537-4356

Motel $68-$113 **Address:** 480 W Deuce of Clubs Ave 85901 **Location:** On US 60 and SR 260. **Facility:** 122 units. 2 stories (no elevator), interior/exterior corridors. **Pool(s):** heated outdoor. **Guest Services:** coin laundry.

HAMPTON INN & SUITES (SHOW LOW/PINETOP)
(928)532-4444

WWWW Hotel $129-$149 Address: 1501 E Woolford Rd 85902 Location: On SR 260, 1.5 mi s of US 60. Facility: 73 units. 3 stories, interior corridors. Terms: 1-7 night minimum stay, cancellation fee imposed. Pool(s): heated indoor. Activities: hot tub, exercise room. Guest Services: valet and coin laundry.

AAA Benefit: Members save up to 10%!

HOLIDAY INN EXPRESS
928/537-5115

WW Hotel. Rates not provided. Address: 151 W Deuce of Clubs Ave 85901 Location: On US 60 and SR 260. Facility: 69 units. 3 stories, interior corridors. Pool(s): heated indoor. Activities: hot tub, exercise room. Guest Services: coin laundry.

K C MOTEL
(928)537-4433

WW WW
Motel
$59-$79

Address: 60 W Deuce of Clubs Ave 85901 Location: On US 60 and SR 260. Facility: 35 units. 1-2 stories (no elevator), exterior corridors. Terms: cancellation fee imposed. Guest Services: coin laundry. Featured Amenity: continental breakfast.

/ SOME UNITS

KIVA MOTEL
(928)537-4542

WW WW
Motel
$58-$68

Address: 261 E Deuce of Clubs 85901 Location: On US 60 and SR 260; center. Facility: 20 units. 1 story, exterior corridors. Terms: 3 day cancellation notice. Activities: sauna, hot tub.

/ SOME UNITS

SUPER 8
(928)532-7323

WW WW
Hotel
$60-$130

Address: 1751 W Deuce of Clubs Ave 85901 Location: 2 mi w of jct US 60 and SR 260, south side. Facility: 66 units. 3 stories, interior corridors. Bath: shower only. Pool(s): heated indoor. Activities: hot tub. Guest Services: coin laundry. Featured Amenity: continental breakfast.

WHERE TO EAT

CATTLEMEN'S STEAKHOUSE AND LOUNGE
928/537-9797

WW WW Steak. Casual Dining. $7-$30 AAA Inspector Notes: A wide selection of broiled beef cuts, along with lobster and fish dishes, gives everyone a favorite choice. Freshly baked bread is served warm, and fixings from the fresh salad bar complete the meal. Features: full bar, happy hour. Address: 1231 E Deuce of Clubs Ave 85901 Location: Jct US 60 and SR 260. [B] [L] [D]

LICANO'S MEXICAN FOOD & STEAK HOUSE
928/537-8220

WW WW Mexican. Casual Dining. $9-$26 AAA Inspector Notes: The attractive dining room resembles that of a stylish steakhouse. Seafood and steak entrées include Alaskan salmon grilled in a lemon butter sauce, slow-roasted prime rib and bacon-wrapped filet mignon, but the classic dishes of Mexico are what are warm and filling here. Guests can count on pleasant service with a friendly smile. Features: full bar. Address: 573 W Deuce of Clubs Ave 85902 Location: On US 60 and SR 260; center. [L] [D]

SIERRA VISTA (G-5) pop. 43,888, elev. 4,600'
• Restaurants p. 240

Sierra Vista has been built upon the historic past of Fort Huachuca (see place listing p. 73), established in 1877. The fort is now the largest single employer in southern Arizona, and most of its personnel live in the area. The scenery makes Sierra Vista special: The city is nestled on the eastern slopes of the Huachuca Mountains and overlooks the San Pedro River Valley. Nature lovers are attracted to nearby Coronado National Memorial (see place listing p. 55), San Pedro Riparian National Conservation Area (6 miles east) and Ramsey Canyon Preserve.

Sierra Vista Visitor Center: 3020 E. Tacoma St., Sierra Vista, AZ 85635. **Phone:** (520) 417-6960 or (800) 288-3861.

FORT HUACHUCA MUSEUM—see Fort Huachuca p. 73.

CANDLEWOOD SUITES
(520)439-8200

WW WW Extended Stay Hotel $110-$149 Address: 1904 S Hwy 92 85635 Location: Jct SR 90 and 92, 1.4 mi s. Facility: 71 efficiencies. 3 stories, interior corridors. Terms: cancellation fee imposed. Pool(s): outdoor. Activities: hot tub, exercise room. Guest Services: valet and coin laundry.

/ SOME UNITS

COMFORT INN & SUITES
(520)459-0515

WWWW
Hotel
$79-$139

Address: 3500 E Fry Blvd 85635 Location: Just w of jct SR 90 and 92. Facility: 65 units. 3 stories, interior corridors. Pool(s): outdoor. Activities: hot tub, limited exercise equipment. Guest Services: coin laundry. Featured Amenity: breakfast buffet.

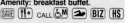

DAYS INN
(520)458-8500

WW WW Hotel $69-$73 Address: 3460 E Fry Blvd 85635 Location: Just w of jct SR 90 and 92. Facility: 40 units. 2 stories (no elevator), exterior corridors. Pool(s): outdoor. Guest Services: valet and coin laundry.

/ SOME UNITS

FAIRFIELD INN & SUITES BY MARRIOTT
(520)439-5900

WWWW Hotel $104-$233 Address: 3855 El Mercado Loop 85635 Location: Jct SR 90, 1.5 mi s on SR 92. Located at Sierra Vista Mall. Facility: 67 units. 3 stories, interior corridors. Pool(s): heated outdoor. Activities: hot tub, picnic facilities, exercise room. Guest Services: valet and coin laundry.

AAA Benefit: Members save 5% or more!

GARDEN PLACE SUITES   (520)439-3300

 Extended Stay Hotel $104 **Address:** 100 N Garden Ave 85635 **Location:** Just n of Fry Blvd. **Facility:** 96 efficiencies. 3 stories, interior corridors. **Terms:** cancellation fee imposed. **Pool(s):** heated outdoor. **Activities:** hot tub, exercise room. **Guest Services:** valet and coin laundry.

GATEWAY STUDIO SUITES   520-458-5555

 Extended Stay Hotel. Rates not provided. **Address:** 203 S Garden Ave 85635 **Location:** Just s of Fry Blvd; just e of main gate to Fort Huachuca. **Facility:** 83 efficiencies. 3 stories, interior corridors. **Pool(s):** heated outdoor. **Activities:** hot tub, picnic facilities, exercise room. **Guest Services:** valet and coin laundry.

HAMPTON INN SIERRA VISTA   (520)439-5400

Hotel
$89-$189

AAA Benefit:
Members save up to
10%!

Address: 4100 Snyder Blvd 85635 **Location:** On SR 92, 1 mi s of SR 90. **Facility:** 58 units. 3 stories, interior corridors. **Terms:** 1-7 night minimum stay, cancellation fee imposed. **Pool(s):** heated indoor. **Activities:** hot tub, bicycles, exercise room. **Guest Services:** valet and coin laundry. **Featured Amenity: breakfast buffet.**

HOLIDAY INN EXPRESS   (520)439-8800

Hotel $99-$249 **Address:** 1902 S Hwy 92 85635 **Location:** Jct SR 90 and 92, 1.4 mi s. **Facility:** 77 units. 3 stories, interior corridors. **Terms:** cancellation fee imposed. **Pool(s):** outdoor. **Activities:** hot tub, picnic facilities, exercise room. **Guest Services:** valet and coin laundry.

QUALITY INN   (520)458-7900

Hotel
$49-$149

Address: 1631 S Hwy 92 85635 **Location:** On SR 92, 1 mi s of jct SR 90. **Facility:** 99 units. 2 stories (no elevator), interior corridors. **Pool(s):** outdoor. **Activities:** hot tub, exercise room. **Guest Services:** valet and coin laundry. **Featured Amenity: full hot breakfast.**

AAA Vacations® packages ...

exciting itineraries

and exclusive values

SIERRA SUITES   (520)459-4221

Hotel
$59-$89

Address: 391 E Fry Blvd 85635 **Location:** Jct SR 90 and 92, 2.2 mi w. **Facility:** 100 units. 2 stories (no elevator), exterior corridors. **Terms:** cancellation fee imposed. **Pool(s):** heated outdoor. **Activities:** hot tub, picnic facilities, exercise room. **Guest Services:** valet and coin laundry. **Featured Amenity: breakfast buffet.**

SUN CANYON INN   (520)459-0610

Hotel $75-$95 **Address:** 260 N Garden Ave 85635 **Location:** Just n of Fry Blvd; just e of main gate to Fort Huachuca. **Facility:** 80 units, some efficiencies. 4 stories, interior corridors. **Terms:** 3 day cancellation notice. **Amenities:** safes. **Pool(s):** heated outdoor. **Activities:** hot tub, exercise room. **Guest Services:** valet and coin laundry.

TOWNEPLACE SUITES BY MARRIOTT   (520)515-9900

Extended Stay Hotel $98-$221 **Address:** 3399 Rodeo Dr 85635 **Location:** Jct SR 90, 1.5 mi s on SR 92, just w on Avenida Cochise, just s on Oakmont Dr, then just e. **Facility:** 71

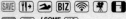
AAA Benefit:
Members save 5%
or more!

efficiencies, some two bedrooms and kitchens. 3 stories, interior corridors. **Pool(s):** heated outdoor. **Activities:** picnic facilities, exercise room. **Guest Services:** valet and coin laundry.

THE WESTERN MOTEL   (520)458-4303

Motel
$40-$45

Address: 43 W Fry Blvd 85635 **Location:** 0.4 mi e of main gate to Fort Huachuca. **Facility:** 25 units, some efficiencies. 1 story, exterior corridors.

WINDEMERE HOTEL & CONFERENCE CENTER   (520)459-5900

Hotel $79-$159 **Address:** 2047 S Hwy 92 85635 **Location:** 1.5 mi s of jct SR 90. **Facility:** 151 units. 3 stories, interior corridors. **Terms:** check-in 4 pm, cancellation fee imposed. **Amenities:** video games. **Pool(s):** heated outdoor. **Activities:** hot tub, exercise room. **Guest Services:** valet and coin laundry.

WHERE TO EAT

THE BREAD BASKET   520/458-8580

 Breads/Pastries. Casual Dining. $4-$9 **AAA Inspector Notes:** This small bakery serves a Continental breakfast, in addition to warm, hearty lunches from 11 am to 2 pm. **Address:** 355 W Wilcox Dr 85635 **Location:** Jct Fry Blvd, just s on Business Rt SR 90 (Buffalo Soldier Tr), just e. B L

GOLDEN DRAGON   520/458-7575

 Chinese. Casual Dining. $5-$21 **AAA Inspector Notes:** Located in a strip mall, the eatery's modest décor gives way to delicious, traditional Chinese favorites like kung pao chicken, Peking duck, and shrimp lo mein. The friendly staff makes you feel right at home. **Features:** full bar. **Address:** 2151 S Hwy 92, Suite 112 85635 **Location:** Jct SR 90, 1.7 mi s. L D

ANA TOKYO JAPANESE RESTAURANT   520/458-1993

▼▼ Japanese. Casual Dining. $11-$60 **AAA Inspector Notes:** his bright and modern eatery has teppan tables and a sushi bar. eatures: full bar. **Address:** 1633 S Hwy 92 85635 **Location:** Jct SR 0 and 92, 1.1 mi s. [L] [D] CALL 🈺

A CASITA MEXICAN RESTAURANT & CANTINA
520/458-2376

▼▼ Mexican. Casual Dining. $7-$19 **AAA Inspector Notes:** heerful Mexican decor pleases the eye, and hearty, traditional ishes satisfy any appetite at this popular spot. **Features:** full bar, appy hour. **Address:** 465 E Fry Blvd 85635 **Location:** 2.1 mi w of t SR 90 and 92. [L] [D]

HE MESQUITE TREE RESTAURANT   520/378-2758

▼▼ American. Casual Dining. $13-$25 **AAA Inspector Notes:** his casual restaurant presents a diverse menu of steaks, prime rib, arbecue foods and seafood, chicken and pasta dishes. When the weather is nice, guests can request a seat on the patio under the nesquite tree. **Features:** full bar, patio dining. **Reservations:** suggested. **Address:** 6398 S Hwy 92 85615 **Location:** 7 mi s of jct SR 0 and 92. [D]

THE OUTSIDE INN   520/378-4645

▼▼▼ International. Casual Dining. $9-$33 **AAA Inspector Notes:** This cozy dining room features creative cuisine from soups, sandwiches and sandwiches for a casual lunch to more refined entrées for dinner. Make sure you ask for the dessert tray after the meal. During ice weather enjoy a meal on the comfortable patio. **Features:** beer & wine, patio dining. **Reservations:** suggested, dinner. **Address:** S Highway 92 85650 **Location:** 5.5 mi s of jct SR 90.
[L] [D]

TANUKI JAPANESE RESTAURANT & SUSHI BAR
520/459-6853

▼▼ Japanese. Casual Dining. $6-$18 **AAA Inspector Notes:** A nice selection of fresh sushi and sashimi can be found at this restaurant. Patrons can choose from teriyaki, tempura or yakitora classics. **Features:** full bar, patio dining. **Address:** 1221 E Fry Blvd 85635 **Location:** Jct SR 90, 1.7 mi w. [L] [D]

SOMERTON (F-1) pop. 14,287, elev. 103'

GAMBLING ESTABLISHMENTS
• **Cocopah Casino,** jct. US 95 (Ave. B) and 15th St. at 15318 S. Ave. B. **Hours:** Daily 24 hours. **Phone:** (928) 726-8066 or (800) 237-5687.

COCOPAH RESORT & CONFERENCE CENTER   928/722-6677

fyi Not evaluated. **Address:** 15268 S Ave B 85350 **Location:** I-8 exit 2 (16th St/US 95), 2.5 mi w to Ave B, then 6.5 mi s. Facilities, services, and décor characterize a mid-scale property. Located just outside of town, this upscale complex features multiple dining and entertainment options and spacious, well-kept guest rooms.

SONOITA pop. 818

SONOITA INN   520/455-5935

fyi Not evaluated. **Address:** 3243 Hwy 82 85637 **Location:** Center. Facilities, services, and décor characterize a mid-scale property.

SONORAN DESERT NATIONAL MONUMENT (E-3)

South of Phoenix in south-central Arizona, Sonoran Desert National Monument comprises mountain ranges, wide valleys and several saguaro cactus forests on 486,000 acres. The functioning desert ecosystem is a habitat for an array of wildlife, including desert bighorn sheep, mule deer, bobcats, desert tortoises, raptors, owls and bats.

It is believed that ancestors of the O'odham, Quechan, Cocopah and other tribes occupied villages in the area, which contains archeological and historical sites. For further information contact the Bureau of Land Management, Phoenix District, 21605 N. 7th Ave., Phoenix, AZ 85027; phone (623) 580-5500.

SPRINGERVILLE (D-6) pop. 1,961, elev. 6,862'

Springerville is in a cattle-ranching area of eastern Arizona. Created by shield volcanoes, the White Mountains neighbor the town, making it a convenient place to stay while enjoying the many outdoor activities offered by the area.

Springerville-Eagar Regional Chamber of Commerce: 418 E. Main St. (in the Springerville Heritage Center), P.O. Box 31, Springerville, AZ 85938. **Phone:** (928) 333-2123 or (866) 733-2123.

SPRINGERVILLE HERITAGE CENTER is at 418 E. Main St. Housed in a restored school building, the center offers a gallery of local art; a sketch by Rembrandt; European antiques dating from the Renaissance to the 18th century; dinosaur fossils found in the area; and access to the ancient ruins at Casa Malpais Pueblo *(see attraction listing).* **Hours:** Mon.-Sat. 8-4. Closed major holidays. **Cost:** Donations. **Phone:** (928) 333-2123.

Casa Malpais Museum, in the Springerville Heritage Center at 418 E. Main St., showcases pottery, artifacts and baskets unearthed at Casa Malpais Archaeological Park, a 15-acre restoration project of Mogollon and ancient pueblo ruins occupied 1250-1400. After watching an orientation film, visitors drive to the pueblo site for a guided walking tour (self-guiding tours are not permitted).

Time: Allow 1 hour, 30 minutes minimum. **Hours:** Museum Mon.-Sat. 8-4. Site tours depart at 9, 11:30 and 2 (weather permitting), Mar.-Nov. Closed Jan. 1, Thanksgiving and Christmas. **Cost:** $10; $8 (ages 60+); $5 (children and students with ID). **Phone:** (928) 333-5375.

SUN CITY (I-2) pop. 37,499, elev. 1,140'
• Hotels & Restaurants map & index p. 154
• Part of Phoenix area — see map p. 126

Twelve miles northwest of Phoenix but part of the metropolitan area of the capital city, Sun City is one of the largest and most popular retirement communities in the country. By 1978 it had reached its population goal of more than 40,000, with most residential property in use. Sun City West, 2.5 miles west via Grand Avenue, offers a similar array of golf courses, stores, restaurants, recreation areas and other services.

Sun City Visitors Center: 16824 N. 99th Ave., Sun City, AZ 85351. **Phone:** (623) 977-5000 or (800) 437-8146.

(See map & index p. 154.)

LITTLE BITE OF ITALY   623/972-3311 6
▼▼ Italian. Casual Dining. $8-$16 **AAA Inspector Notes:** This
casual neighborhood eatery features classic Italian favorites. Friendly
employees enhance the cosy setting. **Features:** full bar, patio dining,
happy hour. **Address:** 15456 N 99th Ave 85351 **Location:** Jct
Greenway Rd. L D CALL M

SUNSET CRATER VOLCANO NATIONAL MONUMENT (B-4)

Lying approximately 12 miles north of Flagstaff via US 89, then 2 miles east on Sunset Crater-Wupatki Loop Road, the 1,000-foot-high cinder cone of Sunset Crater Volcano dominates the surrounding fields of cinders, lava flows and spatter cones. The bright-reddish hues of the decomposed, water-stained sulfuric rock at the summit are in stark contrast with the black basalt of the adjacent rocks. From a distance the mountain appears to be on fire.

Dark at the base, the volcano also has shades of red, orange and yellow leading to the summit and takes on a rosy tint during the hour before sunset. In 1892 John Wesley Powell noted the phenomenon and purportedly gave the cone its name.

Sunset Crater Volcano may have first erupted A.D. 1064-65 and was active intermittently for nearly 200 years. Recent research indicates that the eruption may not have occurred until 1088 and may have lasted only a year. A self-guiding trail leads over the Bonito lava flow; sturdy walking shoes are recommended. A paved road crosses the lava flow and connects the monument with Wupatki National Monument *(see place listing p. 306).* Picnicking is permitted. The Lenox Crater Trail is a steep 1-mile round-trip hike to the top of a nearby volcanic summit.

Fire restrictions may apply. Allow 30 minutes minimum. Visitor center daily 8-5, May-Oct.; 9-5, rest of year. Closed Christmas. Admission $5 per person (includes Wupatki National Monument); free (ages 0-15). Phone (928) 526-0502.

SUPAI (B-3) pop. 208, elev. 3,195'

▼ **HAVASU CANYON** is accessible from Hualapai Hilltop, which is reached from SR 66 via a turnoff 5 miles e. of Peach Springs. There are no services after the turnoff. Most of the 65-mile road from Peach Springs is in good condition.

Havasu Canyon is home to the village of Supai, which serves as the governmental center of the Havasupai Indian Reservation. Automobiles must be left at Hualapai Hilltop; the 8-mile journey to the canyon floor and Havasu Falls can be covered on horseback, helicopter or on foot down a precipitous trail.

Note: The trail is only recommended for experienced hikers in good physical condition. The return climb out of the canyon is very arduous. Summer temperatures may prohibit daytime trips; phone ahead to confirm. Hikers must carry at least two liters of water. Camping is permitted; no open fires are allowed. Swimming is permitted. Horse rental is available.

Hours: Office hours daily 5:30 a.m.-7 p.m., Apr. 1 to mid-Oct.; 8-5, rest of year. **Cost:** Entrance fee $40 (per person). Camping $17 (per person). Helicopter fee $85 (per person, one way). Reservations for horses and campgrounds are required. Helicopter scenic rides have limited availability; reservations are not accepted. **Phone:** (928) 448-2141, or (928) 448-2180 for camping reservations.

SUPERIOR (J-6) pop. 2,837, elev. 2,730'

Although it began as a silver-mining town, Superior owes its existence to its proximity to some of the deepest and richest copper lodes in the country. Near Superior is Apache Leap Cliff, where, according to legend, 75 Apache warriors leaped to their deaths rather than be captured by the cavalry. The town also is near the southern terminus of US 60 (Gila/Pinal Scenic Drive), which travels northward through Tonto National Forest, Salt River Canyon and the Fort Apache Indian Reservation.

Superior Chamber of Commerce: 165 W. Main St., P.O. Box 95, Superior, AZ 85273. **Phone:** (520) 689-0200.

▼ **BOYCE THOMPSON ARBORETUM STATE PARK,** 3 mi. w. on US 60 at Milepost 223, has more than 390 acres of desert plants collected from all over the world; 50 acres are accessible for viewing. Founded in the 1920s by mining magnate Col. William Boyce Thompson, the arboretum has 3 miles of paths and trails leading past towering trees, cacti, mountain cliffs, a streamside forest, a desert lake, hidden canyon and panoramic views.

An interpretive center has educational displays and two greenhouses housing cacti and succulents. **Time:** Allow 1 hour minimum. **Hours:** Daily 8-5, Sept.-Apr.; 6-3, rest of year. Classes, workshops and tours are offered. Closed Christmas. Phone ahead to confirm schedule. **Cost:** $10; $5 (ages 5-12). **Phone:** (520) 689-2811 or (520) 689-2723.

SURPRISE (I-2) pop. 117,517, elev. 1,178'
• Hotels & Restaurants map & index p. 154
• Part of Phoenix area — see map p. 126

In the Sonoran desert, Surprise was founded in 1937 by Homer C. Ludden, a state legislator who named the town after his hometown in Nebraska. Surprise Stadium is the spring training center for the Kansas City Royals and the Texas Rangers. Eight miles southwest is White Tank Mountain Regional Park *(see Recreation Areas Chart),* which offers 22 miles of trails for hiking, horseback riding and mountain biking. Ancestral Desert People petroglyphs and such wildlife as the cactus wren, the official state bird, may be seen.

Surprise Regional Chamber of Commerce: 16126 N. Civic Center Plaza, Surprise, AZ 85374. **Phone:** (623) 583-0692.

(See map & index p. 154.)

COMFORT INN & SUITES OF SURPRISE (623)544-6874 **7**

Hotel $70-$210 **Address:** 13337 W Grand Ave 85374 **Location:** Jct Bell Rd, 0.4 mi se. **Facility:** 86 units. 3 stories, interior corridors. **Pool(s):** heated outdoor. **Activities:** hot tub, picnic facilities, exercise room. **Guest Services:** valet and coin laundry.

DAYS INN & SUITES SURPRISE (623)933-4000 **9**

Hotel $44-$134 **Address:** 12477 W Bell Rd 85374 **Location:** US 60 (Grand Ave), 1.2 mi e. **Facility:** 60 units. 3 stories, interior corridors. **Amenities:** safes. **Pool(s):** heated outdoor. **Activities:** hot tub, picnic facilities. **Guest Services:** coin laundry.

HAMPTON INN & SUITES SURPRISE
(623)537-9122 **4**

Hotel $79-$159

AAA Benefit: Members save up to 10%!

Address: 14783 W Grand Ave 85374 **Location:** Jct Bell Rd, 2 mi nw. **Facility:** 100 units. 4 stories, interior corridors. **Terms:** 1-7 night minimum stay, cancellation fee imposed. **Pool(s):** heated outdoor. **Activities:** hot tub, exercise room. **Guest Services:** coin laundry. **Featured Amenity:** full hot breakfast.

HOLIDAY INN EXPRESS & SUITES 623/975-5540 **5**

Hotel. Rates not provided. **Address:** 16540 N Bullard Ave 85374 **Location:** Jct US 60 (Grand Ave), 1.4 mi w on Bell Rd, then just s. **Facility:** 115 units. 4 stories, interior corridors. **Pool(s):** heated outdoor. **Activities:** hot tub, exercise room. **Guest Services:** valet and coin laundry.

QUALITY INN & SUITES OF SUN CITIES (623)583-3500 **10**

Hotel $59-$209 **Address:** 16741 N Greasewood St 85374 **Location:** US 60 (Grand Ave), 1.2 mi e on Bell Rd, then just s. **Facility:** 69 units. 3 stories, interior corridors. **Amenities:** safes. **Pool(s):** heated indoor. **Activities:** hot tub, exercise room. **Guest Services:** coin laundry.

RESIDENCE INN BY MARRIOTT PHOENIX NW SURPRISE (623)249-6333 **6**

Extended Stay Hotel $113-$280 **Address:** 16418 N Bullard Ave 85374 **Location:** Jct US 60 (Grand Ave), 1.4 mi w on Bell Rd, then just s. **Facility:** 116 units, some two bedrooms, efficiencies and kitchens. 4 stories, interior corridors. **Pool(s):** heated outdoor. **Activities:** hot tub, picnic facilities, exercise room. **Guest Services:** valet and coin laundry.

AAA Benefit: Members save 5% or more!

Remember, car seats, booster seats and seat belts save lives

WINDMILL SUITES IN SURPRISE 623/583-0133 **8**

Hotel
Rates not provided

Address: 12545 W Bell Rd 85378 **Location:** US 60 (Grand Ave), 1 mi e. **Facility:** 126 units. 3 stories, interior corridors. **Terms:** check-in 4 pm. **Pool(s):** heated outdoor. **Activities:** hot tub, bicycles, picnic facilities, limited exercise equipment. **Guest Services:** valet and coin laundry. **Featured Amenity:** full hot breakfast.

WHERE TO EAT

AMUSE BOUCHE 623/322-8881 **1**

American. Casual Dining. $10-$26 **AAA Inspector Notes:** This tiny storefront doubles as a gourmet catering service. Delicious homemade meals are served by a friendly and knowledgeable staff. It is bring your own bottle, so do not forget a favorite bottle of wine. Breakfast is served on the weekend. **Features:** Sunday brunch. **Reservations:** suggested. **Address:** 17058 W Bell Rd 85374 **Location:** Jct Cotton Ln; northeast corner.

MACAYO MEXICAN KITCHEN 623/975-9570

Mexican. Casual Dining. $7-$19 **AAA Inspector Notes:** The colorfully furnished Mexican-style eatery prepares Sonoran Mexican dishes. Friendly and efficient staffers serve traditional and lighter dishes flavored with this place's own chili peppers, which are grown near Tucson. **Features:** full bar, happy hour. **Address:** 15565 W Bell Rd 85379 **Location:** Jct Reems Rd; southwest corner.

SAIGON KITCHEN 623/544-6400 **2**

Vietnamese. Casual Dining. $6-$15 **AAA Inspector Notes:** Classic Vietnamese dishes are served in a stylish setting. The friendly staff helps out with menu options. **Features:** full bar, patio dining. **Address:** 14071 W Bell Rd 85374 **Location:** Jct Grand Ave, 0.8 mi w.

VOGUE BISTRO 623/544-9109 **3**

New American. Casual Dining. $10-$26 **AAA Inspector Notes:** This casual, yet stylish, bistro serves up contemporary American cuisine with a French influence. Try the Tuscan flatbread for starters, followed up by steamed mussels or the hearty meatloaf. **Features:** full bar, patio dining. **Address:** 15411 W Waddell Rd 85379 **Location:** Jct US 60 (Grand Ave), 4.5 mi w; in Marley Park Plaza Shopping Center.

TAYLOR pop. 4,112

RODEWAY INN-SILVER CREEK INN (928)536-2600

Motel $56-$75

Address: 825 N Main St 85939 **Location:** On SR 77. **Facility:** 41 units. 2 stories (no elevator), exterior corridors. **Guest Services:** coin laundry. **Featured Amenity:** full hot breakfast.

TEMPE (J-3) pop. 161,719, elev. 1,159'

- Hotels p. 245 • Restaurants p. 248
- Attractions map p. 138
- Hotels & Restaurants map & index p. 164
- Part of Phoenix area — see map p. 126

Founded as Hayden's Ferry in 1871, Tempe originally was named for Charles Trumbull Hayden, who owned a flour mill and operated a ferry across the

(See map & index p. 164.)

Salt River. The town was renamed Tempe (Tem-PEE) in 1879 for the area's alleged resemblance to the Vale of Tempe in ancient Greece.

In 1886 the dusty cow town became the home of the Arizona Territorial Normal School, later to become Arizona State University *(see attraction listing).* Downtown Tempe has a laid-back college town feel.

ASU Gammage, one of the last major buildings designed by Frank Lloyd Wright, is a performing arts center on the campus of Arizona State University. Phone (480) 965-6912 for information about free guided tours of the center.

Twice a year, crowds head downtown for the ✥ Spring Tempe Festival of the Arts and the ✥ Tempe Fall Festival of the Arts, which feature a live entertainment stage, street performers and more than 350 artists selling handcrafted items. In October, Tempe celebrates its ties to its sister city—Regensburg, Germany—with Oktoberfest at Tempe Town Lake that's complete with beer, brats, bands and family entertainment. Sun Devil Stadium hosts a college bowl game in late December. Then Tempe residents usher in the new year at Mill Avenue's New Year's Eve.

Sports fans can go out to the ball game during spring training, which begins in late February. Fifteen Cactus League teams get ready for the season at Tempe Diablo Stadium; phone (480) 350-5205.

Tempe Tourism Office: 222 S. Mill Ave., Suite 120, Tempe, AZ 85281. **Phone:** (480) 894-8158 or (800) 283-6734.

Shopping: Specialty shops are scattered throughout downtown Tempe, the five-block segment of Mill Avenue between 3rd Street and University Drive. Arizona Mills Mall, I-10 and Baseline Road, is one of the state's largest shopping and attraction complexes. Tempe Marketplace, at McClintock Drive and Rio Salado Parkway, is a popular outdoor shopping and entertainment destination.

Nightlife: Football fans enjoy tasty food and libations as they root on ASU in the sports bars and restaurants on shady Mill Avenue. Gordon Biersch Brewery (420 S. Mill Ave., #201) pours tasty brew and has a second floor terrace overlooking the street action below; phone (480) 736-0033. Blasted Barley Beer Co. (404 S. Mill Ave.) features craft beer and more than 40 flat-screen HDTVs and is usually packed on big game nights; phone (480) 967-5887. Postino Wine Café (615 S. College Ave.), set in a restored, red brick building on the ASU campus, is the place to go before shows at the ASU Gammage auditorium; phone (480) 927-1111.

ARIZONA HISTORICAL SOCIETY MUSEUM AT PAPAGO PARK, 1300 N. College Ave., portrays the history of 20th- and 21st-century Central Arizona through hands-on exhibits about the various people that have inhabited the area. Displays describe the history of transportation in the state, using and conserving water in an arid climate, Arizona's roles in World War II and the rise of a thriving metropolis in the desert. A natural history display contains gems and minerals mined in the Southwest. Educational programs are offered throughout the year.

Hours: Museum Tues.-Sat. 10-4, Sun. noon-4. Closed Jan. 1, July 4, Veterans Day, Thanksgiving and Christmas. **Cost:** $5; $4 (ages 12-18 and 60+). Ages 0-16 must be accompanied by an adult. Prices may vary; phone ahead. **Phone:** (480) 929-9499. 🎦 🏢 Center Pkwy/Washington, 24

ARIZONA STATE UNIVERSITY is at University Dr and Mill Ave. The university's main campus includes the distinctive ASU Gammage, a concert hall designed by Frank Lloyd Wright that is one of his last completed nonresidential designs. The Arboretum at ASU encompasses the entire campus. Self-guiding walking tour brochures are available at the Information Center in the Memorial Union and the Visitors Center. **Hours:** Arboretum open daily dawn-dusk. **Phone:** (480) 965-2100. 🏢 Veterans Way/College, 26

Arizona State University Art Museum is housed on ASU's Tempe campus at 51 E. 10th St. The museum's primary focus is on contemporary art in interactive formats that emphasize new ideas and media. Changing exhibitions and special events also are presented. **Hours:** Tues.-Sat. 11-5 (also Tues. 5-8 during academic year). Closed major holidays. **Cost:** Free. **Phone:** (480) 965-2787. 🏢 Veterans Way/College, 26

ASU Art Museum Ceramics Center and Brickyard Gallery is at 699 S. Mill Ave., Suite 109, on the campus of Arizona State University. The center features more than 4,500 ceramic pieces reflecting the world's social, cultural and historical aspects. **Hours:** Tues.-Sat. 11-5 (also Tues. 5-8 during academic year). Closed major holidays. **Cost:** Free. **Phone:** (480) 727-8170 or (480) 965-2787. 🏢 Mill Ave/3rd St, 25

Gallery of Scientific Exploration is at 781 E. Terrace Mall in Interdisciplinary Science and Technology Building IV on the Arizona State University campus. The gallery features engaging interactive exhibits along with high-definition monitors showing video feeds from satellites and robotic probes. Highlights include a replica of the Mars rover *Curiosity,* a dynamic globe displaying current weather patterns and a panorama of the Martian landscape assembled from images taken by NASA's Mars Exploration Rover *Opportunity.* Astronomy shows in 3D are available; phone for schedule. **Time:** Allow 30 minutes minimum. **Hours:** Mon.-Fri. 8-5. Closed ASU school holidays. **Cost:** Free. **Parking:** $3 per hour. **Phone:** (480) 727-2868 or (480) 727-2538. GT 🏢 University Dr/Rural, 27

(See map & index p. 164.)

BIG SURF, 1500 N. McClintock Rd., provides man-made waves in a wave pool and beaches. There also are 18 waterslides, several volleyball courts and three activity pools. **Hours:** Daily 10-6, Memorial Day-Labor Day. **Cost:** $29.95; $19.95 (under 48 inches tall); $14.95 (ages 55+, police and active military with ID); $2 (ages 0-2). After 3 p.m. $15.95. **Phone:** (480) 994-2297.

IMAX THEATER AT ARIZONA MILLS, off I-10 Baseline Rd. exit at the mall, presents films that are based on both IMAX and IMAX 3D technology. IMAX 3D films require the use of 3D glasses. The lifelike images are projected on a screen that is six stories high. Hollywood feature films are shown. **Hours:** IMAX, IMAX 3D and feature-length films are shown daily. Phone ahead to confirm schedule. **Cost:** $15; $12 (ages 60+); $11 (ages 3-13). **Phone:** (480) 897-4629.

TEMPE HISTORY MUSEUM is off US 60 exit 174 (Rural Rd.), then .4 mi. n. to 809 E. Southern Ave. The museum has four themed areas: College Town, Building Our Community, Living Together and Surviving in the Desert. Reading and computer stations as well as a children's gallery filled with hands-on activities provide educational opportunities. **Hours:** Tues.-Sat. 10-5, Sun. 1-5. Closed major holidays. **Cost:** Donations. **Phone:** (480) 350-5100.

ALOFT HOTEL TEMPE (480)621-3300

Hotel $99-$209

AAA Benefit: Members save up to 15%, plus Starwood Preferred Guest® benefits!

Address: 951 E Playa Del Norte Dr 85281 **Location:** SR 202 (Red Mountain Frwy) exit 7 (Rural Rd), just s on Scottsdale Rd, then just e. Veterans Way/College, 26. **Facility:** 136 units. 5 stories, interior corridors. *Bath:* shower only. **Terms:** cancellation fee imposed. **Amenities:** safes. **Pool(s):** heated outdoor. **Activities:** bicycles, exercise room. **Guest Services:** valet and coin laundry, boarding pass kiosk.

BEST WESTERN INN OF TEMPE (480)784-2233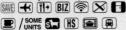

Hotel $69-$149

AAA Benefit: Save 10% or more every day and earn 10% bonus points!

Address: 670 N Scottsdale Rd 85281 **Location:** SR 202 (Red Mountain Frwy) exit 7 (Rural Rd S), just s. Veterans Way/College, 26. **Facility:** 103 units. 4 stories, interior corridors. **Activities:** hot tub, exercise room. **Guest Services:** valet laundry, area transportation.

BEST WESTERN PLUS TEMPE BY THE MALL (480)820-7500

Hotel $70-$140

AAA Benefit: Save 10% or more every day and earn 10% bonus points!

Address: 5300 S Priest Dr 85283 **Location:** I-10 exit 155 (Baseline Rd), 0.4 mi e, then just s. **Facility:** 157 units. 4 stories, interior corridors. **Activities:** hot tub, picnic facilities, exercise room. **Guest Services:** valet and coin laundry, area transportation.

COMFORT SUITES PHOENIX AIRPORT (480)446-9500

Hotel $74-$189

Address: 1625 S 52nd St 85281 **Location:** I-10 exit 153B (Broadway Rd), just s, 0.5 mi e on Broadway Rd, then just n. **Facility:** 92 units. 3 stories, interior corridors. **Pool(s):** heated outdoor. **Activities:** hot tub, exercise room. **Guest Services:** valet and coin laundry.

100% Non-smoking Suites
Free Airport Shuttle from
Sky Harbor Int'l Airport

(See map & index p. 164.)

COUNTRY INN & SUITES BY CARLSON, PHOENIX AIRPORT AT TEMPE   (480)858-9898   **3**
▼▼▼▼ **Hotel** $69-$229 **Address:** 808 N Scottsdale Rd 85281 **Location:** SR 202 (Red Mountain Frwy) exit 7 (Rural Rd S), just n. **Facility:** 83 units. 4 stories, interior corridors. **Pool(s):** heated outdoor. **Activities:** hot tub, exercise room. **Guest Services:** valet and coin laundry, area transportation.

[icons]

COURTYARD BY MARRIOTT-DOWNTOWN TEMPE
                                                  (480)966-2800   **9**

▼▼▼ Hotel $86-$314

COURTYARD *Marriott*
AAA Benefit: Members save 5% or more!

Address: 601 S Ash Ave 85281 **Location:** SR 143 (Hohokam Expwy) exit University Dr, 2.2 mi e, then 0.3 mi n. Mill Ave/3rd St, 25. **Facility:** 160 units. 3 stories, interior corridors. **Parking:** on-site (fee). **Pool(s):** heated outdoor. **Activities:** hot tub, exercise room. **Guest Services:** valet and coin laundry, boarding pass kiosk, area transportation.

[icons]

DAYS INN & SUITES   (480)345-8585   **29**
▼▼ **Hotel** $69-$99 **Address:** 1660 W Elliot Rd 85284 **Location:** I-10 exit 157, just e. **Facility:** 139 units, some efficiencies. 3 stories, exterior corridors. **Pool(s):** heated outdoor. **Activities:** hot tub, picnic facilities. **Guest Services:** coin laundry.

[icons]

DOUBLETREE BY HILTON PHOENIX-TEMPE
                                                  (480)967-1441   **18**

▼▼▼ Hotel $79-$249

DOUBLETREE BY HILTON
AAA Benefit: Members save 5% or more!

Address: 2100 S Priest Dr 85282 **Location:** I-10 exit 153 (Broadway Rd), 0.5 mi e. **Facility:** 270 units. 3 stories, exterior corridors. **Terms:** 1-7 night minimum stay, cancellation fee imposed. **Pool(s):** heated outdoor. **Activities:** hot tub, exercise room, spa. **Guest Services:** valet laundry, area transportation.

[icons]

DRURY INN & SUITES PHOENIX TEMPE (480)940-3700   **30**
▼▼▼ **Hotel** $80-$210 **Address:** 1780 W Ranch Rd 85284 **Location:** I-10 exit 158 (Warner Rd), just e, then just s. **Facility:** 180 units. 7 stories, interior corridors. **Terms:** cancellation fee imposed. **Pool(s):** heated outdoor, heated indoor. **Activities:** hot tub, exercise room. **Guest Services:** valet and coin laundry.

[icons]

Enjoy great member rates and
benefits at AAA/CAA Preferred Hotels

EMBASSY SUITES BY HILTON PHOENIX-TEMPE
                                                  (480)897-7444   **22**
▼▼▼▼ **Hotel** $129-$149 **Address:** 4400 S Rural Rd 85282 **Location:** US 60 (Superstition Frwy) exit 174 (Rural Rd), just s. **Facility:** 224 units. 2-3 stories, exterior corridors. **Terms:** 1-7 night minimum stay, cancellation fee imposed. **Pool(s):** heated outdoor. **Activities:** hot tub, exercise room. **Guest Services:** valet and coin laundry, area transportation.

AAA Benefit: Members save 5% or more!

[icons]

EXTENDED STAY AMERICA-PHOENIX/AIRPORT/TEMPE
                                                  480/557-8880   **12**
▼▼ **Extended Stay Hotel.** Rates not provided. **Address:** 2165 W 15th St 85281 **Location:** I-10 exit 153B (Broadway Rd), 0.3 mi ne, just nw on S 52nd St, then just w. **Facility:** 95 efficiencies. 3 stories, interior corridors. **Pool(s):** heated outdoor. **Activities:** picnic facilities, limited exercise equipment. **Guest Services:** coin laundry.

[icons]

HAMPTON INN & SUITES PHOENIX/TEMPE-ASU AREA
                                                  (480)941-3441   **1**
▼▼▼ **Hotel** $179-$259 **Address:** 1415 N Scottsdale Rd 85281 **Location:** SR 202 Loop (Red Mountain Frwy) exit 7 (Rural Rd S), 0.5 mi n. **Facility:** 117 units. 4 stories, interior corridors. **Terms:** 1-7 night minimum stay, cancellation fee imposed. **Pool(s):** heated outdoor. **Activities:** hot tub, exercise room. **Guest Services:** valet and coin laundry, area transportation.

AAA Benefit: Members save up to 10%!

[icons]

HAWTHORN SUITES BY WYNDHAM
                                                  (480)633-2744   **20**

▼▼▼ Hotel $70-$135

Address: 2301 E Southern Ave 85282 **Location:** SR 101 exit 54 (Southern Ave/Baseline Rd); at southeast corner. **Facility:** 68 units, some efficiencies. 3 stories, interior corridors. **Terms:** cancellation fee imposed. **Amenities:** safes. **Pool(s):** heated outdoor. **Activities:** hot tub, exercise room. **Guest Services:** valet and coin laundry.

[icons]

HOLIDAY INN EXPRESS & SUITES PHOENIX TEMPE-UNIVERSITY   480/966-7202   **16**
▼▼▼ **Hotel.** Rates not provided. **Address:** 1031 E Apache Blvd 85281 **Location:** SR 202 Loop (Red Mountain Frwy) exit 7 (Rural Rd S), 1.5 mi s, then just e. Dorsey/Apache, 28. **Facility:** 72 units. 3 stories, interior corridors. **Terms:** check-in 4 pm. **Pool(s):** heated outdoor. **Activities:** hot tub, exercise room. **Guest Services:** valet and coin laundry, area transportation.

[icons]

HOLIDAY INN EXPRESS HOTEL & SUITES TEMPE ARIZONA MILLS   (480)831-9800   **23**
▼▼▼ **Hotel** $99-$169 **Address:** 1520 W Baseline Rd 85283 **Location:** I-10 exit 155 (Baseline Rd), 0.4 mi e. Adjacent to Arizona Mills Mall. **Facility:** 128 units. 6 stories, interior corridors. **Terms:** 3 day cancellation notice-fee imposed. **Pool(s):** heated outdoor. **Activities:** hot tub, exercise room. **Guest Services:** valet and coin laundry.

[icons]

(See map & index p. 164.)

HOTEL 1333   480/968-3451 **17**

▼▼▼ **Hotel.** Rates not provided. **Address:** 1333 S Rural Rd 85281 **Location:** US 60 (Superstition Frwy) exit 174 (Rural Rd), 2 mi n. Located at southeast area of Arizona State University campus. Dorsey/Apache, 28. **Facility:** 187 units. 4 stories, interior corridors. **Pool(s):** heated outdoor. **Activities:** exercise room. **Guest Services:** valet laundry, area transportation.

HOTEL TEMPE PHOENIX AIRPORT INNSUITES HOTEL & SUITES   480/897-7900 **25**

▼▼ **Hotel.** Rates not provided. **Address:** 1651 W Baseline Rd 85283 **Location:** I-10 exit 155 (Baseline Rd), just e. **Facility:** 160 units, some efficiencies. 2 stories (no elevator), exterior corridors. **Pool(s):** heated outdoor. **Activities:** hot tub, tennis, picnic facilities, exercise room. **Guest Services:** valet and coin laundry, area transportation.

HYATT PLACE TEMPE/PHOENIX AIRPORT
(480)804-9544 **7**

▼▼▼ Hotel $69-$259

HYATT PLACE

AAA Benefit: Members save 10%!

Address: 1413 W Rio Salado Pkwy 85281 **Location:** Just w of Priest Dr. Priest Dr/Washington, 23. **Facility:** 123 units. 6 stories, interior corridors. **Terms:** cancellation fee imposed. **Amenities:** safes. **Pool(s):** heated outdoor. **Activities:** exercise room. **Guest Services:** valet laundry, area transportation. **Featured Amenity:** breakfast buffet.

LA QUINTA INN PHOENIX SKY HARBOR AIRPORT SOUTH
(480)967-4465 **8**

▼▼ **Hotel** $64-$251 **Address:** 911 S 48th St 85281 **Location:** I-10 exit 153B (Broadway Rd) eastbound; exit 153A (University Dr) westbound, 0.8 mi n; on south side of University Dr; east side of SR 143 (Hohokam Expwy). **Facility:** 128 units. 3 stories, interior/exterior corridors. **Pool(s):** heated outdoor. **Activities:** exercise room. **Guest Services:** coin laundry, area transportation.

PHOENIX MARRIOTT TEMPE AT THE BUTTES
(602)225-9000 **19**

▼▼▼ **Resort Hotel** $121-$311

MARRIOTT

AAA Benefit: Members save 5% or more!

Address: 2000 Westcourt Way 85282 **Location:** I-10 exit 153 (Broadway Rd) westbound, 0.8 mi w to 48th St, then 0.3 mi s; exit 48th St eastbound, 0.5 mi s. **Facility:** Ensconced on the side of a mountain, the beautiful resort is enhanced by extensive desert landscaping and sweeping city views. 353 units. 4 stories, interior corridors. **Parking:** on-site (fee) and valet. **Amenities:** safes. **Dining:** 3 restaurants, also, Top of the Rock Restaurant, see separate listing. **Pool(s):** heated outdoor. **Activities:** sauna, hot tub, tennis, lawn sports, exercise room, spa. **Guest Services:** valet laundry, boarding pass kiosk.

RAMADA TEMPE AT ARIZONA MILLS MALL
(480)413-1188 **24**

▼▼▼ Hotel $50-$100

Address: 1701 W Baseline Rd 85283 **Location:** I-10 exit 155 (Baseline Rd), just e. **Facility:** 116 units. 3 stories, exterior corridors. **Pool(s):** heated outdoor. **Activities:** hot tub, picnic facilities, exercise room. **Guest Services:** valet and coin laundry. **Featured Amenity:** full hot breakfast.

RED LION INN & SUITES PHOENIX/TEMPE - ASU
(480)675-9799 **2**

▼▼▼▼ Hotel $79-$159 **Address:** 1429 N Scottsdale Rd 85281 **Location:** SR 202 Loop (Red Mountain Frwy) exit 7 (Rural Rd S), 0.5 mi n. **Facility:** 118 units, some two bedrooms and efficiencies. 1-3 stories, exterior corridors. **Terms:** cancellation fee imposed. **Pool(s):** heated outdoor. **Activities:** hot tub, exercise room. **Guest Services:** valet and coin laundry, area transportation.

RED ROOF INN PHOENIX AIRPORT
(480)449-3205 **13**

▼▼▼ Hotel $49-$118

Address: 2135 W 15th St 85281 **Location:** I-10 exit 153B (Broadway Rd), just nw on S 52nd St, then just w. **Facility:** 125 units. 3 stories, interior corridors. **Amenities:** video games. **Pool(s):** heated outdoor.

RESIDENCE INN BY MARRIOTT TEMPE   (480)756-2122 **21**

▼▼▼ **Extended Stay Hotel** $90-$324 **Address:** 5075 S Priest Dr 85282 **Location:** I-10 exit 155 (Baseline Rd), 0.4 mi e, then just n. Across from Arizona Mills Mall. **Facility:** 126 units,

AAA Benefit: Members save 5% or more!

some two bedrooms, efficiencies and kitchens. 2 stories (no elevator), interior/exterior corridors. **Pool(s):** heated outdoor. **Activities:** hot tub, picnic facilities, exercise room. **Guest Services:** valet and coin laundry.

RESIDENCE INN BY MARRIOTT TEMPE DOWNTOWN/UNIVERSITY
(480)967-2300 **11**

▼▼▼ **Residence Inn Marriott** Extended Stay Hotel $115-$376

AAA Benefit: Members save 5% or more!

Address: 510 S Forest Ave 85281 **Location:** Jct University Dr, just n on Mill Ave, just e; downtown. Veterans Way/College, 26. **Facility:** 173 efficiencies, some two bedrooms. 11 stories, interior corridors. **Parking:** on-site (fee). **Pool(s):** heated outdoor. **Activities:** hot tub, exercise room. **Guest Services:** valet and coin laundry. **Featured Amenity:** breakfast buffet.

(See map & index p. 164.)

SHERATON PHOENIX AIRPORT HOTEL TEMPE
(480)967-6600 **14**

Hotel
$69-$299

Sheraton
HOTELS & RESORTS

AAA Benefit: Members save up to 15%, plus Starwood Preferred Guest® benefits!

Address: 1600 S 52nd St 85281 **Location:** I-10 exit 153B (Broadway Rd) westbound; exit 153A (48th St) eastbound, 0.3 mi ne. Located in a business and industrial park area. **Facility:** 209 units. 4 stories, interior corridors. **Pool(s):** heated outdoor. **Activities:** hot tub, exercise room. **Guest Services:** valet laundry, area transportation.

SPRINGHILL SUITES BY MARRIOTT PHOENIX TEMPE AIRPORT
(480)968-8222 **5**

Hotel
$71-$248

SPRINGHILL SUITES
Marriott

AAA Benefit: Members save 5% or more!

Address: 1601 W Rio Salado Pkwy 85281 **Location:** Just w of Priest Dr. Priest Dr/Washington, 23. **Facility:** 130 units. 6 stories, interior corridors. **Pool(s):** heated outdoor. **Activities:** hot tub, exercise room. **Guest Services:** valet and coin laundry, area transportation. **Featured Amenity: breakfast buffet.**

SPRINGHILL SUITES BY MARRIOTT TEMPE AT ARIZONA MILLS MALL
(480)752-7979 **26**

Hotel $74-$214 **Address:** 5211 S Priest Dr 85283 **Location:** I-10 exit 155 (Baseline Rd), southeast corner of Baseline Rd and Priest Dr. Across from Arizona Mills Mall. **Facility:** 121 units. 3 stories, interior corridors. **Pool(s):** heated outdoor. **Activities:** picnic facilities, exercise room. **Guest Services:** valet and coin laundry, area transportation.

AAA Benefit: Members save 5% or more!

TEMPE MISSION PALMS HOTEL
(480)894-1400 **10**

Hotel
$119-$359

Address: 60 E 5th St 85281 **Location:** Jct University Dr, just n on Mill Ave, just e. Mill Ave/3rd St, 25. **Facility:** In the downtown area surrounded by shops and restaurants, the hotel offers newly renovated, upscale rooms and baths. 303 units. 4 stories, interior corridors. **Parking:** on-site and valet. **Terms:** cancellation fee imposed, resort fee. **Amenities:** safes. **Pool(s):** heated outdoor. **Activities:** hot tub, exercise room, massage. **Guest Services:** valet laundry, boarding pass kiosk, area transportation.

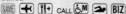

Enjoy peace of mind
with AAA/CAA Insurance products

TOWNEPLACE SUITES BY MARRIOTT TEMPE AT ARIZONA MILLS MALL
(480)345-7889 **28**

Extended Stay Hotel $79-$229 **Address:** 5223 S Priest Dr 85283 **Location:** I-10 exit 155 (Baseline Rd), southeast corner of Baseline Rd and Priest Dr. Across from Arizona Mills Mall. **Facility:** 118 efficiencies, some two bedrooms. 3 stories, interior corridors. **Pool(s):** heated outdoor. **Activities:** picnic facilities, exercise room. **Guest Services:** valet and coin laundry, area transportation.

AAA Benefit: Members save 5% or more!

WHERE TO EAT

BYBLOS RESTAURANT
480/894-1945 **17**

Greek. Casual Dining. $8-$19 **AAA Inspector Notes:** A neighborhood institution for many years, this casual Greek spot serves delicious homemade favorites including moussaka, kebabs and the chef's favorite-an oven-roasted lamb platter. Save room for the homemade desserts. **Features:** full bar. **Address:** 3332 S Mill Ave 85282 **Location:** Just s of Southern Ave.

CAFE ISTANBUL & MARKET
480/731-9499 **11**

Middle Eastern. Casual Dining. $6-$14 **AAA Inspector Notes:** The café's appetizers—including stuffed grape leaves, Lebanese lamb sausage and fava beans seasoned with garlic and lemon—are great lead-ins to marinated meats and poultry, which are gently grilled and served with homemade garlic sauce. Belly dancing enhances the atmosphere on weekends. **Features:** patio dining. **Address:** 1310 E Apache Blvd 85281 **Location:** 0.5 mi e of Rural Rd. Dorsey/Apache, 28.

CAFE LALIBELA
480/829-1939 **5**

Ethiopian. Casual Dining. $6-$15 **AAA Inspector Notes:** Diners eat with their hands by scooping up flavorful vegetable and meat dishes called 'wat', with classic flatbread (inerja). Items can be ordered spicy or mild. Many vegetarian options are available. **Features:** beer & wine. **Address:** 849 W University Dr 85281 **Location:** SR 202 Loop (Red Mountain Frwy) exit 5 (Priest Dr), 1.1 mi s, then 0.5 mi e. Mill Ave/3rd St, 25.

CASEY MOORE'S OYSTER HOUSE
480/968-9935 **6**

American. Casual Dining. $6-$28 **AAA Inspector Notes:** Historic. This historic 1910 house, rumored to be haunted by a trio of ghosts, is a showcase for a casual eatery that serves more than seafood. On the menu such salads as spinach berry, a selection of classic sandwiches and Creole- and Southwestern-influenced dishes, including chipotle chicken and Cajun-style shrimp. **Features:** full bar, patio dining, happy hour. **Reservations:** suggested. **Address:** 850 S Ash Ave 85281 **Location:** Jct Mill Ave, just w on University Dr, then just s. Mill Ave/3rd St, 25.

CLAIM JUMPER
480/831-8200

American. Casual Dining. $10-$30 **AAA Inspector Notes:** Great menu variety makes this place a good stop for parties with diverse tastes. Choices include specialty appetizers, salads, rotisserie chicken and barbecue items, not to mention good comfort foods, such as traditional pot pie. Hearty portions satisfy big appetites. The atmosphere is fun and lively. **Features:** full bar, happy hour. **Address:** 1530 W Baseline Rd 85283 **Location:** I-10 exit 155 (Baseline Rd), just e.

THE DHABA
480/446-2824 **13**

Indian
Casual Dining
$10-$21

AAA Inspector Notes: Savor authentic Indian cuisine while sampling such favorites as tikka masala, paneer with tamarind chutney and freshly baked naan. **Features:** beer & wine. **Address:** 1872 E Apache Blvd 85281 **Location:** Jct Rural Rd, 1.2 mi e. McClintock/Apache, 29.

(See map & index p. 164.)

GORDON BIERSCH BREWERY RESTAURANT
480/736-0033 [1]

WWW American. Casual Dining. $10-$28 **AAA Inspector Notes:** As the name implies this restaurant features fresh, brewed-on-site beer which is crafted in a German tradition. What may not be evident is the wide variety of foods like meal-sized salads, burgers and sandwiches, pizza, pastas, steaks and seafood that is also a huge draw for an upscale, casual dining experience. **Features:** full bar, patio dining, happy hour. **Address:** 420 S Mill Ave 85281 **Location:** Northwest corner of 5th St and S Mill Ave. Mill Ave/3rd St, 25. **Parking:** street only. [L] [D] [♿]

HAJI BABA MIDDLE EASTERN FOOD   480/894-1905 [12]

WW Middle Eastern. Casual Dining. $7-$14 **AAA Inspector Notes:** Enjoy authentic Middle Eastern favorites in this no-frills dining room attached to a market. **Address:** 1513 E Apache Blvd 85281 **Location:** Jct Rural Rd, 0.7 mi e. Dorsey/Apache, 28.

[L] [D] [♿]

HOUSE OF TRICKS   480/968-1114 [3]

WWW American. Casual Dining. $23-$49 **AAA Inspector Notes:** Guests to the "house" can dine on a relaxed shaded patio or inside the quaint bungalow. Offerings include freshly prepared salads, hearty sandwiches and grilled rib-eye or seafood. **Features:** full bar, patio dining, happy hour. **Reservations:** suggested. **Address:** 114 E 7th St 85281 **Location:** Just e of Mill Ave. Veterans Way/College, 26. **Parking:** on-site and street.

[L] [D]

LA BOCCA   480/967-5244 [2]

WW Pizza. Casual Dining. $8-$16 **AAA Inspector Notes:** This stylish, sophisticated pizzeria and wine bar hosts a lively happy hour every day. Sit outside along bustling Mill Avenue and take in the sights and sounds while dining on gourmet pizza and listening to live music. **Features:** full bar, patio dining, happy hour. **Address:** 699 S Mill Ave, Suite 115 85281 **Location:** Jct Mill Ave and 7th St. Mill Ave/3rd St, 25. **Parking:** street only. [L] [D] [♿]

LEMON GRASS THAI CUISINE   480/967-9121 [15]

WW Thai. Casual Dining. $6-$16 **AAA Inspector Notes:** Here diners can enjoy freshly cooked foods including such dishes as pad thai, eggplant and garlic with chicken or seafood combinations cooked in mild to spicy red curry sauce. The neatly kept dining room has charming Thai cottage roof details and wooden carvings. **Features:** beer & wine. **Address:** 818 W Broadway Rd, Suite 108 85282 **Location:** Just e of Priest Rd. [L] [D]

MACAYO MEXICAN KITCHEN   480/966-6677

WW Mexican. Casual Dining. $10-$19 **AAA Inspector Notes:** The colorfully furnished Mexican-style eatery prepares Sonoran Mexican dishes. Friendly and efficient staffers serve traditional and lighter dishes flavored with this place's own chili peppers, which are grown near Tucson. **Features:** full bar, happy hour. **Address:** 300 S Ash Ave 85281 **Location:** I-10 exit 153 (Broadway Rd), 2 mi e, 1.5 mi n on Mill Ave, just w on Fifth St, then just n. Mill Ave/3rd St, 25. [L] [D] [♿]

P.F. CHANG'S CHINA BISTRO   480/731-4600 [4]

WWWW Chinese. Fine Dining. $8-$25 **AAA Inspector Notes:** Trendy, upscale decor provides a pleasant backdrop for New Age Chinese dining. Appetizers, soups and salads are a meal by themselves. Vegetarian plates and sides, noodles, chow meins, chicken and meat dishes are created from exotic, fresh ingredients. **Features:** full bar, patio dining. **Address:** 740 S Mill Ave 85281 **Location:** Corner of Mill Ave and University Dr. Mill Ave/3rd St, 25. **Parking:** street only. [L] [D] [♿]

PITA JUNGLE   480/804-0234 [10]

WW Mediterranean. Casual Dining. $6-$15 **AAA Inspector Notes:** The atmosphere is super-casual in the dining area and on the patio. On the menu is a wide variety of hot and cold pita wraps, pizza, falafel, spanakopita, salads and burgers as well as natural, healthful vegetarian offerings. **Features:** beer & wine, patio dining, Sunday brunch, happy hour. **Address:** 1250 E Apache Blvd, Suite 113 85282 **Location:** 0.4 mi e of jct Rural Rd and Apache Blvd. Dorsey/Apache, 28. [L] [D] [🛏] [♿]

REPUBLIC RAMEN   480/388-3685 [8]

WW WW Asian Noodles. Quick Serve. $6-$8 **AAA Inspector Notes:** Friendly staff at this quick serve will guide you through the Asian noodle-style soup menu, with a choice of different broths and toppings. A full menu of boba (bubble-teas) is available. **Features:** beer & wine, patio dining, happy hour. **Address:** 1301 E University Dr 85281 **Location:** SR 202 Loop (Red Mountain Frwy) exit 7 (Rural Rd), 1 mi s, then 0.5 mi e. Dorsey/Apache, 28.

[L] [D] [♿]

ROYAL TAJ   480/967-5234 [16]

WW Indian. Casual Dining. $9-$17 **AAA Inspector Notes:** Traditional specialties encompass a variety of vegetarian dishes including spinach, eggplant and peas in spiced sauces. The chicken korma is luscious and includes nuts and a spicy cream sauce. **Features:** full bar. **Address:** 1845 E Broadway Rd, Suite 105 85282 **Location:** Just e of McClintock Dr. McClintock/Apache, 29.

[L] [D] [♿]

RUBIO'S FRESH MEXICAN GRILL   480/897-3884

WW Mexican. Quick Serve. $4-$10 **AAA Inspector Notes:** Freshly prepared and healthful foods, bright decor and friendly staff are found in this upscale fast-food spot. A special treat, the salsa bar lines up four styles and flavors. **Features:** beer only, patio dining. **Address:** 1712 E Guadalupe Rd, Suite 107 85281 **Location:** Jct McClintock Dr; northwest corner. [L] [D]

SERRANO'S MEXICAN RESTAURANT   480/345-0044

WWW Mexican. Casual Dining. $7-$17 **AAA Inspector Notes:** A pleasant stop for lunch or dinner, the local chain is known for consistently good food and attractive, upscale Mexican-style décor. The warm bean dip starter stirs the appetite for traditional dishes such as chiles rellenos or seafood enchiladas prepared with fresh ingredients. Service is friendly. **Features:** full bar. **Address:** 6440 S Rural Rd 85283 **Location:** Just s of Guadalupe Rd; west side.

[L] [D]

SUSHI 101   480/317-0101 [7]

WW Sushi. Casual Dining. $5-$25 **AAA Inspector Notes:** This fun, family-owned business offers happy hour all week. Select from classic and inventive rolls, as well as fresh nigiri and sashimi and lunch bento boxes. **Features:** full bar, patio dining, happy hour. **Address:** 920 E University Dr, Suite 101 85281 **Location:** Northeast corner of Rural Rd and University Dr. University Dr/Rural, 27.

[L] [D] [♿]

TASTY KABOB   480/966-0260 [9]

WW Middle Eastern. Casual Dining. $7-$31 **AAA Inspector Notes:** This small eatery is an excellent choice for Persian foods. The owner not only works as the friendly hostess but also prepares the delectable desserts. Diners can choose from varied kebabs or sample walnuts in pomegranate sauce with chicken or beef. **Features:** full bar. **Address:** 1250 E Apache Blvd, Suite 116 85281 **Location:** 0.4 mi e of Rural Rd. Dorsey/Apache, 28.

[L] [D] CALL [🚬♿]

TOM'S BBQ CHICAGO STYLE   480/820-0728 [18]

W Barbecue. Quick Serve. $8-$25 **AAA Inspector Notes:** This unpretentious strip mall eatery displays Chicago memorabilia and serves barbecue beef brisket, pulled pork, smoked chicken, rib tips and sides. Do not miss the delicious homemade pies for dessert. **Address:** 115 E Baseline Rd, Suite 5 85283 **Location:** I-10 exit 155 (Baseline Rd), just e of Mill Ave. [L] [D]

TOP OF THE ROCK RESTAURANT   602/431-2370 [14]

WWWW American. Fine Dining. $14-$35 **AAA Inspector Notes:** This fine-dining establishment treats guests to mountain-top panoramic views. Solid rock juts up and around the casually elegant dining room. An open kitchen affords a hint of what culinary delights await. **Features:** full bar, patio dining, happy hour. **Reservations:** suggested. **Address:** 2000 Westcourt Way 85282 **Location:** I-10 exit 153 (Broadway Rd) westbound, 0.8 mi w to 48th St, then 0.3 mi s; exit 48th St eastbound, 0.5 mi s; in Phoenix Marriott Tempe at the Buttes. **Parking:** on-site and valet. [D]

THATCHER pop. 4,865

SPRINGHILL SUITES BY MARRIOTT THATCHER
(928)428-6900

 Hotel $103-$174 Address: 2855 W Hwy 70 85552 Location: US 191, 2.5 mi w. Facility: 71 units. 3 stories, interior corridors. Pool(s): heated outdoor. Activities: exercise room. Guest Services: coin laundry.

AAA Benefit: Members save 5% or more!

 CALL

COMFORT INN & SUITES-THATCHER
928/348-9500

[fyi] Not evaluated. Address: 2577 W Hwy 70 85552 Location: 2 mi w of jct US 191. Facilities, services, and décor characterize a midscale property.

TOLLESON pop. 6,545
• Hotels & Restaurants map & index p. 154
• Part of Phoenix area — see map p. 126

BEST WESTERN TOLLESON-PHOENIX HOTEL
(623)936-6000　**42**

 Hotel $100

 AAA Benefit: Save 10% or more every day and earn 10% bonus points!

Address: 8421 W McDowell Rd 85353 Location: I-10 exit 135 (83rd Ave), just n, then just w. Facility: 60 units, some two bedrooms. 2 stories (no elevator), interior corridors. Pool(s): outdoor. Activities: hot tub, exercise room. Guest Services: valet and coin laundry.

 / SOME UNITS

PREMIER INNS　623/533-4660　**43**

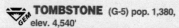 Hotel. Rates not provided. Address: 8399 W Lynwood St 85353 Location: I-10 exit 135 (83rd Ave), just n, then just w. Facility: 132 units. 2 stories (no elevator), exterior corridors. Pool(s): outdoor. Activities: hot tub, game room. Guest Services: coin laundry.

/ SOME UNITS

TOMBSTONE (G-5) pop. 1,380, elev. 4,540'

"The town too tough to die," Tombstone was perhaps the most renowned of Arizona's old mining camps. When Ed Schieffelin came to Camp Huachuca with a party of soldiers and left the fort to prospect, his comrades told him that he would find his tombstone rather than silver. Thus, in 1877 Schieffelin named his first claim Tombstone, and rumors of rich strikes made a boomtown of the settlement that adopted this name.

Over the course of 7 years the mines produced millions of dollars in silver and gold before rising underground waters forced suspension of operations.

Days of lawlessness and violence in Tombstone climaxed with the infamous battle between Wyatt Earp and his brothers against the Clanton brothers, fought at the rear entrance to the O.K. Corral.

Many of Tombstone's historic buildings are within an area bounded by Fremont, 6th, Toughnut and 3rd streets. Among them are St. Paul's Episcopal Church, built in 1882; the Crystal Palace, one of the most luxurious saloons in the West; and the Tombstone Epitaph building, where the oldest continuously published paper in Arizona is still being printed. Western printing history exhibits in the front office are free to the public.

Tombstone Chamber of Commerce: 109 S. 4th St., P.O. Box 995, Tombstone, AZ 85638. **Phone:** (520) 457-9317 or (888) 457-3929.

BIRD CAGE THEATRE, 6th and Allen sts., was built in 1881 and remains virtually unchanged, with the original fixtures, furnishings and interior still intact. A combination theater, saloon and dance hall, the theater was known in its heyday as the bawdiest nightspot between Basin Street and the Barbary Coast. The refrain from the song "Only a Bird in a Gilded Cage" was inspired by this opera house saloon. Various ghost tours of the building are offered. **Time:** Allow 1 hour minimum. **Hours:** Daily 9-6. Family ghost tours depart at 6:30 p.m. Adults-only ghost tour departs at 8 p.m. Closed Christmas. **Cost:** $10; $9 (ages 60+ and military with ID); $8 (ages 8-18); $28 (family). Adult ghost tour $20 (ages 18+). Family ghost tour $15 (ages 12+). Prices may vary; phone ahead. **Phone:** (520) 457-3421 or (800) 457-3423.

BOOTHILL GRAVEYARD, at the w. city limits at 408 SR 80, contains some 250 marked graves of early citizens as well as graves of some of the town's famous and infamous residents. This is reportedly the first cemetery to be called "Boot Hill." **Time:** Allow 1 hour minimum. **Hours:** Daily 8-6:30. Graveyard closes at dusk. Closed Christmas. **Cost:** Donations. **Phone:** (520) 457-3300.

HISTORAMA is next to the main entrance of the O.K. Corral. A 25-minute multimedia presentation narrated by actor Vincent Price offers a look at Tombstone's history. This is a good starting point for a tour of the town. **Hours:** Shows run daily every hour 10-4. Last show at 4:30. Closed Thanksgiving and Christmas. **Cost:** $6; free (ages 0-5). Combination ticket with O.K. Corral (includes gunfight reenactment) $10; free (ages 0-5). **Phone:** (520) 457-3456.

O.K. CORRAL, between 3rd and 4th sts. on Allen St., includes the site where the Gunfight at the O.K. Corral started on Oct. 26, 1881. Re-enactment of the gunfight takes place daily at noon, 2 and 3:30. **Time:** Allow 30 minutes minimum. **Hours:** Daily 9-5. Closed Thanksgiving and Christmas. Phone ahead to confirm schedule. **Cost:** Combination ticket with Historama (includes gunfight reenactment) $10; free (ages 0-5). **Phone:** (520) 457-3456.

Camillus Fly Studio is between 3rd and 4th sts. on Fremont St., entered through the O.K. Corral. This is the re-created studio and boardinghouse of the pioneer photographer. Doc Holliday's room and photographs of early Tombstone and its personalities are displayed. **Time:** Allow 30 minutes minimum.

Hours: Daily 9-5. Closed Thanksgiving and Christmas. **Cost:** O.K. Corral admission (includes Camillus Fly Studio, Historama and gunfight reenactment) $10; free (ages 0-5). **Phone:** (520) 457-3456.

ROSE TREE MUSEUM AND BOOKSTORE, 118 S. 4th St. at the corner of 4th and Toughnut sts., features the world's largest rosebush, which now covers more than 8,000 square feet; the size of the bush is verified by "The Guinness Book of World Records" yearly. The white-blossomed shrub was planted as a cutting sent from Scotland about 1885. Rose slips may be purchased. Exhibits include antique furniture brought to Tombstone by covered wagon in 1880.

Time: Allow 30 minutes minimum. **Hours:** Daily 9-5, Feb.-May; 11-4, rest of year. Closed Thanksgiving and Christmas. **Cost:** $5; $4 (military with ID); free (ages 0-13 with adult). **Phone:** (520) 457-3326.

SCHIEFFELIN HALL is at 4th and Fremont sts. Early Tombstone's theatrical and civic center, Schieffelin Hall is one of the largest adobe structures in the West. **Hours:** closed to the public.

TOMBSTONE COURTHOUSE STATE HISTORIC PARK, 223 E. Toughnut St., was built in 1882. The building contains displays pertaining to the history of Tombstone and Cochise County, using antiques and artifacts to present the lives of former citizens. **Time:** Allow 1 hour minimum. **Hours:** Daily 9-5. Closed Christmas. **Cost:** $5; $2 (ages 7-13). **Phone:** (520) 457-3311.

LANDMARK LOOKOUT LODGE   (520)457-2223

Hotel
$99-$130

Address: 781 N Hwy 80 85638 **Location:** On SR 80, 1 mi n of center. **Facility:** 40 units. 2 stories (no elevator), exterior corridors. **Pool(s):** outdoor. **Featured Amenity:** full hot breakfast.

🆂🆅 🍴➕ 🏊 BIZ 🛜 ✕ 📶
🖥 / SOME UNITS S⬅

THE TOMBSTONE GRAND HOTEL   (520)457-9507

♦♦ Hotel $89-$159 **Address:** 580 W Randolph Way 85638 **Location:** Jct SR 82 and 80, 2 mi s, then just w; 1 mi n of center. **Facility:** 60 units. 2 stories (no elevator), interior corridors. **Terms:** cancellation fee imposed. **Pool(s):** heated outdoor. **Activities:** hot tub, picnic facilities. **Guest Services:** coin laundry.

🍴➕ CALL 🛜 🏊 BIZ HS 🛜 ✕ 📶 🖥
/ SOME UNITS 🖥

TOMBSTONE MONUMENT RANCH   (520)457-8707

♦♦♦ Ranch $109-$450 **Address:** 895 W Monument Rd 85638 **Location:** 2.5 mi nw of center. **Facility:** Situated on more than 250 acres on the outskirts of town, this unique guest ranch features a replica of an old western town, a Native American village, and an abundance of outdoor activities. 18 units. 1 story, exterior corridors. **Terms:** 2 night minimum stay - weekends, 91 day cancellation notice-fee imposed, resort fee. **Pool(s):** outdoor. **Activities:** hot tub, recreation programs, bicycles, game room, trails.

🍴 🍷 🏊 🛜 ✕ 🖥 / SOME UNITS 📶

THE LONGHORN RESTAURANT   520/457-3405

♦♦ ♦♦
American
Casual Dining
$7-$20

AAA Inspector Notes: This historic district corner eatery, popular with locals and tourists, serves a good selection of steak, sandwiches and Mexican entrées in an Old West decor. Desserts, such as deep-dish apple pie and the death by chocolate, are served large enough to share. **Features:** beer & wine. **Address:** 501 E Allen St 85638 **Location:** Corner of 5th St. **Parking:** street only.

B L D

O.K. CAFE   520/457-3980

♦ American. Casual Dining. $6-$16 **AAA Inspector Notes:** The popular eatery can be crowded during breakfast and lunch. Foods are prepared from scratch, and the coffee is said to be the best in town. Hefty buffalo burgers are the specialty. **Features:** patio dining. **Address:** 220 E Allen St 85638 **Location:** Northeast corner of 3rd and Allen sts; center. **Parking:** street only. B L

TONTO NATIONAL FOREST (H-4)

Elevations in the forest range from 1,300 ft. at Apache Junction to 7,900 ft. at the Mogollon Rim in the Payson District. Refer to AAA maps for additional elevation information.

Stretching some 90 miles south from the scenic Mogollon Rim to the city of Scottsdale, the Tonto National Forest encompasses 2.9 million acres of spectacular pine, brush and cactus country, making it one of the largest national forests. Elevations range from 1,300 feet to almost 7,900 feet in the northern pine country. Eight regions have been designated as wilderness areas; the entire forest offers more than 860 miles of trails for backpacking, hiking and horse travel.

Scenic roadways in the area include the Apache Trail (SR 88) *(see Apache Junction p. 38)*, Beeline Highway (SR 87) and Young Highway (SR 288). Some unpaved roads are very rough, so phone ahead for current road condition updates. **Note:** The Apache Trail (SR 88) is a winding road and is not suitable for motor homes or vehicle-towing; nearly 25 miles of the road is unpaved.

Six lakes allow boating, swimming and fishing; Saguaro, Bartlett, Canyon, Apache and Theodore Roosevelt lakes have marina facilities. Tubing is a popular pastime in the summer on the lower Salt River. Campgrounds, picnic sites and other recreational opportunities also are available throughout the forest. A map showing roads, recreation sites and tourist services can be obtained from the local Forest Service office for $10.

For further information contact the Forest Supervisor's Office, Tonto National Forest, 2324 E. McDowell Rd., Phoenix, AZ 85006; phone (602) 225-5200. *See Recreation Areas Chart.*

TONTO NATIONAL MONUMENT (I-6)

Four miles east of Roosevelt Dam on SR 188, Tonto National Monument preserves the most accessible of south-central Arizona's prehistoric cliff dwellings. The remains of a two-story pueblo built in a natural cave are visible from the headquarters parking area. A half-mile-long (one way) paved foot trail ascends 350 feet and leads to cliff dwellings that were occupied by the Salado culture in the 13th and 14th centuries. Summer temperatures are high; wear a hat and suitable shoes and carry sufficient water.

Ranger-conducted, 3-hour tours to the less accessible 40-room Upper Cliff Dwelling are available November through April. Tours are conducted 3 or 4 days a week and are limited to 15 people per day; reservations are required. Phone (928) 467-2241, ext. 8450 for reservations.

A visitor center and museum contain artifacts from the Salado culture, including examples of the pottery and woven textiles for which they are noted. Leashed pets are allowed on the lower trail but not on the Upper Cliff Dwelling tour or in any dwellings. Allow 1 hour, 30 minutes minimum. Park and visitor center open daily 8-5; closed Christmas. Trail to the Lower Cliff Dwelling closes 1 hour before park closing. Picnic area 8-4:45. Admission $3; free (ages 0-15). Phone (928) 467-2241, ext. 8450.

TORTILLA FLAT

TORTILLA FLAT   480/984-1776

▼ American. Casual Dining. $5-$11 **AAA Inspector Notes:** Representative of robust fare are half-pound burgers and varied Mexican dishes, such as enchiladas and killer chili served in a sourdough bowl. The saloon awaits drivers who make the picturesque trip up SR 88 from Apache Junction. **Features:** beer & wine. **Address:** 1 Main St (SR 88) 85290 **Location:** Center. **Parking:** on-site and street.

B L D

TUBAC (G-4) pop. 1,191, elev. 3,200'

Tubac, meaning "sinking water," was a Pima village when Jesuit Eusebio Francisco Kino visited the area in 1691. A presidio and mission were established in 1752 (the first military base in Arizona) shortly after the Pima revolted against Spanish encroachment. Between 1752 and 1856 some 500 people lived at Tubac, but in 1776 the presidio was moved to help fortify the strategically important Tucson. With the Gadsden Purchase in 1853, the town became a part of the United States.

The Mexican War, the California gold rush of 1849 and the raiding Apaches depopulated the town throughout much of the 19th century. However, in 1859 Arizona's first newspaper was printed by a local mining company who revived the town. By 1860 Tubac was the largest town in Arizona, but the Civil War left the town unprotected, and it was deserted once again. Once the Apaches ceded control of the area in the late 1800s, Tubac began to grow, but it never regained its earlier importance.

Next to the old presidio, modern Tubac is a small community of writers and artists. Many of the shops and galleries in town sell the local art.

Tubac Chamber of Commerce: 12 B Tubac Road, P.O. Box 1866, Tubac, AZ 85646. **Phone:** (520) 398-2704.

TUBAC PRESIDIO STATE HISTORIC PARK is off I-19 at 1 Burruel St. Arizona's first state park encompasses the Spanish military site that made Tubac Arizona's first European settlement in 1752. An underground archeological exhibit reveals portions of the captain's house. The museum contains Native American, Spanish, Mexican and American territorial artifacts and the working hand press that printed Arizona's first newspaper in 1859.

Historical buildings include a restored 1885 schoolhouse, a furnished Mexican row house, and Otero Hall, which displays 16 William Ahrendt paintings depicting Arizona history. A living-history program portraying life in Tubac is offered; phone for information. **Time:** Allow 1 hour minimum. **Hours:** Daily 9-5. Closed Christmas. **Cost:** $5; $2 (ages 7-13); free (ages 0-6). **Phone:** (520) 398-2252.

TUBAC GOLF RESORT & SPA   520/398-2211

▼▼▼ Historic Retro Hotel Rates not provided

Address: 1 Otero Rd 85646 **Location:** I-19 exit 40 (Chavez Siding Rd), on east side, then 2 mi s. Located in a quiet area. **Facility:** Set on more than 500 acres, the property's Spanish Colonial architecture and magnificent mountain views provide for a unique and tranquil getaway. 98 units, some two bedrooms and efficiencies. 1 story, exterior corridors. **Terms:** check-in 4 pm. **Amenities:** safes. **Dining:** Stables Ranch Grille, see separate listing. **Pool(s):** heated outdoor. **Activities:** sauna, hot tub, steamroom, regulation golf, tennis, bicycles, lawn sports, exercise room, spa. **Guest Services:** valet and coin laundry.

SAVE ECO ▮▮ 🚶 🍸 🕭 BIZ 🛜 ✕ 📶 ▣
/ SOME UNITS S➡ 🖭

WHERE TO EAT

ELVIRA'S   520/398-9421

▼▼▼ Mexican. Casual Dining. $16-$35 **AAA Inspector Notes:** The executive chef is the son of the owners of the original restaurant in Mexico, and has opened this beautiful establishment which he designed himself. Exquisite mole sauces, homemade tortillas and delectable chile rellenos are some of the offerings. **Features:** full bar, patio dining. **Reservations:** suggested. **Address:** 2221 E Frontage Rd 85646 **Location:** Center. **Parking:** on-site and street.

L D

THE ITALIAN PEASANT   520/398-2668

▼▼ Italian. Casual Dining. $7-$20 **AAA Inspector Notes:** Authentic New York-style is how the owner describes this quaint pizzeria in the heart of artsy Tubac. Try a delicious pie or go for the baked ziti, or eggplant parmigiana. Finish it off with an authentic cannoli. **Features:** full bar, patio dining. **Address:** 50 Avenida Goya 85646 **Location:** I-19 exit 34 (Tubac), just e; downtown. L D

SHELBY'S BISTRO   520/398-8075

▼▼ Regional American. Casual Dining. $11-$26 **AAA Inspector Notes:** Tucked in a courtyard, the brightly decorated bistro serves fresh salads, hearty sandwiches, a selection of steaks and pasta as well as house-made desserts. Patio seating overlooks a fountain. **Features:** full bar, patio dining, happy hour. **Address:** 19 Tubac Rd-Mercado de Baca 85646 **Location:** I-19 exit 34 (Tubac), just e to Frontage Rd, just n to Plaza Rd, then just e.

L D

STABLES RANCH GRILLE   520/398-2678

▼▼▼ American. Fine Dining. $9-$35 **AAA Inspector Notes:** Historic. An elegant atmosphere awaits at this popular Southwestern-style dining room. Choose from grain-fed Prime cuts of beef, dry-aged pork, veal and fresh seafood flown in daily. **Features:** full bar, patio dining. **Reservations:** suggested. **Address:** 1 Otero Rd 85646 **Location:** I-19 exit 40 (Chavez Siding Rd), on east side, then 2 mi s; in Tubac Golf Resort & Spa. B L D

TUBA CITY (B-4) pop. 8,611, elev. 4,936'
• Restaurants p. 254

Tuba City was named after Tuve, a Hopi leader. Natural springs attracted generations of Hopi, Navajo and Paiute Indians to the area. In 1875 the city was laid out and settled by Mormons, who used blocks of dressed stone from nearby prehistoric sites to build structures, some of which still stand.

The town lies on US 160, 10 miles east of US 89 within Arizona's northeastern Native American country, which encompasses the Navajo and Hopi Indian reservations. A variety of Native American crafts are produced in the area, including baskets, pottery and silver products.

MOENKOPI LEGACY INN AND SUITES (928)283-4500

Hotel
$99-$269

Address: 1 Legacy Ln 86045 **Location:** Jct US 160 and SR 264. **Facility:** 100 units, some two bedrooms. 3 stories, interior corridors. **Terms:** cancellation fee imposed. **Pool(s):** heated outdoor. **Activities:** hot tub, exercise room. **Featured Amenity:** full hot breakfast. *(See ad this page.)*

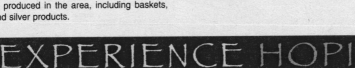

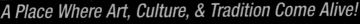

QUALITY INN NAVAJO NATION   (928)283-4545

Hotel
$73-$120

Address: 10 N Main St 86045 **Location:** 1 mi n of US 160. Adjacent to historic Tuba Trading Post. **Facility:** 80 units. 2 stories (no elevator), interior corridors. **Dining:** Hogan Restaurant, see separate listing. **Activities:** exercise room. **Guest Services:** coin laundry. **Featured Amenity:** full hot breakfast.

WHERE TO EAT

HOGAN RESTAURANT   928/283-5260

Southwestern. Family Dining. $8-$22 **AAA Inspector Notes:** This casual restaurant draws a big breakfast crowd from the hotel next door. The service is very basic and slow at times. The menu consist of a mix between Navajo specialties, Mexican and American cuisine. **Address:** 10 N Main St 86045 **Location:** 1 mi n of US 160; in Quality Inn Navajo Nation. B L D

TUUVI CAFE   928/283-4374

Southwestern
Family Dining
$7-$13

AAA Inspector Notes: Do not let the location fool you—this is a basic restaurant that serves simple American and traditional Hopi cuisine. The ingredients are super fresh and tasty. The fry bread and Tuuvi taco are must have items. **Address:** Tuvi Travel Ctr 86045 **Location:** Jct US 160 and SR 264. *(See ad p. 253.)*
B L D

Tucson

Then & Now

Tucson is a culturally-rich city that enjoys a starkly beautiful Sonoran Desert setting and reliably warm weather. It's this tourism trifecta that today draws droves of golfers, hikers, shopaholics, Mexican-food lovers and leisure-wear resort lizards to Arizona's second largest city.

With a population just shy of the half-million mark, Tucson has seen some unfortunate stucco-and-strip-mall suburban sprawl. But make no mistake, this is no Phoenix Junior. With the lovely Santa Catalina Mountains as a backdrop and the towering cacti of Saguaro National Park at its doorstep, Tucson feels connected to its surroundings.

Many of the city's historical adobes were bulldozed back in the 1960s. However, a good number of the low-slung Spanish and Mexican-era structures remain, especially in the Barrio Viejo neighborhood (just south of downtown) and the El Presidio Historic District in the heart of downtown.

When the summer sun isn't blazing, the latter is a nice area for a leisurely stroll, shopping at the Old Town Artisans complex and perhaps a happy hour Cadillac margarita at El Charro Cafe, the city's oldest restaurant.

Downtown's Stone Avenue is home to two of the city's most important houses of worship. The baroque St. Augustine Cathedral looks like it's been plucked straight out of a colonial Mexican town. The historic 1910 Stone Avenue Temple now houses the Jewish History Museum, 564 S. Stone Ave. One of Arizona's first synagogues, it features a mix of neoclassic, Romanesque and Moorish styles; phone (520) 670-9073.

The Tucson skyline at dusk

While the downtown core has long boasted some beautiful public murals and buildings (including the mosaic-tile domed Pima County Courthouse) and the Tucson Museum of Art and Historic Block in addition to two historic neighborhoods, some tourists once complained there's little else to entertain a non-history buff for very long.

But today the area is booming with dozens of restaurants, including several run by nationally acclaimed chefs, and regular food truck and art gallery gatherings. Making it easy to explore Tucson's downtown, the Sun Link streetcar runs from Main Gate Square and the adjacent University of Arizona campus through the 4th Avenue shopping, dining and nightlife district, to the Mercado, Tucson's public market.

On the east side of downtown is the lively Congress Street district. Tourists, Tucson scenesters and college students amble down sidewalks lined with early 20th-century buildings. Amtrak trains rumble into the lovingly restored Railroad Depot Plaza. After dark, indie rock

(Continued on p. 257.)

Destination Tucson

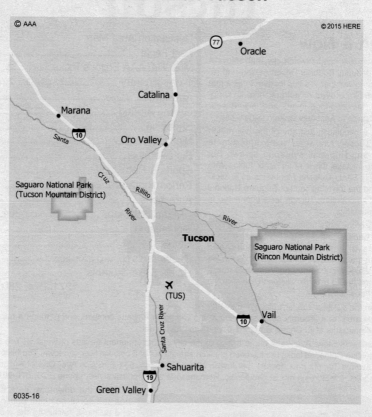

This map shows cities in the Tucson vicinity where you will find attractions, hotels and restaurants. Cities are listed alphabetically in this book on the following pages.

Fast Facts

ABOUT THE CITY

POP: 520,116 ▪ ELEV: 2,389 ft.

MONEY

SALES TAX: Arizona's statewide sales tax is 5.6 percent; an additional 2 percent is levied in Tucson. The tax on a hotel room in Pima County is 13.05 percent, plus an additional $2 per room per night in Tucson. There is a combined state and county rental car tax of 10 percent, plus a Pima County rental car fee of $3.50 per rental; a concession fee of 11.1 percent is added if the car is picked up at the airport, and an additional 2 percent tax is added if the car is picked up off airport property but within the Tucson city limits.

WHOM TO CALL

EMERGENCY: 911

POLICE (non-emergency): (520) 791-4444

HOSPITALS: Carondelet St. Joseph's Hospital, (520) 873-3000 ▪ Carondelet St. Mary's Hospital, (520) 872-3000 ▪ Northwest Medical Center, (520) 742-9000 ▪ Tucson Medical Center, (520) 327-5461 ▪ University Medical Center, (520) 694-0111.

WHERE TO LOOK AND LISTEN

NEWSPAPERS: The major newspaper is the *Arizona Daily Star,* published every morning. The city's free independent paper is *The Tucson Weekly,* published on Thursdays.

RADIO: Tucson radio stations KNST (790 AM) and KVOI (1030 AM) are news/talk radio stations ▪ KUAZ (89.1 FM and 1550 AM) is a member of National Public Radio. Tucson's community radio station is KXCI (91.3 FM).

VISITOR INFORMATION

Visit Tucson: 100 S. Church Ave., Suite 7199, Tucson, AZ 85701. Phone: (520) 624-1817 or (800) 638-8350.

Visit Tucson, in La Placita Village, can provide a variety of information, including the *Visit Tucson Official Destination Guide.* The visitor center is open Mon.-Fri. 9-5, Sat.-Sun. 9-4; closed major holidays.

TRANSPORTATION

AIR TRAVEL: Ten miles south of downtown, Tucson International Airport (TUS), (520) 573-8100, is served by many major passenger airlines. Short-term airport parking costs $1 per half-hour up to $12 per day; long-term parking costs $9 for 24 hours ($2 for the first hour, then $1.50 per half-hour up to $9 per day).

The Arizona Stagecoach, (520) 889-1000, provides van service throughout the Tucson area; prices range from $5-$61. Sunset Limousine, (520) 573-9418, provides limousine service throughout the Tucson area; prices range from $65-$135 per hour. Cab service to downtown averages 20 minutes and costs $27-$30.

RENTAL CARS: Hertz, (520) 573-5201 or (800) 654-3131, offers discounts to AAA members.

RAIL SERVICE: The Amtrak station, 400 N. Toole, accommodates Amtrak rail lines. For advance ticket and schedule information phone (800) 872-7245. Tickets may also be purchased at the station.

BUSES: The terminal for Greyhound Lines Inc. is at 471 W. Congress St.; phone (520) 792-3475 or (800) 231-2222.

TAXIS: There are many independent taxi companies in Tucson. Rates are not regulated by the city. Companies that serve the area include Discount Cab, (520) 388-9000 ▪ VIP Taxi, (520) 300-3000 ▪ and Yellow Cab, (520) 624-6611.

PUBLIC TRANSPORTATION: Sun Tran, (520) 792-9222, operates a fleet of buses running throughout the metro area as well as a streetcar line downtown. *See Getting Around, Public Transportation.*

(Continued from p. 255.)
fans line up under the historic Rialto Theatre's electric pink-and-purple neon marquee for a sold-out gig. It's also here you'll find the 1919 Hotel Congress, home to the hip nightclub Club Congress. On the west end of Congress Street, a former silent-movie house, the Fox Tucson Theatre, is a beautifully restored venue for live performances and classic movie screenings.

Spanish, Mexican and Western heritage play big parts in the city's cultural pageant. But the constant parade of Arizona Wildcats T-shirts on the street will show you that this is a college town as well. The University of Arizona campus sits a few miles northeast of downtown.

Golf and spa resorts and modern shopping centers are ubiquitous in the foothill neighborhoods north of town. Climbing further into the Santa Catalina Mountains you can hit the slopes at Mount Lemmon, one of the country's southernmost ski areas.

A drive up Mount Lemmon, topping out among pine trees at 9,157 feet, also treats you to incredible views of Tucson and its surroundings. Here, the Mount Lemmon SkyCenter takes advantage of the Tucson area's clear skies, clean air and low humidity, as do other internationally known observatories within a couple hours' drive: Kitt Peak and Whipple observatories *(see attraction listings p. 238 and p. 55).*

Must Do: AAA Editor's Picks

- Travel back to New Spain at ⬦ **Mission San Xavier del Bac** (1950 W. San Xavier Rd.). Started in 1692 by the Rev. Eusebio Kino of the Jesuits, today's mission was built 1783-97 by the Franciscans, who continue its ministry. The atmosphere hearkens back to the 18th century, complete with arches and original statuary.

- Explore the diversity of Tucson's ecosystem at the ⬦ **Arizona-Sonora Desert Museum** (2021 N. Kinney Rd.) where you'll find trails, gardens, animals and even an aquarium.

- Embrace the great outdoors at ⬦ **Tucson Mountain Park** (Speedway Blvd. & Kinney Rd.). No visit is complete without experiencing the stark beauty of the desert with its wide horizons and far-reaching saguaros. Whether it's hiking, taking pictures, painting or exploring the area's history, there's plenty to do.

- Indulge in flavors indigenous to Tucson and the Southwest. Thought to have been popularized by **El Charro Cafe** (311 N. Court Ave.) cheese crisps (quesadillas) and chimichangas are good bets at the family-owned restaurant, which has been open since 1922. Also featuring quesadillas, **Teresa's Mosaic Cafe** (2455 N. Silverbell Rd.) is best known for huevos rancheros. Other Tucson favorites: Sonoran hot dogs (bacon-wrapped and loaded with tasty toppings) and fry bread as well as jams and candies made out of cacti.

- Unleash the kids at **Children's Museum Tucson** (200 S. 6th Ave.) where displays are geared toward your youngest family members. STEM—Science, Technology, Engineering and Mathematics—exhibits educate, and kids can get creative in themed activity areas.

- Ride the rails—or imagine you're doing so at the **Southern Arizona Transportation Museum** (414 N. Toole Ave.). Much of the West's growth came from the arrival of railroads, so you'll find the museum beside the former Southern Pacific Railroad Depot—still welcoming passengers. Highlights include a locomotive, sculpture of Doc Holiday and Wyatt Earp, and exhibits highlighting railroad culture.

- View the former site of **El Presidio San Agustin del Tucsón** (196 N. Court Ave.), an adobe established in 1775 by the Spanish. Though the last fort remnant was torn down in 1918, recent conservation efforts re-created portions. You'll see walls, a 20-foot adobe tower called a *torreón* and a mural that explains the rest of the 11-acre site.

- Browse the **Tucson Museum of Art and Historic Block** (140 N. Main Ave.), which sits on a corner of what was once the presidio. Although Art of the American West is understandably a big deal here, the museum features a range of other genres. Shop for handmade creations made by Arizona residents at the museum store and then tour the nearby historic buildings.

- Check out Tucson's many fine music venues. It's up to you whether you hang out at landmark **Hotel Congress** (311 E. Congress St.) for the party-filled ambience or eat with the beat at restaurants such as **Delectables Restaurant & Catering** (533 N. 4th Ave.) or **Cushing Street Bar & Restaurant** (198 W. Cushing St.). For a really unique experience, there's **Sky Bar** (536 N. 4th Ave.), a solar-powered bar that just happens to be a planetarium, too.

- March around the **Arizona Historical Society/Fort Lowell Museum** (2900 N. Craycroft Rd.) grounds to learn about frontier military life. Within the refurbished Commanding Officer's Quarters, you'll find exhibits detailing everything from the Apache Wars to everyday life for soldiers and their families.

- Refresh your memory about the indigenous history of the state and northern Mexico at the ⬦ **Arizona State Museum** (1013 E. University Blvd.). One exhibit features pottery dating back hundreds of years. Other exhibits include photographs, relics and priceless textiles—but all highlight the Southwest's distinctive personality.

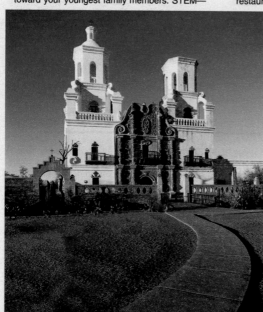

Mission San Xavier del Bac

Tucson 1-day Itinerary

AAA editors suggest these activities for a great short vacation experience.

Morning

- The sun rising over the Sonoran Mountains provides a pleasing light that's perfect for exploring Tucson's rugged terrain. Tread carefully around the prickly saguaros—scene-stealing cacti that dot the landscape and appear on everything from salsa jars to shoot-'em-up Westerns.

- At the ▽ **Arizona-Sonora Desert Museum** (2021 N. Kinney Rd.), you'll find a world-class zoo, museum and botanical garden all rolled into one. Investigate how saguaros provide valuable habitat for wildlife, enjoy a live-animal demonstration or walk one of the desert trails. Start early: Temperatures can climb into the 100-plus range during the summer.

- If you'd like to wander farther than the museum's trails allow, explore ▽ **Tucson Mountain Park** (Speedway Blvd. & Kinney Rd.). With approximately 20,000 acres, the park welcomes hikers, mountain bikers and equestrians alike, and no wonder—the views from Gates Pass Scenic Overlook are superb.

- Did you spot unidentified wildlife? A visit to the **International Wildlife Museum** (4800 W. Gates Pass Rd.) might clear up the mystery. Its interactive displays feature more than 400 species of preserved birds, insects and mammals in natural surroundings.

- The tile-decorated surfaces at **Teresa's Mosaic Cafe** (2455 N. Silverbell Rd.) provide a colorful backdrop for plates of huevos divorciados and huevos rancheros. The latter were even featured on the Food Network's "Throwdown With Bobby Flay," where the chef tried his hand at the dish. Though the egg specialties are hard to beat, try a cheese crisp.

Afternoon

- Sure to inspire your own vacation photographs, the **Center for Creative Photography** (1030 N. Olive Rd.) offers ever-changing exhibits. It's also the museum that noted photographer Ansel Adams co-founded at University of Arizona, so make an appointment to survey its permanent collection.

- The ▽ **Arizona State Museum** (1013 E. University Blvd.), also on campus, highlights the state's indigenous cultures using pottery, textiles and baskets as well as rare field notes and drawings.

- To explain how the state developed, the nearby **Arizona Historical Society/Arizona History Museum** (949 E. 2nd St.) delves into the Spanish and pre-territorial periods.

- Stick to **The Postal History Foundation** (920 N. First Ave.) for your fix of stamps and postal history. The structure—assembled circa 1895 from a prefabricated "post office kit"—was

Arizona-Sonora Desert Museum

moved a few times before serving as a museum. Guests still can mail letters and packages from the full-service post office.

- After licking envelopes and mailing presents, visit **Delectables Restaurant & Catering** (533 N. 4th Ave.) for some finger-licking food. Offering everything from international to vegan and gluten-free fare, the restaurant also features art, music and other events on select days.

- Visualize early Tucson at the **Arizona Historical Society/Downtown History Museum** (140 N. Stone Ave.). History buffs can browse through depictions of houses and other buildings, including police and fire departments, and an old-time barbershop.

Evening

- As the heat of the day settles, head toward the **Tucson Museum of Art and Historic Block** (140 N. Main Ave.) around what was once Spain's **El Presidio San Agustín del Tucsón** (196 N. Court Ave.). An on-site art museum highlights Western and Latin American art as well as rare books and manuscripts.

- A half mile south, across from the Convention Center, the **Cushing Street Bar & Restaurant** (198 W. Cushing St.) is an 1860s landmark serving up cuisine with a Southwestern flair as well as events and live music.

- The atmospheric **Main Dining Room at the Arizona Inn** (2200 E. Elm St.) awaits. Order the Pastry Chef's Selection of Small Bites or a nightcap to end the evening on a warm note.

Arriving
By Car

Tucson's major approach and through-route is I-10, the nation's southernmost transcontinental highway. Primarily an east-west route, it angles into the city from the southeast and the northwest. Northbound, I-10 intersects with I-19 in south Tucson and then continues along the west side of the city, providing access to the downtown area. Once I-10 leaves the city, it proceeds northwest to Phoenix, 120 miles away.

A major approach from the west is I-8, which originates in San Diego and joins with I-10 about midway between Phoenix and Tucson. Because both I-10 and I-8 traverse desert country, some of their sections are subject to dust storms, particularly in spring and early summer. Local radio stations broadcast advisories during these fluctuating weather conditions, and interstate signs with changeable messages warn motorists.

A well-known route reaching Tucson from the north is SR 77. One of the area's oldest two-lane routes, it is especially scenic. South of Tucson, I-19 leads to the Mexican border at Nogales.

Getting Around
Street System

Tucson is laid out in a grid pattern. Numbered streets run east-west to the south of Speedway Boulevard, and numbered avenues run north-south to the west of Euclid Avenue. Address numbers start at the intersection of Broadway, the north-south divider, and Stone, the east-west divider. Unless otherwise posted the speed limit on most streets is 25 to 40 mph.

The Book Stop

Parking

Metered parking is available on many downtown streets, but be sure to check signs and meters for restricted times and limits. There also are a number of commercial garages and lots. Rates average around $2 per hour or $5 per day.

Public Transportation

Sun Link, Tucson's modern streetcar system, began operating July 25, 2014. The 3.9-mile system features 23 stops and connects downtown Tucson with the University of Arizona campus, Main Gate Square, the 4th Avenue Business District and the Mercado District. Several Sun Link stations are decorated with sculptures by various artists, including an eye-catching, 6-foot-tall human head made up of small, steel letters at the E. Helen Street and N. Warren Avenue station.

Riding Sun Link requires either a 1-day SunGo ticket, which costs $4, or a one-way fare of $1.50. Reloadable SunGo Cards, transfers and 30-day tickets also are available. Tickets can be purchased at vending machines at each Sun Link stop, and each ticket must be validated once you are on board by tapping it against one of four validators. Phone (520) 792-9222 for more information.

Sun Tran, Tucson's bus service, operates a fleet of modern buses. The Ronstadt Transit Center, on 6th Avenue between Congress and Pennington streets, is the main downtown station. The fare to all points is $1.50; 50c (ages 65+ with valid ID and the physically impaired); free (ages 0-5). Fares can be paid to the bus driver or at self-serve ticket machines (cash only).

Shopping

If you've come to Tucson itchin' to buy turquoise, Kachina dolls and dream catchers, the world is your oyster. But Southwestern art and crafts are only part of the city's shopping picture. You can also overstuff your carry-on bag or car trunk with goods from funky boutiques, cutting-edge art galleries and high-end shopping malls.

Downtown in the El Presidio district, **Old Town Artisans**, 201 N. Court Ave., is housed in an 1850s adobe building that sits on an entire city block. The half dozen shops and galleries deal mainly in traditional Native and Latin American crafts (pottery, carvings, blankets), but you'll also find some contemporary jewelry and art here.

The Tucson Museum of Art and Historic Block's excellent **Museum Store**, 140 N. Main Ave., carries a nice selection of works by some of the state's best artists (read: expensive), as well as art books and affordable gift items.

Surrounding downtown you'll find a sprinkling of modern art galleries, particularly in the Congress Street district; there are more galleries a few blocks north in the **Warehouse Arts District** (centered at 6th Avenue and 6th Street). **Platform Gallery**, 439 N. 6th Ave., sells visually striking paintings and sculpture by contemporary Southwest artists. For more information on galleries, check hotel brochure racks for the Central Tucson Gallery Association's Downtown Art & Lunch guide map, or phone (520) 629-9759.

Without question, downtown's most eclectic shopping and dining area is 4th Avenue (between 9th Street and University Boulevard). With the exception of a prehistoric Dairy Queen, you won't see a single chain store or restaurant (not even a Starbucks) on the entire strip, which is exactly how Tucson hipsters like it.

This is a college town, so books are big. **Antigone Books,** 411 N. 4th Ave., has a feminist bent. If you need a copy of "Eat Pray Love," there's no danger Antigone is sold out. In addition to edgy, female-focused fare and other off-beat titles, there's a selection of cute gift items. One musty whiff of **The Book Stop,** 214 N. 4th Ave., and you know you've ascended to used-book heaven.

Fashionistas will find two of the street's best clothing boutiques near University Boulevard. The styles at **Zoe Boutique,** 735 N. 4th Ave., range from trendy to funky-casual. Inside an old pale green bungalow home, **Desert Vintage & Costume,** 636 N. 4th Ave., is the place to hunt for 1920s flapper dresses, bellbottoms and poodle skirts.

Tucson's Map & Flag Center, 3239 N. First Ave., is a bit off the beaten path, but a must for backcountry adventurers. The store carries topographic maps for the entire state, plus travel guidebooks and detailed road maps.

As for malls, Tucson isn't in league with Phoenix, but it's no slouch, either. **Tucson Mall,** 4500 N. Oracle Rd., is the city's biggest center followed in size and variety by Park Place Mall, 5870 E. Broadway Blvd. Outlet fanatics can bargain hunt at the **Foothills Mall,** 7401 N. La Cholla Blvd. Shop under blue skies at **La Encanta,** 2905 E. Skyline Dr., an open-air haven with eight diverse eateries, most of them with local roots, and high-end shops (think Brooks Brothers and Louis Vuitton); there's an Apple Store in case your iPod's on the fritz as well as year-round special events.

For a shopping courtyard filled with unique specialty boutiques, try the hacienda-style **St. Philip's Plaza,** at the southeast corner of Campbell Avenue and River Road. The plaza's Bahti Indian Arts specializes in Native American art and crafts. On Sundays the plaza hosts a farmers market.

Nightlife

Tucson's nightlife is mainly concentrated in the downtown area. Whether you choose to catch a live band, sip designer cocktails or guzzle beer alongside UofA students, many spots are within walking distance of one another.

Club Congress, 311 E. Congress St., has been called one of the country's best live music clubs by *Esquire* magazine. Just off the lobby of the historic Hotel Congress, the venue books mostly local and regional alt-rock bands. The stage, backed with red

Watch a show at the Fox Tucson Theatre

velvet drapes and framed by Gothic-style metalwork, overlooks a dance floor that's shoulder-to-shoulder on weekends; phone (520) 622-8848.

If you'd rather skip the club and its surprisingly high cover charge, yet still be able to hear the music, opt for the **Hotel Congress Lobby Bar.** The décor is classic Southwest Deco, the scene is laidback and there's a casual patio out back as well.

Across the street is the **Rialto Theatre,** 318 E. Congress St., a restored 1920 vaudeville and movie palace that now hosts mid-level touring acts (think Bon Iver, Lucinda Williams and Fleet Foxes); phone (520) 740-1000.

The miraculously rehabilitated **Fox Tucson Theatre,** 17 W. Congress St., screens classic movies just as it did back in its 1930s and '40s heyday. Also equipped with a stage and near-perfect acoustics, the Fox books live music acts and ballet performances; phone (520) 547-3040.

Downtown's tiny **Screening Room,** 127 E. Congress St., shows a mix of recent box office smashes and indie fare; phone (520) 882-0204. Even better is **The Loft Cinema,** 3233 E. Speedway Blvd. (a few minutes east of the UofA campus), which has three screens and runs film festival standouts and theme nights like "Mondo Mondays" and "Scream-o-rama"; phone (520) 795-7777.

Fourth Avenue is loaded with casual bars and pubs popular with UofA students. On the upscale side is **Sky Bar,** 536 N. 4th Ave., a sleek space that's a chill-out cafe by day and a hip bar by night. DJs spin techno and house beats on weekends; there's live jazz on Tuesdays. Every night, flatscreen TVs show astronomical images taken from the bar's very own telescope; phone (520) 622-4300.

If it's live music you're after, **The Flycatcher,** 340 E. 6th St. (corner of 4th Ave. and 6th St.) is the neighborhood's best bet. The majority of acts playing this funky club/bar are local indie rock bands, but a quick scan of the schedule will turn up some folk, bluegrass and acoustic singer-songwriter acts as well; phone (520) 798-1298.

For country music you'll need to gas up the F-150 and head to east Tucson. Opened in 1962, **The Maverick Live Country Club,** 6622 E. Tanque Verde Rd., offers live music Tuesday through Saturday; phone (520) 298-0430.

Romantics in the mood to clink wine glasses, hear a jazz pianist and gaze out at the twinkling city lights should head for the hilltop **Hacienda del Sol Guest Ranch Resort,** 5501 N. Hacienda del Sol Rd. Both the elegant Terraza Lounge and the comfy Joesler Room are classy spots for a tête-á-tête; phone (520) 299-1501.

Big Events

In February the city boasts a superlative: the world's largest gem and mineral show with more than 40 shows across town. The focal point of the 🐾 **Tucson Gem and Mineral Show** is at the **Tucson Convention Center,** which is filled with some 250 dealers selling to the public.

If you like horses and cowboys, Tucson is the place to be in mid- to late February during 🐾 **La Fiesta de los Vaqueros,** held at the rodeo grounds. This classic professional rodeo event features a parade with people on foot, on horseback and in every

Go for a hike in Tucson

size and shape of horse-drawn vehicle. The fiesta ends with the rodeo finals, in which some of the best riders and ropers on the circuit compete.

In March and again in December Tucson's 4th Avenue holds a huge street fair filled with artisans selling and demonstrating their crafts. Enhanced by music and food vendor booths, these weekends attract visitors and residents alike. The annual **Tucson International Mariachi Conference** and music festival comes to town in April. Mid-month brings the **Pima County Fair.** In May, the **Tucson Folk Festival** attracts thousands of traditional music fans for a weekend of entertainment by the genre's top acts.

Tucson's fall activities begin in late September and early October with **Oktoberfest on Mount Lemmon.** In early November, a Tucson artists' organization presents the annual **All Souls Procession.** Inspired by Mexico's Día de los Muertos, thousands of people walk 2 miles through the streets of Tucson to commemorate the passing of loved ones, carrying photos of the deceased, wearing the departed's clothing or dressed in skeleton costumes.

Sports & Rec

Tucson is America's **Winter Training Capital,** and an athlete's mid-winter dream. With comfortable temperatures and abundant sunshine, it's almost impossible to lose a training day—no matter what your sport.

Tucson's city parks and Pima County parks offer facilities for almost any activity. A number of **swimming** pools and **tennis, racquetball** and **handball** courts are available as well as picnic areas, playgrounds, and **soccer** and ball fields. For information about facilities and reservations for their use contact the Pima County Parks and Recreation office at 3500 W. River Rd., (520) 877-6000, or Tucson Parks and Recreation at 900 S. Randolph, (520) 791-4873.

Tucson's climate is made to order for **golf** addicts. More than 60 courses are in the region— everything from world-renowned resorts to public access courses. The jaw-dropping topography and rugged desert terrain of the real Southwest have ignited the imaginations of the greatest golf course architects. Some were designed by Robert Cupp, Tom Fazio, Arthur Hill, Robert Trent Jones and Jack Nicklaus along with newcomer Notah Begay III.

Among the courses in Tucson are: Hilton Tucson El Conquistador Golf and Tennis Resort (in Oro Valley), Pusch Ridge Golf Course, (520) 544-5000 or (520) 544-1900, 10000 N. Oracle Rd. and 10555 N. La Cañada Dr.; Omni Tucson National, (520) 297-2271, 2727 W. Club Dr.; Randolph Municipal, (520) 791-4161, 600 S. Alvernon Way; Santa Rita, (520) 762-5620, 16461 S. Houghton Rd.; and Ventana Canyon, (520) 577-1400, 6200 N. Clubhouse Ln. Also in the area is Canoa Hills, (520) 648-1881, at 1401 W. Calle Urbano in Green Valley.

Ranked by several elite **bicycling** publications as one of America's most bike-friendly cities, Tucson also is home to what has been called one of the premier organized rides in the United States—El Tour de Tucson attracts more than 9,000 bicyclists of all ages and abilities each November.

Hiking is probably the best way to get up close and personal with the flora and fauna of the Sonoran Desert. Tucson Mountain Park is laced with hiking trails. The Santa Catalina Mountains offer many areas of unspoiled beauty as well. Hiking permits are required for some areas. Empty vehicles will be fined or towed if a permit is not displayed. For more information about permits and National Forest fee areas, contact the Coronado National Forest office in Tucson; phone (520) 388-8300. Catalina State Park *(see attraction listing p. 266 and Recreation Areas Chart)*, (520) 628-5798, has trails that can challenge the experienced hiker but not intimidate the novice; two longer trails begin at the end of the park's paved road. For more information about hiking phone the county's recreation office at (520) 877-6000. Hike In Tucson directs guided hiking trips along several area trails; phone (520) 477-6867 or (877) 445-3882.

Another great way to see the countryside is on a trail ride. Several stables offer half-day, full-day and overnight **horseback riding** trips into the mountains and desert. Check hotel brochure racks for stables. **Skiing** is available at Mount Lemmon Ski Valley, a scenic 30-mile drive northeast from Tucson. The southernmost ski area in the nation, Mount Lemmon offers both downhill and cross-country skiing. A scenic sky ride on the ski lift is offered during the off-season. Phone (520) 576-1400 for snow condition updates.

The University of Arizona's Wildcats excite crowds during the **football, baseball** and **basketball** seasons. Home football games are played at Arizona Stadium, baseball players batter up at Hi Corbett Field and basketball teams tip off at McKale Memorial Center.

Greyhound racing happens at Tucson Greyhound Park, (520) 884-7576, 2601 S. 3rd Ave. at 36th Street. The dogs race Monday through Saturday, year-round.

Note: Policies concerning admittance of children to pari-mutuel betting facilities vary. Phone for information.

Performing Arts

When it comes to theater, Tucson offers many choices. Top billing is given to the **Arizona Theatre Company,** Arizona's professional state theater. This premier company performs six plays during its September through May season at the **Temple of Music and Art,** (520) 622-2823, 330 S. Scott Ave. A forum for experimental theater is **The Invisible Theatre,** (520) 882-9721, 1400 N. 1st Ave., which stages six plays between September and June.

Entertainment for the entire family is available at the **Gaslight Theatre,** (520) 886-9428, 7010 E. Broadway, where melodramas, comedies and musicals encourage audience participation; reservations

are required. The **University of Arizona** adds to Tucson's theater offerings. The school's resident company, (520) 621-7008, 1025 N. Olive St., presents its offerings of musicals and serious drama in spring, summer and fall, while the UA Presents series brings national touring companies to **Centennial Hall,** (520) 621-3341, 1020 E. University Blvd.

No bit players, Tucson's opera company plays a major part in the performing arts arena. Accompanied by a full orchestra in the **Tucson Convention Center** from October through April, members of the **Arizona Opera,** (520) 293-4336, present five operas.

Completing the cultural scene are the city's orchestras. The **Tucson Symphony Orchestra,** (520) 882-8585, plays both classical and pop music in the **Tucson Music Hall** September to May. Under the desert skies at the **DeMeester Outdoor Performance Center** in Reid Park, the **Tucson Pops Orchestra,** (520) 722-5853, entertains audiences in the spring and fall. From September through May the University of Arizona's Centennial Hall resounds with sounds from Broadway shows to jazz to chamber music performed by guest artists and musicians.

ATTRACTIONS

ARIZONA HISTORICAL SOCIETY/ARIZONA HISTORY MUSEUM, 949 E. 2nd St., features exhibits portraying the daily life of 1870s Native American, Mexican and Anglo families; the life of Apache warrior Geronimo; and various modes of 19th- and early 20th-century transportation. Museum highlights include a full-size replica of a 100-year-old underground copper mine and a hands-on exhibit that describes Tucson's history, land use and environment along the Santa Cruz River. A research library is available.

Time: Allow 1 hour minimum. **Hours:** Museum Mon.-Sat. 10-4. Closed Jan. 1, Martin Luther King Jr. Day, Presidents Day, Memorial Day, July 4, Labor Day, Columbus Day, Veterans Day, Thanksgiving and Christmas. Library hours vary; phone ahead. **Cost:** $8; $6 (ages 65+); $5 (students with ID); $4 (ages 7-17). Prices may vary; phone ahead. Validated parking is available in the garage at E. 2nd Street and N. Euclid Avenue. **Phone:** (520) 628-5774.

ARIZONA HISTORICAL SOCIETY/DOWNTOWN HISTORY MUSEUM, 140 N. Stone Ave., depicts downtown Tucson's history from its origins as a Spanish presidio in 1775 to modern times. Visitors may visit a 19th-century hotel lobby and an old-time barbershop. Explore the history of downtown's police force, firefighters, schools, libraries, businesses and theaters. An exhibit about the 1934 capture of John Dillinger and his gang includes his bulletproof vest.

Time: Allow 30 minutes minimum. **Hours:** Thurs.-Sat. 10-4. Closed Jan. 1, July 4, Veterans Day,

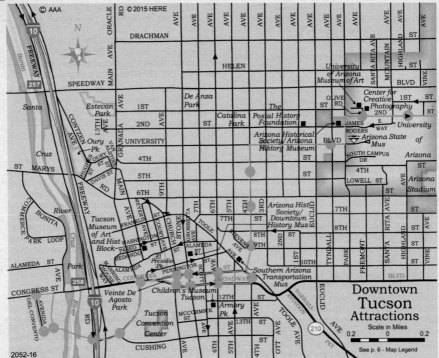

Downtown Tucson Attractions

Thanksgiving and Christmas. **Cost:** $3. Prices may vary; phone ahead. Validated parking is available on lower level of Wells Fargo Bank garage on E. Alameda Street. **Phone:** (520) 770-1473.

ARIZONA HISTORICAL SOCIETY/FORT LOWELL MUSEUM, jct. Fort Lowell and Craycroft rds. at 2900 N. Craycroft Rd. in Fort Lowell Park, features a reconstructed officer's quarters from a military post active 1873-91. Learn about the history of the fort, its soldiers and their families as well as the story of the Apache Indian Wars. Military and horse equipment, uniforms, period furniture and photographs of army life are on display.

Time: Allow 1 hour minimum. **Hours:** Thurs.-Sat. 10-4. Closed Jan. 1, July 4, Veterans Day, Thanksgiving and Christmas. **Cost:** $3. Prices may vary; phone ahead. **Phone:** (520) 885-3832.

ARIZONA HISTORICAL SOCIETY/SOSA-CARRILLO-FRÉMONT HOUSE is at 151 S. Granada Ave., s. of the Tucson Music Hall within the Convention Center Complex. The restored 1880 Mexican-American house is said to be one of Tucson's oldest adobe buildings. Period furnishings, memorabilia of the Sosa, Carrillo and Frémont families, and changing exhibits are displayed.

Time: Allow 30 minutes minimum. **Hours:** Thurs.-Sat. 11-3. **Cost:** Donations. **Phone:** (520) 622-0956 or (520) 628-5774.

ARIZONA-SONORA DESERT MUSEUM, 14 mi. w. in Tucson Mountain Park at 2021 N. Kinney Rd., is an interpretative center showcasing the diversity of the Sonoran Desert region, recognized as the lushest desert on earth. The museum offers a zoo, botanical garden, art gallery, natural history museum and aquarium showcasing the regions' animals, plants, geology, climate and native cultures in a natural environment.

The 21-acre facility features 2 miles of walking paths and houses some 230 animal species, including coatis, javelina, road runners and Mexican wolves. The popular hummingbird aviary features several species of the tiny birds; visitors can see breeding and nesting activity January through May and get close enough to photograph the birds. Sixteen gardens display 1,200 types of plants and 56,000 specimens. The Earth Sciences Center, a simulated walk-through limestone cave, features a collection of regional gems and minerals. Live animal presentations include Live and (sort of) on the Loose (venomous reptiles), Raptor Free Flight (seasonal) showcasing native birds of prey, and Fur, Feathers and Fangs (mammals and birds). **Hours:** Daily 7:30-5, Mar.-Sept. (also Sat. 5-10, June-Aug.); 8:30-5, rest of year. **Cost:** $19.50; $17.50 (ages 65+); $15.50 (ages 13-17 and active military with ID); $6 (ages 4-12). Prices may vary; phone ahead. **Phone:** (520) 883-2702.

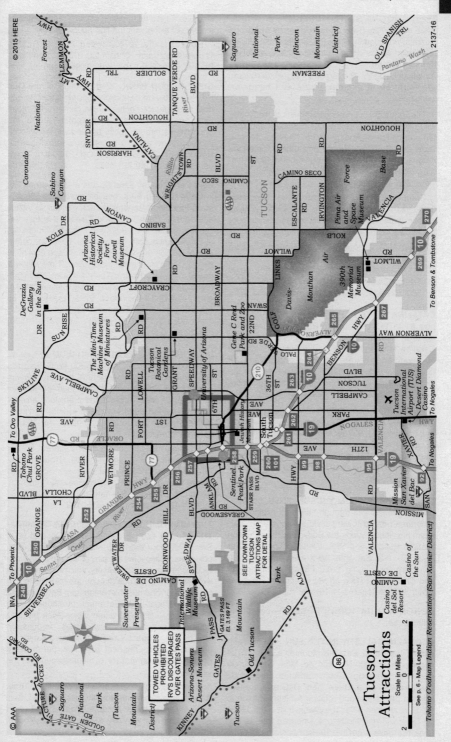

Tucson Attractions

Scale in Miles

See p. 6 - Map Legend

Tohono O'odham Indian Reservation (San Xavier District)

ARIZONA STATE MUSEUM is at 1013 E. University Blvd. on the University of Arizona campus. Founded in 1893, this Smithsonian affiliate reputedly has the world's oldest and largest collections of Southwest Indian pottery and Native American basketry. The region's indigenous cultures are featured in exhibits, tours and hands-on workshops.

The Paths of Life: American Indians of the Southwest exhibit highlights the origin, history and contemporary life of Apache, Hopi, Navajo, Tohono O'odham, Southern Paiute and other indigenous groups. There's a mix of prehistoric artifacts, historical objects, commissioned artwork, video interviews and dioramas.

Southwest Native American pottery spanning 2,000 years is showcased. The library and archives contain more than 90,000 volumes as well as photographs and archeological excavation reports.

Time: Allow 1 hour minimum. **Hours:** Museum Mon.-Sat. 10-5. Library and archives Mon.-Thurs. 10-3. Closed major holidays. **Cost:** $5; free (ages 0-17 and students with ID). **Phone:** (520) 621-6302, or (520) 621-4695 for the library and archives. GT

CATALINA STATE PARK, 9 mi. n. off SR 77 Milepost 81 to 11570 N. Oracle Rd., is home to 5,500 acres of desert plants. At the base of the Santa Catalina Mountains, the park's activities include bird-watching, hiking, camping and horseback riding. A .75-mile interpretive trail winds around the Romero Ruins, the site of a Hohokam village occupied 500-1450. *See Recreation Areas Chart.*

Hours: Park open daily 5 a.m.-10 p.m. Ranger station daily 8-5. **Cost:** $7 (per private vehicle, up to four passengers); $3 (per additional adult passenger in vehicle or individual arriving on foot or bicycle). Camping $15-$25 (per private vehicle). **Phone:** (520) 628-5798, or (520) 586-2283 for camping reservations. ▲ ⛺ ⛩

CHILDREN'S MUSEUM TUCSON, 200 S. 6th Ave., encourages learning through hands-on exhibits and programs geared toward children ages 2-10. Museum highlights include the Bodyology, Investigation Station, Build It and Wee World exhibits. **Hours:** Tues.-Fri. 9-5, Sat.-Sun. 10-5. Last admission 30 minutes before closing. Closed Easter, Thanksgiving and Christmas. Phone ahead to confirm schedule. **Cost:** $8; free (ages 0-1). **Phone:** (520) 792-9985.

CORONADO NATIONAL FOREST—see place listing p. 54.

DEGRAZIA GALLERY IN THE SUN is in the foothills of the Santa Catalina Mountains, 1 mi. n. of Sunrise Dr. at 6300 N. Swan Rd. More than 15,000 ceramics, paintings and sculptures created by Southwestern artist Ettore "Ted" DeGrazia are featured in permanent and rotating exhibits. Mission in the Sun, an open-air adobe chapel built in the 1950s by DeGrazia and his Native American friends, adjoins the gallery on the 10-acre National Historic

site. The artist's final resting place is marked beside the chapel along with the first house he built.

Hours: Daily 10-4. Closed Jan. 1, Easter, Thanksgiving and Christmas. **Cost:** Donations. **Phone:** (520) 299-9191 or (800) 545-2185.

GENE C. REID PARK, 22nd St. and Country Club Rd., is a 160-acre park offering picnic areas, an outdoor performance center, a rose garden, Hi Corbett Field and the Reffkin Tennis Center—one of the Southwest's largest public tennis facilities with 25 lighted courts and 10 lighted racquetball courts. **Hours:** Park open daily 6:30 a.m.-10:30 p.m. **Cost:** Free. **Phone:** (520) 791-4873.

Reid Park Zoo, off 22nd St. just w. of Alvernon Rd. in Gene C. Reid Park, houses more than 500 animals, including elephants, bears, giraffes, ostriches and zebras. Each habitat and species is fully described. Guests may feed and interact with giraffes at Giraffe Encounter, ride a camel, travel the perimeter of the zoo in a train in Reid Park and cool off in Kenya Get Wet, a water playground. **Time:** Allow 2 hours minimum. **Hours:** Daily 9-4, Oct.-May; 8-3, rest of year. Giraffe Encounter daily. Closed Thanksgiving and Christmas. **Cost:** $9; $7 (ages 62+); $5 (ages 2-14). Giraffe Encounter $2. Camel rides $7. Train rides $2. **Phone:** (520) 791-4022 or (520) 791-3204. ⛾

INTERNATIONAL WILDLIFE MUSEUM is 5 mi. w. of I-10 on Speedway Blvd. to 4800 W. Gates Pass Rd. Tucson's interactive natural history museum contains dioramas depicting more than 400 species of mammals, insects, birds and prehistoric animals from around the world. Hands-on exhibits and interactive displays are found throughout the 40,000-square-foot museum.

A 98-seat theater offers hourly natural history films. **Time:** Allow 1 hour minimum. **Hours:** Mon.-Fri. 9-5, Sat.-Sun. 9-6. Last admission 45 minutes before closing. Closed Thanksgiving and Christmas. **Cost:** $9; $7 (ages 62+ and military with ID); $4 (ages 4-12). **Phone:** (520) 629-0100.

THE MINI-TIME MACHINE MUSEUM OF MINIATURES is at 4455 E. Camp Lowell Dr., just w. of Swan Rd. More than 275 miniature houses, room boxes and collectibles are part of this museum's collection. In the History Gallery you'll find miniature exhibits from the 1700s through the mid-1900s. Exploring the World has everything from British pubs to Southwest adobes to Japanese farmhouses. The Enchanted Realm's miniature miscellanea includes haunted mansions, medieval castles, dragons, pirate dioramas and a Christmas-themed exhibit. In addition to the permanent collection, the museum hosts several temporary exhibits throughout the year.

Note: Flash photography is not permitted. **Time:** Allow 1 hour minimum. **Hours:** Tues.-Sat. 9-4, Sun. noon-4. Closed major holidays. **Cost:** $9; $8 (ages 65+ and military with ID); $6 (ages 4-17). **Phone:** (520) 881-0606.

MISSION SAN XAVIER DEL BAC is 9 mi. s. off I-19 exit 92, on San Xavier Rd. in the Tohono O'odham Indian Reservation. Though founded by Jesuit Father Eusebio Francisco Kino before 1700, the present structure was built 1783-97 by the Franciscans. The missionaries were forced to leave San Xavier in 1828 but the Franciscans returned in 1911, and since that time have maintained old San Xavier as the parish church and school of the Tohono O'odham.

This is the only Kino mission in the nation still active in preaching to the Tohono O'odham. Called the "White Dove of the Desert," the structure is an impressive example of Spanish mission architecture. The domes, carvings and arches distinguish it from other missions. The interior murals and the altar are especially noteworthy. The Mission was made a National Historic Landmark in 1963.

A continuous video presentation is shown in the museum, and a self-guiding tour is available. **Hours:** Mission daily 8-5. Museum daily 8-4:30. Guided tours depart every 30 minutes Mon.-Sat. 9:30-12:30. **Cost:** Donations. **Phone:** (520) 294-2624. GT

OLD TUCSON is 12 mi. w. via Speedway Blvd. or Ajo Way in Tucson Mountain Park. Erected in 1939, this replica of 1860s Tucson was the location for the movies "Arizona" and "Tombstone." More than 350 films and TV shows have been filmed here. Highlights include a Native American village, stagecoach rides, live gunfights, stunt demonstrations, Western musical revues, living history presentations and the Film History Museum. Stagecoach tours and trail rides are offered. Nightfall, a month-long Halloween-themed event with haunted houses and live performances, is held in October.

Hours: Daily 10-6, Feb.-Apr.; Sat.-Sun. 10-5, June 1 to mid-Aug.; Fri.-Sat. 6 p.m.-midnight, Thurs. and Sun. 6 p.m.-10 p.m. in Oct. for Nightfall; Fri.-Sun. 10-5 in May and Nov.-Dec.; daily 10-5, in Jan. Closed Thanksgiving, Christmas Eve and Christmas. Phone ahead to confirm schedule. **Cost:**

$17.95; $10.95 (ages 4-11). **Phone:** (520) 883-0100. [¶]

PIMA AIR AND SPACE MUSEUM is at 6000 E. Valencia Rd.; from I-10 take exit 267. Displayed are 300 aircraft, including Air Force One used by Presidents John F. Kennedy and Lyndon B. Johnson. Additional aircraft in five hangars and along pathways include a replica 1903 Wright Flyer and a SR-71 Blackbird. Three hangars are dedicated to World War II. One-hour tram tours of the 80-acre facility are available, as are 75-minute bus tours of the Aircraft Boneyard/Aircraft Maintenance and Regeneration Group (AMARG) facility on Davis-Monthan Air Force Base which features more than 4,400 U.S. military aircraft on 2,600 acres.

Note: Government-issued photo ID is required to enter the base, and visitors are not permitted to leave the bus. **Hours:** Museum daily 9-5. Last admission 1 hour before closing. Tour schedules vary; phone ahead. Closed Thanksgiving and Christmas. **Cost:** Museum $15.50; $12.75 (ages 62+ and military with ID); $9 (ages 7-12). Tram tour $6. Bus tour $7; $4 (ages 7-12). Prices may vary; phone ahead. Advance purchase is recommended for bus and tram tours. **Phone:** (520) 574-0462. GT [¶]

390th Memorial Museum is at 6000 E. Valencia Rd., at the Pima Air and Space Museum. The museum honors the men of the 390th Bombardment Group (Heavy), many of whom died while flying B-17 bombers in World War II. Exhibits include a fully restored B-17 (also known as the "Flying Fortress"), aircraft models, a one-of-a-kind nose art exhibit, flight gear, guns, photos, a Quonset hut, a World War II control tower and other memorabilia. A 54-minute video presentation includes interviews with surviving members and actual film clips from the war.

Time: Allow 30 minutes minimum. **Hours:** Daily 10-4:30. Closed Thanksgiving and Christmas. **Cost:** Pima Air and Space Museum admission (includes 390th Memorial Museum) $15.50; $12.75 (ages 62+ and military with ID); $9 (ages 7-12). Prices may vary; phone ahead. **Phone:** (520) 574-0287.

Sabino Canyon

THE POSTAL HISTORY FOUNDATION, 920 N. First Ave., features stamps, postmarks and books tracing the history of the U.S. Postal Service and caters to serious philatelists and postal historians as well as casual collectors and youth education. Original equipment from the Naco post office as well as antique file cabinets and other memorabilia from Arizona post offices are on display.

An adjacent building houses a research library of philatelic literature and a collection of Civil War memorabilia, books and documents. A working post office is on-site. **Time:** Allow 30 minutes minimum. **Hours:** Mon.-Fri. 8-3. Post Office Mon.-Fri. 8-2:30. Closed major holidays. **Cost:** Donations. **Phone:** (520) 623-6652. GT

SABINO CANYON is at 5900 N. Sabino Canyon Rd., 17 mi. e. via Tanque Verde and Sabino Canyon rds. Part of the Coronado National Forest *(see place listing p. 54),* this desert oasis in the Santa Catalina Mountains offers spectacular panoramic views and a wide range of recreational activities. Visitors can hike along a network of trails; go horseback riding; take a dip in a swimming hole or waterfall; and observe javelinas, roadrunners, white-tailed deer, numerous birds and other native wildlife.

Sabino Canyon Tours offers narrated excursions into the canyon aboard shuttle buses. A shuttle also transports hikers to the Bear Canyon trailhead.

Note: Beware of mountain lions and rattlesnakes within the canyon. Pets are not permitted. **Time:** Allow 1 hour minimum. **Hours:** Visitor reception area Mon.-Fri. 8-4:30, Sat.-Sun. 8:30-4:30. Closed Thanksgiving and Christmas. Phone ahead to confirm schedule. **Cost:** $5 (per private vehicle per day); $7 (per private vehicle per week); free (interagency pass holders and those arriving on foot or bicycle). Admission includes Sabino Canyon, Madera Canyon and Mount Lemmon picnic areas. Sabino Canyon tour $8; $4 (ages 3-12). Bear Canyon shuttle $3; $1 (ages 3-12). Cash only. **Phone:** (520) 749-8700.

SAGUARO NATIONAL PARK—see place listing p. 199.

SENTINEL PEAK PARK, off Broadway w. of I-10 on Sentinel Peak Rd., contains the peak more popularly known as "A" Mountain because of the big "A" annually whitewashed on it by University of Arizona freshmen. It affords an excellent view of Tucson and surrounding mountains. At night the city's lights are particularly captivating from this vantage point. **Hours:** Mon.-Sat. 8-8, Sun. 8-6. **Phone:** (520) 791-5909.

SOUTHERN ARIZONA TRANSPORTATION MUSEUM is at 414 N. Toole Ave. Exhibits at this museum and interpretive center include artifacts and memorabilia relating to the history of the railroad and transportation in southern Arizona. The former Southern Pacific Railroad Depot has been restored to its 1941 design and includes a train depot. A historic 1900 steam locomotive is on display; visitors may go inside to see it close-up.

Time: Allow 30 minutes minimum. **Hours:** Tues.-Thurs. and Sun. 11-3, Fri.-Sat. 10-4. Phone ahead for guided tour schedule. **Cost:** Donations. Guided tours $5. **Phone:** (520) 623-2223. GT

TOHONO CHUL PARK is at 7366 N. Paseo del Norte. Tohono O'odham for "desert corner," Tohono Chul Park is a 49-acre desert preserve set amid a rapidly growing urban area. The park features nature trails, a Geology Wall, a Children's Garden, a greenhouse and changing art exhibits. Displays educate visitors about water conservation, arid lands and the traditions and cultures of the Southwest. Guided and self-guiding tours are available.

Hours: Park open daily 8-5. Exhibit building open daily 9-5. Closed Jan. 1, July 4, Thanksgiving and Christmas. **Cost:** Admission May-Sept. $8; $6 (ages 62+); $5 (active military with ID); $4 (students with ID); $2 (ages 5-12). Admission rest of year $10; $8 (ages 62+); $5 (active military and students with ID); $3 (ages 5-12). **Phone:** (520) 742-6455.

TUCSON BOTANICAL GARDENS, 2150 N. Alvernon Way, covers 5.5 acres and features Zen, children's, herb, historical, iris, sensory, birdwatching and barrio and xeriscape gardens as well as a Native American crop garden. Exhibits include a seasonal tropical butterfly house and art displays. Special events are held throughout the year.

Hours: Daily 8:30-4:30. Closed Jan. 1, July 4, Thanksgiving, Christmas Eve and Christmas. **Cost:**

Oct.-May $13; $12 (students, senior citizens and military with ID); $7.50 (ages 4-12). Rest of year $9; $8 (students, senior citizens and military with ID); $5 (ages 4-12). **Phone:** (520) 326-9686.

TUCSON MOUNTAIN PARK, 8 mi. w. on Speedway Blvd. and Kinney Rd., encompasses approximately 20,000 acres of the Tucson Mountains and adjoining mesa land and embraces one of the largest areas of saguaro and natural desert growth in the Southwest. Camping is available at the Gilbert Ray Campground; firewood is prohibited. Trails for hiking and horseback riding are available.

Hours: Park open daily dawn-dusk. **Cost:** Park free. Camping $10 (tents), $20 (RV) per night. **Phone:** (520) 724-5000.

TUCSON MUSEUM OF ART AND HISTORIC BLOCK is at 140 N. Main Ave. Visitors can view collections of Latin American, Western, Asian, modern and contemporary art. The museum also comprises five homes built 1850-1907 in the El Presidio Historic District, including adobe structures housing Western and Latin American collections; the J. Knox Corbett House, a Mission Revival bungalow with Arts and Crafts *objets d'art* (open October through April); and La Casa Cordova, a Mexican-style adobe home (open November through April). A library and changing art exhibits are featured, and art lectures and classes are offered.

Hours: Museum Tues.-Sat. 10-5 (also Thurs. 5-8), Sun. noon-5. Closed major holidays. **Cost:** Museum $10; $8 (ages 65+ and veterans with ID); $5 (college students with ID); free (ages 0-18, active military with ID and veterans and to all first Sun. of the month). Guided tours included with paid admission. **Phone:** (520) 624-2333. GT

UNIVERSITY OF ARIZONA, bounded by Euclid Ave., E. Helen St., Campbell Ave. and E. 7th St., was founded in 1885 as the state's first institution of higher learning. Today the campus encompasses 380 acres and is one of the nation's top research universities. Campus information and a variety of guided campus walking-tours are available through the UA Visitor Center September through December and February through May. **Hours:** UA Visitor Center Mon.-Fri. 9-5; closed during winter break. Campus tours depart Wed. at 10, Sept.-Dec. and Feb.-May. **Cost:** Free. Reservations are required. **Phone:** (520) 621-5130.

Center for Creative Photography is at 1030 N. Olive Rd., n. of 2nd St. on the University of Arizona campus. The center houses one of the world's largest collections of modern and contemporary photography. The exhibitions in the center's gallery feature works drawn from a collection of more than 90,000 photographs by more than 2,200 photographers, together with material from the archives of many leading American photographers. An additional gallery space exhibits a rotating selection of new acquisitions and collection highlights.

Metered public parking is available in the visitor section of the Park Avenue Garage, just n.e. of Speedway Blvd., with direct pedestrian access to the center's front door. **Hours:** Gallery Mon.-Fri. 9-5, Sat.-Sun. 1-4. Photo Fridays 11:30-3:30. Closed major holidays. Phone ahead to confirm schedule. **Cost:** Donations. **Phone:** (520) 621-7968.

Flandrau Science Center and Planetarium, on the University of Arizona campus at 1601 E. University Blvd., is filled with hands-on, interactive exhibits geared toward school-aged kids. Must-sees include an Apollo display featuring a model of the Saturn V rocket; a raised-relief wall map of the Martian surface; and a rock climbing wall. A planetarium presents astronomy and laser-light shows. The Sky Islands exhibit features the rocks, plants and animals of the Sky Islands, a 70,000-square-mile region of southeastern Arizona, southwestern New Mexico and northwestern Mexico valued for its rich diversity of species and habitats.

Time: Allow 1 hour minimum. **Hours:** Mon.-Wed. 9-5, Thurs. 9-9, Fri. 9 a.m.-10 p.m., Sat. 10-10, Sun. noon-5. Phone for planetarium show options and schedule. Closed major holidays. **Cost:** (Includes University of Arizona Mineral Museum) $7; $5 (ages 4-17). Laser-light show and planetarium $7; $5 (ages 4-17); $3 (each additional show). **Phone:** (520) 621-7827.

University of Arizona Mineral Museum, on the lower level of UA Science: Flandrau at 1601 E. University Blvd., displays fine gems, meteorites and mineral specimens from around the world. The museum specializes in minerals from Arizona and

Ride the trails in Tucson Mountain Park

Mexico. Visitors can use a microscope to see micro-size specimens. **Hours:** Mon.-Wed. 9-5, Thurs. 9-9, Fri. 9 a.m.-10 p.m., Sat. 10-10, Sun. noon-5. Closed major holidays. Phone ahead to confirm schedule. **Cost:** (Includes Flandrau Science Center and Planetarium) $7; $5 (ages 4-17). **Phone:** (520) 621-4227.

University of Arizona Museum of Art, s.e. corner of Park Ave. and Speedway Blvd. in the University of Arizona Fine Arts Complex, features more than 6,000 pieces in the museum's permanent collection comprising both European and American artwork from the 14th century to present day. Six galleries showcase changing exhibitions as well as works by such artists as Rembrandt, Pierre-Auguste Renoir, Pablo Picasso, Andy Warhol and Edward Hopper. Always on view is the 15th-century altarpiece of Ciudad Rodrigo (Spain), old master paintings from the Kress Collection and sculptor Jacques Lipchitz's sketches and models.

Time: Allow 1 hour minimum. **Hours:** Tues.-Fri. 9-5, Sat.-Sun. noon-4, Mon. noon-5, Oct.-May; Tues.-Fri. 9-5, Sat.-Sun. noon-4, rest of year. Closed major university holidays. **Cost:** $5; free (ages 0-18 and students and military with ID). Hourly-rate parking is available; free on weekends. **Phone:** (520) 621-7567.

UNIVERSITY OF ARIZONA-BIOSPHERE 2—see Oracle p. 115.

GAMBLING ESTABLISHMENTS
- **Casino del Sol Resort** is at 5655 W. Valencia Rd. **Hours:** Daily 24 hours. **Phone:** (855) 765-7829.
- **Casino of the Sun,** I-19 Valencia exit, 4.5 mi. w., then .5 mi. s. to 7406 S. Camino de Oeste.

Hours: Daily 24 hours. **Phone:** (520) 838-6506 or (800) 344-9435.
- **Desert Diamond Casino,** I-19 Valencia exit, 1 mi. e., then 1 mi. s. to 7350 S. Nogales Hwy. **Hours:** Daily 24 hours. **Phone:** (520) 294-7777 or (866) 332-9467.

Sightseeing
Bus Tours
Gray Line, (520) 622-8811 or (800) 276-1528, offers sightseeing tours to Tucson's major sites as well as trips to Tombstone and the Grand Canyon. Overnight and multiple-day tours are available.

Walking Tours
For those who prefer to explore the city and its environs on their own, the *Visit Tucson Official Travel Guide,* distributed by the Visit Tucson, 100 S. Church Ave., contains walking tour information; phone (520) 624-1817 or (800) 638-8350 to have a free copy mailed to you before your trip. Visitors may also pick up a destination guide at the Tucson Visitor Center at 110 S. Church Ave., Suite 7199 (in La Placita Village), Mon.-Fri. 9-5, Sat.-Sun. 9-4.

While you're there ask for the free Presidio Trail Historical Walking Tour brochure, which includes a map of the Presidio Trail, a bright turquoise stripe painted on the sidewalks that wind through the heart of downtown Tucson. The 2.5-mile trail begins at the intersection of Church and Washington streets and passes more than 20 numbered historical sites, including the Pima County Courthouse and the Tucson Museum of Art and Historic Block *(see attraction listings).* If you follow the trail without the walking tour brochure and its written descriptions, don't worry; most sites on the tour are marked by plaques.

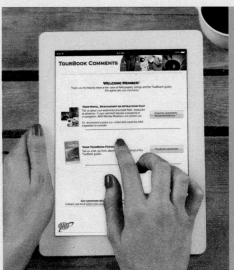

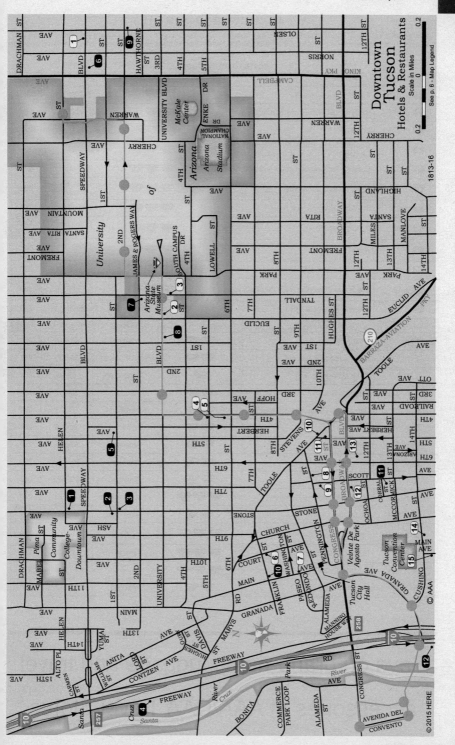

Downtown
Tucson
Hotels & Restaurants

Scale in Miles

0   0.2

0   0.2

See p. 6 - Map Legend

1813-16

© AAA

©2015 HERE

Downtown Tucson

This index helps you "spot" where approved hotels and restaurants are located on the corresponding detailed maps. Hotel daily rate range is for comparison only. Restaurant price range is a combination of lunch and/or dinner. Turn to the listing page for more detailed rate and price information and consult display ads for special promotions.

DOWNTOWN TUCSON

Map Page	Hotels	Diamond Rated	Rate Range	Page
1 p. 271	Econo Lodge University	◆	$43-$160	283
2 p. 271	**BEST WESTERN Royal Sun Inn & Suites**	◆◆◆	$59-$219 SAVE	283
3 p. 271	**University Inn**	◆◆	$49-$149 SAVE	283
4 p. 271	**Country Inn & Suites By Carlson-Tucson City Center**	◆◆◆	$89-$199 SAVE	283
5 p. 271	Catalina Park Inn Bed and Breakfast	◆◆◆	$125-$190	283
6 p. 271	**Aloft Tucson University**	◆◆◆	Rates not provided SAVE	282
7 p. 271	Marriott University Park Hotel	◆◆◆	$99-$247	283
8 p. 271	Peppertrees Inn	◆◆◆	Rates not provided	283
9 p. 271	Adobe Rose Inn	◆◆◆	Rates not provided	282
10 p. 271	El Presidio Bed & Breakfast Inn	◆◆◆	$139-$189	283
11 p. 271	The Royal Elizabeth Bed & Breakfast Inn	◆◆◆	Rates not provided	283
12 p. 271	**Arizona Riverpark Inn**	◆◆	$89-$199 SAVE	283

Map Page	Restaurants	Diamond Rated	Cuisine	Price Range	Page
1 p. 271	Trident Grill	◆◆	American	$8-$16	284
2 p. 271	Pasco Kitchen & Lounge	◆◆	New American	$9-$20	284
3 p. 271	Silver Mine Subs	◆	Sandwiches	$5-$8	284
4 p. 271	Magpie's Gourmet Pizza	◆◆	Pizza	$5-$17	284
5 p. 271	Delectables Restaurant & Catering	◆◆	International	$8-$15	284
6 p. 271	El Charro Cafe	◆◆	Mexican	$8-$19	284
7 p. 271	Café a la C'Art	◆◆	American	$9-$13	284
8 p. 271	Cafe Poca Cosa	◆◆	Mexican	$13-$25	284
9 p. 271	47 Scott	◆◆	American	$12-$22	283
10 p. 271	Maynards Market & Kitchen	◆◆◆	New American	$7-$38	284
11 p. 271	Cup Cafe	◆◆	American	$10-$25	284
12 p. 271	Penca	◆◆	Regional Mexican	$12-$18	284
13 p. 271	DOWNTOWN Kitchen + Cocktails	◆◆◆	American	$15-$28	284
14 p. 271	Cushing Street Bar & Restaurant	◆◆◆	American	$9-$24	284
15 p. 271	El Minuto Cafe	◆◆	Mexican	$7-$17	284

© AAA

Tucson Area
Hotels & Restaurants

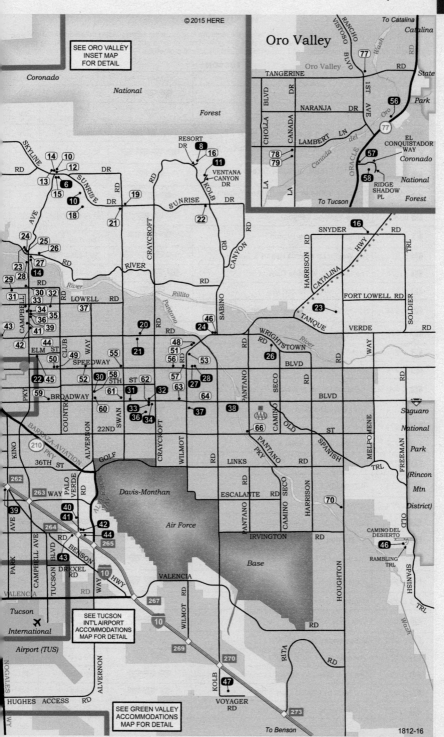

© 2015 HERE

Oro Valley

Catalina

To Catalina

Coronado

National

Forest

SEE ORO VALLEY
INSET MAP
FOR DETAIL

State
Park

TANGERINE

NARANJA DR

LAMBERT LN

EL CONQUISTADOR WAY

Coronado

National

Forest

RIDGE SHADOW PL

To Tucson

RESORT DR

VENTANA CANYON DR

SUNRISE DR

SNYDER RD

FORT LOWELL RD

WRIGHTSTOWN RD

BLVD

BLVD

Saguaro

National

Park

(Rincon

Mtn

District)

CAMINO DEL DESIERTO

RAMBLING TRL

Davis-Monthan

Air Force

Base

SEE TUCSON
INT'L AIRPORT
ACCOMMODATIONS
MAP FOR DETAIL

Tucson
International

Airport (TUS)

VALENCIA

SEE GREEN VALLEY
ACCOMMODATIONS
MAP FOR DETAIL

VOYAGER RD

To Benson

1812-16

Tucson Area

This index helps you "spot" where approved hotels and restaurants are located on the corresponding detailed maps. Hotel daily rate range is for comparison only. Restaurant price range is a combination of lunch and/or dinner. Turn to the listing page for more detailed rate and price information and consult display ads for special promotions.

TUCSON

Map Page	Hotels	Diamond Rated	Rate Range	Page
1 p. 274	Omni Tucson National Resort	◇◇◇	$89-$389	289
2 p. 274	Motel 6 Tucson North #1127	◇	Rates not provided	289
3 p. 274	**Red Lion Inn & Suites Tucson North**	◇◇◇	$69-$219 (SAVE)	289
4 p. 274	**Westward Look Wyndham Grand Resort & Spa** (See ad p. 291.)	◇◇◇◇	$149-$293 (SAVE)	291
5 p. 274	**BEST WESTERN InnSuites Tucson Foothills Hotel & Suites**	◇◇	$79-$159 (SAVE)	285
6 p. 274	**Embassy Suites by Hilton Tucson-Paloma Village**	◇◇◇	$119-$199 (SAVE)	287
8 p. 274	**Loews Ventana Canyon**	◇◇◇◇	$129-$349 (SAVE)	289
9 p. 274	**Candlewood Suites Tucson**	◇◇◇	Rates not provided (SAVE)	285
10 p. 274	**The Westin La Paloma Resort & Spa**	◇◇◇◇	$99-$369 (SAVE)	291
11 p. 274	**The Lodge @ Ventana Canyon**	◇◇◇◇	$95-$799 (SAVE)	289
12 p. 274	Comfort Suites at Tucson Mall	◇◇	$79-$209	286
13 p. 274	Holiday Inn Express Hotel & Suites-Tucson Mall	◇◇◇	Rates not provided	288
14 p. 274	Homewood Suites by Hilton Tucson/St. Philip's Plaza/University	◇◇◇	$119-$209	288
15 p. 274	Casa Tierra Adobe B&B Inn	◇◇◇	$165-$285	285
16 p. 274	Jeremiah Inn Bed & Breakfast	◇◇◇	$130-$160	288
17 p. 274	Holiday Inn Express & Suites-Grant Rd	◇◇◇	Rates not provided	288
18 p. 274	Comfort Inn-Grant Rd	◇◇	$60-$130	286
19 p. 274	Hampton Inn Tucson North	◇◇◇	$69-$199	287
20 p. 274	**Sheraton Tucson Hotel & Suites**	◇◇◇	$69-$309 (SAVE)	290
21 p. 274	Extended Stay America-Tucson Grant Road	◇	Rates not provided	287
22 p. 274	**Arizona Inn**	◇◇◇◇	Rates not provided (SAVE)	285
23 p. 274	Indian Hill Bed & Breakfast	◇◇◇	$150-$200	288
24 p. 274	Comfort Suites at Sabino Canyon	◇◇	$94-$179	286
25 p. 274	**JW Marriott Tucson Starr Pass Resort & Spa**	◇◇◇◇	$146-$377 (SAVE)	288
26 p. 274	The Inns at El Rancho Merlita	◇◇◇	Rates not provided	288
27 p. 274	Sonesta ES Suites	◇◇◇	Rates not provided	290
28 p. 274	**Radisson Suites Tucson**	◇◇◇	$79-$269 (SAVE)	289
29 p. 274	Starr Pass Golf Suites	◇◇◇	Rates not provided	290
30 p. 274	**Lodge on the Desert**	◇◇◇	$99-$329 (SAVE)	289
31 p. 274	**Viscount Suite Hotel**	◇◇	$79-$199 (SAVE)	290
32 p. 274	Embassy Suites by Hilton Tucson-Williams Center	◇◇◇	$109-$264	287
33 p. 274	Courtyard by Marriott-Tucson Williams Centre	◇◇◇	$84-$178	286
34 p. 274	Residence Inn by Marriott Williams Centre	◇◇◇	$118-$221	290
35 p. 274	Super 8 Downtown Tucson Convention Area	◇◇	$65-$130	290

TUCSON (cont'd)

Map Page	Hotels (cont'd)	Diamond Rated	Rate Range	Page
36 p. 274	TownePlace Suites by Marriott Tucson Williams Centre	◆◆◆	$80-$155	290
37 p. 274	Hampton Inn & Suites Tucson East/Williams Center	◆◆◆	$79-$159	287
38 p. 274	**Hilton Tucson East**	◆◆◆	$89-$249 [SAVE]	288
39 p. 274	**Americas Best Value Inn-Tucson**	◆◆	$44-$130 [SAVE]	285
40 p. 274	Clarion Hotel	◆◆◆	$74-$119	286
41 p. 274	**Days Inn Airport**	◆◆	$60-$140 [SAVE]	286
42 p. 274	Fairfield Inn by Marriott Tucson I-10	◆◆	$71-$139	287
43 p. 274	Studio 6 Extended Stay #6002	◆◆	$53-$93	290
44 p. 274	**Red Roof Inn-Tucson South**	◆◆	$39-$120 [SAVE]	289
45 p. 274	**Casino Del Sol Resort**	◆◆◆◆	$109-$349 [SAVE]	285
46 p. 274	Hacienda del Desierto	◆◆◆	$129-$289	287
47 p. 274	Voyager Hotel & RV Resort	◆◆	Rates not provided	291
48 p. 274	TownePlace Suites by Marriott Tucson North	◆◆◆	$76-$184	290
49 p. 274	La Posada Lodge & Casitas	◆◆◆	Rates not provided	289

Map Page	Restaurants	Diamond Rated	Cuisine	Price Range	Page
1 p. 274	Colt's Taste of Texas	◆◆	Steak	$8-$30	292
2 p. 274	Bob's Steak & Chop House	◆◆◆	Steak	$29-$59	292
3 p. 274	Michelangelo Ristorante Italiano	◆◆◆	Italian	$7-$29	294
4 p. 274	Mosaic Cafe Dos	◆◆	Mexican	$8-$14	294
5 p. 274	**Gold**	◆◆◆◆	American	$22-$42	293
6 p. 274	Tohono Chul Park Tea Room	◆◆	American	$12-$16	296
7 p. 274	Wildflower Tucson	◆◆◆	American	$13-$29	296
8 p. 274	Hi Falutin Western Grill	◆◆	American	$12-$29	293
9 p. 274	Sushi on Oracle	◆◆	Sushi	$10-$22	296
10 p. 274	Vivace Restaurant	◆◆◆	Italian	$18-$37	296
11 p. 274	Mr. An's Teppan Steak & Sushi	◆◆	Japanese	$10-$30	294
12 p. 274	Acacia	◆◆◆	New American	$9-$36	291
13 p. 274	Firebirds Wood Fired Grill	◆◆◆	American	$11-$28	293
14 p. 274	NoRTH	◆◆◆	New Italian	$9-$29	294
15 p. 274	Fleming's Prime Steakhouse & Wine Bar	◆◆◆	Steak	$34-$57	293
16 p. 274	Flying V Bar & Grill	◆◆◆	Regional Southwestern	$15-$26	293
17 p. 274	Chantilly Tea Room	◆◆	Specialty Coffee/Tea	$9-$30	292
18 p. 274	**The Grill at Hacienda del Sol**	◆◆◆◆	Southwestern	$28-$50	293
19 p. 274	Bazil's	◆◆◆	Regional Italian	$15-$40	292
20 p. 274	Zona 78	◆◆	Italian	$9-$19	296
21 p. 274	Trattoria Pina	◆◆	Italian	$8-$35	296
22 p. 274	Risky Business	◆◆	American	$8-$23	295
23 p. 274	Sullivan's Steakhouse	◆◆◆	Steak	$20-$65	296

Map Page	Restaurants (cont'd)	Diamond Rated	Cuisine	Price Range	Page
24 p. 274	P.F. Chang's China Bistro	◆◆◆	Chinese	$8-$25	295
25 p. 274	Zinburger	◆◆	Burgers	$9-$15	296
26 p. 274	El Corral Steakhouse	◆◆	Steak	$11-$25	292
27 p. 274	Reforma Cocina & Cantina	◆◆◆	Regional Mexican	$9-$22	295
28 p. 274	Choice Greens	◆◆	Specialty	$6-$10	292
29 p. 274	Guadalajara Grill	◆◆	Mexican	$6-$21	293
30 p. 274	Ghini's French Caffe	◆◆	French	$7-$13	293
31 p. 274	Rosa's Mexican Food	◆◆	Mexican	$8-$15	295
32 p. 274	Cody's Beef 'n Beans	◆◆	Steak	$8-$25	292
33 p. 274	Pastiche Modern Eatery	◆◆◆	American	$8-$29	295
34 p. 274	Beyond Bread	◆◆	American	$5-$11	292
35 p. 274	Lovin' Spoonfuls	◆◆	Vegetarian	$6-$12	294
36 p. 274	Opa! Greek Cuisine & Fun	◆◆	Greek	$9-$17	295
37 p. 274	Le Rendez-vous	◆◆◆	French	$20-$33	293
38 p. 274	Teresa's Mosaic Cafe	◆◆	Mexican	$8-$16	296
39 p. 274	Sauce	◆◆	Italian	$6-$11	296
40 p. 274	Rusty's Family Restaurant & Sports Grille	◆◆	American	$8-$20	295
41 p. 274	India Oven	◆◆	Indian	$10-$17	293
42 p. 274	Blue Willow Restaurant Bakery	◆◆	American	$9-$18	292
43 p. 274	Sher-E-Punjab	◆◆	Indian	$8-$13	296
44 p. 274	Kingfisher	◆◆◆	Seafood	$14-$29	293
45 p. 274	**Main Dining Room at the Arizona Inn**	◆◆◆◆	Continental	$12-$40	294
46 p. 274	The Eclectic Cafe	◆◆	American	$6-$14	292
47 p. 274	Daisy Mae's Steakhouse	◆◆	Steak	$16-$32	292
48 p. 274	Dakota Bar & Grill	◆◆◆	American	$11-$30	292
49 p. 274	May's Counter	◆◆	American	$8-$15	294
50 p. 274	Choice Greens	◆	Specialty	$6-$10	292
51 p. 274	Pinnacle Peak Restaurant	◆	Steak	$8-$27	295
52 p. 274	Feast	◆◆	American	$9-$27	292
53 p. 274	Jonathan's Cork	◆◆◆	Southwestern Steak	$12-$42	293
54 p. 274	**Primo**	◆◆◆◆	Regional Italian	$26-$42	295
55 p. 274	Bushi Traditional Japanese and Asian Cuisine	◆◆	Asian	$9-$27	292
56 p. 274	**Lotus Garden**	◆◆	Chinese	$9-$23	294
57 p. 274	Casa Molina	◆◆	Mexican	$8-$20	292
58 p. 274	Lodge on the Desert	◆◆◆	American	$11-$32	293
59 p. 274	Zemam's	◆◆	Ethiopian	$9-$14	296
60 p. 274	Old Pueblo Grille	◆◆◆	Regional American	$10-$20	294
61 p. 274	**The Hungry Fox Restaurant and Country Store**	◆◆	American	$7-$10	293
62 p. 274	Pita Jungle	◆◆	Mediterranean	$6-$15	295

Map Page	Restaurants (cont'd)	Diamond Rated	Cuisine	Price Range	Page
63 p. 274	Neo Malaysian Kitchen	◆◆	Asian	$7-$20	294
64 p. 274	New Delhi Palace	◆◆	Indian	$8-$14	294
65 p. 274	Mi Nidito Family Restaurant	◆◆	Mexican	$7-$13	294
66 p. 274	Casa del Rio	◆◆	Mexican	$8-$12	292
67 p. 274	Silver Saddle Steakhouse	◆◆	Steak	$7-$28	296
68 p. 274	PY Steakhouse	◆◆◆	Steak	$19-$44	295
69 p. 274	Tequila Factory	◆◆	Mexican	$5-$19	296
70 p. 274	McGraw's Cantina	◆◆	American	$6-$26	294

MARANA

Map Page	Hotels	Diamond Rated	Rate Range	Page
50 p. 274	Comfort Inn & Suites	◆◆◆	$125-$146	106
51 p. 274	La Quinta Inn & Suites NW Tucson Marana	◆◆	$64-$258	106
52 p. 274	Holiday Inn Express & Suites	◆◆◆	Rates not provided	106
53 p. 274	**BEST WESTERN PLUS Gold Poppy Inn**	◆◆◆	$70-$170 [SAVE]	106

Map Page	Restaurants	Diamond Rated	Cuisine	Price Range	Page
73 p. 274	La Olla Mexican Cafe	◆◆	Mexican	$9-$16	107
74 p. 274	Li'l Abner's Steakhouse	◆◆	Steak	$16-$39	107

ORO VALLEY

Map Page	Hotels	Diamond Rated	Rate Range	Page
56 p. 274	Holiday Inn Express Hotel & Suites Oro Valley-Tucson North	◆◆◆	Rates not provided	116
57 p. 274	Fairfield Inn & Suites by Marriott Tucson North/Oro Valley	◆◆◆	$96-$197	116
58 p. 274	**Hilton Tucson El Conquistador Golf & Tennis Resort**	◆◆◆◆	$89-$299 [SAVE]	116

Map Page	Restaurants	Diamond Rated	Cuisine	Price Range	Page
77 p. 274	Dragon Village Restaurant	◆◆	Chinese	$6-$13	116
78 p. 274	Harvest	◆◆◆	Regional American	$9-$21	116
79 p. 274	Caffe Torino Ristorante Italiano	◆◆	Italian	$9-$24	116

© AAA   © 2015 HERE

Tucson International Airport Area Hotels & Restaurants map showing numbered locations 1–16.

1662-16

✈ Airport Hotels

Map Page	**TUCSON INTERNATIONAL** (Maximum driving distance from airport: 1.6 mi)	Diamond Rated	Rate Range	Page
11 p. 280	Baymont Inn & Suites Tucson Airport, 0.7 mi	◆◆	$57-$93	285
9 p. 280	**BEST WESTERN PLUS Tucson Int'l Airport Hotel & Suites, 0.8 mi**	◆◆◆	$79-$139 [SAVE]	285
6 p. 280	**Country Inn & Suites By Carlson-Tucson Airport, 1.0 mi**	◆◆	Rates not provided [SAVE]	286
2 p. 280	**Courtyard by Marriott-Tucson Airport, 1.1 mi**	◆◆◆	$73-$194 [SAVE]	286
14 p. 280	**DoubleTree Suites by Hilton Tucson Airport, 0.5 mi**	◆◆◆	$75-$299 [SAVE]	286
15 p. 280	**Four Points by Sheraton Tucson Airport, 0.6 mi**	◆◆◆	Rates not provided [SAVE]	287
12 p. 280	Hampton Inn Tucson Airport, 0.6 mi	◆◆◆	$79-$149	287
5 p. 280	Hilton Garden Inn Tucson Airport, 1.6 mi	◆◆◆	$99-$219	287
7 p. 280	Holiday Inn Express Tucson Airport, 1.0 mi	◆◆◆	$114-$215	288
10 p. 280	**Hyatt Place Tucson Airport, 0.7 mi**	◆◆◆	$69-$199 [SAVE]	288
13 p. 280	La Quinta Inn & Suites Tucson Airport, 0.6 mi	◆◆◆	$64-$257	289
1 p. 280	**Quality Inn Tucson Airport, 1.6 mi**	◆◆	$70-$120 [SAVE]	289
8 p. 280	Residence Inn by Marriott Tucson Airport, 1.1 mi	◆◆◆	$78-$157	290
3 p. 280	Staybridge Suites Tucson Airport, 1.2 mi	◆◆◆	Rates not provided	290
4 p. 280	TownePlace Suites by Marriott Tucson Airport, 1.3 mi	◆◆◆	$67-$140	290

Tucson International Airport

This index helps you "spot" where approved hotels and restaurants are located on the corresponding detailed maps. Hotel daily rate range is for comparison only. Restaurant price range is a combination of lunch and/or dinner. Turn to the listing page for more detailed rate and price information and consult display ads for special promotions.

Map Page	**TUCSON** Hotels	Diamond Rated	Rate Range	Page
1 p. 280	**Quality Inn Tucson Airport**	◆◆	$70-$120 [SAVE]	289
2 p. 280	**Courtyard by Marriott-Tucson Airport**	◆◆◆	$73-$194 [SAVE]	286
3 p. 280	Staybridge Suites Tucson Airport	◆◆◆	Rates not provided	290
4 p. 280	TownePlace Suites by Marriott Tucson Airport	◆◆◆	$67-$140	290
5 p. 280	Hilton Garden Inn Tucson Airport	◆◆◆	$99-$219	287
6 p. 280	**Country Inn & Suites By Carlson-Tucson Airport**	◆◆	Rates not provided [SAVE]	286
7 p. 280	Holiday Inn Express Tucson Airport	◆◆◆	$114-$215	288
8 p. 280	Residence Inn by Marriott Tucson Airport	◆◆◆	$78-$157	290
9 p. 280	**BEST WESTERN PLUS Tucson Int'l Airport Hotel & Suites**	◆◆◆	$79-$139 [SAVE]	285
10 p. 280	**Hyatt Place Tucson Airport**	◆◆◆	$69-$199 [SAVE]	288
11 p. 280	Baymont Inn & Suites Tucson Airport	◆◆	$57-$93	285
12 p. 280	Hampton Inn Tucson Airport	◆◆◆	$79-$149	287
13 p. 280	La Quinta Inn & Suites Tucson Airport	◆◆◆	$64-$257	289
14 p. 280	**DoubleTree Suites by Hilton Tucson Airport**	◆◆◆	$75-$299 [SAVE]	286
15 p. 280	**Four Points by Sheraton Tucson Airport**	◆◆◆	Rates not provided [SAVE]	287
16 p. 280	**Desert Diamond Casino & Hotel**	◆◆◆	$99-$209 [SAVE]	286

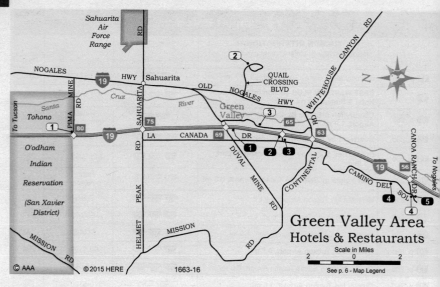

Green Valley Area
Hotels & Restaurants

Scale in Miles

2   0   2

© AAA   © 2015 HERE   1663-16   See p. 6 - Map Legend

Green Valley Area

This index helps you "spot" where approved hotels and restaurants are located on the corresponding detailed maps. Hotel daily rate range is for comparison only. Restaurant price range is a combination of lunch and/or dinner. Turn to the listing page for more detailed rate and price information and consult display ads for special promotions.

GREEN VALLEY

Map Page	Hotels	Diamond Rated	Rate Range	Page
1 this page	Holiday Inn Express	◈◈	Rates not provided	93
2 this page	Comfort Inn	◈◈	$90-$175 SAVE	93
3 this page	BEST WESTERN Green Valley Inn	◈◈◈	$89-$129 SAVE	93
4 this page	Inn at San Ignacio Condo Hotel	◈◈	Rates not provided	94
5 this page	Wyndham Canoa Ranch Resort	◈◈◈	$92-$207 SAVE	94

Map Page	Restaurants	Diamond Rated	Cuisine	Price Range	Page
1 this page	Agave at Desert Diamond Casino	◈◈	Regional American	$10-$28	94
2 this page	Grill at Quail Creek	◈◈◈	American	$8-$29	94
3 this page	Lavender	◈◈◈	French	$10-$29	94
4 this page	Grill on the Green at Canoa Ranch Golf Club	◈◈◈	American	$9-$30	94

DOWNTOWN TUCSON
• Hotels & Restaurants map & index p. 271

ADOBE ROSE INN   520/318-4644   **9**

◈◈◈ **Bed & Breakfast. Rates not provided. Address:** 940 N Olsen Ave 85719 **Location:** I-10 exit 257 (Speedway Blvd), 2.5 mi e, then just s. Located in a quiet residential area. **Facility:** Within walking distance of the university, this 1933 adobe home has a charming courtyard shaded with tall trees and some rooms with a fireplace. 6 units, some kitchens. 1-2 stories (no elevator), interior/exterior corridors. **Parking:** on-site and street. **Terms:** check-in 4 pm. **Pool(s):** outdoor. **Activities:** hot tub, massage. **Guest Services:** complimentary laundry.

ALOFT TUCSON UNIVERSITY   520/908-6800   **6**

◈◈◈
Hotel
Rates not provided

AAA Benefit: Members save up to 15%, plus Starwood Preferred Guest® benefits!

Address: 1900 E Speedway Blvd 85719 **Location:** Southeast corner of Speedway Blvd and Campbell Ave. **Facility:** 154 units. 7 stories, interior corridors. *Bath:* shower only. **Amenities:** safes. **Pool(s):** heated outdoor. **Activities:** exercise room. **Guest Services:** valet and coin laundry, boarding pass kiosk.

(See map & index p. 271.)

ARIZONA RIVERPARK INN (520)239-2300 [12]

Hotel
$89-$199

Address: 777 W Cushing St 85745 **Location:** I-10 exit 258 (Broadway Blvd/Congress St), just w, then 0.4 mi s. **Facility:** 133 units. 2 stories (no elevator), interior/exterior corridors. **Terms:** 3 day cancellation notice. **Amenities:** safes. **Pool(s):** heated outdoor. **Activities:** hot tub, tennis, exercise room. **Guest Services:** valet and coin laundry. **Featured Amenity: full hot breakfast.**

SAVE [TI] [Y] [2v] [BIZ] [HS] [🛜] [🖥] [📷] [📞] / SOME UNITS [🐾]

BEST WESTERN ROYAL SUN INN & SUITES (520)622-8871 [2]

Hotel
$59-$219

AAA Benefit: Save 10% or more every day and earn 10% bonus points!

Address: 1015 N Stone Ave 85705 **Location:** I-10 exit 257 (Speedway Blvd), 0.8 mi e, then just s. **Facility:** 79 units. 2 stories (no elevator), exterior corridors. **Pool(s):** heated outdoor. **Activities:** hot tub, exercise room.

SAVE [ECO] [TI] [Y] [2v] [BIZ] [HS] [🛜] [📷] [🖥] [📞] / SOME UNITS [🐾] [📺]

CATALINA PARK INN BED AND BREAKFAST (520)792-4541 [5]

▼▼▼ **Bed & Breakfast** $125-$190 **Address:** 309 E 1st St 85705 **Location:** I-10 exit 257 (Speedway Blvd), 1 mi e to 5th Ave, just s, then just e; in West University Historic District. **Facility:** The 1927 Spanish Mission-style home is located in a historic residential district and has large, attractively appointed rooms, lush gardens with arbors and lovely porches. 5 units. 1-2 stories (no elevator), interior/exterior corridors. **Parking:** on-site and street. **Terms:** closed 6/1-9/1, check-in 4 pm, 2 night minimum stay - seasonal and/or weekends, age restrictions may apply, 14 day cancellation notice-fee imposed. [BIZ] [🛜] [📷] / SOME UNITS [🐾]

COUNTRY INN & SUITES BY CARLSON-TUCSON CITY CENTER (520)867-6200 [4]

Hotel
$89-$199

Address: 705 N Freeway 85745 **Location:** I-10 exit 257 (Speedway Blvd), just w, then just s. **Facility:** 79 units. 3 stories, interior corridors. **Pool(s):** heated outdoor. **Activities:** hot tub, exercise room. **Guest Services:** valet and coin laundry. **Featured Amenity: breakfast buffet.**

SAVE [TI+] [2v] [BIZ] [HS] [🛜] [📷] [🖥] [📞] [📺] / SOME UNITS [🐾]

ECONO LODGE UNIVERSITY (520)622-6714 [1]

▼ **Motel** $43-$160 **Address:** 1136 N Stone Ave 85705 **Location:** I-10 exit 257 (Speedway Blvd) eastbound, just e, then just n. **Facility:** 48 units. 3 stories (no elevator), exterior corridors. **Pool(s):** outdoor.
[TI+] [2v] [🛜] [📞] [🖥] / SOME UNITS [🐾] [📞]

EL PRESIDIO BED & BREAKFAST INN 520/623-6151 [10]

▼▼▼ **Classic Historic Bed & Breakfast** $139-$189 **Address:** 297 N Main Ave 85701 **Location:** I-10 exit 258 (Broadway Blvd/Congress St), 0.3 mi e, 0.3 mi n on Granada Ave, then just e on Franklin St; in El Presidio Historic District. **Facility:** This 1886 Victorian is located in a charming historic district that is walking distance from museums and the arts district. Nicely decorated rooms surround a quiet, beautifully landscaped courtyard. 4 units, some efficiencies. 1 story, interior/exterior corridors. **Parking:** street only. **Terms:** check-in 4 pm, 2 night minimum stay - seasonal and/or weekends, age restrictions may apply, 14 day cancellation notice.
[TI+] [BIZ] [🛜] [📷] / SOME UNITS [🐾] [📞]

MARRIOTT UNIVERSITY PARK HOTEL (520)792-4100 [7]

▼▼▼ **Hotel** $99-$247 **Address:** 880 E 2nd St 85719 **Location:** I-10 exit 257 (Speedway Blvd), 1.2 mi e to Euclid Ave, then just s. **Facility:** 250 units. 9 stories, interior corridors. **Parking:** on-site (fee) and valet. **Terms:** check-in 4 pm. **Pool(s):** heated outdoor. **Activities:** hot tub, exercise room. **Guest Services:** valet laundry, boarding pass kiosk.

AAA Benefit: Members save 5% or more!

[TI] [🛎] [📶] [🍴] CALL [&M] [2v] [BIZ] [🛜] [📷] [🖥] [📞] / SOME UNITS [SHS] [🖥] [📞]

PEPPERTREES INN 520/622-7167 [8]

▼▼▼ **Bed & Breakfast.** Rates not provided. **Address:** 724 E University Blvd 85719 **Location:** I-10 exit 257 (Speedway Blvd), 1.5 mi e, 0.3 mi s on Euclid Ave, then just w. **Facility:** Southwestern guest houses and two territorial homes dating from 1905 surround a beautifully landscaped courtyard with fountains. In-room dining and special diet meals are available. 6 units, some two bedrooms, kitchens and cottages. 1-2 stories (no elevator), interior/exterior corridors. *Bath:* shower only. **Guest Services:** valet laundry.

[TI+] [🛎] [HS] [🛜] [📷] [🖥] [📞]

THE ROYAL ELIZABETH BED & BREAKFAST INN 520/670-9022 [11]

▼▼▼ **Historic Bed & Breakfast.** Rates not provided. **Address:** 204 S Scott Ave 85701 **Location:** I-10 exit 258 (Broadway Blvd/Congress St), 1 mi e to Scott Ave, then just s. **Facility:** Built in 1878, this Victorian adobe home has been beautifully restored and features large rooms, antiques, and walled patios. Check-in is by appointment. 6 units. 1 story, interior corridors. **Terms:** age restrictions may apply. **Amenities:** safes. **Pool(s):** outdoor. **Activities:** hot tub.

[TI+] [2v] [BIZ] [🛜] [📷] [Z] / SOME UNITS [W] [🖥]

UNIVERSITY INN (520)791-7503 [3]

Motel
$49-$149

Address: 950 N Stone Ave 85705 **Location:** Jct Stone Ave and 1st St, 1 blk s of Speedway Blvd. **Facility:** 38 units. 2 stories (no elevator), exterior corridors. **Terms:** cancellation fee imposed. **Pool(s):** outdoor. **Guest Services:** coin laundry.

SAVE [TI+] [2v] [HS] [🛜] [📷] [🖥] [📞]

HOTEL CONGRESS 520/622-8848

[fyi] Not evaluated. **Address:** 311 E Congress St 85701 **Location:** I-10 exit 258 (Broadway Blvd/Congress St), 0.7 mi e to 5th Ave, then just n. Facilities, services, and décor characterize an economy property. This historic building has kept its ambience of yesteryear with rotary-style phones, quilt bedspreads and antique radios in the guest rooms.

WHERE TO EAT

47 SCOTT 520/624-4747 [9]

▼▼ **American. Gastropub.** $12-$22 **AAA Inspector Notes:** This hip downtown pub serves modern American comfort food in a lively and casual setting. Try the catfish macaroni and cheese or the pork belly with braised apples and cabbage. Wash it all down with one of the hand-crafted cocktails or carefully selected wine choices. **Features:** full bar, patio dining, Sunday brunch, happy hour. **Reservations:** suggested. **Address:** 47 N Scott Ave 85701 **Location:** I-10 exit 258 (Broadway Blvd/Congress St), 0.6 mi e to Scott Ave, then just n. **Parking:** street only. [D]

(See map & index p. 271.)

CAFÉ A LA C'ART   520/628-8533   **7**
▼▼ American. Casual Dining. $9-$13 **AAA Inspector Notes:** Tucked into the side garden of the museum is this delightful café. The chef/owner prepares creative salads and sandwiches, such as grilled salmon on focaccia with chipotle sauce. Dinner is served on weekends. **Features:** patio dining. **Address:** 150 N Main Ave 85701 **Location:** Broadway Blvd/Congress St, just n on Granada Ave, just e on Paseo Redondo, just n on Main Ave to Washington St, then just e; on grounds of Tucson Art Museum. **B   L**

CAFE POCA COSA   520/622-6400   **8**
▼▼▼ Mexican. Casual Dining. $13-$25 **AAA Inspector Notes:** This café's location has an upscale and trendy look. A helpful staff serves an interesting and creative variety of regional Mexican cuisine. The blackboard menu changes twice daily. **Features:** full bar. **Reservations:** suggested. **Address:** 110 E Pennington St 85701 **Location:** I-5 exit Madison St, just e; jct 9th Ave. **Parking:** on-site (fee) and street. **L   D**

CUP CAFE   520/798-1618   **11**
▼▼ American. Casual Dining. $10-$25 **AAA Inspector Notes:** *Classic.* Located in the historic Hotel Congress, the café is a popular spot for breakfast, but the crispy salads, hearty sandwiches and steak dinners have their own following with the lunch and dinner crowd. Homemade desserts spinning in a display case tempt the taste buds. **Features:** full bar, patio dining, happy hour. **Address:** 311 E Congress St 85701 **Location:** I-10 exit 258 (Broadway Blvd/Congress St), 0.7 mi e to 5th Ave, then just n; in Hotel Congress. **B   L   D**

CUSHING STREET BAR & RESTAURANT   520/622-7984   **14**
▼▼▼ American. Casual Dining. $9-$24 **AAA Inspector Notes:** This historic house now is an upscale eatery with an eclectic and casual decor featuring items from a French mansion in Mexico City. Southwestern flavors enhance such traditional offerings as roasted pork loin and shrimp quesadillas. Patio seating is available. **Features:** full bar. **Address:** 198 W Cushing St 85701 **Location:** I-10 exit 258 (Broadway Blvd/Congress St); 0.5 mi e to Church Ave, just s, then just w. **D**

DELECTABLES RESTAURANT & CATERING
                               520/884-9289   **5**
▼▼ International. Casual Dining. $8-$15 **AAA Inspector Notes:** Lively at lunch, this eatery presents a menu of casual, European, gourmet-style dishes. In addition to salads and sandwiches, choices include many vegetarian creations. **Features:** full bar, patio dining, Sunday brunch, happy hour. **Address:** 533 N 4th Ave 85705 **Location:** Just n of 6th St. **L   D**

DOWNTOWN KITCHEN + COCKTAILS   520/623-7700   **13**
▼▼▼ American. Casual Dining. $15-$28 **AAA Inspector Notes:** Local celebrity chef Janos Wilder has created his latest dining destination in the heart of downtown. The stylish eatery features contemporary American cuisine with a Southwestern flair. The varied menu includes nightly specials including beef cheeks with creamy potato puree, buttermilk fried chicken with cheesy grits and seafood gumbo. Try the dark chocolate jalapeno sundae for a distinctive ending. **Features:** full bar, happy hour. **Reservations:** suggested. **Address:** 135 S 6th Ave 85701 **Location:** I-10 exit 258 (Broadway Blvd/Congress St), 0.8 mi e, then just s. **D   CALL&M**

EL CHARRO CAFE   520/622-1922   **6**
▼▼ Mexican. Casual Dining. $8-$19 **AAA Inspector Notes:** *Classic Historic.* This busy, popular restaurant has been operated by the same family since 1922. Several small dining areas and an outdoor cantina add to the charm. Try the famous carne seca—a classic Sonoran-style sun-dried beef specialty of the house. **Features:** full bar, patio dining, happy hour. **Address:** 311 N Court Ave 85701 **Location:** I-10 exit 257A (St. Mary's Rd), 0.7 mi e, then just s; in El Presidio Historic District. **Parking:** street only. **L   D**

EL MINUTO CAFE   520/882-4145   **15**
▼▼ Mexican. Casual Dining. $7-$17 **AAA Inspector Notes:** A short distance from the convention center, this family-owned eatery has been serving traditional Sonoran-style dishes such as chicken or beef enchiladas since 1936. The cheese crisps with such toppings as carne seca or green chiles are popular. **Features:** full bar, patio dining. **Address:** 354 S Main Ave 85701 **Location:** I-10 exit 258 (Broadway Blvd/Congress St), 0.4 mi e on Broadway Blvd, just s on Church Ave, then just w on Cushing St. **L   D**

MAGPIE'S GOURMET PIZZA   520/628-1661   **4**
▼▼▼ Pizza. Casual Dining. $5-$17 **AAA Inspector Notes:** Mouthwatering pizza is made fresh to order at this eatery, and guests can choose from a variety of toppings to create their own gourmet pie. The lunch option of salad and a slice is ample for most appetites. An outdoor patio allows casual dining while watching the street activity. **Features:** beer & wine, happy hour. **Address:** 605 N 4th Ave 85705 **Location:** Just n of 6th St. **Parking:** street only. **L   D**

MAYNARDS MARKET & KITCHEN   520/545-0577   **10**
▼▼▼▼ New American. Fine Dining. $7-$38 **AAA Inspector Notes:** Located inside the historic train depot, this upscale casual bistro is connected to a gourmet market and wine shop. The seasonally changing menu carries a distinct French influence. Items may include a rich bouillabaisse, duck two ways or braised short ribs. Live music is featured on the weekends. **Features:** full bar, Sunday brunch, happy hour. **Reservations:** suggested. **Address:** 400 E Toole Ave 85701 **Location:** Center; at train depot. **Parking:** on-site (fee) and valet. **B   L   D**

PASCO KITCHEN & LOUNGE   520/882-8013   **2**
▼▼ New American. Casual Dining. $9-$20 **AAA Inspector Notes:** Described as urban farm fare, this fun and funky bistro features fresh organic ingredients, many sourced locally, to create delicious comfort food with a modern twist. Try the sloppy joe sliders made with grass-fed beef and seasoned with local chiles, or the steamed quinoa with citrus-grilled white prawns. **Features:** full bar, patio dining, Sunday brunch, happy hour. **Address:** 820 E University Blvd 85719 **Location:** I-10 exit 257 (Speedway Blvd), 1.5 mi e, 0.3 mi s on Euclid Ave, then just e. **Parking:** on-site and street. **L   D   🐄**

PATSY GRIMALDI'S COAL BRICK-OVEN PIZZERIA
                               520/882-6100
▼▼ Pizza. Casual Dining. $9-$18 **AAA Inspector Notes:** Fresh ingredients and a coal-fired brick oven are the features at this New York style pizzeria. **Features:** beer & wine, patio dining. **Address:** 446 N Campbell Ave, Suite 100 85719 **Location:** Southeast corner of 6th St and Campbell Ave. **L   D**

PENCA   520/203-7681   **12**
▼▼▼ Regional Mexican. Casual Dining. $12-$18 **AAA Inspector Notes:** Mexico City-style cuisine is served in a chic and trendy atmosphere. The mole de guajolote with fried plantains is outstanding, and the professional bar staff creates distinctive craft cocktails to complement the food selections. **Features:** full bar, Sunday brunch, happy hour. **Reservations:** suggested. **Address:** 50 E Broadway 85701 **Location:** I-10 exit 258 (Congress St), 0.6 mi e. **Parking:** street only. **L   D**

SILVER MINE SUBS   520/620-6400   **3**
▼ Sandwiches. Quick Serve. $5-$8 **AAA Inspector Notes:** The cold or warm and toasty sandwiches at this casual eatery hit the spot for hungry folks. Choose from chicken, turkey, tuna, roast beef and meatball subs. The chili, thick with meat and beans, is awesome. Delivery is available until 3 am for campus students studying hard. **Address:** 760 N Tyndall Ave 85719 **Location:** Jct University Blvd. **L   D   LATE**

TRIDENT GRILL   520/795-5755   **1**
▼▼ American. Casual Dining. $8-$16 **AAA Inspector Notes:** A nautical theme, a pool table and warm, friendly servers lend to the atmosphere found here. These aspects combine with good sandwiches and salads, such as the applewood BLT and Trident cobb, to make the eatery popular with area college students. **Features:** full bar, happy hour. **Address:** 2033 E Speedway Blvd 85719 **Location:** Just e of Campbell Ave. **L   D   LATE**

TUCSON (F-5)

Restaurants p. 291
Hotels & Restaurants map & index p. 274, 280

AMERICAS BEST VALUE INN-TUCSON
(520)884-5800 **39**

Hotel
$44-$130

Address: 810 E Benson Hwy 85713 **Location:** I-10 exit 262, just s. **Facility:** 98 units. 2 stories (no elevator), exterior corridors. **Terms:** cancellation fee imposed. **Pool(s):** heated outdoor. **Activities:** picnic facilities. **Guest Services:** coin laundry. **Featured Amenity:** continental breakfast.

ARIZONA INN
520/325-1541 **22**

Historic Boutique Hotel

Rates not provided

Address: 2200 E Elm St 85719 **Location:** I-10 exit 257 (Speedway Blvd), 2.5 mi e, 0.5 mi n on Campbell Ave, then just e. Located in a quiet residential area. **Facility:** This historic property, complete with elegant appointments and lush expansive gardens, has kept the integrity of the early 1900s in the style of its rooms. 95 units, some two bedrooms and houses. 1-2 stories (no elevator), interior/exterior corridors. **Parking:** on-site and valet. **Amenities:** safes. **Dining:** Main Dining Room at the Arizona Inn, see separate listing, entertainment. **Pool(s):** heated outdoor. **Activities:** sauna, tennis, bicycles, lawn sports, exercise room, massage. **Guest Services:** valet laundry.

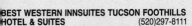

BAYMONT INN & SUITES TUCSON AIRPORT
(520)295-8800 **11**

Hotel $57-$93 **Address:** 6955 S Tucson Blvd 85706 **Location:** Just n of Tucson International Airport. **Facility:** 85 units. 3 stories, interior corridors. **Pool(s):** heated outdoor. **Activities:** hot tub, exercise room. **Guest Services:** valet and coin laundry.

BEST WESTERN INNSUITES TUCSON FOOTHILLS HOTEL & SUITES
(520)297-8111 **5**

Hotel
$79-$159

AAA Benefit: Save 10% or more every day and earn 10% bonus points!

Address: 6201 N Oracle Rd 85704 **Location:** I-10 exit 250 (Orange Grove Rd), 4 mi e, then just s. **Facility:** 159 units, some efficiencies. 2 stories (no elevator), exterior corridors. **Pool(s):** heated outdoor. **Activities:** hot tub, tennis, picnic facilities, exercise room. **Guest Services:** valet and coin laundry.

BEST WESTERN PLUS TUCSON INT'L AIRPORT HOTEL & SUITES
(520)746-3932 **9**

Hotel
$79-$139

AAA Benefit: Save 10% or more every day and earn 10% bonus points!

Address: 6801 S Tucson Blvd 85756 **Location:** Just n of Tucson International Airport. **Facility:** 167 units. 2 stories (no elevator), interior corridors. **Amenities:** safes. **Pool(s):** heated outdoor. **Activities:** hot tub, exercise room. **Guest Services:** valet and coin laundry, area transportation.

CANDLEWOOD SUITES TUCSON
520/373-5799 **9**

Extended Stay Hotel

Rates not provided

Address: 1995 W River Rd 85704 **Location:** I-10 exit 250 (Orange Grove Rd), 0.4 mi e to River Rd, then 2.7 mi se. **Facility:** 89 efficiencies. 4 stories, interior corridors. **Pool(s):** heated outdoor. **Activities:** hot tub, picnic facilities, exercise room. **Guest Services:** complimentary and valet laundry.

CASA TIERRA ADOBE B&B INN
(520)578-3058 **15**

Bed & Breakfast $165-$285 **Address:** 11155 W Calle Pima 85743 **Location:** I-10 exit 257 (Speedway Blvd), 9.5 mi w, 3.8 mi nw on Kinney Rd, 1.4 mi w on Mile Wide Rd, then 0.7 mi s on Camino Del Sapo, follow signs. Located in a quiet, secluded desert area. **Facility:** Built in 1989, this charming adobe home is situated in an isolated desert setting with a central interior courtyard and views across Avra Valley. 4 units, some two bedrooms. 1 story, exterior corridors. **Terms:** closed 6/15-8/15, check-in 4 pm, 2 night minimum stay, 14 day cancellation notice-fee imposed. **Activities:** hot tub, exercise room.

CASINO DEL SOL RESORT
(520)324-9000 **45**

Resort Hotel
$109-$349

Address: 5655 W Valencia Rd 85757 **Location:** I-19 exit 95 (Valencia Rd), 5.8 mi w. **Facility:** Located in a scenic area with Sonoran desert and mountain views, this lodging is a combined upscale resort and entertainment complex. 215 units. 10 stories, interior corridors. **Parking:** on-site and valet. **Terms:** check-in 4 pm, 3 day cancellation notice-fee imposed, resort fee. **Amenities:** safes. **Dining:** 4 restaurants, also, PY Steakhouse, Tequila Factory, see separate listings. **Pool(s):** heated outdoor. **Activities:** hot tub, regulation golf, exercise room, spa. **Guest Services:** valet laundry.

(See maps & indexes p. 274, 280.)

CLARION HOTEL   (520)746-1161 **40**

WWW Hotel $74-$119 Address: 4550 S Palo Verde Blvd 85714 Location: I-10 exit 264 westbound; exit 264B eastbound, 0.5 mi n. Facility: 301 units. 3-6 stories, interior/exterior corridors. Pool(s): heated outdoor. Activities: hot tub, exercise room. Guest Services: valet and coin laundry, boarding pass kiosk, area transportation.

[icons] / SOME UNITS [icons]

COMFORT INN-GRANT RD   (520)547-1755 **18**

WW Hotel $60-$130 Address: 1560 W Grant Rd 85745 Location: I-10 exit 256 (Grant Rd), just w. Facility: 68 units. 3 stories, interior corridors. Pool(s): heated outdoor. Activities: hot tub, exercise room. Guest Services: valet and coin laundry.

[icons]

COMFORT SUITES AT SABINO CANYON (520)298-2300 **24**

WW Hotel $94-$179 Address: 7007 E Tanque Verde Rd 85715 Location: Jct Grand Rd, 0.4 mi ne. Facility: 89 units. 2 stories, exterior corridors. Pool(s): heated outdoor. Activities: hot tub, exercise room. Guest Services: valet and coin laundry.

[icons] / SOME UNITS [icons]

COMFORT SUITES AT TUCSON MALL   (520)888-6676 **12**

WW Hotel $79-$209 Address: 515 W Auto Mall Dr 85705 Location: I-10 exit 254 (Prince Rd), 1.9 mi e, then 1.2 mi n. Facility: 86 units. 3 stories, interior corridors. Amenities: safes. Pool(s): heated outdoor. Activities: hot tub, exercise room. Guest Services: valet and coin laundry.

[icons] / SOME UNITS [icons]

COUNTRY INN & SUITES BY CARLSON-TUCSON AIRPORT   520/741-9000 **6**

WWW
Hotel
Rates not provided

Address: 6681 S Tucson Blvd 85756 Location: 0.4 mi n of Tucson International Airport entrance. Facility: 83 units. 3 stories, interior corridors. Pool(s): heated outdoor. Activities: hot tub, limited exercise equipment. Guest Services: valet and coin laundry. Featured Amenity: full hot breakfast.

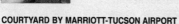
[icons] / SOME UNITS [icons]

COURTYARD BY MARRIOTT-TUCSON AIRPORT
(520)573-0000 **2**

WWW
Hotel
$73-$194

COURTYARD Marriott
AAA Benefit: Members save 5% or more!

Address: 2505 E Executive Dr 85756 Location: On Tucson Blvd, 0.7 mi n of Tucson International Airport entrance. Facility: 149 units. 3 stories, interior corridors. Pool(s): heated outdoor. Activities: hot tub, exercise room. Guest Services: valet and coin laundry, boarding pass kiosk, area transportation.

[icons] / SOME UNITS [icons]

COURTYARD BY MARRIOTT-TUCSON WILLIAMS CENTRE
(520)745-6000 **33**

WWW Hotel $84-$178 Address: 201 S Williams Blvd 85711 Location: Jct Campbell Ave, 3.8 mi e on Broadway Blvd, then just s. Facility: 153 units. 3 stories, interior corridors. Pool(s): heated outdoor. Activities: hot tub, exercise room. Guest Services: valet and coin laundry, boarding pass kiosk.

AAA Benefit: Members save 5% or more!

[icons] / SOME UNITS [icons]

DAYS INN AIRPORT   (520)747-8988 **41**

WWW
Hotel
$60-$140

Address: 4855 S Palo Verde Blvd 85714 Location: I-10 exit 264 westbound; exit 264B eastbound, just n. Facility: 65 units. 2 stories (no elevator), exterior corridors. Pool(s): outdoor. Activities: hot tub. Guest Services: coin laundry.

[icons]

DESERT DIAMOND CASINO & HOTEL
(520)342-3100 **16**

WWW
Hotel
$99-$209

Address: 7350 S Nogales Hwy 85756 Location: I-19 exit 95 (Valencia Rd), 1.4 mi e, then 1 mi s. Facility: The property boasts upscale guest rooms and public areas, which are removed from the hustle and bustle of the casino. A fire pit near the pool offers a cozy spot to unwind. 148 units. 4 stories, interior corridors. Terms: cancellation fee imposed. Amenities: safes. Dining: 3 restaurants. Pool(s): heated outdoor. Activities: hot tub, exercise room. Guest Services: valet laundry.

[icons] / SOME UNITS [icons]

DOUBLETREE SUITES BY HILTON TUCSON AIRPORT
(520)225-0800 **14**

WWW
Hotel
$75-$299

DOUBLETREE BY HILTON
AAA Benefit: Members save 5% or more!

Address: 7051 S Tucson Blvd 85756 Location: At entrance to Tucson International Airport. Facility: 204 units. 3 stories, exterior corridors. Terms: 1-7 night minimum stay, cancellation fee imposed. Amenities: safes. Pool(s): heated outdoor. Activities: hot tub, exercise room. Guest Services: valet and coin laundry, area transportation.

[icons] / SOME UNITS [icons]

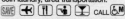

Ask about AAA/CAA Associate membership
to share the benefits you value

(See maps & indexes p. 274, 280.)

EMBASSY SUITES BY HILTON TUCSON-PALOMA VILLAGE (520)352-4000 6

Hotel
$119-$199

AAA Benefit: Members save 5% or more!

Address: 3110 E Skyline Dr 85718 **Location:** Jct Sunrise and Skyline drs; southeast corner. **Facility:** 119 units. 2-3 stories, interior corridors. **Terms:** 1-7 night minimum stay, cancellation fee imposed. **Pool(s):** heated outdoor. **Activities:** hot tub, exercise room. **Guest Services:** valet and coin laundry, area transportation. **Featured Amenity:** full hot breakfast.

EMBASSY SUITES BY HILTON TUCSON-WILLIAMS CENTER (520)745-2700 32

Hotel $109-$264 **Address:** 5335 E Broadway Blvd 85711 **Location:** Jct Campbell Ave, 3.9 mi e. **Facility:** 142 units. 3 stories, interior corridors. **Terms:** 1-7 night minimum stay, cancellation fee imposed. **Pool(s):** heated outdoor. **Activities:** hot tub, exercise room. **Guest Services:** valet and coin laundry, area transportation.

AAA Benefit: Members save 5% or more!

EXTENDED STAY AMERICA-TUCSON GRANT ROAD 520/795-9510 21

Extended Stay Hotel. Rates not provided. **Address:** 5050 E Grant Rd 85712 **Location:** 0.5 mi e of Swan Rd. Located near hospital. **Facility:** 120 efficiencies. 3 stories, exterior corridors. **Guest Services:** coin laundry.

FAIRFIELD INN BY MARRIOTT TUCSON I-10 (520)747-7474 42

Hotel $71-$139 **Address:** 4850 S Hotel Dr 85714 **Location:** I-10 exit 264 westbound; exit 264B eastbound, just n. **Facility:** 65 units. 3 stories, interior corridors. **Pool(s):** heated outdoor. **Activities:** hot tub, limited exercise equipment. **Guest Services:** valet and coin laundry.

AAA Benefit: Members save 5% or more!

Get the App

AAA.com/mobile • CAA.ca/mobile

FOUR POINTS BY SHERATON TUCSON AIRPORT (520)746-0271 15

Hotel
Rates not provided

FOUR POINTS BY SHERATON

AAA Benefit: Members save up to 15%, plus Starwood Preferred Guest® benefits!

Address: 7060 S Tucson Blvd 85756 **Location:** At entrance to Tucson International Airport. **Facility:** 150 units. 2-3 stories, interior corridors. **Pool(s):** heated outdoor. **Activities:** hot tub, exercise room. **Guest Services:** valet laundry, area transportation.

HACIENDA DEL DESIERTO (520)298-1764 46

Bed & Breakfast $129-$289 **Address:** 11770 E Rambling Tr 85747 **Location:** Jct Houghton Rd, 2 mi e on Escalante Rd, 1.3 mi s on Old Spanish Tr, then just w on Camino del Desierto Rd, through security gates. **Facility:** Near Saguaro National Park, guests can lounge on the porch or patio and spy small desert creatures roaming the grounds at this B&B. 4 units, some efficiencies, kitchens and cottages. 1 story, exterior corridors. **Terms:** check-in 4 pm, 2 night minimum stay - seasonal and/or weekends, 7 day cancellation notice-fee imposed. **Activities:** hot tub, trails.

HAMPTON INN & SUITES TUCSON EAST/WILLIAMS CENTER (520)514-0500 37

Hotel $79-$159 **Address:** 251 S Wilmot Rd 85711 **Location:** Jct Broadway Blvd, just s. **Facility:** 101 units. 3 stories, interior corridors. **Terms:** 1-7 night minimum stay, cancellation fee imposed. **Pool(s):** heated outdoor. **Activities:** exercise room. **Guest Services:** valet and coin laundry.

AAA Benefit: Members save up to 10%!

HAMPTON INN TUCSON AIRPORT (520)918-9000 12

Hotel $79-$149 **Address:** 6971 S Tucson Blvd 85756 **Location:** Just n of Tucson International Airport. **Facility:** 126 units. 4 stories, interior corridors. **Terms:** 1-7 night minimum stay, cancellation fee imposed. **Pool(s):** heated outdoor. **Activities:** hot tub, exercise room. **Guest Services:** valet and coin laundry, area transportation.

AAA Benefit: Members save up to 10%!

HAMPTON INN TUCSON NORTH (520)206-0602 19

Hotel $69-$199 **Address:** 1375 W Grant Rd 85745 **Location:** I-10 exit 256 (Grant Rd), just w. **Facility:** 91 units. 5 stories, interior corridors. **Terms:** 1-7 night minimum stay, cancellation fee imposed. **Pool(s):** heated outdoor. **Activities:** hot tub, picnic facilities, exercise room. **Guest Services:** valet and coin laundry.

AAA Benefit: Members save up to 10%!

HILTON GARDEN INN TUCSON AIRPORT (520)741-0505 5

Hotel $99-$219 **Address:** 6575 S Country Club Rd 85706 **Location:** Jct Tucson Blvd, 0.4 mi e on Valencia Rd, just s. **Facility:** 125 units. 3 stories, interior corridors. **Terms:** 1-7 night minimum stay, cancellation fee imposed. **Pool(s):** heated outdoor. **Activities:** hot tub, exercise room. **Guest Services:** valet and coin laundry, area transportation.

AAA Benefit: Members save up to 10%!

(See maps & indexes p. 274, 280.)

HILTON TUCSON EAST (520)721-5600 [38]

Hotel
$89-$249

Hilton
HOTELS & RESORTS

AAA Benefit: Members save 5% or more!

Address: 7600 E Broadway Blvd 85710 **Location:** 0.5 mi e of Kolb Rd. **Facility:** 232 units. 7 stories, interior corridors. **Terms:** 1-7 night minimum stay, cancellation fee imposed. **Amenities:** safes. **Pool(s):** heated outdoor. **Activities:** hot tub, exercise room. **Guest Services:** valet laundry, area transportation.

HOLIDAY INN EXPRESS & SUITES-GRANT RD 520/624-3200 [17]

Hotel. Rates not provided. **Address:** 1564 W Grant Rd 85745 **Location:** I-10 exit 256 (Grant Rd), just w. **Facility:** 92 units. 3 stories, interior corridors. **Pool(s):** heated outdoor. **Activities:** hot tub, picnic facilities, exercise room. **Guest Services:** valet and coin laundry.

HOLIDAY INN EXPRESS HOTEL & SUITES-TUCSON MALL 520/202-5000 [13]

Hotel. Rates not provided. **Address:** 620 E Wetmore Rd 85705 **Location:** Just w of N 1st Ave. **Facility:** 105 units, some efficiencies. 3 stories, interior corridors. **Amenities:** safes. **Pool(s):** heated outdoor. **Activities:** hot tub, picnic facilities, exercise room. **Guest Services:** valet and coin laundry.

HOLIDAY INN EXPRESS TUCSON AIRPORT (520)889-6600 [7]

Hotel $114-$215 **Address:** 2548 E Medina Rd 85756 **Location:** 0.5 mi n of Tucson International Airport entrance. **Facility:** 98 units. 3 stories, interior corridors. **Terms:** 14 day cancellation notice. **Pool(s):** heated outdoor. **Activities:** hot tub, exercise room. **Guest Services:** valet and coin laundry, area transportation.

HOMEWOOD SUITES BY HILTON TUCSON/ST. PHILIP'S PLAZA/UNIVERSITY (520)577-0007 [14]

Extended Stay Hotel $119-$209 **Address:** 4250 N Campbell Ave 85718 **Location:** I-10 exit 254 (Prince Rd), 4 mi e, then 1 mi n. **Facility:** 122 efficiencies. 3 stories, interior corridors. **Terms:** 1-7 night minimum stay, cancellation fee imposed. **Pool(s):** heated outdoor. **Activities:** hot tub, bicycles, picnic facilities, exercise room. **Guest Services:** valet and coin laundry, area transportation.

AAA Benefit: Members save up to 10%!

Turn your road trip dreams

into reality with the

TripTik® Travel Planner

HYATT PLACE TUCSON AIRPORT (520)295-0405 [10]

Hotel
$69-$199

HYATT PLACE®

AAA Benefit: Members save 10%!

Address: 6885 S Tucson Blvd 85756 **Location:** Just n of Tucson International Airport. **Facility:** 120 units. 5 stories, interior corridors. **Terms:** cancellation fee imposed. **Amenities:** safes. **Pool(s):** heated outdoor. **Activities:** exercise room. **Guest Services:** valet laundry, area transportation. **Featured Amenity: breakfast buffet.**

INDIAN HILL BED & BREAKFAST (520)760-4200 [23]

Bed & Breakfast $150-$200 **Address:** 2955 N Tomahawk Tr 85749 **Location:** Jct Speedway Blvd, 1.2 mi n on Houghton Rd, just w on Tanque Verde Rd, then 0.7 mi n. **Facility:** Sweeping views of the mountains surround this modern home, where large rooms have patios and nicely equipped baths. The suite has a barbecue grill. 4 units. 1 story, interior/exterior corridors. *Bath:* shower only. **Terms:** closed 6/1 - 8/31, 2 night minimum stay, 3 day cancellation notice-fee imposed. **Pool(s):** outdoor. **Activities:** bicycles, massage.

THE INNS AT EL RANCHO MERLITA 520/495-0071 [26]

Bed & Breakfast. Rates not provided. **Address:** 1924 N Corte El Rancho Merlita 85715 **Location:** Jct Speedway Blvd and Pantano Rd, 1 mi n to Wrightstown Rd, 0.8 mi e to Corte Tomasin, then just s, stop at call box to open gate, follow signs. **Facility:** Once the winter home of Merle Norman, this tranquil retreat offers beautifully decorated guest rooms surrounded by desert landscaping, nature trails and mountain vistas. 8 units. 1 story, interior/exterior corridors. **Amenities:** safes. **Pool(s):** outdoor. **Activities:** hot tub, game room, massage.

JEREMIAH INN BED & BREAKFAST (520)749-3072 [16]

Bed & Breakfast $130-$160 **Address:** 10921 E Snyder Rd 85749 **Location:** Jct Grant Rd, 3.6 mi ne on Tanque Verde Rd, 3.7 mi ne on Catalina Hwy, then just w. Located in a quiet residential area. **Facility:** The contemporary home with Southwestern architecture is located in a peaceful desert setting at the foothills of the Santa Catalina Mountains. 4 units, some two bedrooms. 1 story, interior corridors. **Pool(s):** outdoor. **Activities:** hot tub. **Guest Services:** complimentary laundry.

JW MARRIOTT TUCSON STARR PASS RESORT & SPA (520)792-3500 [25]

Resort Hotel
$146-$377

JW MARRIOTT.

AAA Benefit: Members save 5% or more!

Address: 3800 W Starr Pass Blvd 85745 **Location:** I-10 exit 259 (Starr Pass Blvd), 4.8 mi w. **Facility:** Carved out of the hillside overlooking the valley, the elegant setting complements the hotel's comfortable upscale rooms and spacious baths. 575 units. 6 stories, interior corridors. **Parking:** on-site and valet. **Terms:** check-in 4 pm, resort fee. **Amenities:** safes. **Dining:** 5 restaurants, also, Primo, see separate listing. **Pool(s):** heated outdoor. **Activities:** hot tub, steamroom, regulation golf, tennis, recreation programs, kids club, bicycles, trails, spa. **Guest Services:** complimentary and valet laundry, boarding pass kiosk, area transportation.

(See maps & indexes p. 274, 280.)

A POSADA LODGE & CASITAS 520/887-4800 **49**

▼▼/▼▼ **Hotel.** Rates not provided. **Address:** 5900 N Oracle Rd 85704 **Location:** 0.5 mi s of Orange Grove Rd. **Facility:** 72 units. 3 stories (no elevator), exterior corridors. **Pool(s):** heated outdoor. **Activities:** hot tub, exercise room. **Guest Services:** valet laundry.

🍴 🍸 🏊 🛜 ✕ 🛎 🖼 🖥 / SOME UNITS 🐕 📶

LA QUINTA INN & SUITES TUCSON AIRPORT
(520)573-3333 **13**

▼▼/▼▼ **Hotel** $64-$257 **Address:** 7001 S Tucson Blvd 85706 **Location:** Just n of Tucson International Airport. **Facility:** 143 units. 4 stories, interior corridors. **Pool(s):** heated outdoor. **Activities:** hot tub, exercise room. **Guest Services:** valet and coin laundry.

🔌 📶+ CALL 🛗M 🏊 BIZ 🛜 🖥 / SOME UNITS 🐕 HS 🛎 🖼

LODGE ON THE DESERT (520)320-2000 **30**

▼▼/▼▼
Hotel
$99-$329

Address: 306 N Alvernon Way 85711 **Location:** I-10 exit 258 (Broadway Blvd/Congress St), 4 mi e, then just n. **Facility:** 103 units. 1-2 stories (no elevator), exterior corridors. **Terms:** 3 day cancellation notice-fee imposed. **Amenities:** Some: safes. **Dining:** restaurant, see separate listing. **Pool(s):** heated outdoor. **Activities:** hot tub. **Guest Services:** valet laundry.

SAVE 🍴 🛎 🍸 BIZ 🛜 ✕ 🛎 🖥 / SOME UNITS 🐕 HS

THE LODGE @ VENTANA CANYON (520)577-1400 **11**

▼▼/▼▼▼
Boutique Resort
Hotel
$95-$799

Address: 6200 N Clubhouse Ln 85750 **Location:** I-10 exit 256 (Grant Rd), 8.6 mi e, 0.6 mi e on Tanque Verde Rd, 2 mi n on Sabino Canyon Rd, then 3.2 mi n on Kolb Rd. Located in a residential resort area. **Facility:** This boutique-style resort, set at the foot of the Santa Catalina Mountains, has spacious rooms and baths, all provided in an intimate setting. 50 kitchen units, some two bedrooms. 2 stories, interior/exterior corridors. **Parking:** on-site and valet. **Terms:** check-in 4 pm, 7 day cancellation notice-fee imposed, resort fee. **Amenities:** safes. **Pool(s):** heated outdoor. **Activities:** sauna, hot tub, steamroom, regulation golf, tennis, recreation programs, exercise room, spa. **Guest Services:** valet and coin laundry, area transportation.

SAVE 🍴 🛎 🍸 CALL 🛗M 🏊 BIZ 🛜 ✕ 🛎 🖼 🖥 / SOME UNITS 📶

LOEWS VENTANA CANYON (520)299-2020 **8**

▼▼/▼▼▼
Resort Hotel
$129-$349

Address: 7000 N Resort Dr 85750 **Location:** I-10 exit 256 (Grant Rd), 8.6 mi e, 0.6 mi ne on Tanque Verde Rd, 2 mi n on Sabino Canyon Rd, then 3.5 mi n on Kolb Rd. Located in a quiet area. **Facility:** The elegant building, reminiscent of a Frank Lloyd Wright design, sits at the base of the Santa Catalina Mountains and is surrounded by full resort facilities. 398 units. 3-4 stories, interior/exterior corridors. **Parking:** on-site (fee). **Terms:** check-in 4 pm, 3 day cancellation notice-fee imposed, resort fee. **Amenities:** safes. **Dining:** 3 restaurants, also, Flying V Bar & Grill, see separate listing. **Pool(s):** heated outdoor. **Activities:** sauna, hot tub, steamroom, regulation golf, tennis, recreation programs, playground, trails, exercise room, spa. **Guest Services:** valet laundry, area transportation.

SAVE ECO 🍴 🛎 🍸 CALL 🛗M 🏊 BIZ SHS 🛜 ✕ 🐾 🛎 🖥 / SOME UNITS 📶

MOTEL 6 TUCSON NORTH #1127 520/744-9300 **2**

▼▼ **Hotel.** Rates not provided. **Address:** 4630 W Ina Rd 85741 **Location:** I-10 exit 248 (Ina Rd), just e to Camino de Oeste, then just n. **Facility:** 117 units. 2 stories, interior corridors. **Pool(s):** outdoor. **Guest Services:** coin laundry.

📶+ 🏊 $🛜 / SOME UNITS 🐕 🛎 🖼

OMNI TUCSON NATIONAL RESORT (520)297-2271 **1**

▼▼/▼▼ **Resort Hotel** $89-$389 **Address:** 2727 W Club Dr 85742 **Location:** I-10 exit 246 (Cortaro Rd), 3.5 mi e, then just n on Shannon Rd. **Facility:** Set on several manicured acres, the resort's guest rooms, suites and haciendas overlook a golf course. An extensive health spa is on site. 128 units, some kitchens. 1-2 stories (no elevator), exterior corridors. **Parking:** on-site and valet. **Terms:** 3 day cancellation notice-fee imposed, resort fee. **Amenities:** safes. **Dining:** 3 restaurants, also, Bob's Steak & Chop House, see separate listing. **Pool(s):** heated outdoor. **Activities:** sauna, hot tub, steamroom, regulation golf, tennis, recreation programs, trails, exercise room, spa. **Guest Services:** valet laundry.

🍴 🛎 🍸 CALL 🛗M 🏊 BIZ 🛜 ✕ 🛎 🖥 / SOME UNITS 📶 SHS 🖼

QUALITY INN TUCSON AIRPORT (520)294-2500 **1**

▼▼/▼▼
Hotel
$70-$120

Address: 2803 E Valencia Rd 85706 **Location:** 1 mi ne of Tucson International Airport; just e of Tucson Blvd. **Facility:** 98 units. 3 stories, interior/exterior corridors. **Amenities:** safes. **Pool(s):** outdoor. **Activities:** hot tub. **Guest Services:** coin laundry. **Featured Amenity:** full hot breakfast.

SAVE 🔌 📶+ 🏊 BIZ HS 🛜 🛎 🖼 🖥 / SOME UNITS 📶

RADISSON SUITES TUCSON (520)721-7100 **28**

▼▼/▼▼
Hotel
$79-$269

Address: 6555 E Speedway Blvd 85710 **Location:** Just e of Wilmot Rd. **Facility:** 299 units. 5 stories, exterior corridors. **Terms:** cancellation fee imposed, resort fee. **Amenities:** Some: safes. **Pool(s):** heated outdoor. **Activities:** hot tub, game room, exercise room. **Guest Services:** valet and coin laundry, area transportation.

SAVE 🔌 🍴 🛎 🍸 🏊 BIZ 🛜 🐾 🛎 🖥 / SOME UNITS 📶 HS

RED LION INN & SUITES TUCSON NORTH
(520)575-9255 **3**

▼▼/▼▼
Hotel
$69-$219

Address: 7411 N Oracle Rd 85704 **Location:** SR 77 (Oracle Rd), just n of Ina Rd. **Facility:** 155 units, some efficiencies. 2-3 stories, exterior corridors. **Terms:** resort fee. **Pool(s):** heated outdoor. **Activities:** hot tub, picnic facilities. **Guest Services:** valet and coin laundry. **Featured Amenity:** full hot breakfast.

SAVE 📶+ CALL 🛗M 🏊 BIZ 🛜 ✕ 🛎 🖼 🖥 / SOME UNITS 📶

RED ROOF INN-TUCSON SOUTH (520)571-1400 **44**

▼▼
Hotel
$39-$120

Address: 3704 E Irvington Rd 85714 **Location:** I-10 exit 264 westbound; exit 264B eastbound. **Facility:** 118 units. 2 stories, exterior corridors. **Amenities:** safes. **Pool(s):** heated outdoor. **Guest Services:** coin laundry.

SAVE 📶+ 🏊 🛜 ✕ 🐾 / SOME UNITS 🐕 🛎 🖼 🖥

(See maps & indexes p. 274, 280.)

RESIDENCE INN BY MARRIOTT TUCSON AIRPORT
(520)294-5522 **8**

◆◆◆ **Extended Stay Hotel** $78-$157 **Address:** 2660 E Medina Rd 85756 **Location:** 0.5 mi n of airport entrance on Tucson Blvd, just e. **Facility:** 124 efficiencies. 3 stories, interior corridors. **Pool(s):** heated outdoor. **Activities:** hot tub, picnic facilities, exercise room. **Guest Services:** valet and coin laundry, area transportation.

AAA Benefit: Members save 5% or more!

RESIDENCE INN BY MARRIOTT WILLIAMS CENTRE
(520)790-6100 **34**

◆◆◆ **Extended Stay Hotel** $118-$221 **Address:** 5400 E Williams Cir 85711 **Location:** Jct Campbell Ave, 3.8 mi e on Broadway Blvd, just s, then just e on Williams Blvd. **Facility:** 120 efficiencies, some two bedrooms. 4 stories, interior corridors. **Pool(s):** heated outdoor. **Activities:** hot tub, picnic facilities, exercise room. **Guest Services:** valet and coin laundry, area transportation.

AAA Benefit: Members save 5% or more!

SHERATON TUCSON HOTEL & SUITES
(520)323-6262 **20**

◆◆◆ Hotel $69-S309

AAA Benefit: Members save up to 15%, plus Starwood Preferred Guest® benefits!

Sheraton HOTELS & RESORTS

Address: 5151 E Grant Rd 85712 **Location:** Jct Campbell Ave, 3.6 mi e. **Facility:** 216 units. 4 stories, interior/exterior corridors. **Terms:** cancellation fee imposed. **Pool(s):** heated outdoor. **Activities:** hot tub, exercise room. **Guest Services:** valet and coin laundry.

SONESTA ES SUITES
520/721-0991 **27**

◆◆◆ **Extended Stay Hotel.** Rates not provided. **Address:** 6477 E Speedway Blvd 85710 **Location:** Just e of Wilmot Rd. **Facility:** 128 units, some two bedrooms, efficiencies and kitchens. 2 stories (no elevator), exterior corridors. **Terms:** check-in 4 pm. **Pool(s):** heated outdoor. **Activities:** hot tub, picnic facilities, exercise room. **Guest Services:** valet and coin laundry, area transportation.

STARR PASS GOLF SUITES
520/670-0500 **29**

◆◆◆ **Condominium.** Rates not provided. **Address:** 3645 W Starr Pass Blvd 85745 **Location:** I-10 exit 259 (Starr Pass Blvd), 3.8 mi w. **Facility:** Surrounded by mountains and golf course fairways, the property's spacious suites offer every amenity desired for a long-term stay. 80 condominiums. 1 story, exterior corridors. **Terms:** check-in 4 pm. **Pool(s):** heated outdoor. **Activities:** hot tub, regulation golf, tennis, exercise room. **Guest Services:** area transportation.

AAA Vacations® packages ...

exciting itineraries and exclusive values

STAYBRIDGE SUITES TUCSON AIRPORT
520/807-1004 **3**

◆◆◆ **Extended Stay Hotel.** Rates not provided. **Address:** 2705 E Executive Dr 85756 **Location:** 0.7 mi n of Tucson International Airport. **Facility:** 97 efficiencies, some two bedrooms. 3 stories, interior corridors. **Pool(s):** heated outdoor. **Activities:** hot tub, picnic facilities, exercise room. **Guest Services:** valet and coin laundry.

STUDIO 6 EXTENDED STAY #6002
(520)746-0030 **43**

◆◆ **Extended Stay Motel** $53-$93 **Address:** 4950 S Outlet Center Dr 85706 **Location:** I-10 exit 264A eastbound; exit 264B westbound, just s, then just nw on Julian Dr. **Facility:** 120 efficiencies. 2 stories (no elevator), exterior corridors. **Pool(s):** heated outdoor. **Activities:** picnic facilities. **Guest Services:** coin laundry.

SUPER 8 DOWNTOWN TUCSON CONVENTION AREA
(520)791-9282 **35**

◆◆ **Motel** $65-$130 **Address:** 715 W Starr Pass Blvd 85713 **Location:** Jct Campbell Ave (22nd St/Starr Pass Blvd), just w. **Facility:** 68 units. 2 stories (no elevator), exterior corridors. **Pool(s):** outdoor. **Activities:** hot tub. **Guest Services:** coin laundry.

TOWNEPLACE SUITES BY MARRIOTT TUCSON AIRPORT
(520)294-6677 **4**

◆◆◆ **Extended Stay Hotel** $67-$140 **Address:** 6595 S Bay Colony Dr 85756 **Location:** 0.7 mi n of Tucson International Airport. **Facility:** 91 efficiencies. 3 stories, interior corridors. **Pool(s):** heated outdoor. **Activities:** picnic facilities, exercise room. **Guest Services:** valet and coin laundry, area transportation.

AAA Benefit: Members save 5% or more!

TOWNEPLACE SUITES BY MARRIOTT TUCSON NORTH
(520)292-9697 **48**

◆◆◆ **Extended Stay Hotel** $76-$184 **Address:** 405 W Rudasill Rd 85704 **Location:** Jct Orange Grove Rd, 0.5 mi s on Oracle Rd, then just e. **Facility:** 76 units, some two bedrooms, efficiencies and kitchens. 3 stories, interior corridors. **Pool(s):** heated outdoor. **Activities:** picnic facilities, exercise room. **Guest Services:** valet and coin laundry.

AAA Benefit: Members save 5% or more!

TOWNEPLACE SUITES BY MARRIOTT TUCSON WILLIAMS CENTRE
(520)747-0720 **36**

◆◆◆ **Extended Stay Hotel** $80-$155 **Address:** 384 S Williams Blvd 85711 **Location:** Jct Campbell Ave, 3.8 mi e on Broadway Blvd, just s. **Facility:** 124 efficiencies. 3-4 stories, interior corridors. **Pool(s):** heated outdoor. **Activities:** picnic facilities, exercise room. **Guest Services:** valet and coin laundry, area transportation.

AAA Benefit: Members save 5% or more!

VISCOUNT SUITE HOTEL
(520)745-6500 **31**

◆◆◆ Hotel $79-$199

Address: 4855 E Broadway Blvd 85711 **Location:** Just e of Swan Rd. **Facility:** 215 units, some two bedrooms. 4 stories, interior corridors. **Terms:** 3 day cancellation notice-fee imposed. **Amenities:** Some: safes. **Pool(s):** heated outdoor. **Activities:** hot tub, exercise room. **Guest Services:** valet and coin laundry. **Featured Amenity:** breakfast buffet.

(See maps & indexes p. 274, 280.)

VOYAGER HOTEL & RV RESORT   520/574-5000 **47**

▼▼ **Hotel.** Rates not provided. **Address:** 8701 S Kolb Rd 85756 **Location:** I-10 exit 270 (Kolb Rd), 0.6 mi s. **Facility:** 36 units, some efficiencies. 2 stories (no elevator), exterior corridors. **Pool(s):** heated outdoor, heated indoor. **Activities:** sauna, hot tub, par 3 golf, tennis, recreation programs, game room, lawn sports, picnic facilities, exercise room, spa. **Guest Services:** coin laundry.

THE WESTIN LA PALOMA RESORT & SPA
(520)742-6000 **10**

Resort Hotel
$99-S369

WESTIN HOTELS & RESORTS **AAA Benefit:** Members save up to 15%, plus Starwood Preferred Guest® benefits!

Address: 3800 E Sunrise Dr 85718 **Location:** SR 77 (Oracle Rd), 4.6 mi e on Ina Rd via Skyline and Sunrise drs, then just s on Via Palomita. **Facility:** In an attractive desert setting, the resort features large rooms with balconies or patios. Guests will enjoy the beautiful pool area with a waterfall, pond, swim-up bar and waterslide. 487 units. 3 stories, exterior corridors. **Parking:** onsite and valet. **Terms:** 3 day cancellation notice-fee imposed, resort fee. **Amenities:** safes. **Dining:** 5 restaurants. **Pool(s):** heated outdoor. **Activities:** sauna, hot tub, steamroom, regulation golf, tennis, recreation programs, kids club, trails, exercise room, spa. **Guest Services:** valet laundry, area transportation.

WESTWARD LOOK WYNDHAM GRAND RESORT & SPA
(520)297-1151 **4**

Resort Hotel
$149-$293

Address: 245 E Ina Rd 85704 **Location:** I-10 exit 248 (Ina Rd), 6 mi e, then just n on Westward Look Dr. Located in a quiet area. **Facility:** Nestled on 80 acres of lush desert terrain, this full-service resort boasts fabulous views of the Santa Catalina Mountains, and features multiple pools, gardens and nature trails. Oversized casita-style rooms each boast 650 sq ft of space. 241 units. 1-2 stories, exterior corridors. **Parking:** on-site and valet. **Terms:** check-in 4 pm, 7 day cancellation notice-fee imposed. **Amenities:** safes. **Dining:** 2 restaurants, also, Gold, see separate listing. **Pool(s):** heated outdoor. **Activities:** hot tub, tennis, recreation programs, bicycles, lawn sports, trails, exercise room, spa. **Guest Services:** valet laundry, boarding pass kiosk, rental car service, area transportation. *(See ad this page.)*

CANYON RANCH   520/749-9000

fyi Not evaluated. **Address:** 8600 E Rockcliff Rd 85749 **Location:** Jct Snyder Rd; 0.8 mi s. Facilities, services, and décor characterize an upscale property.

HACIENDA DEL SOL GUEST RANCH RESORT   520/299-1501

fyi Not evaluated. **Address:** 5601 N Hacienda del Sol Rd 85718 **Location:** Jct SR 77 (Oracle Rd), 5.4 mi e on Ina Rd/Skyline and Sunrise drs, 0.6 mi s to Via Alcalde, then just nw. Facilities, services, and décor characterize a mid-scale property. Built in 1929 as a ranch school for girls, this historic property is set on 34 acres in the Santa Catalina foothills overlooking the desert landscape and city lights below.

TANQUE VERDE RANCH   520/296-6275

fyi Not evaluated. **Address:** 14301 E Speedway Blvd 85748 **Location:** Jct Houghton Rd; 5.5 mi e. Facilities, services, and décor characterize an upscale property. .

ACACIA   520/232-0101 **12**

▼▼▼▼ New American. Fine Dining. $9-$36 **AAA Inspector Notes:** At this restaurant, chef Albert Hall creates delicious dishes such as sustainable salmon with tomato-kiwi salsa. The modern dining room features sweeping views across the city. **Features:** full bar, patio dining, Sunday brunch, happy hour. **Reservations:** suggested. **Address:** 3001 E Skyline Dr 85718 **Location:** Northeast corner of Skyline Dr and Campbell Ave. L D

(See maps & indexes p. 274, 280.)

BAZIL'S   520/577-3322   (19)
WWW Regional Italian. Casual Dining. $15-$40 **AAA Inspector Notes:** Family members pride themselves on their years of friendly service, and the warm ambience of the dining room is a perfect setting. Wonderful traditional dishes, such as chicken rollatini or veal piccata, are popular choices. **Features:** full bar, early bird specials, happy hour. **Reservations:** suggested. **Address:** 4777 E Sunrise Dr, Suite 119 85718 **Location:** Northeast corner of Sunrise Dr and Swan Rd.

BEYOND BREAD   520/322-9965   (34)
WWW American. Quick Serve. $5-$11 **AAA Inspector Notes:** This casual spot prepares hearty breakfasts, homemade soup and luncheon sandwiches to please any taste. The popular eatery features upscale décor that allows for a tempting display of breads and pastries. **Address:** 3026 N Campbell Ave 85719 **Location:** Just s of Fort Lowell Rd. [B] [L] [D]

BLUE WILLOW RESTAURANT BAKERY   520/327-7577   (42)
WWW American. Casual Dining. $9-$18 **AAA Inspector Notes:** Known for its breakfasts--including a variety of omelets and fresh breads--this restaurant also treats guests to relaxed dinners, daily specials and friendly, helpful service. Romance blooms on the charming patio in the evening. **Features:** beer & wine, patio dining. **Address:** 2616 N Campbell Ave 85719 **Location:** Just n of Glenn St. [B] [L] [D]

BOB'S STEAK & CHOP HOUSE   520/877-2377   (2)
WWWW Steak. Fine Dining. $29-$59 **AAA Inspector Notes:** Diners can enjoy this traditional steakhouse in an elegant setting which features Prime steaks, chops and fresh seafood. The patio offers lovely views of the manicured grounds and distant mountains. **Features:** full bar, patio dining, happy hour. **Reservations:** suggested. **Address:** 2727 W Club Dr 85742 **Location:** I-10 exit 246 (Cortaro Rd), 3.5 mi e, then just n on Shannon Rd; in Omni Tucson National Resort. **Parking:** on-site and valet. [D]

BUSHI TRADITIONAL JAPANESE AND ASIAN CUISINE
520/325-6552   (55)
WWW Asian. Casual Dining. $9-$27 **AAA Inspector Notes:** Fresh and innovative cuisine along with an extensive list of sake cocktails are the highlights at this energetic and fun eatery. Chose from a variety of custom rolls, fresh sashimi and noodle dishes. **Features:** full bar. **Address:** 4689 E Speedway Blvd 85712 **Location:** Jct Swan Rd; northwest corner. [L] [D]

CASA DEL RIO   520/308-6896   (66)
WWW Mexican. Casual Dining. $8-$12 **AAA Inspector Notes:** This casual east side eatery has been serving up traditional Sonoranstyle favorites since 1979. Specialties include chimichangas, fajitas and red or green chili con carne. **Features:** full bar. **Address:** 1060 S Pantano Rd 85710 **Location:** Jct E 22nd St, just n. [L] [D]

CASA MOLINA   520/886-5468   (57)
WWW Mexican. Casual Dining. $8-$20 **AAA Inspector Notes:** A Tucson tradition since 1947, this spot serves hearty portions of classic Sonoran-style food. Fresh margaritas accompany dishes like chili con queso, red or green enchiladas and savory carne seca. **Features:** full bar, patio dining, happy hour. **Address:** 6225 E Speedway Blvd 85712 **Location:** Jct Wilmot Rd, just w. [L] [D]

CHANTILLY TEA ROOM   520/622-3303   (17)
WW Specialty Coffee/Tea. Casual Dining. $9-$30 **AAA Inspector Notes:** Elegant duchess tea service, with tiered trays of delectable morsels, is one option at this popular luncheon spot. Salads, quiche, soup and sandwiches round out the menu. **Features:** patio dining. **Reservations:** suggested. **Address:** 5185 N Genematas Dr 85704 **Location:** Jct River Rd, just n on Oracle Rd, then just e. [B] [L]

CHOICE GREENS   520/319-2467   (50)
W Specialty. Quick Serve. $6-$10 **AAA Inspector Notes:** Patrons can create their own made-to-order salads from a vast array of greens, protein, toppings and nearly two dozen dressings. Hearty soups, sandwiches and desserts are also offered. **Features:** wine only. **Address:** 2829 E Speedway Blvd 85716 **Location:** Just w of Country Club Rd. [L] [D] CALL [M]

CHOICE GREENS   520/319-2467   (28)
W Specialty. Quick Serve. $6-$10 **AAA Inspector Notes:** Patrons can create their own made-to-order salads from a vast array of greens, protein, toppings and nearly two dozen dressings. Hearty soups, sandwiches and desserts are also offered. **Features:** beer & wine. **Address:** 4205 N Campbell Ave 85718 **Location:** Jct River Rd, just s. [L] [D]

CLAIM JUMPER   520/795-2900
WWW American. Casual Dining. $10-$30 **AAA Inspector Notes:** Great menu variety makes this place a good stop for parties with diverse tastes. Choices include specialty appetizers, salads, rotisserie chicken and barbecue items, not to mention good comfort foods, such as traditional pot pie. Hearty portions satisfy big appetites. The atmosphere is fun and lively. **Features:** full bar, happy hour. **Address:** 3761 E Broadway Blvd 85716 **Location:** 0.7 mi e of Country Club Rd. [L] [D]

CODY'S BEEF 'N BEANS   520/322-9475   (32)
WW Steak. Casual Dining. $8-$25 **AAA Inspector Notes:** The Cody burger gets raves from the locals but the tender grilled steaks at this eatery are mouthwatering and flavorful. Side dishes, including everything from onion rings and coleslaw, complete the satisfying meal in this small eatery with its Western bunkhouse decor. **Features:** beer & wine. **Address:** 2708 E Fort Lowell Rd 85716 **Location:** Just w of Country Club Rd. [L] [D]

COLT'S TASTE OF TEXAS   520/572-5968   (1)
WW Steak. Casual Dining. $8-$30 **AAA Inspector Notes:** This Northwest Tucson steakhouse is known for its down-home, country-style cooking. On the menu are large cuts of cooked-to-order meats, barbecue, ribs, seafood and enormous desserts sure to satisfy the heartiest appetite. **Features:** full bar, happy hour. **Reservations:** suggested. **Address:** 8310 N Thornydale Rd 85741 **Location:** I-10 exit 246 (Cortaro Rd), 2.5 mi e. [L] [D]

DAISY MAE'S STEAKHOUSE   520/792-8888   (47)
WW Steak. Casual Dining. $16-$32 **AAA Inspector Notes:** Steaks are cooked just as patrons prefer in this casual eatery. Many folks lend to the decor by signing $1 bills and having them hung on the wall. **Features:** full bar, patio dining, happy hour. **Address:** 2735 W Anklam Rd 85745 **Location:** I-10 exit 257A (St. Mary's Rd), 2 mi w.

DAKOTA BAR & GRILL   520/298-7188   (48)
WWWW American. Casual Dining. $11-$30 **AAA Inspector Notes:** Located in Trail Dust Town, this casually decorated dining room and patio are pleasant backdrops for exciting meals. Using cooking styles and food elements from around the world, the menu options blend interesting ingredients in such dishes as prickly pear beef medallions and Jamaican jerk chicken with pineapple coconut sauce. **Features:** full bar, patio dining, Sunday brunch. **Reservations:** suggested. **Address:** 6541 E Tanque Verde Rd 85715 **Location:** Jct Campbell Ave, 5.6 mi e on Grant Rd, just s. [L] [D] [🛒]

THE ECLECTIC CAFE   520/885-2842   (46)
WWW American. Casual Dining. $6-$14 **AAA Inspector Notes:** This storefront eatery has pizazz. On the menu are innovative foods ranging from warm salads made with spicy or cooked meats and cool veggies to hearty sandwiches and a good selection of Mexican classics. **Features:** beer & wine, patio dining, Sunday brunch. **Address:** 7053 E Tanque Verde Rd 85715 **Location:** Jct Grant Rd, 0.5 mi ne.

EL CORRAL STEAKHOUSE   520/299-6092   (26)
WW Steak. Casual Dining. $11-$25 **AAA Inspector Notes:** Historic. Built in the late 1800s, the historic adobe ranch house is a nice spot for casual dining. **Features:** full bar. **Address:** 2201 E River Rd 85718 **Location:** I-10 exit 254 (Prince Rd), 0.4 mi e, 1 mi n on Campbell Ave, then just e. [D]

FEAST   520/326-9363   (52)
WW American. Casual Dining. $9-$27 **AAA Inspector Notes:** Although take-out is a segment of the business, the dine-in option offers friendly staff who see to patrons' every need. The menu centers on such global dishes as cream of asparagus soup, a salad that includes curried chicken, and vegetarian offerings. An extensive wine list is offered. **Features:** full bar, Sunday brunch. **Reservations:** suggested. **Address:** 3719 E Speedway Blvd 85712 **Location:** Just w of Alvernon Way. [L] [D]

(See maps & indexes p. 274, 280.)

FIREBIRDS WOOD FIRED GRILL   520/577-0747   **13**

▼▼▼▼ American. Casual Dining. $11-$28 **AAA Inspector Notes:** The restaurant re-creates the atmosphere of a mountain lodge. Hand-cut steaks and seafood dominate the menu, which also lists a few pork and chicken entrees, as well as elk tenderloin medallions and buffalo meatloaf. The kitchen uses wood grilling, and pizzas bake in a wood-burning oven. Flavorful food, enhanced presentations and a skilled, knowledgeable and attentive staff, together with distinctive physical elements, make this place appealing. **Features:** full bar. **Address:** 2985 E Skyline Dr 85718 **Location:** Jct Campbell Ave; northwest corner; in La Encantada Plaza. L D

FLEMING'S PRIME STEAKHOUSE & WINE BAR
520/529-5017   **15**

▼▼▼▼ Steak. Fine Dining. $34-$57 **AAA Inspector Notes:** The warm, clubby atmosphere is the ideal setting for perfectly grilled steaks and seafood. Side dishes come in hearty portions, and salads are fresh and crisp. More than 100 wine selections are available. **Features:** full bar. **Reservations:** suggested. **Address:** 6360 N Campbell Ave 85718 **Location:** Southeast corner of Skyline Dr and Campbell Ave. **Parking:** on-site and valet. D

FLYING V BAR & GRILL   520/299-2020   **16**

▼▼▼ Regional Southwestern. Casual Dining. $15-$26 **AAA Inspector Notes:** Dry-aged, New York strip steak is one of the 12 signature features at this lakeside dining spot where seafood and meats are custom grilled to meet diners' expectations. The house guacamole, made tableside, garners rave reviews from the local clientele. **Features:** full bar, patio dining, Sunday brunch, happy hour. **Reservations:** suggested. **Address:** 7000 N Resort Dr 85750 **Location:** I-10 exit 256 (Grant Rd), 8.6 mi e, 0.6 mi ne on Tanque Verde Rd, 2 mi n on Sabino Canyon Rd, then 3.5 mi n on Kolb Rd; in Loews Ventana Canyon. D

GHINI'S FRENCH CAFFE   520/326-9095   **30**

▼▼▼ French. Casual Dining. $7-$13 **AAA Inspector Notes:** This busy bistro's breakfast omelets and luncheon salads are prepared in the French country style. Menu offerings are treats either for a celebration or a relaxed meal home with friends. The full-service French bakery allows for take-home goodies. **Features:** beer & wine, patio dining. **Address:** 1803 E Prince Rd 85719 **Location:** Just w of Campbell Ave. B L 🐾

GOLD   520/917-2930   **5**

American
Fine Dining
$22-$42

AAA Inspector Notes: *Classic.* The view over the valley below, which is particularly breathtaking at night, complements the sophisticated fine-dining experience. Sonoran Desert spices and flavors infuse classic and contemporary cuisine. The pastry chef's creations include a poached pear stuffed with pistachio mousse and the delectable ancho chili chocolate bombe. **Features:** full bar, patio dining. **Reservations:** suggested. **Address:** 245 E Ina Rd 85704 **Location:** I-10 exit 248 (Ina Rd), 6 mi e, then just n on Westward Look Dr; in Westward Look Wyndham Grand Resort & Spa. **Parking:** on-site and valet. B L D

THE GRILL AT HACIENDA DEL SOL   520/529-3500   **18**

Southwestern
Fine Dining
$28-$50

AAA Inspector Notes: Both in the main dining room and on the patio, the charming ambience of old Tucson is apparent in this restaurant's décor. Seasonal menu offerings, presented by accomplished servers, are prepared with the freshest ingredients and feature innovative flavor combinations. **Features:** full bar, patio dining, Sunday brunch, happy hour. **Reservations:** suggested. **Address:** 5601 N Hacienda del Sol Rd 85718 **Location:** Jct SR 77 (Oracle Rd), 5.4 mi e on Ina Rd/Skyline and Sunrise drs, 0.6 mi s to Via Alcalde, then just nw; in Hacienda del Sol Guest Ranch Resort. **Parking:** on-site and valet. D

GUADALAJARA GRILL   520/323-1022   **29**

▼▼ Mexican. Casual Dining. $6-$21 **AAA Inspector Notes:** A festive atmosphere awaits at this popular eatery, with live Mariachi music nightly. A choice of salsas is prepared tableside, and the homemade tortillas are always fresh and delicious. **Features:** full bar, happy hour. **Address:** 1220 E Prince Rd 85719 **Location:** I-10 exit 254 (Prince Rd), 3.4 mi e. L D

HI FALUTIN WESTERN GRILL   520/297-0518   **8**

▼▼▼ American. Casual Dining. $12-$29 **AAA Inspector Notes:** The charming Western décor is bright and fun at this grill where Stetson-clad servers are friendly and helpful. Hearty and pleasing eats range from cattle boss pot roast to flat-iron rib-eye. **Features:** full bar. **Address:** 6780 N Oracle Rd 85704 **Location:** Jct Ina Rd, 0.5 mi s. L D

THE HUNGRY FOX RESTAURANT AND COUNTRY STORE   520/326-2835   **61**

American
Casual Dining
$7-$10

AAA Inspector Notes: There may be a wait at this popular breakfast and lunch eatery, but the friendly staff keeps everything running smoothly. Homemade soups, hearty portions and over-sized cinnamon buns are offered. **Address:** 4637 E Broadway Blvd 85711 **Location:** Jct Swan Rd and Broadway Blvd; northwest corner. B L

INDIA OVEN   520/326-8635   **41**

▼▼▼ Indian. Casual Dining. $10-$17 **AAA Inspector Notes:** The menu lists all the classic dishes one might expect, like crisp tandoori chicken, lamb tikka and shrimp masala. Locals pack the daily lunch buffet, and the friendly owner often strolls the open, colorful dining room. **Features:** full bar. **Address:** 2727 N Campbell Ave 85719 **Location:** Just s of Glenn St. L D

JONATHAN'S CORK   520/296-1631   **53**

▼▼▼ Southwestern Steak. Casual Dining. $12-$42 **AAA Inspector Notes:** Chef Landeen flavors his dishes with a Southwestern flair and then may stop by tables with a greeting and to ask about the meal. The dining room is appointed in a casual ranch-style decor. **Features:** full bar, patio dining, happy hour. **Reservations:** suggested. **Address:** 6320 E Tanque Verde Rd 85715 **Location:** Jct Speedway Blvd, 0.5 mi ne. D

KINGFISHER   520/323-7739   **44**

▼▼▼ Seafood. Casual Dining. $14-$29 **AAA Inspector Notes:** Diners can expect a large selection of fresh fish and shellfish as well as pasta, beef and chicken selections. A summer menu centers on regional cuisine. Live entertainment is a draw on Saturday and Monday evenings. **Features:** full bar, happy hour. **Reservations:** suggested. **Address:** 2564 E Grant Rd 85716 **Location:** I-10 exit 256 (Grant Rd), 3.5 mi e. L D LATE

LA PARRILLA SUIZA

▼▼ Mexican. Casual Dining. $8-$22 **AAA Inspector Notes:** The casual atmosphere and friendly, efficient waitstaff contribute to a pleasant outing at the locally popular eatery. Styled as Mexico City cuisine, traditional dishes are prepared with a Continental flair. **Bar:** full bar. L D

For additional information, visit AAA.com

LOCATIONS:
Address: 2720 N Oracle Rd 85705 **Location:** 0.5 mi s of Fort Lowell Rd. **Phone:** 520/624-4300

Address: 4250 W Ina Rd 85741 **Location:** I-10 exit 248 (Ina Rd), 0.5 mi e. **Phone:** 520/572-7200

LE RENDEZ-VOUS   520/323-7373   **37**

▼▼▼ French. Fine Dining. $20-$33 **AAA Inspector Notes:** Patrons of this small, charming restaurant are served elegantly prepared French dishes by the attentive and well-trained waitstaff. Specialties include roasted duck with cherries, coq au vin, and the chateaubriand for two. **Features:** full bar, happy hour. **Reservations:** suggested. **Address:** 3844 E Fort Lowell Rd 85716 **Location:** Jct Oracle Rd, 4 mi e. L D

LODGE ON THE DESERT   520/325-3366   **58**

▼▼▼ American. Casual Dining. $11-$32 **AAA Inspector Notes:** *Classic.* The brightly appointed Southwestern dining room and covered patio are highlights at this casual yet sophisticated restaurant. The seasonal menu prepared by the executive chef includes creative dishes, including citrus-rosemary-glazed chicken. **Features:** full bar, patio dining. **Reservations:** suggested. **Address:** 306 N Alvernon Way 85711 **Location:** I-10 exit 258 (Broadway Blvd/Congress St), 4 mi e, then just n. B L D

(See maps & indexes p. 274, 280.)

LOTUS GARDEN   520/298-3351   56

Chinese
Casual Dining
$9-$23

AAA Inspector Notes: Located in a busy, business area, this eatery is popular with local residents and business people. Although the focus is on preparing Cantonese and Szechuan cuisine, the owners also offer monthly wine tastings with special food. The rose and grey décor is calming and a small patio is available for al fresco dining. A luncheon special offers a choice of more than a dozen entrées accompanied by soup and an egg roll. Mongolian beef and kung pao chicken are two dinner favorites. **Features:** full bar, patio dining. **Reservations:** suggested. **Address:** 5975 E Speedway Blvd 85712 **Location:** Just w of Wilmot Rd.

L   D

LOVIN' SPOONFULS   520/325-7766   35

Vegetarian. Casual Dining. $6-$12 **AAA Inspector Notes:** You will never miss the animal products at this modern vegetarian eatery. Hearty breakfasts, big "bacon" cheeseburgers and "chicken" salad made with tofu taste amazingly like the real deal. **Features:** beer & wine, patio dining, Sunday brunch. **Address:** 2990 N Campbell Ave 85719 **Location:** Just s of Fort Lowell Rd.

B   L   D

MACAYO MEXICAN KITCHEN   520/722-8090

Mexican. Casual Dining. $10-$19 **AAA Inspector Notes:** The colorfully furnished Mexican-style eatery prepares Sonoran Mexican dishes. Friendly and efficient staffers serve traditional and lighter dishes flavored with this place's own chili peppers, which are grown near Tucson. **Features:** full bar, happy hour. **Address:** 7040 E Broadway Blvd 85710 **Location:** Just w of Kolb Rd.

L   D

MAIN DINING ROOM AT THE ARIZONA INN
    520/325-1541   45

Continental
Fine Dining
$12-$40

AAA Inspector Notes: Decorated as it might have been when the inn first opened more than 80 years ago, the restaurant is a nice spot for refined dining. Tall windows overlook the landscaped courtyard, and mirrors and soft lighting create a soothing atmosphere. Diners can savor preparations of seafood, beef and lamb or select from the ever-changing chef's tasting menu. **Features:** full bar, patio dining, Sunday brunch. **Reservations:** suggested. **Address:** 2200 E Elm St 85719 **Location:** I-10 exit 257 (Speedway Blvd), 2.5 mi e, 0.5 mi n on Campbell Ave, then just e; in Arizona Inn. **Parking:** on-site and valet. B   L   D

MAMA'S FAMOUS PIZZA & HEROS

Pizza. Casual Dining. $5-$39 **AAA Inspector Notes:** With four Tucson locations, this popular eatery has been serving New York-style pizza, pasta dishes and sandwiches for nearly three decades. **Bar:** beer & wine. L   D

For additional information, visit AAA.com

LOCATIONS:

Address: 50 S Houghton Rd 85748 **Location:** Southwest corner of Broadway Blvd and Houghton Rd. **Phone:** 520/751-4600

Address: 6996 E 22nd St 85710 **Location:** Southwest corner of 22nd St and Kolb Rd. **Phone:** 520/750-1919

Address: 7965 N Oracle Rd 85704 **Location:** Southwest corner of Oracle and Magee rds. **Phone:** 520/297-3993

Address: 4500 E Speedway Blvd 85712 **Location:** Just w of Swan Rd. **Phone:** 520/319-8856

MAY'S COUNTER   520/327-2421   49

American. Casual Dining. $8-$15 **AAA Inspector Notes:** Chef Aaron May is the culinary talent behind this popular Southern-style diner. Breakfast is the mainstay and is served all day featuring such hearty items as chicken and waffles, chicken-fried steak and a scrambled egg po'boy. Lunch is tempting as well with patty melts, shrimp and grits and pork chops with bourbon apple sauce. **Features:** full bar, patio dining, happy hour. **Address:** 2945 E Speedway Blvd 85716 **Location:** I-10 exit 257 (Speedway Blvd), 3.3 mi e.

B   L   D

MCGRAW'S CANTINA   520/885-3088   70

American. Casual Dining. $6-$26 **AAA Inspector Notes:** Perched on a hill overlooking the valley south of the city is a casual eatery with see forever views. Representative of good home-style cooking are mesquite-barbecue dishes, which locals have enjoyed for 20 years. Servers are friendly. **Features:** full bar, patio dining, happy hour. **Address:** 4110 S Houghton Rd 85730 **Location:** 0.6 mi n of jct Irvington Rd. L   D

MICHELANGELO RISTORANTE ITALIANO   520/297-5775   3

Italian. Casual Dining. $7-$29 **AAA Inspector Notes:** This family-owned and -operated restaurant serves a large selection of classic dishes from veal Marsala to chicken Toscanini served with artichokes and mushrooms over cheese tortellini. Homemade desserts are too tempting to miss. Patio seating is available. **Features:** full bar, patio dining, happy hour. **Address:** 420 W Magee Rd 85704 **Location:** I-10 exit 248 (Ina Rd), 5.5 mi e, then 1 mi n on SR 77 (Oracle Rd). L   D

MI NIDITO FAMILY RESTAURANT   520/622-5081   65

Mexican. Casual Dining. $7-$13 **AAA Inspector Notes:** Mi Nidito means little nest, and guests will be cozy in this one. Hearty portions are served in the bright, welcoming dining room. In the Clinton booth, patrons can taste a dish named after the former president during his visit in 1999. **Features:** beer & wine. **Address:** 1813 S 4th Ave 85713 **Location:** I-10 exit 259 (Starr Pass Blvd), 0.8 mi e on 22nd St, then 0.6 mi s; northeast corner of 29th St and 4th Ave.

L   D

MOSAIC CAFE DOS   520/297-8470   4

Mexican. Casual Dining. $8-$14 **AAA Inspector Notes:** Diners come to this café for delicious, freshly cooked food, as well as the friendly and helpful staff. An added bonus is the patting out and cooking of tortillas right before their eyes. **Features:** full bar, Sunday brunch. **Address:** 7350 N La Cholla Blvd 85741 **Location:** Just n of Ina Rd. B   L   D

MR. AN'S TEPPAN STEAK & SUSHI   520/797-0888   11

Japanese. Casual Dining. $10-$30 **AAA Inspector Notes:** Featuring a sushi bar as well as teppanyaki tables, this eatery offers a very popular happy hour. The Baja roll was very tasty. **Features:** full bar, patio dining, happy hour. **Address:** 6091 N Oracle Rd 85704 **Location:** Jct Orange Grove and Oracle rds, 0.4 mi s. L   D

NEO MALAYSIAN KITCHEN   520/747-7811   63

Asian. Casual Dining. $7-$20 **AAA Inspector Notes:** This casual eatery offers a diverse and flavorful blend of Malaysian and Chinese food from spicy satay skewers of chicken or beef to sambal—a hot and spicy toasted pepper sauce served with a choice of seafood, beef, tofu or chicken. **Features:** full bar, happy hour. **Address:** 6133 E Broadway Blvd 85711 **Location:** Just w of Wilmot Rd. L   D

NEW DELHI PALACE   520/296-8585   64

Indian. Casual Dining. $8-$14 **AAA Inspector Notes:** Local business people come to this eatery for the popular lunch buffet; well-presented evening dinners are every bit as good. Food choices center on traditional preparations of tandoori, curry, seafood and vegetarian ingredients. Desserts are made on the premises, and kulfi is excellent. **Features:** full bar. **Address:** 6751 E Broadway Blvd 85710 **Location:** Jct Wilmot Rd, 0.5 mi e. L   D

NORTH   520/299-1600   14

New Italian. Casual Dining. $9-$29 **AAA Inspector Notes:** Robust Northern Italian foods and attentive servers are hallmarks at this restaurant. Huge windows afford views across the valley. Diners can choose from a wide selection of wines and martinis. **Features:** full bar, patio dining, Sunday brunch, happy hour. **Address:** 2995 E Skyline Dr 85718 **Location:** Jct Campbell Ave; northwest corner; in La Encantada Plaza. L   D

OLD PUEBLO GRILLE   520/326-6000   60

Regional American. Casual Dining. $10-$20 **AAA Inspector Notes:** Whether on the outside walled patio or inside among large cactus plants, diners can enjoy innovative foods with Southwestern flair served by a bright young staff. **Features:** full bar, patio dining, early bird specials, happy hour. **Address:** 60 N Alvernon Way 85711 **Location:** Just n of Broadway Blvd. L   D

(See maps & indexes p. 274, 280.)

OPA! GREEK CUISINE & FUN 520/327-2841 36

Greek. Casual Dining. $9-$17 **AAA Inspector Notes:** Get moderately priced Greek favorites at this busy eatery. The menu lists hearty appetizers like hummus, a crisp, classic Greek salad, moussaka, chicken or beef kebabs and souvlaki. Dine al fresco when the weather permits. **Features:** beer & wine, patio dining. **Address:** 2990 N Campbell Ave, Suite 130 85719 **Location:** Just s of Fort Lowell Rd. L D CALL M

OREGANO'S PIZZA BISTRO

Italian Pizza. Casual Dining. $8-$27 **AAA Inspector Notes:** This high-energy eatery, with its young and attentive waitstaff, serves up hearty, over-sized portions of delicious food including pizza, salads, pasta and baked sandwiches. **Bar:** full bar.

L D

For additional information, visit AAA.com

LOCATIONS:

Address: 4900 E Speedway Blvd 85712 **Location:** 0.6 mi w of Craycroft Rd. **Phone:** 520/327-8955

Address: 100 W Orange Grove Rd 85704 **Location:** Northeast corner of Orange Grove and Oracle rds. **Phone:** 520/229-9999

PASTICHE MODERN EATERY 520/325-3333 33

American. Casual Dining. $8-$29 **AAA Inspector Notes:** The décor, featuring interesting modern art, sets a backdrop for quiet dining. Local products figure significantly in classic, yet creative, dishes such as homemade pumpkin ravioli with fried sage, thyme-crusted sea bass with smoked tomato-caper beurre blanc and champagne cream sauce, and chipotle salmon cakes with corn topped with dill aioli. **Features:** full bar, happy hour. **Reservations:** suggested. **Address:** 3025 N Campbell Ave 85719 **Location:** Just s of Fort Lowell Rd. L D

P.F. CHANG'S CHINA BISTRO 520/615-8788 24

Chinese. Fine Dining. $8-$25 **AAA Inspector Notes:** Trendy, upscale decor provides a pleasant backdrop for New Age Chinese dining. Appetizers, soups and salads are a meal by themselves. Vegetarian plates and sides, noodles, chow meins, chicken and meat dishes are created from exotic, fresh ingredients. **Features:** full bar, happy hour. **Address:** 1805 E River Rd, Suite 100 85718 **Location:** Just w of jct Campbell Ave. L D

PINNACLE PEAK RESTAURANT 520/296-0911 51

Steak. Casual Dining. $8-$27 **AAA Inspector Notes:** In a Western town with a small town square, shops and an opera house, this popular restaurant continues the Western theme in its décor and menu. Diners can count on reliable, down-home fare. Reservations are not accepted and no ties allowed. **Features:** full bar. **Address:** 6541 E Tanque Verde Rd 85715 **Location:** Jct Campbell Ave, 5.6 mi e on Grant Rd, then just s. D

PITA JUNGLE 520/207-6873 62

Mediterranean. Casual Dining. $6-$15 **AAA Inspector Notes:** The atmosphere is hip and super-casual in the dining area and on the patio. The menu offers a wide variety of hot and cold pita wraps, pizza, falafel, spanakopita, salads and burgers, as well as natural, healthful vegetarian offerings. **Features:** full bar, patio dining, happy hour. **Address:** 5340 E Broadway Blvd 85711 **Location:** Jct Craycroft Rd, just w. L D

PRIMO 520/792-3500 54

Regional Italian Fine Dining

$26-$42

AAA Inspector Notes: Chef Melissa Kelly brings a fresh approach to Italian cuisine from delicate side dishes like grilled white and green asparagus with quail egg to the whole roast Mediterranean sea bass with steamed cockles. Luscious desserts vie to bring your attention back to the table from the southern views over the distant valley. **Features:** full bar, patio dining, happy hour. **Reservations:** suggested. **Address:** 3800 W Starr Pass Blvd 85745 **Location:** I-10 exit 259 (Starr Pass Blvd), 4.8 mi w; in JW Marriott Starr Pass Resort & Spa. **Parking:** on-site and valet. D CALL M

PY STEAKHOUSE 520/324-9350 68

Steak. Fine Dining. $19-$44 **AAA Inspector Notes:** Intimate, upscale dining is tucked away inside the busy casino resort. The accomplished staff help guide diners through the extensive wine list and menu consisting of the finest cuts of meat, chops, fresh seafood and the chef-inspired seasonal entrées. **Features:** full bar, happy hour. **Reservations:** suggested. **Address:** 5655 W Valencia Rd 85757 **Location:** I-19 exit 95 (Valencia Rd), 5.8 mi w; in Casino Del Sol Resort. **Parking:** on-site and valet. D

RA SUSHI BAR RESTAURANT 520/615-3970

Japanese Sushi. Casual Dining. $6-$20 **AAA Inspector Notes:** This hip meet-and-greet place prepares fresh and innovative sushi and a selection of bento box meals that make lunch a treat. The gyoza are spicy and delicious, and any of the tempura selections will be sure to please. **Features:** full bar, patio dining, happy hour. **Address:** 2905 E Skyline Dr, Suite 289 85718 **Location:** Jct Campbell Ave; northwest corner; in La Encantada Plaza. L D

REFORMA COCINA & CANTINA 520/867-4134 27

Regional Mexican. Casual Dining. $9-$22 **AAA Inspector Notes:** Intimate and sophisticated, this hot spot focuses on regional, central Mexican cuisine with such specialties as chiles en nogado, cochinita pibil and Guajillo duck confit. The lively bar features Southern Arizona's largest tequila selection. **Features:** full bar, patio dining, happy hour. **Reservations:** suggested. **Address:** 4310 N Campbell Ave 85718 **Location:** Jct River Rd; in St. Philip's Plaza. **Parking:** on-site and valet. L D

RISKY BUSINESS 520/577-0021 22

American. Casual Dining. $8-$23 **AAA Inspector Notes:** This northeast location is full of brightly colored walls, mountain views and such tasty dishes as peppered roast beef sandwich, down-home meatloaf, Greek pasta salad and build-your-own pizza. **Features:** full bar, patio dining. **Address:** 6866 E Sunrise Dr 85750 **Location:** Southwest corner of Kolb Rd and E Sunrise Dr. L D

ROSA'S MEXICAN FOOD 520/325-0362 31

Mexican. Casual Dining. $8-$15 **AAA Inspector Notes:** Family owned and operated for more than 35 years, this Tucson institution packs them in during the lunch rush. The walls are lined with photographs of famous patrons, and one taste of the fresh, authentic homemade food will explain the popularity. The seasoned staff is friendly and helpful. **Features:** full bar. **Address:** 1750 E Fort Lowell Rd 85719 **Location:** Southwest corner of Fort Lowell Rd and Campbell Ave. L D

RUBIO'S FRESH MEXICAN GRILL

Mexican. Quick Serve. $4-$10 **AAA Inspector Notes:** Freshly prepared and healthful foods, stylish decor and friendly staff are found in this upscale fast-food spot. A special treat, the salsa bar lines up four styles and flavors. **Bar:** beer only. L D

For additional information, visit AAA.com

LOCATIONS:

Address: 5870 E Broadway Blvd, #532 85711 **Location:** Just w of Wilmot Rd; in Park Place Mall. **Phone:** 520/514-9166

Address: 2906 N Campbell Ave 85719 **Location:** Jct Glenn St, just n. **Phone:** 520/319-9881

RUSTY'S FAMILY RESTAURANT & SPORTS GRILLE 520/623-3363 40

American. Family Dining. $8-$20 **AAA Inspector Notes:** Depending on the occasion, the front sports bar with banners and 50 TVs is a good place for sandwiches or burgers, while the larger dining room is welcoming to families or groups. Both offer friendly service. **Features:** full bar. **Address:** 2075 W Grant Rd 85745 **Location:** I-10 exit 256 (Grant Rd), 1.1 mi w. L D

SAUCE 520/297-8575

Italian. Casual Dining. $7-$11 **AAA Inspector Notes:** This restaurant's selections could be characterized as gourmet fast food. Among choices are sausage and caramelized onion or chicken and broccoli rabe pizza. Lasagna and fresh salads also are on the menu. A clean modern decor with patio or indoor seating adds to a fun dining experience. **Features:** wine only. **Address:** 7117 N Oracle Rd 85718 **Location:** Just s of Ina Rd. L D

(See maps & indexes p. 274, 280.)

SAUCE   520/514-1122

Italian. Casual Dining. $6-$11 **AAA Inspector Notes:** This restaurant's selections could be characterized as gourmet fast food. Interesting pizzas include chicken Caesar with Parmesan, roasted eggplant and hummus varieties. Lasagna, panini and fresh salads also appear on the menu. A clean, modern decor with patio and indoor seating adds to the fun dining experience. **Features:** wine only. **Address:** 5285 E Broadway, Suite 101 85711 **Location:** Just w of Craycroft Rd. [L] [D]

SAUCE   520/795-0344   39

Italian. Quick Serve. $6-$11 **AAA Inspector Notes:** This restaurant's selections could be characterized as gourmet fast food. Pizza choices include such toppings as chicken Caesar with Parmesan or roasted eggplant and hummus pizzas. Lasagna, various panini and fresh salads are offered. A clean modern décor with patio and indoor seating adds to the fun dining experience. **Location:** Northeast corner of Campbell Ave and Glenn St; in Campbell Plaza Shopping Center. [L] [D]

SHER-E-PUNJAB   520/624-9393   43

Indian. Casual Dining. $8-$13 **AAA Inspector Notes:** The storefront is simple, but the neat, tidy décor welcomes guests to experience the home-style cuisine of India. Try the crisp samosa appetizers full of meat or vegetables. Fragrant curries include chicken, lamb, seafood and beef. The lunch buffet is very popular. **Features:** full bar. **Address:** 853 E Grant Rd 85719 **Location:** Just e of 1st Ave. [L] [D]

SILVER SADDLE STEAKHOUSE   520/622-6253   67

Steak. Casual Dining. $7-$28 **AAA Inspector Notes:** Mesquite wood not only imparts a delicate flavor to meats but also plays a key role in the eatery's decor. The popular grill's bar top is the huge trunk of a mesquite tree that came from Trincheros, Mexico. The friendly staff keeps beverages filled and lets patrons in on all the extras, from sandwiches to vaquero grande, a 1.5-pound T-bone. **Features:** full bar. **Reservations:** suggested. **Address:** 310 E Benson Hwy 85713 **Location:** I-10 exit 261, south side on Frontage Rd, then just e of 6th Ave. [L] [D]

SULLIVAN'S STEAKHOUSE   520/299-4275   23

Steak. Fine Dining. $20-$65 **AAA Inspector Notes:** Named for John L. Sullivan, heavyweight champion of the world in the 1880s, the upscale steakhouse prepares a wide selection of steaks, chops and seafood. The décor features black-and-white photographs of Sullivan, Jack Dempsey and other boxing legends. **Features:** full bar, patio dining, early bird specials, senior menu, happy hour. **Reservations:** suggested. **Address:** 1785 E River Rd 85718 **Location:** Just w of Campbell Ave. **Parking:** on-site and valet. [L] [D] [🐾]

SUSHI ON ORACLE   520/297-3615   9

Sushi. Casual Dining. $10-$22 **AAA Inspector Notes:** Fresh fish can be found at this small, intimate, no-frills sushi bar. House specialties include the caterpillar roll, smelt roe with quail egg and the toro. **Features:** beer & wine, happy hour. **Address:** 6449 N Oracle Rd 85704 **Location:** Northwest corner of Oracle and Orange Grove rds. [L] [D]

TEQUILA FACTORY   520/838-6626   69

Mexican. Casual Dining. $5-$19 **AAA Inspector Notes:** Located just off the casino floor, this fun and casual eatery serves traditional Sonoran-style Mexican favorites along with more than 120 types of tequila. There also is a take-out window for a quick taco to go. Monday is popular for the prime rib special. **Features:** full bar. **Address:** 5655 W Valencia Rd 85757 **Location:** I-19 exit 95 (Valencia Rd), 5.8 mi w; in Casino Del Sol Resort. **Parking:** on-site and valet. [D]

TERESA'S MOSAIC CAFE   520/624-4512   38

Mexican. Casual Dining. $8-$16 **AAA Inspector Notes:** Atop a hill, the friendly spot serves freshly made tortillas that diners may watch being made as they enjoy one of the many classic Mexican dishes. **Features:** full bar, patio dining. **Reservations:** suggested. **Address:** 2455 N Silverbell Rd 85745 **Location:** I-10 exit 256 (Grant Rd), 1 mi w; northwest corner of Silverbell and Grant rds. [B] [L] [D]

TOHONO CHUL PARK TEA ROOM   520/797-1222   6

American. Casual Dining. $12-$16 **AAA Inspector Notes:** Surrounded by Tohono Chul Park, this refreshing stopping place affords desert garden views. Breakfasts and luncheons are locally popular, and afternoon tea, complete with scones, is served daily. **Features:** full bar, patio dining, Sunday brunch. **Address:** 7366 N Paseo Del Norte 85704 **Location:** Jct Oracle Rd, just w on Ina Rd, then just n. [B] [L]

TRATTORIA PINA   520/577-6992   21

Italian. Casual Dining. $8-$35 **AAA Inspector Notes:** Near the base of the Santa Catalina Mountains, the intimate eatery has a charming patio and display kitchen. On the menu are hearty pasta dishes, wood-fired oven pizzas and a wide variety of veal, lamb, beef and seafood preparations. **Features:** full bar, patio dining, happy hour. **Address:** 5541 N Swan Rd 85718 **Location:** Just s of Sunrise Dr. [L] [D]

VIVACE RESTAURANT   520/795-7221   10

Italian. Fine Dining. $18-$37 **AAA Inspector Notes:** Perched high in the foothills, the new location commands impressive views of the city. The popular restaurant employs accomplished staffers who assist diners through a meal that might include classic osso buco or a more contemporary dish, such as crab-filled breaded chicken breast. Selections are prepared with the freshest mix of ingredients. Patio seating is a nice option in good weather. **Features:** full bar, patio dining. **Reservations:** suggested. **Address:** 6440 N Campbell Ave 85718 **Location:** I-10 exit 250 (Orange Grove Rd), 7 mi e to Skyline Dr, 0.5 mi e, then just n. **Parking:** on-site and valet. [L] [D]

WILDFLOWER TUCSON   520/219-4230   7

American. Casual Dining. $13-$29 **AAA Inspector Notes:** In keeping with the restaurant's name, the modern, trendy decor includes oversized photographs of brightly colored flowers, as well as flowers incorporated into some plate presentations. Delectable meat and seafood dishes are prepared in a synthesis of Asian, French and New American cooking styles. **Features:** full bar, patio dining, happy hour. **Reservations:** suggested. **Address:** 7037 N Oracle Rd 85718 **Location:** Just s of Ina Rd. [L] [D]

ZEMAM'S   520/323-9928   59

Ethiopian. Casual Dining. $9-$14 **AAA Inspector Notes:** Spicy Ethiopian dishes are served in a casual atmosphere with leisurely service. Forks are offered, but the traditional style of eating with fingers always is acceptable. For a corking fee, the restaurant allows diners to bring their own bottle of wine. **Address:** 2731 E Broadway Blvd 85716 **Location:** Just e of Tucson Blvd. [L] [D]

ZINBURGER   520/299-7799   25

Burgers. Casual Dining. $9-$15 **AAA Inspector Notes:** Popular with locals, this high-energy bistro serves a selection of gourmet burgers-from Kobe beef to Clint's almost famous veggie option-plus salads, floats and shakes. **Features:** full bar, patio dining. **Address:** 1865 E River Rd 85718 **Location:** Just w of jct Campbell Ave. **Parking:** on-site and valet. [L] [D]

ZONA 78   520/888-7878   20

Italian. Casual Dining. $9-$19 **AAA Inspector Notes:** Innovative pizza with passion, as the chef says, is prepared in stone-fired ovens at this eatery and share menu space with yummy salads, pasta, steaks and such seafood as cedar-plank salmon. A large wine list features ample Italian selections. **Features:** full bar, happy hour. **Address:** 78 W River Rd 85704 **Location:** Just w of jct Stone Ave; northwest corner. [L] [D]

▼ TUMACÁCORI NATIONAL HISTORICAL PARK (G-4)

Approximately 19 miles north of Nogales off I-19 exit 29, Tumacácori National Historical Park preserves the abandoned Mission San Jose de Tumacácori. Once a Pima Indian village, Tumacácori was visited by Jesuit Eusebio Francisco Kino in 1691. In 1767 the Jesuits were expelled from Tumacácori by the King of Spain and replaced by Franciscans. The Franciscans began building the present massive adobe church about 1800, but it was never completed. Apache raids, neglect and a terrible winter contributed to its abandonment in 1848, yet afterward people continued to visit the site.

The area became a national monument in 1908. The 1990 addition of two Spanish mission sites, Guevavi and Calabazas, increased the total acreage to 47. It later was expanded again to include a mile of the Santa Cruz River riparian corridor and mesquite bosque (forest) and now encompasses 360 acres. Guevavi and Calabazas can be visited by reservation only. A historic museum distinguished by architectural features of the Sonora missions unfolds local history and describes mission life.

A self-guiding tour includes the church and cemetery, mortuary chapel, the convent area, a patio garden and a visitor center/museum. Picnic facilities are available. Allow 1 hour minimum. Daily 9-5; closed Thanksgiving and Christmas. Admission $3; free (ages 0-15). Prices may vary; phone ahead. Admission is valid for 7 days. Inter-agency passes are accepted. Phone (520) 398-2341.

TUZIGOOT NATIONAL MONUMENT (C-3)

About 2 miles northwest of Cottonwood via Main Street to Tuzigoot Road, Tuzigoot National Monument preserves the remains of a pueblo that was occupied by Ancestral Puebloan people referred to as the Sinagua culture from about A.D. 1000 until the early 1400s. From more than 110 rooms archeologists have recovered stone and bone tools, textiles, pottery, shell beads and bracelets, which are displayed in the visitor center.

Allow 1 hour minimum. Daily 8-5. Admission $5; free (ages 0-15). Prices may vary; phone ahead. Federal Recreation passes are accepted. Phone (928) 634-5564.

VAIL (F-5) pop. 10,208, elev. 3,225'
• Part of Tucson area — see map p. 256

SAVE **COLOSSAL CAVE MOUNTAIN PARK,** off I-10 exit 279, then 7 mi. n. on Colossal Cave Rd. to 16721 E. Old Spanish Trail, is a 2,200-acre park with what is considered by some to be the world's largest dry cavern. Only partially explored, the cave has chambers and lighted passageways. The park also includes two museums, a butterfly garden and a gemstone sluice as well as wagon rides and horse trails. Guided 45-minute cave tours are offered; extended tours are available. Guided trail rides also are available daily. The Arizona National Scenic Trail runs through the park; several access points and two trailheads within the park offer hiking opportunities.

Hours: Daily 8-5, mid-Mar. to mid-Sept.; 9-5, rest of year. **Cost:** $5 (per private vehicle, up to six passengers); $1 (per additional passenger). Cave tours $13; $11 (military with ID); $6.50 (ages 5-12). **Phone:** (520) 647-7275.

VALLE (B-3) pop. 832

PLANES OF FAME AIR MUSEUM is at the Valle Airport near jct. SR 64 and US 180 at 755 Mustang Way. Covering aviation history from World War I through the supersonic jet age, the museum's collection includes Gen. Douglas MacArthur's personal transport plane *Bataan,* a Lockheed C-121A Constellation. Other aircraft include a Grumman F-11F Tiger formerly used by the Navy's Blue Angels and a 1944 Messerschmitt BF109G-10. A flyby/fly-in is held in August.

Time: Allow 1 hour minimum. **Hours:** Daily 9-6, Apr.-Aug.; 9-5, rest of year. Closed Thanksgiving and Christmas. **Cost:** $6.95; $1.95 (ages 5-11); free (active military with ID). Constellation tour $3. **Phone:** (928) 635-1000.

VERMILION CLIFFS NATIONAL MONUMENT (A-3)

Bounded on the east by Glen Canyon National Recreation Area, on the west by Kaibab National Forest, to the north by the Utah border and to the south by SR 89A, remote Vermilion Cliffs National Monument contains 293,000 acres of unspoiled plateaus, canyons and cliffs. Elevations range from 3,100 to 7,100 feet.

Ancestral Puebloan villages and geologic formations can be found on the monument lands, which were traversed by Spanish explorers and Mormon pioneers. Animal inhabitants include desert bighorn sheep, mule deer, pronghorn and mountain lions. For further information contact the Arizona Strip Field Office, Bureau of Land Management; 345 E. Riverside Dr., St. George, UT 84790; phone (435) 688-3200.

WALNUT CANYON NATIONAL MONUMENT (C-4)

Off I-40 exit 204, 7.5 miles east of Flagstaff, Walnut Canyon National Monument preserves the remains of more than 300 pre-Columbian dwellings built on a series of ledges in the 400-foot-deep gorge. Inhabited by the Walnut Canyon community (archeologists are uncertain of what these inhabitants called themselves) about 1000-1200, the single-family dwellings are visible from the visitor center on the canyon rim.

The self-guiding Island Trail, which descends 185 feet over the course of a half mile, is an interesting but arduous paved path that leads past 25 of the cliff dwelling rooms. The Rim Trail, a pleasant .75-mile round trip, features two overlooks into the canyon as well as access to a small pueblo and pit house. Snow and ice might close both trails at times in winter and spring.

Interpretive programs within the backcountry are available by reservation from Memorial Day through Labor Day. Other ranger-led programs include short hikes and patio talks, which are available year-round, depending on staffing. A museum and picnic facilities are available; however, food is not available. Pets are not allowed on park trails, in buildings or tied to fixed objects.

Note: The Island Trail includes descending/ascending 240 steps and might be cumbersome for the physically challenged and those with heart conditions.

Allow 1 hour, 30 minutes minimum. Daily 8-5, May-Oct.; 9-5, rest of year. Closed Christmas. Last admittance to main trail is 1 hour before closing. Admission $5 per person; free (ages 0-15). Prices may vary; phone ahead. For further information contact the Superintendent, Walnut Canyon National Monument, 6400 N. SR 89, Flagstaff, AZ 86004; phone (928) 526-3367.

WELLTON pop. 2,882

MICROTEL INN & SUITES BY WYNDHAM WELLTON
(928)785-3777

Hotel $67-$95 **Address:** 28784 Commerce Way 85356 **Location:** I-8 exit 30, just s. **Facility:** 93 units. 3 stories, interior corridors. **Pool(s):** outdoor. **Activities:** hot tub, picnic facilities. **Guest Services:** coin laundry.

WENDEN (D-2) pop. 728, elev. 1,869'

ALAMO LAKE STATE PARK, 38 mi. n. of US 60 via a paved road, offers views of the Buckskin and Rawhide mountains from its site on the Bill Williams River. Activities include fishing, camping, boating and hiking. *See Recreation Areas Chart.* **Hours:** Park open daily 24 hours. Visitor center open daily 8-4. Visitor center hours may vary; phone ahead. **Cost:** $7 (per private vehicle, up to four passengers); $3 (per additional adult passenger in vehicle or individual arriving on foot or bicycle). Camping $13-$25 (per private vehicle). **Phone:** (928) 669-2088, or (520) 586-2283 for camping reservations.

WHITERIVER (D-5) pop. 4,104

Center of the Fort Apache Reservation fishing, camping and recreation area, Whiteriver also is the administrative headquarters of the 1,664,874-acre reservation. Four miles south is Fort Apache *(see place listing p. 72)*, an active scout post during the Indian Wars. The fort remained a military post until the early 1920s and is now the site of the Theodore Roosevelt Indian School.

Seven miles west of town via a dirt road are the Kinishba Ruins, a partially restored Pueblo village inhabited 1050-1350; phone (928) 338-4625 to confirm road and weather conditions. Visitors are welcome at both the Alchesay National Fish Hatchery, (928) 338-4901, 4.3 miles north via SR 73, and the Williams Creek Hatchery, (928) 334-2346, 8 miles n. via SR 73 following signs.

Choose real ratings you can trust from professional inspectors who've been there

WHY (F-3)

GAMBLING ESTABLISHMENTS
• **Desert Diamond Casino,** SR 86 Milepost 55. **Hours:** Daily 10 a.m.-midnight. **Phone:** (520) 294-7777 or (866) 332-9467.

WICKENBURG (G-1) pop. 6,363, elev. 2,093'

Nineteen miles southwest of Wickenburg is the Vulture Gold Mine, which yielded more than $20 million in gold during the hectic period following its discovery by Henry Wickenburg in 1863. Allegedly Wickenburg found the gold in one of the rocks he was hurling at his escaping mule.

The gold rush that ensued reached such proportions that by 1866 Wickenburg was the third largest city in Arizona and missed becoming the territorial capital by only two votes. Still standing in the center of town is the old mesquite jail tree to which lawmen chained their prisoners during the early boom years; no one wanted to take time from mining to build a proper jail.

The Hassayampa River, running through town, was called "the river which flows upside down" by Native Americans because it flows 20 feet below ground for most of its length. Along its banks is one of the last and greatest natural riparian areas in the state. The Nature Conservancy's Hassayampa River Preserve protects a portion of this endangered habitat *(see attraction listing this page.)*.

Wickenburg, known for its Old West atmosphere and many dude ranches, brings the past to life in February during Gold Rush Days, when the Desert Caballeros ride into the Bradshaw Mountains to spend several days under the stars; the whole town gathers to bid the horsemen farewell as they ride off into the mountains.

Wickenburg Chamber of Commerce: 216 N. Frontier St., Wickenburg, AZ 85390. **Phone:** (928) 684-5479 or (800) 942-5242.

DESERT CABALLEROS WESTERN MUSEUM, 21 N. Frontier St., contains dioramas depicting the town's history, a re-creation of an early Wickenburg street scene, ancient native artifacts and collections of gems and minerals. A bolo tie collection is on display along with works by such noted Western artists as Frederic Remington and Charles Russell. Cutting-edge contemporary exhibits include the annual Cowgirl Up! Art from the Other Half of the West. Narrated tours via headsets are available.

Time: Allow 1 hour minimum. **Hours:** Mon.-Sat. 10-5, Sun. noon-4, Sept.-May; Tues.-Sat. 10-5, Sun. noon-4, rest of year. Closed Jan. 1, Easter, July 4, Thanksgiving and Christmas. **Cost:** $9.50; $7 (ages 60+); free (ages 0-17, and active military with guest). **Phone:** (928) 684-2272.

THE NATURE CONSERVANCY'S HASSAYAMPA RIVER PRESERVE is 3 mi. s.e. on US 60 near Milepost 114 at 49614 N. US 60. The preserve is home to 280 species of birds, including the zone-tailed hawk, the Harris hawk and the yellow-billed cuckoo. Such animals as the mule deer, bobcat, skink and ring-tailed cat also may be seen. The 4-acre spring-fed Palm Lake attracts other wildlife. The visitor center contains interactive exhibits about preserve ecology. **Hours:** Wed.-Sun. 8-5, mid-Sept. to mid-May; Fri.-Sun. 7 a.m.-11 a.m., rest of year. Trails close 30 minutes before preserve closing. Closed Jan. 1, Thanksgiving, day after Thanksgiving, Christmas Eve, Christmas and Dec. 31. **Cost:** $5; free (ages 0-12). **Phone:** (928) 684-2772. GT

BEST WESTERN RANCHO GRANDE (928)684-5445

Hotel
$67-$104

AAA Benefit:
Save 10% or more every day and earn 10% bonus points!

Address: 293 E Wickenburg Way 85390 **Location:** On US 60; center. **Facility:** 76 units, some efficiencies and kitchens. 1-2 stories (no elevator), exterior corridors. **Pool(s):** heated outdoor. **Activities:** picnic facilities. **Guest Services:** valet laundry.

LOS VIAJEROS INN (928)684-7099
Hotel $75-$165 **Address:** 1000 N Tegner Rd 85390 **Location:** 1 mi n of jct US 60 and 93. **Facility:** 57 units. 2 stories (no elevator), exterior corridors. **Pool(s):** heated outdoor. **Activities:** hot tub. **Guest Services:** valet laundry.

QUALITY INN WICKENBURG (928)684-5461
Hotel $70-$100 **Address:** 850 E Wickenburg Way 85390 **Location:** 1.3 mi se on US 60. **Facility:** 29 units. 2 stories (no elevator), interior corridors. **Pool(s):** outdoor. **Activities:** hot tub. **Guest Services:** coin laundry.

RANCHO DE LOS CABALLEROS (928)684-5484
Historic Ranch $195-$445 **Address:** 1551 S Vulture Mine Rd 85390 **Location:** Jct US 60, 1.8 mi s. **Facility:** Since 1948, this unique ranch resort has been showing Western hospitality to families from around the world. Enjoy horseback rides, trap and skeet shooting, jeep tours and weekend cookouts. 79 units. 1 story, exterior corridors. **Terms:** closed 5/10-10/6, check-in 4 pm, 30 day cancellation notice-fee imposed, resort fee. **Amenities:** safes. **Pool(s):** heated outdoor. **Activities:** regulation golf, tennis, recreation programs, kids club, playground, trails, limited exercise equipment, spa. **Guest Services:** valet and coin laundry, area transportation.

SUPER 8 WICKENBURG (928)684-0808

Motel
$50-$160

Address: 1021 N Tegner St 85390 **Location:** 1 mi n of jct US 60 and 93. **Facility:** 41 units. 2 stories (no elevator), interior/exterior corridors. **Terms:** cancellation fee imposed. **Guest Services:** coin laundry. **Featured Amenity: continental breakfast.**

WHERE TO EAT

ANITA'S COCINA 928/684-5777
Mexican. Casual Dining. $6-$12 **AAA Inspector Notes:** Popular with the locals, this casual eatery serves hearty portions of such classic dishes as cheese enchiladas with rice and beans and chiles rellenos. **Features:** full bar. **Address:** 57 N Valentine St 85390 **Location:** Just n of US 60; center. **Parking:** street only.
B L D

GOLD NUGGET RESTAURANT 928/684-0648
American. Family Dining. $7-$30 **AAA Inspector Notes:** A pleasant staff serves beef, chicken and fish entrees in the historical landmark's dining rooms, which are appointed with turn-of-the-20th-century furnishings. Guests can enjoy an early breakfast in the coffee shop. **Features:** full bar. **Address:** 222 E Wickenburg Way 85390 **Location:** On US 60, just se of jct US 60 and 93; center.
B L D

WILLCOX (F-5) pop. 3,757, elev. 4,156'
• Hotels p. 300 • Restaurants p. 300

Willcox grew from a small cow town into one of the country's major cattle-shipping centers. In days past the large cattle ranches in the surrounding hills and valleys were notorious as refuges for fugitive gunslingers, who often brought their business to town: Wyatt Earp's brother Warren was killed at Headquarters Saloon in 1900. Saloons and other buildings from the late 1800s can be seen in or near the historic district, bounded by Railroad and Haskell avenues and Maley and Stewart streets.

Rex Allen was born and raised in Willcox. Tributes to the cowboy actor include the Rex Allen Arizona Cowboy Museum and Cowboy Hall of Fame (*see attraction listing p. 300*) on Railroad Avenue and a bronze statue in a park across from the museum. A bronze heart imbedded in the statue at Allen's request represents his enduring love for his hometown. The Friends of Marty Robbins Museum has joined Rex Allen on Railroad Avenue and pays tribute to the late singer/actor.

Cattle raising is still important, but added to the contemporary economic mix are the cultivation of apples, peaches, pistachios, onions and tomatoes. At a variety of "U-pick" farms northwest via Fort Grant Road, visitors can pluck fresh produce straight from the orchards and fields July through October.

Thanks to its high desert climate, Willcox also is known for its vineyards, which produce Syrah, Petite Sirah, Zinfandel and Cabernet Sauvignon among several other grape varieties. Maps for a self-guiding wine country tour are available at the Willcox Regional Visitor Center.

Birding is a popular diversion in Sulphur Springs Valley, a mecca for migrating waterfowl and shorebirds as well as wintering raptors. Sandhill cranes arrive in October and stay through February.

Southeast of town at Apache Pass is the isolated Old Fort Bowie National Historic Site. The fort was built in 1862 to guard the Butterfield Overland Trail and to protect pioneers from Apache raids and skirmishes with Native Americans led by Cochise and Geronimo. The site can only be reached by traveling the last 1.5 miles on foot. The high elevation and temperature extremes might make this hike unsuitable for some. Water is available at the fort, but hikers should bring their own canteen. Beware of flash floods, mountain lions and rattlesnakes. All historic items and natural features are strictly protected; metal detectors, digging tools, guns and hunting are prohibited. Phone (520) 847-2500.

Willcox Regional Visitor Center and Chamber of Commerce: 1500 N. Circle I Rd., Willcox, AZ 85643. **Phone:** (520) 384-2272 or (800) 200-2272.

Self-guiding tours: Brochures for a self-guiding walking tour of the historic district and a self-guiding tour of the surrounding wine country are available from the visitor center.

CHIRICAHUA REGIONAL MUSEUM is at 127 E. Maley St. History exhibits cover such topics as the railroad, Butterfield Stage Line, U.S. Cavalry, Apache Indians and development of farming, ranching and mining. The museum is housed in a turn-of-the-20th-century hardware store featuring original wooden floors and a pressed tin ceiling. A research library is across the street (128 E. Maley St.). **Time:** Allow 30 minutes minimum. **Hours:** Mon.-Sat. 10-4. Closed major holidays. **Cost:** Donations. **Phone:** (520) 384-3971.

REX ALLEN ARIZONA COWBOY MUSEUM AND COWBOY HALL OF FAME, 150 N. Railroad Ave., honors the career of Western star Rex Allen, who was born in Willcox in 1920. Allen's life is depicted from his ranching and homesteading years through his radio, television and film career. Through photographs, storyboards, clothing and ranch implements the museum also highlights the pioneers and ranchers who shaped the region. Rex Allen Days take place the first full weekend in October.

Hours: Tues.-Sat. 10-4, Mon. 10-1. Closed major holidays. **Cost:** $2. **Phone:** (520) 384-4583.

DAYS INN (520)384-4222

▼▼▼ Motel $55-$85

Address: 724 N Bisbee Ave 85643 **Location:** I-10 exit 340, just s. Adjacent to shopping center. **Facility:** 73 units. 2 stories (no elevator), exterior corridors. **Pool(s):** outdoor. **Guest Services:** coin laundry. **Featured Amenity: breakfast buffet.**

SAVE [T]• 🛏 BIZ HS 📶 ▦ / SOME UNITS 🏊 🍴 ▦

HOLIDAY INN EXPRESS & SUITES WILLCOX 520/384-3333

▼▼▼ **Hotel.** Rates not provided. **Address:** 1251 N Virginia Ave 85643 **Location:** I-10 exit 340, just n. **Facility:** 100 units. 3 stories, interior corridors. **Pool(s):** heated outdoor. **Activities:** exercise room. **Guest Services:** coin laundry.

[T]• CALL ⬇M 🛏 BIZ HS 📶 ▦ / SOME UNITS 🏊 🍴 ▦

WHERE TO EAT

BIG TEX BAR-B-QUE 520/384-4423

▼▼ Barbecue. Casual Dining. $6-$22 **AAA Inspector Notes:** This old railroad dining car across from the train tracks serves as an interesting spot for sitting down to a hearty lunch or dinner. Outstanding barbecue, including sandwiches served on homemade buns, pairs perfectly with freshly baked fruit pies. **Features:** beer & wine. **Address:** 130 E Maley St 85643 **Location:** Just se of Business Loop I-10; center. **Parking:** on-site and street. [L] [D]

WILLIAMS (C-3) pop. 3,023, elev. 6,752'

• Restaurants p. 303
• Part of Grand Canyon National Park area — see map p. 82

Williams was named after William (Bill) Shirley Williams, the early mountain man who guided trapping parties and expeditions through the wilderness.

Primarily a resort town, Williams marks the beginning of the major entrance route to Grand Canyon National Park (see place listing p. 82). The town is at the base of Bill Williams Mountain and boasts an 18-hole golf course and a ski area offering both downhill and cross-country skiing. In the surrounding Kaibab National Forest (see place listing p. 96), cross-country skiing and hiking are popular. Kaibab Dogtown and White Horse lakes offer camping, picnicking and fishing, while Cataract Lake is open for day use only.

Williams and Forest Service Visitor Center: 200 West Railroad Ave., Williams, AZ 86046. **Phone:** (928) 635-4061 or (800) 863-0546.

BEARIZONA, off I-40 exit 165 at 1500 E. SR 66, is a drive-through wildlife park set in a 160-acre forest. During the 3-mile drive you'll see bison, black bears, deer, elk, American burros, bighorn and Dall sheep, Rocky Mountain goats, wolves and other animals in natural habitats. Afterward you can park your car and walk through Fort Bearizona, an area that's home to young foxes, black bear cubs, bobcats and javelinas. The Wild Ride is a guided bus tour through the park. A birds of prey show is presented several times daily.

Cars are available for visitors arriving on foot or by motorcycle. **Time:** Allow 1 hour minimum. **Hours:** Daily 8-6, June 1-Aug. 15; hours vary, rest of year. Last entry is 90 minutes before closing. Birds of Prey Show daily at 11, 1 and 3, Mar.-Dec. Wild Ride daily at 10, noon, 2 and 4, June 1-Aug. 15. Phone ahead to confirm schedule. **Cost:** $20; $18 (ages 62+); $10 (ages 4-12). Maximum per private vehicle $100. **Phone:** (928) 635-2289. *(See ad p. 86.)*

GRAND CANYON DEER FARM, 6769 E. Deer Farm Rd. off I-40, has several varieties of deer and such other animals as camels, bison, coatimundi, reindeer and wallabies. Visitors are permitted to walk among the deer and feed them. **Hours:** Daily 9-6, mid-Mar. to mid-Oct.; 10-5, rest of year. Closed Thanksgiving and Christmas. **Cost:** $11.50; $10 (ages 62+); $6.75 (ages 3-13). **Phone:** (928) 635-4073 or (800) 926-3337.

GRAND CANYON RAILWAY, .5 mi. s. of I-40 exit 163 (Grand Canyon Blvd.), offers round-trip excursions through grassy plains and pine forests to the South Rim of the Grand Canyon aboard 1950s-era passenger cars powered by vintage diesel locomotives. Strolling musicians, Western characters and a mock train robbery provide entertainment during the ride.

Passengers arrive at the 1910 Grand Canyon Depot, in the historic district at the South Rim; the depot is the only working log depot in the country. A Wild West show takes place daily at 9. Six classes of train service are available. For an additional fee, bus tours of the South Rim with lunch are available.

Refreshments are available in some cars. **Hours:** Train departs daily at 9:30 and returns at 5:45 with a 3.5-hour stopover at the canyon. Closed Christmas Eve and Christmas. Phone ahead to confirm schedule.

Cost: Round-trip coach fare $75; $45 (ages 0-16). One-way fare available; upgraded seats are available for an additional fee. Fare does not include admission to Grand Canyon National Park. Fares may vary; phone ahead. Reservations are recommended. **Phone:** (800) 843-8724.

BEST WESTERN PLUS INN OF WILLIAMS
(928)635-4400

Hotel
$109-$210

AAA Benefit:
Save 10% or more every day and earn 10% bonus points!

Address: 2600 W Route 66 86046 **Location:** I-40 exit 161, just e. **Facility:** 80 units, some two bedrooms and kitchens. 2 stories, interior corridors. **Amenities:** video games. **Dining:** Western View Steakhouse, see separate listing, entertainment. **Pool(s):** heated outdoor. **Activities:** hot tub, trails, exercise room. **Guest Services:** coin laundry. **Featured Amenity:** full hot breakfast.

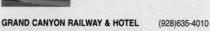

Ideal location between two AZ world destinations-Grand Canyon 50 miles North & Sedona 50 miles South.

COMFORT INN NEAR GRAND CANYON
928/635-4045

Hotel. Rates not provided. **Address:** 911 W Route 66 86046 **Location:** I-40 exit 161, 1 mi e. **Facility:** 74 units. 2 stories, interior corridors. **Pool(s):** heated indoor. **Activities:** hot tub. **Guest Services:** coin laundry.

DAYS INN OF WILLIAMS
(928)635-4051

Motel $70-$170 **Address:** 2488 W Route 66 86046 **Location:** I-40 exit 161, just e. **Facility:** 72 units. 2 stories (no elevator), interior corridors. **Amenities:** safes. **Pool(s):** heated indoor. **Activities:** hot tub. **Guest Services:** coin laundry.

ECONO LODGE
928/635-4085

Motel
Rates not provided

Address: 302 E Route 66 86046 **Location:** I-40 exit 163, 0.5 mi s, then just e. **Facility:** 40 units. 2 stories (no elevator), exterior corridors.

GRAND CANYON RAILWAY & HOTEL
(928)635-4010

Hotel
$109-$219

Address: 235 N Grand Canyon Blvd 86046 **Location:** I-40 exit 163, 0.5 mi s. Located at historic Williams Depot. **Facility:** 298 units. 2 stories, interior corridors. **Terms:** 3 day cancellation notice. **Dining:** 2 restaurants, entertainment. **Pool(s):** heated indoor. **Activities:** hot tub, playground, game room, exercise room. **Guest Services:** coin laundry, area transportation.

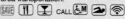

▼ See AAA listing p. 43 ▼

GRAND LIVING BED & BREAKFAST (928)635-4171

 Bed & Breakfast $170-$325 **Address:** 701 Quarter Horse Rd 86046 **Location:** I-40 exit 165 (Williams/Grand Canyon), 1 mi s on Business Loop 40, then just w on Rodeo Rd. Located in a residential area. **Facility:** Located near the center of this small town, this beautifully decorated log cabin-style residence provides comfortable rooms and public areas and features three rooms with a fireplace. 6 units. 1 story, interior/exterior corridors. **Terms:** check-in 4 pm, age restrictions may apply, 11 day cancellation notice-fee imposed, resort fee.

HOWARD JOHNSON EXPRESS INN (928)635-9561

Hotel
$50-$100

Address: 511 N Grand Canyon Blvd 86046 **Location:** I-40 exit 163, just s. **Facility:** 54 units. 2 stories (no elevator), interior corridors. **Terms:** cancellation fee imposed. **Amenities:** safes. **Pool(s):** heated indoor. **Activities:** hot tub. **Featured Amenity:** continental breakfast.

KNIGHTS INN (928)635-1412

Motel
$80-$150

Address: 750 N Grand Canyon Blvd 86046 **Location:** I-40 exit 163, just s. **Facility:** 19 units, some two bedrooms. 2 stories (no elevator), interior corridors. **Terms:** cancellation fee imposed. **Featured Amenity:** continental breakfast.

Closest town to Grand Canyon, 1 mile from Historic Route 66. Hair dryer, Iron & Board. Free parking.

THE LODGE ON ROUTE 66 928)635-4534

 Motel. Rates not provided. **Address:** 200 E Route 66 86046 **Location:** I-40 exit 163, 0.5 mi s, then just e. **Facility:** 19 units. 1 story, exterior corridors. **Terms:** check-in 4 pm.

MOUNTAIN RANCH RESORT AT BEACON HILL
(928)635-2693

Hotel
$119-$259

Address: 6701 E Mountain Ranch Rd 86046 **Location:** I-40 exit 171 (Deer Farm Rd), just s. Located in a scenic country area. **Facility:** 66 units. 2 stories (no elevator), exterior corridors. **Terms:** closed 12/15-3/31, cancellation fee imposed. **Dining:** The Ranch Bar & Grill, see separate listing. **Pool(s):** heated outdoor. **Activities:** hot tub, tennis, exercise room. **Guest Services:** coin laundry. **Featured Amenity:** full hot breakfast.

RAMADA WILLIAMS/GRAND CANYON AREA (928)635-4114

 Hotel $54-$128 **Address:** 950 N Grand Canyon Blvd 86046 **Location:** I-40 exit 163, just s. **Facility:** 120 units, some two bedrooms. 2 stories, interior corridors. **Dining:** Doc Holiday Steakhouse, see separate listing. **Pool(s):** heated indoor. **Activities:** hot tub, exercise room. **Guest Services:** coin laundry.

RODEWAY INN & SUITES DOWNTOWNER MOTEL
(928)635-4041

 **Motel** $100-$170 **Address:** 201 E Route 66 86046 **Location:** I-40 exit 163, 0.5 mi s, then just e. **Facility:** 16 units. 1 story, exterior corridors. **Terms:** check-in 4 pm.

TRAVELODGE WILLIAMS (928)635-2651

Motel
$60-$170

Address: 430 E Route 66 86046 **Location:** I-40 exit 163, 0.5 mi s, then just e. **Facility:** 41 units, some two bedrooms. 2 stories (no elevator), exterior corridors. **Pool(s):** heated outdoor. **Activities:** hot tub. **Guest Services:** coin laundry. **Featured Amenity:** continental breakfast.

FREE Bear Bites Breakfast at newly renovated hotel. Kids 12 and under stay free. Free parking.

CANYON MOTEL & RV PARK 928)635-9371

[fyi] Not evaluated. **Address:** 1900 E Rodeo Rd/Route 66 86046 **Location:** I-40 exit 165 (Williams/Grand Canyon), 1 mi s on Business Loop 40, then just w. Facilities, services, and décor characterize an economy property.

WHERE TO EAT

CAFE 326 928)635-0777

 Coffee/Tea Sandwiches. Quick Serve. $5-$8 **AAA Inspector Notes:** Huge homemade cinnamon rolls and fresh coffee/tea are what attracts guests to this café. Freshly prepared sandwiches are served for lunch. **Features:** Sunday brunch. **Address:** 326 W Route 66 86046 **Location:** Center. **Parking:** street only. B L

CRUISER'S ROUTE 66 BAR & GRILL 928)635-2445

American. Gastropub. $8-$20 **AAA Inspector Notes:** Located in historic downtown, this pleasant family restaurant prepares a variety of Mexican, steak and chicken dishes in a setting reminiscent of the 1950s. Cordial staff members deliver sizzling fajitas, the house specialty. **Features:** full bar, patio dining. **Address:** 233 W Route 66 86046 **Location:** Jct Route 66 and 3rd St. **Parking:** street only.

DARA THAI CAFE 928)635-2201

Thai. Casual Dining. $7-$14 **AAA Inspector Notes:** This small casual restaurant offers traditional Thai cuisine with casual service. The dining room is small so do not be surprised if there is a wait. **Address:** 145 W Route 66 86046 **Location:** Center. **Parking:** street only. L D

DOC HOLIDAY STEAKHOUSE 928)635-4114

Steak. Casual Dining. $8-$29 **AAA Inspector Notes:** This restaurant presents a complete dinner menu with items ranging from steaks to sandwiches. The dining room is filled with Doc Holiday photos and old ranch tools. The lounge is a great place to shoot a game of pool and enjoy a local brew. **Features:** full bar, happy hour. **Address:** 950 N Grand Canyon Blvd 86046 **Location:** I-40 exit 163, just s; in Ramada Williams/Grand Canyon Area. B D CALL

GRAND CANYON COFFEE & CAFE 928)635-4907

International Sandwiches. Casual Dining. $7-$12 **AAA Inspector Notes:** This is a small eatery that offers a mix of Mexican, Chinese and American cuisine which include burgers and sandwiches. Their sauces are made in-house. **Address:** 137 W Railroad Ave 86046 **Location:** I-40 exit 163, 0.5 mi s, then just e. **Parking:** street only. B L

KICKS ON ROUTE 66   928/635-2052

◆◆◆ American. Casual Dining. $9-$30 **AAA Inspector Notes:** Walk into a vibrant grey and green Route 66 oasis with fun American cuisine and a large granite bar serving many local brews. A daily special is offered. Do not forget to grab a souvenir from the gift shop on the way out. **Features:** full bar, patio dining, Sunday brunch, happy hour. **Address:** 2550 W Route 66 86046 **Location:** I-40 exit 161, just e. [L] [D] CALL 🅼M

PANCHO MCGILLICUDDY'S   928/635-4150

◆◆◆ Mexican. Casual Dining. $10-$18 **AAA Inspector Notes:** On the National Register of Historic Places and renovated in 1993, the downtown building once was a boisterous spot along Saloon Row. Railroad workers, cowboys, loggers and rowdy locals came to visit the saloons, gambling houses and houses of ill repute. Now a casual family restaurant, the historic property features attractive Western decor and an authentic Mexican menu with fajitas, enchiladas and chiles rellenos. Expect cordial service from a waitstaff in casual attire. **Features:** full bar, patio dining, happy hour. **Address:** 141 W Railroad Ave 86046 **Location:** I-40 exit 163, 0.5 mi s.

[L] [D]

PINE COUNTRY RESTAURANT   928/635-9718

◆◆◆ American. Casual Dining. $7-$25 **AAA Inspector Notes:** Home-style cooking is at the heart of a menu that includes entrées, soups and salads. No meal, however, is complete without a piece of the delicious, homemade pies. This small storefront is in historic downtown Williams, and its relaxed dining room projects a homelike feel thanks to a number of craft items displayed. Full service is provided by a casually attired, polite staff. **Address:** 107 N Grand Canyon Blvd 86046 **Location:** Cross street Route 66; downtown. **Parking:** on-site and street. [B] [L] [D]

THE RANCH BAR & GRILL   928/635-2693

◆◆◆
American
Casual Dining
$10-$31

AAA Inspector Notes: Only a few minutes from the historic town of Williams, this casual restaurant employs cordial and knowledgeable servers. Menu offerings include steak, seafood and pasta dishes. **Features:** full bar. **Address:** 6701 E Mountain Ranch Rd 86046 **Location:** I-40 exit 171 (Deer Farm Rd), just s; in Mountain Ranch Resort at Beacon Hill. [B] [D]

RED RAVEN RESTAURANT   928/635-4980

◆◆◆ American. Casual Dining. $6-$28 **AAA Inspector Notes:** This small restaurant, located in old downtown, is a surprise to the area by serving contemporary items. Some of the dishes include tempura shrimp, flat-iron steak, Baja tacos, soufflés and crème brûlée. During lunch the menu is a little more basic with such items as Philly cheesesteaks, club sandwich and Reubens. **Features:** full bar. **Address:** 135 W Route 66 86046 **Location:** I-40 exit 163, 0.5 mi s, then just e. **Parking:** street only. [L] [D]

ROD'S STEAK HOUSE   928/635-2671

◆◆◆
Steak
Casual Dining
$8-$25

AAA Inspector Notes: *Classic.* Serving travelers along Historic Route 66, the restaurant has served its specialty steaks-as well as seafood and chicken dishes-since 1946. A must-try is the sugar-dipped charred steak, a surprising delight. **Features:** full bar. **Address:** 301 E Route 66 86046 **Location:** Center. *Menu on AAA.com* [L] [D]

STATION 66 ITALIAN BISTRO   928/635-3992

◆◆◆ Italian. Casual Dining. $10-$20 **AAA Inspector Notes:** This small, family-run restaurant focuses on wood-fired Neapolitan-style pizza and casual, seasonally fresh Italian dishes. The upstairs and downstairs patios are popular in season. It is an amazing place to have a glass of local wine or beer while enjoying the live band on a spring day or evening. **Features:** full bar, patio dining. **Address:** 144 W Route 66 86046 **Location:** I-40 exit 163, 0.5 mi s. **Parking:** street only. [L] [D]

WESTERN VIEW STEAKHOUSE   928/635-4400

◆◆◆
Steak
Casual Dining
$17-$45

AAA Inspector Notes: This small restaurant is located off the hotel lobby and offers an upscale menu featuring Prime steaks, halibut and lamb chops. The portions are large, but the dessert cart is tempting even if guests are full. **Features:** full bar, patio dining. **Address:** 2600 W Route 66 86046 **Location:** I-40 exit 161, just e; in BEST WESTERN PLUS Inn of Williams. [D] CALL 🅼M 🐾

Relaxed dining, forest views, steakhouse & Mexican food

WINDOW ROCK (B-6) pop. 2,712

Window Rock is the capital of the Navajo nation and seat of its tribal government. The elected tribal council meets in the council house at least four times a year. Window Rock also contains the U.S. government's Bureau of Indian Affairs, Navajo Area Office. The headquarters of the Navajo Arts and Crafts Enterprises is just east of the junction of SR 264 and Navajo Route 12.

NAVAJO NATION MUSEUM, at jct. SR 264 and Post Office Loop Rd., contains photographs, jewelry, textiles and other items relating to the history and culture of the Navajo people. One exhibit describes the arduous 1864 ordeal known as the "Long Walk," in which the Navajo were removed from tribal lands and marched some 300 miles to a Fort Sumner, N.M., prison camp. **Hours:** Mon. 8-5, Tues.-Fri. 8-6, Sat. 9-5. Closed Easter. **Cost:** Donations. **Phone:** (928) 871-7941. [🍴]

QUALITY INN NAVAJO NATION CAPITAL (928)871-4108

◆◆◆
Hotel
$70-$120

Address: 48 W Hwy 264 86515 **Location:** Center. **Facility:** 56 units. 2 stories (no elevator), exterior corridors. **Dining:** Diné Restaurant, see separate listing. **Activities:** exercise room. **Guest Services:** coin laundry.

[SAVE] [🍴] [BIZ] [📶] [🔌] [📷] [📺] / SOME UNITS [🛏]

WHERE TO EAT

DINÉ RESTAURANT   928/871-4108

◆◆ Regional American. Family Dining. $10-$20 **AAA Inspector Notes:** Near the center of town and a museum, this family-centered hotel restaurant offers a variety of selections, including steak and seafood, Mexican entrées, Navajo mutton stew and fry bread. **Address:** 48 W Hwy 264 86515 **Location:** Center; in Quality Inn Navajo Nation Capital. [B] [L] [D]

WINKELMAN (E-5) pop. 353, elev. 1,928'

A mining and agricultural center, Winkelman is near the 8.5-mile Aravaipa Canyon, a wilderness retreat that was once the headquarters of the Apache

Indians. The canyon's abundant vegetation, nourished by the year-round flow of Aravaipa Creek, contrasts with the surrounding desert terrain.

Off SR 77, then 13 miles east on a paved and gravel road, the canyon is within the 4,044-acre Aravaipa Canyon Primitive Area. Permits are required to enter the area; contact the Bureau of Land Management's District Office in Safford; phone (928) 348-4400. Visitation to the area is limited; reservations are required.

WINSLOW (C-5) pop. 9,655, elev. 4,856'
• Restaurants p. 306

Winslow was named after Gen. Edward Francis Winslow, a president of the Atlantic and Pacific Railroad. This railroad center is an important shipping and trading site. A two-story mural and bronze statue at Standin' on the Corner Park in downtown Winslow illustrate the Eagles' song "Take It Easy" and its well-known reference to the town. The Apache-Sitgreaves National Forests (see place listing p. 39) lie south of town.

Winslow Chamber of Commerce: 523 W. Second St., Winslow, AZ 86047. **Phone:** (928) 289-2434.

HOMOLOVI STATE PARK, 2 mi n. of I-40 on SR 87, preserves structures and cultural artifacts from the late migration period of the Hopi (1200s-1300s). On the grounds are a visitor center, a museum, various trails and a campground. **Hours:** Daily 8-5. Closed Christmas. **Cost:** $7 (per private vehicle, up to four adult passengers); $3 (each additional adult passenger and individuals arriving by bicycle or on foot). Camping $25 (with electricity), $15-$18 (without electricity). **Phone:** (928) 289-4106, or (520) 586-2283 for camping reservations.

LA POSADA is off I-40 exit 253, then 1 mi. s. to Second St., just e. to 303 E. Second St. (Rte. 66). Designed by Mary Elizabeth Jane Colter and considered her masterpiece, La Posada attracted such luminaries as Howard Hughes, Albert Einstein and Bob Hope. Constructed in 1929 in the style of an 1869 Spanish hacienda, the building has stone and tile floors, glass murals, original furnishings and gardens. Antiques and art from around the globe decorate this working hotel.

Time: Allow 1 hour, 30 minutes minimum. **Hours:** Daily 7 a.m.-10 p.m. **Cost:** Free. **Phone:** (928) 289-4366.

METEOR CRATER, 22 mi. w. on I-40, then 6 mi. s. off exit 233, was formed nearly 50,000 years ago by a meteorite; the crater is 550 feet deep, 2.4 miles in circumference and nearly 1 mile across.

The meteor, estimated to have been 90 feet across and traveling 26,000 mph, slammed into the rocky plain and left a crater that was originally 700 feet deep and more than 4,000 feet across. Because the terrain of the crater is very similar to that of the moon, NASA once trained Apollo astronauts here.

The Discovery Center relays information about the formation of the crater and features interactive displays about meteorites and asteroids. A large-screen theater presents "IMPACT, The Mystery of Meteor Crater." Visitors can view the crater from numerous locations on the rim. Also included are an Astronaut Wall of Fame and an Apollo test capsule.

Guided rim tours of the crater depart daily. **Note:** Inquire about weather policies. **Time:** Allow 2 hours minimum. **Hours:** Daily 7-7, Memorial Day-Labor Day; 8-5, rest of year. Closed Christmas. **Cost:** $18; $16 (ages 60+); $9 (ages 6-17). **Phone:** (928) 289-5898 or (800) 289-5898. *(See ad p. 60.)* GT

ROCK ART RANCH is off I-40 exit 286, 1.5 mi. s. on SR 77 to McLaws Rd., 10.7 mi. w. to Territorial Rd., 7.5 mi. w. to Rock Art Ranch Rd., then 2.2 mi. s.w. to ranch entrance. The working cattle ranch consists of more than 7,000 acres. The restored bunkhouse of the Hashknife Cattle Company, a large 19th-century ranching operation, is featured. Ancestral Puebloan and Hohokam artifacts and pots, some dating to 7,500 years old, are displayed in a barn-like building. Visitors may drive 2 miles with a guide to Chevelon Canyon and examine more than 3,000 petroglyphs, many more than 6,000 years old, on canyon walls.

Note: A descent into a 50-foot-deep canyon is required to view the petroglyphs; appropriate attire and footwear are strongly recommended. The climb and descent are not recommended for the physically impaired, elderly guests and small children. **Time:** Allow 2 hours, 30 minutes minimum. **Hours:** Mon.-Sat. by appointment. Closed major holidays. **Cost:** $35; free (ages 0-12). Prices may vary depending on the number of people on a tour. Reservations for all activities are recommended 2 to 3 days in advance. Reservations are required. **Phone:** (928) 288-3260.

WHERE TO EAT

MOJO COFFEEHOUSE & CAFE   928/289-6656

♦ Coffee/Tea. Quick Serve. $3-$6 **AAA Inspector Notes:** Billboards on either side of Interstate 40 will guide you to this unexpected oasis in the desert featuring burritos, salads, muffins, scones, cheesecake, gourmet cinnamon rolls, bagels, espresso, hot and iced coffee and smoothies with nutritional extras including cool treats for the kids. The wireless Internet, relaxed and comfortable ambience and upbeat music are sure to please. **Address:** 1700 N Park Dr 86047 **Location:** I-40 exit 253, just s. B L

THE TURQUOISE ROOM   928/289-2888

♦♦♦ Southwestern. Fine Dining. $8-$34 **AAA Inspector Notes:** Eight hand-painted glass and tin chandeliers grace the restaurants high beamed ceilings. Elk, quail, salmon, beef, lamb and pork, flavored with home-grown herbs, are always on the menu. Boxed lunches are an option, which include fresh grilled and chilled salmon, herb-roasted chicken breast and fresh breads. **Features:** full bar. **Address:** 303 E 2nd St 86047 **Location:** I-40 exit 253, 1 mi s to Route 66 (2nd St), then just e; in historic downtown; in La Posada Hotel. B L D

▼ WUPATKI NATIONAL MONUMENT (B-4)

Lying about 33 mi. n. of Flagstaff and reached via US 89, 35,253-acre Wupatki National Monument contains more than 2,600 archeological sites, including some 1,000 structures. Thanks to increased rainfall and the water-retaining layer of ash and cinders covering the ground after the late 11th-century eruption of Sunset Crater Volcano (south of the monument), farming became productive enough that at one time the region may have been one of the more densely populated sections of northern Arizona. The original inhabitants of Wupatki are believed to have been ancestors of the Hopi Indians.

The largest and one of the most impressive sites is Wupatki, or "Long-cut House," containing more than 100 rooms. Nearby are a ceremonial amphitheater, ball court and "blow hole." Other important ruins are the Citadel, Nalakihu, Lomaki and the three-story Wukoki, all reachable by short, self-guiding trails. Most of the ruins were inhabited from about 1100-1225. Picnicking is available. Visitors must stay on the trails; the backcountry is closed to unguided travel in order to protect the cultural resources.

Allow 1 hour minimum. Visitor center open daily 9-5; closed Christmas. Ruins and trails open daily dawn-dusk. Admission $5 per person; free ages 0-15. Admission includes Sunset Crater Volcano National Monument *(see place listing p. 242)*. Phone (928) 679-2365.

YARNELL (D-3) pop. 649, elev. 4,800'

Yarnell sprang up as a gold-mining town after a prospector named Harrison Yarnell struck gold on a nearby mountain peak in 1863. Some active mines still produce silver, gold and copper; however, the area's primary industries are cattle raising and tourism. Many vacationers visit Yarnell in the summer to escape the desert heat and to enjoy the many recreational pursuits the area offers.

Yarnell/Peeples Valley Chamber of Commerce: Write P.O. Box 275, Yarnell, AZ 85362. **Phone:** (928) 427-6582.

SHRINE OF ST. JOSEPH OF THE MOUNTAINS, .5 mi. w. off SR 89, is an open-air mountainside shrine with statues that depict scenes of The Last Supper, Garden of Gethsemane, The Way of the Cross and the Risen Christ. Information is available at the shrine or by writing P.O. Box 267, Yarnell, AZ 85362. **Note:** A 2013 fire damaged some of the stations, pathways and statues. **Hours:** Open daily dawn-dusk. **Cost:** Donations. **Phone:** (928) 778-5229.

YOUNGTOWN pop. 6,156

• Hotels & Restaurants map & index p. 154
• Part of Phoenix area — see map p. 126

BEST WESTERN INN & SUITES OF SUN CITY
    (623)933-8211 ㉒

♦♦
Hotel
$69-$159

AAA Benefit: Save 10% or more every day and earn 10% bonus points!

Address: 11201 Grand Ave 85363 **Location:** On US 60, just se of 113th Ave. **Facility:** 97 units, some efficiencies. 2 stories (no elevator), interior/exterior corridors. **Pool(s):** heated outdoor. **Activities:** picnic facilities. **Guest Services:** coin laundry.

SAVE ⊞↑ ⊅ BIZ 🛜 ⊟ ▭
▱ / SOME UNITS 🐾 HS

YUMA (E-1) pop. 93,064, elev. 200'

• Hotels p. 308 • Restaurants p. 310

Tucked into Arizona's southwestern corner, Yuma is on the Arizona-California state line not far from the Mexican border. The town occupies a historically important spot on the Colorado River where it narrows between two granite outcroppings, creating the easiest crossing for many miles.

Although he was not the first white man to visit the area, Father Eusebio Francisco Kino was the first to recognize the Yuma Crossing as the gateway to California. Yet Kino's discovery would not be used for almost a century until Juan Bautista de Anza, presidial captain of Tubac, arrived in search of an overland route to California through Yuma in 1774. The Anza expedition reached Mission San Gabriel, near present-day Los Angeles, in March of that year.

In 1779 two missions were founded at the crossing by Father Francisco Garcés, who, along with all the colonists, was later killed during the last major uprising of the Quechan Indians in 1781. The Spanish retreated and never again tried to dominate the Quechan or control the Yuma Crossing.

After Mexico won its independence from Spain in 1821, the area became part of the new nation's northern territories, but the Mexican government's control over these territories was compromised by economic decline and internal conflict. At the same time, mountain men—American trappers and explorers who acted as guides for settlers heading west—began blazing new trails into the region.

During the Mexican-American War (1846-48), the U.S. Army organized a unit of Mormon volunteers that set out on a difficult march covering nearly 2,000 miles between Council Bluffs, Iowa, and San Diego. In doing so, they blazed a wagon trail that crossed the Colorado River at Yuma. A bronze statue in Yuma's West Wetlands Park, 2200 W. Water St., commemorates the Mormon Battalion's historic trek across the Southwest.

Gold seekers by the thousands poured through Yuma during the California gold rush of 1849, using a rope ferry at present-day Main Street to cross the Colorado River. It wouldn't be until 1873, however, that the city was formally named Yuma, having previously been called Colorado City and later Arizona City.

Pivot Point Interpretive Plaza, 200 N. Madison Ave., preserves the last remnants of the pivoting railroad bridge that once allowed trains to cross the river but also could swing wide to let steamboats pass. The plaza includes a landscaped park with interpretive panels; a 1907 Baldwin locomotive; an audio installation re-creating sounds of a train, a steamboat and the bridge swinging aside; and at night, a light display with twin laser beams tracing the old bridge's route across the river.

The Yuma Art Center & Historic Yuma Theatre, 245 S. Main St., is a downtown cultural center and performing arts venue featuring four visual art galleries and a 650-seat theater. Built in 1911 for vaudeville shows and movies, the theater today hosts a range of events including community theater performances, jazz festivals, film screenings and art lectures. Phone (928) 373-5202.

Yuma is host to a number of outdoor events. The city becomes flooded with dove hunters when hunting season opens September 1 and the population nearly doubles during the winter months as snowbirds arrive to enjoy the sunshine. Golf is a popular pastime with 13 lush golf courses from which to choose. The visitors bureau offers field-to-feast agriculture tours of the area's number one industry, while the Yuma Lettuce Days Festival takes place each March.

Yuma Visitors Bureau: 201 N. 4th Ave., Yuma, AZ 85364. **Phone:** (928) 783-0071 or (800) 293-0071.

Shopping: Yuma Palms Regional Center, 1463 S. Yuma Palms Pkwy., is anchored by Dillard's and JCPenney.

ARIZONA HISTORICAL SOCIETY/SANGUINETTI HOUSE MUSEUM AND GARDENS, 240 S. Madison Ave., was the home of pioneer merchant E.F. Sanguinetti. The house contains late-19th-century period rooms and exhibits about the history of Yuma and the lower Colorado River region. The colorful early-1900s-style gardens combine exotic and local plants.

Hours: Tues.-Sat. 10-4. Closed Jan. 1, July 4, Veterans Day, Thanksgiving and Christmas. **Cost:** $5; $4 (ages 60+); free (ages 0-11). **Phone:** (928) 782-1841.

IMPERIAL NATIONAL WILDLIFE REFUGE encompasses 25,125 acres along the lower Colorado River. The Arizona section of the refuge is 40 mi. n. off US 95 via Martinez Lake Rd., following signs. The remainder of the refuge can be reached best by boat or four-wheel-drive vehicle. Canada geese, ducks, egrets and eagles gather at the refuge. Hiking, hunting, fishing and boating are permitted in designated areas. Maps and public-use regulations are available upon request.

Hours: Daily dawn-dusk. Visitor center open Mon.-Fri. 8-4:30, Sat.-Sun. 9-4, Nov. 15-Mar. 31; Mon.-Fri. 7:30-4, rest of year. Closed Thanksgiving and Christmas. Phone ahead to confirm schedule. **Cost:** Free. **Phone:** (928) 783-3371.

KOFA NATIONAL WILDLIFE REFUGE OFFICE is at 9300 E. 28th St. Serving as the visitor center and headquarters for the 664,327-acre wildlife refuge, the office features exhibits describing the refuge's natural environment and cultural history. You can pick up brochures and schedules of interpretive programs here, and staff members can help you plan your visit to the refuge.

Encompassing the Kofa and Castle Dome mountains 40 miles north of Yuma, the refuge preserves the habitat of desert bighorn sheep. Remote Palm Canyon is 18 miles south of Quartzsite on US 95, then 7 miles east on a maintained gravel road. It is one of the few places in Arizona where native palms grow. They can be seen from a point 200 yards away via a half-mile hike up a moderately steep trail.

Note: The last 200 yards to the palms present a strenuous climb. Refuge roads are rough and are best navigated by four-wheel-drive and high-clearance vehicles. Entering abandoned mines is prohibited. **Hours:** Office Mon.-Fri. 8-4:30. Closed major holidays. Refuge and canyon accessible daily 24 hours. **Cost:** Free. **Phone:** (928) 783-7861.

YUMA QUARTERMASTER DEPOT STATE HISTORIC PARK, I-8 4th Ave. exit to 201 N. 4th Ave., is on a 10-acre site on the s. side of the Colorado River. The park salutes 5 centuries of transportation across the Colorado River. From 1864 through 1883 the U.S. Army Quartermaster Depot stored and distributed supplies for military posts throughout the Southwest. Five restored buildings stand on the site that once comprised the depot. The depot office was built in 1872. **Hours:** Daily 9-4:30, Oct.-May; Tues.-Sun. 9-4:30, rest of year. Closed Thanksgiving and Christmas. **Cost:** $4; $2 (ages 7-13 and active military with ID). **Phone:** (928) 783-0071.

YUMA TERRITORIAL PRISON STATE HISTORIC PARK is off I-8 exit 1 (Giss Pkwy.), on a bluff on the s. side of the Colorado River "meander" (where the river bends). Erected in 1876, the complex of buildings was a prison until 1909. Some of the original structures remain, including the sally port, a main guard tower and various cell blocks. The adobe walls, which no longer stand, were 8 feet thick at the base and 5 feet thick at the top, and at full capacity confined 400 prisoners. Of interest are the cellblocks, the "dark cell" and a museum. Interpretive programs are offered. **Hours:** Daily 9-5, Oct.-May;

Thurs.-Mon. 9-5, rest of year. Closed for maintenance for 2 weeks in August. Closed Thanksgiving and Christmas. Phone ahead to confirm schedule. **Cost:** $6; $3 (ages 7-13). **Phone:** (928) 783-4771.

BEST WESTERN INNSUITES YUMA MALL HOTEL & SUITES   (928)783-8341

Hotel
$79-$159

AAA Benefit: Save 10% or more every day and earn 10% bonus points!

Address: 1450 Castle Dome Ave 85365 **Location:** I-8 exit 2 (16th St/US 95), just e to Yuma Palms Pkwy, just n, then just w. **Facility:** 166 units, some efficiencies. 2-3 stories (no elevator), exterior corridors. **Pool(s):** heated outdoor. **Activities:** hot tub, tennis, picnic facilities, exercise room. **Guest Services:** valet and coin laundry, area transportation.

CANDLEWOOD SUITES   928/726-2800

Extended Stay Hotel. Rates not provided. **Address:** 2036 S Ave 3 E 85365 **Location:** I-8 exit 3, just n, then just w on Frontage Rd. **Facility:** 95 efficiencies. 4 stories, interior corridors. **Activities:** picnic facilities, exercise room. **Guest Services:** complimentary and valet laundry, area transportation.

DAYS INN YUMA   (928)329-7790

Motel
$60-$105

Address: 1671 E 16th St 85365 **Location:** I-8 exit 2 (16th St/US 95), just e. **Facility:** 64 units. 2 stories (no elevator), exterior corridors. **Terms:** 2 night minimum stay - seasonal. **Pool(s):** outdoor. **Activities:** hot tub. **Guest Services:** coin laundry. **Featured Amenity:** breakfast buffet.

FAIRFIELD INN & SUITES BY MARRIOTT   (928)345-1800

Hotel $89-$174 **Address:** 1801 S Sunridge Dr 85365 **Location:** I-8 exit 2 (16th St/US 95), e to Sunridge Dr, then just s. **Facility:** 64 units. 3 stories, interior corridors. **Pool(s):** heated outdoor. **Activities:** hot tub, exercise room. **Guest Services:** valet and coin laundry, area transportation.

AAA Benefit: Members save 5% or more!

HAMPTON INN & SUITES YUMA   (928)329-5600

Hotel
$99-$169

AAA Benefit: Members save up to 10%!

Address: 1600 E 16th St 85365 **Location:** I-8 exit 2 (16th St/US 95), just e, then just n. Adjacent to Yuma Palms Shopping Center. **Facility:** 90 units. 4 stories, interior corridors. **Terms:** 1-7 night minimum stay, cancellation fee imposed. **Pool(s):** heated outdoor. **Activities:** hot tub, exercise room. **Guest Services:** valet and coin laundry. **Featured Amenity:** breakfast buffet.

HILTON GARDEN INN YUMA/PIVOT POINT   (928)783-1500

Hotel $99-$169 **Address:** 310 N Madison Ave 85364 **Location:** I-8 exit 1 (Harold C. Giss Pkwy), w to rotary, then 0.4 mi n. **Facility:** 150 units. 4 stories, interior corridors. **Terms:** 1-7 night minimum stay, cancellation fee imposed. **Pool(s):** heated outdoor. **Activities:** hot tub, exercise room. **Guest Services:** valet and coin laundry, area transportation.

AAA Benefit: Members save up to 10%!

HISTORIC CORONADO MOTOR HOTEL   (928)783-4453

Classic Hotel
$80-$140

Address: 233 4th Ave 85364 **Location:** I-8 exit 172 (4th Ave) eastbound, 0.5 mi s; exit 1 (Harold C. Giss Pkwy) westbound, 1 mi w. **Facility:** This established facility has several Spanish-style buildings spread over a full city block. A variety of room types are available. Take time to visit the Casa de Coronado Museum. 126 units, some two bedrooms and kitchens. 1-2 stories (no elevator), exterior corridors. **Amenities:** safes. **Dining:** Yuma Landing Bar & Grill, see separate listing. **Pool(s):** outdoor, heated outdoor. **Activities:** hot tub, exercise room. **Guest Services:** valet and coin laundry. **Featured Amenity:** full hot breakfast.

HOLIDAY INN EXPRESS & SUITES   928/317-1400

Hotel. Rates not provided. **Address:** 2044 S Ave 3 E 85365 **Location:** I-8 exit 3, just n, then just w on Frontage Rd. **Facility:** 120 units. 4 stories, interior corridors. **Pool(s):** heated outdoor. **Activities:** hot tub, exercise room. **Guest Services:** valet and coin laundry, area transportation.

HOMEWOOD SUITES BY HILTON YUMA   (928)782-4100

Extended Stay Hotel $89-$169 **Address:** 1955 E 16th St 85365 **Location:** I-8 exit 2 (16th St/US 95), 0.4 mi e. **Facility:** 108 kitchen units. 4 stories, interior corridors. **Terms:** 1-7 night minimum stay, cancellation fee imposed. **Pool(s):** heated outdoor. **Activities:** picnic facilities, exercise room. **Guest Services:** valet and coin laundry, area transportation.

AAA Benefit: Members save up to 10%!

LA FUENTE INN & SUITES   (928)329-1814

Hotel
$69-$179

Address: 1513 E 16th St 85365 **Location:** I-8 exit 2 (16th St/US 95), just e. **Facility:** 96 units. 2 stories (no elevator), exterior corridors. **Terms:** cancellation fee imposed. **Pool(s):** heated outdoor. **Activities:** hot tub, picnic facilities, exercise room. **Guest Services:** coin laundry. **Featured Amenity:** full hot breakfast. (See ad p. 309.)

QUALITY INN   (928)782-1200

Hotel $64-$159 **Address:** 1691 S Riley Ave 85365 **Location:** I-8 exit 2 (16th St/US 95), just w. **Facility:** 81 units. 3 stories, interior corridors. **Pool(s):** outdoor. **Activities:** hot tub, picnic facilities, exercise room. **Guest Services:** valet and coin laundry.

RADISSON HOTEL YUMA (928)783-8000

▼▼▼ **Hotel** $99-$180 **Address:** 1501 S Redondo Center Dr 85365 **Location:** I-8 exit 2 (16th St/US 95), just w, then just n. **Facility:** 154 units. 4 stories, interior corridors. **Amenities:** *Some:* safes. **Dining:** Market Seafood & Grill, see separate listing. **Pool(s):** heated outdoor, heated indoor. **Activities:** hot tub, exercise room. **Guest Services:** complimentary and valet laundry, area transportation.

SHILO INN HOTEL & SUITES-YUMA 928/782-9511

▼▼ ▼▼ **Hotel.** Rates not provided. **Address:** 1550 S Castle Dome Ave 85365 **Location:** I-8 exit 2 (16th St/US 95), just e to Yuma Palms Pkwy, just n, then just w. **Facility:** 135 units, some kitchens. 4 stories, interior corridors. **Terms:** check-in 4 pm. **Pool(s):** heated outdoor. **Activities:** sauna, hot tub, steamroom, exercise room. **Guest Services:** valet and coin laundry.

▼ See AAA listing p. 308 ▼

SPRINGHILL SUITES BY MARRIOTT (928)783-7853

◆◆◆ Hotel $98-$174 **Address:**
1825 E 18th St 85365 **Location:** I-8 exit
2 (16th St/US 95), 0.5 mi e to Sunridge
Dr, 0.3 mi s, then just e. **Facility:** 80
units. 3 stories, interior corridors.

AAA Benefit:
Members save 5%
or more!

Pool(s): heated outdoor. **Activities:** hot tub, picnic facilities, exercise room. **Guest Services:** valet and coin laundry, area transportation.

TOWNEPLACE SUITES BY MARRIOTT (928)783-6900

◆◆◆ **Extended Stay Hotel**
$93-$198 **Address:** 1726 S Sunridge Dr
85365 **Location:** I-8 exit 2 (16th St/US
95), just e to Sunridge Dr, then just s. **Fa-**

AAA Benefit:
Members save 5%
or more!

cility: 81 units, some two bedrooms, efficiencies and kitchens. 4 stories, interior corridors. **Pool(s):** heated outdoor. **Activities:** exercise room. **Guest Services:** valet and coin laundry.

WINGATE BY WYNDHAM YUMA (928)783-1400

◆◆◆
Hotel
$99-$139

Address: 1760 S Sunridge Dr 85365
Location: I-8 exit 2 (16th St/US 95), just
e to Sunridge Dr, then just s. **Facility:** 76
units. 3 stories, interior corridors. **Terms:**
cancellation fee imposed. **Amenities:**
safes. **Pool(s):** outdoor. **Activities:** hot
tub, game room, picnic facilities, exercise room. **Guest Services:** coin
laundry. **Featured Amenity:** breakfast
buffet.

YUMA CABANA MOTEL 928/783-8311

◆ **Motel.** Rates not provided. **Address:** 2151 S 4th Ave 85364
Location: I-8 exit 2 (16th St/US 95), 1 mi w, then 0.5 mi s. **Facility:**
63 units, some efficiencies. 2 stories (no elevator), interior corridors.
Bath: shower only. **Pool(s):** outdoor. **Activities:** picnic facilities.
Guest Services: coin laundry.

WHERE TO EAT

AH-SO SUSHI & STEAK RESTAURANT 928/329-7442

◆◆ Japanese. Casual Dining. $9-$24 **AAA Inspector Notes:**
An upbeat eatery with dynamic teppan grill tables, the chefs put on a
show for diners. The range of sushi covers ahi tuna to yellowtail. **Fea-**
tures: full bar. **Address:** 1325 S Yuma Palms Pkwy, Suite B5 85365
Location: I-8 exit 2 (16th St/US 95), just e, then just n; adjacent to
movie theater. L D

BURGERS & BEER 928/783-3987

◆◆ American. Casual Dining. $5-$20 **AAA Inspector Notes:**
Hence the name, this casual sports bar restaurant offers a large variety of gourmet burgers along with American and Mexican favorites,
including breakfast items like the chile relleno omelette. This is a perfect place to watch the game due to the many large flat screen TVs.
Features: full bar, happy hour. **Address:** 321 W 20th St 85364 **Lo-**
cation: I-8 exit 2 (16th St/US 95), 1 mi w, 0.4 mi s on 4th Ave, then
just e. B L D

THE CROSSING RESTAURANT 928/726-5551

◆◆ American. Casual Dining. $7-$19 **AAA Inspector Notes:**
The owners of this local institution use the freshest ingredients for
their hearty, family-style meals. Flame-broiled chicken and the openfaced hot prime rib sandwich are popular choices. **Features:** full bar,
patio dining, happy hour. **Address:** 2690 S 4th Ave 85364 **Location:**
I-8 exit 2 (16th St/US 95), 1 mi w, then 1.5 mi s. L D

THE GARDEN CAFE 928/783-1491

◆◆ American. Casual Dining. $9-$12 **AAA Inspector Notes:**
Relax in a true garden setting, with trees overhead for shade, terraced areas for dining, a charming gazebo and cages of singing
birds. The menu offers freshly prepared salads, soups and sandwiches, including a tri-tip sandwich, perfect for heartier appetites,
along with Virginia ham and chicken selections. **Features:** patio
dining, Sunday brunch. **Reservations:** suggested. **Address:** 250
Madison Ave 85364 **Location:** I-8 exit 1 (Harold C. Giss Pkwy), 0.4
mi w, then just n. **Parking:** street only. B L

HUNTER STEAKHOUSE 928/783-1166

◆◆◆ Steak. Casual Dining. $18-$40 **AAA Inspector Notes:**
Classic. A local institution for decades, the dark wood masculine interior sets the stage for hearty cuts of steak, ribs, lamb chops, chicken
and seafood specialties, all served by a friendly and attentive staff.
Features: full bar, happy hour. **Reservations:** suggested. **Address:**
2355 S 4th Ave 85364 **Location:** I-8 exit 2 (16th St/US 95), 1 mi w,
then 0.8 mi s. L D

JACK & ROSIE'S STEAKHOUSE 928/783-9172

◆◆ Steak. Casual Dining. $14-$28 **AAA Inspector Notes:**
Classic. Since 1935, locals and visitors alike have been flocking to
this fun and casual tavern that serves expertly prepared steaks,
crispy fried chicken and fresh seafood. The friendly staff makes
diners feel right at home. **Features:** full bar. **Address:** 1551 5th St
85364 **Location:** Southeast corner of 16th Ave and 5th St.
D

JULIEANNA'S PATIO CAFE 928/317-1961

◆◆ American. Casual Dining. $9-$30 **AAA Inspector**
Notes: Located near a major medical center, this café has a colorfully
decorated dining room and a large, outdoor patio with brightly
painted, wrought-iron furnishings and metal sculptures. The young
and friendly waitstaff are watchful that guests should lack for nothing.
Features: full bar, patio dining, happy hour. **Address:** 1951 W 25th
St 85364 **Location:** I-8 exit 3 (SR 280), jct 24th St and 19th Ave, then
just s. L D

KNEADERS BAKERY & CAFE 928/783-4099

◆ Deli. Quick Serve. $7-$9 **AAA Inspector Notes:** Fresh
kneaded and baked bread is prepared on-site along with pastries,
salads and soups-all served in a comfortable country decor. **Ad-**
dress: 1651 E Castle Dome Ave 85364 **Location:** I-8 exit 2 (16th
St/US 95), just e. B L D

LA FONDA TORTILLA FACTORY 928/783-6902

◆◆ Mexican. Casual Dining. $9-$15 **AAA Inspector Notes:**
This casual restaurant serves authentic, Sonoran-style Mexican cuisine which makes it one of the most popular in Yuma. The homemade tamales are a local favorite. **Features:** beer & wine. **Address:**
1095 S 3rd Ave 85364 **Location:** Jct W 11th St. **Parking:** on-site and
street. B L D

LUTES CASINO 928/782-2192

◆ American. Casual Dining. $4-$7 **AAA Inspector Notes:** Not
really a casino, this is the oldest pool hall in Arizona, now serving
dogs and burgers with all the fixings. There still are some tables
where patrons can practice billiards amid movie poster-clad walls and
pictures (some a bit risqué), game machines and such ceiling art as
a large model helicopter and a full-size Schwinn bike. **Features:** full
bar, patio dining. **Address:** 221 S Main St 85364 **Location:** Just n of
Harold C. Giss Pkwy; center. L D

MARKET SEAFOOD & GRILL 928/783-8000

◆◆◆ American. Casual Dining. $10-$25 **AAA Inspector**
Notes: This bright and vibrant restaurant offers a popular lounge and
wine bar. The menu include items such as fresh fish, filet mignon,
scallops, lamb and calamari. **Features:** full bar, patio dining, happy
hour. **Reservations:** suggested. **Address:** 1501 S Redondo Center
Dr 85365 **Location:** I-8 exit 2 (16th St/US 95), just w, then just n; in
Radisson Hotel Yuma. B D

MOSTLY MUFFINS BAKERY & CAFE 928/783-7484

◆ Breads/Pastries Sandwiches. Quick Serve. $4-$8 **AAA In-**
spector Notes: In the wee hours of the morning, the kitchen staff is
busy making special treats for breakfast and hearty sandwiches and
soups for lunch. A casual atmosphere, good coffee and low-fat to
decadent muffins help diners start their day. **Features:** patio dining.
Address: 2451 W 16th St 85364 **Location:** I-8 exit 2 (16th St/US
95), 2.4 mi w. B L

NINJA SUSHI   928/782-4000

♦♦ Sushi. Casual Dining. $11-$30 **AAA Inspector Notes:** Diners can find fresh, tasty sushi in the middle of the desert, as this fun and popular spot proves. Other Japanese favorites such as teriyaki, udon and tempura also are available. **Features:** full bar. **Address:** 1400 E 16th St 85365 **Location:** I-8 exit 2 (16th St/US 95), just e. [L] [D]

PRISON HILL BREWING COMPANY   928/276-4001

♦♦ American. Casual Dining. $9-$14 **AAA Inspector Notes:** A local favorite, this friendly downtown spot features tasty and interesting eats like the yard bird and waffles, along with a good selection of burgers and salads. There always are a couple of home-brewed ales, plus more than a dozen rotating guest taps. **Features:** full bar, patio dining. **Address:** 278 S Main St 85364 **Location:** I-8 exit 1 (Giss Pkwy), 0.5 mi nw, then just n; downtown. **Parking:** on-site and street. [L] [D]

RIVER CITY GRILL   928/782-7988

♦♦ Seafood. Casual Dining. $18-$35 **AAA Inspector Notes:** Bright, eclectic decor and a friendly vibe sets the mood. Fresh fish are flown in from the Northwest. Try wild salmon with polenta blueberry jus or mustard-crusted halibut, but don't forget to leave room for homemade desserts like chocolate bread pudding. **Features:** full bar, patio dining. **Reservations:** suggested. **Address:** 600 W 3rd St 85364 **Location:** I-8 exit 1 (Harold C. Giss Pkwy), 1 mi w. **Parking:** on-site and street. [L] [D]

YUMA LANDING BAR & GRILL   928/782-7427

♦♦♦
American
Casual Dining
$5-$18

AAA Inspector Notes: *Historic.* On the historic site of the first plane landing in Arizona in 1911, this restaurant displays early city memorabilia throughout the dining rooms. Representative of the diverse selection of American, Mexican and Italian entrées are barbecue ribs, fried shrimp and fettuccine Alfredo. **Features:** full bar, happy hour. **Address:** 195 S 4th Ave 85364 **Location:** I-8 exit 172 (4th Ave) eastbound, 0.5 mi s; exit 1 (Harold C. Giss Pkwy) westbound, 1 mi w; in Historic Coronado Motor Hotel. [B] [L] [D]

YUMA PALACE   928/726-6669

♦♦♦ Asian Sushi. Casual Dining. $9-$25 **AAA Inspector Notes:** This restaurant is located on the business loop of the Interstate through town and close to the airport. Mandarin and Szechuan cuisine plus a wide variety of sushi dominate the offerings. The friendly staff provide attentive service. **Features:** full bar. **Address:** 350 E 32nd St 85364 **Location:** I-8 exit 2 (16th St/US 95) southbound, 0.5 mi w, then 2 mi s on Arizona Ave; exit 3 northbound, 1 mi s, then 2 mi w on I-8 business loop. [L] [D]

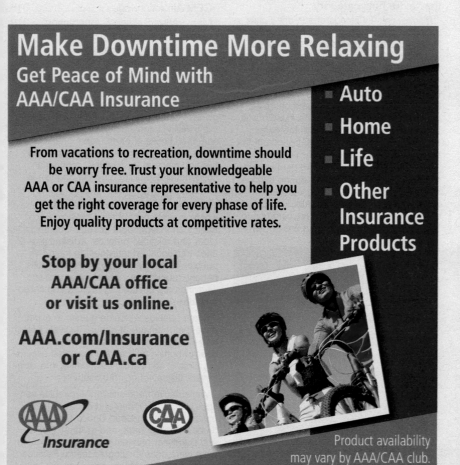

Bisti/De- Na-Zin Wilderness, Farmington

New Mexico

Welcome to New Mexico, deemed the home of the world's finest chile peppers, where you can fire up your taste buds with 10-plus varieties—most in the "extra hot" category.

Ristras, colorful strings of sun-dried chile peppers, drape café entryways and residential doorways. They're said to ward off evil, welcome visitors and alert guests to the fiery delicacies served there.

But chile isn't the only thing that heats things up. The radiant symbol that has come to represent New Mexico (found on its license plate and flag) is the Zia Pueblo sign for sun. Four rays extend from the center, signifying directions, seasons, periods of the day and stages of life.

Hundreds of rainbow-colored gentle giants fill the sunny sky with hot air during balloon festivals held statewide. The selection is anything but ordinary at the Albuquerque International Balloon Fiesta: It's common to see such diverse shapes as a castle, parrot,

Colorful pottery

spare tire, cola can, corncob and yes, even Dumbo, everyone's favorite flying elephant.

From the basket of a balloon you can glimpse centuries-old, flat-roofed houses and cliff dwellings constructed of adobe—sun-dried bricks of earth, sand, charcoal and grass. This mixture served as the primary building material for pueblos, communal settlements established by the Spanish in the 16th century.

Working pueblos remain at Taos and elsewhere in north-central New Mexico. Each retains an independent government, social order and religious practice. Artisans produce traditional art individual to their own pueblo: Turquoise jewelry, storyteller dolls, pottery, drums, carvings, Navajo rugs and weavings are coveted by visitors and collectors alike.

Some pueblos welcome guests to experience their heritage at annual festivals held in honor of the pueblo's patron saint. Corn, deer or buffalo dances are executed according to strict standards, culminating in a flamboyant display of colorful costumes.

While native traditions at the pueblos continue, only stark stone and adobe walls remain at the uninhabited Chaco Culture National Historical Park, and at Aztec Ruins and Bandelier national monuments. Explore what were once thriving Ancestral Puebloan communities; multistory cliff dwellings with remnants of hundreds of rooms, kivas (ceremonial meeting halls) and petroglyphs offer a warm welcome into the state's rich cultural past.

Sizzling Secrets

Southeastern New Mexico was a hotbed of controversy when, in 1947, a farmer discovered exotic metal debris on a sheep ranch. Some say it was the wreckage of a flying saucer, while others believe it to be the result of tests performed by the U.S. Air Force.

The mysteries surrounding what was dubbed the "Roswell Incident" make the International UFO Museum & Research Center in Roswell all the more intriguing. Don't miss the annual Roswell UFO Festival—held in July—where aliens are the hot ticket.

Or you can learn more about another top-secret scientific development—the Manhattan Project. Los Alamos was chosen as the hot spot for a weapons laboratory that developed and tested the atomic bomb during World War II. Visit the Bradbury Science Museum and peruse artifacts from the project.

If you can't stand the heat, pack a jacket and head for the cool solace of Carlsbad Caverns. At 830 feet below ground, the three-level Big Room begs exploration. Arguably one of the world's biggest underground chambers, it encompasses 8 acres—and at 56 F, it's definitely cool.

Recreation

From snow-clad mountains and sandy desert lowlands to rusty looking canyons and verdant timbered forests, the New Mexico landscape is a tapestry of colors and shapes that can be enjoyed in any season.

North-central New Mexico is *the* place for snow skiing. Sandia Peak Ski Area, just east of Albuquerque in the Cibola National Forest, packs a variety of trails, bowls and catwalks into a wedge of mountain.

Santa Fe Ski Area, north of Santa Fe, attracts families and first-timers to its groomed slopes for downhill skiing. With runs for beginning, intermediate and advanced skiers as well as freestyle areas for both snowboarding and skiing, Angel Fire Resort, east of Taos, is another family favorite.

Alpine skiing is the winter sport of choice at Taos Ski Valley, where snowfall averages more than 300 inches per year—the most in the state—and the vertical drop exceeds 2,600 feet.

Enchanted Forest, east of Red River; Sugarite Canyon State Park, on the Colorado border near Raton; and Manzano Mountain State Park, southeast of Albuquerque, welcome cross-country skiers.

When the snow melts, shift gears and explore the state by bicycle. Trails in southern New Mexico are as varied as the terrain. Fresnal Canyon Loop traverses the Sacramento Mountains foothills, just northeast of Alamogordo, passing through villages and orchards. Race the jackrabbits on a 4.5-mile loop around Tortugas Mountain, 1 mile southeast of Las Cruces. This desertlike area's riding surface comes in three textures: rocky, sandy and smooth.

Bicycling on paved surfaces can be a family event at Chaco Culture National Historical Park, in the northwest. An easy 9-mile circle tour begins at the visitor center and offers stops at several archeological ruins. The king of the road-rides may well be a 70-mile round-trip excursion via state and forest roads from Carlsbad to Sitting Bull Falls, in Lincoln National Forest.

With some 1,500 miles of trails, Gila National Forest, in the southwest, invites camping, hiking and backpacking. State parks, too, cater to this trinity of outdoor activities. Strike camp beside Elephant Butte Lake in that state park; walk among the aspens in Hyde Memorial; or press deep into primitive Morphy Lake State Park's backwoods.

The spring thaw creates a flood of whitewater rafting opportunities in northern New Mexico, especially on the Rio Grande and Rio Chama.

Albuquerque International Balloon Fiesta

Historic Timeline

1598	Conquistador Juan de Oñate takes possession of New Mexico for Spain.
1680	The victorious Pueblo Rebellion expels Spanish rule.
1850	New Mexico becomes a U.S. territory.
1862	Key Civil War battles are waged at Glorieta Pass and Valverde.
1864	Col. Kit Carson forces more than 8,000 Navajos to make the 300-mile Long Walk to Bosque Redondo.
1912	New Mexico is admitted to the Union as the 47th state.
1916	The United States invades Mexico after Pancho Villa attacks Columbus.
1945	The United States tests the first atomic bomb at Trinity Site.
1947	Reports of a crashed UFO spark media interest in Roswell.
1986	The United States' deepest limestone cave is discovered in Carlsbad Caverns National Park.
2010	Santa Fe celebrates its 400th anniversary.

What To Pack

Temperature Averages Maximum/Minimum	JANUARY	FEBRUARY	MARCH	APRIL	MAY	JUNE	JULY	AUGUST	SEPTEMBER	OCTOBER	NOVEMBER	DECEMBER
Albuquerque	47/23	53/27	59/32	70/41	80/51	89/60	92/65	90/63	83/58	72/45	57/32	47/25
Carlsbad	61/27	65/31	73/38	81/46	88/54	95/63	95/66	94/65	89/59	79/47	69/35	59/27
Clayton	47/19	50/22	55/25	66/36	74/46	83/55	87/60	86/60	80/51	69/40	60/28	49/21
Las Cruces	57/28	64/31	70/37	79/45	88/53	96/61	97/67	95/66	91/59	82/47	67/33	59/29
Roswell	55/21	61/25	68/31	78/42	86/50	94/60	95/64	93/62	86/54	77/42	69/29	57/22
Santa Fe	40/19	43/23	51/29	59/35	68/43	78/52	80/57	79/56	73/49	62/39	50/28	41/20

From the records of The Weather Channel Interactive, Inc.

Good Facts To Know

ABOUT THE STATE

POPULATION: 2,059,179.

AREA: 121,590 square miles; ranks 5th.

CAPITAL: Santa Fe.

HIGHEST POINT: 13,161 ft., Wheeler Peak.

LOWEST POINT: 2,842 ft., Red Bluff Reservoir.

TIME ZONE(S): Mountain. DST.

GAMBLING

MINIMUM AGE FOR GAMBLING: 21.

REGULATIONS

TEEN DRIVING LAWS: No more than one passenger under the age of 21 is permitted (family members exempt). Driving is not permitted midnight-5 a.m. The minimum age for an unrestricted driver's license is 16 years, 6 months. Phone (888) 683-4636 for more information about New Mexico's driver's license regulations.

SEAT BELT/CHILD RESTRAINT LAWS: Seat belts required for driver and all passengers 18 and older. Children ages 7 through 17 must use child restraints or seat belts. Appropriate child restraints are required for children under age 7 or under 60 pounds. AAA recommends the use of seat belts and appropriate child restraints for the driver and all passengers.

CELLPHONE RESTRICTIONS: All drivers are prohibited from text messaging while driving. Instruction and provisional license holders may not use any wireless device while driving. In Santa Fe and Las Cruces drivers are also prohibited from using hand-held cell phones.

HELMETS FOR MOTORCYCLISTS: Required for riders under 18.

RADAR DETECTORS: Permitted.

MOVE OVER LAW: Driver is required to slow down and vacate the lane nearest stopped police, fire and rescue vehicles using audible or flashing signals.

FIREARMS LAWS: Vary by state or county. Contact New Mexico Department of Public Safety, 6301 Indian School Rd. N.E., Suite 310, Albuquerque, NM 87110; phone (505) 841-8053.

HOLIDAYS

HOLIDAYS: Jan. 1 ▪ Martin Luther King Jr. Day, Jan. (3rd Mon.) ▪ Memorial Day, May (last Mon.) ▪ July 4 ▪ Labor Day, Sept. (1st Mon.) ▪ Columbus Day, Oct. (2nd Mon.) ▪ Veterans Day, Nov. 11 ▪ Thanksgiving, Nov. (4th Thurs.) ▪ Presidents Day (observed day after Thanksgiving) ▪ Christmas, Dec. 25.

MONEY

TAXES: New Mexico has a 5.13 percent gross receipts tax, with a local option for additional increments of up to 3.5 percent.

VISITOR INFORMATION

INFORMATION CENTERS: State welcome centers that provide maps, weather information, brochures and information about attractions, accommodations, historic sites, parks and events are at I-10W near Anthony ▪ US 64/84 at Chama ▪ I-40 exit 22 at Gallup ▪ I-40W near Glenrio ▪ I-10E exit 20 at Lordsburg ▪ I-25 exit 451 near Raton ▪ I-25 mile marker 269, 17 miles south of Santa Fe, near the Santo Domingo Indian Reservation ▪ at 491 Old Santa Fe Tr. in downtown Santa Fe ▪ and at US 60/70/84 near Texico.

ROAD CONDITIONS: The State Department of Transportation provides current information about road closures and conditions; phone (800) 432-4269.

SPECIAL NOTE: Plague bacilli, a condition promoted by fleas, is endemic to New Mexico. Pet owners are advised to provide flea protection for their animals.

FURTHER INFORMATION FOR VISITORS:
New Mexico Department of Tourism
Lamy Building
491 Old Santa Fe Tr.
Santa Fe, NM 87501-2753
(505) 827-7336
(800) 545-2070

NATIONAL FOREST INFORMATION:
Southwestern Region
333 Broadway Blvd. S.E.
Albuquerque, NM 87102
(505) 842-3293
(877) 444-6777
TTY (505) 842-3198 (reservations)

FISHING AND HUNTING REGULATIONS:
Department of Game and Fish
1 Wildlife Way
Santa Fe, NM 87507
(505) 476-8000

RECREATION INFORMATION:
State Parks Division
1220 S. St. Francis Dr.
Santa Fe, NM 87505
(505) 476-3200
(888) 667-2757

New Mexico Annual Events
Please call ahead to confirm event details.

JANUARY

- Souper Bowl / Albuquerque
505-349-2052
- Taos Winter Wine Festival
Taos Ski Valley
505-946-8506
- New Mexico Filmmakers
Showcase / Albuquerque
505-476-5671

FEBRUARY

- For the Love of Art Month
Las Cruces
575-523-6403
- ARTFeast / Santa Fe
505-992-2787
- Mount Taylor Winter
Quadrathlon / Grants
505-285-3542

MARCH

- Rio Grande Arts and Crafts
Festival / Albuquerque
505-292-7457
- Rockhound Roundup
Deming
575-544-9019
- National Fiery Foods and
Barbecue Show
Albuquerque
505-873-8680

APRIL

- American Indian Week
Albuquerque
505-843-7270
- Park 'N the Park
Rio Rancho
505-891-5015
- Gathering of Nations
Powwow / Albuquerque
505-836-2810

MAY

- Northern New Mexico Fine
Arts and Crafts Guild
Cathedral Park Show
Santa Fe
505-473-5590
- Blessing of the Field
Las Cruces
505-522-4100
- Truth or Consequences
Fiesta / Truth Or
Consequences
505-740-7542

JUNE

- New Mexico Arts and
Crafts Fair / Albuquerque
505-884-9043
- Rodeo de Santa Fe
Santa Fe
505-471-4300
- Fine Art and Wine Festival
Red River
575-754-2366, ext. 1

JULY

- Fiestas de Taos / Taos
800-732-8267
- Freedom Days / Farmington
505-326-7602
- Santa Fe International Folk
Art Market / Santa Fe
505-467-1197

AUGUST

- Inter-Tribal Indian
Ceremonial / Gallup
505-863-3896
- Great Southwestern
Antiques Show
Albuquerque
505-255-4054
- Hot Chili Days, Cool
Mountain Nights / Red River
254-968-8505

SEPTEMBER

- Santa Fe Wine and Chile
Fiesta / Santa Fe
505-438-8060
- New Mexico State Fair
Albuquerque
505-222-9700
- Chile Festival / Hatch
505-252-0431

OCTOBER

- Albuquerque International
Balloon Fiesta
Albuquerque
505-821-1000
- Lincoln County Cowboy
Symposium
Ruidoso Downs
575-378-4431
- Harvest Festival / Santa Fe
505-471-2261

NOVEMBER

- Renaissance ArtsFaire
Las Cruces
575-523-6403
- River of Lights
Albuquerque
505-768-2000
- Las Cruces International
Mariachi Concerts and
Festival / Las Cruces
575-525-1735

DECEMBER

- New Mexico Bowl
Albuquerque
505-925-5999
- WinterFest / Los Alamos
505-661-4844
- Old-Fashioned Christmas
Truth Or Consequences
575-740-3902

Chile peppers, Santa Fe

Historic Route 66

White Sands National
Monument

San Francisco de Asis Church, Taos

Welcome to Roswell

Index: Great Experience for Members

AAA editor's picks of exceptional note

Chimney Rock

Gila Cliff Dwellings
National Monument

San Miguel Chapel

Anderson-Abruzzo
Albuquerque
International Balloon
Museum

See Orientation map on p. 326 for corresponding grid coordinates, if applicable.

Trust the recommendations of AAA/CAA
travel experts to make a good trip great

New Mexico
Atlas Section

ROADS/HIGHWAYS
- INTERSTATE
- CONTROLLED ACCESS
- CONTROLLED ACCESS TOLL
- TOLL ROAD
- PRIMARY DIVIDED
- PRIMARY UNDIVIDED
- SECONDARY DIVIDED
- SECONDARY UNDIVIDED
- LOCAL DIVIDED
- LOCAL UNDIVIDED
- UNPAVED ROAD
- UNDER CONSTRUCTION
- TUNNEL
- PEDESTRIAN ONLY
- AUTO FERRY
- PASSENGER FERRY
- SCENIC BYWAY
- DISTANCE BETWEEN MARKERS
- EXIT NUMBER-FREE/TOLL
- INTERCHANGE FULL/PARTIAL
- WELCOME/INFORMATION CENTER
- REST AREA/ SERVICE CENTER

ROAD SHIELDS
- INTERSTATE/BUSINESS
- U.S./STATE/COUNTY
- FOREST/INDIAN
- TRANS-CANADA
- PROVINCIAL AUTOROUTE/ KING'S HIGHWAY
- MEXICO
- HISTORIC ROUTE 66
- REFERENCE PAGE INDICATOR

POINTS OF INTEREST
- TOWN
- NATIONAL CAPITAL
- STATE/PROVINCIAL CAPITAL
- AAA/CAA CLUB LOCATION
- FEATURE OF INTEREST
- COLLEGE/UNIVERSITY
- CAMPGROUND INFORMATION PROVIDED BY WOODALL'S ®
- CUSTOMS STATION
- HISTORIC
- LIGHTHOUSE
- MONUMENT/MEMORIAL
- STATE/PROVINCIAL PARK
- NATIONAL WILDLIFE REFUGE
- SKI AREA
- SPORTS COMPLEX
- DAM

AREAS OF INTEREST
- INDIAN
- MILITARY
- PARK
- FOREST
- GRASSLANDS
- HISTORIC
- INT'L/REGIONAL AIRPORT
- INCORPORATED CITY

BOUNDARIES
- INTERNATIONAL
- STATE
- COUNTY
- TIME ZONE
- CONTINENTAL DIVIDE

CITIES/TOWNS
are color-coded by size, showing where to find AAA Approved and Diamond rated lodgings or restaurants listed in the AAA TourBook guides and on AAA.com:
- Red – major destinations and capitals; many listings
- Black – destinations; some listings
- Grey – no listings

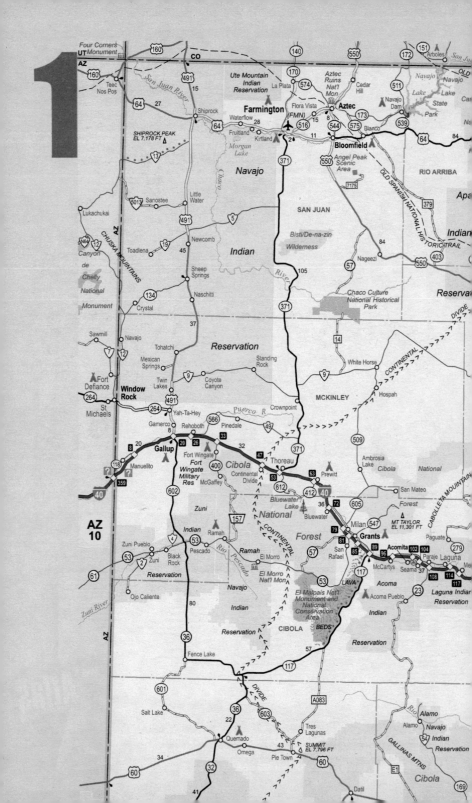

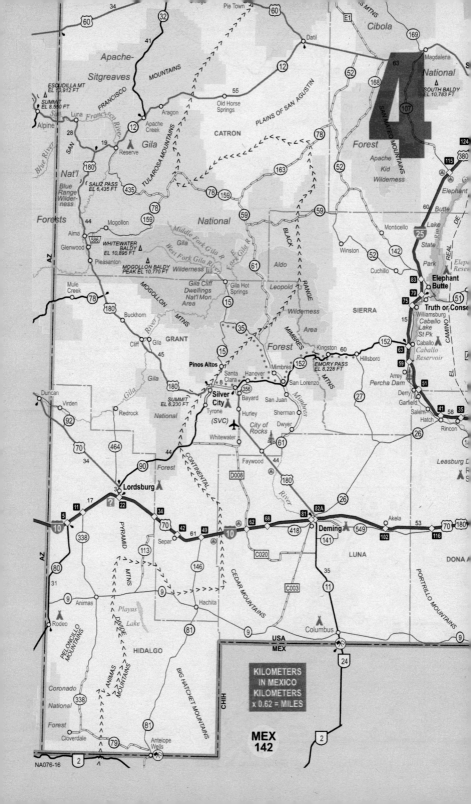

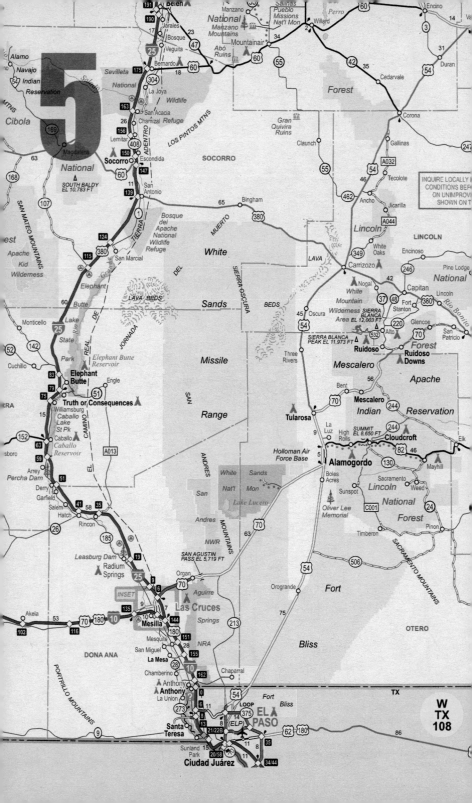

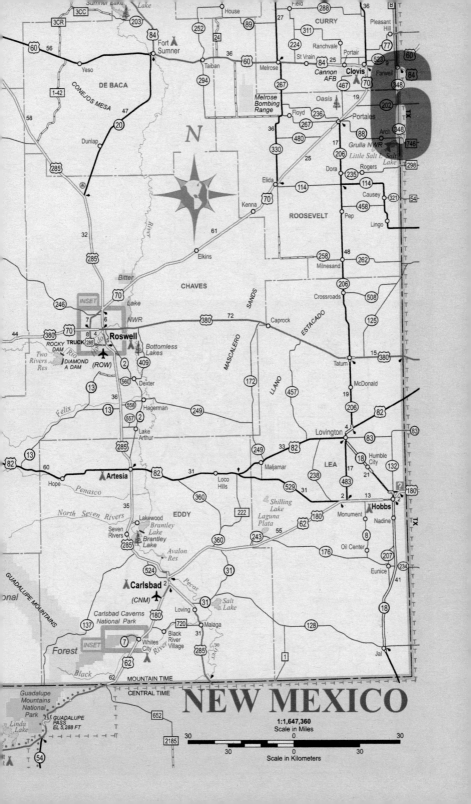

NEW MEXICO

1:1,647,360
Scale in Miles

30   30

Scale in Kilometers

30   0   30

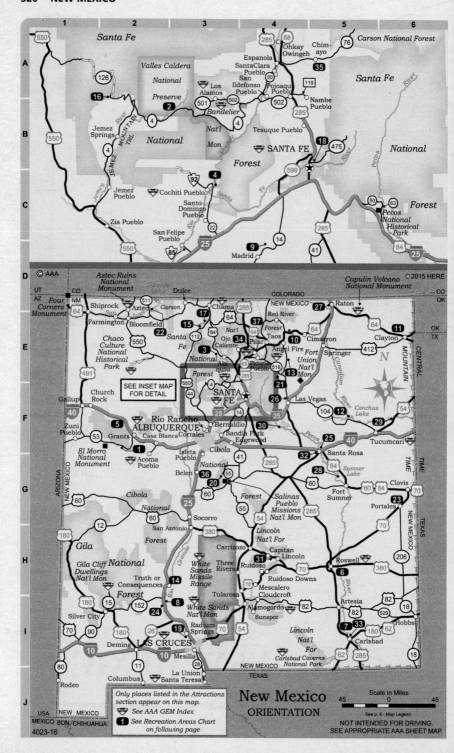

New Mexico
ORIENTATION

Scale in Miles
45   0   45

See p. 6 - Map Legend

NOT INTENDED FOR DRIVING.
SEE APPROPRIATE AAA SHEET MAP.

Only places listed in the Attractions section appear on this map.
☙ See AAA GEM Index
❶ See Recreation Areas Chart on following page

4023-16

Recreation Areas Chart

The map location numerals in column 2 show an area's location on the preceding map.

	MAP LOCATION	CAMPING	PICNICKING	HIKING TRAILS	BOATING	BOAT RAMP	BOAT RENTAL	FISHING	SWIMMING	PETS ON LEASH	BICYCLE TRAILS	WINTER SPORTS	VISITOR CENTER	LODGE/CABINS	FOOD SERVICE
NATIONAL PARKS *(See place listings.)*															
Chaco Culture (E-2) 33,974 acres. Northwest New Mexico.		•	•	•						•	•		•		
NATIONAL FORESTS *(See place listings.)*															
Carson (D-4) 1,500,000 acres. North-central New Mexico.		•	•	•				•		•	•	•	•		
Cibola (G-2) 1,625,542 acres. Central New Mexico.		•	•	•				•	•	•	•	•	•		
Gila (H-1) 3,321,000 acres. Southwestern New Mexico.		•	•	•	•	•		•	•	•	•	•	•		
Lincoln (H-4) 1,103,441 acres. South-central New Mexico. Horse rental.		•	•	•				•		•	•	•	•		•
Santa Fe (A-5) 1,600,000 acres. North-central New Mexico between the San Pedro Mountains and the Sangre de Cristo Mountains.		•	•	•				•		•	•	•	•	•	
NATIONAL CONSERVATION AREAS															
El Malpais (F-2) 376,000 acres 23 mi. s. of I-40 via SRs 53 and 117. *(See Grants p. 386.)*	❶	•	•	•						•	•		•		
Valles Caldera (B-2) 89,000 acres 18 mi. w. of Los Alamos off SR 4. *(See Los Alamos p. 396.)*	❷			•				•			•	•	•		
ARMY CORPS OF ENGINEERS															
Abiquiu Lake (E-3) 4,015 acres 7 mi. n.w. of Abiquiu via US 84. Water skiing. *(See Abiquiu p. 329.)*	❸	•	•	•	•	•		•	•	•			•		
Cochiti Lake (C-3) 1,200 acres 5 mi. n. of Pea Blanca on SR 22. Golfing, sailing, windsurfing. *(See Cochiti Pueblo p. 374.)*	❹	•	•	•	•	•	•	•	•	•			•		
STATE															
Bluewater Lake (F-2) 3,000 acres 28 mi. n.w. of Grants off I-40.	❺	•	•	•	•	•		•	•	•		•	•		
Bottomless Lakes (H-5) 1,400 acres 12 mi. s.e. of Roswell via US 380, then 3 mi. s. on SR 409. *(See Roswell p. 404.)*	❻	•	•	•	•			•	•	•			•		
Brantley Lake (I-5) 3,000 acres 12 mi. n. of Carlsbad off US 285.	❼	•	•		•	•		•	•	•			•		
Caballo Lake (I-3) 11,610 acres 16 mi. s. of Truth or Consequences off I-25. *(See Truth or Consequences p. 450.)*	❽	•	•		•	•		•	•	•			•		
Cerrillos Hills (D-4) 1,116 acres 4 mi. n. of Madrid on CR 59. Mountain biking; horse rental.	❾		•	•							•		•		
Cimarron Canyon (E-4) 33,000 acres 12 mi. w. of Cimarron via US 64. *(See Cimarron p. 371.)*	❿	•	•	•				•		•			•		
Clayton Lake (E-6) 471 acres 12 mi. n. of Clayton on SR 370. *(See Clayton p. 372.)*	⓫	•	•	•	•			•		•			•		
Conchas Lake (F-5) 290 acres 34 mi. n.w. of Tucumcari via SR 104. *(See Tucumcari p. 451.)*	⓬	•	•		•	•	•	•	•	•			•	•	
Coyote Creek (E-4) 80 acres 17 mi. n.e. of Mora on SR 434.	⓭	•	•	•				•		•			•		
Elephant Butte Lake (H-3) 40,056 acres 5 mi. n. of Truth or Consequences off I-25. *(See Truth or Consequences p. 450.)*	⓮	•	•	•	•	•	•	•	•	•			•	•	
El Vado Lake (E-3) 1,730 acres 4 mi. n.e. of El Vado off SR 112.	⓯	•	•	•	•	•		•	•	•			•	•	
Fenton Lake (A-1) 700 acres 38 mi. w. of Los Alamos via SRs 4 and 126. Canoeing, cross-country skiing; horse trails. Boats with electric motors only.	⓰	•	•		•	•		•		•		•	•		
Heron Lake (E-3) 4,107 acres 11 mi. w. of Tierra Amarilla via US 84 and SR 95.	⓱	•	•	•	•			•		•			•	•	
Hyde Memorial (B-5) 350 acres 8 mi. n.e. of Santa Fe on Hyde Park Rd.	⓲	•	•							•		•	•		•
Leasburg Dam (I-3) 240 acres 15 mi. n.w. of Las Cruces via I-25 and SR 157. Canoeing; playground. Non-motorized boats only.	⓳	•	•		•			•	•	•			•		
Manzano Mountains (G-3) 160 acres 16 mi. n.w. of Mountainair via SR 55.	⓴	•	•	•						•		•	•		
Morphy Lake (F-4) 30 acres 25 mi. n. of Las Vegas off SR 518. *(See Las Vegas p. 393.)*	㉑	•	•	•	•	•		•		•					
Navajo Lake (E-2) 21,000 acres 23 mi. n.e. of Bloomfield on SR 511. *(See Bloomfield p. 363.)*	㉒	•	•	•	•	•	•	•	•	•	•	•	•	•	

Recreation Areas Chart

The map location numerals in column 2 show an area's location on the preceding map.

	MAP LOCATION	CAMPING	PICNICKING	HIKING TRAILS	BOATING	BOAT RAMP	BOAT RENTAL	FISHING	SWIMMING	PETS ON LEASH	BICYCLE TRAILS	WINTER SPORTS	VISITOR CENTER	LODGE/CABINS	FOOD SERVICE
Oasis (G-6) 193 acres 6.5 mi. n. of Portales off SR 467. *(See Portales p. 402.)*	23	•	•	•				•		•	•		•		
Percha Dam (I-2) 84 acres 21 mi. s. of Truth or Consequences via I-25. Playground.	24	•	•					•	•	•			•		
Santa Rosa Lake (F-5) 500 acres 7 mi. n. of Santa Rosa via SR 91. Water skiing; nature trail. *(See Santa Rosa p. 437.)*	25	•	•	•	•	•		•	•	•	•		•		
Storrie Lake (F-4) 83 acres 4 mi. n. of Las Vegas off SR 518. Windsurfing. *(See Las Vegas p. 393.)*	26	•	•	•	•			•	•	•			•		
Sugarite Canyon (D-5) 3,600 acres 10 mi. n.e. of Raton via SR 72. Historic. Canoeing, cross-country skiing, mountain climbing, snowmobiling; horse trails. *(See Raton p. 403.)*	27	•	•	•	•			•		•		•	•		
Sumner Lake (G-5) 6,700 acres 16 mi. n.w. of Fort Sumner on US 84.	28	•	•	•	•	•		•	•	•	•		•		
Ute Lake (F-6) 1,500 acres 2 mi. s.w. of Logan on SR 540. *(See Tucumcari p. 451.)*	29	•	•		•	•	•	•	•	•			•		
Villanueva (F-4) 1,679 acres 31 mi. s.w. of Las Vegas via I-25 and SR 3.	30	•	•	•				•	•	•			•		
OTHER															
Fort Stanton (H-4) 24,000 acres 7.7 mi. w. of Lincoln on US 380, then 1 mi. s. on SR 220. Caving; horse trails. *(See Lincoln p. 394.)*	31	•	•	•							•				
Janes-Wallace Memorial (G-4) 1 mi. s. of Santa Rosa on SR 91. *(See Santa Rosa p. 437.)*	32	•	•					•		•					
Lake Carlsbad (I-5) In Carlsbad on Park Dr. Water skiing. *(See Carlsbad p. 364.)*	33	•	•		•	•			•				•		
Orilla Verde (E-4) 2,840 acres 6 mi. n of Pilar on SR 570.	34	•	•	•	•			•		•	•		•		
Santa Cruz Lake (A-5) 2,543 acres 14 mi. e. of Española via SRs 76 and 4.	35	•	•	•	•	•		•		•					
Sen. Willie M. Chavez (G-3) 150 acres on the Rio Grande at Belen.	36	•	•	•				•		•	•				
Wild Rivers (E-4) 20,300 acres 5 mi. w. of Questa off SR 378.	37	•	•	•	•	•		•		•	•		•		

ABIQUIU (E-3) pop. 231, elev. 6,063'

In the mid-18th century Abiquiu (AH-be-cue) was one of several settlements the Spanish government provided for *Genízaros,* people of mixed blood who were either the Spaniards' own prisoners or captives ransomed from the Comanches or Apaches and later released from slavery. By 1778 the community was a stop on the Old Spanish Trail, which led westward to an infant coastal hamlet called Los Angeles.

Abiquiu was the birthplace of Padre Antonio José Martínez, the priest credited with the establishment of the Southwest's first coeducational school. His lifelong crusade to educate his people took him to Taos in 1826, then into politics.

The area is known for its colorful, rugged rock formations and other scenic features. Abiquiu Lake *(see Recreation Areas Chart),* 7 miles northwest via US 84, provides opportunities for water sports while controlling downstream flooding and sedimentation. The Carson and Santa Fe national forests surround the lake.

As anyone who has seen her landscapes would conclude, artist Georgia O'Keeffe spent winters and springs in Abiquiu and summers and autumns at nearby Ghost Ranch. Along US 84 are some of the views O'Keeffe captured in her work. Guided tours of the Georgia O'Keeffe Home and Studio are available only by reservation mid-March through November. Tours, which accommodate 12 people, require advanced payment and depart from the nearby Abiquiu Inn; phone (505) 685-4539. The artist's ashes were scattered at Pedernal, the flat-topped mountain to the south of Ghost Ranch.

GHOST RANCH is 12 mi. n.w. on US 84. Georgia O'Keeffe owned a summerhouse and painted familiar scenes at this 21,000-acre former ranch, now a Presbyterian education and retreat center. In addition to the spectacular climb to Chimney Rock, hikers can tackle Box Canyon (a 4-mile round trip that reaches elevations of 6,900 feet) and the more difficult Kitchen Mesa trail, a 5-mile trek that takes several hours to complete.

Also at the site are a meditation labyrinth and two museums. O'Keeffe Landscape Trail Rides are offered year-round; reservations are required. Georgia O'Keeffe at Ghost Ranch Landscape Tours are given mid-March through Thanksgiving weekend. **Hours:** Ranch open Mon.-Sat. 7-7, Sun. 9-5. O'Keeffe Trail Ride departs daily at 10 and 2 (sunset trail rides depart Fri.-Sat. at 6:10 p.m.). Landscape Tours are given Tues.-Fri. at 1:30 and 3. **Cost:** Grounds and conservation fee $3. Landscape tour $29. Walking tour $39. O'Keefe Trail Ride $85. **Phone:** (505) 685-1000 or (877) 804-4678. 🍴 🏕

Chimney Rock is 12 mi. n.w. on US 84. The trailhead is located at the arroyo behind the Ghost Ranch museums and past the Corral Block complex.

This is the most popular of several hiking trails at Ghost Ranch, and deservedly so; it's an absolute stunner. The well-marked trail ascends a ridge to the top of a red rock mesa that is within striking distance of Chimney Rock, a tall, spire-shaped rock. Along the way you'll see drought-tolerant vegetation like cholla, prickly pear cactus, saltbush and piñon pine.

After reaching the top of the mesa hikers approach Chimney Rock from behind, getting close enough for a dizzying look at the valley floor below. Spectacular 360-degree vistas take in the Piedra Lumbre basin, Mt. Pedernal on the western horizon and an array of multicolored sandstone and gypsum formations. The views as the trail climbs from 6,500 to 7,100 feet are splendid.

Note: The round-trip distance is 3 miles. Hikers should check in at the Ghost Ranch Welcome Center office before and after hiking. Wear hiking boots or non-slip athletic shoes and a hat (there's no shade) and bring water. Stay on the marked trail and do not attempt to climb any of the rock formations or get close to the soft rock edge. **Time:** Allow 2 hours minimum. **Hours:** Daily 8-5. **Cost:** $3 conservation fee. **Phone:** (505) 685-1000 or (877) 804-4678.

Florence Hawley Ellis Museum of Anthropology is 12 mi. n.w. on US 84. Part of the Ghost Ranch Education and Retreat Center, the museum features exhibits depicting 12,000 years of civilization within the Chama-Rio Grande region. Contemporary Southwestern art also is displayed. **Time:** Allow 30 minutes minimum. **Hours:** Mon.-Sat. 9-5, Sun. 1-5. **Cost:** (includes Ruth Hall Museum of Paleontology) $4; $3 (ages 60+); $2 (ages 2-12). **Phone:** (505) 685-1000, ext. 4118.

Ruth Hall Museum of Paleontology is 12 mi. n.w. on US 84. The museum at the Ghost Ranch Education and Retreat Center documents the area's rich fossil record, including the 1947 discovery of a small, predatory dinosaur named *Coelophysis,* the state fossil, and *Tawa hallae,* one of the oldest North American dinosaurs to have a complete skeleton. **Time:** Allow 30 minutes minimum. **Hours:** Mon.-Sat. 9-5, Sun. 1-5. **Cost:** (includes Florence Hawley Ellis Museum of Anthropology) $4; $3 (ages 60+); $2 (ages 2-12). **Phone:** (505) 685-1000.

THE ABIQUIU INN   505/685-4378

fyi Not evaluated. **Address:** 21120 Hwy 84 87510 **Location:** On US 84, 3 mi n of jct SR 554. Facilities, services, and décor characterize a mid-scale property.

GHOST RANCH B&B   505/685-4333

fyi Not evaluated. **Address:** HC 77, Box 11 87510 **Location:** On US 84, 12 mi n; between MM 224 and 225, 1 mi e on Private Dr 1708, follow signs. Facilities, services, and décor characterize an economy property.

WHERE TO EAT

CAFE ABIQUIU   505/685-4378

♦♦ Southwestern. Casual Dining. $10-$21 **AAA Inspector Notes:** This charming restaurant has a creative menu that includes selections from Mediterranean pizza to trout tacos. The dessert tray presentation will tempt with luscious creations from the summer berry pudding is a must-try. **Features:** beer & wine. **Address:** 21120 Hwy 84 87510 **Location:** On US 84, 3 mi n of jct SR 554.

 B L D

ACOMA PUEBLO (G-2) elev. 6,550'

One of the oldest continuously inhabited settlements in the country—evidence dates it from A.D. 1150—Acoma was well established when Francisco Vázquez de Coronado explored New Mexico in 1540. Inhabitants of Sky City, as the pueblo was known, worked fields on the plains 357 feet below their village and climbed back atop the mesa each night. Acoma afforded protection through decades of warfare, but the numerical superiority of the Spaniards proved too much. A final battle in 1599 vanquished the community.

Today only a few dozen Acomans live year-round on the mesa top; others live in nearby villages but return to Sky City for cultural observances. Visitors must register at the Sky City Cultural Center and Haak'u Museum at the base of the mesa, where permits and guided tours are available.

About 3 miles northeast is Enchanted Mesa, which looms 430 feet above the surrounding plain. According to Acoma tribal folklore, this was an ancestral settlement, but access to it was wiped out by a violent storm, leaving several Acoma women and children to starve on the mesa top.

ACOMA PUEBLO (SKY CITY) is off I-40 exit 102, then 16 mi. s. on R.R. 30/32 to the Sky City Mesa. Occupied by the Acomans since the second century, this 367-foot-high mesa is topped by one of the largest adobe structures in North America, the 1629 Spanish mission San Esteban del Rey. Building materials, including great log beams hand cut on Mount Taylor some 30 miles north, were manually carried to the summit by Acoman laborers.

The first Native American site to be designated as such by the National Trust for Historic Preservation, Acoma Pueblo is the 28th National Trust Historic Site. More than 15 Acoma families live on the mesa in dwellings without running water or electricity while observing the customs and traditions of their ancestors. Pottery makers showcasing their works for sale outside their homes are observed on guided walking tours featuring the pueblo, the plaza and the mission church, with its ecclesiastic art, tapestries and hand-carved woodwork.

Visitors to the mesa must arrange for a guide at the Sky City Cultural Center and Haak'u Museum, located at the base of the pueblo. Videotaping is not allowed on the mesa; a permit for still photography may be acquired at the cultural center. **Time:** Allow 3 hours minimum. **Hours:** Daily 8-5, Mar.-Oct.; Sat.-Sun. 9-4, rest of year. Tours given 8:30-3:30. Closed June 24 and 29, July 9-14 and 25, first weekend in Oct., first Sat. of Dec. and other days without notice. Phone ahead to confirm schedule. **Cost:** Guided tours $23; $20 (ages 60+, active military and college students with ID); $15 (ages 6-17); still-camera photography fee without tour $13. **Phone:** (505) 552-7869, or (800) 747-0181 for information about guided tours. ⊤⊤

Sky City Cultural Center and Haak'u Museum, off I-40 exit 102, then 16 mi. s. to the Sky City Mesa, features two galleries with temporary displays.

Note: Revealing clothing, video cameras and cell phones are not permitted. **Time:** Allow 1 hour minimum. **Hours:** Daily 8-5, Mar.-Oct.; Sat.-Sun. 9-4, rest of year. Tours given 8:30-3:30. Closed June 24 and 29, July 9-14 and 25, first weekend in Oct., first Sat. of Dec. and other days without notice. Phone ahead to confirm schedule. **Cost:** Guided tours $23; $20 (ages 60+, active military and college students with ID); $15 (ages 6-17); still-camera photography fee without tour $13. **Phone:** (505) 552-7869, or (800) 747-0181 for information about guided tours. ⊤⊤

ALAMOGORDO (I-4) pop. 30,403, elev. 4,335'

A ready water supply from the looming Sacramento Mountains prompted the town's founding as a railroad terminal in 1898. Alamogordo—Spanish for "fat cottonwood"—grew quickly as ranching, lumber production, farming and tourism were added to its assets. Nevertheless, modern development has been due primarily to the Holloman Air Force Base. Diversified industry, much of it related to space, also contributes to the economy.

The Air Force Missile Development Center conducts rocket and allied research at the base, while the National Solar Observatory in Sunspot *(see attraction listing p. 441)* works to advance knowledge of the sun. The nearby White Sands Missile Range *(see place listing p. 452)* administers the testing, evaluating, researching and assessing of military systems and commercial products.

Tularosa Basin Historical Society Museum, 1301 N. White Sands Blvd., focuses on local and regional history; phone (575) 434-4438. Leading eastward to Cloudcroft, US 82 passes through the state's only highway tunnel.

In July, Alamogordo hosts the Southern New Mexico Festival of Quilts.

Alamogordo Chamber of Commerce and Aubrey Dunn Sr. Visitor Center: 1301 N. White Sands Blvd., Alamogordo, NM 88310. **Phone:** (575) 437-6120 or (800) 826-0294.

ALAMEDA PARK AND ZOO is at 1321 N. White Sands Blvd., jct. US 54 and 10th St. The 7-acre zoo is home to 90 species of American and exotic wildlife including herd animals, cougars, bears, wolves and birds. Shaded lawns, recreation facilities and a playground are offered. **Hours:** Daily 9-5. Closed Jan. 1 and Christmas. **Cost:** $2.50; $1.50 (ages 3-11 and 60+). **Phone:** (575) 439-4290. ⊕

NEW MEXICO MUSEUM OF SPACE HISTORY is 2 mi. e. of US 54/70 at jct. Indian Wells Rd. and Scenic Dr. This large complex includes the museum, Stapp Air and Space Park, Astronaut Memorial Garden, International Space Hall of Fame and the Daisy Track. Exhibits honor pioneers from many nations and include international space program items. A special display chronicles the pivotal role that New Mexico plays in the ongoing race to space. A Smithsonian affiliate, the museum serves as the archive for Spaceport America.

At the Clyde W. Tombaugh IMAX Dome Theater and Planetarium, films are projected on a 40-foot wraparound dome screen. The Air & Space Park feature a high-speed sled, rocket engines and missiles.

Time: Allow 2 hours minimum. **Hours:** Daily 9-5; closed Thanksgiving and Christmas. IMAX films are shown daily on the hour 10-5, Memorial Day-Labor Day. **Cost:** Museum $6; $5 (ages 60+ and active military with ID); $4 (ages 3-12). IMAX admission $6; $5.50 (ages 60+, military with ID and New Mexico residents); $4.50 (ages 3-12). Combination ticket $10; $9 (ages 60+, military with ID and New Mexico residents); $7 (ages 3-12). IMAX admission may be higher for certain movies. **Phone:** (575) 437-2840 or (877) 333-6589, ext. 41153.

OLIVER LEE MEMORIAL STATE PARK is 12 mi. s. on US 54. A green oasis flourishes here around the springs of Dog Canyon, a deep ravine on the west-facing flank of the Sacramento Mountains. The park features historical exhibits and the restored 19th-century house of rancher Oliver Milton Lee. **Hours:** Park daily 24 hours. Visitor center daily 9-4. One-hour ranch house tours are given Sat.-Sun. at 3. **Cost:** $5 per private vehicle. **Phone:** (575) 437-8284.

TOY TRAIN DEPOT is 1 mi. n. on US 70/54 to 1991 N. White Sands Blvd. Hundreds of models and toy train displays are housed in an old depot. Built in 1898, a narrow-gauge train ride runs outdoors through neighboring Alameda Park. **Time:** Allow 30 minutes minimum. **Hours:** Depot Wed.-Sun. noon-4:30. Train departs Wed.-Sun. 12:30-4. **Cost:** $4. Train $4. Combination ticket $6. **Phone:** (575) 437-2855 or (888) 207-3564.

FAIRFIELD INN & SUITES BY MARRIOTT ALAMOGORDO
(575)437-4000

 Hotel $99-$160 **Address:** 300 Panorama Blvd 88310 **Location:** 1.6 mi s of jct US 82/70 and 54, just e. **Facility:** 73 units, some efficiencies. 4 stories, interior corridors. **Pool(s):** heated indoor. **Activities:** hot tub, exercise room. **Guest Services:** valet and coin laundry.

> **AAA Benefit:** Members save 5% or more!

HOLIDAY INN EXPRESS HOTEL & SUITES
(575)434-9773

 Hotel $103-$139 **Address:** 100 Kerry Ave 88310 **Location:** 1.6 mi s of jct US 54 and 70, just e on Panorama Blvd, just s. **Facility:** 80 units. 3 stories, interior corridors. **Terms:** cancellation fee imposed. **Pool(s):** heated indoor. **Activities:** hot tub, exercise room. **Guest Services:** valet and coin laundry.

MAGNUSON HOTEL AND SUITES ALAMOGORDO
575/437-2110

Motel
Rates not provided

Address: 1021 S White Sands Blvd 88310 **Location:** 1.6 mi s of jct US 82/70 and 54. **Facility:** 92 units, some kitchens. 2 stories (no elevator), exterior corridors. **Pool(s):** heated outdoor. **Activities:** exercise room. **Guest Services:** valet and coin laundry. **Featured Amenity: full hot breakfast.**

QUALITY INN
(575)434-4200

 Hotel $80 **Address:** 1020 S White Sands Blvd 88310 **Location:** 1.6 mi e of jct US 82/70 and 54. **Facility:** 91 units, some efficiencies and kitchens. 2 stories (no elevator), exterior corridors. **Pool(s):** heated outdoor. **Activities:** hot tub, exercise room. **Guest Services:** valet and coin laundry.

SUPER 8-ALAMOGORDO
(575)434-4205

Hotel
$59-$80

Address: 3204 N White Sands Blvd 88310 **Location:** Just s of jct US 54/70 and 82. Across from mall and adjacent to fairgrounds. **Facility:** 51 units. 2 stories (no elevator), interior corridors. **Guest Services:** coin laundry. **Featured Amenity: continental breakfast.**

WHITE SANDS MOTEL
575/437-2922

Motel
$59-$99

Address: 1101 S White Sands Blvd 88310 **Location:** 1.6 mi s of jct US 54/70 and 82. **Facility:** 24 units. 1 story, exterior corridors. **Featured Amenity: continental breakfast.**

WHERE TO EAT

MARGO'S MEXICAN FOOD
575/434-0689

 Regional Mexican. Family Dining. $5-$15 **AAA Inspector Notes:** This long-time restaurant serves heaping plates of fresh-made, traditional New Mexican favorites. **Features:** beer & wine. **Address:** 504 1st St 88310 **Location:** Just e of White Sands Blvd; downtown. [B] [L] [D]

MEMORIES RESTAURANT
575/437-0077

 American. Family Dining. $8-$25 **AAA Inspector Notes:** Set in a historic turn-of-the-twentieth-century Victorian home, this restaurant offers traditional American favorites served in a cozy atmosphere. The extensive menu includes homemade soups, salads, and a variety of beef, chicken and fish entrées. Save room for the luscious lemon meringue pie. **Features:** beer & wine. **Reservations:** suggested. **Address:** 1223 New York Ave 88310 **Location:** In historic downtown. **Parking:** on-site and street.

[L] [D] CALL

ALBUQUERQUE (F-3) pop. 545,852, elev. 4,957'

• Hotels p. 347 • Restaurants p. 350
• Attractions map p. 334
• Hotels & Restaurants map & index p. 339, 342

The Duke City. Burque. ABQ. They're all nicknames for New Mexico's largest city, and etymologically speaking, you wonder if it isn't because the full name (pronounced "AL-buh-kur-kee") isn't a bit of a tongue twister. While Burque and ABQ are simply shorter versions, the Duke City is a tribute to Don Francisco Fernández de la Cueva, the 8th Duke of Alburquerque of Spain—and somewhere along the way the first "r" got dropped.

Albuquerque was founded in 1706 as a Spanish colonial outpost and farming community along the Rio Grande. The town was laid out in traditional Spanish fashion: a central plaza bordered by a church on one side and government buildings on the other. Following the Mexican War in 1846-47 the U.S. government established a federal garrison to protect American settlers during the period of westward expansion, and the town became a major supply depot.

The arrival of the Atchison, Topeka and Santa Fe Railroad in 1880 ushered in a more modern era. The plaza, however, was bypassed; the rail yards were built 2 miles to the east. The area languished, but fortunately for the benefit of future visitors it didn't lose its trademark Spanish character; today Old Town is a tourist hot spot.

The city fills a wide valley between the Sandia Mountains to the east and the sweeping plateau country paralleling the north-south flowing Rio Grande to the west. It's a big city that doesn't look like one. The modest downtown skyline is no match for the twin summits of the Sandias (10,678-foot Sandia Crest and 9,702-foot South Sandia Peak). This small mountain range—running about 17 miles north to south and 4 to 8 miles east to west—is nevertheless steep and rugged, and gives Albuquerque a prominent backdrop. *Sandia* is the Spanish word for watermelon, and dramatic Southwestern sunsets often cast a pinkish hue over the mountains. The ponderosa pines growing along the top of the range even suggest (if you have an active imagination) a watermelon's green rind.

Adding a great deal more color are the fanciful shapes of hot-air balloons. Balloonists from all over the world come here to fly, especially during the 9-day 🎈 Albuquerque International Balloon Fiesta in the first full weekend of October. Not only are morning temperatures cool at this time of year, but an atmospheric effect known as the "Albuquerque Box" makes precision flying possible. The "box" is a set of predictable wind patterns that balloon navigators can take advantage of to change direction by varying their altitude, thus staying within a confined area.

The most dramatic sight at this major annual event is the mass ascensions, hundreds of spherical, brilliantly hued balloons taking to the air at once in coordinated flights. The spectacle is a photographer's dream. Also popular is the Special Shape Rodeo, when cows, pigs, soft drink cans and other nontraditional balloon shapes have their turn aloft. During evening Balloon Glows, pilots fire up their propane burners and masses of balloons are illuminated from within. The Anderson-Abruzzo Albuquerque International Balloon Museum in Balloon Fiesta Park is a great place to learn more about hot-air ballooning.

The high desert landscape in and around Albuquerque is a study in shades of brown. This region averages a meager 9 inches of rain a year, so the predominant vegetation is drought-tolerant sagebrush, which forms distinctive silvery-green clumps. Desert plants like yucca and juniper thrive. The sunlight is piercing, the sky huge. The wind often blows.

But it's hardly desolate. Wildlife abounds in the wetlands bordering the Rio Grande, as do cottonwood trees, which form a green ribbon along the river's course. Cottonwoods like water; their presence was a welcome sight to 19th-century pioneers traveling across the Great Plains, since a grove of cottonwoods meant shade, wood and a water supply.

Mexican heritage is evident in the prevalence of terra cotta and turquoise; the two colors even adorn concrete abutments along I-25. But New Mexican cuisine is more of a state affair. It's not Tex-Mex, and it's not California-style Mexican. The chief difference boils down to chile peppers.

New Mexico chiles come in two varieties, green and red (the color depends on the stage of ripeness when picked). They're served roasted or chopped, but usually as a sauce—and at many restaurants in town you're more likely to be asked "Green or red?" than "Sweet or unsweet tea?" If you want both, the proper response is "Christmas." A green chile-slathered cheeseburger is a local delicacy, along with blue corn enchiladas and sopaipillas, puffy pieces of fried bread that should be drizzled liberally with honey.

East-west Central Avenue navigates downtown Albuquerque, passes the University of New Mexico and runs through the funky Nob Hill district. The avenue is better known to out-of-towners as Historic Route 66, an icon for American auto travel.

During its golden era in the 1930s and '40s a slew of whimsically designed motels, diners and service stations opened along Route 66, beckoning motorists to stop. The completion of I-40 in 1959 was a blow, allowing drivers to zip along without being bogged down by stop signs and traffic lights. Most of the roadside architecture is gone, although you'll still see the occasional pueblo-inspired building and Art Deco storefront, reminders of the Duke City's good old days.

Albuquerque Convention and Visitors Bureau: 20 First Plaza N.W., Suite 601, Albuquerque, NM 87125. **Phone:** (505) 842-9918 or (800) 284-2282.

(See maps & indexes p. 339, 342.)

Self-guiding tours: Brochures of driving tours through Albuquerque and nearby communities are available from the convention and visitors bureau.

Shopping: The most interesting shopping isn't in chain stores; it's at places where you can immerse yourself in the distinctive culture of the Southwest. And there's no better place to start than Old Town's enticing collection of shops, galleries and artist studios.

You'll find Native American pottery, weavings, turquoise and silver jewelry, *retablos* (religious paintings), tinwork, custom-made furniture and more. The Aceves Old Town Basket & Rug Shop (301 Romero St. in Plaza Don Luis) is a treasure trove of ceramic figures, decorative tiles, knickknacks and hand-woven textiles; items are literally packed to the rafters here. Southwestern Handcrafts & Gifts (1919 Old Town Rd. in Plaza Hacienda) is a general store that carries everything from stoneware, Kachina dolls and decorated vases to Route 66 and Roswell alien souvenirs.

The Penfield Gallery of Indian Art (2043 S. Plaza) has Navajo rugs, sand paintings, and fetish and storyteller figures. Oaxacan wood carvings and finely crafted turquoise earrings are on display at the Tanner Chaney Gallery (323 Romero St. in Plazuela Sombra).

In addition to T-shirts, beads and the ubiquitous *ristras* (strings of dried red chiles), search out the unusual. For Mexican folk art (think *calavera* skeleton figures, tin ornaments and all things Frida Kahlo), check out Hispaniae (410 Romero St.). And no shopping trip to Old Town is complete without a stop at The Candy Lady (424 San Felipe St. NW, near The Albuquerque Museum of Art & History). Chile brittle, homemade fudge, a wall devoted to black licorice—it's all here, including sugar-free chocolate truffles for those feeling a bit guilty.

Nob Hill-Highland is another area with an offbeat selection of shops lining Central Avenue (Route 66). Antiques and collectibles dealers display their wares at the Antique Specialty Mall (4516 Central Ave.). As the name implies, Cowboys and Indians Antiques (4000 Central Ave.) features Indian baskets, Zuni fetishes, spurs, horse figure clocks and turquoise jewelry. Lilly Barrack (3205 Central Ave.) specializes in contemporary silver jewelry, often in designs paired with uncut gemstones.

Astro-Zombies (3100 Central Ave.) has a huge collection of comics (DC, Marvel, Dark Horse, Japanese manga), graphic novels and collectible toys from Star Wars characters to Godzilla. Next door is Masks Y Mas (Masks and More), where much of the merchandise revolves around Mexico's Day of the Dead celebration—skeleton figures, bizarre-looking masks and lots of original art. Even if you don't buy anything, the wildly colorful wall murals at both of these establishments are worth a look.

In downtown Albuquerque, TrendBenderz (311-B Gold Ave.) is a funky little boutique with vintage clothing, handmade jewelry and art created by New Mexico artists. There's more art (paintings, painted furniture, pet portraits), plus unusual jewelry and decorative home and office accessories, at Patrician Design (216 Gold Ave.).

A block north, Skip Maisel's Indian Jewelry & Crafts (510 Central Ave.) is in a historic building complete with a neon Indian chief sign. This large emporium is crammed with pottery, rugs, Hopi dolls, opal jewelry and cool items like the feather-bedecked charms called dream catchers. You also can observe Native American crafters at work in the store.

Another one-stop destination for quality arts and crafts is the Bien Mur Indian Market Center at Sandia Pueblo (I-25 to exit 234, then east on Tramway Road to Rainbow Road). The circular building's kiva-shaped showroom displays authentic Native American items like war bonnets, moccasins, musical instruments (flutes, rattles, drums), Zuni fetishes, Hopi and Navajo jewelry, Kachina carvings, rugs and pottery. An added attraction is the 107-acre buffalo preserve established by the pueblo—a section of which borders the parking lot—where you can observe these magnificent beasts in a natural setting.

Albuquerque's mall of choice is ABQ Uptown (Louisiana Boulevard and Indian School Road), an outdoor mix of retailers and restaurants that includes the usual suspects (Anthropologie, Eddie Bauer, Pottery Barn). Nearby at Louisiana and Menaul boulevards is the Coronado Center, with anchors JCPenney, Macy's and Sears as well as some 130 additional stores and eateries.

Nightlife: The KiMo Theatre (423 Central Ave. at 5th Street) opened in 1927 as a movie palace, boasting an architectural style dubbed "Pueblo Deco." This is one of only a handful of theaters in the country that incorporate Native American design motifs (ceiling beams that resemble logs, rows of buffalo skulls with glowing eyes), all carefully restored since the theater was rescued from the brink of demolition in the 1970s. Performances run the gamut from music to film showings to special events; for event information phone (505) 768-3522.

Burt's Tiki Lounge, downtown at 313 Gold Ave., is a small club with faux-tropical decor, a pool table and a no-cover-charge policy that brings in a variety of local bands from rock and punk to hip-hop and alt-country. DJs spin tunes on Wednesdays and Thursdays; it's closed on Sunday. Phone (505) 247-2878.

Shows at the Launchpad, 618 Central Ave. (look for the silver sputnik above the door) lean toward punk, hardcore and metal, with occasional appearances by national bands; phone (505) 764-8887. Blues, blues-rock and country-rock musicians take the stage for shows at Low Spirits, 2823 2nd St. (two blocks north of Menaul Boulevard in the Near North Valley neighborhood). The bar has an open mic happy hour weekdays from 4-8. For ticket information phone (505) 344-9555.

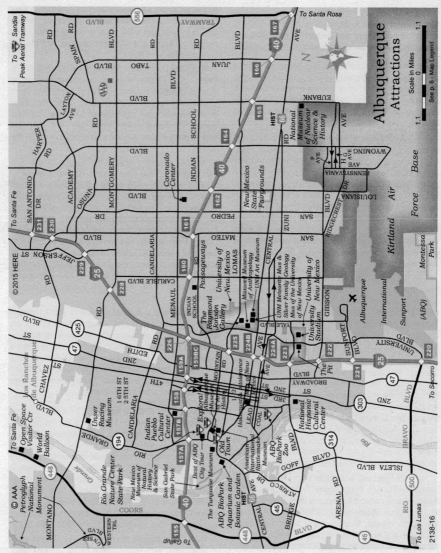

Albuquerque Attractions

Scale in Miles

See p. 6 - Map Legend

To Santa Rosa

©2015 HERE

2138-16

(See maps & indexes p. 339, 342.)

Q Bar, in the Hotel Albuquerque at Old Town (800 Rio Grande Blvd.), is a swanky lounge with a piano bar, plush seating areas and a billiards room. The cocktails here are pricey but expertly made. There's live music—mostly jazz—Tuesday through Saturday evenings; for table reservations phone (505) 225-5928. More casual is O'Niell's Irish Pub (4310 Central Ave. in Nob Hill), where local musicians play on Sunday at 4. Phone (505) 255-6782.

Vernon's Jazz Club is an intimate lounge that seats just 50 and aims to replicate the speakeasies of the Prohibition era, at least in ambience (subdued lighting, black walls, red stage curtains). It's the kind of atmosphere that will appeal to serious jazz fans.

There's a cover charge of $10 and a one-drink minimum per set. The club is inside Vernon's Hidden Valley Steakhouse, 6855 4th St. (in the northern suburb of Los Ranchos). Patrons are urged to "dress well." Reservations are recommended; phone (505) 341-0831.

Sandia Resort & Casino (north on I-25 to exit 234, then east a quarter mile on Tramway Road) provides the necessary sparkle for a glitzy evening out. This expansive resort sits on Sandia Pueblo land and has outstanding views of the Sandia Mountains. The casino features more than 2,100 slots, a bevy of table games (blackjack, craps, roulette, mini baccarat), live keno and a nonsmoking poker room. Big-name concerts take place at the resort's outdoor

(See maps & indexes p. 339, 342.)

amphitheater from late May to mid-September; for ticket and schedule information phone (800) 745-3000.

ABQ BIOPARK AQUARIUM AND BOTANIC GARDEN are at 2601 Central Ave. N.W. Marine habitats of the Gulf of Mexico and other ecosystems are presented at the aquarium. Tanks contain stingrays, jellyfish, eels, sharks and other aquatic life. The botanic garden features Mediterranean and desert conservatories, a children's fantasy garden, water and plant exhibits, demonstration gardens, the PNM Butterfly Pavilion, a butterfly-hummingbird garden, the Rio Grande Heritage Farm and the Sasebo Japanese Garden.

Time: Allow 1 hour, 30 minutes minimum. Hours: Daily 9-5 (also Sat.-Sun. 5-6, June-Aug.). Last admission 30 minutes before closing. Closed Jan. 1, Thanksgiving and Christmas. Cost: $12.50; $9 (New Mexico residents); $5.50 (ages 65+); $4.50 (New Mexico residents ages 65+); $4 (ages 3-12). Combination ticket with ABQ BioPark Zoo (Tues.-Sun. 9-noon) $20; $15 (New Mexico residents); $10 (ages 65+); $8 (New Mexico residents ages 65+); $6 (ages 3-12). **Phone:** (505) 768-2000.

ABQ BIOPARK ZOO is at 903 Tenth St. S.W. The zoo houses more than 1,000 animals representing some 250 species in a variety of naturalistic habitats. Popular residents include chimpanzees, gorillas, elephants, polar bears, giraffes, hippos, Komodo dragons, jaguars and zebras. Tropical America features toucans, spider monkeys, tamarins, tarantulas and colorful bromeliads. The 6-acre Africa Exhibit is home to warthogs, cheetahs, rhinos and Marabou storks. Seal and sea lion feedings take place daily in a 350,000-gallon tank.

Hours: Daily 9-5 (also Sat.-Sun. 5-6, June -Aug.). Last admission 30 minutes before closing. Closed Jan. 1, Thanksgiving and Christmas. Cost: $12.50; $9 (New Mexico residents); $5.50 (ages 65+); $4.50 (New Mexico residents ages 65+); $4 (ages 3-12). Combination ticket with ABQ BioPark Aquarium and Botanic Garden (Tues.-Sun. 9-noon) $20; $15 (New Mexico residents); $10 (ages 65+); $8 (New Mexico residents ages 65+); $6 (ages 3-12). Ages 0-12 must be with an adult. **Phone:** (505) 768-2000.

THE ALBUQUERQUE MUSEUM OF ART & HISTORY is at 2000 Mountain Rd. N.W. The museum features national and international exhibits and art of the Southwest and explores 400 years of Albuquerque history through permanent displays, exhibitions and guided walking tours of Old Town. The collection includes works from major New Mexican artists from the early 20th century to the present. A sculpture garden also is featured.

Time: Allow 2 hours minimum. Hours: Tues.-Sun. 9-5. Thirty-minute gallery tours depart Tues.-Sun. at 2. Sculpture garden tours depart Tues.-Sat. at 10, Mar.-Nov. Old Town walking tours depart Tues.-Sun. at 11, Mar. 1 to mid-Dec. Closed Jan. 1,

Thanksgiving and Christmas. Phone ahead to confirm schedule. Cost: $4; $2 (ages 65+); $1 (ages 4-12); free (Sun. 9-1, first Wed. of the month and 5-8:30 third Thurs. of the month). Special fees may apply. **Phone:** (505) 243-7255.

AMERICAN INTERNATIONAL RATTLESNAKE MUSEUM is at 202 San Felipe St. N.W. More than 30 species of live rattlesnakes are displayed at the museum, which offers films and information about snakes and other reptiles. Artwork featuring snakes, herpetological fossils and skeletons, and other items also are featured. Time: Allow 30 minutes minimum. Hours: Mon.-Sat. 10-6, Sun. 1-5, June-Aug., Mon.-Fri. 11:30-5:30, Sat. 10-6, Sun. 1-5, rest of year. Cost: $5; $4 (ages 60+ and students, teachers and active military with ID); $3 (ages 3-12). **Phone:** (505) 242-6569.

ANDERSON-ABRUZZO ALBUQUERQUE INTERNATIONAL BALLOON MUSEUM is at 9201 Balloon Museum Dr. N.E. Embrace the spirit of adventure through interactive exhibits about balloon flight, which dates to the early 1700s. In addition to highlighting the history of ballooning, exhibits also reveal the many uses of balloons in the scientific realm, from weather forecasting to the development of Project Strato-Lab, a U.S. Navy program designed to gather data about human physiology in the stratosphere and a precursor to space exploration.

Other exhibit topics include recreational ballooning and lighter-than-air craft used in conflicts ranging from the Civil War to World War II. Colorful balloons of all shapes and sizes are suspended throughout the two-story grand hall, and some can be viewed up close from a catwalk. Collections include gondolas, balloon systems, books, ephemera and decorative arts.

The museum is named after pioneering balloonists and Albuquerque natives Maxie Anderson and Ben Abruzzo, who, along with a third pilot, were the first to cross the Atlantic Ocean in a gas balloon.

Time: Allow 1 hour minimum. Hours: Tues.-Sun. 9-5. Closed Jan. 1, Thanksgiving, Christmas and Mon. holidays. Cost: $4; $2 (ages 65+); $1 (ages 4-12). Free (Sun. 9-1 and first Fri. of the month). **Phone:** (505) 768-6020.

BEST OF ABQ CITY TOUR departs from the Hotel Albuquerque at 800 Rio Grande N.W. Narrated 85-minute tours on a distinctively Albuquerque trolley include such sights as Old Town, Route 66, historic neighborhoods, Museum Row, the Railyards, the University of New Mexico and the ABQ BioPark Zoo.

Note: Sunscreen or a light jacket may be necessary in some months. Time: Allow 1 hour, 30 minutes minimum. Hours: Tours depart Tues.-Sat. at 11 and 1, Sun. at 1. Hours vary seasonally and on holidays. Phone ahead to confirm schedule. Cost: $25; $15 (ages 0-12). **Phone:** (505) 240-8000.

(See maps & indexes p. 339, 342.)

EXPLORA! is at 1701 Mountain Rd. N.W. Visitors wander through a maze of personal learning centers at this innovative museum featuring more than 250 hands-on science, technology and art exhibits. Giant bubbles, hair-raising demonstrations of static electricity and a laminar-flow fountain entertain children and adults alike while encouraging independent thinking, exploration and experimentation. **Time:** Allow 1 hour minimum. **Hours:** Mon.-Sat. 10-6, Sun. noon-6. Closed Jan. 1, July 4, week after Labor Day, Thanksgiving and Christmas. **Cost:** $8; $5 (ages 65+); $4 (ages 1-11). **Phone:** (505) 224-8323.

HOLOCAUST & INTOLERANCE MUSEUM OF NEW MEXICO is at 616 Central Ave. S.W. Dedicated to combating hate and intolerance and promoting understanding through education, the museum's documents, photographs and artifacts illustrate how ethnic intolerance engenders global conflict. Exhibits depict the Holocaust, Native American persecution, slavery in America and the Rwandan, Armenian and Greek genocides. **Time:** Allow 1 hour minimum. **Hours:** Tues.-Sat. 11-3:30. Closed major holidays. **Cost:** Donations. **Phone:** (505) 247-0606. GT

INDIAN PUEBLO CULTURAL CENTER is at 2401 12th St. N.W. The center depicts the history, art and culture of New Mexico's 19 American Indian pueblos. The main museum features an extensive collection of artifacts, and an intergenerational learning classroom and programs offer hands-on learning about the Pueblo people. Traditional dances take place weekly. An exhibit gallery highlights the work of traditional and contemporary artists.

Time: Allow 30 minutes minimum. **Hours:** Daily 9-5. Closed Jan. 1, Memorial Day, July 4, Labor Day, Thanksgiving and Christmas. **Cost:** $6; $5.50 (ages 62+); $3 (ages 5-17 and college students with ID). **Phone:** (505) 843-7270 or (866) 855-7902.

NATIONAL HISPANIC CULTURAL CENTER is at 1701 Fourth St. S.W. Mayan temples, Spanish haciendas and adobe pueblos influenced the architecture of this 51-acre site, which features an art museum, a theater complex, a library and a genealogy center. Cultural programs and activities are offered throughout the year, many accompanied by children's events. **Time:** Allow 30 minutes minimum. **Hours:** Museum open Tues.-Sun. 10-5. Library open Tues.-Sat. 10-5. Closed Jan. 1, Thanksgiving and Christmas. **Cost:** Museum $3; $2 (ages 60+); free (ages 0-15 and to all Sun.). **Phone:** (505) 246-2261.

NATIONAL MUSEUM OF NUCLEAR SCIENCE & HISTORY is at 601 Eubank Blvd. S.E. The nation's official museum for the history and science of the Nuclear Age features replicas of the world's first two atomic weapons, Little Boy and Fat Man. Exhibits cover such topics as atomic theory, the Cold War, pioneers in nuclear science, uranium processing, radiation facts and the testing of the first atomic bomb. A hands-on physics lab for children also is available. Numerous airplanes and other large artifacts are installed in Heritage Park. Films relating to the history of nuclear development are shown daily.

Time: Allow 2 hours minimum. **Hours:** Daily 9-5. Closed Jan. 1, Easter, Thanksgiving and Christmas. **Cost:** $12; $10 (ages 6-17 and 60+); $8 (retired military with ID); $7 (active military with ID). **Phone:** (505) 245-2137.

NEW MEXICO MUSEUM OF NATURAL HISTORY & SCIENCE is .5 mi. s. of I-40 on Rio Grande Blvd., then 2 blks. e. to 1801 Mountain Rd. N.W. The origins and geological history of the Southwest are explored through full-scale dinosaur models, a walk-through volcano model, an ice age cave replica, a time machine and a fossil preparation area. A saltwater tide pool, a hands-on naturalist center, botanical exhibits and planetarium shows also are offered. The Lockheed Martin DynaTheater presents giant-screen film adventures to exotic locales.

Time: Allow 1 hour minimum. **Hours:** Daily 9-5. DynaTheater films are shown on the hour 10-5; other show schedules vary. Closed Jan. 1, Thanksgiving and Christmas. **Cost:** Museum or planetarium show $7; $6 (ages 60+); $4 (ages 3-12). DynaTheater $10; $8 (ages 60+); $6 (ages 3-12). Combination tickets are available. **Phone:** (505) 841-2800.

OLD TOWN is .5 mi. s. of I-40 exit 157A via Rio Grande Blvd. Albuquerque began where Old Town stands today, and the focal point of community life in the city's beginnings remains a place where people come to meet, sightsee and above all, shop. It doesn't look much like it did some 3 centuries ago, but Old Town's narrow streets, winding brick walkways, hidden patios and wrought-iron benches do invite visitors to relax and stay awhile.

The focal point of this village-like setting is a tree-shaded plaza with a gazebo, the scene of frequent impromptu musical performances. Standing on the plaza's north side is the San Felipe de Neri Church, founded in 1706 by Fray Manuel Moreno, a Franciscan priest. The original church building collapsed during the very rainy summer of 1792; the present adobe structure, in the shape of a cross and with walls 5 feet thick, dates from 1793. The church's rose garden is a lovely, quiet spot to relax.

Surrounding the plaza is a pedestrian-friendly district (bounded north/south by Mountain Road and Central Avenue and east/west by Rio Grande Boulevard and 19th Street) containing more than 150 shops, boutiques, galleries and artist studios. Browsers will find all things Southwestern, of course, but Old Town shops offer everything from handmade Native American jewelry, Oaxacan woodcarvings and Mata Ortiz pottery to painted ponies, Christmas ornaments and Route 66 memorabilia.

(See maps & indexes p. 339, 342.)

Across from the plaza's east side, in the 200 block of San Felipe Road, vendors and local artists display their wares on blankets under the building *portal* (porch). And it's a sure bet that before you leave you'll see a couple of *ristras,* those hanging strings of dried red chile peppers that all but shout out "New Mexico."

Pick up a free Old Town map at the information center in Plaza Don Luis (303 Romero St.). **Hours:** Guided 75-minute historical walking tours depart daily at noon, Mar.-Nov., from the ticket window at Plaza Don Luis (ticket window opens 15 minutes prior to the tour start time). Video or audio recording is not permitted. Ghost tour departs nightly at 8 p.m. (at 10 p.m. on full moon nights). Advance reservations are required for all tours. **Cost:** Tour fee $20; $18 (ages 55+, active military and college students with ID); $16 (ages 13-17); $10 (ages 6-12). **Phone:** (505) 246-8687. GT ⊓

OPEN SPACE VISITOR CENTER is at 6500 Coors Blvd., N.W. The center offers information and resources about Albuquerque's Open Space Program with exhibits interpreting the natural and cultural resources protected by city-wide program. An art gallery, agricultural fields that draw a variety of wildlife and beautiful views of the Sandia Mountains are offered. Comfortable indoor and outdoor viewing areas are available to watch sandhill cranes and other migratory birds during their fall and winter migratory season. There are 3 miles of walking trails along the Paseo del Bosque trail accessible from the visitor center. **Time:** Allow 1 hour minimum. **Hours:** Tues.-Sun. 9-5. Closed major holidays. Phone ahead to confirm schedule. **Cost:** Free. **Phone:** (505) 897-8831. ⊠ 🚻

PETROGLYPH NATIONAL MONUMENT is at 4001 Unser Blvd. Boca Negra Canyon, Rinconada Canyon and Piedras Marcadas Canyon all afford opportunities for viewing petroglyphs by way of self-guiding trails. A visitor center offers trail guides and park information. **Time:** Allow 1 hour minimum. **Hours:** Daily 8-5. Closed Jan. 1, Thanksgiving and Christmas. **Cost:** Free. **Parking:** Mon.-Fri. $1; Sat.-Sun. $2 at Boca Negra Canyon. **Phone:** (505) 899-0205, ext. 335.

RIO GRANDE NATURE CENTER STATE PARK is at 2901 Candelaria Rd. N.W. On the central Rio Grande flyway, the park provides a winter refuge for migrating sandhill cranes and other waterfowl. Trails along the Rio Grande, classrooms, a library and visitor center exhibits are offered. **Time:** Allow 30 minutes minimum. **Hours:** Park daily 8-5. Visitor center daily 10-5. Closed Jan. 1, Thanksgiving and Christmas. **Cost:** $3 (per private vehicle); $15 (vehicles with eight or more people). Exact change is required. **Phone:** (505) 344-7240.

SAN AGUSTÍN DE LA ISLETA MISSION—see Isleta Pueblo p. 388.

SANDIA CREST—see Cibola National Forest p. 371.

▼◆◆ **SANDIA PEAK AERIAL TRAMWAY** is off I-25 exit 234, then 6 mi. e. on Tramway Rd. N.E. The 2.7-mile tramway, one of the world's longest, transports visitors above the deep canyons and spectacular terrain of the western Sandia Mountains in the Cibola National Forest. A Forest Service visitor center is in the upper tram terminal. Restaurants operate at the base and summit.

Sandia Peak is a popular recreation spot. Skiers frequent the 10,378-foot peak from mid-December to mid-March. In summer 24 miles of trails are available for mountain biking. Bicycle rentals are available weekends and holidays, Memorial Day weekend through Labor Day, and in October during the Albuquerque International Balloon Fiesta.

Hours: Trams depart every 20-30 minutes daily 9-9, Memorial Day-Labor Day and during the Albuquerque International Balloon Fiesta; Wed.-Mon. and holidays 9-8, Tues. 5-8, rest of year. The tram is closed for 10 days in Apr. and Nov. for maintenance. **Cost:** Round-trip tram fare $20; $17 (ages 13-20, ages 62+ and active military with ID); $12 (ages 5-12). **Phone:** (505) 856-7325 or (505) 856-6419.

THE TURQUOISE MUSEUM is at 2107 Central Ave. N.W. A mine tunnel provides entrance to this museum, which features rare turquoise specimens from around the world. Interactive silversmith and lapidary demonstrations are presented. **Hours:** Guided 90-minute tours are given Mon.-Sat. at 11 and 1. Closed major holidays. **Cost:** $10; $8 (ages 5-17 and 55+). Reservations are required. **Phone:** (505) 247-8650. GT

UNIVERSITY OF NEW MEXICO is 2 mi. e. on Central Ave./US 66. New Mexico's flagship research university occupies an 800-acre campus and enrolls approximately 36,700 students. College buildings feature Pueblo Revival architecture, and the grounds are designated as a National College Arboretum. Of particular interest are several museums and libraries as well as Popejoy Hall, home to ballet, musicals, lectures and the New Mexico Symphony Orchestra.

Some 3,000 Native American dancers and singers participate in the ▼◆◆ Gathering of Nations Powwow, held at University Arena in April. In December the ▼◆◆ New Mexico Bowl takes place at University Stadium; teams representing the Mountain West and Western Athletic conferences compete for a 20-inch Zia Pueblo pottery trophy. **Hours:** Academic buildings open Mon.-Fri. 8-5. **Phone:** (505) 277-1989.

Maxwell Museum of Anthropology is on Redondo Dr. just e. of University Blvd. on the University of New Mexico campus. The museum explores the cultures of the world with a special emphasis on the heritage of the Southwest. Permanent exhibits include People of the Southwest and Ancestors. Changing exhibits also are presented. **Hours:**

(See maps & indexes p. 339, 342.)

Tues.-Sat. 10-4. Closed major holidays. **Cost:** Donations. **Phone:** (505) 277-4405.

Silver Family Geology Museum of the University of New Mexico is at 221 Yale Blvd. (Northrop Hall) in the Earth and Planetary Sciences Building. Various types of minerals, the geology of the Earth and New Mexico fossils are depicted in more than 20 exhibits. Guided tours are offered by appointment. **Time:** Allow 30 minutes minimum. **Hours:** Mon.-Fri. 8-noon and 1-4:30. Closed major holidays. **Cost:** Donations. **Phone:** (505) 277-4204.

UNM Art Museum is at Cornell St. and Redondo Dr. N.E. on the University of New Mexico campus, inside the Center for the Arts. The permanent collection includes some 30,000 pieces of photography, prints and paintings spanning the 16th through the 21st centuries. **Time:** Allow 1 hour minimum. **Hours:** Tues.-Fri. 10-4, Sat. 10-8. Closed major holidays. **Cost:** Donations. **Phone:** (505) 277-4001.

UNM Meteorite Museum, part of the Institute of Meteoritics, is on the first floor of the Earth and Planetary Sciences Building, 221 Yale Blvd. (106 Northrop Hall) on the University of New Mexico campus. The institute is a center for the teaching and research of space and planetary sciences, and is the home of one of the world's largest collections of meteorites. Hundreds of meteorites discovered throughout the world are displayed, including the 1,000 kg Norton County stony meteorite. **Note:** The museum is temporarily closed for renovations and is expected to reopen in early 2015; phone ahead for updates. **Time:** Allow 30 minutes minimum. **Hours:** Mon.-Fri. 9-4. Closed major and university holidays. Phone ahead to confirm schedule. **Cost:** Free. **Phone:** (505) 277-2747.

UNSER RACING MUSEUM is at 1776 Montano N.W. The museum traces the history of the Unser family in racing from the early 1900s to the present. Exhibits—some interactive—include antique cars, trophies and uniforms. The Indy simulator is sure to get your engine going. Changing exhibits also are offered. **Time:** Allow 1 hour minimum. **Hours:** Daily 10-4. **Cost:** $10; $6 (ages 60+ and military with ID); free (ages 0-16 with adult). **Phone:** (505) 341-1776.

RECREATIONAL ACTIVITIES
Hot Air Ballooning

- ● [SAVE] **Rainbow Ryders, Inc.** departs from various locations for flights over the Rio Grande Valley. **Hours:** Daily at dawn. **Phone:** (505) 823-1111. or (800) 725-2477. *(See ad this page.)*
- **World Balloon** meets at 6390 Coors Blvd. N.W. **Hours:** Departures daily beginning at sunrise (weather permitting). Office hours daily 7-6. Closed Jan. 1, Thanksgiving and Christmas. **Phone:** (505) 293-6800.

White-water Rafting

- **Passageways** departs El Vado Ranch at the base of El Vado Dam and Lower Chama Canyon. **Hours:** Daily July-Aug. **Phone:** (505) 265-4542.

GAMBLING ESTABLISHMENTS

- **Isleta Resort & Casino** is at 11000 Broadway S.E. **Hours:** Mon.-Thurs. 8 a.m.-4 a.m., Fri.-Sun. and holidays 24 hours. **Phone:** (505) 724-3800 or (877) 747-5382.
- **Sandia Resort & Casino** is at 30 Rainbow Rd. N.E. **Hours:** Mon.-Thurs. 8 a.m.-4 a.m., Fri.-Sun. 24 hours. **Phone:** (505) 796-7500 or (800) 526-9366.

▼ *See AAA listing this page* ▼

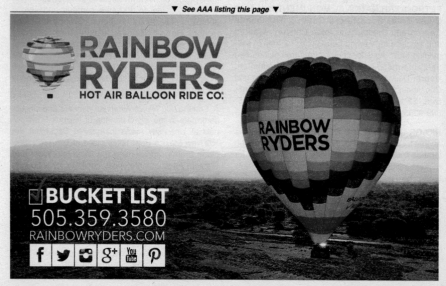

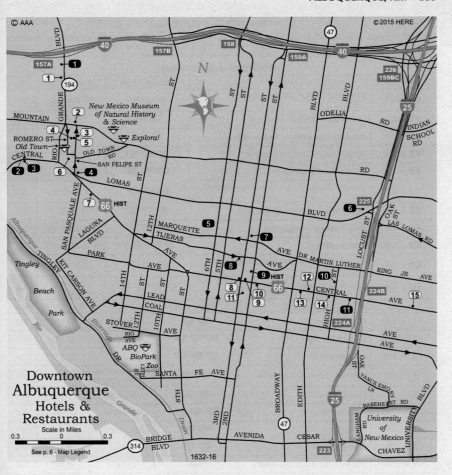

Downtown Albuquerque

This index helps you "spot" where approved hotels and restaurants are located on the corresponding detailed maps. Hotel daily rate range is for comparison only. Restaurant price range is a combination of lunch and/or dinner. Turn to the listing page for more detailed rate and price information and consult display ads for special promotions.

DOWNTOWN ALBUQUERQUE

Map Page	Hotels	Diamond Rated	Rate Range	Page
1 p. 339	BEST WESTERN PLUS Rio Grande Inn *(See ad p. 349.)*	◈◈◈	$94-$221 SAVE	347
2 p. 339	Econo Lodge Old Town Albuquerque	◈◈	$55-$100	348
3 p. 339	Monterey Non-Smokers Motel-Old Town	◈◈	$58-$100 SAVE	350
4 p. 339	Bottger Mansion Bed and Breakfast	◈◈◈	$115-$179	348
5 p. 339	Mauger Bed & Breakfast Inn	◈◈◈	$99-$204	350
6 p. 339	Embassy Suites by Hilton Albuquerque Hotel & Spa	◈◈◈	$129-$259	348
7 p. 339	DoubleTree by Hilton Albuquerque	◈◈◈	$109-$189 SAVE	348
8 p. 339	Hyatt Regency Albuquerque	◈◈◈	$109-$299 SAVE	350
9 p. 339	Hotel Andaluz	◈◈◈◈	$139-$269 SAVE	348
10 p. 339	Albuquerque Downtown Historic Bed & Breakfast	◈◈◈	$89-$209 SAVE	347
11 p. 339	Hotel Parq Central	◈◈◈◈	Rates not provided SAVE	348

Map Page	Restaurants	Diamond Rated	Cuisine	Price Range	Page
① p. 339	St. Clair Winery & Bistro	◈◈	American	$9-$20	350
② p. 339	Seasons Rotisserie & Grill	◈◈◈	American	$8-$32	351
③ p. 339	La Crepe Michel	◈◈◈	French	$8-$21	350
④ p. 339	High Noon Restaurant & Saloon	◈◈	Regional American	$11-$37	350
⑤ p. 339	Church Street Cafe	◈◈	Mexican	$9-$15	350
⑥ p. 339	Antiquity Restaurant	◈◈◈	Continental	$20-$32	350
⑦ p. 339	Vinaigrette	◈◈	Natural/Organic	$11-$18	351
⑧ p. 339	Q Burger	◈◈	Burgers	$8-$12	350
⑨ p. 339	JC's New York Pizza Department	◈	Italian	$8-$20	350
⑩ p. 339	Tucanos Brazilian Grill	◈◈◈	Brazilian	$16-$23	351
⑪ p. 339	Gold Street Caffé	◈◈	American	$9-$14	350
⑫ p. 339	The Artichoke Cafe	◈◈◈	New American	$12-$38	350
⑬ p. 339	Standard Diner	◈◈	American	$10-$20	351
⑭ p. 339	The Grove Cafe & Market	◈◈	American	$7-$12	350
⑮ p. 339	66 Diner	◈◈	Burgers Desserts	$6-$12	350

Keep your focus safely

on the road when driving

Take Your *Imagination* to New Destinations

Use AAA Travel Guides online to explore the possibilities.

> Tour popular places in the U.S., Canada, Mexico and the Caribbean from the comfort of your home.

> Read what AAA's professional inspectors say about area hotels, restaurants and attractions.

> Check out the best stuff to see and do, with itineraries to ensure you won't miss a thing.

 Go to AAA.com/travelguide today to discover your next destination.

AAA Mobile App
CAA Mobile App

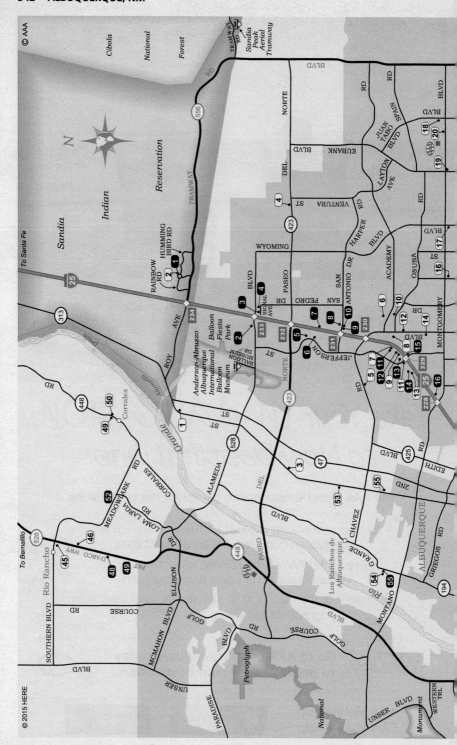

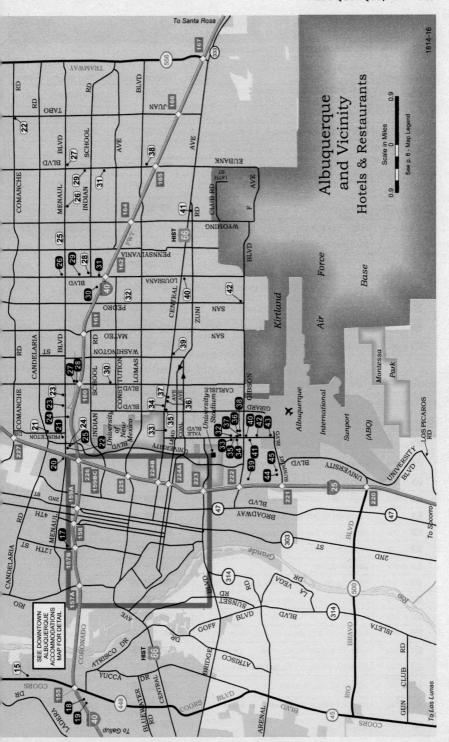

✈ Airport Hotels

Map Page	ALBUQUERQUE INTERNATIONAL SUNPORT (Maximum driving distance from airport: 2.2 mi)	Diamond Rated	Rate Range	Page
42 p. 342	**BEST WESTERN Airport Albuquerque InnSuites Hotel & Suites, 1.0 mi**	◆◆	$69-$149 SAVE	351
33 p. 342	**Comfort Inn Airport, 1.5 mi**	◆◆◆	$75-$84 SAVE	352
35 p. 342	**Courtyard by Marriott Airport, 1.4 mi**	◆◆◆	$83-$185 SAVE	352
36 p. 342	Days Inn & Suites Albuquerque Airport, 1.5 mi	◆◆	$62-$87	352
37 p. 342	Fairfield Inn & Suites by Marriott Airport, 1.4 mi	◆◆◆	$67-$122	352
39 p. 342	GuestHouse Inn & Suites Albuquerque Airport, 2.2 mi	◆◆	Rates not provided	353
34 p. 342	Holiday Inn Express & Suites, 1.4 mi	◆◆◆	Rates not provided	353
45 p. 342	**Hyatt Place Albuquerque Airport, 1.4 mi**	◆◆◆	$74-$179 SAVE	354
40 p. 342	La Quinta Inn Albuquerque Airport, 1.2 mi	◆◆	$64-$235	354
32 p. 342	Residence Inn by Marriott Albuquerque Airport, 1.5 mi	◆◆◆	$103-$206	355
43 p. 342	**Sheraton Albuquerque Airport Hotel, 0.7 mi**	◆◆◆	Rates not provided SAVE	356
44 p. 342	Staybridge Suites Albuquerque Airport, 1.5 mi	◆◆◆	Rates not provided	356
41 p. 342	Super 8 Albuquerque Airport, 1.2 mi	◆◆	$49-$149	356
38 p. 342	TownePlace Suites by Marriott, 1.5 mi	◆◆◆	$79-$138	356

Albuquerque and Vicinity

This index helps you "spot" where approved hotels and restaurants are located on the corresponding detailed maps. Hotel daily rate range is for comparison only. Restaurant price range is a combination of lunch and/or dinner. Turn to the listing page for more detailed rate and price information and consult display ads for special promotions.

ALBUQUERQUE

Map Page	Hotels	Diamond Rated	Rate Range	Page
1 p. 342	**Sandia Resort & Casino** (See ad p. 355.)	◆◆◆◆	$179-$299 SAVE	355
2 p. 342	Holiday Inn Express Hotel & Suites	◆◆◆	Rates not provided	353
3 p. 342	Comfort Inn & Suites by Choice Hotels	◆◆	$65-$101	352
4 p. 342	Staybridge Suites Albuquerque North	◆◆◆	$95-$240	356
5 p. 342	**Courtyard by Marriott Journal Center**	◆◆◆	$81-$150 SAVE	352
6 p. 342	**Albuquerque Marriott Pyramid North**	◆◆◆	$97-$175 SAVE	351
7 p. 342	Quality Inn & Suites Albuquerque	◆◆	$55-$200	355
8 p. 342	**Comfort Suites**	◆◆◆	$79-$124 SAVE	352
9 p. 342	Hilton Garden Inn Albuquerque Journal Center	◆◆◆	$99-$159	353
10 p. 342	Homewood Suites by Hilton-Journal Center	◆◆◆	$119-$139	353
11 p. 342	Residence Inn by Marriott North	◆◆◆	$104-$182	355
12 p. 342	Hampton Inn & Suites Albuquerque North I-25	◆◆◆	$119-$170	353
13 p. 342	Drury Inn & Suites-Albuquerque	◆◆◆	$90-$155	352
14 p. 342	TownePlace Suites by Marriott Albuquerque North	◆◆◆	$93-$176	356
15 p. 342	Holiday Inn Hotel & Suites	◆◆◆	Rates not provided	353
16 p. 342	**BEST WESTERN PLUS Executive Suites**	◆◆◆	$99-$149 SAVE	351
17 p. 342	Holiday Inn Express Hotel & Suites Albuquerque Historic Old Town	◆◆◆	Rates not provided	353

ALBUQUERQUE (cont'd)

Map Page	Hotels (cont'd)	Diamond Rated	Rate Range	Page
18 p. 342	La Quinta Inn & Suites Albuquerque West	◆◆◆	$64-$224	354
19 p. 342	Hampton Inn & Suites	◆◆◆	$99-$139	353
20 p. 342	**ClubHouse Inn & Suites**	◆◆◆	Rates not provided [SAVE]	351
21 p. 342	La Quinta Inn & Suites Albuquerque Midtown	◆◆◆	$97-$240	354
22 p. 342	**Fairfield Inn by Marriott Albuquerque-University Area**	◆◆◆	$68-$118 [SAVE]	352
23 p. 342	Candlewood Suites	◆◆◆	$90-$190	351
24 p. 342	Holiday Inn Express Albuquerque Midtown	◆◆◆	Rates not provided	353
25 p. 342	**Crowne Plaza Albuquerque**	◆◆◆	Rates not provided [SAVE]	352
26 p. 342	**Albuquerque Sheraton Uptown Hotel** *(See ad p. 348.)*	◆◆◆	$89-$299 [SAVE]	351
27 p. 342	**Hampton Inn University-Midtown**	◆◆◆	$104-$169 [SAVE]	353
28 p. 342	Econo Lodge Midtown	◆◆	$55-$100	352
29 p. 342	**Hyatt Place Albuquerque Uptown**	◆◆◆	$95-$229 [SAVE]	354
30 p. 342	Hilton Garden Inn Albuquerque Uptown	◆◆◆	$99-$199	353
31 p. 342	The Albuquerque Marriott Hotel	◆◆◆	$95-$247	351
32 p. 342	Residence Inn by Marriott Albuquerque Airport	◆◆◆	$103-$206	355
33 p. 342	**Comfort Inn Airport**	◆◆◆	$75-$84 [SAVE]	352
34 p. 342	Holiday Inn Express & Suites	◆◆◆	Rates not provided	353
35 p. 342	**Courtyard by Marriott Airport**	◆◆◆	$83-$185 [SAVE]	352
36 p. 342	Days Inn & Suites Albuquerque Airport	◆◆	$62-$87	352
37 p. 342	Fairfield Inn & Suites by Marriott Airport	◆◆◆	$67-$122	352
38 p. 342	TownePlace Suites by Marriott	◆◆◆	$79-$138	356
39 p. 342	GuestHouse Inn & Suites Albuquerque Airport	◆◆	Rates not provided	353
40 p. 342	La Quinta Inn Albuquerque Airport	◆◆	$64-$235	354
41 p. 342	Super 8 Albuquerque Airport	◆◆◆	$49-$149	356
42 p. 342	**BEST WESTERN Airport Albuquerque InnSuites Hotel & Suites**	◆◆	$69-$149 [SAVE]	351
43 p. 342	**Sheraton Albuquerque Airport Hotel**	◆◆◆	Rates not provided [SAVE]	356
44 p. 342	Staybridge Suites Albuquerque Airport	◆◆◆	Rates not provided	356
45 p. 342	**Hyatt Place Albuquerque Airport** *(See ad p. 354.)*	◆◆◆	$74-$179 [SAVE]	354

Map Page	Restaurants	Diamond Rated	Cuisine	Price Range	Page
1 p. 342	El Pinto	◆◆	Mexican	$8-$27	357
2 p. 342	Bien Shur Restaurant	◆◆◆	International	$26-$50	356
3 p. 342	Casa de Benavidez New Mexican Restaurant	◆◆	Mexican	$9-$22	356
4 p. 342	Jinja Bar & Bistro	◆◆◆	Asian	$10-$18	357
5 p. 342	Vic's Daily Cafe	◆◆	American	$6-$10	359
6 p. 342	**Trombino's Bistro Italiano**	◆◆◆	Italian	$8-$26	359
7 p. 342	P.F. Chang's China Bistro	◆◆◆	Chinese	$8-$25	358
8 p. 342	Saigon Restaurant	◆◆	Vietnamese	$8-$20	359
9 p. 342	Pars Cuisine	◆◆◆	Mediterranean	$10-$28	358

Map Page	Restaurants (cont'd)	Diamond Rated	Cuisine	Price Range	Page
⑩ p. 342	Monroe's Restaurant	◆◆	Mexican	$9-$17	358
⑪ p. 342	Nick & Jimmy's Restaurant & Bar	◆◆◆	Mediterranean Steak Seafood	$12-$30	358
⑫ p. 342	Siam Cafe	◆◆	Thai	$8-$11	359
⑬ p. 342	Chama River Brewing Company	◆◆	American	$10-$28	356
⑭ p. 342	Azuma	◆◆	Japanese	$9-$30	356
⑮ p. 342	Mimmo's Ristorante & Pizzeria	◆◆	Italian Pizza	$8-$18	357
⑯ p. 342	Weck's	◆◆	American	$8-$10	359
⑰ p. 342	Range Cafe	◆◆	American	$8-$18	358
⑱ p. 342	Flying Star Cafe	◆◆	American	$9-$13	357
⑲ p. 342	Scarpa's Brick Oven Pizza	◆◆	Italian Pizza	$8-$15	359
⑳ p. 342	Savoy Bar & Grill	◆◆◆	American	$9-$38	359
㉑ p. 342	Milly's Restaurant	◆◆	American	$5-$10	357
㉒ p. 342	Garcia's Kitchen	◆◆	Mexican	$5-$15	357
㉓ p. 342	Richard's Mexican Restaurant	◆◆	Mexican	$6-$10	358
㉔ p. 342	**Rancher's Club of New Mexico**	◆◆◆	Steak	$26-$78	358
㉕ p. 342	Krung Thai	◆◆	Thai	$7-$10	357
㉖ p. 342	Los Cuates del Norte	◆◆	Mexican	$9-$16	357
㉗ p. 342	Papa Felipe's	◆◆	Mexican	$8-$17	358
㉘ p. 342	Marcello's Chophouse	◆◆◆	Steak	$8-$65	357
㉙ p. 342	Paisano's Italian Restaurant	◆◆	Italian	$8-$26	358
㉚ p. 342	**Taj Mahal Cuisine of India**	◆◆	Indian	$10-$18	359
㉛ p. 342	Ming Dynasty	◆◆	Chinese	$6-$12	358
㉜ p. 342	Christy Mae's	◆◆	American	$9-$11	357
㉝ p. 342	Frontier Restaurant	◆	American	$5-$12	357
㉞ p. 342	Zinc Wine Bar & Bistro	◆◆◆	American	$17-$32	359
㉟ p. 342	Mannie's Family Restaurant	◆◆	American	$6-$9	357
㊱ p. 342	Nob Hill Bar & Grill	◆◆◆	American	$11-$25	358
㊲ p. 342	Kelly's Brewery & Restaurant	◆◆	American	$8-$14	357
㊳ p. 342	The Owl Cafe	◆◆	American	$5-$12	358
㊴ p. 342	Loyola's Family Restaurant	◆◆	Mexican	$4-$10	357
㊵ p. 342	May Cafe	◆◆	Vietnamese	$8-$15	357
㊶ p. 342	The Town House Dining Room	◆◆◆	American	$8-$25	359
㊷ p. 342	**Cervantes Restaurant & Lounge**	◆◆	Regional Mexican	$9-$26	356

RIO RANCHO

Map Page	Hotels	Diamond Rated	Rate Range	Page
㊽ p. 342	Hilton Garden Inn Albuquerque North/Rio Rancho	◆◆◆	$89-$189	404
㊾ p. 342	Extended Stay America Albuquerque-Rio Rancho	◆◆	Rates not provided	404

Map Page	Restaurants	Diamond Rated	Cuisine	Price Range	Page
㊺ p. 342	O'Hare's Grille & Pub	◆◆	American	$7-$25	404
㊻ p. 342	Federico's Mexican Food	◆	Mexican	$3-$12	404

CORRALES

Map Page	Hotel	Diamond Rated		Rate Range	Page
52 p. 342	The Chocolate Turtle Bed & Breakfast	▼▼▼		$129-$169	375

Map Page	Restaurants	Diamond Rated	Cuisine	Price Range	Page
49 p. 342	Indigo Crow Cafe	▼▼▼	American	$9-$34	375
50 p. 342	Hannah & Nate's Market Cafe	▼▼	American	$8-$13	375

LOS RANCHOS DE ALBUQUERQUE

Map Page	Hotel	Diamond Rated		Rate Range	Page
56 p. 342	Los Poblanos Historic Inn & Organic Farm	▼▼▼		Rates not provided	397

Map Page	Restaurants	Diamond Rated	Cuisine	Price Range	Page
53 p. 342	Vernon's Hidden Valley Steakhouse	▼▼▼	Steak Seafood	$30-$80	397
54 p. 342	La Merienda at Los Poblanos	▼▼▼	International	$20-$36	397
55 p. 342	Sadie's Dining Room	▼▼	Mexican	$7-$20	397

DOWNTOWN ALBUQUERQUE
- **Restaurants p. 350**
- **Hotels & Restaurants map & index p. 339**

ALBUQUERQUE DOWNTOWN HISTORIC BED & BREAKFAST
505/842-0223

Historic Bed & Breakfast
$89-$209

Address: 207 & 209 High St NE 87102 **Location:** I-25 exit 224A northbound; exit 224B southbound, just w, then just n. **Facility:** This property is comprised of two beautifully restored homes nestled in what was once Albuquerque's first subdivision. The Spy House and Heritage House offer a glimpse of historic local intrigue. 10 units, some kitchens. 1-2 stories (no elevator), interior corridors. **Parking:** on-site and street. **Terms:** check-in 4 pm, 7 day cancellation notice-fee imposed. **Activities:** hot tub. **Guest Services:** complimentary and valet laundry.

BEST WESTERN PLUS RIO GRANDE INN
(505)843-9500 **1**

Hotel
$94-$221

AAA Benefit:
Save 10% or more every day and earn 10% bonus points!

Address: 1015 Rio Grande Blvd NW 87104 **Location:** I-40 exit 157A (Rio Grande Blvd), just s. **Facility:** 173 units. 4 stories, interior corridors. **Terms:** cancellation fee imposed. **Pool(s):** heated outdoor. **Activities:** hot tub, exercise room. **Guest Services:** valet and coin laundry, area transportation. *(See ad p. 349.)*

  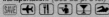 

▼ See AAA listing p. 355 ▼

(See map & index p. 339.)

BOTTGER MANSION BED AND BREAKFAST
505/243-3639 **4**

▼▼▼▼ **Historic Bed & Breakfast** $115-$179 **Address:** 110 San Felipe St NW 87104 **Location:** I-40 exit 157A (Rio Grande Blvd), 1.5 mi s, then just e; off Central Ave. **Facility:** Located in the historic Old Town area, the classic Victorian home features period furnishings and artifacts. A hearty breakfast is served daily. 7 units. 2 stories (no elevator), interior corridors. **Terms:** 7 day cancellation notice-fee imposed. 🛎️⊕ BIZ 🛜 ✕ / SOME UNITS 🛏️

DOUBLETREE BY HILTON ALBUQUERQUE
(505)247-3344 **7**

Hotel
$109-$189

DOUBLETREE
BY HILTON

AAA Benefit: Members save 5% or more!

Address: 201 Marquette Ave NW 87102 **Location:** I-25 exit 224B (Central Ave), 0.8 mi w to 2nd St, then just n. **Facility:** 295 units. 15 stories, interior corridors. **Parking:** on-site (fee). **Terms:** 1-7 night minimum stay, cancellation fee imposed. **Amenities:** video games. **Pool(s):** heated outdoor. **Activities:** exercise room. **Guest Services:** valet laundry, area transportation.

SAVE ✈️ 🍴 🧖 🍸 CALL 🅂M 🏊 BIZ 🛜 ✕ 📠 / SOME UNITS 🛏️

ECONO LODGE OLD TOWN ALBUQUERQUE
(505)243-8475 **2**

▼▼▼ **Hotel** $55-$100 **Address:** 2321 Central Ave NW 87104 **Location:** I-40 exit 157A, 0.6 mi s on Rio Grande Blvd, then 0.4 mi w. **Facility:** 43 units. 2 stories (no elevator), exterior corridors. **Pool(s):** heated indoor. **Activities:** hot tub. **Guest Services:** area transportation.

✈️ 🍴⊕ 🏊 BIZ HS 🛜 🛏️ 📷 📠 / SOME UNITS 🛏️

EMBASSY SUITES BY HILTON ALBUQUERQUE HOTEL & SPA
(505)245-7100 **6**

▼▼▼ **Hotel** $129-$259 **Address:** 1000 Woodward Pl NE 87102 **Location:** I-25 exit 224B, just w. **Facility:** 261 units. 9 stories, interior corridors. **Terms:** 1-7 night minimum stay, cancellation fee imposed. **Amenities:** safes. **Pool(s):** heated indoor. **Activities:** hot tub, exercise room, spa. **Guest Services:** valet and coin laundry.

AAA Benefit: Members save 5% or more!

🍴 🧖 🍸 CALL 🅂M 🏊 BIZ sHS 🛜 ✕ 📷 🛏️ 📷 📠

HOTEL ANDALUZ
(505)242-9090 **9**

▼▼▼ ▼▼▼
Historic Hotel
$139-$269

Address: 125 2nd St NW 87102 **Location:** I-25 exit 224A northbound; exit 224B southbound, jct Copper Ave and 2nd St. Located in a commercial area. **Facility:** This historic hotel has been completely renovated with stylish Andalusian-influenced décor throughout. Guest rooms feature modern, upscale appointments and amenities. 107 units. 10 stories, interior corridors. **Parking:** on-site (fee) and valet. **Terms:** cancellation fee imposed. **Amenities:** safes. **Activities:** recreation programs, massage. **Guest Services:** valet laundry.

SAVE 🍴 🧖 🍸 BIZ HS 🛜 ✕ 🛏️ / SOME UNITS 🛏️ 📠

HOTEL PARQ CENTRAL
505/242-0040 **11**

▼▼▼ ▼▼▼
Boutique Vintage Hotel
Rates not provided

Address: 806 Central Ave SE 87102 **Location:** I-25 exit 224A northbound; exit 224B southbound, just w. **Facility:** In a renovated 1926 hospital, the property reflects a blend of historic elegance and contemporary comfort with chic stylish décor. 74 units. 4 stories, interior corridors. **Amenities:** safes. **Activities:** hot tub, recreation programs, exercise room, massage. **Guest Services:** valet and coin laundry, area transportation. **Featured Amenity:** continental breakfast.

SAVE ✈️ 🍴 🧖 🍸 CALL 🅂M BIZ HS 🛜 ✕ 🛏️ / SOME UNITS 🛏️ 📠

▼ See AAA listing p. 347 ▼

OLD TOWN CHARM

Enjoy your Albuquerque experience at our ideal location, within walking distance of Old Town Plaza, five museums, and dozens of restaurants, shops, and galleries. Just minutes away are the Albuquerque Zoo, and Bio Park, Indian Pueblo Cultural Center and Downtown Business District. Exit 157A off I-40 at Rio Grande Blvd.

Best Western PLUS

RIO GRANDE INN

1015 Rio Grande Blvd NW
Albuquerque, New Mexico 87104
505.843.9500
Reservations:
800.959.4726
www.riograndeinn.com

Savor Southwest cuisine in the Albuquerque Bar and Grill. Our pool and spa are open year round. We have free wireless Internet and a business center.

AAA Approved ♦♦♦

(See map & index p. 339.)

(See map & index p. 339.)

HYATT REGENCY ALBUQUERQUE (505)842-1234 8

Hotel
$109-$299

AAA Benefit: Members save 10%!

Address: 330 Tijeras Ave NW 87102 **Location:** I-25 exit 224B (Central Ave), 0.5 mi w. **Facility:** 395 units. 20 stories, interior corridors. **Parking:** on-site (fee) and valet. **Terms:** cancellation fee imposed. **Amenities:** video games. **Dining:** 2 restaurants. **Pool(s):** heated outdoor. **Activities:** sauna, hot tub, recreation programs, exercise room, massage. **Guest Services:** valet laundry.

MAUGER BED & BREAKFAST INN (505)242-8755 5

Historic Bed & Breakfast $99-$204 **Address:** 701 Roma Ave NW 87102 **Location:** I-25 exit 225, 1 mi w, then just s on 7th Ave. **Facility:** Centrally located in the downtown area, the restored Queen Anne-style residence features rooms with high ceilings and gorgeous woodwork. 8 units. 3 stories (no elevator), interior corridors. *Bath:* shower only. **Terms:** check-in 4 pm, 10 day cancellation notice-fee imposed.

MONTEREY NON-SMOKERS MOTEL-OLD TOWN
(505)243-3554 3

Motel
$58-$100

Address: 2402 Central Ave SW 87104 **Location:** I-40 exit 157A (Rio Grande Blvd), 0.5 mi s, then 0.3 mi w. **Facility:** 15 units. 1 story, exterior corridors. **Pool(s):** heated outdoor. **Guest Services:** coin laundry.

WHERE TO EAT

66 DINER 505/247-1421 15

Burgers Desserts. Family Dining. $6-$12 **AAA Inspector Notes:** Patrons can return to the 1950s for some of the best burgers and American comfort food in town. Delicious desserts will please as well. **Address:** 1405 Central Ave NE 87106 **Location:** Jct Central Ave and University Blvd, just w. L D

ANTIQUITY RESTAURANT 505/247-3545 6

Continental. Fine Dining. $20-$32 **AAA Inspector Notes:** This cozy, intimate restaurant specializes in steak dishes and is perfect for that special occasion or a romantic dinner for two. A fine selection of wines suits the most discriminating palate. This place is popular with the tourists who frequent Old Town, as well as local steak connoisseurs. **Features:** beer & wine. **Reservations:** suggested. **Address:** 112 Romero St NW 87104 **Location:** I-40 exit 157A, 0.5 mi s to Romero St, just n of Central Ave; just s of Old Town Plaza; in Old Town. **Parking:** street only. D

THE ARTICHOKE CAFE 505/243-0200 12

New American. Fine Dining. $12-$38 **AAA Inspector Notes:** This establishment features new American cuisine prepared with a Southwestern flair, using many local organic products. Creativity marks the appetizers, salads and entrées. Diners will find a sophisticated selection of wines and luscious desserts. **Features:** full bar, happy hour. **Reservations:** suggested. **Address:** 424 Central Ave SE 87102 **Location:** I-25 exit 224B, just s to Central Ave, then just w; jct Edith Blvd. L D

CHURCH STREET CAFE 505/247-8522 5

Mexican
Casual Dining
$9-$15

AAA Inspector Notes: This 1706 adobe house also contains an art gallery. Tasty Mexican dishes, such as tamales, chiles rellenos and burritos, as well as a selection of sandwiches, are served in the dining room and on the patio. **Features:** beer & wine, patio dining. **Address:** 2111 Church St NW 87104 **Location:** I-40 exit 157A (Rio Grande Blvd), 0.5 mi s to Mountain Rd, then just e; in Old Town. **Parking:** street only. B L D

GOLD STREET CAFFÉ 505/765-1633 11

American. Casual Dining. $9-$14 **AAA Inspector Notes:** A popular spot for morning coffee drinkers, this cozy café also serves imaginative daily luncheon specials. Delicious pastries are popular with folks from nearby downtown offices and businesses. **Features:** patio dining. **Address:** 218 Gold Ave SW 87102 **Location:** I-25 exit 224B, 1 mi w, just s, then just w. **Parking:** on-site (fee). B L

THE GROVE CAFE & MARKET 505/248-9800 14

American. Casual Dining. $7-$12 **AAA Inspector Notes:** This popular bustling café recently was voted Albuquerque's best breakfast and brunch spot. The highest quality seasonal ingredients are used including local and organic produce, fresh baked breads, artisanal cheese plus preservative-free meats. The market features high-quality gourmet items and foodie gifts. **Features:** Sunday brunch. **Address:** 600 Central Ave SE 87102 **Location:** I-25 exit 224A northbound; exit 224B southbound, just w. B L

HIGH NOON RESTAURANT & SALOON 505/765-1455 4

Regional American. Casual Dining. $11-$37 **AAA Inspector Notes:** *Historic.* An eclectic menu offers selections of wild game, certified Angus beef steak, seafood and New Mexican cuisine. Its decor features tri-cultures of northern New Mexico, and part of its structure is the original 250-year-old adobe building. Dining here is leisurely paced. **Features:** full bar. **Reservations:** suggested. **Address:** 425 San Felipe NW 87104 **Location:** I-40 exit 157A, 0.5 mi s to Mountain Rd, then just e; in Old Town. L D

JC'S NEW YORK PIZZA DEPARTMENT 505/766-6973 9

Italian. Quick Serve. $8-$20 **AAA Inspector Notes:** This downtown restaurant's patio affords a good view of busy Central Avenue. A good selection of pizza can be prepared with all the expected toppings. Also on the menu are salads and pasta dishes. **Features:** beer & wine, patio dining. **Address:** 215 Central Ave NW, Suite B 87102 **Location:** Jct 2nd St, just w. **Parking:** street only. L D LATE

LA CREPE MICHEL 505/242-1251 3

French. Casual Dining. $8-$21 **AAA Inspector Notes:** Off the beaten path, this well-known Old Town café serves fine French cuisine. The crepes are fabulous. **Features:** beer & wine. **Address:** 400 San Felipe St NW, Unit C-2 87104 **Location:** Jct San Felipe St and Central Ave, just n; in Old Town. **Parking:** street only. L D

Q BURGER 505/224-2747 8

Burgers. Casual Dining. $8-$12 **AAA Inspector Notes:** Featuring grass-fed, hormone- and antibiotic-free beef from New Mexico ranches, the menu offers creative and delicious burgers, especially when topped by fire-roasted New Mexico green chile. A great selection of salads and sides, all accompanied by locally crafted beer and wine, makes for a great Southwestern meal. **Features:** beer & wine. **Address:** 301 Central Ave NW 87102 **Location:** Jct 3rd St. **Parking:** street only. L D

ST. CLAIR WINERY & BISTRO 505/243-9916 1

American. Casual Dining. $9-$20 **AAA Inspector Notes:** This lively bistro features creative comfort food along with a lush patio for outdoor dining with live music. Wine tasting is available with an excellent selection of New Mexico wines. A good selection of local craft beers are also featured. **Features:** beer & wine. **Reservations:** suggested. **Address:** 901 Rio Grande Blvd NW, Suite B100 87104 **Location:** I-40 exit 157A (Rio Grande Blvd), just s. L D

(See map & index p. 339.)

SEASONS ROTISSERIE & GRILL   505/766-5100 2

 American. Fine Dining. $8-$32 **AAA Inspector Notes:** The young, affluent clientele comes to this trendy, contemporary spot to see and be seen. Inspired by the changing seasons, the menu features imaginative culinary creations and fine wines chosen to complement them. Sunset views are spectacular from rooftop outdoor tables. **Features:** full bar, patio dining, happy hour. **Reservations:** suggested. **Address:** 2031 Mountain Rd NW 87104 **Location:** Just n of Old Town; in San Felipe Plaza. [L] [D]

STANDARD DINER   505/243-1440 13

American. Casual Dining. $10-$20 **AAA Inspector Notes:** Flashback in time at this upscale retro diner with a modern creative twist on comfort food favorites. The standard mac and cheese and finer loaf are house specialties along with country fried tuna with wasabi guacamole and mouthwatering fish tacos. Also on the menu are creative salads, sandwiches and burgers. **Features:** beer & wine, Sunday brunch. **Address:** 320 Central Ave SE 87102 **Location:** I-25 exit 224A northbound; exit 224B southbound, just w; jct Central Ave and Arno St. **Parking:** on-site and street. [L] [D]

TUCANOS BRAZILIAN GRILL   505/246-9900 10

Brazilian. Casual Dining. $16-$23 **AAA Inspector Notes:** This downtown restaurant caters to meat lovers. Casually attired servers bring multiple courses consisting of freshly cooked beef, pork, chicken and sausage to the table on long, swordlike skewers. The extensive salad bar adds to this place's popularity. **Features:** full bar, patio dining, senior menu, Sunday brunch. **Address:** 110 Central Ave SW 87102 **Location:** Jct 1st St. **Parking:** on-site and street. [L] [D]

VINAIGRETTE   505/842-5507 7

Natural/Organic. Casual Dining. $11-$18 **AAA Inspector Notes:** This vibrant fresh food restaurant features creative salads, soups and sandwiches with ingredients grown on the chef/owner's 10-acre organic garden. Start with the incredibly flavorful wild mushroom stew with fried olive bread. Then try the omega avocado-pinon or nutty pear-fessor salads. A selection of grilled meats or seafood can be added to any salad. Daily fresh baked desserts plus homemade ice cream are a treat. **Features:** beer & wine, patio dining. **Address:** 1828 Central Ave SW 87104 **Location:** Just se of jct San Pasquale Ave SW. [L] [D]

ALBUQUERQUE (F-3)
- **Restaurants p. 356**
- **Hotels & Restaurants map & index p. 342**

THE ALBUQUERQUE MARRIOTT HOTEL   (505)881-6800 31

Hotel $95-$247 **Address:** 2101 Louisiana Blvd NE 87110 **Location:** I-40 exit 162 westbound; exit 162B eastbound, just n; in Northeast Heights.

AAA Benefit: Members save 5% or more!

Facility: 411 units. 17 stories, interior corridors. **Amenities:** video games. **Pool(s):** heated outdoor, heated indoor. **Activities:** exercise room. **Guest Services:** valet and coin laundry, area transportation.

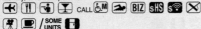

ALBUQUERQUE MARRIOTT PYRAMID NORTH
                                    (505)821-3333 6

Hotel $97-$175

AAA Benefit: Members save 5% or more!

Address: 5151 San Francisco Rd NE 87109 **Location:** I-25 exit 232, just w, then 1 mi s on Pan American Frwy NE. **Facility:** 310 units. 10 stories, interior corridors. **Pool(s):** heated outdoor, heated indoor. **Activities:** exercise room. **Guest Services:** valet and coin laundry.

ALBUQUERQUE SHERATON UPTOWN HOTEL
                                    (505)881-0000 26

Hotel $89-$299

AAA Benefit: Members save up to 15%, plus Starwood Preferred Guest® benefits!

Address: 2600 Louisiana Blvd NE 87110 **Location:** I-40 exit 162, 0.8 mi n; in Northeast Heights. **Facility:** 295 units. 8 stories, interior corridors. **Terms:** cancellation fee imposed. **Amenities:** safes. **Pool(s):** heated indoor. **Activities:** hot tub, exercise room. **Guest Services:** valet laundry, area transportation. *(See ad p. 348.)*

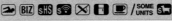

BEST WESTERN AIRPORT ALBUQUERQUE INNSUITES
HOTEL & SUITES   (505)242-7022 42

Hotel $69-$149

AAA Benefit: Save 10% or more every day and earn 10% bonus points!

Address: 2400 Yale Blvd SE 87106 **Location:** I-25 exit 222 (Gibson Blvd) northbound; exit 222A southbound, 1 mi e, then just s. **Facility:** 101 units. 2 stories (no elevator), interior corridors. **Pool(s):** heated outdoor. **Activities:** hot tub. **Guest Services:** valet and coin laundry, area transportation. **Featured Amenity:** breakfast buffet.

BEST WESTERN PLUS EXECUTIVE SUITES
                                    (505)830-0900 16

Hotel $99-$149

AAA Benefit: Save 10% or more every day and earn 10% bonus points!

Address: 4630 Pan American Frwy NE 87109 **Location:** I-25 exit 228 (Montgomery Blvd), just e, then just n. **Facility:** 89 units. 3 stories, interior corridors. **Pool(s):** heated indoor. **Activities:** sauna, hot tub, exercise room. **Guest Services:** valet and coin laundry.

CANDLEWOOD SUITES   (505)888-3424 23

Extended Stay Hotel $90-$190 **Address:** 3025 Menaul Blvd NE 87107 **Location:** I-40 exit 160, just n to Menaul Blvd, then 0.5 mi w. **Facility:** 123 efficiencies. 3 stories, interior corridors. **Terms:** cancellation fee imposed. **Activities:** exercise room. **Guest Services:** valet and coin laundry.

CLUBHOUSE INN & SUITES   505/345-0010 20

Hotel
Rates not provided

Address: 1315 Menaul Blvd NE 87107 **Location:** I-25 exit 227A southbound, 1.5 mi s to Menaul Blvd, then just w; exit 225 northbound, 1.8 mi n, then just w. **Facility:** 136 units. 2 stories (no elevator), interior corridors. **Pool(s):** heated outdoor. **Activities:** hot tub, exercise room. **Guest Services:** valet and coin laundry, area transportation. **Featured Amenity:** full hot breakfast.

(See map & index p. 342.)

COMFORT INN AIRPORT
(505)242-0036 **33**

Hotel
$75-$84

Address: 1801 Yale Blvd SE 87106 **Location:** I-25 exit 222 (Gibson Blvd) northbound; exit 222A southbound, 1 mi e on Gibson Blvd, then just n. **Facility:** 72 units. 3 stories, interior corridors. **Pool(s):** heated indoor. **Activities:** hot tub, exercise room. **Guest Services:** valet and coin laundry. **Featured Amenity: full hot breakfast.**

COMFORT INN & SUITES BY CHOICE HOTELS
(505)822-1090 **3**

Hotel $65-$101 **Address:** 5811 Signal Ave NE 87113 **Location:** I-25 exit 233 (Alameda Blvd), just e. 68 units. 3 stories, interior corridors. **Amenities:** safes. **Pool(s):** heated indoor. **Guest Services:** coin laundry.

COMFORT SUITES
(505)797-0850 **8**

Hotel
$79-$124

Address: 5251 San Antonio Dr NE 87109 **Location:** I-25 exit 231 (San Antonio Dr), just e. **Facility:** 69 units. 3 stories, interior corridors. **Pool(s):** heated indoor. **Activities:** hot tub, exercise room. **Guest Services:** valet and coin laundry. **Featured Amenity: full hot breakfast.**

COURTYARD BY MARRIOTT AIRPORT
(505)843-6600 **35**

Hotel
$83-$185

COURTYARD *Marriott*
AAA Benefit: Members save 5% or more!

Address: 1920 Yale Blvd SE 87106 **Location:** I-25 exit 222 (Gibson Blvd) northbound; exit 222A southbound, 1 mi e, then just n. **Facility:** 150 units. 4 stories, interior corridors. **Pool(s):** heated indoor. **Activities:** hot tub, exercise room. **Guest Services:** valet and coin laundry.

COURTYARD BY MARRIOTT JOURNAL CENTER
(505)823-1919 **5**

Hotel
$81-$150

COURTYARD *Marriott*
AAA Benefit: Members save 5% or more!

Address: 5151 Journal Center Blvd NE 87109 **Location:** I-25 exit 232, just s on Pan American Frwy NE. **Facility:** 150 units. 1-4 stories, interior corridors. **Pool(s):** heated indoor. **Activities:** hot tub, exercise room. **Guest Services:** valet and coin laundry, area transportation.

CROWNE PLAZA ALBUQUERQUE
505/884-2500 **25**

Hotel
Rates not provided

Address: 1901 University Blvd NE 87102 **Location:** I-40 exit 160, just n to Menaul Blvd, then 1.1 mi w. **Facility:** 261 units. 2-12 stories, interior corridors. **Parking:** on-site and valet. **Dining:** 2 restaurants, also, Rancher's Club of New Mexico, see separate listing. **Pool(s):** heated outdoor. **Activities:** hot tub, exercise room. **Guest Services:** valet laundry.

DAYS INN & SUITES ALBUQUERQUE AIRPORT
(505)247-1500 **36**

Hotel $62-$87 **Address:** 2331 Centre Ave SE 87106 **Location:** I-25 exit 222 (Gibson Blvd) northbound; exit 222A southbound, 1 mi e to Yale Blvd, at northeast jct of Gibson and Yale blvds, then just e. **Facility:** 56 units. 3 stories, interior corridors. **Pool(s):** heated indoor. **Activities:** hot tub, exercise room. **Guest Services:** coin laundry.

DRURY INN & SUITES-ALBUQUERQUE
(505)341-3600 **13**

Hotel $90-$155 **Address:** 4310 The 25 Way NE 87109 **Location:** I-25 exit 229 (Jefferson St); northwest quadrant of exchange. **Facility:** 164 units. 6 stories, interior corridors. **Terms:** cancellation fee imposed. **Pool(s):** heated indoor. **Activities:** hot tub, exercise room. **Guest Services:** valet and coin laundry.

ECONO LODGE MIDTOWN
(505)880-0080 **28**

Hotel $55-$100 **Address:** 2412 Carlisle Blvd NE 87110 **Location:** I-40 exit 160, just n. **Facility:** 37 units. 2 stories (no elevator), exterior corridors.

FAIRFIELD INN & SUITES BY MARRIOTT AIRPORT
(505)247-1621 **37**

Hotel $67-$122 **Address:** 2300 Centre Ave SE 87106 **Location:** I-25 exit 222 (Gibson Blvd) northbound; exit 222A southbound, 1 mi e to Yale Blvd; northeast jct Gibson and Yale blvds. **Facility:** 118 units. 4 stories, interior corridors. **Pool(s):** heated outdoor. **Activities:** hot tub, exercise room. **Guest Services:** valet and coin laundry, area transportation.

AAA Benefit: Members save 5% or more!

FAIRFIELD INN BY MARRIOTT ALBUQUERQUE-UNIVERSITY AREA
(505)889-4000 **22**

Hotel
$68-$118

FAIRFIELD INN & SUITES *Marriott*
AAA Benefit: Members save 5% or more!

Address: 1760 Menaul Blvd NE 87102 **Location:** I-40 exit 160, just n to Menaul Blvd, then 1 mi w. **Facility:** 189 units. 3 stories, interior corridors. **Pool(s):** heated indoor. **Activities:** sauna, hot tub, exercise room. **Guest Services:** valet and coin laundry. **Featured Amenity: continental breakfast.**

(See map & index p. 342.)

GUESTHOUSE INN & SUITES ALBUQUERQUE AIRPORT
505/246-9600 **39**

▼▼ Hotel. Rates not provided. **Address:** 2601 Mulberry St SE 87106 **Location:** I-25 exit 222 (Gibson Blvd), just e. **Facility:** 80 units. 3 stories, interior corridors. **Pool(s):** heated outdoor. **Activities:** exercise room. **Guest Services:** valet and coin laundry, area transportation.

HAMPTON INN & SUITES (505)833-3700 **19**

▼▼▼ Hotel $99-$139 **Address:** 6150 Iliff Rd NW 87121 **Location:** I-40 exit 155, 0.6 mi s, then just w. **Facility:** 88 units. 4 stories, interior corridors. **Terms:** 1-7 night minimum stay, cancellation fee imposed. **Pool(s):** heated indoor. **Activities:** hot tub, exercise room. **Guest Services:** valet and coin laundry.

AAA Benefit: Members save up to 10%!

HAMPTON INN & SUITES ALBUQUERQUE NORTH I-25
(505)345-4500 **12**

▼▼▼ Hotel $119-$170 **Address:** 4412 The 25 Way 87109 **Location:** I-25 exit 229 (Jefferson St), just w, then just n. **Facility:** 79 units. 5 stories, interior corridors. **Terms:** 1-7 night minimum stay, cancellation fee imposed. **Amenities:** Some: safes. **Pool(s):** heated indoor. **Activities:** hot tub, exercise room. **Guest Services:** valet and coin laundry.

AAA Benefit: Members save up to 10%!

HAMPTON INN UNIVERSITY-MIDTOWN
(505)837-9300 **27**

▼▼▼ Hotel $104-$169

AAA Benefit: Members save up to 10%!

Address: 2300 Carlisle Blvd NE 87110 **Location:** I-40 exit 160, just w, then just n. **Facility:** 126 units. 4 stories, interior corridors. **Terms:** 1-7 night minimum stay, cancellation fee imposed. **Pool(s):** heated outdoor. **Activities:** hot tub, exercise room. **Guest Services:** valet and coin laundry. **Featured Amenity: full hot breakfast.**

HILTON GARDEN INN ALBUQUERQUE JOURNAL CENTER
(505)314-0800 **9**

▼▼▼ Hotel $99-$159 **Address:** 5320 San Antonio Dr NE 87109 **Location:** I-25 exit 231 (San Antonio Dr), just e. **Facility:** 94 units. 4 stories, interior corridors. **Terms:** 1-7 night minimum stay, cancellation fee imposed. **Amenities:** video games, safes. **Pool(s):** heated indoor. **Activities:** hot tub, exercise room. **Guest Services:** valet and coin laundry.

AAA Benefit: Members save up to 10%!

Discover a wealth of savings and offers on the AAA/CAA travel websites

HILTON GARDEN INN ALBUQUERQUE UPTOWN
(505)944-0300 **30**

▼▼▼ Hotel $99-$199 **Address:** 6510 Americas Pkwy 87110 **Location:** I-40 exit 162, just n, then just w; in Northeast Heights. **Facility:** 149 units. 7 stories, interior corridors. **Terms:** 1-7 night minimum stay, cancellation fee imposed. **Amenities:** video games, safes. **Pool(s):** heated indoor. **Activities:** hot tub, exercise room. **Guest Services:** valet and coin laundry.

AAA Benefit: Members save up to 10%!

HOLIDAY INN EXPRESS ALBUQUERQUE MIDTOWN
505/881-0544 **24**

▼▼▼ Hotel. Rates not provided. **Address:** 2500 Menaul Blvd NE 87107 **Location:** I-40 exit 160, just n to Menaul Blvd, then 0.6 mi w. **Facility:** 122 units. 6 stories, interior corridors. **Pool(s):** heated outdoor. **Activities:** exercise room. **Guest Services:** valet and coin laundry, area transportation.

HOLIDAY INN EXPRESS & SUITES 505/338-5255 **34**

▼▼▼ Hotel. Rates not provided. **Address:** 1921 Yale Blvd SE 87106 **Location:** I-25 exit 222 (Gibson Blvd) northbound; exit 222A southbound, 1 mi e, then just n. **Facility:** 100 units. 4 stories, interior corridors. **Pool(s):** heated indoor. **Activities:** hot tub, exercise room. **Guest Services:** valet and coin laundry, area transportation.

HOLIDAY INN EXPRESS HOTEL & SUITES
505/797-2291 **2**

▼▼▼ Hotel. Rates not provided. **Address:** 5401 Alameda Blvd NE 87113 **Location:** I-25 exit 233 (Alameda Blvd), just w. **Facility:** 62 units. 3 stories, interior corridors. **Amenities:** safes. **Pool(s):** heated indoor. **Activities:** hot tub, exercise room. **Guest Services:** valet and coin laundry.

HOLIDAY INN EXPRESS HOTEL & SUITES ALBUQUERQUE HISTORIC OLD TOWN 505/842-5000 **17**

▼▼▼ Hotel. Rates not provided. **Address:** 2300 12th St NW 87104 **Location:** I-40 exit 157B eastbound; exit 158 westbound; just s of Menaul Blvd. **Facility:** 108 units. 4 stories, interior corridors. **Pool(s):** heated indoor. **Activities:** hot tub, exercise room. **Guest Services:** valet and coin laundry.

HOLIDAY INN HOTEL & SUITES 505/944-2222 **15**

▼▼▼ Hotel. Rates not provided. **Address:** 5050 Jefferson St NE 87109 **Location:** I-25 exit 229 northbound, just n on east frontage road; exit 229 southbound, s on west frontage road to Jefferson St, then just e. **Facility:** 122 units. 6 stories, interior corridors. **Parking:** winter plug-ins. **Amenities:** safes. **Pool(s):** heated indoor. **Activities:** hot tub, exercise room. **Guest Services:** valet and coin laundry.

HOMEWOOD SUITES BY HILTON-JOURNAL CENTER
(505)998-4663 **10**

▼▼▼ Extended Stay Hotel $119-$139 **Address:** 5400 San Antonio Dr NE 87109 **Location:** I-25 exit 231 (San Antonio Dr), just e. **Facility:** 63 efficiencies. 3 stories, interior corridors. **Terms:** 1-7 night minimum stay, cancellation fee imposed. **Pool(s):** heated indoor. **Activities:** hot tub, exercise room. **Guest Services:** valet and coin laundry.

AAA Benefit: Members save up to 10%!

(See map & index p. 342.)

HYATT PLACE ALBUQUERQUE AIRPORT
(505)242-9300 **45**

Hotel
$74-$179

HYATT PLACE

AAA Benefit: Members save 10%!

Address: 1400 Sunport Pl SE 87106 **Location:** I-25 exit 221, 0.3 mi e to University Blvd exit, then just n to Woodward Rd. **Facility:** 127 units. 6 stories, interior corridors. **Terms:** cancellation fee imposed. **Amenities:** video games, safes. **Pool(s):** heated outdoor. **Activities:** exercise room. **Guest Services:** valet laundry, area transportation. **Featured Amenity:** breakfast buffet. *(See ad this page.)*

HYATT PLACE ALBUQUERQUE UPTOWN
(505)872-9000 **29**

Hotel
$95-$229

HYATT PLACE

AAA Benefit: Members save 10%!

Address: 6901 Arvada Ave NE 87110 **Location:** I-40 exit 162, 0.7 mi n. **Facility:** 126 units. 6 stories, interior corridors. **Terms:** cancellation fee imposed. **Amenities:** video games. *Some:* safes. **Pool(s):** heated outdoor. **Activities:** exercise room. **Guest Services:** valet laundry. **Featured Amenity:** breakfast buffet.

ISLETA RESORT & CASINO
505/724-3800

Resort Hotel. Rates not provided. **Address:** 11000 Broadway SE 87105 **Location:** I-25 exit 215, 0.5 mi s of Isleta Pueblo. **Facility:** This popular resort has everything for a relaxing, fun-filled stay from the casino to luxurious spa, 27-hole golf course, six restaurants and fishing lakes. 201 units. 6 stories, interior corridors. **Parking:** on-site and valet. **Amenities:** safes. **Dining:** 6 restaurants, nightclub, entertainment. **Pool(s):** heated outdoor, heated indoor. **Activities:** hot tub, steamroom, fishing, regulation golf, playground, game room, picnic facilities, trails, exercise room, spa. **Guest Services:** coin laundry, area transportation.

LA QUINTA INN ALBUQUERQUE AIRPORT
(505)243-5500 **40**

Hotel $64-$235 **Address:** 2116 Yale Blvd SE 87106 **Location:** I-25 exit 222 (Gibson Blvd) northbound; exit 222A southbound, 1 mi e. **Facility:** 105 units. 3 stories, exterior corridors. **Pool(s):** heated outdoor. **Activities:** exercise room. **Guest Services:** valet and coin laundry, area transportation.

LA QUINTA INN & SUITES ALBUQUERQUE MIDTOWN
(505)761-5600 **21**

Hotel $97-$240 **Address:** 2011 Menaul Blvd 87107 **Location:** Jct University and Menaul blvds, just e. **Facility:** 72 units. 3 stories, interior corridors. **Pool(s):** heated indoor. **Activities:** hot tub, exercise room. **Guest Services:** valet and coin laundry.

LA QUINTA INN & SUITES ALBUQUERQUE WEST
(505)839-1744 **18**

Hotel $64-$224 **Address:** 6101 Iliff Rd NW 87121 **Location:** I-40 exit 155, just sw. **Facility:** 118 units. 5 stories, interior corridors. **Pool(s):** heated outdoor. **Activities:** hot tub, exercise room. **Guest Services:** valet and coin laundry.

▼ See AAA listing this page ▼

Say YES to ERS text updates to stay posted when your tow truck is on the way

(See map & index p. 342.)

QUALITY INN & SUITES ALBUQUERQUE (505)823-1300 **7**

◥◥ ◥◥ Hotel $55-$200 Address: 7620 Pan American Frwy NE 87109 Location: I-25 exit 231 (San Antonio Dr), 0.8 mi n on frontage road. Facility: 168 units. 3 stories, interior corridors. Amenities: safes. Pool(s): heated outdoor. Activities: exercise room. Guest Services: valet and coin laundry.

CALL ⎙M ⇌ BIZ 🛜 ✕ ⬛ /SOME UNITS 🖪 📠

RESIDENCE INN BY MARRIOTT ALBUQUERQUE AIRPORT
(505)242-2844 **32**

◥◥ ◥◥ Extended Stay Hotel
$103-$206 Address: 2301 International
Dr SE 87106 Location: I-25 exit 222
(Gibson Blvd) northbound; exit 222A
southbound, 1 mi e, just n of jct Yale

AAA Benefit:
Members save 5%
or more!

Blvd. Facility: 110 units, some two bedrooms, efficiencies and kitchens. 4 stories, interior corridors. Pool(s): heated indoor. Activities: hot tub, exercise room. Guest Services: valet and coin laundry.

✚ ⬆ CALL ⎙M ⇌ BIZ HS 🛜 ✕ 🖪 📠 ⬛ /SOME UNITS 🖪

RESIDENCE INN BY MARRIOTT NORTH (505)761-0200 **11**

◥◥ ◥◥ Extended Stay Hotel
$104-$182 Address: 4331 The Lane at
25 NE 87109 Location: I-25 exit 229
(Jefferson St), just w, just n to The Lane
at 25 NE, then just e. Facility: 90 units,

AAA Benefit:
Members save 5%
or more!

some two bedrooms, efficiencies and kitchens. 3 stories, interior corridors. Pool(s): heated outdoor. Activities: hot tub, exercise room. Guest Services: valet and coin laundry.

⬆ CALL ⎙M ⇌ BIZ HS 🛜 ✕ 🖪 📠 ⬛ /SOME UNITS 🖪

Trust the recommendations
of AAA/CAA travel experts
to make a good trip great

ROUTE 66 CASINO HOTEL   505/352-7866

◥◥ ◥◥ ◥
Hotel
$99-$139

Address: 14500 Central Ave SW 87121 Location: I-40 exit 140, just w. Facility: This casino property sports a fun Route 66 décor along with newly renovated guest rooms. 154 units. 6 stories, interior corridors. Parking: on-site and valet. Terms: check-in 4 pm, cancellation fee imposed. Amenities: safes. Dining: 4 restaurants, also, Thunder Road, see separate listing, nightclub, entertainment. Pool(s): heated indoor. Activities: hot tub, game room, exercise room. Guest Services: coin laundry. (See ad p. 347.)

SAVE 🐾 🍴 ⛉ CALL ⎙M ⇌ BIZ HS 🛜 🎦 🖪 ⬛ /SOME UNITS 📠

SANDIA RESORT & CASINO   (505)796-7500 **1**

◥◥ ◥◥ ◥◥
Resort Hotel
$179-$299

Address: 30 Rainbow Rd NE 87113 Location: I-25 exit 234, just e. Facility: In a beautiful setting at the foot-hills of the Sandia Mountains, this resort offers plush guest rooms that welcome you for a restful night after enjoying the abundance of on-site activities. 228 units, some two bedrooms. 9 stories, interior corridors. Terms: check-in 4 pm, cancellation fee imposed. Amenities: video games, safes. Dining: 8 restaurants, also, Bien Shur Restaurant, see separate listing, nightclub, entertainment. Pool(s): heated outdoor. Activities: sauna, hot tub, steamroom, regulation golf, recreation programs, exercise room, spa. Guest Services: valet laundry, area transportation. (See ad this page.)

SAVE 🐾 ✚ 🍴 🖧 ⛉ CALL ⎙M ⇌ BIZ HS 🛜 🎦 🖪 ⬛

▼ See AAA listing this page ▼

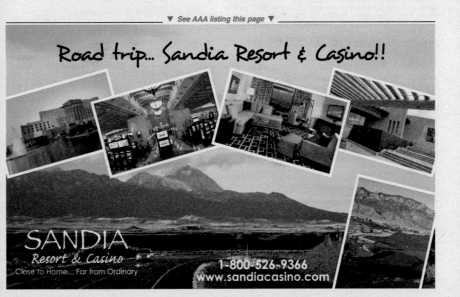

(See map & index p. 342.)

SHERATON ALBUQUERQUE AIRPORT HOTEL
505/843-7000

Hotel
Rates not provided

AAA Benefit: Members save up to 15%, plus Starwood Preferred Guest® benefits!

Address: 2910 Yale Blvd SE 87106 **Location:** I-25 exit 222 (Gibson Blvd) northbound; exit 222A southbound, 1 mi e, then 0.5 mi s. **Facility:** 276 units. 15 stories, interior corridors. **Amenities:** video games. **Pool(s):** outdoor. **Activities:** exercise room. **Guest Services:** valet and coin laundry, area transportation.

STAYBRIDGE SUITES ALBUQUERQUE AIRPORT
505/338-3900 **44**

Extended Stay Hotel. Rates not provided. **Address:** 1350 Sunport Pl SE 87106 **Location:** I-25 exit 221, 0.3 mi e to University Blvd exit, then just n to Woodward Rd. **Facility:** 100 efficiencies, some two bedrooms. 4 stories, interior corridors. **Pool(s):** heated outdoor. **Activities:** hot tub, exercise room. **Guest Services:** valet and coin laundry, area transportation.

STAYBRIDGE SUITES ALBUQUERQUE NORTH
(505)266-7829 **4**

Extended Stay Hotel $95-$240 **Address:** 5817 Signal Ave NE 87113 **Location:** I-25 exit 233 (Alameda Blvd), just e; jct Alameda Blvd and Signal Ave. **Facility:** 90 efficiencies, some two bedrooms. 3 stories, interior corridors. **Amenities:** Some: safes. **Pool(s):** heated indoor. **Activities:** hot tub, exercise room. **Guest Services:** complimentary and valet laundry, area transportation.

SUPER 8 ALBUQUERQUE AIRPORT
(505)246-2255 **41**

Hotel $49-$149 **Address:** 2231 Yale Blvd SE 87106 **Location:** I-25 exit 222 (Gibson Blvd) southbound; exit 222 (Gibson Blvd) northbound, 1 mi e, then just n. **Facility:** 62 units. 3 stories, exterior corridors. **Pool(s):** heated indoor. **Activities:** hot tub, exercise room. **Guest Services:** valet laundry.

TOWNEPLACE SUITES BY MARRIOTT
(505)232-5800 **38**

Extended Stay Hotel $79-$138 **Address:** 2400 Centre Ave SE 87106 **Location:** I-25 exit 222 (Gibson Blvd) northbound; exit 222A southbound, 1 mi e to Yale Blvd, at northeast jct of Gibson and Yale blvds, then just e. **Facility:** 107 efficiencies, some two bedrooms and kitchens. 4 stories, interior corridors. **Pool(s):** heated outdoor. **Activities:** hot tub, exercise room. **Guest Services:** valet and coin laundry, area transportation.

AAA Benefit: Members save 5% or more!

Take your imagination to new destinations with the online AAA/CAA Travel Guides

---

TOWNEPLACE SUITES BY MARRIOTT ALBUQUERQUE NORTH
(505)345-3131 **14**

Extended Stay Hotel $93-$176 **Address:** 5511 Office Blvd NE 87109 **Location:** I-25 exit 229 (Jefferson St), just s. **Facility:** 91 units, some two bedrooms, efficiencies and kitchens. 4 stories, interior corridors. **Pool(s):** heated outdoor. **Activities:** exercise room. **Guest Services:** valet and coin laundry.

AAA Benefit: Members save 5% or more!

HILTON GARDEN INN ALBUQUERQUE AIRPORT
505/765-1000

fyi Hotel Did not meet all AAA rating requirements for locking devices in some guest rooms at time of last evaluation. **Address:** 2601 Yale Blvd SE 87106 **Location:** I-25 exit 222 (Gibson Blvd) northbound; exit 222A southbound, 1 mi e, then just s. Facilities, services, and décor characterize a mid-scale property.

AAA Benefit: Members save up to 10%!

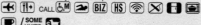
WHERE TO EAT

AZUMA
505/880-9800 **14**

Japanese. Casual Dining. $9-$30 **AAA Inspector Notes:** A tasty meal, this restaurant's dragon roll has artistic appeal. The presentation of appetizers and entrées shows careful attention to visual detail. **Features:** beer & wine. **Address:** 4701 San Mateo Blvd NE 87109 **Location:** Jct Montgomery and San Mateo blvds, just n.

BIEN SHUR RESTAURANT
505/796-7500 **2**

International. Fine Dining. $26-$50 **AAA Inspector Notes:** At the top of the Sandia Resort, the tasteful restaurant and bar offers spectacular views of the Sandia Mountains and golf course to the east or the city of Albuquerque to the west. Outdoor seating is available on the ninth-floor terrace. The creative menu offers a variety of fish, poultry, fowl, game and steaks. The excellent dessert cart presentation is difficult to resist. **Features:** full bar, patio dining, happy hour. **Reservations:** suggested. **Address:** 30 Rainbow Rd NE 87113 **Location:** I-25 exit 234, just e; in Sandia Resort & Casino.

CASA DE BENAVIDEZ NEW MEXICAN RESTAURANT
505/898-3311 **3**

Mexican. Casual Dining. $9-$22 **AAA Inspector Notes:** The garden patio setting, with a pond and lush foliage, is ideal for relaxing with a margarita and generous portions of New Mexican specialties. Although the salsa gets most of the buzz, the green chile is also great. **Features:** full bar, patio dining. **Reservations:** suggested. **Address:** 8032 4th St NW 87114 **Location:** Jct 4th St and El Pueblo Rd, just s.

CERVANTES RESTAURANT & LOUNGE
505/262-2253 **42**

Regional
Mexican
Casual Dining
$9-$26

AAA Inspector Notes: Well-prepared New Mexican dishes-including excellent carne adovada, chiles rellenos and homemade tamales-are featured at this locally popular restaurant. Served as an appetizer with tortilla chips, salsa commands real authority. This place is near Kirtland Air Force Base. **Features:** full bar. **Address:** 5801 Gibson Rd SE 87108 **Location:** Jct San Pedro Dr.

CHAMA RIVER BREWING COMPANY
505/342-1800 **13**

American. Casual Dining. $10-$28 **AAA Inspector Notes:** A Santa Fe atmosphere, along with Northern New Mexico cuisine, give this impressive restaurant and brewery its personality. The menu lists a good selection of sandwiches. **Features:** full bar. **Address:** 4939 Pan American Frwy NE 87109 **Location:** I-25 exit 229, just w.

(See map & index p. 342.)

CHRISTY MAE'S   505/255-4740   32
▼ American. Family Dining. $9-$11 **AAA Inspector Notes:** This unpretentious family operation prepares home-style cooking, including a good selection of soups, salads, sandwiches and pot pies. Breads and desserts, such as carrot cake, are prepared in house. **Address:** 1400 San Pedro Dr NE 87110 **Location:** I-40 exit 162 westbound; exit 162A eastbound, 0.5 mi s on Louisiana Blvd to Lomas Blvd, 0.5 mi w to San Pedro Dr, then just n; corner of Mountain and San Pedro drs. L D

EL PINTO   505/898-1771   1
▼▼ Mexican. Family Dining. $8-$27 **AAA Inspector Notes:** Southwestern decor, fireplaces and indoor waterfalls add visual interest to the many rooms of the local favorite established in 1962. The roomy patio, which seats 600, is believed to be the state's largest. The menu focuses on basic New Mexican fare, including enchiladas, burritos and carne adovada. The flavorful assortment of salsas are available in jars for purchase. **Features:** full bar, patio dining, Sunday brunch, happy hour. **Address:** 10500 4th St NW 87114 **Location:** I-25 exit 234 (Tramway Blvd), 1.5 mi w to SR 556 (which becomes 4th St), then just s. L D CALL M

FLYING STAR CAFE   505/275-8311   18
▼▼ American. Family Dining. $9-$13 **AAA Inspector Notes:** This eatery has a trendy coffee-shop setting with an area for reading magazines while enjoying quiche, pizza, salad, stir-fry, sandwiches, baguettes and dessert. Sustainable, local and organic products are featured. They have a good range of coffees and Italian soda, and seating on the outside deck. **Features:** beer & wine, patio dining. **Address:** 4501 Juan Tabo Blvd NE 87111 **Location:** Just n of jct Montgomery Blvd. B L D

FRONTIER RESTAURANT   505/266-0550   33
▼ American. Quick Serve. $5-$12 **AAA Inspector Notes:** Right across the street from the University of New Mexico campus, the well-known dining spot prepares jumbo homemade sweet rolls and a large selection of Southwestern dishes, burgers and sandwiches. Students love this place, which has been in business since 1971. **Address:** 2400 Central Ave SE 87106 **Location:** Corner of Central and Harvard aves, just e. B L D LATE

GARCIA'S KITCHEN   505/275-5812   22
▼▼ Mexican. Casual Dining. $5-$15 **AAA Inspector Notes:** Green chile and carne adovada addictions have been born at this casual spot. And many tortilla worshipers make a pilgrimage here or to any of the Garcia's locations on a regular basis. This bright and flashy restaurant serves breakfast all day long. **Features:** beer & wine. **Address:** 3601 Juan Tabo Blvd NE 87111 **Location:** Southwest corner of Juan Tabo Blvd and Comanche Rd. B L D

HIGH FINANCE   505/243-9742
▼▼ American. Casual Dining. $9-$38 **AAA Inspector Notes:** Patrons enjoy a great view of the city from the restaurant's vantage point atop the 10,378-foot Sandia Peak. Ticket prices to ride the aerial tramway, the only way to access this place, are reduced for those who make reservations. It is wise to be prepared for a time-consuming meal. **Features:** full bar. **Reservations:** suggested. **Address:** 40 Tramway Rd 87122 **Location:** I-25 exit 234 (Tramway Rd), 5.5 mi e to Sandia Peak Tramway base terminal. **Parking:** on-site (fee). L D

IL VICINO WOOD OVEN PIZZA   505/271-0882
▼ Pizza Sandwiches. Quick Serve. $6-$11 **AAA Inspector Notes:** Wood-oven pizza is the signature dish, but great sandwiches and salads also are served. Wine complements the meal. **Features:** beer & wine. **Address:** 11225 Montgomery Blvd NE 87111 **Location:** Jct Montgomery and Juan Tabo blvds. L D CALL M

JINJA BAR & BISTRO   505/856-1413   4
▼▼▼ Asian. Casual Dining. $10-$18 **AAA Inspector Notes:** The diverse menu at this bistro gives plenty of opportunities for diners to sample several cuisine styles with a menu that includes Japanese, Thai, Chinese and Vietnamese choices. Subtle sophistication marks the casual dining room. **Features:** full bar, patio dining, happy hour. **Address:** 8900 Holly Ave NE, Suite B 87122 **Location:** I-25 exit 232, 1.8 mi e on Paseo del Norte, just n on Barstow St; in Ventura Place. L D

KELLY'S BREWERY & RESTAURANT   505/262-2739   37
▼▼ American. Casual Dining. $8-$14 **AAA Inspector Notes:** A sunny street side patio area greets guests at this pleasant setting, the perfect spot for drinks or dining with friends. Pub-style food is served with a grand selection of microbrewed beers. **Features:** full bar, patio dining, Sunday brunch. **Address:** 3222 Central Ave SE 87106 **Location:** Jct Central and Wellesley aves. **Parking:** street only. B L D

KRUNG THAI   505/292-9319   25
▼▼ Thai. Family Dining. $7-$10 **AAA Inspector Notes:** Well-prepared traditional Thai cuisine can be ordered as spicy or mild as desired. Thai iced tea is a popular beverage. **Address:** 7923 Menaul Blvd NE 87110 **Location:** Jct Wyoming and Menaul blvds, just w. L D

LOS CUATES DEL NORTE   505/237-2800   26
▼▼ American. Casual Dining. $9-$16 **AAA Inspector Notes:** Waits are commonplace at this large and locally popular restaurant, where New Mexican specialties include fajitas, dark red and spicy salsa, hefty burger-filled burritos, chicken enchiladas on corn tortillas and refried beans and rice. **Features:** full bar, patio dining. **Address:** 8700 Menaul Blvd NE 87112 **Location:** Jct Menaul and Wyoming blvds, just w. L D

LOYOLA'S FAMILY RESTAURANT   505/268-6478   39
▼▼ Mexican. Family Dining. $4-$10 **AAA Inspector Notes:** Patrons can dine on both American and New Mexican fare. Reasonable prices, generous portions and exceptional red chile are hallmarks of this neighborhood eatery. **Address:** 4500 Central Ave SE 87108 **Location:** Jct Central and Adams aves. B L

MANNIE'S FAMILY RESTAURANT   505/265-1669   35
▼▼ American. Casual Dining. $6-$9 **AAA Inspector Notes:** This long-time favorite has been serving folks in the University of New Mexico area for more than 30 years. Moderately priced American and New Mexican food is plated in generous portions. Service is fast. **Features:** beer & wine. **Address:** 2900 Central Ave SE 87106 **Location:** Jct Central Ave and Girard Blvd. B L D

MARCELLO'S CHOPHOUSE   505/837-2467   28
▼▼▼ Steak. Fine Dining. $8-$65 **AAA Inspector Notes:** Attentive service at this upscale steakhouse makes for an enjoyable dining experience. The freshest steaks and chops plus excellent fish and shellfish top the menu. A creative twist on comfort sides include truffled macaroni and cheese and green chile mashed potatoes. The hot chocolate cake is a definite treat. **Features:** full bar, patio dining, happy hour. **Reservations:** suggested, for dinner. **Address:** 2201 Q St, Suite B 87110 **Location:** I-40 exit 162, 0.5 mi n; in Uptown Center. L D CALL M

MAY CAFE   505/265-4448   40
▼▼ Vietnamese. Casual Dining. $8-$15 **AAA Inspector Notes:** Excellent lemon grass chicken is one of many well-prepared entrées at this ethnically decorated restaurant. **Features:** beer & wine. **Address:** 111 Louisiana Blvd SE 87108 **Location:** Jct Central Ave and Louisiana Blvd, just s. L D

MILLY'S RESTAURANT   505/884-0707   21
▼▼ American. Family Dining. $5-$10 **AAA Inspector Notes:** Hearty breakfasts and lunches are priced moderately at this family spot. Enticing daily specials such as meatloaf are served with mashed potatoes, gravy and a vegetable. The sandwich selection is substantial. Brownies make a great dessert. **Address:** 2100 Candelaria Rd NE 87107 **Location:** Jct Candelaria Rd and Princeton Ave. B L

MIMMO'S RISTORANTE & PIZZERIA   505/831-4191   15
▼▼ Italian Pizza. Family Dining. $8-$18 **AAA Inspector Notes:** This restaurant sets up a daily luncheon buffet with an array of tasty choices, including lasagna and pizza. The menu offers a wide selection of Italian specialties. **Features:** beer & wine. **Address:** 3301 Coors Blvd NW 87120 **Location:** I-40 exit 155, just n; in Ladera Shopping Center. L D

(See map & index p. 342.)

MING DYNASTY 505/296-0298 31
WW WW Chinese. Casual Dining. $6-$12 **AAA Inspector Notes:** The traditional American-style Chinese restaurant is complete with a dim sum lunch and a comfortable, ethnically decorated dining room. **Features:** beer & wine. **Address:** 1551 Eubank Blvd NE 87112 **Location:** Jct Eubank Blvd and Indian School Rd, just s.
L D

MONROE'S RESTAURANT 505/881-4224 10
WW WW Mexican. Casual Dining. $9-$17 **AAA Inspector Notes:** Long a popular dining spot for those who enjoy New Mexican food, this restaurant produces local favorites, as well as some seafood dishes popular along the Mexican coast. **Features:** beer & wine. **Address:** 6051 Osuna Rd NE 87109 **Location:** I-25 exit 230 (San Mateo Blvd), 0.4 mi s, then just e. L D

NICK & JIMMY'S RESTAURANT & BAR 505/344-9169 11
WW WW WW Mediterranean Steak Seafood. Fine Dining. $12-$30 **AAA Inspector Notes:** This bustling restaurant, popular with local business clientèle offers professional and attentive staff. Plentiful servings of Mediterranean favorites are offered along with Prime steaks and seafood. **Features:** full bar, happy hour. **Reservations:** suggested. **Address:** 5021 S Pan American West Frwy 87109 **Location:** I-25 exit 229 (Jefferson St) southbound, just s; exit northbound, just w, then just s. L D

NOB HILL BAR & GRILL 505/266-4455 36
WW WW WW American. Casual Dining. $11-$25 **AAA Inspector Notes:** An upscale joint is the theme of this trendy and hip hangout. The lively atmosphere is where the in-crowd is to be seen enjoying great food and cocktails. **Features:** full bar, patio dining, Sunday brunch, happy hour. **Address:** 3128 Central Ave SE 87106 **Location:** Jct Girard Blvd, southwest corner. **Parking:** street only.
L D

THE OWL CAFE 505/291-4900 38
WW WW American. Casual Dining. $5-$12 **AAA Inspector Notes:** This café delivers its distinctive green-chile cheeseburgers in a 1950s diner setting complete with tableside jukeboxes and soda-jerk malts. It also offers a wide-ranging menu of stir-fry veggies, red-chile pork tamales and chicken-fried steak. **Features:** beer & wine, patio dining, senior menu. **Address:** 800 Eubank Blvd NE 87123 **Location:** I-40 exit 165 (Eubank Blvd), just n. B L D

PAISANO'S ITALIAN RESTAURANT 505/298-7541 29
WW WW Italian. Casual Dining. $8-$26 **AAA Inspector Notes:** Patrons can unwind in the cozy dining room or on the romantic patio to nosh on colorful traditional dishes, such as eggplant parmigiana accented by tasty red marinara sauce. The wine selection is good and housemade desserts are luscious. **Features:** beer & wine, patio dining. **Address:** 1935 Eubank Blvd NE 87112 **Location:** I-40 exit 165 (Eubank Blvd), 1.4 mi n. L D

PAPA FELIPE'S 505/292-8877 27
WW WW Mexican. Casual Dining. $8-$17 **AAA Inspector Notes:** A welcoming cantina lounge and pleasant, ethnic look are combined with well-prepared food and efficient service at this long-popular dining spot. Try the fresh sopaipillas, and save room for flan. **Features:** full bar, senior menu, happy hour. **Address:** 9800 Menaul Blvd NE 87112 **Location:** Jct Eubank and Menaul blvds, just e.
L D

PAPPADEAUX SEAFOOD KITCHEN 505/345-0240
WW WW Cajun Seafood. Casual Dining. $11-$50 **AAA Inspector Notes:** A seafood lover's delight, the restaurant taps into a little bit of New Orleans with its Cajun dishes and elaborate menu selections. Patrons might start off with a creative choice of blackened oyster and shrimp fondeaux with crayfish and let the feast begin. While music plays in the background, patrons can dig into dirty rice or spicy gumbo loaded with seafood. Well-seasoned shrimp and fish are prepared in varied ways. **Features:** full bar, happy hour. **Address:** 5011 Pan American Frwy NE 87109 **Location:** I-25 exit 229 (Jefferson St), just s. L D

PARS CUISINE 505/345-5156 9
WW WW WW Mediterranean. Casual Dining. $10-$28 **AAA Inspector Notes:** This popular restaurant's exotic decor evokes a typical Middle Eastern villa. Persian and Greek dishes include chelo-kebab barg and lamb souvlaki, prepared in the traditional manner. Live entertainment, including belly dancing, is featured on weekends. **Features:** beer & wine, patio dining. **Reservations:** suggested. **Address:** 4320 The 25 Way NE, Suite 100 87109 **Location:** I-25 exit 229 (Jefferson St), just e. L D

P.F. CHANG'S CHINA BISTRO 505/344-8282 7
WW WW WW Chinese. Fine Dining. $8-$25 **AAA Inspector Notes:** Trendy, upscale decor provides a pleasant backdrop for New Age Chinese dining. Appetizers, soups and salads are a meal by themselves. Vegetarian plates and sides, noodles, chow meins, chicken and meat dishes are created from exotic, fresh ingredients. **Features:** full bar, patio dining, happy hour. **Reservations:** suggested. **Address:** 4440 The 25 Way NE 87109 **Location:** I-25 exit 230, just w. L D

QUARTERS BAR-B-QUE 505/299-9864
WW WW Barbecue. Casual Dining. $8-$23 **AAA Inspector Notes:** A homey, rustic look is what diners find at this popular eatery. Widely known for barbecue spare ribs, beef and hot links, don't pass up the chance to try the Alaskan king crab legs. Plan to save room for dessert—especially tempting to those with a sweet tooth are the mud pie and cheesecake. **Features:** full bar, patio dining. **Address:** 4516 Wyoming Blvd NE 87111 **Location:** I-40 exit 164 eastbound, 3 mi n; exit 164C westbound, 0.5 mi w on Lomas Blvd, then 3.3 mi n.
L D

RANCHER'S CLUB OF NEW MEXICO
505/889-8071 24
WW WW WW
Steak
Fine Dining
$26-$78
AAA Inspector Notes: A fine dining restaurant with an elegant lounge and dining room that, at the same time, reflects a ranch motif yet displays a cultivated, upscale ambience. The house specializes in the finest steak and seafood available, grilled over exotic woods and served by a professional staff that is well known for polished and refined service. **Features:** full bar. **Reservations:** required. **Address:** 1901 University Blvd NE 87102 **Location:** I-40 exit 160, just n to Menaul Blvd, then 1.1 mi w; in Crowne Plaza Albuquerque. **Parking:** on-site and valet. *Menu on AAA.com*
D

RANGE CAFE 505/293-2633 17
WW WW American. Casual Dining. $8-$18 **AAA Inspector Notes:** This colorful café features some of the best dishes of two cultures. In addition to spicy New Mexican food, such as green chile enchiladas, the menu includes good old American food and sandwiches. **Features:** beer & wine, Sunday brunch. **Address:** 4401 Wyoming Blvd NE 87111 **Location:** Jct Montgomery and Wyoming blvds, just s.
B L D CALL M

RICHARD'S MEXICAN RESTAURANT 505/881-1039 23
WW WW Mexican. Casual Dining. $6-$10 **AAA Inspector Notes:** Heart-healthy New Mexican cuisine is the specialty here, and traditional favorites are prepared to be low in cholesterol and fat but high on flavor and taste. Try the green chile chicken enchiladas or Huevos Rancheros with fresh red chile sauce. **Features:** beer & wine. **Address:** 3301 Menaul Blvd NE, Suite 1 87107 **Location:** Jct Carlisle Blvd, just w; in American Square.

RUDY'S COUNTRY STORE AND BAR-B-QUE
WW Barbecue. Quick Serve. $7-$19 **AAA Inspector Notes:** This small, informal barbecue chain has a twist: The tasty food is ordered by the pound. Guests can mix and match and order three-quarters of a pound of beef with a half-pound of turkey or pork, for example. Desserts and coleslaw are prepackaged, and precooked beans accompany the meat. A drive-through window is available at most locations. **Bar:** beer only. B L D

For additional information, visit AAA.com
LOCATIONS:
Address: 2321 Carlisle Blvd NE 87110 **Location:** I-40 exit 160, just n. **Phone:** 505/884-4000

Address: 10136 Coors Blvd NW 87114 **Location:** Just s of jct Alameda Blvd NW. **Phone:** 505/890-7113

(See map & index p. 342.)

SAIGON RESTAURANT   505/884-0706 8

▼▼ Vietnamese. Casual Dining. $8-$20 **AAA Inspector Notes:** Patrons experience the subtle, exotic flavors of Vietnam at the family-owned café, where traditional menu offerings are served in generous portions. **Features:** beer & wine. **Address:** 6001 San Mateo Blvd NE, Suite D4 87109 **Location:** I-25 exit 230 (San Mateo Blvd), 0.4 mi s; jct San Mateo Blvd and Osuna Rd; in Fiesta Norte Center. L   D

SANDIAGO'S MEXICAN GRILL AT THE TRAM   505/856-6692

▼▼ ▼▼ Mexican. Casual Dining. $8-$24 **AAA Inspector Notes:** Dazzling evening city views are available from either the patio or dining room. The fish specialties are prepared in an authentic Mexican style; try the plantain-wrapped halibut for a little bit of Mexico. Save room for the heavenly chocolate flan. **Features:** full bar, patio dining. **Address:** 40 Tramway Rd NE 87122 **Location:** At eastern end of tramway access road; in same building as tram departure point. L   D

SAVOY BAR & GRILL   505/294-9463 20

▼▼ ▼▼ American. Fine Dining. $9-$38 **AAA Inspector Notes:** This open and airy space features sophisticated décor and showcases a wine-friendly atmosphere. The demonstration kitchen produces a creative menu of local products including organic produce, cheese and meats. **Features:** full bar, patio dining, Sunday brunch, happy hour. **Reservations:** suggested. **Address:** 10601 Montgomery Blvd NE 87111 **Location:** Between Juan Tabo Blvd and Morris St. L   D 🐾

SCARPA'S BRICK OVEN PIZZA   505/323-0222 19

▼▼ Italian Pizza. Casual Dining. $8-$15 **AAA Inspector Notes:** Options for topping your thin, crispy pie range from old faves like pepperoni and fresh basil to artichoke hearts and oak-grilled chicken in the popular pizzeria, where the busy buzz is from the locals, who also drop by for beer on tap, pasta and gourmet salads. **Features:** beer & wine. **Address:** 9700 Montgomery Blvd NE 87111 **Location:** Jct Montgomery and Eubank blvds; southeast corner.
L   D

SIAM CAFE   505/883-7334 12

▼▼ ▼▼ Thai. Family Dining. $8-$11 **AAA Inspector Notes:** The menu here features subtle or spicy flavors of traditional Thai cuisine. **Address:** 5500 San Mateo Blvd NE, Suite 101 87109 **Location:** I-25 exit 230 (San Mateo Blvd), 0.6 mi s; jct Osuna Rd and San Mateo Blvd, just s. L   D

TAJ MAHAL CUISINE OF INDIA   505/255-1994 30

Indian
Casual Dining
$10-$18

AAA Inspector Notes: On the menu at this eatery are such traditional dishes as curries, tandoori, masalas, kormas and saegs. **Features:** beer & wine. **Address:** 1430 Carlisle Blvd NE 87110 **Location:** I-40 exit 160, 0.5 mi s.
Menu on AAA.com

L   D

THE TOWN HOUSE DINING ROOM   505/255-0057 41

▼▼ ▼▼ American. Casual Dining. $8-$25 **AAA Inspector Notes:** Steaks and Greek food are specialties at the long-popular Central Avenue dining spot. Patrons are likely to find this place suitable for enjoying a relaxed dinner with friendly hosts. **Features:** beer & wine. **Address:** 9018 Central Ave SE 87123 **Location:** Jct Central Ave and Carlisle Blvd, just e. L   D

THUNDER ROAD   505/352-7888

▼▼ Southwestern Steak. Casual Dining. $12-$28 **AAA Inspector Notes:** This lively casual steakhouse, open to the casino, features a fun and unique Route 66 theme with wall hung vintage cars. **Features:** full bar, happy hour. **Address:** 14500 Central Ave SW 87121 **Location:** I-40 exit 140, just w; in Route 66 Casino Hotel. D CALL 🖬 🔲

TROMBINO'S BISTRO ITALIANO   505/821-5974 6

Italian
Casual Dining
$8-$26

AAA Inspector Notes: Well-prepared and delicious entrées-including pasta, veal, poultry, seafood and aged steaks-are served in this locally popular restaurant's Mediterranean atmosphere. Fresh ingredients, tasty homemade breads, sauces, pizza and tempting desserts complete the menu. **Features:** full bar, happy hour. **Reservations:** suggested. **Address:** 5415 Academy Rd NE 87109 **Location:** I-25 exit 230 (Osuna Rd), just s on San Mateo Blvd to Academy Rd, then just e. D

VIC'S DAILY CAFE   505/341-9710 5

▼▼ ▼▼ American. Family Dining. $6-$10 **AAA Inspector Notes:** The café is well-known for its green chile sauce, which can be had with breakfast or lunch—it is a nice accompaniment to chicken enchiladas. For those who prefer an American entrée, blue ribbon meatloaf is sure to please. **Address:** 3600 Osuna Rd NE, Unit 105 87109 **Location:** I-25 exit 230 (Osuna Rd), 0.5 mi w. B   L

WECK'S   505/881-0019 16

▼▼ ▼▼ American. Casual Dining. $8-$10 **AAA Inspector Notes:** Although traditional American breakfasts are on the menu, this restaurant's morning specialties are huevos rancheros, carne adovada and burritos served with lots of red or green chile. Portions are generous. **Address:** 3913 Louisiana Blvd NE 87110 **Location:** Corner of Louisiana and Montgomery blvds; just s of Montgomery Blvd.
B   L

ZINC WINE BAR & BISTRO   505/254-9462 34

▼▼ ▼▼ ▼▼ American. Fine Dining. $17-$32 **AAA Inspector Notes:** A stylish place to be seen, this bistro presents a finer-than-casual menu with French rotisserie meats as a highlight. The wine selection is legend. **Features:** full bar, Sunday brunch. **Reservations:** suggested. **Address:** 3009 Central Ave NE 87106 **Location:** Jct Central Ave and Monte Vista Blvd, just e. **Parking:** street only. D

ZACATECAS TACOS + TEQUILA   505/255-8226

fyi Not evaluated. Great margaritas and creative tacos make for a fun atmosphere at this trendy café. **Address:** 3423 Central Ave NE 87106 **Location:** Jct Amherst Dr.

ALGODONES pop. 814

HACIENDA VARGAS BED AND BREAKFAST INN
                              505/867-9115

▼▼ ▼▼ Historic Bed & Breakfast. Rates not provided. **Address:** 1431 SR 313 (El Camino Real) 87001 **Location:** I-25 exit 248, 0.3 mi w, then 0.3 mi s. Located beside train tracks. **Facility:** Set along the Royal Road that once led from Santa Fe to Mexico City, this 18th-century hacienda features adobe-style architecture. The lush gardens make for a romantic wedding venue. 7 units. 1 story, interior corridors. **Terms:** check-in 4 pm.
📶 ✕ W 🕿 / SOME UNITS 🔥

ANGEL FIRE (E-4) pop. 1,216, elev. 8,415'

Tucked into the Moreno Valley and surrounded by the imposing Sangre de Cristo Mountains, Angel Fire gained its name from two different natural phenomena—bright afternoon sunlight reflecting off alpine peaks, and (according to 19th-century mountain man and Indian fighter Kit Carson) early morning winter sunlight glinting on ice-covered tree branches. At different points in time this ruggedly scenic region has been home to Moache Ute Indians, miners, ranchers, trappers, pioneers and cowboys.

Angel Fire was a filming location for the 1989 TV mini-series "Lonesome Dove," and you can still visit the cabin built for this critically acclaimed and immensely popular Western starring Robert Duvall and

Tommy Lee Jones, in which New Mexico stood in for Montana.

A year-round outdoor activity mecca, Angel Fire offers summer boating, fishing, hunting, golfing, hiking, mountain biking and horseback riding. Torchlight parades, races and a web of runs (from beginner to advanced) keep boarders, skiers and snowshoers busy during the winter months.

Duffers looking to improve their game will find that golf balls travel up to 10 percent farther due to the high altitude. Angel Fire Resort Golf Course, N. Angel Fire Road and Miller Lane, is one of the area's premier public courses; phone (800) 633-7463.

Culturally, the Music from Angel Fire festival brings chamber music to the mountain community from late August to early September.

Angel Fire Chamber of Commerce: 3407 Mountain View Blvd., Centro Plaza, P.O. Box 547, Angel Fire, NM 87710. **Phone:** (575) 377-6661 or (800) 446-8117.

 **VIETNAM VETERANS MEMORIAL STATE PARK** is at 34 Country Club Rd. This curvilinear structure originally was built as one family's memorial to a young son killed in an enemy ambush in Vietnam. President Ronald Reagan proclaimed it "a memorial of national significance" in November 1987. The chapel is dedicated to Vietnam War casualties. Its hilltop vantage affords views of the Sangre de Cristo Mountains and the broad Moreno Valley. **Hours:** Chapel and grounds are open daily 24 hours. Visitor center daily 9-5 Apr.-Oct.; Thurs.-Mon. 9-5 rest of year. Closed Thanksgiving and Christmas. **Cost:** Donations. **Phone:** (575) 377-2293 (park office), or (575) 377-6900 (foundation).

ARROYO SECO pop. 1,785
• Hotels & Restaurants map & index p. 447

ADOBE AND STARS B & B   575/776-2776   [10]

Bed & Breakfast. Rates not provided. **Address:** 584 State Hwy 150 87571 **Location:** 1.1 mi ne of Arroyo Seco village, at Valdez Rd. Located in a rural area. **Facility:** This B&B offers wonderful views of Taos Mountain. The moving sculptures in the gardens and the visual elements surrounding and filling the rooms add an artsy flavor. 7 units. 1-2 stories (no elevator), interior/exterior corridors. **Terms:** check-in 4 pm, age restrictions may apply.

WHERE TO EAT

ACEQ RESTAURANT   575/776-0900   [16]

Northern American. Casual Dining. $13-$25 **AAA Inspector Notes:** This family-owned, farm-to-table restaurant serves creative comfort food in a cozy, neighborhood atmosphere. The menu relies on fine local, seasonal, wild and organic products. **Features:** beer & wine, patio dining, Sunday brunch. **Reservations:** suggested. **Address:** 480 SR 150 87514 **Location:** Center of village.

ARTESIA (I-5) pop. 11,301, elev. 3,379'

Artesia was named for its huge underground water supply, which is pumped to the surface via numerous artesian wells. The water irrigates thousands of acres of area farmland.

Another underground resource—oil—was discovered in 1924. This, coupled with reserves of natural gas, has bolstered Artesia's economy and made it one of New Mexico's most productive oil centers. The city also claims what was once the first underground school in the country, built to shelter about 500 students and 2,000 other citizens in the event of a nuclear attack.

Artesia Chamber of Commerce and Visitors Center: 107 N. First St., Artesia, NM 88210. **Phone:** (575) 746-2744 or (800) 658-6251.

ARTESIA HISTORICAL MUSEUM AND ART CENTER is at 505 W. Richardson Ave. The historic Moore-Ward House, built at the beginning of the 20th century, contains historical and cultural displays. The museum, devoted to local heritage, displays equipment used in industrial development as well as such Western paraphernalia as saddles, barbed wire and clothing. The art center next to the museum offers traveling exhibits, special events and work by area artists. **Time:** Allow 30 minutes minimum. **Hours:** Tues.-Fri. 9-noon and 1-5, Sat. 1-5. Closed major holidays. **Cost:** Free. **Phone:** (575) 748-2390.

ARTESIA INN   575/746-9801

Motel. Rates not provided. **Address:** 1820 S 1st St 88210 **Location:** 1.5 mi s on US 285. **Facility:** 34 units. 1 story, exterior corridors. **Pool(s):** outdoor.

BEST WESTERN PECOS INN   (575)748-3324

Hotel
$159-$199

 AAA Benefit: Save 10% or more every day and earn 10% bonus points!

Address: 2209 W Main St 88210 **Location:** 1.5 mi w on US 82. **Facility:** 82 units, some two bedrooms and kitchens. 2 stories (no elevator), interior corridors. **Pool(s):** heated indoor. **Activities:** hot tub, exercise room. **Guest Services:** valet and coin laundry.

COMFORT INN & SUITES ARTESIA   (575)616-2000

Hotel $119-$259 **Address:** 115 N 26th St 88210 **Location:** 1.5 mi w on US 82, then just n. **Facility:** 66 units. 3 stories, interior corridors. **Pool(s):** heated indoor. **Activities:** hot tub, exercise room. **Guest Services:** coin laundry.

HOTEL ARTESIA   (575)746-2066

Hotel. Rates not provided. **Address:** 203 N 2nd St 88210 **Location:** Jct US 285 and Main St, just n. **Facility:** 51 units. 2 stories, interior corridors. **Amenities:** safes. **Guest Services:** coin laundry.

LA QUINTA INN & SUITES ARTESIA   (575)736-2400

Hotel. Rates not provided. **Address:** 2207 W Main St 88210 **Location:** 1.5 mi w on US 82. **Facility:** 67 units. 3 stories, interior corridors. **Pool(s):** heated outdoor. **Activities:** hot tub, exercise room. **Guest Services:** coin laundry.

WHERE TO EAT

LA FONDA RESTAURANT   575/746-9411

♥♥ Mexican. Family Dining. $7-$17 **AAA Inspector Notes:** This family restaurant combines a Southwestern atmosphere with American fare. Also on the menu are regional and Mexican selections, including flautas, chimichangas and tacos. Portions are large. The luncheon buffet is a popular offering. **Address:** 210 W Main St 88210 **Location:** Center. ⬜L ⬜D

AZTEC (D-2) pop. 6,763, elev. 5,623'

In 1948 an investigator named Frank Scully gathered information from a variety of sources about a purported alien crash-landing in the area. While there is no evidence a real-life Mulder assisted Scully in the investigations, modern-day "X-Files" enthusiasts gather to swap alien stories and theories at the annual Aztec UFO Symposium in March. Tours of the nearby crash site are available during the symposium.

Nearby Aztec Ruins National Monument is a popular day trip. The Aztec Arches were considered sacred by the Puebloan Indians. One of the most impressive of these natural sandstone features is the Cox Canyon Arch, which has an estimated span of 43 feet. While the rock formations are uniformly amazing, they're not all easy to find. The Aztec Visitor Center, 110 N. Ash Ave., can provide driving directions on how to reach some of the more accessible arches; phone (505) 334-9551 or (888) 543-4629.

Aztec Chamber of Commerce: 110 N. Ash St., Aztec, NM 87410. **Phone:** (505) 334-7646.

Self-guiding tours: Information on walking tours of the city's historic sites is available from the Aztec Museum & Pioneer Village.

AZTEC MUSEUM & PIONEER VILLAGE is 1 mi. s. of Aztec Ruins National Monument at 125 N. Main Ave. Visitors can explore 14 original and replicated structures dating back to the 1880s. An outdoor oil and gas exhibit depicts the history of the industry. Farm and ranch equipment used by early settlers also is displayed. **Hours:** Tues.-Sat. 10-4, Memorial Day-Sept. 30. Closed major holidays. **Cost:** $5; $3 (ages 0-9). **Phone:** (505) 334-9829.

MICROTEL INN & SUITES BY WYNDHAM   (505)334-4014

♥♥ Hotel $53-$89 **Address:** 623 Phoenix Ct 87410 **Location:** Jct SR 516 and US 550, 3 mi s. **Facility:** 70 units. 4 stories, interior corridors. **Pool(s):** heated outdoor. **Activities:** hot tub, picnic facilities, exercise room. **Guest Services:** coin laundry.

 / SOME UNITS

WHERE TO EAT

THE MAIN STREET BISTRO   505/334-0109

♥ American. Quick Serve. $6-$12 **AAA Inspector Notes:** This cheerful café offers a variety of tasty sandwiches, soups and salads in a relaxed atmosphere. Rich, chocolate brownies and other baked goods are a must. **Features:** patio dining. **Address:** 122 N Main St 87410 **Location:** US 550, follow signs to historic downtown; jct Main and Blanco sts. ⬜B ⬜L ⬜✗

◆ AZTEC RUINS NATIONAL MONUMENT (D-2)

In the northwest corner of New Mexico, just north of Aztec on US 516 to Ruins Road, is one of the best preserved Ancestral Pueblo ruins in the Southwest. The misnomer Aztec was given by early settlers who incorrectly identified the builders of these sandstone pueblos.

Although smaller than the site preserved at Chaco Culture National Historical Park, the structures here make up for that in terms of detail. Especially noteworthy is the Great Kiva, a ceremonial building that is the only reconstruction of its kind in North America.

The largest of these sandstone pueblos, the West Ruin, was built about 1110; it contained more than 500 rooms, some of which remain intact. Several smaller structures adjoin the main ruin. Among the architectural features are original roofs that have amazingly withstood the test of time.

The visitor center displays artifacts uncovered during excavations, and a 15-minute video offers background information and historical context. Monument open daily 8-6, Memorial Day-Labor Day; 8-5, rest of year. Closed Jan. 1, Thanksgiving and Christmas. Admission (valid for 7 days) $5; free (ages 0-15). Phone (505) 334-6174.

◆ BANDELIER NATIONAL MONUMENT (B-3)

About 50 miles northwest of Santa Fe via US 285 to Pojoaque, then west on SR 502 and south on SR 4, this 50-square-mile site sits on the Pajarito Plateau in northern New Mexico's rugged canyon and mesa country. Pueblo and cliff dwellings constitute the remnants of an Ancestral Puebloan community established 7 to 8 centuries ago.

The most accessible sites consist of cave rooms hewn out of the soft tuff rock, houses built on the talus slopes and a circular community village. Bandelier also contains 33,000 acres of designated wilderness, including 70 miles of hiking trails. Offering views of archeological sites, the 1.2-mile round-trip paved Main Loop Trail starts at the visitor center. Free permits, required for overnight back-country travel, can be obtained at the visitor center. Pets or bicycles are not permitted on any trails in the monument.

In summer a variety of ranger-led activities are offered including guided walks, interpretive programs and craft demonstrations. The Nightwalk tour of archeological sites is conducted largely in silence, which underscores nighttime's magnificent solitude. An introductory slide program and a small museum in the visitor center provide background orientation.

One- and 2-hour self-guiding walking tours of the principal sites start at the visitor center. Monument open daily dawn-dusk. Visitor center open daily 8-6, Memorial Day-Labor Day; 9-5:30, mid-Mar. to day before Memorial Day and day after Labor Day-early Oct.; 9-4:30, rest of year. Closed Jan. 1 and

Christmas. Admission $12 per private vehicle. Visitor center free. Nightwalk tours (cash only) $6; $3 (ages 6-15); reservations are required. Visitors are advised to phone ahead for current road conditions before visiting the site. Phone (505) 672-3861, ext. 517.

BELÉN (G-3) pop. 7,269, elev. 4,808'

Belén, which in Spanish means "Bethlehem," was founded by Capt. Don Diego Torres and Antonio Salazar in 1740. By the late 19th century, the farming community was a major hub on the Atchison, Topeka and Santa Fe Railroad.

BELEN HARVEY HOUSE MUSEUM is at 104 N. First St. The building served as a restaurant for Santa Fe Railroad passengers 1910-39. Exhibits depict railroad and town history. A model train display and changing exhibits are offered. One of the last remaining Harvey Houses, this chain of restaurants offered meals for railroad passengers. **Time:** Allow 1 hour, 30 minutes minimum. **Hours:** Wed.-Sat 12:30-4, Tues 9-4. Closed major holidays. **Cost:** Donations. **Phone:** (505) 861-0581.

HOLIDAY INN EXPRESS   505/861-5000
▼▼▼ **Hotel.** Rates not provided. **Address:** 2110 Camino del Llano 87002 **Location:** I-25 exit 191, just w. **Facility:** 63 units. 2 stories, interior corridors. **Pool(s):** heated outdoor. **Activities:** exercise room. **Guest Services:** coin laundry.

[icons]

BERNALILLO (F-3) pop. 8,320, elev. 5,052'

Bernalillo's (bern-a-LEE-oh) first settlers arrived at the turn of the 18th century and were descendants of Bernal Díaz del Castillo, who chronicled Hernando Cortés' conquest of Mexico. Reminders of times past include the pueblo of Santa Ana and the Spanish-American village of San Ysidro, both northwest of town.

The Santa Ana Pueblo Mission, one of the oldest missions in the United States, is open to visitors on feast day, July 26. It is believed to have been built by Spanish missionary Fray Juan de Rosas, who accompanied Spanish explorer Juan de Oñate on his expedition to New Mexico in 1598.

At the end of August Bernalillo hosts the 3-day 🍷 New Mexico Wine Festival, which features wine tastings, food vendors, live music and arts and crafts. A fee is charged to enter the festival, and those under 21 must be accompanied by a legal-age guardian.

Sandoval County Visitor Center: 264 S. Camino del Pueblo, P.O. Box 40, Bernalillo, NM 87004. **Phone:** (505) 867-8687 or (800) 252-0191.

CORONADO HISTORIC SITE is 2 mi. w. on US 550 (old SR 44) to 485 Kuaua Rd. The 98-acre site includes ruins of the Tiwa pueblo of Kuaua. Lured by the Rio Grande's fertile land, an ancient tribe first

settled Kuaua around 1300. The area is named for Francisco Vázquez de Coronado, whose army camped here in 1540 while searching for the fabled Cities of Gold. A kiva excavated in the 1930s features many layers of pre-Columbian art, some of which is displayed in the visitor center.

Hours: Wed.-Mon. 8:30-5. Closed major holidays. **Cost:** $3; free (ages 0-16). Combination ticket with Jémez Historic Site (see Jémez Springs p. 389) $5. **Phone:** (505) 867-5351.

DAYS INN BERNALILLO   (505)771-7000

▼▼ ▼▼
Hotel
$65-$95

Address: 107 N Camino del Pueblo 87004 **Location:** I-25 exit 242, just w. **Facility:** 56 units. 3 stories, interior corridors. **Amenities:** safes. **Pool(s):** heated indoor. **Activities:** hot tub, exercise room. **Guest Services:** coin laundry. **Featured Amenity:** full hot breakfast.

[icons]

HOLIDAY INN EXPRESS-BERNALILLO   (505)867-1600
[fyi] Hotel $80-$200 Under major renovation, scheduled to be completed July 2015. **Last Rated:** ▼▼ ▼▼ **Address:** 119 Bell Ln 87004 **Location:** I-25 exit 242, just w. **Facility:** 70 units. 3 stories, interior corridors. **Terms:** 3 day cancellation notice-fee imposed. **Pool(s):** heated indoor. **Activities:** hot tub, exercise room. **Guest Services:** valet and coin laundry.

[icons]

HYATT REGENCY TAMAYA RESORT AND SPA
(505)867-1234

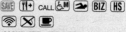
▼▼▼ ▼▼▼
Resort Hotel
$119-$309

HYATT REGENCY

AAA Benefit: Members save 10%!

Address: 1300 Tuyuna Tr 87004 **Location:** I-25 exit 242, 1 mi w on US 550 to Tamaya Blvd, then 1 mi n, follow signs. **Facility:** This upscale resort in a tranquil setting offers a strong Native American feel. Activities for the entire family include a luxurious spa, 18-hole golf course and Camp Hyatt. 350 units. 4 stories, interior corridors. **Parking:** on-site and valet. **Terms:** check-in 4 pm, 3 day cancellation notice-fee imposed, resort fee. **Amenities:** safes. **Dining:** 4 restaurants. **Pool(s):** heated outdoor. **Activities:** sauna, hot tub, steamroom, regulation golf, tennis, recreation programs, kids club, bicycles, playground, trails, exercise room, spa. **Guest Services:** valet laundry, area transportation.

[icons]

WHERE TO EAT

ABUELITA'S NEW MEXICAN RESTAURANT 505/867-9988

Mexican. Casual Dining. $7-$11 **AAA Inspector Notes:** Abuelita means grandma in Spanish, and this unpretentious cafe uses Grandma's recipes for its traditional New Mexican dishes. Tamales, enchiladas and carne adovada are good enough to eat every day. **Features:** beer & wine, senior menu. **Address:** 621 S Camino del Pueblo 87004 **Location:** I-25 exit 242, 0.5 mi w on US 550, then 0.7 mi s. B L D

PRAIRIE STAR 505/867-3327

Northern American. Fine Dining. $17-$35 **AAA Inspector Notes:** Ideal for special occasions, the restaurant affords guests breathtaking views of the Sandia Mountains and Rio Grande Valley. Imaginative, skillfully prepared cuisine blends nouvelle American and Asian influences, as well as the flavors and spices used in traditional New Mexican cuisine. The result is an exciting and unforgettable fine dining experience. **Features:** full bar, patio dining, happy hour. **Reservations:** suggested. **Address:** 288 Prairie Star Rd 87004 **Location:** I-25 exit 242, 2.2 mi w on US 550 to Tamaya Blvd, then 0.5 mi n. D

THE RANGE CAFE 505/867-1700

American. Casual Dining. $9-$16 **AAA Inspector Notes:** This colorful, lively eatery features a Hoosier tenderloin, New Mexican food, pasta preparations and good ol' American favorites, as well as a fine selection of sandwiches. This spot is a good meeting place for coffee and scrumptious made-in-house desserts. **Features:** full bar. **Address:** 925 Camino del Pueblo 87004 **Location:** I-25 exit 240, 0.5 mi w on E Avenida Bernalillo, then just n. **Parking:** street only. B L D

BLOOMFIELD (E-2) pop. 8,112, elev. 5,453'

Bloomfield was settled around 1876 and quickly morphed into an all-but-lawless Wild West town, complete with a gang of rustlers headed by the ex-sheriff. The brazen gang operated openly, marketing stolen beef through its own butcher shop. Blancett's Saloon was a hangout for gunslingers from every corner of the San Juan Basin.

By the early 20th century, however, residents were more interested in stimulating agriculture through irrigation, an endeavor that persists in this arid region. The Navajo Reservoir, 25 miles northeast via US 64 and SR 511, is the source of much of the area's water. Navajo Lake State Park surrounds the reservoir and offers recreational opportunities, including world-class fly fishing *(see Recreation Areas Chart)*.

Bloomfield Chamber of Commerce: 224 W. Broadway, Bloomfield, NM 87413. **Phone:** (505) 632-0880.

SALMON RUIN is 2 mi. w. on US 64. The site was built in the late 11th century by people from the Chaco culture *(see Chaco Culture National Historical Park p. 368)*. The E-shaped masonry complex measuring 450 feet along the back wall and 150 feet along the arms features an elevated kiva in the center of the pueblo and an excavated great kiva. Some of the more than 1 million artifacts recovered are displayed in San Juan County Archaeological Research Center and Library, next to the ruin.

Hours: Mon.-Fri. 8-5, Sat.-Sun. 9-5, May-Oct.; Mon.-Fri. 8-5, Sat. 9-5, Sun. noon-5, rest of year. Closed Jan. 1, Thanksgiving and Christmas. **Cost:** (includes Heritage Park) $4; $3 (ages 60+); $1 (ages 6-16). **Phone:** (505) 632-2013.

Heritage Park is 2 mi. w. on US 64 at 6131 US 64 at Salmon Ruin. Offering a glimpse into the lifestyles and cultures of the San Juan Valley, the park features Navajo log homes, Apache teepees and a basket maker pit house—a semi-underground house that conserved heat in winter and remained cool in summer. Visitors can examine ancient figures etched into stone and view the unusual construction of the Salmon homestead, built about 1900. **Hours:** Mon.-Fri. 8-5, Sat.-Sun. 9-5, May-Oct.; Mon.-Fri. 8-5, Sat. 9-5, Sun. noon-5, rest of year. Closed Jan. 1, Thanksgiving and Christmas. **Phone:** (505) 632-2013.

BEST WESTERN TERRITORIAL INN & SUITES
(505)632-9100

Hotel
$105

AAA Benefit: Save 10% or more every day and earn 10% bonus points!

Address: 415 S Bloomfield Blvd 87413 **Location:** Just s of jct US 64 and 550. **Facility:** 65 units. 3 stories, interior corridors. **Pool(s):** heated indoor. **Activities:** hot tub, exercise room. **Guest Services:** coin laundry. **Featured Amenity:** full hot breakfast.

SUPER 8 (505)632-8886

Motel
$79-$94

Address: 525 W Broadway 87413 **Location:** Jct of US 64 and 550. **Facility:** 42 units. 2 stories (no elevator), interior corridors. **Terms:** 3 day cancellation notice-fee imposed. **Guest Services:** coin laundry. **Featured Amenity:** continental breakfast.

WHERE TO EAT

ROADSIDE RESTAURANT 505/632-9940

American. Family Dining. $8-$16 **AAA Inspector Notes:** This down-home restaurant is a favorite of locals and travelers alike. An interesting and extensive collection of Coca-Cola collectibles is showcased. Menu items include burgers, sandwiches and Mexican dishes. **Features:** wine only. **Address:** 319 S Bloomfield Blvd 87413 **Location:** Just s of jct US 64 and 550. B L D

CAPITAN (H-4) pop. 1,489, elev. 6,351'

Capitan began to flourish in 1897 when the El Paso and Northeastern Railway built a line to nearby coal reserves. After the mines became depleted and the railroad abandoned its branch, the town became a commercial center for farmers and ranchers, and it also serves as a base for visitors taking advantage of the recreational opportunities offered by the Lincoln National Forest *(see place listing p. 395)*.

SMOKEY BEAR HISTORICAL PARK is on US 380. Exhibits and a 10-minute film trace the history of Smokey Bear and the government's efforts to combat forest fires. After surviving a devastating fire in 1950, the bear cub was found clinging to a burned tree in the Lincoln National Forest and became the national symbol for wildfire prevention. Smokey died in 1976 and is buried in the park. **Hours:** Daily 9-5. Closed Jan. 1, Thanksgiving and Christmas. **Cost:** $2; $1 (ages 7-12). **Phone:** (575) 354-2748.

CAPULIN VOLCANO NATIONAL MONUMENT (D-5)

Three miles north of US 64/87 and Capulin on SR 325, Capulin Volcano National Monument contains one of the best examples of a volcanic cinder cone in the nation. About 60,000 years ago ash, cinders and lava erupted and formed a classic cinder cone that stands more than 1,000 feet above the surrounding prairie. Today, a 2-mile road winds up the volcano, and five trails lead into the crater and around the rim. The view from the summit includes the Rocky Mountains, volcanic features of the Raton-Clayton Volcanic Field, and the distant horizons of Colorado, Oklahoma and Texas. Ranger-led programs are offered in summer.

The visitor center offers information and a 10-minute video program. Pets are not allowed on trails. The road to the crater rim, park and visitor center is open daily 8-5:30, Memorial Day weekend-Labor Day; 8-4:30, rest of year. Phone ahead to confirm schedule. Closed Jan. 1, Thanksgiving and Christmas. Admission (valid for 7 days) $5 per private vehicle. Phone (575) 278-2201.

CARLSBAD (I-5) pop. 26,138, elev. 3,111'

The fields of cotton, alfalfa and veggies that surround Carlsbad are made possible by the U.S. Bureau of Reclamation's system of dams and canals, which irrigates 25,000 acres. Carlsbad Caverns National Park *(see place listing p. 365)* is nearby, and Lake Carlsbad *(see Recreation Areas Chart)* offers fishing, boating and water sports.

Homeowners along the Pecos River decorate their houses, yards and docks with Christmas lights for Christmas on the Pecos, an annual celebration lasting from Thanksgiving weekend through New Year's Eve. Nighttime pontoon boat tours make it impossible to *not* get into the holiday spirit.

Carlsbad Chamber of Commerce: 302 S. Canal St., Carlsbad, NM 88220. **Phone:** (575) 887-6516.

CARLSBAD MUSEUM AND ART CENTER is 1 blk. w. of Canal St. (US 285) at 418 W. Fox St. in Halagueno Arts Park. Established in 1931, this municipal museum houses local and regional history displays, archeological specimens, contemporary and Southwestern art, Peruvian and Pueblo pottery

and pioneer ranching artifacts. The McAdoo Room features paintings by the founders of the Taos Society of Artists. Changing exhibits range from works by local artists to 3D photography of local cave explorations and cultural exhibits produced by the Smithsonian Institution. **Time:** Allow 1 hour minimum. **Hours:** Mon.-Sat. 10-5. Closed major holidays. **Cost:** Free. **Phone:** (575) 887-0276.

LIVING DESERT ZOO AND GARDENS STATE PARK stands atop the Ocotillo Hills off US 285. Dedicated to the interpretation of the Chihuahuan Desert, this zoo displays some 60 native animal species and hundreds of succulents from around the world. Endangered Mexican gray wolves are featured as part of a species conservation exhibit. **Hours:** Daily 8-5, Memorial Day weekend-Labor Day; 9-5, rest of year. Last admission 90 minutes before closing. Closed Christmas. **Cost:** $5; $3 (ages 7-12). **Phone:** (575) 887-5516.

HAMPTON INN & SUITES   (575)725-5700

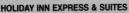 Hotel $229-$499 **Address:** 120 Esperanza Cir 88220 **Location:** Jct US 285. **Facility:** 85 units. 4 stories, interior corridors. **Terms:** 1-7 night minimum stay, cancellation fee imposed. **Pool(s):** heated indoor. **Activities:** hot tub, exercise room. **Guest Services:** valet and coin laundry.

AAA Benefit:
Members save up to 10%!

HOLIDAY INN EXPRESS & SUITES   (575)234-1252

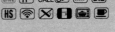
Hotel
$259-$329

Address: 22101 W Pierce St 88220 **Location:** N on US 285. **Facility:** 80 units. 3 stories, interior corridors. **Terms:** cancellation fee imposed. **Pool(s):** heated indoor. **Activities:** hot tub, exercise room. **Guest Services:** coin laundry. **Featured Amenity:** full hot breakfast.

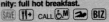

Close to Caverns. Indoor pool & spa, fitness center and 40" plasma TV's. Next to mall & restaurants.

THE TRINITY HOTEL   575/234-9891

 **Historic Boutique Country Inn** $189-$209 **Address:** 201 S Canal St 88220 **Location:** Jct Fox St. **Facility:** This unique downtown property in a renovated historic building provides upgraded guest amenities and a great restaurant. All rooms have a wine chiller. 9 units. 2 stories (no elevator), interior/exterior corridors. **Amenities:** safes. **Dining:** The Trinity Restaurant, see separate listing.

U.S. TRAVELERS INN & SUITES   575/887-1994

Hotel. Rates not provided. **Address:** 2429 W Pierce St 88220 **Location:** N on US 285. Across from medical center. **Facility:** 54 units. 2 stories (no elevator), interior corridors. **Activities:** limited exercise equipment.

SLEEP INN & SUITES   (575)941-2300

Hotel
$159-$189

Address: 3825 National Parks Hwy 88220 **Location:** 2 mi s of jct US 62 and 180. **Facility:** 64 units. 3 stories, interior corridors. **Terms:** cancellation fee imposed. **Activities:** exercise room. **Guest Services:** coin laundry. **Featured Amenity:** full hot breakfast.

New hotel with free hot breakfast, fitness center & indoor pool. Closest AAA rated hotel to Caverns.

THE FLUME RESTAURANT   575/887-2851

American. Casual Dining. $6-$27 **AAA Inspector Notes:** Although prime rib is the specialty, this restaurant also offers a choice of seafood, Mexican and pasta dishes. The salad bar is served with each entrée. **Features:** full bar. **Address:** 1829 S Canal St 88220 **Location:** 1 mi s on US 62, 180 and 285; in BEST WESTERN Stevens Inn. B L D CALL M

RED CHIMNEY PIT BAR-B-Q   575/885-8744

Barbecue. Casual Dining. $6-$14 **AAA Inspector Notes:** This fun restaurant features a lodge theme with plentiful portions of barbecue favorites. **Features:** beer & wine. **Address:** 817 N Canal St 88220 **Location:** On US 285, just n of Church St. L D

THE STOCK EXCHANGE   575/725-5444

American. Fine Dining. $15-$30 **AAA Inspector Notes:** Located in the Old City Hall, this restaurant features a changing seasonal menu with a creative Southwest twist. Portions are plentiful but save room for fresh baked desserts—the lemon meringue pie is luscious. **Features:** beer & wine. **Address:** 220 W Fox St 88220 **Location:** Jct Canal St; center. D

THE TRINITY RESTAURANT   575/234-9891

American. Casual Dining. $10-$34 **AAA Inspector Notes:** *Historic.* The chic atmosphere in this renovated bank building features tall ceilings and sparkling chandeliers. The menu offers a selection of entrées and pasta dishes plus a luscious tiramisu. Daily wine tasting is offered 3-5 pm. **Features:** beer & wine. **Reservations:** suggested. **Address:** 201 S Canal St 88220 **Location:** Jct Fox St; in The Trinity Hotel. B L D

YELLOWBRIX RESTAURANT   575/941-2749

American. Casual Dining. $11-$36 **AAA Inspector Notes:** This quaint café serves up a modern twist of American favorites, best enjoyed with a glass of wine from a thoughtfully put together wine list, or a craft-brewed beer. Save room for gourmet gelato to put a fine finish on a great, casual meal. The spacious patio features live music in season. **Features:** beer & wine, patio dining. **Address:** 201 N Canal St 88220 **Location:** Jct Stevens St. L D

CARLSBAD CAVERNS NATIONAL PARK (I-4)

Elevations in the park range from 3,596 ft. in the southeastern corner to 6,368 ft. in the southwestern region. Refer to AAA maps for additional elevation information.

Carlsbad Caverns National Park is 20 miles southwest of Carlsbad off US 62/180. The park covers 46,776 acres in the rugged foothills of the Guadalupe Mountains, with miles of caves cutting through a Permian-age fossil reef. Among more than 117 known caves is Lechuguilla, thought to be the nation's deepest limestone cavern. The park's showpiece is Carlsbad Cavern, a series of enormous rooms that make up one of the world's largest caves.

Unlike most limestone caves that form when surface water flows through cracks in the rock, these passageways in the Guadalupe Mountains are the rare product of sulfuric acid. A hydrogen sulfide gas solution rose from petroleum deposits thousands of feet below the surface and mixed with the water table to create an aggressive chemical that dissolved holes in the subterranean limestone. As the mountains rose over a period of 20 million years, ground water drained from the caves, revealing the wonders of Carlsbad.

366 CARLSBAD CAVERNS NP, NM

A steep, paved trail leads into the cavern's natural entrance, which measures 90 feet wide and 40 feet high. The cavern has more than 30 miles of surveyed subterranean corridors and great chambers. Formations range from small, delicate growths resembling plants to massive stalagmites, stalactites and columns. Many are tinted by iron and other minerals present in the limestone. Highlights include Bat Cave, Devil's Spring, Iceberg Rock, Green Lake Overlook and the Boneyard, a maze of limestone rock reminiscent of Swiss cheese.

The 8-acre Big Room, one of the most impressive chambers, has a 255-foot ceiling. Its clear pools contain limestone masses resembling lily pads. Other formations evoke an atmosphere of snow-banked forests, adding to the tranquil beauty of the cavern.

Every evening from mid-May to mid-October, hundreds of thousands of bats emerge from Carlsbad Cavern's uppermost chamber at dusk to feed on flying insects. Park rangers give a pre-flight talk in an amphitheater at the mouth of the cave. The flight outward lasts a half-hour to 2 hours; the bats return near dawn. Cameras, cellular phones and other electronic devices are prohibited. During the day, bats hang head down from the walls and ceilings of a portion of the cavern not open to visitors. At the ⛣ Carlsbad Caverns Bat Flight Breakfast in mid-summer, visitors gather at the park just before dawn to watch the bats' spectacular return flight.

General Information and Activities

The park is open all year, except Christmas. The visitor center is open daily 8-7 (cave tours are offered 8:30-5), Memorial Day weekend-Labor Day; 8-5 (cave tours are offered 8:30-3:30), rest of year. Last cave entry via natural entrance is 1 hour, 30 minutes before closing. Visitors may explore Carlsbad Cavern on two self-guiding routes, the Natural Entrance and the Big Room, and return to the surface by elevator. The Big Room route is recommended for visitors who are short on time or who prefer a less strenuous walk.

A brief orientation is presented prior to tours. Interpretive signs explain cavern features, history and geology, and an audio guide providing descriptive commentary is available to rent. Additional activities include ranger talks, self-guiding nature trails and a desert automobile drive.

Guided cave tours (see Carlsbad Caverns Guided Tours attraction listing) are led by park rangers and range from easy walks to difficult crawls and climbs. These tours fill quickly in the summer and are available by reservation only.

The visitor center includes educational exhibits about the area's geology, biology, history and archeology; works of art depicting cave features; and original Ansel Adams photographs. A half-mile self-guiding desert nature trail begins near the cave entrance.

The 9.5-mile Walnut Canyon Desert Drive, a one-way loop drive over a graded gravel road, offers views of Rattlesnake Canyon and upper Walnut Canyon; the loop is not maintained for low-clearance vehicles. A permit is required for overnight back-country trips; inquire at the visitor center for hiking information. See Recreation Areas Chart.

The temperature underground is a constant 56 F. A sweater and flat-heeled shoes with rubber soles are recommended. Baby strollers are not permitted inside the caves. Flash and time-exposure photography is allowed, but all photographs must be taken from paved trails. Food is available but is not permitted on cave trails. **Note:** To prevent the spread of fungus that causes a deadly disease to bats, visitors entering park caves may be screened; some clothing and equipment may not be permitted or disinfection may be required.

ADMISSION to the park area and the visitor center without entrance to the caves is free. Cave admission (valid for 3 days) including the Natural Entrance and Big Room self-guiding routes $6; free (ages 0-15). Ranger-led tours $7-$20; $3.50-$10 (ages 3-15); age restrictions may apply. Audio guide rental $4. **PETS** (except Seeing Eye dogs) are not permitted inside caves. The visitor center provides kennels for $6 per pet.

ADDRESS inquiries to the Superintendent, Carlsbad Caverns National Park, 3225 National Parks Hwy., Carlsbad, NM 88220; phone (575) 785-2232.

CARLSBAD CAVERNS GUIDED TOURS depart from various sites in Carlsbad Caverns National Park. Offered in addition to the Natural Entrance and Big Room self-guiding tours of Carlsbad Caverns are six guided tours led by park rangers. Tours range from easy to difficult, and participants must supply their own equipment, batteries and flashlights for some routes. **Note:** Sturdy hiking boots are required. Tours fill quickly in the summer. **Hours:** Departure times and tour lengths vary. **Cost:** Fees, group sizes and age restrictions vary. Reservations are required. **Phone:** (575) 785-2232, or (877) 444-6777 for reservations.

Hall of the White Giant Tour departs from the Carlsbad Caverns Visitor Center 7 mi. off US 62/180. This strenuous 4-hour guided tour leads to a remote chamber. Participants must crawl long distances, squeeze through crevices such as the tight Matlock's Pinch and climb a slippery passage. **Note:** Hiking boots or other sturdy shoes, kneepads, gloves and three new AA batteries are required; a long-sleeved shirt and long pants are recommended. Backpacks are not permitted. Headlamps are provided. The tour is limited to eight participants. **Hours:** Tours depart Mon. at 8:30, late May-early Aug; at 10, early March-late May. Guests should arrive 15 minutes prior to departure. **Cost:** (In addition to cavern admission) $20; $10 (ages 12-15). Ages 0-11 are not permitted. Reservations are required. **Phone:** (877) 444-6777.

King's Palace Tour departs from the underground rest area in Carlsbad Cavern. This 1.5-hour tour covers 1 mile and descends to the deepest part of the cave open to the public, 830 feet below the surface. Cave formations include helictites, draperies, columns and soda straws. **Note:** The tour is limited to 55 participants. **Hours:** Tours depart daily at 10:30 and 1:30, early March-late May; Sat.-Sun., Tues. and Thurs. at 10:30, noon, 1:30 and 3, late May-early Aug. Guests should arrive 15 minutes prior to departure. **Cost:** (In addition to cavern admission) $8; $4 (ages 4-15). Ages 0-3 are not permitted. Reservations are recommended. **Phone:** (877) 444-6777.

Left Hand Tunnel Tour departs from the Carlsbad Caverns Visitor Center 7 mi. off US 62/180. This 2-hour lantern tour highlights cavern history and geology along a half-mile route. Sights along this easy tour include cave pools and fossils. **Note:** Walking shoes are required. Backpacks are not permitted. Lanterns are provided. The tour is limited to 15 participants. **Hours:** Tours depart Mon., Wed. and Fri. at 1:30, late May-early Aug.; Sun. and Wed. at 1:30, early March-late May. Guests should arrive 15 minutes prior to departure. **Cost:** (In addition to cavern admission) $7; $3.50 (ages 6-15). Ages 0-5 are not permitted. Reservations are required. **Phone:** (877) 444-6777.

Lower Cave Tour departs from the Carlsbad Caverns Visitor Center 7 mi. off US 62/180. Entered by descending a 10-foot rope and 50 feet of ladders, this area of the cavern contains beautiful formations and evidence of early exploration. The Rookery is a showcase for cave pearls. **Note:** The 3-hour tour involves ladder climbing and heights and is moderately strenuous. Hiking boots, three new AA batteries and gloves are required; helmets and headlamps are provided. Backpacks are not permitted. The tour is limited to 12 participants. **Hours:** Tours depart Sat.-Sun., Tues. and Thurs. at 10:30, late May-early Aug.; Sat., Tues. and Thurs. at 10:30, early March-late May. Guests should arrive 15 minutes prior to departure. **Cost:** (In addition to cavern admission) $20; $10 (ages 12-15). Ages 0-11 are not permitted. Reservations are required. **Phone:** (877) 444-6777.

Slaughter Canyon Cave Tour departs from the Carlsbad Caverns Visitor Center 7 mi. off US 62/180 to CR 418, following signs to the cave entrance. Dramatic formations in this undeveloped cave include the 89-foot-high Monarch, the sparkling Christmas Tree column and the delicate Chinese Wall.

Note: An unpaved, half-mile trail leads from the parking area to the cave, climbing 500 feet; allow 45 minutes to make this steep and strenuous climb. Hiking boots or other sturdy shoes, two C-cell flashlights with new batteries and water are required. The 2-hour tour is limited to 25 participants. **Hours:** Tours depart Fri. at 8:30 a.m., Memorial Day weekend-Labor Day. Hikers should arrive at the cave entrance 15 minutes prior to tour time. **Cost:** $15; $7.50 (ages 8-15). Ages 0-7 are not permitted. Reservations are required. **Phone:** (877) 444-6777.

Spider Cave Tour departs from the Carlsbad Caverns Visitor Center 7 mi. off US 62/180. This three-dimensional maze includes tight crawlways, canyonlike passages and bizarre formations. Highlights include the Mace and Medusa rooms and Cactus Spring. **Note:** Hiking boots or other sturdy shoes, gloves, kneepads and four new AA batteries are required for this strenuous tour; a long-sleeved shirt, long pants and water are recommended. Backpacks are not permitted. Helmets and headlamps are provided. The 4-hour tour is limited to eight participants. **Hours:** Tours depart Fri. at 8:30, early March-late May; Wed. at 8:30, late May-early Aug. Guests should arrive 15 minutes prior to departure. **Cost:** Fee $20; $10 (ages 12-15). Ages 0-11 are not permitted. Reservations are required. **Phone:** (877) 444-6777.

CARRIZOZO (H-4) pop. 996, elev. 5,426'

Once a shipping and commercial center for area ranches, Carrizozo now is a busy county seat and tourist center. In addition to its own parks and recreational facilities, it offers easy access to the northern portion of Lincoln National Forest *(see place listing p. 395).* Established in 1899 as a division point on the El Paso & Northeastern Railroad, the community takes its name from *carrizo,* a regional grass.

Nine miles northeast via US 54 and SR 349 is the ghost town of White Oaks. For 20 years after the original gold strike on nearby Baxter Mountain in 1879, White Oaks was a substantial community with stone buildings, two banks, four churches, four newspapers and more than 50 established businesses. Although White Oaks faded with the gold market in the 20th century, one of the first strikes—the Old Abe Mine—produced $3 million in gold until it closed around 1960.

Carrizozo Chamber of Commerce: P.O. Box 567, Carrizozo, NM 88301. **Phone:** (575) 648-2732.

VALLEY OF FIRES RECREATION AREA is 4 mi. w. on US 380, immediately adjacent to the Malpais (badlands) Lava Flow. About 5,000 years ago, Little Black Peak erupted and flowed 44 miles into the Tularosa Basin, filling the basin with molten rock. The resulting lava flow is 4-6 miles wide, 160 feet thick and covers 125 square miles. This lava flow is considered to be one of the youngest lava flows in the Continental United States. A three-quarter-mile walking trail winds through the lava beds.

Hours: Daily 24 hours. Visitor center daily 8-4. **Cost:** $3 per person or $5 per private vehicle. Admission is half-price for Golden Age and Golden Access pass holders. Camping $7-$18. **Phone:** (575) 648-2241. 🅐 📷

CARSON NATIONAL FOREST (D-4)

Elevations in the forest range from 6,000 ft. in the Pinon Juniper Tree region to 13,161 ft. at Wheeler Peak. Refer to AAA maps for additional elevation information.

In north central New Mexico, Carson National Forest encompasses 1,500,000 acres. Its scenic and recreational focus is in the districts that encompass the Sangre de Cristo and the San Juan mountains flanking the upper Rio Grande Valley.

Five wilderness areas—Wheeler Peak, Latir Peak, Cruces Basin, the northern portion of the Pecos and Chama wildernesses and an 8-mile-long section of the Rio Grande Wild River—preserve the region's pristine beauty.

Enchanted Circle Scenic Byway is an 84-mile drive offering panoramic views of the southern Rocky Mountains, including Wheeler Peak. It loops from Taos east to Eagle Nest, then north to Questa via SR 38, and south on SR 522 back to Taos.

The curved cliff side of Echo Amphitheater, 9 miles south of Canjilon on US 84, is a prime spot for photography. Summer and winter recreation is available. Trails for bicycling, hiking, horseback riding, snowmobiling and cross-country skiing traverse the forest.

For further information contact Carson National Forest, 208 Cruz Alta Rd., Taos, NM 87571; phone (575) 758-6200. *See Recreation Areas Chart.*

CHACO CULTURE NATIONAL HISTORICAL PARK (E-2)

Located in northwestern New Mexico, the recommended park access is from the north via the US 550 exit at CR 7900—entry is about 3 miles southeast of Nageezi and approximately 50 miles west of Cuba. Follow signs to the park for 21 miles. This route has 8 miles of paved road (CR 7900) and 13 miles of dirt road (CR 7950). The road is only lightly maintained, and may be impassable during or after inclement weather. Phone the park visitor center at (505) 786-7014, ext. 221 for current road conditions. Unless you are planning to camp in the park, it is not recommended that you drive a motor home on the access roads.

Chaco Culture National Historical Park preserves the remains of 13 major great houses, or monumental public buildings, and several thousand smaller sites that exemplify the culture of the Ancestral Puebloan people A.D. 850-1250.

By about A.D. 500 the Ancestral Puebloan people gradually exchanged their nomadic ways for agriculture and permanent settlements. They began to build Pueblo Bonito at the base of the northern canyon wall, 4 miles west of the headquarters area, during the mid-9th century. By the late 12th century Pueblo Bonito had attained a height of at least 4 stories and contained more than 600 rooms and kivas (ceremonial rooms).

In addition to the large public buildings, numerous smaller village sites in the canyon attest to the settlement's sizable and diverse populations, which were greater than those found in the area today. It is one of the most imposing cultural sites in the Southwest.

Not content with building great public buildings and an elaborate irrigation system of gates and canals that diverted runoff from summer storms into their cornfields, the Chacoans also constructed a vast road network. These straight, 30-foot-wide corridors linked the canyon settlements with more than 150 satellite communities, some as distant as the present-day states of Arizona, Colorado and Utah.

One route, the Great North Road, runs from Pueblo Alto near Pueblo Bonito to a point near Salmon Ruin *(see Bloomfield p. 363)* and may continue as far as Aztec Ruins National Monument *(see place listing p. 361).*

Another major Chacoan achievement was a highly sophisticated solstice marker. High on the isolated Fajada Butte, a sliver of noontime sunlight slashes between stone slabs onto two spiral petroglyphs, precisely timing the equinoxes and solstices on which the people based crop planting and ceremonial observances. The butte is closed to the public due to its fragile condition.

As Chaco's influence waned, new centers emerged at Aztec and Mesa Verde, and by 1250 only the wind whispered among the colossal masonry walls of Pueblo Bonito and its sister cities. The Chacoans were assimilated into the existing populations in the Zuni, Hopi, Acoma and Rio Grande pueblos, but their descendants continue to return and honor these sacred places.

Note: Due to the park's remote location and its extensive ruins and trails, it may be worthwhile to plan 2 or 3 days for the visit. A full day is required for travel and to see a portion of the park. A second or third day is necessary to view the entire site.

There are no lodgings or food service facilities within the park. Gallo Campground, which is open year-round, is located 1 mile east of the park visitor center and has 49 campsites (15 for tent camping) available for $15 per night (maximum of 14 days). This is primitive camping with no shade; each site has a picnic table and fire grate, but gathering wood is prohibited and no firewood is available in the park. There are no showers or hook-ups; drinking water is available in the visitor center parking area. Trailers and RVs more than 35 feet in length may not be accommodated. April through October are the busiest months. Advance reservations are required; phone (877) 444-6777.

Because points of interest are accessible only over dirt roads that are rough, towing trailers more than 35 feet long is not advised. There are no gas stations or other services within the park. Campers must bring their own wood or charcoal. Drinking water and dump station facilities are available year round.

Self-guiding trails explore seven major sites, including Pueblo Bonito, Chetro Ketl, Pueblo del Arroyo, Casa Rinconada and three village sites. Allow 1 hour minimum per trail. Four other back-country trails for day hiking lead to more distant sites; free permits, which can be obtained at the visitor center and at trailheads, are required.

Tours, hikes and evening programs are offered April through October. The Chaco Night Sky Program features astronomy-related activities and solar viewing April through October. Picnicking is permitted in designated areas. *See Recreation Areas Chart.*

CHACO CULTURE NATIONAL HISTORICAL PARK VISITOR CENTER is 2.5 mi. from the park entrance. A short film about the region is shown. **Note:** New exhibits are scheduled to be installed in late 2015 or early 2016; phone ahead for updates. **Hours:** Visitor center open daily 8-5. Closed Jan. 1, Thanksgiving and Christmas. Trails and park sites open daily 7 a.m.-dusk, year-round. **Cost:** (valid for 7 days) $8 (per private vehicle), $4 (per person arriving by other means). **Phone:** (505) 786-7014, ext. 221.

CHAMA (D-3) pop. 1,022, elev. 7,875'
• Restaurants p. 370

Like the railroad that is its most popular attraction, Chama sprang up during the silver mining boom of the 1880s. Old railroad yards, shops, a roundhouse and one of the last coal tipples in the nation remain as relics of that era.

Chama Valley Chamber of Commerce: 2732 SR 17, Chama, NM 87566. **Phone:** (575) 756-2306 or (800) 477-0149.

CUMBRES & TOLTEC SCENIC RAILROAD is on SR 17. The 64-mile railroad, built in 1880, is jointly owned by the states of New Mexico and Colorado, with trips originating from Antonito, Colo., and Chama, New Mexico. All-day trips on the vintage, narrow-gauge, coal-burning trains afford spectacular views of the rugged San Juan and Sangre de Cristo mountain ranges.

Osier, an old stagecoach stop, is the transfer and lunch point for those making the complete trip and returning by bus, as well as the turnaround and lunch point for passengers making the round-trip to their point of origin.

AAA offices in New Mexico and Colorado can make reservations. **Hours:** Trains depart from Chama and Antonito daily at 10, Memorial Day weekend to mid-Oct. Phone ahead to confirm schedule. **Cost:** Fares (including lunch) $79-$189; $29-$69 (ages 2-12). Reservations are recommended. **Phone:** (575) 756-2151 in N.M. or (888) 286-2737. *(See ad this page.)*

GANDY DANCER INN B & B   (575)756-2191

Bed & Breakfast
$79-$149

Address: 299 Maple Ave 87520 **Location:** Just w of SR 17 via 3rd St. **Facility:** 7 units. 2 stories (no elevator), interior corridors. **Terms:** check-in 4 pm, age restrictions may apply, 14 day cancellation notice-fee imposed. **Activities:** hot tub, recreation programs in season, picnic facilities. **Guest Services:** complimentary laundry. **Featured Amenity:** full hot breakfast.

▼ See AAA listing this page ▼

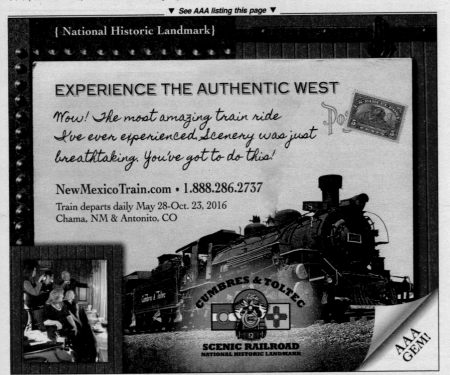

VISTA DEL RIO LODGE 575/756-2138

Motel
$80-$200

Address: 2595 US Hwy 84/64 87520 **Location:** 0.5 mi s of SR 17. Located in a quiet area. **Facility:** 19 units. 1 story, exterior corridors. **Terms:** cancellation fee imposed. **Activities:** fishing.

SAVE 🛗 📶 ❌ 🛢 🔲
/ SOME UNITS 🔲

WHERE TO EAT

HIGH COUNTRY RESTAURANT AND SALOON 575/756-2384

American. Casual Dining. $6-$25 **AAA Inspector Notes:** Near the town center, this eatery features casual service in a turn-of-the-20th-century saloon atmosphere. Among New Mexican favorites are tamales, steak asada, red and green chile and house specialties of garlic shrimp con pequin, seasoned to the diner's taste, and trucha con piñon, mountain trout in butter and piñon sauce. **Features:** full bar, Sunday brunch. **Reservations:** required. **Address:** 2281 Hwy 17 87520 **Location:** SR 17, just n of jct US 64 and 84.

L D

CHIMAYÓ (A-5) pop. 3,177, elev. 6,075'

The Spanish village of Chimayó is the home of the softly colored Chimayó blankets and rugs woven by Ortega and Trujillo family members. Throughout the village winding dirt roads lead past adobe houses. Vibrant colors decorate the village each autumn as the golden foliage of cottonwood trees provides a backdrop for garlands of red chile peppers drying in the sun.

Chimayó was founded near the end of the 17th century and for the next 100 years was the easternmost outpost of the Province of New Mexico, the frontier place of banishment. The conquest of the rebellious Pueblo and Apache in 1692 initiated a new settlement in the western foothills of the Sangre de Cristo Mountains, and Spaniards were granted permission to settle along the Santa Cruz River.

In 1740 the Plaza of San Buenaventura de Chimayó—Chimayó of the Good Venture—was built. Now called Plaza del Cerro, it is one of the oldest of Spanish colonial origin surviving in the Southwest; many surrounding structures are homes of the settlers' descendants.

East of Chimayó on SR 76—a route known as the High Road to Taos—are two other well-known craft villages. Cordova maintains a tradition of excellence in woodcarving, in which the Lopez family is most prominent. Beyond Cordova, Truchas is the home of the Cordova family of master weavers. Visitors are welcome to browse during daylight hours in the workshops scattered throughout the villages.

Shopping: Galleria Ortega and Rancho Manzana, in the Plaza del Cerro, offer weavings, pottery and furnishings. Centinela Traditional Arts specializes in handwoven wool products.

EL SANTUARIO DE CHIMAYÓ is at the s.e. end of town via SR 76 and CR 98. In 1810 Bernardo Abeyta, a farmer, was praying and claimed to see a light emanating from the soil. Upon investigation he found a cross, which is now kept inside the chapel. Legend maintains that the earth surrounding this cross has healing power. Many pilgrims come to touch the dirt in a pit inside the chapel, where castoff crutches and braces line the walls. **Hours:** Daily 9-6, May-Sept.; 9-5, rest of year. **Cost:** Free. **Phone:** (505) 351-4360.

CASA ESCONDIDA BED & BREAKFAST (505)351-4805

Bed & Breakfast $119-$179 **Address:** 64 CR 100 87522 **Location:** Jct SR 76 and 98, just w on SR 76, then 0.5 mi ne, follow signs; 7.5 mi e of Espanola on SR 76. Located in a rural area. **Facility:** 8 units, some efficiencies. 2 stories (no elevator), interior/exterior corridors. **Terms:** check-in 4 pm, 14 day cancellation notice-fee imposed.

🛗 BIZ 📶 ❌ 🅿 🔲
/ SOME UNITS 🔲 🔲 🛢 🔲 🔲

WHERE TO EAT

RANCHO DE CHIMAYO 505/351-4444

Regional Mexican. Casual Dining. $7-$21 **AAA Inspector Notes:** A scenic drive off the beaten path leads to this lovely setting. Enjoy a leisurely meal in the historic, renovated farmhouse. Friendly staffers will tempt diners with a wide selection of hearty regional favorites. The spicy chile rellenos topped with green chile sauce is a must and the homemade flan is the perfect palate pleaser. **Features:** full bar, patio dining. **Address:** 300 CR 98 87522 **Location:** 0.6 mi s on CR 98 from jct SR 76. L D 🐄

CHURCH ROCK (F-1) pop. 1,128, elev. 6,765'

Church Rock, which received its name from a prominent sandstone formation, was called *Kinlitsoh sinili* by the Navajo, or "place of yellow houses." This small settlement was the unlikely site of a nuclear disaster in 1979, when a dam containing uranium waste collapsed, spilling millions of gallons of radioactive water into the Puerco River.

RED ROCK PARK is off I-40 exit 26/33 via SR 566. Red sandstone cliffs provide a striking backdrop for this 640-acre park, which features hiking and nature trails, a rodeo arena, a convention center, campgrounds and a museum. Archeological evidence of ancient Pueblo dwellings dates to the third century. Red Rock Museum traces prehistoric habitation and the modern-day culture of Zuni, Hopi and Navajo tribes through displays of artwork and crafts.

Hours: Park open daily 24 hours. Museum open Mon.-Fri. 8-4:30. Phone ahead to confirm schedule. **Cost:** Park free. Museum by donation. **Phone:** (505) 722-3839. 🎫

CIBOLA NATIONAL FOREST (G-2)

Elevations in the forest range from 5,000 ft. in the Magdalena district to 11,301 ft. at Mt. Taylor. Refer to AAA maps for additional elevation information.

The forest comprises scattered mountain ranges rising from the desert east and south of Albuquerque and stretching west to Arizona. Cibola National Forest's 1,625,542 acres encompass four wilderness areas: Sandia, Manzano, Apache Kid and The Withington. Recreational opportunities include camping, fishing and hiking. *See Recreation Areas Chart.*

The rugged Canadian River Canyon west of Roy provides another type of beauty within Kiowa National Grassland. The forest also administers Black Kettle National Grassland, in neighboring western Oklahoma and the Texas panhandle. Camping and fishing center on the grassland's five lakes. In some areas, hunting is available in season, and there is skiing at Sandia Peak Ski Area.

A chairlift carries visitors to the northeastern face of Sandia Peak. The lift may be accessed via the Sandia Peak Aerial Tramway *(see attraction listing p. 337)* or by automobile, taking I-40 exit 175 north to SR 536. It operates Sat.-Sun. 10-4, Memorial Day through Labor Day and during the Albuquerque International Balloon Fiesta. It also transports mountain bikes for cyclists who wish to explore the peak's upper trails; phone (505) 856-7325.

SANDIA CREST is 16 mi. e. of Albuquerque on I-40, 6 mi. n. on SR 14, then 14 mi. n.w. on the Sandia Crest National Scenic Byway (SR 536). At the observation deck atop the 10,678-foot crest, the panorama encompasses 15,000 square miles. A self-guiding nature trail begins here and loops for a half-mile. The byway is a 14-mile spur of the Turquoise Trail, a scenic stretch of SR 14 that links Albuquerque and Santa Fe. Volcanic formations, mountains, desert landscapes and the Rio Grande are visible.

Snowboarding and downhill and cross-country skiing are available in winter; hiking and mountain biking are popular in summer. Equipment can be rented in both seasons. Food is available at the top of the crest. **Cost:** $3 recreation amenity fee. **Parking:** $1 at the base of the tramway. **Phone:** (505) 281-3304, (505) 856-1532 Tram, or (505) 242-9052 Ski area.

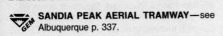 **SANDIA PEAK AERIAL TRAMWAY**—see Albuquerque p. 337.

CIMARRON (E-4) pop. 1,021, elev. 6,428'
• Hotels p. 372 • Restaurants p. 372

Meaning "wild" or "untamed," Cimarron was fitting for both the brawling stream and the settlement that developed on its banks. Although Eagle Nest Lake ultimately tamed the river, nothing could contain the activities in town from the late 1860s to about 1880. The Las Vegas *Gazette* once reported,

"Things are quiet in Cimarron; nobody has been killed in three days."

Clay Allison, Billy the Kid, Bob Ford and Black Jack Ketchum were among notorious part-time residents. Gunfights killed 26 men, and New Mexico's first printing press was dumped into the Cimarron River before the range wars ended and the town ceased to be a magnet for every outlaw in the Southwest.

Cimarron languished after losing the county seat to Springer in 1880 but revived in the early 1900s with the arrival of two railroads and the lumber industry. The modern-day city serves nearby ranches, some logging operations and a lively tourist trade. Standing as reminders of a boisterous past are the old jail and the St. James Hotel at 617 S. Collison St., where Annie Oakley joined Buffalo Bill Cody's Wild West Show. Four miles south on SR 21 is Philmont Scout Ranch, a high-adventure camp for members of the Boy Scouts.

Sizable populations of eagles, hawks and falcons inhabit the 3,700-acre Maxwell National Wildlife Refuge, 30 miles east off I-25. Part of Carson National Forest, Valle Vidal offers 100,000 acres of rugged back country for backpacking, hunting and fishing. It is 4 miles north on scenic US 64, then 21 miles northwest on Valle Vidal Road, following signs. Cimarron Canyon State Park, 12 miles west on US 64, offers brown trout fishing, hiking and camping *(see Recreation Areas Chart).*

Cimarron Chamber of Commerce: 104 N. Lincoln Ave., P.O. Box 604, Cimarron, NM 87714. **Phone:** (575) 376-2417 or (888) 376-2417.

Self-guiding tours: A walking tour map available from the chamber of commerce describes 14 historic buildings in the old town of Cimarron.

OLD MILL MUSEUM is s. of US 64 in Old Town on SR 21. An 1864 building houses four floors of artifacts relating to county history. Included are Native American arts and crafts, furnishings, historic items, vintage clothing and books. Placards explain the mill's original workings, which are partially intact. **Time:** Allow 1 hour minimum. **Hours:** Daily 10-4, Memorial Day-Labor Day. Phone ahead to confirm schedule. **Cost:** Donations. **Phone:** (575) 376-2417 (Cimarron Chamber of Commerce).

PHILMONT SCOUT RANCH is 5 mi. s. off SR 21 at 17 Deer Run Rd. The 137,493-acre national camping center is operated by the National Council of the Boy Scouts of America. More than 20,000 Scouts from around the world visit each summer. Villa Philmonte, the summer home of Tulsa oilman Waite Philips, benefactor of Philmont Scout Ranch, can be toured.

Hours: Library and museum daily 8-5:30, June-Aug.; Mon.-Fri. 8-5, rest of year. Villa tours by appointment, Mar.-Oct. Last tour begins 30 minutes before closing. Reservations are required. **Cost:** Donations. **Phone:** (575) 376-1136.

Philmont Museum is 5 mi. s. off SR 21 at 17 Deer Run Rd. Rotating exhibits focus on Southwestern art, culture and history. The museum also contains the Seton Memorial Library, named for artist, naturalist and Boy Scouts of America co-founder Ernest Thompson Seton. **Hours:** Daily 8-5:30, June-Aug.; Mon.-Fri. 8-5, rest of year. **Cost:** Free. **Phone:** (575) 376-1136.

CASA DEL GAVILAN
575/376-2246

Historic Bed & Breakfast
$120-$180

Address: 570 Hwy 21 S 87714 **Location:** SR 21, 5.7 mi s of US 64, follow signs. Located in a secluded area. **Facility:** The remote hacienda-style structure dates from 1905 and is in a serene setting with very fine mountain views. 5 units, some two bedrooms. 1 story, interior corridors. **Terms:** closed 11/15-3/15, 7 day cancellation notice-fee imposed.

CIMARRON INN & RV PARK
575/376-2268

Motel
$49-$75

Address: 212 10th St 87714 **Location:** On US 64. **Facility:** 15 units, some kitchens, cabins and cottages. 1 story, exterior corridors. **Terms:** cancellation fee imposed.

EXPRESS ST. JAMES HOTEL
575/376-2664

[fyi] Not evaluated. **Address:** 617 S Collison Ave 87714 **Location:** Center. Facilities, services, and décor characterize a mid-scale property. The renovated historic hotel has a haunted past.

WHERE TO EAT

ST. JAMES RESTAURANT
575/376-2664

American Casual Dining
$6-$32

AAA Inspector Notes: In the historic St James Hotel, this dining room features Western décor and many antiques related to the local ranching community. Patio dining is available in season. **Features:** full bar, patio dining. **Reservations:** suggested. **Address:** 617 S Collison Ave 87714 **Location:** Center; in Express St. James Hotel. [B] [L] [D]

CLAYTON (E-6) pop. 2,980, elev. 5,053'

So numerous were the herds of cattle driven through this small farming community in the mid-1880s that the Denver & Fort Worth Railroad established the settlement as a division point. As a railhead and trading center, Clayton underwent a Wild West phase. Celebrated train robber Black Jack Ketchum was hanged from a gallows enclosed in a stockade to foil yet another rescue by his gang.

Clayton, at the foot of the Rabbit Ear Mountains, is still a cattle town; some of the largest feedlots in the region are just to the north. It also is one of the world's largest producers of carbon dioxide, which is used for recovering oil in the Permian Basin in New Mexico and Texas.

Livestock studies are conducted at Clayton Livestock Research Center, 5 miles east in the Kiowa and Rita Blanca National Grasslands. The University of New Mexico and the U.S. Forest Service investigate problems related to the health, nutrition and management of cattle. Phone (575) 374-2566.

Recreational opportunities abound at Clayton Lake State Park *(see Recreation Areas Chart)*, known for its excellent trout, catfish, walleye and bass fishing. Dinosaur tracks were first discovered on the spillway of the dam in 1982; since then more than 500 tracks have been plotted.

Clayton-Union County Chamber of Commerce: 1103 S. First St., P.O. Box 476, Clayton, NM 88415. **Phone:** (575) 374-9253 or (800) 390-7858.

THE HERZSTEIN MEMORIAL MUSEUM is at 22 S. Second St. Offering a glimpse into the local area's rich history, the collection is wide-ranging and includes pioneer artifacts, paintings and antique furniture. **Time:** Allow 1 hour minimum. **Hours:** Tues.-Sat. 10-4. Closed major holidays. **Cost:** Donations. **Phone:** (575) 374-2977.

BEST WESTERN KOKOPELLI LODGE
(575)374-2589

Hotel
$110-$135

AAA Benefit: Save 10% or more every day and earn 10% bonus points!

Address: 702 S 1st St 88415 **Location:** US 87, 0.5 mi se of jct US 56 and 64. **Facility:** 50 units. 2 stories (no elevator), exterior corridors. **Pool(s):** heated outdoor. **Activities:** exercise room.

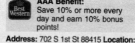

DAYS INN & SUITES
(575)374-0133

Hotel $105-$145 **Address:** 1120 S 1st St 88415 **Location:** US 87, 1 mi s of jct US 56 and 64. **Facility:** 41 units. 2 stories, interior corridors. **Terms:** cancellation fee imposed. **Pool(s):** heated indoor. **Activities:** hot tub, limited exercise equipment. **Guest Services:** coin laundry.

CLOUDCROFT (I-4) pop. 674, elev. 8,663'

A resort and recreation center at the summit of the Sacramento Mountains, Cloudcroft offers skiing and other fun in the snow in winter and summer camping and hiking in the Lincoln National Forest *(see place listing p. 395).*

This high, wide country was settled when the Southern Pacific Railroad ran a spur from Alamogordo to tap the timber reserves in the Sacramento Mountains. To lure excursion passengers the railroad built an elaborate resort, The Lodge, in 1901. Although the last freight train arrived in 1947, the resort still operates. Today's visitors enjoy hiking, bicycling and skiing along trails where trains once traveled. Local artisans create a variety of crafts. Shopping, dining and entertainment venues are along downtown's historic Burro Avenue.

The Sacramento Mountains Historical Museum, on US 82, recalls the town's settlement days. Within the museum complex is Cloudcroft Pioneer Village, where visitors can see antique farm equipment and historic buildings furnished in period, including a granary, barn, chapel, one-room schoolhouse and train depot. Phone (575) 682-2932.

Cloudcroft Chamber of Commerce: 1001 James Canyon Hwy., P.O. Box 1291, Cloudcroft, NM 88317. **Phone:** (575) 682-2733.

SACRAMENTO MOUNTAINS HISTORICAL MUSEUM & PIONEER VILLAGE is at 1000 US 82. Self-guiding tours are offered for visitors to explore 19th century buildings, including a one-room school house, railroad depot, chapel, tack barn, train caboose and blacksmith shop. The buildings and exhibits feature items relating to the time period. **Time:** Allow 1 hour minimum. **Hours:** Mon.-Tues. and Fri.-Sat. 10-4, Sun. 1-4, Memorial Day weekend through Oct. 31; Fri.-Sat. 10-4, Sun. 1-4, rest of year. Phone ahead for special events. Closed Jan. 1, Thanksgiving and Christmas. **Cost:** $5; $4 (military with ID); $3 (ages 6-12). Cash or check only. **Phone:** (575) 682-2932. 🐾

THE LODGE RESORT   (575)682-2566

Historic Hotel
$125-$335

Address: 601 Corona Pl 88317 **Location:** US 82, 0.3 mi s on Curlew Pl/Corona Pl. **Facility:** Constructed in 1899 as a luxurious mountain retreat, this enchanting historic hotel features well-appointed guest rooms, spa services and a nine-hole golf course spread over lush green hillsides. 59 units. 3 stories (no elevator), interior corridors. **Terms:** check-in 4 pm, 14 day cancellation notice-fee imposed. **Dining:** Rebecca's, see separate listing. **Pool(s):** heated outdoor. **Activities:** sauna, hot tub, regulation golf, exercise room, spa.

SAVE ❚¶✚ 🍸 🏌 ➿ BIZ 📶
✕ 💻 / SOME UNITS 🔌 🖥 🖨

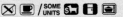

WHERE TO EAT

BIG DADDY'S DINER   575/682-1224

🍷 American. Family Dining. $7-$27 **AAA Inspector Notes:** Big Daddy might watch over the dining room but it is Little Mama who oversees the kitchen and turns out generous portions of country favorites. The hand-cut, fresh sweet potato fries are especially tasty. **Address:** 1705 James Canyon Hwy 82 88317 **Location:** Just e.

B L D ⌂

REBECCA'S   575/682-2566

American
Casual Dining
$8-$38

AAA Inspector Notes: Located in a lovely hotel that dates back to 1899, Rebecca's wonderful stained-glass porch windows enhance the mountain views. Lunch offers sandwiches or pasta. Dinner features piano music, steak, seafood, and well-known, tasty fruit cobbler. **Features:** full bar, patio dining, Sunday brunch. **Reservations:** suggested. **Address:** 601 Corona Pl 88317 **Location:** US 82, 0.3 mi s on Curlew Pl/Corona Pl; in The Lodge Resort.

Menu on AAA.com   B L D 🐾

CLOVIS (G-6) pop. 37,775, elev. 4,266'
• Restaurants p. 374

On the high plains of eastern New Mexico in the heart of cattle country, Clovis is a ranching, farming and dairy center. Six miles west is Cannon Air Force Base, a major contributor to the local economy.

Buddy Holly recorded his 1957 hit "Peggy Sue" at the Norman Petty Recording Studio, 1313 W. 7th St. The facility contains original recording equipment and music memorabilia; a visit will take you back to the glory days of early rock 'n roll. Guided tours are available by appointment only and must be made at least 1 month in advance; phone (575) 763-3435.

Clovis/Curry County Chamber of Commerce: 105 E. Grand Ave., Clovis, NM 88101. **Phone:** (575) 763-3435 or (800) 261-7656.

HILLCREST PARK ZOO is at 10th and Sycamore sts. and is home to some 500 animals. Some of the residents at the 25-acre zoo include a Bengal tiger, common tamarins, black bears, giraffes, spotted hyenas and bison. **Time:** Allow 1 hour minimum. **Hours:** Tues.-Sun. 9-3:30. Closed major holidays. **Cost:** $4; $3 (ages 60+); $2 (ages 3-11). **Phone:** (575) 769-7873. 🏧

COMFORT INN & SUITES   (575)762-4536

▽▽▽ Hotel $90-$130 **Address:** 201 Schepps Blvd 88101 **Location:** Jct US 60/70/84, just n. **Facility:** 66 units, some two bedrooms. 3 stories, interior corridors. **Pool(s):** heated indoor. **Activities:** hot tub, exercise room. **Guest Services:** valet and coin laundry.
❚¶✚ ➿ BIZ HS 📶 🖥 🖨 💻 / SOME UNITS 🔌

FAIRFIELD INN & SUITES BY MARRIOTT   (575)762-1411

▽▽▽ Hotel $94-$169 **Address:** 4305 N Prince St 88101 **Location:** 2.5 mi n of jct US 60/84. **Facility:** 69 units. 3 stories, interior corridors. **Pool(s):** heated outdoor. **Activities:** hot tub, exercise room. **Guest Services:** valet and coin laundry.

AAA Benefit: Members save 5% or more!

❚¶✚ CALL 🔊 ➿ BIZ HS 📶 ✕ 🖥 🖨 💻

HAMPTON INN   (575)763-3300

▽▽▽ Hotel $110-$170 **Address:** 2212 Mabry Dr 88101 **Location:** Jct US 60/70/84, 1.1 mi e. **Facility:** 55 units. 2 stories, interior corridors. **Terms:** 1-7 night maximum stay, cancellation fee imposed. **Pool(s):** heated indoor. **Activities:** hot tub, exercise room. **Guest Services:** valet and coin laundry.

AAA Benefit: Members save up to 10%!

❚¶✚ CALL 🔊 ➿ BIZ 📶 ✕ 🖥 🖨 💻

HOLIDAY INN EXPRESS & SUITES   575/935-8777

▽▽▽ Hotel. Rates not provided. **Address:** 4728 N Prince St 88101 **Location:** Jct US 60/84, 3 mi n. **Facility:** 80 units. 3 stories, interior corridors. **Pool(s):** heated indoor. **Activities:** hot tub, exercise room. **Guest Services:** valet and coin laundry.
CALL 🔊 ➿ BIZ HS 📶 ✕ 🖥 🖨 💻

LA QUINTA INN & SUITES CLOVIS   (575)763-8777

▽▽▽ Hotel $86-$176 **Address:** 4521 N Prince St 88101 **Location:** Jct US 60/84, 3 mi n. **Facility:** 66 units. 3 stories, interior corridors. **Pool(s):** heated indoor. **Activities:** hot tub, exercise room. **Guest Services:** valet and coin laundry.
CALL 🔊 ➿ BIZ HS 📶 ✕ 🖥 🖨 💻
/ SOME UNITS 🐾

SUPER 8 CLOVIS   (575)762-5600

▼▼ **Hotel** $68-$73 **Address:** 2912 Mabry Dr 88101 **Location:** 1.8 mi e on US 60/70/84. **Facility:** 96 units, some efficiencies. 2 stories (no elevator), exterior corridors. **Pool(s):** heated outdoor. **Activities:** hot tub, exercise room. **Guest Services:** valet and coin laundry.

🍴➕ 🛍 BIZ HS 🛜 🖥 📁 🖨 💻 /SOME S📶

WHERE TO EAT

COTTON PATCH CAFE   575-762-2233

▼▼ American. Family Dining. $6-$16 **AAA Inspector Notes:** This family friendly restaurant features a variety of sandwiches, burgers, salads and comfort food entrées. Save room for the peach cobbler a la mode. **Address:** 2604 N Prince St 88101 **Location:** Jct Parkland Dr; across from mall. L D

DAKOTA'S STEAKHOUSE   575-935-3535

▼▼ Steak. Casual Dining. $10-$38 **AAA Inspector Notes:** Enjoy great steaks, seafood and burgers served in a casual atmosphere by a friendly staff. Desserts include a selection of sugar-free and gluten-free cakes. **Reservations:** suggested. **Address:** 816 Lexington Rd 88101 **Location:** Jct Prince St, just e. L D

RIB CRIB BBQ AND GRILL   575-742-0200

▼▼ Barbecue. Casual Dining. $6-$15 **AAA Inspector Notes:** Most guests need extra napkins to tackle the ribs, brisket, ham, pork and chicken selections. The menu also lists sandwiches and wraps, along with tempting sides and large desserts. The decor is decidedly Western. **Features:** beer & wine. **Address:** 4020 N Prince St 88101 **Location:** Jct US 84 W and Prince St, 2.6 mi n. L D

TACO BOX   575-935-8226

▼ Mexican. Quick Serve. $3-$7 **AAA Inspector Notes:** This popular quick service restaurant features tacos, burritos and burgers for dining in or taking out. This is a favorite stop on the New Mexico Green Chile Cheeseburger Trail. Complimentary Wi-Fi is offered. **Address:** 136 W 21st St 88101 **Location:** Just w of jct Main St. B L D

COCHITÍ PUEBLO (C-3) pop. 528, elev. 5,258'

West of the Rio Grande and a few miles southwest of Cochiti Dam, this ancient Keresan pueblo retains few of its old landmarks. The mission church, San Buenaventura de Cochiti, was built in 1628. The tribe leases land to the community of Cochiti Lake, where a recreation area offers boating, camping, fishing, sailing, windsurfing and nature trails *(see Recreation Areas Chart)*. Visitors to the pueblo are welcome dawn to dusk. Drawing, painting, photography or tape recording is not permitted.

KASHA-KATUWE TENT ROCKS NATIONAL MONUMENT is roughly midway between Albuquerque and Santa Fe. From Albuquerque, take I-25 n. to exit 259, then SR 22 w. to Cochiti Pueblo and follow signs to the national monument. From Santa Fe, take I-25 s. to exit 264, then SR 16 w. about 8 mi. to SR 22 and follow signs. Located on north-central New Mexico's Pajarito Plateau, Tent Rocks is a remarkable wonderland of cone-shaped rock formations, the product of volcanic eruptions that occurred millions of years ago. The pumice, ash and tuff deposits left behind were subsequently shaped by wind, water and erosion.

Boulder caps perch precariously atop many of these tapering formations—which range in height from a few to more than 90 feet—protecting the softer rock below. Another fascinating geologic feature are the slot canyons, narrow, twisting passageways carved over time by rushing water. Ponderosa and piñon pines grow along with desert plants like Indian paintbrush and Apache plume.

The area's austere beauty can be explored on two hikes. The 1.2-mile Cave Loop Trail is an easy trek that leads to an above-ground cave. The more strenuous Canyon Trail (3 miles round-trip) ascends a narrow canyon with a steep 630-foot elevation gain. The trail ends atop a mesa that offers breathtaking 360-degree views of the tent rocks below, the Rio Grande Valley and the Sangre de Cristo, Jémez and Sandia mountains looming in the distance.

Note: The trailhead is 5 miles from the monument entrance gate via a bumpy dirt-gravel road. Some hands-free climbing is required on the Canyon Trail; steps built into the trail in a couple of places help facilitate the ascent. Wear hiking boots or nonslip athletic shoes and a hat, and bring water. Stay on the designated trail; climbing on the tent rocks is prohibited. There are parking areas and restrooms at the trailhead. Dogs are not permitted. **Time:** Allow 2 hours, 30 minutes minimum. **Hours:** Daily 7-7, Mar. 11-Oct. 31; 8-5, rest of year. Last admission 1 hour before closing. Closed Jan. 1, Thanksgiving, Christmas Eve and Christmas. **Cost:** $5 per private vehicle. **Phone:** (505) 761-8797. 🅣

COLUMBUS (J-2) pop. 1,664, elev. 4,064'

Just before dawn on Mar. 9, 1916, the revolutionary activities of Pancho Villa and his 500 guerrillas spilled over the international border into drowsy Columbus and its military outpost—the first attack on U.S. soil since the War of 1812. The raiders seized livestock, burned the town and killed 18 Americans, eliciting immediate retaliation from President Woodrow Wilson.

Within a week Gen. John "Black Jack" Pershing marched his 6,000 troops, accompanied by motorized vehicles and airplanes, into Mexico to mark the first mechanized U.S. military action. Pershing's forces pursued the rebel leader for 11 months but never captured him; Villa was assassinated in 1923.

COLUMBUS HISTORICAL SOCIETY MUSEUM is at jct. SRs 9 and 11. Chronicling local history from the pioneer era to modern times, the museum is housed in a 1902 El Paso and Southwestern Railroad depot that stood witness to Pancho Villa's raid on the city. This attack and the U.S. Army's subsequent retaliation are depicted with photographs, military artifacts and a 20-minute film. Displays include Mexican pottery and beads, pioneer implements and railroad memorabilia. **Time:** Allow 30 minutes minimum. **Hours:** Daily 10-4, Sept.-Apr.; Mon.-Fri. 10-1, Sat.-Sun. 10-4, rest of year. Closed Christmas. **Cost:** Donations. **Phone:** (575) 531-2620.

PANCHO VILLA STATE PARK is at jct. SRs 9 and 11. The site of Pancho Villa's raid into American territory is preserved at the park, which commemorates the event with historical exhibits, including pre-World War I vehicles used by Gen. John Pershing's men in their pursuit of Villa. The 61-acre park includes a visitor center, a 7,000-square-foot exhibit hall, buildings from Camp Furlong, nature trails, a playground and an exotic botanical garden with some 30 varieties of cacti. **Hours:** Daily 24 hours. Visitor center daily 9-4. **Cost:** $5 per private vehicle. Camping $8-$14. **Phone:** (575) 531-2711, or (575) 531-2119 for visitor center.

CORRALES (F-3) pop. 8,329, elev. 5,023'
• Hotels & Restaurants map & index p. 342

Corrales, about half an hour north of downtown Albuquerque via I-40 exit 155, is not only a pleasant escape from the city but a step back in time to an earlier New Mexico. For a dozen or so miles after leaving the interstate, Coors Boulevard is solid suburban sprawl—walled-in housing developments, strip centers, car dealerships, Starbucks outlets. But once you bear right onto Corrales Road (SR 448), and especially after crossing the Sandoval County line, the scene abruptly changes.

Suddenly you're in the country. Cottonwood trees line the roadside—credit the nearby presence of the Rio Grande for that. The landscape is greener. The two-lane road winds past adobes and (in fall) produce stands selling fresh apple cider. Sample the bounty from local farmers—everything from arugula to green chiles to tomatillos—at the Corrales Growers' Market. It sets up at the Recreation Center at Jones and Corrales roads (south of the post office) Sundays 9-noon, April through October (also Wednesday afternoons from 3-6, mid-July through late October). The rest of the year it is open the first Sunday of the month from 11 to 1; phone (505) 898-7927.

Sunday in Corrales, the third Sunday of the month from May through September, offers family-friendly events like Art in the Park, where local painters, potters, metalworkers, jewelers and sculptors exhibit their wares under the shade of cottonwood trees. Kids can engage in activities like making bread and crafting mosaic art out of glass. It all happens at La Entrada Park (corner of Corrales and La Entrada roads).

Poke around the shops and galleries scattered along Corrales Road. Artist-owned Corrales Bosque Gallery (in the Mercado de Maya) displays landscape paintings, sculpture, ceramic pieces and collage art by New Mexico artists working in a variety of media (everything from clay to torn paper). Local artwork adorns The Oasis (in the Village Plaza Center at 4940 Corrales Rd.), where you can relax with a barista-brewed coffee or iced specialty concoction in the cool green surroundings of an indoor garden.

Explore the village's history at Casa San Ysidro at 973 Old Church Road (just off Corrales Road; watch for the sign). This partially reconstructed 19th-century adobe displays Spanish Colonial furnishings, hand-woven floor coverings, iron tools and an authentic 18th-century loom. The house is open for tours February through November; phone (505) 897-8828 for information. Behind it is a country cemetery with interesting statues and headstones and a view framed by the Sandia Mountains. Don't be surprised if a jackrabbit lopes by in this serene rural setting.

Across the street is the Old Church (Iglesia de San Ysidro), which dates from around 1868. Shaped like a cross, it features massive adobe walls nearly 3 feet thick. Twin bell towers were added in the 1930s to help support the weakening facade. Today this historic structure serves as a venue for community activities and music programs.

WINERIES
• **Corrales Winery** is at 6275 Corrales Rd. Tours and tastings are offered. **Hours:** Wed.-Sun. noon-5. **Phone:** (505) 898-5165. GT

THE CHOCOLATE TURTLE BED & BREAKFAST
(505)898-1800 52
▼▼▼▼ **Bed & Breakfast** $129-$169 **Address:** 1098 W Meadowlark Ln 87048 **Location:** I-25 exit 233 (Alameda Blvd), 4 mi w to Corrales Rd, 1 mi n to Meadowlark Ln, then 1 mi w. **Facility:** The B&B features a large, colorful, Southwestern-style living room and attractively decorated guest rooms. A patio and garden provide nice views and is a romantic setting for small weddings.. 4 units. 1 story, interior corridors. **Terms:** 2 night minimum stay - seasonal and/or weekends, age restrictions may apply, 14 day cancellation notice-fee imposed. CALL &M BIZ 🛜 ✕ 🅦 🄕

WHERE TO EAT

HANNAH & NATE'S MARKET CAFE   505/898-2370 50
▼▼ ▼ American. Casual Dining. $8-$13 **AAA Inspector Notes:** In addition to hearty breakfasts, guests can sample from an eclectic selection of sandwiches and delectable cakes, pies and cookies produced in the in-house bakery of this cafe. **Address:** 4512 Corrales Rd 87048 **Location:** Center. B L

INDIGO CROW CAFE   505/898-7000 49
▼▼▼▼ American. Casual Dining. $9-$34 **AAA Inspector Notes:** A dining room with territorial charm, a patio surrounded by a Mexican-style wall and an imaginative menu are some of the features of this café in the center of town. The tasty Cobb salad is gigantic. **Features:** beer & wine, patio dining, Sunday brunch. **Reservations:** suggested. **Address:** 4515 Corrales Rd 87048 **Location:** Center. L D

DEMING (I-2) pop. 14,855, elev. 4,337'

Fields of chiles flourish in the river valley around Deming, along with secondary crops cotton, onions, pecans, grapes and sorghum. The water that sustains them is the subsurface flow of the Mimbres River, which vanishes underground north of the city and reappears at the surface as a lake in the Mexican state of Chihuahua. Southeast of this growing retirement center the Little Florida (flo-REE-da) Mountains yield agates, fire opals, jasper and semiprecious stones.

Deming-Luna County Chamber of Commerce and Visitors Center: 103 E. Ash St., P.O. Box 8, Deming, NM 88031. **Phone:** (575) 546-2674.

Self-guiding tours: A walking-tour brochure listing 16 historic buildings and sites is available from the Deming-Luna County Chamber of Commerce and Visitors Center.

CITY OF ROCKS STATE PARK is 30 mi. n.w. via US 180, then 3 mi. n.e. on SR 61. Millions of years ago wind and water shaped volcanic rock into the curious monolithic formations that give this 680-acre park its name. The Mimbres Indians and Spanish conquistadors left evidence of their visits. A cactus garden, hiking trails, interpretive exhibits and visitor center also are featured. **Hours:** Daily 7 a.m.-9 p.m. Visitor center open daily 8:30-noon and 1-3:30 during daylight saving time; 9:30-noon and 1-4:30, rest of the year (when staff is available). Phone ahead to confirm visitor center schedule. **Cost:** $5 per private vehicle. Camping $10-$14. **Phone:** (575) 536-2800.

DEMING LUNA MIMBRES MUSEUM is at 301 S. Silver St. The museum depicts Southwest history with an 1853 customs house, pioneer artifacts, military items from early cavalry days through World War II, railroad and cowboy memorabilia, gems and minerals, and a Mimbres Indian pottery exhibit. The transportation annex features street scenes and antique automobiles representing Deming's past. **Hours:** Mon.-Sat. 9-4. Closed Jan. 1, Easter, Thanksgiving and Christmas. **Cost:** Donations. **Phone:** (575) 546-2382.

ROCKHOUND STATE PARK is 14 mi. s.e. off SR 11. Abundant agate and quartz crystals are found within this park on the western slope of the Florida Mountains. Up to 15 pounds of rock may be collected, making it a favorite spot for rockhounds. **Hours:** Gate open daily 7-dusk. Visitor Center daily 10-noon and 1-4. Office daily 7-4. **Cost:** $5 per private vehicle. Camping $10-$18. **Phone:** (575) 546-6182, or (877) 664-7787 for reservations.

BEST WESTERN MIMBRES VALLEY INN   (575)546-4544

Hotel
$85-$150

 AAA Benefit: Save 10% or more every day and earn 10% bonus points!

Address: 1500 W Pine St 88030 **Location:** I-10 exit 81, just e. **Facility:** 40 units. 1 story, exterior corridors. **Pool(s):** outdoor. **Guest Services:** coin laundry. **Featured Amenity:** full hot breakfast.

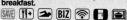

DAYS INN   (575)546-8813

Motel
$57-$72

Address: 1601 E Pine St 88030 **Location:** I-10 exit 85, 2 mi w on business loop; exit 81 eastbound, 1 mi e on business loop. **Facility:** 57 units. 2 stories (no elevator), exterior corridors. **Pool(s):** outdoor. **Featured Amenity:** full hot breakfast.

GRAND MOTOR INN

Hotel
$46-$69

(575)546-2632

Address: 1721 E Pine St 88030 **Location:** I-10 exit 85, 2 mi w on business loop; exit 82 eastbound, 1 mi e on business loop. **Facility:** 58 units. 2 stories (no elevator), interior/exterior corridors. **Terms:** cancellation fee imposed. **Pool(s):** outdoor. **Guest Services:** valet and coin laundry. *(See ad this page.)*

HAMPTON INN

(575)546-2022

Hotel $89-$129 **Address:** 3751 E Cedar St 88030 **Location:** I-10 exit 85, just s to Cedar St, then just w. **Facility:** 75 units. 3 stories, interior corridors. **Terms:** 1-7 night minimum stay, cancellation fee imposed. **Pool(s):** heated indoor. **Activities:** hot tub, exercise room. **Guest Services:** coin laundry.

AAA Benefit: Members save up to 10%!

HOLIDAY INN EXPRESS & SUITES

575/545-6500

Hotel. Rates not provided. **Address:** 3801 E Cedar St 88030 **Location:** I-10 exit 85, just s to Cedar St, then just w. **Facility:** 84 units. 4 stories, interior corridors. **Pool(s):** heated indoor. **Activities:** hot tub, exercise room. **Guest Services:** valet and coin laundry.

LA QUINTA INN & SUITES DEMING

Hotel
$71-$174

(575)546-0600

Address: 4300 E Pine St 88030 **Location:** I-10 exit 85, just w. **Facility:** 58 units, some kitchens. 3 stories, interior corridors. **Pool(s):** outdoor. **Activities:** hot tub, limited exercise equipment. **Guest Services:** coin laundry.

WHERE TO EAT

EL MIRADOR

575/544-7340

Mexican. Family Dining. $7-$16 **AAA Inspector Notes:** This modest cafe is very busy at lunch time. Diners will find Mexican food here which is prepared in the traditional way, including carefully prepared enchiladas, tacos and burritos. **Address:** 510 E Pine St 88030 **Location:** Center. [B] [L] [D]

RANCHER'S GRILL

575/546-8883

American. Casual Dining. $9-$25 **AAA Inspector Notes:** Great steaks and a well-stocked salad bar are hallmarks of the busy eatery. Lots of Western memorabilia and decor entertain and amuse. The restaurant is equally popular with travelers and locals who visit frequently. **Features:** beer & wine. **Address:** 316 E Cedar St 88030 **Location:** I-10 exit 82B (US 180), just e. [L] [D]

▼ See AAA listing this page ▼

AAA Vacations® packages ...

exciting itineraries and exclusive values

DULCE (D-3) pop. 2,743, elev. 6,769'

Dulce is the capital and principal town of Jicarilla Apache Indian Reservation. The Jicarillas (hek-a-REH-yas), whose name means "little baskets," are renowned for woven baskets and other ornate craftwork. Visitors may watch artisans at work at the Jicarilla Arts and Crafts Museum on the reservation.

The town, at the northeastern corner of the reservation, is a popular provision point with hunters and anglers. The 14,500-acre Horse Lake Mesa Game Park is one of the country's largest elk enclosures.

Jicarilla Apache Nation, Public Relations Department: P.O. Box 507, Dulce, NM 87528. **Phone:** (575) 759-3242.

WILD HORSE CASINO & HOTEL   575/759-3663

Hotel
$95

Address: 13603 US Hwy 64 87528 **Location:** Center. **Facility:** Colorful paintings by local artists brighten up the public areas and guest room décor. Planning a special event? Take advantage of the large, on-site ballroom. 41 units. 2 stories (no elevator), interior corridors. **Activities:** exercise room. **Guest Services:** coin laundry.

EDGEWOOD (F-3) elev. 6,645'

A relative newcomer in state history, the farming community of Edgewood was settled in the 1930s and incorporated in 1999.

WILDLIFE WEST NATURE PARK is off I-40 exit 187 to 87 N. Frontage Rd. The 122-acre native wildlife zoo contains animals and plants native to New Mexico. Trails allow visitors to see elk, black bears, Mexican wolves, mountain lions, pronghorn antelope, foxes, raccoons, raptors and other birds and wildlife. Hayrides are offered Saturday summer evenings prior to the Chuckwagon Dinner Show, which features barbecue and Western musical entertainment. Several festivals are offered throughout the year.

Time: Allow 1 hour, 30 minutes minimum. **Hours:** Park daily 10-6, mid-Mar. to early Nov.; noon-4, rest of year. Dinner show is offered Sat. at 6 p.m., mid-June through Labor Day. **Cost:** $9; $7 (ages 60+); $5 (ages 5-11). Dinner show $25; $23 (ages 60+); $12 (ages 5-11); reservations required by 2 p.m. on day of show. **Phone:** (505) 281-7655.

ELEPHANT BUTTE pop. 1,431

ELEPHANT BUTTE INN & SPA   (575)744-5431

Hotel
$80-$140

Address: 401 Hwy 195 87935 **Location:** I-25 exit 83, 4 mi e. **Facility:** 45 units. 2 stories (no elevator), exterior corridors. **Terms:** cancellation fee imposed. **Pool(s):** heated outdoor. **Activities:** spa. **Guest Services:** valet laundry. **Featured Amenity:** continental breakfast.

EL MORRO

CIMARRON ROSE BED & BREAKFAST   505/783-4770

[fyi] Not evaluated. **Address:** 689 Oso Ridge Rt 87321 **Location:** 12 mi e; on SR 53, between MM 56 and 57. Facilities, services, and décor characterize a mid-scale property.

EL MORRO NATIONAL MONUMENT (F-2)

El Morro National Monument is 43 miles southwest of Grants via SR 53. The central features of the 1,278-acre monument are 200-foot-high Inscription Rock and the water hole fed by snowmelt and rainfall pouring off the rock. The Spanish called the sandstone mesa *El Morro,* meaning "the bluff" or "the headland."

Carved into the soft rock are centuries-old petroglyphs. The first known European inscription was left in 1605 by Juan de Oñate, governor and colonizer of New Mexico. Others include those of Gov. Manuel de Silva Nieto in 1629; a soldier in 1632; Don Diego de Vargas, leader of the 1692 reconquest; and Lt. Edward Beale, who passed by with a camel caravan in 1857. Other soldiers and settlers making their way west added their names and dates.

Two Ancestral Puebloan villages once thrived atop this mesa. Remains of an 875-room dwelling from about the 13th century have been partly excavated.

Self-guiding tours are available. A half-mile trail and a 2-mile trail take about 45 minutes and 1.5 hours, respectively. A 15-minute video presentation in the visitor center offers a glimpse into the cultural and natural history of the area. A small campground is available on a first-come, first-served basis. For further information contact the Superintendent, El Morro National Monument, HC 61, Box 43, Ramah, NM 87321.

Visitor center daily 9-5; phone for extended summer hours. Closed Jan. 1 and Christmas. Last admission to hiking trails 1 hour before closing. Phone (505) 783-4226.

ESPAÑOLA (A-4) pop. 10,224, elev. 5,589'

In the northern Rio Grande Valley between the Jémez Mountains and Truchas Peaks, Española was founded in 1598 by the Spaniards as the first capital of New Mexico.

The town assumed its present role as a trading and distribution center when the Denver and Rio Grande Western Railroad built its Chili Line between Española and Antonito, Colo., in the late 1870s. In late summer garlands of *ristras*—strings of scarlet chile peppers drying in the sun—decorate houses and fences.

Española is the central point for visiting the eight northern pueblos and Hispanic villages selling arts and crafts, including Nambé, Picurís, Pojoaque, San Ildefonso, Ohkay Owingeh, Santa Clara, Taos and Tesuque *(see place listings)*.

Española Valley Chamber of Commerce: 1 Calle de las Españolas, Suites F and G, P.O. Box 190, Española, NM 87532-0190. **Phone:** (505) 753-2831.

INN AT THE DELTA   505/753-9466
▼▼▼ **Bed & Breakfast.** Rates not provided. **Address:** 243 Paseo de Onate 87532 **Location:** US 84 and 285, 1 mi n of jct SR 68; 0.3 mi n of jct SR 30. **Facility:** Hand-carved wooden furniture, original artwork and a kiva fireplace fill each spacious room of this tranquil inn. 10 units. 1-2 stories (no elevator), exterior corridors. **Activities:** massage.

[icons]

SANTA CLARAN HOTEL CASINO   505/367-4900
▼▼▼ **Hotel.** Rates not provided. **Address:** 464 N Riverside Dr 87532 **Location:** SR 68; center. **Facility:** This hotel is adjacent to Big Rock Casino. Guests will enjoy spacious and well-appointed rooms and an excellent, new indoor swimming pool. 124 units. 7 stories, interior corridors. **Terms:** check-in 4 pm. **Dining:** 2 restaurants. **Pool(s):** indoor. **Activities:** hot tub, regulation golf, exercise room. **Guest Services:** coin laundry.

[icons]

WHERE TO EAT

ANGELINA'S RESTAURANT   505/753-8543
▼▼ Mexican. Casual Dining. $6-$18 **AAA Inspector Notes:** Locals flock to this restaurant for traditional New Mexican food. Popular dishes include the chile rellenos, fajitas, enchiladas, and burritos. Local farmers raise lamb especially for Angelina's and many of this restaurant's most famous dishes include this specialty item. **Features:** beer & wine. **Address:** 1226 N Railroad Ave 87532 **Location:** Jct SR 30 and US 84/285, 1.4 mi n, then 4 mi e on Fairview Dr.

[B] [L] [D]

EL PARAGUA   505/753-3211
▼▼▼ Mexican. Casual Dining. $8-$28 **AAA Inspector Notes:** Since 1966, locals have come to this restaurant to experience true northern New Mexican culture and cuisine. Guests will find generous portions of authentic northern New Mexican dishes, mesquite wood-grilled steaks and fish in addition to traditional, homemade desserts. **Features:** full bar. **Reservations:** suggested. **Address:** 603 Santa Cruz Rd 87532 **Location:** SR 76, just e of SR 68. [L] [D]

LA COCINA RESTAURANT & CANTINA   505-753-3016
▼▼▼ Mexican. Casual Dining. $7-$14 **AAA Inspector Notes:** Enjoy generous portions of flavorful northern New Mexican cuisine at this lively eatery. A longtime local favorite, the eatery starts each meal with complimentary fresh tortilla chips with salsa then ends the meal with a puffy sopaipilla with honey. **Features:** beer & wine, patio dining, senior menu. **Address:** 415 Santa Clara Bridge Rd 87532 **Location:** Just e of jct SR 30 and US 84.

[B] [L] [D] [icon]

FARMINGTON (E-2) pop. 45,877, elev. 5,292'
• Hotels p. 380 • Restaurants p. 380

Apple orchards replaced saloons and coal miners ousted card sharks as Farmington evolved into the major commerce and industrial center of the Four Corners region in northwestern New Mexico.

Navajo Mine, west of town, is one of the largest coal mining operations in the world. Its output fuels the adjacent Four Corners Power Plant, which in turn heats the waters used by windsurfers on nearby Morgan Lake. Anglers favor the San Juan River and Farmington and Jackson lakes.

West of town the vast Navajo Indian Reservation extends into Arizona. The convention and visitors bureau distributes a list of trading posts.

Forty miles south via SR 371 is the Bisti/De-Na-Zin Wilderness, an area of weirdly eroded hoodoos and slate-topped *mesitas*—geological formations made up of sandstone and shale that have become eroded by wind and rain. Angel Peak Scenic Area lies 30 miles southeast via SR 550. Once considered by the Navajos as the dwelling place of sacred ones, the colorful sandstone formations crowning the peak were shaped over millions of years.

Changing exhibits by area artists are displayed at San Juan College Fine Arts Center. Outdoor theatrical performances are offered mid-June to mid-August in the Lions Wilderness Park, a natural sandstone amphitheater.

Farmington Convention and Visitors Bureau: 3041 E. Main St., Farmington, NM 87402. **Phone:** (505) 326-7602 or (800) 448-1240.

FARMINGTON MUSEUM is at 3041 E. Main St. Permanent exhibits depict local history, including the region's oil and gas industry, through such items as clothing, photographs, tools and equipment. The facility hosts year-round lectures, educational programs and art shows highlighting regional heritage and culture. An atrium affords excellent views of the Animas River. **Time:** Allow 30 minutes minimum. **Hours:** Mon.-Fri. 8-5, Sat. 8-8. Closed Jan. 1, Thanksgiving and Christmas. **Cost:** Free. **Phone:** (505) 599-1174.

Children's Museum & Science Center, part of the Farmington Museum complex, is just n. of jct. Main and Orchard sts. Permanent and changing science exhibits encourage interactive learning for kids. Children under 5 years of age can practice early motor skills at Tot's Turf. **Time:** Allow 30 minutes minimum. **Hours:** Tues.-Sat. 10-5 and by appointment. **Cost:** Free. **Phone:** (505) 599-1425.

FARMINGTON PUBLIC LIBRARY is at 2101 Farmington Ave. In addition to its state-of-the-art technological facilities, the building is notable for architectural elements that represent the Four Corners region's Native American cultures. Distinctive features include a counterclockwise layout and a spacious central rotunda designed in part to resemble a kiva, the underground chamber used by Puebloan Indians for spiritual ceremonies. Earth-tone colors reflect the natural environment, and glass wall panels let in lots of natural light. **Hours:** Mon.-Sat. 9-5 (also Mon.-Thurs. 5-7), Sun. 1-5. **Cost:** Free. **Phone:** (505) 599-1270.

BEST WESTERN PLUS THE FOUR CORNERS INN
(505)564-8100

Hotel
$99-$149

 AAA Benefit: Save 10% or more every day and earn 10% bonus points!

Address: 4751 Cortez Way 87402 **Location:** On US 550 at Cortez Way. **Facility:** 65 units. 3 stories, interior corridors. **Pool(s):** heated indoor. **Activities:** hot tub, exercise room. **Guest Services:** valet and coin laundry.

COMFORT INN
(505)325-2626

Hotel
$83-$104

Address: 555 Scott Ave 87401 **Location:** 1 mi e on SR 516 (Main St), just s. **Facility:** 59 units. 2 stories (no elevator), interior corridors. **Pool(s):** heated outdoor. **Guest Services:** valet laundry. **Featured Amenity: full hot breakfast.**

COMFORT SUITES
(505)325-9414

Hotel $115-$160 **Address:** 1951 Cortland Dr 87401 **Location:** 1.6 mi e on US 64 (Bloomfield Blvd), just past jct Broadway; on Frontage Rd. **Facility:** 73 units. 3 stories, interior corridors. **Pool(s):** heated indoor. **Activities:** picnic facilities, exercise room. **Guest Services:** complimentary and valet laundry.

COURTYARD BY MARRIOTT
(505)325-5111

Hotel $72-$153 **Address:** 560 Scott Ave 87401 **Location:** 1 mi e on SR 516 (Main St), just s. **Facility:** 125 units. 4 stories, interior corridors. **Pool(s):** heated indoor. **Activities:** hot tub, exercise room. **Guest Services:** valet and coin laundry, boarding pass kiosk.

AAA Benefit: Members save 5% or more!

HAMPTON INN & SUITES
(505)564-3100

Hotel $94-$149 **Address:** 1500 Bloomfield Blvd 87401 **Location:** 0.3 mi e of jct E Broadway and Scott Ave. **Facility:** 73 units. 4 stories, interior corridors. **Terms:** 1-7 night minimum stay, cancellation fee imposed. **Pool(s):** heated indoor. **Activities:** hot tub, exercise room. **Guest Services:** coin laundry.

AAA Benefit: Members save up to 10%!

HOLIDAY INN EXPRESS
505/325-2545

Hotel. Rates not provided. **Address:** 2110 Bloomfield Blvd 87401 **Location:** 1.6 mi e on US 64 (Bloomfield Blvd), just past jct Broadway; on Frontage Rd. **Facility:** 101 units. 3 stories, interior corridors. **Pool(s):** heated indoor. **Activities:** hot tub, picnic facilities, exercise room. **Guest Services:** valet and coin laundry.

TOWNEPLACE SUITES BY MARRIOTT
(505)327-2442

Extended Stay Hotel $85-$173 **Address:** 4200 Sierra Vista Dr 87402 **Location:** 5 mi e on SR 516 (E Main St), just s. **Facility:** 117 units, some two bedrooms, efficiencies and kitchens. 5 stories, interior corridors. **Pool(s):** heated indoor. **Activities:** hot tub, picnic facilities, exercise room. **Guest Services:** valet and coin laundry.

AAA Benefit: Members save 5% or more!

WHERE TO EAT

BLUE MOON DINER
505/324-0001

American. Family Dining. $9-$16 **AAA Inspector Notes:** This 1950s theme diner is a true blast from the past. Enjoy all the favorites from burgers, fries and a shake to chicken-fried steak. For dessert, enjoy any one of the twenty flavors of homemade ice cream or a slice of pie. **Address:** 1819 E 20th St 87401 **Location:** Jct Sullivan St, just e; adjacent to movie theater. [B] [L] [D]

KB DILLON'S BAR & GRILLE
505/325-0222

American. Casual Dining. $7-$33 **AAA Inspector Notes:** Appealing to those seeking a hearty meal, this restaurant has rustic surroundings on the outside and a warm, boisterous atmosphere inside. The menu lists steak, poultry, fish and veal choices, as well as several seafood selections. **Features:** full bar. **Address:** 101 W Broadway 87401 **Location:** On US 64 (Bloomfield Blvd); downtown. [L] [D]

LOS HERMANITOS RESTAURANT
505/326-5664

Mexican. Casual Dining. $7-$20 **AAA Inspector Notes:** This family-owned restaurant serves traditional Mexican favorites in a relaxed atmosphere. Hearty portions and quick service have guests fed and on their way in no time. **Address:** 3501 E Main St 87401 **Location:** 3 mi nw of historic town center. [B] [L] [D]

LOS RIOS CAFE
505/325-5699

Mexican. Casual Dining. $8-$11 **AAA Inspector Notes:** This family-owned eatery offers flavorful New Mexican cuisine in a casual setting. Try the hand-breaded rellenos and chicken enchiladas smothered in slightly spicy green chile. **Features:** beer & wine. **Address:** 915 Farmington Ave 87401 **Location:** Jct Main St, just n. [L] [D]

PIZZA 9
505/325-6463

Pizza Sandwiches. Casual Dining. $6-$12 **AAA Inspector Notes:** This eatery offers deep-dish and thin-crust pizzas. If you like a little heat, try the Fire Eater, which comes with pepperoni, jalapeños, green chiles and hot giardiniera. You can build your own pizza or calzone. Desserts include creamy tiramisu, cheesecake and brownies. **Address:** 685 Scott Ave 87401 **Location:** 1 mi e on SR 516 (Main St), just s. [L] [D]

ST. CLAIR WINERY & BISTRO   505/325-0711

WW WW American. Casual Dining. $8-$19 **AAA Inspector Notes:**
The menu at this bistro features French-country dishes paired with
award-winning New Mexico wines served in a charming dining room
and seasonal outdoor patio. Enjoy live jazz music Thursday through
Sunday nights. **Features:** beer & wine, patio dining. **Address:** 5150
E Main St, Suite 101 87402 **Location:** 5.5 mi e on SR 516 (E Main
St). [L] [D]

SI SEÑOR RESTAURANT   505/324-9050

WW WW Southwestern. Casual Dining. $11-$24 **AAA Inspector
Notes:** You can expect homemade tortillas, posole and chile sauces.
The menu includes tamales, rellenos, enchiladas and other New
Mexican favorites as well as steaks. You might become addicted to
the creamy jalapeño dip served with the chips and salsa. **Features:**
full bar, Sunday brunch. **Address:** 4015 E 30th St 87402 **Location:**
3.8 mi e; jct SR 516 (E Main St) and E 30th St. [L] [D]

THREE RIVERS EATERY AND BREW HOUSE   505/324-2187

WW WW American. Casual Dining. $8-$30 **AAA Inspector Notes:**
This popular and lively local eatery features an extensive list of
award-winning, handcrafted beers and a menu that includes sandwiches, steaks, burgers, ribs, pork and fish. Located in the renovated
Andrews Building in the historic downtown, the building features antiques salvaged during construction as part of the décor, plus the
state's largest collection of beer labels and beer coasters. **Features:**
beer & wine. **Address:** 101 E Main St 87401 **Location:** Jct Orchard
St; downtown. **Parking:** street only. [L] [D]

FORT SUMNER (G-5) pop. 1,031, elev. 4,049'

The agricultural potential of the Pecos River bottomlands surrounding this quiet farming and
ranching center so impressed Maj. James Carleton
that in 1852 he recommended the site for an Army
post. A decade later, as brigadier general, he realized his dream. He established Fort Sumner and
made it the core of a permanent reservation for the
Navajos and Apaches, whose resettlement was
being supervised by Col. Kit Carson.

In 1864 Carson forced more than 8,000 Navajos
to make the 300-mile Long Walk from Fort Defiance,
Ariz., to the 1,024,000-acre reservation at Fort
Sumner. The fort was abandoned in 1868, and the
Navajos returned to their tribal lands.

After he was sentenced to death in Lincoln (see
place listing p. 394), the notorious Billy the Kid fa-
tally shot his guards and fled the town's courthouse
on April 28, 1881. Nearly 3 months after the escape,
a pistol-packing sheriff named Pat Garrett tracked
down and killed the outlaw in Fort Sumner. Billy the
Kid's grave, flanked by those of cronies Tom
O'Folliard and Charlie Bowdre, sticks out like a sore
thumb in Old Fort Sumner Cemetery, 3.5 miles
south off Billy the Kid Road; all three tombs are surrounded by a big steel cage built after the Kid's foot-
stone was stolen and recovered twice.

Fort Sumner Chamber of Commerce: 707 N.
Fourth St., P.O. Box 28, Fort Sumner, NM 88119.
Phone: (575) 355-7705.

FORT SUMNER STATE MONUMENT is 3 mi. e. on
US 60, then 3 mi. s. on Billy the Kid Rd. The site
marks the former Bosque Redondo Indian Reserva-
tion, where some 9,000 Navajo and Mescalero
Apache Indians were interned in the 1860s after the
U.S. government removed them from tribal lands.
Troops led by Kit Carson marched the Navajo more

than 400 miles to the prison camp, a grueling ordeal
that came to be known as the "Long Walk." Exhibits
and artifacts at the Bosque Redondo Memorial re-
count 5 years of starvation, disease and forced labor
before the Navajo were allowed to return to their
homes.

Hours: Wed.-Sun. 8:30-4:30. Closed Jan. 1,
Easter, Thanksgiving and Christmas. **Cost:** $3; free
(ages 0-16). **Phone:** (575) 355-2573.

FORT UNION NATIONAL MONUMENT (E-4)

Eight miles northwest of Watrous on SR 161 (off
I-25 exit 366), ranks of chimneys are stark reminders of the days when Fort Union was one of the
largest military posts on the Southwestern frontier.
From 1851 until 1891 Fort Union was the chief quartermaster depot for all garrisons throughout the region as well as the primary station for troops
assigned to protect settlers and Santa Fe Trail
travelers.

The site was well chosen, for the two branches of
the Santa Fe Trail—the Mountain Branch and the
Cimarron—pass through the Fort Union Valley. In
addition, the remote location put the soldiers closer
to the tribes and farther from towns that might dis-
tract them from their duties.

A group of log buildings west of Wolf Creek con-
stituted the first Fort Union. For a decade it served
as a way station on the Santa Fe Trail and as a
headquarters for battling the Utes, Jicarilla Apaches,
Comanches and Kiowas.

The outbreak of the Civil War abruptly turned the
Army's attention away from these conflicts. The
second Fort Union, an earthwork defense bastion,
was built east of the creek in late 1861. It was constructed by local volunteers just before Confederate
forces from Texas, eager to control Colorado's mineral resources and Fort Union's supplies, swept up
the Rio Grande Valley. After their supply train was
destroyed in the Battle of Glorieta, the Confederate
troops retreated and headed for home.

The third fort dates from the mid-1860s; its garrison, quartermaster depot and arsenal still stand
today. For the next 15 years the Indian wars occupied the military, while tons of goods flowed through
the depot. Gradually local tribes were subdued. The
Santa Fe Railway reached New Mexico in 1879,
making travel safer. Fort Union was abandoned in
1891.

Interpretive signs relay the history of the fort and
the local area. A self-guiding 1.6-mile interpretive
trail explores 100 acres of adobe ruins. A half-mile
trail also is an option. A visitor center containing a
museum relates fort history. Living-history demonstrations and other events are offered during
summer. Daily 8-6, Memorial Day-Labor Day; 8-4,
rest of year. Closed Jan. 1, Thanksgiving and
Christmas. Admission $3, free (ages 0-15). Phone
(505) 425-8025.

GALLUP (F-1) pop. 21,678, elev. 6,508'
• Restaurants p. 385

The Atchison, Topeka & Santa Fe Railway pushed into this red rock mesa region in 1881 to use area coal deposits for its engines. Until then mostly stockmen had lived in the area; Gallup was a stage stop with nothing more than a saloon/general store called the Blue Goose. Coal mining and the presence of the railroad attracted settlers from other nations, giving the city an unusually cosmopolitan heritage.

The city is best known as the principal Navajo trading center—their vast reservation extends north and west into Arizona—as well as for the residents of nearby Zuni Pueblo *(see place listing p. 453)*. Gallup has more than 100 trading posts, shops and galleries; at many trading posts handmade articles ranging from rugs and baskets to turquoise jewelry are sold.

Gallup Chamber of Commerce and Convention and Visitors Bureau: 106 W. Hwy. 66, Gallup, NM 87301. **Phone:** (505) 722-2228.

GALLUP CULTURAL CENTER is at 201 US 66E. Southwest American Indian history is presented within the setting of a restored Santa Fe Railroad depot. Audio-narrated exhibits include vintage photographs, sand paintings, ancient pottery and a 10-foot bronze statue honoring World War II Navajo code talkers. The Kiva Cinema presents films about Native American culture. **Time:** Allow 30 minutes minimum. **Hours:** Mon.-Sat. 8-4. **Cost:** Free. **Phone:** (505) 863-4131. GT ⊞ ⊞

▼ See AAA listing this page ▼

COMFORT SUITES (505)863-3445

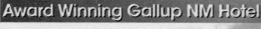

Hotel
$99-$134

Address: 3940 E Hwy 66 87301 Location: I-40 exit 26, just e. Facility: 66 units. 3 stories, interior corridors. Pool(s): heated indoor. Activities: hot tub, exercise room. Guest Services: valet and coin laundry. Featured Amenity: full hot breakfast. (See ad this page.)

HOLIDAY INN EXPRESS & SUITES (505)722-7500

Hotel $120-$190 Address: 3850 E Hwy 66 87301 Location: I-40 exit 26, just e. Facility: 91 units. 4 stories, interior corridors. Terms: cancellation fee imposed. Amenities: Some: safes. Pool(s): heated indoor. Activities: hot tub, exercise room. Guest Services: coin laundry. (See ad this page.)

LA QUINTA INN & SUITES GALLUP (505)722-2233

Hotel $92-$210 Address: 3880 E Hwy 66 87301 Location: I-40 exit 26, just e. Facility: 67 units. 3 stories, interior corridors. Pool(s): heated indoor. Activities: hot tub, steamroom, exercise room. Guest Services: coin laundry.

▼ See AAA listing this page ▼

▼ See AAA listing this page ▼

MICROTEL INN BY WYNDHAM GALLUP   (505)722-2600

Hotel
$65-$85

Address: 3270 W Hwy 66 87301 **Location:** I-40 exit 16, just e. **Facility:** 53 units. 2 stories (no elevator), interior corridors. **Terms:** age restrictions may apply, 3 day cancellation notice. **Featured Amenity: continental breakfast.**

QUALITY INN & SUITES   (505)726-1000

Motel
$99-$169

Address: 1500 W Maloney Ave 87301 **Location:** I-40 exit 20, just n on Muñoz Dr, then just w. **Facility:** 69 units. 2 stories (no elevator), interior/exterior corridors. **Pool(s):** heated indoor. **Activities:** sauna, hot tub. **Guest Services:** valet and coin laundry. **Featured Amenity: full hot breakfast.**

RED ROOF INN - GALLUP   (505)722-7765

Motel
$40-$110

Address: 3304 W Hwy 66 87301 **Location:** I-40 exit 16, just se. Adjacent to RV/truck parking. **Facility:** 103 units. 2 stories (no elevator), exterior corridors. **Pool(s):** heated outdoor. **Activities:** sauna, exercise room. **Guest Services:** coin laundry. **Featured Amenity: continental breakfast.** *(See ad this page.)*

HAMPTON INN & SUITES   505/726-0900

[fyi] Not evaluated; management refused inspection. **Address:** 1460 W Maloney Ave 87301 **Location:** I-40 exit 20, 1 mi w. Facilities, services, and décor characterize a mid-scale property.

AAA Benefit:
Members save up to 10%!

▼ *See AAA listing this page* ▼

Red Roof Inn Gallup

- Free Continental Breakfast
- Refrigerator, Microwave and Coffee in all rooms
- Outdoor Pool (Seasonal)
- Fitness Center
- Pets Welcome
- Truck Parking in Rear

10% Discount For AAA members

AAA Approved

3304 W Hwy 66 • Gallup, NM 87301
505.722.7765 • redroofinngallup.com • 888.681.6035

ENJOY THE FREEDOM

Extend your safe driving years.

SENIORDRIVING.AAA.COM   SENIORSDRIVING.CAA.CA

WHERE TO EAT

ANGELA'S CAFE CON LECHE   505/722-7526

◆◆ American. Casual Dining. $6-$14 **AAA Inspector Notes:** Nestled in the historic train depot, this comfy café is a local favorite serving excellent homemade soups, salads and sandwiches. **Features:** beer & wine. **Address:** 201 E Hwy 66 87301 **Location:** I-40 exit 22, just s to US 66, then just w; in historic train depot.

B L

BADLANDS GRILL   505/722-5157

◆◆◆ Steak. Casual Dining. $10-$38 **AAA Inspector Notes:** This Western theme dining room features a wide variety of steaks that have been wet-aged for 21 days. Wild game, seafood and pasta plus tempting desserts round out the menu. **Features:** beer & wine. **Reservations:** suggested. **Address:** 2201 W Hwy 66 87301 **Location:** I-40 exit 16, 2.7 mi e. D

EARL'S FAMILY RESTAURANT   505/863-4201

◆◆

American
Family Dining
$8-$17

AAA Inspector Notes: *Classic.* Since 1947, this landmark family restaurant has served a wide variety of American and Mexican dishes. The favorite steak and enchiladas is a blend of the two cuisines. A long held tradition allows Native American artists to sell jewelry and crafts directly to dining patrons inside and at tables outside the eatery. **Address:** 1400 E Hwy 66 87301 **Location:** I-40 exit 22, just s to US 66, then e. B L D

EL SOMBRERO   505/863-4554

◆◆ Mexican. Casual Dining. $7-$15 **AAA Inspector Notes:** Along famous Route 66, this restaurant has a Southwestern feel with informal service and easy-going hospitality. Although American dishes are available, Mexican foods reign supreme. **Features:** beer & wine. **Address:** 1201 W US 66 87301 **Location:** I-40 exit 20, just w. B L D

KING DRAGON   505/863-6300

◆◆ Chinese. Casual Dining. $6-$15 **AAA Inspector Notes:** Specializing in Mandarin, Szechuan and Hunan dishes, this restaurant also lays out a popular buffet at lunch. In addition to beef, pork and chicken entrees, the menu lists a good choice of soups. Portions are generous. **Features:** full bar. **Address:** 1212 N Hwy 491 87301 **Location:** I-40 exit 20, 1.5 mi n. L D

SAMMY C'S ROCK'N SPORTS PUB, GRILLE & COFFEE BAR   505/863-2220

◆◆

American
Casual Dining
$9-$20

AAA Inspector Notes: This family-friendly restaurant features Wi-Fi, a coffee bar and many sporting events broadcasted on flat-screen TVs. The varied menu, including a separate and fun child's menu, offers four daily soup choices, Cobb and chef salads, juicy burgers, a variety of pasta dishes, grilled trout and tempting desserts. **Features:** full bar. **Address:** 107 W Coal Ave 87301 **Location:** I-40 exit 20, between 1st and 2nd sts; downtown. L D

 GILA CLIFF DWELLINGS NATIONAL MONUMENT (H-2)

Gila Cliff Dwellings National Monument is a minimum 2-hour drive 44 miles north of Silver City via SR 15; vehicles pulling trailers 20 feet or longer should use SR 35 north from San Lorenzo. In this rough and desolate country near the west fork of the Gila (HEE-la) River, seven natural cavities indent the face of a cliff some 175 feet above the canyon floor. Five of these hollows contain rooms constructed during the late 13th century by people of the Mogollon culture—these remain the focus of the monument.

A 1-mile hiking trail loops from the contact station to the dwellings. The Gila Visitor Center is 2 miles south of the monument entrance. Guided 1-hour tours of the cliff dwellings depart daily at 1 from the dwellings themselves (allow 30 minutes to walk from the trailhead). Pets are not permitted on the monument trails; free kennels are available.

Park open daily 8:30-5, Memorial Day weekend-Labor Day; 9-4, rest of year. Visitor center open daily 8-5, Memorial Day weekend-Labor Day; 8-4:30, rest of year. Admission $3; free (ages 0-15 and Federal Recreational Lands Pass holders); $10 (family). Exact change is required and may be obtained at the visitor center. Self-guiding trail pamphlets and travel guide brochures are available at no cost. Phone (575) 536-9461.

GILA NATIONAL FOREST (H-1)

Elevations in the forest range from 4,000 ft. in the desert to 11,000 ft. at Whitewater Baldy. Refer to AAA maps for additional elevation information.

In southwestern New Mexico, Gila (HEE-la) National Forest occupies 3,321,000 acres of forest and rangeland. The smaller of its two units extends north from Lordsburg along the Big Burro Mountains. The main unit, north of Silver City *(see place listing p. 439)*, embraces the Black, Mogollon, Tularosa and Diablo mountains. These wild ranges and remote canyons were the stronghold of such Apache warriors as Geronimo and Mangas Coloradas.

Much of the Mogollon Mountains lies within the Gila Wilderness, the first area in the nation to be so designated. Instrumental in its 1924 establishment was Aldo Leopold, the forester and naturalist whose "Sand County Almanac" and other writings have become classics of environmental literature.

A plaque 9 miles south of Glenwood on US 180 at the Aldo Leopold Overlook marks the Leopold Vista Historical Monument. The Gila, Blue Range and Aldo Leopold wilderness areas as well as Gila Cliff Dwellings National Monument are north of Silver City.

In the 1870s the region was the center of a mining boom, of which ghost towns and old mine structures are silent reminders. The half-mile-long Catwalk National Recreation Trail passes through the steep walls of Whitewater Canyon. A metal suspension bridge carries hikers across a creek that once provided water to a nearby mill. Now a popular recreation area, it is reached via SR 174 from US 180. A $3 fee per private vehicle is charged to access the Catwalk National Recreation Area.

Note: The Catwalk National Recreation Area is currently closed due to flooding and is expected to reopen in the spring or summer of 2016. For the latest updates, contact the Glenwood Ranger District office; phone (575) 539-2481.

The 110-mile Trail of the Mountain Spirits Scenic Byway travels from Silver City east to San Lorenzo, through the Mimbres Valley, down Sapillo Creek, past Clinton P. Anderson Vista to Gila Cliff Dwellings

National Monument, and returns to Silver City over the Pinos Altos Range. Overlooks along the byway provide perspective on the magnitude of the cliffs and the surrounding countryside.

There are numerous developed recreation areas in the forest. Stream and lake fishing and big game hunting are available in season. *See Recreation Areas Chart.*

GILA VISITOR CENTER is 3.5 mi. n. of Gila Hot Springs via SR 15; vehicles pulling trailers 20 feet or longer should use SR 35 north from San Lorenzo. It contains displays of cultural artifacts and exhibits about the Apache and Mogollon people and the Gila Wilderness. A 15-minute video is shown. You can also pick up information about all Gila National Forest recreational activities. **Hours:** Daily 8-4:30. Phone ahead during winter months for road condition updates. **Cost:** $5; free (ages 0-15). **Phone:** (575) 536-9461.

GRANTS (F-2) pop. 9,182, elev. 6,450′

Operated by the Cibola County Historical Society, the Western New Mexico Aviation Heritage Museum honors the pioneer aviators who flew the then-remote Amarillo to Los Angeles stretch of the Mid-continental Airway, established by Charles Lindbergh for Transcontinental Air Transport. The route was equipped with generator-powered beacon towers spaced approximately every 10 to 15 miles to aid pilots flying mail delivery planes at night. A 30-minute guided walking tour of the restored airway beacon at the Grants-Milan Airport is offered Sat. 9-1; from I-40, take exits 79 or 81 to Airport Road.

Grants/Cibola County Chamber of Commerce: 100 N. Iron Ave., Grants, NM 87020. **Phone:** (505) 287-4802 or (800) 748-2142.

EL MALPAIS NATIONAL MONUMENT is 23 mi. s.w. of I-40 via SRs 53 and 117. The monument preserves 376,000 acres of *mal país*, or badlands, a landscape of lava flows, volcanoes and lava tube caves. Primitive camping, hiking, caving (equipment needed) and mountain biking are permitted. Information is available at the National Park Information Center, 23 mi. south of Grants on SR 53; the Northwest New Mexico Visitor Center, off I-40 exit 85 at 1900 E. Santa Fe Ave. in Grants; and the Bureau of Land Management Ranger Station, 9 mi. s. of I-40 on SR 117. *See Recreation Areas Chart.*

Note: Use heavy footgear and extreme care when hiking on the sharp lava. **Hours:** Daily 24 hours. Visitor center daily 8-5. Closed Jan. 1, Thanksgiving and Christmas. **Cost:** Free. **Phone:** (505) 783-4774 for the El Malpais Information Center, (505) 280-2918 for the Bureau of Land Management Ranger Station, or (505) 876-2783 for the Northwest New Mexico Visitor Center.

ICE CAVE AND BANDERA VOLCANO is 25 mi. s.w. of Grants on SR 53, w. of El Malpais National Monument. A partially collapsed lava tube formed the cave, which contains perpetual formations of ice. At an elevation of 8,000 feet, the temperature never rises above 31 F. The dormant Bandera Volcano, which erupted 10,000 years ago with massive lava flows, rises above the mountain valley. Self-guiding tours depart from the trading post located a half mile south of SR 53.

Comfortable shoes are recommended. Gem stone mining also is available. **Time:** Allow 1 hour minimum. **Hours:** Daily 9-5 (weather permitting). Closed Thanksgiving and Christmas. **Cost:** $12; $11 (ages 65+); $6 (ages 5-12). **Phone:** (505) 783-4303 or (888) 423-2283. 🎫

NEW MEXICO MINING MUSEUM is 2 mi. w. off I-40 exit 85 at 100 N. Iron Ave. Exhibits chronicle the discovery of uranium on Haystack Mountain in 1950 by a local Navajo rancher, the subsequent transformation of Grants from farming community to mining town and the end of an era due to an early 1980s recession that forced the closure of mills and mines. Beneath the museum and reached by elevator is a replica of a mine complete with equipment. **Time:** Allow 30 minutes minimum. **Hours:** Mon.-Sat. 9-4. Closed major holidays. **Cost:** $3; $2 (ages 7-18 and 60+). **Phone:** (505) 287-4802 or (800) 748-2142.

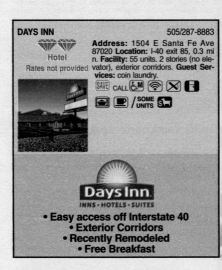

HOLIDAY INN EXPRESS   (505)287-9252

▽▽▽▽
Hotel
$115-$139

Address: 1512 E Santa Fe Ave 87020 **Location:** I-40 exit 85, just n. **Facility:** 76 units. 3 stories, interior corridors. **Pool(s):** heated indoor. **Activities:** hot tub, limited exercise equipment. **Guest Services:** valet and coin laundry. **Featured Amenity: full hot breakfast.**

SAVE 〖ᵀ↑〗 ≈ 〖BIZ〗 〖HS〗 🛜 ✕ 〖✕〗 🛄 🖼 💻

Contemporary hotel featuring triple sheets, 32" flat TV, WiFi, microfridge, free hot breakfast, & pool

QUALITY INN & SUITES   (505)285-4676

▽▽▽▽
Hotel
$80-$90

Address: 1496 E Santa Fe Ave 87020 **Location:** I-40 exit 85, 0.3 mi n. **Facility:** 58 units. 2 stories (no elevator), interior corridors. **Pool(s):** heated indoor. **Activities:** hot tub, limited exercise equipment. **Guest Services:** valet and coin laundry. **Featured Amenity: full hot breakfast.**

SAVE 〖ᵀ↑〗 ≈ 〖BIZ〗 🛜 ✕ 🛄 🖼 💻 / SOME UNITS 🛏

Free Hot Breakfast, Wi-Fi, Microfridge, Indoor Pool, Fitness Ctr. Easy I-40 access. Pet Friendly w/fee.

RED LION HOTEL GRANTS   505/287-7901

▽▽▽▽ **Hotel.** Rates not provided. **Address:** 1501 E Santa Fe Ave 87020 **Location:** I-40 exit 85, just w. **Facility:** 126 units. 2 stories (no elevator), interior corridors. **Pool(s):** heated indoor. **Activities:** hot tub, exercise room. **Guest Services:** valet and coin laundry.

〖ᵀ↑〗 ≈ 🛜 💻 / SOME UNITS 🛏 🛄 🖼

WHERE TO EAT

CANTON CAFE   505/287-8314

▽ Chinese. Family Dining. $6-$13 **AAA Inspector Notes:** Locals keep this eatery busy for lunch and dinner. The buffet lines up a good selection of traditional items along the lines of sweet and sour pork, Szechuan shrimp and kung pao chicken, in addition to salads and desserts. **Address:** 1212 E Santa Fe Ave 87020 **Location:** I-40 exit 85, 0.8 mi w on Business Loop 40 (Santa Fe Ave). 〖L〗 〖D〗

Enjoy peace of mind

with AAA/CAA

Insurance products

EL CAFECITO   505/285-6229

▽ New Mexican. Casual Dining. $5-$20 **AAA Inspector Notes:** Convenient to Interstate 40, this friendly and colorful cafe offers drive-through service and is open for breakfast and lunch. Examples of New Mexican cuisine include stuffed sopaipillas, chimichangas and a signature fritta frutta topped with ice cream. **Address:** 820 E Santa Fe Ave 87020 **Location:** I-40 exit 85, 1.5 mi w on Business Loop 40 (Santa Fe Ave). 〖B〗 〖L〗 〖D〗

LA VENTANA RESTAURANT   505/287-9393

▽▽ American. Casual Dining. $9-$42 **AAA Inspector Notes:** The city's business community flocks to the relaxed restaurant's comfortable Southwestern setting. A full-service bar complements tempting selections of great steak, salad and tasty desserts. Good choices include the succulent prime rib, fresh seafood and well-seasoned Mexican favorites. **Features:** full bar, patio dining, Sunday brunch. **Reservations:** suggested. **Address:** 110 1/2 Geis St 87020 **Location:** Just n of Santa Fe Ave; just e of First St, jct High St; center. 〖L〗 〖D〗

HOBBS (I-6) pop. 34,122, elev. 3,621'
• Hotels p. 388 • Restaurants p. 388

Oil and water mix in the economy of Hobbs, a modern city on the western edge of the flat Llano Estacado. Grasslands first attracted farmers and cattlemen to this region in the early 20th century; one of them, James Hobbs, gave his name to the community. A vast underground reserve of water provided irrigation for bountiful crops of cotton, alfalfa, vegetables and grain.

In 1928, however, the discovery of another kind of well changed pastoral Hobbs into a boomtown. Within a decade the city was the home of some 10,000 citizens, most associated with tapping the oil field that still produces 90 percent of the state's petroleum. Many oil companies operating in the area have headquarters in Hobbs.

History buffs will want to check out the Thelma A. Webber Southwest Heritage Room in the Scarborough Memorial Library at the University of the Southwest, 6610 Lovington Hwy. It has a small exhibit of prehistoric Native American artifacts, art pieces and pioneer collectibles; phone (800) 530-4400.

Hobbs Chamber of Commerce: 400 N. Marland Blvd., Hobbs, NM 88240. **Phone:** (575) 397-3202.

CENTER FOR THE ARTS is at 122 W. Broadway St. Displays feature changing art exhibits of local artisans. Highlights include photography, multimedia prints and Southwestern art. The center offers visual and literary programs for all ages. **Hours:** Tues.-Fri. 11-7, Sat. 10-4. **Cost:** Donations. **Phone:** (575) 397-2787.

WESTERN HERITAGE MUSEUM AND LEA COUNTY COWBOY HALL OF FAME is about 4 mi. n. to 5317 Lovington Hwy./SR 18, on the New Mexico Junior College campus. Well-known Lea County ranchers and rodeo performers are honored. Exhibits depict the cultures—Native American to pioneer—that shaped the area over some 150 years. **Time:** Allow 30 minutes minimum. **Hours:** Tues.-Sat. 10-5, Sun. 1-5. Closed major holidays. **Cost:** $3; $2 (ages 6-18 and 65+). **Phone:** (575) 392-6730.

BEST WESTERN EXECUTIVE INN (575)397-7171

Hotel
$85-$125

AAA Benefit:
Save 10% or more every day and earn 10% bonus points!

Address: 309 N Marland Blvd 88240 **Location:** US 62, 180 and Snyder St. **Facility:** 62 units. 2 stories (no elevator), exterior corridors. **Terms:** cancellation fee imposed. **Amenities:** safes. **Pool(s):** outdoor.

SAVE 🛎️ 🏊 BIZ HS 🛜 🔒 🖥️ 💻 / SOME UNITS 🐾

COMFORT SUITES-HOBBS (575)492-1000

▼▼▼ Hotel $99-$219 **Address:** 2708 W Scenic Dr 88240 **Location:** Jct SR 18 N (Lovington Hwy) and W Millen Dr, 0.8 mi s. **Facility:** 75 units, some efficiencies. 4 stories, interior corridors. **Amenities:** safes. **Pool(s):** heated indoor. **Activities:** exercise room. **Guest Services:** valet and coin laundry.

🛎️ CALL 🆖M 🏊 BIZ HS 🛜 ✖️ 🔒 🖥️ 💻

COUNTRY INN & SUITES BY CARLSON HOBBS NEW MEXICO (575)391-0282

Hotel
$99-$199

Address: 5220 N Lovington Hwy 88240 **Location:** Jct SR 18 N (Lovington Hwy) and W Millen Dr, just n. **Facility:** 64 units. 3 stories, interior corridors. **Terms:** 7 day cancellation notice. **Pool(s):** heated indoor. **Activities:** hot tub, exercise room. **Guest Services:** coin laundry. **Featured Amenity:** full hot breakfast.

SAVE 🛎️ CALL 🆖M 🏊 BIZ HS 🛜 ✖️ 🔒 🖥️ 💻

FAIRFIELD INN & SUITES BY MARRIOTT (575)393-0667

▼▼▼ Hotel $101-$278 **Address:** 1350 W Joe Harvey Blvd 88242 **Location:** 0.4 mi n on Grimes St to Joe Harvey Blvd, just w. **Facility:** 94 units. 4 stories, interior corridors. **Pool(s):** heated outdoor. **Activities:** hot tub, exercise room. **Guest Services:** valet and coin laundry.

AAA Benefit:
Members save 5% or more!

🛎️ CALL 🆖M 🏊 BIZ HS 🛜 ✖️ 🔒 🖥️ 💻

HAMPTON INN & SUITES (575)492-6000

▼▼▼ Hotel $119-$229 **Address:** 5420 Lovington Hwy 88242 **Location:** Jct SR 18 N (Lovington Hwy) and W Millen Dr, just n. **Facility:** 67 units. 3 stories, interior corridors. **Terms:** 1-7 night minimum stay, cancellation fee imposed. **Pool(s):** heated indoor. **Activities:** exercise room. **Guest Services:** valet and coin laundry.

AAA Benefit:
Members save up to 10%!

CALL 🆖M 🏊 BIZ HS 🛜 ✖️ 🔒 🖥️ 💻

HOLIDAY INN EXPRESS & SUITES 575/391-8777

▼▼▼ Hotel. Rates not provided. **Address:** 4000 N Lovington Hwy 88240 **Location:** Jct SR 18 N (Lovington Hwy) and W Millen Dr, 1.1 mi s. **Facility:** 80 units. 3 stories, interior corridors. **Amenities:** safes. **Pool(s):** heated indoor. **Activities:** hot tub, exercise room. **Guest Services:** valet and coin laundry.

CALL 🆖M 🏊 BIZ HS 🛜 ✖️ 🔒 🖥️ 💻

LA QUINTA INN & SUITES HOBBS (575)397-8777

▼▼▼ Hotel $97-$229 **Address:** 3312 N Lovington Hwy 88240 **Location:** SR 18 N (Lovington Hwy), just s of jct Joe Harvey Blvd. **Facility:** 68 units. 3 stories, interior corridors. **Pool(s):** heated indoor. **Activities:** hot tub, exercise room. **Guest Services:** coin laundry.

🛎️ CALL 🆖M 🏊 BIZ HS 🛜 ✖️ 🔒 🖥️ 💻 / SOME UNITS 🐾

QUALITY INN & SUITES (575)392-8777

▼▼▼ Hotel $99-$179 **Address:** 3610 N Lovington Hwy 88240 **Location:** SR 18 N (Lovington Hwy), just s of jct Joe Harvey Blvd. **Facility:** 65 units. 3 stories, interior corridors. **Pool(s):** heated indoor. **Activities:** hot tub, exercise room. **Guest Services:** valet and coin laundry.

🛎️ CALL 🆖M 🏊 BIZ HS 🛜 🔒 🖥️ 💻

SLEEP INN & SUITES (575)393-3355

▼▼▼ Hotel $169-$229 **Address:** 4630 N Lovington Hwy 88240 **Location:** Jct SR 18 N (Lovington Hwy) and W Millen Dr, 0.8 mi s. **Facility:** 67 units. 3 stories, interior corridors. **Pool(s):** heated indoor. **Activities:** hot tub, exercise room. **Guest Services:** coin laundry.

CALL 🆖M 🏊 BIZ HS 🛜 ✖️ 🔒 🖥️ 💻 / SOME UNITS 🐾

WHERE TO EAT

CATTLE BARON STEAK & SEAFOOD 575/393-2800

▼▼▼ American. Casual Dining. $9-$27 **AAA Inspector Notes:** A scrumptious array of menu selections includes steak, seafood, chicken and prime rib as well as desserts such as caramel apple pie. An upscale Western decor includes wood trim and distinctive chandeliers made from deer antlers. **Features:** full bar. **Address:** 1930 N Grimes St 88240 **Location:** Jct Broadway and Grimes St, 1.3 mi n; downtown. L D CALL 🆖M

PACIFIC RIM 575/392-0030

▼▼▼ Pacific Rim. Casual Dining. $11-$45 **AAA Inspector Notes:** Enjoy a wide variety of seafood, beef and chicken entrées, plus custom-made stir-fry and pasta entrées. Vegetarian selections and sushi options are available, as are luscious house-made desserts. **Features:** beer & wine. **Reservations:** suggested. **Address:** 1309 Joe Harvey Blvd 88240 **Location:** SR 18 N (Lovington Hwy), just e of jct Joe Harvey Blvd. L D CALL 🆖M

TIA JUANA'S MEXICAN GRILLE & CANTINA 575/392-0500

▼▼▼ Mexican. Casual Dining. $8-$21 **AAA Inspector Notes:** Hearty portions of flavorful Mexican favorites are served in a colorful and lively atmosphere. The homemade flour tortillas are a must-try item. **Features:** full bar, patio dining. **Address:** 3510 N Lovington Hwy 88240 **Location:** SR 18 N (Lovington Hwy), just s of jct Joe Harvey Blvd. L D

ISLETA PUEBLO (G-3) elev. 4,887'

Thirteen miles south of Albuquerque in the Rio Grande Valley, Isleta Pueblo was established in the 14th century. Its name in Spanish means "little island."

SAN AGUSTÍN DE LA ISLETA MISSION is s. of Isleta Blvd., following signs. The heavily buttressed structure was erected in 1613 by Spanish missionary Fray Juan de Salas. During the Pueblo Rebellion the mission was burned partially and then used as a corral. The church, restored after the 1692 reconquest, has been in constant use since. **Hours:** Mon.-Fri. 10-3. **Cost:** Donations. **Phone:** (505) 869-3398.

JÉMEZ PUEBLO (C-2) pop. 1,788, elev. 5,604'

When European explorers arrived in 1541, the Jémez nation was one of the most powerful pueblo cultures in the Southwest. With an estimated population of 30,000, the Towa-speaking people lived in numerous villages spread far across the high mountain mesas. Clashes between the two cultures eventually ensued and the Jémez defended their land for some 80 years.

Eventually defenses were broken by gunfire, but through perseverance Jémez traditions, religion and language have remained alive. Today many tribal descendants live within the pueblo community of Walatowa.

The Walatowa Visitor Center, 7413 SR 4, contains cultural exhibits, photographs and pottery displays. Visitors also can see a reconstructed field house and go on nature walks. Guided 1.5-hour hikes to the scenic Jémez Red Rocks are conducted when the pueblo is open; the fee is $7 per person, plus a $5 camera permit. The visitor center is open daily 8-5, Apr.-Dec.; Wed.-Sun. 10-4, rest of year. Phone (575) 834-7235.

An open-air market takes place the second weekend in October, offering a great opportunity to meet the artists that create Jémez pottery. Special events are held at various times throughout the year. For additional information, including dates the pueblo is open to the public, contact the visitor center.

Note: In order to preserve privacy and culture, the pueblo is closed to the public except on selected feast days, when ceremonial dances are performed. Photography, video or audio recording, sketching or painting is prohibited.

The Jémez Mountain Trail (SR 44/US 550) is a National Scenic Byway that runs through the Jémez and Zia reserves between Cuba and San Ysidro.

JÉMEZ SPRINGS (B-2) pop. 250, elev. 6,200'

About 13 miles north of Jémez Pueblo, the hot mineral waters at Jémez Springs attracted Spanish explorers, pueblo dwellers, cowboys, miners and pioneers. A bath house built here in the 1870s continues to serve weary travelers. Five miles north are the Soda Dam and Battleship Rock formations; there are picnic facilities at Battleship Rock, and trout fishing is available.

JÉMEZ HISTORIC SITE is 1 mi. n. on SR 4. The site preserves the 700-year-old stone ruins of Giusewa Pueblo, ancestral home of the present-day Jémez people. About 1621 the Spanish built the fortress-like San Jose de los Jémez Mission; its massive walls still stand. A visitor center offers interpretive history exhibits and information about self-guiding tours. Special events are scheduled throughout the year. **Hours:** Wed.-Sun. 8:30-5. Closed major holidays. **Cost:** $3; free (ages 0-16). Combination ticket with the Coronado Historic Site $5 *(see Bernalillo p. 362)*. **Phone:** (575) 829-3530.

CAÑON DEL RIO RIVERSIDE INN   575/829-4377
▼▼▼ **Bed & Breakfast.** Rates not provided. **Address:** 16445 Hwy 4 87025 **Location:** 1 mi s of center. **Facility:** Known for great massage treatments and retreat-like luxuries, the inn is situated along the river at the base of dramatic cliffs. 5 units. 1 story, interior/exterior corridors. **Terms:** age restrictions may apply. **Pool(s):** heated outdoor. **Activities:** sauna, hot tub, cross country skiing, spa.
🐾 BIZ 🛜 ✕ 🅽 🆉

WHERE TO EAT

LOS OJOS RESTAURANT & SALOON   575/829-3547
▼▼▼ American. Casual Dining. $9-$20 **AAA Inspector Notes:** Rustic decor and vintage Western memorabilia sets the stage in this village restaurant, popular for its northern New Mexico cuisine, generous one-third-pound burgers and the weekend prime rib dinner. Vegetarians will find plenty of selections. The fresh-baked fruit of the forest pie is a must for dessert. Live music is presented every Monday, Wednesday and Saturday. **Features:** full bar, Sunday brunch. **Address:** 17596 Hwy 4 87025 **Location:** Center.
L D LATE

LAGUNA PUEBLO (C-2) elev. 5,807'

Rich in history, Laguna Pueblo consists of six villages; Old Laguna Village has served as the capital since the early 1300s. Casa Blanca is a tourist and commercial center for the reservation, which is known for its traditional crafts, pottery and jewelry.

After the completion of the mission church, the Spanish government recognized the pueblo as one of the largest Keresan pueblos. Completed in 1699, the Mission of the Pueblo of Laguna is a long, narrow stone structure notable for its bright and unusual interior design.

The pueblo can be visited dawn to dusk weekdays; weekend religious ceremonies are closed to the public. Photographing, sketching, painting or recording pueblo ceremonies is not permitted.

Governor's Office of Pueblo-Laguna: 22 Capital Rd., P.O. Box 194, Laguna Pueblo, NM 87026. **Phone:** (505) 552-6654.

Shopping: Browse for pottery and traditional Indian crafts at the Dancing Eagle Supermarket, off I-40.

GAMBLING ESTABLISHMENTS

• **Dancing Eagle Casino** is off I-40 exit 108 at 167 Casa Blanca Rd. **Hours:** Thurs.-Sat. 24 hours, Sun.-Wed. 8 a.m.-4 a.m. **Phone:** (505) 552-7777 or (877) 440-9969.

LA MESA pop. 728

CHOPE'S BAR & CAFE   575/233-3420
▼▼ Mexican. Casual Dining. $4-$10 **AAA Inspector Notes:** This legendary cafe and bar has been serving locals since 1915 and has become a favorite pilgrimage for many fans from across the country. The chile rellenos are a must along with the green chile enchiladas. Be sure to save room for the fluffy sopaipillas with honey. **Features:** full bar. **Address:** 16145 S Hwy 28 88044 **Location:** Center. L D

LAS CRUCES (I-3) pop. 97,618, elev. 3,908'
• Hotels p. 391 • Restaurants p. 392

A little forest of crosses marking the graves of members of a caravan ambushed by Mescalero Apaches soon came to identify this spot on El Camino Real at the foot of the Organ Mountains. By the mid-19th century Las Cruces—the crosses—was a major supply point for mining operations and forts that protected the trade routes to Santa Fe and points west. The largest of these posts was Fort Selden in nearby Radium Springs *(see place listing p. 402)*.

The Mesquite Street Historic District, east of Main Street, preserves 22 blocks of the original town site, which was plotted out in 1849 using rawhide ropes. Many of the small adobe houses, painted vibrant shades of pink, blue and green, are at least a century old.

Irrigated by the Rio Grande, the surrounding Mesilla Valley is a leading producer of alfalfa, chile peppers, onions, corn, cotton and pecans. About 25 miles northeast of town on US 70/82, then 4 miles south, is White Sands Missile Range *(see place listing p. 452)*, where experimental rockets are tested.

Las Cruces hosts ▽ The Whole Enchilada Fiesta in late September. This festive 3-day gathering features live music, a car show, a parade, carnival rides, an enchilada-eating contest and the crowning of a fiesta queen. In early November thousands flock to Young Park, 1905 Nevada Ave., for the ▽ Renaissance ArtsFaire. In addition to spotlighting the creativity of local and regional artists, this popular event offers live entertainment, food and an appearance by Magellan the dragon.

Surrounding Las Cruces is the nation's newest national monument, Organ Mountains-Desert Peaks National Monument. Officially designated in May 2014, it encompasses 466,330 acres and includes four distinct geologic areas: the Organ Mountains, the Desert Peaks, the Potrillo Mountains and the Doña Ana Mountains.

The Potrillo Mountains, the most remote section, is a volcanic landscape of cinder cones, lava flows and craters pockmarking broad desert plains. The Desert Peaks include the Doña Ana Mountains, an isolated cluster of steep and jagged peaks; they offer an extensive network of hiking, mountain biking and equestrian trails as well as rock climbing areas.

The Robledo Mountains cover a much larger area characterized by peaks that rise sharply from the flat desert plain. Farther to the northwest are the Sierra de las Uvas, masses of volcanic rock punctuated by cliffs. For day visitors the Organ Mountains region is not only the most developed portion, but the easiest to reach.

For more information about Organ Mountains-Desert Peaks National Monument, contact the Bureau of Land Management's Las Cruces District office, 1800 Marquess St., Las Cruces, NM 88005; phone (575) 525-4300.

Las Cruces Convention and Visitors Bureau: 211 N. Water St., Las Cruces, NM 88001. **Phone:** (575) 541-2444.

BRANIGAN CULTURAL CENTER is on the n. end of downtown at 501 N. Main St. Traveling and permanent exhibits highlight regional history. **Time:** Allow 30 minutes minimum. **Hours:** Tues.-Sat. 9-4:30. Closed major holidays. **Cost:** Free. **Phone:** (575) 541-2154.

Las Cruces Museum of Art is at 491 N. Main St., next to the Branigan Cultural Center. The 3,000-square-foot gallery features changing exhibits of contemporary art, many featuring local artists. **Time:** Allow 30 minutes minimum. **Hours:** Tues.-Sat. 9-4:30. **Cost:** Free. **Phone:** (575) 541-2000.

LAS CRUCES MUSEUM OF NATURE AND SCIENCE is at 411 N. Main St. Permanent and temporary exhibits relate to the area's natural history, science and environment. More than 50 live animals and hands-on displays are included. **Time:** Allow 30 minutes minimum. **Hours:** Tues.-Sat. 9-4:30. Closed major holidays. **Cost:** Donations. **Phone:** (575) 522-3120.

◤GEM **NEW MEXICO FARM & RANCH HERITAGE MUSEUM** is off I-25 exit 1, then 1.5 mi. e. to 4100 Dripping Springs Rd. New Mexico's rural life and 3,000-year-old farming history are presented with interactive displays and demonstrations. The 47-acre site includes a working cattle ranch where daily milking and blacksmith techniques are showcased. Other residents include horses, donkeys, goats and sheep. Also featured are a greenhouse, gardens and a theater.

Hours: Mon.-Sat. 9-5, Sun. noon-5. Closed Jan. 1, Thanksgiving and Christmas. **Cost:** $5; $4 (ages 60+); $3 (ages 4-17); $2 (active military and U.S. veterans with ID). **Phone:** (575) 522-4100. *(See ad p. 391.)* 🍽 🏕

ORGAN MOUNTAINS-DESERT PEAKS NATIONAL MONUMENT surrounds Las Cruces. Visitors wishing to check out the nation's newest national monument should head to the Organ Mountains, the most easily accessible of its four areas. The name refers to the needle-like spires resembling organ pipes that jut dramatically from the Chihuahuan Desert floor and reach heights of up to 9,000 feet. Other features of this ruggedly scenic environment are narrow canyons and open woodlands. The Organ Mountains offer numerous opportunities for hiking, horseback riding, mountain biking, camping, wildlife viewing and landscape photography.

Dripping Springs Natural Area is one of several designated recreation areas within the national monument. More than 4 miles of easy hiking trails wind past desert scrub and woods of juniper and oak trees. Bird watchers will spot red-tailed hawks, golden eagles and Gambel's quail, among other species; wildlife includes desert mule deer, coyotes and the occasional mountain lion.

The Dripping Springs Visitor Center is about 10 miles east of Las Cruces; from I-25 exit 1, take University Avenue/Dripping Springs Road east to the end. Interpretive displays provide information about the Organ Mountains. **Hours:** Entrance gate open daily 8-7, Apr.-Sept.; 8-5, rest of year. Visitor center open daily 8-5; closed Jan. 1, Thanksgiving and Christmas. **Cost:** Day use fee $5 per private vehicle. **Phone:** (575) 522-1219.

UNIVERSITY MUSEUM is on the New Mexico State University campus in Kent Hall at Solano Dr. and University Ave. The museum on this 15,500-student campus presents changing exhibits about the archeology, history and culture of southern New Mexico and northern Mexico. **Time:** Allow 30 minutes minimum. **Hours:** Tues.-Sat. noon-4. Closed major holidays. **Cost:** Donations. **Phone:** (575) 646-5161. GT

BEST WESTERN MISSION INN (575)524-8591

Hotel
S90-$130

AAA Benefit:
Save 10% or more every day and earn 10% bonus points!

Address: 1765 S Main St 88005 **Location:** I-10 exit 142 (University Ave), 1 mi n. **Facility:** 68 units. 2 stories (no elevator), exterior corridors. **Pool(s):** outdoor.

SAVE [↑→] [≈] [BIZ] [◉] [▯] [▤] [▣] / SOME UNITS [S↱]

Best Western

Free Hot Breakfast Buffet, Outdoor Pool, Pets Welcome, 5 minutes from NMSU & historic Old Mesilla.

COMFORT INN & SUITES DE MESILLA (575)527-1050

Hotel $79-$117 **Address:** 1300 Avenida de Mesilla 88005 **Location:** I-10 exit 140, just s. **Facility:** 50 units. 2 stories, interior corridors. **Amenities:** safes. **Pool(s):** heated indoor. **Activities:** hot tub, limited exercise equipment. **Guest Services:** coin laundry.
[↑→] CALL [&M] [≈] [HS] [◉] [▯] [▤] [▣] / SOME UNITS [S↱]

Trust the recommendations of AAA/CAA

travel experts to make a good trip great

COMFORT SUITES BY CHOICE HOTELS (575)522-1300

Hotel $79-$99 **Address:** 2101 S Triviz Dr 88001 **Location:** I-25 exit 1 (University Ave), just w, then just n. **Facility:** 61 units. 3 stories, interior corridors. **Amenities:** safes. **Pool(s):** heated indoor. **Activities:** hot tub, limited exercise equipment. **Guest Services:** valet and coin laundry.
[↑→] CALL [&M] [≈] [BIZ] [◉] [✕] [▯] [▤] [▣] / SOME UNITS [S↱]

DAYS INN LAS CRUCES (575)526-8311

Hotel
$46-$70

Address: 755 Avenida de Mesilla 88005 **Location:** I-10 exit 140, just e. **Facility:** 117 units. 2 stories (no elevator), exterior corridors. **Terms:** check-in 4 pm, cancellation fee imposed. **Amenities:** video games. **Pool(s):** outdoor. **Activities:** exercise room. **Guest Services:** valet laundry. **Featured Amenity:** full hot breakfast.

SAVE [↑→] [≈] [BIZ] [◉] [▯] [▤] [▣] / SOME UNITS [S↱]

DRURY INN & SUITES LAS CRUCES (575)523-4100

Hotel $85-$160 **Address:** 1631 Hickory Loop 88005 **Location:** I-10 exit 140, just e. **Facility:** 73 units. 4 stories, interior corridors. **Terms:** cancellation fee imposed. **Pool(s):** heated indoor. **Activities:** hot tub, exercise room. **Guest Services:** valet and coin laundry.
[↑→] CALL [&M] [≈] [HS] [◉] [▯] [▤] [▣] / SOME UNITS [S↱]

HAMPTON INN & SUITES (575)527-8777

Hotel $104-$159 **Address:** 2350 E Griggs Ave 88001 **Location:** I-25 exit 3 (Lohman Ave), just w, just n on Walton Blvd, then just e. **Facility:** 73

AAA Benefit:
Members save up to 10%!

units. 4 stories, interior corridors. **Terms:** 1-7 night minimum stay, cancellation fee imposed. **Pool(s):** heated indoor. **Activities:** hot tub, exercise room. **Guest Services:** valet and coin laundry.
[↑→] CALL [&M] [≈] [BIZ] [HS] [◉] [▯] [▣]

▼ See AAA listing p. 390 ▼

HILTON GARDEN INN LAS CRUCES — 575/522-0900
WWWW **Hotel.** Rates not provided. **Address:** 2550 S Don Roser Dr 88011 **Location:** I-25 exit 1 (University Ave), just e. **Facility:** 114 units. 4 stories, interior corridors. **Pool(s):** heated outdoor. **Activities:** hot tub, exercise room. **Guest Services:** valet and coin laundry.

AAA Benefit: Members save up to 10%!

HOLIDAY INN EXPRESS & SUITES — (575)522-0700
WWWW **Hotel** $124-$169 **Address:** 2142 Telshor Ct 88011 **Location:** I-25 exit 6 (US 70), just s. **Facility:** 80 units. 4 stories, interior corridors. **Terms:** cancellation fee imposed. **Amenities:** *Some:* safes. **Pool(s):** heated indoor. **Activities:** hot tub, exercise room. **Guest Services:** valet and coin laundry.

HOLIDAY INN EXPRESS HOTEL & SUITES — (575)527-9947
WWWW **Hotel** $99-$299 **Address:** 2635 S Valley Dr 88005 **Location:** I-10 exit 142 (University Ave), just n. **Facility:** 87 units. 4 stories, interior corridors. **Terms:** cancellation fee imposed. **Pool(s):** heated indoor. **Activities:** hot tub, exercise room. **Guest Services:** valet and coin laundry.

HOTEL ENCANTO DE LAS CRUCES — (575)522-4300
WWWW Hotel $129-$179

Address: 705 S Telshor Blvd 88011 **Location:** I-25 exit 3 (Lohman Ave), just e, then just s. **Facility:** 204 units. 7 stories, interior corridors. **Terms:** cancellation fee imposed, resort fee. **Pool(s):** heated outdoor. **Activities:** hot tub, exercise room. **Guest Services:** valet laundry, area transportation.

LA QUINTA INN & SUITES LAS CRUCES ORGAN MOUNTAIN — (575)523-0100
WW **Hotel** $64-$147 **Address:** 1500 Hickory Dr 88005 **Location:** I-10 exit 140, just se of jct I-25 and Avenida de Mesilla. **Facility:** 87 units. 4 stories, interior corridors. **Pool(s):** outdoor. **Guest Services:** coin laundry.

LUNDEEN'S INN OF THE ARTS — (575)526-3326
WW **Historic Bed & Breakfast** $79-$125 **Address:** 618 S Alameda Blvd 88005 **Location:** Jct Lohman Ave, just s; center. Located in historic district. **Facility:** The restored century-old territorial inn also incorporates a gallery that displays an interesting collection of art. 7 units, some kitchens. 2 stories (no elevator), interior corridors. **Terms:** 3 day cancellation notice-fee imposed.

RAMADA PALMS DE LAS CRUCES — (575)526-4411
WW **Hotel** $79-$199 **Address:** 201 E University Ave 88005 **Location:** I-10 exit 142 (University Ave), just n. **Facility:** 114 units. 2 stories (no elevator), interior corridors. **Terms:** cancellation fee imposed. **Pool(s):** heated indoor. **Activities:** exercise room, massage. **Guest Services:** valet and coin laundry.

SPRINGHILL SUITES BY MARRIOTT — (575)541-8887
Hotel $86-$163

AAA Benefit: Members save 5% or more!

Address: 1611 Hickory Loop 88005 **Location:** I-10 exit 140, just ne. **Facility:** 101 units. 3 stories, interior corridors. **Pool(s):** heated outdoor. **Activities:** hot tub, exercise room. **Guest Services:** valet and coin laundry. **Featured Amenity: breakfast buffet.**

STAYBRIDGE SUITES — 575/521-7999
WWW **Extended Stay Hotel.** Rates not provided. **Address:** 2651 Northrise Dr 88011 **Location:** I-25 exit 6 (US 70), just e. **Facility:** 115 efficiencies, some two bedrooms. 4 stories, interior corridors. **Amenities:** safes. **Pool(s):** heated outdoor. **Activities:** hot tub, exercise room. **Guest Services:** valet and coin laundry.

SUPER 8 EAST WHITE SANDS AREA — (575)382-1490
WW Hotel $55-$109
Address: 3405 Bataan Memorial W 88012 **Location:** US 70, exit Rinconda, just w. **Facility:** 55 units. 3 stories (no elevator), interior corridors. **Pool(s):** outdoor. **Guest Services:** coin laundry.

TOWNEPLACE SUITES BY MARRIOTT LAS CRUCES — (575)532-6500
WWW **Extended Stay Hotel** $93-$189 **Address:** 2143 Telshor Ct 88011 **Location:** I-25 exit 6 (US 70), just s. **Facility:** 81 kitchen units, some two bedrooms. 3 stories, interior corridors. **Pool(s):** heated outdoor. **Activities:** hot tub, exercise room. **Guest Services:** valet and coin laundry.

AAA Benefit: Members save 5% or more!

QUALITY INN & SUITES — 575/524-4663
fyi Not evaluated. **Address:** 2200 S Valley Dr 88005 **Location:** I-10 exit 142 (University Ave), 2 blks w. Facilities, services, and décor characterize a mid-scale property.

WHERE TO EAT

AQUA REEF EURO ASIAN CUISINE — 575/522-7333
WW Asian. Casual Dining. $6-$19 **AAA Inspector Notes:** A distinctive dining experience can be found in this cozy contemporary Asian eatery. Menu highlights showcase dim sum, sushi and creatively presented entrées. The sushi bar features boats floating along a stream of water carrying plates of sushi from the kitchen. **Features:** beer & wine. **Reservations:** suggested, Dinner. **Address:** 900-B S Telshor Blvd 88011 **Location:** Just s of jct E Lohman Ave.

BOBA CAFE 575/647-5900

Sandwiches Soup. Casual Dining. $7-$13 **AAA Inspector Notes:** Offering friendly service, this lively café is popular with nearby university staff and students. The creative soups, sandwiches and salads feature an Asian twist. Arrive hungry as the portions are very generous. **Features:** beer & wine, patio dining. **Address:** 1900 S Espina St, Suite 8 88001 **Location:** Just n of jct University Ave.

L D

CATTLE BARON STEAK & SEAFOOD 575/522-7533

American. Casual Dining. $9-$29 **AAA Inspector Notes:** A scrumptious array of menu selections includes steak, seafood, chicken and prime rib as well as desserts such as caramel apple pie. An upscale Western decor includes wood trim and distinctive chandeliers made from deer antlers. **Features:** full bar. **Address:** 790 S Telshor Blvd 88011 **Location:** I-25 exit 3 (Lohman Ave), just e, then just s. L D

CHILITOS 575/526-4184

Mexican. Family Dining. $7-$14 **AAA Inspector Notes:** It is the heaping platters of flavorful, authentic Mexican favorites that keeps the locals coming back to this eatery. Be sure not to fill up on the complimentary homemade salsa and chips--take-out jars are available for purchase. **Features:** beer & wine, senior menu. **Address:** 2405 S Valley Dr 88005 **Location:** I-10 exit 142 (University Ave), just n; jct S Valley Dr and S Main St. B L D

DE LA VEGA'S PECAN GRILL & BREWERY 575/521-1099

American. Casual Dining. $7-$35 **AAA Inspector Notes:** Enjoy Prime beef, chicken and fish cooked over a state-of-the-art pecan wood grill. Specialty brewed beers are on tap to accompany the house-smoked ribs. Sandwiches, burgers and a variety of soups and salads round out the menu. Gluten-free options are available. **Features:** full bar, patio dining, Sunday brunch, happy hour. **Address:** 500 S Telshor Blvd 88011 **Location:** I-25 exit 3 (Lohman Ave), just e. L D LATE CALL M

EL SOMBRERO PATIO CAFE 575/524-9911

Mexican. Family Dining. $7-$15 **AAA Inspector Notes:** This bustling local favorite has been serving traditional New Mexico cuisine since 1956. Generous portions of steak, chicken and salads are served up. Many of the dishes come with flavorful sauces. **Features:** beer & wine. **Address:** 363 S Espina St 88001 **Location:** I-25 exit 3 (Lohman Ave), 2 mi w on Lohman and Amador aves; jct Espina St. L D

FARLEY'S 575/522-0466

American. Casual Dining. $7-$15 **AAA Inspector Notes:** The menu at this laid-back restaurant includes hot dogs, pizza and grilled cheese for the kids, as well as choices for mom and dad, including ribs, sandwiches, steak, fajitas, soups, salads, beer and fantastic margaritas. **Features:** full bar, patio dining. **Address:** 3499 Foothills Rd 88011 **Location:** I-25 exit 3 (Lohman Ave), 0.3 mi e to Nacho Dr, then 0.3 mi s. L D

HIGH DESERT BREWING CO. 575/525-6752

American. Casual Dining. $6-$11 **AAA Inspector Notes:** This very popular gathering spot for locals features award-winning, hand-crafted brews and a menu of hearty pub fare. Live music is offered in the evenings on Thursdays and Saturdays. **Features:** beer only. **Address:** 1201 W Hadley Ave 88005 **Location:** Just e of jct Valley Dr. **Parking:** on-site and street. L D

INTERNATIONAL DELIGHTS CAFE 575/647-5956

Mediterranean. Quick Serve. $7-$15 **AAA Inspector Notes:** This popular local eatery has a variety of Mediterranean dishes from creamy hummus and flavorful soups to delectable desserts. Free Wi-Fi and specialty coffee keeps this a favorite late night hangout for university students. **Address:** 1245 El Paseo Rd 88001 **Location:** Jct Idaho Ave; in Brazito Plaza.

B L D LATE

LORENZO'S 575/521-3505

Italian. Casual Dining. $8-$24 **AAA Inspector Notes:** Authentic Sicilian dishes are served here, which offers pasta dishes with flavorful sauces, hand-tossed pizza with unusual combinations including green chile, and my favorite eggplant parmigiana that is not breaded. The eggplant parmigiana is Vince's grandmother's special recipe. Finish with an imported tiramisù, spumoni or cheesecake. **Features:** beer & wine. **Address:** 1753 E University Ave 88001 **Location:** I-25 exit 1 (University Ave), just sw. L D

MIX PACIFIC RIM CUISINE 575/532-2042

Asian. Casual Dining. $9-$24 **AAA Inspector Notes:** The cozy and contemporary restaurant presents an extensive menu of sushi prepared with a Southwest twist, as well as Asian fusion entrées and bento box specials. Worth a try are tempura green chile and the Mexico roll. Creative sake cocktails are served in fun decanters. **Features:** beer & wine. **Address:** 1001 E University Ave, Suite D4 88001 **Location:** Jct Espina St, just e. L D

OLD MESILLA PASTRY CAFE-THE SHED RESTAURANT 575/525-2636

American. Family Dining. $8-$13 **AAA Inspector Notes:** This busy café with casual service features breakfast offerings ranging from huevos rancheros and eggs Benedict to pancakes and omelets. The wood-burning oven produces pizza, calzone and house bread. Such vegetarian delights as garden burgers and grilled eggplant sandwiches also are served. **Features:** beer & wine. **Address:** 810 S Valley Dr 88005 **Location:** I-10 exit 142 (University Ave), just e, then 1 mi nw. B L

ST. CLAIR WINERY & BISTRO 575/524-0390

American. Casual Dining. $7-$22 **AAA Inspector Notes:** This lively neighborhood bistro prepares creative comfort food, which guests can enjoy with an excellent selection of New Mexico wines. Wine tastings are popular here, as is the lush dining patio. **Features:** beer & wine, patio dining. **Reservations:** suggested. **Address:** 1720 Avenida de Mesilla 88004 **Location:** I-10 exit 135, just w. L D CALL M

SI ITALIAN BISTRO 575/523-1572

Italian. Casual Dining. $7-$21 **AAA Inspector Notes:** This restaurant presents an extensive menu of Italian entrées, as well as pasta, salads, sandwiches and wood-fired pizza, which guests can enjoy with beer or wine. The talented pastry chef creates exceptional eat-in or take-out desserts in an open bakery. **Features:** beer & wine. **Address:** 523 E Idaho Ave 88001 **Location:** Jct El Paseo Rd, just e. L D

SI SEÑOR RESTAURANT 575/527-0817

Mexican. Family Dining. $8-$17 **AAA Inspector Notes:** Come hungry for generous portions of authentic New Mexican cuisine served in a lively atmosphere. The tortillas and flavorful chile sauce both are house-made. Be sure to try a selection from the extensive margarita menu. **Features:** full bar, patio dining. **Address:** 1551 Amador Ave 88001 **Location:** I-25 exit 3 (Lohman Ave), 1 mi w. L D

ZEFFIRO PIZZERIA NAPOLETANA 575/525-6757

Pizza. Casual Dining. $7-$13 **AAA Inspector Notes:** Fresh-baked artisan bread is the specialty at this bustling café and bakery. Friendly servers greet patrons with a basket of warm bread and a dish of olive oil seasoned with herbs. This is a popular lunch spot for delicious hand-tossed pizza, salads, soups and sandwiches. Before leaving, diners can purchase a loaf of bread from the adjacent Popular Artisan Bread Bakery. **Features:** beer & wine. **Address:** 136 N Water St 88001 **Location:** Downtown; in historic Main Street area. L D

LAS VEGAS (F-4) pop. 13,753, elev. 6,430'
• Hotels p. 394 • Restaurants p. 394

The faint wagon wheel ruts still visible outside Las Vegas attest to the town's era as a mercantile center on the Santa Fe Trail. Las Vegas also was a military post until Fort Union (see Fort Union National Monument p. 381) was built. During the 1880s it was known as one of the roughest towns on the frontier, frequented by such desperadoes as Billy the Kid and Doc Holliday. The arrival of the Santa Fe Railroad in 1879 brought commercial prosperity, and hundreds of historic buildings still stand.

Recreational activities can be enjoyed at Storrie Lake State Park, 4 miles north off SR 518 (see Recreation Areas Chart); Morphy Lake State Park, 25 miles north off SR 518 (see Recreation Areas Chart); and in the Sangre de Cristo Mountains, which rise to the west (see Santa Fe National Forest p. 437).

City of Las Vegas Visitors Center: 500 Railroad Ave., Las Vegas, NM 87701. **Phone:** (505) 425-3707 or (800) 832-5947.

Self-guiding tours: A brochure describing walking and driving tours is available from the visitors center.

CITY OF LAS VEGAS MUSEUM AND ROUGH RIDER MEMORIAL COLLECTION is just n. of I-25 exit 345 at 727 Grand Ave. The museum illustrates the cultural heritage of the town through its collection. Exhibits include the Rough Riders, the first U.S. Volunteer Cavalry regiment led by Theodore Roosevelt in the Spanish-American War; the Santa Fe Trail; and railroad history. **Time:** Allow 30 minutes minimum. **Hours:** Tues.-Sat. 10-4. Closed major holidays. **Cost:** Donations. **Phone:** (505) 426-3205.

LAS VEGAS NATIONAL WILDLIFE REFUGE is 6 mi. s.e. via SRs 104 and 281. Covering 8,672 acres of prairie bordered by the timbered canyons of the Gallinas River and Vegosa Creek, the refuge has more than 300 species of wildlife and is noted for its birds of prey. In season, bald eagles, hawks and kestrels are seen. Brochures, an auto loop map and nature-trail permits are available at the refuge office. Allow 1 hour minimum for the driving tour, 2 hours minimum for the nature trail. **Hours:** Auto loop drive open daily 24 hours. Office Mon.-Fri. 8-4. Closed major holidays. **Cost:** Free. **Phone:** (505) 425-3581.

BEST WESTERN PLUS MONTEZUMA INN & SUITES
(505)426-8000

Hotel
$90-$160

AAA Benefit: Save 10% or more every day and earn 10% bonus points!

Address: 2020 N Grand Ave 87701 **Location:** I-25 exit 347, just sw. **Facility:** 67 units. 3 stories, interior corridors. **Terms:** cancellation fee imposed. **Pool(s):** heated indoor. **Activities:** sauna, hot tub, exercise room. **Guest Services:** coin laundry.

HOLIDAY INN EXPRESS HOTEL & SUITES (505)426-8182
Hotel $100-$130 **Address:** 816 S Grand Ave 87701 **Location:** I-25 exit 343, just n. **Facility:** 68 units. 3 stories, interior corridors. **Terms:** check-in 4 pm. **Pool(s):** heated indoor. **Activities:** hot tub, exercise room. **Guest Services:** coin laundry.

WHERE TO EAT

DICK'S RESTAURANT 505/454-8084
American. Casual Dining. $7-$26 **AAA Inspector Notes:** This hidden gem is a favorite of locals. You'll enjoy a large selection of regional specialties plus some creative entrées. Start with an excellent margarita and then enjoy the spicy chipotle shrimp on spinach and cool off with the homemade flan, a true burst of flavors. **Features:** full bar, happy hour. **Address:** 705 Douglas Ave 87701 **Location:** Jct 7th St; center. L D

LA UNION (J-3) pop. 1,106, elev. 3,795'

WINERIES

• **La Viña Winery** is off I-10 exit 2, 4 mi. w. to SR 28, then 1 mi. n. Tours and tastings are offered. **Hours:** Thurs.-Tues. noon-5. Tours are given at 11:30 by appointment. Closed major holidays. **Phone:** (575) 882-7632. GT

LINCOLN (H-4) elev. 5,715'

Lincoln's historical claim to fame is tied to an Old West gunslinger born to Irish immigrant parents. William Henry McCarty, Jr.—better known as Billy the Kid—was tried, convicted and sentenced to hang as retribution for a life of rustling and murder, but instead he killed his guards and escaped from the Lincoln County Courthouse. Sheriff Pat Garrett tracked him to Fort Sumner, where two shots ended the outlaw's life on July, 14, 1881 at the young age of 21.

Fort Stanton Recreation Area, approximately 9 miles west of town off US 380, comprises 24,000 acres of BLM-managed lands in the foothills of the Sierra Blanca Mountains. Mountain streams, rolling hills, flat-topped mesas and open bottomlands offer a variety of outdoor activities (see Recreation Areas Chart).

FORT STANTON HISTORIC SITE is w. of Lincoln on US 380, then s. on SR 220. Established in 1855 to protect settlers against Apache raids, the fort was later occupied by Confederate soldiers, John J. "Blackjack" Pershing, New Mexico volunteers under "Kit" Carson, and the Buffalo Soldiers. The Army abandoned the fort in 1896. An interpretive center chronicles the fort's history. Living-history events take place the third Saturday of each month (except July); among the re-enactment sites are an Apache encampment and the fort bakery and blacksmith. **Time:** Allow 1 hour minimum. **Hours:** Grounds daily dawn-dusk. Museum Mon.-Sat. 10-4, Sun. noon-4, Apr.-Dec.; Mon.-Thurs. 11-3, rest of year. **Cost:** Donations. **Phone:** (575) 354-0341.

LINCOLN HISTORIC SITE covers the half-mile stretch of town. Nearly a dozen 19th-century stone and adobe buildings are preserved as they appeared during the 1878-81 Lincoln County War, a violent era in the state's history. The Tunstall Store and the Lincoln County Courthouse Museum contain exhibits. Other buildings include the Montaño Store and the San Juan Mission Church. The Anderson Freeman Museum houses Native American, settler, cowboy and war exhibits.

Time: Allow 1 hour minimum. **Hours:** Daily 8:30-4:30. Closed major holidays. **Cost:** $5; free (ages 0-16 with adult). **Phone:** (575) 653-4372.

WORTLEY DINING ROOM   575/653-4300
[fyi] Not evaluated. This famous dining room served many participants of the Lincoln County War, including Pat Garrett and Billy the Kid. The last meal of Marshall Bob Ollinger was interrupted by the escape of The Kid; Ollinger was gunned down as he tried to enter the jail during the battle. **Address:** Hwy 380 88338 **Location:** Center of town; in Wortley Hotel.

LINCOLN NATIONAL FOREST (H-4)

Elevations in the forest range from 4,440 ft. at Grapevine Canyon to 11,580 ft. at Lookout Mountain. Refer to AAA maps for additional elevation information.

In south central New Mexico, most of the Sacramento, Jicarilla, Guadalupe and Capitan mountains lie within the three districts of Lincoln National Forest. Covering 1,103,441 acres of pine, juniper and fir timber lands, the terrain in this vast region ranges from desert to subalpine.

Within the Smokey Bear Ranger District are two wilderness areas offering unspoiled back country for hikes and horseback rides. The district office is located in Ruidoso (see place listing p. 407), a popular recreation center and resort.

The Smokey Bear Ranger District also was home to the original Smokey Bear, the living symbol of fire prevention. The Smokey Bear Historical Park in Capitan, north of Ruidoso, displays memorabilia about the tiny cub and information about wildfire prevention along with the town's original train depot. In fire season from April through July, campfires and charcoal grills may be prohibited. Points of interest and a bevy of scenic vistas along Billy the Kid National Scenic Byway make it a drive well worth exploring.

The Sacramento Ranger District is located in and around the mountain community of Cloudcroft (see place listing p. 372). Shaded by tall pines, it's a haven for those wishing to escape the desert heat below. At an elevation of 9,000 feet, the nine-hole golf course at The Lodge Resort & Spa is not only one of the highest courses in the nation but offers challenging terrain as well (picture a 150-foot vertical drop at the first hole tee-off). The course is open April through October, and calling ahead for a tee time is recommended; phone (800) 395-6343.

In addition to golf, the area around Cloudcroft offers camping, hiking, fishing, horseback riding, hunting, skiing and off-road ATV trails. Take a drive along the Sunspot Scenic Highway (SR 6563) and marvel at spectacular views of the Tularosa Basin and the dunes of White Sands National Monument (see place listing p. 453).

The southern Guadalupe Ranger District encompasses the relatively less-traveled Guadalupe Mountains. A 150-foot waterfall, an uncommon feature in this semi-arid region, is the scenic centerpiece of an oasis in the otherwise desert-like environment at Sitting Bull Falls Picnic Area, 49 miles southwest of Carlsbad via US 285, SR 137 and FR 276. The area is open Fri.-Mon. noon-6; phone ahead to confirm. Admission $5 per private vehicle (exact change is required), free for Federal Recreational Lands Pass holders. Phone (575) 885-4181.

Numerous caves can be explored; permits are issued on a first-come, first-served basis. For further information contact the Lincoln Forest Supervisor's Office, 3463 Las Palamos Rd., Alamogordo, NM 88310. It's advisable to check current road and trail conditions before planning a visit, especially during the winter months; phone (575) 434-7200. See Recreation Areas Chart.

LORDSBURG pop. 2,797

COMFORT INN & SUITES   (575)542-3355

♦♦♦ Hotel $89-$114 Address: 400 W Wabash St 88045 Location: I-10 exit 22, just n, then w. Facility: 64 units. 3 stories, interior corridors. Pool(s): heated indoor. Activities: sauna, hot tub, exercise room. Guest Services: coin laundry.

[†+] CALL [&M] [≈] [BIZ] [HS] [◊] [🖥] [🖨] [▭]
/ SOME UNITS [🔌]

HAMPTON INN   (575)542-8900

♦♦♦ Hotel $84-$114 Address: 412 W Wabash St 88045 Location: I-10 exit 22, just w. Facility: 64 units. 3 stories, interior corridors. Terms: 1-7 night minimum stay, cancellation fee imposed. Pool(s): heated indoor. Activities: hot tub, exercise room. Guest Services: coin laundry.

AAA Benefit: Members save up to 10%!

[†+] CALL [&M] [≈] [BIZ] [HS] [◊] [✕] [🖥] [🖨] [▭]
/ SOME UNITS [🐾]

MOTEL-6 LORDSBURG   575/542-8807

♦♦
Motel
Rates not provided

Address: 1303 S Main St 88045 Location: I-10 exit 22, just s. Facility: 40 units. 1 story, exterior corridors. Pool(s): heated outdoor. Guest Services: coin laundry.

[SAVE] [†+] [≈] [BIZ] [◊] [🖥] [🖨]
[▭] / SOME UNITS [HS]

WHERE TO EAT

KRANBERRY'S FAMILY RESTAURANT   575/542-9400

♦♦ American. Family Dining. $7-$15 AAA Inspector Notes: In an atmosphere much like that found at well-known pancake house chains, this restaurant serves generous breakfasts, lunches and dinners. The menu lists a good selection of good old American food, including burgers, sandwiches and cooked-to-order dinners. Just off the interstate, the clean, bright setting appeals to motorists and locals alike. Address: 1405 S Main St 88045 Location: I-10 exit 22, just s. [B] [L] [D] CALL [&M]

LOS ALAMOS (A-3) pop. 12,019, elev. 7,320'

In 1943 the federal government selected Los Alamos Ranch School as the top secret, maximum security site for the Manhattan Project, an atomic bomb research and testing program where Little Boy and Fat Man—the atomic bombs that ended World War II—were built. By 1945, when the first atomic device was detonated at Trinity Site *(see White Sands Missile Range p. 452)*, more than 3,000 civilian and military personnel were working at the laboratory.

Los Alamos National Laboratory continues to apply science to issues of national security, economic strength and energy security. Its staff of nearly 9,000 conducts extensive research about technology associated with nuclear weapons, deterrence and other defense applications, energy production, health, safety and environmental concerns, astrophysics and life sciences.

Explosions of another sort created the rugged setting that was so essential for maintaining the secrecy of the Manhattan Project. About a million years ago the volcanic vents that had built the Jémez Mountains issued 100 cubic miles of ash and pumice and then collapsed. The result is Valle Grande, one of the largest measured calderas on Earth. Covering 148 square miles, the depression has a rim that averages some 500 feet in height above its floor.

SR 4, about 15 miles west of Los Alamos, follows the crater's southern curve and makes it possible to view the vast, grassy bowl. Over time erupting ash hardened into a layer of tuff, the Pajarito Plateau, which seems even more remote because it is protected by a series of finger-like canyons serrating its edges.

Within the plateau is Bandelier National Monument *(see place listing p. 361)*, the site of extensive Ancestral Puebloan ruins. Guided hiking trips, wagon rides and van tours of Valles Caldera National Preserve *(see Recreation Areas Chart)* offer opportunities to explore the region's geology, archeology and wildlife; phone (505) 661-3333 for information, (866) 382-5537 for reservations.

Los Alamos Chamber of Commerce and Visitor Center: 109 Central Park Sq., Los Alamos, NM 87544. **Phone:** (505) 662-8105 or (800) 444-0707.

Self-guiding tours: A guidebook available at the visitor center and the Los Alamos County Historical Museum outlines a walking tour of local historical sites.

BRADBURY SCIENCE MUSEUM is at 1350 Central Ave. It features films and interactive exhibits interpreting Los Alamos National Laboratory's contributions to modern science, research and technology, including its role in the Manhattan Project and current mission in national security. **Hours:** Tues.-Sat. 10-5, Sun.-Mon. 1-5. **Cost:** Free. **Phone:** (505) 667-4444.

LOS ALAMOS HISTORICAL MUSEUM is next to Fuller Lodge on Central Ave. This restored log and stone cottage once served as the infirmary and guest house for the Los Alamos Ranch School. Exhibits relate the region's history, including the Manhattan Project, and include newspaper articles, military uniforms and photographs of bomb tests. Also on display are an ancestral Tewa site dating from the 13th century and a relocated homesteader's cabin.

Hours: Mon.-Fri. 9:30-4:30, Sat.-Sun. 11-4, Apr.-Oct.; Mon.-Fri. 10-4, Sat.-Sun. 11-4, rest of year. Closed Jan. 1, Thanksgiving and Christmas. **Cost:** Donations. **Phone:** (505) 662-6272 or (505) 662-4493.

HOLIDAY INN EXPRESS & SUITES   505/661-2646

 Hotel. Rates not provided. Address: 60 Entrada Dr 87544 Location: Jct Airport Basin Dr and SR 502. Facility: 86 units, some efficiencies. 4 stories, interior corridors. Pool(s): heated indoor. Activities: hot tub, exercise room. Guest Services: valet and coin laundry.

CALL ⬛ ➤ BIZ HS 🛜 ✕ ▣ / SOME UNITS ⬛ ▤ ▣

WHERE TO EAT

THE BLUE WINDOW BISTRO   505/662-6305

 International. Casual Dining. $9-$29 AAA Inspector Notes: This vibrant eatery has a pleasant, cheerful atmosphere that appeals to business people, tourists and staffers at the Los Alamos National Laboratory. On the menu is a good selection of popular New Mexican dishes, sandwiches, salads and desserts. Features: beer & wine, patio dining. Address: 813 Central Ave 87544 Location: 0.5 mi w of jct SR 502 and Central Ave. L D 🖿

LOS LUNAS pop. 14,835

WESTERN SKIES INN & SUITES   (505)865-0001

Hotel
$65-$95

Address: 2258 Sun Ranch Village Loop 87031 Location: I-25 exit 203, just w. Facility: 57 units. 3 stories, interior corridors. Terms: 3 day cancellation notice. Pool(s): heated indoor. Activities: exercise room. Guest Services: coin laundry.

SAVE ⬛ CALL ⬛ ➤ BIZ 🛜 ▤ ▣ ▣ / SOME UNITS ⬛

WHERE TO EAT

TEOFILOS RESTAURANTE   505/865-5511

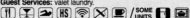 Mexican. Casual Dining. $9-$18 AAA Inspector Notes: New Mexican cuisine is served in a renovated adobe house that dates back to the 1800s. Red chile enchiladas are fantastic. Features: beer & wine, Sunday brunch. Address: 144 Main St NW 87031 Location: I-25 exit 203, 1.5 mi e. L D

LOS RANCHOS DE ALBUQUERQUE
pop. 6,024
• Hotels & Restaurants map & index p. 342

LOS POBLANOS HISTORIC INN & ORGANIC FARM
505/344-9297 55

 Historic Country Inn. Rates not provided. Address: 4803 Rio Grande Blvd NW 87107 Location: I-40 exit 157A (Rio Grande Blvd), 3.3 mi n. Facility: Mornings are kicked off with a full breakfast prepared using organic ingredients from the on-site garden and from other local growers. 22 units, some kitchens and cottages. 1 story, exterior corridors. Terms: check-in 4 pm. Dining: La Merienda at Los Poblanos, see separate listing. Pool(s): heated outdoor. Activities: recreation programs, bicycles, exercise room, massage. Guest Services: valet laundry.

⬛ 🍸 ➤ HS 🛜 ✕ ▣ / SOME UNITS ⬛ ▤

WHERE TO EAT

LA MERIENDA AT LOS POBLANOS   505/344-9297 54

 International. Fine Dining. $20-$36 AAA Inspector Notes: This restaurant features a creative and ever-changing seasonal menu using farm fresh ingredients and artisanal products from New Mexican purveyors. Attentive service and the romantic country farm setting makes for a memorable dining experience. Features: beer & wine, patio dining. Reservations: suggested. Address: 4803 Rio Grande Blvd NW 87107 Location: I-40 exit 157A (Rio Grande Blvd), 3.3 mi n; in Los Poblanos Historic Inn & Organic Farm.

D

SADIE'S DINING ROOM   505/345-5339 55

 Mexican. Casual Dining. $7-$20 AAA Inspector Notes: This is a popular restaurant, with some of the hottest New Mexican food around, so expect a wait to be seated here. The chicken enchiladas are wonderful. The interior is decorated in the traditional Southwestern pink and turquoise. Features: full bar. Address: 6230 4th St NW 87107 Location: 0.5 mi s of jct Osuna Rd. L D

VERNON'S HIDDEN VALLEY STEAKHOUSE
505/341-0831 53

Steak Seafood. Fine Dining. $30-$80 AAA Inspector Notes: The fun starts at the time of your reservation. Take a trip to the Prohibition era; a password is needed to enter this "speakeasy," so don't be intimidated by the mobster at the secret door. The menu is taken seriously here with fine quality steaks, chops and game, plus a selection of fresh seafood. The lounge is the place to be seen in this city and features nightly live entertainment from pianos to jazz. Features: full bar, Sunday brunch. Reservations: required. Address: 6855 4th St NW, Suite A 87107 Location: Just n of Osuna Rd.

D

MADRID (D-4) pop. 204, elev. 6,020'
• Restaurants p. 398

Madrid couldn't be more different from the Spanish capital it shares a name with, starting with its pronunciation (say "MAH-drid"). This spot of a hamlet in the high desert country of central New Mexico has had several incarnations over the course of approximately 2 centuries: coal mining boomtown, home of the Madrid Miners minor league baseball team, all-but-deserted "ghost town," offbeat artists' collective. The last one describes Madrid today and is one reason why it's one of the state's most distinctive small communities.

The nearby, mineral-rich Ortiz Mountains ensured Madrid's early success. By 1892 coal was being extracted from mines with shafts as deep as 2,500 feet. A company town of wood-framed cabins rose up, supplying coal for the Santa Fe Railway and the U.S. Government. Beginning in the early 1920s, Madrid became famous for its big Fourth of July parade and a lavish Christmastime display of lights, powered by electricity provided by coal-fed generators. Baseball games were played in the first lighted ballpark in the West.

But the development of cheaper and cleaner fuels brought about Madrid's decline. By the end of the 1950s the mines had closed and only a handful of people were left. Rebirth began in the early 1970s, when artists and craftspeople who didn't mind roughing it started converting old miners' cabins into funky little galleries and shops.

Today there are reminders of Madrid's past in names like the Mine Shaft Tavern and the Ghost Town Trading Post. There's a definite hippie sensibility—a stone gargoyle here, a whiff of incense there. And more recently a biker contingent has made its presence known. The 2007 hit movie "Wild Hogs," a comedy about a group of suburbanites (led by Will Ferrell and Tim Allen) turned wannabe bikers, was partially filmed in town; Maggie's Diner, built specifically for the film, was left standing.

Another blink-and-you'll-miss-it town is Cerrillos, a couple of miles north of Madrid off SR 14 (watch for the signed turnoff). As early as 1,000 B.C., prehistoric people using stone axes and antler picks worked the surrounding region for turquoise, that beautifully hued mineral long prized as a gem and ornamental stone. Cerrillos turquoise even ended up adorning the crown jewels of Spain. Gold, silver, lead and zinc also were extracted from area mines that reached their peak in the 1880s, when the town boasted four hotels and more than 20 saloons.

Today's Cerrillos is a far cry from its boisterous past, but there's still a rustic Old West look to the cottonwood-shaded dirt streets and adobe houses. While "sleepy" is an accurate description, there are a couple of shops and artist studios for visitors to explore. The Cerrillos Turquoise Mining Museum (17 Waldo St.; watch for the signs) has an interesting collection of rocks, Cerrillos turquoise, bottles, curios, tools, coffee cans, hand grinders and antiques amassed by the owners, plus an adjacent fenced enclosure where you can feed llamas, goats and chickens. The museum is open daily 9-5; phone (505) 438-3008.

The stretch of SR 14 between I-40 exit 175 and I-25 exit 278 is called the Turquoise Trail National Scenic Byway. Tijeras is the gateway to this popular alternate route between Albuquerque and Santa Fe. The natural setting is grand—forests of juniper and piñon pine, sagebrush-speckled hills, rolling prairies, vistas of the Sandia Mountains. The Turquoise Trail scenery is particularly spectacular from the village of Golden north to Madrid. Just north of Cerrillos is the Garden of the Gods, a grouping of vertical sandstone and mudstone rocks. While not as large, impressive or famous as the towering red sandstone formations at Garden of the Gods Park in Colorado Springs, they were shaped by the same geological forces.

Shopping: Narrow, winding SR 14, Madrid's main—and only—drag, is lined with an eclectic collection of art galleries and little shops housed in fancifully decorated wooden houses. Parking is a do-it-yourself affair; in other words, grab a spot wherever you can along the road or in one of the few gravel lots. Some establishments are open seasonally or have reduced hours during the winter months.

Galleries like the Chumani Gallery (2839 SR 14), Spirit in Art (just off SR 14 on Firehouse Road), Johnsons of Madrid (2843 SR 14) and Indigo (2854 SR 14) deal in contemporary paintings, Navajo jewelry, Mata Ortiz pottery, Cerrillos turquoise and fiber art. For souvenirs, Madrid T-shirts and Route 66-themed gifts check out Tumbleweeds (just off SR 14 on Firehouse Road). Cowgirl Red (2865 SR 14) has Wild West art, antiques and vintage cowboy boots. Heaven (2853 SR 14) is a Victorian-style boutique selling clothing, jewelry, hats and gifts. Hanuman's (2872 SR 14) calls itself a "world gallery" and carries cool items like tribal and sacred objects, metal sculpture, and Native American and world music CDs.

Madrid's meeting place is the Java Junction (2855 SR 14), where you can mingle with the locals over coffee or a smoothie before checking out the kitschy array of novelty coffee mugs, kitchen magnets and T-shirts, as well as a killer selection of hot sauces and regional salsas.

MADRID OLD COAL TOWN MUSEUM is at 2846 SR 14. Several buildings reflecting Madrid's ghost town past display old mining equipment and vintage vehicles. There are exhibits pertaining to Madrid's famous Christmas lights and the Madrid Miners baseball team, as well as a 1901 Richmond Steam locomotive. The Engine House Theatre offers music and many special events on weekends in season.

Time: Allow 1 hour minimum. **Hours:** Sat.-Sun. 10-6. Closed Christmas. Phone ahead to confirm schedule. **Cost:** $5; $3 (children and senior citizens). **Phone:** (505) 438-3780. GT

MINE SHAFT TAVERN   505/473-0743
American. Casual Dining. $11-$26 **AAA Inspector Notes:** Originally built for coal miners' entertainment, this rustic watering hole serves a good selection of sandwiches, lunch and dinner specials and spirits to please its jovial clientele. **Features:** full bar, patio dining. **Reservations:** suggested. **Address:** 2846 SR 14 87010 **Location:** Center. L D

MESCALERO (H-4) pop. 1,338, elev. 6,600'

Mescalero is the largest town within the Mescalero Apache Reservation and serves as its headquarters. The more than 460,000-acre tract embraces the Sierra Blanca Mountains and their wealth of timber, grazing lands and scenic beauty. Among the last American Indians to lay down arms against the U.S. government, the tribe now operates as a federally chartered corporation.

INN OF THE MOUNTAIN GODS RESORT & CASINO
575/464-7777
Resort Hotel
Rates not provided

Address: 287 Carrizo Canyon Rd (Rt 4) 88340 **Location:** Jct Sudderth Dr, 3.4 mi w, follow signs. **Facility:** This combination resort-casino on the Mescalero Apache Reservation features a breathtaking view of the nearby lake and a pristine natural setting. A new outdoor feature is a zip line over the lake. 273 units. 6 stories, interior corridors. **Parking:** on-site and valet. **Amenities:** safes. **Dining:** 4 restaurants, also, Wendell's, see separate listing. **Pool(s):** heated indoor. **Activities:** sauna, hot tub, steamroom, fishing, regulation golf, downhill skiing, snowmobiling, snowboarding, recreation programs, playground, game room, trails, exercise room, massage. **Guest Services:** valet laundry, area transportation. (See ad p. 408.)

WHERE TO EAT

WENDELL'S   575/464-7777
Steak. Fine Dining. $8-$44 **AAA Inspector Notes:** This fine dining restaurant, offering spectacular lake and mountain views, presents locally grown and harvested elk as well as fine beef cuts, fowl and seafood dishes. The professional staff will create a memorable occasion. **Features:** full bar, patio dining, Sunday brunch. **Reservations:** suggested. **Address:** 287 Carrizo Canyon Rd 88340 **Location:** Jct Sudderth Dr, 3.4 mi w, follow signs; in Inn of the Mountain Gods Resort & Casino. B L D CALL

MESILLA (I-3) pop. 2,196, elev. 3,886'

Mesilla's founding dates from 1848, when residents of a nearby community that had become part of the United States as a result of the Treaty of Guadalupe Hidalgo elected to relocate in order to retain Mexican citizenship. They were awarded a Mexican land grant in 1850, but in 1854 the Gadsden Purchase transferred nearly 30,000 square miles west of the Rio Grande back to the United States.

Productive farmland and a strategic location spurred growth. By the time the Butterfield Trail Overland mail route established a stagecoach stop in 1858, Mesilla was the largest town in the southern New Mexico Territory, which included present-day Arizona; El Paso, Texas, and neighboring Las Cruces *(see place listing p. 389)* were mere hamlets in contrast. Another historical footnote: Billy the Kid was tried and sentenced in Mesilla, the territorial capital.

Mesilla Plaza, designated a state monument in 1957, is the scene of cultural events throughout the year, notably Cinco de Mayo and Mexican Independence Day celebrations (on May 5 and Sept. 16, respectively) and Day of the Dead (Día de Los Muertos) festivities at the beginning of November. On Christmas Eve the plaza gets a magical touch courtesy of thousands of luminaria lights lining streets and sidewalks. Refurbished 19th-century buildings surrounding the plaza house shops, art galleries and restaurants.

The Gadsden Museum, 1875 Boutz Rd., has exhibits relating to Colonel Albert Jennings Fountain and five generations of Fountain family as well as local history. It is open by appointment only; phone (575) 526-6293.

Mesilla (J. Paul Taylor) Visitor Center: 2231 Avenida de Mesilla, P.O. Box 10, Mesilla, NM 88046. Phone: (575) 524-3262, ext. 117.

MESON DE MESILLA BOUTIQUE HOTEL   575/652-4953
[fyi] Not evaluated. Address: 1803 Avenida de Mesilla 88046 Location: Just ne of jct SR 28 and 292. Facilities, services, and décor characterize a mid-scale property. Walking distance to historic Old Mesilla.

WHERE TO EAT

ANDELE! RESTAURANTE   575/526-9631
Mexican. Casual Dining. $7-$15 AAA Inspector Notes: Authentic New Mexican cuisine is served at this popular neighborhood cafe. Came adovada is excellent, as is the salsa. Flan satisfies for dessert. Features: beer & wine, senior menu. Address: 1950 Calle del Norte 88046 Location: Jct Calle del Norte and Avenida de Mesilla; in Onate Plaza Shopping Center. B L D

DOUBLE EAGLE RESTAURANT   575/523-6700
Steak. Fine Dining. $23-$48 AAA Inspector Notes: *Historic.* On the National Register of Historic Places, this formal restaurant is decorated with Baccarat crystal and 19th-century art. Features: full bar, Sunday brunch. Reservations: suggested. Address: 2355 Calle de Guadalupe 88046 Location: In The Plaza; in Old Mesilla. D

JOSEPHINA'S OLD GATE   575/525-2620
Sandwiches. Casual Dining. $7-$12 AAA Inspector Notes: Enjoy a relaxing lunch or a cup of tea at this quaint little restaurant, just a short stroll from The Plaza. This is a popular subject for local photographers and painters. Features: wine only, patio dining. Address: 2261 Calle de Guadalupe 88046 Location: North of The Plaza. Parking: street only. B L

LA POSTA DE MESILLA   575/524-3524
 Mexican Casual Dining $10-$17 AAA Inspector Notes: *Historic.* Once a stagecoach stop, the 1840s adobe structure now houses an atrium of shops and Southwestern gourmet foods. This busy, popular restaurant serves traditional New Mexican meals, all cooked to order. Enchilada plates which come with a choice of tasty green chile or thick, rich red chile sauce are especially tasty. Features: full bar, patio dining, Sunday brunch. Address: 2410 Calle de San Albino 88046 Location: I-10 exit 142; on eastern edge of The Plaza. *Menu on AAA.com* L D

MESON DE MESILLA RESTAURANT   575/652-4953
American. Casual Dining. $9-$28 AAA Inspector Notes: Casually elegant atmosphere featuring steak, seafood and pasta. A well-priced wine list can be ordered from in the dining room or at the wine bar. Features: full bar. Address: 1803 Avenida de Mesilla 88046 Location: Just ne of jct SR 28 and 292; in Meson de Mesilla Boutique Hotel. L D CALL M

PAISANO CAFE   575/524-0211
Regional Mexican. Casual Dining. $9-$21 AAA Inspector Notes: This bustling restaurant serves Old Mexico classics with a creative local flair. An enjoyable selection of flavorful homemade moles is the focus of the menu. Features: beer & wine. Address: 1740 Calle de Mercado 88046 Location: I-40 exit 140 (La Mesilla), just s; in Mesilla Mercado shopping complex. B L D

SAVOY DE MESILLA   575/527-2869
International. Casual Dining. $8-$26 AAA Inspector Notes: Innovative cuisine with a global influence is served here in a casual and relaxed atmosphere which provides for an enjoyable dining experience. The liquid nitrogen ice cream is a must after dinner treat. Features: beer & wine, patio dining, Sunday brunch. Reservations: suggested. Address: 1800 Avenida de Mesilla 88005 Location: I-10 exit 140, 1 mi sw on SR 28. L D

MORIARTY pop. 1,910

AMERICAS BEST VALUE INN   (505)832-4457

Hotel
$52-$85

Address: 1316 Route 66 W 87035 **Location:** I-40 exit 194, 0.5 mi se on US 66 and I-40 business loop. Located in a commercial area. **Facility:** 26 units. 2 stories (no elevator), interior corridors. **Terms:** cancellation fee imposed. **Activities:** exercise room. **Featured Amenity: continental breakfast.**

BEST WESTERN MORIARTY HERITAGE INN
                                              (505)832-5000

Hotel
$99

AAA Benefit:
Save 10% or more every day and earn 10% bonus points!

Address: 111 Anaya Blvd 87035 **Location:** I-40 exit 194, 0.4 mi e. **Facility:** 70 units. 2 stories, interior corridors. **Pool(s):** heated indoor. **Activities:** hot tub, exercise room. **Guest Services:** coin laundry. **Featured Amenity: full hot breakfast.**

COMFORT INN   (505)832-6666

Hotel $75-$109 **Address:** 119 Route 66 E 87035 **Location:** I-40 exit 196, just s, then just e. **Facility:** 59 units. 2 stories (no elevator), interior corridors. **Amenities:** safes. **Pool(s):** heated indoor.

SUPER 8   (505)832-6730

Hotel
$62-$108

Address: 1611 W Old Route 66 87035 **Location:** I-40 exit 194, 0.5 mi e on Central Ave. **Facility:** 66 units. 2 stories (no elevator), interior corridors. **Terms:** cancellation fee imposed. **Guest Services:** coin laundry.

SHORTY'S BAR BE CUE   505/832-0400

Barbecue. Casual Dining. $4-$15 **AAA Inspector Notes:** This modest eatery is a favorite of the locals as well as travelers. Try the house specialties, barbecue beef or the succulent fried chicken. Save room for ice cream! **Address:** 1204 Main St 87035 **Location:** Center. L D

NAMBÉ PUEBLO (A-4) elev. 6,058'

NAMBÉ PUEBLO is 8 mi. s. of Española on US 84, then 2 mi. e. on SR 503. Established in the 14th century, Nambé Pueblo (in the Tewa language, the name means "people of the round earth") was a hub of cultural, economic and religious activity when Spanish colonists arrived in the 17th century. The Nambé took part in the Pueblo Revolt of 1680, an attempt to drive the colonists out of the province. Above the pueblo, Nambé Falls Recreation Area is a popular spot for camping, hiking, picnicking and boating.

Note: Still-camera photography and sketching is permitted in the recreation area but not within the pueblo. **Hours:** Pueblo open to visitors daily 8-noon and 1-5. Recreation area open Thurs.-Sun. 7-7. Phone ahead to confirm schedule. **Cost:** Pueblo free. Recreation area day use fee $10. Still-camera photography fee $5. Contact the ranger station for fees for other recreational activities. **Phone:** (505) 455-2304 for the ranger station, or (505) 455-2036 for the tribal office.

OHKAY OWINGEH (A-4) elev. 5,660'

Explorer and New Mexico colonial governor Juan de Oñate established the first Spanish capital of New Mexico in 1598 at the Tewa settlement of *O'ke*, where villagers gave the *conquistador* a hospitable welcome. Oñate named the pueblo San Juan de los Caballeros in honor of his horsemen. A traditional meeting ground, the pueblo became so powerful that only an *O'ke* native had the authority to declare war for the Pueblo Indians.

Today Ohkay Owingeh is one of the largest of the state's Tewa-speaking communities. Before Oñate's arrival, the village was named Ohkay Owingeh (O-keh o-WEENG-eh); in September 2005 the pueblo's tribal council restored the traditional name.

OHKAY OWINGEH is 4 mi. n.e. of Española off SR 68. Some 2,000 inhabitants of Ohkay Owingeh—headquarters for the Eight Northern Indian Pueblos Council—the pueblo is home to some 2,000 residents who farm and produce red pottery, beadwork and embroidery. Ceremonial dances are held throughout the year, and most are open to the public. The Dance of the Matachines is performed on Christmas day. **Hours:** Pueblo open to visitors Mon. -Fri. 8 -5. Phone ahead to confirm schedule. **Cost:** Pueblo entry free; inquire regarding photography restrictions and applicable fees. **Phone:** (505) 852-4400.

OHKAY CASINO RESORT HOTEL   505/747-1668

Hotel. Rates not provided. **Address:** Hwy 68 87566 **Location:** 3.4 mi n of jct US 84 and 285, 1 mi n of Española, then right at light. **Facility:** Spacious rooms with custom-made furniture, authentic Native American artwork and good clothes storage await you. The art centers of Santa Fe and Taos are each a short drive away. 101 units. 3 stories, interior corridors. **Terms:** check-in 4 pm. **Dining:** nightclub. **Pool(s):** heated outdoor. **Activities:** exercise room. **Guest Services:** valet laundry.

OJO CALIENTE (E-3) elev. 6,257'

First sought out by Native Americans and later by Spanish settlers for the alleged therapeutic qualities, Ojo Caliente Mineral Springs are still providing relief to bathers. Fueled by a volcanic aquifer, five springs each supply a different mineral: iron, sodium sulphate, lithium, soda and arsenic.

And don't discount the potential of the sacred; according to Tewa tradition, the spiritual being Poseyemo returns to the waters each year to visit her grandmother. The Tewa believed that the springs were a window from the outer world to the below world, where the people originated. Fittingly, *ojo caliente* means "hot eye." Numerous bathing facilities and pools are open to the public; for more information phone (505) 583-2233 or (800) 222-9162.

OJO CALIENTE MINERAL SPRINGS RESORT & SPA
505/583-2233

Not evaluated. **Address:** 50 Los Baños Dr 87549 **Location:** Jct US 285, just w. Facilities, services, and décor characterize a mid-scale property. Deemed sacred by Native Americans, Ojo Caliente Mineral Springs has been a gathering place for hundreds of years and is one of the oldest natural health resorts in the U.S.

WHERE TO EAT

THE ARTESIAN RESTAURANT
505/583-2233

Southwestern. Casual Dining. $10-$29 **AAA Inspector Notes:** Serving breakfast, lunch and dinner, the restaurant's creative menu features a variety of fresh, healthful, organic selections from granola and pancakes to salads, sandwiches and pasta. **Features:** beer & wine. **Address:** 50 Los Baños Dr 87549 **Location:** Jct US 285, just w; in Ojo Caliente Mineral Springs Resort & Spa.

B L D

PECOS NATIONAL HISTORICAL PARK (C-5)

Two miles south of Pecos on SR 63, Pecos National Historical Park preserves the ruins of one of the state's largest ancient pueblos as well as two mission churches built by Franciscans in the 17th and 18th centuries. After famine, diseases and emigration contributed to a population decline over the years, in 1838 the remaining Pecos people moved to Jémez Pueblo *(see place listing p. 388)*.

Visitors can explore the ruins via a 1.2-mile self-guiding trail or the 2.25-mile Civil War Battle of Glorieta Pass Trail. Guided 1- to 2-hour tours are conducted (reservations are required), and narrated van tours also are offered. The visitor center has displays of hand-carved furniture, artifacts from excavations, tin chandeliers and original artwork. You can also watch a film about Pecos history.

Picnicking is permitted. Allow 1 hour, 30 minutes minimum. Trails open daily 8-6, Memorial Day weekend-Labor Day; 8-5, rest of year. Visitor center open daily 8-6, Memorial Day weekend-Labor Day; 8-4:30, rest of year. Phone ahead to confirm winter hours. Closed Jan. 1, Thanksgiving and Christmas. Admission $7; free (ages 0-15 and Federal Recreational Lands pass holders); van tour $2. Phone (505) 757-7241.

PENASCO pop. 589

SUGAR NYMPHS BISTRO
575/587-0311

American. Casual Dining. $7-$15 **AAA Inspector Notes:** On the scenic drive between Santa Fe and Taos, this off-the-beaten-path restaurant occupies a charming old adobe mercantile and movie theater in the center of a village that feels as if it is torn from a history book. The menu focuses on fresh salads, sandwiches and fabulous baked goods. **Features:** Sunday brunch. **Address:** 15046 Hwy 75 87553 **Location:** On SR 75; center. L

PICURÍS PUEBLO (E-4) pop. 68, elev. 7,320'

Once one of the largest Tewa pueblos, Picurís (or *We-Lai*) is now among the smallest. Tribal leaders estimate the number of "people of the hidden valley" at less than 300. Picurís pottery is known for its sparkling bronze finish, which comes from mica in the regional clay.

PICURÍS PUEBLO is about 30 mi. n.e. of Española off SR 75. Believed to have been built in 1150, the pueblo was a site of unrest during the revolts of the late 17th century. Mission of San Lorenzo, erected after the 1692 reconquest, has been in use for more than 2 centuries. **Hours:** Pueblo Mon.-Fri. 8-5. Closed major holidays. **Cost:** Fees apply for sketching, filming and still-camera photography. **Phone:** (575) 587-2519.

PILAR (E-4) elev. 6,082'

The Rio Grande flows through a deep gorge between Pilar and Taos, making this one of New Mexico's prime white-water rafting areas. The presence of hot springs is evidence of ongoing seismic activity along the Rio Grande Rift, which stretches from Colorado to Mexico.

RECREATIONAL ACTIVITIES
White-water Rafting

- **Big River Raft Trips** departs from various locations. **Hours:** Daily at 9 and 1, Mar.-Sept. **Phone:** (575) 758-9711 or (800) 748-3746.
- **Far Flung Adventures** departs from Pilar Café. **Hours:** Daily late Apr.-Sept. 30. **Phone:** (575) 758-2628 or (800) 359-2627.
- **New Wave Rafting Co.** departs from either the Rio Grande Gorge Visitor Center or the County Line Meeting Place on US 68, depending on the trip. **Hours:** Daily Mar. 1-late Aug. **Phone:** (505) 579-0075 or (800) 984-1444.

AAA.com/TourBook Comments

Let Your Voice Be Heard

If your visit to a TourBook-listed property doesn't meet your expectations, tell us about it.

AAA.com/TourBookComments

PINOS ALTOS pop. 198

BEAR CREEK MOTEL & CABINS   575/388-4501

WWW **Cabin** $99-$269 **Address:** 88 Main St 88053 **Location:** 1 mi n of town on SR 15. **Facility:** 15 cabins, some kitchens. 2 stories (no elevator), exterior corridors. **Terms:** 7 day cancellation notice-fee imposed. **Activities:** hot tub.

🛜 🍴 🛏 🖥 📺 / SOME UNITS 🔌

WHERE TO EAT

THE BUCKHORN SALOON   575/538-9911

WWWW Steak. Fine Dining. $10-$38 **AAA Inspector Notes:** Historic. This original 1870s saloon makes diners feel like a real cowboy when they belly-up for a cocktail. Dinner is a little more elegant and romantic in the dining room with a fireplace, but the service remains very casual and attentive. The specialty is cooked-to-order steaks and just plain good food with portions large enough to share. Some nights there is live music in the bar. **Features:** full bar. **Reservations:** suggested. **Address:** 32 Main St 88053 **Location:** Center.

D

POJOAQUE PUEBLO (A-4) pop. 1,907, elev. 5,852'

At the joining of three rivers, Pojoaque (po-WALK-ee) was named "the water-drinking place" by the Tewa tribe. Smallpox wiped out the settlement twice before it was abandoned in 1915. Tribal members returned in the 1930s, and casino gambling now drives the local economy.

POJOAQUE PUEBLO is 8 mi. s. of Española on US 84 to SR 502 at 96 Cities of Gold Rd. The Pojoaque people's Tewa ancestors migrated to the Four Corners region in the first millennium. The Poeh Cultural Center, 78 Cities of Gold Rd., presents centuries of culture through art, archeological artifacts and history exhibits. Photography is not permitted. **Hours:** Gallery Mon.-Sat. 8-5. **Cost:** Free. **Phone:** (505) 819-2277.

PORTALES (G-6) pop. 12,280, elev. 4,009'

The discovery of shallow groundwater in 1890 ensured the prosperity of Portales. Wells provide irrigation for thousands of acres of peanuts, sorghum, cotton and other crops. Set among cottonwood trees on the eastern New Mexico high plains is Oasis State Park (see Recreation Areas Chart), 6.5 miles north on SR 467, then 2 miles west; fishing and camping are popular activities.

Blackwater Draw Archaeological Site, 7 miles northeast of Portales via US 70 to SR 467, has yielded evidence of Paleo-Indian habitation stretching back more than 11,000 years. Exhibits from the dig can be seen at the Blackwater Draw Museum on US 70; phone (575) 562-2202. The museum is maintained by Eastern New Mexico University, off US 70 at the southern edge of town. On campus is the Roosevelt County Museum, which has exhibits focusing on late 19th and early 20th-century local history; phone (575) 562-2592.

If you're looking to generate some energy, drive past the Dalley Windmill Collection, off SR 70 at 1506 S. Kilgore St. Bill Dalley began collecting windmills more than 30 years ago, and has amassed one of the largest such collections in the country. On a good windy day the turning, twirling blades of some 75 windmills are a sight to behold.

Roosevelt County Chamber of Commerce: 100 S. Ave. A, Portales, NM 88130. **Phone:** (575) 356-8541 or (800) 635-8036.

SUPER 8 PORTALES   (575)356-8511

WWW **Hotel** $50-$80 **Address:** 1805 W 2nd St 88130 **Location:** 1 mi s. **Facility:** 45 units. 2 stories (no elevator), interior corridors. **Guest Services:** coin laundry.

BIZ 🛜 🛏 🖥 📺 / SOME UNITS 🔌

RADIUM SPRINGS (I-3) pop. 1,699, elev. 3,980'

As the name suggests, Radium Springs first became a travel destination because of hot mineral waters (averaging a toasty 127 F). Apache Indians considered springs in the vicinity to be sacred, and it's said that Chief Geronimo camped here. Soldiers stationed at Fort Selden once frequented a bath house near the springs' source, a rhyolite dome along the Rio Grande. In the 1930s the Santa Fe Railroad carried weekend travelers from El Paso to the Radium Hot Springs Resort.

FORT SELDEN HISTORIC SITE is at 1280 Ft Selden Rd. The Mogollón farmed this site long before Civil War forces arrived and later became a Spanish baraje on the Camino Real. Crumbling adobe walls are all that remain of the 1865 fort which protected travelers and settlers in the Mesilla Valley from desperados and Apache Indians. After the war, African-American Buffalo Soldiers occupied the fort. As a boy in the 1880s, Gen. Douglas MacArthur also lived here while his father served as post commander. A visitor center displays military artifacts. Frontier Days at Fort Selden is celebrated the second weekend in September with period encampments and re-enactments.

Hours: Wed.-Mon. 8:30-5. Living-history demonstrations are offered the second weekend of the month. Closed Jan. 1, Easter, Thanksgiving and Christmas. **Cost:** $3; free (ages 0-16). **Phone:** (575) 526-8911.

RANCHOS DE TAOS pop. 2,518
• **Hotels & Restaurants map & index p. 447**

TRADING POST CAFE   575/758-5089 19

WW Italian. Casual Dining. $8-$38 **AAA Inspector Notes:** Italian dishes are prepared with the freshest ingredients and served in the cozy dining room or on the breezy patio at this casual dining spot. The wine list includes many good-value choices. Accomplished servers are prompt and friendly. Homemade desserts are simply a must, so be sure to save room. **Features:** beer & wine, patio dining, early bird specials. **Address:** 4179 Hwy 68 87557 **Location:** On SR 68, jct SR 518. L D

RATON (D-5) pop. 6,885, elev. 6,680'

In 1866 Uncle Dick Wootton, an enterprising local, completed 27 miles of road over Raton Pass, set up a tollgate at his ranch near the summit and charged $1.50 per wagon to use his Santa Fe Trail improvement. As the trail was the main route to the Southwest, Wootton fared well; his bank deposits were allegedly whiskey kegs full of silver dollars.

By 1880 the stopover 7 miles south of the summit of Raton (ra-TONE) Pass had evolved into a full-fledged community. Surviving Victorian-style buildings along First Street are a reminder of Raton's late 19th-century mining and railroad heyday; one example is the 1890s-era Palace Hotel is at First and Cook streets.

Sugarite Canyon State Park *(see Recreation Areas Chart)*, 10 miles northeast via SR 72, offers lakes and picnic sites.

Raton Chamber and Economic Development Council, Inc.: 100 Clayton Rd., Raton, NM 87740. **Phone:** (575) 445-3689.

Self-guiding tours: Brochures detailing tours of the city's historic district are available from the chamber and economic development council.

NRA WHITTINGTON CENTER is 4 mi. w. of I-25 exit 446 on US 64. This 33,300-acre shooting facility offers a number of gun ranges. An unaltered section of the Santa Fe Trail cuts through the complex. A museum also is on site. **Time:** Allow 1 hour minimum. **Hours:** Ranges open daily dawn-dusk. Museum Mon.-Fri. 8-5, Sat.-Sun. 9-4. Phone ahead for holiday schedule. Closed major holidays. **Cost:** Visitor center free. Gun ranges $20. Other fees may apply. **Phone:** (575) 445-3615 or (800) 494-4853.

RATON MUSEUM is at 108 S. Second St. Photographs, household articles, railroad and coal camp memorabilia and other items depict 19th-century life. **Hours:** Tues.-Sat. 9-5, Memorial Day-Labor Day; Wed.-Sat. 10-4, rest of year. Closed major holidays. **Cost:** Free. **Phone:** (575) 445-8979.

BEST WESTERN PLUS RATON HOTEL   (575)445-8501

Hotel
$119-$179

AAA Benefit:
Save 10% or more every day and earn 10% bonus points!

Address: 473 Clayton Rd 87740 **Location:** I-25 exit 451, just w. **Facility:** 72 units. 2 stories, interior/exterior corridors. **Dining:** Mulligan's, see separate listing. **Pool(s):** heated indoor. **Activities:** exercise room. **Guest Services:** coin laundry.

HOLIDAY INN EXPRESS HOTEL & SUITES   (575)445-1500
WWW **Hotel** $140-$190 **Address:** 101 Card Ave 87740 **Location:** I-25 exit 450, just w. **Facility:** 80 units. 2 stories, interior corridors. **Amenities:** *Some:* video games. **Pool(s):** heated indoor. **Activities:** hot tub, exercise room. **Guest Services:** coin laundry.

RATON PASS INN   575/445-3641
[fyi] Not evaluated. **Address:** 308 Canyon Dr 87740 **Location:** I-25 exit 454, 0.8 mi s. Facilities, services, and décor characterize an economy property.

WHERE TO EAT

K-BOB'S STEAKHOUSE   575/445-2548
WW **Steak. Casual Dining.** $8-$19 **AAA Inspector Notes:** The steakhouse prepares a great variety of plump, juicy fillets. A fireplace opens up into both dining rooms, and antique clocks decorate the walls. Rustic wagon-wheel chandeliers illuminate the room. **Features:** beer & wine. **Address:** 1228 S 2nd St 87740 **Location:** Jct US 87 N and 2nd St, just w. [L] [D]

MULLIGAN'S   575/445-8501
WW **American. Casual Dining.** $7-$26 **AAA Inspector Notes:** This restaurant features a contemporary atmosphere with a center bar and an expansive view. A casual menu lists salads, sandwiches, burgers, barbecue, pizzas and pasta. **Features:** full bar. **Address:** 473 Clayton Rd 87740 **Location:** I-25 exit 451, just w; in BEST WESTERN PLUS Raton Hotel. [B] [L] [D]

PAPPAS SWEET SHOP RESTAURANT   575/445-9811
WW **American. Casual Dining.** $7-$28 **AAA Inspector Notes:** This restaurant's well-rounded menu offers spaghetti, steak, seafood and sandwiches. Diners also find displays of antiques, collectibles and items related to the family-owned restaurant and its early years of candy and ice cream making. **Features:** wine only. **Reservations:** suggested, in season. **Address:** 1201 S 2nd St 87740 **Location:** I-25 exit 451, 0.5 mi w on US 64 and 87, then just s on US 64. [L] [D]

THE SANDS RESTAURANT   575/445-4024
WW **Mexican. Family Dining.** $7-$21 **AAA Inspector Notes:** Sharing space on the menu are generous portions of Mexican favorites and seafood and steak dishes. **Features:** beer & wine. **Address:** 350 Clayton Rd 87740 **Location:** I-25 exit 451, just w. [L] [D]

RED RIVER (E-4) pop. 477, elev. 8,650'
• Hotels p. 404 • Restaurants p. 404

Gold drew early settlers to this former frontier town on the northeastern face of Wheeler Peak. Today's visitors are drawn by the prospect of fun; skiing and snowmobiling are popular winter pursuits, with hiking, fishing and mountain biking taking over in the summer.

Red River Visitor Center: 101 W. River St., P.O. Box 870, Red River, NM 87558. **Phone:** (575) 754-3030 or (877) 754-1708.

RECREATIONAL ACTIVITIES
Skiing

• **Enchanted Forest Cross Country Ski Area** is 3 mi. e. of downtown. **Hours:** Daily mid-Nov. to late Mar. **Phone:** (575) 754-6112 for ski area.

• **Red River Ski & Summer Area** is at 400 Pioneer Rd. **Hours:** Daily 7:30-5. Lift operates 9-4, Memorial Day-Labor Day; Mon.-Fri. 9-4, Sat.-Sun. 9-5, rest of year (weather permitting). **Phone:** (575) 754-2223.

BEST WESTERN RIVERS EDGE   (575)754-1766

Hotel
$89-$199

AAA Benefit:
Save 10% or more every day and earn 10% bonus points!

Address: 301 W River St 87558 **Location:** 1 blk s of W Main St (SR 38); center. **Facility:** 31 units, some kitchens. 2 stories (no elevator), exterior corridors. **Parking:** winter plug-ins. **Terms:** 7 day cancellation notice, resort fee. **Activities:** hot tub, fishing, downhill & cross country skiing, snowmobiling. **Guest Services:** coin laundry. **Featured Amenity: continental breakfast.**

THE RIVERSIDE LODGE & CABINS   575/754-2252

Historic Motel. Rates not provided. **Address:** 201 E Main St 87558 **Location:** On SR 38; center. **Facility:** Along the Red River guests can choose from individual or duplex housekeeping cabins and apartments. Some lodge rooms are available, many with fireplaces. 38 units, some two bedrooms, three bedrooms and kitchens. 1-2 stories (no elevator), exterior corridors. **Parking:** winter plug-ins. **Activities:** hot tub, fishing, downhill & cross country skiing, snowmobiling, playground. **Guest Services:** coin laundry.

WHERE TO EAT

CAPO'S   575/754-6297

Italian. Family Dining. $10-$28 **AAA Inspector Notes:** Hearty portions of Italian favorites are featured at this family restaurant. **Features:** beer & wine, patio dining. **Address:** 110 Pioneer Rd 87558 **Location:** Jct River St; across from ski lift. **Parking:** on-site and street. [L] [D]

MOUNTAIN TREASURES BISTRO   575/754-2700

Sandwiches. Quick Serve. $5-$11 **AAA Inspector Notes:** The fragrance of fresh-baked bread lures patrons in for homemade soups, sandwiches and baked goods. Also on the menu are great smoothies and an excellent selection of gourmet coffee. **Address:** 121 E Main St 87558 **Location:** Center. [B] [L]

RIO RANCHO (F-3) pop. 87,521, elev. 5,550'
• Hotels & Restaurants map & index p. 342

J&R VINTAGE AUTO MUSEUM is off I-25 exit 242, 2.4 mi. w. on US 550, then .5 mi. s. to 3650A SR 528. More than 65 restored vintage cars are displayed, including several that have competed in the Great American Race. Highlights include a 1917 Marmon, a 1928 Model A Ford and a 1932 Packard. **Time:** Allow 30 minutes minimum. **Hours:** Mon.-Sat. 10-5. Closed major holidays. **Cost:** $6; $5 (ages 55+); $3 (ages 6-12). **Phone:** (505) 867-2881.

Request roadside assistance

in a click — online or using

the AAA or CAA apps

EXTENDED STAY AMERICA ALBUQUERQUE-RIO RANCHO
                                                505/792-1338

Extended Stay Motel. Rates not provided. **Address:** 2608 The American Rd NW 87124 **Location:** Corner of SR 528 and Cottonwood Dr, just n, just w. **Facility:** 101 efficiencies. 3 stories, interior corridors. **Guest Services:** coin laundry.

HILTON GARDEN INN ALBUQUERQUE NORTH/RIO RANCHO
                                                (505)896-1111

Hotel $89-$189 **Address:** 1771 Rio Rancho Blvd 87124 **Location:** I-25 exit 233 (Alameda Blvd), then n (which becomes SR 528/Rio Rancho Blvd). Across from Intel; convenient to retail area. **Facility:** 129 units. 4 stories, interior corridors. **Terms:** 1-night minimum stay, cancellation fee imposed. **Pool(s):** heated indoor. **Activities:** hot tub, exercise room. **Guest Services:** valet and coin laundry.

AAA Benefit:
Members save up to 10%!

WHERE TO EAT

FEDERICO'S MEXICAN FOOD   505/891-7218

Mexican. Quick Serve. $3-$12 **AAA Inspector Notes:** This quick-serve restaurant, which offers a great variety of Mexican drinks dishes up hearty portions of such specialties as the shrimp cocktail chunks of avocado, cucumbers and tomatoes in a spicy broth. **Address:** 1590 Deborah Rd SE 87124 **Location:** Jct SR 528 and Barbara Loop SE, just e. [L] [D]

O'HARE'S GRILLE & PUB   505/896-0123

American. Casual Dining. $7-$25 **AAA Inspector Notes:** Guests can unwind in this busy, cheerful place with a meal complemented by a choice from the large selection of beers and spirits. The friendly pub attracts folks who work in the neighborhood. A short lunchtime wait is typical. **Features:** full bar. **Address:** 4100 Southern Blvd SE 87124 **Location:** Jct SR 528 and Southern Blvd; in Rio Rancho Shopping Center. [L] [D] CALL

RODEO (J-1) pop. 101, elev. 4,128'

The passing of the El Paso and Southwestern Railroad resulted in many ghost towns along the former line, but Rodeo was one of the few that survived. Built in 1902 to connect El Paso with copper mines in Bisbee, Ariz., the trains stopped running in 1952.

CHIRICAHUA GALLERY is at 5 Pine St. Works by local artists and artisans include paintings, photographs, ceramics, basketry, woodwork, quilted items, leather work, silver jewelry and pottery. **Time:** Allow 30 minutes minimum. **Hours:** Tues.-Sat. 10-4 closed Thanksgiving, Christmas and Dec. 31. **Cost:** Free. **Phone:** (575) 557-2225.

ROSWELL (H-5) pop. 48,366, elev. 3,573'
• Hotels p. 406 • Restaurants p. 407

Roswell's economy is based on agriculture manufacturing, oil production—and little green men. Long fueled by reports of flying saucers, tourism is big business. The city's primary intergalactic port the International UFO Museum & Research Center showcases a variety of exhibits documenting what has come to be known as the "Roswell Incident"—the military's supposed recovery (and subsequent cover-up) of extraterrestrial debris from a local ranch in 1947.

Additionally, each July the Roswell UFO Festival attracts curious earthlings with 4 days of alien-inspired activities, including a costume contest, a parade, and lectures given by UFO investigators and witnesses.

While it's *possible* you'll have your own close encounter of the third kind in the self-proclaimed "Alien Capital of the World," you're more likely to meet a few undergrads than a bug-eyed space creature. Roswell is home to a branch of Eastern New Mexico University as well as the prestigious New Mexico Military Institute, a 4-year high school and 2-year junior college founded in 1891. The latter institution boasts such alumni as journalists Sam Donaldson and Chuck Roberts, founder of the Hilton Hotels chain Conrad Hilton and Pulitzer Prize-winning author Paul Horgan.

The Roswell Symphony Orchestra contributes to the cultural scene. Many performances take place at Pearson Auditorium, 426 N. Main St. For schedule information, phone (575) 623-5882.

While your eyes will likely be fixed on the skies much of the time, be sure to take a breather from stargazing to explore some of the region's alluring Blue Planet landscapes. A handful of bicycle trails highlight scenic views, including the 1.5-mile Hondo River Recreation Trail, accessed via the western terminus just east of Hendricks and S. Main streets or the eastern terminus off E. Second Street.

The 5-mile Spring River Recreation Trail runs between Enchanted Lands Park, 306 N. Sycamore Ave., and Spring River Park and Zoo. There are pretty, tree-lined 1- and 2-mile bicycle paths at Cielo Grande Recreational Area, off W. College Boulevard.

Established in 1933, Bottomless Lakes State Park *(see Recreation Areas Chart)* is 15 miles southeast via US 380 and SR 409. New Mexico's first state park comprises a series of water-filled sinkholes ranging in depth from 17 to 90 feet and bordered by high red bluffs. The deepest, Lea Lake, is suitable for swimming and scuba diving. It's stocked with rainbow trout in winter, and in summer you can traverse the lake's greenish-blue waters aboard a rented paddleboat. Other recreational pursuits at the park include camping, hiking and wildlife viewing.

Roswell Chamber of Commerce: 131 W. Second St., Roswell, NM 88201. **Phone:** (575) 623-5695.

ANDERSON MUSEUM OF CONTEMPORARY ART is at 409 E. College Blvd. The museum displays the collective work of the Roswell Artist-In-Residence Program, which attracts visual artists from around the world. The permanent collection includes more than 400 paintings, sculptures, photographs and mixed-media pieces. **Time:** Allow 1 hour minimum. **Hours:** Mon.-Fri. 9-4, Sat.-Sun. 1-5. Closed major holidays. **Cost:** Free. **Phone:** (575) 623-5600.

BITTER LAKE NATIONAL WILDLIFE REFUGE is 7 mi. e. to 4200 E. Pine Lodge Rd. The refuge occupies more than 24,000 acres of grassland, ponds and desert shrubs. A 6-mile drive tour offers glimpses of wintering waterfowl, sandhill cranes, roadrunners, quails and more than 300 other species of birds. Salt Creek Wilderness can be entered only on foot or horseback; the access point is off US 70 near the Pecos River. The best time for viewing large waterfowl is October through November.

The refuge also supports one of the most diverse populations of dragonflies in North America, and the Dragonfly Festival is celebrated every year in September. **Hours:** Daily dawn-dusk (weather permitting). Visitor center Mon.-Sat. 8-4. **Cost:** Free. **Phone:** (575) 625-4011.

INTERNATIONAL UFO MUSEUM & RESEARCH CENTER is at 114 N. Main St. The center is dedicated to the study of Unidentified Flying Objects (UFOs) thought to be from other planets. Exhibits include paintings, murals and dioramas depicting the purported 1947 crash of a UFO in Roswell along with other alleged sightings of alien beings and their spacecraft. On the premises is a research library with extensive works dealing with UFOs. **Time:** Allow 1 hour, 30 minutes minimum. **Hours:** Daily 9-5. **Cost:** $5; $3 (ages 65+ and military with ID); $2 (ages 5-15). **Phone:** (575) 625-9495.

LT. GEN. DOUGLAS L. MCBRIDE MUSEUM is at W. College Blvd. and N. Main St., on the campus of New Mexico Military Institute. Displays examine the history of the New Mexico Military Institute, founded in 1891. Also featured are exhibits pertaining to the historical service of New Mexicans as well as the institute's graduates. **Hours:** Mon.-Fri. 7:30-4:30, Oct.-May; 7:30-3:30, rest of year. Closed major holidays. **Cost:** Donations. **Phone:** (575) 624-8380.

ROSWELL MUSEUM AND ART CENTER is in the Civic Center Plaza at 11th and Main sts. Known for its New Mexico modernism collection, the museum showcases Southwestern culture through historical artifacts and fine art. Highlights include works by Andrew Dasburg, Stuart Davis, Marsden Hartley, Victor Higgins, Georgia O'Keeffe, Roswell landscape artist Peter Hurd and the Rogers and Mary Ellen Aston Collection of the American West.

The Goddard wing has a re-creation of Dr. Robert Goddard's early laboratory with displays about rocketry and space. The Robert H. Goddard Planetarium presents monthly astronomy programs and multimedia presentations. **Hours:** Mon.-Sat. 9-5, Sun. and holidays 1-5. Closed Jan. 1, Thanksgiving and Christmas. **Cost:** Donations. A fee is charged for special events. **Phone:** (575) 624-6744.

SPRING RIVER PARK AND ZOO is 1 mi. e. off US 285/Main St. on College Blvd., or 1 mi. n. of US 380/Second St. on Atkinson St. More than 150 animals and birds represent 60 species. Within the 36-acre zoo are a wooden-horse carousel, a miniature train ride and a children's fishing lake. **Time:** Allow 1 hour minimum. **Hours:** Daily 10-dusk. Train rides offered Wed.-Sun. 1-6, late May to mid-Aug.; Sat.-Sun and Mon. holidays 1-6, Easter-late May and mid-Aug. through Sept. 30. Closed Christmas. **Cost:** Free. Train rides and antique carousel 50c. **Phone:** (575) 624-6760.

BEST WESTERN EL RANCHO PALACIO (575)622-2721

Hotel
$80-$110

AAA Benefit:
Save 10% or more every day and earn 10% bonus points!

Address: 2205 N Main St 88201 **Location:** Jct US 70 and 285, 1.8 mi n. **Facility:** 45 units. 2 stories (no elevator); exterior corridors. **Pool(s):** heated outdoor.

BEST WESTERN SALLY PORT INN & SUITES
(575)622-6430

Hotel
$109-$149

AAA Benefit:
Save 10% or more every day and earn 10% bonus points!

Address: 2000 N Main St 88201 **Location:** Jct US 70 and 285, 1.5 mi n. **Facility:** 124 units. 2 stories (no elevator), interior corridors. **Terms:** cancellation fee imposed. **Pool(s):** heated indoor. **Activities:** sauna, hot tub, exercise room. **Guest Services:** valet and coin laundry.

CANDLEWOOD SUITES ROSWELL (575)623-4300
Extended Stay Hotel $109-$159 **Address:** 4 Military Heights Dr 88201 **Location:** Jct US 70 and 285, just n of US 385. **Facility:** 87 efficiencies. 4 stories, interior corridors. **Terms:** cancellation fee imposed. **Pool(s):** heated outdoor. **Activities:** hot tub, exercise room. **Guest Services:** valet and coin laundry.

COMFORT INN (575)623-4567

Hotel
$89-$94

Address: 3595 N Main St 88201 **Location:** Jct US 70 and 285, 3 mi n. **Facility:** 55 units. 2 stories (no elevator), interior corridors. **Amenities:** safes. **Pool(s):** heated indoor. **Activities:** hot tub. **Guest Services:** valet and coin laundry. **Featured Amenity:** continental breakfast.

COMFORT SUITES ROSWELL (575)623-5501
Hotel $89-$129 **Address:** 3610 N Main St 88201 **Location:** Jct US 70 and 285 N, 1 mi s. **Facility:** 68 units. 3 stories, interior corridors. **Amenities:** safes. **Pool(s):** heated indoor. **Activities:** hot tub, exercise room. **Guest Services:** valet and coin laundry.

DAYS INN (575)623-4021

Hotel
$70-$110

Address: 1310 N Main St 88201 **Location:** Jct US 70 and 285, 0.8 mi n. **Facility:** 62 units. 2 stories (no elevator), exterior corridors. **Pool(s):** outdoor. **Activities:** limited exercise equipment. **Featured Amenity: breakfast buffet.**

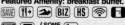

FAIRFIELD INN & SUITES BY MARRIOTT (575)624-1300
Hotel $103-$198 **Address:** 1201 N Main St 88201 **Location:** Jct US 380 and 285, 0.7 mi n. **Facility:** 67 units. 3 stories, interior corridors. **Pool(s):** heated outdoor. **Activities:** hot tub, exercise room. **Guest Services:** valet and coin laundry.

AAA Benefit:
Members save 5% or more!

HAMPTON INN & SUITES BY HILTON (575)623-5151

Hotel
$109-$189

Hampton
by HILTON

AAA Benefit:
Members save up to 10%!

Address: 3607 N Main St 88201 **Location:** Jct US 70 and 285 N, 1 mi s. **Facility:** 70 units. 3 stories, interior corridors. **Terms:** 1-7 night minimum stay, cancellation fee imposed. **Amenities:** video games. **Pool(s):** heated indoor. **Activities:** sauna, hot tub, exercise room. **Guest Services:** valet and coin laundry. **Featured Amenity: full hot breakfast.**

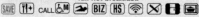

HOLIDAY INN 575/623-3216
Hotel. Rates not provided. **Address:** 3620 N Main St 88201 **Location:** Jct US 70 and 285 N, 1 mi s. **Facility:** 93 units. 4 stories, interior corridors. **Pool(s):** heated indoor. **Activities:** hot tub, exercise room. **Guest Services:** valet and coin laundry.

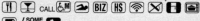

HOLIDAY INN EXPRESS & SUITES 575/627-9900
Hotel. Rates not provided. **Address:** 2300 N Main St 88201 **Location:** Jct US 70 and 285, 1.8 mi n. **Facility:** 80 units, some efficiencies. 3 stories, interior corridors. **Pool(s):** heated indoor. **Activities:** sauna, hot tub, exercise room. **Guest Services:** valet and coin laundry.

TOWNEPLACE SUITES BY MARRIOTT (575)622-5460
Extended Stay Hotel $98-$209 **Address:** 180 E 19th St 88201 **Location:** Jct Main St, just e. **Facility:** 71 kitchen units, some two bedrooms. 3 stories, interior corridors. **Pool(s):** heated outdoor. **Activities:** exercise room. **Guest Services:** valet and coin laundry.

AAA Benefit:
Members save 5% or more!

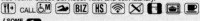

WHERE TO EAT

CATTLE BARON STEAK & SEAFOOD   575/622-2465

▼▼▼ American. Casual Dining. $8-$27 **AAA Inspector Notes:** A scrumptious array of menu selections includes steak, seafood, chicken and prime rib as well as desserts such as caramel apple pie. An upscale Western decor includes wood trim and distinctive chandeliers made from deer antlers. **Features:** full bar. **Address:** 1113 N Main St 88201 **Location:** US 380 and 285, 0.7 mi n.

L D

GALACTIC SUSHI   575/910-1959

▼▼▼ Sushi. Casual Dining. $15-$50 **AAA Inspector Notes:** Star Trek fans will appreciate the memorabilia lining the walls and the TV showing movies and reruns. Sushi fans will appreciate the fine quality of fish prepared before your eyes by skilled Japanese chefs. **Features:** beer & wine. **Address:** 4311C N Main St 88201 **Location:** Jct US 70 and 285 N, just s.   L D

LEMON GRASS THAI CUISINE   575/208-0411

▼▼▼ Thai. Casual Dining. $7-$15 **AAA Inspector Notes:** Enjoy authentic Thai cuisine at this restaurant. The green curry is especially savory and loaded with spicy peppers. The banana and coconut dessert egg roll, served with a side of chocolate sauce, is delightful. **Features:** beer & wine. **Address:** 610 S Main St 88201 **Location:** Just s of jct McGaffey St; center.   L D

LOS CERRITOS   575/622-4919

▼▼▼ Mexican. Casual Dining. $7-$17 **AAA Inspector Notes:** Your meal begins with fresh, homemade tortilla chips and out-of-this-world salsa. The menu features a large selection of favorites, from tacos, burritos and enchiladas to a variety of Mexican-style seafood. A cool and light flan is a nice finish. **Features:** beer & wine, happy hour. **Address:** 2103 N Main St 88201 **Location:** 1.8 mi n on US 70 and 285.   B L D

PASTA CAFE ITALIAN BISTRO   575/624-1111

▼▼▼ Italian. Casual Dining. $10-$22 **AAA Inspector Notes:** The menu at this bistro comprises tasty classic pasta dishes, pizza selections and hot appetizers, as well as a limited number of steak, veal, seafood and pork entrées. Two types of fresh bread tempt patrons. A small bar area is off the dining room and features an excellent selection of wines by the glass. **Features:** full bar, early bird specials. **Address:** 1208 N Main St 88201 **Location:** Jct N Main and 12th sts.   L D CALL ⬚M

PEPPERS GRILL & BAR   575/623-1700

▼▼▼ American. Casual Dining. $7-$18 **AAA Inspector Notes:** This restaurant prepares a good variety of appetizers, burgers, salads, pasta, sandwiches and traditional Mexican dishes, as well as steak and seafood entrées. Entertainers perform on the patio Friday and Saturday in summer. **Features:** full bar, patio dining, senior menu, happy hour. **Address:** 500 N Main St 88201 **Location:** US 70 and 285; corner of Main and 6th sts.   L D

RIB CRIB BBQ AND GRILL   575/625-1200

▼▼▼ Barbecue. Casual Dining. $6-$17 **AAA Inspector Notes:** Most guests need extra napkins to tackle the ribs, brisket, ham, pork and chicken selections. The menu also lists sandwiches and wraps, along with tempting sides and large desserts. The decor is decidedly Western. **Features:** beer & wine. **Address:** 4495 N Main St 88202 **Location:** Just s of SR 48.   L D

TIA JUANA'S MEXICAN GRILLE & CANTINA   575/627-6113

▼▼▼ Mexican. Casual Dining. $7-$21 **AAA Inspector Notes:** Hearty portions of flavorful Mexican favorites are served in a colorful and lively atmosphere. The homemade flour tortillas are a must. **Features:** full bar. **Address:** 3601 N Main St 88201 **Location:** On US 70 and 285, 3 mi n.   L D

TINNIE'S MERCANTILE & DELI   575/622-2031

▼ Deli. Quick Serve. $5-$9 **AAA Inspector Notes:** This casual café features house-baked breads and pastries, hearty sandwiches, delectable salads and comforting soups. Enjoy shopping the mercantile offering a wide selection of quality merchandise. **Features:** patio dining. **Address:** 412 W 2nd St 88201 **Location:** Just w of Main St.

L

RUIDOSO (H-4) pop. 8,029, elev. 6,720'
• **Restaurants p. 409**

With skiing in winter, golfing, horseback riding, camping, hiking and fishing in spring and summer and the fall foliage beauty of aspen trees highlighting autumn, Ruidoso is among New Mexico's premier year-round mountain playgrounds. It's such a popular destination, in fact, that making travel reservations several months in advance is advisable for holiday weekends.

The natural backdrop—the heavily forested Sacramento Mountains within Lincoln National Forest *(see place listing p. 395)*—is sublime. The resort community that now extends for 10 miles along the Ruidoso River had inauspicious beginnings in the 1890s as a trading post, and an old waterwheel from that era still stands on Main Street.

Ruidoso Valley Chamber of Commerce and Visitors Center: 720 Sudderth Dr., Ruidoso, NM 88345. **Phone:** (575) 257-7395 or (877) 784-3676.

RECREATIONAL ACTIVITIES
Skiing
- **Ski Apache** is 16 mi. n.w. at the end of SR 532. **Hours:** Daily 9-4, Thanksgiving-early Apr. **Phone:** (575) 464-3600, or (575) 464-1234 for ski conditions.

BEST WESTERN PLUS RUIDOSO INN   (575)257-3600

▼▼▼▼ Hotel $69-$209

 AAA Benefit: Save 10% or more every day and earn 10% bonus points!

Address: 97 Camelot Dr 88345 **Location:** US 70, just w of jct Sudderth Dr, just n. **Facility:** 57 units. 3 stories, interior corridors. **Terms:** check-in 4 pm, cancellation fee imposed. **Pool(s):** heated indoor. **Activities:** hot tub, playground, picnic facilities, exercise room. **Guest Services:** coin laundry.

COMFORT INN-RUIDOSO   (575)257-2770

▼▼▼ Hotel $69-$214

Address: 2709 Sudderth Dr 88345 **Location:** On SR 48, just w, then s. **Facility:** 54 units. 3 stories, interior corridors. **Amenities:** safes. **Activities:** hot tub, exercise room. **Guest Services:** coin laundry. **Featured Amenity:** full hot breakfast.

CROWN POINT CONDOMINIUMS   (575)257-7641

▼▼▼ Condominium $125-$225 **Address:** 220 Crown Dr 88355 **Location:** US 70 W; at entrance to Camelot subdivision. **Facility:** Perched on a high mountain ridge, the attractive vacation condos offer spectacular views of the town below as well as the pine-covered mountains. 60 condominiums. 2 stories (no elevator), exterior corridors. **Terms:** check-in 4 pm, 2 night minimum stay, 3 day cancellation notice-fee imposed. **Pool(s):** heated indoor. **Activities:** hot tub, tennis, exercise room. **Guest Services:** coin laundry.

HOTEL RUIDOSO-MIDTOWN (575)257-2007

▽▽▽ Hotel $69-$209

Address: 110 Chase St 88345 **Location:** Just s of jct Sudderth Dr. **Facility:** 55 units. 3 stories, interior corridors. **Terms:** cancellation fee imposed. **Pool(s):** heated indoor. **Activities:** hot tub, exercise room. **Guest Services:** coin laundry. **Featured Amenity:** full hot breakfast.

SAVE ▮▮+ CALL ⬥M ⟲ BIZ HS
🛜 ✕ ▯ ▭ ▱

THE LODGE AT SIERRA BLANCA (575)258-550▮

▽▽▽▽ **Hotel** $119-$239 **Address:** 107 Sierra Blanca Dr 8834▮ **Location:** Jct Sudderth Dr. **Facility:** 118 units, some two bedroom and efficiencies. 3 stories, interior corridors. **Terms:** 2 night minimur stay - seasonal and/or weekends, cancellation fee imposed, reso▮ fee. **Pool(s):** heated indoor. **Activities:** hot tub, regulation gol▮ tennis, playground, exercise room, massage. **Guest Services:** coi▮ laundry.

🍽 CALL ⬥M ⟲ BIZ 🛜 ✕ 🎥 ▮ ▭ ▱
/ SOME UNITS 🅢▮

RUIDOSO MOUNTAIN INN 575/257-373▮

▽▽ **Hotel.** Rates not provided. **Address:** 400 W Hwy 7▮ 88345 **Location:** US 70, just w of jct Sudderth Dr. **Facility:** 102 units 3 stories, interior corridors. **Pool(s):** heated outdoor. **Activities:** h▮ tub. **Guest Services:** coin laundry.

CALL ⬥M ⟲ BIZ 🛜 ▮ ▭ ▱ / SOME UNITS 🅢▮

▼ See AAA listing p. 398 ▼

VILLAGE LODGE
(575)258-5442

▼▼▼
Condominium
$89-$199

Address: 1000 Mechem Dr 88345 **Location:** 2 mi n on SR 48. **Facility:** The facility consists of spacious units with living rooms and full kitchens. Guests will have access to the clubhouse. 30 condominiums. 2 stories (no elevator), exterior corridors. **Terms:** check-in 4 pm, 2 night minimum stay - weekends, 7 day cancellation notice-fee imposed. **Activities:** hot tub, massage. **Guest Services:** coin laundry.
SAVE 🛜 ✕ 🛢 🖥 💻

WHISPERING PINE CABINS
575/257-4311

▼▼▼ **Cabin.** Rates not provided. **Address:** 422 Main Rd 88345 **Location:** 0.9 mi w of jct SR 48 and Sudderth Dr. **Facility:** 42 cabins, some kitchens. 1 story, exterior corridors. **Activities:** hot tub, fishing.
🛜 🛢 🖥 💻 / SOME UNITS 🔲 ⚿

RUIDOSO LODGE CABINS
575/257-2510

fyi Not evaluated. **Address:** 300 Main Rd 88345 **Location:** 0.7 mi w on Upper Canyon Rd. Facilities, services, and décor characterize a mid-scale property.

STORY BOOK CABINS
575/257-2115

fyi Not evaluated. **Address:** 410 Main Rd 88345 **Location:** 1 mi w on Upper Canyon Rd. Facilities, services, and décor characterize a mid-scale property.

WHERE TO EAT

BLUE GOOSE CAFE
575/257-8652

▼▼ Sandwiches Soup. Casual Dining. $7-$12 **AAA Inspector Notes:** This bustling café offers hearty sandwiches, made-from-scratch soups and colorful salads. The homemade desserts are worth a visit and the lemon pie is especially luscious. **Address:** 201 Eagle Dr 88345 **Location:** Jct Sudderth Dr, just n. L

CAFE RIO
575/257-7746

▼ Italian. Casual Dining. $5-$20 **AAA Inspector Notes:** This main-street cafe serves pizza, salads, jambalaya and a fine selection of sandwiches. There is a great selection of ice cream and desserts, including cakes baked on site. **Address:** 2547 Sudderth Dr 88345 **Location:** Center. **Parking:** street only. L D

CASA BLANCA
575/257-2495

▼▼ Mexican. Casual Dining. $10-$27 **AAA Inspector Notes:** A local favorite, the restaurant features generous portions of flavorful Mexican specialties. A frosty margarita will definitely cool the taste buds after a mouthful of spicy salsa and warm tortilla chips or the house favorite, green chile chicken enchiladas. Save room for the sopaipilla. **Features:** full bar. **Address:** 501 Mechem Dr 88345 **Location:** 1 mi n on SR 48 (Mechem Dr). B L D

CATTLE BARON STEAK & SEAFOOD
575/257-9355

▼▼ American. Casual Dining. $9-$28 **AAA Inspector Notes:** A scrumptious array of menu selections includes steak, seafood, chicken and prime rib as well as desserts such as caramel apple pie. An upscale Western decor includes wood trim and distinctive chandeliers made from deer antlers. **Features:** full bar. **Address:** 657 Sudderth Dr 88345 **Location:** 1.3 mi s. L D

CORNERSTONE BAKERY CAFE
575/257-1842

▼▼ Breads/Pastries. Family Dining. $8-$12 **AAA Inspector Notes:** The bakery and cafe has a bright, clean look. Sandwiches, soups and desserts are perfect for a casual lunch. Bakery items, such as the strawberry-filled croissant, are exceptional. **Address:** 359 Sudderth Dr 88345 **Location:** 1 mi n of jct US 70 and Sudderth Dr. B L

GRACE O'MALLEY'S IRISH PUB
575/630-0219

▼▼ Irish. Casual Dining. $7-$25 **AAA Inspector Notes:** This large pub is lively with locals and visitors alike, featuring a menu of authentic Irish pub fare. Guinness on tap and Guinness ice cream are treats. **Features:** full bar, patio dining. **Address:** 2331 Sudderth Dr 88345 **Location:** Center. L D LATE CALL 🅶M

GRILL CALIENTE
575/630-0224

▼▼▼ Mexican. Casual Dining. $16-$30 **AAA Inspector Notes:** Popular with locals, this lively café serves modern interpretations of regional specialties. The chile relleno stuffed with cheese and roasted vegetables is a flavorful vegetarian creation and the grilled peaches with ice cream is a delicious summer treat. **Features:** beer & wine, patio dining. **Address:** 2800 Sudderth Dr 88345 **Location:** Just e of Mechem Dr; downtown. L D 🍴

K-BOB'S STEAKHOUSE
575/378-0025

▼▼ Steak. Casual Dining. $7-$23 **AAA Inspector Notes:** The steakhouse prepares a great variety of plump, juicy fillets. A fireplace opens up into both dining rooms, and antique clocks decorate the walls. Rustic wagon-wheel chandeliers illuminate the room. **Features:** beer & wine. **Address:** 157 W Hwy 70 88345 **Location:** Jct US 70 and SR 48, just e. L D

LINCOLN COUNTY GRILL
575/257-7669

▼ American. Casual Dining. $8-$14 **AAA Inspector Notes:** This bustling mom-and-pop café is well known for hearty breakfasts or juicy burgers and homemade sweet potato french fries. A thick chocolate milk shake is a special treat. **Features:** beer & wine, patio dining. **Address:** 2717 Sudderth Dr 88345 **Location:** Jct Chase St; center. B L D

LUCY'S MEXICALI RESTAURANT & CANTINA
575/257-8754

▼▼ Mexican. Casual Dining. $8-$20 **AAA Inspector Notes:** The house margarita is a good pick among 25 tasty recipes, all of which go well with excellent New Mexican specialties. A mariachi band plays once a week at this spot, which has been in operation for more than 30 years. **Features:** full bar, happy hour. **Address:** 2408 Sudderth Dr 88345 **Location:** Center. L D

MICHELENA'S ITALIAN RESTAURANT
575/257-5753

▼▼ Italian. Family Dining. $6-$18 **AAA Inspector Notes:** This bustling family restaurant offers a good value and serves up plentiful helpings of your favorite Italian specialties. **Features:** Sunday brunch. **Address:** 2703 Sudderth Dr 88345 **Location:** Center. **Parking:** on-site and street. L D

THE RANCHERS STEAK AND SEAFOOD
575/257-7540

▼▼▼ Steak Seafood. Casual Dining. $9-$45 **AAA Inspector Notes:** A thoughtfully crafted menu features a fine selection of steaks and seafood cooked to perfection, served by friendly staff in a comfortable and inviting atmosphere. The cozy, intimate bar serves creative cocktails by an expert mixologist. The jalapeño martini is a kick! **Features:** full bar, happy hour. **Reservations:** required. **Address:** 2822 Sudderth Dr 88345 **Location:** Jct Mechem Dr.
L D

TEXAS CLUB
575/258-3325

▼▼ Steak. Casual Dining. $13-$37 **AAA Inspector Notes:** Guests interested in meeting real Texans and noshing on great steaks will find the lively, fun restaurant just the ticket. On the menu is a good selection of pasta, chicken and fish dishes. **Features:** full bar. **Address:** 212 Metz Dr 88345 **Location:** Jct SR 48 and Sudderth Dr, 2 mi n, just e. D

TINA'S CAFE
575/257-8903

▼▼ American. Casual Dining. $7-$15 **AAA Inspector Notes:** This bustling and popular café offers quaint indoor seating or patio dining next to the river. Portions are plentiful and served by a friendly staff. Unique offerings include "pig candy," a cinnamon roll with bacon. **Features:** patio dining. **Address:** 522 Sudderth Dr 88345 **Location:** East end of town; just w of Junction Rd. B L

THE VILLAGE BUTTERY
575/257-9251

▼▼ Sandwiches Soup. Quick Serve. $6-$9 **AAA Inspector Notes:** This cozy neighborhood café is a favorite local lunch spot. The healthy menu features homemade soups, pasta salads, green salads and quiche. Save room for the luscious Granny Guthrie's buttermilk pie, famous throughout the county. **Features:** patio dining. **Address:** 2107 Sudderth Dr 88345 **Location:** Center. **Parking:** street only. L 🍴

RUIDOSO DOWNS (H-4) pop. 2,815, elev. 6,420'
• Hotels p. 410

From humble origins in a mountain field in 1947, Ruidoso Downs Race Track—also the site of the

Racehorse Hall of Fame—is a premier facility for quarter horse and Thoroughbred racing. The All-American Futurity is held on Labor Day, the final day of the racing season. Famed as the world's richest quarter horse race (the purse exceeds $2 million), it is the final leg of quarter horse racing's Triple Crown. It is preceded by the Ruidoso Quarter Horse Futurity and the Rainbow Futurity, which take place in June and July, respectively. For more information phone (575) 378-4431.

The 84-mile-long Billy the Kid National Scenic Byway more than lives up to its name in terms of impressive mountain vistas. Maps and information are available from the scenic byway interpretive center on US 70, next to the Hubbard Museum of the American West.

Events at the Lincoln County Cowboy Symposium, held the second full weekend in October, include cowboy poetry readings, musical performances, roping demonstrations, a chuck wagon cook-off and displays of Western arts and crafts.

HUBBARD MUSEUM OF THE AMERICAN WEST is 1 mi. e. of the racetrack off US 70. The museum displays horse-related items from the Anne C. Stradling Collection. Included are life-size models, saddles, wagons and carriages, harnesses and paintings. There also is an interactive area for kids. On the grounds is a monumental horse sculpture, "Free Spirits at Noisy Water."

Time: Allow 1 hour minimum. **Hours:** Thurs.-Mon. 9-5. Closed 1 day in July (date varies), Thanksgiving and Christmas. **Cost:** $7; $5 (ages 60+ and military with ID); $2 (ages 6-16). **Phone:** (575) 378-4142.

BEST WESTERN PINE SPRINGS INN   (575)378-8100

Hotel
$69-$209

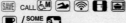

AAA Benefit: Save 10% or more every day and earn 10% bonus points!

Address: 111 Pine Springs Dr 88346 **Location:** Just e of jct US 70 and SR 48. Across from racetrack. **Facility:** 98 units. 2 stories (no elevator), exterior corridors. **Terms:** check-in 4 pm, cancellation fee imposed. **Pool(s):** heated outdoor. **Activities:** hot tub. **Guest Services:** coin laundry.

SALINAS PUEBLO MISSIONS NATIONAL MONUMENT (G-3)

Salinas Pueblo Missions National Monument is the site of three geographically and historically related pueblos and 17th-century Spanish Franciscan missions. The park includes the former Gran Quivira National Monument and two former state monuments, Abó and Quarai.

Because there was no further resettlement after the Spaniards and the Tompiro and Tewa Indians

abandoned the site in the late 17th century, the masonry ruins are remarkably intact. A visitor center is near Mountainair, on US 60 a block west of SR 55, and is open daily 8-5. All three pueblo sites open daily 9-6, Memorial Day weekend-Labor Day; 9-5, rest of year. Sites closed Jan. 1, Thanksgiving and Christmas. Free. Phone (505) 847-2585.

ABÓ RUINS are 9 mi. w. of Mountainair on US 60, then .7 mi. n. on SR 513. Once a large pueblo, this Tompiro Indian village was abandoned in the 1670s. The ruins of San Gregorio de Abó, a medieval-style church built in 1620 that has a 40-foot-tall buttressed curtain wall, rise curiously from the desert floor. **Time:** Allow 1 hour minimum. **Hours:** Open daily 9-6, Memorial Day-Labor Day; 9-5, rest of year. Closed Jan. 1, Thanksgiving and Christmas. **Cost:** Free. **Phone:** (505) 847-2585.

GRAN QUIVIRA RUINS are 26 mi. s. of Mountainair on SR 55 to 102 S. Ripley Ave. Historians estimate that at its height the Gran Quivira pueblo was home to more than 2,000 people. Some 20 limestone house mounds date from 1300 to about 1670; approximately 300 rooms and six kivas can be explored. Also preserved are the 17th-century ruins of San Isidro and San Buenaventura. **Time:** Allow 1 hour minimum. **Hours:** Ruins daily 9-6, Memorial Day-Labor Day; 9-5, rest of year. Closed Jan. 1, Thanksgiving and Christmas. **Phone:** (505) 847-2585.

QUARAI RUINS are 8 mi. n. of Mountainair on SR 55, then 1 mi. w. on a hard-surfaced road. At the site are 10 large unexcavated pueblo house mounds. The remains of the 1630 church and convent of Nuestra Señora de La Purísma Concepción de Cuarac include impressive sandstone walls nearly 40 feet tall. The ruins of another, smaller church dating from before 1820 also can be seen. **Hours:** Ruins daily 9-6, Memorial Day-Labor Day; 9-5, rest of year. Closed Jan. 1, Thanksgiving and Christmas. **Phone:** (505) 847-2585.

SAN ANTONIO (H-3) pop. 165, elev. 4,568'

Founded in 1629 as a mission, San Antonio is a trading center for nearby farms and ranches. Corn and alfalfa thrive in the fields along the Rio Grande Valley. But to the southeast, beyond the river valley, lies a 35-mile-wide, 90-mile-long stretch of merciless desert. In the days when settlers trudged westward along the El Camino Real—The Royal Road—the desert earned the name Jornada del Muerto, or Journey of the Dead.

Some 21 miles south across the Rio Grande from San Marcial is Valverde Battlefield, scene of the first Civil War engagement in New Mexico. Confederate forces led by Gen. H.H. Sibley beat back Union troops from nearby Fort Craig in a daylong battle in February 1862, and went on to occupy Albuquerque. Eroded remnants of the fort survive and are accessible by way of a 5-mile gravel road; the battlefield, however, is not.

San Antonio is the birthplace of famed hotelier Conrad Hilton. The ruins of the Hilton family's mercantile boardinghouse and home are at Sixth and Main streets, west of SR 1 and 1 mile south of US 380.

BOSQUE DEL APACHE NATIONAL WILDLIFE REFUGE is 8 mi. s. of I-25 exit 139 at US 380 and SR 1. It features a 12-mile auto tour route along which are six observation decks, 10 hiking trails and a scenic overlook providing access to marsh, grassland and desert upland habitats. A visitor center contains exhibits pertaining to wildlife that inhabit or visit the refuge, including sandhill cranes, snow geese and more than 380 other bird species as well as coyotes, mountain lions, deer, elk, javalina, turkeys and rattlesnakes. Wildlife observation is best from September through May.

The Laura Jean Deal Desert Arboretum has one of the Southwest's most complete collections of cacti, succulents and native trees and plants. The peak bloom period is April through August.

Fishing and hunting are permitted in designated areas during regulated seasons. **Time:** Allow 2 hours minimum. **Hours:** Refuge daily 1 hour before dawn-1 hour after dusk. Visitor center daily 8-4, Sept.-May; Thurs.-Mon 8-4. rest of year. Closed Jan. 1, July 4, Thanksgiving and Christmas. **Cost:** Auto tour route $5 per private vehicle. **Phone:** (575) 835-1828. 🎫 🛉

SANDIA PARK (F-3) pop. 237, elev. 7,159'

Sandia Park, about 25 miles east of Albuquerque, is on the Turquoise Trail National Scenic Byway, a desert highland route that runs past Sandia Mountain and winds through the Cibola National Forest *(see place listing p. 371).*

TINKERTOWN MUSEUM is 1 mi. w. on SR 536 to 121 Sandia Crest Rd. The museum displays the life's work of New Mexican folk artist Ross Ward, whose carved and hand-painted miniatures include an animated Western town and a three-ring circus. A wall made of more than 50,000 glass bottles surrounds the museum. **Hours:** Daily 9-6, Apr. 1-Nov. 1. Last admission 30 minutes before closing. **Cost:** $3.50; $3 (ages 62+); $1 (ages 4-16). **Phone:** (505) 281-5233.

SAN FELIPE PUEBLO (D-3) pop. 2,404, elev. 5,130'

Founded in 1706, San Felipe Pueblo is the most culturally conservative of the Keresan-speaking communities. Villagers are protective of ancient traditions and permit visitors only during the Green Corn Dance in May, when hundreds of men, women and children dance in traditional costumes, and during Christmas Eve service and the traditional dances that follow. An arts and crafts show is held in October.

GAMBLING ESTABLISHMENTS
• **San Felipe's Casino Hollywood** is at 25 Hagen Rd. **Hours:** Mon.-Thurs. 8 a.m.-4 a.m., Fri.-Sun. 24 hours. **Phone:** (505) 867-6700 or (877) 529-2946.

SAN ILDEFONSO PUEBLO (A-4) pop. 524, elev. 5,550'

About 23 miles north of Santa Fe, San Ildefonso sits in the shadow of Black Mesa; this natural mountain stronghold helped the Pueblo people withstand a Spanish attack in 1694.

SAN ILDEFONSO PUEBLO is at 74 Povi Kaa, 13 mi. s. of Española via SR 30/502. For the past century this Tewa village has been at the forefront of a Pueblo arts revival. It is best known as the home of Maria Martinez, celebrated potter and the creator of black-on-black pottery that is prized by collectors. Today family members and other potters continue the tradition she began. Shops in the main plaza display and sell her work, and a museum depicts pottery-making techniques.

Hours: Daily 8-5. Hours may vary. Closed major holidays. Phone ahead to confirm schedule. **Cost:** Pueblo entry fee $10 per private vehicle. Additional fees for drawing ($25), filming ($20) and still-camera photography ($10). **Phone:** (505) 455-3549.

SAN PATRICIO

HURD-LA RINCONADA GALLERY & GUEST HOMES
575/653-4331

[fyi] Not evaluated. **Address:** 105 La Rinconada Ln 88348 **Location:** US 70 at MM 281. Facilities, services, and décor characterize a mid-scale property.

SANTA CLARA PUEBLO (A-4) elev. 5,605'

In the 12th century, ancestors of the present-day Santa Clara Pueblo carved primitive dwellings into the cliffs above Santa Clara Canyon, where they hunted and farmed. Today visitors can view the Puye Cliff Dwellings, two levels of cliff and cave dwellings. The tribe migrated east to the Rio Grande Valley and the present pueblo site around 1600.

PUYE CLIFF DWELLINGS TOUR is at SR 30 and Santa Clara Canyon Rd. Located atop the Pajarito Plateau at an elevation of nearly 7,000 feet is the ancestral home of the Santa Clara Pueblo people. This was once a multi-story complex built around a large central plaza. The southern portion contained 173 rooms on the ground floor. Guided tours offer both breathtaking views and an in-depth cultural and spiritual appreciation of pueblo life. The Harvey House displays pueblo-related exhibits, and during the summer local artisans display their work.

The tour requires walking on steep slopes at a high elevation. **Time:** Allow 1 hour minimum. **Hours:** Daily 9-6, mid-Apr. through Sept. 30; 9:30-3, rest of year (weather permitting). Closed the week before Easter, June 13, Aug. 12 and Christmas. **Cost:** Tour fees range from $20-$35; $18-$33 (ages 0-14 and 55+). Harvey House $7; $5 (ages 0-14 and 55+). Reservations are recommended. **Phone:** (505) 917-6650 or (888) 320-5008. GT 🍴

SANTA CLARA PUEBLO is 2 mi. s. of Española on SR 30. Established in 1550, this Tewa-speaking pueblo traces its ancestry to the Puye cliff dwellers. Santa Clara artists are noted for their glossy black and red pottery adorned with meticulously incised designs as well as for their paintings and sculpture. **Hours:** Daily 8-4:30. **Cost:** Free. Photography fee $5 per camera. **Phone:** (505) 753-7326.

SANTA FE (F-4) pop. 67,947, elev. 6,989'

Having celebrated its 400th birthday in 2010, you'd think Santa Fe would stop, take a deep breath and rest on that considerable achievement. Not a chance. While this city treats preservation of the past as paramount, there's always something new to discover. You can return a dozen times and still leave with new discoveries and experiences under your belt.

The high desert country that surrounds New Mexico's capital city, however, is timeless. Undulating hills that stretch to the horizon in all directions are a study in shades of buff, beige and brown. The landscape is speckled with clumps of *Artemisia tridentate*—more commonly known as sagebrush—a hardy shrub with silvery-gray leaves, a pungent fragrance and a tolerance for arid conditions. In the distance, mountains stand like sentinels—the Jemez range to the northwest, the Sangre de Cristos to the northeast. It's an austere but awesome natural setting heightened by remarkably clear air and the intense azure blue of the vast New Mexico sky.

Surely it's a setting that captivated Spanish explorer Juan de Oñate. In 1598 he led the initial effort to colonize the region that was claimed for the Spanish Crown as the province of Santa Fé de Nuevo México. Ten years later the newly appointed Spanish governor, Don Pedro de Peralta, founded a city that was to be the seat of power for all imperial holdings north of the Rio Grande. Peralta lived up to the Spanish penchant for cumbersome titles, naming it La Villa Real de la Santa Fé de San Francisco de Asis—the Royal Town of the Holy Faith of St. Francis of Assisi.

In 1610 Santa Fe became the provincial capital. It's a designation the city has retained ever since, except for a brief period during the Pueblo Revolt of 1680 when Indian villages banded together to expel the colonizers. That same year a mission was established to serve as headquarters for a second power in the region: the church. Franciscan fathers fanned out to usher the Indians into the Christian fold; according to a 1617 report, 14,000 souls had been converted. Four hundred years later the sturdy walls

of the San Miguel Mission Church *(see attraction listing p. 418)* are still intact.

Spanish colonists adopted a tried-and-true method of construction for their own churches, government buildings and other structures. The Pueblo Indians used adobe, a mixture of earth, straw and water that was shaped into bricks and dried in the sun. The bricks were stacked and bonded together with more adobe. Pueblo walls were frequently several feet thick, with entry to their dwellings through an opening in the rooftop accessed via ladder. These walls efficiently kept the interiors cool in summer and warm in winter.

Innovations like mud-brick fireplaces and *hornos* (outdoor ovens) were added. A few buildings from this era survive today. The Oldest House on E. De Vargas Street (across from the San Miguel Mission Church) was built around 1646; although the "oldest" title also is claimed by houses in Connecticut, Florida and Massachusetts, this is the only one made of adobe. Another place to see adobe dwellings in their original state (minus doors and windows that were added later) is at Taos Pueblo *(see attraction listing p. 446)*.

Question: What's a non-authentic adobe? Answer: Most of the buildings in town. In 1912 a code was passed requiring the use of a style called Spanish Pueblo Revival. It incorporated the defining features of local architecture, which included earth-toned, flat-topped buildings, wood-beamed ceilings (*vigas*), and door and window frames painted white or turquoise. But the majority of houses and commercial structures in the city have stucco surfaces that mimic adobe, referred to amusingly as "Santa Fake" and faux-dobe (foe-dough-bee).

Authentic adobe or not, Santa Fe still looks like no other place in the country. "The City Different" prides itself on the cultivation of "Santa Fe style." It's a term that goes beyond decorative details like clay pots, cow skulls, Southwestern blankets and Native American artifacts (there are plenty of those).

Santa Fe style embraces the use of natural materials to enhance the stark natural beauty of the landscape. That's why you'll see, along with the omnipresent adobe, weathered stone walls and picturesque fences made from tree branches lashed together. And everything is suffused with the elusive quality of light that has long attracted painters and photographers, a constant interplay between piercing sun and flickering shadow that's downright mesmerizing.

It's all a nice backdrop for a packed social calendar. One event that has been drawing crowds since 1949 is the annual 🏇 Rodeo de Santa Fe in late June, when hundreds of cowboys and cowgirls compete in barrel racing, bull riding, calf roping and steer wrestling. The 🏇 Santa Fe International Folk Art Market in July showcases the work of artists from some 35 countries.

Both the 🏇 Traditional Spanish Market in late July and the 🏇 Winter Spanish Market in early December celebrate Hispanic heritage through art,

(See maps & indexes p. 420, 423.)
music and dance. The Indian Market in mid-August is Santa Fe's oldest and largest market, celebrating emerging and established artists from some 100 tribes.

By Spanish decree the original town was laid out around a central square, bordered on one side by the seat of government (the Palace of the Governors, which looks much the same now as it did 4 centuries ago), and on the other by a church (the present-day Cathedral Basilica of St. Francis of Assisi). A grid of narrow streets and alleyways radiated out from this central point. Today, of course, these streets are lined with a plethora of shops, restaurants, art galleries and museums, forming a compact downtown core just meant to be strolled.

A magnet for residents and visitors alike, The Plaza is a meeting place morning, noon and evening. It has tree-shaded green lawns and plenty of benches where you can relax and take in the scene. Street musicians contribute a frequent soundtrack. In summer flower baskets hang from the ornamental wrought-iron lampposts, and during the Christmas holidays walkways and rooftops glow with the soft light from *farolitos,* small paper bags holding sand and a single lit candle. The Plaza is Santa Fe's heart, a perfect starting point for exploring a city that's different in the most delightful way.

Guided downtown walking tours, led by docents from the New Mexico History Museum, depart from the blue gate at the Palace of the Governors April to October; phone (505) 476-5200. Historic Walks of Santa Fe also offer guided walking tours departing from various hotels; phone (505) 986-8388.

Tourism Santa Fe: 201 W. Marcy St., Santa Fe, NM 87504. **Phone:** (505) 955-6200 or (800) 777-2489.

Shopping

Shopping is a favorite way to while away the time in Santa Fe, but where you go depends on your agenda. Downtown is shopping central, with stores and boutiques catering to just about every taste (and disposable income level). Serious art collectors for whom money is no object head for Canyon Road, while the up-and-coming Railyard District offers additional shopping opportunities.

Many shops traffic in the usual T-shirts and Southwestern-themed souvenirs, but you also can find more offbeat and specialized merchandise. The mini-malls are as good a place as any to start. Plaza Mercado (entrances on San Francisco, Galisteo and Water streets) has more than 30 specialty retailers.

The Santa Fe Arcade (60 E. San Francisco St. on the south side of The Plaza) is a sleek three-level indoor mall with trendy shops specializing in stylish Western wear, custom-made boots, home accessories and gold and silver jewelry. Malouf on the Plaza specializes in pricey, high-end clothing and accessories: designer fashions, handbags, jewelry and shoes for her; shirts, ties, sportswear and tailored apparel for him.

Art galleries are scattered throughout downtown. POP Gallery (125 Lincoln Ave., next to the New Mexico History Museum) displays photography, jewelry and modern art and sculpture in varied media. Most of the items are expensive, but there are some reasonable deals to be had. D R Fine Art Santa Fe (123 Galisteo St.) sells contemporary Southwest landscape paintings by David Rothermel. Moon Rabbit Toys (112 W. San Francisco St.) stocks toys from all over the world, an eclectic array of stuffed animals, high-quality jigsaw puzzles and the latest must-owns for serious gamers.

The Shops at La Fonda at the La Fonda Hotel (100 E. San Francisco St.) offer clothing, designer jewelry, handmade textiles, folk art and kitchen accessories. Also at the hotel is Señor Murphy's candy shop, where you can sample goodies like chocolate piñon nut clusters. Across the street is the O'Farrell Hat Shop, selling customized cowboy hats and "Santa Fe sticks," locally handcrafted canes and walking sticks made from fine hardwoods.

The buildings surrounding Sena Plaza (125 E. Palace Ave. opposite The Plaza) were once part of one big single-family residence, with multiple rooms for family members as well as various tradesmen. The shops here sell pottery, ceramics and touristy gifts. A courtyard (accessible only through two narrow entryways on Palace Avenue) has shade trees, benches, a fountain and an arbor; it's a secluded little spot to relax for a spell.

Few cities in the country offer a better selection of Native American art. Ortega's on the Plaza (101 W. San Francisco St.) carries Navajo weavings, Zuni fetishes, traditional turquoise jewelry, silver-studded belts, pottery and other treasures, along with a beautiful array of beadwork.

For a more personalized shopping experience, wander among the displays of traditional and contemporary jewelry, arts and crafts, pottery, sand paintings and other handmade items sold under the *portal* (porch) of the Palace of the Governors (105 W. Palace Ave.). Vendors spread their wares on blankets on the sidewalk outside this long adobe building. Although the casual setting might imply that haggling is acceptable, prices are usually fixed (though often a bargain compared with many shops). And it's fun to meet the artists and learn about their work.

Within walking distance of downtown, Canyon Road (between East Alameda Street and Acequia Madre) is the upscale center of the Santa Fe art scene. The 10 or so blocks between Paseo de Peralta and Palace Avenue constitute a "gallery row" of festively decorated adobes trading in all manner of fine art, from paintings and sculpture to rugs, jewelry and custom-designed furniture.

Galleries dealing in contemporary works include Adieb Khadoure Fine Art (613 Canyon Rd.), Patricia Carlisle Fine Art (554 Canyon Rd.) and the Waxlander Gallery & Sculpture Garden (622 Canyon Rd.). At the Wiford Gallery (403 Canyon Rd.) there's an outdoor garden with Utah artist Lyman Whitaker's

(See maps & indexes p. 420, 423.)

contemporary wind sculptures, delicate-looking copper and stainless steel creations that twirl whenever there's a breeze. Western-themed paintings by artists representing the early Taos and Santa Fe schools are displayed at the Nedra Matteucci Galleries (1075 Paseo de Peralta).

The Railyard District (along Guadalupe Street between Paseo de Peralta and Montezuma Avenue) is also worth investigating. Casa Nova (530 S. Guadalupe St.) has a little bit of everything—vibrantly colorful furniture, dinnerware, baskets, wall decorations and handicrafts, mostly created by African artists.

For Southwestern agricultural specialties like locally grown white corn, cactus honey and an incredible variety of heirloom tomatoes and dried chiles, check out the Santa Fe Farmers Market in the Railyard (Guadalupe Street at Paseo de Peralta). The Saturday market sets up 7 a.m.-noon during the summer months, 8-1 the rest of the year; a Tuesday market is open 8-1, May through late November. Everything from pottery to hand-blown glass can be found at the Railyard Artisan Market, held in the Farmers Market Pavilion building Sundays 10-4, year-round.

Nightlife

Given Santa Fe's close relationship with the fine arts, it's no surprise that highbrow cultural events top the social calendar. First and foremost is the Santa Fe Opera, where classics like "Madame Butterfly," contemporary works and world premieres are performed in a state-of-the-art, open-air venue that has the Sangre de Cristo and Jemez mountains as a backdrop. This may be the only opera company in the world that has to compete with a spectacular sunset for the audience's attention. The show actually begins a couple of hours earlier, when opera goers begin arriving with lavish tailgate picnics in tow. Attendees also can take advantage of a preview buffet set up on the landscaped rehearsal grounds.

Some 40 performances are offered in July and August. Single ticket prices start at $33-$280, depending on the seating section and performance date, and are nonrefundable. A roof covers all seating areas, but evenings can occasionally be cool, rainy or both. The facility is located 7 miles north of downtown Santa Fe on the west side of US 84/285 (exit 168). The box office is open Mon.-Fri. 9-5 (Mon.-Sat. 9-5 during the season); phone (505) 986-5900 or (800) 280-4654.

A variety of events—from the Santa Fe Chamber Music Festival, performances by the Santa Fe Symphony Orchestra and the Aspen Santa Fe Ballet, and popular music headliners to theater, ballet and classic film festivals—take place at the Lensic Performing Arts Center (211 W. San Francisco St.). The Lensic opened in 1931 as a movie palace and vaudeville theater; a major renovation in 2001 retained the building's distinctive Spanish-style facade and rooftop line of undulating sea serpents. Phone (505) 988-1234 for the box office.

The Pink Adobe (406 Old Santa Fe Tr. across from the San Miguel Mission Church) has been around since 1944, when Rosalea Murphy opened the doors of her restaurant. Locals refer to it as "the Pink," and the restaurant's Dragon Room Lounge is a popular hangout with the artsy crowd. The ambience is classy: dim lighting, walls decorated with carved wood dragons, and a bar with elm trees growing through the roof. Live music runs to jazz, salsa and flamenco, and the specialty margaritas pack a potent punch. Phone (505) 983-7712.

More raucous is dive bar Evangelo's (200 W. San Francisco St.). In the basement (Underground at Evangelo's) local rock and reggae bands tear it up several nights a week. The mahogany bar dispenses a variety of imported brews. Cowgirl BBQ (319 S. Guadalupe St.) has a big outdoor patio with a lantern-festooned tree, country bands, Cowgirl Karaoke nights and—parents take note—a Kid Corral to keep the young 'uns happy.

Or you could just take a downtown evening stroll. Weather permitting (meaning if it isn't too chilly), The Plaza is a pretty, peaceful spot to relax on a bench, enjoy an ice cream cone and people watch. You may even be treated to an impromptu concert by a couple of jamming musicians.

INSIDER INFO:
Pueblo Etiquette

When Spanish conquistadors arrived in northern New Mexico in the 1500s, they encountered a vast network of Indian villages dating back centuries. The Spaniards referred to Native Americans as Pueblo Indians, after the Spanish word for town. About 25 pueblos remain today, and many of the people who live on these lands still adhere to traditional ways and speak the Tewa language in addition to Spanish or English.

Visiting a pueblo is a wonderful way to experience a different culture. One of the most accessible for tourists is Taos Pueblo, right outside of Taos. The ceremonial village—the only section of the pueblo open to visitors—is considered sacred, and about 150 Taos Indians choose to live here as their ancestors did, without benefit of conveniences like electricity and plumbing.

Primitive-looking yet ingenious devices are scattered throughout the village. Lattice-like drying racks were used for harvested corn, pumpkin, squash and bean crops, and to cure wild game meat for food and animal hides for clothing. Beehive-shaped, outdoor adobe ovens called *hornos* are still used to bake Indian fry bread.

Most pueblos celebrate annual feast days coinciding with a Catholic patron saint designated by the early Spanish missionaries. A blend of ancient harvest traditions and Catholic religious practices, they combine traditional dances with singing and drumming; some also incorporate private ceremonies, processions and masses.

Taos Pueblo celebrates the San Geronimo Feast Day on Sept. 30 with traditional pole climbing. The

(See maps & indexes p. 420, 423.)

Buffalo and Deer Dance is performed on the Jan. 23 feast day at San Ildefonso Pueblo. One of the smallest pueblos, but one with a very rich heritage, is Tesuque Pueblo, where the Corn Dance takes place the first weekend in June and the Feast Day of San Diego is celebrated on Nov. 12.

Nambé Pueblo, about 18 miles north of Santa Fe, sits at the base of the Sangre de Cristo Mountains; the Nambé Falls Ceremonial on July 4, which includes dances and an arts and crafts fair, is a popular event with both pueblo residents and tourists. Some pueblos also hold celebrations on Christmas Day, and most celebrate Día de El Rey (King's Day) on Jan. 6.

Many pueblos are open to the public, and visitors are usually welcome on feast days. It's advisable to confirm if the pueblo is open on the day you plan to visit; contact the Eight Northern Indian Pueblos Council at (505) 747-1593, or inquire at Tourism Santa Fe.

Feast day or not, it's important to follow commonsense etiquette. Most pueblos have strict rules regarding photography, filming and even sketching, so ask regarding what type of cameras are allowed and if fees are required. Ignoring these rules could result in the confiscation of your equipment.

Laptops, iPads and cell phones are usually not welcome on pueblo grounds. Refrain from photographing religious sites (chapels or kivas), and always ask if you can photograph tribal members or their personal property before doing so. If you happen to receive an invitation to someone's home accept graciously, but refrain from offering payment or a tip.

Ceremonial dances are no different than any religious rite. The participants are in a prayerful state, and quiet, respectful behavior is expected. Refrain from loud talking, clapping, dancing along or wandering around during a dance. If photographing dancers, keep a respectful distance during the ceremony and between dances.

You are a guest while on pueblo land; do not enter or peek into a resident's home unless a sign on the door welcomes visitors. Children should not climb on walls or look into windows. Kivas and cemeteries are generally off limits; also heed all signs that designate restricted access areas. Different pueblos have different rules (for example, wading is forbidden in Red Willow Creek at Taos Pueblo), so make sure you're familiar with them before you set off exploring.

BATAAN MEMORIAL MILITARY MUSEUM & LIBRARY is at 1050 Old Pecos Tr. The museum houses exhibits from early Mexican wars to the present. Artifacts include uniforms, equipment and original artwork relating to the captivity of the 200th Coast Artillery Regiment in the Philippine Islands. **Time:** Allow 30 minutes minimum. **Hours:** Tues.-Fri. 10-4; closed holidays except Bataan Memorial Day. **Cost:** Free. **Phone:** (505) 474-1670.

CATHEDRAL BASILICA OF ST. FRANCIS OF ASSISI is 1 blk. e. of The Plaza on Cathedral Pl. Built to serve the fledgling settlement's Catholic community, this became the first church in New Mexico to attain the status of cathedral basilica. The parish was founded in 1610; the present church, built in 1869, is one of Santa Fe's most widely recognized landmarks.

Bordered by a lovely tree-shaded park, it's also one of the few downtown buildings that isn't an adobe. The cathedral's sharp, French Romanesque lines provide a striking contrast to the rounded contours of its neighbors, making it a popular subject to photograph.

Archbishop J.B. Lamy, who inspired Willa Cather's novel "Death Comes for the Archbishop," is buried beneath the main altar beside missionary priests Fray Zarate and Fray Gerónimo de la Lama. When services are not being held visitors may view a display of ecclesiastical art in the sanctuary. **Hours:** Mon.-Fri. 9:30-4:30. Services are held on Saturday night and throughout the day on Sunday. **Cost:** Free. **Phone:** (505) 982-5619.

THE CENTER FOR CONTEMPORARY ARTS AND CCA CINEMATEQUE is at 1050 Old Pecos Tr. The center is a forum for contemporary art exhibits, independent and foreign films, theater, lectures and workshops. **Time:** Allow 30 minutes minimum. **Hours:** Gallery open Thurs.-Sun. noon-5. Movies presented daily; film times vary. Phone ahead to confirm schedule. **Cost:** Donations; fee varies for films. **Phone:** (505) 982-1338.

CRISTO REY CHURCH is at Canyon Rd. and Cristo Rey St. One of the largest adobe structures in the country, the church contains a hand-carved stone *reredos* (altar screen) dating from 1761. **Hours:** Daily 8:30-4:30. **Cost:** Donations. **Phone:** (505) 983-8528.

CUSTOM TOURS BY CLARICE departs from corner of Lincoln and West Palace aves. on The Plaza as well as from several area hotels. The narrated, open-air tram tour transports guests past such historic sites as the Cathedral Basilica of St. Francis of Assisi and the Loretto Chapel. Passengers also receive an insider's guide with restaurant and shopping recommendations.

Time: Allow 1 hour, 30 minutes minimum. **Hours:** Tours are given daily at 10, noon, 2 and 4, Apr.-Oct. No tours are offered during inclement weather or when under 50 F. Phone ahead to confirm schedule. **Cost:** $20. Cash only when boarding tram without reservations; credit cards accepted with 24-hour notice. Reservations are required. **Phone:** (505) 438-7116, or (505) 690-8741 (mobile number).

EL RANCHO DE LAS GOLONDRINAS is off I-25 exit 276, following signs to 334 Los Pinos Rd. The living-history museum's name means "The Ranch of

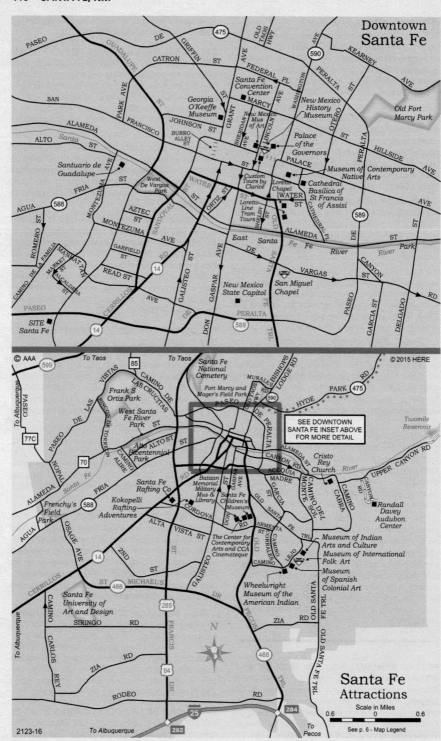

Downtown Santa Fe

PASEO DE GRIFFIN ST
CATRON ST
GUADALUPE ST
DE FEDERAL PL
475
590
KEARNEY
OLD TAOS HWY
AVE
WASHINGTON AVE
PERALTA ST
AVE
SAN FRANCISCO
PARK AVE
Santa Fe Convention Center
MARCY
Georgia O'Keeffe Museum
JOHNSON ST
GRANT ST
New Mexico Mus of Art
OTERO
New Mexico History Museum
Old Fort Marcy Park
ALAMEDA
ALTO ST
Santa
Santuario de Guadalupe
FRIA
588
AGUA
ROMERO ST
MONTEZUMA ST
West De Vargas Park
WATER ST
BURRO ALLEY ST
SHERIDAN
SANDOVAL ST
Palace of the Governors
PALACE
Custom Tours by Clarice
Loretto Chapel
WATER
Cathedral Basilica of St Francis of Assisi
Museum of Contemporary Native Arts
HILLSIDE AVE
PERALTA ST
589
AVE
ST
AZTEC ST
Loretto Line Tram Tours
ORTIZ ST
OLD SANTA FE TRL
CATHEDRAL PL
DE
MONTEZUMA AVE
East Santa Fe Fe River River Park
ALAMEDA
ST
MANHATTAN ST
MARKET ST
VALCADSA ST
GARFIELD ST
READ ST
GALISTEO ST
GASPAR AVE
DON
DE
VARGAS
SAN SANTA FE TRL
CANYON ST
GARCIA ST
DELGADO
14
CERRILLOS AVE
New Mexico State Capitol
San Miguel Chapel
PASEO
PERALTA
589
SITE Santa Fe
14

© AAA   © 2015 HERE

Santa Fe Attractions

599 To Taos   85   To Taos
CAMINO DE LAS CRUCITAS
Santa Fe National Cemetery
Fort Marcy and Mager's Field Park
MURALES RD
BISHOPS LODGE RD
590
HYDE PARK RD
475
To Albuquerque
PASEO DE LAS VISTAS
Frank S Ortiz Park
West Santa Fe River Park
PASEO
77C
NOPAL
DE
RINCON DE TORREON
CAMINO ALIRE
West Alto ST Alto St Bicentennial Park
PASEO
Twomile Reservoir
Santa Fe
70
ALAMEDA
FRIA
588
AGUA
Frenchy's Field Park
Santa Fe Rafting Co
Kokopelli Rafting Adventures
ALTA VISTA ST
CORDOVA RD
Bataan Memorial Military Mus & Library
GASPAR AVE
Santa Fe Children's Museum
DON
CANYON RD
ACEQUIA MADRE
GARCIA ST
CAMINO DEL MONTE SOL
OLD SANTA FE
Cristo Rey Church
River
UPPER CANYON RD
CAMINO CABRA
CANYON RD
Randall Davey Audubon Center
14
2ND ST
ST MICHAEL'S DR
466
The Center for Contemporary Arts and CCA Cinemateque
GALISTEO ST
ARMENTA
CAMINO CORRALES
CAMINO
LEJO
FE TRL RD
OLD SANTA FE TRL
Museum of Indian Arts and Culture
Museum of International Folk Art
Museum of Spanish Colonial Art
Santa Fe University of Art and Design
SIRINGO RD
285
FRANCIS DR
PECOS
Wheelwright Museum of the American Indian
ZIA
CAMINO
CARLOS REY
ZIA RD
RODEO RD
84
466
N
282
25
To Albuquerque
284
To Pecos

SEE DOWNTOWN SANTA FE INSET ABOVE FOR MORE DETAIL

Scale in Miles
0.6   0   0.6
See p. 6 - Map Legend

2123-16

(See maps & indexes p. 420, 423.)

the Swallows." It was once a stopping place on El Camino Real (The Royal Road) from Mexico City to Old Santa Fe. Exhibits depict Spanish colonial life in New Mexico. Restored buildings include an 18th-century *placita* house with a defensive tower as well as a mill, smithy, schoolhouse and church. A 1.5-mile path leads to the buildings.

Time: Allow 1 hour, 15 minutes minimum. **Hours:** Wed.-Sun. 10-4, June-Sept. Guided tours are offered daily by reservation, Apr.-Oct. **Cost:** $6; $4 (ages 13-18, ages 62+ and military with ID). Additional fees for special events may apply. **Phone:** (505) 471-2261.

GEORGIA O'KEEFFE MUSEUM is at 217 Johnson St. The artist's best-known works include many pieces inspired by New Mexico's stark beauty. More than half of O'Keeffe's lifetime output of paintings, drawings and sculptures comprise the permanent collection, which spans 7 decades. Special exhibits combine O'Keeffe's paintings with other works from the American Modernism Movement.

Time: Allow 1 hour minimum. **Hours:** Daily 10-5 (also Fri. 5-7). Guided tours are given at 10:30 and 2. Closed Jan. 1, Easter, Thanksgiving, Christmas and between some exhibits. Phone ahead to confirm schedule. **Cost:** $12; $10 (students 18 and over with ID); $8 (New Mexico residents); free (ages 17 and under). Audio tour rental fee $5. **Phone:** (505) 946-1000. GT

LORETTO CHAPEL is at 207 Old Santa Fe Tr. The "Miraculous Staircase" to the chapel's choir loft has two 360-degree turns and no visible means of support. An anonymous carpenter is said to have fashioned the spiral steps in 1878 using only wooden pegs. Legend suggests that St. Joseph, the patron saint of carpenters, inspired the work.

Time: Allow 30 minutes minimum. **Hours:** Mon.-Sat. 9-5, Sun. 10:30-5. Chapel may close part of a day for weddings and other special events. Phone ahead to confirm schedule. **Cost:** $3; $1 (ages 0-6). **Phone:** (505) 982-0092.

LORETTO LINE TRAM TOURS departs near Loretto Chapel at 211 Old Santa Fe Tr. Passengers board an open-air tram for a guided 1.5-hour historical tour of Santa Fe. **Hours:** Tours depart daily from Loretto Chapel at 10, noon and 2 and from La-Fonda Hotel at 10:30, 12:30 and 2:30, mid-March.-Oct. (weather-permitting). **Cost:** Fare $15; $10 (ages 0-11). **Phone:** (505) 982-0092.

MUSEUM OF CONTEMPORARY NATIVE ARTS is at 108 Cathedral Pl. The museum organizes contemporary art exhibitions devoted exclusively to the display of dynamic and diverse arts practices representative of Native North America. **Time:** Allow 1 hour minimum. **Hours:** Wed.-Sat. and Mon. 10-5, Sun. noon-5. Closed Jan. 1, Easter, Thanksgiving and Christmas. **Cost:** $10; $5 (ages 62+ and students with ID); free (ages 0-16, Native Americans and veterans with ID). **Phone:** (505) 983-8900.

MUSEUM OF INDIAN ARTS AND CULTURE is on Museum Hill off Old Santa Fe Tr. The museum has an inclusive collection of New Mexican and Southwestern archeological and anthropological artifacts. Objects include pottery, basketry, textiles, jewelry and contemporary arts. One permanent exhibition examines the comprehensive story of the Navajo, Apache and Pueblo peoples in their own words and voices, and the other focuses on 4 centuries of pueblo pottery.

Time: Allow 1 hour minimum. **Hours:** Daily 10-5 May-Oct.; Tues.-Sun. 10-5, rest of year. Closed Jan. 1, Easter, Thanksgiving and Christmas. **Cost:** $9; $8 (students with ID); $6 (New Mexico residents); free (ages 0-16, New Mexico residents with ID on Sun. and New Mexico senior citizens with ID on Wed.). **Phone:** (505) 476-1269.

MUSEUM OF INTERNATIONAL FOLK ART, on Museum Hill off Old Santa Fe Tr., houses the world's largest collection of international folk art. The Girard Wing features folk art, toys and miniature scenes of marketplaces and villages from 100 countries. Textiles are exhibited in the Neutrogena Wing, which also features a behind-the-scenes look at museum storage and conservation activities.

The Bartlett, Neutrogena and Hispanic Heritage wings offer changing exhibitions and hands-on activities, while the Gallery of Conscience presents exhibits that explore important social issues. For youngsters there's the Tree of Life play area.

Time: Allow 1 hour minimum. **Hours:** Daily 10-5 (also Fri. 5-8), Memorial Day-early Oct.; Tues.-Sun. 10-5, rest of year. Docent-led guided tours are given at 10:30, 11:30 and 2. Closed Jan. 1, Easter, Thanksgiving and Christmas. **Cost:** $9; $8 (students with ID); $6 (New Mexico residents with ID); free (ages 0-16 and to all on Sun., mid-May to mid-Sept.). **Phone:** (505) 476-1200, or (505) 476-1217 to confirm guided tour times.

MUSEUM OF SPANISH COLONIAL ART is 2 mi. s.e. of The Plaza at 750 Camino Lejo. Housed in a 1930 Pueblo Revival building designed by architect John Gaw Meem, the museum presents traditional Spanish art produced throughout the world since the start of Spanish colonization. The collection of some 3,500 objects includes painted images of saints, sculpture, textiles, metal work, ceramics, furniture and books. **Time:** Allow 1 hour minimum. **Hours:** Daily 10-5, Memorial Day-Labor Day; Tues.-Sun. 10-5, rest of year. Closed Jan. 1, Easter, Thanksgiving and Christmas. **Cost:** $8; $4 (New Mexico residents with ID); free (ages 0-15 and for New Mexico residents with ID on Sun.). **Phone:** (505) 982-2226.

NEW MEXICO HISTORY MUSEUM, 113 Lincoln Ave. on The Plaza, combines the state's oldest and newest museums. Permanent and changing exhibits focus on the history of New Mexico—Native Americans, Spanish colonists, Mexican rule, the Santa Fe Trail, the railroad era, statehood, World War II and the present day.

(See maps & indexes p. 420, 423.)

The museum serves as the anchor of a campus complex. The Palace Press, situated in the rooms adjoining the courtyard, is a working exhibit dedicated to the history of the state's printing techniques. The *portal* (porch) is a gathering place for artisans who sell jewelry, pottery, weavings and crafts. The Fray Angelico Chavez History Library has a collection of some 40,000 titles, while a photo archives contains more than 750,000 images dating back to the early 1850s.

Time: Allow 3 hours minimum. **Hours:** Museum daily 10-5 (also Fri. 5-8), May-Oct.; Tues.-Sun. 10-5 (also Fri. 5-8), rest of year. Library Tues.-Fri. 1-5 (also Wed. 5-8). Photo archives Tues.-Fri. 1-5. Closed Jan. 1, Easter, Thanksgiving and Christmas. **Cost:** (includes Palace of the Governors) $9; $8 (students with ID); $6 (New Mexico residents with ID); free (ages 0-16, New Mexico residents with ID on Sun., New Mexico senior citizens with ID on Wed., and to all Fri. 5-8). **Phone:** (505) 476-5200. GT

Palace of the Governors is on The Plaza at 105 W. Palace Ave. Built in 1610, this long, low adobe structure is a National Historic Landmark and is considered to be one of the oldest public buildings in the United States. It functioned as the seat of government under Spanish, Pueblo Indian, Mexican and U.S. territorial rule until 1909, when the building became the state history museum.

Four-foot-thick walls enclose period rooms with displays that chronicle nearly 400 years of New Mexico History. There are several open-pit excavation sites showing layers of foundations, different types of wall constructions and middens. Among the artifacts exhibited are ceramics, glassware, metal utensils, buttons, jewelry and weapons. The chapel room is a replica of a mid-19th century chapel with a simple, brightly colored altarpiece made in 1830.

Time: Allow 2 hours minimum. **Hours:** Daily 10-5 (also Fri. 5-8), May-Oct.; Tues.-Sun. 10-5 (also Fri. 5-8), rest of year. Closed Jan. 1, Easter, Thanksgiving and Christmas. **Cost:** (includes New Mexico History Museum) $9; $8 (students with ID); $6 (New Mexico residents with ID); free (ages 0-16, New Mexico residents with ID on Sun., New Mexico senior citizens with ID on Wed., and to all Fri. 5-8). **Phone:** (505) 476-5100. GT

NEW MEXICO MUSEUM OF ART is just off The Plaza at 107 W. Palace Ave. The museum, completed in 1917, houses contemporary and traditional American art. Changing exhibits focus on Southwestern artists from the 19th century to the present, including the Santa Fe and Taos masters. **Time:** Allow 1 hour minimum. **Hours:** Daily 10-5 (also Fri. 5-8), Memorial Day-Labor Day; Tues.-Sun. 10-5 (also Fri. 5-8), rest of year. Closed Jan. 1, Easter, Thanksgiving and Christmas. **Cost:** $9; $8 (students with ID); $6 (New Mexico residents with ID); free (ages 0-16, for New Mexico residents with ID on Sun., New Mexico senior citizens with ID on Wed.,

and to all Fri. 5-8). Combination tickets are available with the Museum of Indian Arts and Culture, the Museum of International Folk Art and the New Mexico History Museum/Palace of the Governors. **Phone:** (505) 476-5072.

NEW MEXICO STATE CAPITOL is at 490 Old Santa Fe Tr. at the jct. of Paseo de Peralta, 4 blks. s. of The Plaza. The capitol building is designed in the shape of the state's official emblem, the Zia sun symbol, and features a permanent collection of contemporary artwork and furnishings handcrafted by New Mexicans. Galleries on the second floor permit views of the house and senate chambers. **Hours:** Self-guiding tours Mon.-Fri. 7-6. Guided tours are given Mon.-Fri. by appointment. Closed Jan. 1, Easter, Labor Day, Thanksgiving, Christmas Eve and Christmas. **Cost:** Free. **Phone:** (505) 986-4589.

RANDALL DAVEY AUDUBON CENTER is 3 mi. e. of The Plaza at the end of Upper Canyon Rd. This 135-acre preserve in the Santa Fe Canyon hosts more than 130 bird species as well as bears, bobcats, coyotes, deer and foxes. The site includes an education center and nature trails. The Historic Randall Davey House, originally an 1847 sawmill, was converted into a home by the noted painter. It contains his studio, antiques and art work. **Time:** Allow 1 hour minimum. **Hours:** Mon.-Sat. 8-4, Feb.-Dec. Guided house tours are offered Fri. at 2. Guided bird walks depart Sat. at 8. Phone ahead to confirm hours and tour times. **Cost:** Audubon center by donation. House tours $5; free (ages 0-12). Guided bird walks free. **Phone:** (505) 983-4609.

SAN MIGUEL CHAPEL is 3 blks. s. of The Plaza at 401 Old Santa Fe Tr. (at E. De Vargas St.). A feeling of timelessness emanates from this simple mission church, built by Tlaxcala Indians under the direction of Franciscan *padres* (priests). Constructed around 1610, it is thought to be the nation's oldest active church. Records of its early history were burned during the Pueblo Indian Rebellion of 1680, but the thick, sturdy adobe walls remained unscathed; stone buttresses were subsequently added to strengthen the walls and bell tower.

The sanctuary has wooden pews and massive timber roof beams *(vigas)*. The hand-carved wooden *reredos* (altar screen) dates from 1798. Paintings of saints and Christ the Nazarene surround a gilded and painted wooden statue of St. Michael the Archangel, brought from Mexico in the early 18th century. In the rear of the church is a painting of Our Lady of Guadalupe. The 780-pound San Jose Bell that once hung in the bell tower now is displayed in the gift shop, and visitors are welcome to ring it; according to legend, those who do are destined to return to Santa Fe.

Hours: Mon.-Fri. 10-2, Sat. 11-3. The church is occasionally closed for special events; phone ahead to confirm. Closed Christmas. **Cost:** $1; free (ages 0-5). **Phone:** (505) 983-3974.

(See maps & indexes p. 420, 423.)

SANTA FE CHILDREN'S MUSEUM is 1 mi. s. of The Plaza at 1050 Old Pecos Tr. Geared to children ages 0-12, interactive exhibits focus on the arts, sciences and humanities. Among the highlights are an outdoor garden learning environment, bubble exhibits, a rock climbing wall and water works. Artists, scientists and environmental educators conduct hands-on activities; phone ahead for schedule. **Hours:** Wed.-Sat. 10-5 (also Thurs. 5-6:30), Sun.-Tues. noon-5, early June-early Oct.; Wed.-Sat. 10-5 (also Thurs. 5-6:30), Sun. noon-5, rest of year. Closed major holidays. **Cost:** Tues.-Sat. $7.50; $6 (New Mexico residents with ID). Admission Sun. $5; $2 (New Mexico residents with ID). **Phone:** (505) 989-8359.

SANTA FE NATIONAL CEMETERY is 1.5 mi. n. of The Plaza on US 285 at 501 N. Guadalupe St. Originally the military post cemetery, the site contains the graves of soldiers from the Indian Wars as well as those killed in the battles of Pigeon's Ranch and Valverde during the Civil War. It also is the final resting place for nine Congressional Medal of Honor recipients. **Hours:** Gates open daily dawn-dusk; office open Mon.-Fri. 8-4:30. **Cost:** Free. **Phone:** (505) 988-6400.

SANTUARIO DE GUADALUPE is 4 blks. w. of The Plaza at Agua Fria and Guadalupe sts. This 18th-century church is thought of as the nation's oldest shrine dedicated to Our Lady of Guadalupe. An interior highlight is the 1783 oil-on-canvas altar painting by Mexican baroque artist José de Alzibar. A meditation chapel contains religious-themed woodcarvings, and there is also a pictorial history room. On the grounds is the Plants of the Holy Land botanical garden. An 18th-century mission is at the end of El Camino Real. **Hours:** Mon.-Fri. 9-noon and 1-4; call for mass schedule. **Cost:** Donations. **Phone:** (505) 983-8868, ext. 21.

SITE SANTA FE is at 1606 Paseo de Peralta. This contemporary arts organization provides exhibit space for national, international, local and regional artists. Different collections are typically showcased three times a year; visitors should phone ahead to confirm. **Time:** Allow 1 hour minimum. **Hours:** Thurs. and Sat. 10-5, Fri. 10-7, Sun. noon-5 (also Wed. 10-5, July-Aug.). **Cost:** $10; $5 (ages 60+ and students with ID); free (ages 0-18 and to all Fri. 10-7 and Sat. 10-noon). **Phone:** (505) 989-1199.

SOUTHWEST SAFARIS departs from and returns to the Santa Fe Airport. Full-day air/land combination tours travel to the Grand Canyon, Monument Valley, Canyon de Chelly, Arches/Canyonlands and Mesa Verde. The expeditions include exploration of landmarks, pueblos, cliff dwellings and ruins. Regional geology, archeology and history are explained. Local scenic flights and half-day air/land adventures also are available. **Hours:** Tour lengths range from 30 minutes to 8 hours; some include lunch. **Cost:** Fares $99-$999. Reservations are required. **Phone:** (505) 988-4246 or (800) 842-4246.

TESUQUE PUEBLO—see place listing p. 450.

WHEELWRIGHT MUSEUM OF THE AMERICAN INDIAN is 2 mi. s.e. of The Plaza at 704 Camino Lejo on Museum Hill. Reminiscent of an eight-sided Navajo hogan, the museum offers historic and contemporary art exhibits with emphasis on the Southwest. Displays include pottery, jewelry, rugs and baskets. **Hours:** Daily 10-5. Closed Jan. 1, Thanksgiving and Christmas. **Cost:** $5; free (ages 0-11 and students with ID). **Phone:** (505) 982-4636 or (800) 607-4636. GT

RECREATIONAL ACTIVITIES
White-water Rafting

- **Kokopelli Rafting Adventures** departs from various locations. **Hours:** Daily Apr.-Oct. **Phone:** (505) 983-3734 or (800) 879-9035.
- **New Mexico River Adventures** departs from 2217 SR 68. Other activities are available. **Hours:** Daily Apr.-Sept. **Phone:** (505) 983-7756 or (800) 983-7756.
- **Santa Fe Rafting Co.** is 1.5 mi. s.w. of the Plaza on Cerrillos Rd. **Hours:** Daily Apr.-Sept. **Phone:** (505) 988-4914 or (888) 988-4914.

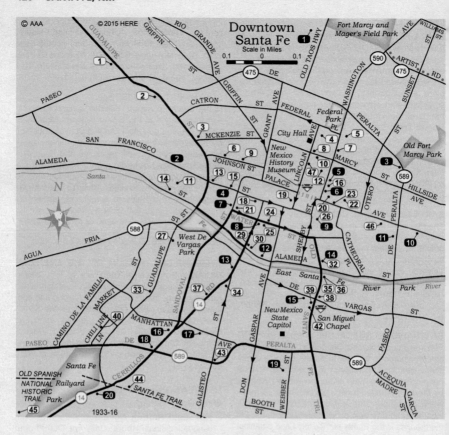

Downtown
Santa Fe
Scale in Miles

Downtown Santa Fe

This index helps you "spot" where approved hotels and restaurants are located on the corresponding detailed maps. Hotel daily rate range is for comparison only. Restaurant price range is a combination of lunch and/or dinner. Turn to the listing page for more detailed rate and price information and consult display ads for special promotions.

DOWNTOWN SANTA FE

Map Page	Hotels	Diamond Rated	Rate Range	Page
1 p. 420	Casa Cuma B & B	◆◆◆	Rates not provided	425
2 p. 420	Las Palomas	◆◆◆	Rates not provided	428
3 p. 420	Inn on the Paseo	◆◆◆	Rates not provided	427
4 p. 420	**Eldorado Hotel & Spa** *(See ad p. 426.)*	◆◆◆◆	$149-$419 SAVE	425
5 p. 420	**Hotel Chimayó de Santa Fe**	◆◆◆	Rates not provided SAVE	426
6 p. 420	Rosewood Inn of the Anasazi	◆◆◆◆	Rates not provided	428
7 p. 420	**Hilton Santa Fe Historic Plaza**	◆◆◆	$109-$299 SAVE	425
8 p. 420	Otra Vez en Santa Fe	◆◆◆	$165-$215	428
9 p. 420	**La Fonda On the Plaza**	◆◆◆◆	$159-$599 SAVE	427
10 p. 420	**La Posada de Santa Fe, A Luxury Collection Resort & Spa**	◆◆◆◆	Rates not provided SAVE	427
11 p. 420	The Drury Plaza Hotel in Santa Fe	◆◆◆	$130-$340	425
12 p. 420	Inn of the Governors	◆◆◆	$99-$309	427
13 p. 420	**The Old Santa Fe Inn**	◆◆◆	$99-$390 SAVE	428
14 p. 420	**The Inn & Spa at Loretto**	◆◆◆◆	$189-$599 SAVE	427
15 p. 420	The Inn of The Five Graces	◆◆◆◆	$425-$2500	427
16 p. 420	Santa Fe Motel & Inn	◆◆	$99-$249	428
17 p. 420	**El Paradero Bed & Breakfast**	◆◆◆	$100-$200 SAVE	425
18 p. 420	Hotel Santa Fe, The Hacienda & Spa	◆◆◆	$119-$600	426
19 p. 420	Four Kachinas Inn	◆◆◆	$140-$250	425
20 p. 420	**Santa Fe Sage Inn & Suites** *(See ad p. 428.)*	◆◆◆	Rates not provided SAVE	428

Map Page	Restaurants	Diamond Rated	Cuisine	Price Range	Page
1 p. 420	Jinja Bar & Bistro	◆◆◆	Asian	$9-$18	429
2 p. 420	Clafoutis	◆◆	French	$5-$13	429
3 p. 420	Bumble Bee's Baja Grill	◆	Regional Mexican	$7-$13	429
4 p. 420	**Osteria d'Assisi**	◆◆◆	Northern Italian	$10-$33	430
5 p. 420	**Santacafe**	◆◆◆	New American	$10-$35	430
6 p. 420	Shohko Cafe	◆◆◆	Japanese	$15-$37	431
7 p. 420	El Meson	◆◆◆	Spanish	$22-$36	429
8 p. 420	Il Piatto	◆◆◆	Italian	$11-$30	429
9 p. 420	Georgia	◆◆◆	Northern American	$20-$35	429
10 p. 420	La Boca	◆◆◆	International Small Plates	$9-$24	430
11 p. 420	Vanessie	◆◆◆	American	$16-$45	431
12 p. 420	The Bull Ring	◆◆◆	Steak	$10-$48	429
13 p. 420	Thai Cafe	◆◆	Thai	$10-$16	431

Map Page	Restaurants (cont'd)	Diamond Rated	Cuisine	Price Range	Page
⑭ p. 420	Bouche French Bistro	▽▽▽	French	$16-$30	429
⑮ p. 420	**Old House**	▽▽▽	Regional Southwestern	$11-$36	430
⑯ p. 420	Anasazi Restaurant	▽▽▽	Regional American	$12-$38	428
⑱ p. 420	Tia Sophia's	▽	Southwestern	$7-$11	431
⑲ p. 420	Plaza Cafe	▽▽	American	$8-$25	430
⑳ p. 420	The Burrito Company	▽	Regional Mexican	$6-$9	429
㉑ p. 420	Blue Corn Cafe & Brewery	▽▽	Southwestern	$9-$18	429
㉒ p. 420	La Casa Sena Restaurant	▽▽▽	Regional American	$12-$40	430
㉓ p. 420	The Shed	▽▽	Regional Mexican	$8-$20	431
㉔ p. 420	Cafe Pasqual's	▽▽▽	Regional American	$12-$29	429
㉕ p. 420	Coyote Cafe	▽▽▽	Southwestern	$28-$56	429
㉖ p. 420	La Plazuela at La Fonda	▽▽▽	Regional American	$11-$30	430
㉗ p. 420	Cowgirl Bar and Grill	▽▽	Regional American	$8-$23	429
㉙ p. 420	Galisteo Bistro & Wine Bar	▽▽▽	International	$21-$29	429
㉚ p. 420	L'Olivier	▽▽▽	French	$19-$36	430
㉜ p. 420	Luminaria Restaurant & Patio	▽▽▽	New American	$20-$45	430
㉝ p. 420	Tomasita's Restaurant	▽▽	Regional Mexican	$7-$15	431
㉞ p. 420	Saveur	▽▽	French	$6-$16	431
㉟ p. 420	315 Restaurant & Wine Bar	▽▽▽	French	$24-$36	428
㊱ p. 420	Santa Fe Bite	▽▽	Burgers	$6-$27	430
㊲ p. 420	Yin Yang	▽▽	Chinese	$8-$26	431
㊳ p. 420	Upper Crust Pizza	▽	Pizza	$4-$22	431
㊴ p. 420	The Pink Adobe	▽▽▽	American	$18-$30	430
㊵ p. 420	Second Street Brewery at the Railyard	▽▽	American	$9-$15	431
㊷ p. 420	Rio Chama	▽▽▽	Steak	$11-$46	430
㊸ p. 420	Restaurant Martin	▽▽▽	New American	$10-$36	430
㊹ p. 420	Vinaigrette	▽▽	Natural/Organic	$10-$19	431
㊺ p. 420	La Choza	▽▽	Regional Mexican	$9-$18	430
㊻ p. 420	Eloisa	▽▽▽	New Southwestern	$13-$36	429
㊼ p. 420	Taberna	▽▽▽	Spanish Small Plates	$8-$22	431

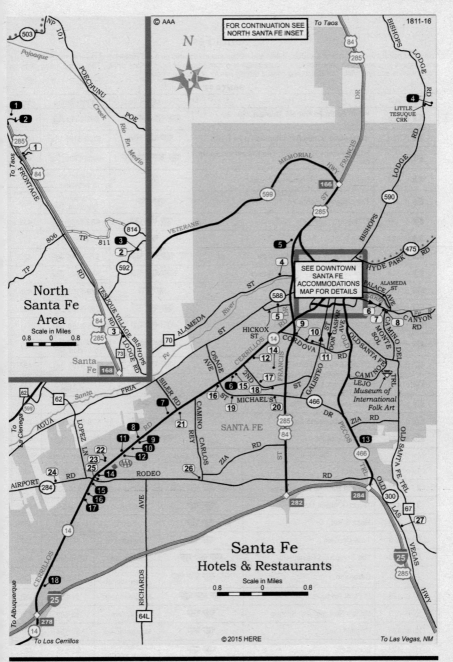

Santa Fe
Hotels & Restaurants

Santa Fe

This index helps you "spot" where approved hotels and restaurants are located on the corresponding detailed maps. Hotel daily rate range is for comparison only. Restaurant price range is a combination of lunch and/or dinner. Turn to the listing page for more detailed rate and price information and consult display ads for special promotions.

SANTA FE

Map Page	Hotels	Diamond Rated	Rate Range	Page
❶ p. 423	Hilton Santa Fe Buffalo Thunder (See ad p. 433.)	◆◆◆◆	$99-$399 [SAVE]	433
❷ p. 423	Homewood Suites By Hilton-Santa Fe North	◆◆◆	$109-$189 [SAVE]	435
❸ p. 423	Four Seasons Resort Rancho Encantado Santa Fe	◆◆◆◆	$209-$909 [SAVE]	433
❹ p. 423	Bishop's Lodge Ranch Resort & Spa	[fyi]	Rates not provided	432
❺ p. 423	The Lodge at Santa Fe	◆◆	Rates not provided [SAVE]	435
❻ p. 423	El Rey Inn (See ad p. 432.)	◆◆◆	$89-$265 [SAVE]	433
❼ p. 423	Motel 6-150	◆	$45-$75	435
❽ p. 423	Courtyard by Marriott-Santa Fe	◆◆◆	$79-$144 [SAVE]	432
❾ p. 423	Comfort Suites by Choice Hotels	◆◆◆	$89-$199 [SAVE]	432
❿ p. 423	Holiday Inn Express-Santa Fe	◆◆	$79-$199 [SAVE]	435
⓫ p. 423	Hampton Inn Santa Fe	◆◆◆	$89-$189 [SAVE]	433
⓬ p. 423	BEST WESTERN PLUS Inn of Santa Fe	◆◆◆	$95-$150 [SAVE]	431
⓭ p. 423	Pecos Trail Inn	◆◆	Rates not provided [SAVE]	435
⓮ p. 423	DoubleTree by Hilton Santa Fe	◆◆◆	$99-$199 [SAVE]	432
⓯ p. 423	Baymont Inn & Suites	◆◆	Rates not provided	431
⓰ p. 423	La Quinta Inn Santa Fe	◆◆	$64-$218	435
⓱ p. 423	Hyatt Place Santa Fe	◆◆◆	$79-$249 [SAVE]	435
⓲ p. 423	Inn at Santa Fe	◆◆◆	$79-$249 [SAVE]	435

Map Page	Restaurants	Diamond Rated	Cuisine	Price Range	Page
① p. 423	Gabriel's	◆◆	Mexican	$9-$20	436
② p. 423	Terra at Rancho Encantado	◆◆◆◆	Southwestern	$18-$39	437
③ p. 423	Tesuque Village Market	◆◆	American	$10-$40	437
④ p. 423	Masa Sushi	◆◆	Sushi	$9-$26	436
⑤ p. 423	Tune-Up Cafe	◆◆	International	$9-$15	437
⑥ p. 423	The Compound Restaurant	◆◆◆	American	$18-$45	436
⑦ p. 423	Geronimo	◆◆◆◆	Regional International	$28-$50	436
⑧ p. 423	El Farol Restaurant	◆◆◆	Mediterranean	$8-$52	436
⑨ p. 423	Maria's New Mexican Kitchen	◆◆	Mexican	$9-$25	436
⑩ p. 423	Pyramid Cafe	◆◆	Mediterranean	$9-$24	437
⑪ p. 423	Body Cafe	◆◆	Natural/Organic Raw Foods	$9-$15	435
⑫ p. 423	Mu Du Noodles	◆◆	Asian	$12-$25	436
⑭ p. 423	Sweetwater Harvest Kitchen	◆◆	Natural/Organic	$7-$20	437
⑮ p. 423	The Pantry	◆◆	Regional American	$7-$16	436
⑯ p. 423	Jambo Cafe	◆◆	African	$9-$15	436

Map Page	Restaurants (cont'd)	Diamond Rated	Cuisine	Price Range	Page
⑰ p. 423	Midtown Bistro	▽▽▽	Northern Mexican	$10-$32	436
⑱ p. 423	Chocolate Maven Bakery & Cafe	▽▽▽	American	$10-$15	435
⑲ p. 423	Pizzeria Espiritu	▽▽	Italian	$10-$25	437
⑳ p. 423	Chow's Asian Bistro	▽▽▽	Asian	$9-$20	436
㉑ p. 423	Dr. Field Goods Kitchen	▽▽	Regional American	$8-$15	436
㉒ p. 423	Santa Fe Capitol Grill	▽▽▽	International	$8-$27	437
㉓ p. 423	Cleopatra's Cafe	▽	Mediterranean	$6-$16	436
㉔ p. 423	Puerto Penasco	▽▽	Mexican Seafood	$7-$15	437
㉕ p. 423	Blue Corn Cafe & Brewery	▽	Southwestern	$9-$18	435
㉖ p. 423	Joe's Diner and Pizza	▽▽	American	$9-$27	436
㉗ p. 423	Harry's Roadhouse	▽▽	American	$8-$22	436

DOWNTOWN SANTA FE
- Restaurants p. 428
- Hotels & Restaurants map & index p. 420

CASA CUMA B & B 505-216-7516 **1**

▽▽▽ **Bed & Breakfast.** Rates not provided. **Address:** 105 Paseo de la Cuma 87501 **Location:** Just w off Old Taos Hwy. **Facility:** Near Cross of the Martyrs, this 1950s adobe-style B&B offers well-appointed guest rooms, a lush patio with a fire pit and an outdoor hot tub with beautiful mountain views. 6 units, some kitchens, houses and cottages. 1 story, interior/exterior corridors. **Terms:** age restrictions may apply. **Activities:** hot tub, massage. **Guest Services:** valet laundry.

THE DRURY PLAZA HOTEL IN SANTA FE
(505)424-2175 **11**

▽▽▽ **Hotel** $130-$340 **Address:** 828 E Paseo de Peralta 87501 **Location:** At Palace Ave. **Facility:** 182 units. 5 stories, interior corridors. **Parking:** valet only. **Terms:** cancellation fee imposed. **Dining:** Eloisa, see separate listing. **Pool(s):** heated outdoor. **Activities:** hot tub, exercise room, massage. **Guest Services:** valet and coin laundry.

ELDORADO HOTEL & SPA   (505)988-4455 **4**

▽▽▽ ▽▽▽
Hotel
$149-$419

Address: 309 W San Francisco St 87501 **Location:** Just w of The Plaza; at Sandoval St. **Facility:** Custom contemporary Southwestern décor marks the hotel's public facilities. The property is centrally located for an easy day of shopping, museum gazing and gallery hopping. 219 units. 5 stories, interior corridors. **Parking:** on-site (fee) and valet. **Terms:** check-in 4 pm, 3 day cancellation notice-fee imposed. **Amenities:** video games, safes. **Dining:** Old House, see separate listing. **Pool(s):** heated outdoor. **Activities:** sauna, hot tub, steam-room, exercise room, spa. **Guest Services:** valet laundry.
(See ad p. 426.)

EL PARADERO BED & BREAKFAST
(505)988-1177 **17**

▽▽▽
Historic Bed & Breakfast
$100-$200

Address: 220 W Manhattan Ave 87501 **Location:** 0.3 mi s on Cerrillos Rd, 1/2 blk e. **Facility:** Within walking distance of the Guadalupe and Railyard shopping districts, this early 1800s farmhouse serves tea under a cherry tree or in the cheerful breakfast room. 15 units, some two bedrooms and efficiencies. 1-2 stories (no elevator), interior/exterior corridors. **Terms:** 2 night minimum stay - seasonal and/or weekends, age restrictions may apply, 14 day cancellation notice-fee imposed. **Guest Services:** valet laundry.

FOUR KACHINAS INN   (505)988-1631 **19**

▽▽▽ **Bed & Breakfast** $140-$250 **Address:** 512 Webber St 87505 **Location:** Jct Cerrillos Rd and Paseo de Peralta, 4 blks e, then just s. **Facility:** Rooms appointed with Spanish-Colonial reproductions enhance the inn's appeal. Breakfast is served in a room that opens to a sunlit patio. 6 units. 1-2 stories (no elevator), interior/exterior corridors. **Terms:** 2 night minimum stay - weekends, 15 day cancellation notice-fee imposed. **Guest Services:** valet laundry.

HILTON SANTA FE HISTORIC PLAZA
(505)988-2811 **7**

▽▽▽
Hotel
$109-$299

AAA Benefit: Members save 5% or more!

Address: 100 Sandoval St 87501 **Location:** Just sw of The Plaza; between San Francisco and W Alameda sts. **Facility:** 158 units, some two bedrooms. 3 stories, interior/exterior corridors. **Parking:** on-site (fee). **Terms:** 1-7 night minimum stay, cancellation fee imposed. **Amenities:** safes. **Dining:** 2 restaurants. **Pool(s):** heated outdoor. **Activities:** hot tub, exercise room. **Guest Services:** valet laundry.

(See map & index p. 420.)

HOTEL CHIMAYÓ DE SANTA FE   505/988-4900

Hotel
Rates not provided

Address: 125 Washington Ave 87501 **Location:** Just ne of The Plaza; center. **Facility:** 56 units, some efficiencies. 2-3 stories, interior/exterior corridors. **Parking:** on-site (fee). **Terms:** check-in 4 pm. **Guest Services:** valet laundry.

HOTEL SANTA FE, THE HACIENDA & SPA
(505)982-1200 **18**

Hotel $119-$600 **Address:** 1501 Paseo de Peralta 87501 **Location:** At Cerrillos Rd, 0.6 mi s of The Plaza. **Facility:** 163 units. 3 stories, interior corridors. **Terms:** check-in 4 pm, 3 day cancellation notice-fee imposed, resort fee. **Amenities:** safes. **Pool(s):** heated outdoor. **Activities:** hot tub, exercise room, spa. **Guest Services:** valet and coin laundry, area transportation.

▼ See AAA listing p. 425 ▼

(See map & index p. 420.)

THE INN & SPA AT LORETTO   (505)988-5531

Hotel
$189-$599

Address: 211 Old Santa Fe Tr 87501 **Location:** Just s of The Plaza. Located in the historic district. **Facility:** This is a cozy retreat after a day spent in the galleries, museums, sightseeing and shopping, all available just a short walk away. 136 units, some kitchens. 5 stories, interior corridors. **Parking:** on-site (fee) and valet. **Terms:** check-in 4 pm, 3 day cancellation notice-fee imposed, resort fee. **Dining:** Luminaria Restaurant & Patio, see separate listing. **Pool(s):** heated outdoor. **Activities:** exercise room, spa. **Guest Services:** valet laundry.

THE INN OF THE FIVE GRACES   (505)992-0957

Historic Retro Country Inn $425-$2500 **Address:** 150 E DeVargas St 87501 **Location:** Jct Old Pecos Trail. **Facility:** Classic Santa Fe architecture is blended with imported antique furniture and tapestries to create an almost dream-like ambiance. This inn sets the standard for unique style and eclectic décor. 24 units, some two bedrooms, kitchens and houses. 1-2 stories (no elevator), interior/exterior corridors. **Parking:** valet only. **Terms:** check-in 4 pm, 2-3 night minimum stay - seasonal and/or weekends, age restrictions may apply, 7 day cancellation notice-fee imposed. **Amenities:** safes. **Activities:** exercise room, massage. **Guest Services:** valet laundry, area transportation.

INN OF THE GOVERNORS   (505)982-4333

Hotel $99-$309 **Address:** 101 W Alameda St 87501 **Location:** Between Ortiz St and Don Gaspar Ave; center. Located in the historic district. **Facility:** 100 units. 2-3 stories, interior/exterior corridors. **Terms:** check-in 4 pm, cancellation fee imposed. **Amenities:** safes. **Pool(s):** heated outdoor. **Guest Services:** valet laundry.

INN ON THE PASEO   505/984-8200

Boutique Bed & Breakfast. Rates not provided. **Address:** 630 Paseo de Peralta 87501 **Location:** I-25 exit 282, 2 mi e; jct St. Francis Dr. **Facility:** Located within walking distance of the historic plaza, this charming B&B offers true Southwestern hospitality. Enjoy a complimentary afternoon refreshment after a long day of exploring Santa Fe. 18 units, some two bedrooms. 2 stories (no elevator), interior/exterior corridors. **Terms:** check-in 4 pm. **Guest Services:** valet laundry.

LA FONDA ON THE PLAZA   (505)982-5511

Historic Hotel
$159-$599

Address: 100 E San Francisco St 87501 **Location:** On The Plaza. **Facility:** The current building dates to the 1920s, but there has been an inn on this site since 1620. Impressive and recently renovated, the inn maintains its historic charm but with modern conveniences. 180 units. 5 stories, interior corridors. **Parking:** on-site (fee). **Terms:** cancellation fee imposed. **Amenities:** safes. **Dining:** 3 restaurants, also, La Plazuela at La Fonda, see separate listing, entertainment. **Pool(s):** heated outdoor. **Activities:** hot tub, steamroom, exercise room, spa. **Guest Services:** valet laundry.

LA POSADA DE SANTA FE, A LUXURY COLLECTION RESORT & SPA   505/986-0000

Resort Hotel
Rates not provided

Address: 330 E Palace Ave 87501 **Location:** Jct Paseo de Peralta and E Palace Ave. **Facility:** This is a classic Santa Fe resort that blends the Old World New Mexico style of the original house with elegant contemporary luxury amenities. 157 units, some two bedrooms. 1-2 stories (no elevator), exterior corridors. **Parking:** valet only. **Terms:** check-in 4 pm. **Amenities:** safes. **Dining:** 3 restaurants, entertainment. **Pool(s):** heated outdoor. **Activities:** hot tub, steamroom, recreation programs, exercise room, spa. **Guest Services:** valet laundry, area transportation.

(See map & index p. 420.)

LAS PALOMAS   505/982-5560 **2**

▼▼▼ **Boutique Hotel.** Rates not provided. **Address:** 460 W San Francisco St 87501 **Location:** Just w of jct Guadalupe St. **Facility:** Circa 1870s, these restored adobe casitas provide an excellent Southwestern ambiance with such in-room extras as a cappuccino/espresso maker and a kiva fireplace or gas-burning stove. 63 units, some efficiencies and condominiums. 2 stories (no elevator), exterior corridors. **Activities:** exercise room, massage. **Guest Services:** valet and coin laundry.

THE OLD SANTA FE INN   (505)995-0800 **13**

▼▼▼▼

Motel
$99-$390

Address: 320 Galisteo St 87501 **Location:** Just sw of The Plaza; center. **Facility:** 43 units. 1-2 stories (no elevator), interior/exterior corridors. **Terms:** check-in 4 pm, 3 day cancellation notice-fee imposed. **Amenities:** safes. **Activities:** exercise room. **Guest Services:** valet laundry.

OTRA VEZ EN SANTA FE   (505)988-2244 **8**

▼▼▼▼ **Condominium** $165-$215 **Address:** 202 Galisteo St 87501 **Location:** Just s of The Plaza; center. **Facility:** Offered are well-appointed, fully equipped condo units with typical Santa Fe décor. Some units have a fireplace. Take a convenient stroll to the historic Plaza. 18 condominiums. 3 stories, interior/exterior corridors. **Terms:** check-in 4 pm, 3 night minimum stay - seasonal and/or weekends, 3 day cancellation notice-fee imposed. **Guest Services:** complimentary laundry.

ROSEWOOD INN OF THE ANASAZI   505/988-3030 **6**

▼▼▼ ▼▼▼ **Hotel.** Rates not provided. **Address:** 113 Washington Ave 87501 **Location:** Just ne of The Plaza. **Facility:** Guest rooms showcase contemporary Southwestern style with traditional ceilings of vigas and latillas. All have cozy fireplaces. Its plaza location is convenient to many museums, shops and galleries. 58 units. 3 stories, interior corridors. **Parking:** valet only. **Terms:** check-in 4 pm. **Amenities:** safes. **Dining:** Anasazi Restaurant, see separate listing. **Activities:** massage. **Guest Services:** valet laundry.

SANTA FE MOTEL & INN   (505)982-1039 **16**

▼▼▼ **Motel** $99-$249 **Address:** 510 Cerrillos Rd 87501 **Location:** 4 blks sw of The Plaza. **Facility:** 23 units, some efficiencies. 1-2 stories (no elevator), exterior corridors. **Terms:** 2 night minimum stay - seasonal and/or weekends, 3 day cancellation notice-fee imposed. **Guest Services:** valet laundry.

SANTA FE SAGE INN & SUITES   505/982-5952 **20**

▼▼▼▼

Hotel
Rates not provided

Address: 725 Cerrillos Rd 87505 **Location:** 0.4 mi ne of St. Francis Dr (US 84). **Facility:** 145 units. 2 stories (no elevator), exterior corridors. **Parking:** on-site (fee). **Terms:** check-in 4 pm. **Pool(s):** heated outdoor. **Activities:** exercise room. **Guest Services:** valet and coin laundry, area transportation. **Featured Amenity:** continental breakfast. (See ad this page.)

WHERE TO EAT

315 RESTAURANT & WINE BAR   505/986-9190 **35**

▼▼▼ French. Fine Dining. $24-$36 **AAA Inspector Notes:** Excellent French and American preparations such as pate, steak and seafood are the focus of the seasonal menu, which also includes splendid desserts such as warm tarte tatin with crème fraiche. Several cozy dining rooms with original art and white table coverings provide an intimate setting; a small patio area at the entrance allows for seasonal dining. A professional, knowledgeable staff provides service. **Features:** full bar, patio dining. **Reservations:** suggested. **Address:** 315 Old Santa Fe Tr 87501 **Location:** 0.5 mi s of The Plaza; at De Vargas St. **Parking:** street only. **D**

ANASAZI RESTAURANT   505/988-3236 **16**

▼▼▼ Regional American. Fine Dining. $12-$38 **AAA Inspector Notes:** Located in a downtown inn near the Plaza's many shops, guests can be treated to a superior meal in this upscale, casual restaurant. The chef offers innovative preparation methods of stylish Western cuisine featuring organic produce, free-range meats and fresh fish. **Features:** full bar, Sunday brunch. **Reservations:** suggested. **Address:** 113 Washington Ave 87501 **Location:** Just ne of The Plaza; in Rosewood Inn of the Anasazi. **Parking:** valet only. **B L D**

▼ See AAA listing this page ▼

(See map & index p. 420.)

BLUE CORN CAFE & BREWERY   505/984-1800   21
WWW Southwestern. Casual Dining. $9-$18 **AAA Inspector Notes:** Just off The Plaza, this upstairs restaurant beckons diners to feast on ample servings of New Mexican cuisine with an American twist. Watch passersby on Water and Galisteo streets as you sip a cool libation-perhaps one of the daily margarita specials or a selection from an extensive list of brewery choices-and indulge your appetite. The staff is friendly and attentive. **Features:** full bar. **Address:** 133 W Water St 87501 **Location:** Jct Galisteo St; center. **Parking:** street only. L D

BOUCHE FRENCH BISTRO   505/982-6297   14
WWWW French. Fine Dining. $16-$30 **AAA Inspector Notes:** This cozy bistro has an authentic neighborhood atmosphere and features traditional French country fare expertly prepared and presented by award-winning chef Charles Dale and his skilled staff. Dinner here will transport you to the streets of Paris. **Features:** beer & wine, patio dining. **Address:** 451 W Alameda St 87501 **Location:** Jct Guadalupe St, just w; parking and entrance on Water St. D

THE BULL RING   505/983-3328   12
WWW Steak. Fine Dining. $10-$48 **AAA Inspector Notes:** Steaks arrive sizzling in hot butter, potatoes are served seven ways and servers are hometown-friendly in this steakhouse offering entrées served a la carte including lamb chops, salmon and Prime beef. The bank's parking garage is made available fee-free for patrons in the evenings. **Features:** full bar, patio dining, early bird specials, happy hour. **Reservations:** suggested. **Address:** 150 Washington Ave 87501 **Location:** Just n of The Plaza; in Wells Fargo Bank building. **Parking:** street only. L D

BUMBLE BEE'S BAJA GRILL   505/820-2862   3
W Regional Mexican. Quick Serve. $7-$13 **AAA Inspector Notes:** This café is the place to head when in a hurry, where guests can dine in or drive through. A local favorite for fresh, healthy fast food served in very generous portions. Enjoy the cheerful dining area while munching on such dishes as grilled mahi mahi tacos with chunks of avocado, or low-carb naked burritos without the tortilla. **Features:** beer & wine. **Address:** 301 Jefferson St 87501 **Location:** Jct Guadalupe St. L D

THE BURRITO COMPANY   505/982-4453   20
W Regional Mexican. Quick Serve. $6-$9 **AAA Inspector Notes:** Just off The Plaza, this laid-back restaurant is near shopping, museums and several lodgings. The cheerful interior offers plenty of colorful Mexican folk art and the patio is complete with umbrellas for seasonal dining. Self service for those wanting a quick meal with generous portions at a good value. **Features:** beer & wine, patio dining. **Address:** 111 Washington Ave 87501 **Location:** Between Marcy St and Palace Ave; downtown. **Parking:** street only. B L

CAFE PASQUAL'S   505/983-9340   24
WWW Regional American. Casual Dining. $12-$29 **AAA Inspector Notes:** If the line is long at this small and charming spot one block from the downtown plaza, join the community table for good coffee, local chat and such dishes as breakfast quesadillas with applewood smoked bacon or huevos motulenos with grilled bananas. Dinner features a creative changing seasonal menu with a distinctive twist on Latin American favorites. This farm to table restaurant strives to serve only organic food products including produce and chicken plus naturally raised beef and pork. **Reservations:** required, for dinner. **Address:** 121 Don Gaspar Ave 87501 **Location:** Just sw of The Plaza; center. **Parking:** street only. B L D

CLAFOUTIS   505/988-1809   2
WW French. Casual Dining. $5-$13 **AAA Inspector Notes:** This small café, featuring typical French bistro fare, is a favorite of local Santa Feans for its strong coffee and delectable homemade pastries. **Features:** patio dining. **Address:** 402 N Guadalupe St 87501 **Location:** Just s of jct Paseo de Peralta; in DeVargas area. B L

COWGIRL BAR AND GRILL   505/982-2565   27
WWW Regional American. Casual Dining. $8-$23 **AAA Inspector Notes:** Downhome dining amid the kitschy cowgirl memorabilia at this rustic eatery near The Plaza includes ribs, great salsa and Mexican favorites. It is a prime place for people-watching while sipping on a very good house margarita and listening to eclectic live music on the pleasant patio. **Features:** full bar, patio dining, Sunday brunch. **Reservations:** suggested. **Address:** 319 S Guadalupe St 87501 **Location:** 2 blks s of Alameda St; jct Aztec St. **Parking:** street only. L D

COYOTE CAFE   505/983-1615   25
WWW Southwestern. Casual Dining. $28-$56 **AAA Inspector Notes:** A block from the downtown plaza, the now-iconographic restaurant has a creative seasonal menu and contemporary atmosphere. Diners can enjoy a signature cocktail or fine wine from the extensive wine list. **Features:** full bar, patio dining. **Reservations:** suggested. **Address:** 132 W Water St 87501 **Location:** Just sw of The Plaza; between Ortiz and Galisteo sts. **Parking:** street only. D

EL MESON   505/983-6756   7
WWW Spanish. Casual Dining. $22-$36 **AAA Inspector Notes:** Authentic Spanish cuisine and tapas are featured at this restaurant where chef David Huertas showcases many traditional family recipes. Tapas are available in the lounge where live entertainment includes music and dancing. **Features:** full bar. **Reservations:** suggested. **Address:** 213 Washington Ave 87501 **Location:** Just ne of main plaza, jct Marcy St. **Parking:** street only. D

ELOISA   505/982-0083   46
WWW New Southwestern. Casual Dining. $13-$36 **AAA Inspector Notes:** This new trendy dining room features an open kitchen where you can watch the staff in action. A creative Southwestern menu showcases local fresh and organic farm-to-table cuisine. **Features:** full bar, patio dining. **Reservations:** suggested. **Address:** 228 E Palace Ave 87501 **Location:** At Palace Ave and Paseo de Peralta; in The Drury Plaza Hotel in Santa Fe. **Parking:** on-site and valet. L D CALL M

GALISTEO BISTRO & WINE BAR   505/982-3700   29
WWW International. Casual Dining. $21-$29 **AAA Inspector Notes:** Chef owned and operated, this open kitchen concept features a creative international menu from tapas to seasonal bistro entrées. Ingredients are fresh, local and organic, when possible. **Features:** beer & wine. **Reservations:** suggested. **Address:** 227 Galisteo St 87501 **Location:** Jct Alameda St, just n. **Parking:** street only. D

GEORGIA   505/989-4367   9
WWW Northern American. Fine Dining. $20-$35 **AAA Inspector Notes:** A creative twist of familiar comfort foods is featured here, with no trace of chile. Beautiful, contemporary décor and refined service make for an excellent dining experience. **Features:** full bar, patio dining. **Reservations:** suggested. **Address:** 225 Johnson St 87501 **Location:** Northwest of historic plaza; adjacent to Georgia O'Keeffe museum. **Parking:** valet and street only. D

IL PIATTO   505/984-1091   8
WWW Italian. Casual Dining. $11-$30 **AAA Inspector Notes:** In the heart of the downtown historic district and only one block from the Plaza, this restaurant tempts patrons with seasonal and ever-changing farm fresh specialties. Pasta is made fresh daily. The lunch or dinner prix fixe menu is an excellent value as is half-priced appetizers for happy hour. **Features:** beer & wine, patio dining, happy hour. **Reservations:** suggested, for dinner. **Address:** 95 W Marcy St 87501 **Location:** Between Lincoln Ave and Washington St; just n of The Plaza. **Parking:** street only. L D

JINJA BAR & BISTRO   505/982-4321   1
WWW Asian. Casual Dining. $9-$18 **AAA Inspector Notes:** This cafe appeals to diners who do not want to limit themselves to one style of cuisine. Thai, Japanese, Chinese and Vietnamese dishes are served in an elegant but relaxed atmosphere. **Features:** full bar, senior menu. **Reservations:** suggested. **Address:** 510 N Guadalupe St, Suite P 87501 **Location:** Just nw of Paseo de Peralta; in DeVargas Center Mall. L D

(See map & index p. 420.)

LA BOCA
505/982-3433 [10]

International Small Plates. Casual Dining. $9-$24 **AAA Inspector Notes:** Creative tapas make this a fun and lively dining experience. A variety of items for sharing includes many vegetarian options. The grilled asparagus with smoked salmon and goat cheese is a must. **Features:** full bar, patio dining, Sunday brunch, happy hour. **Reservations:** suggested. **Address:** 72 W Marcy St 87501 **Location:** Just n of historic central plaza. **Parking:** on-site (fee) and street.
[L] [D]

LA CASA SENA RESTAURANT
505/988-9232 [22]

Regional American. Fine Dining. $12-$40 **AAA Inspector Notes:** *Historic.* This restaurant features an extensive wine list and excellent regional preparations of traditional menu selections. Servers are attentive and knowledgeable, and a large outdoor dining area is available. For a fun treat enjoy dessert and after-dinner drinks in the bar area that features waitstaff performing Broadway show tunes. **Features:** full bar, patio dining, Sunday brunch. **Reservations:** suggested. **Address:** 125 E Palace Ave 87501 **Location:** Just e of The Plaza. **Parking:** street only.
[L] [D]

LA CHOZA
505/982-0909 [45]

Regional Mexican. Casual Dining. $9-$18 **AAA Inspector Notes:** The folks who own The Shed, a popular downtown restaurant, also operate this casual eatery in Santa Fe's up-and-coming Railyard District. Offerings feature the same satisfying New Mexican dishes, including the outstanding sopaipilla-puffy fried bread served with warm honey. **Features:** full bar. **Address:** 905 Alarid St 87505 **Location:** Just e of jct Cerrillos Rd and St. Francis Dr; adjacent to Railyard Park.
[L] [D]

LA PLAZUELA AT LA FONDA
505/982-5511 [26]

Regional American. Casual Dining. $11-$30 **AAA Inspector Notes:** Bright blue-, orange- and yellow-colored table settings delight the eye and set the stage. The dinner menu includes steak and seafood dishes prepared with a Southwestern accent, as well as several Mexican entrées. **Features:** full bar, senior menu, happy hour. **Address:** 100 E San Francisco St 87501 **Location:** On The Plaza; in La Fonda On the Plaza. **Parking:** on-site (fee).
[B] [L] [D]

L'OLIVIER
505/989-1919 [30]

French. Fine Dining. $19-$36 **AAA Inspector Notes:** Featuring fine French cuisine with a Southwestern flair, chef Grenet has created a unique menu. Find seasonal local and organic produce including piquant peppers plus flavorful piñon nuts and pumpkin seeds (pepitas) enhancing grass-fed beef, wild game, fowl and fresh seafood. **Features:** beer & wine, patio dining. **Reservations:** suggested. **Address:** 229 Galisteo St 87501 **Location:** Jct W Alameda St; sw of historic plaza. **Parking:** street only. [D]

LUMINARIA RESTAURANT & PATIO
505/984-7915 [32]

New American. Fine Dining. $20-$45 **AAA Inspector Notes:** Modern American cuisine prepared with market-fresh organic vegetables and meats, flavorful sauces and creative desserts plus professional staff make this a memorable dining experience. **Features:** full bar, Sunday brunch. **Reservations:** suggested. **Address:** 211 Old Santa Fe Tr 87501 **Location:** Just s of The Plaza; in The Inn & Spa at Loretto. **Parking:** on-site (fee) and valet.
[B] [L] [D] CALL [M]

OLD HOUSE
505/988-4455 [15]

Regional Southwestern Casual Dining
$11-$36

AAA Inspector Notes: Just a short walk from downtown Santa Fe, this gem is a cozy and intimate spot with Southwestern flair. The menu features aged beef plus a selection of seafood. **Features:** full bar, Sunday brunch, happy hour. **Reservations:** suggested. **Address:** 309 W San Francisco St 87501

Location: Just w of The Plaza; at Sandoval St; in Eldorado Hotel & Spa. **Parking:** valet only. *Menu on AAA.com*
[B] [L] [D]

OSTERIA D'ASSISI
505/986-5858 [4]

Northern Italian Casual Dining
$10-$33

AAA Inspector Notes: This convenient, busy restaurant near both the business and cultural centers of the city serves up delicious Northern Italian cuisine to tourists and business people in comfortable surroundings near the Federal Courthouse. Some gluten-free pasta dishes are available. **Features:** full bar, happy hour. **Reservations:** suggested. **Address:** 58 S Federal Pl 87501 **Location:** 1 blk n of The Plaza. **Parking:** street only.
Menu on AAA.com [L] [D]

THE PINK ADOBE
505/983-7712 [39]

American. Casual Dining. $18-$30 **AAA Inspector Notes:** Established in 1944 and known for its pink adobe look, this restaurant is located in what was previously a 350-year-old home just a short walk from The Plaza. The restaurant is popular with locals and visitors alike and frequented by famous actors and politicians. Several intimate dining rooms, each with a fireplace, enhance the dining experience. Patio seating is available in season. **Features:** full bar, patio dining. **Reservations:** suggested. **Address:** 406 Old Santa Fe Tr 87501 **Location:** Just s of The Plaza. **Parking:** street only.
[D]

PLAZA CAFE
505/982-1664 [19]

American. Family Dining. $8-$25 **AAA Inspector Notes:** This popular retro-style café on the plaza serves hearty portions for all meals. For a true breakfast favorite, try the blue corn piñon pancakes with thick sugar-cured bacon. **Features:** beer & wine. **Address:** 54 Lincoln Ave 87501 **Location:** On the west side of historic plaza. **Parking:** no self-parking.
[B] [L] [D] CALL [M]

RESTAURANT MARTIN
505/820-0919 [43]

New American. Fine Dining. $10-$36 **AAA Inspector Notes:** Well-known chef Martin Rios presents an innovative menu featuring progressive American cuisine. Showcasing local, seasonal and organic ingredients, dishes range from flavorful soups and creative salads to sandwiches and creative entrées. Save room for the luscious desserts. **Features:** beer & wine, patio dining, Sunday brunch. **Reservations:** suggested. **Address:** 526 Galisteo St 87501 **Location:** Jct Paseo de Peralta and Galisteo St; center.
[L] [D] 🐾

RIO CHAMA
505/955-0765 [42]

Steak. Casual Dining. $11-$46 **AAA Inspector Notes:** In the heart of the downtown historic district and next door to the state capitol (Roundhouse), this restaurant is a favorite of government officials especially during the annual legislative session. A menu of Prime and Choice dry-aged steaks, prime rib, chops and seafood are presented. The atmosphere is casual, yet dignified, in the intimate dining rooms. **Features:** full bar, patio dining, Sunday brunch, happy hour. **Reservations:** suggested. **Address:** 414 Old Santa Fe Tr 87501 **Location:** 2 blks s of The Plaza; center.
[L] [D] [N]

SANTACAFE
505/984-1788 [5]

New American Fine Dining
$10-$35

AAA Inspector Notes: *Historic.* This upscale restaurant caters to tourists and locals seeking fine dining with a trendy twist. Crisp linens and fine wines are the order of the day, with American nouvelle cuisine served in a refined ambience. Classic Santa Fe architecture inside a grand old hacienda circa 1854. **Features:** full bar, patio dining, Sunday brunch, happy hour. **Reservations:** suggested. **Address:** 231 Washington Ave 87501 **Location:** Just ne of The Plaza; between Marcy St and Paseo de Peralta. *Menu on AAA.com* [L] [D]

SANTA FE BITE
505/982-0544 [36]

Burgers. Casual Dining. $6-$27 **AAA Inspector Notes:** The famous green chile cheeseburger is well regarded as one of the top in the United States. This bustling casual eatery also serves excellent salads, sandwiches and tacos. Be prepared for a wait, as this is one of the most popular places in town. **Features:** beer & wine. **Address:** 311 Old Santa Fe Trail 87501 **Location:** Just s of the Plaza; jct Alameda St. [B] [L] [D] CALL [M]

(See map & index p. 420.)

SAVEUR
505/989-4200 (34)

▼ French. Casual Dining. $6-$16 **AAA Inspector Notes:** This casual restaurant is set up much like a traditional bistro, but the food is healthier and of considerably higher quality. Diners can choose from an impressive salad buffet, gourmet sandwiches and even fresh French entrées. **Features:** beer & wine, patio dining. **Address:** 204 Montezuma Ave 87501 **Location:** Jct Galisteo St, Cerrillos Rd and Montezuma Ave; downtown. B L ☂

SECOND STREET BREWERY AT THE RAILYARD
505/989-3278 (40)

▼ American. Casual Dining. $9-$15 **AAA Inspector Notes:** This sister to the original Second Street Brewery offers a fun atmosphere, great food and award-winning craft beers in a modern setting. Patio and open air seating in season plus regularly scheduled live music. **Features:** beer & wine, happy hour. **Address:** 1607 Paseo de Peralta, Suite 10 87501 **Location:** Just w of Guadalupe St; north end of the farmer's market building. **Parking:** street only.
L D

THE SHED
505/982-9030 (23)

▼▼ Regional Mexican. Casual Dining. $8-$20 **AAA Inspector Notes:** *Historic.* Red and green chile enchiladas and mocha cake are the specialties at this restaurant, located in a 17th-century fortified hacienda. The menu features Northern New Mexican dishes. This is a popular and busy restaurant, so reservations are a must. **Features:** full bar. **Reservations:** suggested. **Address:** 113 &1/2 E Palace Ave 87501 **Location:** Just e of The Plaza. **Parking:** street only.
L D

SHOHKO CAFE
505/982-9708 (6)

▼▼▼ Japanese. Casual Dining. $15-$37 **AAA Inspector Notes:** Diners are in for a relaxing meal with friendly service in a quaint adobe-style setting. Established in 1976, this restaurant is known for its fresh sushi, sashimi, bento box meals, rice bowls and noodle dishes. Ingredients such as soft-shell crab, eel, tuna, mackerel, salmon, shrimp, yellowtail and albacore are used to create the various sushi rolls. Sushi specials are skillfully prepared by Chef Shohko. **Features:** beer & wine. **Reservations:** suggested. **Address:** 321 Johnson St 87501 **Location:** Just e of jct W San Francisco St.
L D

TABERNA
505/988-7102 (47)

▼▼ Spanish Small Plates. Casual Dining. $8-$22 **AAA Inspector Notes:** The sister restaurant of the adjacent La Boca has created a new, fun vibe and features an ever-changing menu of creative small plates. There are so many plates to share...or not! The vibrant flavors of Latin America are showcased, from the delicately sliced octopus carpaccio to the grilled artichokes with pancetta. Finish with tres leches cake with mango sauce. **Features:** beer & wine, patio dining, happy hour. **Reservations:** suggested. **Address:** 125 Lincoln St 87501 **Location:** Jct Marcy St, just s. **Parking:** street only. D LATE

THAI CAFE
505/982-3886 (13)

▼▼ Thai. Casual Dining. $10-$16 **AAA Inspector Notes:** Guests can take a short walk from The Plaza to enter another realm at this café, which uses colorful Asian decor to add a refreshing twist to the traditional Santa Fe adobe building. Flavorful Thai favorites are served in large portions. **Features:** beer & wine. **Address:** 329 W San Francisco St 87501 **Location:** 3 blks w of The Plaza; jct Guadalupe St. L D

TIA SOPHIA'S
505/983-9880 (18)

▼ Southwestern. Casual Dining. $7-$11 **AAA Inspector Notes:** A short walk from The Plaza, this restaurant specializes in traditional New Mexican cuisine. Particularly worth trying are huevos rancheros for breakfast and the flavorful chiles rellenos for lunch. **Address:** 210 W San Francisco St 87501 **Location:** Just w of The Plaza. **Parking:** street only. B L

TOMASITA'S RESTAURANT
505/983-5721 (33)

▼▼ Regional Mexican. Casual Dining. $7-$15 **AAA Inspector Notes:** A restored mid-1800s train station is the setting for this bustling restaurant. The menu is lined with generous portions of traditional Northern New Mexican cuisine, including specialty burritos, blue corn enchiladas and rellenos. Locals and visitors alike frequent the place. **Features:** full bar, patio dining. **Address:** 500 S Guadalupe St 87501 **Location:** From The Plaza, just w on Alameda St, then just s. L D

UPPER CRUST PIZZA
505/982-0000 (38)

▼ Pizza. Quick Serve. $4-$22 **AAA Inspector Notes:** Not far from The Plaza, this eatery prepares fresh, made-to-order meals that satisfy patrons with light appetites and lean budgets. Seating can be had on the porch, on the back patio or inside. Among favorites are the build-a-pizza, calzones and sandwiches that come with a choice of bread. **Features:** beer & wine, patio dining, happy hour. **Address:** 329 Old Santa Fe Tr 87501 **Location:** 0.5 mi s of The Plaza; at De Vargas St. L D

VANESSIE
505/982-9966 (11)

▼▼▼ American. Fine Dining. $16-$45 **AAA Inspector Notes:** Serving the best of beef and lamb dishes for many years, this restaurant upholds the tradition of attentive service, pleasing flavors and hearty portions. Enjoy the popular piano bar before or after dinner. **Features:** full bar, patio dining. **Reservations:** suggested. **Address:** 427 W Water St 87501 **Location:** Just w of Guadalupe St; parking entrance just w on Water St. D

VINAIGRETTE
505/820-9205 (44)

▼▼ Natural/Organic. Casual Dining. $10-$19 **AAA Inspector Notes:** This vibrant, fresh-food restaurant features creative salads, soups and sandwiches with ingredients grown in the chef/owner's 10-acre organic garden. Start with the incredibly flavorful wild mushroom stew with fried olive bread followed by the omega AKA avocado-piñon or nutty pear-fessor salad. A selection of grilled meats or seafood can be added to any salad. Daily fresh-baked desserts plus homemade ice cream are a treat. **Features:** beer & wine, patio dining. **Address:** 709 Don Cubero Alley 87505 **Location:** Just e of jct Cerrillos Rd and Guadalupe St, just w of jct Cerrillos Rd and Paseo de Peralta.
L D CALL ☕ ☂

YIN YANG
505/986-9279 (37)

▼▼ Chinese. Casual Dining. $8-$26 **AAA Inspector Notes:** This Chinese restaurant features Hunan- and Peking-style comfort food. A wide selection of seafood, beef, chicken and vegetarian options are offered. A lunch buffet with a variety of popular items is available in addition to the menu. **Features:** beer & wine. **Address:** 418 Cerrillos Rd 87501 **Location:** Just sw of The Plaza; near jct Montezuma Ave, Galisteo St and Cerrillos Rd; in Design Center.
L D

SANTA FE (F-4)
- Restaurants p. 435
- Hotels & Restaurants map & index p. 423

BAYMONT INN & SUITES
505/474-4442 (15)

▼▼ Hotel. Rates not provided. **Address:** 4150 Cerrillos Rd 87505 **Location:** I-25 exit 278, 2 mi n. **Facility:** 55 units. 2 stories (no elevator), interior corridors. **Pool(s):** heated indoor. **Guest Services:** valet laundry.

🛏 CALL ☕ ⊇ BIZ HS 📶 ✕ 🔌 📺 🖥

BEST WESTERN PLUS INN OF SANTA FE
(505)438-3822 (12)

Hotel
$95-$150

 AAA Benefit: Save 10% or more every day and earn 10% bonus points!

▼▼▼ **Address:** 3650 Cerrillos Rd 87507 **Location:** I-25 exit 278, 2.8 mi n. **Facility:** 95 units. 3 stories, interior corridors. **Pool(s):** heated indoor. **Activities:** hot tub, exercise room. **Guest Services:** valet and coin laundry.

SAVE 🛏 CALL ☕ ⊇ BIZ 📶 ✕ 🖥 / SOME UNITS ☂ 🔌 📺

(See map & index p. 423.)

BISHOP'S LODGE RANCH RESORT & SPA
505/983-6377 **4**

fyi **Resort Hotel.** Rates not provided. Under major renovation, scheduled to be completed October 2016. **Last Rated:** ♥♥♥ **Address:** 1297 N Bishop's Lodge Rd 87501 **Location:** 3.5 mi n of jct Paseo de Peralta. Located in a quiet area. **Facility:** Expansive landscaped grounds surround the 1800s ranch-style resort, situated in the foothills of the Sangre de Cristo Mountains. 91 units, some two bedrooms, kitchens and houses. 1-3 stories (no elevator), interior/exterior corridors. **Terms:** check-in 4 pm. **Amenities:** safes. **Pool(s):** heated outdoor. **Activities:** hot tub, tennis, sledding, recreation programs, kids club, bicycles, playground, trails, exercise room, spa. **Guest Services:** valet laundry, area transportation.

COMFORT SUITES BY CHOICE HOTELS
(505)473-9004 **9**

♥♥♥
Hotel
$89-$199

Address: 3348 Cerrillos Rd 87507 **Location:** I-25 exit 278, 2 mi n; jct Avenida de las Americas. **Facility:** 60 units. 3 stories, interior corridors. **Pool(s):** heated indoor. **Activities:** hot tub, exercise room. **Guest Services:** valet laundry. **Featured Amenity:** full hot breakfast.

COURTYARD BY MARRIOTT-SANTA FE
(505)473-2800 **8**

♥♥♥♥
Hotel
$79-$144

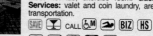

COURTYARD Marriott

AAA Benefit: Members save 5% or more!

Address: 3347 Cerrillos Rd 87507 **Location:** I-25 exit 278, 3.2 mi n. **Facility:** 209 units. 3 stories, interior/exterior corridors. **Pool(s):** heated indoor. **Activities:** hot tub, exercise room. **Guest Services:** valet and coin laundry, area transportation.

DOUBLETREE BY HILTON SANTA FE
(505)473-4646 **14**

♥♥♥♥
Hotel
$99-$199

DOUBLETREE BY HILTON

AAA Benefit: Members save 5% or more!

Address: 4048 Cerrillos Rd 87507 **Location:** I-25 exit 278, 2.3 mi n; just n of Rodeo Dr. **Facility:** 130 units. 4 stories, interior corridors. **Terms:** 1-7 night minimum stay, cancellation fee imposed. **Pool(s):** heated outdoor, heated indoor. **Activities:** hot tub, exercise room. **Guest Services:** valet and coin laundry, area transportation.

▼ See AAA listing p. 433 ▼

Use travel time to share driving tips
and rules of the road with your teens

(See map & index p. 423.)

EL REY INN

(505)982-1931

Hotel
$89-$265

Address: 1862 Cerrillos Rd 87505
Location: I-25 exit 278, 6 mi nw. **Facility:** 86 units, some two bedrooms, efficiencies and kitchens. 1-2 stories (no elevator), exterior corridors. **Terms:** 3 day cancellation notice-fee imposed. **Amenities:** safes. **Pool(s):** heated outdoor. **Activities:** sauna, hot tub, playground, exercise room. **Guest Services:** coin laundry. **Featured Amenity:** continental breakfast. (See ad p. 432.)

SAVE ⬇ 🛏 🚭 BIZ 🛜 ✖ 📶 🖥 / SOME UNITS 📺

FOUR SEASONS RESORT RANCHO ENCANTADO SANTA FE

(505)946-5700 **3**

Resort Hotel
$209-$909

Address: 198 State Road 592 87506 **Location:** US 285/84 N exit 172 (CR 73/Tesuque), 0.5 mi se to SR 592, then 2 mi ne. **Facility:** Guest rooms are spacious and luxuriously appointed, and they each have a private terrace or patio with grand vistas. 65 units. 1-2 stories (no elevator), exterior corridors. **Parking:** on-site and valet. **Terms:** check-in 4 pm, 3 day cancellation notice-fee imposed. **Amenities:** safes. **Dining:** Terra at Rancho Encantado, see separate listing. **Pool(s):** heated outdoor. **Activities:** sauna, hot tub, steamroom, recreation programs, trails, exercise room, spa. **Guest Services:** valet laundry, area transportation.

SAVE 🚶 🛏 👶 🍽 🎣 CALL ♿ 🚭 BIZ HS 🛜 ✖ 📶 🖥 / SOME UNITS

Check DrivingLaws.AAA.com for local motor vehicle laws when traveling

HAMPTON INN SANTA FE

(505)474-3900 **11**

Hotel
$89-$189

AAA Benefit:
Members save up to 10%!

Address: 3625 Cerrillos Rd 87505 **Location:** I-25 exit 278, 2.5 mi n. **Facility:** 81 units. 2 stories, interior corridors. **Terms:** 1-7 night minimum stay, cancellation fee imposed. **Pool(s):** heated indoor. **Activities:** hot tub, exercise room. **Guest Services:** valet and coin laundry. **Featured Amenity:** full hot breakfast.

SAVE 🛏 CALL ♿ 🚭 BIZ 🛜 ✖ 📶 🖥 🖵 / SOME UNITS 🐾

HILTON SANTA FE BUFFALO THUNDER

(505)455-5555 **1**

Resort Hotel
$99-$399

 Hilton
HOTELS & RESORTS

AAA Benefit:
Members save 5% or more!

Address: 20 Buffalo Thunder Tr 87506 **Location:** N on US 285 exit Buffalo Thunder Rd, just e. **Facility:** The luxurious resort property has activities for all interests, from an award-winning golf course, casino, spa and shopping to fine dining, which all adds up to a fun, relaxing stay. 393 units. 6 stories, interior corridors. **Parking:** valet and street only. **Terms:** check-in 4 pm, 1-7 night minimum stay, cancellation fee imposed. **Amenities:** video games, safes. **Dining:** 8 restaurants, nightclub, entertainment. **Pool(s):** heated outdoor, heated indoor. **Activities:** sauna, hot tub, steamroom, regulation golf, tennis, recreation programs in season, game room, exercise room, spa. **Guest Services:** valet laundry, area transportation. (See ad this page.)

SAVE 🚭 🚶 🛏 👶 🍽 CALL ♿ 🚭 BIZ SHS 📶 ✖ 🐾 📶 🖥 / SOME UNITS 🐾

▼ See AAA listing this page ▼

HILTON
HHONORS

MAP YOUR NEXT ADVENTURE FROM OUR BALCONY.

AAA Four Diamond Hilton Buffalo Thunder offers stunning vistas of New Mexico's natural beauty. Play our 27 hole Towa golf course, dine in elegance at Red Sage or relax at Wo'P'in spa. Gaming enthusiasts are in their element in the expansive Las Vegas-style casino.

Rates from $99-$399 Single/Double Based on Availability

For reservations visit BuffaloThunderResort.com or call 505-455-5555
20 Buffalo Thunder Trail | Santa Fe | NM 87506 | USA

Keep Your Children Safe in the Car

AAA has teamed up with two beloved HarperCollins Children's Books characters, and 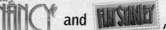, to promote child passenger safety.

For car seat guidelines, visit **SafeSeats4Kids.AAA.com** and go to SeatCheck.org or call 866-SEAT-CHECK (732-8243) for installation information.

In Canada, visit the Child Safety section of Transport Canada's website: **tc.gc.ca**

Remember—car seats, booster seats and seat belts save lives

FANCY NANCY © 2014 by J. O'Connor and R.P. Glasser.
FLAT STANLEY ® is a registered trademark of the
Trust u/w/o Richard C. Brown f/b/o Duncan Brown.

(See map & index p. 423.)

HOLIDAY INN EXPRESS-SANTA FE   (505)474-7570 **10**

Hotel
$79-$199

Address: 3450 Cerrillos Rd 87507 **Location:** I-25 exit 278, 3 mi n. **Facility:** 76 units. 3 stories, interior corridors. **Terms:** cancellation fee imposed, resort fee. **Pool(s):** heated outdoor. **Activities:** exercise room. **Guest Services:** coin laundry. **Featured Amenity:** breakfast buffet.

SAVE (TI+) CALL (&M) (➜) (BIZ) (🛜)
(✕) (🛏) (🖥) (🖨) / SOME UNITS (🔒)

HOMEWOOD SUITES BY HILTON-SANTA FE NORTH
(505)455-9100 **2**

Extended Stay Hotel
$109-$189

AAA Benefit: Members save up to 10%!

Address: 10 Buffalo Thunder Tr 87506 **Location:** US 84/285 exit 177, just e. **Facility:** 81 efficiencies, some two bedrooms. 3 stories, interior/exterior corridors. **Terms:** 1-7 night minimum stay, cancellation fee imposed. **Amenities:** video games. **Pool(s):** heated outdoor. **Activities:** regulation golf, exercise room. **Guest Services:** valet and coin laundry, area transportation.

SAVE (TI+) CALL (&M) (➜) (BIZ) (🛜) (✕) (🎮) (🛏) (🖨)
(🖥) / SOME UNITS (🔒)

HYATT PLACE SANTA FE   (505)474-7777 **17**

Hotel
$79-$249

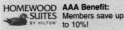
HYATT PLACE
AAA Benefit: Members save 10%!

Address: 4320 Cerrillos Rd 87507 **Location:** I-25 exit 278, 2 mi e. **Facility:** 92 units. 3 stories, interior corridors. **Terms:** cancellation fee imposed. **Pool(s):** heated indoor. **Activities:** hot tub, exercise room. **Guest Services:** valet and coin laundry, area transportation. **Featured Amenity:** breakfast buffet.

SAVE (🏋) (TI) (🍽) CALL (&M) (➜)
(BIZ) (HS) (🛜) (✕) (🎮) (🛏) (🖥) (🖨)
/ SOME UNITS (🔒) (🖥)

INN AT SANTA FE   (505)474-9500 **18**

Hotel
$79-$249

Address: 8376 Cerrillos Rd 87507 **Location:** I-25 exit 278, 0.3 mi n. Adjacent to Santa Fe Premium Outlet stores. **Facility:** 98 units. 3 stories, interior corridors. **Terms:** cancellation fee imposed. **Amenities:** safes. **Pool(s):** heated outdoor. **Activities:** sauna, hot tub, exercise room. **Guest Services:** valet and coin laundry. **Featured Amenity:** full hot breakfast.

SAVE (🏋) (TI) (🍽) CALL (&M) (➜)
(BIZ) (HS) (🛜) (✕) (🛏) (🖨) (🖥)
/ SOME UNITS (🔒)

LA QUINTA INN SANTA FE   (505)471-1142 **16**

Hotel $64-$218 **Address:** 4298 Cerrillos Rd 87507 **Location:** I-25 exit 278, 1.8 mi n. **Facility:** 131 units. 3 stories, interior/exterior corridors. **Pool(s):** heated outdoor. **Guest Services:** valet and coin laundry.

(TI+) CALL (&M) (➜) (BIZ) (🛜) (🖥)
/ SOME UNITS (🐾) (🖨) (🖥)

THE LODGE AT SANTA FE   505/992-5800 **5**

Hotel
Rates not provided

Address: 750 N St. Francis Dr 87501 **Location:** Jct of Cerrillos Rd and St. Francis Dr (US 84/285), 1.1 mi nw to Alamo Dr, just w, then just n. **Facility:** 126 units. 1-3 stories, interior/exterior corridors. **Terms:** check-in 4 pm. **Dining:** entertainment. **Pool(s):** heated outdoor. **Activities:** hot tub, exercise room. **Guest Services:** valet and coin laundry, area transportation.

SAVE (TI) (➜) (&M) (BIZ) (🛜) (✕)
(🖥) / SOME UNITS (🔒) (🖨) (🖥)

MOTEL 6-150   (505)473-1380 **7**

Motel $45-$75 **Address:** 3007 Cerrillos Rd 87507 **Location:** I-25 exit 278, 3.8 mi n. **Facility:** 104 units. 2 stories (no elevator), exterior corridors. *Bath:* shower only. **Pool(s):** heated outdoor.
(TI+) CALL (&M) (➜) (🛰) / SOME UNITS (🐾) (🖨) (🖥)

PECOS TRAIL INN   505/982-1943 **13**

Motel
Rates not provided

Address: 2239 Old Pecos Tr 87505 **Location:** I-25 exit 284, 0.8 mi n on CR 466 (Old Pecos Tr). **Facility:** 23 units, some two bedrooms and kitchens. 1 story, exterior corridors. **Pool(s):** heated outdoor.

SAVE (TI) (🍽) CALL (&M) (➜) (🛜)
(✕) (🖥) / SOME UNITS (🔒) (🖨) (🖥)

INN ON THE ALAMEDA   505/984-2121

[fyi] Not evaluated. **Address:** 303 E Alameda St 87501 **Location:** Just e of The Plaza; jct Paseo de Peralta. Facilities, services, and décor characterize a mid-scale property.

WHERE TO EAT

BLUE CORN CAFE & BREWERY   505/438-1800 **25**

Southwestern. Casual Dining. $9-$18 **AAA Inspector Notes:** Across the street from Villa Linda Mall on the southern outskirts of town, this café provides the same menu and tastes as its sister downtown restaurant. Northern New Mexican cuisine, great margaritas and handcrafted microbrews are served. The spicy crab dip with fresh-fried tortilla wedges will serve a crowd. **Features:** full bar, patio dining, happy hour. **Address:** 4056 Cerrillos Rd 87505 **Location:** I-25 exit 278, 2 mi n, jct Rodeo Rd; northwest corner.
(L) (D)

BODY CAFE   505/986-0362 **11**

Natural/Organic Raw Foods. Casual Dining. $9-$15 **AAA Inspector Notes:** This eatery focuses on organic and healthy food choices. Vegetarian and raw food dishes dominate the menu. Dining room entrées include pasta, grains and in-season wild fish. Turkey and tuna sandwiches are available in the deli. Visitors also can enjoy specialty coffees, fruit smoothies, fresh juices and elixirs. **Features:** beer & wine, patio dining. **Address:** 333 W Cordova Rd 87505 **Location:** I-25 exit 282, 2.3 mi n on St. Francis Dr, then just e.
(B) (L) (D)

CHOCOLATE MAVEN BAKERY & CAFE   505/984-1980 **18**

American. Casual Dining. $10-$15 **AAA Inspector Notes:** Those looking for an escape from the hustle and bustle of downtown should seek out this cozy and distinctive café. Soups, salads, sandwiches, pizza and baked goods are made from the freshest ingredients. The friendly and attentive staff enhances the dining experience. **Features:** beer & wine, Sunday brunch. **Reservations:** suggested, for dinner. **Address:** 821 W San Mateo Rd, Suite C 87505 **Location:** Jct St. Michaels Dr and Cerrillos Rd, just n on Cerrillos Rd to 2nd St, then 0.6 mi e; in industrial building.
(B) (L) (D)

(See map & index p. 423.)

CHOW'S ASIAN BISTRO   505/471-7120   20

Asian. Casual Dining. $9-$20 **AAA Inspector Notes:** This local hideaway is off the beaten path and the place to go for creative and flavorful Asian dishes. Attentive service keeps people coming back. **Features:** beer & wine. **Address:** 720 St. Michael's Dr 87501 **Location:** Jct St. Francis Dr, just w. L D

CLEOPATRA'S CAFE   505/474-5644   23

Mediterranean. Quick Serve. $6-$16 **AAA Inspector Notes:** A local favorite, this eatery offers generous portions of flavorful Mediterranean specialties such as organic, New Mexico-raised lamb. Vegetarians will find plenty of offerings. **Features:** beer & wine. **Address:** 3482 Zafrano Dr 87507 **Location:** I-25 exit 278 (Cerrillos Rd), 2.5 mi n; jct Cerrillos Rd and Zafarano Dr; in San Isidro Plaza. L D

THE COMPOUND RESTAURANT   505/982-4353   6

American. Fine Dining. $18-$45 **AAA Inspector Notes:** In an adobe-style hacienda in the fashionable Canyon Road area, this restaurant prepares a variety of contemporary American cuisine. The menu includes classic sweetbreads and foie gras starters. Entrées include a variety of seafood, steak, lamb and chicken dishes. Grilled beef tenderloin with Italian crepe O'Brien potatoes and foie gras hollandaise is a must for beef lovers. **Features:** full bar, patio dining. **Reservations:** suggested. **Address:** 653 Canyon Rd 87501 **Location:** From Paseo de Peralta, 0.4 mi e. L D

DR. FIELD GOODS KITCHEN   505/471-0043   21

Regional American. Casual Dining. $8-$15 **AAA Inspector Notes:** The high-energy, open kitchen restaurant is a bit outside of the tourist area, hence its popularity with locals. The farm-to-table philosophy employs fresh, local, organic and sustainable food products to create unique sandwiches, salads, daily specials and wood-fired pizzas with a Southwestern twist. **Features:** beer & wine, patio dining. **Address:** 2860 Cerrillos Rd 87505 **Location:** Just e of jct Siler Rd. L D

EL FAROL RESTAURANT   505/983-9912   8

Mediterranean. Casual Dining. $8-$52 **AAA Inspector Notes:** In the fashionable Canyon Road area, this restaurant occupies an old, adobe-style building with a rustic interior. The menu contains a variety of Spanish beef, lamb, veal and seafood preparations. On the wine list is a good variety of Spanish and New World wines, several available by the glass. **Features:** full bar. **Reservations:** suggested. **Address:** 808 Canyon Rd 87501 **Location:** From Paseo de Peralta, 0.5 mi e. **Parking:** on-site (fee). L D

GABRIEL'S   505/455-7000   1

Mexican. Casual Dining. $9-$20 **AAA Inspector Notes:** Cold margaritas and guacamole prepared tableside and served with a basket of warm chips make great starters at this roadside restaurant which is a popular place to have lunch on the way to Taos or for dinner before attending a performance at the Santa Fe Opera. **Features:** full bar. **Reservations:** suggested. **Address:** US 285/84 87501 **Location:** US 84/285 exit 176 (Cuyamungue), just n. L D

GERONIMO   505/982-1500   7

Regional International Fine Dining $28-$50

AAA Inspector Notes: Whether you choose to dine on the porch to watch the art gallery aficionados and gift shoppers pass by, or inside in the quietly elegant surroundings, the polished and attentive service will smooth your dining experience. The Southwestern-style cuisine highlights fresh seafood dishes, spicy pan-roasted quail and the signature grilled black pepper elk tenderloin. Don't plan to skip dessert—the Meyer lemon crepe is not to be missed. **Features:** full bar, patio dining. **Reservations:** suggested. **Address:** 724 Canyon Rd 87501 **Location:** 0.5 mi e of jct Paseo de Peralta. **Parking:** on-site and valet. D

HARRY'S ROADHOUSE   505/989-4629   27

American. Casual Dining. $8-$22 **AAA Inspector Notes:** The friendly, casual staff give attentive service. You may dine inside, on the porch, or in the garden surrounded by flowers. Next comes menu choices-grilled fish tacos, blue corn turkey enchiladas or the ever popular buffalo burger. The homemade desserts are mouthwatering-bread and rice pudding, lemon meringue pie or ice cream sandwiches. **Features:** full bar, patio dining. **Address:** 96B Old Las Vegas Hwy 87505 **Location:** I-25 exit 284 (Old Pecos Tr), 0.8 mi se on Frontage Rd (Old Las Vegas Hwy). ECO B L D

JAMBO CAFE   505/473-1269   16

African. Casual Dining. $9-$15 **AAA Inspector Notes:** This restaurant, a local favorite, serves flavorful Afro-Caribbean cuisine in a cozy atmosphere with great background music and a friendly staff. The succulent New Mexico lamb with sweet potato fries and curry dipping sauce is a satisfying meal. End the meal with a palate-cooling coconut sorbet. **Features:** beer & wine. **Address:** 2010 Cerrillos Rd 87505 **Location:** Jct St. Michaels Dr, just sw; downtown. L D

JOE'S DINER AND PIZZA   505/471-3800   26

American. Casual Dining. $9-$27 **AAA Inspector Notes:** This diner's classic décor provides a blast to the past with lots of chrome, black-and-white tile floors and booths with red vinyl upholstery. A family-friendly neighborhood restaurant, this spot offers fresh and creative specialties using organic and locally raised produce and meats. Try one of the favorite mesquite-grilled burgers made from organic grass-fed beef, lamb or buffalo. The build-your-own pizza utilizes fresh dough and sauce made daily. The luscious fruit pies are homemade. **Features:** beer & wine, Sunday brunch. **Address:** 2801 Rodeo Rd 87507 **Location:** 1.7 mi w of US 84/285. B L D

MARIA'S NEW MEXICAN KITCHEN   505/983-7929   9

Mexican. Casual Dining. $9-$25 **AAA Inspector Notes:** A local favorite, this kitchen has been cooking and serving New Mexican fare for generations. A casual atmosphere and friendly service make it a great place to kick back with an outstanding margarita and the house specialty carne adovada (roasted pork in a spicy red chile sauce). **Features:** full bar. **Reservations:** suggested. **Address:** 555 W Cordova Rd 87505 **Location:** Just e of jct St. Francis Dr. L D

MASA SUSHI   505/982-3334   4

Sushi. Casual Dining. $9-$26 **AAA Inspector Notes:** Japanese and Korean specialties are served at this neighborhood eatery, including a sushi bar featuring the chef's creations. **Features:** beer & wine. **Address:** 927 W Alameda St 87501 **Location:** Just w of US 285. L D

MIDTOWN BISTRO   505/820-3121   17

Northern Mexican. Fine Dining. $10-$32 **AAA Inspector Notes:** This carefully crafted menu showcases fresh ingredients with a slight Southwestern twist. Find a seat in the chic, contemporary dining room, or al fresco among many stone water features. **Features:** full bar, patio dining, Sunday brunch. **Reservations:** suggested. **Address:** 901 W San Mateo, Suite A 87501 **Location:** Jct 2nd St; southeast of railroad tracks. L D

MU DU NOODLES   505/983-1411   12

Asian. Casual Dining. $12-$25 **AAA Inspector Notes:** Do as the locals and hit this spot for flavorful Asian specialties featuring market fresh and organic ingredients. The emerald sautee with seared scallops, green tea noodles and fresh local vegetables shouldn't be missed. Many vegetarian and vegan items are on the menu. **Features:** beer & wine, patio dining. **Address:** 1494 Cerrillos Rd 87505 **Location:** 1 mi w of St. Francis Dr; downtown. **Parking:** on-site and street. D

THE PANTRY   505/986-0022   15

Regional American. Casual Dining. $7-$16 **AAA Inspector Notes:** Genuine New Mexican cuisine draws locals and tourists to this laid-back restaurant. The menu consists of traditional favorites: enchiladas, burritos, green chile stew and much more. The hearty portions are worth the wait. **Features:** beer & wine. **Address:** 1820 Cerrillos Rd 87505 **Location:** I-25 exit 278, 6 mi nw, jct 5th St. B L D

(See map & index p. 423.)

PIZZERIA ESPIRITU   505/424-8000   (19)

▼▼ Italian. Casual Dining. $10-$25 **AAA Inspector Notes:** In addition to the pizza, this pizzeria prepares a variety of fresh pasta dishes, sandwiches and soups. Rich Old World decor adds a touch of elegance to an otherwise casual meal. Diners can look up at the ceiling to see a whimsical take on Michelangelo's mural of "The Creation of Adam," in which God and Adam share a slice of pizza. **Features:** beer & wine. **Address:** 1722-A St. Michael's Dr 87505 **Location:** Jct Cerrillos Rd, just se of Llano St; in strip mall.

(L) (D)

PUERTO PENASCO   505/438-6622   (24)

▼▼ Mexican Seafood. Casual Dining. $7-$15 **AAA Inspector Notes:** A friendly staff is welcoming at this lively, family-run eatery where the essence of true Mexican seaside cuisine is showcased. Start with a typical shrimp cocktail in a cool tomato broth with diced avocados, cilantro and cucumbers. The spicy seafood soup can really warm diners up on a cold day. The Discata Tierra y Mar, served in a mini tabletop disc, allows guests to make their own tacos. Save room for the decadent homemade tres leches cake. **Features:** beer & wine. **Address:** 4681 Airport Rd, Suite 1 87507 **Location:** SR 14 (Cerrillos Rd), 1.6 mi w. (L) (D)

PYRAMID CAFE   505/989-1378   (10)

▼▼ Mediterranean. Casual Dining. $9-$24 **AAA Inspector Notes:** This Mediterranean restaurant features Tunisian specialties made with all natural ingredients containing no preservatives, no antibiotics and no hormones. Lunch includes menu offerings and a buffet. As a perk, this spot also offers Wi-Fi access. **Features:** beer & wine. **Address:** 505 W Cordova Rd 87505 **Location:** Just e of St. Francis Dr. (L) (D) CALL (⅃M)

SANTA FE CAPITOL GRILL   505/471-6800   (22)

▼▼▼ International. Casual Dining. $8-$27 **AAA Inspector Notes:** Fun and friendly service can be found in this lively bistro. From savory appetizers to creative salads and sandwiches, enjoy a quick meal before the movies or a cocktail and leisurely meal afterward. **Features:** full bar, patio dining, happy hour. **Address:** 3462 Zafarano Dr 87507 **Location:** Northwest of jct Cerrillos Rd; in San Isidro Plaza. (L) (D) (🐾)

SWEETWATER HARVEST KITCHEN   505/795-7383   (14)

▼▼ Natural/Organic. Casual Dining. $7-$20 **AAA Inspector Notes:** Offering a creative menu for breakfast, lunch and dinner using farm-fresh natural, organic and sustainable ingredients, the menu is very conscious of gluten-free, vegetarian and vegan diets. There is something delicious available for everyone, and all items are carefully prepared, setting a leisurely pace for the meal. **Features:** beer & wine, Sunday brunch. **Reservations:** suggested, for dinner. **Address:** 1512 Pacheco St, Bldg B 87505 **Location:** Just w of St Francis Dr; just n of Camino de Monte Rey. (B) (L) (D)

TERRA AT RANCHO ENCANTADO   505/946-5800   (2)

▼▼▼ ▼▼▼▼
Southwestern
Fine Dining
$18-$39

AAA Inspector Notes: This upscale dining combined with a contemporary ambience contribute to the start of a memorable dining experience. Consider one of the creatively prepared desserts to end your meal. **Features:** full bar, patio dining, Sunday brunch. **Reservations:** suggested. **Address:** 198 State Road 592 87506 **Location:** US 285/84 N exit 172 (CR 73/Tesuque), 0.5 mi se to SR 592, then 2 mi ne; in Four Seasons Resort Rancho Encantado Santa Fe. **Parking:** on-site and valet. (B) (L) (D)

TESUQUE VILLAGE MARKET   505/988-8848   (3)

▼▼ American. Casual Dining. $10-$40 **AAA Inspector Notes:** This Santa Fe institution is well worth a beautiful leisurely drive along Bishop's Lodge Road, where you'll find funky charm, friendly locals and, most importantly, hearty servings of traditional and creative Southwestern cuisine. **Features:** full bar, patio dining. **Address:** 138 Tesuque Village Rd 87506 **Location:** US 285 exit 168, just s.

(B) (L) (D)

TUNE-UP CAFE   505/983-7060   (5)

▼▼ ▼▼ International. Casual Dining. $9-$15 **AAA Inspector Notes:** This local café has a true neighborhood feel with counter service, funky decor, shared tables and patio seating. A flavorful menu features many El Salvadoran items such as pupusas and banana leaf tamales. A creative breakfast menu includes pan-fried trout with poached eggs and huevos rancheros. The desserts are excellent. **Features:** beer & wine, patio dining, Sunday brunch. **Address:** 1115 Hickox St 87505 **Location:** 0.5 mi w of St. Francis Dr. **Parking:** on-site and street. (B) (L) (D)

SANTA FE NATIONAL FOREST (A-5)

Elevations in the forest range from 5,300 ft. to 13,103 ft. at Truchas Peak. Refer to AAA maps for additional elevation information.

In the north central part of the state, some 1,600,000 acres of forest and rangeland lie within Santa Fe National Forest. The southern Sangre de Cristo Range, with several 12,000- to 13,000-foot peaks, dominates the eastern half. Within the forest are Pecos Wilderness, the headwaters of the Pecos River and the Santa Fe Basin winter sports area. The 18-mile trip along SR 63 between Cowles and Pecos provides outstanding views of the forest's eastern section.

In the portion west of the Rio Grande are the Jémez Mountains, San Pedro Parks Wilderness, Chama River Canyon Wilderness and Dome Wilderness. Developed recreation sites and day-use picnic areas are near streams, trailheads and other scenic highlights. Recreational opportunities include hiking, fishing, horseback riding and such winter sports as cross-country skiing and snowshoeing. Fees are required for some developed areas.

For information and maps contact the Supervisor, Santa Fe National Forest, 11 Forest Ln., Santa Fe, NM 87508; phone (505) 438-5300 (Public Information Officer). *See Recreation Areas Chart.*

SANTA ROSA (F-5) pop. 2,848, elev. 4,599'
• Hotels p. 438 • Restaurants p. 438

Santa Rosa is surrounded by parcels of land with property lines that were established by Spanish land grants. Many residents are descended from the exploration party that accompanied Francisco Vázquez de Coronado in 1540.

Ironically, this semi-desert region also has artesian springs and spring-fed lakes. Blue Hole, an artesian spring 81 feet deep, is a half-mile west of Park Lake. Scuba divers can explore the 64-degree water; a diving permit is required. Fishing and scuba diving are also good at Perch Lake.

Other nearby lakes, such as Park Lake and the lake in Janes-Wallace Memorial Park *(see Recreation Areas Chart)*, yield catches of trout, crappie and walleye. Anglers fish for channel catfish in the Pecos River. Rock Lake State Fish Hatchery, 2 miles south of town on River Road, raises rainbow trout and walleye.

Scenic SR 91 follows the Pecos River south for 10 miles to Puerto de Luna, one of several abandoned Spanish settlements in this region. A marker indicates where Coronado camped while a make-shift bridge was built so the river could be crossed. Another scenic is SR 91; 7 miles north of Santa Rose is Santa Rosa Lake State Park *(see Recreation Areas Chart)*. A nature trail and recreational facilities are adjacent to the dam and reservoir.

Santa Rosa Visitors Information Center: 1085 Blue Hole Rd., P.O. Box 429, Santa Rosa, NM 88435. **Phone:** (575) 472-3763.

BEST WESTERN SANTA ROSA INN   (575)472-5877

Motel
$89-$150

AAA Benefit: Save 10% or more every day and earn 10% bonus points!

Address: 2491 Historic Route 66 88435 **Location:** I-40 exit 275, 0.5 mi w. **Facility:** 44 units. 1 story, exterior corridors. **Pool(s):** heated outdoor. **Guest Services:** coin laundry.

DAYS INN & SUITES   (575)472-3446

Hotel
$70-$75

Address: 2255 Historic Route 66 88435 **Location:** I-40 exit 275, just w. **Facility:** 58 units. 1-2 stories (no elevator), exterior corridors. **Pool(s):** heated outdoor. **Guest Services:** coin laundry. **Featured Amenity: continental breakfast.**

HAMPTON INN   (575)472-2300

Hotel
$120-$135

AAA Benefit: Members save up to 10%!

Address: 2475 Historic Route 66 88435 **Location:** I-40 exit 277, 1 mi w. **Facility:** 64 units. 3 stories, interior corridors. **Terms:** 1-7 night minimum stay, cancellation fee imposed. **Pool(s):** heated indoor. **Activities:** hot tub, game room, exercise room. **Guest Services:** coin laundry. **Featured Amenity: full hot breakfast.**

HOLIDAY INN EXPRESS   575/472-5411

Hotel. Rates not provided. **Address:** 2516 Historic Route 66 88435 **Location:** I-40 exit 277, 0.4 mi w. **Facility:** 73 units. 3 stories, interior corridors. **Pool(s):** heated indoor. **Activities:** hot tub, game room, exercise room. **Guest Services:** coin laundry.

QUALITY INN   575/472-5570

Hotel $85-$95 **Address:** 2533 E Historic Route 66 88435 **Location:** I-40 exit 277, 0.3 mi w. **Facility:** 45 units. 2 stories (no elevator), exterior corridors. **Pool(s):** heated indoor. **Activities:** hot tub. **Guest Services:** coin laundry.

SUPER 8-SANTA ROSA   (575)472-5388

Motel $53-$96 **Address:** 2075 Historic Route 66 88435 **Location:** I-40 exit 275, just w. **Facility:** 88 units. 2 stories (no elevator), interior corridors. **Guest Services:** coin laundry.

LA QUINTA INN SANTA ROSA   575/472-4800

Hotel Did not meet all AAA rating requirements for locking devices in some guest rooms at time of last evaluation on 06/18/2015. **Address:** 2277 Historic Route 66 88435 **Location:** I-40 exit 275, just e. Facilities, services, and décor characterize a mid-scale property.

WHERE TO EAT

JOSEPH'S BAR & GRILL   575/472-3361

Southwestern. Casual Dining. $7-$22 **AAA Inspector Notes:** This family-run restaurant has been serving travelers on Route 66, The Mother Road, since 1956. From well-prepared New Mexican cuisine to salads, burgers and steaks, this eatery has something for every appetite. This includes the luscious, fresh-baked lemon meringue pie. **Features:** full bar. **Address:** 1775 Historic Route 66 88435 **Location:** I-40 exit 275, just w.

SANTA FE GRILLE   575/472-5568

American. Casual Dining. $7-$18 Under major renovation, scheduled to be completed January 2016. Last rated: AAA **Inspector Notes:** Traditional, homemade New Mexican cuisine and American specialties are featured at this casual and friendly restaurant. **Features:** beer & wine, senior menu. **Address:** 2249 Historic Route 66 88435 **Location:** I-40 exit 275, just e.

SANTA TERESA (J-3) pop. 4,258, elev. 4,100'

Santa Teresa is on the western edge of the El Paso/Ciudad Juárez metropolitan area. Since it bypasses Ciudad Juárez, Santa Teresa is the recommended crossing point for tourists and other travelers who are driving to Chihuahua and beyond or otherwise headed for interior Mexico. Banjercito offices at this border crossing and at the 30-kilometer (19-mile) mark on Mex. 45 (the Juárez-Chihuahua Highway) can process the paperwork necessary for vehicle travel into the interior.

Dollars or pesos are accepted when entering or departing Mexico or the United States. Baggage may be inspected at the customs offices. Both Mexican and U.S. Customs and Border Protection offices are open daily 24 hours at Ciudad Juárez; daily 6 a.m.-midnight at Santa Teresa. AAA/CAA members can obtain Mexican automobile insurance at AAA Texas offices.

WAR EAGLES AIR MUSEUM is off I-10 exit 8, 7.5 mi. w. on Airport Rd. to Santa Teresa Airport. The museum features restored aircraft from the World War II era and jet fighters used in the Korean Conflict. Fighters include the P-51 Mustang, the P-38 Lightning, the P-40 Warhawk, a twin-engine Invader bomber and a Fieseler Storch.

Among the 1950s jets are a T-33 Silver Star and MiG-15. Additional displays feature women aviators, flight equipment and 46 vintage automobiles. **Time:** Allow 1 hour minimum. **Hours:** Tues.-Sun. 10-4. Last admission 30 minutes before closing. Closed major holidays. **Cost:** $5; $4 (ages 65+ and military

with ID); free (ages 0-11 and students with ID).
Phone: (575) 589-2000.

BILLY CREWS   575/589-2071
▼▼▼ American. Casual Dining. $15-$40 **AAA Inspector Notes:** This dining room is well known for excellent cuts of aged beef and prime rib plus a very extensive wine list. A casual lunch is served in the lounge. **Features:** full bar, patio dining, happy hour. **Reservations:** suggested. **Address:** 1200 Country Club Rd 88008 **Location:** Jct SR 273 (McNutt Rd) and 184 (Country Club Rd), just e.

L D

SANTO DOMINGO PUEBLO (C-3)
pop. 2,456, elev. 5,185'

Santo Domingo received its name in 1691 when missionaries began renaming New Mexican pueblos for Catholic saints. Keresan people had inhabited the site since the 1200s. The pueblo's actual location has changed over the years with flooding of the Rio Grande. The town of Santo Domingo became a stopover on the way to Peña Blanca during Spanish colonial times; it later served as a stage stop on the road between Albuquerque and Santa Fe. The 1883 Santo Domingo Trading Post is one of the largest in the area.

SANTO DOMINGO PUEBLO is off I-25 exit 259, then 2.5 mi. w. Because of their proximity to the ancient Cerrillos turquoise mines, the Keresan artisans of Santo Domingo earned a reputation for fine jewelry, beadwork and mosaics. Their *heishe* beads are prized today. A community center offers visitors a glimpse into tribal life and traditions. Some 350 artists gather for an arts and crafts festival on Labor Day weekend.

The Church of the Pueblo of Santo Domingo dates from 1886 and replaced a mission that was carried away by Rio Grande floodwaters. Visitors can see historical records and paintings by Native American artists. Photography, sketching and painting are not permitted. **Hours:** Daily 8-5. **Cost:** Donations. **Phone:** (505) 465-2214.

SHIPROCK (E-1) pop. 8,295, elev. 4,900'

Within the Navajo Indian Reservation, 15 miles southwest via US 491 and Red Rock Road, is the geological formation Shiprock. The basalt core of an old volcano, the rock rises more than 1,700 feet above the desert floor. At sunset it appears to shimmer and float.

Because the Navajo consider Shiprock to be a sacred place, the tribe does not permit climbers to scale it. Scenic Indian Route 33 runs between Shiprock and Red Rock on the Arizona border.

FOUR CORNERS MONUMENT, 33 mi. n.w. off SR 597, is the only place in the country where four states meet. The juncture of Arizona, Utah, Colorado and New Mexico is marked by a concrete monument bearing each state's seal. Navajo and Ute artists sell their wares near the site. **Hours:** Daily 8-7, May-Sept.; 8-5, rest of year. Closed Jan. 1, Thanksgiving and Christmas. **Cost:** $5; free (ages 0-6). Cash only. **Phone:** (928) 206-2540.

SILVER CITY (I-2) pop. 10,315, elev. 5,938'
• Hotels p. 440 • Restaurants p. 440

The discovery of silver in the late 1860s led to the founding of appropriately named Silver City, while the establishment of Western New Mexico University in 1893—the same year the bottom dropped out of the silver market—ensured its continued existence. This was also the boyhood home of one William Bonney, who achieved notoriety at a young age as outlaw Billy the Kid.

Mining processes can be viewed from an open pit copper mine 15 miles east on SR 152. The huge pit, 1.7 miles across and 1,000 feet deep, has produced mountains of ore since the discovery of the deposits in 1800. One of the largest operations of its type in the United States, Chino Mine shows evidence of Spanish and Mexican workings. Chino Mines Co. provides an observation point and a picnic area.

Twelve miles south on SR 90, another vast open-pit mine yields some 50,000 tons of copper ore a day from the original site of Tyrone. Built in 1915 by Phelps-Dodge Corp. to house miners and their families, it was a beautifully designed city until declining markets caused the closure of the mine in 1921. Reactivation in the mid-1960s resulted in a new Tyrone 4.5 miles south of Silver City.

Silver City provides access to the 110-mile Trail of the Mountain Spirits, which leads to Gila Cliff Dwellings National Monument *(see place listing p. 385)* via US 180 and SRs 152, 35 and 15, then crosses the Pinos Altos Range back to Silver City. Contact the visitor center at Gila National Forest *(see place listing p. 385)* at (575) 536-9461.

Silver City/Grant County Chamber of Commerce: 500 18th St., Silver City, NM 88061. **Phone:** (575) 538-3785 or (800) 548-9378.

Self-guiding tours: Pocket guides describing walking tours of three historic neighborhoods—Capilla, Gospel Hill and the historic business district—can be purchased at the Silver City Museum.

SILVER CITY MUSEUM is at 312 W. Broadway St. Exhibits in the 1881 H.B. Ailman house explore the history of southwest New Mexico. Collections include 19th- and 20th-century regional history objects and photographs, Southwestern artifacts and objects from an early 20th-century mining camp. **Time:** Allow 1 hour minimum. **Hours:** Tues.-Fri. 9-4:30, Sat.-Sun. 10-4. Closed Jan. 1, Thanksgiving and Christmas. **Cost:** Donations. **Phone:** (575) 538-5921, or (877) 777-7947 out of state.

WESTERN NEW MEXICO UNIVERSITY MUSEUM is .5 mi. s.w. of US 180 at 10th and West sts., in Fleming Hall. Information about the prehistoric Mimbres culture includes displays of pottery, stone tools and jewelry. The collection also features Casas Grandes pottery and mining artifacts. Temporary exhibitions are presented as well. **Hours:** Mon.-Fri. 9-4:30, Sat.-Sun. 10-4; closed university holidays. **Cost:** Donations. **Phone:** (575) 538-6386.

COMFORT INN

▼▼ ▼▼
Hotel
$80-$100

Address: 1060 E Hwy 180 88061 **Location:** Just e of jct SR 15. **Facility:** 52 units. 2 stories (no elevator), interior corridors. **Pool(s):** heated indoor. **Activities:** hot tub. **Guest Services:** valet and coin laundry.

SAVE ❙❙➕ ⊕ BIZ 📶 ✖ 🛏
🖨 💻 / SOME UNITS 🐕

ECONO LODGE SILVER CITY   (575)534-1111

▼▼ ▼▼ Hotel $75-$120 **Address:** 1120 Hwy 180 E 88061 **Location:** 1.5 mi ne on US 180 and SR 90. **Facility:** 61 units. 3 stories, interior corridors. **Amenities:** safes. **Pool(s):** heated indoor. **Activities:** hot tub, exercise room. **Guest Services:** valet and coin laundry.

❙❙➕ CALL 🔒📶 ⊕ BIZ 📶 🛏 🖨 💻 / SOME UNITS 🐕

HOLIDAY INN EXPRESS   (575)538-2525

▼▼▼ ▼ Hotel $130-$154 **Address:** 1103 Superior St 88061 **Location:** 3 mi ne on US 180 and SR 90. **Facility:** 73 units. 3 stories, interior corridors. **Terms:** cancellation fee imposed. **Pool(s):** heated outdoor. **Activities:** limited exercise equipment. **Guest Services:** valet and coin laundry.

❙❙➕ ⊕ BIZ HS 📶 ✖ 🛏 🖨 💻
/ SOME UNITS 🐕

MURRAY HOTEL   575/956-9400

fyi Not evaluated. **Address:** 200 W Broadway St 88061 **Location:** Center. Facilities, services, and décor characterize a mid-scale property. Currently under renovation, this unique historic hotel reflects its original, classic Art Deco style.

WHERE TO EAT

THE CURIOUS KUMQUAT   575/534-0337

▼▼ ▼▼ American. Casual Dining. $6-$35 **AAA Inspector Notes:** Featuring local farm-raised and foraged foods, this eatery also offers an excellent beer and wine list all in an eclectic setting. The gourmet market showcases local items including meats and cheese. **Features:** beer & wine. **Address:** 111 E College Ave 88061 **Location:** Just e of jct Hudson St (SR 90), n of Bullard St. L D

DIANE'S RESTAURANT   575/538-8722

▼▼ ▼▼ International. Fine Dining. $8-$30 **AAA Inspector Notes:** This popular local eatery presents a menu listing a good selection of appetizers, such as spanakopita, as well as tasty soups and fish, poultry and beef entrées. Vegetarian and some gluten-free items also are available. **Features:** beer & wine, Sunday brunch. **Address:** 510 N Bullard St 88061 **Location:** Center; in historic downtown. **Parking:** street only. L D

JALISCO CAFE   575/388-2060

▼▼ ▼▼ Mexican. Family Dining. $7-$28 **AAA Inspector Notes:** Flavorful Mexican favorites are served in hearty portions at this popular eatery. For a tropical treat, try the crab tostadas with mango. A house specialty, the mandarin orange cake is luscious. **Features:** beer & wine. **Address:** 103 S Bullard St 88061 **Location:** Center; in historic downtown. **Parking:** street only. L D

SHEVEK & CO RESTAURANT   575/534-9168

▼▼▼ ▼▼
Mediterranean
Casual Dining
$9-$30

AAA Inspector Notes: This distinctive dining experience features traditional Mediterranean and Mediterranean fusion dishes. Tapas size allows a diner to experience many flavors. An extensive beer and wine selection is offered with most wines available by the glass. **Features:** beer & wine. **Address:** 602 N Bullard St 88061 **Location:** Center. **Parking:** street only.
Menu on AAA.com D

TRE ROSAT CAFE   575/654-4919

▼▼▼ ▼▼ French. Fine Dining. $9-$26 **AAA Inspector Notes:** The well thought-out menu showcases fine French specialties in addition to many dishes with an international flair. Great service, a good wine list and a comfortable ambience round out an excellent dining experience. **Features:** beer & wine. **Reservations:** suggested. **Address:** 304 N Bullard St 88061 **Location:** Just n of Broadway; downtown. **Parking:** street only. L D

SOCORRO (G-3) pop. 9,051, elev. 4,605'

Socorro was the largest—and wildest—city in New Mexico during the 1880s. After the Panic of 1893 sent silver prices plunging, local mines produced zinc and other ores until these reserves became depleted. The mining era also produced the New Mexico School of Mines, founded in 1889 and later renamed the New Mexico Institute of Mining and Technology.

Socorro County Chamber of Commerce: 101 Plaza, P.O. Box 743, Socorro, NM 87801. **Phone:** (575) 835-0424.

Self-guiding tours: A brochure outlining a walking tour of historic buildings and places, most within walking distance of the central plaza, is available from the chamber.

EL CAMINO REAL HISTORIC TRAIL SITE is about 35 mi. s. of Socorro off I-25S exit 115, then 1.5 mi. s. on SR 1, then 3 mi. e. on CR 1598 (just past marker 24). Used by traders, settlers and Native Americans for some 300 years, El Camino Real de Tierra Adentro (The Royal Road to the Interior) brought the first Spanish and Mexican colonists to what is now New Mexico. The trail not only provided a means of travel through a vast region but served as a means of introducing livestock, agricultural products, cultural ideas, religion and literature.

Exhibits at the visitor center include a re-creation of the main plaza in Zacatecas, Mexico, a hand-hewn *carreta* (cart) that carried people and their belongings along the trail, a *tienda* (store) and such artifacts as tools and leather water jugs. **Time:** Allow 1 hour minimum. **Hours:** Wed.-Sun. 8:30-5. Closed Jan. 1, Easter, Thanksgiving and Christmas. **Cost:** $5; free (ages 0-16, military with ID, New Mexico residents with ID on Sun. and New Mexico senior citizens with ID on Wed.). **Phone:** (575) 854-3600.

MINERAL MUSEUM is at Olive Ln. and Canyon Rd., on the campus of the New Mexico Institute of Mining and Technology. An extensive mineral collection includes more than 2,000 specimens indigenous to the region and from around the world, as well as artifacts and memorabilia related to mining and minerals. Exhibits change periodically. **Hours:** Mon.-Fri. 8-5, Sat.-Sun. 10-3. Closed major holidays. **Cost:** Free. **Phone:** (575) 835-5140.

SAN MIGUEL MISSION is n. of the plaza at 403 El Camino Real. Its long history dates back to 1598, when Franciscan priest Juan de Oñate lead a band of several hundred colonists north from Mexico; the mission he founded was named Nuestra Señora del

ocorro (Our Lady of Perpetual Help). The twin-
owered adobe church, built in the early 19th cen-
ury, remains an active parish; the original church
vas abandoned following the Pueblo Rebellion of
680 and fell into ruins.

Changes to the building over the years include
ne addition of stained-glass windows and a side
hapel. Hand-carved ceiling beams highlight the
ewly restored main sanctuary. The church cel-
orated its 400th anniversary in 2015. A collection of
rtifacts is displayed in the adjoining office. **Hours:**
hurch daily 8-6. Office Mon.-Thurs. 8:30-4:30, Fri.
:30-noon. Mass is held Sat. at 5, Sun. at 8 and 10
.m. **Cost:** Donations. **Phone:** (575) 835-2891.

ERY LARGE ARRAY (VLA) RADIO TELESCOPE
 50 mi. w. on US 60. One of the world's premier
adio telescope observatories, the VLA consists of
7 radio telescopes, each weighing 230 tons. The
arabolic dish portion of the antenna measures 82
et in diameter. For optimum tracking, the antennas
re maneuvered along a Y-shaped grid of railroad
acks that stretch for miles across the desert floor.
elf-guiding walking tours to a working antenna start
t the visitor center, which provides an orientation
lm and educational exhibits. **Note:** Phone ahead in
oring, early summer and fall for possible closure
ue to high-altitude snowfall. **Time:** Allow 1 hour
inimum. **Hours:** Self-guiding tours available 8:30-
usk. Visitor center open daily 8:30-dusk. Guided
urs are offered Sun. at 1 and on the first Sat. of the
onth at 11, 1 and 3. Guests should arrive 15 min-
tes before departure time. **Cost:** Free. $6, $5
senior citizens), free (ages 0-17). **Phone:** (575)
35-7410, or (505) 515-5780 to schedule a tour.

EST WESTERN SOCORRO HOTEL & SUITES

(575)838-0556

Hotel
$90-$105

AAA Benefit:
Save 10% or more every
day and earn 10% bonus
points!

Address: 1100 California Ave NE 87801
Location: I-25 exit 150, just s. **Facility:**
120 units. 2 stories (no elevator),
interior/exterior corridors. **Terms:** cancellation fee imposed, resort fee.
Pool(s): heated indoor. **Activities:**
sauna, hot tub, game room, exercise
room. **Guest Services:** coin laundry.
**Featured Amenity: continental
breakfast.**

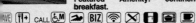

SOME
UNITS

Get maps, travel information

and road service with the

AAA and CAA Mobile apps

COMFORT INN & SUITES   (575)838-4400

Hotel $83-$105 **Address:** 1259 Frontage Rd NW 87801
Location: I-25 exit 150, just nw. **Facility:** 66 units. 3 stories, interior
corridors. **Activities:** hot tub, exercise room. **Guest Services:** coin laundry.

ECONO LODGE   (575)835-1500

Motel
$65-$99

Address: 713 California St NW 87801
Location: I-25 exit 150, just s. **Facility:**
66 units. 1-2 stories (no elevator), exterior corridors. **Pool(s):** heated outdoor.
Activities: sauna, hot tub, exercise
room. **Featured Amenity: continental
breakfast.**

HOLIDAY INN EXPRESS   575/838-4600

[fyi] Not evaluated. **Address:** 1040 N California St 87801 **Location:**
I-25 exit 150, just s. Facilities, services, and décor characterize a mid-
scale property.

WHERE TO EAT

EL SOMBRERO   575/835-3945

Mexican. Casual Dining. $8-$20 **AAA Inspector Notes:**
Located at the edge of town, this popular bright and cheerful local
café is convenient to the interstate. All the traditional New Mexican
dishes are featured here: carne adovada, flat enchiladas, tamales
and sopaipillas stuffed with meat, beans and chicken. **Features:** beer
& wine. **Address:** 210 Mesquite St 87801 **Location:** I-25 exit 150,
just e. [L] [D]

SOCORRO SPRINGS RESTAURANT AND BREWERY
575/838-0650

American. Casual Dining. $9-$23 **AAA Inspector Notes:**
Near the central plaza, this brew pub satisfies patrons with well-made
suds in several varieties, as well as pizza and sandwiches. Also
tempting are a number of good desserts. A Southwestern look
complements the location. **Features:** beer & wine. **Address:** 1012 N
California St 87801 **Location:** I-25 exit 150, 0.3 mi s.
[L] [D]

SPRINGER (E-5) pop. 1,047, elev. 5,832'

Springer was named for Frank Springer, who
came to New Mexico from Iowa in 1873, settled in
Cimarron and became a prominent lawyer and pale-
ontologist. His legacy is the New Mexico Museum of
Art *(see attraction listing p. 418),* of which he was a
founder.

The Santa Fe Trail Interpretive Center and Museum, housed in the old county courthouse at 606
Maxwell Ave., displays household items, clothing,
period furniture and the only electric chair ever put
to use in New Mexico to carry out the death penalty;
phone (575) 483-5554.

**Springer Chamber of Commerce and Visitor
Center:** P.O. Box 323, Springer, NM 87747. **Phone:**
(575) 643-6401.

SUNSPOT (I-4) elev. 9,200'

NATIONAL SOLAR OBSERVATORY is on Sacramento Peak. At an elevation of 9,200 feet, this research facility conducts high-resolution observations

of the sun. There are exhibits and interactive displays at the Sunspot Astronomy and Visitor Center, at the end of the Sunspot Scenic Byway (SR 6563). The observatory also offers views of the Tularosa Basin. A brochure and map are available for self-guiding tours.

Time: Allow 1 hour minimum. **Hours:** Daily 9-5, May-Sept.; otherwise varies. Guided tours are given daily at 2, June-Aug. (weather permitting). Phone ahead to confirm schedule. **Cost:** $3; $1.50 (ages 55+ and active military); free (ages 0-9); $10 (family). Guided tours $3; $1.50 (ages 55+ and active military with ID); $1 (ages 10-17). **Phone:** (575) 434-7190. GT

TAOS (E-4) pop. 5,716, elev. 6,952'
• Hotels p. 449 • Restaurants p. 449
• Hotels & Restaurants map & index p. 447

Originally named Don Fernando de Taos by the Spanish, this northeastern New Mexico jewel has long been a lure. The natural setting in the shadow of the lofty Sangre de Cristo Mountains is glorious. There's a mystical quality that finds its most evocative expression through art. And how many other towns can you name that have a history embracing the Athabascans, Kit Carson and Dennis Hopper?

The Athabascan people (now referred to as Apaches and Navajos) began settling this area almost a thousand years ago. Adobe dwellings were constructed as early as 1350 A.D. at Taos Pueblo, which has the distinction of being considered the nation's oldest continuously inhabited community as well as being the only UNESCO Living World Heritage Site in the United States. The pueblo's two largest structures appear much as they did in 1540, when the first Spanish explorers arrived. Searching for the "seven cities of gold" that supposedly contained unlimited riches, the Spaniards unfortunately came face to face with a very early urban legend.

Christopher Houston "Kit" Carson is a major figure in Taos lore. The Missouri-born frontiersman was a fur trapper before gaining renown as the guide for John C. Frémont's successful 1840s exploration of the Continental Divide—a trek that set off a flurry of expeditions charting the American West.

Carson later became a Taos rancher and a U.S. Army general who was instrumental in quelling a Navajo uprising in New Mexico. His legendary status grew from the publication of many dime store novels and pulp magazine stories. You can brush up on the "fighting trapper's" life at the Kit Carson Home and Museum and visit his grave in Kit Carson Park.

Flash back to a more recent time—the 1960s—when hippie communes began springing up in the region's spectacular high desert country. Actor/filmmaker Dennis Hopper came to New Mexico to scout locations for "Easy Rider," a 1969 cult classic that vividly depicts the counterculture

vibe of the time, partially filmed in and around Taos. Hopper returned and lived here for 12 years. A 201 memorial service for the two-time Oscar nomine was held at the historic San Francisco de As Church in Ranchos de Taos. Hopper is burie nearby.

What always has attracted people is the shee beauty of the land. Adventurous sketch and wate color artists in search of inspiration arrived alon with railroad survey teams in the 1870s. The pro posed Río del Norte and Santa Fe Railroad neve came to fruition, and later efforts to bring rail servic to town also failed. This has left Taos somewhat de lightfully isolated despite the inevitable presence c modern highways.

It was illustrator Ernest Blumenschein who reall got the town's artistic ball rolling. On a covere wagon trip to the Southwest in 1898, he and col league Bert Phillips were forced to stop in Taos t repair a broken wheel. They became enthralled wit the surroundings during their brief stay, and bot eventually settled in permanently. In 1915 Blumen schein helped form the Taos Society of Artists, whic established the town as an artists' colony with a ber for the eccentric; creative types have gravitated her ever since.

The heart of Taos is Taos Plaza, just off Paseo de Pueblo Norte between Kit Carson Road and Camin de la Placita. It dates back to the late 18th centur and has long been a local meeting place. A big co tonwood tree stands in the center of this small plaza in spring and summer its shiny green leaves flutte in the slightest breeze and then turn bright yellow i the fall, providing a lovely contrast to the azure blu sky.

The plaza's gazebo was donated by Mabe Dodge, a transplanted New York socialite and a connoisseur who came to town in 1918, marrie Taos Indian Tony Luhan and championed New Mexi co's Indian culture and natural beauty to contempo raries like Georgia O'Keeffe, D.H. Lawrence an Ansel Adams. This is a perfect spot to relax and se your internal clock to a more laid-back rhythm.

Taos also provides plenty of outdoor action for ac tive types who aren't content to sit and contemplate The nearby Rio Grande makes the area a popula starting point for river rafting excursions. Durin high-water season, from late April to mid-June, th thrills range from relatively gentle to pulse poundin (the latter courtesy of the infamous Taos Box, 1 miles of wilderness gorge and physically demandin rapids). Outfitters are based in town and in Sant Fe.

Mountain bikers and hikers meet their match o the trails that traverse 13,161-foot Wheeler Peak and Wheeler Peak Wilderness Area offers summe fishing and camping. Winter sports enthusiasts floc to Taos Ski Valley's world-class downhill facilities phone (575) 586-0520 for snow conditions and year round recreational activities.

ee map & index p. 447.)

SRs 522 and 38 and US 64—the Enchanted
ircle Scenic Byway—encircle Wheeler Peak, of-
ring a multitude of spectacular vistas. About a half
our's drive north of Taos via SR 522 is the tiny, his-
ric village of Questa, one of a long string of vil-
ges scattered up the Rio Grande into southern
olorado. Founded in 1842, the isolated settlement
as subject to Ute raids for generations. The loca-
on still feels remote, and thankfully its beauty re-
ains unspoiled.

The focal point of the community is a thick-walled
dobe church that gave the village its original name,
an Antonio del Río Colorado. "Questa" was an
ngtlo attempt at simplification that became an offi-
al misspelling of the Spanish *cuesta,* or ridge,
here the church plaza was built.

Lovely scenery surrounds Questa. Hiking trails
escend into the Rio Grande Gorge and wind
round lakes nestled in the Sangre de Cristo Moun-
ins. Thanks to a location between the Carson Na-
nal Forest and the Rio Grande del Norte National
onument, this region offers outdoor recreation ga-
re, from mountain biking and fishing to horseback
ding excursions and hiking treks with a llama-riding
uide.

The Questa Visitor Center, in the center of the vil-
ge on SR 38 just after the SR 522 turn-off, is open
hurs.-Sun. 9:30-5 (also holiday and mid-summer
ondays), Memorial Day-Labor Day; phone (575)
13-2852. For information about recreational oppor-
nities within Rio Grande del Norte National Monu-
ent contact the Bureau of Land Management Taos
eld office; phone (575) 758-8851.

own of Taos Visitor Center: 1139 Paseo del
ueblo Sur, Taos, NM 87571. **Phone:** (575)
58-3873 or (800) 732-8267.

Self-guiding tours: A walking tour map of the city's
historic district and Taos Plaza is available from the
visitor center.

Shopping: Many shops at Taos Plaza veer more
toward souvenirs, T-shirts and knickknacks than fine
art, but it's such a relaxed hangout that you'll want
to poke around anyway. Indulge your sweet tooth at
the Rocky Mountain Chocolate Factory (next to La-
Fonda Hotel) before browsing the merchandise at
places like the Taos Trading Co. or Mesa's Edge
Jewelry.

There's more browsing at the John Dunn House
Shops, a tree-shaded, open-air lane of shops be-
tween Taos Plaza and Bent Street. Monet's Kitchen
has Southwest table and kitchen accessories; Leth-
erwerks sells handmade belts, hats and jackets.
Rock hounds should check out the La Tierra Mineral
Gallery (fossils, crystals, jewelry). Moby Dickens
Bookshop has a good Southwest selection.

Taos Blue (101 Bent St., just off Paseo del Pueblo
Norte) offers finely handcrafted Southwestern and
northern New Mexico art—pottery, jewelry, beadwork, medicine bags, Kachina dolls and the like. The
gallery also sells fetishes, which are small carvings
of animals made from turquoise, mother of pearl and
other materials. Created by the Zuni for ceremonial
purposes, they're prized by collectors of contemporary Native American art.

The town's thriving art scene, in fact, lures collectors from around the country. Ledoux Street, a block
southwest of the plaza, is lined with galleries like
203 Fine Art (203 Ledoux St.), the Baumann Gallery
(136C Paseo de Pueblo Norte), the Inger Jirby Gallery (207 Ledoux St.) and the R.C. Gorman Navajo
Gallery (210 Ledoux St.). The Ledoux Art Stroll, held
the third Saturday of the month June through August, is a popular way to experience what the local

(See map & index p. 447.)

artist community offers. Local merchants usher in the holiday season with Lighting of Ledoux, held the second Saturday in December.

There are more galleries along Kit Carson Road just east of the plaza. Parsons Gallery of the West (122-D Kit Carson Rd.) features vintage Western art, while the Timothy O. Sutherland Gallery (140 Kit Carson Rd.) specializes in fine art photography. The Thom Wheeler Studio Gallery (939 Kit Carson Rd.) has paintings and sculptures. Cowboy collectibles and Western-style furnishings are on display at Horse Feathers (109 Kit Carson Rd. next to the Kit Carson Home and Museum).

Take home a bit of Taos history from the El Rincón Trading Post (114 Kit Carson Rd.). Established in 1909, it actually was a trading post back in the day. In addition to Indian pottery, baskets and rugs, this is a great place to hunt for old turquoise jewelry pawned more than a century ago. The store also has a museum with a collection of Western and Indian artifacts—everything from buckskin britches to peyote fans (used for powwow ceremonial dances).

Ancient traditions live on at Taos Pueblo. Tourism contributes to the local livelihood, and many of the adobe dwellings contain gift shops that sell items like clay pottery, tanned buckskin moccasins and handcrafted pipes. Family-run Wahleah's Taos Pueblo Gallery has five rooms filled with rugs, deerskin drums, beautiful turquoise jewelry and traditional crafts. Even Wahleah's T-shirts, imprinted with lovely nature scenes and cool-looking Indian symbols, are works of art. And don't leave without trying some Indian fry bread, baked in an outdoor adobe oven.

Nightlife: Taos isn't known for frenetic nightlife; options here are mellow and mostly revolve around live music. The Adobe Bar (125 Paseo del Pueblo Norte in The Historic Taos Inn), fondly known as "the living room of Taos," is *the* place to go if you want to mingle with Taoseños. There's live music every night of the week—everything from jazz, bluegrass and alt-country to flamenco, Celtic and native folk music. Better yet, there's no cover charge. The list of creative margaritas includes the inn's famous "Cowboy Buddha."

The Alley Cantina (just off the plaza at 121 Teresina Ln.) is a lively restaurant and bar where singles congregate at happy hour and diners scarf down the highly regarded fish and chips. This is said to be the oldest building in Taos, although only parts of the walls can make that claim. Legend also has it that Teresina Bent, daughter of 19th-century territorial governor Charles Bent, haunts the premises. Local bands play several nights a week.

More local talent—from guitarists to oboe players to stand-up comics—takes the stage on open mic nights (Mondays beginning at 6:30 at the Adobe Bar, Wednesdays at 9:30 at the Alley Cantina). Caffe Tazza (122 Kit Carson Rd.) has weekend open mic nights that bring young performers and mos acoustic music to this cozy coffeehouse.

Another popular nightspot is the Anaconda B (317 Kit Carson Rd. in the El Monte Sagrado R sort), where the decor includes a snake sculptu slithering across the ceiling and a massive saltwa aquarium. Live entertainment takes place Frid and Saturday evenings beginning at 10.

Or you could just hang out in Taos Plaza. Wh the weather's warm the plaza becomes a magnet locals and tourists alike. But it's Taos Plaza Li (every Thursday evening from late May to early Se tember) that brings out the crowds. Two bands pe form at each show, and the musical lineup eclectic: rock, jazz, blues, country, traditional Ne Mexican and Native American. Performances sta at 6; admission is free.

E.L. BLUMENSCHEIN HOME AND MUSEUM is blks. w. of historic Taos Plaza on Ledoux St. T artist and co-founder of the original Taos Society Artists made this his permanent home in 1919. Po tions of the adobe house were built in 1797; oth sections were purchased by Blumenschein. The r stored 13-room house contains original furnishin and serves as a showcase for works by Ernest a Mary Blumenschein, their daughter, Helen, a other Taos painters. **Hours:** Mon.-Sat. 10-5, Su noon-5, Apr.-Sept. Phone for winter hours. **Cost:** $ $4 (ages 5-16). Combination ticket with Martine Hacienda $12. Combination ticket with Harwoo Museum of Art, Martinez Hacienda, Millicent Roge Museum and Taos Art Museum $25. **Phone:** (57 758-0505.

HARWOOD MUSEUM OF ART is at 238 Ledoux S Taos art from the 18th century to the present i cludes paintings, sculpture and Hispanic religio art. The Agnes Martin Gallery presents seven pai ings by this foremost American abstract arti Changing exhibits focus on Taos artists. **Hour** Mon.-Sat. 10-5, Sun. noon-5, May-Oct.; Tues.-S 10-5, Sun. noon-5, rest of year. Closed Jan. Thanksgiving and Christmas. **Cost:** $10; $8 (age 60+ and students with ID); free (ages 0-12). Comb nation ticket with E.L. Blumenschein Home and M seum, Martinez Hacienda, Millicent Rogers Museu and Taos Art Museum $25. **Phone:** (575) 758-982

HISTORIC TAOS TROLLEY TOURS depart fro the Taos County Visitors Center at 1139 Paseo c Pueblo Sur, and from Atira's Southwest gift shop 102-A S. Taos Plaza. Visitors can choose betwee two narrated tours aboard a trolley-style bus. T Taos Pueblo Excursion includes a 1-hour visit to centuries-old pueblo, plus stops at Taos Plaza ar the San Francisco de Asis Church. The History a Culture Tour includes Taos Plaza, the Millice Rogers Museum and the Martinez Hacienda.

Note: Another site is substituted if the puebl closes for the day without prior notice. **Time:** Allo 3 hours minimum. **Hours:** Taos Pueblo Excursic departs the visitor center Tues.-Sat. at 10:30 and

See map & index p. 447.)

May-Oct. (also departs 15 minutes later from Ati-
a's). History and Culture Tour departs the visitor
enter Sun.-Mon. at 2, May-Oct. (also departs 15
minutes later from Atira's). **Cost:** (includes admission to attractions) $33; $10 (ages 6-12). A gas sur-
harge is added to ticket prices. Tickets can be
urchased daily 10:30-5:30 at Atira's. **Phone:** (505)
50-5612.

KIT CARSON HOME AND MUSEUM is at 113 Kit
Carson Rd. Located within the home of Christopher
Houston "Kit" Carson and his wife Josefa and their
children, the museum focuses on the history of the
Carson family. Kit Carson was a well-known mountain man, guide, army officer and Mason. Exhibits
reflect the life of the home's occupants during the
mid-1800s. A 20-minute video presentation about
Carson also is shown. **Time:** Allow 1 hour minimum.
Hours: Daily 10-5, Mar.-Oct.; 10-4, rest of year.
Closed Jan. 1, Thanksgiving and Christmas. Phone
ahead to confirm schedule. **Cost:** $7; $6 (ages 62+
and military with ID); $5 (ages 13-19). **Phone:** (575)
758-4945.

KIT CARSON PARK is 2 blks. n. of Taos Plaza. The
park contains the cemetery where Kit Carson, Padre
Martinez and other historic figures are buried.
Hours: Daily 8-8, Apr.-Oct.; 8-5, rest of year. **Cost:**
Free. **Phone:** (575) 758-8234. 🎟

MARTINEZ HACIENDA is 2 mi. w. of Taos Plaza at
708 Hacienda Way. This restored *hacienda* was built
in 1804 by Don Antonio Severino Martinez, a merchant and *alcalde* (mayor) of Taos. The fortress-like
house has 21 rooms built around two large courtyards. Furnished in period, it contains exhibits of
Spanish colonial life and culture. Living-history demonstrations are presented periodically. **Hours:** Mon.-
Sat. 10-5, Sun. noon-5, Apr.-Oct.; Mon.-Tues. and
Fri.-Sat. 10-4, Sun. noon-4, rest of year. Phone
ahead to confirm schedule. **Cost:** $8; $4 (ages
4-16). Combination ticket with E.L. Blumenschein
Home and Museum $12. Combination ticket with
E.L. Blumenschein Home and Museum, Harwood
Museum of Art, Millicent Rogers Museum and Taos
Art Museum $25. **Phone:** (575) 758-1000.

MILLICENT ROGERS MUSEUM is 4 mi. n. of Taos
Plaza near US 64. The adobe house contains dis-
plays relating to the art, history and culture of the
Southwest. Emphasis is given to the Indian, Hispanic and Anglo art of Taos and northern New
Mexico. A highlight among the 15 galleries is the collection of pottery by Maria Martinez, a San Ildefonso
Pueblo potter whose career spanned some 85
years. **Time:** Allow 1 hour minimum. **Hours:** Daily
10-5, Apr.-Oct.; Tues.-Sun. 10-5, rest of year.
Closed Jan. 1, Easter, Memorial Day, July 4, Labor
Day, San Geronimo Day, Thanksgiving and
Christmas. **Cost:** $10; $8 (ages 60+); $6 (students
and active and retired military with ID); $2 (ages
6-16). Combination ticket with E.L. Blumenschein

Home and Museum, Harwood Museum of Art, Martinez Hacienda and Taos Art Museum $25. Prices
may vary; phone ahead. **Phone:** (575) 758-2462.

PICURÍS PUEBLO—see place listing p. 401.

RIO GRANDE GORGE BRIDGE is 10 mi. w. of Taos
on US 64. Built in 1965, this continuous steel deck
truss bridge is 1,272 feet long and spans the gorge
some 650 feet above the Rio Grande. A raised sidewalk allows daredevils to walk out to the mid-span
observation deck for a dizzying look down—the
gorge is spectacularly deep at this point—with
rugged cliff walls zigzagging to the water far below.
If you suffer from acrophobia even hanging on to the
guardrail for dear life won't be enough, but the views
still are spectacular (and not as vertigo-inducing)
from the side of the highway.

There are parking areas on both sides of the
highway at the east end of the bridge, and vendors
set up tables to sell jewelry, T-shirts and other items.
The 20-minute drive from Taos is a scenic one, running through a flat, sagebrush-speckled valley
framed by the Sangre de Cristo Mountains to the
east and the San Juan range to the northwest.
Hours: Daily 24 hours. **Cost:** Free.

SAN FRANCISCO DE ASIS CHURCH is 4 mi. s. on
SR 68 in St. Francis Plaza. Built by Franciscan
priests and completed in 1772, this heavily buttressed structure with twin bell towers exemplifies
Spanish colonial architecture. Its rounded contours
inspired the imaginations of Ansel Adams and
Georgia O'Keeffe, among other artists.

You can still see straw glinting in the sunlight on
the massive adobe walls. Inside are wood pews, two
large, carved *reredos* (altar screens) divided into
painted panels, paintings of saints and a ceiling of
wood beams *(vigas)*. The church's simple dignity is
best appreciated from the arched portal entrance
that overlooks a walled courtyard.

Photography is not permitted inside the church. In
the parish hall across the plaza is Henri Ault's
mysterious—some say miraculous—luminescent
painting "The Shadow of the Cross."

Hours: Open to visitors Wed.-Sun. 10-4. Mass
given Sun. at 8 a.m. (in Spanish) and 10 a.m.
Weekday Communion Masses Mon.-Tues. at 6:45
a.m. Phone ahead to confirm mass schedule. **Cost:**
Church free. Parish hall admission $3; free (ages
0-9). **Phone:** (575) 758-2754.

TAOS ART MUSEUM is at 227 Paseo del Pueblo
Norte. Housed in the historic home of Russian-born
artist Nicolai Fechin, the permanent collection includes paintings by the Taos Society of Artists and
the Taos Moderns. The Fechin Home, designed and
reconstructed in the 1930s, is considered an architectural masterpiece. It is filled with Fechin's hand-
carved doors, windows, furniture and art. **Time:**
Allow 30 minutes minimum. **Hours:** Tues.-Sun.
10-5, May-Oct.; Tues.-Sun. 10-4, rest of year. Phone
ahead to confirm schedule. **Cost:** $10; $9 (ages 65+

(See map & index p. 447.)

and military with ID); $6 (students with ID). Combination ticket with E.L. Blumenschein Home and Museum, Harwood Museum of Art, Martinez Hacienda and Millicent Rogers Museum $25. **Phone:** (575) 758-2690.

TAOS PUEBLO is 2 mi. n. of the plaza via Paseo del Pueblo Norte, then about half a mile n. on the entrance road to the parking/registration area. Located at the base of Taos Mountain, this is one of the oldest continuously inhabited communities in North America.

Stepping onto pueblo land is like taking a big step backward in time. Buildings are constructed entirely of adobe; roofs are supported by *vigas* (large wood timbers). The only modern additions are simple doors and windows. The two largest structures are composed of individual dwellings with common walls but no connecting doorways. About 150 Taos Indians choose to live in the sacred village as their ancestors did, without conveniences like electricity or plumbing; drinking water comes from Red Willow Creek, which flows through the center of the pueblo.

A cemetery with primitive wood crosses contains a bell tower, all that remains of the original San Geronimo Church, erected in the early 17th century by Spanish priests overseeing Indian labor. The present church dates from 1850 and has a simple dignity; a central altar figure of the Virgin Mary also

represents Mother Nature in the blend of Catholi and native religious iconography.

Registration is required to enter the pueblo. Visi tors must heed all signs designating restricted ac cess. **Time:** Allow 1 hour minimum. **Hours:** Mon. Sat. 8-4:30, Sun. 8:30-4:30, Memorial Day-late Oct Mon.-Sat. 8-4, Sun. 8:30-4, rest of year. Closed fo approximately 10 weeks from late winter to earl spring. Phone ahead to confirm schedule. **Cos** $16; $14 (ages 60+ and students with ID); fre (ages 0-10). **Phone:** (575) 758-1028. GT

RECREATIONAL ACTIVITIES
Skiing
- **Taos Ski Valley** is in the Sangre de Cristo Moun tains in Carson National Forest *(see place listin p. 367).* **Hours:** Daily Thanksgiving-early Apr **Phone:** (575) 776-2291 or (866) 968-7386.

White-water Rafting
- **Cottam's Rio Grande Rafting** departs from 207-A Paseo del Pueblo Sur. Other activities ar available. **Hours:** Daily May-Sept. **Phone:** (575 758-2822 or (800) 322-8267.
- **Far Flung Adventures** departs from 15 SR 522N **Hours:** Daily late Apr.-Sept. 30. **Phone:** (575 758-2628 or (800) 359-2627.
- **Los Rios River Runners** departs from various lo cations. **Hours:** Daily Mar.-Oct. **Phone:** (575 776-8854 or (800) 544-1181.

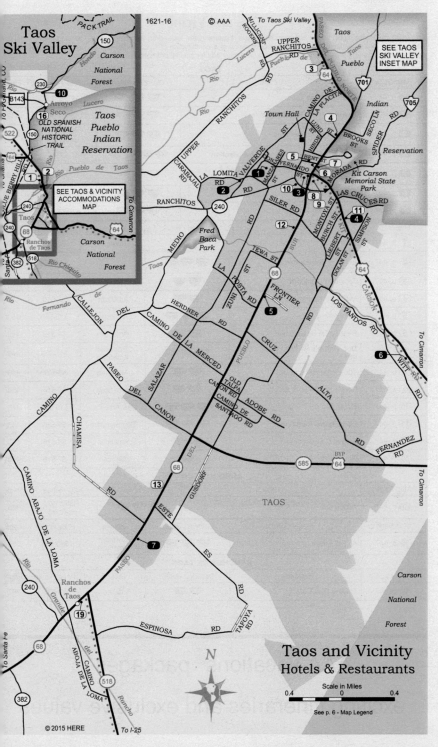

Taos and Vicinity
Hotels & Restaurants

Taos and Vicinity

This index helps you "spot" where approved hotels and restaurants are located on the corresponding detailed maps. Hotel da
rate range is for comparison only. Restaurant price range is a combination of lunch and/or dinner. Turn to the listing page f
more detailed rate and price information and consult display ads for special promotions.

TAOS

Map Page	Hotels	Diamond Rated	Rate Range	Page
❶ p. 447	**La Posada de Taos**	◈ ◈ ◈	$149-$250 SAVE	449
❷ p. 447	**Dreamcatcher Bed & Breakfast**	◈ ◈ ◈	$140-$200 SAVE	449
❸ p. 447	Hotel La Fonda De Taos	◈ ◈ ◈	Rates not provided	449
❹ p. 447	**El Monte Sagrado, Autograph Collection**	◈ ◈ ◈ ◈	$161-$354 SAVE	449
❺ p. 447	**American Artists Gallery House Bed & Breakfast**	◈ ◈ ◈	$119-$250 SAVE	449
❻ p. 447	An Inn On The Rio	◈ ◈ ◈	$110-$175	449
❼ p. 447	Hampton Inn	◈ ◈ ◈	$109-$189	449

Map Page	Restaurants	Diamond Rated	Cuisine	Price Range	Page
① p. 447	Orlando's New Mexican Cafe	◈ ◈	Mexican	$8-$12	450
② p. 447	El Meze Restaurant	◈ ◈ ◈	Regional Spanish	$16-$28	450
③ p. 447	Taos Pizza Outback	◈ ◈	Italian	$4-$29	450
④ p. 447	Michael's Kitchen	◈ ◈	American	$7-$10	450
⑤ p. 447	Lambert's of Taos	◈ ◈ ◈	American	$10-$40	450
⑥ p. 447	Bent Street Deli & Cafe	◈ ◈	American	$4-$12	449
⑦ p. 447	**Doc Martin's At The Historic Taos Inn**	◈ ◈ ◈	Regional American	$11-$28	449
⑧ p. 447	The Gorge Bar and Grill	◈ ◈	American	$9-$27	450
⑨ p. 447	Eske's Brew Pub & Eatery	◈ ◈	American	$8-$14	450
⑩ p. 447	Byzantium	◈ ◈ ◈	New American	$16-$28	449
⑪ p. 447	**De la Tierra Restaurant**	◈ ◈ ◈	Southwestern	$9-$35	449
⑫ p. 447	Station Cafe 3 one 6	◈ ◈	American	$8-$16	450
⑬ p. 447	Guadalajara Grill	◈	Mexican	$7-$16	450

ARROYO SECO

Map Page	Hotel	Diamond Rated	Rate Range	Page
⑩ p. 447	Adobe and Stars B & B	◈ ◈ ◈	Rates not provided	360

Map Page	Restaurant	Diamond Rated	Cuisine	Price Range	Page
⑯ p. 447	ACEQ Restaurant	◈ ◈ ◈	Northern American	$13-$25	360

RANCHOS DE TAOS

Map Page	Restaurant	Diamond Rated	Cuisine	Price Range	Page
⑲ p. 447	Trading Post Cafe	◈ ◈	Italian	$8-$38	402

AAA Vacations® packages ...

exciting itineraries and exclusive values

(See map & index p. 447.)

AMERICAN ARTISTS GALLERY HOUSE BED & BREAKFAST
(575)758-4446 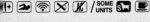 **5**

WWWW
Bed & Breakfast
$119-$250

Address: 132 Frontier Ln 87571 **Location:** 1 mi s of jct US 64 and Taos Plaza, 0.3 mi e. **Facility:** Local artwork decorates the gallery and walls of every room and represents the three diverse cultures that meet in Taos. 9 units, some kitchens and cottages. 1 story, interior/exterior corridors. **Terms:** 2-3 night minimum stay - seasonal and/or weekends, 14 day cancellation notice-fee imposed. **Featured Amenity: full hot breakfast.**

(SAVE) [符↑] [BIZ] 🛜 ✕ 🎿 💻 / SOME UNITS 🐾 🏊 🍴 🖥

INN ON THE RIO
(575)758-7199 **6**

WWW Bed & Breakfast $110-$175 **Address:** 910 Kit Carson Rd 87571 **Location:** US 64, 1.5 mi e of jct SR 68 and Taos Plaza. Located in a residential area. **Facility:** This charming B&B features friendly hosts and homemade breakfasts. Two renowned, local folk artists created exterior and interior murals and hand-painted furniture. 12 units. 1 story, exterior corridors. **Terms:** 14 day cancellation notice-fee imposed. **Pool(s):** heated outdoor. **Activities:** hot tub, picnic facilities.

[符↑] 🛖 🛜 ✕ 🎿 / SOME UNITS 🐾 💻

DREAMCATCHER BED & BREAKFAST
(575)758-0613 **2**

WWWW
Bed & Breakfast
$140-$200

Address: 416 La Lomita Rd 87571 **Location:** From Taos Plaza, 0.5 mi sw on Don Fernando St (which becomes La Loma St), just w on San Antonio St. **Facility:** Relaxing is encouraged at this B&B, which offers hammocks in the large garden, a selection of board games and comfortable beds. 7 units, some two bedrooms. 1 story, exterior corridors. **Terms:** check-in 4 pm, 2 night minimum stay - seasonal and/or weekends, age restrictions may apply, 15 day cancellation notice-fee imposed. **Featured Amenity: full hot breakfast.**

(SAVE) 🛜 ✕ 🎿 🖥 🍴 💻

EL MONTE SAGRADO, AUTOGRAPH COLLECTION
(575)758-3502 **4**

WWWW
Hotel
$161-$354

AUTOGRAPH COLLECTION® HOTELS

AAA Benefit: Members save 5% or more!

Address: 317 Kit Carson Rd 87571 **Location:** 0.5 mi e of jct US 64 and SR 68. **Facility:** Select from several adobe-style cottage units, some with mountain views and a fireplace. A large patio area is available. 84 units, some two bedrooms. 2 stories, interior/exterior corridors. **Parking:** valet only. **Terms:** check-in 4 pm, 3 day cancellation notice. **Amenities:** safes. **Dining:** De la Tierra Restaurant, see separate listing. **Pool(s):** heated indoor. **Activities:** sauna, hot tub, steamroom, game room, exercise room, spa. **Guest Services:** valet laundry, area transportation.

(SAVE) [符↑] 👥 🍴 🛖 [BIZ] [SHS] 🛜 ✕ 📷 🖥 💻 / SOME UNITS 🐾

HAMPTON INN
(575)737-5700 **7**

WWW Hotel $109-$189 **Address:** 515 Paseo del Pueblo Sur 87571 **Location:** SR 68, 3 mi s of Taos Plaza. **Facility:** 71 units. 2 stories, interior corridors. **Terms:** 1-7 night minimum stay, cancellation fee imposed. **Pool(s):** heated indoor. **Activities:** hot tub, exercise room. **Guest Services:** coin laundry.

AAA Benefit: Members save up to 10%!

[CALL] 🔥M 🛖 [BIZ] 🛜 💻 / SOME UNITS 🍴 🖥

HOTEL LA FONDA DE TAOS
575/758-2211 **3**

WWWW Historic Hotel. Rates not provided. **Address:** 108 S Taos Plaza 87571 **Location:** Center. **Facility:** Located on Taos Plaza, this updated circa 1820s hotel is home to the scandalous D.H. Lawrence "Forbidden Art" collection banned from England in 1929. 25 units, some kitchens. 3 stories, interior corridors. **Activities:** massage. [符↑] [BIZ] [HS] 🛜 ✕ / SOME UNITS 🍴

LA POSADA DE TAOS
(575)758-8164 **1**

WWWW
Historic Bed & Breakfast
$149-$250

Address: 309 Juanita Ln 87571 **Location:** From Taos Plaza, just w on Don Fernando St, just s on Manzanares St, then just w. **Facility:** This B&B has a shady courtyard garden, a bright sunroom and many historic architectural elements that enhance the décor. 6 units. 1 story, interior/exterior corridors. **Terms:** check-in 4 pm, 2 night minimum stay - seasonal and/or weekends, 14 day cancellation notice-fee imposed. **Featured Amenity: full hot breakfast.**

(SAVE) [符↑] 🛜 ✕ 🎿 / SOME UNITS 🐾 🎿 💻

BURCH STREET CASITAS
575/737-9038

[fyi] Not evaluated. **Address:** 310 Burch St 87571 **Location:** US 64, just e of jct SR 68, then just s. Facilities, services, and décor characterize a mid-scale property.

WHERE TO EAT

BENT STREET DELI & CAFE
575/758-5787 **6**

WW American. Casual Dining. $4-$12 **AAA Inspector Notes:** A block off Taos Plaza, this eatery's patio seating is a nice good-weather option. **Features:** beer & wine, patio dining, Sunday brunch. **Address:** 120-M Bent St 87571 **Location:** Just n of Taos Plaza, just w of US 64. **Parking:** street only. [B] [L] 🎿

BYZANTIUM
575/751-0805 **10**

WWW New American. Casual Dining. $16-$28 **AAA Inspector Notes:** A visit to Taos is not complete without a meal at the distinctive restaurant. All of the dishes are creative, attractively presented and wonderful in taste. Friendly staff take good care of patrons. **Features:** beer & wine. **Reservations:** required. **Address:** 112 Camino de la Placitas 87571 **Location:** Just s of Taos Plaza; in Courtyard at Ledoux and La Placita. [D] 🎿

DE LA TIERRA RESTAURANT
575/758-3502 **11**

WWWW
Southwestern Fine Dining
$9-$35

AAA Inspector Notes: The cuisine is primarily Southwestern at this upscale restaurant, with such exotic game offerings as elk and quail as well as halibut, salmon, beef and lamb. Diners will find an extensive selection of wines to complement main courses. **Features:** full bar. **Reservations:** suggested. **Address:** 317 Kit Carson Rd 87571 **Location:** 0.5 mi e of jct US 64 and SR 68; in El Monte Sagrado, Autograph Collection. **Parking:** on-site and valet. [L] [D]

DOC MARTIN'S AT THE HISTORIC TAOS INN
575/758-1977 **7**

WWW
Regional American Fine Dining
$11-$28

AAA Inspector Notes: *Historic.* New American and New Mexican cuisine is featured at this historic spot. Tempting desserts are too luscious to miss. Watch the world go by on the outside patio, a local gathering spot. **Features:** full bar, patio dining, Sunday brunch. **Reservations:** suggested, for dinner & Sunday brunch. **Address:** 125 Paseo del Pueblo Norte 87571 **Location:** On US 64, just n of jct SR 68 and Taos Plaza; center; in The Historic Taos Inn. *Menu on AAA.com* [L] [D]

(See map & index p. 447.)

EL MEZE RESTAURANT   575/751-3337 ②
▼▼▼▼ Regional Spanish. Casual Dining. $16-$28 **AAA Inspector Notes:** Expect a well prepared, creative New Mexico twist on Spanish Mediterranean cuisine. The Andalusian-style chicharrónes are a great starter or plate for sharing, and the green chilesmothered buffalo tamale is savory and filling. **Features:** beer & wine, patio dining. **Reservations:** suggested. **Address:** 1017 Paseo del Pueblo Norte 87571 **Location:** 1.2 mi n of plaza.

D 🐂

ESKE'S BREW PUB & EATERY   575/758-1517 ⑨
▼▼ American. Casual Dining. $8-$14 **AAA Inspector Notes:** Bright, cheery and smoke-free, this is a great place to sample beer and root beer brewed on site, or nosh on such pub favorites as the club sandwich: a hearty stack of meat between two slices of beer-battered oat bread. **Features:** beer only, patio dining. **Address:** 106 Des Georges Ln 87571 **Location:** Just w of Taos Plaza.

L D Ⓚ

THE GORGE BAR AND GRILL   575/758-8866 ⑧
▼▼ American. Casual Dining. $9-$27 **AAA Inspector Notes:** The contemporary setting and lively atmosphere of this establishment offers an excellent view for people watching on the plaza below while enjoying a great meal and cocktail from the extensive beverage list. **Features:** full bar, patio dining, happy hour. **Address:** 103-I E Plaza 87571 **Location:** On the Plaza, upstairs in The Shops @103. **Parking:** street only. L D CALL ⅏M

GUADALAJARA GRILL   575/751-0063 ⑬
▼ Mexican. Quick Serve. $7-$16 **AAA Inspector Notes:** This Mexican restaurant packs its menu with all the staples, including tacos, burritos and seafood enchiladas, but the specialty is shrimp prepared in a variety of traditional ways. Orders are taken at the counter, and cordial servers deliver them to the table. **Features:** beer & wine, patio dining. **Address:** 1384 Paseo del Pueblo Sur 87571 **Location:** SR 68, 2.7 mi s of Taos Plaza. L D

LAMBERT'S OF TAOS   575/758-1009 ⑤
▼▼▼ American. Fine Dining. $10-$40 **AAA Inspector Notes:** Find friendly and attentive service at this restaurant just a short walk from the plaza and surrounded by trees and a small garden. Choose from dishes like pepper-crusted lamb loin with red wine demi-glace or the daily fresh fish special. Decadent chocolate mousse with raspberry sauce is large enough to share. Take time to peruse the outstanding wine list for the perfect selection to accompany your fine meal. **Features:** full bar, patio dining, Sunday brunch, happy hour. **Reservations:** suggested. **Address:** 123 Bent St 87571 **Location:** Just n of Taos Plaza, just w of US 64. L D

MICHAEL'S KITCHEN   575/758-4178 ④
▼▼ American. Family Dining. $7-$10 **AAA Inspector Notes:** Just north of Taos Plaza and a short distance from the pueblo, the bustling eatery has a rustic atmosphere and an on-site bakery. All-day breakfast items are served alongside standards such as nachos, tamales, burgers, chicken tacos, salads and enchiladas. **Address:** 304C Paseo del Pueblo Norte 87571 **Location:** US 64, 0.3 mi n of jct SR 68 and Taos Plaza. B L

ORLANDO'S NEW MEXICAN CAFE   575/751-1450 ①
▼▼ Mexican. Casual Dining. $8-$12 **AAA Inspector Notes:** This lively and colorful spot offers cozy inside seating or popular umbrella tables outdoors. Fresh Mexican eats include burritos, enchiladas, tamales, chiles rellenos, chimichangas, tacos and yummy nacho dishes. **Features:** beer & wine, patio dining. **Address:** 1114 Don Juan Valdez Ln 87571 **Location:** 1.8 mi n on US 64.

L D

STATION CAFE 3 ONE 6   575/737-0316 ⑫
▼▼ American. Casual Dining. $8-$16 **AAA Inspector Notes:** A fun atmosphere is what you'll find in this contemporary café, which sports a creative biker theme in its décor and serves up great pub food. **Features:** beer & wine, patio dining, happy hour. **Address:** 316 Paseo del Pueblo Sur 87571 **Location:** Just s of Siler Rd.

L D

TAOS PIZZA OUTBACK   575/758-3112 ③
▼▼ ▼▼ Italian. Casual Dining. $4-$29 **AAA Inspector Notes:** A the heart of the menu at this eatery are freshly made pizza, calzone and pasta dishes. The quaint restaurant proudly serves local and organic produce, which means the salads are mighty tasty. Desserts are displayed near the entrance so diners can plan ahead. **Features** beer & wine, patio dining. **Address:** 712 Paseo de Pueblo Norte 87571 **Location:** Just nw of jct Camino de la Placita.

L D

TESUQUE PUEBLO (B-4) elev. 6,365'

Named by the Tewa-speaking people for the "village at the narrow place of the cottonwood trees," Tesuque (te-SOO-kay) rests in the foothills of the Sangre de Cristo Mountains. The pueblo is just south of Camel Rock, one of many unusual sandstone formations in the area.

TESUQUE PUEBLO is off US 84/285. Tewa-speaking people founded the present settlement in the late 17th century, although habitation dates to 1200 A.D. The 1915 San Diego Mission, designed in the shape of a crucifix, stands on the main plaza. The Pueblos, who have retained their traditional language and culture, hold Three Kings Day festivities in January, a ceremonial Corn Dance the first Saturday in June and the Feast of San Diego on Nov. 12. Photography and sketching are not permitted. **Hours:** The pueblo closes to the public on certain days. Phone ahead to confirm schedule. **Cost:** Free. **Phone:** (505) 983-2667.

THREE RIVERS (H-3) elev. 4,568'

Watered by runoff from the surrounding mountains, the grazing lands of the upper Tularosa Valley attracted cattle barons in the 1870s. Three Rivers once a railroad shipping point, maintains a ranching and farming economy.

THREE RIVERS PETROGLYPH SITE is 5 mi. e. on CR B30 from US 54 following signs. A large group of prehistoric picture writings includes more than 21,000 individual petroglyphs. The Jornada branch of the Mogollon culture is thought to have inscribed them A.D. 900-1400. A trail links many petroglyph sites. **Hours:** Daily 8-7, Apr.-Sept.; 8-5 rest of year **Cost:** $5 (per private vehicle). **Phone:** (575) 525-4300 weekdays only. ▲ ⌂

TRUTH OR CONSEQUENCES (H-3)
pop. 6,475, elev. 4,242'

Playing host to a live broadcast of the radio program "Truth or Consequences" changed not only Hot Springs' future but also its name. So pleased were residents with the publicity engendered by Ralph Edwards' popular show that they adopted the program's name in 1950.

The fire of the chile peppers—one of the Rio Grande Valley's major crops—is nearly matched by the thermal springs that bubble to the surface in Truth or Consequences (their average temperature is 110 F). The Apaches took advantage of the water's legendary curative properties, and bath-houses operated in the vicinity of the springs in the early 20th century.

Both Elephant Butte Lake State Park in Elephant Butte and Caballo Lake State Park in Caballo offer water-oriented recreation. *See Recreation Areas Chart.*

Geronimo Trail Scenic Byway Interpretive Visitors Center: 301 S. Foch St., Truth or Consequences, NM 87901. **Phone:** (575) 894-1968.

GERONIMO SPRINGS MUSEUM is 211 Main St. The museum houses American Indian artifacts; prehistoric Mimbres pottery; ranching, military and mining items; paleontological and geological finds; a reconstructed log cabin; Southwestern art; and mementos of Ralph Edwards, originator of the "Truth or Consequences" radio show. **Time:** Allow 1 hour, 30 minutes minimum. **Hours:** Mon.-Sat. 9-5, Sun. noon-5. Closed Jan. 1, Easter, July 4, Thanksgiving and Christmas. **Cost:** $6; $5 (ages 55+ and active and retired military with ID); $3 (ages 6-18); $15 (family). **Phone:** (575) 894-6600.

HOLIDAY INN EXPRESS & SUITES   (575)894-3900
Hotel $90-$99 **Address:** 2201 FG Amin St 87901 **Location:** I-25 exit 79, just e. **Facility:** 63 units. 3 stories, interior corridors. **Pool(s):** heated indoor. **Activities:** hot tub, exercise room. **Guest Services:** valet and coin laundry.

SIERRA GRANDE LODGE & SPA   575/894-6976
Boutique Hotel $145-$395 **Address:** 501 McAdoo St 87901 **Location:** Just w of Foch St; center. **Facility:** Tastefully restored, this neo-rustic downtown hotel features an elegant western flair. The spa offers spring mineral baths and holistic treatments. 18 units, some two bedrooms. 2 stories (no elevator), interior/exterior corridors. **Activities:** hot tub, recreation programs, exercise room, spa.

COMFORT INN & SUITES   575/894-1660
fyi Not evaluated. **Address:** 2205 N Date St 87901 **Location:** I-25 exit 79, just e. Facilities, services, and décor characterize a mid-scale property.

WHERE TO EAT

CAFE BELLALUCA   575/894-9866
Italian. Casual Dining. $8-$38 **AAA Inspector Notes:** The eatery's casual contemporary atmosphere is inviting and the service welcoming. The menu includes creative hand-tossed pizza and calzones, plus a mouth-watering selection of pasta and Italian entrées. The wild mushroom ravioli or grilled pizza with roasted garlic, goat cheese and onion marmalade are menu favorites. **Features:** beer & wine, patio dining, Sunday brunch. **Address:** 303 Jones St 87901 **Location:** Center.

LA COCINA RESTAURANT   575/894-6499
Mexican. Casual Dining. $6-$30 **AAA Inspector Notes:** The sign out front says "hot stuff," and sure enough the New Mexican cuisine has real authority in the chile department. Red and green varieties are made from fresh ingredients, making all dishes burst with originality and flavor. Interesting artistic accents—such as tabletops and hand-crafted chairs—are rustic yet elegant. **Features:** beer & wine, patio dining. **Address:** 1 Lakeway Dr 87901 **Location:** I-25 exit 79, just e; jct Date St.

LOS ARCOS   575/894-6200
Steak. Casual Dining. $14-$60 **AAA Inspector Notes:** This local favorite serves a wide variety of steaks and prime rib along with a selection of seafood. One of the steak and seafood combinations is just the ticket for a special occasion. Also good are the salads and desserts. **Features:** full bar. **Reservations:** suggested. **Address:** 1400 N Date St 87901 **Location:** I-25 exit 83, 0.5 mi e.

TUCUMCARI (F-5) pop. 5,363, elev. 4,086'
• Hotels p. 452 • Restaurants p. 452

Tucumcari, named for 4,999-foot Tucumcari Mountain—utilized by Comanche Indians as a lookout point, or *tucumcari*—is another town that came into being by way of a rail line (in this case, the Rock Island Railroad). Legend traces the origin of the name to an ill-fated romance between the warrior Tocom and Kari, the daughter of a chief. When Tocom died in a fight for Kari's hand she stabbed the victor, then herself. Witnessing the tragedy, her father also ended his life with a dagger, crying out "Tocom-Kari."

In the 1920s Tucumcari became the first New Mexico stop for westbound travelers on new federal highway Route 66. Stretching 2,448 miles from Chicago to Los Angeles, it played a major role in early transcontinental auto travel. The interstate highway system eventually supplanted Route 66, and it was officially decertified in 1985.

You'll still see a few neon-lit motor courts, kitschy reminders of a bygone era, along the Tucumcari stretch of Route 66. Another local landmark is Tee Pee Curios, known for its teepee-shaped entrance and elaborate neon sign. It opened in 1944 as a Gulf gas station and souvenir shop.

Two Canadian River reservoirs not only provide necessary irrigation but opportunities for outdoor recreation. Conchas Lake is 34 miles northwest of town via SR 104; Ute Lake is 23 miles northeast via SR 54 to Logan. *See Recreation Areas Chart.*

Tucumcari-Quay County Chamber of Commerce: 404 W. Rte. 66, P.O. Drawer E, Tucumcari, NM 88401. **Phone:** (575) 461-1694.

MESALANDS COMMUNITY COLLEGE'S DINOSAUR MUSEUM AND NATURAL SCIENCES LABORATORY is at 222 E. Laughlin Ave. The Exhibit Hall showcases original and replicated fossils and skeletons from the Mesozoic era, the "Age of Dinosaurs." The centerpiece is a 40-foot-long skeleton of a Torvosaurus, a rare carnivorous relative of the Tyrannosaurus rex. **Time:** Allow 1 hour minimum. **Hours:** Tues.-Sat. 10-6, Mar. 1-Labor Day; Tues.-Sat. noon-5, rest of year. Closed Jan. 1, Thanksgiving and Christmas. **Cost:** $6.50; $5.50 (ages 65+); $4.50 (students with ID); $4 (ages 5-11). **Phone:** (575) 461-3466.

TUCUMCARI HISTORICAL MUSEUM is at 416 S. Adams St. A 1903 schoolhouse contains three floors of regional artifacts and memorabilia. Thematic exhibits include a pioneer kitchen, general store, bunkhouse, courtroom room, barn, firehouse with a

1926 fire truck and a tribute to the Armed Forces. Native landscaping surrounds the museum and provides the setting for outdoor exhibits, among them a railroad caboose. **Hours:** Tues.-Sat. 9-3. Closed major holidays. **Cost:** $5; $4 (ages 65+); $1 (ages 6-15). **Phone:** (575) 461-4201.

BEST WESTERN DISCOVERY INN   (575)461-4884

Hotel
$69-$149

AAA Benefit:
Save 10% or more every day and earn 10% bonus points!

Address: 200 E Estrella Ave 88401 **Location:** I-40 exit 332, just n. **Facility:** 80 units. 2 stories (no elevator), exterior corridors. **Pool(s):** heated outdoor. **Activities:** exercise room. **Guest Services:** coin laundry. **Featured Amenity:** full hot breakfast.

  CALL

DAYS INN   (575)461-3158

Hotel $60-$102 **Address:** 2623 S 1st St 88401 **Location:** I-40 exit 332, just n. **Facility:** 40 units. 2 stories (no elevator), interior/exterior corridors.

HOLIDAY INN EXPRESS HOTEL & SUITES   (575)461-3333

Hotel
$110-$199

Address: 2624 S Adams St 88401 **Location:** I-40 exit 332, just n. **Facility:** 80 units. 3 stories, interior corridors. **Terms:** cancellation fee imposed. **Pool(s):** heated indoor. **Activities:** sauna, hot tub, game room, exercise room. **Guest Services:** coin laundry. **Featured Amenity:** full hot breakfast.

LA QUINTA INN & SUITES TUCUMCARI   575/461-2233

[fyi] **Hotel** Did not meet all AAA rating requirements for locking devices in some guest rooms at time of last evaluation on 06/17/2015. **Address:** 2516 S Adams St 88401 **Location:** I-40 exit 332, just n. Facilities, services, and décor characterize a mid-scale property.

WHERE TO EAT

DEL'S RESTAURANT   575/461-1740

American. Casual Dining. $8-$18 **AAA Inspector Notes:** Colorful Southwestern decor punctuates the dining room at this casual, family restaurant located on Historic Route 66. Established in 1956, this spot is a local favorite that features American and Mexican dishes. Check out the gift area offering interesting Route 66 and New Mexico souvenirs. **Address:** 1202 E Route 66 88401 **Location:** I-40 exit 333, 1.5 mi n on Mountain Rd, then 0.5 mi w. [L] [D]

KIX ON 66 COFFEE SHOP & EATERY   575/461-1966

American. Casual Dining. $5-$9 **AAA Inspector Notes:** This retro diner serves generous breakfasts and lunch sandwiches. Ice cream sundaes, shakes and floats are a specialty. **Address:** 1102 E Route 66 Blvd 88401 **Location:** I-40 exit 332, 1.5 mi n on Mountain Rd, then just e. [B] [L]

POW-WOW RESTAURANT   575/461-258

American. Casual Dining. $6-$24 **AAA Inspector Note:** On Historic Route 66, this local favorite offers cocktails plus a wid variety of steaks, chicken, seafood and Mexican food entrées. Sav room for luscious homemade pies. **Features:** full bar, happy hou **Address:** 801 W Tucumcari Blvd 88401 **Location:** I-40 exit 332, 1 n to Tucumcari Blvd, then 1 mi w. [B] [L] [D]

ROCKIN' YS' ROADHOUSE   575/461-994

American. Casual Dining. $6-$15 **AAA Inspector Note:** Favored by locals this casual spot offers a variety of American an Mexican specialties. **Features:** beer & wine. **Address:** 1806 E Rou 66 88401 **Location:** I-40 exit 333, 0.5 mi n; jct US 54 and Histor Route 66. [L] [D]

TULAROSA (H-4) pop. 2,842, elev. 4,508'

WINERIES

- **Tularosa Vineyards** is at 23 Coyote Canyon R Tastings offered. Tours are given by appointmen phone ahead. **Hours:** Mon.-Sat. 9-5, Sun noon-5. **Phone:** (575) 585-2260 or (800 687-4467. [GT]

CASA DE SUEÑOS   575/585-349

Mexican. Casual Dining. $8-$17 **AAA Inspector Notes** Flavorful Mexican dishes and generous portions make this a favorit stop for locals and travelers alike. The dining room features a live and colorful atmosphere. **Features:** beer & wine, patio dining. **Ad dress:** 35 St. Francis Dr 88352 **Location:** Just s on US 54/70. [L] [D]

WHITE ROCK pop. 5,725

HAMPTON INN & SUITES LOS ALAMOS   (505)672-383

Hotel $99-$144 **Address:** 124 SR 4 87544 **Location:** Center. **Facility:** 72 units, some kitchens. 3 stories, interior corridors. **Terms:** check-in 4 pm, 1-7 night minimum stay, cancellation fee imposed. **Activities:** sauna, exercise room. **Guest Services:** vale and coin laundry.

AAA Benefit:
Members save up to 10%!

WHITE SANDS MISSILE RANGE (H-3)
elev. 4,295'

On July 16, 1945, in a remote section of Whit Sands Missile Range, the first man-made atomic ex plosion sent a huge multicolored cloud surging to a altitude of 40,000 feet. The resultant sloping crate at Trinity Site is evidence of the beginning of th Atomic Age.

The desert environment proved ideal for rocke testing and, in the 1960s, testing for the luna module engines that propelled Apollo astronauts o the moon's surface. Today the world-class test facili ties are used by the U.S. Army as well as private in dustry and foreign nations for laser, radar and fligh research.

Vehicle passes are issued at the main gate; a valid driver's license, registration and proof of insur ance are required. A photo ID is required for all ve hicle occupants over age 16. Trinity Site is open the first Saturday in April and October. For more infor mation contact the Public Affairs Office, Bldg. 1782

White Sands Missile Range, NM 88002; phone (575) 678-8800 or (575) 437-6120 (Alamogordo Chamber of Commerce).

WHITE SANDS MISSILE RANGE MUSEUM

is 19 mi. n.e. of Las Cruces on US 70/80, then 4 mi. e. to just inside the main gate. The history of the nation's missile program and the Atomic Age is chronicled via artifacts, displays and photographs depicting early rocket launches and the first atomic bomb test at Trinity Site.

An outdoor park displays some 60 rockets and missiles, including a restored German V-2 rocket exhibited horizontally to reveal its interior. There also are exhibits about Paleo-Indian culture as well as 19th-century mining and ranching. **Time:** Allow 30 minutes minimum. **Hours:** Mon.-Fri. 8-4, Sat. 10-3. Missile park open daily dawn-dusk. Closed major holidays. **Cost:** Free. **Phone:** (575) 678-8800.

WHITE SANDS NATIONAL MONUMENT (I-3)

About 15 miles southwest of Alamogordo on US 70, White Sands National Monument is the source of rare gypsum sands that form snow-white dunes rising up to 60 feet above the Tularosa Basin floor.

Covering 275 square miles, the massive dunes are created when rain and melting snow dissolve gypsum from the surrounding mountains and carry it into Lake Lucero, a seasonal lake, or *playa*. Desert heat evaporates the water, causing gypsum crystals to form. Dry winds expose the crystals, eroding them into sand-sized particles that are blown into the dune field.

Much of this wide sea of dunes is bare of vegetation. A few species of plants exhibit remarkable adaptation to the shifting sands; the stem of the soaptree yucca stretches up to 30 feet to keep the plant from being buried.

Drinking water is available only at the visitor center; covered picnic sites and restrooms are in the heart of the dunes area. Interactive exhibits at the visitor center describe the origin and history of White Sands, and a video is shown every half hour.

Ranger-guided sunset strolls are offered daily 1 hour before sunset, except on Christmas. There are several hiking trails; brochures describing desert hiking safety can be obtained at the visitor center. On full-moon nights from May through October, the park remains open until 11 p.m. so visitors can witness celestial light reflecting off the dunes. Ranger-led hikes are given; advance reservations are required. Music and educational programs pertaining to New Mexico's heritage and the monument's geology, plants and animals also are presented on full-moon nights.

Scenic, 16-mile round-trip Dunes Drive can be entered daily 7 a.m.-9 p.m., Memorial Day weekend-Labor Day; 8 a.m.-dusk, rest of year. It is subject to closures of up to 3 hours during missile testing. Visitors must exit the park by 1 hour after dusk, except on full-moon nights May-Oct. Visitor center open daily 9-5; closed Christmas. Admission (valid for 7 days) $3; free (ages 0-15). Phone (575) 479-6124.

ZIA PUEBLO (C-2) pop. 737, elev. 5,470'

This Rio Grande pueblo is famous for its pottery. Zia potters utilize geometric designs as well as plant and animal motifs on a white background. The thin-walled pieces adorned with the Zia bird symbol are highly prized by collectors.

ZIA PUEBLO AND MISSION is off US 550 at 135 Capital Square Dr. Settled in the 13th century, the pueblo stands on a barren mesa, seemingly blending into the natural terrain. The pueblo's ancient sun symbol was chosen to adorn the state flag. The Zia Cultural Center displays and sells traditional crafts.

Photography, sketching and recording are not permitted. A permit is required to fish in Zia Lake. **Hours:** Pueblo open by appointment. Cultural center open Mon.-Fri. 8-5; hours may vary. Closed to visitors during some ceremonial events. Phone ahead to confirm schedule. **Cost:** Free. **Phone:** (505) 867-3304.

ZUNI PUEBLO (F-1) pop. 6,302, elev. 6,282'

About 30 miles south of Gallup *(see place listing p. 382)* via SRs 602 and 53, Zuni is the only surviving settlement of the Seven Cities of Cíbola sought by Spanish explorer Francisco Vázquez de Coronado in his quest for gold. Today it is among the largest of New Mexico's inhabited pueblos.

Zuni artisans are master carvers renowned for such techniques as jewelry inlaid with silver and turquoise, finely cut turquoise needlepoint work and carved animal fetishes. Ancient rites and traditions are still honored, and ceremonial dances are held at the pueblo throughout the year.

Photography, filming, sketching and hiking within the pueblo are allowed by permit only; permits must be obtained from the Zuni visitor center. For information about permits as well as guided walking tours phone (505) 782-7238. Additional information is available at the Zuni A:shiwi A:wan Museum and Heritage Center, 02E Ojo Caliente Rd., Zuni, NM 87327; phone (505) 782-4403.

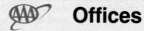

Offices

Main office listings are shown in **BOLD TYPE** and toll-free member service numbers appear in *ITALIC TYPE*.
All are closed Saturdays, Sundays and holidays unless otherwise indicated.
The addresses, phone numbers and hours for any AAA/CAA office are subject to change.
The type of service provided is designated below the name of the city where the office is located:

✚ Auto travel services, including books and maps, and on-demand TripTik ® routings.
● Auto travel services, including selected books and maps, and on-demand TripTik ® routings.
▬ Books/maps only, no marked maps or on-demand TripTik ® routings.
▲ Travel Agency Services; cruise, tour, air, car and rail reservations; domestic and international hotel reservations; passport photo services; international and domestic travel guides and maps; travel money products; and International Driving Permits. In addition, assistance with travel related insurance products including trip cancellation, travel accident, lost luggage, trip delay and assistance products.
✪ Insurance services provided. If only this icon appears, only insurance services are provided at that office.
◖ Car Care Plus Facility provides car care services.
▣ Electric vehicle charging station on premises.

AAA NATIONAL OFFICE: 1000 AAA DRIVE, HEATHROW, FLORIDA 32746-5063, (407) 444-7000

ARIZONA

CHANDLER—AAA ARIZONA, 301 N ARIZONA AVE, 85225.
WEEKDAYS (M-F) 7:00-6:00, SAT 8:00-4:00. (602) 230-3960 ◖

CHANDLER—AAA ARIZONA, 4040 W RAY RD STE 2, 85226.
WEEKDAYS (M-F) 8:30-5:30. (602) 230-3601 ✚▲✪▣

CHANDLER—AAA ARIZONA, 6205 W CHANDLER BLVD, 85226.
WEEKDAYS (M-F) 8:00-4:00. (602) 230-3600 ◖

GOODYEAR—AAA ARIZONA, 14175 W INDIAN SCH RD A-8, 85395. WEEKDAYS (M-F) 8:30-5:30. (602) 230-3170 ✚▲✪

MESA—AAA ARIZONA, 4126 E VALLEY AUTO DR, 85206.
WEEKDAYS (M-F) 7:00-6:00, SAT 8:00-4:00. (602) 241-3900 ◖ ▣

MESA—AAA ARIZONA, 4126 E VALLEY AUTO DR, 85206.
WEEKDAYS (M-F) 8:30-5:30, SAT 9:00-3:00. (602) 241-3901 ✚▲✪

PEORIA—AAA ARIZONA, 7422 W THUNDERBIRD RD, 85381.
WEEKDAYS (M-F) 7:00-6:00, SAT 8:00-4:00. (602) 230-3100 ◖ ▣

PEORIA—AAA ARIZONA, 7422 W THUNDERBIRD RD, 85381.
WEEKDAYS (M-F) 8:30-5:30, SAT 9:00-3:00. (602) 230-3101 ✚▲✪

PHOENIX—AAA ARIZONA, 1050 E CAMELBACK RD, 85014.
WEEKDAYS (M-F) 7:00-6:00, SAT 8:00-4:00. (602) 230-3401 ◖ ▣

PHOENIX—AAA ARIZONA, 15439 N 40TH ST, 85032.
WEEKDAYS (M-F) 7:00-6:00, SAT 8:00-4:00. (602) 230-3200 ◖ ▣

PHOENIX—AAA ARIZONA, 2375 E CAMELBACK RD #500, 85016. WEEKDAYS (M-F) 8:00-5:00, MON 8:00-7:00, THU 8:00-7:00. (602) 650-2700, *(800) 352-5382.* ✪

PHOENIX—AAA ARIZONA, 4046 E GREENWAY RD, 85032.
WEEKDAYS (M-F) 8:30-5:30. (602) 230-3201 ✚▲✪◖

PHOENIX—AAA ARIZONA, 742 E GLENDALE AVE #182, 85020
WEEKDAYS (M-F) 8:30-5:30. (602) 285-6241 ✚▲✪

PRESCOTT—AAA ARIZONA, 172 E SHELDON ST #C-100, 86301
WEEKDAYS (M-F) 8:30-5:30. (928) 541-8600 ✚▲✪

SCOTTSDALE—AAA ARIZONA, 15509 N HAYDEN RD, 85260.
WEEKDAYS (M-F) 7:00-6:00, SAT 8:00-4:00. (602) 248-3700 ◖

SUN CITY WEST—AAA ARIZONA, 19802 R H JOHNSON BL #141, 85375. WEEKDAYS (M-F) 8:00-5:00. (602) 230-3301 ✚▲✪

TUCSON—AAA ARIZONA, 3870 W RIVER RD, 85741.
WEEKDAYS (M-F) 7:00-6:00, SAT 8:00-4:00. (520) 258-7708 ◖

TUCSON—AAA ARIZONA, 6950 N ORACLE RD, 85704.
WEEKDAYS (M-F) 8:30-5:30. (520) 258-0505 ✚▲✪▣

TUCSON—AAA ARIZONA, 8204 E BROADWAY, 85710.
WEEKDAYS (M-F) 8:30-5:30. (520) 258-0504 ✚▲✪

NEW MEXICO

ALBUQUERQUE—AAA NEW MEXICO, 10501 MONTGOMERY BLVD NE, 87111. WEEKDAYS (M-F) 9:00-5:30, SAT 10:00-2:00. (505) 291-6611, *(877) 222-1020.* ✚▲✪

ALBUQUERQUE—AAA NEW MEXICO, 9231 COORS RD NW STE 5-7, 87114. WEEKDAYS (M-F) 9:00-5:30, SAT 10:00-2:00. (505) 792-1938, *(877) 222-1020.* ✚▲✪

LAS CRUCES—AAA NEW MEXICO, 3991 E LOHMAN AVE STE #A, 88011. WEEKDAYS (M-F) 9:00-5:30, SAT 10:00-2:00. (575) 523-5681, *(877) 222-1020.* ✚▲✪

SANTA FE—AAA NEW MEXICO, 3517 ZAFARANO DR STE D, 87507. WEEKDAYS (M-F) 9:00-5:30, SAT 10:00-2:00. (505) 471-6620, *(877) 222-1020.* ✚▲✪

Metric Equivalents Chart

TEMPERATURE

To convert Fahrenheit to Celsius, subtract 32 from the Fahrenheit temperature, multiply by 5 and divide by 9.
To convert Celsius to Fahrenheit, multiply by 9, divide by 5 and add 32.

ACRES

1 acre = 0.4 hectare (ha)   1 hectare = 2.47 acres

MILES AND KILOMETERS

Note: A kilometer is approximately 5/8 or 0.6 of a mile.
To convert kilometers to miles multiply by 0.6.

Miles/Kilometers		Kilometers/Miles	
15	24.1	30	18.6
20	32.2	35	21.7
25	40.2	40	24.8
30	48.3	45	27.9
35	56.3	50	31.0
40	64.4	55	34.1
45	72.4	60	37.2
50	80.5	65	40.3
55	88.5	70	43.4
60	96.6	75	46.6
65	104.6	80	49.7
70	112.7	85	52.8
75	120.7	90	55.9
80	128.7	95	59.0
85	136.8	100	62.1
90	144.8	105	65.2
95	152.9	110	68.3
100	160.9	115	71.4

LINEAR MEASURE

Customary	Metric
1 inch = 2.54 centimeters	1 centimeter = 0.4 inches
1 foot = 30 centimeters	1 meter = 3.3 feet
1 yard = 0.91 meters	1 meter = 1.09 yards
1 mile = 1.6 kilometers	1 kilometer = .62 miles

LIQUID MEASURE

Customary	Metric
1 fluid ounce = 30 milliliters	1 milliliter = .03 fluid ounces
1 cup = .24 liters	1 liter = 2.1 pints
1 pint = .47 liters	1 liter = 1.06 quarts
1 quart = .95 liters	1 liter = .26 gallons
1 gallon = 3.8 liters	

Celsius °   Fahrenheit °

Celsius		Fahrenheit
100	BOILING	212
37		100
35		95
32		90
29		85
27		80
24		75
21		70
18		65
16		60
13		55
10		50
7		45
4		40
2		35
0	FREEZING	32
-4		25
-7		20
-9		15
-12		10
-15		5
-18		0
-21		-5
-24		-10
-27		-15

WEIGHT

If You Know:	Multiply By:	To Find:
Ounces	28	Grams
Pounds	0.45	Kilograms
Grams	0.035	Ounces
Kilograms	2.2	Pounds

PRESSURE

Air pressure in automobile tires is expressed in kilopascals. Multiply pound-force per square inch (psi) by 6.89 to find kilopascals (kPa).

24 psi = 165 kPa   28 psi = 193 kPa
26 psi = 179 kPa   30 psi = 207 kPa

GALLONS AND LITERS

Gallons/Liters			Liters/Gallons			
5	19.0	12	45.6	10	2.6	40	10.4
6	22.8	14	53.2	15	3.9	50	13.0
7	26.6	16	60.8	20	5.2	60	15.6
8	30.4	18	68.4	25	6.5	70	18.2
9	34.2	20	76.0	30	7.8	80	20.8
10	38.0	25	95.0	35	9.1	90	23.4

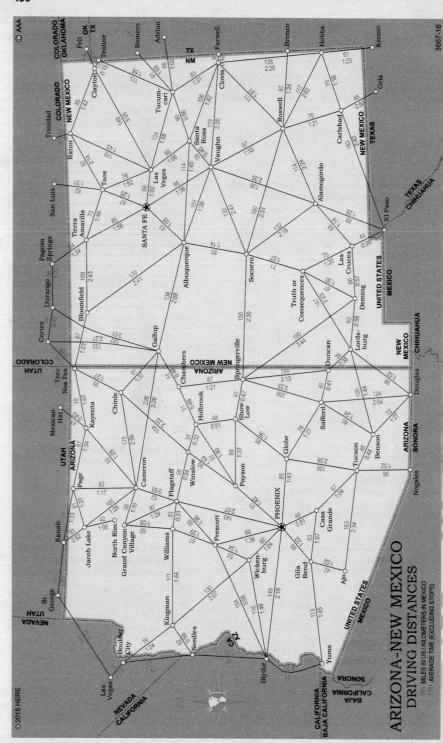

ARIZONA–NEW MEXICO
DRIVING DISTANCES

MILES IN US / KILOMETERS IN MEXICO
AVERAGE TIME (EXCLUDING STOPS)

© 2015 HERE

© AAA

3667-16

Border Information

Traveling to Mexico

FOR U.S. AND CANADIAN RESIDENTS TRAVELING TO MEXICO

AAA recommends that travelers consult online U.S. State Department travel advisories when planning travel abroad. Find this information at http://travel.state.gov/content/passports/english/alertswarnings/mexico-travel-warning.html.

Border crossing requirements: Travelers are required to present proper travel documents for travel to Mexico and to return to the United States.

Air travel: U.S. and Canadian citizens traveling between the United States and Mexico by air are required to show a valid passport.

Land or sea travel: A passport or passport card, or other U.S. official ID (not including a state-issued driver's license), is required to enter Mexico by land or sea. U.S. citizens returning to the United States from Mexico by land or sea are required to present proper travel documents according to the Western Hemisphere Travel Initiative. Approved documents include a passport or passport card, Enhanced Driver's License or Trusted Traveler program card; for more information refer to the U.S. Department of

State's website travel.state.gov. Canadian citizens should refer to the Canada Border Services Agency website cbsa-asfc.gc.ca for requirements to re-enter Canada.

Children: Minors under age 18 traveling alone or with someone other than a parent or legal guardian are required to present a notarized letter of consent from at least one absent parent giving permission to travel only if the minor is departing (not entering) Mexico, is traveling by air or sea or is using Mexican documents to travel. However, because airline or Mexican immigration officials may request a notarized letter of consent under other circumstances as well, the U.S. Embassy in Mexico City recommends that any minor traveling without both parents carry a notarized consent letter at all times. For more information contact the embassy, the nearest Mexican consulate or the Mexican National Immigration Institute (INM).

Automobile insurance: Full coverage from a reliable Mexican insurance company is required, including property damage and public liability. AAA offices in border states (along with offices in Nevada and Utah) can provide Mexican automobile insurance to members. U.S. or Canadian automobile insurance is not valid in Mexico.

Tourist permits: When traveling to Mexico as a tourist you must obtain an FMM tourist permit. You must show a valid passport or passport card to obtain a permit.

Permits are issued at immigration offices at official points of entry and at some Mexican tourism offices. You must have a valid tourist permit if you remain within the border zone—the area within 20 to 30 kilometers (12 to 19 miles) of the U.S. border, depending on the Mexican state—for more than 72 hours, or if you travel beyond the border zone.

The permit costs approximately $24.50 (U.S.), which must be paid at a Mexican bank (see the list of banks on the back of the permit form) or at a bank window at the border. You are required to show the "Fee Paid" stamp on your tourist permit when leaving Mexico. It is recommended that you obtain your tourist permit before leaving the United States and pay the fee at the border.

If traveling by air, the permit is distributed on the flight and the fee is included in the airline ticket price. If arriving by cruise ship, the fee is collected when disembarking or is included in the cruise fare if the stay is longer than 72 hours.

Exemptions:

- Visitors traveling by sea, staying less than 72 hours and remaining in the seaport.
- Visitors traveling by land to destinations within the border zone and staying less than 72 hours.
- Visitors traveling by land beyond the border zone, staying less than 72 hours and limiting their visit to the following destinations/tourist corridors: Tijuana to Ensenada, Baja California; Sonoyta to Puerto Peñasco, Sonora; Ciudad Juárez to Paquime, Chihuahua; Piedras Negras to Santa Rosa, Coahuila; and Reynosa to Presa Cuchillo, Nuevo León.
- Business travelers with a business visa; students (as defined by Mexican immigration laws) with a student visa (contact a Mexican consulate for business/student visa information).

Permit validity:

- The permit is valid for up to 180 days.
- A multiple-entry permit allows unlimited visits into and out of Mexico within the 180-day period.
- In Baja California a tourist permit is good for a maximum of 180 days per year and 30 days per visit.
- A tourist permit not used within 90 days of issue becomes void.
- Visitors should carry their tourist permit with them at all times while in Mexico.
- If a permit is lost, obtain a duplicate from local immigration officials (write down the tourist permit number and keep it separate from the permit to expedite this process).
- Permits are required to be turned in to Mexican immigration officials at the border when you depart the country.
- If you choose to remain in Mexico beyond the permit validity period an extension must be requested from immigration authorities prior to the expiration date.
- Violation of the laws governing tourist permits may result in subsequently being refused entry into Mexico and/or incurring a substantial fine.

Vehicle travel beyond the border zone requires a government-issued temporary vehicle importation permit and a promise to return vehicle form. These two documents are not required in Baja California unless the vehicle is put on a ferry bound for the mainland. They also are not required for travel to the following destinations in the state of Sonora: Rocky Point (Puerto Peñasco), Guaymas, San Carlos, Bahía Kino and other locations west of Mex. 15, as well as cities along Mex. 15 (Magdalena, Santa Ana, Hermosillo).

An Only Sonora permit is acceptable if driving is confined within the state east of Mex. 15 as well as south of Empalme (about 350 miles south of the U.S. border). The permit can be obtained at Banjercito offices in Agua Prieta (opposite Douglas, Ariz.), Cananea (on Mex. 2 southwest of Agua Prieta) and Empalme (on Mex. 15 at Km marker 98, just south of the Guaymas bypass).

To obtain the temporary vehicle importation permit and promise to return vehicle form at an official point of entry (immigration checkpoint), the vehicle owner must have a valid (unexpired) tourist permit, a valid international major credit card and a current vehicle license/registration receipt (the original and two copies). Information on the application for temporary vehicle importation and on the promise to return form must match; the same requirements apply to both.

An administration fee plus tax must be paid with a major international credit card (American Express, Mastercard or Visa) at the official point of entry (mainland border crossing or ferry crossing from Baja California to the mainland) in order to receive a temporary importation permit windshield sticker. The credit card must be in the vehicle owner's name and issued by a U.S. or Canadian bank or lending institution. Vehicle owners who don't have a major credit card must post a bond ($200 to $400 based on vehicle value) with a Mexican bonding firm (Afianzadora) at the point of entry. Cash, checks, money orders or credit cards issued by a Mexican bank are not accepted.

More about temporary importation permits:

- Generally issued for 180 days, the same length as the tourist permit.
- Only one permit will be issued per person, for one motorized vehicle at a time.
- Carry the permit with you; do not leave it in the vehicle.
- Return permit, promise to return vehicle form and windshield sticker to Mexican customs officials at the Banjercito office

at the border before or on the expiration date shown on the form, or be subject to a fine.
- If the permit or form is lost or stolen, Mexican customs offices can issue replacement documentation provided you obtain a certified document attesting to the loss from your homeland (U.S. or Canada) embassy or consulate.
- If you remain in Mexico beyond the authorized time period and without the proper documentation, your car will be immediately confiscated.

Pets: U.S. visitors may bring a dog, cat or bird into Mexico with government approval. A pet health certificate signed not more than 15 days before the animal enters Mexico and a pet vaccination certificate showing proof of treatment for rabies, hepatitis and leptospirosis are required at the border for each animal. A pet permit fee is charged at the time of entry.

Leaving Mexico

FOR U.S. AND CANADIAN RESIDENTS LEAVING MEXICO

When leaving the country:
- FMM tourist permits, temporary vehicle importation permits, promise to return vehicle forms and windshield stickers must be returned to Mexican immigration and customs officials at the departure or border checkpoint (or at an interior inspection point).

- Those entering Mexico with a motor vehicle must leave the country with the vehicle.
- At highway stations near the U.S. border, Mexican agricultural officials will inspect vehicles traveling north that are carrying any fruits, vegetables, houseplants and other plant matter.
- You must have an export certificate to take official cultural artifacts (excluding handicrafts) out of the country.
- Religious or archeological artifacts may not be taken out of the country.

Returning to the United States or Canada:

U.S. citizens returning from Mexico by land or sea are required to present proper travel documents; refer to the U.S. Department of State website for the most current information. Canadian citizens entering the United States are subject to the rules governing entry to the U.S. by foreign nationals; refer to the Canadian Border Services Agency website for requirements to re-enter Canada.

U.S. exemptions:
- You may bring back duty-free articles not exceeding $800 in retail value from a stay abroad of at least 48 hours.
- The exemption is allowed once every 30 days.
- A family (related persons living in the same household) may combine exemptions; i.e., a family of six would be entitled to $1,600 worth of goods duty-free on one declaration, even if the articles claimed by one member exceed that individual's $800 amount.
- Duty must be paid on all items in excess of the exemption amount.
- Payment of duty is required upon arrival.
- Gifts taken across the U.S./Mexico border are considered to be for personal use and are included in the $800 exemption.
- Articles purchased and left behind for alterations or other reasons do not qualify for the $800 exemption when shipped at a later date.
- The $800 exemption may include no more than 1 liter of alcoholic beverages and no more than 200 cigarettes and 100 cigars.

Restricted or prohibited articles: An agricultural quarantine bans the importation of certain fruits, vegetables, plants, livestock, poultry and meats. All food products brought into the United States must be declared. The U.S. Department of Agriculture also prohibits bringing back any type of pet. Visit the Animal and Plant Health Inspection Service (APHIS) website or U.S. Customs at cbp.gov for more information.

One foreign-made article carrying a protected U.S. trademark (i.e., camera, binoculars, musical instrument, jewelry or watch) may normally be brought into the United States under your personal exemption, provided it is for your private use and not sold within 1 year of importation.

The following are prohibited: narcotics and dangerous drugs, drug paraphernalia, obscene articles and publications, seditious or treasonable matter, lottery tickets, hazardous items (fireworks, dangerous toys, toxic or poisonous substances) and switchblade knives. Goods originating in the following embargoed countries are prohibited: Western Balkans, Burma, Ivory Coast, Cuba, Democratic Republic of Congo, Iran, Iraq, Liberia, Sierra Leone, Sudan, Syria and Zimbabwe.

If you plan to bring back items made of fur or whalebone, any animal skin other than cowhide leather, or any product manufactured wholly or in part from any type of wildlife, contact the U.S. Fish and Wildlife Service's Office of Law Enforcement, 4401 N. Fairfax Dr., MS-LE-3000, Arlington, VA 22203. Phone (703) 358-1949 for regulations; fws.gov/le.

Alcoholic beverages: Both federal and state laws apply. If regulations conflict, state laws regarding import limits supersede.

U.S. residents 21 years of age or older may bring into the United States 1 liter of alcohol duty-free once every 30 days. However, if you arrive in a state that permits a lesser amount than what you have legally brought into the United States, state law prevails.

Gifts: Gifts in packages with a total retail value not exceeding $100 may be sent to friends or relatives in the United States free of U.S. customs duty or tax, provided no recipient receives more than one gift shipment per day. Gifts may be sent to more than one person in the same package if they are individually wrapped and labeled with each recipient's name. Perfumes valued at more than $5 retail, tobacco products or alcoholic beverages may not be included in gift packages, which should be clearly marked with the designation "Unsolicited Gift," the gift giver's name and the retail value of the contents.

Duties: A flat rate duty of 3 percent is applied to the first $1,000 (fair retail value) worth of merchandise in excess of the $800 customs exemption. A sales receipt constitutes proof of value. Family members residing in one household and traveling together may group articles for application of the flat-duty rate, which may be taken once every 30 days. Articles must accompany you to the U.S. border.

Canadian exemptions: Citizens who have been outside Canada at least 48 hours may bring back duty- and tax-free goods not exceeding $400 (CAN) in retail value. The exemption can be claimed any number of times a year. Citizens who have been outside Canada 7 days or more may bring back duty- and tax-free goods not exceeding $750 (CAN) in retail value. The $750 exemption can be claimed regardless of any $400 exemption taken on a previous trip and requires a written declaration. The two exemptions may not be combined.

Citizens may claim duty- and tax-free entry for articles (excluding tobacco products or alcoholic beverages) not exceeding $50 (CAN) in retail value when returning from a trip abroad of at least 24 hours. Items brought into Canada under a personal exemption must be for personal or household use, souvenirs or gifts.

Canadian limitations (on either the $400 or $750 exemption): 50 cigars, 200 cigarettes, 200 tobacco sticks, 200 grams (6.4 ounces) of tobacco, 40 ounces (1.1 liters) of liquor, 53 imperial ounces of wine and 300 ounces (8.5 liters) of beer or ale (equivalent to 24 12-ounce bottles/cans). All exemptions are individual and may not be combined with that of another person to cover an article valued at more than the maximum exemption. You may be asked to prove the length of your visit outside Canada. Dated sales receipts for goods or services constitute valid proof.

All declared goods associated with the $400 personal exemption must accompany the purchaser to the Canadian border. Declared goods associated with the $750 personal exemption may follow the purchaser by mail.

While AAA makes every effort to provide accurate and complete information, AAA makes no warranty, express or implied, and assumes no legal liability or responsibility for the accuracy or completeness of any information contained herein.

Points of Interest Index

 Attractions appear at the top of each category
and offer a Great Experience for Members®.

Index Legend

CHILDREN'S ACTIVITIES

OUTDOORS & SCIENCE

SHOPPING & NIGHTLIFE

SPORTS & RECREATION

TOURS & SIGHTSEEING

Photo Credits

Page numbers are in bold type. Picture credit abbreviations are as follows:
- (i) numeric sequence from top to bottom, left to right ▪ (AAA) AAA Travel library.

- (Cover) Monument Valley Navajo Tribal Park, AZ / © Heeb Christian / age fotostock
- **2** (i) Courtesy of Desert Botanical Garden
- **2** (ii) © iStockphoto.com / David Sucsy
- **2** (iii) © Erik Harrison / Shutterstock.com
- **12** (i) Courtesy of Berry Manor Inn
- **12** (ii) © Chris Dew / Killarney Lodge
- **12** (iii) Courtesy of Hyatt Hotels
- **12** (iv) Courtesy of Montpelier Plantation and Beach
- **12** (v) © Elisa Rolle / Wikimedia Commons
- **12** (vi) Courtesy of The Shores Resort & Spa
- **12** (vii) Courtesy of All Star Vacation Homes
- **12** (viii) Courtesy of Bryce View Lodge
- **12** (ix) Courtesy of Vista Verde Guest Ranch
- **13** Courtesy of Divi Resorts
- **18** (i) © Erik Harrison / Shutterstock.com
- **18** (ii) Courtesy of Scottsdale Convention & Visitors Bureau
- **19** © SCPhotos / Alamy
- **20** (i) Courtesy of Wikimedia Commons
- **20** (ii) Courtesy of Wikimedia Commons
- **23** (i) © iStockphoto.com / David Sucsy
- **23** (ii) © EpicStockMedia / Shutterstock.com
- **23** (iii) © Dennis Frates / Alamy
- **23** (iv) Courtesy of Petrified Forest National Park
- **23** (v) Courtesy of Grand Canyon Railway
- **24** (i) © Gage Skidmore / flickr
- **24** (ii) Courtesy of Heard Museum
- **24** (iii) Courtesy of Musical Instrument Museum
- **24** (iv) Courtesy of Phoenix Art Museum
- **125** © iStockphoto.com / David Sucsy
- **128** Courtesy of Desert Botanical Garden
- **129** © neilsetchfield.com / Alamy
- **130** © Fotosearch RM / age fotostock
- **131** © Robert Harding World Imagery / Alamy
- **132** © ClassicStock / Alamy
- **133** © Igor Mojzes / Fotolia.com
- **134** Courtesy of Scottsdale Convention & Visitors Bureau
- **141** © Action Sports Photography / Shutterstock.com
- **255** © Frontpage / Shutterstock.com
- **258** © Lane Erickson / 123RF.com
- **259** © All Canada Photos / Alamy
- **260** © Mira / Alamy
- **261** © Ilene MacDonald / Alamy
- **262** © hessianmercenary / Shutterstock.com
- **268** © Ron Niebrugge / Alamy
- **269** © Norma Jean Gargasz / Alamy
- **312** (i) © Erik Harrison / Shutterstock.com
- **312** (ii) © iStockphoto.com / kman59
- **313** © Steve Bower / Shutterstock.com
- **314** (i) Courtesy of Wikimedia Commons
- **314** (ii) Courtesy of Wikimedia Commons
- **317** (i) © H. Mark Weidman Photography / Alamy
- **317** (ii) © sumikophoto / Shutterstock.com
- **317** (iii) © trekandshoot / Shutterstock.com

476

(cont'd)

- **317** (iv) © Jon Arnold Images Ltd / Alamy
- **317** (v) © VStock / Alamy
- **318** (i) © Larry Lamsa / flickr
- **318** (ii) © Buddy Mays / Alamy
- **318** (iii) © LizCoughlan / Alamy
- **318** (iv) © jay goebel / Alamy
- **457** © Garry Gay / Alamy
- **459** © Barry Singleton / Shutterstock.com

© LifeJourneys / Getty Images

Maximize Your Membership